Strategies for Quality Improvement

Strategies for Quality Improvement

TQM, Reengineering, and ISO 9000

Second Edition

Harry Ivan Costin

Endicott College
International Organization New Acropolis

THE DRYDEN PRESS
HARCOURT BRACE COLLEGE PUBLISHERS
FORT WORTH PHILADELPHIA SAN DIEGO NEW YORK AUSTIN ORLANDO SAN ANTONIO
TORONTO MONTREAL LONDON SYDNEY TOKYO

Acquisitions Editor: John Weimeister
Product Manager: Lisé Johnson
Development Editor: Ellen Hostetler
Project Editor: Lisa Cooper & Rebecca Dodson
Art Director: Linda Beaupré
Production Manager: Lois West
Permissions Editor: Adele Krause

Cover image: Copyright © 1998 Marc Brown

ISBN: 0-03-024611-3

Library of Congress Catalog Card Number: 98-73894

Portions of this work were published in previous editions.

Address for editorial correspondence:
The Dryden Press
301 Commerce Street, Suite 3700
Fort Worth, TX 76102

Address for domestic orders:
The Dryden Press
6277 Sea Harbor Drive
Orlando, FL 32887-6777
1-800-782-4479

Address for international orders:
International Customer Service
The Dryden Press
6277 Sea Harbor Drive
Orlando, FL 32887-6777
407-345-3800
(fax) 407-345-4060
(e-mail) hbintl@harcourtbrace.com

Website address: http://www.hbcollege.com

Printed in the United States of America

7 8 9 0 1 2 3 4 5 6 066 9 8 7 6 5 4 3 2 1

The Dryden Press
Harcourt Brace College Publishers

I dedicate this book to

PHILIP DARGIE

friend, partner, and teacher.

The Dryden Press Series in Management

Anthony, Perrewé, and Kacmar
Strategic Human Resource Management
Second Edition

Bereman, Lengnick-Hall, and Mark
Compensation Decision Making: A Computer-Based Approach
Second Edition

Bergmann, Scarpello, and Hills
Compensation Decision Making
Second Edition

Boone and Kurtz
Contemporary Business
Ninth Edition

Bourgeois
Strategic Management: From Concept to Implementation

Bracker, Montanari, and Morgan
Cases in Strategic Management

Brechner
Contemporary Mathematics for Business and Consumers

Calvasina and Barton
Chopstick Company: A Business Simulation

Costin
Readings in Total Quality Management

Costin
Managing in the Global Economy: The European Union

Costin
Economic Reform in Latin America

Costin
Management Development and Training: A TQM Approach

Costin
Readings in Strategy and Strategic Management

Czinkota, Ronkainen, and Moffett
International Business
Fourth Edition

Czinkota, Ronkainen, Moffett, and Moynihan
Global Business
Second Edition

Daft
Management
Fourth Edition

Daft and Marcic
Understanding Management
Second Edition

DeSimone and Harris
Human Resource Development
Second Edition

Foegen
Business Plan Guidebook
Revised Edition

Gatewood and Feild
Human Resource Selection
Fourth Edition

Gold
Exploring Organizational Behavior: Readings, Cases, Experiences

Greenhaus and Callanan
Career Management
Second Edition

Higgins and Vincze
Strategic Management: Text and Cases
Fifth Edition

Hodgetts
Modern Human Relations at Work
Sixth Edition

Hodgetts and Kroeck
Personnel and Human Resource Management

Hodgetts and Kuratko
Effective Small Business Management
Sixth Edition

Holley and Jennings
The Labor Relations Process
Sixth Edition

Holt
International Management: Text and Cases

Jauch and Coltrin
The Managerial Experience: Cases and Exercises
Sixth Edition

Kindler and Ginsburg
Strategic & Interpersonal Skill Building

Kirkpatrick and Lewis
Effective Supervision: Preparing for the 21st Century

Kuratko and Hodgetts
Entrepreneurship: A Contemporary Approach
Fourth Edition

Kuratko and Welsch
Entrepreneurial Strategy: Text and Cases

Lengnick-Hall, Cynthia, and Hartman
Experiencing Quality

Lewis
Io Enterprises Simulation

Long and Arnold
The Power of Environmental Partnerships

Morgan
Managing for Success

Ryan, Eckert, and Ray
Small Business: An Entrepreneur's Plan
Fourth Edition

Sandburg
Career Design Software

Vecchio
Organizational Behavior
Third Edition

Walton
Corporate Encounters: Law, Ethics, and the Business Environment

Weiss
Business Ethics: A Stakeholder and Issues Management Approach
Second Edition

Zikmund
Business Research Methods
Fifth Edition

Brief Table of Contents

Contents

Preface

This book was originally planned as the second edition of *Readings in Total Quality Management,* which was published in 1994. The first edition of the book was well received, possibly because it attempted to map the entire field of Total Quality. Five years later, as I worked on this new edition, several important trends became evident to me:

1. Many of the original TQM principles and tools have since gone mainstream, and are being widely used.
2. TQM as a "buzzword" has begun to fade.
3. Two other approaches to quality improvement, the ISO 9000 series of Standards for Quality Systems, and Reengineering, have enjoyed worldwide popularity.
4. The visibility of the Baldrige Award has decreased, but many new quality awards have been instituted at the state level and also internationally.
5. A growing body of literature has explored the implementation of the different models for quality improvement in diverse industries and companies.
6. Bibliographic resources on quality issues have become widely available on the worldwide Web. These resources include the guidelines for different quality awards, such as the Baldrige and the European Quality Award.

CHANGES IN THIS EDITION

In light of these trends and in the spirit of continuous improvement, I have made the following editorial decisions:

1. To change the title of the book to *Strategies for Quality Improvement,* since ISO 9000, QS 9000, and Reengineering are also covered in this new edition.

2. To strengthen the book conceptually. The book now includes substantial readings on ISO 9000 and Reengineering. Many case studies on how diverse companies approach quality improvement are now available for free online downloading, but a substantial overview of models and concepts is often lacking. This book attempts to fill that gap.

3. To eliminate the appendix on quality awards. The guidelines to several quality awards (including the Baldrige and the European Quality Award) and profiles of award winning companies are now available online (URLs are included in the book).

4. To include a list of suggested online resources that allows for further research.

Introduction: Quality 2000

As I set out to prepare this second edition of the book originally titled *Readings in Total Quality Management,* I not only had the opportunity to review the current literature, but also my own thinking influenced by 10 years of consulting in quality, training, and research in the United States, Europe, and Latin America. I will present some of my current views in a summarized form and relate them to what I see as the major trends in the quality field over the last 10 years.

The selection of a 10-year period for a review is not arbitrary, since 1987 was indeed a *very good year.* The Malcolm Baldrige National Quality Award was established by Public Law in 1987, and the first edition of the ISO 9000 international Standards for Quality Systems was published the same year. The Baldrige Award guidelines and the ISO 9000 series have since become the most important benchmarks for quality systems internationally. The Baldrige Award, which has a more quantitative orientation than the Japanese Deming Award, was the first in a series of quality awards at the state level in the United States, and at national and regional levels internationally. It has served as a model to the internationalization of quality models and the measurement of quality progress.

In a parallel development, ISO 9000 has provided a foundation for quality, first in Europe, then in the United States, and recently at a global level. What often remains unrecognized is that the ISO 9000 series of standards for quality systems was not only based upon the existing international experience with quality standards, but also was developed with a Total Quality framework in mind. The relationship between ISO 9000 and TQM is more clear in the QS 9000 standards, the guidelines for quality systems based on ISO 9000 developed by the automotive industry (Chrysler, Ford, and GM) and first published in 1994. QS 9000 focuses on preventive and corrective action and integrates systematically different TQM-related disciplines for problem solving and product and process design, such as team-based problem-solving using the seven quality control tools, or quality function deployment (QFD).

The growth of quality awards at the national and international levels and the wide acceptance of the ISO 9000 series is a clear indication of the global trend of the quality movement, and that is that *quality has gone mainstream.* Today, although

TQM as a buzzword might be on its way out, concepts such as teamwork, empowerment, continuous improvement, and quality improvement through process redesign have become permanent features of the management landscape.

AND THEN THERE WAS DILBERT. . .

The wide diffusion of quality models and the introduction of quality improvement programs in many companies and industries, with more or less understanding and success, led to often justified criticism of some quality programs. In a particularly poignant manner, the "Dilbert"[1] cartoon highlighted some of the sheer nonsense that was going on in some organizations. I must confess that as a quality consultant, I have witnessed many a crime committed in the name of TQM and ISO 9000, often with the best of intentions, but it should not be forgotten that *the road to Hell is paved with good intentions.* On the other hand, we have all benefited from the quality movement to the extent that today we take significant improvements in quality and service for granted. Most of this improvement has been the result of hard work by individuals and teams at all organizational levels, rather than of "technological miracles."

TO REENGINEER OR NOT TO REENGINEER?

Quite a bit of Scott Adams's (the creator of "Dilbert") astute criticism of the excesses of quality programs has been directed to reengineering. The best known form of reengineering was popularized by Hammer and Champy in 1993[2], who argued that "American corporations must undertake nothing less than a radical reinvention of how they do their work." In theory their claim was similar to Drucker's contention for the need to periodically reevaluate what he called the "theory of business,"[3] (1) the assumptions about the environment of the organization: society and its structure, the market, the customer, and technology; (2) the assumptions about the specific mission of the organization; and (3) the assumptions about the core competencies needed to accomplish the organization's mission. In practice, Hammer and Champy offered a step-by-step model for reengineering, which they defined as "the fundamental rethinking and radical redesign of business processes to achieve dramatic improvements in critical, contemporary measures of performance, such as cost, quality, service, and speed."

It is difficult to argue against such lofty and sound goals. However, *the devil is in the details.* Hammer and Champy argued, without going into specifics, that essentially most critical manufacturing and service processes are outdated. One reason for generalized "out of synch" industrial phenomenon is the emergence of radically new technologies such as IT, which allows us to do work in ways we could not even dream of before. In light of this trend, according to Hammer and Champy, tweaking outdated processes (or "paving old cow paths," as Hammer and Champy would say) makes no sense. Companies have to start over! If they do, they will reap dramatic benefits from the "heavy blasting."

The implementation of reengineering has been met with deep disappointment in many organizations (some have estimated over a 70 percent failure rate of reengineering efforts), and in all fairness, this cannot be blamed on Hammer and Champy, who were cautious enough not to get into devilish details, but said only that

> If a company falls 10 percent short of where it should be, if its costs come in 10 percent too high, if its quality is 10 percent too low, if its customer performance needs a 10 percent boost, that company does not need reengineering. More conventional methods, from exhorting the troops to establishing incremental quality programs, can dig a company out of a 10 percent hole. Reengineering should be brought in only when a need exists for heavy blasting. Marginal improvement requires fine tuning; dramatic improvement demands blowing up the old and replacing it with something new[4] (33–34).

In other words, reengineering is not for the faint of heart. However, those companies that dare to embark upon this adventure that even Rambo would find challenging, will reap extraordinary benefits. In a nation that does not accept second bests it is no wonder that many executives choose only to hear the promise of multi-fold improvement as opposed to the trivial results (by comparison) of continuous improvement programs.

I have taken the liberty to elaborate on reengineering because of a generalized perception that "reengineering is in and TQM is out." There is nothing wrong with the basic tenets of reengineering, but, in my opinion the reengineering hoopla has caused significant damage to organizations and to the quality movement at large, since the high failure rate of reengineering programs does throw a negative light upon process improvement efforts in general.

On a theoretical-practical level, my own ideas about reengineering can be summarized as follows: Reengineering is necessary in industries and companies that are suffering because of what I refer to as disruptive technologies—radically new and more productive ways to perform value-added activities linked through processes. The wide range of information technology processes in knowledge-intensive industries is one example. Today, it would be difficult to conceive everyday life without ATMs, faxing, or word processing. It is, therefore, not surprising that industries such as banking have engaged heavily in reengineering efforts.

On the other hand, there is the organizational capital represented by experience and learning (the learning and experience curves are famous models related to the improvement of productivity). When an organization embarks upon reengineering, the accumulated capital represented by experience and learning becomes "sunk." Unfortunately, the cost-benefit analysis of reengineering projects (productivity measures before and after) does not consider in the decision making process the cost implicit in losing what people already know. For example, organizations upgrading software have become keenly aware of the high costs related to starting over. In other words, my claim is that when, as reengineering advocates argue, we start over, we do lose much of what we have, which may not be reflected on any balance sheet. And most of what we lose is knowledge capital—the most important form of capital in modern society.

CONCLUSION

Today, some of the most prominent members of the quality landscape are TQM, ISO 9000, QS 9000, and Reengineering. These four approaches to quality improvement share a fundamental common feature: that improvement comes from the understanding, adjustment, and when necessary, complete redesign of *organizational processes*. In other words, the great winner of the last decade is the concept of process improvement and process redesign as a foundation for quality. I consider this concept to be the fundamental claim to fame of the quality movement. Further, process improvement/redesign can be linked to other concepts and implementation approaches such as customer-driven value-added design of products and services, teamwork, team-based problem-solving, or statistical process control.

Those familiar with systemic organizational models such as Senge's "learning organization" or the Baldrige Award model may disagree with me and claim that systemic thinking is the greatest contribution of the quality movement. My own experience suggests that models such as Senge's learning organization, a vision for an organization that practices what he refers to as the five disciplines, have provided increased depth and richness to organizational analysis, but have also been a source of confusion. On a personal level, I find myself enthralled by glorious organizational utopias, but as a practitioner, I have learned that process improvement works even in organizational environments (most of those I have been exposed to) where such utopias remain a distant dream. I am grateful to systemic thinkers such as Senge who have provided me with much inspiration, but I often have not found their advice to be practical, for example, their call for visionary leaders.

Time will tell whether TQM or reengineering are simply buzzwords and management fads. What cannot be denied is that the quality movement has had a significant impact upon management thinking, one that hopefully will become a source of *continuous improvement* at all organizational levels.

Notes

1. Adams, Scott. *The Dilbert Principle.* New York: Harper Business, 1996.
2. Hammer, Michael and James Champy. *Reengineering the Corporation.* New York: Harper Business, 1993.
3. Drucker, Peter F. "The Theory of Business" in *Managing in a Time of Great Change.* New York: Truman Talley Books/Dutton, 1995.
4. Hammer and Champy, pp. 33–34.

Strategies for Quality Improvement

part

1

What Is Total Quality Management?

The readings in Part 1 address the basic question: What is Total Quality Management (TQM)?[1] An attempt has been made to provide an answer from a historic perspective and by examining the key concepts related to the quality field.

Historically, it should be noted that quality as a concept has evolved from the focused definitions of quality as inspection and quality control to the almost all-encompassing concept of "quality" of the '90s. Today, quality implies product and service quality as perceived by the customer, quality of processes, and even the societal and environmental impact of products and business activity.

As quality concepts have become generalized, two reasons for concern have developed. A first danger is that quality is becoming such an overused concept as to become vague and unfocused, the very criticism the quality movement has applied to preceding management approaches. A second danger lies in taking a particular "quality guru" or "party line" as an exclusive interpretation of what TQM is or is not. The key benefits of the diverse writings included under the generic heading of TQM lie in the diversity of approaches used and the emphasis on a reality check of our activities, such as learning from our mistakes and experiences. In other words, our understanding of quality should evolve with our ongoing learning as we implement diverse quality programs.

Conceptually, current definitions and processes related to "total quality" can be interpreted as an interplay of three fields and approaches:

1. **Efficiency concerns** rooted in process analysis, related to such traditions as process engineering, operations management, operations research, and statistical process control.
   From this perspective, the key concepts are **efficient resource utilization** and **continuously improving processes** for product and service delivery.
2. Concerns about quality of work life, collaborative management-labor relations, and synergy through **teamwork.** This approach is closely related to the human relations school of management thought and the fields of organizational behavior and organizational design.
   Some of the key concepts related to this approach are **teamwork, synergy,** and **empowerment.**
3. Concerns about the goals of any business—survival, profits, market share, and sustainable competitive advantage in an increasingly hostile and competitive global environment. This requires the formulation and implementation of a coherent **strategy** and a **shared vision.** This perspective is the most recent one in the United States and European implementations of total quality and is closely linked to the field of strategy or management policy.
   The key concepts related to this approach are **strategy, mission, vision,** and **benchmarking.**

Conceptually, and also in its implementation, total quality should integrate strategic, human, and operational concerns. In practice though, because of the complexities involved, there are few theorists or practitioners writing about or implementing total quality who have enough experience in all three fields to integrate them effectively.

Consequently, several quality efforts under the banner of TQM have been criticized with good reason. The shortcomings of specific TQM programs can often be traced back to the professional background and orientation of those involved in their planning and implementation stages. Among the thinkers and practitioners who often fail to integrate effectiveness, efficiency, and motivation concerns in the application of TQM are:

- Engineers and other practitioners with experience in process optimization efforts who are also advocates of teamwork and shared decision making but have difficulties grasping the complexities and uncertainties inherent in a strategic approach. Their efforts are most likely to fail in high velocity strategic environments.

- Other advocates of a humane work environment and of teamwork who do not understand the demands of a global competitive environment and do not like to get involved in the details of process analysis, improvement, and redesign.
- Managers focusing on strategic and marketing issues who take efficient processes for granted.

If total quality is to be *total* and live up to the lofty expectations of its advocates, it will have to integrate **strategy, process efficiency, effectiveness, teamwork,** and **shared decision making concerns,** both conceptually and practically. Otherwise, total quality management will be, as its critics argue, "more of the same with a new and more complex jargon."

The next step in terms of the conceptual development of total quality lies in extending *total* to include not only the internal and external customers and society at large, but also to address specifically the environmental impact of the creation, delivery, and recycling of products. Some companies are beginning to study the full product life cycle and to plan ultimate disposal of their products from their very inception and design.

Notes

1. Other approaches to quality improvement, such as reengineering and ISO 9000, are discussed in later sections.

Reading 1

Exploring the Concepts Underlying Total Quality Management

By Harry Costin

The purpose of this paper is to offer a brief overview of the key concepts underlying the management approach that has come to be known as "Total Quality Management," or, until recently, as "Total Quality Control." The main themes of the quality literature will be presented in a historically significant sequence followed by an analysis of a few predominant models. Finally, suggestions will be offered for a conceptual enrichment of the field.

KEY TOTAL QUALITY MANAGEMENT CONCEPTS

Although there is no perfect consensus in terms of what all the key concepts of Total Quality Management are, the following themes pervade the literature (most of the following have been suggested by Marchese [1991] as core ideas of the TQM movement):

1. Excellence is ascribed to customer-driven organizations that systematically integrate customer feedback into their strategic planning and delivery of products and services.
2. Customer-driven organizations have a strong focus on quality, with quality being defined as both the measurable dimensions of products and services and the perceptions of internal and external customers.
3. Continuous improvement is the result of a focus on quality.
4. Improvement means making processes work better.
5. There is a strong need to extend the existing mind-set and shift to paradigms that see organizational and individual success as a result of collaboration rather than cutthroat competition.

6. Decisions should be data driven. Previous experience needs to be systematically documented and analyzed to achieve continuous improvement.
7. Teamwork is the practical application of "collaboration." In order to be effective, teams need to be trained in creative and analytical problem-solving techniques.
8. People should be empowered, i.e., have real input and decision-making power in job design and organizational policies that affect them.
9. Training and recognition are essential (according to Ishikawa TQM begins and ends with education).
10. A vision (what Senge has termed a "shared vision," which needs to be known and shared by all employees and managers) is the key to give any organization a unified direction and avoid wasteful duplication of efforts and infighting.
11. Organizational change is only possible through effective leadership by example. Empty promises and speeches only make existing problems worse.

Historical foundations

This management approach and theory has been strongly influenced by the ideas of a few American and Japanese scholars and practitioners. Among the most widely credited "founding fathers" of the so-called TQM (Total Quality Management) movement we find Feigenbaum, Deming, Juran, Crosby, Ishikawa, Kano, Imai, Mizuno, and others. The core concepts of TQM can be found in the writings of these thinkers, who have made a lasting contribution to management theory and practice worldwide.

The term "Total Quality Control" was first introduced by Armand Feigenbaum in the November–December 1956 issue of *Harvard Business Review.* His original exploration of what he referred to as a "way out of the dilemma imposed on businessmen by increasingly demanding customers and by ever-spiraling costs of quality, . . . a new kind of quality control, which might be called **total quality control**" already integrated some of the key concepts of what today is known as TQM. Quoting Feigenbaum, Ishikawa defined "total quality control" as

> an effective system for integrating the quality development, quality maintenance, and quality improvement efforts of the various groups in an organization so as to enable production and service at the most economic levels which allow for full customer satisfaction. (1985, 90)

Further, for Ishikawa "TQC requires participation of all divisions, including the divisions of marketing, design, manufacturing, inspection, and shipping." This integration was explained by Feigenbaum in the 1956 HBR article in the following terms:

> The underlying principle of this total quality view—and its basic difference from all other concepts—is that, to provide genuine effectiveness, control must start with the

> design of the product and end only when the product has been placed in the hands of a customer who remains satisfied.
>
> The reason for this breadth of scope is that the quality of any product is affected at many stages of the industrial cycle:
>
> 1. Marketing evaluates the level of quality customers want and for which they are willing to pay.
> 2. Engineering reduces this marketing evaluation to exact specifications.
> 3. Purchasing chooses, contracts with, and retains vendors for parts and materials.
> 4. Manufacturing engineering selects the jigs, tools, and processes for relay production.
> 5. Manufacturing supervision and shop operators exert a major quality influence during parts making, subassembly, and final assembly.
> 6. Mechanical inspection and functional test check conformance to specifications.
> 7. Shipping influences the caliber of the packaging and transportation.
>
> In other words, the determination both of quality and of quality costs actually takes place throughout the entire industrial cycle. This is the reason why real quality control cannot be accomplished by concentrating on inspection alone, or design alone, or reject trouble-shooting alone, or operator education alone, or statistical analysis alone—important as each of these individual elements is.
>
> The breadth of the job makes quality control a new and important business management function. Just as the theme of the historical inspection activity was "they (i.e., bad parts) shall not pass," the theme of this new approach is "make them right the first time." Emphasis is on defect prevention so that routine inspection will not be needed to as large an extent. The burden of quality proof rests, not with inspection, but with the makers of the part—machinist, assembly foreman, vendor, as the case may be. (1956, 94)

What Feigenbaum calls the "industrial cycle" was popularized in the business literature of the 1980s as "value chain" by Porter (1985). In hindsight, the principles expounded by Feigenbaum may not appear as revolutionary, since today they are part of mainstream thinking. But in an era obsessed by "control" and mass production using Frederick Taylor's management approach, they were.

Some of the key concepts that can be recognized in Feigenbaum's early writings and that have profoundly influenced the TQM movement are:

- To perceive the production process (and later, service delivery) as an integrated system that originates with the customer (what the customer wants) and ends with the customer (customer satisfaction).
- The need to redefine the role of the inspection function (defect prevention and line workers' responsibility for quality in order to reduce the need for inspection), the consequent reduction in costs of quality by building quality into the product ("quality by design"), and the usefulness of statistical quality tools (later to be known as "Statistical Process Control").

The idea of translating customer demands and needs and chosen quality levels into a product "by design" is the basic underlying concept of what is likely the second most widely used TQM process after SPC (Statistical Process Control): Quality Function Deployment, or QFD for short. This is a product or service design process using cross-functional teams that often include customers, marketing and purchasing representatives, and design and manufacturing engineers.

- To define quality as a management function. Deming and Juran elaborated further this concept assigning responsibility for quality to everybody in the organization.
- The important role of the purchasing function in the industrial cycle (or value chain). In modern industrial applications, companies implementing TQM programs favor the introduction of "vendor partnership programs" whereby the vendors commit to the delivery of consistent quality (e.g., implementing SPC processes), thus reducing the need for incoming inspection (Just-in-Time systems).

TQM as a management system

Dr. W. Edwards Deming, the best-known father of the Quality movement, is widely credited with extending the quality concerns to management practice as a whole rather than simply considering them a domain of action of "quality engineers." Two key concepts developed by Dr. Deming, management responsibility and intrinsic motivation of workers and their relationship to statistical process control, deserve attention:

> Competent men in every position, from top management to the humblest worker, if they are doing their best, know all there is to know about their work **except how to improve it**. Help toward improvement can come **only from some other kind of knowledge**. Help may come from outside the company, or from better use of knowledge and skills already within the company, or both. (1975, 6)

According to Dr. Deming, only management has the power to change "systems," which are responsible for 85 percent of all defects:

> Another roadblock is management's supposition that the production workers are responsible for all trouble: that there would be no problems in production or in service if only the workers would do their jobs in the way they were taught. Pleasant dreams. The workers are handicapped by the system.

Using statistical terminology, he makes further reference to management's responsibility in the reduction of variation:

> It is good management to reduce the variation of any quality characteristic. . . . Reduction in variation means greater uniformity and dependability of product, greater output per hour, greater output per unit of raw material, and better competitive position.
>
> Causes of variation and of high cost, with loss of competitive position, may be usefully subsumed under two categories:

- **Faults of the system (common or environmental causes) 85 percent:**
  These faults stay in the system until reduced by management. Their combined effect is usually easy to measure. Some individual causes must be isolated by judgment. Others may be identified by experiment: some by records on operations and materials suspected of being offenders.
- **Special causes 15 percent:**
  These causes are specific to a certain worker or to a machine. A statistical signal detects the existence of a special cause, which the worker can usually identify and correct. (1975, 6)

Statistical tools allow workers to keep the process in control, once management has provided them a system capable of running in control. Management's responsibility is to provide adequate training and to continuously strive to improve the existing systems. Supervision and inspection is thereby replaced by training and education.

Dr. Deming is also a firm believer in the workers' intrinsic motivation in a job well done. His "14 points" call for an "elimination of numerical quotas," and throughout his writings he further advocates the need for an educational system that from childhood fosters collaboration rather than competition.

An example of his clearly defined position on this issue can be found in his introduction to Peter Senge's book on the learning organization, *The Fifth Discipline:*

> The prevailing system of management has destroyed our people. People are born with intrinsic motivation, self-esteem, dignity, curiosity to learn, joy in learning. The forces of destruction begin with the toddlers—a prize for the best Halloween costume, grades in school, gold stars—and on up through the university. On the job, people teams, divisions are ranked—reward for the one at the top, punishment for the one at the bottom.

JURAN'S QUALITY TRILOGY

Dr. J. M. Juran, whose impact on the quality movement in Japan was second only to Deming's, developed a useful framework to what he referred to as "a universal thought process—a universal way of thinking about quality, which fits all functions, all levels, all product lines." He called it the "quality trilogy": (1986)

> The underlying concept of the quality trilogy is that managing for quality consists of three basic quality-oriented processes:
>
> - Quality planning
> - Quality control
> - Quality improvement
>
> The starting point is quality planning—creating a process that will be able to meet established goals and do so under operating conditions. . . . Following the planning, the process is turned over to the operating forces. Their responsibility is to run the process at optimal effectiveness [this includes corrective action] . . . the zone defined by the "quality control" limits.

Finally, quality improvement is "the process for breaking through to unprecedented levels of performance." But quality improvement

> does not happen of its own accord. It results from purposeful action taken by upper management to introduce a new managerial process into the system of managers' responsibilities—the quality improvement process. This quality improvement process is superimposed on the quality control process—a process implemented in addition to quality control, not instead of it.

Juran's approach is essentially the same as Deming's. Quality is a management responsibility that needs to be performed systematically to achieve "continuous improvement" (when it is performed over time).

This is the same basic idea behind the so-called PDCA or Shewhart cycle, known in Japan as the Deming cycle, considered to be the essence of the Japanese approach to Total Quality Control:

Plan: The basic planning process described by Juran.

Do: The implementation of the plan.

Check: Evaluation of performance according to critical measures.

Act: Quality improvement efforts based on the lessons learned from experience. These experiences feed into the new plan, since PDCA is a cyclical process.

Defining quality

One of the most widely used terms and concepts in the quality literature is, of course, **quality**. Definitions of quality range from narrowly defined, "primary operating characteristics" of a manufactured product (e.g., acceleration or cruising speed for a car) to customer-defined quality (emphasized as "core" definition of quality by most writers in the field, i.e., it is the customer who defines what quality is).

Ishikawa, one of the best known Japanese pioneers of the Quality movement, makes a distinction between a narrow and a broad definition of quality:

> Narrowly interpreted, quality means quality of product. Broadly interpreted, quality means quality of work, quality of service, quality of information, quality of process, quality of division, quality of people, including workers, engineers, managers, and executives, quality of system, quality of company, quality of objectives, etc. (1985, 45)

Garvin (1988) has identified eight dimensions or categories of quality that apply for the most part to manufactured products:

- *Performance* It refers to the primary operating characteristics of a product (like clarity, color, and the ability to receive distant stations on a color television set).
- *Features* The "bells and whistles" of a product (like a remote control for the television set).

- *Reliability* The probability of a product's malfunctioning or failing within a specific period of time.
- *Conformance* The degree to which a product's design and operating characteristics meet pre-established standards (a definition of quality often used by Phil Crosby, one of the best known U.S. "quality gurus").
- *Durability* A measure of product life that has both economic and technical dimensions.
- *Serviceability* The speed, courtesy, competence, and ease of repair. Attempts have been made to identify "measurable" characteristics of serviceability (like speed of response) as opposed to the more elusive elements of customer satisfaction.
- *Aesthetics* A user-defined, subjective set of attributes, based on individual preferences, of a product—how a product looks, feels, sounds, tastes, or smells according to the customer.
- *Perceived quality* "Consumers do not always possess complete information about a product or a service's attributes. Frequently, indirect measures are the only basis for comparing brands. A product's durability, for example, can seldom be observed directly; it usually must be inferred from various tangible and intangible aspects of a product."

Juran defined quality as "fitness to use," i.e., the users of a product or service should be able to count on it for what they needed or wanted to do with it (March 1986). He further identifies five dimensions of fitness for use: quality of design, quality of conformance, availability, safety, and field use.

A narrower approach to defining quality is used by Crosby:

> Requirements must be clearly stated so that they cannot be misunderstood. Measurements are then taken continually to determine conformance to those requirements. The nonconformance detected is the absence of quality. Quality problems become nonconformance problems; and quality becomes definable. . . . If a Cadillac conforms to all the requirements of a Cadillac, then it is a quality car. If a Pinto conforms to all the requirements of a Pinto, then it is a quality car. Luxury or its absence is spelled out in specific requirements, such as carpeting or rubber mats. (1980, 15)

Crosby also popularized the concept of "zero defects," a further definition of quality to be found in the literature, and the ultimate goal of quality improvement efforts. "Zero defects" were to be achieved through prevention rather than after-the-fact inspection.

It is evident from these definitions, that most of them refer to tangible manufactured products. Definitions of service quality have been mostly derived from definitions of product quality, with specific emphasis on measurable attributes and the translation of vague customer-based notions of service quality into terms that can be expressed through sophisticated instruments of market research, like scales of customer satisfaction that compare consumer perceptions of competing products.

Even though specific attempts are made to render quality measurable, it is ultimately the customer who defines what it is and what it is not. In the TQM literature, the concept of customer embraces both the "internal" and the "external" customers. Internal customers are the next process in the manufacturing or service delivery value-added chain. External customers include the end user (the "key" customer), suppliers, and even society at large. Many uses of the word "customer" in the TQM literature make us think of the concept of "stakeholders," commonly found in the management policy literature. In a broad sense, customers are all those affected by what we do.

Evolution of the quality movement

The evolution of quality concepts, including the development of the concept of quality from a narrowly defined set of product attributes to the nearly all-embracing modern definitions of quality, is closely related to the different eras of the modern quality movement.

Garvin has attempted to map the evolution of the quality movement in the United States and described it in terms of four distinct "quality eras": inspection, statistical quality control, quality assurance, and strategic quality management.

The first stage, the introduction of formal inspection in the industrial process, was the necessary consequence of mass production in the early nineteenth century, while the second stage, Quality Control, can be traced back to the early twentieth century:

> Inspection activities were linked more formally to quality control in 1922 with the publication of G. S. Radford's *The Control of Quality in Manufacturing*. For the first time quality was viewed as a distinct management responsibility and as an independent function. (1988, 5)

During the Quality Control era the essential mathematical and statistical tools of the quality movement were developed. These included the Shewhart cycle and analysis of variability, statistical sampling techniques, and Statistical Process Control (SPC). SPC was used extensively during WWII with phenomenal results (this is one of the reasons why it was so well received in Japan in the 1950s) but came into disuse after the war ended.

The third era, Quality Assurance, includes, according to Garvin, the Total Quality Control approach initiated by Feigenbaum:

> During the period of quality assurance, quality evolved from a narrow, manufacturing-based discipline to one with broader implication for management. Problem prevention remained the primary goal, but the profession's tools expanded far beyond statistics. Four separate elements were involved: quantifying the costs of quality, total quality control, reliability engineering, and zero defects. (12)

The fourth era, Strategic Quality Management, implies a new emerging "vision":

> It embodies a dramatic shift in perspective. For the first time, top managers at the levels of the presidents and chief executive officers have expressed an interest in quality. They have linked it with profitability, defined it from the customer's point of view, and required its inclusion in the strategic planning process. In the most radical departure of all, many have insisted that quality be viewed as an aggressive competitive weapon. (21)

This author disagrees with Garvin's contention that this is new, at least conceptually. Garvin's description adequately defines the key elements of the modern Total Quality Management movement, but the basic underlying concepts can be traced back to the original writings of the founders of the movement, including Deming, Feigenbaum, and Juran. Nevertheless, it is true that the implementation of the strategic perspective to quality is recent, particularly the integration of quality principles and strategic planning in the United States. In Japan, this integration began in 1962 at Bridgestone Tire (Akao 1991) and is known as **Hoshin Kanri** or "Policy Deployment."

Another interpretation of the role of the quality movement in the context of management and organizational theory has been advanced by Senge (1992):

> I believe that the quality movement as we have known it up to now in the United States is in fact the first wave in building "learning organizations"—organizations that continually expand their ability to shape the future.
>
> The roots of the quality movement lie in assumptions about people, organizations, and management that have one unifying theme: to make continual learning a way of organizational life, especially improving the performance of the organization as a total system. This can only be achieved by breaking with the traditional authoritarian command and control hierarchy where the top thinks and the local acts to merge thinking and acting at all levels.
>
> This represents a profound re-orientation in the concerns of management—a shift from a predominant concern with controlling to a predominant concern with learning.

Senge further recognizes three waves in the evolution of learning organizations. While the United States is in the first wave (the quality movement as we have known it), Japan has moved on to the second:

> In the first wave, the primary focus of change was frontline workers. Management's job was to
>
> - Champion continual improvement.
> - Remove impediments (like quality control experts and unnecessary bureaucracy) that disempowered local personnel.
> - Support new practices like quality training and competitive benchmarking that drive process improvement.
>
> In the second wave, the focus shifts from improving work processes to improving how we work—fostering ways of thinking and interacting conducive to continual learning about the dynamic, complex, conflictual issues that determine systemwide performance. In the second wave, the primary focus of change is the managers themselves.

> The third wave of quality . . . These two ways of thinking will, I believe, gradually merge into a third, in which learning becomes "institutionalized" as an inescapable way of life for managers and workers alike (if we even bother maintaining that distinction).

Senge's analysis is useful to understand potential conceptual shortcomings of existing TQM models and possible ways to enrich them. We will explore three models that are representative of current approaches to Total Quality Management: the TQM Wheel Model, the Baldrige Award Criteria, and the European Model for Quality.

Exhibit 1.1 *The GOAL/QPC TQM wheel model*

The Total Quality Management Wheel, shown on page 17, was developed by GOAL/QPC as a holistic model to illustrate the elements of TQM. It depicts the orientation of TQM—customers—and the interrelationship among systems, people, and tools within an organization implementing TQM.

Looking at the top of the wheel, unit optimization is used to describe the "who, what, and how" of daily management. The term encompasses the concept of continuous improvement, the individuals and teams who are involved, and the methods or tools that can be used most effectively. Unit optimization is typically the first phase of TQM implementation, and it refers to the identification, measurement, improvement, and standardization of the processes that make up daily work. This initial step, often summarized by the Deming or Shewhart Cycle (Plan-Do-Check-Act), involves a variety of individuals, working singly and in teams, in using the Seven Basic Quality Control tools to manage their day-to-day responsibilities.

Moving clockwise on the wheel, the TQM practitioner next focuses on the vertical alignment phase of TQM implementation. Vertical alignment is a term used to describe the "who, what, and how" of Hoshin Planning. Hoshin Planning is a method used to ensure that the mission, vision, goals, and annual objectives of an organization are communicated to and implemented by everyone, from the executive level to the "frontline" level. Senior managers use the Seven Management and Planning Tools to facilitate the sharing of critical information among all members of the organization and to assist in the organizational planning process.

After making gains in Daily Management and Hoshin Planning, senior managers generally face the need for Cross-Functional Management, which requires an integration of quality improvement efforts across the functional areas of an organization. Top-level managers use the advanced TQM tool Quality Function Deployment (QFD) to elicit the involvement of customer/supplier teams. QFD is a method for integrating the "voice of the customer" into the design of services, and provides the means to analyze and prioritize customer demands. QFD clarifies the actions that are most important to meeting or exceeding customer demands. QFD may also be used at earlier stages of implementation as needed. Additionally, managers use a variety of audit tools to assess how well the organization has incorporated TQM principles and broken down departmental barriers. Strategic information systems can be helpful at this phase to integrate all useful data in the effort to improve quality, cost, delivery, and employee morale.

THE TQM WHEEL MODEL

The Wheel Model (Exhibit 1.1) was developed by researchers of GOAL/QPC, a leading research and publishing organization in the field of Total Quality with significant input from representatives of large organizations implementing TQM, like GM, Ford, and Hewlett Packard. It represents a systematic effort to integrate all dimensions and processes of TQM around a "Customer-Driven Master Plan" (Moran et al., 1991):

> The Customer-Driven Total Quality Master Plan begins by involving all employees in an organization with the identification of their customers' needs. . . . Total Quality Management begins with a long-term plan (commitment) rooted in the organization's customers. This plan emphasizes thorough understanding of the customers and their needs along with continual improvement of customer satisfaction.

EXHIBIT 1.1 ***(continued)***

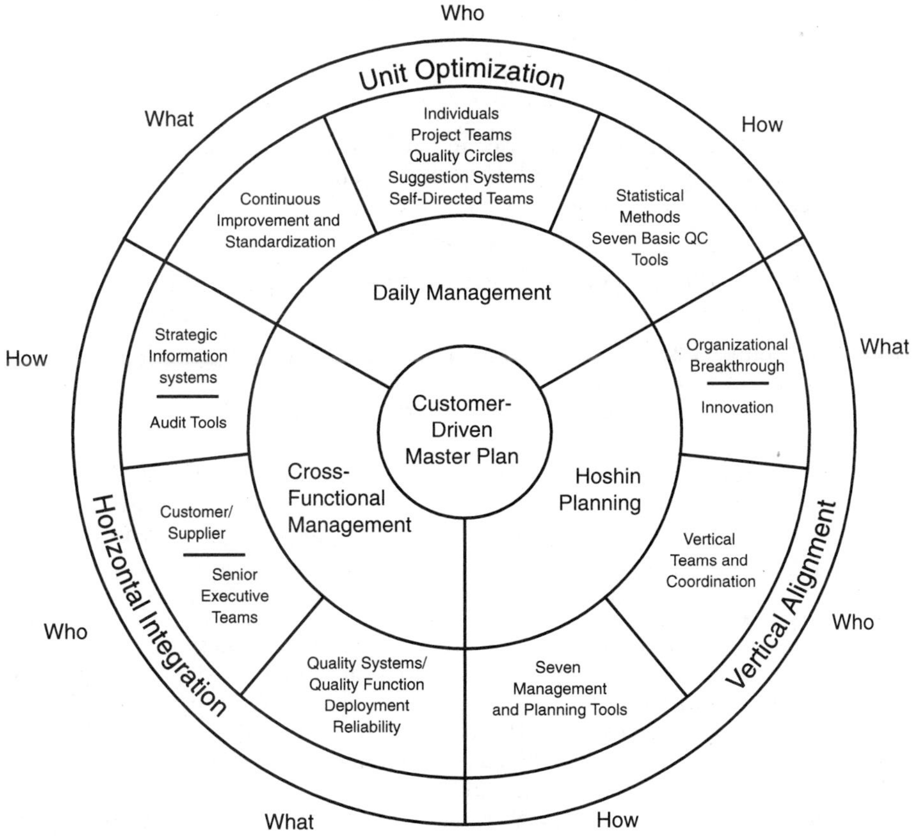

SOURCE: GOAL/QPC TQM in Health Care Research Report, 1992.

The implementation of the plan occurs along three dimensions or Macro-processes: Daily Management (elsewhere called a "bottom-up" approach), Cross-Functional Management ("side-by-side"), and Hoshin Planning ("top-down").

Most references made to Total Quality (e.g., Statistical Process Control and Quality Circles) relate to Daily Management (e.g., Kaizen = continuous improvement). Its purpose is the implementation of a daily control, continuous improvement, and standardization system of best practices with the direct involvement of line workers working as teams under the "coaching" of their supervisors, or as self-directed teams. Daily Management involves the identification of critical processes and the use of systematic data collection and group problem-solving methods (definition of key indicators and use of the 7 QC = "Quality Control" tools to do root cause analysis).

The second key element of the wheel model is "Cross-Functional Management":

> Whether establishing a Customer-Driven Master Plan, a Daily Management system, or Hoshin Planning, all require horizontal integration of many persons and teams. This integration across the organization is known as Cross-Functional Management.

Cross-Functional Teams have different roles:

> Teams may establish organization-wide quality systems. Another cross-functional system, Quality Function Deployment, helps the organization utilize customer and competitive data in planning the best possible products and services.

Quality Function Deployment (QFD) has been widely hailed for reducing new product introduction time, translating customer requirements into actual products, and promoting a dialogue among suppliers, design and manufacturing engineers, and marketing analysts. After SPC and the different types of quality teams (e.g., Quality Circles and Quality Improvement Teams), it is the most popular implementation of the TQM processes.

The third element of the model is Hoshin Planning, a strategy planning and implementation process only recently introduced in large U.S. organizations, like FP&L and Hewlett Packard, but in existence in Japan since the 1970s and pioneered by Bridgestone Tire in 1962:

> When the magnitude of a needed process improvement is widespread and permeates the entire organization, a Daily Management system may not be sufficient to bring about the needed major improvement. In this case, a 'breakthrough' planning system may be needed. One such system, Hoshin Planning is defined as a policy management system. . . . Hoshin Planning is directed by top management but may involve teams throughout the organization. . . . The Hoshin Planning system focuses the energy of the entire organization on achieving a major improvement in a specific area of critical importance. The improvement may be needed to ensure long-term competitiveness or even the survival of the organization.

THE MALCOLM BALDRIGE AWARD

A second model, which in this case defines "excellence" in terms of overall quality of an organization (in terms similar to Ishikawa's broad definition of quality), can be found in the guidelines of the Malcolm Baldrige Award. These guidelines are being used extensively by organizations trying to understand and implement "quality" as a key internal driving force to achieve competitive advantage.

The Baldrige Award defines core values and concepts—a "framework" or model establishing the relationships between the "driver, system, goal, and measures of progress"—and an implicit hierarchy of priorities and values (points assigned to each category of the award, which add to a total of 1,000).

The guidelines recognize explicitly the following core values and concepts:

Customer-Driven Quality Quality is judged by the customer. All product and service attributes that contribute value and lead to customer satisfaction and preference must be the foundation for a company's quality system. . . . Customer-driven quality is thus a strategic concept.

Leadership A company's senior leaders must create clear and visible quality values and high expectations. Reinforcement of the values and expectations requires their substantial personal commitment and involvement. The leaders' basic values and commitment need to include areas of public responsibility and corporate citizenship. The leaders must take part in the creation of strategies, systems, and methods for achieving excellence.

Continuous Improvement Achieving the highest levels of quality and competitiveness requires a well-defined and well-executed approach to continuous improvement. The term "continuous improvement" refers to both incremental and "breakthrough" improvement. A focus on improvement needs to be part of all operations and of all work unit activities of a company.

Employee Participation and Development A company's success in meeting its quality and performance objectives depends increasingly on work force quality and involvement. The close link between employee satisfaction and customer satisfaction creates a "shared fate" relationship between companies and employees. For this reason, employee satisfaction measurement provides an important indicator of the company's efforts to improve customer satisfaction and operating performance. . . . Companies need to invest in the development of the work force and to seek new avenues to involve employees in problem solving and decision making.

Fast Response Success in competitive markets increasingly demands ever-shorter cycles for a new or improved product and service introduction. Also, faster and more flexible response to customers is now a more critical requirement of business management.

Design Quality and Prevention Quality systems should place strong emphasis on design quality—problem and waste prevention achieved through building quality into products and services and into the processes through which they are produced.

Long-Range Outlook Achieving quality and market leadership requires a company to have a strong future orientation and a willingness to make long-term commitments to customers, employees, suppliers, stockholders, and the community.

Management by Fact Pursuit of quality and operational performance goals of the company requires that process management be based upon reliable information, data, and analysis. Facts and data needed for quality improvement and quality assessment are of many types, including: customer, product and service performance, operations, market, competitive comparisons, supplier, employee-related, and cost and financial.

Partnership Development Companies should seek to build internal and external partnerships to better accomplish their overall goals. Internal partnerships might include those that promote labor-management cooperation such as agreements

EXHIBIT 1.2 ***Baldrige Award criteria framework***

The framework has four basic elements:

Driver
Senior executive leadership creates the values, goals, and systems, and guides the sustained pursuit of customer value and company performance improvement.

System
System comprises the set of well-defined and well-designed processes for meeting the company's customer, quality, and performance requirements.

Measures of Progress
Measures of progress provide a results-oriented basis for channeling actions to delivering ever-improving customer value and company performance.

Goal
The basic aim of the quality process is the delivery of ever-improving value to customers.

The seven Criteria categories shown in the figure are subdivided into Examination Items and Areas to Address. These are described on page 21.

Examination Items
There are a total of 28 Examination Items in the seven Examination Categories. Each Item focuses on a major quality system requirement. All information submitted by applicants is in response to the Item requirements. Item titles and Examination point values are given on page 22.

Areas to Address
Each Examination Item includes a set of Areas to Address (Areas). The Areas serve to illustrate and clarify the intent of the Items and to place emphasis on the types and amounts of information the applicant should provide. Areas are not assigned individual point values, because their relative importance depends upon factors such as the applicant's type and size of business and quality system.

with unions. . . . Examples of external partnerships include those with customers, suppliers, and education organizations.

Corporate Responsibility and Citizenship A company's customer requirements and quality system objectives should address corporate responsibility and citizenship. Corporate responsibility refers to basic expectations of the company—business ethics and protection of public health, public safety, and the environment. . . . Corporate citizenship refers to leadership and support—within reasonable limits of a company's resources—of publicly important purposes. . . . Such purposes might include education, resource conservation, community services, improving industry and business practices, and sharing of nonproprietary quality-related information.

These core values and concepts are embodied in the seven categories integrated in the Baldrige Award Criteria Framework (Exhibit 1.2), which is the quality model of the award:

Exhibit 1.2 ***(continued)***

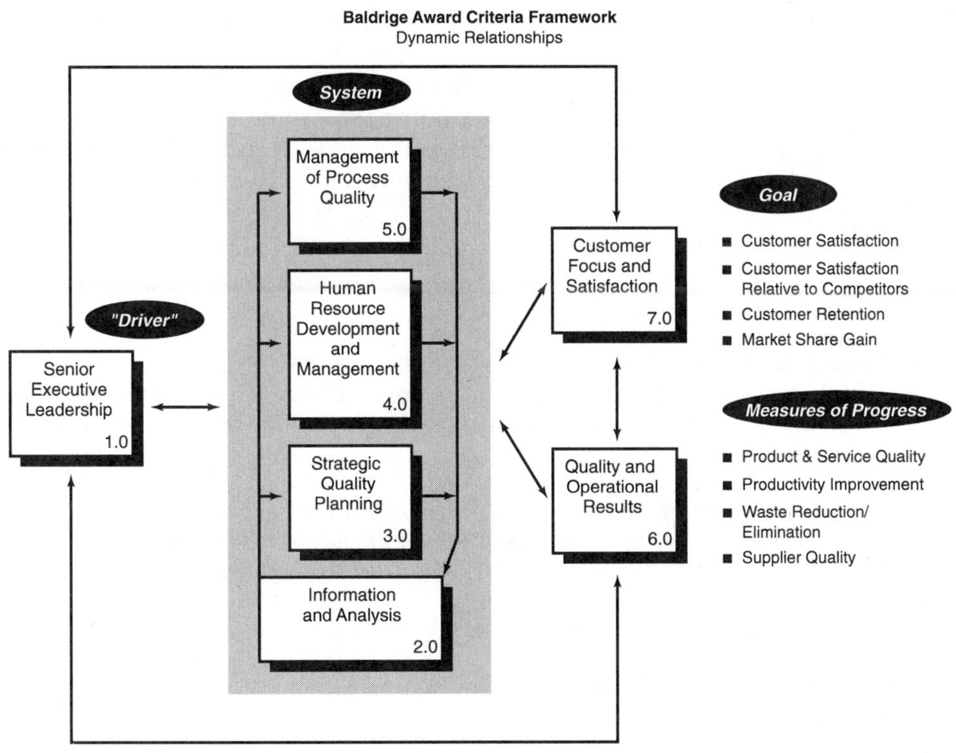

Source: U.S. Department of Commerce.

1.0	Leadership	95 points
2.0	Information and Analysis	75 points
3.0	Strategic Quality Planning	60 points
4.0	Human Resource Development and Management	150 points
5.0	Management of Process Quality	140 points
6.0	Quality and Operational Results	180 points
7.0	Customer Focus and Satisfaction	300 points
		1,000 points

The relative number of points assigned to each category establishes a hierarchy of importance of "quality values." It is to be noted that the category with the strongest weight is "Customer Focus and Satisfaction," the key principle to be found throughout the quality literature.

THE EUROPEAN QUALITY AWARD

Based on both the Deming and Baldrige Awards, the European Community, under the auspices of the Commission and the European Foundation for Quality Management, have recently instituted The European Quality Award, which was awarded for the first time in October 1992 to companies demonstrating excellence in the implementation of Total Quality Management.

The European model, which "was developed as a framework for the European Quality Award, jointly sponsored by the European Commission, the European Foundation for Quality Management, and the European Organization for Quality" (Exhibit 1.3) has nine elements that link "enablers" with "results":

> Processes are the means by which the organization harnesses and releases the talents of its people to produce results. In other words, the processes and the people are the ENABLERS, which provide RESULTS.
>
> **Customer Satisfaction, People (employee) Satisfaction,** and **Impact on Society** are achieved through **Leadership,** which drives **Policy and Strategy, People Management, Resources**, and **Processes** leading ultimately to excellence in **Business Results.**
>
> Each of the nine elements shown in the model is a criterion that can be used to appraise the organization's progress towards Total Quality Management.
>
> The Results aspects are concerned with **what** the organization has achieved and is achieving.
>
> The Enablers are concerned with how results are being achieved.

A particular feature of the model is also the integration of "Impact on Society" as one of the nine elements:

> In the 1990s it is vital that the organization achieves positive results in terms of the community at large. The criterion "Impact on Society" is included in the Model for this reason.

Exhibit 1.3 *The European model for quality*

The European Model

Processes are the means by which the organization harnesses and releases the talents of its people to produce results. In other words, the processes and the people are the ENABLERS, which provide the RESULTS.

Expressed graphically, the principle looks like this:

This model was developed as a framework for The European Quality Award, jointly sponsored by the European Commission, the European Foundation for Quality Management, and the European Organization for Quality. Essentially the model tells us that:

Customer Satisfaction, People (employee) Satisfaction, and *Impact on Society** are achieved through *Leadership* which drives
Policy and Strategy, People Management, Resources, and *Processes* leading ultimately to excellence in *Business Results.*

Each of the nine elements shown in the model is a criterion that can be used to appraise the organization's progress toward Total Quality Management.

The Results aspects are concerned with *what* the organization has achieved and is achieving.

The Enablers aspects are concerned with *how* results are being achieved.

The objective of a comprehensive quality management self-appraisal and self-improvement program is to regularly review each of these nine criteria and, thereafter, to adopt relevant improvement strategies.

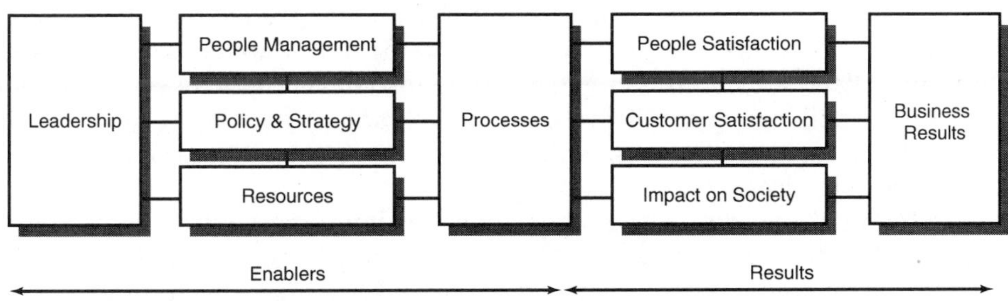

Notes:

*In the 1990s it is vital that the organization achieves positive results in terms of the community at large. The criterion "Impact on Society" is included in the model for this reason.

Source: European Foundation for Quality Management.

This element includes explicitly an environmental dimension, "the organization's approach to quality of life, the environment, and . . . the preservation of global resources," a consideration largely absent in U.S. quality definitions and models.

Opportunities for conceptual enrichment and model building

This paper has explored some of the predominant concepts and models of the quality literature. Many of these concepts are key to rethinking the role of management in the 1990s and understand opportunities for cooperative relationships between management and labor, and businesses and society at large.

As the field evolves, the need for further conceptual clarity and model building becomes evident. In most of the current literature, the following conceptual shortcomings, or rather "opportunities for improvement" by building on paradigms of other fields, can be found:

1. The underlying concept of **organization** is not clearly defined. From a point of view of organizational theory, the organization seems largely conceived as a rational unitary decision maker (organizations that succeed or fail) or as a series of interlocking teams (management team, teams of workers, etc.). What is absent is any systematic exploration of the concept of "informal organization" and its implications for the decision-making process. This key concept was already analyzed by Barnard in the 1940s.

   Network theories of organizations would provide useful insights as the quality literature insists on the need to build networks between suppliers, customers, companies, educational institutions, etc. Applications of TQM, like Just-in-Time, are built on the assumption of efficiently working networks.

2. A second perspective largely absent in the literature are political views of organizations. It is insisted (e.g., Baldrige Award) that Management and Labor should collaborate, but the simple insistence on collaboration does not provide adequate guidance to conflict resolution. U.S. unions have been suspicious of TQM implementation efforts, which they have seen as a clear threat to establish labor practices.

   If TQM fails to acknowledge the political realities of organizations and of its models to integrate political concepts, it will continue to provide weak guidelines for implementation in turbulent industrial environments or times of economic distress. Political views of organizations begin addressing questions of values, power, and legitimacy, and at the implementation level, the basic concern expressed by Pfeffer and Salancick in their landmark study on *The External Control of Organizations* (1978): What matters more to organizational success—**efficiency** (largely embraced by the quality definitions) or **effectiveness** (the political maneuvers to co-opt collaboration and resources from the external environment)?

3. One of the key contributions of the writings of quality gurus like Deming and Ishikawa may also constitute one of the potential shortcomings of the literature—

the normative approach to management theory of these writings, i.e., the insistence on value-driven management practices (empowerment, teamwork, and so on). The attempt to construct organizational reality may lead to ignoring reality as it is, a key problem during implementation of TQM programs. We are reminded of Mintzberg (1973), who decided to research what managers "actually do" rather than "what they are supposed to do." The richness of well-designed case analysis may be a prerequisite to design the value-driven organizations hailed in the quality literature.

CONCLUSION

The concepts on which Total Quality thinking is based imply basic values of respect for the individual and a sense of social responsibility. Efficiency is seen as a natural result of our intrinsic motivation and desire to learn. Continuous improvement based on collaboration is a never ending process to be extended to all facets of individual life and societal action.

It is the responsibility of all to make these noble desires a reality, but this can only be achieved through the clear understanding of the complexities inherent in the activities of individuals, groups, and organizations and their interactions in society at large.

Bibliography

Akao, Yoki, ed. *Hoshin Kanri: Policy Deployment for Successful TQM.* Cambridge, MA: Productivity Press, 1991.

Akao, Yoki, ed. *Quality Function Deployment: Integrating Customer Requirements into Product Design.* Cambridge, MA: Productivity Press, 1990.

Barnard, Chester. *The Functions of the Executive.* Cambridge, MA: Harvard University Press, 1968.

Crosby, Philip. *Quality Is Free.* New York, NY: Mentor Books, 1980.

Deming, W. Edwards. "On some Statistical Aids Toward Economic Production." *Interfaces.* Vol. 3, N. 4, August 1975.

Deming, W. Edwards. *Out of the Crisis.* Cambridge, MA: MIT Press, 1982.

U.S. Department of Commerce. *Malcolm Baldrige National Quality Award: 1993 Award Criteria.*

Dertouzos, et al. *Made in America.* Cambridge, MA: MIT Press, 1989.

Ernst & Young and American Quality Foundation. *International Quality Study.* 1991.

European Foundation for Quality Management. *Total Quality Management: The European Model for Self-Appraisal 1992.* Eindhoven, Netherlands, 1992.

Feigenbaum, Armand V. "Total Quality Control." *Harvard Business Review.* Nov.–Dec. 1956, Vol. 34, N. 6.

Feigenbaum, Armand. "Total Quality Control & Customer Satisfaction." *Performance Management.* Fall/Winter, 1984.

Hosotani, Katsuya. *Japanese Quality Concepts: An Overview.* New York, NY: Quality Resources, 1992.

Ishikawa, Kaoru. *What Is Total Quality Management: The Japanese Way.* Englewood Cliffs, NJ: Prentice Hall, 1985.

Juran, J. M. "The Quality Trilogy," *Quality Progress.* August 1986, pp. 19–24.

King, Bob. *Better Designs in Half the Time: Implementing QFD in America.* Methien, MA: GOAL QPC, 1989.

Marchese, Ted. "TQM Reaches the Academy," *American Association for Higher Education Bulletin.* November 1991, pp. 13–18.

Mizuno, Shigeru, ed. *Management for Quality Improvement: The Seven New QC Tools.* Cambridge, MA: Productivity Press, 1988.

March, Artemis. "A Note on Quality: The Views of Deming, Juran and Crosby." Note 9.687-011. Harvard Business School. Cambridge, MA, 1986.

Mintzberg, Henry. *The Nature of Managerial Work.* New York, NY: Harper & Row, 1973.

Moran, Jack, et al. *Daily Management.* Methuen, MA: GOAL QPC, 1990.

Morgan, Gareth. *Images of Organization.* Newbury Park, CA: Sage Publications, 1986.

Neave, Henry R. *The Deming Dimension.* Knoxville, TN: SPC Press, 1990.

Nemoto, Masao. *Total Quality Control for Management: Strategies and Techniques from Toyota and Toyoda Gosei.* Englewood Cliffs, NJ: Prentice Hall, 1987.

Perrow, Charles. *Complex Organizations.* 3rd Ed. New York, NY: Random House, 1986.

Pfeffer, Jeffrey, and Gerald Salanzick. *The External Control of Organizations.* New York, NY: Harper & Row, 1978.

Porter, Michael. *Competitive Advantage: Creating and Sustaining Superior Performance.* New York, NY: The Free Press, 1985.

Reich, Robert B. *Tales of a New America.* New York, NY: Times Books, 1987.

Schoenberger, Richard J. "Is Strategy Strategic? Impact of Total Quality Management on Strategy," *The Executive.* Vol. VI, N. 3, August 1992.

Senge, Peter M. *The Fifth Discipline: The Art and Practice of the Learning Organization.* New York, NY: Doubleday Currency, 1990.

Senge, Peter. "Building Learning Organizations," *Journal for Quality and Participation.* March 1992.

Smircich, Linda, et al., eds. "New Intellectual Currents in Organization and Management Theory." Theory Development Forum. Special Issue. *Academy of Management Review.* Vol. 17, N. 3, July 1992.

Thompson, James. *Organizations in Action.* New York, NY: McGraw-Hill, 1967.

Young, S. Mark. "A Framework for Successful Adoption and Performance of Japanese Manufacturing Practices in the United States," *Academy of Management Review* Vol. 17, N. 4, October 1992, pp. 647–676.

Reading 2

History and Evolution of the Quality Movement

BY DAVID A. GARVIN

As a concept, quality has been with us for millennia. Only recently has it emerged as a formal management function. The discipline is still evolving. In its original form, it was reactive and inspection-oriented; today, quality-related activities have broadened and are seen as essential for strategic success. Once the exclusive province of manufacturing and operations departments, quality now embraces functions as diverse as purchasing, engineering, and marketing research, and commands the attention of chief executive officers.

How have these changes come about? Most modern approaches to quality have emerged gradually, arriving through steady evolution rather than dramatic breakthroughs. They are the product of a series of discoveries stretching back over a century. In the United States, these discoveries can be organized into four distinct "quality eras": inspection, statistical quality control, quality assurance, and strategic quality management.[1]

THE RISE OF INSPECTION

In the eighteenth and nineteenth centuries, quality control as we know it today did not yet exist. Most manufacturing was performed by artisans and skilled craftsmen or by journeymen and apprentices who were supervised by masters at the trade.[2] Goods were produced in small volumes; parts were matched to one another by hand, and after-the-fact inspection to ensure high quality was conducted informally, if at all. A well-performing product was viewed as the natural outgrowth of reliance on skilled tradesmen for all aspects of design, manufacturing, and service.[3]

Formal inspection became necessary only with the rise of mass production and the need for interchangeable parts. As volumes increased, parts could no longer be fitted to one another by hand: The process required a large pool of skilled labor and was both costly and time-consuming. Prices were often beyond the reach of the average consumer, especially for machinery and equipment. Nor was the federal government able to purchase large quantities of high-quality firearms at low cost.

These pressures gave rise to what has been called the American system of manufacturing: the use of special-purpose machinery to produce interchangeable parts by following a preestablished sequence of operations.[4] Most initial efforts were connected with the military's demand for armaments and were closely coordinated by the United States Ordnance Department, the national armory at Springfield, Massachusetts, and the Harpers Ferry Armory. In consumer products, the Singer Company, which manufactured sewing machines, and the McCormick Harvesting Company, which made farm equipment, later adopted the same techniques.

From a quality control standpoint, the key breakthrough was the development of a rational jig, fixture, and gauging system in the early 1800s.[5] Jigs and fixtures are devices that position tools or hold parts while they are being worked on, keeping them fixed to the equipment so that machining operations can be performed accurately and precisely. Since every part that is worked on is held in place in exactly the same way—all jigs and fixtures having been designed from a standard model of the product to be manufactured—a high degree of interchangeability is assured. Nevertheless, parts may still deviate from one another: They may have been mounted improperly during machining, built from imperfect raw materials, or made on worn tooling. To minimize problems at final assembly, when parts are matched together for the first time, accurate inspection is required during the process of manufacture. A system of gauges is often used for that purpose; like jigs and fixtures, gauges are based on a standard model of the product to ensure uniformity.

By 1819, an elaborate gauging system was in place at the Springfield Armory. It gave inspection a new respectability, for activities that were previously conducted by eye were replaced by a more objective, verifiable process.[6] Two inspectors using a gauge were much more likely to reach the same result than two who were relying on personal judgment alone.

As the American system of manufacturing matured, gauging became more refined, and inspection became even more important. In the early 1900s, Frederick W. Taylor, the father of "scientific management," gave the activity added legitimacy by singling it out as an assigned task for one of the eight functional bosses (foremen) required for effective shop management:

> The inspector is responsible for the quality of the work, and both the workmen and the speed bosses [who see that the proper cutting tools are used, that the work is properly driven, and that cuts are started in the right part of the piece] must see that the work is

finished to suit him. This man can, of course, do his work best if he is a master of the art of finishing work both well and quickly.[7]

Inspection activities were linked more formally to quality control in 1922, with the publication of G. S. Radford's *The Control of Quality in Manufacturing*.[8] For the first time, quality was viewed as a distinct management responsibility and as an independent function. The book even touched on a number of principles regarded as central to modern-day quality control: the need to get designers involved early in quality activities, the need for close coordination among the various departments affecting quality, and the association of quality improvement with increased output and lower costs. Its primary focus, however, was inspection. Nine of the book's twenty-three chapters were devoted to that subject alone. Topics included the purpose of inspection (to "exercise the duty of viewing the work closely and critically so as to ascertain the quality, detect the errors, and present them to the attention of the proper persons in such a way as to have the work brought up to standard")[9]; the evolution of inspection (from visual to dimensional checks); types of inspection (material, office, tool, and process); sampling methods (including 100 percent and random sampling, but without any statistical foundation); gauging techniques; and the organization of the inspection department. Throughout, the emphasis was on conformance and its link with inspection; according to Radford, the purchaser's "principal interest in quality [was] that evenness or uniformity which results when the manufacturer adheres to his established requirements."[10]

Here matters stood for several years. Quality control was limited to inspection and to such narrow activities as counting, grading, and repair. Troubleshooting was considered beyond the reach of the average inspection department.[11] In the next decade, however, the role of the quality professional would be redefined. The stimulus for change was research conducted at Bell Telephone Laboratories; the result was what is today called statistical quality control.

STATISTICAL QUALITY CONTROL

The year 1931 marked a watershed for the quality movement. W. A. Shewhart's *Economic Control of Quality of Manufactured Product* was published that year, giving the discipline a scientific footing for the first time.[12] Much of modern-day quality control can be traced to that single volume. In it, Shewhart gave a precise and measurable definition of manufacturing control, developed powerful techniques for monitoring and evaluating day-to-day production, and suggested a variety of ways of improving quality.

Shewhart was in fact part of a larger group at Bell Telephone Laboratories that was investigating problems of quality. The group's research was prompted by the concerns of engineers at Western Electric, the manufacturing arm of the Bell System, who were seeking greater standardization and uniformity in the nationwide telephone network. Most attention was focused on the complex equipment being built at the company's Hawthorn Works. How, the engineers wondered, could the maximum amount of information about the quality of these units be extracted from the minimum amount of inspection data? And how should that data be presented? In 1924, an Inspection Engineering Department was established at Western Electric to address such questions; it later became the Quality Assurance Department of Bell Laboratories. The group, which included such luminaries as Shewhart, Harold Dodge, Harry Romig, G. D. Edwards, and later Joseph Juran, was largely responsible for creating the present-day discipline of statistical quality control.[13]

Process control

The initial breakthrough was Shewhart's. He was the first to recognize that variability was a fact of industrial life and that it could be understood using the principles of probability and statistics. Shewhart observed that no two parts were likely to be manufactured to precisely the same specifications. Raw materials, operator skills, and equipment would all vary to some degree. Even the same part produced by a single operator on a single machine was likely to show variation over time. From a management standpoint, this required a rethinking of the problem of quality. The issue was no longer the existence of variation—it was certain to continue at some level no matter what actions were taken—but how to distinguish acceptable variation from fluctuations that indicated trouble.

The entire analysis grew out of Shewhart's concept of statistical control:

> A phenomenon will be said to be controlled when, through the use of past experience, we can predict, at least within limits, how the phenomenon may be expected to vary in the future. Here it is understood that prediction means that we can state, at least approximately, the probability that the observed phenomenon will fall within the given limits.[14]

Shewhart then developed simple statistical techniques for determining these limits, as well as graphic methods for plotting production values to assess whether they fell within the acceptable range. The result, the process control chart illustrated in Figure 2.1, is one of the most powerful tools used by today's quality professionals.[15] By segregating abnormal (assignable) causes of variation from those that are inherent in a production process, it ensures that genuine problems are distinguished from those due purely to chance. Moreover, it does so by drawing samples of output during the course of production, rather than waiting until after a unit has been fully assembled.

At the same time that Shewhart was pursuing his work on process control, other researchers at Bell Laboratories were advancing the practice of sampling, the second critical element in the growth of statistical quality control. Harold Dodge and Harry Romig were the prime movers in this effort.

FIGURE 2.1 *A typical process control chart*

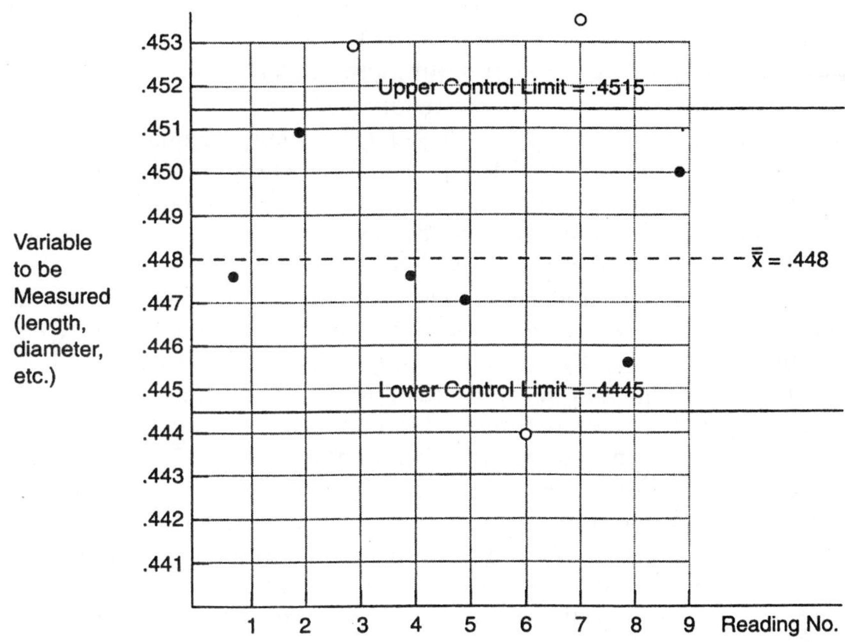

NOTES:

Upper and lower control limits are statistically determined limits of control.

All readings are taken at preset intervals using samples of output (e.g., five parts in a row).

$\bar{\bar{X}}$ = grand average of all readings.

● = readings falling within limits (variations due to chance).

○ = readings falling outside limits (assignable causes to be corrected).

Sampling

Sampling techniques start from the simple premise that 100 percent inspection is an inefficient way of sorting good products from bad. Checking a limited number of items in a production lot, then deciding on that basis whether the entire lot is acceptable, is clearly an alternative. The process, however, entails certain risks. Because samples are never fully representative, one may occasionally accept a production lot that in reality contains a large number of defective items. A related error is also possible: one may reject a production lot that is actually of perfectly acceptable quality.

Dodge and Romig recognized these problems, called consumer's and producer's risk, and devised plans for dealing with them systematically. They were able to develop sampling plans that ensured that for a given level of defects, the probability of unwittingly accepting an unsatisfactory lot would be limited to a certain percentage.[16] A certain number of items would be checked for a specified lot size. If according to the sampling tables the number of defective items in that group exceeded the number allowable, the entire lot would be rejected.

Useful as it was, the method was limited in application. It applied only to individual production lots, rather than to the overall level of quality produced by a manufacturing process. A new concept, the average outgoing quality limit (AOQL), was developed to meet that deficiency. It indicated the maximum percentage of defective units that a process would produce under two conditions: sampling inspection by lots, and the individual separation of good from bad items in all lots that had already been rejected on the basis of sampling.[17] A typical AOQL sampling table, showing the relationship between process quality, lot size, sampling rules, and outgoing quality, is illustrated in Figure 2.2.

These breakthroughs were instrumental in improving the quality of telephone equipment and service. Inspection costs fell, quality improved, and with fewer defects to correct, employees became more productive. Surprisingly, however, neither sampling techniques nor process control charts had much of an immediate impact outside the Bell System. Most of the original research was published in technical journals with limited circulation. Only with the advent of World War II and the need to produce munitions in large volumes did the concepts of statistical quality control gain a wider audience.

The impact of World War II

In December 1940, a committee was formed by the War Department to draft standards in the area of quality. The standards were published in 1941 and 1942. Their primary focus was the development and use of control charts. At roughly the same time, the Ordnance Department of the U.S. Army was facing the problem of how to get large quantities of arms and ammunition from multiple suppliers at acceptable levels of quality. Two alternatives were under consideration: extensive training of contractors in the use of process control charts and the development of a system of acceptance sampling procedures to be applied by government inspectors. The second approach won out, and in 1942 a Quality Control section was established in the War Department, staffed largely by statisticians from Bell Laboratories.[18]

This group soon developed a new set of sampling tables based on the concept of acceptable quality levels (AQL): The poorest quality (maximum percent defective) that a supplier could maintain over time and still be considered satisfactory. Two kinds of inspection were involved. Normal inspection, which required fewer checks, was used when the products under review had recently proved to have a defect rate lower than or equal to the AQL. Tightened inspection was used when

FIGURE 2.2 *A typical AOQL single sampling table*

AVERAGE OUTGOING QUALITY LIMIT = 0.75%

Process Average %	0–.015			.016–.15			.16–.30			.31–.45			.46–.60			.61–.75		
Lot Size	n	c	P_t%	n	c	P_t%	n	c	P_t%	n	c	P_t%	n	c	P_t%	n	c	P_t%
1–25	All	0	—	All	0	—	All	0	—	All	0	—	All	0	—	All	0	—
26–50	25	0	6.4	25	0	6.4	25	0	6.4	25	0	6.4	25	0	6.4	25	0	6.4
51–100	33	0	5.6	33	0	5.6	33	0	5.6	33	0	5.6	33	0	5.6	33	0	5.6
101–200	39	0	5.2	39	0	5.2	39	0	5.2	39	0	5.2	39	0	5.2	39	0	5.2
201–300	42	0	5.0	42	0	5.0	42	0	5.0	42	0	5.0	42	0	5.0	42	0	5.0
301–400	44	0	4.9	44	0	4.9	44	0	4.9	44	0	4.9	90	0	4.0	90	1	4.0
401–500	45	0	4.8	45	0	4.8	45	0	4.8	90	1	4.1	90	1	4.1	90	1	4.1
501–600	45	0	4.9	45	0	4.9	45	0	4.9	95	1	3.9	95	1	3.9	95	1	3.9
601–800	46	0	4.9	46	0	4.9	100	1	3.8	100	1	3.8	100	1	3.8	100	1	3.8
801–1,000	47	0	4.8	47	0	4.8	100	1	3.8	100	1	3.8	100	1	3.8	155	2	3.2
1,001–2,000	48	0	4.7	48	0	4.7	105	1	3.7	105	1	3.7	170	2	3.1	170	2	3.1
2,001–3,000	48	0	4.7	110	1	3.5	110	1	3.5	170	2	3.1	170	2	3.1	240	3	2.8
3,001–4,000	48	0	4.7	110	1	3.5	110	1	3.5	175	2	3.1	245	3	2.7	315	4	2.5
4,001–5,000	49	0	4.6	110	1	3.6	175	2	3.1	175	2	3.1	245	3	2.7	320	4	2.5
5,001–7,000	49	0	4.6	110	1	3.6	180	2	3.0	250	3	2.7	325	4	2.5	400	5	2.3
7,001–10,000	49	0	4.6	110	1	3.7	180	2	3.0	255	3	2.6	405	5	2.3	560	7	2.1
10,001–20,000	49	0	4.6	110	1	3.7	255	3	2.6	335	4	2.4	495	6	2.1	750	9	1.9
20,001–50,000	110	1	3.7	180	2	3.0	260	3	2.6	420	5	2.2	675	8	1.9	1,130	13	1.6
50,001–100,000	110	1	3.7	185	2	2.9	335	4	2.4	590	7	2.0	955	11	1.7	1,720	19	1.5

NOTES:

n = size of sample. Entry of "All" indicates that each piece in lot is to be inspected.

c = allowable defect number for sample. If more than this number of defects is found, the lot should be rejected.

P_t = lot tolerance percent defective corresponding to a consumer's risk (Pc) = 0.10. This means that under the given sampling plan, the probability of inadvertently accepting a lot whose quality (measured in percent defective) is P_t, is at most 10 percent.

Process average = the average percentage of defective units produced by the manufacturing process.

SOURCE: H. F. Dodge, "Notes on the Evolution of Acceptance Sampling Plans, Part I," *Journal of Quality Technology*, April 1969, p. 85. Copyright © 1969 American Society for Quality Control. Reprinted with permission.

the defect rate had recently exceeded the AQL. The tables also contained rules showing when to switch from one method of inspection to the other.[19]

These techniques were immensely successful. The primary bottleneck slowing the production of war materials had occurred in inspection; it was soon eliminated.[20] In the first eight months after the methods were introduced on a large scale, inspectors were able to process far higher volumes. The number of Ordnance Department inspectors per million dollars of accepted material dropped from 42 to 12.[21] Substantial improvements in quality were realized as well.

Meanwhile, additional training programs were being organized by the Office of Production Research and Development (OPRD) of the War Production Board. Researchers at Bell Laboratories again played a leading role, this time in cooperation with major universities. Walter Shewhart, for example, was instrumental in selling the initial proposal to OPRD. At the time, the techniques of statistical quality control had still seen little application outside the telephone company. As one of the early academic participants in the program remarked: "What we professors had at the time was faith—faith that statistical techniques would prove to be widely useful in the control of quality in many different kinds of manufacturing."[22] The aim of the programs that were finally developed was the rapid dissemination of these techniques to other branches of industry.

Courses were first offered at the Carnegie Institute of Technology of 1941 and Stanford in 1942. By the end of the war, institutions in twenty-five states were involved. A total of 8,000 people were trained in courses ranging from one-day executive programs to intensive eight-day seminars for engineers, inspectors, and other quality control practitioners.[23]

Most early trainees made little effort to apply the techniques they had learned. Statistical concepts were still something of a novelty, with only a brief track record. A few companies, however, achieved spectacular gains; these were reported in follow-up seminars and proved instrumental in inducing other companies to experiment with process control and sampling methods.[24]

Soon the students who had attended the courses began to form local societies for quality control. In October 1945, thirteen of these groups banded together to become the Society of Quality Engineers; a year later they merged with another federation to become the American Society for Quality Control (ASQC). Today the ASQC remains the field's dominant professional group. Meanwhile, the first U.S. journal on the subject, *Industrial Quality Control,* was published in July 1944 by the Buffalo Society of Quality Control Engineers. It later became *Quality Progress,* the official magazine of the ASQC.[25]

By the late 1940s, then, quality control was established as a recognized discipline. Its methods were primarily statistical, however, and its impact was confined largely to the factory floor. Little would change until several key works were published in the 1950s and early 1960s. These ushered in the next major quality era, that of quality assurance.

QUALITY ASSURANCE

During the period of quality assurance, quality evolved from a narrow, manufacturing-based discipline to one with broader implications for management. Problem prevention remained the primary goal, but the profession's tools expanded far beyond statistics. Four separate elements were involved: quantifying the costs of quality, total quality control, reliability engineering, and zero defects.

Costs of quality

Until the 1950s, most efforts to improve quality were based on the unstated assumption that defects were costly. How costly was a matter of conjecture, for few companies had gone to the trouble of tallying up the expenses they incurred because products were not built right the first time. In the absence of such a yardstick, managers accustomed to making decisions on the basis of hard numbers had little to go on. For them, a critical question remained: How much quality was enough?

In 1951 Joseph Juran tackled the question in the first edition of his *Quality Control Handbook,* a publication that would shortly become the profession's bible.[26] Its initial chapter discussed the economics of quality and proposed the now famous analogy to "gold in the mine." Juran observed that the costs of achieving a given level of quality could be divided into avoidable and unavoidable costs. The latter were the costs associated with prevention—inspection, sampling, sorting, and other quality control initiatives. Avoidable costs were those of defects and product failures—scrapped materials, labor hours required for rework and repair, complaint processing, and financial losses resulting from unhappy customers. Juran regarded failure costs as "gold in the mine" because they could be reduced sharply by investing in quality improvement. The payoff from these efforts could be substantial: At the time, Juran estimated that avoidable quality losses were typically in the range of $500 to $1,000 per productive operator per year.[27]

Managers now had a way of deciding how much to invest in quality improvement. Additional expenditures on prevention were likely to be justified as long as failure costs remained high. The concept also illustrated another important principle: that decisions made early in the production chain—for example, when engineers first sketched out a new product's design—had implications for the level of quality costs incurred later on, in both the factory and the field.

Total quality control

In 1956 Armand Feigenbaum took this principle a step further by proposing "total quality control." High-quality products, he argued, were unlikely to be produced if the manufacturing department was forced to work in isolation:

> The underlying principle of this total quality view . . . is that, to provide genuine effectiveness, control must start with the design of the product and end only when the product has been placed in the hands of a customer who remains satisfied . . . the first principle to recognize is *that quality is everybody's job*.[28]

Feigenbaum noted that all new products, as they moved from design to market, involved roughly the same activities. From a quality standpoint, they could be grouped into three categories: new design control, incoming material control, and product or shop floor control. The first, for example, involved preproduction assessments of a design's "manufacturability" as well as the debugging of new manufacturing techniques through pilot runs. To be successful, these activities required the cooperation of multiple departments. In fact, as products moved through the three principal stages, groups as varied as marketing, engineering, purchasing, manufacturing, shipping, and customer service had to become involved. Otherwise, mistakes might be made early in the process that would cause problems to appear later—during assembly or, worse yet, after the product was in a customer's hands.

To make the system work, many companies developed elaborate matrices, like the one in Figure 2.3, listing departmental responsibilities across the top and required activities down the left-hand side. The matrices typically showed considerable overlap among functions, for few activities were likely to be error free if they were assigned to a single department or were pursued seriatim. Interfunctional teams therefore became essential: They ensured that diverse viewpoints were represented and that otherwise autonomous departments worked together. Top management was ultimately responsible for the effectiveness of the system; to maintain its interest, Feigenbaum, like Juran, proposed careful measurement and reporting of the costs of quality.

The two experts also agreed on the need for a new type of quality professional. Statistical methods were still important—both authors devoted large sections of their books to explanations of process control and sampling—as were traditional techniques of inspection and gauging. But the quality system now included new product development, vendor selection, and customer service, in addition to manufacturing control. To deal with these responsibilities, both Feigenbaum and Juran argued that a new function, quality control engineering, was necessary.[29] It would be involved in high-level quality planning, coordinating the activities of other departments, setting quality standards, and providing quality measurements. These activities required a mix of management skills. They implied that a statistics background was no longer enough to guarantee competence as a quality professional.

Reliability engineering

Yet, at about the same time that Feigenbaum and Juran were making these arguments, another branch of the discipline was emerging that relied even more heavily on probability theory and statistics: reliability engineering, which had as its

FIGURE 2.3 *A typical matrix of quality responsibilities*

	GROUP OR DEPARTMENT							
Activity or Function	**General management**	**Finance**	**Marketing**	**Engineering**	**Manufacturing**	**Quality control**	**Purchasing**	**Service**
Establish product reliability and quality policies	x	o	o	o	o	o	o	o
Analyze quality costs	o	x				x		
Perform in-process quality audits				o	o	x		
Ensure that new product designs meet the test of manufacturability and ease of service			x	x	o		x	
Establish specifications for purchased parts and materials and qualify vendors				x		o	x	

NOTES:

x indicates the departments primarily responsible for an activity.

o indicates other departments that should be involved in an activity.

SOURCE: Adapted from A. V. Feigenbaum, *Total Quality Control* (New York: McGraw-Hill, 1961), p. 65. Reprinted with permission.

objective the assurance of acceptable product performance over time.[30] The field was closely aligned with the postwar growth of the aerospace and electronics industries in the United States; as a result, the military was a prime supporter. In 1950 the Department of Defense formed an Ad Hoc Group on Reliability of Electronic Equipment, and in 1957 a major report was issued on the subject.[31] The report eventually resulted in a number of military specifications setting out the requirements for a formal reliability program.

These efforts were stimulated by the plummeting reliability of military components and systems. In 1950 only one-third of the Navy's electronic devices were working properly at any given time. A study by the Rand Corporation at the time estimated that every vacuum tube the military had plugged in and working was backed by nine others in warehouses or on order. Equally serious problems were encountered with missiles and other aerospace equipment.[32]

Clearly, greater attention needed to be paid to product performance over time. The first step was to define reliability more precisely—as "the probability of a product's performing a specified function without failure, for a given period of time, under specified conditions."[33] Coupled with the tools of modern probability theory, this definition led to formal methods for predicting equipment performance over time. It also resulted in techniques for reducing failure rates while products were still in the design stage.

Much of the analysis rested on the concept of a probability distribution. This was no more than a mathematical relationship specifying a product's reliability (or inversely, its failure rate) as a function of time. Engineers soon found that different operating conditions and different products were better approximated by different mathematical forms. Among the most popular were the exponential life function, which assumed that a product's failure rate remained relatively unchanged over its entire operating life; the Weibull distribution, which allowed failure rates to increase or decrease over time as products improved or deteriorated with age; and the "bathtub curve"—so called because of its distinctive shape which dropped the assumption that failure rates were constant or changed steadily over time and argued instead for a break-in period (when failure rates were high), a normal operating period (when failure rates were constant and relatively low), and a wear-out phase (when failures rose steadily as the product deteriorated).[34] These relationships were then coupled with careful testing programs designed to simulate extreme operating conditions, to estimate reliability levels even before products reached full-scale production.

Prediction, however, was only the first step. The discipline's real goal was to improve reliability and reduce failure rates over time. To accomplish these ends, a variety of techniques were employed: failure mode and effect analysis (FMEA), which systematically reviewed the ways a product could fail and on that basis proposed alternative designs; individual component analysis, which computed the probability of failure of key components and then tried to eliminate or strengthen the weakest links; derating, which required that parts be used below their specified stress levels; and redundancy, which involved the use of parallel systems to ensure that backups were available whenever an important component or subsystem failed.[35] An effective reliability program also required close monitoring of field failures. Otherwise, engineers would be denied vital information—a product's actual operating experience—useful for planning new designs. Field failure reporting normally involved comprehensive systems of data collection as well as efforts to ensure that failed parts were returned to the laboratory for further testing and analysis.[36]

Like total quality control, reliability engineering was aimed at preventing defects from happening in the first place. It too emphasized engineering skills and attention to quality throughout the design process. Zero defects, the last significant development in the quality assurance era, took a different tack: It focused on management expectations and the human relations side of the equation.

Zero Defects

Zero defects had its genesis at the Martin Company in 1961–62.[37] At the time, Martin was building Pershing missiles for the U.S. Army. Their quality, though generally good, was achieved only through massive inspection. Incentives were offered to workers to lower the defect rate still further; together with even more intensive inspection and testing, these efforts led, on December 12, 1961, to the delivery of a Pershing missile to Cape Canaveral with zero discrepancies.

A defect-free missile could therefore be made, although it was likely to require extensive debugging before shipment. A month later, Martin's general manager in Orlando, Florida, accepted a request from the U.S. Army's missile command to deliver the first field Pershing one month ahead of schedule. He went even further—he promised that the missile would be perfect, with no hardware problems, no document errors, and all equipment set up and fully operational ten days after delivery (the norm was ninety days or more). Two months of feverish activity followed. Since little time was available for the usual inspection and after-the-fact correction of errors, all employees were asked to contribute to building the missile exactly right the first time. The result was still a surprise: In February 1962 a perfect missile was delivered. It arrived on time and was fully operational in less than twenty-four hours.

This experience was an eye-opener for Martin. After careful review, management concluded that the project's success was primarily a reflection of its own changed attitude: "The reason behind the lack of perfection was simply that perfection had not been expected. The one time management demanded perfection, it happened!"[38] Similar reasoning suggested a need to focus on workers' motivation and awareness. Of the three most common causes of worker errors—lack of knowledge, lack of proper facilities, and lack of attention—management concluded that the last had been least often addressed. It set out to design a program whose overriding goal was to promote a constant, conscious desire to do a job (any job) right the first time."[39]

The resulting program was called zero defects. It was very heavy on philosophy, motivation, and awareness, and much leaner when it came to specific proposals and problem-solving techniques. A key step, in fact—the identification of problems at their source and the design of remedial efforts (called error cause removal)—was developed by the Small Engine Department of General Electric, an early adopter of the program, and not by Martin. Martin's contribution lay primarily in articulating a philosophy—that the only acceptable quality standard was zero defects—and in showing how it could be instilled in the work force through training, special events, the posting of quality results, goal-setting, and personal feedback. That was no small achievement. Since the prevailing quality ethic at the time was acceptable quality levels (AQL)—the idea, associated with sampling techniques, that some non-zero level of defects was good enough—Martin was fighting nearly thirty years of quality control history. Even today, the debate continues. One of the most popular—and controversial—recent books on quality is *Quality Is Free,* written by Philip B. Crosby, an advocate of zero defects who worked at Martin in the 1960s.[40] Crosby's claim that perfect quality is both technically possible and economically desirable has rekindled many of the old arguments about how much quality is enough.

EVOLUTION AND CHANGE

Zero defects was the last major movement in the quality assurance era. Together with reliability engineering, total quality control, and the costs of quality, it helped expand the boundaries of the quality profession. Design, engineering, planning, and service activities were now as relevant as statistics and manufacturing control. New management skills were required, especially in the area of human relations. Interfunctional coordination became a primary concern, and quality professionals shifted their attention to program design, standard setting, and monitoring the activities of other departments.

Table 2.1 charts the evolution from inspection to quality assurance in more detail. It shows how quality management in the United States has expanded in ever widening circles, each era incorporating elements of the one that preceded it. Quality assurance, for example, acknowledged the role of statistical analysis while placing it in the larger context of the production chain, just as quality control saw gauging and measurement as a small part of the problem of efficient inspection. Early breakthroughs were seldom rejected; rather, they were subsumed within larger categories.

The resulting pattern of change reflects, in microcosm, the evolution of U.S. industry and the escalating demand it faced for technically sophisticated products. When American manufacturing involved only simple fabrication and assembly and low production volumes, informal inspection was enough to ensure high quality. Larger volumes, however, required tighter control and led to separate inspection departments and precise systems of gauging. The nationwide telephone network resulted in a further leap forward. It involved still more complex equipment and even higher degrees of standardization; both enhanced the desirability of statistical methods. Scale effects played a role in the discipline's later evolution as well. The war years were a fertile period for quality control for just this reason.

Table 2.1 *From inspection to quality assurance*

	Stage of the Quality Movement		
Identifying characteristics	**Inspection**	**Statistical quality control**	**Quality assurance**
Primary concern	Detection	Control	Coordination.
View of quality	A problem to be solved	A problem to be solved	A problem to be solved, but one that is attacked proactively.
Emphasis	Product uniformity	Product uniformity with reduced inspection	The entire production chain, from design to market, and the contribution of all functional groups, especially designers, to preventing quality failures.
Methods	Gauging and measurement	Statistical tools and techniques	Programs and systems.
Role of quality professionals	Inspection, sorting, counting, and grading	Troubleshooting and the application of statistical methods	Quality measurement, quality planning, and program design.
Who has responsibility for quality	The inspection department	The manufacturing and engineering departments	All departments, although top management is only peripherally involved in designing, planning, and executing quality policies.
Orientation and approach	"Inspects in" quality	"Controls in" quality	"Builds in" quality.

Quality assurance continued these trends. It was born of necessity: the need to meet the tightened specifications and performance criteria demanded by the country's military, electronics, and space programs. Product design became more exacting, giving rise to reliability engineering and the need for better coordination among departments before new products were released. At the same time, a number of new ideas were emerging in American thinking about human resource management. Such concepts as Theory Y and the Scanlon Plan encouraged companies to offer greater autonomy to workers.[41] The zero defects movement, with its emphasis on motivation and employee initiative, was remarkably similar in spirit.

Yet, in spite of these changes, approaches to quality remained largely defensive throughout this period. The main objective of the quality department was still the prevention of defects. Even though a proactive approach was not being pursued, quality was still viewed negatively—as something that could hurt a company if ignored—rather than as a possible basis for competition. That view finally changed in the 1970s and 1980s, when the strategic aspects of quality were recognized and embraced.

Notes

1. A number of authors have divided the history of the quality movement into distinct periods, although they have frequently used only two categories, quality control and quality assurance. See Robert A. Abbott and David C. Leaman, "Quality Control and Quality Assurance," in Carl Heyel, ed., *The Encyclopedia of Management,* Third Edition (New York: Van Nostrand Reinhold, 1982), pp. 998–1009; Everett Adam, Jr., "Quality Assurance Broadens the Concept of Quality Control," *The Pulse Report,* American Productivity Center, January 1984, p. 4; "ASQC: 40 Years of Growth and Change," *Quality Progress,* May 1986, pp. 56–67; Lawrence R. Dorsky, "Management Commitment to Japanese Apple Pie," *Quality Progress,* February 1984, pp. 14–18; Debra A. Owens, "QA/QC and ASQC History," unpublished paper, American Society for Quality Control, undated; and Jack Reddy, "Incorporating Quality in Competitive Strategies," *Sloan Management Review,* Spring 1980, pp. 53–60.
2. Alfred D. Chandler, Jr., *The Visible Hand* (Cambridge, Mass.: Belknap Press, Harvard University Press, 1977), pp. 50–64.
3. J. M. Juran, "Consumerism and Product Quality," *Quality Progress,* July 1970, p. 20, and Debra A. Owens, Director, Technical Programs, American Society for Quality Control, personal communication, April 18, 1984.
4. William J. Abernathy and John E. Corcoran, "Relearning from the Old Masters: Lessons of the American System of Manufacturing," *Journal of Operations Management,* August 1983, pp. 155–68; David A. Hounshell, *From the American System to Mass Production, 1800–1932* (Baltimore: Johns Hopkins Press, 1984), pp. 15–17; and Merritt Roe Smith, *Harpers Ferry Armory and the New Technology* (Ithaca, N.Y.: Cornell University Press, 1977), esp. chs. 3–5. While the initial breakthroughs involving interchangeable parts have often been associated with Eli Whitney, recent research suggests that his role has been overstated. See Robert S. Woodbury, "The Legend of Eli Whitney and

Interchangeable Parts," *Technology and Culture,* Summer 1960, pp. 235–53, as well as the above sources.

5. Hounshell, *From American System,* pp. 6, 34–35.
6. *Ibid.,* p. 34.
7. Frederick Winslow Taylor, *Shop Management* (New York: Harper & Brothers, 1919), p. 101. See also Chandler, *Visible Hand,* pp. 275–77, and Frank Barkley Copley, *Frederick W. Taylor: Father of Scientific Management* (New York: Harper & Brothers, 1923), I:324.
8. G. S. Radford, *The Control of Quality in Manufacturing* (New York: Ronald Press, 1922). The book is predated by an earlier article on the subject by the same author. See G. S. Radford, "The Control of Quality," *Engineering Magazine,* October 1917.
9. Radford, *Control of Quality in Manufacturing,* p. 36.
10. *Ibid.,* p. 5.
11. Charles A. Bicking, "The Technical Aspects of Quality Control," *Industrial Quality Control,* March 1958, p. 7.
12. W. A. Shewhart, *Economic Control of Quality of Manufactured Product* (New York: D. Van Nostrand Company, 1931).
13. Abbott and Leaman, "Quality Control" (note 1), p. 1000, and Harold F. Dodge, "Notes on the Evolution of Acceptance Sampling Plans, Part I," *Journal of Quality Technology,* April 1969, p. 77.
14. Shewhart, *Economic Control of Quality,* p. 6.
15. Shewhart in fact developed two charts: the X or average chart, and the σ or standard deviation chart. The former measured the average level around which dispersion was to be controlled; the latter, the degree of dispersion itself. Standard deviations, however, proved to be difficult to compute and were shortly replaced by range charts (R), developed in England by Leonard Tippett. See Abbott and Leaman, "Quality Control," pp. 1000–1001, for further discussion of this development. For more on the application of process control charts, see such standard texts as J. M. Juran and Frank M. Gryna, Jr., *Quality Planning and Analysis* (New York: McGraw-Hill, 1980), esp. chs. 12, 13, and 14, and E. L. Grant and R. S. Leavenworth, *Statistical Quality Control,* Fifth Edition (New York: McGraw-Hill, 1980), chs. 2–11. For a more succinct treatment, see *Constructing and Using Process Control Charts* (Boston: Harvard Business School Case Services 9-684-073, 1984).
16. These plans were based on two technical concepts: operating characteristic (OC) curves and lot tolerance percent defective (LTPD). For further discussion, see Dodge, "Notes, Part I," pp. 78–81; Juran and Gryna, *Quality Planning and Analysis,* ch. 17; and Grant and Leavenworth, *Statistical Quality Control,* chs. 12 and 13.
17. Dodge, "Notes, Park I," pp. 82–84, and Harold F. Dodge and Harry G. Romig, *Sampling Inspection Tables* (New York: John Wiley & Sons, 1944).
18. H. F. Dodge, "Notes on the Evolution of Acceptance Sampling Plans, Part II," *Journal of Quality Technology,* July 1969, pp. 155–56.
19. *Ibid.,* pp. 156–59. After years of refinement and revision, these techniques led to Military Standard 105D (MIL-STD-105D), the most widely used acceptance sampling plan in the world. See H. F. Dodge, "Notes on the Evolution of Acceptance Sampling Plans, Part III," *Journal of Quality Technology,* October 1969, pp. 229–32.

20. Abbott and Leaman, "Quality Control," p. 1001.
21. H. F. Safford, "The U.S. Army Ordnance Department Use of Quality Control," *Industrial Quality Control,* January 1946, p. 4. W. Edwards Deming, who would later play a leading role in introducing statistical quality control in Japan, was involved in this effort as Adviser in Sampling to the Chief of Army Ordnance.
22. Eugene L. Grant, "Industrialists and Professors in Quality Control: A Look Back and a Look Ahead," *Industrial Quality Control,* July 1953, p. 31.
23. Holbrook Working, "Statistical Quality Control in War Production," *Journal of the American Statistical Association,* December 1945, pp. 425, 433, 439.
24. One initiator of the OPRD programs has observed that had it not been for the early successes of the Ontario Works of General Electric in applying the techniques of statistical quality control, he might have recommended that the program be curtailed. See Grant, "Industrialists and Professors," p. 33.
25. Abbott and Leaman, "Quality Control," pp. 1001–2; Dodge, "Notes, Part III," p. 228; *Industrial Quality Control,* July 1944; Owens, "QA/QC" (note 1).
26. J. M. Juran, ed., *Quality Control Handbook* (New York: McGraw-Hill, 1951).
27. *Ibid.,* p. 37.
28. Armand V. Feigenbaum, "Total Quality Control," *Harvard Business Review,* November–December 1956, pp. 94, 98 (italics in original). See also Armand V. Feigenbaum, *Total Quality Control* (New York: McGraw-Hill, 1961).
29. Feigenbaum, *Total Quality Control,* pp. 54–57, and Juran, *Quality Control Handbook,* pp. 170–72, 174–77, 281–82.
30. Thomas A. Budne, "Reliability Engineering," in Carl Heyel, ed., *The Encyclopedia of Management,* Third Edition (New York: Van Nostrand Reinhold Company, 1982), p. 1023, and George A. W. Boehm, "'Reliability' Engineering," *Fortune,* April 1963, pp. 124–27, 181–82, 184, 186.
31. *Reliability of Military Electronic Equipment,* Report by the Advisory Group on Reliability of Electronic Equipment, Office of the Assistant Secretary of Defense (Research and Engineering) (Washington, D.C.: U.S. Government Printing Office, 1951). This was the so-called AGREE report.
32. Boehm, "'Reliability' Engineering," p. 127.
33. Budne, "Reliability Engineering," p. 1024. For reasons of clarity, Budne's definition, which parallels that of the AGREE report, has been slightly reworded. See Grant and Leavenworth, *Statistical Quality Control* (note 15), pp. 536–37, for a number of similar definitions.
34. Boehm, "'Reliability' Engineering," pp. 181–82; Budne, "Reliability Engineering," pp. 1024–25; Juran and Gryna, *Quality Planning and Analysis* (note 15), ch. 8; and J. M. Juran, *Quality Control Handbook,* Third Edition (New York: McGraw-Hill, 1974), pp. 22-26–22-27. For an introduction to probability distributions, see any basic statistics text, e.g., Richard I. Levin, *Statistics for Management* (Englewood Cliffs, N.J.: Prentice-Hall, 1978), pp. 136–38.
35. Boehm, "'Reliability' Engineering," pp. 182, 184; Budne, "Reliability Engineering," p. 1026; and Juran and Gryna, *Quality Planning and Analysis,* pp. 182–84.
36. Budne, "Reliability Engineering," p. 1028.

37. The discussion of zero defects is based on James F. Halpin, *Zero Defects* (New York: McGraw-Hill, 1966). At the time the book was written, Halpin was Director of Quality at the Martin Company. He had been one of the founders of its zero defects program.
38. *Ibid.*, p. 15.
39. *Ibid.*, p. 5. See also Captain E. R. Pettebone, "'Zero Defects' Type Programs: Basic Concepts," in Office of the Assistant Secretary of Defense (Installations and Logistics), *Zero Defects: The Quest for Quality* (Washington, D.C.: U.S. Government Printing Office, 1968), pp. 45–60.
40. Philip B. Crosby, *Quality Is Free* (New York: Mentor/New American Library, 1979). For an interesting comparison of Crosby's approach with those of other quality experts, see Charles H. Fine and David H. Bridge, "Managing Quality Improvement," Working Paper 1607-84, Sloan School of Management, Massachusetts Institute of Technology, November 1984, mimeographed.
41. See, for example, Douglas McGregor, *The Human Side of Enterprise* (New York: McGraw-Hill, 1960), and Frederick G. Lesieur, ed., *The Scanlon Plan* (Cambridge, Mass., and New York: Technology Press, John Wiley & Sons, 1958).

Reading 3

Continuous Incremental Improvement: An Operations Strategy for Higher Quality, Lower Costs, and Global Competitiveness

BY HAROLD L. GILMORE

Conventional wisdom holds that product and service quality is costly and that the relevant activities behave in an interdependent manner. Their behavior for a particular organization depends to a great extent on the mission, objectives, and ultimately, the operational strategy pursued by management in an effort to achieve its objectives.

This paper presents the notion that under certain operating conditions improving product or service quality can lead to steep short-run reductions in quality expenditures and to substantial long-run reductions in total operating costs. Concurrently, higher levels of product and service quality and customer satisfaction will be achieved. An operations strategy of continuous incremental improvement is suggested as the way to establish the appropriate operating conditions.

DEFINITIONS

Two important terms are defined next as an aid to this discussion. The first insert defines the concept of continuous improvement. It is important to recognize that this concept is comprehensive and therefore not restricted to a specific activity or function in an organization. Operating improvements can be implemented in office and support activities as well as on the production line. Identifying improvements

SOURCE: Reprinted from the Winter 1990 issue of *SAM Advanced Management Journal* with the permission of the author.

need not be restricted to management or supervision but should be an important part of everyone's responsibility.

Given an organizational philosophy and structure equipped with appropriate improvement techniques, the opportunity for improving operations is infinite.

Improved quality is a major source of increased competitiveness and quality expenditure reduction. Traditionally, quality control activities focused on the conformance of products or services to preestablished standards. The degree to which this is achieved is called conformance quality.

Continuous improvement

The integration of organizational philosophy, techniques, and structure to achieve sustained performance improvements in all activities on an uninterrupted basis.

Conformance quality[1]

The degree to which a specific product or service conforms to a design or specification.

The continuous incremental improvement concept represents a significant extension of the traditional concept of conformance quality since it includes product and service design in addition to production, delivery, and end use. The concept is not constrained by the idea of standards. While standards are likely to exist, they are viewed as merely a temporary guide to present activity. Over time, standards will yield to the changes introduced as a result of continuous improvement and, therefore, will always be changing. Improvements may come from anywhere, internally or externally to the organization. Irrespective of the source, improvements have a significant and measurable effect on an organization's quality assurance activities.

QUALITY ASSURANCE ACTIVITIES

Quality assurance can be viewed as a subsystem of operations composed of three main activities: prevention, appraisal, and defect/failure correction. Total quality expenditures are the sum of organizational expenditures on these interrelated and interdependent activities. The quality control subsystem is depicted in Figure 3.1.

Some research has focused on the extent to which management resource allocations conform with theory, i.e., are in line with the optimum allocation of prevention, appraisal, and defect and failure correction activity to ensure product or service conformance to preestablished quality levels.[2] These activities and their associated "costs" have the following widely accepted definitions (Figure 3.2).

Interestingly quality cost research to date has been limited in quantity and scope.[1] Researchers have found that, for proprietary reasons, organizations utilizing quality costs for managerial purposes are reluctant to disclose cost data. However, it is even more likely that organizations do not have a complete picture of their quality expenditures, and what data they do have are of limited use for decision making.

FIGURE 3.1 ***Quality assurance subsystem***

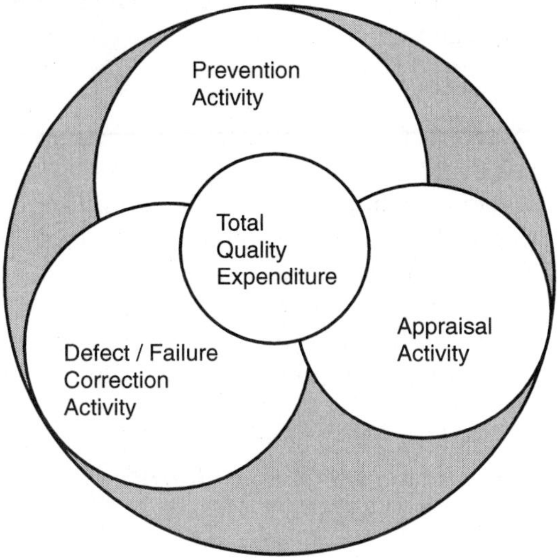

Prevention Activity

Total Quality Expenditure

Appraisal Activity

Defect / Failure Correction Activity

FIGURE 3.2 ***Quality activity definitions***

Prevention Activities or actions undertaken to provide a product or service which meets with customer satisfaction and organizational standards of quality. Included here are quality engineering, process planning and design of equipment for quality assurance purposes, training, delivery system, and equipment maintenance to assure proper performance.

Appraisal Activities or actions undertaken to determine the actual level of quality achieved relative to desired levels of customer satisfaction and organizational standards of quality. Specifically included are all inspection and tests costs, such as product destruction, utilities consumed, audits, external evaluation.

Defect/Failure Correction Activities or actions undertaken to correct products or services that fail to satisfy the customer or do not conform to organizational standards of quality. Included are refunds, recalls, scrap, rework, vendor produced defects, customer complaints and adjustments, customer service costs due to defects.

ALLOCATION MODEL

The traditional economic model for the allocation of resources to quality activities assumes that the objective of management is to achieve conformance quality (at a given quality level) at minimum total conformance quality expenditures. Management achieves or approaches this minimum through the prudent commitment of resources to prevention, appraisal, and defect/failure correction activities.

Most people believe that the emphasis in achieving product or service quality should be on prevention rather than appraisal or defect/failure correction activities. As the old adage suggests, "An ounce of prevention is worth a pound of cure." Others have suggested building quality in or doing the job right the first time.

Figures 3.3 and 3.4 depict, for the purpose of discussion, nonparametric quality expenditure models based on the foregoing concepts. They diagram the interrelated activities of prevention, appraisal, and defect/failure correction.

Figure 3.3 shows prevention and appraisal expenditure behavior as a function of prevention appraisal activity. Prevention expenditures are shown rising linearly as prevention activity is increased. The appraisal cost curve illustrates that as prevention activity is increased, the expenditure can be expected to decrease, but at a decreasing rate. This curve is asymptotic as prevention activity increases, which

FIGURE 3.3 ***Prevention and appraisal expenditure model (quality level fixed)***

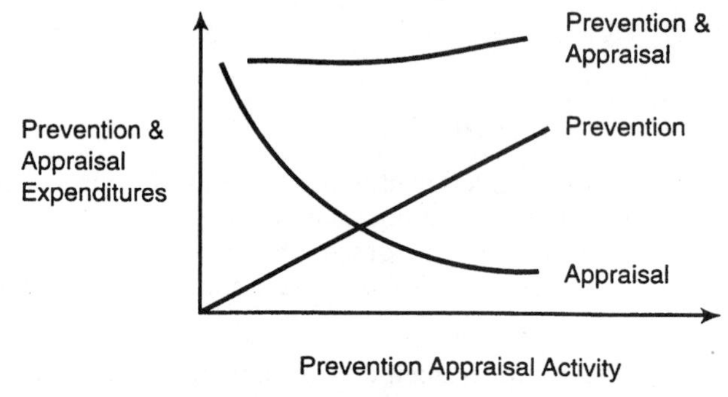

FIGURE 3.4 ***Conformance expenditure model (quality level fixed)***

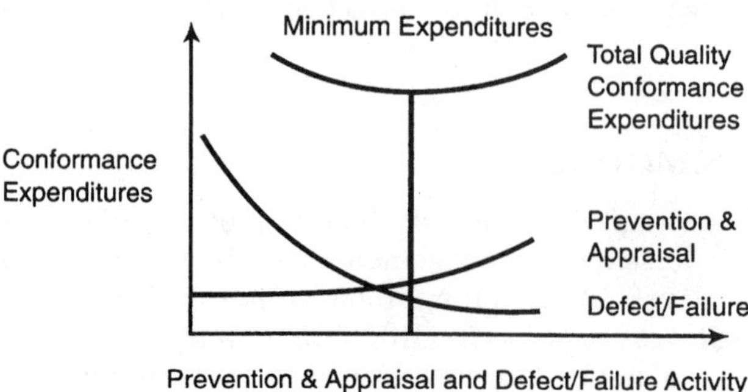

reflects the reality that the complete elimination of appraisal activity (expenditures) is highly unlikely. There will always be some measurement required to determine the extent to which the product or service meets specifications and satisfies customers. In addition, this curve indicates that some finite amount of appraisal activity (expenditure) exists even when little or no prevention activity is performed. In that situation, the firm would be engaged in determining what the quality level of the output actually was.

The sum of the prevention and appraisal expenditure curves results in a curve depicting the cost of assuring that the desired quality or customer satisfaction has been achieved.

Figure 3.4 illustrates conformance quality control total expenditures as a function of prevention, appraisal, and defect/failure correction activity. The prevention and appraisal cost curve as depicted in Figure 3.3 is duplicated in Figure 3.4, along with the resulting expected relationship to defect/failure correction expenditures.

Defect/failure correction expenditures are shown decreasing and asymptotically approaching the abscissa as the combination of prevention and appraisal activities are increased. The defect/failure correction curve is shown as an asymptote in order to reflect the idea that the complete elimination of defects is unlikely. There are bound to be some scrap, rework, or customer service "call backs" in any operation, for a variety of personnel and material-related causes. The curve also indicates that some finite value of defect/failure correction expenditure exists when little or no quality assurance (prevention or appraisal) activity is performed.

The total conformance quality control expenditure curve is the sum of the two other cost curves. It takes the familiar U-shape of the cost curves depicted by economic theorists—technically a quadratic cost function. The bottom point of the curve indicates the minimum cost combination of prevention, appraisal, and defect/failure correction activity. It should be noted that a firm may have to operate at a quality cost level higher than the minimum cost point due to customer requirements. However, a firm seeking to maximize profits would not be justified in operating at any lower prevention and appraisal level. To do so would result in larger expenditures than necessary at a lower level of conformance quality (higher defect/failure expenditures).

Maximizing profits from a conformance quality control point of view is equivalent to minimizing total conformance quality control expenditures. According to Figure 3.4, this occurs approximately where the prevention, appraisal, and defect/failure correction cost curves intersect. A firm operating at minimum total conformance quality control expenditure should employ the indicated mix of prevention, appraisal, and defect/failure correction activity. In terms of minimum conformance quality control cost, the combined cost of prevention and appraisal activity should approximately equal defect/failure correction related activity.

Having reviewed popular views and the assumptions associated with the behavior of quality assurance activities and related expenditures, let's review some recent strategic management developments and their likely impact on the foregoing.

CONTINUOUS INCREMENTAL IMPROVEMENT

It is no secret that American industry is experiencing competitive difficulty. The story has been presented by the media time and again. Even in the face of overwhelming evidence, domestic businesses cling to the ways of the past. However, some noteworthy companies such as Nucor Steel, Nashua Corporation, AT&T, Campbell Soup, Ford Motor Company, and General Motors, to name a few examples, have brought themselves back from the brink of disaster and to a state of global competitiveness. In fact it was the sense of impending disaster that motivated them to undertake organization-wide change to alter the direction they were traveling. By implementing strategic and systemic changes via continuous incremental improvements, these troubled firms sought to improve customer satisfaction, raise quality, lower operating costs, and regain a competitive advantage.

The philosophy of continuous incremental improvement differs significantly from the programmatic management approaches taken in the past. Over the years, American business has been the scene of one technological love affair after another. Commencing in the 1930s with the Human Relations movement and more recently with such programs as Statistical Quality Control (SQC), Zero Defects (ZD), Management by Objectives (MBO), Quality Circles, Job Enrichment, Job Enlargement, Just in Time (JIT), Material Requirements Planning (MRP II), Computer Aided Design (CAD), Computer Aided Manufacturing (CAM), Computer Aided Inspection (CAI), and various other participatory management schemes, the search has been on to find a road map to world class competition. The most recent popular approach is Statistical Process Control (SPC).[2]

The organizations mentioned earlier seem to have found the way. A study of their practices discloses they have skillfully and innovatively crafted total organizational change processes which involve relevant facets of the above.[3,4] These processes focus on management philosophy, the dignity of the individual, close attention to customer needs and to process details. Such a comprehensive and enduring approach has significant impact on quality assurance activities, especially with respect to who does them and for what reason. Several notable characteristics of these organizations are:

- Customer driven
- Employee involved
- Continuous improvement oriented
- Process focused
- Internationally sensitive

A moment of reflection on these characteristics reveals a substantial shift from a *primary concern for output* to one that is directed toward 1) the *recipient* of the goods or services; 2) the process which generated them; and 3) a *sustained* concern for *improving the level of satisfaction and value* the goods and services provided. A more subtle characteristic of continuous improvement is a redefinition of the customer. The most advanced organizations have defined the customer as the next person or step in the *process*—again reflecting a focus on the total process rather than exclusively on output or an external customer.

From a quality expenditure allocation perspective, the impact is clearly a stress on prevention activity and an enhancement of appraisal activity so as to continuously raise the level of customer satisfaction, value, and quality. Thus, the earlier discussion of predetermined fixed quality levels achieved via a combination of prevention, appraisal, and failure activity appears passé. The process focus coupled with continuous improvement suggests a significant change in management philosophy and emphasis.

Where prevention and appraisal activities are still practiced, they are becoming far more pervasive in the work force. The search for continuous improvement is not the purview of a select few individuals. Nor is some predetermined level of quality established and maintained for all time. The new objective is to seek ever higher levels of quality, value, and customer satisfaction by analyzing process capability and eliminating the causes and amounts of process variation. The ultimate objective is *perfection,* a state previously thought unattainable due to the general acceptance of defects and the widely held view that you cannot please everyone.

How is the continuous incremental improvement strategy reflected in quality expenditure behavior? Figure 3.5 depicts the familiar total quality expenditure relationships discussed earlier but reflects the concept of continuous incremental improvement over time. The assumption that product or service imperfections are removed by appraisal activity no longer pertains. Continuous improvement is brought about by identifying breakthroughs (e.g., process controls, improved raw materials, training, equipment improvements) that permit incremental changes in product or service performance, added value, and customer satisfaction. Every step of the process must add value from a customer perspective. Failure to do so results in change or elimination. If the customer will not pay for it, do not do it.

The quality expenditure behavior depicted in Figure 3.5 is based on many examples. One of the 1988 National Quality Award Winners, Motorola, has reported a \$250 million reduction in appraisal expenditures as a result of their

FIGURE 3.5 ***Quality expenditure reduction relationships***

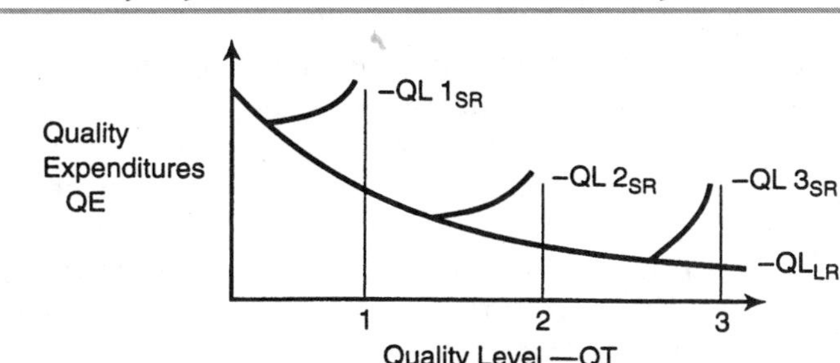

management's quest for quality improvements. Motorola's quality improvements focused on "six sigma quality." Statistically this measure translates into a benchmark of no more than 3.4 defects per million products, customer services included. The company found that, contrary to conventional thinking, as the number of defects during production were reduced the cost of manufacture decreased to less than one percent. No longer was there a need to maintain production capacity for rework and repair activity. In addition, failures in use were found to be closely associated with products that had undergone repair or rework. Another source of both tangible and intangible cost was eliminated by discontinuing repair and rework activity.

Similarly, Globe Metallurgical adopted a statistical process control strategy in 1985 which has resulted in their becoming the nation's lowest cost, highest quality producer of feroalloys and silicon metal. Like Motorola, Globe's achievement was recognized with the National Quality Award.

Many more success stories could be recounted, all of which would have the same characteristics: predisposition to change for the better, willingness to tap heretofore unused capacity, and a sense of urgency. Robert H. Schaffer[5] recounts the experiences of numerous other companies which have used the strategy of continuous incremental improvements to achieve the behavior reflected in Figure 3.5.

The family of short run curves illustrates the behavioral relationship of quality expenditures to the level of quality. The short run curves ($QL1_{sr}$, $QL2_{sr}$, $QL3_{sr}$) rise as the limit of existing technology is reached and incremental expenditures exceed quality level gains. But at this point, breakthroughs occur, and the opportunity exists for incremental gains to exceed the inputs. The cycle begins again. Since the search is continuous, there is no end to this cycle of improved quality, value, and customer satisfaction. Of additional importance is the long run phenomena of lowered total quality expenditures (QL_{lr}), increased level of quality, and reallocation of quality resources to prevention and away from appraisal and defect/failure correction activities. This ability to focus increased resources on incremental improvement (prevention) facilitates additional breakthroughs and sustains the process.

CONCLUSION

We have outlined the impact on total quality expenditures and customer satisfaction of a continuous improvement operating strategy. Implementation of this strategy promises to usher in a new era of organizational behavior—one that holds out the promise of world market preeminence once again for American businesses.

The quality assurance professional should emphasize process capability and control rather than output and continuous improvement rather than the setting and maintaining quality standards. Quality expenditures should be increasingly allocated to prevention-related activities, not appraisal. As perfection is approached, the need for defect/failure correction activity will be extinguished. The measure of corporate success will not be simply an acceptable quality level but increased customer satisfaction, improved process capability, decreased process variation, and lowered operating costs. The widespread adoption of continuous improvement philosophy offers American businesses the opportunity to return to global competitiveness.

Notes

1. Gilmore, Harold L., Herbert C. Schwartz, *Integrated Product Testing and Evaluation: A Systems Approach to Improved Reliability and Quality,* Rev. Ed., Marcel Dekker, Inc., New York and Basel; ASQC Quality Press, Milwaukee, 1986.
2. Walton, Mary, *The Deming Management Method.* Dodd, Mead & Company, New York, 1986.
3. Peters, Thomas J., Robert H. Waterman, Jr., *In Search of Excellence: Lessons from America's Best-Run Companies,* Harper & Row Publishers, New York, 1982.
4. Takeuchi, Hirotaka, John A. Quelch, "Quality Is More Than Making a Good Product," *Harvard Business Review,* (July–August 1983) pages 139–145.
5. Shaffer, Robert H., *The Breakthrough Strategy,* Ballinger Publishing Company, Cambridge, MA, 1988.

Additional Sources

Buetow, Richard C. Director of Quality, Motorola Inc., Address 1989 ASQC Quality Congress, Toronto, Canada, May 9, 1989.

Garvin, David A., "Quality on the Line," *Harvard Business Review,* (September–October 1983) pages 65–75.

Gitlow, Howard S., Paul T. Hertz, "Product Defects and Productivity," *Harvard Business Review,* (September–October 1983) pages 131–141.

Leach, Kenneth E., Vice President, Administration and Chief Quality Officer, Globe Metallurgical Inc., Address to 1989 ASQC Quality Congress, Toronto, Canada, May 9, 1989.

Reading 4

Building Learning Organizations

By Peter Senge

Why do many leaders of the so-called "quality movement" hate the term "the quality movement"? The man most often identified as the father of total quality management, Dr. W. Edwards Deming, takes offense at the assumed parentage. "The term is counterproductive," says Dr. Deming, the man who first taught the Japanese statistical quality control. "My work is about a transformation in management and about the profound knowledge needed for the transformation. Total quality stops people from thinking."

"Neither 'total quality' nor 'total quality management' describes what this approach to management is all about," says Dr. Edward Baker, director of Ford's corporate quality office. "It's about improving the total behavior of organizations, about developing the capability of a system to do what its members actually want it to do—anywhere in life."

Without a unifying conceptual framework, the quality movement in the United States risks being fragmented into isolated initiatives and slogans. *The voice of the customer, fix the process not the people, competitive benchmarking, continuous improvement, policy deployment, leadership*—the more we hear, the less we understand.

"Trying to put together the alphabet soup coming out of Japan of SPC, JIT, QIP, QFD, and so on can be hopelessly confusing without a unifying theme," says Analog Devices CEO Ray Stata.

It is not surprising that, for many, it doesn't add up to much more than management's latest *flavor of the month* that must be endured until the next fad comes along.

Even those firms where there has been significant commitment to quality management for several years are encountering slowing rates of improvement. "We've picked all the low hanging fruit," as one Detroit executive put it recently. "Now, the difficult changes are what's left."

Source: Excerpt from "Building Learning Organizations" from *Journal For Quality and Participation*, March 1992, by Peter Senge. Reprinted with the permission of Peter Senge.

The "difficult changes" are unlikely without a coherent picture of where we are trying to take our organizations through the quality management process.

Our global competitors Equally troubling, the best of our international competitors are not fragmenting, they are building—steadily advancing an approach to improving quality, productivity, and profitability that differs fundamentally from the traditional authoritarian, mechanical management model.

"Total quality [TQ] is not a closed-ended methodology; its an open-ended methodology," says Shoji Shiba, of Japan's Tsukuba University. "TQ continues to develop according to the needs of society."

The tools American corporations are racing to master today, the frontier of the quality movement in Japan in the 1960s, are no longer the frontier. The "thought revolution in management," as quality pioneer Ishikawa called it, is still evolving.

Learning organizations I believe that the quality movement as we have known it up to now in the United States is in fact the first wave in building *learning organizations*—organizations that continually expand their ability to shape their future.

The roots of the quality movement lie in assumptions about people, organizations, and management that have one unifying theme: to make continual learning a way of organizational life, especially improving the performance of the organization as a total system. This can only be achieved by breaking with the traditional authoritarian, command and control hierarchy where the top thinks and the local acts, to merge thinking and acting at all levels.

This represents a profound reorientation in the concerns of management—a shift from a predominant concern with controlling to a predominant concern with learning. Failure to come to grips with this shift plagues the efforts of many U.S. firms eager to jump on the quality bandwagon.

Learning organizations in Japan Our Japanese competitors have no trouble with this shift. "Japan's greatest long-term comparative advantage is not its management system, Japan Inc., or quality," says C. Jackson Grayson Jr., of the American Productivity and Quality Center in Houston. "It's the Japanese commitment to learning."

More specifically, as management practices in Japan have evolved over the past 40 years, there has been a steady spread of the commitment to learning—starting with statistical process control (SPC) for small groups of quality experts, to teaching quality improvement tools to frontline workers throughout the organization, to developing and disseminating tools for managerial learning.

> "If we fail to grasp the deeper messages of the quality movement, we will one day awake to discover ourselves chasing a receding target."

Learning waves The evolution of learning organizations can be best understood as a series of waves. What most managers think of as quality management focuses on improving tangible work processes. This is the first wave.

The first wave of quality In the first wave, the primary focus of change was frontline workers. Management's job was to:

- Champion continual improvement
- Remove impediments (like quality control experts and unnecessary bureaucracy) that disempowered local personnel
- Support new practices like quality training and competitive benchmarking that drive process improvement.

The second wave of quality In the second wave, the focus shifts from improving work processes to improving how we work—fostering ways of thinking and interacting conducive to continual learning about the dynamic, complex, conflictual issues that determine system wide performance. In the second wave, the primary focus of change is the managers themselves.

The third wave of quality These two ways will, I believe, gradually merge into a third, in which learning becomes *institutionalized* as an inescapable way of life for managers and workers alike (if we even bother maintaining that distinction).

We are still in the first wave American industry is, with a few exceptions, primarily operating in the first wave. "Despite all our improvements, the basic behavior of our managers, especially our senior managers, hasn't really changed much," laments the head of a major corporation's quality office.

Japan and the second wave By contrast, the second wave is well under way in Japan, driven by their *seven new tools for management,* as distinct from their traditional *seven quality tools* that drove the first wave.

America's challenge The challenge today, as American companies endeavor to master the basic tools and philosophy of quality management, is not to be caught short-sighted with mechanical "quality programs."

If we fail to grasp the deeper messages of the quality movement, we will one day awaken to discover ourselves chasing a receding target.

THE ROOTS OF THE QUALITY MOVEMENT

A close look at the roots of the quality movement shows that it has always been about learning.

"The prevailing system of management has destroyed our people," says Dr. Deming. "People are born with intrinsic motivation, self-esteem, dignity, curiosity to learn, joy in learning."

Intrinsic versus extrinsic motivation Intrinsic motivation lies at the heart of Deming's management philosophy. By contrast, extrinsic motivation is the bread and butter of Western management.

The holiest of holy for the American manager, "People do what they are rewarded for," is actually antithetical to the spirit of quality management. This doesn't imply that rewards are irrelevant. Rather, it implies that no set of rewards, neither carrots nor sticks, can ever substitute for intrinsic motivation to learn. A corporate commitment to quality that is not based on intrinsic motivation is a house built on sand.

Motivate* them *or loose* their *own motivation? Consider, for example the goal of continuous improvement, which remains an elusive target for most American corporations.

Motivate them From an extrinsic perspective, the only way to get continuous improvement is to find ways to continually motivate people to improve, because people only modify their behavior when there is some external motivation to do so. Otherwise, they will just sit there—or worse, slide backwards. This leads to what workers perceive as management continually raising the bar to manipulate more effort from them.

Loose their motivation with information and appropriate tools However, from an intrinsic perspective, there is nothing mysterious at all about continuous improvement. If left to their own devices, people will naturally look for ways to do things better. What they need is adequate information and appropriate tools.

From the intrinsic perspective people's innate curiosity and desire to experiment, if unleashed, creates an engine for improvement that can never be matched by external rewards.

Learning and intrinsic motivation to learn have always been the roots of quality A management system based on intrinsic motivation to learn is as befuddling to Western economists as it is to Western managers.

Princeton economist Alan Blinder recently cited an impressive list of Japanese "violations" of economic orthodoxy—tolerated monopolies and cartels, single suppliers, salary scales that do not differentiate adequately between ranks, keeping promising young managers waiting too long for promotion, and "almost nothing gets you fired."

"We did the opposite of what American economists said," Blinder quotes a top Ministry of International Trade & Industry (MIT) official. "We violated all the normal rules." But the puzzle of how a nation that does so many things *wrong* can get so many things right dissolves when we realize that Western economic theories, from Adam Smith on, are based solely on extrinsic motivation.

The way we thought it was Adam Smith's *homo economicus* is presumed to maximize his income, not his learning. The following are some maxims of *U.S. homo economicus:*

- If there is no opportunity for significant salary increase by climbing the corporate ladder, he will have little motivation to do his best or to improve.
- If there is no fear of dismissal, there will be nothing to drive him to be productive.
- If his company, made up of lots of greedy little buggers just like him, does not have to compete against other companies, they will have no motivation to continually lower costs of production, nor to improve their products.

In short, no competition, no innovation. But, if the drive to innovate comes from within, all this changes—especially if a management system can nurture and harness this drive.

Shewhart's and Dewey's roots to quality But we don't have to look just to subtleties like intrinsic motivation to see that the quality movement has always been about learning.

PDCA The famous PDCA cycle is evidence enough. No one ever gets far into any introduction to total quality management without learning about Plan-Do-Check-Act, the never-ending cycle of experimentation that structures all quality improvement efforts. Deming called it the *Shewhart cycle* when he introduced it to the Japanese in 1950, in honor of his mentor Walter Shewhart of Bell Labs. Eventually the Japanese called it the *Deming cycle.*

Of John Dewey, learning and quality But the roots of the PDCA cycle go back further than Deming or Shewhart, at least as far as the educator, John Dewey.

Dewey posited that all learning involves a cycle between four basic stages:

- Discover: the discovery of new insights, invent, creating new options for action.
- Produce: producing new actions.
- Observe: seeing the consequences of those actions, which leads to new discoveries, continuing the cycle.

This is how we learned to walk, to talk, to ride a bicycle, to act skillfully wherever we have achieved some proficiency. The young child first must discover that they want to walk, invent ways of getting started, act, and observe the consequences of her or his action.

Interrupting the cycle interrupts the learning. If the toddler is supported so they do not fall, they also do not learn.

Learning is moving from thought to action In effect, Dewey canonized the simple fact that all real learning occurs over time, as we move between the world of thought and the world of action. Learning is never simply an intellectual exercise. Nor is it a matter of changing behavior. It is an interactive process linking the two, in a spiral of continually expanding our capabilities.

It is not altogether irrelevant to note that this is a far cry from the common image of *learning* inculcated in the schoolroom, where most of us conclude that learning is synonymous with *taking in information* and being able to produce the *right answer* on cue—little wonder that for most adults, the word *learning* does not quicken the pulse.

The PDCA cycle takes Dewey's theory of learning one step further, saying, in effect, that in an organization it is often wise to distinguish *small actions* from widespread adoption of new practices.

The *do* stage then becomes pilot tests from which new data can be collected and analyzed (*checked*). Gradually, a series of such pilots results in more general learnings and the *act* stage moves to broader and broader application of new practices.

PDCA American style While simple in concept, the PDCA cycle is often practiced quite differently in the United States and in Japan.

Impatient for quick results, American managers often jump from *plan* to *act.*

The rush to act undermines efforts We conceive new programs and then begin rolling them out throughout the organization. In fact, that's exactly what many U.S. firms are doing with their total quality programs.

While rolling out new programs makes us feel good about doing something (*acting*) to improve things in our business, in fact we are actually undermining possibilities for learning. Who can learn from an experiment involving thousands of people that is only run one time?

PDCA Japanese style By contrast the Japanese are masters of organizational experimentation. They meticulously design and study pilot tests, often with many corporations participating cooperatively.

Through repeated cycles, new knowledge gradually accumulates. By the time for organization-wide changes, people adopt new practices more rapidly because so many more have been involved in the learning.

For Americans, this whole process often seems unnecessarily time consuming and costly. As one manager pointed out to me recently, the statement "I'm running an experiment" in most American companies is a code word for "Don't hold me accountable for the results." Consequently, while we may go through the motions of quality improvement, we often get the facade without the substance. At best, we get limited bursts of learning.

IMPROVING HOW WE WORK

The first wave Improving tangible work processes (from the production line, to order entry, to responding to customer inquiries or coordinating the typing queue) was the predominant theme of the first wave in building learning organizations.

The initial tools were derived primarily from statistics, including SPC, and related methods for diagramming, analyzing, and redesigning work processes to reduce variability and enable systematic improvement.

As the first wave was unfolded, the focus has broadened to include more complex processes like product development. By and large, the customer was outside the system of production and the system was designed to meet customer needs.

First wave strength The strength of the first wave lay in achieving measurable improvements in cost, quality, and customer satisfaction through rigorous and reproducible processes of improvement.

First wave limitation The limitation lay in the relatively passive role of management and the limited impact on the larger *systems* whereby processes interact—for example, how sales, order entry, manufacturing, and customer satisfaction interact.

The second wave unfolds The initial profile of the second wave could be seen in Japan as early as the 1960s when leading firms began to undertake mass deployment of quality tools. Previously, only small groups of quality control experts learned how to analyze work processes, reduce variation, and improve quality and cost.

Japanese quality circles and learning "Beginning with quality circles," says Massachusetts Institute of Technology's Alan Graham, "that changed. Everyone began to participate in quality improvement." This was the time when *kaizan* (organization-wide commitment to continuous improvement) was born. This also was the time when Japanese organizations began extensive training in team learning skills, to develop the norms and capabilities needed if quality circles were to be effective.

U.S. quality circles and a lack of emphasis on learning Interestingly, when U.S. firms began to organize production workers in quality circles, 10 to 15 years later, the emphasis was on forming teams, not on developing team learning skills. Consequently, "The skills and practices, both among workers and managers, necessary for QC circles to be effective," according to Graham, "were not present in the introduction of QC circles in the United States. This has been typical of the general underemphasis here on skills and practices, as opposed to official programs and management goals."

The result was that many initial efforts at quality control circles in the United States failed to generate lasting commitment or significant improvement. "Mid-level managers," says USC's Ed Lawler, "saw QC circles as a threat to their authority, and workers saw them as a gimmick to elicit increased effort and undermine union influence."

The second wave arrives In Japan, the second wave arrived in full force with the introduction of the *seven new tools for management* in 1979.

The seven new tools These tools, the work of a committee of the Society for QC Technique Development that operated from 1972 to 1979, focus specifically on how managers think and interact. They particularly emphasize developing better communication and common understandings of complex issues, and relating that understanding to operational planning.

"There are a lot of methodologies for measuring, analyzing, and testing quantitative data," says the leader of the group that developed the new tools, Professor Shiba, "but the area of qualitative methodologies, how to create hypotheses, is very weak. Professor Jiro Kawakita, a Japanese anthropologist, developed methods for analyzing non-numerical data and making sense of that data."

For example, the *KJ method* or affinity diagram, as taught by Professor Shiba and other experts on the *seven management tools,* helps teams gather large amounts of non-quantitative data and organize it into groupings based on natural relationships or affinities. Other tools help to clarify interrelationships, establish priorities, and think through and plan the complex tasks required for accomplishing an agreed upon goal.

A new perspective of the customer Along with these new tools for thinking and interacting, a new orientation toward the customer has gradually emerged. The new perspective moved from *satisfying the customer's expressed requirements* to *meeting the latent needs of the customer.*

The Miata as a second wave example As one Detroit executive put it, "You could never produce the Mazda Miata from market research. You have to understand what the customer would value if he experienced it." In the second wave, the customer becomes part of the system. There is an interplay between what the firm seeks to produce and what the customer desires.

The second wave in America Today, a small number of American companies are starting to experiment with the seven new management tools.

They are discovering a whole new territory for increasing organizational capabilities—how we think and interact around complex, potentially conflictual issues. This is the real message of the second wave—leverage ultimately lies in improving us, not just improving our work processes.

Engelbart's* A, B *and* C *work "There are three levels of work in organizations," says computer pioneer and inventor of the *mouse* Douglas Engelbart, who has spent the better part of 20 years studying the nature of collaborative work.

"The most obvious level, *A work,* involves the development, production, and sale of a firm's products and services. Most of a company's people and resources are focused at this level.

Effective *A work* would be impossible, however, without the next level, *B work,* which involves designing the systems and processes that enable a company to develop, produce, and sell its products and services.

But, the subtlest and potentially most influential level is *C work,* improving how we think and interact. Ultimately, the quality of *C work* determines the quality of systems and processes we design and the products and services we provide."

The first wave and B work The major contribution of quality management in the first wave was to focus time and energy systematically on Engelbart's *B work,* especially on improving processes, and to provide tools for the task.

The second wave and C work The major contribution of the second wave will be to systematically focus on Engelbart's *C work.* This, too, will require appropriate tools. But, before such tools can be developed, we must first understand the *core competencies of learning organizations,* those distinctive capabilities in thinking and interacting which will enable us to "continually improve the total behavior of organizations."

Core competencies for learning organizations The seven new tools point in the right direction. But our work suggests that they are only a start to developing an organization's capabilities in:

Building shared vision There is no substitute for organizational resolve, conviction, commitment, and clarity of intent. They create the need for learning and the collective will to learn. Without shared visions, significant learning occurs only when there are crises, and the learning ends when the crises end.

Personal mastery Shared vision comes from personal visions. Collective commitment to learning comes from individual commitment to learning. An organization that is continually learning how to create its future must be made up of individuals who are continually learning how to create more of what truly matters to them in their own lives.

Working with mental models Organizations become frozen in inaccurate and disempowered views of reality because we lack the capability to *see our assumptions,* and to continually challenge and improve those assumptions. This requires fostering managerial skills in *balancing inquiry and advocacy* in organizations that have been traditionally dominated by advocacy.

Team learning Ultimately, the learning that matters is the learning of *groups of people who need one another to act* (the real meaning of team). The only problem is that we've lost the ability to talk with one another. Most of the time we are limited to *discussion,* which comes from the same roots as percussion and concussion and literally means *to heave one's views at the other.* What is needed also is dialogue, which comes from the Greek *dia logos* and literally means when a group of people talk with one another such that the meaning (*logos*) moves through (*dia*) them.

Systems thinking It's not just how we learn, but what we learn. The most important learning in contemporary organizations concerns gaining shared insight into complexity and how we can shape change. But, since early in life, we've been taught to break apart problems.

The resulting fragmentation has left us unable to see the consequences of our own actions, creating an illusion that we are victims of forces outside our control and that the only type of learning that is possible is learning to react more quickly. Systems thinking is about understanding wholes, not parts, and learning how our actions shape our reality.

Creating an organizational symphony The intrinsic limitations to each of these capabilities is only overcome if they are developed in concert:

- Empowering people (an organization-wide commitment to personal mastery) empowers the organization, but only if individuals are deeply aligned around a common sense of purpose and shared vision.
- Shared vision will energize and sustain an organization through thick and thin, but only if people think systemically: once people are able to see how their actions shape their reality, they begin to understand how alternative actions could create a different reality.
- Individual skills in reflection and inquiry mean little if they cannot be practiced when groups of people confront controversial issues.
- Systems thinking will become the province of a small set of *systems experts* unless it is tied to an organization wide commitment to improving mental models, and even then nothing much will change without shared visions.
- A commitment to seeing the larger system only matters when there is a commitment to the long-term. In the short run, everyone can just fix their piece. Only with a long-term view can an organization see that optimizing the parts, one at a time, can lead to sub-optimizing the whole.

A SHORT STUDY ON LEARNING AS A WAY OF ORGANIZATIONAL LIFE

In 1970, Royal/Dutch Shell was arguably the weakest of the *big seven* oil companies. Today, it is one of the strongest. A key to Shell's ascent has been reconceiving *planning as learning,* a conscious process of bringing operating managers' mental models to the surface and challenging those models.

Shell's scenario planning This conceptual shift has been operationalized by tools like scenario planning. Through its use of scenarios, Shell's planners help managers continually think through how they would manage under multiple possible futures. Today, it is hard for a Shell manager to do business planning without engaging in a conscious learning process.

Shell has become perhaps the first global corporation to realize the leverage the institutionalizing learning as the most effective approach to strategy in a turbulent world. "The corporate one-track mind," says former planning chief Arie de Geus, "is the single primary reason why so many once successful corporations fail to survive beyond their infancy."

From a foreboding view to a new form of planning Shell's innovations in institutional learning were driven by necessity. As early as 1971, Shell's planners became convinced that major shocks in supply and price were becoming a possibility in world oil markets. But, they were unable to convince managers conditioned by the stability of world markets in the 50s and 60s.

This led the planners to develop scenario planning *exercises,* wherein managers thought through how they would manage if there were a shift from a buyer's market to a seller's market, where sudden changes in price would be a part of life, regardless of whether or not they expected such a change.

Prepared for change in the '70s When OPEC did become a reality and the first oil shocks hit in the winter of 1973 and 1974, Shell responded differently than any other big oil company. It increased local operating company control rather than increasing corporate control. It accelerated development of reserves, especially in its North Sea fields. While the other major oil companies saw a sudden, unexpected crisis and acted accordingly, Shell's managers perceived a sea change in the basic nature of the business, and acted differently.

Shell's scenario planning and the '80s The discipline of thinking in terms of alternative futures served Shell equally well in the '80s. Shell planners created a *$15 a barrel oil scenario* in 1983, at a time when prices averaged around $30. They considered two alternative futures:

Alternative future one As managers considered how they would manage in a depressed price world, they quickly concluded that many of their present production processes would have to be shut down because they were too costly.

Alternative future two A few engineers suggested that radical redesign of their oil platforms using new miniaturization technologies could make them operable at prices as low as $11 per barrel.

As they considered the plan, it soon became obvious that such a redesign was in fact more desirable under any possible scenario.

Their production people went ahead with the new design concepts. And when prices did fall, hitting an unbelievable $8 per barrel in 1984, Shell was, once again, one step ahead of its competitors.

Organizational learning alternatives Institutionalizing learning as part of the planning process is one of many possible approaches. It's clear that many Japanese companies have institutionalized learning around quality improvement teams and related innovations.

There is no shortage of ways by which learning may become an inescapable aspect of organizational life, once the nature of the commitment to learning is understood, and once appropriate tools are available.

Institutionalized experimentation "Institutionalizing experimentation can make an enormous difference," says Harvard's Dave Garvin. "For example, Allegheny Ludlum, one of the most profitable American steel companies, treats its entire production process as a laboratory for experimenting with new processes and technologies. Production managers can designate experiments they want to conduct and an entirely different set of measures and standards are used to evaluate their efforts."

Managerial microworlds Another means to institutionalizing learning, the focus of our research at MIT, involves developing *managerial microworlds,* practice fields for management teams.

A financial services microworld For example, in a microworld designed for a leading property and liability insurance company, managers discover how many of their most trusted practices, when they interact in the larger systems of which they are a part, actually contribute to runaway settlement and litigation costs.

Using a computerized *management flight simulator,* they are then able to freely experiment, in ways that would be difficult in real insurance offices, with a wide range of alternative personnel, workflow, and quality management practices to find where there may be leverage in reversing the growing insurance crisis.

Eventually, we envision such microworlds being as common place in organizations as meeting rooms. There will be places where we gather to think through complex issues and learn through experimentation when trial and error learning is impossible in the real system.

Activity-based cost accounting Another potential breakthrough lies in changing managerial accounting practices to reinforce learning rather than controlling.

"Managers and manufacturing engineers," says Harvard's Robert Kaplan "frequently comment that considerable operating improvements they achieve go unrecognized in their financial results."

If the emphasis is on continuous, system wide improvement, how can we have accounting practices based on historically determined standards? "Traditional cost accounting measures fail when they focus on small, local (but not system wide) measures of efficiency and productivity."

WHY BECOMING A LEARNING ORGANIZATION MATTERS

Seeing quality management as part of a deeper and even more far reaching shift leads to several realizations into why the unfolding changes in American management practices may not produce an enduring transformation.

First wave quality is still not well understood in the United States Despite enormous attention, public commitment by prominent corporations, and even a national award, there is a distinct possibility that American management still does not understand what the quality movement is really all about.

Specifically, we lack understanding of what is required for even first wave quality management practices to take root, and why they often fail to take root in American firms.

Confusion over the connections between learning, teams, standards, motivations, and innovation The total quality management task force at one of America's most successful high-tech manufacturing firms recently came unglued around a question of standards.

The external consultant brought in to help develop and implement the TQM strategy argued that standards and standardization were vital to gain better control of the organization's production processes, so that they could be improved. But, to some of the firm's managers, standardization meant rigidity, and a loss of freedom and respect for workers' creativity and individuality.

"Everything becomes vanilla," argued one manager. "We will kill the spark of individual creativity that has made this company what it is."

"If you're not operating in a learning orientation," observed MIT's Dan Kim, "you hear *standardization* differently than if you are. People internalize the need to improve as, *I must be deficient.* Naturally, they then resist what they perceive as an effort to make their deficiencies in public and *fix them.*"

Confusion over the meaning of continuous *and* control The same happens with continuous improvement. Within a learning culture, continuous improvement is a natural by-product of people's commitment and empowerment. Within a controlling culture it is an admission of deficiency. "Why must I improve, unless I'm not good enough now?"

From such a view point, continuous improvement is about becoming less deficient. It is not about learning. This is why it is so deeply resisted by workers in many U.S. companies.

In response to this resistance, managers with good intentions resort to exhortation and to driving *highly mechanized* quality programs through their organizations. This creates a vicious cycle of increasing exhortation and increasing resistance. What is needed is understanding and changing the source of the resistance, which stems from bringing tools for learning into a managerial system based on controlling.

We still believe controlling people is more important than creating a learning environment The second realization is that there is nothing in the American bag of quality tools today that will cause the shift to a learning orientation. And causing such a shift is exactly what is needed in most American corporations. Without a shift of mind from controlling to learning, or as Kim puts it, from "protect and defend" to "create and learn," we "get the tools for quality management without the substance."

Learning cannot be switched on Creating such a shift is an organic process, not a mechanical one. It demands penetrating to deep levels of the corporate psyche and unearthing and examining deep fears.

What will it take to change? To put it bluntly, the shift will not occur if it is not within us. It cannot be faked. It cannot be achieved by public declarations. If at some basic level, we do not genuinely value and truly desire to live life as learners, it will not happen.

My experience is that it can only be caused by small groups of thoughtful leaders who truly desire to build an organization where people are committed to a larger purpose and to thinking for themselves.

Such thoughtful groups then must be willing to become models of continually learning, with all the vulnerability and uncertainty that implies. They become lead users of new learning tools and approaches.

Public and organizational learning/education are linked The last, and potentially most important, realization is that the transformation in corporate and public education may be linked.

"Humans are the learning organism *par excellence,*" according to anthropologist Edward T. Hall. "The drive to learn is as strong as the sexual drive—it begins earlier and lasts longer."

If the drive to learn is so strong, why is it so weak in our corporations? What happened to our "intrinsic joy in learning," as Dr. Deming puts it. The answer according to Deming, Hall, and many educators lies, surprisingly, as much in the classroom as on the factory floor. "The forces of destruction begin with toddlers," says Deming, " . . . a prize for the best Halloween costume, grades in school, gold stars—and on up through the university."

Performing versus learning The young child in school quickly learns that the name of the game is not learning, it is *performing*. Mistakes are punished, correct answers rewarded. If you don't have the right answer, keep your mouth shut.

If we had operated under that system as two-year olds, none of us would have ever learned to walk. Is it any wonder the manager or worker shows little intrinsic motivation to *learn*—that is, to experiment and discover new insights from *mistakes,* outcomes that don't turn out according to plan.

If the conditioning toward performing for others rather than learning is so deeply established in schools, it may not be possible to reverse it on the job. If knowledge is always something somebody else has and I don't, then learning becomes embedded in deep instincts of self-protection not free experimentation.

If the identification of *boss* with *teacher,* the authority figure who has the answers and is the arbiter of our performance is so firmly anchored, we may never be able to roll up our sleeves and all become learners together.

Today, there is no lack of corporate concern for the erosion in our public education. But, there is a lack of vision as to what is truly needed. It is not enough to go back to the 3R's. We must revolutionize the school experience so that it nurtures and deepens our love of learning, develops new skills of integrative or systemic thinking, and helps us learn how to learn, especially together.

FINAL THOUGHTS

I recently asked Dr. Deming if he thought it was possible to fully implement his philosophy of management without radical reform in our schools, as well as in our corporations. "No" was his answer.

However, if we come to a deeper understanding of the linkage between school and work in the 21st century, we may be able to generate a wholly new vision and commitment to the vital task of rethinking both. This may be the real promise of the *learning organization.*

part 2

Total Quality Management Classics

Readings in Part 2 are selections from some of the best-known founding fathers of the modern quality movement. The first reading, by Armand Feigenbaum, introduced the concept of total quality control in a systematic way in 1957. It is striking, from a late 1990s perspective, how insightful and comprehensive Dr. Feigenbaum's ideas were at such an early period of evolution of the quality movement.

The readings by Deming, Juran, and Crosby illustrate some of the original ideas of the three best known American representatives of the quality movement. Over time their ideas have evolved and been extended to new fields of application.

Japanese quality thinking is represented by Kaoru Ishikawa, whose book *Total Quality Control* remains one of the most lucid, clear, and comprehensive texts in the field. A further reading by a well-known Japanese quality expert, Mizuno, can be found in Part 3 and is dedicated to quality improvement tools. Many names are still missing. Among these are Shingo, Taguchi, Kano, Ouchi, and others. Their writings are often highly technical and focused on specific applications (e.g., Taguchi's writings on experimental design) and beyond the scope of this book. Ouchi's analysis of *Theory Z* is widely known and readily accessible. What is less known is that psychologist Abraham Maslow (who developed a comprehensive model to explain human motivation) also offered a very clear exposition of a humanistic theory of motivation which he called *Theory Z,* building on McGregor's *Theory X-Y* model.

SUGGESTIONS IN READING AND STUDY

The readings in this section should be complemented by recent writings of both American and Japanese quality "gurus." Some books, like Deming's *Out of the Crisis,* go beyond the narrow field of manufacturing quality applications and examine broad societal issues. Others focus on highly technical applications. A literature review of this sort is useful to understand the historic development of quality concepts, their practical applications, and to discover fruitful areas for applied research. Such effort is best undertaken in the context of teams who survey a particular field or set of readings and provide the larger group with annotated bibliographies and executive summaries.

Reading 5

Total Quality Control

By Armand V. Feigenbaum

To design, process, and sell products competitively in the 1956 market place, American businessmen must take full account of these crucial trends:

Customers—both industrial and consumer—have been increasing their quality requirements very sharply in recent years. This tendency is likely to be greatly amplified by the intense competition that seems inevitable in the near future.

For example, the electrical relay that could command the lion's share of the 1950 industrial market is no longer acceptable for 1956 operating needs. Consumers are progressively more minute in their examination of the finish of appliances, or in their judgment of the tone of a radio or television set. Even for military products on which quality has always been the major consideration—e.g., jet engines, airborne electronics, and ordnance—specifications are continually being made more rigorous.

As a result of this increased customer demand for higher quality products, present in-plant quality practices and techniques are now, or soon will be, outmoded.

Thus, the machined part that could once be checked with a pocket scale or a pair of micrometers must now be carefully measured with an air gauge; and material that could once be visually accepted if it were "reddish brown and shiny" must now be carefully analyzed both chemically and physically to assure that it is beryllium copper instead of phosphor bronze. At the same time, automation, in which rapid quality evaluation is a pivotal point, has magnified the need for mechanization of inspection and test equipment—much of which is now in the hand-tool

Source: Reprinted by permission of *Harvard Business Review*. From "Total Quality Control," by Armand V. Feigenbaum, November–December 1956.

stage. Indeed, the quality control content of the manufacturing equipment investment dollar may well double in the next decade to purchase the benefit of this mechanization.

Quality costs have become very high. For many companies they may be much too high if these companies are to maintain and improve their competitive position over the long run.

In fact, quality costs (inspection, testing, laboratory checks, scrap, rework, customer complaints, and similar expenses) have crept up to become a multimillion-dollar item. For many businesses they are comparable in degree with total direct labor dollars, with distribution dollars, or with purchased material dollars! While I can find no documented research on the subject, evidence points strongly to the fact that many businesses have quality-cost expenditures representing 7 percent, 8 percent, 10 percent, and even more of their cost of sales!

Taken together, these three trends spell out the twin quality objective that 1956 competitive conditions present to American business management: (a) considerable improvement in the quality of many products and many quality practices, and, at the same time, (b) substantial reductions in the over-all costs of maintaining quality.

Under these conditions, if quality must be not only maintained but upgraded, the wave of the future looks like an expensive one to ride. How many of the frailer business craft will be able to avoid getting swamped?

BROAD SCOPE

Fortunately, there is a way out of the dilemma imposed on businessmen by increasingly demanding customers and by ever-spiraling costs of quality. This "way out" seems to lie in a new kind of quality control, which might be called "total quality control."

The underlying principle of this total quality view—and its basic difference from all other concepts—is that, to provide genuine effectiveness, control must start with the design of the product and end only when the product has been placed in the hands of a customer who remains satisfied.

The reason for this breadth of scope is that the quality of any product is affected at many stages of the industrial cycle:

1. Marketing evaluates the level of quality which customers want and for which they are willing to pay.
2. Engineering reduces this marketing evaluation to exact specifications.
3. Purchasing chooses, contracts with, and retains vendors for parts and materials.
4. Manufacturing engineering selects the jigs, tools, and processes for relay production.
5. Manufacturing supervision and shop operators exert a major quality influence during parts making, subassembly, and final assembly.

6. Mechanical inspection and functional test check conformance to specifications.
7. Shipping influences the caliber of the packaging and transportation.

In other words, the determination both of quality and of quality cost actually takes place throughout the entire industrial cycle. This is the reason why real quality control cannot be accomplished by concentrating on inspection alone, or design alone, or reject trouble-shooting alone, or operator education alone, or statistical analysis alone—important as each of these individual elements is.

The breadth of the job makes quality control a new and important business management function. Just as the theme of the historical inspection activity was "they (i.e., bad parts) shall not pass," the theme of this new approach is "make them right the first time." Emphasis is on defect prevention so that routine inspection will not be needed to as large an extent. The burden of quality proof rests, not with inspection, but with the makers of the part—machinist, assembly foreman, vendor, as the case may be.

Like traditional inspection, the quality control function in this total quality view is still responsible for assurance of the quality of products shipped, but its broader scope places a major addition on this responsibility. Quality control becomes responsible for quality assurance *at optimum quality costs.*

The total quality view sees the prototype quality control man, not as an inspector, but as a quality control engineer—with an adequate background of the applicable product technology and with training in statistical methods, in inspection techniques, and in other useful tools for improving and controlling product quality.

Compared with other views

It may serve further to clarify the character of the total quality view if we compare it with other quality control concepts. Actually, there have been and are today a great many different concepts both of the meaning of the term "quality control" and of what the principal elements of the quality control activity are. The two most widely accepted of these concepts may be described as the "modern inspection view" and the "statistical view."

Historically, quality control meant nothing more than the activity of traditional factory inspection, which was intended to protect the customer by screening bad material from good prior to shipment. In the *modern inspection view,* quality control means this traditional inspection function updated and made more efficient by the use of certain statistical methods and work-in-process inspection routines. Thus:

Statistically verified sampling plans assure the quality of outgoing lots better and more economically than do the older 100 percent inspection or hit-or-miss spot check procedures.

In-process sampling inspections detect quality errors before too many bad parts have been produced, and are consequently more effective than concentration on final inspection with its risk of producing a large number of bad parts.

An impressive weight of dollars-and-cents evidence demonstrates that such techniques represent a great improvement over old-fashioned practices. Probably most systems of quality control in American business today are examples of this modern inspection point of view. That is, they see the prototype quality control man as a well-grounded inspection specialist who has had training in useful statistical methods.

The *statistical view,* in turn, reflects the major and increasing contributions which probability methods are making to the improvement of industrial decision making. It is a view that predominates both in the literature of quality control and in professional meetings on the subject. It sees the prototype quality control man as an industrial statistician, who works on problems ranging from the design of laboratory experiments, through the establishment of control charts for production processes, on to the analysis of manufacturing rejects. It sees him, in other words, as capable of making contributions in fields not directly connected with product quality, such as time study and safety.

These modern inspection and statistical concepts of quality control have been and are highly useful in the areas of product quality which they cover. But, compared with total quality control, their scope is much too limited; they are able to provide only a partial grasp of the overall quality problem that faces American businessmen. They simply are not geared to the fact that quality considerations are involved in every phase of industrial activity, and are not equipped to keep overall costs of quality at a minimum.

Effect of cost accounting

If the burden and sharp upward trend of these quality costs—and the need for genuinely broad quality control effort—are only now becoming recognized in some businesses, part of the reason must be ascribed to traditional industrial cost accounting practices. Cost accounting methods often have not identified and grouped quality costs in a form suitable for the development of adequate controls. The magnitude of the quality cost sum has tended to be obscured by the piecemeal identification of certain individual quality cost elements: for example, scrap and spoilage, or field complaint expense. Most often, quality cost has been conceived as the cost of the company inspection activity—actually just a fraction of overall quality cost—and controls have been established on this fragmentary basis.

Regardless of the source of the fault, the only clear answer to the quality cost problem seems to lie in the new concept of total quality control.

Operation of the function

The work of this total quality control function may be classified into four broad categories, as follows (see Exhibit 5.1 for elaboration):

EXHIBIT 5.1 *Quality control in the quality activity cycle*

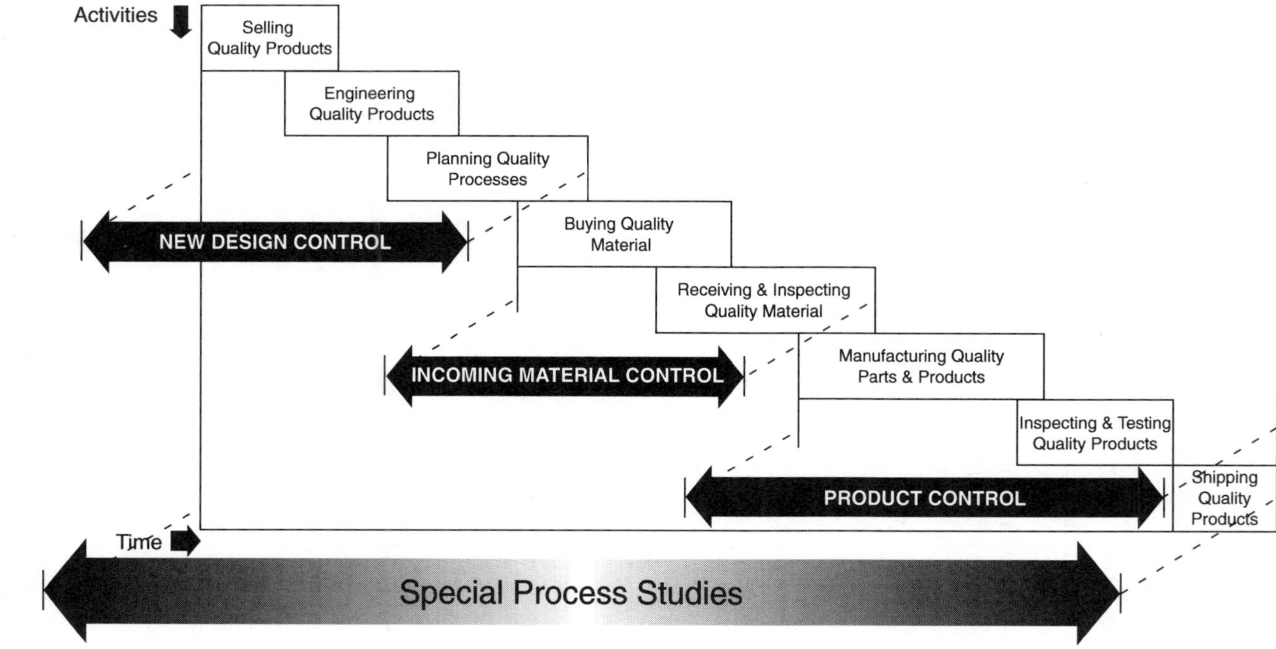

1. New design control, or the planning of controls for new or modified products prior to the start of production.
2. Incoming material control, or the control of incoming purchased parts and materials.
3. Product control, or the shop floor control of materials, parts, and batches from machines, processes, and assembly lines.
4. Special process studies, or the conducting of special analyses of factory and processing problems.

In this work, the two basic responsibilities of the quality control function are: (1) to provide quality assurance for the company's product—i.e., simply, to be sure that the products shipped are right; and (2) to assist in assuring optimum quality costs for those products. It fulfills these responsibilities through its subfunctions: *quality control engineering, inspection,* and *test,* which operate a continuous feedback cycle:

1. Quality control engineering does *quality planning;* this establishes the basic framework of the quality control system for the firm's products.
2. Inspection and test do *quality measuring;* this determines, in accordance with the quality plan, the conformance and performance of parts and products with engineering specifications.
3. There is rapid feedback to quality control engineering for *quality analysis,* which results in new quality planning, thus completing the cycle. (This analysis also fosters corrective action for product quality deviations.)

ENGINEERING COMPONENT

The true nerve center of the total quality control function is the engineering component. Its activities in each of the four broad quality control jobs deserve examination in some detail.

New design control

In this area, quality control engineering provides three main activities:

1. *Preproduction service to design engineering and manufacturing engineering in analyzing the quality-ability of new products and production processes, and in debugging quality problems*—This assures a product which will be as defect-free as possible prior to the start of production. Among the new technical tools which the quality control engineer brings to this effort are process quality capability studies, tolerance analysis technique, pilot run practice, and a wide variety of statistical methods.

2. *Planning of inspections and tests to be carried on when production is under way on the new product*—This is to establish continuous control of in-process quality. It involves determining the following:

   - Dimensions and characteristics of the parts to be checked.
   - Degree to which they are to be checked.
   - In-process and final production points at which checks are required.
   - Methods and procedures to be used—including statistical sampling plans, control charts, and so on.
   - Personnel who will make the checks—that is, production operators or people from the inspection and test subfunctions.

3. *Design of genuinely modern inspection and testing equipment, which, to the fullest possible extent, is physically integrated with manufacturing equipment to permit the machine to check its own work*—The aim of this activity is economical investment expenditures, maximum equipment utilization, and fullest practical mechanization and automation both of operations and of quality control paper work.

Incoming material control

In this area, quality control engineering must assist in the establishment of good quality relationships with suppliers. It contributes to this objective in the following ways:

By planning the periodic rating of the quality performance of present suppliers, it provides facts which assist the purchasing function in quickly bringing satisfactory or unsatisfactory quality performance to the attention of vendors.

By evaluating the quality capability of potential suppliers, it provides facts which assist purchasing to select good quality vendors.

By working with the vendors, it assists them in understanding the quality control requirements of the purchase contracts they have won.

By establishing quality certification programs, it places the burden of quality proof on the vendor rather than on an extensive, expensive in-plant incoming inspection effort.

Product control

In this area, quality control engineering carries on the cost measurement and quality cost reduction project activity required for overall quality cost control and reduction, and it works closely with the inspection and test subfunctions which perform the actual measuring work. It also performs process quality capability studies to determine the quality limits within which a machine or process may be expected to operate. The aim is to make sure that parts will be routed to equipment which is capable of economically maintaining engineering specifications.

Special process studies

In this area, the job of quality control engineering is to analyze complex, in-process quality problems which have been fed back to it by inspection and test. These studies are directed both to the elimination of defects and to the development of possible improvements in present quality levels.

SPECIALIZED ACTIVITY

Certain elements of this quality control engineering work have previously been performed on a sporadic or divided basis. But the quality control engineer himself is something new under the sun. For quality control engineering is not merely a new label for the inspection planning package, nor a fresh designation for the test equipment engineer, nor yet a technologically flavored title for the industrial statistician. It is, instead, a specialized activity with a character all its own, calling for a unique combination of skills.

Quality control engineering work is the product of the cross-fertilization of modern developments in several fields—in statistical methodology, in fast-response high-precision inspection and testing equipment, in management understanding of the nature of the control function in modern business. Altogether, it has the attributes of a genuinely new sector of the engineering profession.

In experience, education, aptitude, and attitude, the man entering quality control engineering work today is, in fact, not very different from the man entering other longer established major technical fields as, for example, product engineering or manufacturing engineering. He must possess, or have the capacity to acquire, the necessary product and process background. He must have the personal characteristics to work effectively in a dynamic atmosphere with people of diverse interests. He must possess the technical background which will enable him to acquire, if he does not already have it, a growing body of quality control engineering knowledge. Finally, he needs the analytical ability to use this knowledge in solving new and different quality problems.

Inspection and test

The planning and analysis work of the quality control engineer makes a new, more positive type of inspection and test both possible and necessary in the modern quality control function. Instead of policing the manufacturing process, this type of inspection and test becomes a direct *part* of that process by assisting in the production of good quality products.

Thus, during incoming material control and product control, the inspection and test subfunctions are responsible not only for fully establishing that the materials received and the products in-process and shipped are of the specified quality, but also for thoroughly and promptly feeding back facts for preventing the purchase and production of poor quality material in the future.

This positive quality measuring requires only a very minimum of routine hand-sorting inspection and test. In product control, for example, this result is made possible through a continuous sequence of engineering work to assure that with the facilities provided production operators can make parts right the first time, know that they can, and have the necessary equipment and gauges to check their own work. On this basis, then, inspection and test can provide genuine assistance in the production of the right quality by:

- Becoming auditors of the good quality practices that have been established.
- Providing as much as possible on-the-spot, shop floor analysis of defects.
- Feeding back facts about these defects for corrective analysis and action elsewhere.

Such quality assurance effort has been termed *control-audit* inspection and test. Inevitably it means the upgrading of traditional inspection and test; it requires considerably fewer but much more highly qualified and more specialized personnel—those who have genuine ability to be helpful in making the right quality. An instance in point is the arc-welding inspector who now not only knows whether or not weld penetration on a part is satisfactory but also, in the case of defective welds, may be able to counsel the shop on the reasons why the penetration has been unsatisfactory.

ORGANIZATIONAL PROBLEM

In organizing a modern quality control function, the first principle to recognize is *that quality is everybody's job.*

In defiance of this principle, there have been many business experiments over the years which have attempted to make the quality activity cycle less of a decentralized, Tinkers-to-Evers-to-Chance sequence. Often these attempts have taken the form of centralizing all quality responsibility by organizing a component whose job was handsomely described as "responsibility for all factors affecting product quality."

These experiments have had a life span of as long as six months—when the job incumbent had the advantage of a strong stomach, a rhinoceros hide, and a well-spent and sober boyhood. Others not similarly endowed did not last even that long.

The simple fact of the matter is that the marketing man is in the best position to evaluate adequately customer's quality preferences; the design engineer is the only man who can effectively establish specification quality levels; the shop supervisor is the individual who can best concentrate on the building of quality. Total quality control programs therefore require, as a first step, top management's reemphasis on the responsibility and accountability of *all* company employees in new design control, incoming material control, product control, and special process studies.

The second principle of total quality control organization is a corollary to the first one. It is *that because quality is everybody's job, it may become nobody's job*. Thus, the second major step required in total quality programs becomes clear. Top management must recognize that the many individual responsibilities for quality will be exercised most effectively when they are buttressed and serviced by a well-organized, genuinely modern management function whose only area of specialization is product quality, and whose only area of operation is in the quality control job.

Location of the function

In view of these two organizational principles, where should the quality control function be placed in the larger structure of company organization? Should it be part of marketing, of engineering, of manufacturing? Should it report direct to general management?

While these are crucial questions, they are not susceptible to categorical answers. Certainly, quality control in any company should report high enough so that it can implement its responsibilities for quality assurance at optimum costs. Certainly, also, it should be close enough to the firing line so that it will be able to fulfill its technological role. However, companies vary widely in their objectives, their character, their philosophy of organization structure, and their technology. The answer to the question of where to locate quality control will necessarily vary also.

It may be worthwhile, however, to report one firm's approach to this issue. In the General Electric Company's product departments, each of which operates as a decentralized business with profit and loss accountability reposing with the department general manager, the cycle of basic quality responsibility is as follows:

The marketing component is responsible for evaluating customers' quality preferences and determining the prices these customers are willing to pay for the various quality levels.

The engineering component is responsible for translating marketing's requirements into exact drawings and specifications.

The manufacturing component is responsible for building products to these drawings, and for knowing that it has done so.

Within this structure of responsibility, quality control clearly emerges as a *manufacturing* function. Thus, in the General Electric product department, the quality control manager reports to the chief manufacturing executive in that department—the manufacturing manager—and operates at the same organization level as the production superintendents, the managers of materials, and the managers of manufacturing engineering.

THE RESULTS

Experience in an increasing number of companies shows that operation of a total quality control program has paid off in six ways:

1. Improved product quality.
2. Reduced scrap, complaint, inspection, and other quality costs.
3. Better product design.
4. Elimination of many production bottlenecks.
5. Improved processing methods.
6. Development of a greater spirit of quality-mindedness on the production shop floor.

Certainly our experience with this program has been highly satisfactory in the General Electric Company, where we have been developing the concept and procedure for some years.

Total quality control has thus, in actual practice, been successful in meeting the dual objective of better quality at lower quality costs. The reason for the satisfactory better-quality result is fairly clear from the very nature of the prevention-centered, step-by-step, technically thorough program. But the explanation may not be nearly so obvious for the accompanying by-product of lower overall quality cost. This needs to be spelled out, especially since it includes, in the long run, lower expenses for the quality control activities themselves as compared with the costs of traditional inspection and test.

Costs of quality

The reason for the favorable cost result of total quality control is that it cuts the two *major* cost segments of quality (which might be called failure and appraisal costs) by means of much smaller increases in the third and *smallest* segment (prevention costs). Why this is possible can be seen as soon as the character of these three categories is considered:

1. Failure costs are caused by defective materials and products that do not meet company quality specifications. They include such loss elements as scrap, spoilage, rework, field complaints, etc.
2. Appraisal costs include the expenses for maintaining company quality levels by means of formal evaluations of product quality. This involves such cost

elements as inspection, test, quality audits, laboratory acceptance examinations, and outside endorsements.

3. Prevention costs are for the purpose of keeping defects from occurring in the first place. Included here are such costs as quality control engineering, employee quality training, and the quality maintenance of patterns and tools.

In the absence of formal nationwide studies of quality costs in various businesses, it is impossible to generalize with any authority about the relative magnitude of these three elements of quality cost. However, I believe it would not be far wrong to assert that failure costs may represent from one-half to three-quarters of total quality costs, while appraisal costs probably range in the neighborhood of one-quarter of this total. Prevention costs, on the other hand, probably do not exceed one-tenth of the quality cost total in most businesses. Out of this 10 percent, usually 8–9 percent are directed into such traditional channels as pattern and tool maintenance and the specification-changing or interpreting work of product engineering. This leaves only 1 or 2 percent that is spent for elements of quality control engineering work.

It is a significant fact that, historically, under the traditional inspection function, failure and appraisal costs have tended to move upward together, and it has been difficult to pull them down once they have started to rise. The reason for this relationship is that:

As defects increase—thus pushing up failure costs—the number of inspectors has been increased to maintain the "they shall not pass" screen to protect the customer. This, in turn, has pushed up appraisal costs.

For the reasons mentioned earlier in this article, screening inspection does not have much effect in eliminating the defects, nor can it completely prevent some of the defective products from leaving the plant and going into the hands of complaining customers.

Appraisal costs thus stay up as long as failure costs remain high. In fact, the higher these failure and appraisal costs go, the higher they are likely to go without successful preventive activity.

Once these two main elements of quality cost have started to rise—as they seem to have throughout industry generally today—the one best hope for pulling them to earth again seems to be spending more on the third and smallest element, namely, prevention cost. The 10 percent now spent may well need to be doubled, much of the increase going for quality control engineering as well as for improved methods of inspection and test equipment automation.

At first glance such increases in prevention costs may not seem to be in the interest of quality cost improvement, but this objection is rapidly dispelled as soon as results are considered. Translated into quality cost terms, the operation of total quality control has the following sequence of results:

1. A substantial cut in failure costs—which has the highest cost reduction potential of all quality cost elements—occurs because of the reduced number of defects and the improvements in product quality brought about by modern quality control practice.
2. Fewer defects mean somewhat less need for routine inspection and test, causing a reduction in appraisal costs.
3. Better inspection and test equipment and practices, and the replacement of many routine operators by less numerous but more effective *control audit* inspectors and testers, bring about additional reductions in appraisal costs.
4. Because the new *control-audit* inspection and test is effective in preventing defects, appraisal dollars for the first time begin to exercise a positive downward pull on failure costs.

The ultimate end result is that total quality control brings about a sizable reduction in overall quality costs, and a major alteration in the proportions of the three cost segments. No large, long-term increase in the size of the quality control function is required as a necessary condition for quality cost improvement. Instead, quality control expense, as a proportion of total company expense, will be down in the long run. Improvements of one-third or more in overall quality costs are not unusual.

Quality dollar budgeting

It is worth noting that this identification and analysis of quality costs permits a major forward step in the business budgeting process. That is, it makes feasible determining the dollars needed for quality control, not on the basis of historical inspection cost experience, but on the basis of current company objectives in product quality and quality costs.

Quality needs and problems differ so much from company to company that it is not realistic to generalize about the specific mix of quality costs that should be budgeted under total quality control. But the direction of budgetary trends may be suggested by an example, which embodies current industrial experience in this area. Exhibit 5.2 shows how one company expects to cut its quality costs by switching from a mild version of the inspection view to total quality control. The company anticipates that total quality expenses will drop from the current high of 7 percent of sales to 5 percent with declines achieved both in failure and appraisal costs while prevention costs increase from only 0.70 percent of sales to a still modest 1.25 percent. In this example, the cost savings budgeted are rather moderate, owing to the presence of complicating factors such as the following:

EXHIBIT 5.2 ***Budgeted quality costs and savings under total quality control (assuming sales increase from $50 million to $75 million)***

	Total dollars		Percent of sales		Percent of total quality cost	
Quality cost element	**Present**	**5-year goal**	**Present**	**5-year goal**	**Present**	**5-year goal**
Failure	$2,275,000	$2,062,500	4.55%	2.75%	65%	55%
Appraisal	875,000	750,000	1.75	1.00	25	20
Prevention	350,000	937,500	0.70	1.25	10	25
Total	$3,500,000	$3,750,000	7.00%	5.00%	100%	100%

- An anticipated 50 percent increase in sales over the next five years—from $50 million to $75 million.
- Planned additions to a product line that is already highly technical and diversified, hence accompanied by major quality problems.

Such a planned 30 percent improvement in quality cost ratios is feasible, indeed conservative, with a successful total quality control program—even with a 50 percent business expansion and even with counterbalancing quality cost increases brought about by the introduction of new products. While the company in the example may not be typical (probably there is no such thing as a typical business enterprise), it is at least illustrative of the good results that can be achieved even when circumstances pose unusual difficulties.

CONCLUSION

Total quality control thus represents another forward step in management science. Its integration of design-through-shipment control of the many elements in the quality picture makes it much more effective than the unlinked fragmentary controls of the past. As a major new business management activity, it provides professional effort in meeting the objective of assured product quality at minimum quality cost.

With this concept, inspection and test have a chance to develop in the direction that conscientious inspectors and testers have always sought; that is, into an activity with a positive role in assisting other members of the manufacturing, engineering, and marketing team toward quality improvement and quality cost control. No longer are inspection and test confined to essentially a negative, fist-shaking role in sorting bad parts from good, a role placing them continually on the defensive and evoking the hostility of other managers.

Further, those tools of statistical methodology that have proved practical and useful can now be brought to their fullest effectiveness. With the quality control engineers as tool builders, and the control-audit inspectors as tool users, statistical techniques can be put to work in a down-to-earth fashion that welds them into regular day-by-day controls. No longer will these techniques be treated—as too often in the past—merely as curiosities, to be employed in special situations on a pinch-hitting basis.

With equipment for inspection and test a direct and major responsibility of the quality control function, more use can be made of equipment specialists who wish to concentrate their skills on the great needs, opportunities, and unique complexities of today's quality control equipment field.

Total quality control thus welds this new technology into a strong yet flexible weapon, capable of successfully coming to grips with the three major quality problems that modern business must face and solve: the upward customer pressure on quality levels, the resulting rapid obsolescence of quality practices, the very high level of quality costs.

While delivery and other factors may sell a product the first time, it is usually quality which keeps the product sold and which keeps the customer coming back a second and a third time. Quality cost—perhaps 8 percent or more of cost of sales—is one of the major elements of product cost that must be made right to permit the setting of the right price to the customer. Helping to assure this right quality at this right quality cost is the way the new *total quality control* can serve its company in the years ahead.

Reading 6

On Some Statistical Aids toward Economic Production[1]

By W. Edwards Deming

Abstract

This paper covers management's responsibility for (1) design of product; (2) specification of service offered; (3) measurement by simple statistical methods of the amount of trouble with product or with service that can be ascribed to causes that only management can act on; (4) action on the causes so indicated. It shows by principle and by example how management may observe week by week the effects of guided effort toward reduction of trouble. The paper upsets a number of commonly accepted principles of administration. For example, a job description, for best economy, should require the production worker to achieve statistical control of his work; to meet specifications without paying the high cost of inspection, rework, and replacement. Statistical evidence of performance replaces opinion of foreman and supervisor.

As a second principle, it is demoralizing and costly to call the attention of a production worker to a defective item when he is in a state of statistical control. The fault for the defective item is not chargeable to the worker, but to the system. Fewer defectives can come only from a change in the system, not from efforts of the production worker.

Third, it is better to shift to a totally different job a worker that has developed statistical control of bad habits in his present job.

Source: Reprinted by permission: W. Edwards Deming, "On Some Statistical Aids Toward Economic Production," *Interfaces*, Volume 5, Number 4, August 1975.

All variation in quality characteristics (dimension, hardness, color) causes loss, whether the variation results in defective product or not. Economies in manufacture are a natural consequence of reduction in the variation of a quality characteristic. The author divides causes of variation into two sources: (1) the system (common causes), the responsibility of management; (2) special causes, which are under the governance of the individual employee. In the author's experience, losses from the system overshadow losses from special causes. The same principles apply to sales and to service.

PURPOSE AND SCOPE OF THIS PAPER

One purpose of this paper is to present a number of new principles of training and administration that upset generally accepted conventions. The new principles had their origin in the author's work in Japan, which commenced in 1950 [1], [2].

Another purpose is to point out to management that most of the trouble with faulty product, recalls, high cost of production and service, is chargeable to the system and hence to management. Effort to improve the performance of workers will be a disappointment until the handicap of the system is reduced.

The principles explained here will apply to any company, large or small, whether engaged in production of manufactured items or in service (hotel, hospital, restaurant, retail store, wholesale, railway, motor freight, delivery service, communication, including the postal service), agricultural or industrial, whether owned by private investment or by the government, and in any country, whether it be developed, underdeveloped, or overdeveloped.

Many causes have contributed to devaluation of the dollar and to our precarious balance of payments, but one contributor, steadfastly avoided by economists, is that the quality of many American products is no longer competitive, here or abroad. Statisticians have failed in America to explain to people in management the impact that statistical methods could make on quality, production, marketing, labor-relations, and competitive position. Schools of business teach words and goals, but not methods.

The reader will note, I hope, that I write as a statistician, working with management on problems in industry and in research in many disciplines. I am not a consultant in management. I am not an economist.

ROADBLOCKS TO QUALITY IN AMERICA

An obstacle that ensures disappointment is the supposition all too prevalent that quality control is something that you install, like a new Dean, or a new carpet, or new furniture. Install it and you have it. This supposition is unfortunately force-fed by the common language of quality control engineers, some of whom offer to install a quality control system. Actually, quality control, to be successful in any company, must be a learning-process, year by year, from the top downward and from the bottom up, with accumulation of knowledge and experience, under competent tutelage.

Another roadblock is management's supposition that the production workers are responsible for all trouble: that there would be no problems in production or in service if only the workers would do their jobs in the way that they were taught. Pleasant dreams. The workers are handicapped by the system.

In my experience, it is something new and incomprehensible to a man in an executive position that management could be at fault in the production end. Production and quality, in the view of management, are the responsibilities of the production worker. Research into faults of the system, to be corrected by management, is not what a manager is trained for. Result: The faults of the system stay put, along with rejections and high costs of production.

Management usually discharges its responsibilities (sweeps them under the rug) by turning the job over to a department of quality control. This would be a happy solution and good administration if it solved anything, but it seldom does: the job lands on people that try hard but have not the necessary competence, and the management never knows the difference.

As a result, one finds in most companies not quality control, but guerrilla sniping—no provision nor appreciation for the statistical control of quality in the broad sense of this paper.

People in management need to know enough about quality control to be able to judge whether their quality control departments are doing the job.

Statements by management of aims desired in quality and production are not quality control, nor are they action on improvement of the system. Neither are periodic reviews and evaluations of quality and production. They are necessary but not sufficient.

Exhortations, pleas, and platitudes addressed to the rank and file in an organization are not very effective instruments for the improvement of quality. Something more is required.

I should mention here also the costly fallacy held by many people in management that a technical man (a statistician, for example) must know all about a process and all about the business in order to work in the company. All evidence points to the contrary. Competent men in every position, from top management to the humblest worker, if they are doing their best, know all there is to know about their work *except how to improve it.* Help toward improvement can come *only from some other kind of knowledge*. Help may come from outside the company, or from better use of knowledge and skills already within the company, or both.

LOSS FROM VARIATION: TWO SOURCES OF VARIATION

It is good management to reduce the variation of any quality characteristic (thickness, or measure of performance), whether this characteristic be in a state of control or not, and even when no or few defectives are produced. Reduction in variation means greater uniformity and dependability of product, greater output per hour, greater output per unit of raw material, and better competitive position [5], [7].

Causes of variation and of high cost, with loss of competitive position, may be usefully subsumed under two categories:

Faults of the System (Common or Environmental Causes)
85%

These faults stay in the system until reduced by management. Their combined effect is usually easy to measure. Some individual causes must be isolated by judgment. Others may be identified by experiment: some by records on operations and materials suspected of being offenders (see reference to Juran).

Special Causes
15%

These causes are specific to a certain worker or to a machine. A statistical signal detects the existence of a special cause, which the worker can usually identify and correct.

Both types of cause[s] require attention of management. Common causes get their name from the fact that they are common to a whole group of workers: they belong to the system [2].

No improvement of the system, nor any reduction of special causes of variation and trouble, will take place unless management attacks common causes with as much science and vigor as the production-workers and engineers attack special causes [3].

The percentages shown are intended only to indicate that, in my experience, problems of the system overshadow special causes. The percentages will fluctuate as special causes are eliminated one by one, and as faults of the system are reduced or eliminated.

Confusion between the two types of cause[s] leads to frustration at all levels and leads to greater variability and to higher costs—exactly contrary to what is needed.

Fortunately, this confusion can be eliminated with almost unerring accuracy. Simple statistical techniques, distributions, run-charts, Shewhart control charts, all explained in many books, provide signals that tell the operator when to take action to improve the uniformity of his work. They also tell him when to leave it alone. Results of inspection, without signals, lead to frustration and dissatisfaction of any conscientious worker.

What is not in the books, nor known generally amongst quality-control engineers, is that the same charts that send statistical signals to the production worker also indicate the totality of fault that belongs to the system itself, correction of which is management's responsibility [2]. The production worker can observe from his charts whether attempts by management to improve the system have had an effect. Management can give themselves the same test. Examples appear further on.

Removal of a special cause of variation, important though it be, is not improvement of the system: It merely reduces the variation to a level that identifies the system, but leaves it unimproved.

Mechanical feedbacks that hold dimensions and other quality characteristics within bounds are sometimes helpful but may be wasteful of material and of machine time. They do not improve the system. Better understanding of the function of feed-back systems, so as to use them effectively, and to supplement them, will be an important step for management.

"We rely on our experience," is the answer that came from the manager of quality in a large company recently, when I inquired how he distinguishes between the two kinds of trouble, and on what principles. This answer is self-incriminating: It is a guarantee that this company will continue to pile up about the same amount of trouble as in the past. Why should it change?

"Bill," I asked of the manager of a large company engaged in motor freight, "how much of this trouble (shortage and damage, 7,911 examples in one terminal alone in 1974) is the fault of the drivers?" His reply, "All of it," is again a guarantee that this level of loss will continue until statistical methods detect some of the sources of trouble with the system for Bill to work on.

The QC-Circle movement in Japan (3 million members; 4 to 8 workers to a circle) gives employees the chance to study and revise the system of production at the local level, for greater output and better quality. Japanese workers are not handicapped by the rigidity of the American production line. The QC-Circles represent partial decentralization of management's responsibility to find local faults in the system, and to take action on them. The QC-Circles in Japan bear no relationship to suggestion boxes, common everywhere.

The boost in morale of the production worker, if he were to perceive a genuine attempt on the part of management to improve the system and to hold the production worker responsible only for what the production worker is responsible for and can govern, and not for handicaps placed on him by the system, would be hard to overestimate. It has not been tried, I believe, outside Japan.

It is now clear that the term zero defects can only be a theatrical catchword, a nostrum. The management of many concerns have adopted it outright or in equivalent form and have posted it all over the plant for everyone to see, especially visitors, expecting magic. Empty words they are till the management acknowledges responsibility toward reduction of common causes. One company that I know of reduced their defects by eliminating 8 inspectors out of 10. This is a successful approach until the defectives start coming back with claims attached.

THUMBNAIL SKETCH OF THE STATE OF STATISTICAL CONTROL

Some understanding of the concept of statistical control, invented by Shewhart [6] is necessary as background. A state of statistical control is a state of randomness. Simple tests of randomness are the Shewhart charts—run charts, $\bar{x}$-charts, R-charts. The up and down movements on a chart are to be disregarded by the production-worker unless there is indication of a special cause. A point that falls outside the control limits is a statistical signal that indicates the existence of a special cause of variation. This the production worker can almost always identify readily and correct.

Control limits are not specification limits. Control limits are set by simple statistical calculations from the output itself. What the control limits do is to send out signals that if heeded will minimize the net loss from the two kinds of mistakes that the production worker can make:

1. Adjust his work process when it would be better to leave it alone.
2. Fail to adjust his work process when it needs adjustment. The only rational and economic guide to minimum loss is statistical signals.

The production worker himself may in most cases plot the statistical charts that will tell him whether and when to take action on his work. He requires only a knowledge of simple arithmetic. But the production worker cannot by himself start his own chart, and still less a movement for use of charts. Management must start the movement, and stay on the job.

Some processes in nature exhibit statistical control. Radioactive disintegration is an example. The distribution of time to failure of vacuum tubes and of many other pieces of complex apparatus furnish further examples. But a state of statistical control is not a natural state for a work process. It is instead an achievement, arrived at by elimination one by one, by determined effort, of special causes of excessive variation.

Figure 6.1 shows the results of inspection from a process that is not in statistical control. The upper panel ($\bar{x}$) average of 5 successive items indicates the existence of special causes. There are points below the lower control limit and too many points on the border of the upper control limit. The lower panel (range (R) shows a downward trend, which, although it may indeed be a trend toward greater uniformity, indicates nevertheless also the existence of one or more (possibly additional) special causes, which again the worker must discover and correct. The charts thus indicate the existence of special causes, elimination or reduction of which is the responsibility of the operator. The reader may turn to Figures 6.2 and 6.4 to see a state of statistical control.

A process has an identity only if it is in a state of statistical control. The control limits, and the size of the sample, then enable management to predict rationally the level and range of variation of product that will be produced tomorrow. The same principles and rules are applicable to service organizations.

Statistical control thus provides a basis for doing business in a rational way. The manufacturer knows what quality he can produce, and at what cost. He will not walk into heavy loss by taking a contract for uniformity that he cannot meet, or can meet only by inspection and rework, always costly and unsatisfactory. He can make no rational prediction about his product and costs when his processes are not in statistical control.

Results of inspection are too often unreliable—worse, are sources of strife—because of mistrust of the measurements whether made by use of instruments or

FIGURE 6.1 ***A control chart showing the existence of special causes of variation***

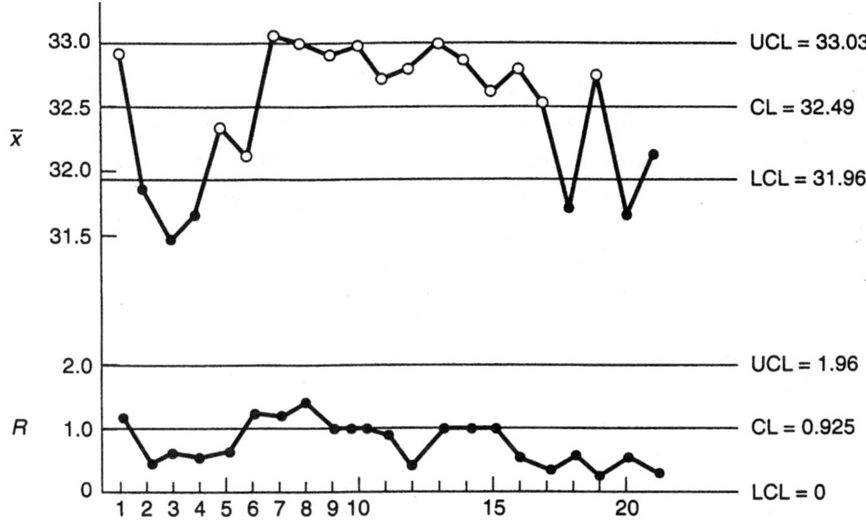

by visual inspection. Measurement must be viewed as a process, the product of which is figures. A method of measurement cannot be dignified as a method, unless, with some operators at least, it shows a state of statistical control. A control chart is a powerful scientific tool.

The first step is to achieve reasonably good statistical control of some of the main operations, including inspection. The next step is for management to work on the common causes of variation and of defective products.

Textbooks on quality control (except for Juran [3]) teach only detection of special causes (Shewhart's assignable causes) and acceptance sampling (for disposition of product already on hand). These are important statistical methods, but acceptance sampling does not build quality that is not already there; and removal of special causes stops short of the main part of the problem, namely, faults of the system.

The explanation is simple. The usual terminology, following Shewhart [6] himself, is that the remaining sources of variation, lumped together, once control is established, constitute "chance causes," variation to leave to chance. This is the correct view for the production-worker in a state of control: He should indeed leave the remaining variation to chance. Likewise for a group of workers, or a line, or a process: ups and downs in a state of control are not a basis for action on the process.

The contribution that I am trying to make here is that management must take a different view: Management *must not* leave the remaining variation to chance.

FAMILIAR CONSEQUENCES OF FAULTS OF THE SYSTEM

Recalls of automobiles, electrical apparatus, and of other items, familiar enough to people in America, for possible hazards from failure of components and assemblies, or from contamination, are signs of faults in design. Failure to carry out adequate tests of components and assemblies over the ranges of jolt, stress, dust, speeds, voltages, corrosion, likely to be met in practice, or failure to heed the results of such tests, is chargeable to the system; hence to management. Or, as sometimes happens, management sometimes goes ahead with production, test or no test, to beat a competitor to the marketplace. No amount of care and skill on the part of the production worker can overcome a fault in design. Where is the statistician's report on the performance of parts and assemblies that give rise to trouble and to recalls?

If one enquires whether more experimentation in advance would have overpaid its cost, or whether it is better business to rush into the marketplace and take a chance, I would offer the following remarks: (a) no dollar value can be placed on the unhappiness of a customer and the loss of future business over a defective item of an unsatisfactory service call; (b) the costliest experimentation on the performance of a product is the tests the customer carries out for himself; and (c) cost-benefit analysis has important uses, but also serious limitations. If the Japanese manufacturers had depended on cost-benefit analysis in 1949 to decide whether to learn and use the statistical control of quality, they would, I surmise, have given it a negative vote, or would still be studying the matter.

PARTIAL LIST OF USUAL FAULTS OF THE SYSTEM (COMMON OR ENVIRONMENTAL CAUSES OF VARIATION)

The reader may make additions and subtractions to suit his own situation.

1. Hasty design of component parts and assemblies. Inadequate tests of prototypes. Hasty production.
2. Inadequate testing of incoming materials. Specifications that are too stringent, or too loose, or meaningless. Waiving specifications.
3. Failure to know the capabilities of processes that are in a state of statistical control, and to use this information as a basis for contracts, both for quantity and quality.
4. Failure to provide production workers with statistical signals that will tell them how they are doing and when to make some change.

5. Failure to use these charts as a measure of the faults of the system, and of the effect of action taken by management to reduce them.
6. Failure to write job descriptions that take account of the capability of the process.
7. Inadequate training of workers, with the help of statistical controls.
8. Settings of machines chronically inaccurate (fault of the crew responsible for settings).
9. Instruments and tests not reliable. Consequent demoralization and loss from false reports and false signals. Loss from needless retesting.
10. Smoke, noise, unnecessary dirt, poor light, humidity confusion.

The production worker is helpless to reduce any of these causes of trouble. Economic considerations must of course govern the decision of management to reduce or eliminate a fault of the system. An easy way out is to say that it would cost too much.

A WORD ON DUE CARE

Statistical control and its consequences, if explained by statisticians to the legal profession in industry and in government, would clear up many problems about safety and reliability. The most that a manufacturer can put into the uniformity and dependability of a device is (a) to achieve and maintain statistical control, at the right level and spread, of the most important quality characteristic of the main outgoing components and assemblies, and incoming ingredients, and (b) to be able to demonstrate by adequate statistical records and charts, along with action taken on special causes and on common causes, that he has done so.

In spite of scrupulous care and intelligent use of statistical controls, it is inevitable that a defective item will get out now and then. An unfortunate freak of this kind cannot be viewed as an act of carelessness on the part of the manufacturer. He can do no more than to exercise due care.

SOME NEW PRINCIPLES IN ADMINISTRATION

This paper upsets some well-accepted principles of administration, which when examined under the logic of statistical inference turn out to be bad practice—that is, demoralizing to the rank and file of production workers, and costly. For example, it turns out to be bad practice to draw the attention of a production worker to a defect in his work when he is in a state of statistical control. Why? The production worker is helpless: He cannot do better. It is as if he were drawing blindfolded handfuls from a mixture of black and white beans. The number of black beans in a handful may be 0, or it may be 1, or 2, or more. The laws of chance apply. He cannot alter these laws, once he achieves statistical control. He will only make

FIGURE 6.2 *Average scores in golf for an experienced golfer, before and after lessons*

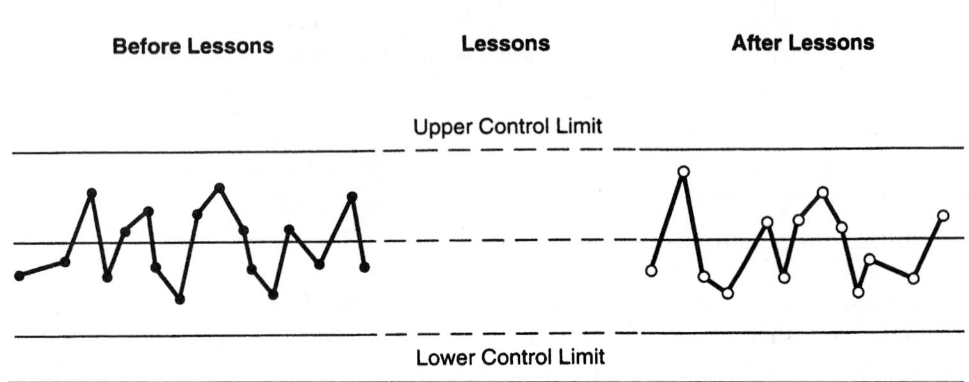

things worse (increase the proportion of black beans) if he tries to adjust his work except on statistical signal. To draw his attention to an error or to hold him on the job until he corrects it is to charge him with a fault of the system.

Yet it is common practice in industry, whether it be production or service, to bring to the attention of a man any output that is discovered to be defective. In an example that I could cite, a production worker, whether in a state of statistical control or not, reworks on his own time all the defectives that inspection discovered in the product that he turned out during his shift. This is what some people call quality control. The reason given to me upon enquiry is that this procedure is a continual reminder to the production worker that defectives will not be toler-

FIGURE 6.3 *Average weekly scores in golf for a beginner who took lessons before he reached a state of statistical control*

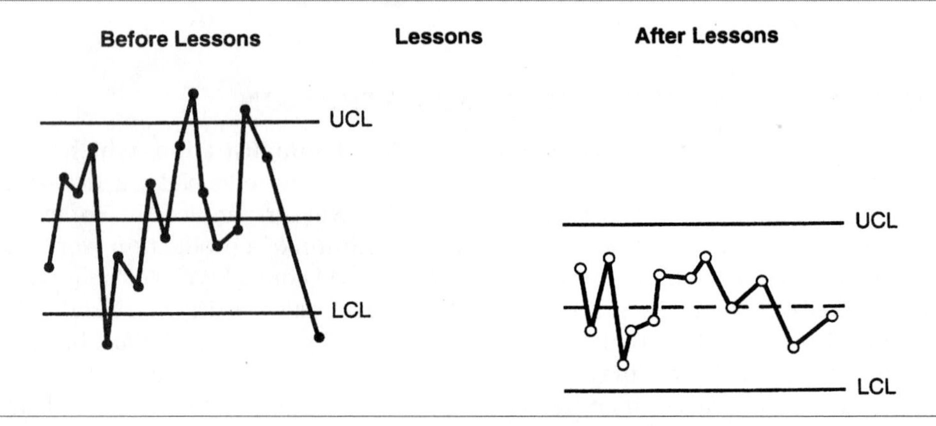

ated; that he is responsible for the work that he turns out. How can he improve if he doesn't know about his mistakes?

Like so many obvious solutions to problems, this one is also wrong. The fallacy in this principle is demonstrated by dependable day-to-day figures on rejections.

A job description, for best economy, should require achievement of statistical control of a dimension [4]. Under this requirement, the production worker is in charge of his own process, and can achieve in his work maximum economic uniformity and output. This is very different from asking a production worker to force a dimension of individual pieces to stay within specified limits.

An economic level and spread of the control limits would produce a distribution for individual pieces that rarely if ever extends beyond the specification and produces a defective item. It is the responsibility of the foreman or higher supervision to remove obstacles to an economic level and spread. This might mean better setting of the machine, or better maintenance, or incoming materials better suited to the right spread. None of this refinement in job descriptions will take place without understanding and action on the part of management (see Example 1).

A state of statistical control can exist in a climate of mild but uniform carelessness. This degree of carelessness is part of the system, the climate. In my experience, workers seldom know the cost of carelessness nor the cost of a mistake (see Example 2). Only management can teach them.

To call to the attention of a worker to a careless act, in a climate of general carelessness, is a waste of time and can only generate hard feelings, because the condition of general carelessness belongs to everybody and is the fault of management, not of any one worker, nor of all workers.

A general reminder, posted in a factory so that everyone can see it, to explain to the workers the cost of a defective item, or the cost of a mistake, may be helpful in improving the system. Meetings illustrated with moving pictures to show how defects are made, caught in the act, are also helpful.

Continuing education on the job to rehearse principles of the job and the cost of defective work belong in the system. This is management's job: workers cannot institute it.

A worker who is in a state of control but whose work is unsatisfactory presents a difficult problem. It is usually uneconomical to try to retrain him on this same job. It is more economical to put him into a new job in which the training may be more expert than it was in his present job.

Figure 6.2 provides an illustration. An experienced man in golf hoped to improve his score by taking lessons. The chart shows that the lessons accomplished nothing. His techniques were engrained: His teacher was unsuccessful in dislodging them and replacing them with better ones.

Curiously, so long as a man has not reached a state of statistical control, there is hope. Figure 6.3 shows average scores ($\bar{x}$) in golf for a beginner. His scores, before the lessons, were obviously not in a state of control, there are points outside the control limits. Then came lessons. His scores thereupon showed a state of statistical control with the desired results, viz., an average score considerably below what his average was before the lessons. Here, lessons changed the system.

Ten production workers may all be in statistical control as individuals, all at different levels. Their combined output will also be in control. *Improvement comes about by studying the individual workers, transferring to another job with a fresh start anyone that is out of line on the side of poor performance.*

It is my observation that training in industry is deplorable. A new employee simply goes to work. Written instructions for the job, if they exist, are in many cases incomprehensible. What happens is that the new worker gives up on the instructions for fear of being further confused. His coworkers come to the rescue, instructions or no instructions, and in a few days he is running along with the herd. The service industries (restaurants, hotels, laundries, etc.) provide horrible examples. The argument is that instruction and training are too costly, and that it is all lost if an employee quits the job.

In contrast, a girl that runs a lift in Japan, or is conductor on a bus, spends two months in training on how to handle people, this in spite of her genteel background of culture.

Training or the lack of it is part of the system. Training can be improved only by management, certainly not by the workers.

Example 1

This example illustrates how a small change in the system could virtually eliminate the possibility of defective items. The ordinates in Figure 6.4 are the means ($\bar{x}$) of samples of $n = 3$ for tests of uniformity of finished wheels. The test is the running balance of the wheel. Observations:

1. The production worker is in a state of control with respect to his own work (which is the only work that he is responsible for). No point falls outside the control limits.
2. He is under the handicap of the system. He cannot beat the system and the capability of his process: He will once in a while produce a defective wheel, even though he is a good worker and in a state of control.
3. He is meeting the requirements of his job. He can do no more. He has nothing further to offer.
4. The main trouble lies in the system. The central line in Figure 6.4, which fall at about 125 gram-cms, represents the contribution of the system to the total trouble. This handicap is built in. If the faults of the system were reduced to 75 percent of their present level, the upper tail of the distribution of individual pieces would drop well below the specification limit, and the entire production would be accepted; economies in production would be realized.

The reaction of management on the above paragraphs was the usual one, namely, that they did not have in mind this kind of quality control when they went into it. They were looking for everything to clear up, once the production workers put their best efforts into the job. Eventually, however, patience paid off.

Charts like Figure 6.4 are to be seen almost anywhere, but interpretation of them in terms of a quantitative measure of the faults of the system are rare.

FIGURE 6.4 *Chart for $\overline{X}$ for test of uniformity of wheels turned out by a production worker*

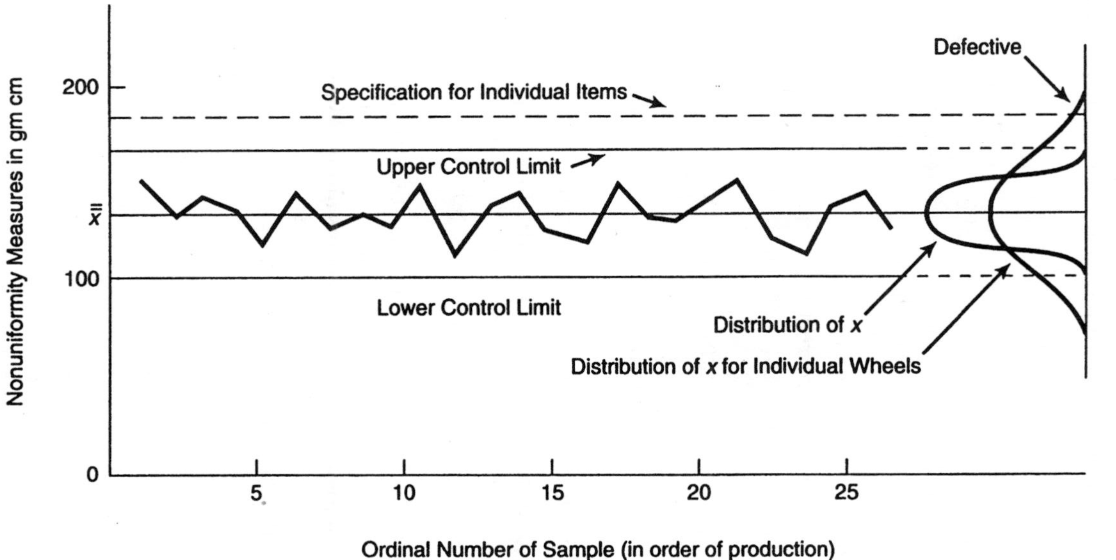

Example 2

The second example deals with a service industry, motor freight. Drivers of trucks pick up shipments and bring them into a terminal for reload and onward movement. Other drivers deliver. A large company in motor freight may have anywhere from ten to forty terminals in or near large cities. There is a long chain of operations between the request of a shipper to the carrier (usually by telephone) to come and pick up a shipment, and placement of the shipment on the platform of the carrier, ready for reload and line haul to the terminal that serves the destination of the shipment. Every operation offers a chance for the driver to make a mistake. The table shows 6 types of mistakes, plus all others. Although the frequency of mistakes is low, the total loss is substantial.

In mistake No. 1, the driver signs the shipping order for 10 cartons, but someone else finds, later on in the chain of operations, that there are only 9 cartons; one carton missing. Where is it? There may have been only 9 cartons in the first place; the shipping order was written incorrectly; or, more usual, the driver left one carton on the shipper's premises. Let us list some of the sources of loss from mistake No. 1:

1. It costs about $25 to search the platform for the missing carton, or to find the truck (by now out on the road) and to search it.
2. It costs $15 on the average to send a driver back to the shipper to pick up the missing carton.
3. It costs $10 to segregate and hold the 9 cartons for the duration of the search.
4. If the carrier does not find the carton, then the shipper may legitimately put in a claim for it. The carrier is responsible for the 10th carton. Its value may be anywhere from $10 to $1,000, with the possibility of an amount even greater.

It is obvious that mistake No. 1 may be costly. Any one of the 7 mistakes will on the average lead to a loss of $50. There were a total of 617 mistakes on the record, and they caused a loss of $31,000 for claims alone. Multiplied by 20, for 20 terminals, the total loss from the 7 mistakes was $620,000. (This amount is a minimum. It does not include the expenses of searches nor administration. Moreover, some mistakes are not included in the total of 617, but they nevertheless cause loss.)

THE 7 TYPES OF MISTAKES

Type of mistake	Description
1	Short on pick up
2	Over on pick up
3	Failure to call in (by telephone) on over, short, and damaged cartons on delivery
4	Incomplete bill of lading
5	Improperly marked cartons
6	Incomplete signature on delivery-receipt
7	Other

There were 150 drivers that worked all year long. Figure 6.5 shows the distribution of the 150 drivers by number of mistakes, all 7 mistakes combined.

We postulate the following mechanism, which will distribute errors at random to drivers. We imagine a huge bowl of black and white beads, thoroughly mixed. Each driver scoops up a sample of 1,000 or more (the number of trips that an average driver makes in a year), and returns the beads to the bowl for more mixing. The number of black beads in a scoop will be a random variable, following the Poisson distribution. The total number of mistakes in Figure 6.5 is 617, and there were 150 drivers. An estimate of the mean number of mistakes per driver would be is seen in Figure 6.5.

The upper and lower 3-sigma limits for these samples would be easy to calculate by use of the square-root-transformation, by which

$$(\sqrt{4.1} + 1.5)^2 = 12 \text{ [Upper Limit]}$$
and
$$(\sqrt{4.1} - 1.5)^2 = 0 \text{ [Lower Limit]}$$

One may perform the same calculations instantly by use of the Mosteller-Tukey double square-root paper [8].

We interpret the upper limit to mean that a driver that made 12 or more mistakes in the year is not part of the system. He contributes more than his share. He is a special cause of loss. I may add here that other statistical models that I have tried lead to about the same conclusions.

Drivers that made 0, 1, 2, 3, or 4 mistakes are far more numerous than the Poisson distribution would allow. I accordingly consolidate the drivers that made 0, 1, 2, 3, or 4 mistakes, and postulate that they too form a separate group. There are then three groups of drivers:

A. Drivers that made 12 or more mistakes.

B. Drivers that made between 5 and 11 mistakes.

C. The extra careful group, drivers that made 0, 1, 2, 3, or 4 mistakes.

What have we learned from this simple statistical model?

1. The 7 drivers with 12 or more mistakes accounted for 112/617, or 18 percent of the mistakes. They could reduce their rates of mistakes to average if they knew that they were outliers.
2. Drivers that made 5 to 11 mistakes measure the losses that arise from the system itself. They make the system what it is. They account for (425 − 112)/617 or about 51 percent of the mistakes. Clearly, about half the losses from the 7 types of mistake[s] arise from the system as it is.
3. The 102 drivers of Group C accounted for only 192/617 = 31 percent of the mistakes. This Group C is worth studying: How do they do it? Did they have easy routes or easy conditions (e.g., day-time pick-ups, inside pick-ups), or do

FIGURE 6.5 *The distribution of drivers by number of mistakes, all 7 errors combined*

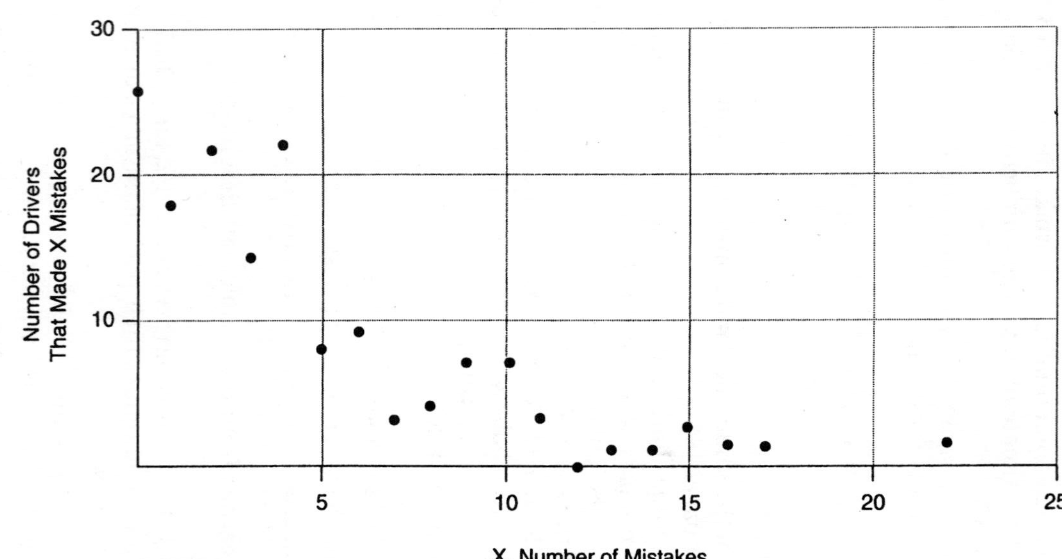

> they have a system of their own? These are questions to pursue. If these men have a system of their own, then they should teach the others. (Enquiry turned up no evidence of easy routes.)

No problem with people is simple. It would be wise for the management to defer criticism of Group A, to determine first whether these drivers worked unusually difficult routes, or whether they had achieved excessive mileage (high productivity). As it turned out, they had.

Here we encounter an important lesson in administration. This company had been sending a letter to a driver at every mistake. It made no difference whether this was the one mistake of the year for this driver, or the 15th: The letter was exactly the same. A letter sent to a driver in Group B or C is demoralizing: The driver's interpretation thereof—and he is absolutely correct—is that he is blamed for faults of the system.

The management had failed to see that they face three distinct types of problem[s]. What was needed was a separation of responsibilities for improvement—special causes, to be corrected by the drivers of Group A; the system itself, to be improved by the management; study of Group C; and examination of the accuracy of their records of mistakes.

One might pause here in passing to ask two questions: (1) what does the manager of the terminal think of the driver to whom he has sent in one year 15 warnings of disciplinary action? More important, (2) what does the driver think of the manager?

Example 3

A small manufacturer of shoes was having trouble with his sewing machines, rent of which was very costly. The operators were spending a lot of their time rethreading the machines, a serious loss.

The key observation was that the trouble was common to all machines and to all operators. The obvious conclusion was that the trouble, whatever it was, was common, environmental, affecting all machines and all operators. A few tests showed that it was the thread that caused the trouble. The owner of the shop had been purchasing poor thread at bargain prices. The loss of machine-time had cost him hundreds of times the difference between good thread and what he had been buying. Bargain prices for thread turned out to be a costly snare.

Better thread eliminated the problem. Only the management could make the change. The operators could not go out and buy better thread, even if they had known where the trouble lay. They work in the system. The thread was part of the system.

Prior to the simple investigation that found the cause, pedestrian but effective, the owner had supposed that his troubles all came from inexperience and carelessness of the operators.

Example 4

The work of every one of 50 production workers on a certain production line is in statistical control. The manager of personnel came forth with a plan, immediately hailed by the management, to award monthly a prize and half a day off to the operator on this line whose production the month before showed the smallest proportion of defective product.

Was this a good idea? What was wrong? Why should the statistician advise the management to drop the idea? The answer is that it would not improve the performance of the workers, nor improve quality.

Why not? Every operator has already put into the job all that he has to offer: The work of each one is in a state of control.

This award would not be an award of merit. What harm would come from it? It would produce frustration and dissatisfaction amongst conscientious workers. Their efforts to find out what they are doing that is wrong, and why their work is not as good as that of the man that won the prize, would be a fruitless chase. They would try out changes in their operations, the only effect of which would be greater variability, not less.

The award would be a lottery. There would be no harm that I know of in introducing a lottery for excitement, provided management calls it a lottery, not an award of merit.

This is an example of administration without statistical judgment. The plan seemed to be a great idea until examined by the theory of probability, with reference to special causes and common causes.

What the personnel man could do, if he wishes to offer a prize and be effective, is to reward a man that contrives ways to improve the system, to decrease the percent defective for the group by some stated amount of economic importance.

Management could make good use of the figures on defectives for the 50 workers, but not to award a prize. The 50 proportions of defectives furnish a basis, by use of the simple statistical technique called chart for fraction defective, to discover which worker if any ought to be transferred and trained in other jobs. The same chart, even if the 50 workers were not in statistical control with each other, would indicate how much of the overall fraction defective arises from the system itself, beyond reach of the workers, and correctable only by management.

CONCLUDING REMARKS

The principles expounded here, and the examples of application, are all simple, yet the economic gains from corrective action by management are considerable. The examples all belong to the statistical control of quality. Did the solutions require a statistician? Couldn't other people have done as well? One answer is that other people had their chance.

Some people would call this work operations research. Some would call it systems analysis, others, industrial engineering. To me, it is just a statistician trying to be positive and helpful in the use of statistical methods.

When will schools of business and other academic departments get into the business of teaching modern principles of administration and management? Without statistical logic, management learns words and goals, but not methods by which to reach these goals, nor meaningful language by which to describe a goal or to measure advancement toward it or away from it.

References

1. W. Edwards Deming, *Elementary Principles in the Statistical Control of Quality,* Union of Japanese Scientists and Engineers, Tokyo, 1950.
2. W. Edwards Deming, "On the Use of Theory," *Industrial Quality Control,* vol. xiii, no. 1, July 1956. "On Some Statistical Logic in the Management of Quality," *All India Congress on Quality Control,* New Delhi, 17 March 1971.
3. J. M. Juran, *Quality Control Handbook,* McGraw-Hill, New York, 1951, 1962; pages 11, 4–5; 26, 10–11, and other pages in this book listed under Pareto. (The pages cited belong to the 3rd edition.) I strongly recommend the whole book for people of all responsibilities and disciplines. See also Hy Pitt, "Pareto Re-visited," *Quality Progress,* vol. vii, no. 2, pp. 29–30.
4. This procedure was first described, so far as I know, by J. M. Juran in a meeting of the American Society for Quality Control in New York at least 20 years ago. It was formalized by Irving Burr. "Specifying the Desired Distribution Rather than Maximum and Minimum Limits," *Industrial Quality Control,* vol. 24, no. 2, 1967: pp. 94–101.
5. Kenichi Koyanagi, *Statistical Quality Control in Japanese Industry,* Proceedings of the American Society for Quality Control, Rochester, 1952.
6. Walter A. Shewhart, *The Economic Control of Manufactured Product,* Van Nostrand, New York, 1931. *Statistical Method from the Viewpoint of Quality Control,* The Graduate School, Department of Agriculture, Washington, 1939.
7. An easy reference for the nonstatistician is my chapter entitled, "Making Things Right," in the book, Judith Tanner, et al., *Statistics, Guide to the Unknown,* Holden-Day, 1972.
8. See almost any textbook in statistical methods. The original reference is Frederick Mosteller and John W. Tukey, "The Uses and Usefulness of Binomial Probability Paper," *Journal of the American Statistical Association,* vol. 44, 1949: pp. 174–212. The double square-root paper is manufactured by the Codex Book Company of Norwood, Mass.

Notes

1. This paper is based on principles taught in Japan since 1950. I am indebted to the editor and to referees, and to students at New York University, for many helpful suggestions in presentation.

Reading 7

The Quality Trilogy: A Universal Approach to Managing for Quality

By J. M. Juran

Several premises have led me to conclude that our companies need to chart a new direction in managing for quality. These premises are as follows.

1. There is a crisis in quality. The most obvious outward evidence is the loss of sales to foreign competition in quality and the huge costs of poor quality.
2. The crisis will not go away in the foreseeable future. Competition in quality will go on and on. So will the impact of poor quality on society. In the industrialized countries, society lives behind protective quality dikes.
3. Our traditional ways are not adequate to deal with the quality crisis. In a sense, our adherence to those traditional ways has helped to create the crisis.
4. To deal with the crisis requires some major breaks with tradition. A new course must be charted.
5. Charting a new course requires that we create a universal way of thinking about quality—a way applicable to all functions and to all levels in the hierarchy, from the chief executive officer to the worker in the office or the factory.
6. Charting a new course also requires extensive personal leadership and participation by upper managers.

Source: J. M. Juran is chairman of Juran Institute, Inc., Wilton, Conn. The Institute offers consulting and management training in quality. An ASQC Honorary Member, Juran is the editor in chief of *The Quality Control Handbook,* author of *Managerial Breakthrough,* and co-author with Frank Gryna of *Quality Planning and Analysis.* Excerpt from "The Quality Trilogy: A Universal Approach to Managing for Quality" from *Quality Progress,* August 1986 by J. M. Juran.

7. An obstacle to participation by upper managers is their limited experience and training in managing for quality. They have extensive experience in management of business and finance but not in managing for quality.
8. An essential element in meeting the quality crisis is to arm upper managers with experience and training in how to manage for quality, and to do so on a time scale compatible with the prevailing sense of urgency.
9. Charting a new course also requires that we design a basis for management of quality that can readily be implanted into the company's strategic business planning, and that has minimal risk of rejection by the company's immune system.

A company that wants to chart a new course in managing for quality obviously should create an all-pervasive unity so that everyone will know which is the new direction, and will be stimulated to go there. Creating such unity requires dealing with some powerful forces which resist a unified approach. These forces are for the most part due to certain non-uniformities inherent in any company. These non-uniformities include:

- The multiple functions in the company: product development, manufacture, office operations, etc. Each regards its function as something unique and special.
- The multiple levels in the company hierarchy, from the chief executive officer to the nonsupervisory worker. These levels differ with respect to responsibility, prerequisite experience and training, etc.
- The multiple product lines: large and complex systems, mass production, regulated products, etc. These product lines differ in their markets, technology, restraints, etc.

Such inherent non-uniformities and the associated beliefs in uniqueness are a reality in any company, and they constitute a serious obstacle to unity of direction. Such an obstacle can be overcome if we are able to find a universal thought process—a universal way of thinking about quality—which fits all functions, all levels, all product lines. That brings me to the concept of the "quality trilogy."

(Let me add parenthetically that my colleagues in Juran Institute have urged me to let them call it the "Juran Trilogy." Their reasons are purely mercenary. I have yielded to their wishes. In Juran Institute we also need unity.)

The underlying concept of the quality trilogy is that managing for quality consists of three basic quality-oriented processes.

- Quality planning.
- Quality control.
- Quality improvement.

Each of these processes is universal; it is carried out by an unvarying sequence of activities. (A brief description of each of these sequences appears in the box on page 117.) Furthermore, these universal processes are interrelated in ways we can depict on a simple diagram. (See Figure 7.1.)

The starting point is quality planning—creating a process that will be able to meet established goals and do so under operating conditions. The subject matter of the planning can be anything: an office process for producing documents; an engineering process for designing products; a factory process for producing goods; a service process for responding to customers' requests.

Following the planning, the process is turned over to the operating forces. Their responsibility is to run the process at optimal effectiveness. Due to deficiencies in the original planning, the process runs at a high level of chronic waste. That waste has been planned into the process, in the sense that the planning process failed to plan it out. Because the waste is inherent in the process, the operating forces are unable to get rid of the chronic waste. What they do instead is to carry out "quality control"—keep the waste from getting worse. If it does get worse (sporadic spike), a fire fighting team is brought in to determine the cause or causes of this abnormal variation. Once the cause(s) has been determined, and corrective action is taken, the process again falls into the zone defined by the "quality control" limits.

Figure 7.1 also shows that in due course the chronic waste falls to a much lower level. Such a reduction does not happen of its own accord. It results from purposeful action taken by upper management to introduce a new managerial process into the system of managers' responsibilities—the quality improvement

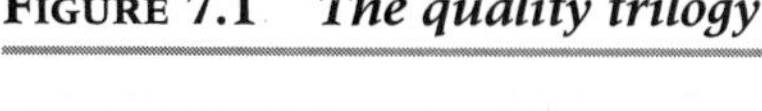

FIGURE 7.1 ***The quality trilogy***

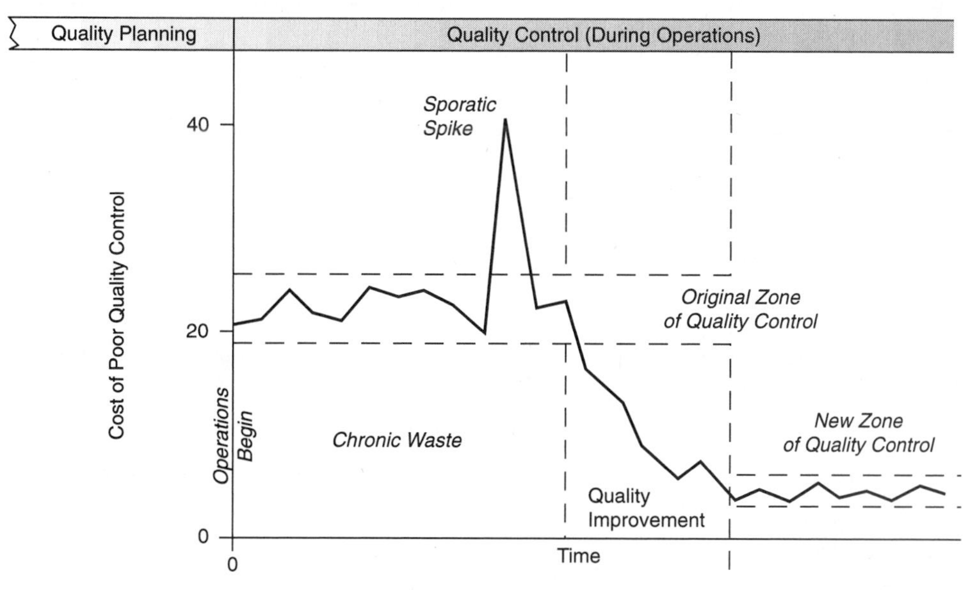

process. This quality improvement process is superimposed on the quality control process—a process implemented in addition to quality control, not instead of it.

We can now elaborate the trilogy descriptions somewhat as follows.

Process: Quality planning—the process for preparing to meet quality goals.

End Result: A process capable of meeting quality goals under operating conditions.

Process: Quality control—the process for meeting quality goals during operations.

End Result: Conduct of operations in accordance with the quality plan.

Process: Quality improvement—the process for breaking through to unprecedented levels of performance.

End Result: Conduct of operations at levels of quality distinctly superior to planned performance.

The trilogy is not entirely "new." If we look sideways at how we manage finance, we notice some interesting parallels, as shown in Figure 7.2. (I have often used the financial parallels to help explain the trilogy to upper managers. It does help.)

In recent seminars, I have been collecting upper managers' conclusions on their companies' performance relative to the basic processes of the trilogy. The results are quite similar from one seminar to another, and they can be summarized as shown in Figure 7.3.

FIGURE 7.2 ***Quality and finance: parallels***

Trilogy processes
Quality planning
Quality control
Quality improvement
Financial processes
Budgeting
Cost control; expense control
Cost reduction; profit improvement

FIGURE 7.3 ***Quality process performance***

	UPPER MANAGERS' RATINGS OF THEIR COMPANIES' PERFORMANCE		
Trilogy processes	**Good**	**Passing**	**Not passing**
Quality planning	13%	40%	47%
Quality control	44	36	20
Quality improvement	6	39	55

These summarized data point to several conclusions.

1. The managers are not happy with their performance relative to quality planning.
2. The managers rate their companies well with respect to quality control, i.e., meeting the established goals. Note that since these goals have traditionally been based mainly on past performance, the effect is mainly to perpetuate past performance—the very performance which is at the root of the quality crisis.
3. The managers are decidedly unhappy with their performance relative to quality improvement.

My own observations of company performance (during consultations) strongly confirm the above self-assessment by company managers. During my visits to companies, I have found a recurring pattern of priorities and assets devoted to the processes within the trilogy. This pattern is shown in Figure 7.4.

As Figure 7.4 shows, the prevailing priorities are not consistent with the managers' self-assessment of their own effectiveness. That assessment would suggest that they should put the control process on hold while increasing the emphasis on quality planning and especially on quality improvement.

To elaborate on the need for raising the priority on quality improvement, let me present several baffling case examples.

1. Several years ago the executive vice president of a large multinational rubber company made a round-the-world trip with his chairman. They made the trip in order to visit their major subsidiaries with a view to securing inputs for strategic business planning. They found much similarity with respect to productivity, quality, etc., except for Japan. The Japanese company was outperforming all others, and by a wide margin. Yet the Americans were completely mystified as to why. The Americans had toured the Japanese plant, and to the Americans' eyes the Japanese were using the same materials, equipment, processes, etc., as everyone else. After much discussion the reason emerged: The Japanese had been carrying out many, many quality improvement projects year after year. Through the resulting improvements they made *more and better products from the same facilities.* The key point relative to "ignorance" is that the Americans did not know what to look for.
2. A foundry that made aluminum castings had an identical experience. The foundry was losing share of market to a Japanese competitor, mainly for quality

FIGURE 7.4 ***Priorities for quality processes***

Trilogy processes	Self-assessment by upper managers	Prevailing priorities
Quality planning	Weak	Limited priority
Quality control	Very strong	Top priority, by a wide margin
Quality improvement	Very weak	Very low priority

reasons. Arrangements were made for a delegation of Americans to visit the Japanese factory. The delegation came away completely mystified. The Japanese were using the same types of equipment and processes as were used by the Americans. Yet the Japanese results in quality and productivity were clearly superior. To this day the Americans don't know why.

3. A few years ago I conducted research into the yields of the processes that make large scale integrated circuits. To assure comparability, I concentrated on a single product type—the 16K random access memory (16K RAM). I found that Japanese yields were two to three times the Western yields despite similarity in the basic processes. It came as no surprise to me that the Japanese have since become dominant in the market for 64K RAMs and up.
4. My final example relates to the steel industry. The managers of American steel companies report that their cost of poor quality (just for factory processes) runs at about 10–15 percent of sales. Some of these steel companies have business connections with Japanese steel companies, and the respective managers exchange visits. During these visits the Americans learn that in Japanese steel mills, which use comparable equipment and processes, the cost of poor quality runs at about 1–2 percent of sales. Again the American managers don't know why. Some of them don't even believe the Japanese figures.

My own explanation is that the Japanese, since the early 1950s, have undertaken to improve quality at a pace far greater than that of the West. The slopes of those two lines (Figure 7.5) are an index of the rate of improvement. That rate is

FIGURE 7.5 ***World competition in quality***

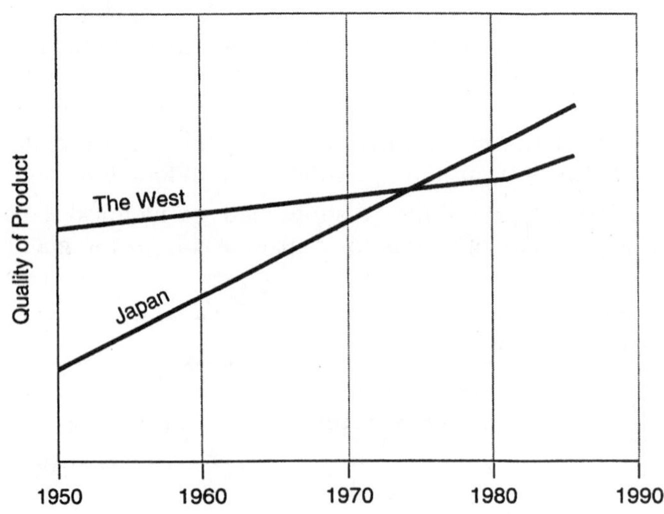

in turn dependent on the number of quality improvement projects completed. (A project is a problem scheduled for solution.) My estimate is that in terms of numbers of improvement projects completed, the Japanese pace has been exceeding that of the West by an order of magnitude, year after year.

It seems clear that we must change our priorities with regard to the three quality processes. This change in priorities represents a new course. Underlying this new course is the quality trilogy. As a universal way of thinking about quality, the trilogy offers a unified approach for multiple purposes. Let us look at two of these purposes: training in managing for quality and strategic quality planning.

With respect to training, many of our companies have decided to break with tradition. In the past, their training in managing for quality has been limited to managers and engineers in the quality department. The break with tradition is to extend such training to all functions. Since this is a sizable undertaking, the companies have set up corporate task forces to plan the approach.

Basic quality processes

Quality planning:

Identify the customers, both external and internal.
Determine customer needs.
Develop product features that respond to customer needs. (Products include both goods and services.)
Establish quality goals that meet the needs of customers and suppliers alike, and do so at a minimum combined cost.
Develop a process that can produce the needed product features.
Prove process capability—prove that the process can meet the quality goals under operating conditions.

Control:

Choose control subjects—what to control.
Choose units of measurement.
Establish measurement.
Establish standards of performance.
Measure actual performance.
Interpret the difference (actual versus standard).
Take action on the difference.

Improvement:

Prove the need for improvement.
Identify specific projects for improvement.
Organize to guide the projects.
Organize for diagnosis—for discovery of causes.
Diagnose to find the causes.
Provide remedies.
Prove that the remedies are effective under operating conditions.
Provide for control to hold the gains.

These task forces have run into serious obstacles due to those same systems of variables mentioned earlier. It is hopeless to establish numerous training courses in managing for quality, each specially designed to fit specific functions, specific levels in the hierarchy, specific product lines, etc. Instead, the need is for a universal training course that will apply to all audiences, but with provision for plugging in special case examples as warranted. The trilogy concept meets that need.

The training courses then consist of fleshing out the three sequences of steps described in the box on page 117. Those sequences have been field tested and proven to be applicable to all functions, levels, and product lines.

We have already seen that the trilogy parallels our approach to strategic business planning. Our companies are experienced in business planning; they are familiar and comfortable with the concepts of financial budgets, cost control, and cost reduction. We can take advantage of all that experience by grafting the quality trilogy onto the existing business planning structure. Such a graft reduces the risk that the implant will be rejected by the company's immune system.

The usual starting point is to set up a quality planning council to formulate and coordinate the activity companywide, The council membership consists of high ranking managers—corporate officers. The chairman is usually the chief executive officer or an executive vice president. The functions of this council parallel closely the functions of the company's finance committee, but apply to quality instead of finance.

The council prepares a written list of its responsibilities. These typically involve the following:

- Establish corporate quality policies.
- Establish corporate quality goals; review quality goals of divisions and major functions.
- Establish corporate quality plans; review divisional and functional plans.
- Provide the infrastructure and resources needed to carry out the plans.
- Review quality performance against plans and goals.
- Revise the managerial merit rating system to reflect performance against quality goals.

It is all quite logical, and some companies are already securing gratifying benefits from going into strategic quality planning. However, other companies are failing to get results, and the main reasons for these failures are becoming evident. They relate to some areas which I will now discuss: goal setting; providing the infrastructure; providing resources; upper management leadership.

Setting goals Goal setting has traditionally been heavily based on past performance. This practice has tended to perpetuate the sins of the past. Failure-prone designs were carried over into new models. Wasteful processes were not challenged if managers had met the budgets—budgets which had in turn assumed that the wastes were a fate to be endured.

All this must change. Goals for parameters that affect external customers must be based on meeting competition in the marketplace. Goals for parameters that affect internal customers must be based on getting rid of the traditional wastes.

Infrastructure Strategic quality planning requires an infrastructure to be set up. The nature of this is evident when we look sideways at the infrastructure needed for strategic business planning: a budgetary process; an accounting system to evaluate performance; associated procedures, audits, etc.

Much of this structure has long been in place to serve various local needs: divisions, functions, factories, etc. This structure must now be supplemented to enable it to meet strategic quality needs as well. This is especially the case in large corporations which traditionally have delegated matters of quality to the autonomous divisions. The quality crisis has caused some large corporations to revise this delegation. They now require corporate review of divisional quality goals, plans, and reports of performance. The new approach has required revision of the infrastructure.

Resources It takes resources to carry out plans and meet goals. To date, companies have exhibited a selective response to this need. Let us look at several areas that require such resources.

- Training. Here the response of companies has generally been positive. Companies have invested heavily in training programs for special areas such as quality awareness, statistical process control, and QC circles. To go into strategic quality planning will require extensive training in the trilogy—how to think about quality. One can hope the response will continue to be positive.
- Measurement of quality. The quality crisis has required a major change in the basis for goal setting—the new basis requires measurement of market quality on an unprecedented scale. For example, some companies now have a policy that new products may not go on the market unless their reliability is at least equal to that of leading competitive products. Such a policy cannot be made effective unless resources are provided to evaluate the reliability of competing products.

Beyond the need to expand quality-oriented marketing research, there are other aspects of measurement which require resources: establishing the scorekeeping associated with strategic quality planning (the quality equivalent of the financial profit statements, balance sheets, etc.); extending measures of quality to the nonmanufacturing processes; and establishing means for evaluating the quality performance of managers, and fitting these evaluations into the merit rating system.

- Quality improvement. Here we have some puzzling contradictions. An emerging database tells us that quality improvement projects provide a higher return on investment than virtually any other investment activity. Yet many companies have not provided the needed resources.

To be specific, that database comes mainly from the companies that have presented papers at the annual IMPRO conferences—conferences on quality improvement. Those published papers and related unpublished information indicate that in large organizations—sales of $1 billion or more—the average quality improvement project yields about $100,000 of cost reduction.[1]

The same database indicates that to complete a project requires from $5,000 to $20,000 in resources. These resources are needed to diagnose the cause of the problem and to provide the remedy. The return on investment is obviously attractive. Nevertheless, many companies—too many—have failed to provide the resources and hence have failed to get the results.

To go into strategic quality planning will require companies to create, for the quality function, a new role—a role similar to that of the financial controller. In all likelihood this new role will be assigned to the quality managers.

In part this new role will involve assisting the company managers to prepare the strategic quality goals—the quality equivalent of the financial budget. In addition the new role will involve establishing the continuing means of reporting performance against quality goals. This role parallels the financial reporting role of the financial controller.

Collateral with those two new responsibilities will be others, also of a broad business nature.

- Evaluation of competitive quality and of trends in the marketplace.
- Design and introduction of needed revisions in the trilogy of processes: quality planning, quality control, and quality improvement.
- Conduct of training to assist company personnel in carrying out the necessary changes.

For many quality managers such a new role will involve a considerable shift in emphasis: from technology to business management; from quality control and assurance to strategic quality planning. But such is the wave of the future. Those quality managers who choose to accept that responsibility, if and when it comes, can look forward to the experience of a lifetime. They will be participating fully in what will become the most important quality development of the century.

References

1. Eighteen case examples are cited in "Charting the Course," *The Juran Report,* Number 4 (Winter 1985).

Reading 8

Quality Is Free: The Art of Making Quality Certain

BY PHILIP B. CROSBY

COST OF QUALITY

Let's eavesdrop on the management monthly status review of our favorite company. The comptroller is providing his overview:

"Inventory increased $270,358 this month for a total of $21,978,375.18. This is still $9,981 below budget, but I think it requires a good look because the rate of increase is getting steeper."

"Good point," says the boss, who then directs purchasing to see if they are bringing material in quicker than needed and asks material control to give him a detailed report on in-process versus finished-goods inventory.

"Sales are directly on budget except for the hotel operation, where occupancy is falling off. During the week occupancy is running 98 percent, but this is dragged down by the weekend rate of 35 percent."

"Hmmm," says the boss. "Marketing better get hopping on putting together some weekend specials. 'Take the little lady away from it all' sort of thing. Give them a special rate and a bottle of bubbly. That should take care of it."

"Employee compensation is overbudget. We've been paying too much overtime in the foundry and electronic test operations. This is caused by delinquent schedules in the assembly group. They got two days late last month and haven't been able to catch up."

"Production," frowns the boss, "hasn't been paying enough attention to scheduling. I think it's all due to that new and expensive computer operation. Set up a task team to find out what's wrong and give me a daily report."

"Our quality is falling off—we've had several customer complaints."

> "There's no excuse for low quality. The quality department has to get on the ball," growls the boss. "Maybe we need a new quality manager. I want high quality. Meeting adjourned."

Now you'll notice that everything in the above report is quite precise, even down to the last 18 cents of inventory. All things are measured, evaluated calmly, and dispositioned. All, that is, except quality, which is merely "falling off." How come that portion of the company is not reported in numbers? Why is it left dangling in midair? Why is the quality manager suddenly considered inadequate when the other functional managers who have troubles are not? Why wasn't he there?

How come there wasn't a report on *quality*? Something like this:

> "Our receiving inspection rejection rate has climbed from 2.5 to 4 percent in the last month. This is due to purchase orders on standard hardware not calling out the proper plating requirements. Printed circuit board rejections have risen from 4 to 6 percent due to untrained assemblers being placed on the line. Production has pulled them back for training. Customer returns have dropped from 3 to 1.2 percent, but this has cost us $35,491 in overtime due to the additional testing required. An engineering error was responsible for the defect. Changes have been issued and the problem will be corrected by the 18th of next month. The cost of quality is running at 6.1 percent of sales, and we plan to meet the year-end objective of 5.9 percent."
>
> "Great," beams the boss. "As long as we can find these situations early and take action, we will be able to have confidence in our conformance. Quality is doing a fine job."

Quality is free, but no one is ever going to know it, if there isn't some sort of agreed-on system of measurement. Quality has always suffered from the lack of an obvious method of measurement in spite of the fact that such a method was developed by General Electric in the 1950s as a tool for determining the need for corrective action on a specific product line. I remember a case history in a course I took that compared two product lines using the cost of quality as the basis of comparison.

The quality profession, however, clings to the very management concepts that allow them to be inadequate, so cost-of-quality measurement was never really implemented except by a radical here and there. The first instance of using a companywide quality measurement, actually calculated and reported by the comptroller was probably in the ITT program we instituted in the mid-1960s.

By bringing together the easily assembled costs like rework, scrap, warranty, inspection, and test, we were able to show an accumulation of expense that made the line management listen to us. This led us to install more sophisticated quality management programs, which uncovered costs in areas such as change notices, installation, and supplier in-plant operations. At present we are learning how to measure "service" costs of quality. This applies not only to operations like insurance or hotels, where there are no milling machines or printed circuit assembly areas, but to manufacturing plants themselves. It took a long time to get around to the realization that half the people in the most manufacturing of manufacturing plants never touch the product. And, of course, as individuals we are all service people. Unless we are blood donors—then we are manufacturing plants.

A detailed explanation of how to use the cost of quality to get an improvement team moving is given in Chapters 10 and 11. Here I cover some general details on the things that go into the cost of quality (hereafter often referred to as COQ).

All you really need is enough information to show your management that reducing the cost of quality is in fact an opportunity to increase profits without raising sales, buying new equipment, or hiring new people. The first step is to put together the fully loaded costs of (1) all efforts involved in doing work over, including clerical work; (2) all scrap; (3) warranty (including in-plant handling of returns); (4) after-service warranty; (5) complaint handling; (6) inspection and test; and (7) other costs of error, such as engineering change notices, purchasing change orders, etc. It is normal to obtain only one-third of the real cost the first time you try it.

Many quality management people start out with the thought that it is a good thing for them personally if the company has a very low figure for cost of quality. They tend to come up with readings like 1.3 percent of sales. Then they run to the boss for applause. A few years later their successor finds that it is really 12.6 percent of sales and embarks on a well-rewarded campaign to reduce this needless waste. The first person just refused to understand that the cost of quality has little to do with the operation of the quality department.

To make the total calculation more understandable to other managements, it is a good idea to relate it to a significant base. Most people use a percent of sales. However, if you are in a company where there are unusually high costs of distribution like the food industry, you may want to measure COQ as a percentage of cost of sales, or just plain manufacturing costs. In insurance, banks, hotels, and similar businesses the cost of operations makes a good base. What is really important is that the number be something that quality management can use to communicate the importance of the concept. That is what the whole business of COQ is all about.

Many managers wait, and fiddle, and never really do get a workable COQ system installed. They collect endless lists and classifications of things that should be considered. They are too concerned with trying to obtain an exact cost figure, and don't really understand the reason for doing the calculation in the first place.

All this just delays the rest of their program. As I said, the purpose of calculating COQ is really only to get management's attention and to provide a measurement base for seeing how quality improvement is doing. If managers spend all their time getting ready and attending endless conferences searching for the secret, they will be disappointed.

Once an operation knows its COQ, or a good approximation, goals for reducing that cost can be set. Ten percent a year is a good, attainable goal that people can relate to. As you go along, and become more adept in determining things that belong in the COQ, you will find the base number growing. This means that you must go back and apply this information to figures obtained in the past if you want apples to look like apples.

All calculations should be produced by the accounting department; that ensures the integrity of the operation. Naturally, they are going to ask you for a list of those costs which must be included. The following list should be of some help, although you will have to add any items that are unique to your business. These three categories should be sufficient at first; don't search for additional details until you absolutely need them. That is what creates bureaucracy.

PREVENTION COSTS

Prevention costs are the cost of all activities undertaken to prevent defects in design and development, purchasing, labor, and other aspects of beginning and creating a product or service. Also included are those preventive and measurement actions conducted during the business cycle. Specific items are:

Design Reviews
Product Qualification
Drawing Checking
Engineering Quality Orientation
Make Certain Program
Supplier Evaluations
Supplier Quality Seminars
Specification Review
Process Capability Studies
Tool Control
Operation Training
Quality Orientation
Acceptance Planning
Zero Defects Program
Quality Audits
Preventive Maintenance

APPRAISAL COSTS

These are costs incurred while conducting inspections, tests, and other planned evaluations used to determine whether produced hardware, software, or services conform to their requirements. Requirements include specifications from marketing and customer, as well as engineering documents and information pertaining to procedures and processes. All documents that describe the conformance of the product or service are relevant. Specific items are:

Prototype Inspection and Test
Production Specification Conformance Analysis
Supplier Surveillance
Receiving Inspection and Test
Product Acceptance
Process Control Acceptance
Packaging Inspection
Status Measurement and Reporting

FAILURE COSTS

Failure costs are associated with things that have been found not to conform or perform to the requirements, as well as the evaluation, disposition, and consumer-affairs aspects of such failures. Included are all materials and labor involved. Occasionally a figure must be included for lost customer credibility. Specifics are:

Consumer Affairs
Redesign
Engineering Change Order
Purchasing Change Order
Corrective Action Costs
Rework
Scrap
Warranty
Service after Service
Product Liability

Once you and the comptroller have calculated the COQ for your operation, the next step is to figure out what to do with it. This calculation is the only key you will ever have to help your company properly implement quality management. Seize an opportunity and make a speech like the following:

> A prudent company makes certain that its products and services are delivered to the customer by a management system that does not condone rework, repair, waste or nonconformance of any sort. These are expensive problems. They must not only be detected and resolved at the earliest moment, they must be prevented from occurring at all. To give you an idea of how expensive these problems are, let me show you some of the actual costs we are incurring at this moment. (At this point, show them.)
>
> To remove these costs and to prove that quality is free, we must implement our quality management system to its fullest. That way we can turn what is sometimes considered

a necessary evil into a profit center. Our cost of quality is now *X* percent of sales. It only needs to be *Y* percent of sales. The difference is pretax profit.

Thank you.

Used as a management tool for the purpose of focusing attention on quality management the COQ is a positive blessing and serves a unique purpose. Used as an accounting measurement, like the calculation of nuts-and-bolts inventory, it becomes a useless pain. When the concern becomes which operation has come up with the most accurate figures, the purpose of keeping the figures gets lost. It is like someone on a tight budget keeping neat records of overspending. Make certain you keep your eye on the true reason for the calculation. Don't get lost in statistical swamps.

QUALITY IMPROVEMENT PROGRAM

The most difficult lesson for the crusader to learn is that real improvement just plain takes a while to accomplish. The urgency of the need, the obviousness of the cause, and the clarity of the solution have little to do with getting things straightened out.

That is why government programs almost always fail and are scrapped whenever a new administration takes over. The disappointment and disillusionment of the previous administrator are all too obvious. The administrator blames a lack of funds, cooperation, timing, or whatever for the failure. Yet no matter what the program was, or however well it was directed, its success potential hinged on events entirely separate from the executive's efforts.

Quality improvement programs have similar problems. Because quality improvement sounds like such a great idea, and because it is usually so necessary, managers often feel that merely announcing its conception is the signal for arranging a victory dinner.

I have yet to attend a quality meeting where someone didn't comment to me that they had been unable to "really reach their management," or "get the people motivated," in order to put quality improvement over the top. They claim that they have taken the actions any well-oriented professional would expect, and yet they are disappointed. Those colleagues who have faithfully implemented the fourteen-step quality improvement program worry about an inevitable falloff in "enthusiasm," and search for new means of keeping the program on a high intensity level.

Each time I hear these things I am shocked. I am always surprised that they are surprised. Why should quality be different from the real world? After all, the method of preventing smallpox had been discovered and tested many years before the devastation of plagues ceased. Why wouldn't people take the necessary steps to protect themselves from such a painful and ugly disease? Why did they ignore the simple and inexpensive act of vaccination in the face of absolute evidence that it worked? Why do people continue to smoke tobacco when even the tobacco companies admit it is a clear danger? I smoked for thirty years, enjoying every puff, before being forced to quit. Now that I am free I recognize what a truly messy business smoking is and am not tempted to return to it. But that may be hindsight. Basically, we are slow to change because we reject newness. The world is a complicated and unsettled place. Each individual treasures the few things he or she can depend upon. "Perhaps it is better to take my chances on the pox rather than go over and let these strange people scratch me." If you think this is old-fashioned, just consider how much difficulty the government has had in getting people to take flu shots. Why? Well, for one thing we know for a fact that the flu shot is going to make us ill for a while. And we might not catch the flu even if we don't get the shot (particularly if everyone else takes it).

Take another example: urban redevelopment. It has cost more money than any domestic program in the history of the United States except defense. However, you could say that both operations have similar effects: the subjugation of cities and their populations. The difference is in the location of the cities.

Obviously the goals of urban redevelopment are above reproach. Tear out the old and inefficient and replace it with the new and different. Create jobs in the process and improve our way of life. Very rarely has that happened. Poor people have been uprooted, middle-class people have fled the cities, and the urban patterns built up by centuries of slow development and real living have been destroyed in a few years. Whose fault has it been? Not the politicians—they really didn't have time to do it right because they had to get reelected or they had to spend this year's budget this year.

There is always some reason given for failure, but it is rarely the real one. The real one is that you have to lead people gently toward what they already know is right. Otherwise they just will not cooperate. If you have any doubts, ask those who have tried to stamp out the "adult entertainment" sections in cities, assuming that the population is against such things. But the basic assumption is wrong. The population isn't against adult entertainment. It just doesn't want it next door. After all, nothing lives unless the people support it. It is not the "kooks" who support such enterprises, it is real people with real money.

The most practical way to establish your frame of reference when you decide to start an improvement program is to put it in very personal terms. Pretend that you are a company. Presumably you know yourself well enough to know how you will react under certain circumstances. Then announce to yourself that for your own good you must take up a new sport. Let us say that you have selected golf. Millions of people play the game, there are courses everywhere, and there is probably more information available about the details of this sport than any other. Perhaps someone has even written a book on the fourteen steps of golf improvement through defect prevention. In that case it is only necessary to announce your commitment, agree upon the measurement criteria, and go forth to meet your goals. Maybe you can even have some banners made in order to "motivate" yourself.

You could set up goals based on improvement, and could reward yourself for achievement. But it is going to take a while. There is a lot more to golf than having the equipment and the intent. You must work hard at it, and you must stay at the wheel for a long time, if you ever want to play a really good game of golf.

A company quality improvement effort has a lot of the same elements. It must be well thought out, and it must be implemented according to a plan, over a long period of time. It requires a "culture" change; it must become part of your lifestyle. And it requires that you never relax your attention. You have to stay at it continually.

You as a manager have an obligation to demand continual quality improvement from your operation, whether you are in the accounting business or a machine shop. You as a manager have an obligation to provide thoughtful and imaginative leadership. What you put out is what you get back.

It is not possible to take shortcuts in an attempt to keep from involving yourself. Everyone can tell whether or not you are being sincere. Experiments in "job enrichment" have shown this clearly. The technique of having one group of individuals completely assemble a car, in order to build their pride in their work, did not noticeably improve quality, interest, or productivity. The people knew they were being used.

People who have to put improvement programs of any kind into their company always feel that others are not for it. This is entirely normal, and reflects the natural shyness of the organization bird. We don't really like to get out front with too much unless we are absolutely certain it will be properly received. But my experience has been that improvement efforts, properly explained, are always received correctly. It's the "proper explanation" that takes some effort. So in searching for a way to convince the quality manager at ITT, I came up with the Quality Management Maturity Grid. The Grid has its own uses, as described in the previous chapters. But in the case of the quality improvement program it is even more important just for itself. The question you have to ask yourself is: "What would the boss, and the rest of the managers who report to him or her, have to do to convince you that they really want a quality improvement program?" The answer, of course, is that they would have to convince you that they personally feel the need for improvement in the operation. And that is what you use the Grid for. Send them a copy, ask them to read it, and then go see them to discuss it. Have each of them rate the company as they see it according to the Grid. Don't be too heavy with them. If they think something is Wisdom and you think it is Awakening, don't argue too much. Just leave room for improvement.

Once you have discussed all their judgments on an individual basis, you can bring them together to discuss the overall program. And if anyone is reluctant, you can point out that their personal evaluation showed the need for improvement.

At this time it is a good idea to move right into the basics of quality. Help them to understand what real quality means, emphasizing the absolutes of quality management:

- Quality means conformance, not elegance.
- There is no such thing as a quality problem.
- There is no such thing as the economics of quality; it is always cheaper to do the job right the first time.
- The only performance measurement is the cost of quality.
- The only performance standard is Zero Defects.

Explain the Zero Defects concept. Have them take the test, and leave out nothing. Answer all their questions, and keep it all simple and untechnical. Tell them again that quality is free.

They really want to believe, and they really want it to happen. But their life is one continual scene of people bringing them plans and schemes that will help them succeed, cut costs, fly to the moon, and a thousand other things. Like you, they know that most things don't work like they are supposed to work.

The main task you have at this key moment is to show them that the program has worked for other companies and it will work for yours, if they participate. But you also have to help them understand that although there will be instant improvement as soon as you start the effort, it will be a long while before it becomes permanent. It is hard and rewarding work. It will bring recognition to all of them.

As for yourself, remember that the product that you are selling, and they are buying, is quality improvement. The result of quality improvement is improved everything else, from sales to absenteeism. But it is a result. So don't tie in a bunch of marketing motivation activities, the blood bank, the savings bond drive, or the annual barbecue. Keep quality improvement in the front of your mind each time a decision has to be made.

THE FOURTEEN STEPS

Step one: management commitment

Action Discuss the need for quality improvement with management people, with an emphasis on the need for defect prevention. There are plenty of movies, visual aids, and other material available to support this communication. (Do not confuse "communication" with "motivation." The results of communication are real and long-lasting; the results of motivation are shallow and short-lived.) Prepare a quality policy that states that *each individual is expected to "perform exactly like the requirement or cause the requirement to be officially changed to what we and the customer really need."* Agree that quality improvement is a practical way to profit improvement.

Accomplishment Helping management to recognize that they must be personally committed to participating in the program raises the level of visibility for quality and ensures everyone's cooperation so long as there is some progress.

Step two: quality improvement team

Action Bring together representatives of each department to form the quality improvement team. These should be people who can speak for their department in order to commit that operation to action. (Preferably, the department heads should participate—at least on the first go-around.) Orient the team members as to the content and purpose of the program. Explain their role—which is to cause the necessary actions to take place in their department and in the company.

Accomplishment All the tools necessary to do the job now are together in one team. It works well to appoint one of the members as the chairman of the team for this phase.

Step three: quality measurement

Action It is necessary to determine the status of quality throughout the company. Quality measurements for each area of activity must be established where they don't exist and reviewed where they do. Quality status is recorded to show where improvement is possible, where corrective action is necessary, and to document actual improvement later on.

Nonmanufacturing measurements, which are sometimes difficult to establish, might include the following:

Accounting:
- Percentage of late reports
- Computer input incorrect
- Errors in specific reports as audited

Data processing:
- Keypunch cards thrown out for error
- Computer downtime due to error
- Reruntime

Engineering:
- Change orders due to error
- Drafting errors found by checkers
- Late releases

Finance:

Billing errors (check accounts receivable overdues)

Payroll errors

Accounts payable deductions missed

Hotel front desk:

Guests taken to unmade rooms

Reservations not honored

Manufacturing engineering:

Process change notices due to error

Tool rework to correct design

Methods improvement

Marketing:

Contract errors

Order description errors

Plant engineering:

Time lost due to equipment failures

Callbacks on repairs

Purchasing:

Purchase order changes due to error

Late receipt of material

Rejections due to incomplete description

There are innumerable ways to measure any procedure. The people doing the work will respond with delight to the opportunity to identify some specific measurements for their work. If a supervisor says her area is completely immeasurable, she can be helped by asking how she knows who is doing the best work, how she knows whom to keep and whom to replace.

Accomplishment Formalizing the company measurement system strengthens the inspection and test functions and assures proper measurement. Getting the paperwork and service operations involved sets the stage for effective defect prevention where it counts. Placing the results of measurement in highly visible charts establishes the foundation of the entire quality improvement program.

Step four: cost of quality evaluation

Action Initial estimates are likely to be shaky (although low), and so it is necessary now to get more accurate figures. The comptroller's office must do this.

They should be provided with detailed information on what constitutes the cost of quality. The cost of quality is not an absolute performance measurement: It is an indication of where corrective action will be profitable for a company. The higher the cost, the more corrective action that needs to be taken.

Accomplishment Having the comptroller establish the cost of quality removes any suspected bias from the calculation. More important, a measurement of quality management performance has been established in the company's system.

Step five: quality awareness

Action It is time now to share with employees the measurements of what non-quality is costing. This is done by training supervisors to orient employees, and by providing visible evidence of the concern for quality improvement through communication material such as booklets, films, and posters. Don't confuse this with some get-motivated-quick scheme. It is a sharing process, and does not involve manipulating people. This is an important step. It may be the most important step of all. Service and administrative people should be included just like everybody else.

Accomplishment The real benefit of communications is that it gets supervisors and employees in the habit of talking positively about quality. It aids the process of changing, or perhaps clarifying, existing attitudes toward quality. And it sets the basis for the corrective-action and error-cause-removal steps.

Step six: corrective action

Action As people are encouraged to talk about their problems, opportunities for correction come to light, involving not just the defects found by inspection, audit, or self-evaluation, but also less obvious problems—as seen by the working people themselves—that require attention. These problems must be brought to the supervision meetings at each level. Those that cannot be resolved are formally passed up to the next level of supervision for review at their regular meeting. If a specific functional area does not hold such meetings, the team should take action to establish them in that department.

Accomplishment Individuals soon see that the problems brought to light are being faced and resolved on a regular basis. The habit of identifying problems and correcting them is beginning.

Step seven: establish an ad hoc committee for the zero defects program

Action Three or four members of the team are selected to investigate the Zero Defects concept and ways to implement the program. The quality manager must be clear, right from the start, that Zero Defects is *not* a motivation program. Its purpose is to communicate to all employees the literal meaning of the words *zero defects* and the thought that everyone should do things right the first time. This must be transmitted to every member of the team. In particular, the ad hoc group should seek out ways to match the program to the company's personality.

Accomplishment Improvement comes with each step of the overall program. By the time ZD day is reached, as much as a year may have gone by and the initial improvement will be flattening out. At that point the new commitment to an explicit goal takes over, and the improvement begins again. Setting up the ad hoc committee to study and prepare the implementation ensures that the goals of the program will be firmly supported by the company's thought leaders.

Step eight: supervisor training

Action A formal orientation with all levels of management should be conducted prior to implementation of all the steps. All managers must understand each step well enough to explain it to their people. The proof of understanding is the ability to explain it.

Accomplishment Eventually all supervision will be tuned into the program and realize its value for themselves. Then they will concentrate their action on the program.

Step nine: zero defects day

Action The establishment of ZD as the performance standard of the company should be done in one day. That way, everyone understands it the same way. Supervisors should explain the program to their people, and do something different in the facility so everyone will recognize that it is a "new attitude" day.

Accomplishment Making a "day" of the ZD commitment provides an emphasis and a memory that will be long lasting.

Step ten: goal setting

Action During meetings with employees each supervisor requests that they establish the goals they would like to strive for. Usually, there should be 30-, 60-, and 90-day goals. All should be specific and capable of being measured.

Accomplishment This phase helps people learn to think in terms of meeting goals and accomplishing specific tasks as a team.

Step eleven: error cause removal

Action Individuals are asked to describe any problem that keeps them from performing error-free work on a simple, one-page form. This is not a suggestion system. All they have to list is the problem; the appropriate functional group (e.g., industrial engineering) will develop the answer. It is important that any problems listed be acknowledged quickly—within twenty-four hours. Typical inputs might be:

- This tool is not long enough to work right with all the parts.
- The sales department makes too many errors on their order entry forms.
- We make a lot of changes in response to telephone calls, and many of them end up having to be done all over again.
- I don't have any place to put my pocketbook.

Accomplishment People now know that their problems can be heard and answered. Once employees learn to trust this communication, the program can go on forever.

Step twelve: recognition

Action Award programs are established to recognize those who meet their goals or perform outstanding acts. It is wise not to attach relative values to the identification of problems. Problems identified during the error-cause-removal stage should all be treated the same way because they are not suggestions. The prizes or awards should not be financial. Recognition is what is important.

Accomplishment Genuine recognition of performance is something people really appreciate. They will continue to support the program whether or not they, as individuals, participate in the awards.

Step thirteen: quality councils

Actions The quality professionals and team chairpersons should be brought together regularly to communicate with each other and to determine actions necessary to upgrade and improve the solid quality program being installed.

Accomplishment These councils are the best source of information on the status of programs and ideas for action. They also bring the professionals together on a regular basis.

Step fourteen: do it over again

Action The typical program takes a year to eighteen months. By that time turnover and changing situations will have wiped out much of the education effort. Therefore, it is necessary to set up a new team of representatives and begin again. ZD day, for instance, should be marked as an anniversary. Nothing more than the notification may be necessary. Or a special lunch for all employees might be given. The point is that the program is never over.

Accomplishment Repetition makes the program perpetual and, thus, "part of the woodwork." If quality isn't ingrained in the organization, it will never happen.

Reading 9

A Note on Quality: The Views of Deming, Juran, and Crosby

By Artemis March

During the 1980s, concerns about American competitiveness steered many U.S. companies to a new interest in quality. Most were likely to be introduced to quality concepts by one of the three leading "quality gurus"—W. Edwards Deming, Joseph Juran, and Philip Crosby. Each was an active consultant, lecturer, and author, with years of experience. Deming and Juran were in their eighties, and had been enormously influential in Japan; Crosby was in his sixties, and had worked previously at ITT as vice president of quality. Each of the three had developed his own distinctive approach to quality management.

DEMING

W. Edwards Deming was widely credited with leading the Japanese quality revolution. The Japanese began to heed his advice on statistical process control and problem-solving techniques (SPC) in 1950, but it was another thirty years before American businesses began to respond. By then, Deming's message to managers was blunt: "The basic cause of sickness in American industry and resulting unemployment is failure of top management to manage."[1] Known to dismiss client companies that did not change, he stated, "I give 'em three years. I've got to see a lot happen."[2] Best efforts were not enough; a program was needed, and it had to be adopted wholeheartedly:

> Everyone doing his best is not the answer. It is necessary that people know what to do. Drastic changes are required. The responsibility for change rests on management. The first step is to learn how to change.[3]

What Deming then expected from his clients was summarized in a 14-point program (see Exhibit 9.1).

To begin, managers had to put aside their preoccupation with today to make sure there was a tomorrow. They had to orient themselves to constant improvement of products and services to meet customers' needs and stay ahead of the competition. They had to innovate constantly, and commit resources to supporting innovation and continuous quality improvement. They had to build quality in.

EXHIBIT 9.1 ***Deming's 14 points***

1. *Create Constancy of Purpose for Improvement of Product and Service.*[a] Management must change from a preoccupation with the short run to building for the long run. This requires dedication to innovation in all areas, to best meet the needs of customers.

2. *Adopt the New Philosophy.* Shoddy materials, poor workmanship, defective products, and lax service must become unacceptable.

3. *Cease Dependence on Mass Inspection.* Inspection is equivalent to planning for defects; it comes too late and is ineffective and costly. Instead, processes must be improved.

4. *End the Practice of Awarding Business on Price Tag Alone.* Price has no meaning without a measure of the quality being purchased. Therefore, the job of purchasing will change only after management establishes new guidelines. Companies must develop long-term relationships and work with fewer suppliers. Purchasing must be given statistical tools to judge the quality of vendors and purchased parts. Both purchasing and vendors must understand specifications; but they must also know how the material is to be used in production and by the final customer.

5. *Constantly and Forever Improve the System of Production and Service.* Waste must be reduced and quality improved in every activity: procurement, transportation, engineering, methods, maintenance, sales, distribution, accounting, payroll, customer service, and manufacturing. Improvement, however, does not come from studying the defects produced by a process that is in control, but from studying the process itself. Most of the responsibility for process improvement rests with management.

6. *Institute Modern Methods of Training on the Job.* Training must be restructured and centered on clearly defined concepts of acceptable work. Statistical methods must be used for deciding when training has been completed successfully.

7. *Institute Modern Methods of Supervising.* Foremen must be empowered to inform upper management about conditions that need correction; once informed, management must take action. Barriers that prevent hourly workers from doing their jobs with pride must be removed.
8. *Drive Out Fear.* Because of the tremendous economic losses caused by fear on the job, people must not be afraid to ask questions, to report problems, or to express ideas.

They had to break down department and worker–supervisor barriers. They had to rid themselves of numerical targets and quotas, and concentrate instead on improving processes, giving workers clear standards for what constitutes acceptable work, plus the tools needed to achieve it. And, they had to create a climate free of fingerpointing and fear, which block cooperative identification and solution of problems.

If management committed itself to this new order, Deming argued, it would improve productivity as well as quality. Contrary to conventional wisdom in the United States, quality and productivity were not to be traded off against each other. Rather, productivity was a by-product of quality, and of doing things right the first time:

Exhibit 9.1 ***(Continued)***

9. *Break Down Barriers between Departments.* Members of the research, design, procurement, sales, and receiving departments must learn about problems with raw materials and specifications in production and assembly. Each discipline must stop optimizing its own work, and work together as a team for the company as a whole. Multidisciplinary quality-control circles can help improve design, service, quality, and costs.

10. *Eliminate Numerical Goals for the Work Force.* Targets, slogans, pictures, and posters urging people to increase productivity must be eliminated. Most of the necessary changes are out of workers' control, so such exhortations merely cause resentment. Although workers should not be given numerical goals, the company itself must have a goal: never-ending improvement.

11. *Eliminate Work Standards and Numerical Quotas.* Quotas focus on quantity, not quality. Therefore, work standards practically guarantee poor quality and high costs. Work standards that state percentage defective or scrap goals normally reach those targets, but never exceed them. Piecework is even worse, for it pays people for building defective units. But if someone's pay is docked for defective units, that is unfair, for the worker did not create the defects.

12. *Remove Barriers That Hinder the Hourly Workers.* Any barrier that hinders pride in work must be removed, including not knowing what good work is, supervisors motivated by quotas, off-gauge parts and material, and no response to reports of out-of-order machines.

13. *Institute a Vigorous Program of Education and Training.* Because quality and productivity improvements change the number of people needed in some areas and the jobs required, people must be continually trained and retrained. All training must include basic statistical techniques.

14. *Create a Structure in Top Management That Will Push Every Day on the above 13 Points.*

Notes:

[a]Italicized headings are in Deming's words. The remainder of each paragraph paraphrases his discussions.

> Improvement of the process increases uniformity of product, reduces rework and mistakes, reduces waste of manpower, machine-time, and materials, and thus increases output with less effort. Other benefits of improved quality are lower costs, . . . happier people on the job, and more jobs, through better competitive position of the company.[4]

Because management was responsible, in Deming's view, for 85 percent of quality problems, management had to take the lead in changing the systems and processes that created those problems. For example, consistent quality of incoming materials and components could not be expected where buyers were told to shop for price, or were not given the tools for assessing a supplier's quality. Management had to take the lead in developing long-term relationships with vendors, working with vendors to improve and maintain quality, training its own purchasing department in statistical quality control, requiring statistical evidence of quality from vendors, and insisting that specifications be complete, including an understanding of how the material actually worked in manufacturing. Only when management had changed purchasing systems and procedures could buyers be expected and able to do their job in a new way. Once top management was seriously committed to quality, lower-level personnel would be more likely to take action on problems that were within their control.

Accordingly, Deming delineated two means of process improvement: changing the "common causes" that were systemic (and were thus shared by numerous operators, machines, or products), and removing the "special causes" that produced nonrandom variation within systems (and were usually confined to individual employees or activities). Common causes included poor product design, incoming materials not suited to their use, machines out of order, improper bills of materials, machinery that would not hold tolerances, poor physical conditions, and so on. Special causes included lack of knowledge or skill, worker inattention, or a poor lot of incoming materials. Common causes were the responsibility of management and special causes the responsibility of operators:

> The discovery of a special cause of variation and its removal, are usually the responsibility of someone who is connected directly with some operation. . . . In contrast, there are common causes of defectives, of errors, of low rates or production, of low sales, of accidents. These are the responsibility of management. . . . The worker at a machine can do nothing about causes common to all machines. . . . He can not do anything about the light; he does not purchase raw materials; the training, supervision, and the company's policies are not his.[5]

The key tool Deming advocated to distinguish between systemic and special causes—and indeed, the key to quality management in general—was statistical process control. Developed by Walter Shewart while at Bell Labs in the 1930s and later refined by Deming in a well-known paper, "On the Statistical Theory of Errors," SPC was an inevitable fact of industrial life. It was unlikely that two parts, even when produced by the same operator at the same machine, would ever be identical. The issue, therefore, was distinguishing acceptable variation from variation that could indicate problems. The rules of statistical probability provided a method for making this distinction.

Probability rules could determine whether variation was random or not—i.e., whether it was due to chance. Random variation occurred within statistically determined limits. If variation remained within those limits, the process was a stable one, and said to be in control. As long as nothing changed the process, future variation could be easily predicted, for it would remain indefinitely within the same statistical limits.

Data of this sort were normally collected and plotted on control charts kept by the operators themselves. Such charts graphically plotted actual performance readings (e.g., the outside diameters of pistons) on graphs that also depicted the upper and lower control limits for that characteristic, which were statistically determined (see Figure 9.1). As long as the readings, taken on a small sample of units at predetermined intervals (such as every half-hour), fell between limits or did not show a trend (or "run"), the process was in control and no intervention was required, despite the obvious variation in readings. Readings that either fell outside the limits or produced a run indicated a problem to be investigated.

The practical value of distinguishing random from nonrandom variation was enormous. Operators now knew when to intervene in a process and when to leave it alone. Further, because readings were taken during the production

FIGURE 9.1 *A typical control chart*

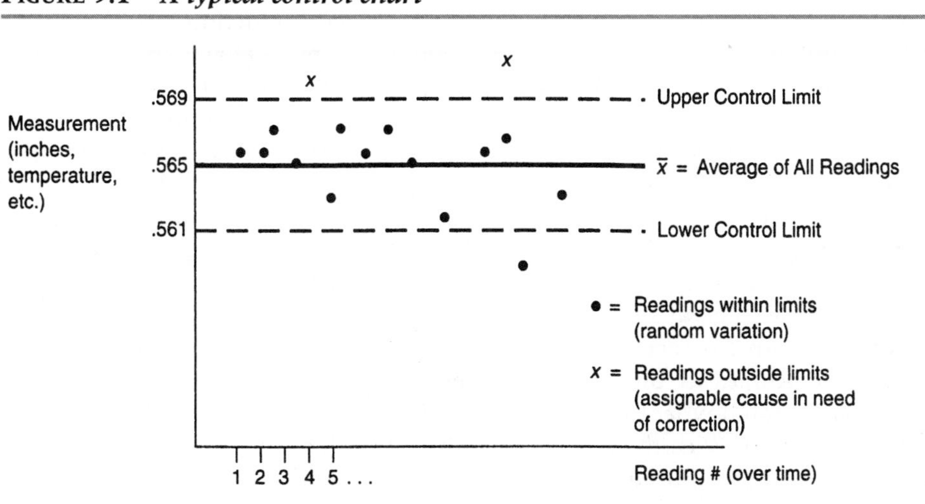

process itself, unacceptable variation showed up early enough for corrective action, rather than after the fact.

Once a process was in control, readings that fell outside the limits indicated a special cause. When the cause of such nonrandom variation was found and removed, the system returned to its stable state. For example, if a particular lot of goods showed yields that were below control limits, further analysis might determine that raw materials peculiar to that lot were the cause. The removal of such special causes, however, did not improve the system (i.e., raise yield levels), but simply brought it back under control at the preexisting yield.

To improve the system itself, common causes had to be removed. Simply because a system was in statistical control did not mean it was as good as it could be. Indeed, a process in control could produce a high proportion of defects. Control limits indicated what the process was, not what it should or could be. To move the average (yield, sales, defects, returns, etc.) up or down—and thus also move the control limits up or down—typically required the concerted efforts of engineering, research, sales, manufacturing, and other departments. To narrow the range of variation around the target point could consume even more effort. In both cases, control charts would readily document the improvements in the process.

Deming viewed training in the use of control charts as essential if workers were to know what constituted acceptable work. He was adamant that quotas, piecework, and numerical goals be eliminated. Instead, workers had to be shown what good work was, and given the tools to do it. Such tools would also allow them to monitor their own work and correct it in real time, rather than find out about problems days or weeks later.

Control charts were but one part of the statistical approach to quality. Because 100 percent testing was inefficient, sampling techniques had been developed to provide a scientific basis on which to accept or reject production lots based on a limited number of units. Although sampling and control charts could indicate problems, they could not by themselves identify their causes. For that purpose, other statistical techniques were needed, such as Pareto analysis, Ishikawa ("fishbone") cause-and-effect diagrams, histograms, flowcharts, and scatter diagrams.

By 1986, Deming's lectures concentrated more on management than SPC, but SPC remained the core of his approach. Many U.S. firms had sought him out, and some, such as the Ford Motor Company, had adopted his approach throughout the company, with great success. Deming, who still worked out of the basement of his home with his secretary of thirty years, was hardly sanguine about the prospects of American business. He believed it would take thirty years for Americans to match what the Japanese had done, and that the United States was still falling behind. With the spectre of a lower standard of living, he concluded, "We should be pretty scared."[6]

JURAN

Joseph M. Juran's impact on Japanese quality was usually considered second only to Deming's. At 82, he had enjoyed a varied and distinguished career, including periods as a business executive, government administrator, lecturer, writer, and consultant. After years of independent activity, he established the Juran Institute in 1979 to serve as a base for the seminars, consulting, conferences, and videotapes long associated with his name. In recent years, clients had included Texas Instruments, DuPont, Monsanto, and Xerox.

Juran defined quality as "fitness to use," meaning that the users of a product or service should be able to count on it for what they needed or wanted to do with it. For example, a manufacturer should be able to process a purchased material or component to meet the demands of its customers while achieving high yields and minimal downtime in production; a wholesaler should receive a correctly labeled product, free from damage during shipment and easy to handle and display; and a consumer should receive a product that performed as claimed and did not break down—or, if it did, receive prompt and courteous adjustment of his claim.

Fitness for use had five major dimensions: quality of design, quality of conformance, availability, safety, and field use.[7] Quality of design was what distinguished a Rolls Royce from a Chevrolet; it involved the design concept and its specification. Quality of conformance reflected the match between actual product and design intent; it was affected by process choices, ability to hold tolerances, workforce training and supervision, and adherence to test programs. Availability referred to a product's freedom from disruptive problems; it reflected both reliability (the frequency or probability of failure) and maintainability (the speed or ease of repair). Safety could be assessed by calculating the risk of injury due to product hazards. And field use referred to a product's conformance and condition after it reached customers' hands. It was affected by packaging, transportation, storage, and field service competence and promptness.

To achieve fitness for use, Juran developed a comprehensive approach to quality that spanned a product's entire life—from design through vendor relations, process development, manufacturing control, inspection and test, distribution, customer relations, and field service. Each area was carefully dissected, and approaches were proposed to specify and quantify its impact on the various elements of fitness for use. A broad range of statistical techniques was included to assist in the analysis.

Juran's approach to reliability provides a representative example. His reliability program began by establishing reliability goals. It then apportioned these among product components; identified critical components, identified possible modes, effects, and causes of failures; and developed solutions for those most critical to successful product operation and safety. Juran also discussed the setting of realistic tolerances, design reviews, vendor selection, and testing of designs. Statistical methods for improving reliability included analysis of various types of failure rates, analysis of relationships between component and system reliability, and setting of tolerance limits for interacting dimensions. The aims of these activities were quantified reliability goals, a systematic guide for achieving them, and a measurement and monitoring system for knowing when they had been achieved.

Although Juran's analytical methods could identify areas needing improvement and could help make and track changes, they were in the language of the shop floor: defect rates, failure modes, not within specification, and the like. Juran recognized that such measures were not likely to attract top management attention; for this reason, he advocated a cost of quality (COQ) accounting system. Such a system spoke top management's language: money. Quality costs were costs "associated solely with defective product—the costs of making, finding, repairing, or avoiding defects."[8] They were of four types: internal failure costs (from defects discovered before shipment); external failures costs (from defects discovered after shipment); appraisal costs (for assessing the condition of materials and product); and prevention costs (for keeping defects from occurring in the first place). See Exhibit 9.2A. In most companies, external and internal failure costs together accounted for 50–80 percent of COQ. When these were converted to dollars, or presented as a percentage of sales or profits, top management usually took notice.

EXHIBIT 9.2A *Categories of quality costs*[a]

Internal Failure Costs = Costs from product defects prior to shipment to customer. They include:

- *Scrap*—Net losses in labor and material resulting from defective goods that cannot economically be repaired or used.
- *Rework*—Cost of correcting defective products to make them usable.
- *Retest*—Cost of reinspection and retesting of products that have been reworked.
- *Downtime*—Cost of idle facilities, equipment, and labor due to defective products.
- *Yield Losses*—Cost of process yields lower than could be attained through improved process control.
- *Disposition*—The time of those involved in determining whether nonconforming products are usable and what should be done with them.

External Failure Costs = Costs associated with defects found after shipment to customer. They include:

- *Complaint Adjustment*—Costs of investigating and responding to complaints due to defective product, faulty installation, or improper instructions to users.
- *Returned Material*—Costs associated with receiving and replacing defective product returned from the field.
- *Warranty Charges*—Costs of services and repairs performed under warranty contracts.
- *Allowances*—Income losses due to downgrading products for sale as seconds, and to concessions made to customers who accept substandard products as is.

Exhibit 9.2A *(Continued)*

Appraisal Costs = Costs associated with discovering the condition of products and raw materials. They include:

- *Incoming Materials Inspection*—Costs associated with determining the quality of vendors' products.
- *Inspection and Test*—Costs of checking product conformance throughout design and manufacture, including tests done on customer's premises.
- *Maintaining Accuracy of Test Equipment*—Costs of operating and maintaining measuring instruments.
- *Materials and Services Consumed*—Costs of products consumed in destructive tests; also materials and services (e.g., electric power) consumed in testing.
- *Evaluation of Stocks*—Costs of testing products in storage to assess their condition.

Prevention Costs = Costs associated with preventing defects and limiting failure and appraisal costs. They include:

- *Quality Planning*—Costs of creating and communicating plans and data systems for quality, inspection, reliability, and related activities; includes the costs of preparing all necessary manuals and procedures.
- *New Products Review*—Costs of preparing bid proposals, evaluating new designs, preparing test and experimentation programs, and related quality activities associated with launching new products.
- *Training*—Costs of developing and conducting training programs aimed at improving quality performance.
- *Process Control*—Costs of process control aimed at achieving fitness for use, as distinguished from productivity (a difficult distinction to make in practice).
- *Quality Data Acquisition and Analysis*—Costs of operating the quality data system to get continuing data on quality performance.
- *Quality Reporting*—Costs of bringing together and presenting quality data to upper management.
- *Improvement Projects*—Costs of building and implementing breakthrough projects.

Notes:

[a]This is a summary and rewording of Juran and Gryna, pp. 14–16.

COQ not only provided management with a dollar cost for defective products, it also established the goal of quality programs: to keep improving quality until there was no longer a positive economic return. This occurred when the total

EXHIBIT 9.2B ***Minimizing the costs of quality***[a]

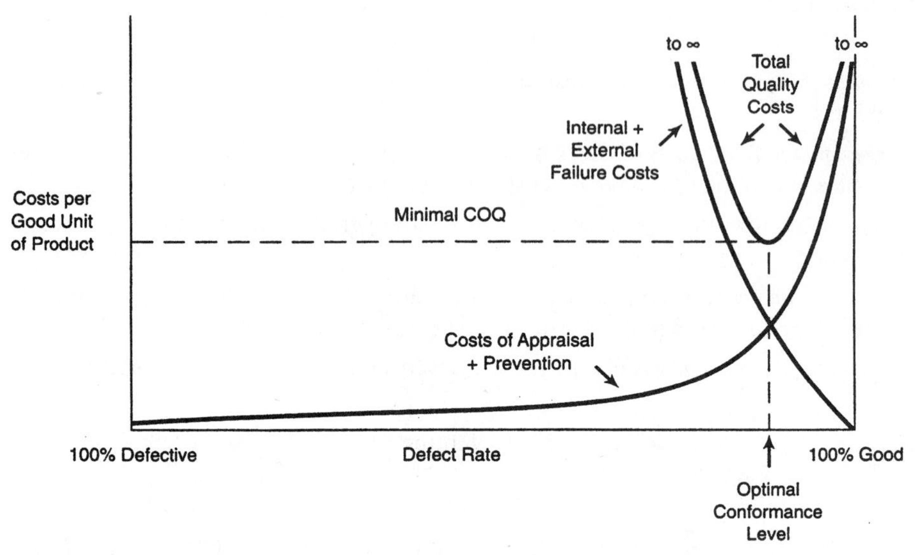

NOTES:

[a]This figure adapted from Juran and Gryna, p. 27.

costs of quality were minimized. (See Exhibit 9.2B). Two assumptions were built into this analysis: that failure costs approached zero as defects became fewer and fewer, and that prevention and appraisal costs together approached infinity as defects were reduced to lower and lower levels. COQ minimization therefore occurred at the point where additional spending on prevention and appraisal was no longer justified, because it produced smaller savings in failure costs.

This approach had important practical implications. It implied that zero defects was not a practical goal, for to reach that level, prevention and appraisal costs would have to rise so substantially that total costs of quality would not be minimized. As long as prevention and appraisal costs were cheaper (on a per-unit basis) than failure costs, Juran argued that resources should continue to go to prevention and testing. But when prevention activities started to pull COQ unit costs up rather than down, it was time to maintain quality rather than attempt to reduce it further.

To reach and maintain this minimum cost of quality, Juran proposed a three-pronged approach: breakthrough projects, the control sequence, and annual quality programs. In the early stages, when a firm's failure costs greatly exceeded its prevention and appraisal costs, there were significant opportunities for breakthrough projects, aimed at chronic problems. Such problems were adverse situations of long standing, such as the need to revise tolerances, ignored because they were neither dramatic nor thought to be solvable. The "breakthrough sequence" involved identifying the "vital few" projects, selling them to management, organizing to analyze the issues and to involve the key people who were needed for implementation, and overcoming resistance to change (see Exhibit 9.3). Juran

EXHIBIT 9.3 ***Juran's breakthrough sequence***[a]

1. *Breakthrough in Attitudes.* Managers must first prove that a breakthrough is needed, and then create a climate conducive to change. To demonstrate need, data must be collected to show the extent of the problem; the data most convincing to top management are usually cost-of-quality figures. To get the resources required for improvement, expected benefits can be monetized and presented in terms of return on investment.
2. *Identify the Vital Few Projects.* Pareto analysis is used to distinguish the vital few projects from the trivial many, and to set priorities based on problem frequency.
3. *Organize for Breakthrough in Knowledge.* Two organizational entities should be established—a steering group and a diagnostic group. The steering group, composed of people from several departments, defines the program, suggests possible problem causes, gives the authority to experiment, helps overcome resistance to change, and implements the solution. The diagnostic group, composed of quality professionals and, sometimes, line managers, is responsible for analyzing the problem.
4. *Conduct the Analysis.* The diagnostic group studies symptoms, develops hypotheses, and experiments to find the problem's true causes. It also tries to determine whether defects are primarily operator-controllable or management-controllable. (A defect is operator-controllable only if it meets three criteria: operators know what they are supposed to do, have the data to understand what they are actually doing, and are able to regulate their own performance.) Theories can be tested using past data and current production data, and by conducting experiments. With this information, the diagnostic group then proposes solutions to the problem.
5. *Determine How to Overcome Resistance to Change.* The need for change must be established in terms that are important to the key people involved. Logical arguments alone are insufficient. Participation is therefore required in both the technical and social aspects of change.
6. *Institute the Change.* Departments that must take corrective action must be convinced to cooperate. Presentations to these departments should include the size of the problem, alternative solutions, the cost of recommended changes, expected benefits, and efforts taken to anticipate the change's impact on employees. Time for reflection may be needed, and adequate training is essential.
7. *Institute Controls.* Controls must be set up to monitor the solution and see that it works, and to keep abreast of unforeseen developments. Formal follow-up is provided by the control sequence used to monitor and correct sporadic problems.

NOTES:

[a]This summary adapted from Juran and Gryna, pp. 100–129, and Juran, 1964.

claimed that most breakthrough analyses found that over 80 percent of the problems (e.g., defect rates, scrap rates) were under management control and less than 20 percent were caused by operators.

After successive breakthrough projects, a firm reached the point of optimal quality—in Juran's formulation, the bottom of the COQ curve. It then needed to employ the control sequence to preserve its gains. This sequence was actually a large feedback loop. One first chose an objective to control, then defined a unit of measure, set a numerical standard or goal, created a means of measuring performance, and mobilized the organization to report the measurements. After these preparatory steps, an action cycle was repeated over and over: Actual performance was compared with standard, and action was taken (if needed) to close the gap.[9]

The control sequence was also used to attack sporadic problems—sudden, usually dramatic changes in the status quo, such as a worn cutting tool. Eliminating sporadic problems only returned processes to their historical levels; to improve them to optimum levels, breakthrough teams were needed because chronic problems were involved. Juran's contrast between these two types of problems is illustrated in Figure 9.2.

Both the control and breakthrough processes demanded sophisticated analysis and statistics. The comprehensiveness of Juran's program—it ran from vendor relations through customer service, and covered all the functions in between—required high-level planning and coordination as well. For this reason, Juran argued that a new group of professionals—quality control engineers—was needed. This department would be involved in high-level quality planning, coordinating the activities of other departments, setting quality standards, and providing quality measurements. But Juran also believed that top management

FIGURE 9.2 ***Juran's sporadic and chronic problems***[a]

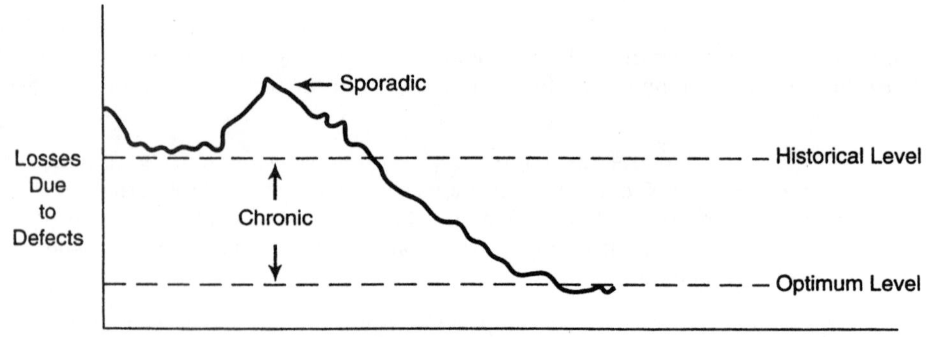

NOTES:

[a]This figure adapted from Juran and Gryna, p. 100.

had to give overall leadership and support to quality improvement if it were to succeed.

Juran's major vehicle for top-management involvement was the annual quality program. Akin to long-range financial planning and the annual budget process, this program gave top management quality objectives. It was especially important for internalizing the habit of quality improvement and ensuring that complacency did not set in.

CROSBY

Philip B. Crosby had started in industry as an inspector; eventually he rose through the ranks at several companies to become vice president of quality at ITT. In 1979, he left ITT to found Philip Crosby Associates, Inc. and with it, the Crosby Quality College, which by 1986 had been attended by some 35,000 executives and managers. General Motors owned over 10 percent of Crosby stock, and had set up its own Crosby school, as had such companies as IBM, Johnson & Johnson, and Chrysler.

Crosby's message was directed at top management. He sought to change their perceptions and attitudes about quality. Typically, top managers viewed quality as intangible, or else to be found only in high-end products. Crosby, however, spoke of quality as "conformance to requirements," and believed that any product that consistently reproduced its design specifications was of high quality. In this sense, a Pinto that met Pinto requirements was as much a quality product as a Cadillac that conformed to Cadillac requirements.

American managers must pursue quality, Crosby argued, because it would help them compete. In fact, he believed that if quality were improved, total costs would inevitably fall, allowing companies to increase profitability. This reasoning led to Crosby's most famous claim: that quality was "free."[10]

Ultimately, the goal of quality improvement was zero defects, to be achieved through prevention rather than after-the-fact inspection. Crosby had popularized the zero defects movement, but it had actually originated in the United States at the Martin Company in the 1960s, where Crosby was employed. The company had promised and delivered a perfect missile, with limited inspection and rework, and its managers had concluded that perfection was possible if it was in fact expected. The company then developed a philosophy and program to support that goal.

Crosby elaborated on this approach. He believed that the key to quality improvement was changing the thinking of top management. If management expected imperfection and defects, it would get them, for workers would bring similar expectations to their jobs. But if management established a higher standard of performance, and communicated it thoroughly to all levels of the company, zero defects was possible. Thus, according to Crosby, zero defects was a management standard, and not simply a motivational program for employees.

Exhibit 9.4 *The quality management maturity grid*[a]

Measurement categories	Stage I: uncertainty	Stage II: awakening	Stage III: enlightenment	Stage IV: wisdom	Stage V: certainty
Management Understanding and Attitude	Fails to see quality as a management tool.	Supports quality management in theory, but is unwilling to provide the necessary money or time.	Learning about quality management and becoming supportive.	Participates personally in quality activities.	Regards quality management as essential to the company's success.
Quality Organization Status	Quality activities are limited to the manufacturing or engineering department, and are largely appraisal and sorting.	A strong quality leader has been appointed, but quality activities remain focused on appraisal and sorting, and are still limited to manufacturing and engineering.	Quality department. reports to top management and its leader is active in company management.	Quality manager is an officer of the company. Prevention activities have become important.	Quality manager is on the board of directors. Prevention is the main quality activity.

Measurement categories	Stage I: uncertainty	Stage II: awakening	Stage III: enlightenment	Stage IV: wisdom	Stage V: certainty
Problem Handling	Problems are fought as they occur and are seldom fully resolved; "firefighting" dominates.	Teams are established to attack major problems, but the approach remains short term.	Problems are resolved in an orderly fashion and corrective action is a regular event.	Problems are identified early in their development.	Except in the most unusual cases, problems are prevented.
Cost of Quality as Percent of Sales	Reported: unknown Actual: 20%	Reported: 5% Actual: 18%	Reported: 8% Actual: 12%	Reported: 6.5% Actual: 8%	Reported: 2.5% Actual: 2.5%
Quality Improvement Actions	No organized activities.	Activities are motivational and short term.	Implementing the 14-step program with full understanding.	Continuing the 14-step program and starting Make Certain.	Quality improvement is a regular and continuing activity.
Summation of Company Quality Posture	"We don't know why we have quality problems."	"Must we always have quality problems?"	"Because of management commitment and quality improvement programs, we are identifying and resolving our quality problems."	"We routinely prevent defects from occurring."	"We know why we don't have quality problems."

Notes:

[a]This chart is adapted from Crosby, pp. 32–33.

To help managers understand the seriousness of their quality problems, Crosby provided two primary tools: cost of quality measures and the management maturity grid (see Exhibit 9.4). Costs of quality, which Crosby estimated to be 15–20 percent of sales at most companies, were useful for showing top management the size of their quality problem and the opportunities for profitable improvement. The management maturity grid was used for self-assessment. It identified five states of quality awareness: uncertainty (the company failed to recognize quality as a management tool); awakening (quality was recognized as important, but management put off taking action); enlightenment (management openly faced and addressed quality problems by establishing a formal quality program); wisdom (prevention was working well, problems were identified early, and corrective action was routinely pursued); and certainty (quality management was an essential part of the company, and problems occurred only infrequently). For each of these five stages, Crosby also examined the status of the quality organization, problem-handling procedures, reported and actual costs of quality as percentages of sales, and quality improvement actions.

Once companies had positioned themselves on the management maturity grid, Crosby offered a 14-point program for quality improvement (see Exhibit 9.5). It emphasized prevention over detection, and focused on changing corporate culture rather than on analytical or statistical tools. The program was designed as a guide for securing management commitment and gaining employees' involvement through actions such as Zero Defects day. Crosby believed every company should tailor its own defect-prevention program; nevertheless, the goal should always be zero defects. In this process, top management played a leadership role; quality professionals played a modest but important role as facilitators, coordinators, trainers, and technical assistants; and hourly workers were secondary.

EXHIBIT 9.5 *Crosby's 14-point program*[a]

1. *Management Commitment.* Top management must become convinced of the need for quality improvement, and must make its commitment clear to the entire company. This should be accompanied by a written quality policy, stating that each person is expected to "perform exactly like the requirement, or cause the requirement to be officially changed to what we and the customers really need."

2. *Quality Improvement Team.* Management must form a team of department heads (or those who can speak for their departments) to oversee quality improvement. The team's role is to see that needed actions take place in its departments and in the company as a whole.

3. *Quality Measurement.* Quality measures appropriate to every activity must be established to identify areas needing improvement. In accounting, for example, one measure might be the percentage of late reports; in engineering, the accuracy of drawings; in purchasing, rejections due to incomplete descriptions; and in plant engineering, time lost because of equipment failures.

Exhibit 9.5 ***(Continued)***

4. *Cost of Quality Evaluation.* The controller's office should make an estimate of the costs of quality to identify areas where quality improvements would be profitable.

5. *Quality Awareness.* Quality awareness must be raised among employees. They must understand the importance of product conformance and the costs of nonconformance. These messages should be carried by supervisors (after they have been trained) and through such media as films, booklets, and posters.

6. *Corrective Action.* Opportunities for correction are generated by Steps 3 and 4, as well as discussions among employees. These ideas should be brought to the supervisory level and resolved there, if possible; they should be pushed up further if that is necessary to get action.

7. *Zero Defects Planning.* An ad hoc zero defects committee should be formed from members of the quality improvement team. This committee should start planning a zero defects program appropriate to the company and its culture.

8. *Supervisor Training.* Early in the process, all levels of management must be trained to implement their part of the quality improvement program.

9. *Zero Defects Day.* A Zero Defects day should be scheduled to signal to employees that the company has a new performance standard.

10. *Goal Setting.* To turn commitments into action, individuals must establish improvement goals for themselves and their groups. Supervisors should meet with their people and ask them to set goals that are specific and measurable. Goal lines should be posted in each area, and meetings held to discuss progress.

11. *Error Cause Removal.* Employees should be encouraged to inform management of any problems that prevent them from performing error-free work. Employees need not do anything about these problems themselves; they should simply report them. Reported problems must then be acknowledged by management within 24 hours.

12. *Recognition.* Public, nonfinancial appreciation must be given to their quality goals or perform outstandingly.

13. *Quality Councils.* Quality professionals and team chairpersons should meet regularly to share experiences, problems, and ideas.

14. *Do It All over Again.* To emphasize the never-ending process of quality improvement, the program (Steps 1–13) must be repeated. This renews the commitment of old employees and brings new ones into the process.

Notes:

[a]This summary is adapted from Crosby, pp. 132–139, 175–259.

Notes

1. W. Edwards Deming, *Quality, Productivity, and Competitive Position,* Cambridge: Massachusetts Institute of Technology, Center for Advanced Engineering Study, 1982, p. i.
2. Jeremy Main, "The Curmudgeon Who Talks Tough on Quality," *Fortune,* June 25,1984, p. 122.
3. Deming, 1982, p. ii. This note has been prepared by Associate for Case Development Artemis March, under the supervision of Associate Professor David A. Garvin, as the basis for class discussion.
4. Ibid., p. 1.
5. Ibid., p. 116.
6. Main, 1984, p. 122.
7. The key parameters of fitness for use, as well as their dimensions, vary somewhat in Juran's writings over a 35-year period. Their comprehensiveness and their spanning the entire product life cycle, however, are constants. The present discussion draws most heavily on Joseph M. Juran and Frank M. Gryna, Jr., *Quality Planning and Analysis,* New York: McGraw-Hill Book Company, 1980.
8. Juran and Gryna, p. 13.
9. This description of the control sequence is based on Joseph M. Juran, *Managerial Breakthrough,* New York: McGraw-Hill Book Company, 1964, pp. 183–187.
10. Philip B. Crosby, *Quality Is Free* (New York: McGraw-Hill Book Company, 1979).

Reading 10

What Is Total Quality Control? The Japanese Way

BY KAORU ISHIKAWA

WHAT IS TOTAL QUALITY CONTROL?

Companies and individuals may give different interpretations, but broadly speaking, total quality control means management control itself.

The concept of "total quality control" was originated by Dr. Armand V. Feigenbaum, who in the 1950s variously served as company manager of quality control and company-wide manager of manufacturing operations and quality control at General Electric staff headquarters in New York City. His article on total quality control was published in the May 1957 issue of *Industrial Quality Control* and was followed by a book in 1961, entitled *Total Quality Control: Engineering and Management.*

According to Feigenbaum, total quality control (TQC) may be defined as "an effective system for integrating the quality development, quality maintenance, and quality improvement efforts of the various groups in an organization so as to enable production and service at the most economical levels which allow for full customer satisfaction." TQC requires participation of all divisions, including the divisions of marketing, design, manufacturing, inspection, and shipping. Fearing that quality which is everybody's job in a business can become nobody's job, Feigenbaum suggested that TQC be buttressed and serviced by a well-organized management function whose only area of specialization is product quality and whose only area of operation is in the quality control jobs. His Western-type professionalism led him to advocate TQC conducted essentially by QC specialists.

SOURCE: Excerpt from *What Is Total Quality Control? The Japanese Way* by Kaoru Ishikawa, translated by David J. Lu. Copyright © 1985. Reprinted with permission of Prentice Hall.

The Japanese approach has differed from Dr. Feigenbaum's approach. Since 1949 we have insisted on having all divisions and all employees become involved in studying and promoting QC. Our movement has never been an exclusive domain of QC specialists. This has been manifested in all of our activities, including the basic QC course for engineers, Dr. Deming's seminars for top and middle management (1950), the course for foremen broadcast in 1956, and the advocation of QC circle activities in 1962. We have promoted these under various names, such as integrated quality control, total quality control, all member participation quality control, and the like. The term "total quality control" has been the most frequently used. Yet when this term is used overseas, people may think that we are imitating Dr. Feigenbaum's approach, which we are not. So I have called ours Japanese-style total quality control, but found it too cumbersome. At the 1968 QC symposium, we agreed to use the term companywide quality control to designate the Japanese approach.

Quality control participated in by all divisions

What do I mean by companywide or total quality control? It simply means that everyone in every division in the company must study, practice, and participate in quality control. Merely to assign QC specialists in every division as suggested by Feigenbaum is not enough. In Japan the vertical line authority relationship is too strong for staff members such as QC specialists to have much voice in the operation of each separate division. To counter this situation, our approach has always been to educate everyone in every division and to let each person implement and promote QC. Our QC courses are now well defined, and separate courses are available for different divisions. For example, there are QC courses for the marketing divisions and for the purchasing divisions. After all, "QC begins with education and ends with education."

Quality control participated in by all employees

Our own definition of companywide quality control has undergone certain changes. Initially total participation extended only to the company president, directors, middle management, staff, foremen, line workers, and salesmen. But in recent years, the definition has been expanded to include subcontractors, distribution systems, and affiliated (*keiretsu*) companies. This system, developed in Japan, is quite different from what is being practiced in the West. In China, Chairman Mao spoke of the inadequacy of control through specialists and advocated combining efforts of the workers, specialists, and leaders. This approach is closer to that of ours. There seems to be a common thread in the way of thinking in the Orient.

Integrated quality control

In effecting integrated quality control, control of quality is central, but at the same time cost control (profit control and price control), quantity control (amount of production, of sales, of stock), and control of delivery date are to be promoted. This method is based on the fundamental assumption of QC that a manufacturer must develop, produce, and sell commodities that satisfy the needs of consumers. In conducting QC, unless one knows the cost no quality planning and design can be effected. If cost control is tightly managed, one can know how much profit could be realized if certain trouble spots were eliminated. In this manner, the effects of QC can also be easily anticipated.

As to quantity, unless the exact amount is known, neither the percent defective nor the rate of reworks can be obtained and QC cannot progress. Conversely, unless QC is actively promoted—and unless standardization, the standard yield rate, standard rate of operation, and a standard workload are determined—there can be no way of finding standard cost, and consequently no cost control can be effected. Similarly, if percent defective varies too widely and if there are many rejected lots, neither production control nor control of the delivery date can be effected. In short, management must be done on an integrated basis. QC, cost (profit) control, and quantity (delivery date) control cannot be effected independently of one another. We do our integrated quality control at the core of all efforts, and that is the reason we also call this method integrated quality control. When each of the divisions (design, purchasing, manufacturing, and marketing) engages in QC activities, it must always follow this integrated approach.

In the West the definition of "quality control" has always included control of the quality of both products and services. Thus QC has been practiced in department stores, airlines, and banks. This is a sound approach. In Japan, by translating the term "quality control" into *hinshitsu kanri,* with the term *hin* connoting products, we may have unwittingly created quality control primarily for our manufacturing sector. In the past three decades Japan has emphasized quality of products, manufacturing them inexpensively and exporting them successfully, resulting in a rise in the level of Japan's living standards. In retrospect, then, it has been good to have the term *hin* (products) placed in the word designating quality.

However, I want to emphasize that the term quality means quality, and that the term extends to the quality of work in offices, in the service-related industries and in the financial sector.

I often use a diagram to explain this concept. (See Diagram 10.1.) The essence of TQC is found in the central ring, which contains quality assurance narrowly defined, which means doing QC well for the company's new products. In the service industry where no manufactured goods are involved, quality assurance means assuring the quality of services rendered. In developing new services, such as new deposit accounts or new insurance contracts, quality must be assured.

Once the meanings of QC and of good quality and good services become clear, the second ring comes into play. The ring represents control of quality that is defined more broadly, including the questions of how to bring about good sales activities, how to make salesmen better, how to make office work more efficient, and how to deal effectively with subcontractors.

If the meaning is broadened even further, the third ring will be formed. This ring stresses that control of all phases of work is to be done effectively. It utilizes

DIAGRAM 10.1 COMPANYWIDE QUALITY CONTROL

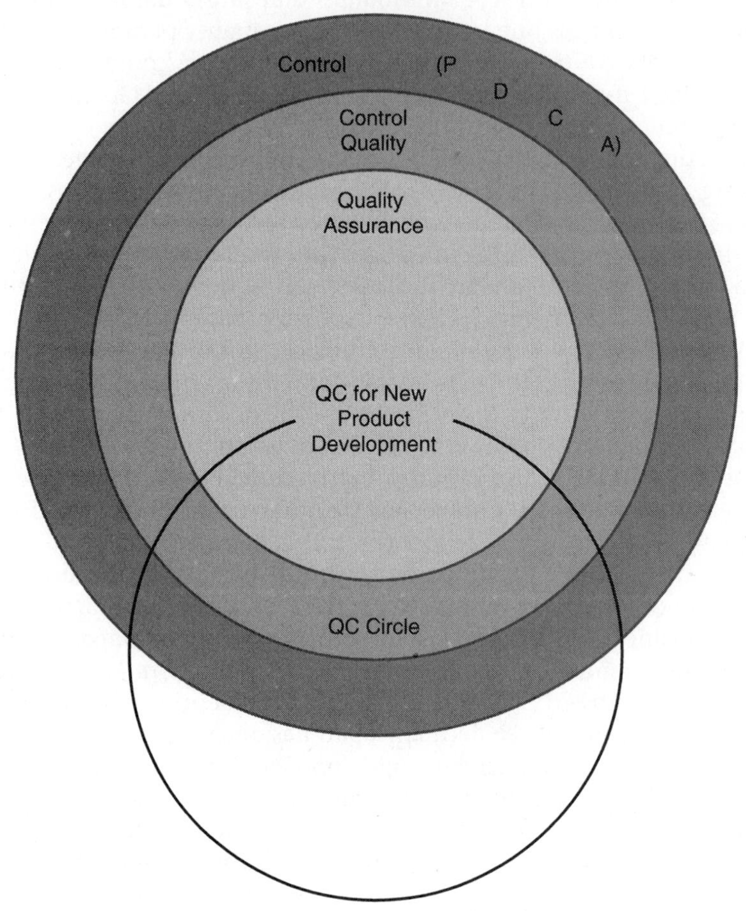

the PDCA (plan, do, check, action) circle, turning its wheel over and over again to prevent recurrence of defects at all levels. This work involves the entire company, each division and each function. Each individual must also be actively involved.

Japanese QC has been fortunate in that in its history, once quality has been improved, control has been done effectively by turning the wheel of the PDCA circle. This has contributed effectively to the prevention of recurrence.

How far can a company's QC go in relation to the above three rings? That determination must be made by the chief executive officer taking into account the nature of the company. He must then communicate his decision to the entire company. Otherwise, within the company people may start debating unnecessarily about the QC definition. Some companies in Japan use the second and third rings with broader definitions. Other companies are confined to the central ring with quality assurance as the core. These can still claim to practice total quality control. One note of caution to those companies that use the broader definitions. Whatever you do, you must not forget the very essence of QC, which is found in quality assurance and in QC for development of new products.

Incidentally, QC circle activities must always be conducted as part of companywide quality control activities. The QC circle is to be regarded as a ring that intersects all other rings. QC circle activities alone will not bring about TQC. Without participation by top and middle management and by the staff, QC circle activities cannot last. All over the world many companies are following the Japanese example in instituting QC activities. I fear many of them will not last unless they take the concept of companywide quality control seriously and involve their top and middle management and their staff members in QC.

The above is what we call companywide quality control or total quality control. The two terms can be used interchangeably.

ADVANTAGES OF TOTAL QUALITY CONTROL

Why do companies decide to institute TQC? I have given my answers in the April 1980 issue of *Engineers,* in a report entitled "Management Ideals of Companies Receiving the Deming Prize." The companies that have received the Deming Application Prize are all in the forefront of total quality control in Japan. Reproduced below is a summary of my report, outlining the reasons these companies decided to engage in TQC:

- To make our company recession proof, with true sales and technological capabilities (Ricoh Co., Ltd., recipient of the prize, 1975).
- To secure profit for the benefit of our employees, and to secure quality, quantity, and cost to obtain the confidence of our customers (Riken Forge Co., Ltd., 1975).
- To build quality into products that can always satisfy our customers. As a means of doing this, we engage in QC with (1) full employee participation, (2) emphasis on problem solving that can contribute to our profit picture, and (3) utilization of statistical approaches and methods (Tokai Chemical Industries, Ltd., 1975).
- To establish a company whose corporate health and character allow its steady growth by combining the creative energies of all of its employees, with attainment of the highest quality in the world as our goal. To develop the most up-to-date products, and to improve our quality assurance system (Pentel Co., Ltd., 1976).
- To create a cheerful workplace and show respect for humanity through QC circles with all-member participation. To supply in Japan and abroad automatic transmissions of impeccable quality, superior to the international standards but

lower in cost, which takes into account fully the requirements of customers and users. To bring about prosperity of the company through improvement in management control, and thus contribute to the welfare of regional society (Aisin-Warner Limited, 1977).

- To improve the corporate health and character of our company, to upgrade quality of our products, and to raise our profit picture (Takenaka Komuten Co., Ltd., 1979).
- To establish a company whose corporate health and character are competitive and viable in any business environment change (Sekisui Chemical Co., Ltd., 1979).
- To attain the following goals: (a) Securing quality control development—To implement product goals according to company policy in a timely manner, the efforts of all employees are to be combined and organized; (b) Strengthening of control—Everyone must put into practice what he has learned about the methods and approaches of quality control and bring about improvement in the quality of control in every aspect of company activities; and (c) Nurturing human resources—To show respect for each employee as an individual, the company is to create a workplace that is worthy of everyone's labor through the nurturing and utilization of human resources and through teamwork (Kyushu Nippon Electric, 1979).

Space does not permit me to go on with other individual examples. In general, companies that have received the Deming Prize—including those not mentioned above—have the following purposes in common:

1. *Improving the corporate health and character of the company*—Almost all companies are serious about this point. Japan has entered a period of steady but less accelerated economic growth. So most companies feel that they must begin again from the beginning and utilize TQC to strengthen the corporate health and character of the company. Some set specific goals. Others do not spell them out. As I have often said, QC is not an act of cheerleading. Employees cannot act if they are given nothing but abstract instructions. Top management must make clear the goals it has in mind, pointing out which part of the company's character requires modification, or which aspect must be improved.
2. *Combining the efforts of all employees, achieving participation by all, and establishing a cooperative system*—Control by specialists does not work in Japan. All employees in all divisions must be actively involved and combine their efforts.
3. *Establishing the quality assurance system and obtaining the confidence of customers and consumers*—Quality assurance being what it is, the very essence of QC, most companies announce such assurance to be their goal or ideal. The difference between new-style QC and old-style management is that QC does not seek short-term profit. Its primary goal is "quality first." By doing quality assurance well, QC can gain customer confidence, which will eventually lead to long-term profit.

4. *Aspiring to achieve the highest quality in the world and developing new products for that purpose*—As a corollary to this, many companies speak of development of creativity, or of improvement and establishment of technology. Japan is a resource-poor country. For Japan to be able to survive in international competition, it must in a short period of time develop highly reliable products with the highest quality.
5. *Establishing a management system that can secure profit in times of slow growth and can meet various challenges*—After the two oil shocks, many Japanese companies attempted a number of new approaches. They included saving resources and energy, casting off debt financing of the company, and encouraging belt-tightening management. To these companies, adoption of QC brings very desirable results. Do not go through the motion of observing perfunctory QC, but consider QC to be your ally in making money. If QC is carried out effectively profit is always assured.
6. *Showing respect for humanity, nurturing human resources, considering employee happiness, providing cheerful workplaces, and passing the torch to the next generation*—A company is no better or no worse than the employees it has. All of the goals presented here can be accomplished through active pursuance of QC activities in the workplace, where respect for humanity must prevail. As for middle management and staff members, delegate to them as much authority as you can. Let them become "managers" in their own right. Proven competence in QC circle activities opens the way for performing well in other management roles.
7. *Utilization of QC techniques*—Some people are mesmerized by the term "total quality control" and do not fully utilize the statistical methods. That is a mistake. Statistical methods form the basis of QC. Whether they be those seven simple QC tools or advanced techniques, people in the appropriate divisions must be able to master them and use them.

These seven items are the goals and accomplishments of those companies that undertook total quality control and accepted the challenge of the Deming Application Prize. I cannot be sure if they all reached 100 percent of the goals they set for themselves—the passing grade for the Deming Prize is seventy out of a possible 100—but I trust that these companies did reach 70 percent of their goals.

WHAT IS MANAGEMENT?

Goals of management

My view of management is as follows. (See Table 10.1.)

1. People In management, the first concern of the company is the happiness of people who are connected with it. If the people do not feel happy and cannot be made happy, that company does not deserve to exist.

TABLE 10.1 OBJECTIVES AND TECHNIQUES OF MANAGEMENT

Goals		People	
		Price	Quantity
		Cost &	Date of
Techniques	**Quality**	**Profit**	**Delivery**
Physics			
Chemistry			
Electrical Engineering			
Mechanical Engineering			
Civil Engineering			
Architecture			
Metallurgy			
Mathematics			
Statistical Methods			
Computer			
Automatic Control			
Production Engineering			
Industrial Engineering			
Time Study			
Motion Study			
Market Survey			
Operation Research			
Value Engineering/Value Analysis			
Standardization			
Inspection			
Education			
Material Control			
Equipment Control			
Measurement Control			
Metallurgical Tool Control			

The first order of business is to let the employees have adequate income. Their humanity must be respected, and they must be given an opportunity to enjoy their work and lead a happy life. The term "employees" as used here includes those employees of subcontractors and affiliated sales and service organizations.

Consumers come next. They must feel satisfied and pleased when they buy and use goods and services. If a television just bought breaks immediately, or if an electric heater is the cause of fire and injury, then the company that sold it has done enormous disservice. Also, if at the time of purchase the salesman does not treat the customer with courtesy or fails to explain fully how the merchandise is supposed to work, the customer will not be satisfied.

The welfare of shareholders must also be taken into consideration. Japan is a capitalist society, and each company must make sufficient profit to provide stock dividends for shareholders.

Companies exist in a society for the purpose of satisfying people in that society. This is the reason for their existence and should be their primary goal. We must now deal with the question of how to reach this goal.

There are three basic means which enable us to reach this primary goal. They are quality, price (including cost and profit), and quantity (including the date of delivery). I shall call these three our secondary goals. Controlling these three must be considered the goal of a given company, a process I shall call goal control.

2. *Quality* I have discussed quality repeatedly. Defective products will not only inconvenience consumers but also hinder sales. If a company makes too many products that cannot be sold, it will waste raw materials and energy. This waste will also be a loss for society. A company must always supply products with the qualities the consumers demand. Consumers' requirements usually get higher and higher year after year as society advances. What was good last year may not be adequate the following year. In QC narrowly defined, QC means controlling carefully the supplying of quality products that have good sales points.

3. *Price, Cost, and Profit* Everything has to do with money. No matter how inexpensive a product, if its quality is poor, no one will buy it. Similarly, no matter how high the quality, if the price is too steep, again no one will buy it. The consumer's main demand is for a just quality at a just price.

It is said that in a capitalist society, making profits is the goal of a company. On the other hand, there are some people who say that profit is sinful. These two statements represent extreme positions and both of them are wrong. If there is no profit, there can be no development of new products and new technology. Nor can there be investment in equipment modernization. Without profit, no salaries can be paid, and good people will not come to work for the company. In the end the company will be bankrupt, inconveniencing the very society it is supposed to serve.

Profit is actually the means to maintain a company permanently. A company without profits cannot even pay its fair share of taxes and cannot fulfill its social obligations.

To raise profits, cost control must be practiced effectively. First, there must be a cost plan. At each stage of the development of a new product, the wheel of the PDCA circle must be turned in the right direction.

Generally, if QC is conducted effectively, defectives will decrease, and waste of materials and time will also decrease. This will lead to a rise in productivity and as a result will bring cost down. Through this process, products can be supplied to consumers at just prices. Incidentally, the price of a product is not determined by the cost but rather by value of true quality.

4. Quantity and Date of Delivery A company must manufacture products in the amount required by the consumers and it must supply them to the consumers prior to the specified delivery date.

Quantity control includes control of the following: amount purchased, amount of production, amount of materials and products in stock (including amount of products in the production process), amount of sales, and date of delivery. If the company is overstocked with a certain commodity, a lot of resources and capital are not being utilized. Not only are they wasted, but they also push up the production cost. Of course if the amount of stock is too low, the company will not be able to meet adequately the requirements of consumers. The famed *kanban* (just-in-time delivery) system at Toyota takes this factor into account. It is a system that has been completed after effective implementation of QC and various forms of quantity control have taken place. Without these safeguards and effective control, a premature introduction of the *kanban* system can spell disaster, causing a complete shutdown of a factory.

On the other hand, if people, quality, cost, and quantity are effectively controlled, management can proceed smoothly.

Techniques and tools of reaching management goals

There are many techniques and tools that can be used to reach management goals. The items listed vertically in Table 10.1 are these techniques or tools.

For example, physics, chemistry, mathematics, and mechanical engineering are all tools. At the annual convocation of my Institute, I often say to my students, "You are going to study many subjects, such as physics, chemistry, mathematics, electrical engineering, and mechanical engineering. You are engineering students, but to study these subjects must not in itself be the purpose of your entering this institute. You are to study these subjects as a means of serving society, the nation, and the world. In your learning, never make the mistake of confusing the true goal with the means."

Misperceptions are found not only among students but also among their professors. They study statistical methods and computers, but the study becomes the end in itself. In the case of quality control, when it was first introduced in Japan, there was a similar tendency. Some people thought quality control existed for the sake of statistical methods, while others thought that it existed for standardization. They confused the goals with the tools. Japan's quality control has become what it is today only after it has learned to correct past mistakes.

The tools of quality control are often divided into two categories, proper techniques and control techniques. I do not particularly like this differentiation. In Table 10.1, items such as mechanical engineering, electrical engineering, architecture, civil engineering, metallurgy, physics, and mathematics are proper techniques, and statistical methods and the items listed below are considered control techniques. In my view, they are proper techniques as well.

To attain the four goals described earlier, we must utilize all proper techniques at our disposal and produce high quality goods inexpensively to serve our society.

I ask all applied scientists and engineers to acquire technology which is more like A than B in Diagram 10.2. I call B the well-type technology and A the cone-shaped technology. When products become complex and technology becomes highly specialized as in today's world, the well-type technology becomes structurally frail. It dries up too quickly and cannot contribute to true technical development or to the development of new products. One must acquire cone-shaped technology, which develops a greater width as one digs in deeper. For example, a mechanical engineer must possess a general knowledge of electrical engineering, electronics, metallurgy, chemistry, statistical methods, and computers. If an engineer has only well-type knowledge, he cannot move from project *c* to project *d.* However, if he has cone-shaped knowledge, once he succeeds in new product development in *a,* he can transfer that knowledge to new product development in *b.*

Let us try another example. What makes good engine specialists? Obviously engine specialists must be good mechanical engineers, but they must also know

DIAGRAM 10.2

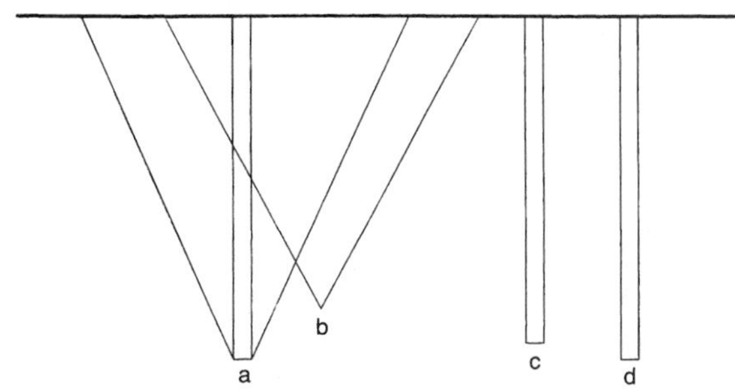

metallurgy and casting to appreciate how raw materials for the engine are made. They must be familiar with the principle of engine operations and must be able to utilize some degree of technical knowledge in the following areas: machine processing technique, fuel and lubricants, packing, ignition, electronics, statistical methods, computers, standardization, etc.

Similarly, to create the highest quality products, we must utilize all tools and proper techniques available to us.

I am often asked, "What is the relationship between quality control, industrial engineering, and operation research?" My answer is simple: "To create a quality product, we utilize all tools at our disposal, including industrial engineering and operation research." The so-called QC techniques (statistical methods) are, of course, the tools. However, QC itself must be treated as one of the basic objectives of the company. "Do not confuse the objectives with the tools."

part

3

Quality Improvement Tools

Part 3 describes quality improvement tools commonly used in TQM and Reengineering processes. The section includes an overview of the well-known *quality control tools* and *management and planning tools.* Their origin lies in fields and applications as diverse as engineering, psychology, anthropology, and project management. In the United States and Japan the tools presented here are complemented by other creative and analytical tools such as brainstorming and force field analysis.

Use of the tools is one of the essential components of TQM training for line workers and managers alike. Most of the tools are particularly well suited for team-based problem solving and planning. They allow teams to gather, develop, and organize significant amounts of information using creative and analytical approaches.

The tools are easy to understand conceptually but are not always easy to use. The mechanics of teamwork are complex, and the role of a trained facilitator is key in team-based problem solving. Herein lies one of the greatest difficulties related to the use of tools in problem solving. The tools do not provide answers in and of themselves. They are to be carefully chosen depending upon various factors like the task at hand, the amount and kind of information that can be accessed, the number and experience of the group members, the time available, and the culture of the organization.

Nevertheless, the tools remain one of the most appealing practical features of TQM approaches: the systematic effort to integrate creativity and analysis in team-based problem solving and planning.

Reading 11

Going with the Flow(chart)

BY JOHN T. BURR

- Before you try to solve a problem, define it.
- Before you try to control a process, understand it.
- Before trying to control everything, find out what is important.
- Start by picturing the process.

Making and using flowcharts are among the most important actions in bringing process control to both administrative and manufacturing processes. While it is obvious that to control a process one must first understand that process, many companies are still trying to solve problems and improve processes without realizing how important flowcharts are as a first step.

The easiest and best way to understand a process is to draw a picture of it—that's basically what flowcharting is. There are many styles that can be used to draw a flowchart. Some people use pictures, some use engineering symbols, and others just use squares or rectangles for the whole diagram. There really is no right or wrong way to display the information. The true test of a flowchart is how well those who create and use it can understand it.

CONSTRUCTING FLOW DIAGRAMS

Every process is supplied with services and products from some suppliers. Likewise, every process provides products or services to some other process—its customer(s). Figure 11.1 shows a generic process. Using this figure as a guide, making a flowchart is simple as long as the designer(s) follows these roles:

Rule 1 The most important rule is that the right people must be involved in making the chart. This includes those who actually do the work of the process,

FIGURE 11.1 ***Generic process/product improvement model***

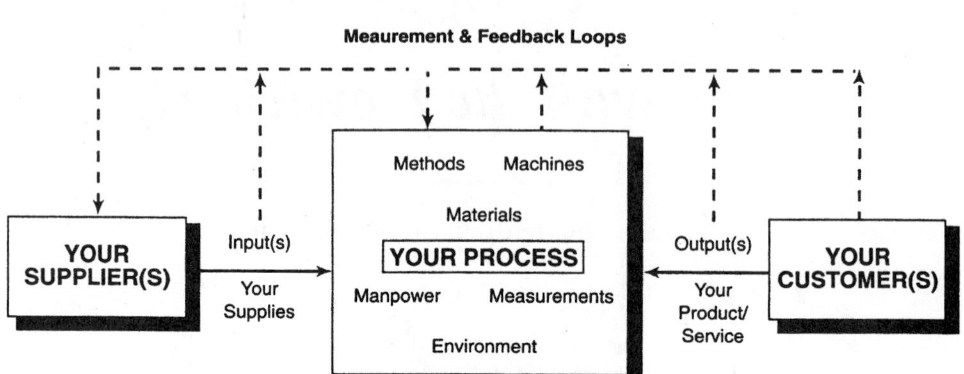

suppliers to the process, customers of the process, the supervisor of the area within which the process functions, and an independent facilitator.

Rule 2 All members of the group must participate. To that end, the use of an independent facilitator will be a great benefit for several reasons. There will be less chance of one member of the group having undue influence on the outcome. Second, a facilitator is trained to ask the right questions, seek input from everyone, and resolve any conflicts that arise. Finally, a facilitator can save the group members from the drudgery of writing down all the information. Their time is better spent discussing and charting the process.

Rule 3 All data must be visible to all the people all the time. I have found that the use of newsprint and masking tape is imperative for a good flowcharting session. As one sheet is completed, it is taped on the wall in sequence with previous work. Rarely is a session completed without at least some rework of previous parts of the flowchart as the group members reflect on the information in front of them.

Avoid using transparencies, because that allows only a segment of the chart to be displayed at one time. This reduces the opportunity for the group to rethink earlier decisions. The use of a chalkboard or white board also limits the space available and requires that someone keep a running record of the diagram on paper as it is made.

Rule 4 Enough time must be allotted. Experience shows that much more time is required to make a flowchart than is usually expected. More than one session might be required. It might even be desirable, since group members will have more time to obtain more information on the functioning of the process.

Rule 5 The more questions everyone asks, the better. Questions are the key to the flowcharting process. There are many questions that can be asked by both the facilitator and the group members. What is the first thing that happens? What is the next thing that happens? Questioning should continue throughout the process. Questions that will be helpful at certain times during the process include:

- Where does the (service, material) come from?
- How does the (service, material) get to the process?
- Who makes the decision (if one is needed)?
- What happens if the decision is "yes"? What happens if the decision is "no"?
- Is there anything else that must be done at this point?
- Where does the (product, service) of this operation go?
- What tests are performed on the product at each part of the process?
- What tests are performed on the process?
- What happens if the test is out of tolerance?

Even more questions will arise during the session(s). One caution, however: It's usually not a good idea to ask the question "Why?" This question might make one of the team members feel defensive. In very specific situations it might be helpful to ask that question, but only if the team needs the information.

APPLICATIONS

There are many ways to use flowcharts on the factory floor—for example, for equipment diagrams, pipe diagrams, etc. Figure 11.2 shows one example. Employees should get used to working with flowcharts. The charts can be even more helpful if employees ask the questions listed earlier, particularly the questions about what could be measured.

While flowcharts are important in manufacturing, the most substantial improvements can be made by using them in staff or administrative functions. One company I visited recently had almost every staff function flowcharted—including traffic control, billing, accounting, and purchasing. The employees were excited about their jobs; they controlled the process.

One process flowchart with which I've had a lot of fun teaching is shown in Figure 11.3. If a process as mundane as getting to work can be flowcharted, any process can be flowcharted!

FIGURE 11.2 ***Manufacture of photographic film and paper***

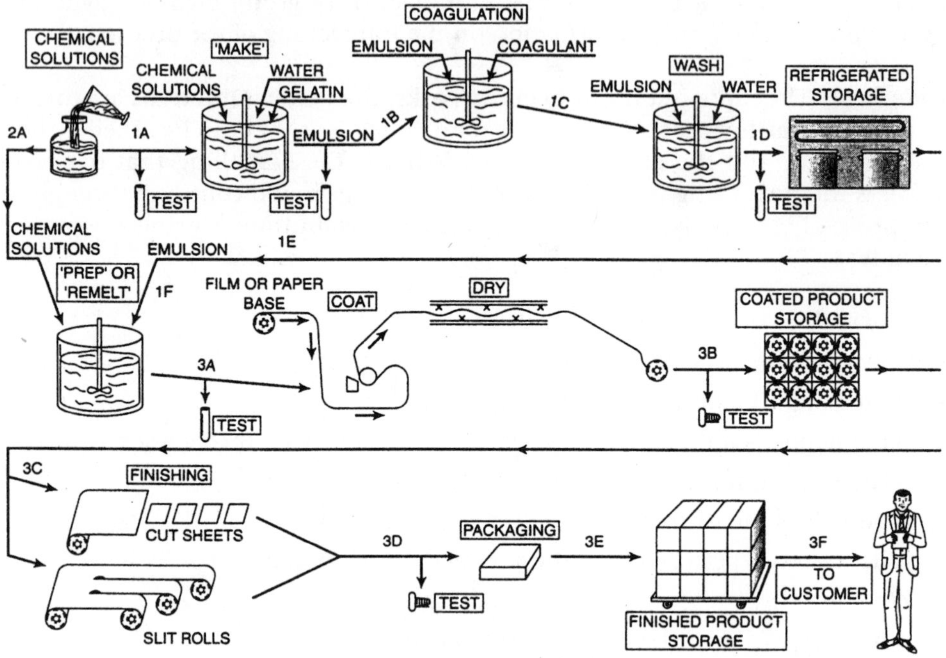

THE BENEFITS OF FLOWCHARTS

Companies that use process flowcharting reap many benefits, including the following:

- The people who work in the process understand the process. They begin to control it—instead of being victims of it.
- Once the process can be seen objectively in the flowchart, improvements can be easily identified.
- Employees realize how they fit into the overall process, and they visualize their suppliers and customers as a part of that overall process. This leads directly to improved communication between departments and work areas.
- The people who participate in flowcharting sessions become enthusiastic supporters of the entire quality effort. They will continue to provide suggestions for even further improvement.
- Process flowcharts are valuable tools in training programs for new employees.

In short, perhaps the most important benefit of using process flowcharts is that the people in the process will all understand it in the same terms. That under-

FIGURE 11.3 ***Getting to work in the morning***

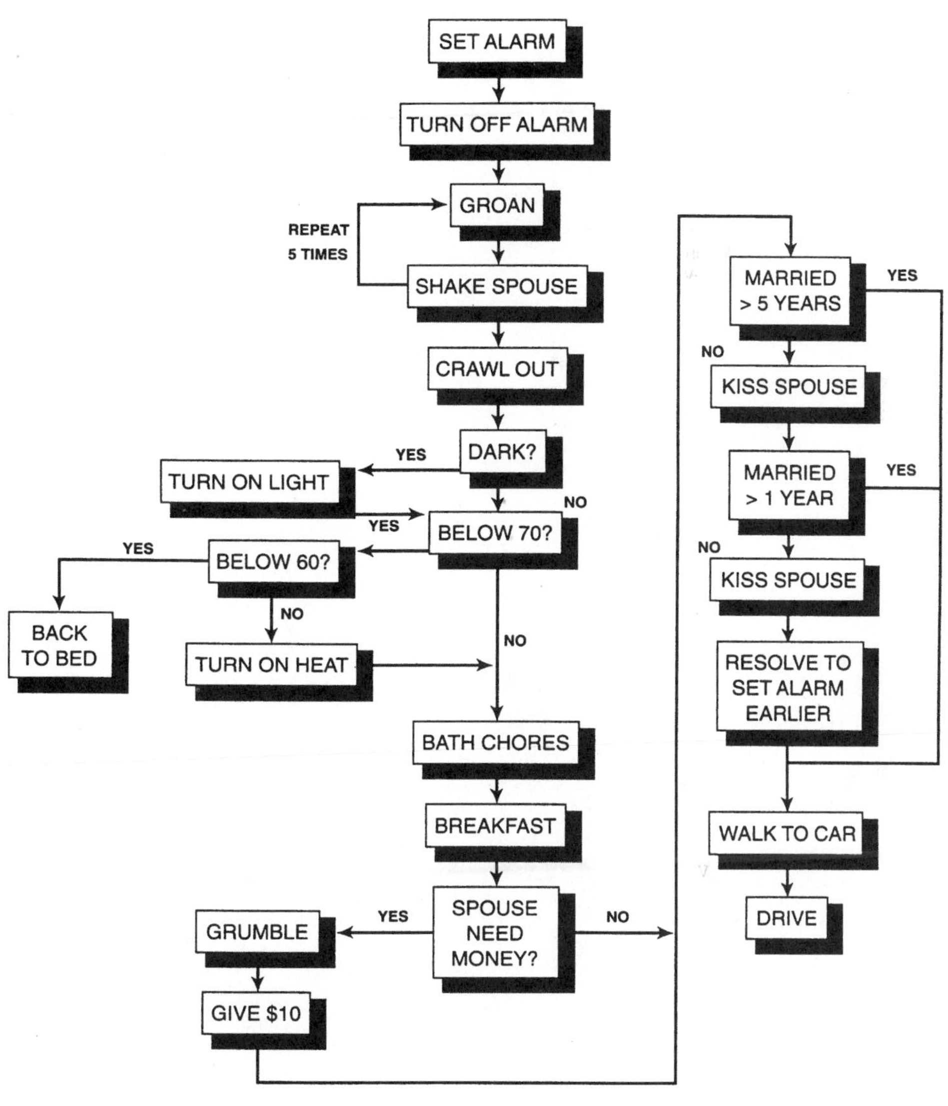

standing leads to happier employees who can control their destinies, more economical processes, less waste in administrative functions, and better customer-supplier relationships between departments.

Reading 12

Cause-and-Effect Diagrams

By J. Stephen Sarazen

"Quality begins with education and ends with education." These words, attributed to the late Kaoru Ishikawa, sum up a principal philosophy of quality. To improve processes, you must continuously strive to obtain more information about those processes and their output.

One unique and valuable tool for accomplishing this goal is the cause-and-effect diagram. This tool was first developed in 1943 by Ishikawa at the University of Tokyo; he used it to explain to a group of engineers from the Kawasaki Steel Works how various factors could be sorted and related.

The cause-and-effect diagram is a method for analyzing process dispersion. The diagram's purpose is to relate causes and effects. It is also known as the Ishikawa diagram and the fishbone diagram (because the completed diagram resembles the skeleton of a fish). Whatever it's called, the tool is certainly one of the most elegant and widely used of the so-called seven QC tools.

It has been my experience that this tool is not only invaluable for virtually any issue requiring attention, but can be easily learned by people at all levels of the organization and applied immediately.

There are three basic types of cause-and-effect diagrams: dispersion analysis, production process classification, and cause enumeration. Figure 12.1 depicts the basic format for the cause-and-effect diagram. Note the hierarchical relationship of the effect to the main causes and their subsequent relationship to the sub-causes. For example, Main Cause A has a direct relationship to the effect. Each of the sub-causes is related in terms of its level of influence on the main cause.

While a cause-and-effect diagram can be developed by an individual, it is best when used by a team. (Considering how well-suited this tool is for team applications, it is not surprising that Ishikawa is the father of quality circles.) One of the most valuable attributes of this tool is that it provides an excellent means to

FIGURE 12.1 ***The basic cause-and-effect diagram***

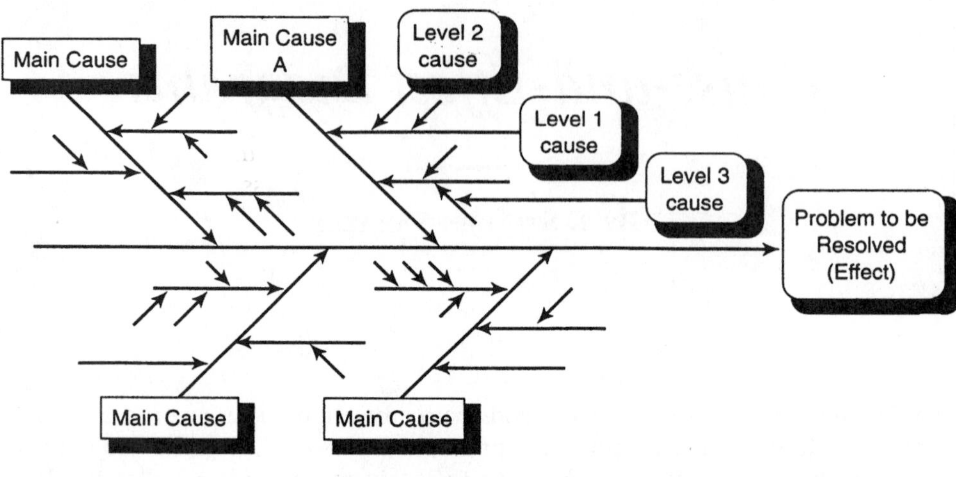

facilitate a brainstorming session. It will focus the participants on the issue at hand and immediately allow them to sort ideas into useful categories, especially when the dispersion analysis or process classification methods are used.

DISPERSION ANALYSIS

Let's assume you are having difficulties with customer complaints. Let us further assume that you are able to pull together about seven individuals from various functions throughout the organization. Each of these individuals has sound knowledge of the overall business as well as an area of specific expertise. This team will provide a good example of the way to construct a cause-and-effect diagram using the dispersion analysis methods. There are three steps:

Step 1 It is quite simple to construct the diagram. First, determine the quality characteristic you wish to improve—perhaps customer satisfaction. You must be certain there is consensus when you write the problem statement. For example: "Customers are dissatisfied."

Write this brief statement of fact on a large sheet of paper, a white board, or similar area. Write it on the right side, center of the page, and draw a box around it with an arrow running to it. This problem statement constitutes the effect.

In a manufacturing process, you might use a specific characteristic of a product as the effect, such as a problem with paste thickness in a surface mount line, poor paint coverage, or welding errors. In an administrative or service area, you might use customer complaints, decreased sales volume, or increased accounts receivable past due.

Step 2 Now the team must generate ideas as to what is causing the effect, contributing to customer dissatisfaction. The causes are written as branches flowing to the main branch. Figure 12.2 shows the main cause headings resulting from an actual session in a service/distribution business. In this case, the team determined five areas—product quality, service, order processing system, distribution system, and order fulfillment—as the main potential causes of dissatisfied customers. If there is difficulty in determining the main branches or causes, use generic headings—such as method, machine, people, materials, environment, or training—to help start the team.

Step 3 The next step is to brainstorm all the possible causes of problems in each of the major cause categories. These ideas are captured and applied to the chart as sub-causes. It is important to continually define and relate causes to each other. It is acceptable to repeat sub-causes in several places if the team feels there is a direct, multiple relationship. This effort will ensure a complete diagram and a more enlightened team.

Returning to Figure 12.2, you can see that the team identified five main causes of customer dissatisfaction. Now the team members must ask themselves, "What could contribute to each of these five main causes?" Once several sub-causes have been identified, the team continues asking the same question until the lowest-level causes are discovered.

Figure 12.3 shows the completed portion of the diagram for one of the main causes: service. The team identified reliability issues, carrier issues (e.g., a trucking company), poor communications, and lack of, or poor, training.

FIGURE 12.2 ***The main cause headings***

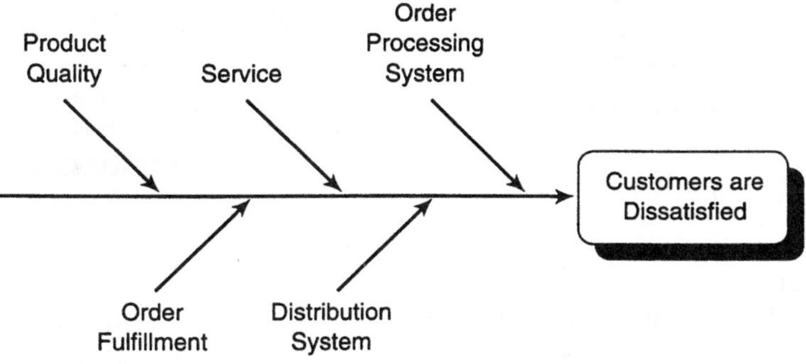

FIGURE 12.3 ***A detailed look at one main course***

Version 1

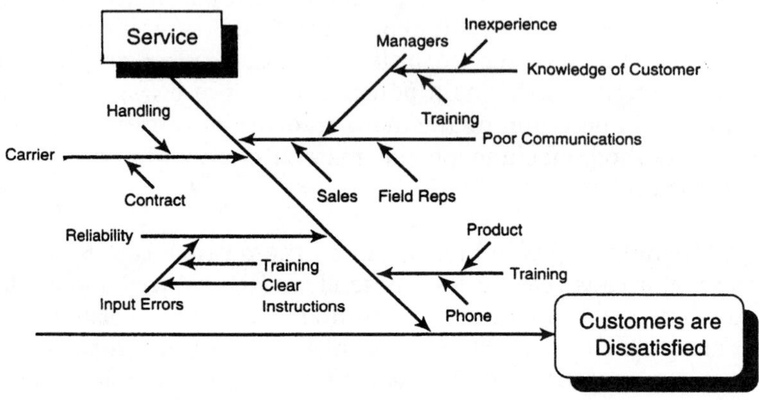

Version 2

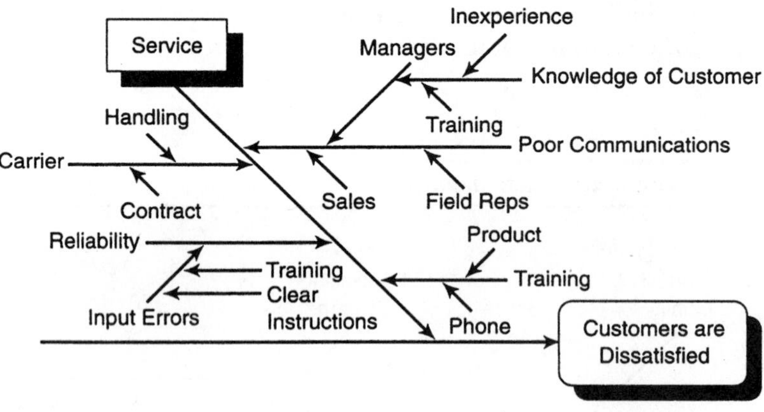

The next level of causes is identified by asking the question, "What could cause a problem in these areas?" In the case of the poor communications, the team focused on functions and jobs—sales people, field representatives, and managers—as potential causes. You can see that lack of knowledge of the customer can cause managers to communicate poorly. Subsequently you can see that inexperience and training can be two key contributors to a manager's lack of customer knowledge. Thus, there are six levels of causes in this example.

PROCESS CLASSIFICATION

Another type of diagram is known as the process classification diagram. I prefer to eliminate the word "production" from the chart title because it has a manufacturing ring to it. From my experience, this tool is as valuable in service-based businesses as it is in manufacturing companies. After all, every product or service is the result of a process.

Although the basic process for constructing this type of diagram is similar to the one used for dispersion analysis, there are some differences. These differences are driven by the application. For the process classification method, you identify the flow of the process you wish to improve and then list key quality-influencing characteristics at each of the steps.

Step 1 Identify the process and develop a flow diagram of the primary sequential steps. For example, in a generic selling process, the following steps might be identified: make initial customer contact, develop an understanding of customer needs, provide information to the customer, follow up, close the sale, and follow up on the sale.

Step 2 Now add all the things that might influence the quality of each step. Use the method described in the previous section. Brainstorming with a team of knowledgeable people will make the finished diagram more like the actual process.

Figure 12.4 is an example of a completed process classification diagram. As you can see, the intent is to take the cause and effect to the lowest level to understand all the contributing factors to improve the process.

FIGURE 12.4 ***A completed process classification diagram***

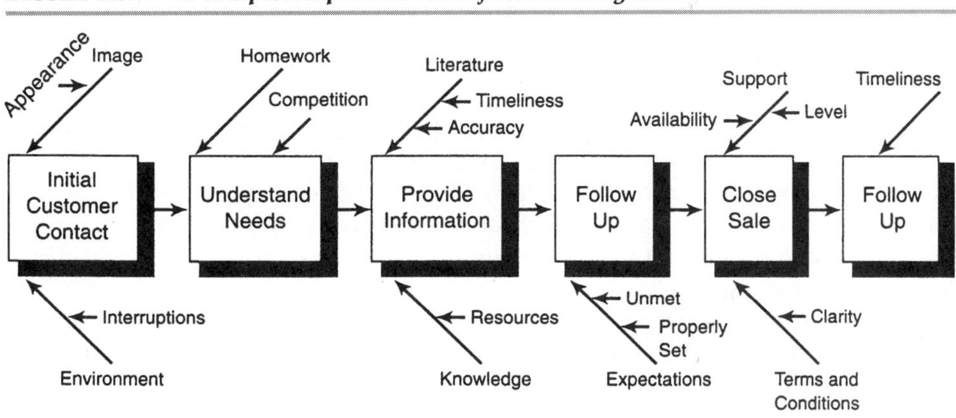

It is also advisable to consider the connecting steps from process step to process step. Everywhere there is a handoff from one step to the next, there are likely to be possible causes of dispersion. Many opportunities for improvement can be found in these areas.

CAUSE ENUMERATION

The cause enumeration method involves simply brainstorming all possible causes and listing them in the order they are offered. Once the brainstorm has exhausted itself, the team begins the process of grouping the causes as it did for the dispersion analysis diagram. The end result looks exactly the same.

I have found this process can be enhanced dramatically using the affinity diagram process. It is a valuable method for gaining insight and organization of ideas. Basically, the brainstorm is conducted by capturing all ideas on cards or those handy little notepads with the gum on one end. Each card should contain only one idea. The cards are then arranged in groups and subgroups. Cards that have an affinity for one another are placed together. Once it is completed, the affinity diagram provides the basis for the cause-and-effect diagram.

FILLETING THE FISH

Understanding processes, using teams, and identifying areas of opportunity are excellent ways to move toward continuous improvement while solving some of today's tough issues. But they are only the beginning. To obtain the full value from the cause-and-effect diagram, it must be turned into action. It is therefore wise to quantify the problem and as many of the causes as possible. Once this has been done, the business can determine the priority areas to be addressed and can track improvements.

In the earlier example, the business was able to quantify the problem of customer dissatisfaction by measuring several key parameters, including number of calls about problems, number of requests to return material for specific reasons, and receivables aging.

In the areas where sub-causes were identified, various parts of the organization were surveyed to determine the primary areas of opportunity for addressing the causes identified by the cause-and-effect diagram. For example, one need was for training in simple statistical problem-solving methods. This need was quantified not only by the number of people needing training, but also by the results of the training applications.

As the team and business move to quantify the causes, other tools play key roles. Pareto analysis, histograms, control charts, scatter plots, and multivariate analysis might be particularly valuable.

HINTS AND CREATIVE USES

Here are some helpful hints for facilitating or participating in a cause-and-effect exercise.

1. **Consider the big picture.** When constructing a cause-and-effect diagram, think about the issue at hand in its broadest sense. Consider the environment, inside the business and externally; politics, including government policies if appropriate; employee issues; and external factors, such as the local or national

The benefits and weaknesses of each cause-and-effect diagram

- Diagram Type: Dispersion analysis
  Key Benefits:
  1. Helps organize and relate factors.
  2. Provides a structure for brainstorming.
  3. Involves everyone.
  4. It's fun.

  Potential drawbacks:
  1. Might be difficult to facilitate if developed in true brainstorming fashion.
  2. Might become very complex; requires dedication and patience.
- Diagram Type: Process classification
  Key Benefits:
  1. Provides a solid sequential view of the process and the factors that influence each step.
  2. Might help determine functional ownership for the work to be done in improvement.

  Potential drawback:
  1. It is sometimes difficult to identify or demonstrate interrelationships.
- Diagram Type: Cause enumeration
  Key Benefits:
  1. Easy to facilitate.
  2. Provides in-depth list of all possible causes.

  Potential drawbacks:
  1. The added step of creating an affinity diagram might add time to the process.
  2. The final diagram might be difficult to draw because of the random output of the brainstorming session.

economy. Granted, some of these areas are well beyond the control of the team. Nevertheless, there is a benefit to understanding the impact of such factors.

2. **Facilitation.** Facilitating a cause-and-effect session is very challenging. It is similar to facilitating any brainstorming session except that the thoughts must be written in a particular place as opposed to being listed. The facilitator must listen to the ideas of the participants, capture those thoughts in only one or two words, and write them in the appropriate position on the chart. This last step is the tricky part. My recommendation is to have the participants decide where the cause should be written. This approach helps ensure that the correct location is chosen and removes some of the burden from the facilitator.

3. **Review and embellishment.** To ensure that the diagram is complete, have each member of the team review it the next day or have them show it to one or two additional people to obtain their opinion. Use your discretion in deciding whether to use second parties on very technical issues or problems unique to a particular job or area.

4. **Broad-based participation.** If you want to add a creative flair to your development effort and, at the same time, encourage broad-based participation from your group or organization, try this. Hang a large white board or sheet of butcher paper in an accessible location. Ask the group or a manager to identify a problem that needs to be addressed. Write that problem statement in the "head of the fish" and draw the arrow to it. Now invite the entire organization to participate in developing the diagram over a certain time frame—say two weeks. You will be amazed how many people will really get into working and understanding the process.

   The obvious drawback to this approach is that you miss the brainstorming opportunity. However, reading what others have written in the diagram will generate ideas. The commitment that must be made is to take the input and act on it.

   While this might sound a little out of the ordinary, I can tell you from first-hand experience that it works. I trained a vice president's staff in the use of cause-and-effect diagrams several years ago and suggested this approach. We hung a large white board outside his office and began writing a new issue on it every couple of weeks. Some of his people had been trained in the technique; many had not. The end result was that more than 100 people contributed to the first few diagrams and his staff was provided with invaluable information, insight, and suggestions for improving processes.

5. **Working toward the desired result.** I have found it very useful to state the desired result—rather than a problem—in the head of the fish. For example, instead of writing "Customers are dissatisfied," write "100% customer satisfaction." The exercise now focuses on finding means to achieve this goal rather than working the problem. Many of the findings will be the same but some unique approaches might find their way onto the chart.

The work could also be stated as "how to" arrive at some desired result. A few years ago, I trained a group of elementary teachers in the use of cause-and-effect diagrams. They needed to get students to perform as a team. Rather than trying to solve the problem of why students didn't perform as a team, we developed a cause-and-effect diagram using the statement "What makes an effective/winning team?"

Many of the teachers returned to their classes and used this exercise with students. The students wanted to be winners. Now they were asked to identify all the attributes of a winning team, and they were able to do so. They learned that it takes a lot of hard work and dedication.

The teachers then posted the completed diagram every day and when the students did not demonstrate the behavior required to be a winner (in their own words), the diagram served as a reminder. This process had also worked for business issues such as how to improve competitiveness and how to ensure SPC applications will follow training.

UNDERSTANDING PROCESSES

In the past decade, quality has gained recognition as the competitive imperative for all businesses. The root of all quality improvement lies in understanding processes. Many existing tools assist managers, engineers, and others in this work. You need not always look for the newest tool, software, or management theory to construct a sound foundation on which to build improvements. If you are looking for a tool that fosters team work, educates users, identifies lowest-level issues on which to work, helps show a true picture of the process, guides discussion, can be used for virtually any issue your business might face, and is fun, look no further than this 46-year-old tool called the cause-and-effect diagram.

Bibliography

Ishikawa, Kaoru, *Guide to Quality Control*. Tokyo: Asia Productivity Organization, 1986.

Wadsworth, Harrison M., Kenneth S. Stephens, and A. Blanton Godfrey, *Modern Methods for Quality Control and Improvement*. New York: John Wiley & Sons, Inc., 1986.

Reading 13

Control Charts

By Peter D. Shainin

Even the best automatic machine tools cannot make every unit exactly the same. Better tools are followed by new product designs offering lower cost, better performance, or both; both these improved designs often require tighter tolerances. Thus, the luxury of improved machine capability soon becomes the necessity. So, the ability to operate to a tight tolerance without producing defects becomes a major business advantage.

A diligent operator, adjusting the machine settings often to stay within this tight tolerance, will make many scrap pieces. The more diligent the operator, the worse the result—proof of Murphy's law.

W. Edwards Deming does a very dramatic demonstration of this phenomenon using a funnel and a marble as shown in Figure 13.1. The funnel, mounted on a stand, is placed so its spout is directly over a target. The marble is dropped through the funnel, hits the target, and rolls some distance to one side. The target represents the nominal value (halfway between the tolerance limits), and the final resting place of the marble represents the value of the final product. The direction and distance the marble rolls represents random variation from the manufacturing process. The diligent operator now measures the distance by which the marble missed the target and moves the funnel that distance in the opposite direction. The marble is dropped a second time and again the operator measures the distance by which it missed the target and adjusts the funnel position.

After several drops of the marble, it becomes obvious that the final resting place of the marble is actually moving farther from the target rather than closer. The operator's diligence is making the variation worse!

If we collect all the pieces that could ever be made with this process, this machine, and its specific settings, tooling, raw material, etc. and we measure an important characteristic (such as a dimension) on each piece, we could arrange

FIGURE 13.1

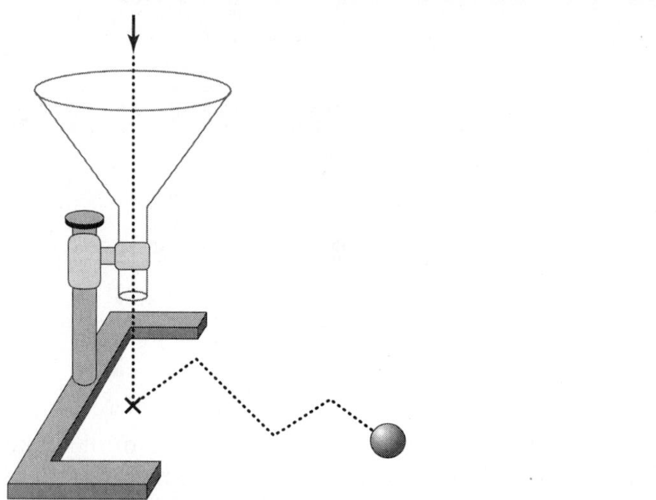

FIGURE 13.2

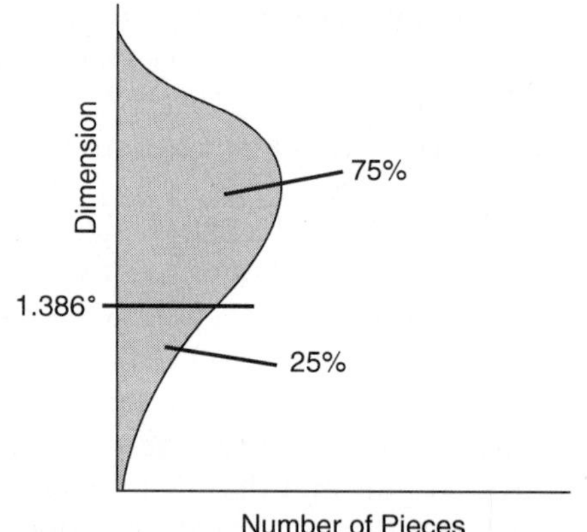

these numbers in a frequency plot like Figure 13.2. The vertical axis is the value of the dimension. The horizontal axis is the number of pieces that have each value. The frequency plot in Figure 13.2 is the distribution of the dimension produced by this particular process. The distribution gives us a picture of the random variation represented by the rolling marble.

Statistical process control (SPC) uses statistics to tell the operator when to adjust the process and when to leave it alone. SPC recognizes that some random variation always exists. It helps us control the distribution rather than the individual piece dimensions. Control charts are a method of SPC.

PROBABILITIES AND CONTROL

The shaded area in Figure 13.2 represents all pieces that will ever be made by this process. Because 75 percent of the area is above 1.386 inches, three-quarters of the time a piece made by this process will be larger than 1.386 inches. Said another way, the probability of producing pieces larger than 1.386 inches is 0.75. If the distribution is normal or Gaussian shaped and we know its mean and standard deviation, we can find the probability of producing pieces beyond any specific dimension. We could pick a dimension on each side of the distribution with only a very small probability of being exceeded and call them control limits. If the process makes pieces beyond these control limits, we can be quite confident the distribution has changed.

CONTROL CHARTS

In about 1926, Walter Shewhart of Bell Labs worked out a way to take data from a process that allows us to tell if the process variation is from a stable distribution, to transform that distribution into a normal shape, and to estimate its mean and standard deviation. We usually set control limits so that pieces from the stable distribution will exceed them only 0.26 percent of the time. Any pieces made beyond these control limits indicate the distribution has changed. Shewhart was successful in finding the causes that changed the distribution but was unable to discover the causes of variation within the distribution. He theorized that variation within the distribution was from chance or undiscoverable causes and that changes in the distribution were from assignable causes.

Since Shewhart completed his work, a number of techniques have been developed that will discover both chance and assignable causes of variation. The most universally useful of these is Multi-Varied. Although control charts are no longer useful to decide when a process can or cannot be improved, they can reduce overadjustment by telling an operator when to adjust the process and when to leave it alone. They can also tell us when a process is good enough that we should direct our improvement resources to more pressing needs.

In general, if the distribution is narrower than the tolerance and within the tolerance, the process should not be adjusted. If the distribution changes so at least some portion of it is out of tolerance, the process must be adjusted immediately or defective work will be produced, as shown in Figure 13.3. To define the distribution and sense any changes, Shewhart relied on the central limit theorem, central to statistics, which was codified by Pierre Simon Laplace in about 1800. There are three aspects of the theorem relevant to control charts:

1. If samples are taken from a distribution in groups, called subgroups, and the individual items are averaged, the distribution of the averages will approach a normal or Gaussian shape as the subgroups become larger.

FIGURE 13.3

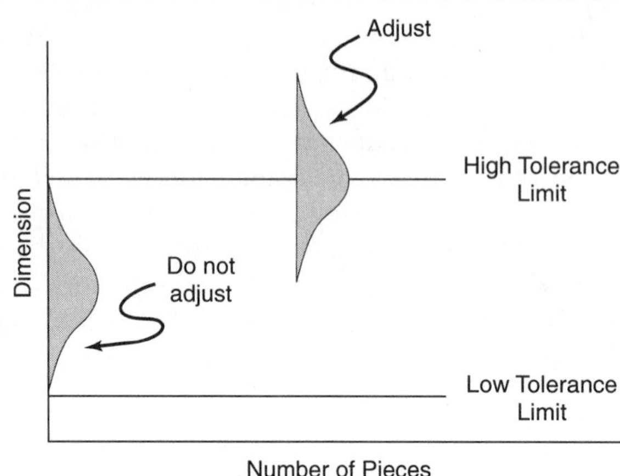

2. The distribution of averages will have the same mean as the distribution of individuals.
3. The standard deviation of the distribution of averages will be narrower than the distribution of individuals. In fact, their relationship will be:

$$\sigma_{\bar{x}} = \sigma_x / \sqrt{n}$$

Where $\sigma_{\bar{x}}$ is the standard deviation of a distribution of averages, σ_x is the standard deviation of a distribution of individuals, and n is the number of individuals used to make up each average.

The distribution of averages can be treated as normal for the purposes of control charts provided each subgroup consists of at least four pieces. If we take at least 25 subgroups, we can use the average of all their ranges to estimate $\sigma_{\bar{x}}$. The preceding formula allows us to calculate σ_x and compare the distribution of individual pieces to the tolerance limits.

Making control charts

The upper and lower control limits for averages are customarily set at the mean ±3 standard deviations. Because this includes 99.74 percent of the area to the left of the distribution, the probability of obtaining a subgroup average from this distribution, which is outside the control limits, is only 0.26 percent. Occasionally, ±2 standard deviation limits are used. In that case, the probability of an average falling beyond the control limits is about 5 percent. We find control limits by taking 25 subgroups consisting of a minimum of four pieces each. We calculate the average and range of each subgroup, then the grand average, $\bar{x}$, and the average

FIGURE 13.4

SAMPLE #	1	2	3	4	5	6	7	8	9	10	11	12	13
	14.5	13.5	10.5	11.5	12	9	12	17	17	11	19	16	15
	10	12.5	10.5	16	9	9.5	11.5	14.5	12	10	14	12	18
	10.5	16	10.5	15	11	8	8	12	11	14	13.5	14.5	14
	14	9	11	16	10.5	12	9	16	19	16	17	11	11
$\bar{x}$	12.25	12.75	10.63	14.63	10.63	9.63	10.13	14.88	14.75	12.75	15.88	13.38	14.50
R	4.50	7.00	0.50	4.50	3.00	4.00	4.00	5.00	8.00	6.00	5.50	5.00	7.00

SAMPLE #	14	15	16	17	18	19	20	21	22	23	24	25
	15	17	17	15.5	14	13.5	15	19	15	14	11.5	15
	19	15	14.5	19	19	15	19	18	11.5	17	14	13
	10	14	9.5	18	18	18	18.5	14	9	16	15	14
	12	16	14.5	19	16.5	14.5	18	13	17	12	10	17
$\bar{x}$	14.00	15.50	13.88	17.88	16.88	15.25	17.63	16.00	13.13	14.75	12.63	14.75
R	9.00	3.00	7.50	3.50	5.00	4.50	4.00	6.00	8.00	5.00	5.00	4.00

range, $\bar{R}$. Figure 13.4 is a spread sheet convenient for this purpose. The grand average, $\bar{x}$, will be the central line of our $\bar{x}$ chart.

For $\bar{x}$:
Upper control limit $= \bar{x} + A_2 \times \bar{R}$
Lower control limit $= \bar{x} - A_2 \times \bar{R}$
$\bar{R}$ will be the central line for the R chart.

For R:
Upper control limit $= D_4 \times \bar{R}$
Lower control limit $= D_3 \times \bar{R}$

A_2, D_3, and D_4 are factors that depend on subgroup size, n. Values for some typical subgroup sizes are given in Table 13.1. We draw the charts for $\bar{x}$ and R as shown in Figure 13.5. The central line and control limits for the data shown in Figure 13.4 are:

Central line for $\bar{x}$ chart $= \bar{x} = 13.96$
Upper control limit for $\bar{x} = 13.96 + 0.73 \times 5.14 = 17.7$
Lower control limit for $\bar{x} = 13.96 - 0.73 \times 5.14 = 10.2$
Central line for R chart $= \bar{R} = 5.14$
Upper control limit for $R = 2.28 \times 5.14 = 11.7$
Lower control limit for $R = 0 \times 5.14 = 0.0$

TABLE 13.1

n	A_2	D_3	D_4
4	0.73	0	2.28
5	0.58	0	2.11

FIGURE 13.5

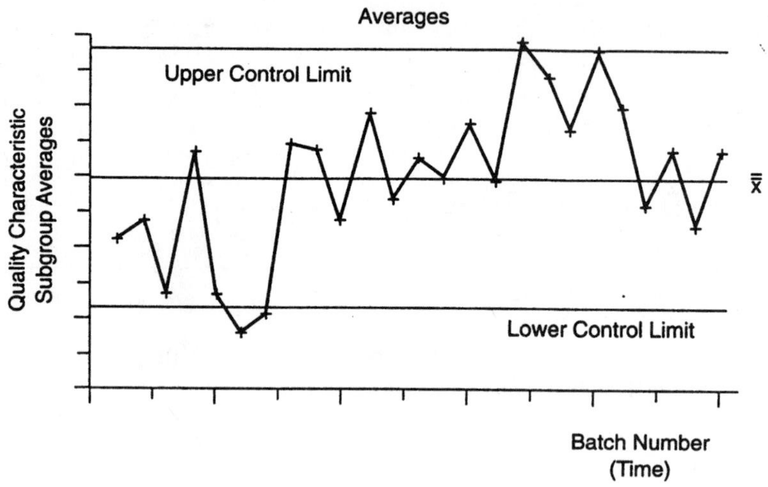

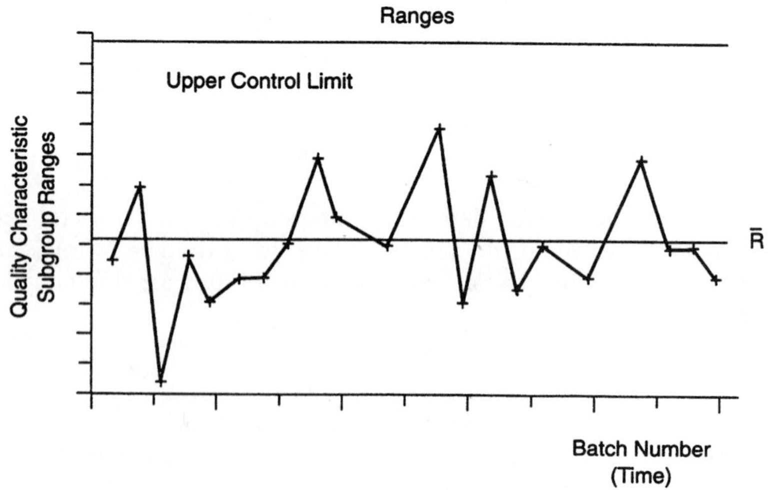

All the average and range values used to calculate the control limits must be plotted on their respective charts. If any points fall outside either set of control

FIGURE 13.6

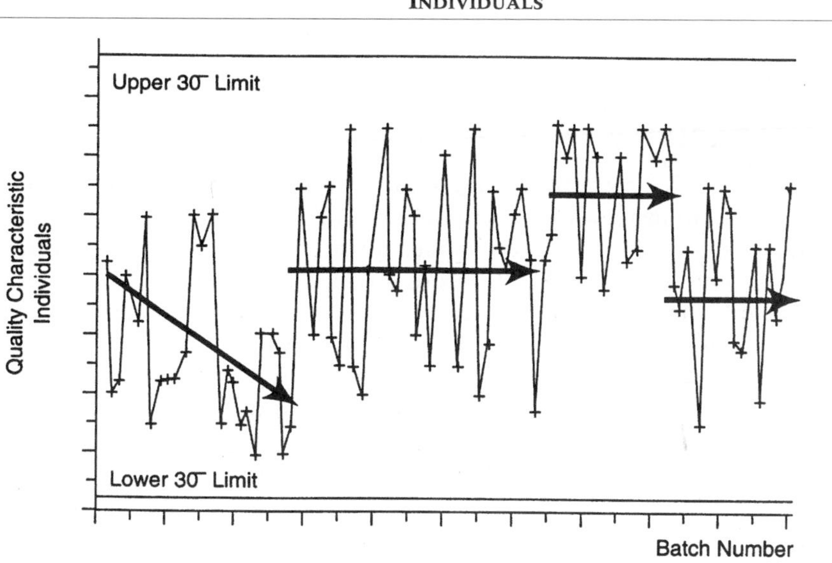

limits, the distribution was not stable and the control limits are inflated. The reason for this instability must be discovered and controlled or eliminated. A new set of 25 subgroups must be taken and a new set of control limits calculated. The X bar chart of Figure 13.5 has three points beyond the control limits. The assignable cause must be discovered and these 100 data points retaken. Figure 13.6 is a plot of the individuals from Figure 13.4. Overlaid arrows show the shifts in the distribution. Notice, the distribution changed both its mean and standard deviation several times while the control limits were being calculated. If the assignable causes of this shift and width change were discovered and eliminated or controlled, this process could be held to a much narrower variation.

The time and effort required to retake all 100 data points is often so burdensome that many practitioners just delete the subgroups that fall outside of the control limits and recalculate the control limits. Figure 13.4 demonstrates just how unsatisfactory that practice really is.

INTERPRETING THE RESULTS

After obtaining a good set of control limits, we can take subgroups periodically and plot their average and range on the appropriate chart. If an average falls outside either control limit, the distribution has either moved or gotten wider. If a range falls outside either control limit, the distribution has changed width. In either case, the process is not stable and is said to be out of control. The assignable cause must be discovered and eliminated or controlled in order to control this distribution. Control charts can only warn us of an assignable cause of variation. They are not very good at finding the cause and they cannot eliminate or control it. Process engineers and operators must use other tools to do that.

PROCESS CAPABILITY

A process distribution that stays stable and within control limits is satisfactory only if the control limits are inside the tolerance. The control limits apply to the distribution of averages, and the tolerance applies to the distribution of individuals. These distributions are in terms of two different scales. Their relationship is given by the central limit theorem above. If we wish to compare the tolerance to the control limits, we must first divide the tolerance by the square root of n; so, if the subgroup size is four, we will first divide the tolerance by two. Process capability, Cp, is the scaled tolerance width divided by the width of the control limits. Most processes can be operated satisfactorily if their Cp is 1.33 or greater.

CAUTIONS

I want to issue two cautions. The first involves tolerance limits. It is not a good idea to show scaled tolerance limits on the averages chart. Points beyond the control limits require action even if they are beyond the tolerance limits. Operators are likely to become confused and use tolerance limits instead of control limits. After all, only work outside of tolerance is unsatisfactory.

My second caution involves stability. Many processes do not remain stable for very long. A change in raw material, tooling, or any number of process operating conditions can change the process distribution. New control limits must be calculated for each such change if the control charts are to maintain their effectiveness. Process capability can change as often as several times a day. Management efforts to catalog process capability for all processes in a facility are, therefore, a waste of resources.

Reference

1. Leonard Seder, "Diagnosis with Diagrams," *Industrial Quality Control*, January 1950.

Bibliography

A more complete treatment of control charts, including different types of charts and alternative methods of SPC, can be found in *Juran's Quality Control Handbook*, Fourth Edition, McGraw-Hill Book Company, 1988, chapter 24. Peter D. Shainin, along with Dorian Shainin, are the coauthors of that chapter.

Reading 14

Histograms

ADAPTED FROM THE QUALITY IMPROVEMENT TOOLS WORKBOOK SET PUBLISHED BY THE JURAN INSTITUTE, INC.

A histogram is a graphic summary of variation in a set of data. The pictorial nature of the histogram enables us to see patterns that are difficult to see in a simple table of numbers.

The development of the histogram is credited to the French statistician A. M. Guerry. In 1833 Guerry introduced a new kind of bar graph to describe his analysis of crime data. Guerry's bar graphs were unique in that he arranged the bars to show the number of crimes corresponding to various categories of continuous variables such as the age of the criminal. Since Guerry presented the data pictorially, rather than as simple columns of numbers, it was easier for his readers to "see" his conclusions about crime in France. Guerry's work won him the medal of the French Academy, and his histograms became a standard tool for summarizing, analyzing, and displaying data.

THE CASE OF "COULDN'T HEAR"

We stress the importance of using data and facts in our problem-solving and quality improvement efforts. But sometimes the data can seem overwhelming or of little value to us as we tackle the problem at hand. Consider the following example.

A manufacturer of electronic telecommunications equipment was receiving complaints from the field about low volume on long-distance connections. Aunt Millie in California couldn't hear Cousin Bill in Florida.

A string of amplifiers manufactured by the company was being used to boost the signal at various points along the way. The boosting ability of the amplifiers (engineers call it the "gain") was naturally the prime suspect in the case.

The design of the amplifiers had called for a gain of 10 decibels (dB). This means that the output from the amplifier should be about 10 times stronger than the input signal. This amplification makes up for the natural fading of the signal over the long-distance connection. Recognizing that it is difficult to make every amplifier with a gain of exactly 10 dB, the design allowed the amplifiers to be considered acceptable if the gain fell between 7.75 dB and 12.2 dB. These permissible minimum and maximum values are sometimes called the specification (or spec) limits. The expected value of 10 dB is the nominal value. Because there were literally hundreds of amplifiers boosting the signal on a long connection, low-gain amplifiers should have been balanced by high-gain amplifiers to give an acceptable volume level.

The quality improvement team investigating the "couldn't hear" condition arranged to test the gain of 120 amplifiers. The results of the tests are listed in Figure 14.1.

This table of data is certainly formidable; there are 120 numbers to examine. More important, since the gain of all the amplifiers fell within the specification limits, the team was tempted to conclude, based on a quick glance at the numbers, that the data were of little value. The testing and data gathering done by the team obviously represented a dead end in their investigation of the case. Or did it?

The team decided to construct a histogram to give them a better "picture" of the 120 data point. They divided the specification range into nine intervals of 0.5 dB each and counted the number of data points that fell in each interval. They found that there were 24 amplifiers whose gain reading fell between 7.75 dB and 8.24 dB, 28 amplifiers between 8.25 dB and 8.74 dB, and so on.

This histogram of the data is shown in Figure 14.2. The height of each bar on the histogram represents the number of amplifiers with gain readings that fell within the dB range that the bar covers on the horizontal axis. For example, the histogram indicates that 19 amplifiers had a gain reading between 9.25 dB and 9.74 dB.

FIGURE 14.1 ***Data on amplifier gain***

GAIN OF 120 TESTED AMPLIFIERS									
8.1	10.4	8.8	9.7	7.8	9.9	11.7	8.0	9.3	9.0
8.2	8.9	10.1	9.4	9.2	7.9	9.5	10.9	7.8	8.3
9.1	8.4	9.6	11.1	7.9	8.5	8.7	7.8	10.5	8.5
11.5	8.0	7.9	8.3	8.7	10.0	9.4	9.0	9.2	10.7
9.3	9.7	8.7	8.2	8.9	8.6	9.5	9.4	8.8	8.3
8.4	9.1	10.1	7.8	8.1	8.8	8.0	9.2	8.4	7.8
7.9	8.5	9.2	8.7	10.2	7.9	9.8	8.3	9.0	9.6
9.9	10.6	8.6	9.4	8.8	8.2	10.5	9.7	9.1	8.0
8.7	9.8	8.5	8.9	9.1	8.4	8.1	9.5	8.7	9.3
8.1	10.1	9.6	8.3	8.0	9.8	9.0	8.9	8.1	9.7
8.5	8.2	9.0	10.2	9.5	8.3	8.9	9.1	10.3	8.4
8.6	9.2	8.5	9.6	9.0	10.7	8.6	10.0	8.8	8.6

FIGURE 14.2 ***Histogram of amplifier gain data figure***

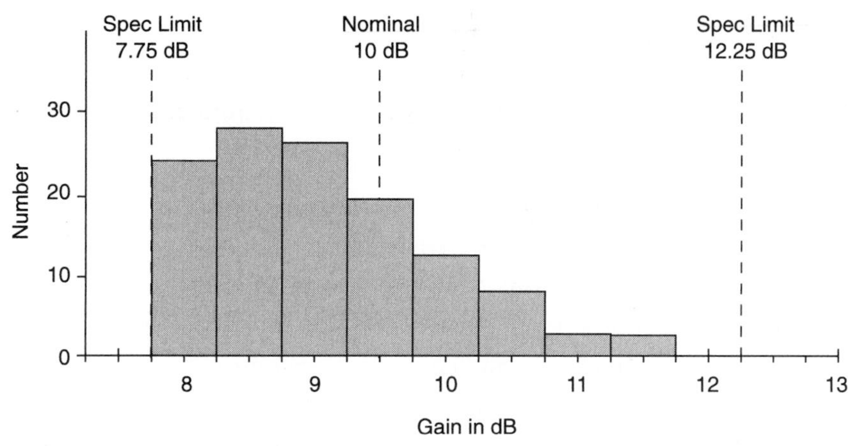

The histogram of the data gave the team a very different view of the situation. While all the amplifiers fell within the specification limits, the readings were certainly not evenly distributed around the nominal 10 dB value. Most of the amplifiers had a lower-than-nominal value of gain. This pattern was hard to see in the table of data, but the histogram clearly revealed it.

If most of the amplifiers in the series on a long-distance connection boost the signal a little bit less than expected, the result will be a low volume level—Aunt Millie in California won't be able to hear Cousin Bill in Florida.

The histogram gave the team a clearer and more complete picture of the data. Their testing, data gathering, and analysis were not a dead end. They could now concentrate their investigation in the factory to find out why the manufacturing line was not producing more amplifiers closer to the nominal value.

HISTOGRAMS IN PROBLEM SOLVING

As this example illustrates, the histogram is a simple but powerful tool for elementary analysis of data. Let us look again at the example and summarize some key concepts about data and the use of histograms in problem solving.

CONCEPT 1: Values in a set of data almost always show variation. Although the amplifiers were designed for a nominal value of 10 dB gain, very few of them actually had a measured gain of 10 dB. Furthermore, very few amplifiers had exactly the same gain. This variation is due to small differences in literally hundreds of factors surrounding the manufacturing process—the exact values of the component parts, the nature of the handling that each amplifier receives, the accuracy and repeatability of the test equipment, even the humidity in the factory on the day the amplifier was made.

Variation is everywhere. It is inevitable in the output of any process: manufacturing, service, or administrative. It is impossible to keep all factors in a constant state all the time.

Consider these examples of variation. Will the measurement be a constant or will there be some variation in the data?

- The height of 10-year-old boys
- The number of pieces of candy in a 1-pound bag
- The exact weight of a 2-foot-by-2-foot piece of sheet steel
- The exact volume of product in a container
- The time required to repair an appliance for a customer
- The number of passengers on a 747 airplane
- The number of minutes required to process an invoice

In each case, the measurement will show some variation; few values will be exactly the same.

CONCEPT 2: Variation displays a pattern. In the amplifier example, the pattern of variation [is] shown in Figure 14.2 and a number of characteristics. For example:

- All values fell within the specification limits.
- Most of the values fell between the nominal and the lower specification limit.
- The values of gain tended to bunch up near the lower specification limit.
- More values fell in the range of 8.25 dB to 8.75 dB than in any other 0.5 dB category.
- The number of values in each 0.5 dB category decreased uniformly for values of gain greater than 8.75 dB.

Different phenomena will have different variation, but there is always some pattern to the variation. For example, we know that the height of most 10-year-old boys will be close to some average value and that it would be relatively unusual to find an extremely tall or extremely short boy. If we gathered the data on the time required to repair an appliance for a customer, or the time required to process paperwork, or the time required to complete a transaction at a bank, we would expect to see some similar pattern in the numbers.

These patterns of variation in data are called "distributions." There are books available with good introductory discussions on distributions.[1,2]

For our purposes, we simply want to point out that there are usually discernible patterns in the variation and that these patterns often tell us a great deal about the cause of a problem. Identifying and interpreting these patterns are the most important topics discussed here. There are three important characteristics of a histogram: its center, width, and shape.

CONCEPT 3: Patterns of variation are difficult to see in simple tables of numbers. Again, recall the amplifier example and the table of data in Figure 14.1. Looking at the table of numbers, we could see that no values fall outside the specification limits, but we cannot see much else. While there is a pattern in the data, it is difficult for our eyes and minds to see it. It is easy to conclude erroneously, as the team almost did, that the data represent a dead end in the problem-solving effort.

CONCEPT 4: Patterns of variation are easier to see when the data are summarized pictorially in a histogram. The histogram in Figure 14.2 gave the team more insight into how to improve the quality of long-distance telecommunications service and made it easier for the team to draw conclusions.

The histogram is a useful tool when a team is faced with the task of analyzing data that contain variation. We know intuitively that the variation will usually follow some pattern, but the pattern is often hard to see from the table of numbers. Because it is a "picture" of the data, a histogram enables us to see this pattern of variation.

TYPICAL PATTERNS OF VARIATION

Figure 14.3 shows common patterns of variation. The following list contains general explanations of each type and provides suggestions for further analysis.

The bell-shaped distribution: a symmetrical shape with a peak in the middle of the range of data. This is the normal, natural distribution of data from a process. Deviations from this bell shape might indicate the presence of complicating factors or outside influences. While deviations from a bell shape should be investigated, such deviations are not necessarily bad. As we will see, some non-bell distributions are to be expected in certain cases.

The double-peaked distribution: a distinct valley in the middle of the range of the data with peaks on either side. This pattern is usually a combination of two bell-shaped distributions and suggests that two distinct processes are at work.

There is more than one possible interpretation for this pattern. Trying various stratification schemes to isolate the distinct processes or conditions is one method of further analysis.

The plateau distribution: a flat top with no distinct peak and slight tails on either side. This pattern is likely to be the result of many different bell-shaped distributions with centers spread evenly throughout the range of data.

Diagram the flow and observe the operation to identify the many different processes at work. An extreme case occurs in organizations that have no defined processes or training—everyone does the job his or her own way. The wide variability in process leads to the wide variability observed in the data. Defining and implementing standard procedures will reduce this variability.

The comb distribution: high and low values alternating in a regular fashion. This pattern typically indicates measurement error, errors in the way the data were grouped to construct the histogram, or a systematic bias in the way the data were rounded off. A less likely alternative is that this is a type of plateau distribution.

Review the data collection procedures and the construction of the histogram before considering possible process characteristics that might cause the pattern.

The skewed distribution: an asymmetrical shape in which the peak is off center in the range of data and the distribution tails off sharply on one side and gently on the others. The illustration in Figure 14.3 is called a positively skewed distribution because the long tail extends rightward, toward increasing values.

FIGURE 14.3 *Common histogram patterns*

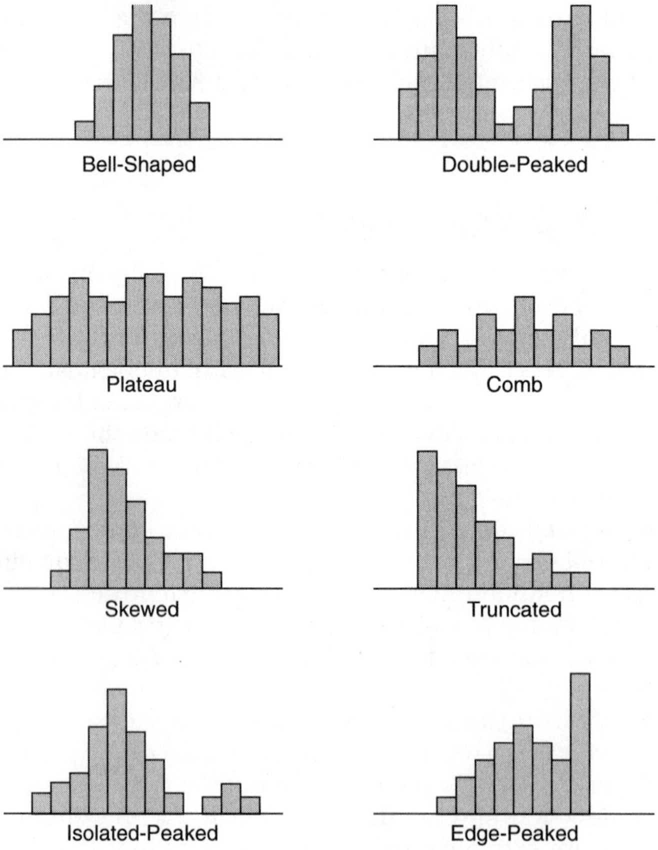

A negatively skewed distribution would have a long tail extending leftward, toward decreasing values.

The skewed pattern typically occurs when a practical limit, or a specification limit, exists on one side and is relatively close to the nominal value. In these cases, there simply are not as many values available on one side as there are on the other. Practical limits occur frequently when the data consist of time measurements or counts of things.

For example, tasks that take a very short time can never be completed in zero or less time. Those occasions when the task takes a little longer than average to complete create a positively skewed tail on this distribution of task time.

The number of weaving defects per 100 yards of fabric can never be less than zero. If the process averages about 0.7 defects per 100 yards, then sporadic occurrences of three of four defects per 100 yards will result in a positively skewed distribution.

One-sided specification limits (a maximum or minimum value only) also frequently give rise to skewed distributions.

Such skewed distributions are not inherently bad, but a team should question the impact of the values in the long tail. Could they cause customer dissatisfaction (e.g., long waiting times)? Could they lead to higher costs (e.g., overfilling containers)? Could the extreme values cause problems in downstream operations? If the long tail has a negative impact on quality, the team should investigate and determine the causes for those values.

The truncated distribution: an asymmetrical shape in which the peak is at or near the edge of the range of the data, and the distribution ends very abruptly on one side and tails off gently on the other. The illustration in Figure 14.3 shows truncation on the left side with a positively skewed tail. Of course, one might also encounter truncation on the right side with a negatively skewed tail. Truncated distributions are often smooth, bell-shaped distributions with a part of the distribution removed, or truncated, by some external force such as screening, 100 percent inspection, or a review process. Note that these truncation efforts are an added cost and are, therefore, good candidates for removal.

The isolated peaked distribution: a small, separate group of data in addition to the larger distribution. Like the double-peaked distribution, this pattern is a combination and suggests that two distinct processes are at work. But the small size of the second peak indicates an abnormality, something that doesn't happen often or regularly.

Look closely at the conditions surrounding the data in the small peak to see if you can isolate a particular time, machine, input source, procedure, operator, etc. Such small isolated peaks in conjunction with a truncated distribution might result from the lack of complete effectiveness in screening out defective items. It is also possible that the small peak represents errors in measurements or in transcribing the data. Recheck measurements and calculations.

The edge-peaked distribution: a large peak is appended to an otherwise smooth distribution. This shape occurs when the extended tail of the smooth distribution has been cut off and lumped into a single category at the edge of the range of the data. This shape very frequently indicates inaccurate recording of the data (e.g., values outside the "acceptable" range are reported as being just inside the range).

POTENTIAL PITFALLS IN INTERPRETATION

There are three important pitfalls that a quality improvement team should be aware of when interpreting histograms:

1. Before you state your conclusions from the analysis of a histogram, make sure that the data are representative of typical and current conditions in the process. If the data are old (i.e., the process has changed since the data were collected), or if there is any question about bias or incompleteness in the data, it is best to gather new data to confirm and enhance your conclusions.
2. Don't draw conclusions based on a small sample. As we pointed out earlier, the larger the sample, the more confidence we have that the peaks, spread, and shape of our histogram of the sample data are representative of the total process or group of products. As a rule of thumb, if you intend to construct before-and-after or stratified histograms to examine differences in variability or the location of peaks, use a sample large enough to give you 40 or more observations for each histogram you intend to construct. For example, if you plan to stratify the data into three groups, your minimum sample size should be around 120 (3×40). If this is not practical, consult a statistical adviser to design an appropriate sampling and hypothesis-testing scheme.
3. It is important to remember that your interpretation of the histogram is often merely a theory that must still be confirmed through additional analysis and direct observation of the process in question. The first conclusion and interpretation might not be correct—even if it sounds perfectly reasonable. Always take time to think of alternative explanations for the pattern seen in the histogram.

WHAT DO WE DO NEXT?

The key accomplishments of our analysis of a histogram are:

1. We have quantified some aspect of the process; we are managing by facts, not opinions.
2. We have a better understanding of the variability inherent in the process; we have a more realistic view of the ability of the process to produce acceptable results consistently.
3. We have new ideas and theories about how the process operates or about the causes of a problem; we have set the stage for additional investigative efforts.

Because histograms almost always provide eye-opening information in a format that is easy to explain to managers and coworkers, there is a certain exhilaration that team members feel as they explain their theories and conclusions.

Unfortunately, this feeling of exhilaration tends to make one think that the work is over, the problem is solved. It is not, of course. Usually, all we have are theories that must still be confirmed before we can be sure that any proposed solutions would be effective.

Our next steps should be to:

- Clarify and agree on what we have learned.
- Acknowledge that all we have at this point are theories to guide subsequent investigative efforts.
- Plan for direct observation of the process and additional collection, stratification, and analysis of data to confirm our theories before we begin implementing remedies.
- Continue the diagnostic and remedial journeys.

References

1. Juran, J.M. and Frank M. Gryna Jr., *Quality Planning and Analysis,* second edition (New York: McGraw-Hill Publishing Co., 1980), Chapter 3.
2. Wadsworth, Harrison M., Kenneth S. Stephens, and A. Blanton Godfrey, *Modern Methods for Quality Control and Improvement* (New York: John Wiley & Sons, 1986), Chapter 3.

Reading 15

Check Sheets

ADAPTED FROM THE QUALITY IMPROVEMENT TOOLS WORKBOOK SET PUBLISHED BY THE JURAN INSTITUTE, INC.

Quality improvement is an information-intensive activity. We need clear, useful information about problems and their causes to make improvements. In many cases, the absence of relevant information is the major reason why problems go unsolved for so long.

Most organizations have vast stores of data and facts about their operations. However, when quality improvement teams begin working on a project, they often find that the information they need does not exist. To resolve this apparent paradox, we need to understand some basic concepts about the difference between data and information:

- Data = facts.
- Information = answers to questions.
- Information includes data.
- Data does not necessarily include information.

Quality improvement teams are seeking the answers to questions: "How often does the problem occur?" or "What is causing the problem?" In other words, they are seeking information. But, while good information is always based on data (the facts), simply collecting data does not necessarily ensure that a team will have useful information. The data may not be relevant or specific enough to answer the question at hand.

The key issue, then, is not "How do we collect data?" but rather "How do we generate useful information?" Figure 15.1 presents a model for generating useful information.

Information generation begins and ends with questions. To generate information, we need to:

- Formulate precisely the question we are trying to answer.
- Collect the data and facts relating to that question.
- Analyze the data to determine the factual answer to the question.
- Present the data in a way that clearly communicates the answer to the question.

Learning to ask the right questions is the key skill in effective data collection. Accurate, precise data collected through an elaborately designed statistical sampling plan are useless if they do not clearly address a question that someone cares about.

PLANNING TO COLLECT DATA

Planning for good data collection should proceed along the following lines:

- What question do we need to answer?
- How will we recognize and communicate the answers to the question?
- What data analysis tools (Pareto diagram, histogram, bar graph, etc.) do we envision using, and how will we communicate the results?

FIGURE 15.1 ***Generating information***

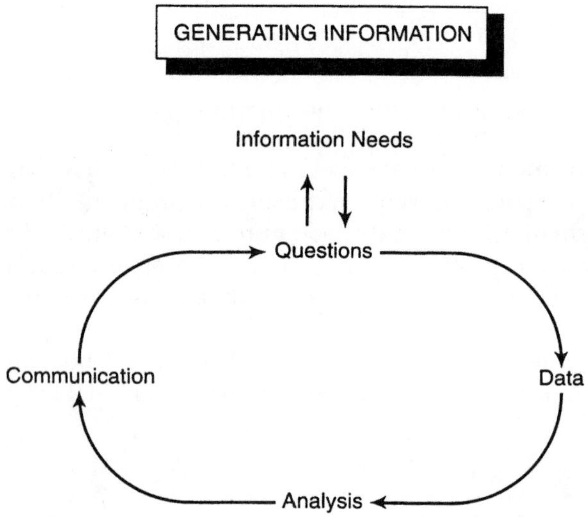

- What type of data do we need in order to construct this tool and answer the question?
- Where in the process can we get these data?
- Who in the process can give us these data?
- How can we collect these data from these people with minimum effort and chance of error?
- What additional information do we need to gather for future analysis, reference, and traceability?

Notice how this planning process essentially works backward through the model in Figure 15.1. We start by defining the question. Then, rather than diving into the details of data collection, we consider how we might communicate the answer to the question and what types of analysis we will need to perform. This helps us define our data needs and clarifies what characteristics are most important in the data. With this understanding as a foundation, we can deal more coherently with the where, who, how, and what else issues of data collection.

Of course, like most planning processes, some iteration might be required to complete the design of a good data collection system. For example, the discussion about where in the process to collect the data might require going back and restating the question more precisely.

We will look at the elements of this data-collection planning process in more detail later. First, we will look at some examples of when data collection is necessary and how it is used.

TYPES OF DATA COLLECTION

Three types of data collection forms are commonly used by quality improvement teams: check sheets, data sheets, and checklists. While these three types of forms are quite different, the similarity in their names often leads to confusion.

A check sheet is a simple data recording form that has been specially designed to readily interpret results from the form itself. Figure 15.2 shows an example of a simple check sheet for recording temperatures in a manufacturing process. Notice that the form was designed to allow the operator to enter the temperatures on a time versus temperature grid. Because of this, the form does more than simply provide a record of the data—it allows the simultaneous analysis of trends in the data.

Data sheets are also used to gather data. They differ from check sheets, however, in that data are recorded in a simple tabular or columnar format. Specific bits of data—numbers, words, or marks (e.g., *X*)—are entered in spaces on the sheet. As a result, additional processing is typically required after the data are collected to construct the tool needed for analysis. Figure 15.3 shows an example of a data sheet for collecting temperatures.

FIGURE 15.2 *A check sheet*

SOLDER BATH TEMPERATURE

- Read temperature to nearest degree off meter number 5.
- Plot the temperature and time on the grid using a dot (●). Connect the dots with a line.
- Reading should be taken on the hour (± 5 minutes).
- Use the "Notes" section to record anything unusual.

Date: 6-7-88

Line #: 13

Inspector: Ginny Smith

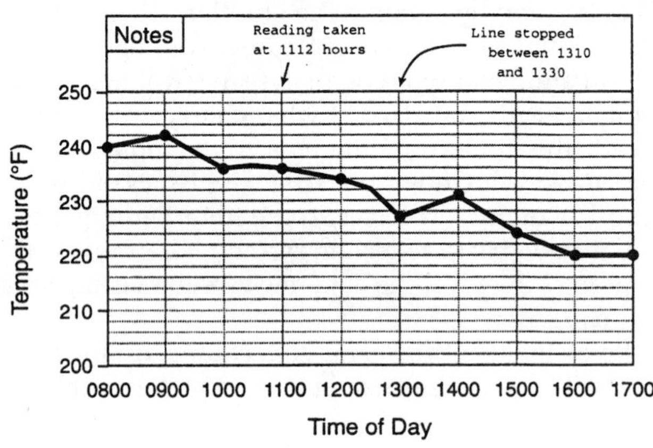

A checklist contains items that are important or relevant to a specific issue or situation. Checklists are used under operational conditions to ensure that all important steps or actions have been taken. Although completed checklists might be analyzed by a quality improvement team, their primary purpose is for guiding operations, not for collecting data. Checklists are therefore more commonly used in the remedial journey and holding-the-gains phases of problem solving; they are part of the solution. The preflight checklist that a commercial airline pilot must complete is a good example.

Much of the material in this article focuses on check sheets for two reasons: Data sheets and checklists are straightforward and need little explanation; and check sheets are typically not used that often.

OBTAINING GOOD DATA

Collected data must be accurate. Inaccurate data might give the wrong answer to information questions. Most collected data are not perfect, but there are techniques that keep inaccuracies to a minimum. The most serious types of data inaccuracies are called biases.

FIGURE 15.3 *A data sheet*

SOLDER BATH TEMPERATURE

- Read temperature to nearest degree off meter number 5. Date: 6-7-88
- Record the temperature in the table below.
- Reading should be taken on the hour (± 5 minutes). Line # 13
- Use the "Notes" section to record anything unusual. Inspector: Ginny Smith

* Questions? Contact Larry Fine x2222

Time of Day	Temperature (°F)
0800	240
0900	242
1000	236
1100	236
1200	234

Time of Day	Temperature (°F)
1300	227
1400	230
1500	224
1600	220
1700	220

Notes: - 1100 hours reading taken at 1112
- The line was stopped between 1310 and 1330

Biases can come from many sources, including the design of the data collection instrument, the collection procedures, and the perceptions of the persons collecting the data. For some types of bias, it is helpful to conduct an audit of the data collection process while the data are being collected. As you study the following examples, notice how some of the teams considered and dealt with issues of bias.

REDUCING WARRANTY COSTS

A few years ago, a television manufacturer introduced a line of television sets that was a big commercial success. The style of the cabinet was attractive, the price was competitive, and the set offered a number of features that the public appreciated. As time went by, however, the company discovered that reliability was poor. A high percentage of television sets came back to be repaired within the 12-month warranty period.

A quality improvement project team was chartered to determine the causes of this problem, which was increasing warranty costs for the company to an unacceptable level. The team formulated the following information questions to guide the analysis of the symptoms:

How to collect data

Data collection is a type of production process itself and, like any process, needs to be understood and improved. Generally speaking, 10 points must be addressed when collecting data:

1. Formulate good questions that relate to the specific information needs of the project. It is much easier to get others to help collect data if they believe those in charge know precisely what they are looking for and that they are going to do something with the collected information.

2. Use the appropriate data analysis tools and be certain the necessary data are being collected. Whenever practical, collect continuous variable data. A few minutes of thought before gathering data can often prevent having to recollect data because they are incomplete or answer the wrong question.

3. Define comprehensive data collection points. The ideal is to set the collection point where the job flow suffers minimum interruption. An accurate flowchart of the work process can help immensely.

4. Select an unbiased collector. The collector should have the easiest and most immediate access to the relevant facts.

5. Understand data collectors and their environment. The training and experience of the collectors determine whether they can handle this additional assignment.

- How many total components are replaced under warranty in each of the three existing models of the set (model numbers 1013, 1017, and 1019)?
- How many integrated circuits, capacitors, resistors, transformers, commands (i.e., switches), and CRTs are replaced under warranty in each of the three models?

These questions could be answered with a bar graph or Pareto diagram if the team had simple tallies of the number of each type of component replaced in each model during a typical week. The repair shop where all the sets came for warranty repairs was the obvious data collection point. Since the repair technicians were the closest to the facts of each repair and had no reason to bias the data, they were selected as the data collectors. The team designed a check sheet, showed it to two

6. Design data collection forms that are simple; reduce opportunities for error; capture data for analysis, reference and traceability; are self-explanatory; and look professional. The KISS (keep it simple, stupid) principle applies here.

7. Prepare the instructions for use. In some cases, a special training course might be necessary for data gatherers. In other cases, a simple sheet of instructions will suffice.

8. Test the forms and instructions. Try out the forms on a limited basis to make sure they are filled out properly. If they aren't, the forms or instructions might need revision.

9. Train the data collectors. Training should include the purpose of the study, what the data will be used for, a properly completed form, and a discussion about the importance of complete and unbiased information.

10. Audit the collection process and validate the results. Randomly check completed forms and observe data collection during the process. Look for missing or unusual data, and be wary of variations in the data that might result from biases in the data collection process.

of the technicians, made some modifications based on their comments, spent 15 minutes describing the study and the final form to the entire group, and then implemented the data collection system. Figure 15.4 is an example of the check sheet given to each workshop technician to record the components replaced during a one-week period.

It was immediately evident that there was a problem with capacitors. This problem was present in all three models. Model 1017 also had a specific problem associated with its command components. The on-off switch for that model failed much more often than did the switch in the other two models.

USING A LOCATION PLOT

When the data to be recorded refer to positions on the surface of an item, a variation of the check sheet called a location plot (or concentration diagram) is ideal in terms of ease of use and ability to transform data into information (Figure 15.5).

FIGURE 15.4 *Check sheet for TV component failures*

COMPONENTS REPLACED BY LAB
Enter a mark for each component replaced. Mark like the following: / // /// //// ~~////~~
TIME PERIOD: *22 Feb to 27 Feb 1988*
REPAIR TECHNICIAN: Bob

TV SET MODEL 1013

Integrated circuits	~~////~~
Capacitors	~~////~~ ~~////~~ ~~////~~ ~~////~~ ~~////~~ //
Resistors	//
Transformers	////
Commands	
CRT	/

TV SET MODEL 1017

Integrated circuits	//
Capacitors	~~////~~ ~~////~~ ~~////~~ ~~////~~ ~~////~~ //
Resistors	/
Transformers	//
Commands	~~////~~ ~~////~~ ~~////~~ //
CRT	/

TV SET MODEL 1019

Integrated circuits	/
Capacitors	~~////~~ ~~////~~ ~~////~~ ~~////~~ ///
Resistors	/
Transformers	//
Commands	
CRT	/

This check sheet was designed by a quality improvement project team to answer the question "Are certain areas on our household range more prone to chipped enamel damage during transportation?" It is clear from Figure 15.5 that the corners were the areas most prone to damage. This information was invaluable in indicating that certain corners of the appliances required more protection for safe transportation.

INTEGRATED CIRCUIT YIELD

The manufacture of integrated circuits begins with silicon slices that, after a sequence of complex operations, will contain hundreds or thousands of chips on

FIGURE 15.5 ***Location plot of chipped enamel on range***

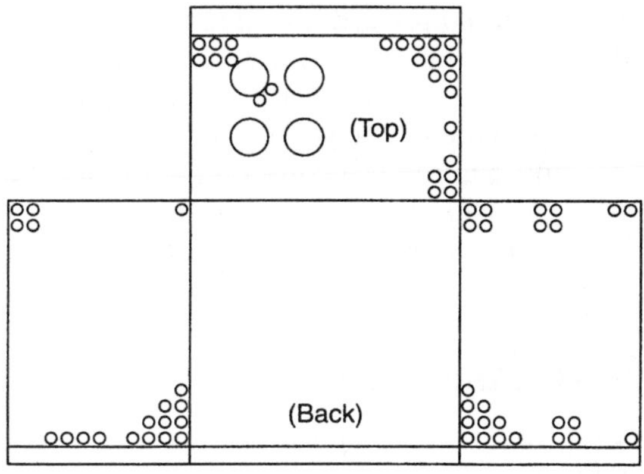

FIGURE 15.6 ***Location plot of chip rejects***

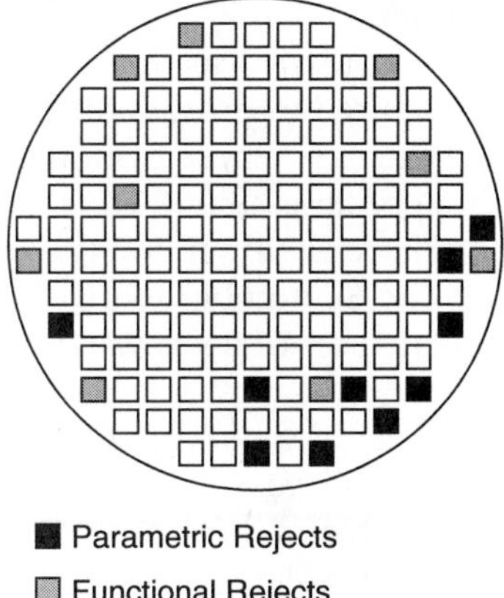

their surfaces. Each chip must be tested to establish whether it functions properly. During slice testing, some chips are found to be defective and are rejected. To reduce the number of rejects, it is necessary to know not only the percentage but also the locations and the types of defects. There are normally two major types of defects: functional and parametric. A functional reject occurs when a chip does not perform one of its functions. A parametric reject occurs when the circuit functions properly, but a parameter of the chip, such as speed or power consumption, is not correct.

Figure 15.6 is an example of a check sheet showing the location of rejected chips within the integrated circuit. Only those chips that had five or more defects during the testing of 1,000 circuits are colored in. The information shows that parametric rejects are mostly concentrated on the lower right of the slice, while functional rejects are distributed toward the edges.

This is an unusual check sheet because it takes advantage of the automated testing equipment. Chip failures are recorded by the test equipment for each circuit and displayed on the video screen attached to the test equipment. In addition, the results of each test are stored in the test computer, and the results of hundreds or thousands of tests can be quickly summarized in the form shown in Figure 15.6. Such computerized applications, when available, should not be overlooked.

PROCESSING PURCHASE ORDERS

When a company wants to buy raw material, piece parts, services, or other items from an outside supplier, a purchase requisition form must be filled out. After management approves the purchase, this request goes to the purchasing department. It will obtain offers from several different potential suppliers before one is selected and a purchase order is used. At this point, with all the internal processing steps completed, the purchase order is sent to the selected supplier and a copy of it to the originator of the order.

A quality improvement project team was appointed to speed up this process. The team analyzed the time required to process purchase orders. The question of interest was "How many working days elapse from the date of the originator's signature to the date the purchase order is sent?" The team used a histogram to analyze the distribution of the total processing time in order to obtain insight into the structure of the process. (See the September issue of *Quality Progress* for the article about histograms.) The needed set of data was the elapsed time in days for 40 or more purchase orders.

Asking purchasing clerks to record when they send out purchase orders is the obvious, ideal approach. However, it raises the issue of potential bias because the clerks might fear they would be blamed for delays. In this case, great care was taken to explain to the clerks that no blame was being placed. Furthermore, it was carefully explained that, unless they followed their normal routines during the study period, the data would be biased and things would never get better permanently. To make sure that this was understood, one of the clerks was enlisted to conduct casual interviews with her peers. These interviews confirmed that the study could be conducted using the clerks as collectors. The clerk was also relieved of some of her normal workload so that she could observe and audit the data collection process during the study period. A completed check sheet from the study is shown in Figure 15.7.

The design of the check sheet makes the distribution of times immediately obvious, and the distribution can be analyzed as discussed in the section on histograms without any additional processing. Note one nice feature of this check sheet: by providing boxes to mark in, the results will be easier to interpret. If the

FIGURE 15.7 ***Check sheet for elapsed processing time***

WORKING DAYS

1		3		5		7		9		11		13		15		17		19		21		23		25	
											X	X	X												
											X	X	X												
										X	X	X	X	X											
									X	X	X	X	X	X											
									X	X	X	X	X	X	X										
								X	X	X	X	X	X	X	X										
								X	X	X	X	X	X	X	X	X									
							X	X	X	X	X	X	X	X	X	X									
		X				X	X	X	X	X	X	X	X	X	X	X	X	X				X		X	X

Enter an X in the lowest unoccupied box under the number of working days from the date of the originator's signature to the date the purchase order was sent out.

horizontal lines had not been provided, variations in the size and placement on the x's might make interpretation less exact.

While the use of a check sheet in this case was a good, quick way to obtain some initial insight, the team members realized that the check sheet had limitations when compared to a complete data sheet. For example, they would not be able to differentiate among the times required for different types of materials being purchased.

INTERPRETING DATA, VALIDATING RESULTS

Before starting to draw conclusions from collected data, the team should verify that the data are appropriate. It is helpful to review the questions that were originally asked. Does the data collected still appear to answer those questions?

Look at the results of any audits of the data collection phase. Is there any evidence of bias in the collection process? Is the number of observations collected the number specified? If not, why not?

Are there any missing observations or responses? These can be a major source of error. Identify missing data for special treatment. In a survey of customers, for example, dissatisfied customers who are taking their business to your competitor might be the least likely to respond. But their views are vital. Never assume that missing data will, on average, look like the collected data. Generally, it will not.

Do some comparative tabulations of the data. For example, do the data gathered by each collector look, on average, about the same? If not, why not? Is the variability of the results from each data collector about the same? Excessively high or very low variability by one or two data collectors might indicate problems with the data collection process—or falsified data.

GREAT EXPECTATIONS

Do not expect too much from the data. The data should indicate the answer to the question asked during the design of the collection process. It might not be able to answer other unanticipated questions. Do not try to make inferences from the data that they will not support. Usually a check sheet, with its simple collection and analysis format, is intended for a quick answer to a single question. It will not usually support further analysis or stratification. A good complete data sheet, however, will often support many levels of analysis and stratification if they have been anticipated in the design.

For example, the team looking at enamel chips on kitchen ranges might later develop a theory that the location of the chips might also be, in part, related to the shipping method used—a particular railroad or truck line. The data in Figure 15.5 would not help test that theory.

INTERPRETATION PITFALLS

Most of the interpretation pitfalls relate to the application of specific tools to the data, but a few are generic to all collected data. The following biases might cause problems:

Exclusion bias The results will be biased if they are intended to represent the entire process and some part of the process being investigated has been left out. Data should be collected from all the places, times, and conditions under which the process operates.

Interaction bias The process of collecting the data itself might affect the process being studied. For example, a team was trying to improve the speed with which promotions were processed by a personnel office. Team members began to collect data on the process, but while they were collecting the data, the speed of processing increased by a factor of four.

Perception bias The attitudes and beliefs of the data collectors can sometimes color what they see and how they record it.

Operational bias Failure to follow the established procedures is the most common operational bias. This bias usually arises because the instructions, training, and/or forms were not adequately prepared and tested in an operational environment. The transcribing and processing of the collected data can create additional errors.

Nonresponse bias Missing data can bias the results. As we noted above, it is not safe to assume that missing data, on average, look like the collected data. The fact that they are missing is a clue that they are different from the rest in some way.

Estimation bias The formulas and methods used to calculate statistics from the collected data might give certain types of biases. These biases are beyond the scope of this article; however, estimation bias must be understood when using tools other than the simple ones described here.

KNOW THE QUESTION

Most quality improvement tools depend on reliable, accurate data. If such data are not available, they must be collected. The data collection process must be driven by the information from questions that we formulate based on our needs. In short, know what question is to be answered before collecting data.

Reading 16

Pareto Charts

By John T. Burr

The Pareto principle is several things. It is a state of nature, the way things happen around us. It is also a way of managing projects. Finally, it is a process—a way of thinking about problems that affect us.

STATE OF NATURE

The Pareto principle was first defined by Joseph Juran in 1950.[1] During his early work, Juran found that there was a "maldistribution of quality losses." Not liking such a long name, he named the principle after Vilfredo Pareto, a 19th-century Italian economist. Pareto found that a large share of the wealth was owned by relatively few people—a maldistribution of wealth.

Juran found this was true in many areas of life, including quality technologies. In 1975, he published a retraction of his use of Pareto's name in an article called "The Non-Pareto Principle; Mea Culpa."[2] Nevertheless, the term "Pareto principle" is here to stay.

In simplest terms, the Pareto principle suggests that most effects come from relatively few causes. In quantitative terms, 80 percent of the problems come from 20 percent of the machines, raw materials, or operators. Also, 80 percent of the wealth is controlled by 20 percent of the people. It is well-known that 80 percent of the funds contributed to charity come from only 20 percent of the possible sources. Finally, 80 percent of scrap or rework quality costs come from 20 percent of the possible causes.

In the quality technologies, Juran calls the 20 percent of the causes the "vital few."[3] He originally called the rest of the causes the "trivial many." However, he and other quality professionals came to understand that there are no trivial problems on the manufacturing floor and that all problems deserve management's attention. Juran has since renamed the trivial many the "useful many."[4,5] But no matter the labels, the Pareto principle is one of the most powerful decision tools available.

A MANAGEMENT TOOL

Data can be collected on the state of scrap, rework, warranty claims, maintenance time, raw material usage, machine downtime, or any other cost associated with manufacturing a product or providing a service. In the case of providing a service, for example, data can be collected on wasted time, number of jobs that have to be redone, customer inquiries, and number of errors. The data should be organized as illustrated in Figure 16.1. The most frequent (highest cost) cause is placed on the left, and the other causes are added in descending order of occurrence.

Figures 16.2 and 16.3 are examples of the Pareto diagram. It is quite obvious which causes or problems have to be reduced or eliminated to have any real impact on the system.

A double Pareto diagram, as in Figure 16.4, can be used to contrast two products, areas, or shifts, or to look at a system before and after improvement.

In 1984, Jeffery Kalin, the manufacturing manager of a Hewlett Packard plant in Colorado Springs, stated that no one in his plant worked on a problem until they had developed a Pareto diagram. The diagram had to show that the problem being worked on by the team or the supervisor was the most important one at that time.[6]

FIGURE 16.1 *Generalized Pareto diagram*

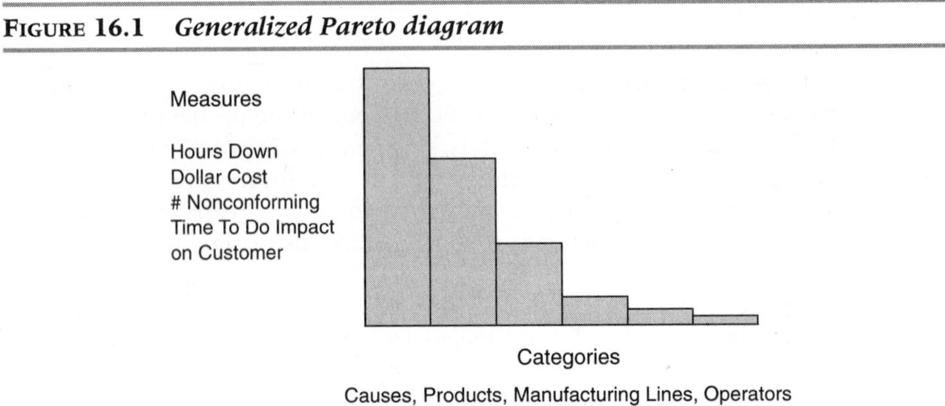

FIGURE 16.2 ***Strut rod rejects***

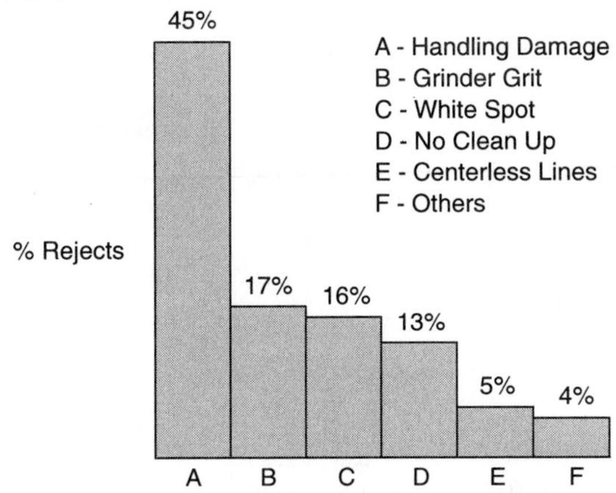

FIGURE 16.3 ***Information systems***

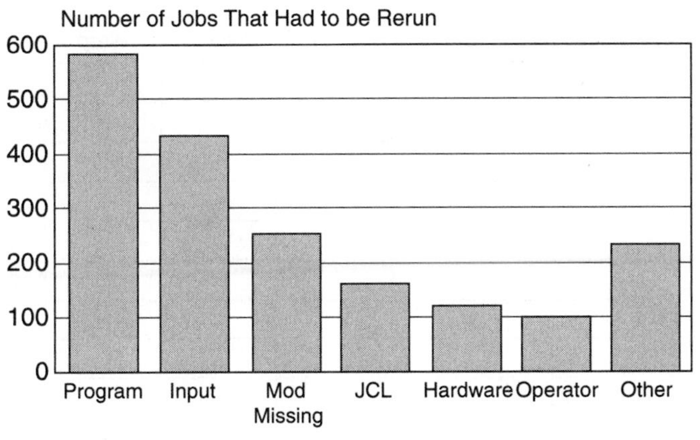

A WAY OF THINKING

Figure 16.5 is not a Pareto diagram, but a set of data on problems encountered with boxes used to package a number of different products. The most frequent problem is on only one of the box types. Talking to the supplier about the specific problem (warping on box style no. 3) will solve almost half of the difficulties. This

FIGURE 16.4 ***Poor golf shots***

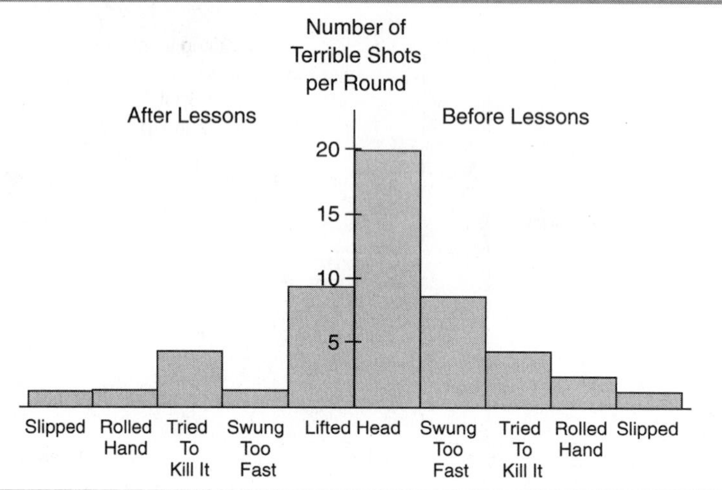

FIGURE 16.5 ***Problems with supplied boxes***

Product	Labels	Liner	Glue	Score	Warp	
A	2		8			10
B	1		4			5
C		1		7	28	36
D		2			4	6
E	3		11			14
F	1				1	2
G	1					1
H				2		2
I	2					2
	10	3	23	9	33	

(Problem columns: Labels, Liner, Glue, Score, Warp)

would also probably lead to less warping of box style no. 4, particularly if the boxes are made on the same line.

The next most frequent problem is glue. The problem occurs over several box types. Are they made on a common line? Is the glue or glue lot the same among these? If so, then a common cause has been identified and should be eliminated. The "mess" of incoming box supply problems will be reduced 80 percent by solving the two problems that have the most impact on quality. Of course, the improvement process is not stopped. The box manufacturing process should be continually analyzed using the Pareto diagram and the other tools of quality.

GETTING DATA FOR A PARETO DIAGRAM

American industries, manufacturing or service, are some of the greatest collectors of data in the world. Computers store vast amounts of data. Wastebaskets receive data daily. Data are there for the asking. The trick is to recognize what data are useful.

Occasionally data are not available. The situation might come up, for example, when a group must define a problem or look for a cause. With a process flow diagram and a cause-and-effect program visible and understandable to the group, each member must identify what he or she feels are the most important causes of the problem. This can be done in three ways:

1. Each person votes on the major categories in the cause-and-effect diagram. It might also be helpful to have each person explain why he or she is voting for a particular category. Often, consensus can be quickly reached; otherwise, a Pareto diagram of the votes should be made.
2. Each person has five votes and can place them anywhere on the cause-and-effect diagram. It is good to do this in conjunction with a break so that each person has time to come to the diagram to make the marks. By the way, a person could give all five votes to one cause if he or she felt very strongly about it. A Pareto diagram of the results should be made.
3. There is a nominal technique that is more involved and particularly useful when there is a large number of possible causes and a good deal of uncertainty of which is important. This technique requires a large supply of 3 by 5 cards. All members get 10 cards (or five for shorter lists of causes). They write each of their top 10 choices on separate cards. They then pick the most likely cause. This card gets a 10. Next they pick the least likely cause and give it a 1. Then the next least likely cause is selected, a 2. Then the next most likely cause, a 9. This process is repeated back and forth until all the causes are ranked. (It is easier to select the most and the least likely causes than to distinguish among the ones in the middle.) The numbers are then compiled for each cause and a Pareto diagram is constructed. This same technique can be used giving each person 100 points to distribute among the ranked cards. The seam process of compiling is then used.

The Pareto principle describes the way causes occur in nature and human behavior. It can be a very powerful management tool for focusing personnel's effort on the problems and solutions that have the greatest potential payback.

References

1. Juran, Joseph M., "Pareto, Lorenz, Cournot, Bernoulli, Juran and Others," *Industrial Quality Control,* October 1950, p. 5.
2. Juran, Joseph M., "Then and Now in Quality Control," *Quality Progress,* May 1975, p. 8.
3. Juran, Joseph M., editor, *Quality Control Handbook,* 4th edition, McGraw-Hill Book Co., 1989.
4. Juran, Joseph M., *Juran on Planning of Quality* (New York: The Free Press, 1988).
5. Juran, Joseph M., *Juran on Leadership for Quality* (New York: The Free Press, 1989).
6. Kalin, Jeffery, Presentation to the Rochester Section, ASQC, on September 6, 1984.

Reading 17

Scatter Diagrams

By John T. Burr

In many situations we have data that might be related to some product characteristic or to other data. These data might come from manufacturing, service, or administrative sources. For example, we might want to know whether the thickness of paperboard will predict its ability to withstand punctures when used, or whether work backlog affects the error rate of computer data entry. These relationships can be nonmathematically evaluated by using a scatter diagram. The data are plotted on graph paper; each axis is used for one of the two sets of data being compared. The y axis is usually reserved for the characteristic we would like to predict, e.g., burst strength of paperboard and error rate. The x axis is used for the variable that we are using to make the prediction, e.g., thickness of the paperboard and the work backlog.

To show how this works, let us review an example from a recent publication.[1] The color of the bread (how well it is toasted) is what we want to predict, so it is assigned to the y axis. The number 1 equals uncooked and 9 equals burnt. The age of the bread is what will be used to predict the color, so it is assigned to the x axis. The data pairs (one number for the color and another for the age) are plotted on the graph paper as a scatter diagram (Figure 17.1). Is there a relationship? Does it require statistical calculation to see the relationship? There is variability in the measurement or in other process parameters because bread that is the same age does not always have the exact same color. In Figures 17.2–4, we can see that there are various degrees to which data can be related to each other.

However, it is important to note that, just because two variables appear to be related, it does not mean they are. There might be other reasons why two variables seem to be related. In Figure 17.5, it would appear that food and housing prices are related to each other, but they are, in fact, both related to inflation or the rising cost of production.

FIGURE 17.1 *Toast color*

Also, just because there is an apparent graphical relationship between two variables, it does not mean that one causes the other to change. For example, one such diagram related the Dow Jones Index to the height of Lake Superior from 1925 to 1965. There is obviously no relationship between the two, but data can be much more subtle. Don't fall into this trap.

FIGURE 17.2 ***Example of a scatter diagram between variable numbers 8 and 9 of a recent experiment on plastic sheeting***

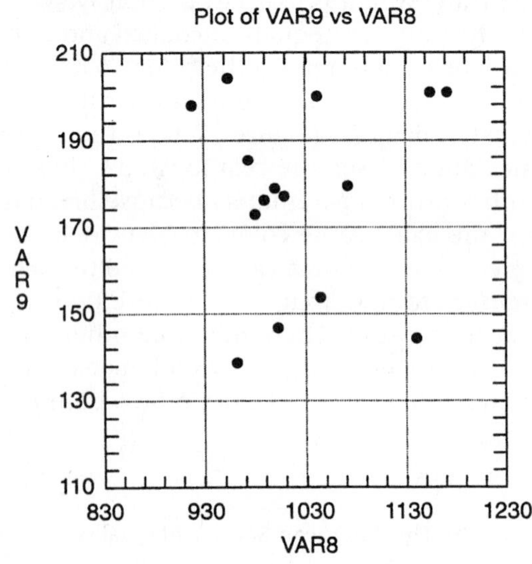

FIGURE 17.3 ***Example of a scatter diagram between variable numbers 6 and 7 of a recent experiment on plastic sheeting***

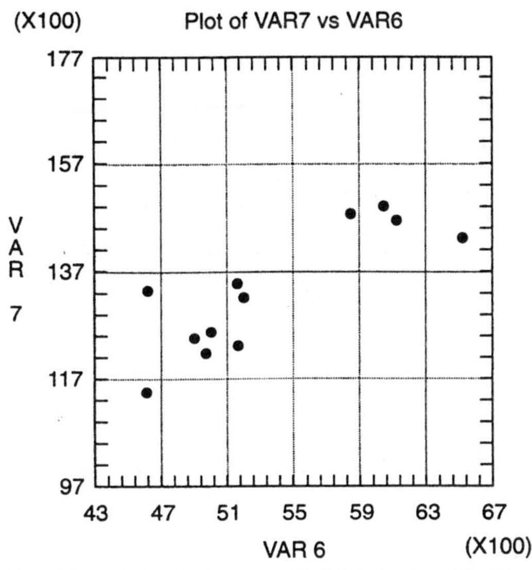

FIGURE 17.4 ***Example of a scatter diagram between the flow rate of a liquid and the voltage applied to a valve***

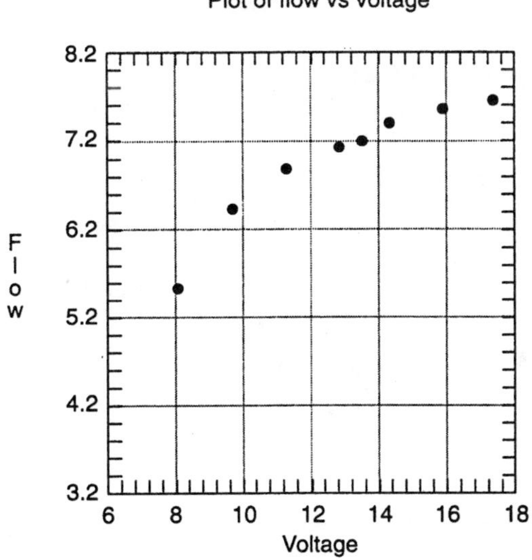

FIGURE 17.5 ***Relationship between food and housing prices***

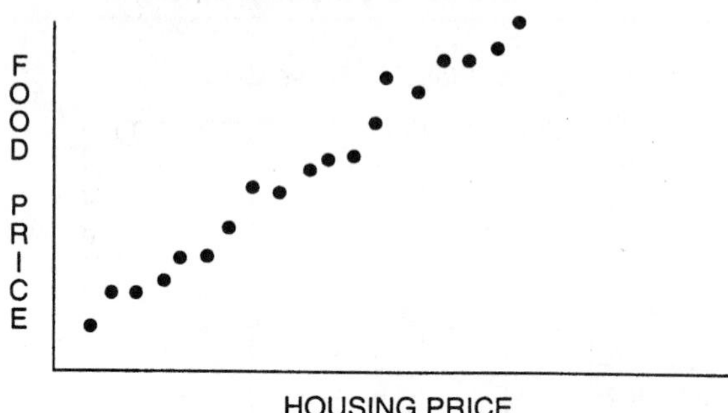

FIGURE 17.6 ***Height versus age of seventh graders***

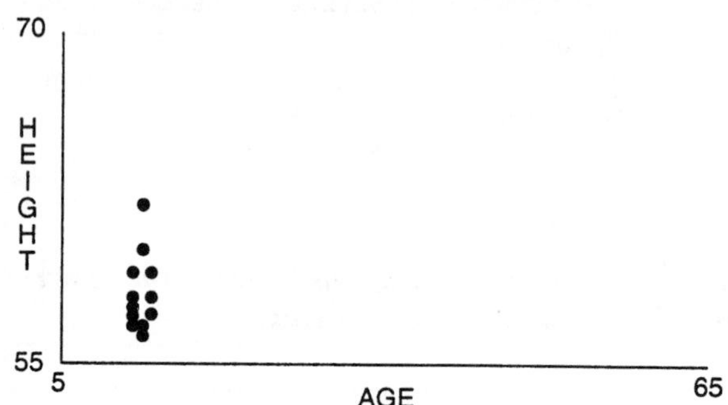

FIGURE 17.7 ***Gas mileage versus fuel additive***

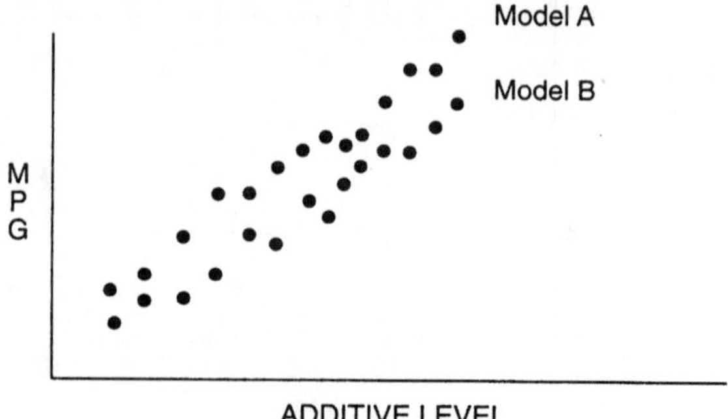

FIGURE 17.8 ***Seal strength versus sealing temperature***

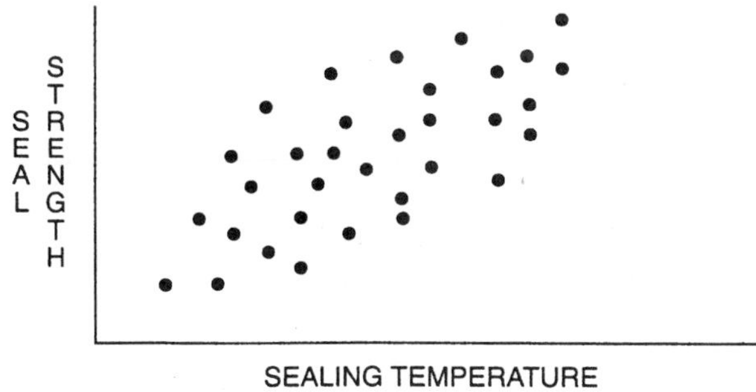

If the data do not appear to have a relationship, it does not mean they are not related. There might be a variety of reasons for this, as seen in Figures 17.6–8. In Figure 17.6, we have taken data from too small a range of persons; we need to find some children from other grades in the school. In Figure 17.7, there might be more than one model of automobile used to obtain the data. We would need to make several diagrams, one for each automobile used in the study. In Figure 17.8, a large measurement error is concealing the relationship.

Like any of the SPC tools, the scatter diagram is very powerful, but it can easily be misused. The diagram must be evaluated by those who know most about the product or the process, e.g., the operators, engineers, supervisors, and maintenance personnel.

Reference

1. John T. Burr, *SPC Tools for Operators* (Milwaukee, WI: Quality Press, 1989).

Reading 18

Seven New Quality Control Tools

EDITED BY SHIGERU MIZUNO

OVERVIEW OF THE SEVEN METHODS

This section will introduce only the fundamentals of each method.

The relations diagram method

This is a technique developed to clarify intertwined causal relationships in a complex problem or situation in order to find an appropriate solution.

The method In order to analyze problems with a complex network of cause-and-effect relationships, a relations diagram is constructed by indicating the logical relationships that exist between the causal factors (Figure 18.1). Such a diagram facilitates solutions to problems by allowing the whole problem to be viewed from a broad perspective.

To solve problems using the relations diagram method, a team composed of as many members as necessary should draft diagrams several times. By constructing diagrams in this way, the team generates new ideas that may lead to an effective solution.

Uses The relations diagram method can be used to

- Determine and develop quality assurance policies.
- Establish promotional plans for TQC introduction.

FIGURE 18.1 ***Abstract relations diagram***

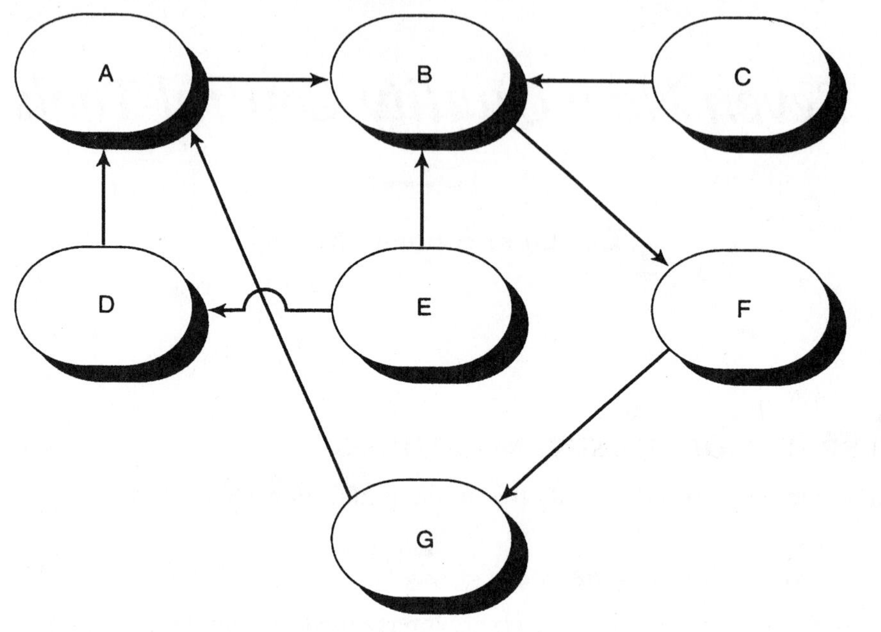

- Design steps to counter market complaints.
- Improve quality in the manufacturing process (especially in planning to eliminate latent defects).
- Promote quality control in purchased or ordered items.
- Provide measures against troubles related to payment and process control.
- Effectively promote small group activities.
- Reform administrative and business departments.

Applications

Example 1. At the first symposium on quality control, a survey was conducted on the major items necessary for the introduction and promotion of total quality control. The items obtained from this study are presented in the relational diagram pictured in Figure 18.2. This diagram clarifies the important items that companies might consider in their promotion of total quality control.

Example 2. Company U investigated the causes of a chronic deficiency in its assembly line of a certain product by using a relational diagram (Figure 18.3). As a result of drawing the relational diagram, the staff's preconceptions regarding the causes of the deficiency were corrected and countermeasures were taken that result in a drastic reduction in the defective rate.

Figure 18.2 *Relations diagram depicting the group of items important in the promotion of total quality control*

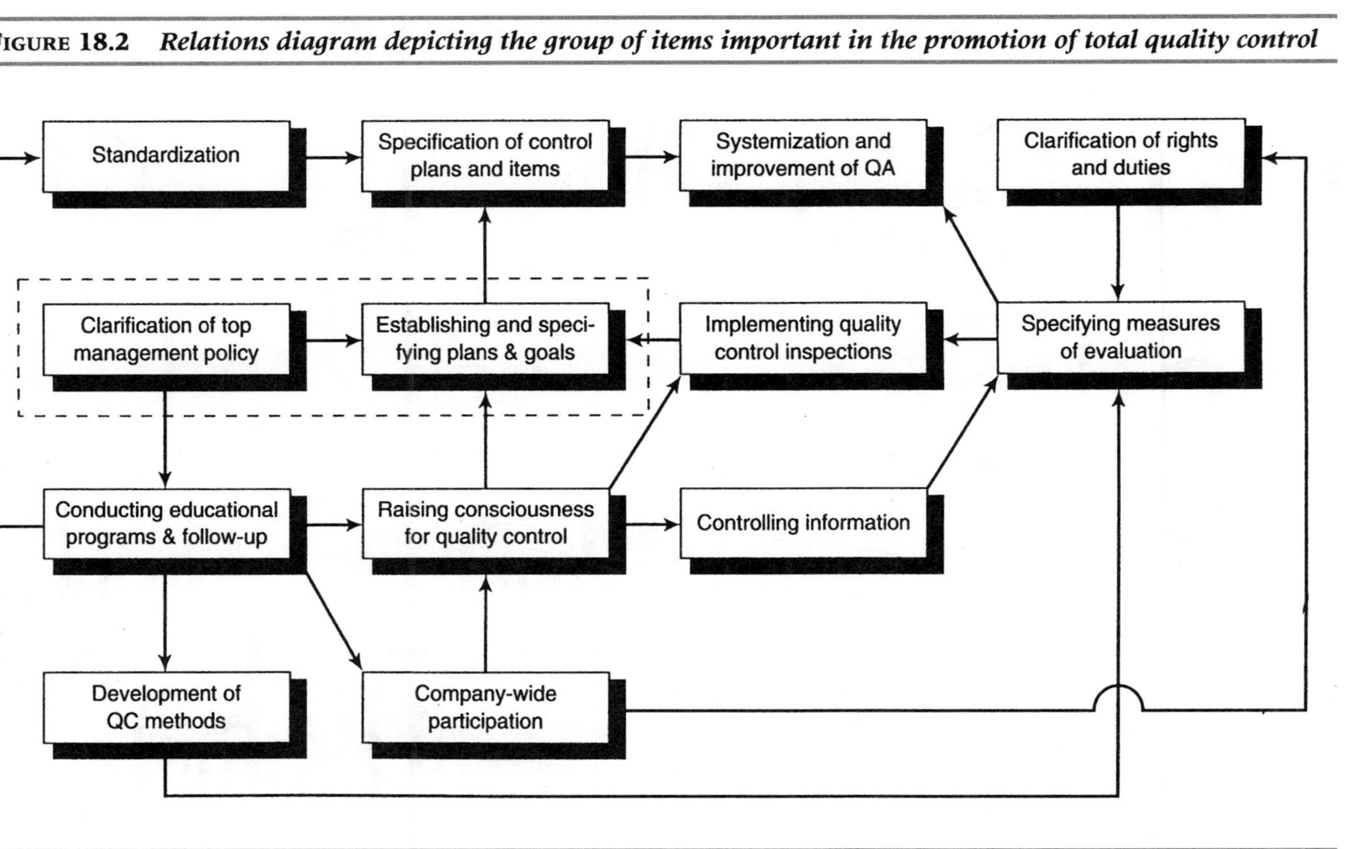

FIGURE 18.3 *Relations diagram examining the causes of a deficiency in assembly-line production*

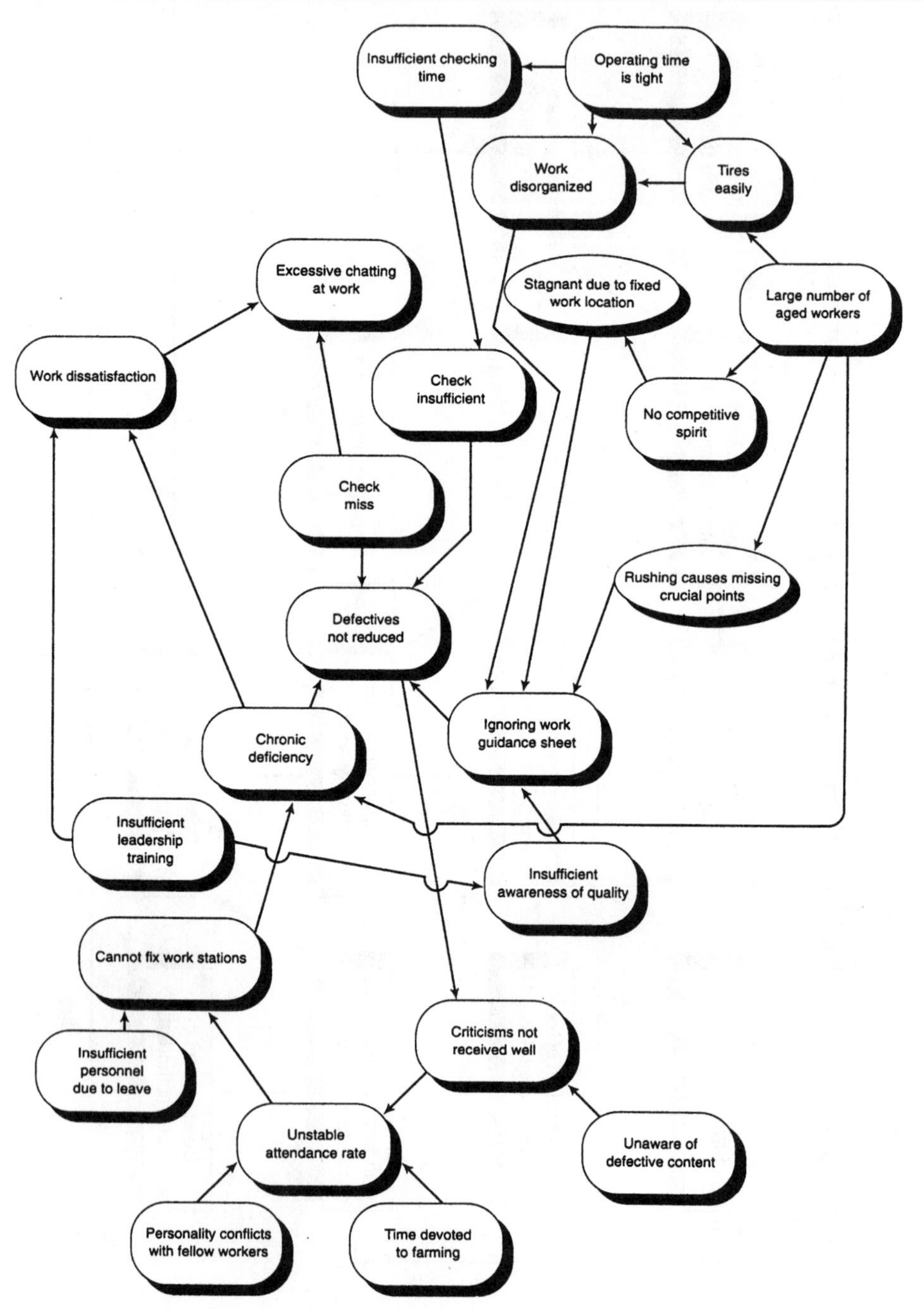

TABLE 18.1 ***KJ method versus statistical techniques***

Statistical techniques	The KJ method
1. Oriented for testing hypotheses	1. Oriented for discovering problems
2. Quantifies and transforms an event into numerical data	2. Expresses data in language and symbols without quantifying
3. Capable of analytic understanding; ability to stratify	3. Overall understanding possible; harmonizes heterogeneous elements
4. Can grasp by reasoning	4. Can grasp through feeling
5. Western way of thinking introduced through translation	5. Thinking based on Japanese language (said not to be amenable with language written horizontally)

*The KJ Method**

This technique clarifies important but unresolved problems by collecting verbal data from disordered and confused situations and analyzing that data by mutual affinity.

The method The KJ method attempts to clarify the nature, shape, and extent of problems that affect the near and distant future in fields where there is little or no prior knowledge and/or experience. This technique consists of gathering ideas and opinions in the form of verbal data and drawing a complete diagram based on the common relationships and similarities found among the data.

The KJ method is an organizational technique based on "participatory group formation." Problems are solved through the creation of teams that gather the opinions, ideas, and experiences of diverse people and then coordinate and organize those data in terms of mutual affinity.

The KJ method was originally conceived, developed, and promoted by Kawakita Jiro. Mr. Kawakita attempts to solve all problems by cumulatively using the affinity diagram. Contrasting the KJ method with statistical techniques (Table 18.1 and Figure 18.4) highlights its effectiveness as one of the seven new tools in solving problems in conjunction with other methods.

Uses The KJ method can be used to

- Establish a QC policy for a new company or a new factory and to implement that plan.
- Establish a QC policy concerning new projects, new products, or new technology and to implement that plan.
- Conduct quality assurance market surveys when entering a new untested market.

*The KJ method is a trademark registered by the founder of the Kawayoshida Research Center. The trademark is still held by the center. We gratefully acknowledge the center's permission to use its materials in this chapter.

FIGURE 18.4 *Similarities between statistical quality control and the KJ Method*

What are the similarities between statistical quality control and the KJ method?

KJ method is an external exploration method

Emphasis on external exploration and observation

Treasures the smell of the earth

Listens with the third ear (sensitive to hidden meanings)

The term "external" used in the KJ method is similar to the terms "on-site" or "actual goods" used in statistical quality control

Emphasize thinking based on fact

QC has to be fact control-oriented

Go out to site and become familiar with it

Make objective judgments based on data

Observe the site carefully

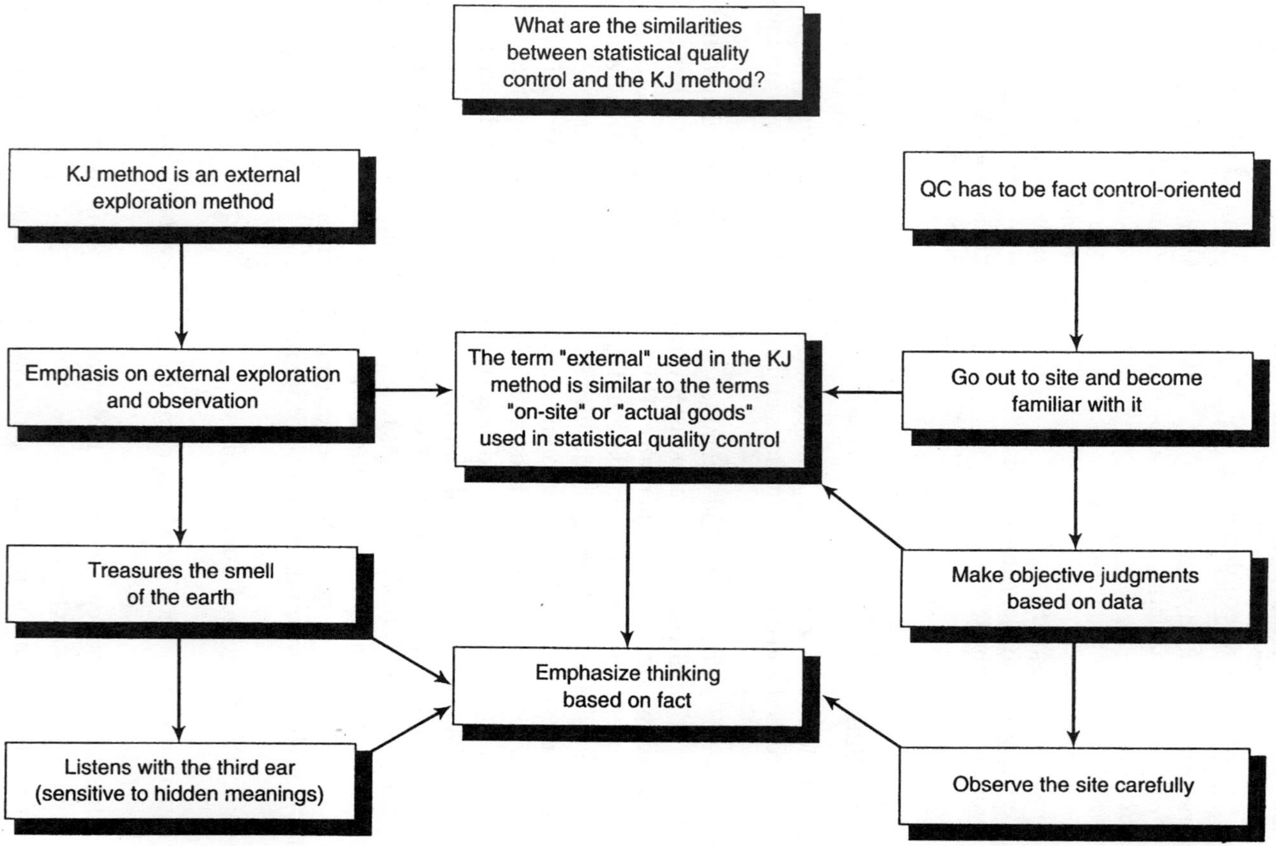

- Find a starting point for TQC promotion by creating a consensus among people with varying opinions regarding the problems that arise within each department.
- Invigorate project teams and QC circles and promote team work within various groups.

Applications

Example 1. Shown in Figure 18.5 is a portion of the affinity diagram obtained from the second round of cumulative KJ method discussions on the topic of "Where and how should our research and development proceed from here?" This discussion was conducted by a 10-member team of engineers and research managers from heterogeneous fields. Since the members were from different fields, the synthesis of their opinions led to a conclusion that will have wide applicability.

The systematic diagram method

This technique searches for the most appropriate and effective means of accomplishing given objectives.

The method The systematic diagram method searches for techniques that will be most suitable for attaining established objectives by systematically clarifying important aspects of the problem. Such systematic diagrams enable workers to have an overview of the whole situation at one glance, effectively delineating the means and measures necessary for achieving the desired objectives (Figure 18.6).

Systematic diagrams can be divided into two types: The *constituent-component-analysis* diagram breaks down the main subject into its basic elements and depicts their relationships to the objectives and means of attaining those objectives. The *plan-development* diagram systematically shows the means and procedures necessary to successfully implement a given plan.

Uses The systematic diagram method can be used to

- Deploy a design-quality plan in the development of a new product.
- Depict the relationship between a QC production process chart and the development of certified levels of quality designed to improve the accuracy of quality assurance activities.
- Create a cause-effect diagram.
- Develop ideas in order to solve problems dealing with quality, cost, and delivery that arise in new businesses.
- Develop objectives, policies, and implementation steps.
- Pursue the specification of increased efficiency in parts and control functions.

Applications

Example 1. A systematic diagram of the plan-development type is shown in Figure 18.7. This diagram illustrates the development of design-quality and implementation steps necessary for production of a UHF tuner for a television.

Figure 18.5 ***Portion of affinity diagram depicting the discussion of "Where and how should R and D proceed from here?"***

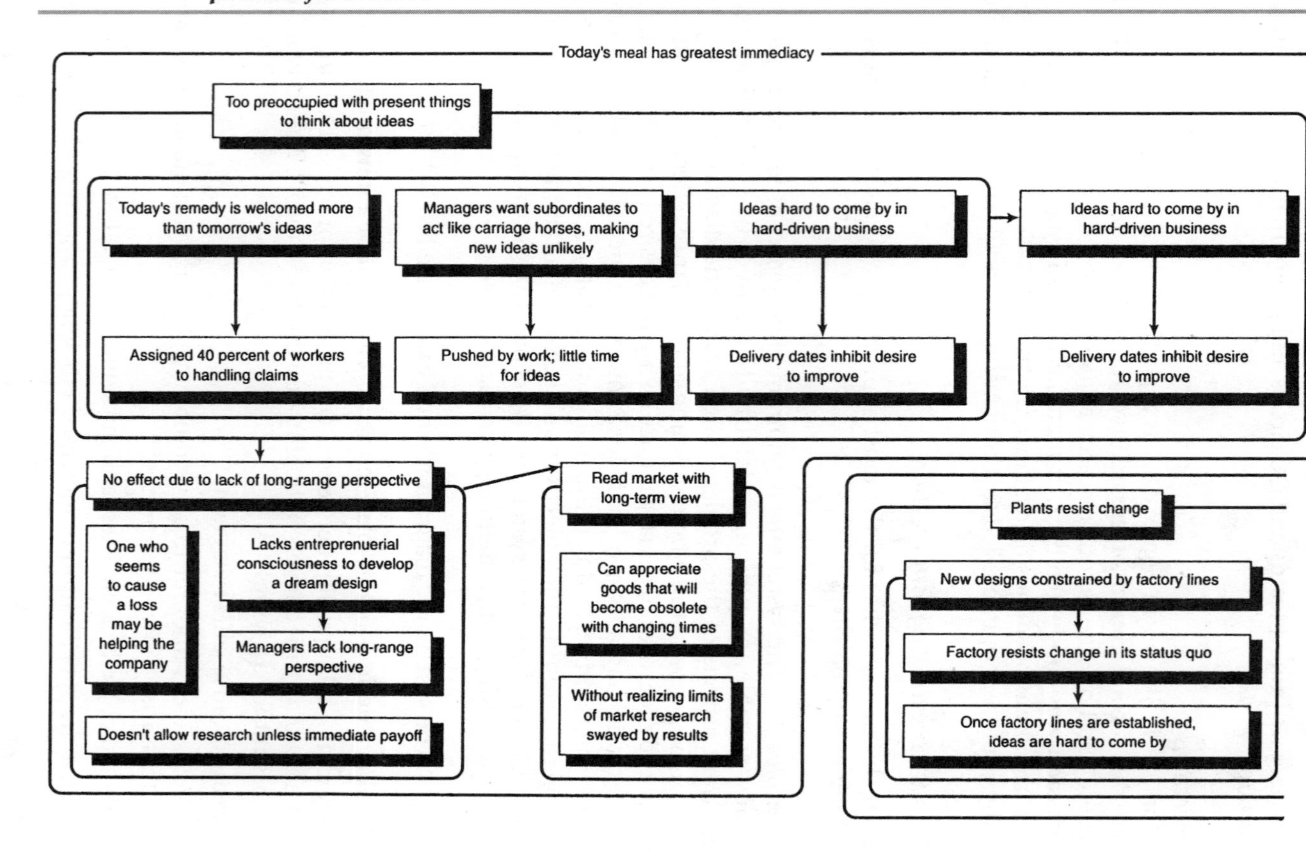

FIGURE 18.6 ***Conceptual systematic diagram***

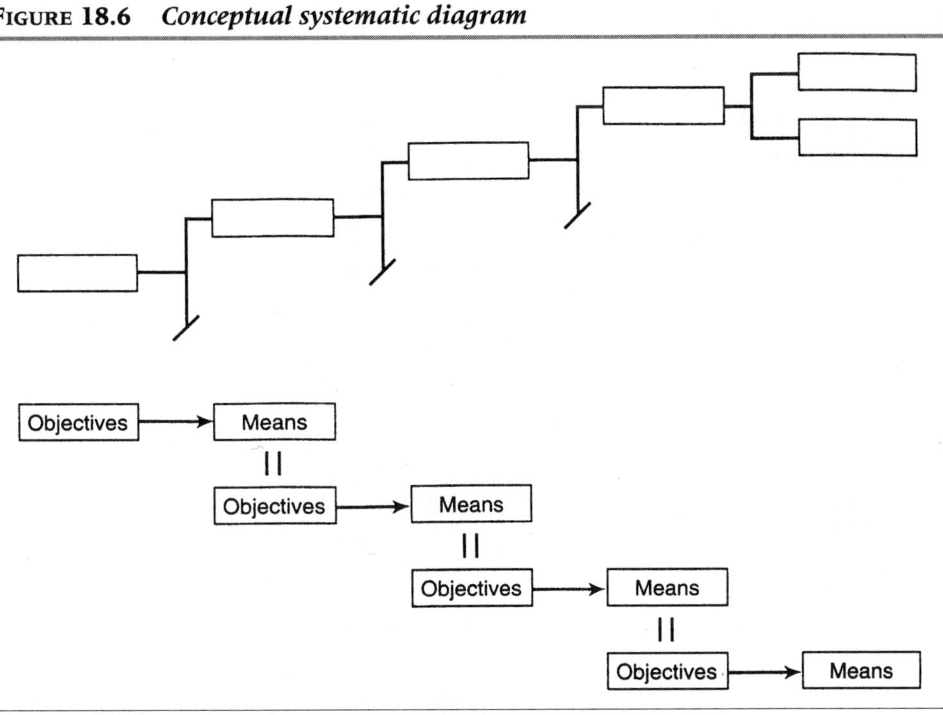

The matrix diagram method

This technique clarifies problematic spots through multidimensional thinking.

The method The matrix diagram method identifies corresponding elements involved in a problem situation or event. These elements are arranged in rows and columns on a chart (Figure 18.8) that shows the presence or absence of relationships among collected pairs of elements. Hopefully, this method will assist in specifying (with a two-way layout) the nature and/or location of problems, enabling idea conception on the basis of two-dimensional relationships. Effective problem solving is facilitated at the intersection points, also referred to as "idea conception points."

Matrix diagrams are classified on the basis of their pattern into five different groups: (1) the L-type matrix, (2) the T-type matrix, (3) the Y-type matrix, (4) the X-type matrix, and (5) the C-type matrix.

Uses Matrix diagrams can be used to

- Establish idea conception points for the development and improvement of system products.
- Achieve quality deployment in product materials.

FIGURE 18.7 ***Systematic diagram for design quality for a television UHF tuner***

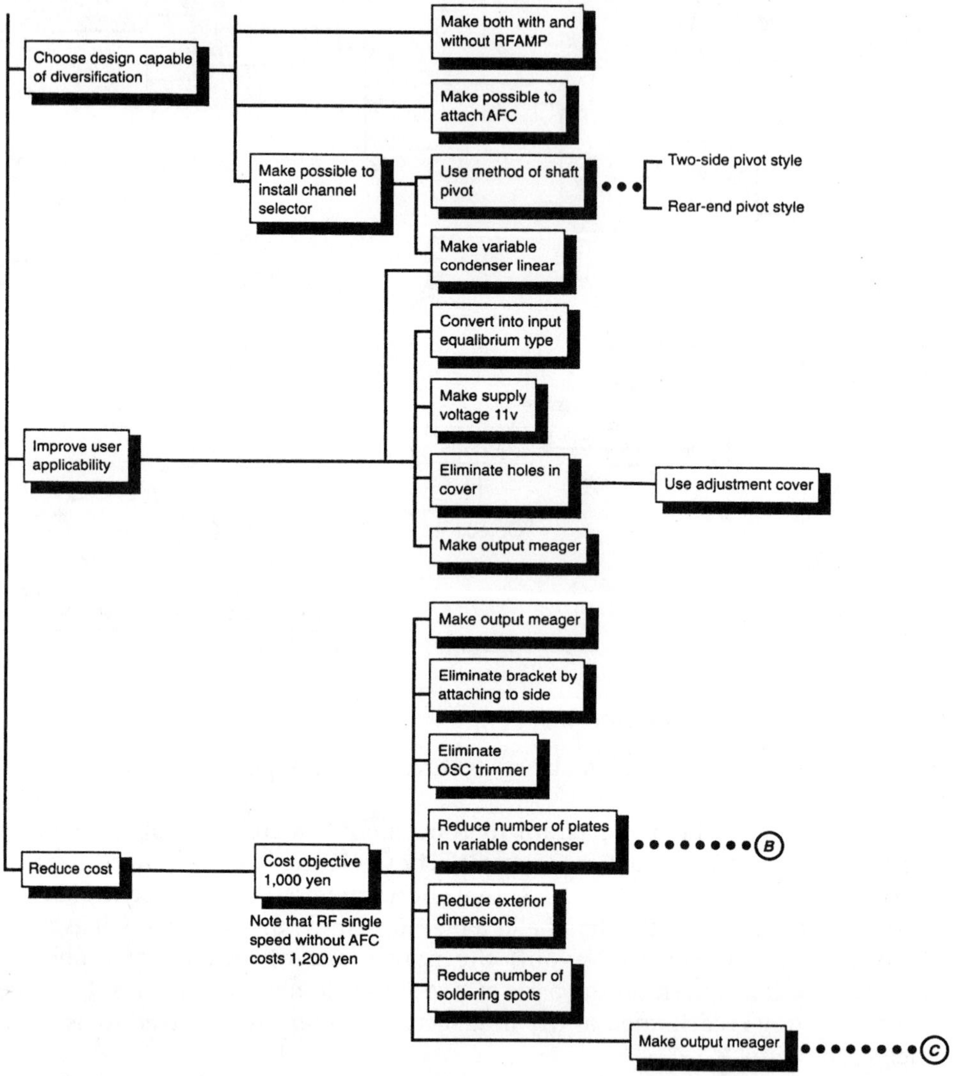

- Establish and strengthen the quality assurance system by linking certified levels of quality with the various control functions.
- Reinforce and improve the efficiency of the quality evaluation system.
- Pursue the causes of nonconformities in the manufacturing process.
- Establish strategies about the mix of products to send to market by evaluating the relationships between the products and market situations.

FIGURE 18.8 ***Conceptual matrix diagram method***

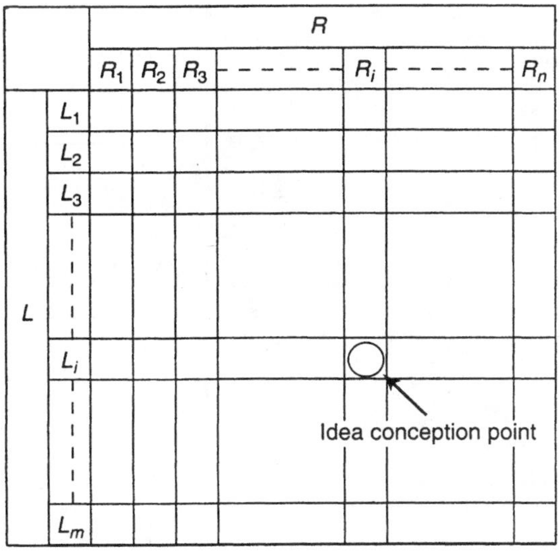

- Clarify the technical relationships among several projects.
- Explore the application potential of currently available technology and raw materials.

Applications As Figure 18.9 indicates, a T-type matrix was constructed in the investigation of smearing during the production of printed cloth. The matrix helped to clarify the relationships between nonconformities and their causes. Based on the results of this matrix, a list of countermeasures was produced, and their implementation considerably reduced smears.

The matrix data-analysis method

This technique arranges data presented in a matrix diagram so that the large array of numbers can be visualized and comprehended easily.

The method The matrix data-analysis method quantifies and arranges matrix diagram data so that the information is easy to visualize and comprehend. The relationships between the elements shown in a matrix diagram are quantified by obtaining numerical data for intersection cells.

Of the seven new QC tools, this is the only numerical analysis method. The results of this technique, however, are presented in diagram form. One major technique that this method also utilizes is known as principal-component

FIGURE 18.9 ***T-type matrix searching for causes of smears in printing of cloth***

Production process (causes)		Appearances / Causes	Oil	Rust	Soot	Dust	Trough	Source	Oiled yarn	Dew dropping	Dregs	Hair	Hand grease	Cardboard	Paper	Black paint	Static electricity	Dust
		Chafe blemish	△					△					○	○				
		Color change	**○**	**○**	**○**	**○**		○	○	△	○	**○**			△	○	○	△
		Shade change					△				○	○						
		Stain	△	△				○		○								
		Black spot	**○**	**○**	**○**	**○**									○	○	○	○
Pigment condition		Mixer	○	**○**	○													
		Drum can		**○**														
		Raw material				○												
		Operation																
Transportation & storage																		
Pigment covering	Machine	Roller	○	○									○	○	○	○	**○**	
		Pump hose		○	○	○												
		Coating roll		○			○			○	○					○		
		Guiding roll	○							○	○							
		Cylinder			**○**	**○**					○							
		Handle	○	**○**						○	○							
		Cuer	○	**○**	**○**	**○**				○			○	○			○	
	Environment	Ceiling			**○**	**○**				○								
		Floor			**○**	**○**											○	
		Frame	○	**○**	**○**	**○**				○								
		Pipe	○	○	○	○				○								
		Cooling water	○							○	○							
Transportation & storage					○	○				○			○			○		
Finishing	Machine	Dew sprayer	○	○						○		○				○		
		Water mangle		**○**	**○**								○	○		○		
		Presser	○	○	**○**	**○**				○	○						○	
		Dew eliminator	○		○	○				○				○				
		Roll	**○**		**○**	**○**										○	○	
	Environment																	
Cutting	Machine	Single cutter	○		○												○	
		Guillotine	○															
		SE	○		○													○
	Environment floor																	○

○ : Strong relationship ○ : Relationship △ : Likely relationship

analysis, one of the multivariate analysis techniques. The matrix data-analysis method has been included as one of the seven new QC tools so that managers and staff can become more familiar with multivariate analysis techniques.

As an example of how this technique is used, Table 18.2 is presented as a data matrix showing the relationships between 40 uses of cloth and their desired qualities. Suppose that a new material, material *A*, is developed. The data in Table 18.2 does not readily provide information about the potential uses of material *A;* however, the matrix data-analysis method does offer answers by analyzing the data in Table 18.2.

Uses The matrix data-analysis method can be used to

- Analyze production processes where factors are complexly intertwined.
- Analyze causes of nonconformities that involve a large volume of data.
- Grasp the desired quality level indicated by the results of a market survey.
- Classify sensory characteristics systematically.
- Accomplish complex quality evaluations.
- Analyze curvilinear data.

Applications A principal-component analysis is performed on the matrix data provided in Table 18.2. The resulting first and second principal components are shown graphically in Figure 18.10. This figure reveals that the new material *A* would probably be better suited for skirts and trousers than for sports wear, work uniforms, or gloves.

The PDPC method

This technique helps determine which processes to use to obtain desired results by evaluating the progress of events and the variety of conceivable outcomes.

The method Implementation plans do not always progress as anticipated. When problems, technical or otherwise, arise, solutions are frequently not apparent.

The PDPC (process decision program chart) method, in response to these kinds of problems, anticipates possible outcomes and prepares countermeasures that will lead to the best possible solutions. By anticipating potential outcomes of events, this technique allows process adjustments in light of actual progress.

If an unanticipated event occurs, then it becomes necessary to rewrite the process decision program chart (PDPC) at once so that adjustive countermeasures can be taken.

The PDPC method[1] is borrowed from the operations research field for use in quality control.

TABLE 18.2 *Product uses and their desired qualities*

Uses	Desirable qualities						
	1 **Resists fading**	**2** **Washable**	**3** **Resists perspiration**	…	**23** **Flame retardant**	**24** **Chemical resistant**	**25** **Non-irritating to skin**
1. Men's summer suits	x_{1-1}	x_{1-2}	x_{1-3}	…	x_{1-23}	x_{1-24}	x_{1-25}
2. Men's all-season suits	x_{2-1}	x_{2-2}	x_{2-3}	…	x_{2-23}	x_{2-24}	x_{2-25}
3. Ladies' summer dresses	x_{3-1}	x_{3-2}	x_{3-3}	…	x_{3-23}	x_{3-24}	x_{3-25}
4. Ladies' all-season dresses	x_{4-1}	x_{4-2}	x_{4-3}	…	x_{4-23}	x_{4-24}	x_{4-25}
5. Skirts	x_{5-1}	x_{5-2}	x_{5-3}	…	x_{5-23}	x_{5-24}	x_{5-25}
6. Trousers	x_{6-1}	x_{6-2}	x_{6-3}	…	x_{6-23}	x_{6-24}	x_{6-25}
7. Overcoats	x_{7-1}	x_{7-2}	x_{7-3}	…	x_{7-23}	x_{7-24}	x_{7-25}
8. Raincoats	x_{8-1}	x_{8-2}	x_{8-3}	…	x_{8-23}	x_{8-24}	x_{8-25}
9. Office wear	x_{9-1}	x_{9-2}	x_{9-3}	…	x_{9-23}	x_{9-24}	x_{9-25}
10. Work clothes	x_{10-1}	x_{10-2}	x_{10-3}	…	x_{10-23}	x_{10-24}	x_{10-25}
11. Sportswear	x_{11-1}	x_{11-2}	x_{11-3}	…	x_{11-23}	x_{11-24}	x_{11-25}
12. Student wear	x_{12-1}	x_{12-2}	x_{12-3}	…	x_{12-23}	x_{12-24}	x_{12-25}
13. Home wear	x_{13-1}	x_{13-2}	x_{13-3}	…	x_{13-23}	x_{13-24}	x_{13-25}
14. Baby wear	x_{14-1}	x_{14-2}	x_{14-3}	…	x_{14-23}	x_{14-24}	x_{14-25}
15. Dress shirts	x_{15-1}	x_{15-2}	x_{15-3}	…	x_{15-23}	x_{15-24}	x_{15-25}
⋮ ⋮	⋮	⋮	⋮	⋮	⋮	⋮	⋮
40. Foot warmer blankets	x_{40-1}	x_{40-2}	x_{40-3}	…	x_{40-23}	x_{40-24}	x_{40-25}
Material *A*	x_1	x_2	x_3	…	x_{23}	x_{24}	x_{25}

FIGURE 18.10 ***Searching for uses of new material A***

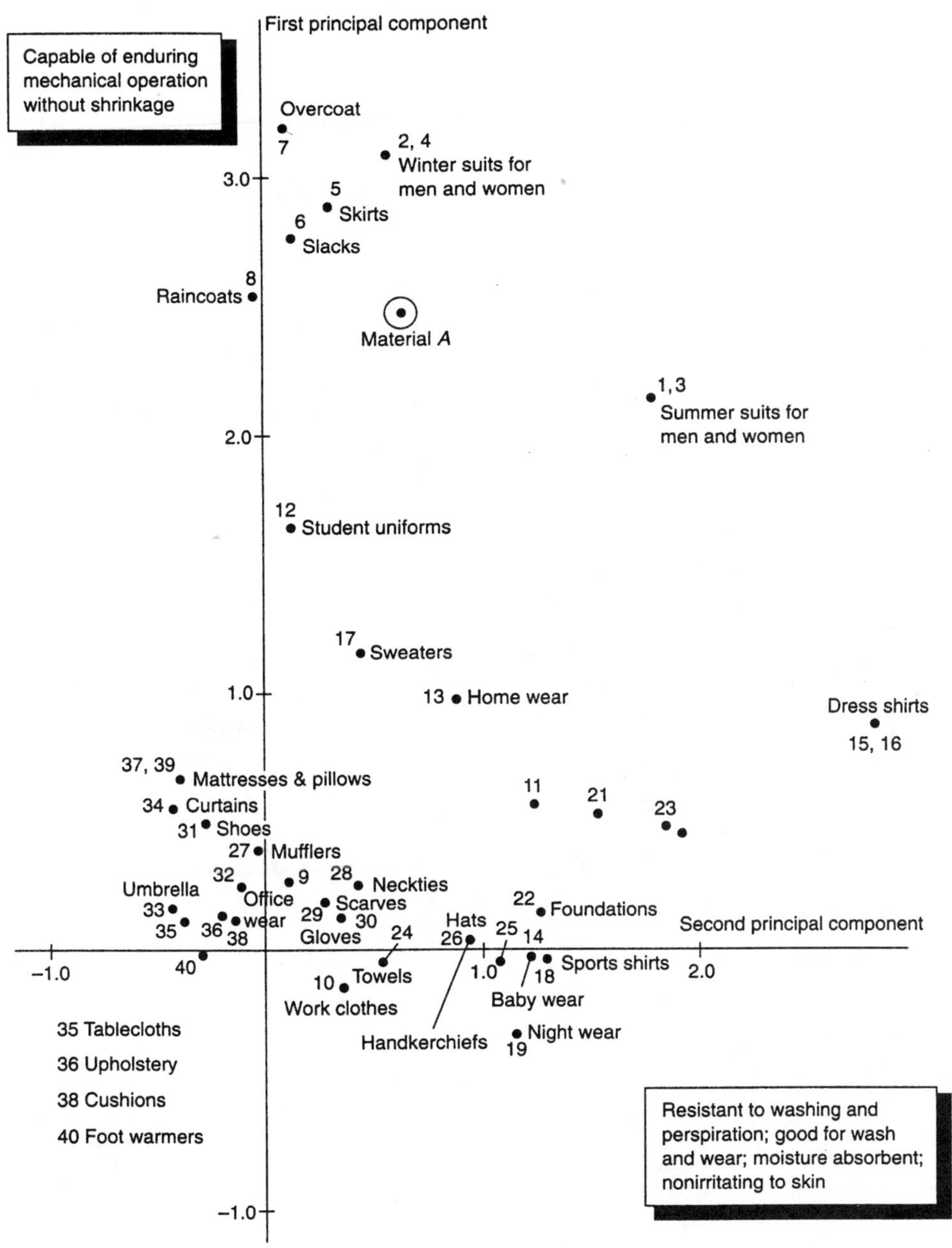

Uses The PDPC method can be used to

- Establish an implementation plan for management by objectives.
- Establish an implementation plan for technology-development themes.
- Establish a policy of forecasting and responding in advance to major events predicted in the system.
- Implement countermeasures to minimize nonconformities in the manufacturing process.
- Set up and select adjustment measures for the negotiating process.

Applications Suppose that a company's objective is to deliver a fragile item to an addressee in a developing country. The company must anticipate various contingencies from shipment time to delivery, and address all the problems that might arise as a result of transportation and landing. The company must then develop countermeasures to avoid possible mishaps. The PDPC method approach to this hypothetical example and the results are shown in Figure 18.11.

FIGURE 18.11 ***Delivery of fragile item (pattern II)***

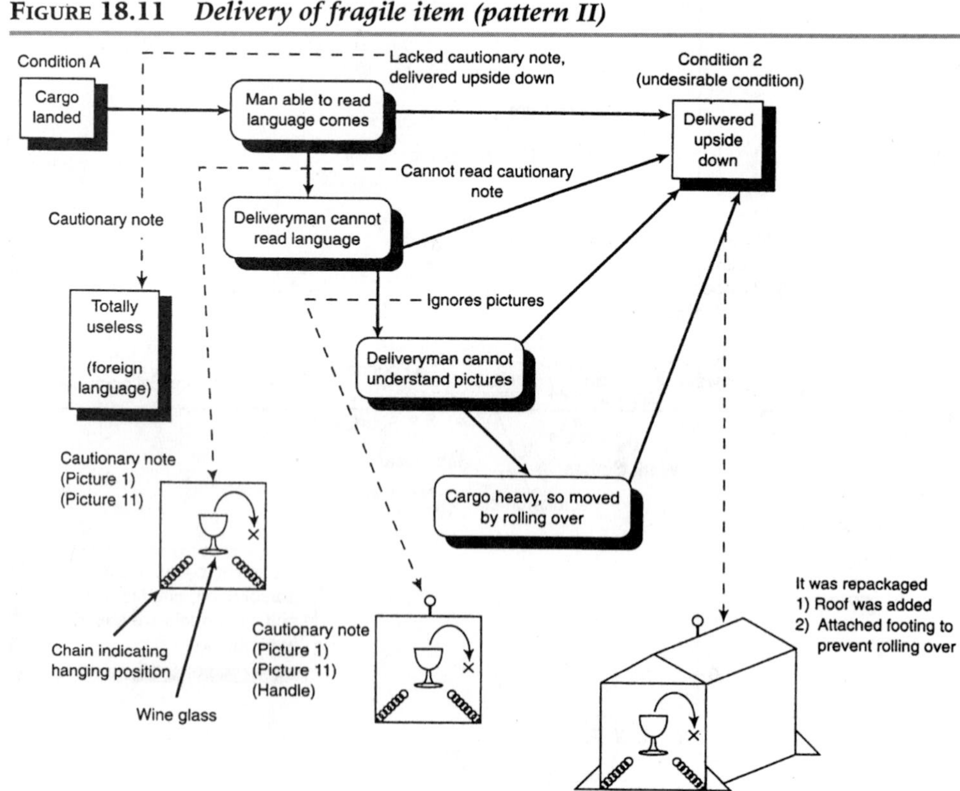

The arrow diagram method

This technique establishes the most suitable daily plan and monitors its progress efficiently.

The method The arrow diagram method, utilized by PERT and CPM, is a network diagram for daily plans. It illustrates the network of lines that connect all the elements related to plan execution, as shown in Figure 18.12.

Use of the arrow diagram method in advancing and monitoring daily plans has the following advantages:

1. It establishes a finely tuned plan.
2. It establishes the most suitable daily plan, since changes can be made easily during the early planning stages.
3. It allows one to cope easily with changes that occur in a given situation or during plan execution.
4. It expedites necessary action by quickly providing information on the impact delays in certain subparts will have on the operation as a whole.
5. It is increasingly useful in proportion to the size of the plans.
6. It controls the process efficiently because the progress highlights are easily discernible.

The control of daily plans is extremely important in the promotion of QC activities. An efficient method of constructing and utilizing arrow diagrams that employs cards will be introduced mainly to assist staff members.

Uses The arrow diagram method can be used to

- Implement plans for new product development and its follow-up.
- Develop product-improvement plans and follow-up activities.

FIGURE 18.12 ***Elements of an arrow diagram***

Elements of an Arrow Diagram

Operation

Fusion Point

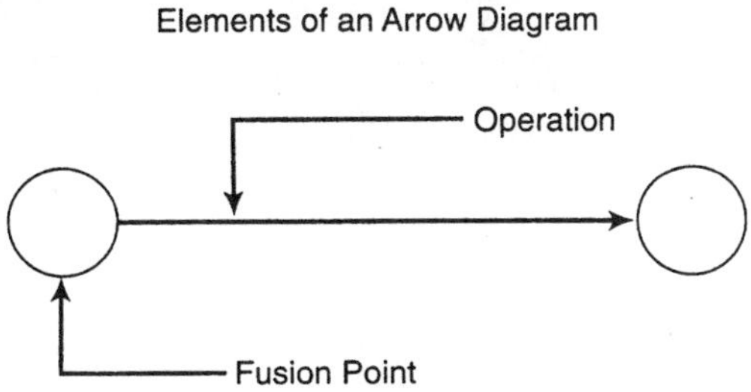

FIGURE 18.13 *Experimental trials and quality confirmation plan for VE improvement of special resistor electrodes*

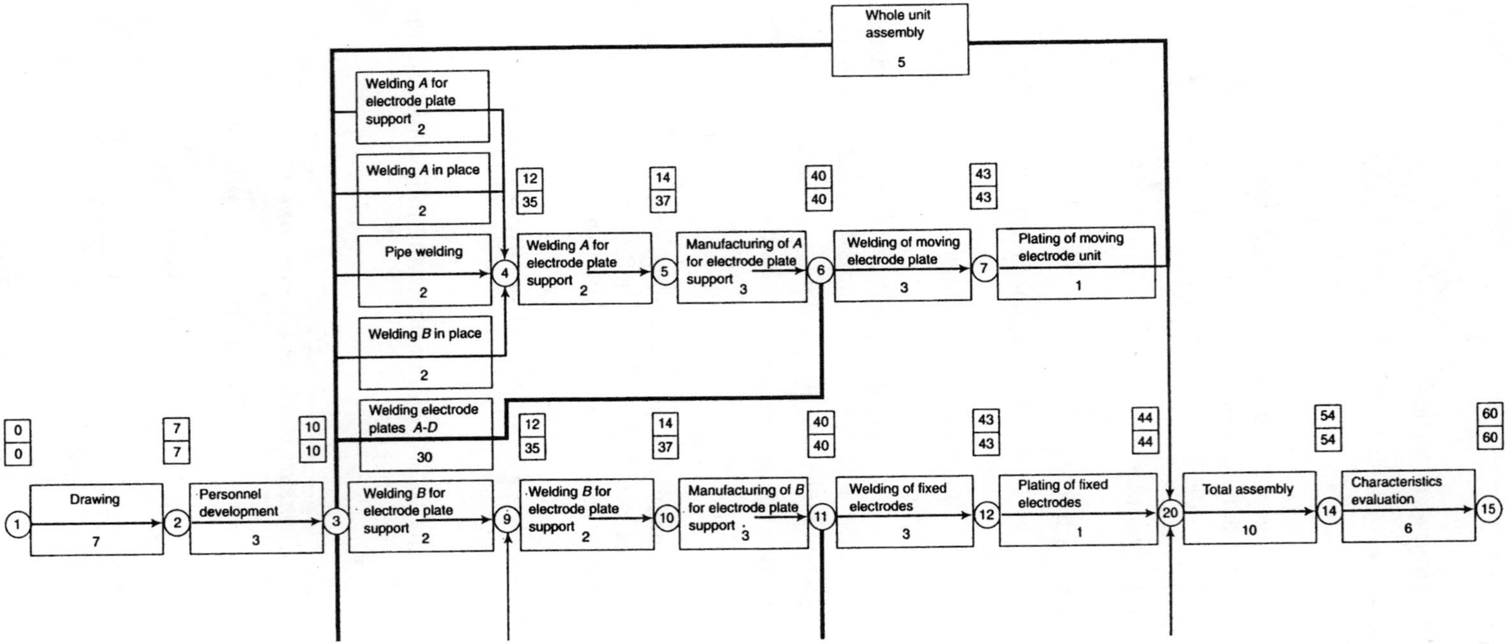

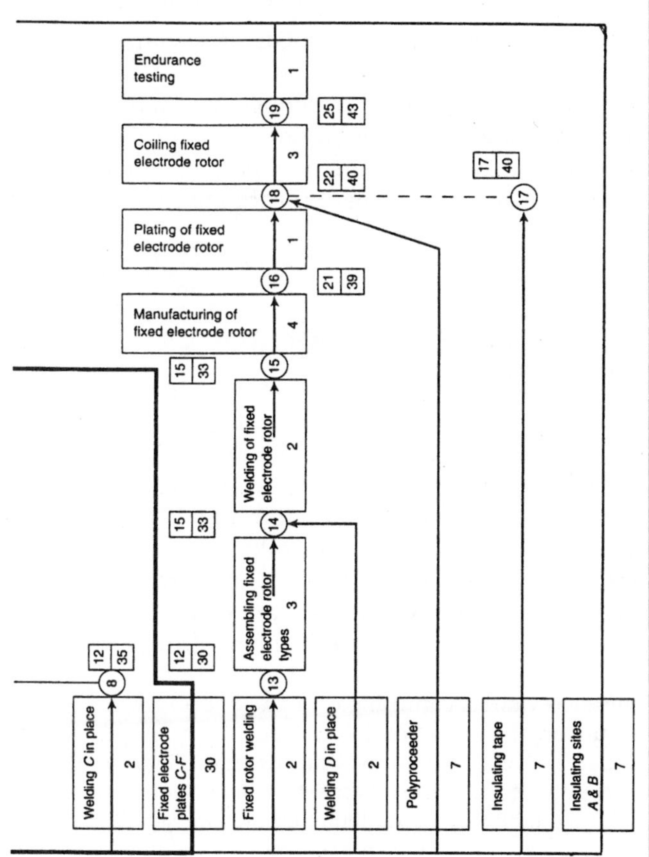

Endurance testing
1
Coiling fixed electrode rotor
3
Plating of fixed electrode rotor
1
Manufacturing of fixed electrode rotor
4
Welding of fixed electrode rotor
2
Assembling fixed electrode rotor types
3
Welding C in place
2
Fixed electrode plates C-F
30
Fixed rotor welding
2
Welding D in place
2
Polyproceeder
7
Insulating tape
7
Insulating sites A & B
7
8
12
35
12
30
13
14
15
15
33
15
33
16
21
39
18
22
40
19
25
43
17
17
40

- Establish daily plans for experimental trials and follow-up activities.
- Establish daily plans for increases in production and their follow-up.
- Synchronize the preceding plans with QC activities.
- Develop plans for a facility move and for monitoring follow-up.
- Implement a periodic facility maintenance plan and its follow-up.
- Analyze a manufacturing process and draw up plans for improved efficiency.
- Plan and follow up QC inspections and diagnostic tests.
- Plan and follow up QC conferences and QC circle conference.

Applications In a low-cost project to produce special resistor electrodes used in a starter for an electric motor, value engineering (VE) experimental trials and quality confirmation tests were implemented based on an arrow diagram (Figure 18.13) of daily plans constructed using the "card method." This diagram made the trials and tests possible.

THE ROLE OF THE SEVEN NEW QC TOOLS IN QUALITY CONTROL

The seven new tools proposed fulfill the planning steps often mentioned in the "plan, do, check, act" (PDCA) TQC cycle. Figure 18.14 graphically demonstrates the placement of various QC techniques applied in the *plan* and *do* stages to solve an important problem. If an adequate amount of past quantitative data is available, the traditional seven tools would probably suffice; however, this is not always the case in TQC problem solving. Therefore, Figure 18.14 should be viewed as relating to a situation where data are relatively scarce.

The plan stage can be divided into the following three phases:

Plan 1: This phase reviews a confusing event and arranges the information so to clarify the underlying nature of the problem.

Plan 2: This phase searches for various means that might be employed to solve the problem and identifies the relationships between the objectives and the means.

Plan 3: This phase establishes an implementation strategy in a time-order sequence in order to increase the chance for success.

During the plan 1 phase, the relations diagram and the KJ methods are used. During plan 2, the systematic diagram and matrix diagram methods, as well as the cause-and-effect diagram and matrix data-analysis methods are used. The plan 3 phase relies on the arrow diagram and the PDPC methods. The arrow diagram method is most often used when the sequence of steps is relatively fixed and predetermined, as in the construction of a building or in shortening the delivery time of a product. However, in QC-related activities, the original readings or plans frequently must be modified because of an unexpected development or occurrence. Whenever there is an unexpected development, information collected up to that point must be analyzed, underlying causes must be understood, and appropriate

FIGURE 18.14 *Relationship of seven new QC tools to traditional QC techniques*

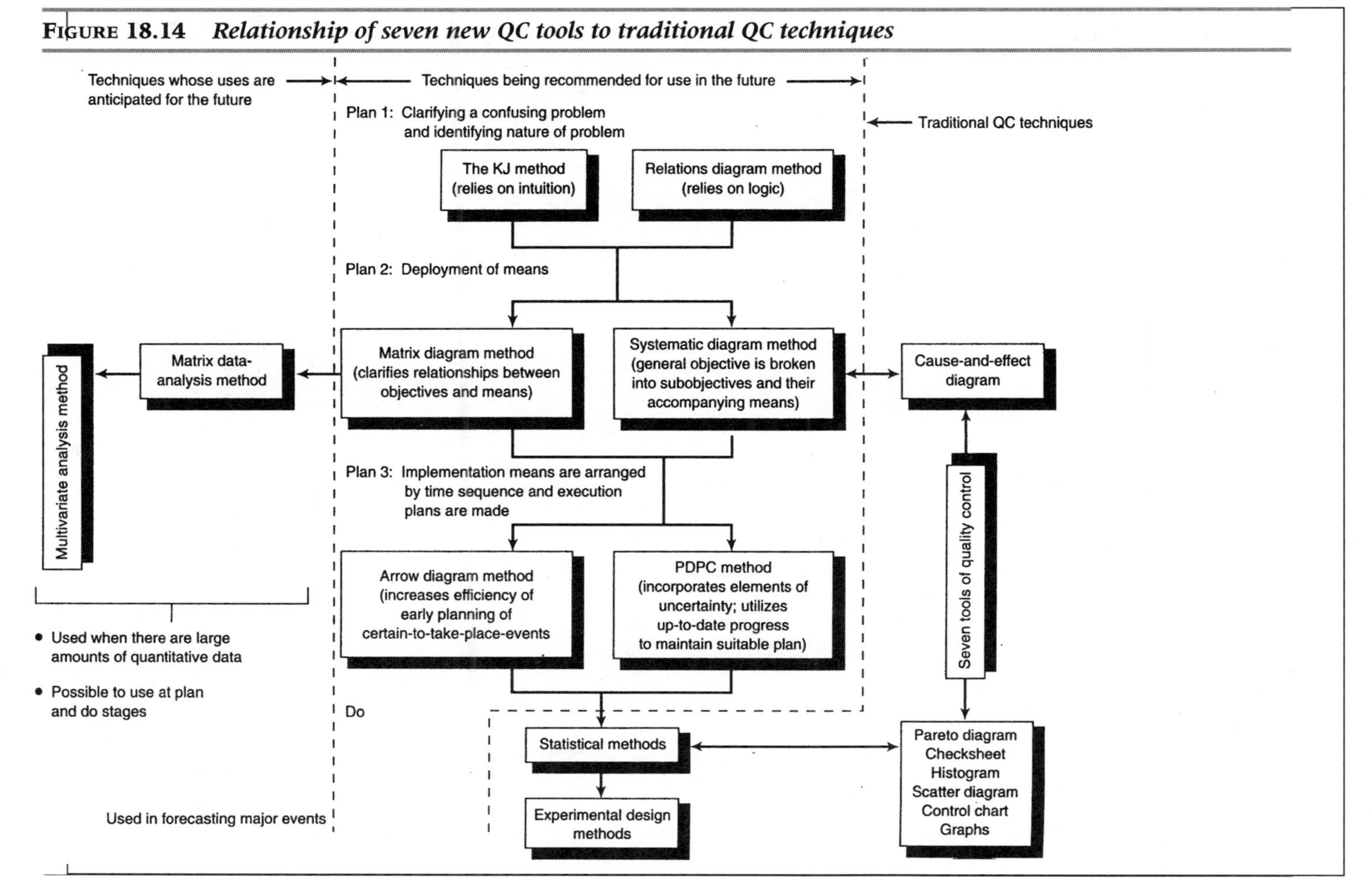

changes in plans must be made in order to achieve the overall objectives. The PDPC method is an extremely useful technique in such situations, and the PDPC method also can be used to forecast major accidents in such related areas as environmental hazards and product liability.

During the *do* stage, other statistical and experimental design methods are selected from the traditional seven tools depending on the particular circumstances of implementation.

Although the *check* and *act* stages of the PDCA cycle are not shown in Figure 18.14, they proceed from the outcome of the *do* stage. But in Figure 18.14 it is clear that the following six of the seven new tools should be used in every stage of TQC promotion in the future:

- Relations diagram method
- KJ method
- Systematic diagram method
- Matrix diagram method
- PDPC method
- Arrow diagram method

The matrix diagram method provides a readily comprehensible graphic representation of complex data when each cell in the matrix is given a numerical value. It corresponds to the principal-component analysis method, one of the multivariate analysis methods. Hopefully, the matrix diagram method will be accepted as a tool that can simplify and bring order to numerical or quantitative confusion.

During product planning and process-improvement activities, situations are frequently encountered in which numerous intertwined causes must be untangled. Keeping pace with the development of computers, many businesses have aggressively introduced this method with good results. Even though this technique should be brought to the attention of managers and staff, it should not necessarily be overused.

To prevent misunderstandings about the origin of the seven new QC tools, five points should be highlighted:

1. The seven methods described here do not necessarily exhaust the list. Selection of these seven tools came after much hesitation and thought. Actually, it is hoped that these techniques enrich QC techniques even further. Even people who use the traditional seven tools use them differently over time. Therefore, some modifications and revisions of the seven new tools in response to future developments are necessary. There is also nothing sacred about the number seven. What is essential is that one's toolbox contain all the useful and necessary tools.
2. Most of the techniques described above are already known and were not recently created as QC methods. This also applies to the traditional seven

tools, such as the histogram, Pareto chart, scatter diagram, and other statistical methods. Some of these even appear in elementary school textbooks. However, because of their promotion, along with the cause-and-effect diagram, as part of the seven tools for quality control, they have come to be used extensively in QC activities. By christening the preceding methods as the seven new QC tools, it is hoped that they too will receive the attention necessary to allow the development of diverse applications in fields concerned with quality control.

3. There are two important reasons for using the seven new tools as a group. One is that, as previously mentioned, the seven tools act like an organically integrated set; it would be hard to expect excellent results if they were used independently. The seven new tools should be used in combination, for best results in solving problems. The second reason is that the seven new tools are best used when promoted in all facets of operation under the direction of the company or department head. Effects are limited if the tools are used sporadically in isolated divisions or units.
4. The pioneers who promoted quality control deserve our thanks for having introduced various techniques and for having successfully completed the original seven QC tools, the statistical and experimental design methods for quality control. Unfortunately, however, over the course of the past decade or so, few innovative proposals similar to the ones promoted by the first-generation pioneers have been set forth. As the succeeding generation, though, it is important for us to gather all the seedlings and fruit of the preceding generation, develop them as much as possible in a systematic fashion, and pass them on to the next generation.
5. All the techniques described here have been used previously in various fields and have demonstrated some level of effectiveness. Although not unique to quality control, the requirements for using these tools include a keen awareness of the problem at hand, an incessant desire for improvement, and an enhanced spirit and thought process. Without these kinds of mental preparation, the tools cannot be used effectively. Anyone who expects a tool to do all the work cannot expect good results and cannot really be considered a "user."

THE SEVEN NEW QC TOOLS AND THE BASICS OF GRAPHICS-LANGUAGE THEORY[2]

As discussed earlier, the seven new tools make considerable use of graphics. Table 18.3 presents a classification system developed by T. Kahn[3] that shows the differences between language and graphics as they apply to manner of recognition and relative ease of understanding. When viewing graphics, we first comprehend the overall structure (pattern, balance, and trends of dots and lines) and then reach out for that which is interesting.

TABLE 18.3 *Differences between graphics and language*

	Graphics	Language
Manner of recognition:	First, the whole is grasped. Next, the elements are analyzed.	First, elements are recognized. Next, whole is constructed.
Ease of understanding:	Understood by almost anybody immediately (pictures).	If rules are not understood, then it is incomprehensible (foreign languages).

Regardless of nationality and race, any person can understand pictures. Language, however, presupposes an understanding of preexisting rules, without which the language is totally incomprehensible, for example, when a non-Japanese speaking person tries to make sense of Japanese characters. The understanding of graphics and language is analogous to the human developmental process. Infants start out as "contact beings," whose exchanges of information with others, including their mother, occur through physical contact. These contact beings later grow into "picture beings," who are able to understand information based on pictures, drawings, and graphics of various sorts. Finally, these picture beings turn into "character beings," who are capable of information transmission through written characters. The recent popularity of commercial drawings and comic books may be viewed as an extension of the picture-being stage. In other words, the human capability to understand graphic forms easily seems to be a developmental characteristic. It should be evident that tools anchored in graphics will emerge as powerful techniques in the promotion of company-wide total quality control because of their ready comprehension by all concerned.

Computer graphics theorists distinguish pictures that contain characters, such as the seven new tools, from graphics that contain only drawings by calling them "graphics language." The graphics-language group is further divided into the following four types:

1. Relational system
2. Network system
3. Column-row system
4. Coordinate system

A further explanation of these system types is contained in *Computer Graphics Theory.* However, their names alone suggest their meanings. Of the four types listed, the coordinate system has been in use the longest. Table 18.4 shows the seven new and seven "old" tools classified into the different graphics-language types. Notice that the "old" tools are primarily coordinate-based, while the new tools rely primarily on the relational or network systems.

Experience has shown that the ease or difficulty involved in constructing graphics for the seven new tools varies from one person to another. The graphics tools used can also be divided into two groups:

TABLE 18.4 ***The seven new tools and the traditional seven tools classified by graphics-language systems***

Graphics-language system	Seven new tools	Traditional seven tools
Relational system	KJ method	—
Network system	Relations diagram method Systematic diagram method Arrow diagram method PDPC method	Cause-and-effect diagram
Column-row system	Matrix diagram method	Checksheet
Coordinate system	Matrix data-analysis method	Pareto chart Histogram Scatter diagram Control chart Graphs

Soft graphic tools: The KJ method, the relations diagram method, and the PDPC method offer a relatively greater degree of freedom in graphics construction.

Hard graphic tools: The systematic diagram method, the matrix diagram method, and the arrow diagram method have considerably less freedom in graphics construction.

Even though the former may appear to be the easier to people just starting to use the new tools, they are actually more difficult because they allow a greater degree of freedom. Nevertheless, some beginners have produced outstanding graphics.

A necessary step in company-wide QC activities is for all employees to become thoroughly acquainted with pictorial or graphic thinking. This is accomplished by practicing the construction of various graphics and through the cooperation of everyone involved. All employees should be exposed to a wide variety of graphics so they may identify their own weak areas and learn to construct the diagrams properly. Only this kind of total exposure will make the combined use of all the seven new tools feasible.

Notes

1. Kondo Jiro, *Operations Research* (Tokyo: JUSE Press, Ltd., 1973), pp. 128–136.
2. This section relies heavily on information in Chaps. 2 and 3 of *Computer Graphics Theory,* by Yoshikawa Hiroyuki, published by JUSE Press in 1977. Grateful acknowledgment is due.
3. Yoshikawa Hiroyuki, *Computer Graphics Theory* (Tokyo: JUSE Press, Ltd., 1977).

Reading 19

Decision and Planning Tools

BY GLEN D. HOFFHERR AND NORMAN W. YOUNG

In our daily business we face many situations for which we do not have detailed factual information. We are forced to make decisions on what we think rather than on what we know. We then apply the accumulation of our experiences, knowledge, and possibly the recommendations of our associates to make the decision. We are generally thought to have good judgment if the results of our decisions are good for the organization. Decisions that do not bring about the desired results may cause our judgment to be called into question. The tools in this article will help you make better decisions by focusing on the information you have.

There is a group of tools often called the *7 New QC tools,* or the *7 Management and Planning tools.* These names do not describe the power of these tools or who should use them. They would more accurately be called decision and planning tools. This article lists and describes the authors' favorite decision and planning tools. They are used most effectively to make decisions and plans when you do not have hard data or facts. There is no right or wrong way to use any of these tools. Remember that the purpose of any tool is to enable you to make a better decision. These tools are powerful vehicles for gathering, organizing, examining, and presenting the collective judgments of you and your coworkers. They will improve the quality of the decisions you make and increase your success at solving problems and achieving goals.

Many of these tools can be used in multiple ways. Some have facets that predispose them to certain situations. As you work with the tools, you will find that you use some every day and others infrequently. You will develop comfort and expertise with the tools you use most often.

SOURCE: Much of the information contained in this article is taken from *The Toolbook: Decision Making & Planning for Optimum Results* and the courseware that is associated with it. The authors gratefully acknowledge the publisher, Markon Inc., for granting permission to use excerpts from these two works.

In our zeal to develop the science of leadership and decision making, we often overuse tools and techniques. The result is that we lose sight of the goal that we are trying to accomplish or miss an opportunity through analysis paralysis. Thus, it is most important to know when not to use tools. When the proper decision is clear to all concerned, when you have adequate resources, and everyone is in agreement—ACT! You will, however, want to employ the tools when:

- you are having difficulty analyzing complex alternatives,
- you disagree with coworkers and must find a way to come to consensus,
- you need to organize large volumes of data,
- you have limited resources and must set priorities, or
- you want to develop a complete plan including priorities, schedules, and contingency plans.

These tools organize judgmental or soft data into clear pictures that promote effective decision making. Successful decision making begins with the proper mindset. In traditional organizations, we have assumed that one person, the manager, has all the answers. As our world has become more complex, so have the decisions we face. Today everyone in the organization must be able to make good decisions; they must have the appropriate tools to be able to function adequately in their jobs.

Today good decisions involve the consideration of many alternatives. Through the participation of others, we search for every possible option. We try to consider what could go wrong. Our attitudes towards others and the process we use will affect the value we receive. To receive the most benefit from these tools:

- value the differences of others; they can offer a different point of view,
- value the ideas of others; this will keep creative ideas flowing,
- embrace ambiguity; it promotes creativity,
- be flexible; this will lead to more effective planning,
- trust your (and others') initial reactions; it may prevent making fundamental mistakes, and
- use them only when they are needed, not because you think you should.

Each tool is different, but there are some common guidelines that make all the tools more effective.

- Get the right people to form the group—diverse, willing, and skilled.
- Empower the group by defining operating limits, granting the authority to make changes, providing protection, support, and resources, and defining measures of accountability.
- Clearly define the opportunity or goal.

- Allow time to complete the process.
- Include new ideas at any time.
- Make decisions only by consensus. Majority vote creates winners and losers. The time required to reach consensus will be offset by the speed of implementation.
- **Make the tool work for you, do not work for the tool.**

These tools are known by many different names. The name listed first is the authors' choice. The tools that will be covered in this article are brainstorming, forced choice, card sort (affinity diagram), cause and effect map (relationship diagram, ID), selection window, tree diagram, force field analysis, matrices, problem prevention plan (contingency plan, PDPC), and PERT chart (CPM, arrow diagram).

BRAINSTORMING

Brainstorming is the most commonly used method for the generation of a large number of ideas in a group setting. Despite its widespread usage, there remains a body of empirical data that indicates that its use by individuals or nominal groups (groups that never physically meet) may be more effective than its use by people in a meeting-type setting. We think brainstorming is most effective when used by a group of four to nine people.

Like many commonly used tools, there is some confusion regarding the source of brainstorming. Mizuno in the *7 New QC Tools* (1979), indicated that it was introduced to Japan in 1952. Donelson Forsyth in *An Introduction To Group Dynamics* (1983) cites the following version.

> Brainstorming was developed in 1957 by Alex F. Osborne, an advertising executive. He defined four traits which contributed to the generation of new alternatives or ideas. Virtually all brainstorming work today is based on the traits of expressiveness, non-evaluative, quantity, and building as described below.
>
> Osborne recommended:
>
> - recording all of the ideas in full view of participants,
> - stimulating ideas by asking open-ended questions,
> - utilizing a turn-taking procedure if interaction becomes unequal,
> - evaluating ideas at a later session.
>
> In 1974, Rickards added the idea of warm up exercises to 'break the ice' and get discussion started.
>
> Experience has shown that training in brainstorming procedures, practicing brainstorming, and allowing the participants to record their ideas after the brainstorming session improves the group's proficiency.

The cornerstone of judgmental decision making is the generation of creative alternatives. Virtually every decision and planning tool requires such alternatives.

As a freewheeling vehicle for getting new ideas, brainstorming can help a group break through existing patterns of thought and generate new options. Often, however, we fail to get the results we need by omitting one of the few **but critical** rules of brainstorming. Remember, creativity is the result of productive controversy. The following rules apply to any type of group creative process, including brainstorming.

1. **Expressiveness.** Each individual in the group must have complete freedom to express any idea that comes to mind, no matter how strange, wild, or fanciful. Freewheeling ideas are encouraged, and constraint is avoided.
2. **Non-evaluative.** Ideas are not to be evaluated in any way during the generation phase. All ideas are valuable, and criticizing another's viewpoint is not allowed. A negative comment can stifle the energy and creativity of a group so that the exercise becomes useless.
3. **Quantity.** The goal of the generation process is to create as many ideas as possible. Even the most unrealistic idea can provide the stimulus or basis for a totally new and valuable idea. Having many new ideas increases the possibility of generating excellent solutions.
4. **Building.** Brainstorming is conducted in a group so that participants can draw from one another. We draw from each other by modifying and adding to our ideas. This will create mental bridges to new opportunities.

To complete a brainstorming session, first select a purpose. Be as specific as possible, but consider the resources available to the group. Be sure everyone in the group fully understands and agrees with the purpose. Next, organize your group. Decide who will write, and where the ideas will be placed for best visibility. Be sure to place only one idea on a card and write clearly so that everyone can read the cards. Be wild! Impossible ideas can stimulate spontaneity and help to suspend critical judgment. Finally, set a time limit. The pressure of a time limit helps to put evaluation on hold. It is the creative, right side of the brain that has the ability to react, while the evaluative left brain requires time to think through any new idea. The output of a typical brainstorming session is shown in Figure 19.1.

FORCED CHOICE

Forced choice is an adaptation of a forced choice matrix from a training course taught by M. B. Bryce Associates in the late 1960s. It relies on a basic pairwise comparison to aid the user in sorting large lists, or lists where there is little difference between the options presented. In its matrix form, the forced choice was cumbersome to use and required the use of special preprinted matrix forms.

The free form adaptation described here was developed by N. W. Young in 1981 when he created a list-based pairwise comparison in a basic language computer program. It was further refined for use in a facilitated group setting to aid the group in reaching consensus on the priority of options in a list.

FIGURE 19.1 ***Results of brainstorming***

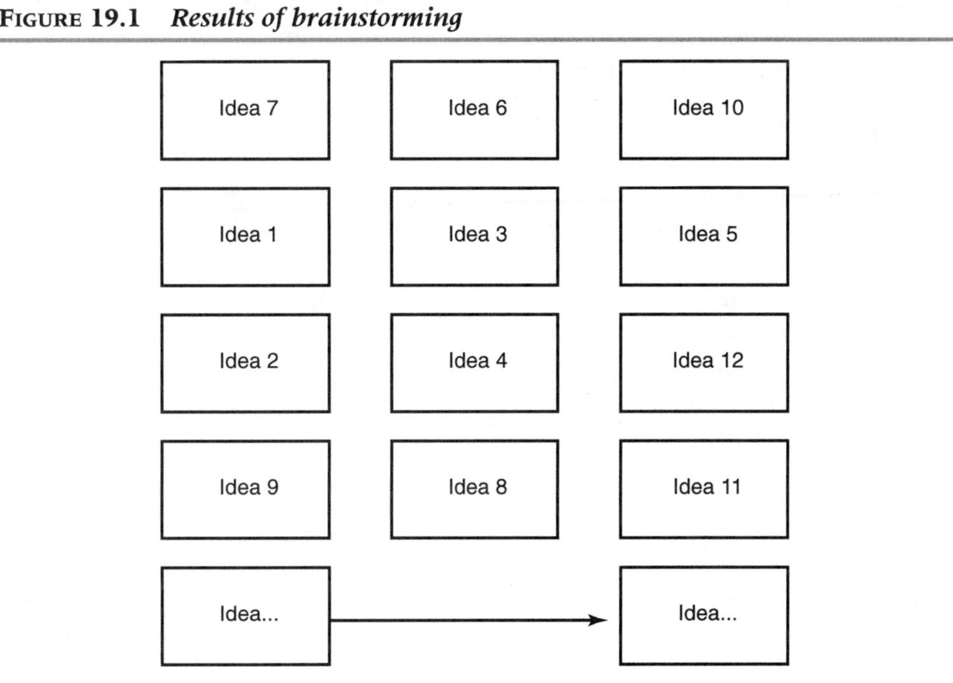

The forced choice requires a list of items or alternatives to be sorted against an agreed-upon standard. Each alternative is measured against the standard. It also requires a method of marking the choices made during a sort. Completing the forced choice can help you make choices in complex situations, as well as to help defuse difficult political situations by helping a group make choices together. It is most effective in defining areas of inconsistency in logic and is easily completed individually or in a group.

To complete a forced choice, select a list to be sorted or ranked. This list can be the product of a creative effort, such as brainstorming or any other situation that produces alternatives to be sorted. Write the list where everyone can see it. Leave a blank area or column to the right. Draw a line to separate the area on the right from the list and additional lines to separate each of the alternatives. This is not required, but it will simplify the necessary record keeping. Now define a standard for the sort. When selecting standards, consider customer impact, satisfaction, time, cost, level of quality, and so on. The standard must be clearly voiced.

Then perform a pairwise comparison to isolate a single choice among many choices. The comparison will focus all resources on the single choice and simplify the process of selection. Since the number of comparisons required to sort or rank a list grows rapidly as the list gets longer, the use of the pairwise comparison is limited only by time. Begin the pairwise comparison of each item in the list with every other item in the list. Form a sentence using the items being compared and the standard of comparison. Make a mark in the right-hand column for the item that wins the comparison. Continue using the same comparison until each possible pairwise comparison has been made once. To ensure that no possible comparisons are missed and none are performed more than once, use the following methodology.

a. Compare the **1st** item with each item below it in the list, that is, compare item 1 with item 2, compare item 1 with item 3, compare item 1 with item 4, and so on until you reach the end of the list.
b. Compare the **2nd** item with each item below it in the list, that is, compare item 2 with item 3, compare item 2 with item 4, and so on until you reach the end.
c. Compare the **nth** item with each item below it in the list, that is, compare item n with item n+1, compare item n with item n+2, and so on.
d. The last comparison will be the next to last item with the last item.

After you have completed all comparisons, summarize and analyze the results by adding the number of marks each item received and writing that number at the end of the row. The item, or option, with the highest number has best met the standard. Those with lower numbers have met the standard to a lesser degree. Understanding of the results will be improved for larger lists by rewriting the list in numerical order from the top to the bottom.

Beware of items that have the same numerical value. This points out areas where the results of your comparisons were inconsistent or circular reasoning was used. Such inconsistencies near the bottom of your list (after reordering) will have little effect on your future efforts. Inconsistencies at or near the top of the reordered list suggest fuzzy comprehension of the most important items. Further discussion and more research may be necessary before you are ready to take action, based on the results of the forced choice. Figure 19.2 shows how to complete a forced choice.

CARD SORT (AFFINITY DIAGRAM)

The card sort is a generic name for a tool that uses the creativity of a group to organize large amounts of information or complex situations into manageable order. It begins with a clearly defined purpose to keep the group on track. It then uses creative techniques, such as brainstorming or mind mapping, to generate a large volume of ideas. Finally, silent sorting promotes group interaction without criticism.

The card sort has a long history and is known by several other names and variations including the following:

The **person card sort** was used in anthropological work in the 1930s to sort information about artifacts. It was also used to some advantage during the Watergate investigations and to plan the Apollo moon landings.

FIGURE 19.2 ***Forced choice using brainstormed list***

GREATEST IMPACT ON REDUCED SALES

Out of Control Processes	///	3
Flexibility to Customer Needs	//	2
Customer Communication Difficulties	////	(4)
Product Quality Is Lacking	/	1
Product Shipping Problems		0

The **KJ Method** is the registered trademark of Jiro Kawakita who is credited with creating the card sort as we know it today. In the 1960s this Japanese anthropologist developed the rules that allow us to sift efficiently through large amounts of data and to allow new patterns of information to rise to the surface.

The **affinity diagram** is a variation of the KJ Method first documented in *The 7 New QC Tools* by Shigeru Mizuno.

The **Shiba method** is a creation of Shobi Shiba, a Japanese consultant who was a student of Dr. Kawakita. He uses a new rule set, popularized at the Center for Quality in Boston, Massachusetts, based on logical rather than intuitive methods.

The **whole brain affinity model** was developed by Glen Hoffherr, John Moran, and Richard Talbot and published in GOAL/QPC's *Competitive Times Newsletter.* The whole brain affinity takes the power and strength of the traditional card sort and adds Ned Herrmann's brain dominance model. The Herrmann brain dominance model is a metaphorical interpretation of how we think. This seminal work on problem solving combines the two into a colorful implementation of the card sort that shows the cognitive styles of the participant group.

The card sort combines techniques from the variations to produce an integrated tool that performs the task in a straightforward manner.

The card sort is a technique to bring order and structure to a large number of ideas. It helps a group reach consensus. Its primary strength is that it promotes interaction without criticism and facilitates building a plan. It can provide the synergy to break through old paradigms that might have prevented progress in the past as well as unite a group that has been divided on an issue. The card sort works best with a diverse group of four to nine people that contains at least one content expert. It begins with a clear statement of purpose to focus the group's energy. Materials such as 3″ × 5″ cards or Post-it® notes to facilitate the gathering and movement of ideas are a must.

To complete a card sort, first select a purpose. Be as specific as possible, but consider the resources available to the group. The purpose may be assigned, result from the use of some other tool or method, or evolve from your current discussion. Be sure the purpose is worded clearly and everyone in the group fully understands and agrees. Write the purpose where it can be clearly seen by the entire group. The more important the purpose, the easier it is to motivate the group to generate ideas.

Headline the purpose and record ideas, leaving ample space to list more ideas. Generate a list of ideas typically through brainstorming. There are a number of other creative techniques, including mind mapping and dialogue, that can help generate the list. (The list may already exist from some other source, in which case simply transfer it to the card sort medium.)

Each idea should be expressed in at least three words, including a noun and a verb. Place only one idea on a card and write clearly. As each idea is placed where everyone can see it, someone should read it aloud. When the group has posted all of the ideas, it is time to begin sorting.

The sorting process is a group activity. The idea cards must be accessible to all members of the group. Sort the cards by picking up a card and placing it next to another card that you feel is related. Cards can be moved several times and put in a new cluster. The sorting is done in silence by all members of the group at the same time. Continue sorting in silence until the sorting visibly slows down. This will normally require about 15 to 20 minutes. Each cluster of cards should contain no more than nine.

The next step is to develop headers. During this part of the card sort, there is opportunity for much interaction and discussion. The group must generate a header for each cluster. The header ideally summarizes and compresses all the ideas of the cards in the cluster. Any card that does not fit within a cluster should be set to the side for later consideration. Each header statement needs at least three words, including a noun and a verb. Headers should be as specific as possible to reduce the chance for misinterpretation. The group reaches consensus on the theme and wording of each header. When a header has been defined and accepted, place it above the cards in the cluster. This header card should be clearly marked to distinguish it from the idea cards. The group may choose to use an idea card as a header. If this is done, be sure it is clearly marked as a header. Each card in a cluster should also be marked with the identification of the header. This can be a letter, number, color, or even a word if the cards are large enough. Figure 19.3 shows how a completed card sort would appear.

FIGURE 19.3 ***Card sort using brainstormed list***

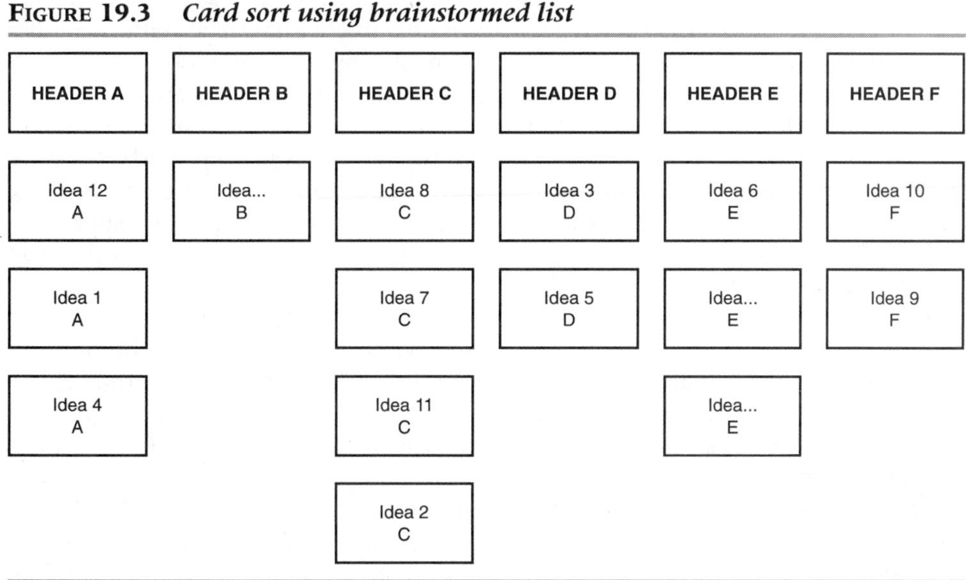

CAUSE AND EFFECT MAP (RELATIONSHIP DIAGRAM, ID)

In *The 7 New QC Tools* Shigeru Mizuno describes the "Relations Diagram Method" as having been developed by The Society for QC Technique Development in 1979. It was based on the work of T. Brown in a 1977 paper titled, "Inquiry into the Relation of Cause and Effect," Delmar, New York: Scholar's Facsimiles and Reprints. The method was created to:

- analyze problems with a complex network of causes and effects, and
- view the whole problem from a broad perspective.

Another name for the tool is *interrelationship digraph* or *ID*. The authors have not been able to find any reason for this choice of name and no adequate definition of *digraph* has been unearthed.

Cause and effect relationships exist when the action of one item determines or creates conditions (effects) in another item. Understanding cause and effect relationships allows groups to focus resources where they are most likely to produce results. They also provide a beginning point for developing the order of tasks and process steps, balancing resource distribution to prevent overloading, and isolating root causes to focus continuous improvement efforts in any planning process. Cause and effect networks are complex sets of relationships.

The cause and effect map is a technique to display graphically this type of relationship, invoking the intuitive right side of the brain. This method helps determine cause and effect relationships by providing a way to visually identify key driving forces as root causes, as well as point out key bottlenecks (major effects). The cause and effect map can help a group effectively analyze situations with a complex network of cause and effect relationships by providing a broad perspective. Key drivers are primary, or root causes, that are having the greatest impact on the network. They are often the most effective place to concentrate efforts to resolve the entire situation. Bottlenecks are the restraints in a network. They are effected by the most causes and usually cannot be resolved by themselves. The cause and effect map requires a set of interrelated options, ideas, or issues to be analyzed. It is best completed by a group of four to nine people, drawing the map where everyone can see it.

To complete the cause and effect map, begin by identifying the topic or purpose for the map and putting it at the top of the work area. Now write the options, ideas, or issues to be analyzed in a circular pattern. Write large enough that everyone can read the options. After placing the options around a circular pattern, number them to make the process of comparison easier to track. Numbering is particularly important with larger option lists.

When the options have been placed on the map, it is time to begin the process of pairwise comparisons. Each option must be compared just once with each of the other options to determine if there is a cause and effect relationship. When such a relationship is found, draw a line with an arrow pointing to the effect. If no relationship is found, simply proceed to the next pair. (To keep track of the comparisons, it helps to proceed in an orderly fashion. Compare option one with option two, then option one with option three, and so on until you have traversed the entire circle of options.)

When option one has been compared to each of the others, then start with option two and compare it with option three and all of the other options except option one. The cause and effect relationship between option two and option one was already examined. After completing the option two comparisons, continue around the circle comparing each option with every other option just once until you have a map of options connected by their relationships.

Analyze the map by counting the number of incoming arrows and outgoing arrows for each option and note the numbers for in and out beside the option as shown in Figure 19.4. The option or options with the highest number of outgoing arrows are the primary drivers or root causes. Changes in these options will affect the majority of the other options. Therefore, resources applied to these areas can produce pronounced change.

The option or options that are receiving the most incoming arrows are key bottlenecks. These outcomes are affected by many other options and may even be inhibiting other options from proceeding as they should. Mark visibly the key drivers and bottlenecks to further clarify your map in complex networks.

Be certain to examine only cause and effect relationships. If the group stays with this criteria, it is probable that only about 50 percent of the relationships will have arrows. In addition, this tool forces a group to make a decision since it does not allow for two-way arrows. Figure 19.4 shows a completed cause and effect map.

FIGURE 19.4 *Cause and effect map using card sort headers*

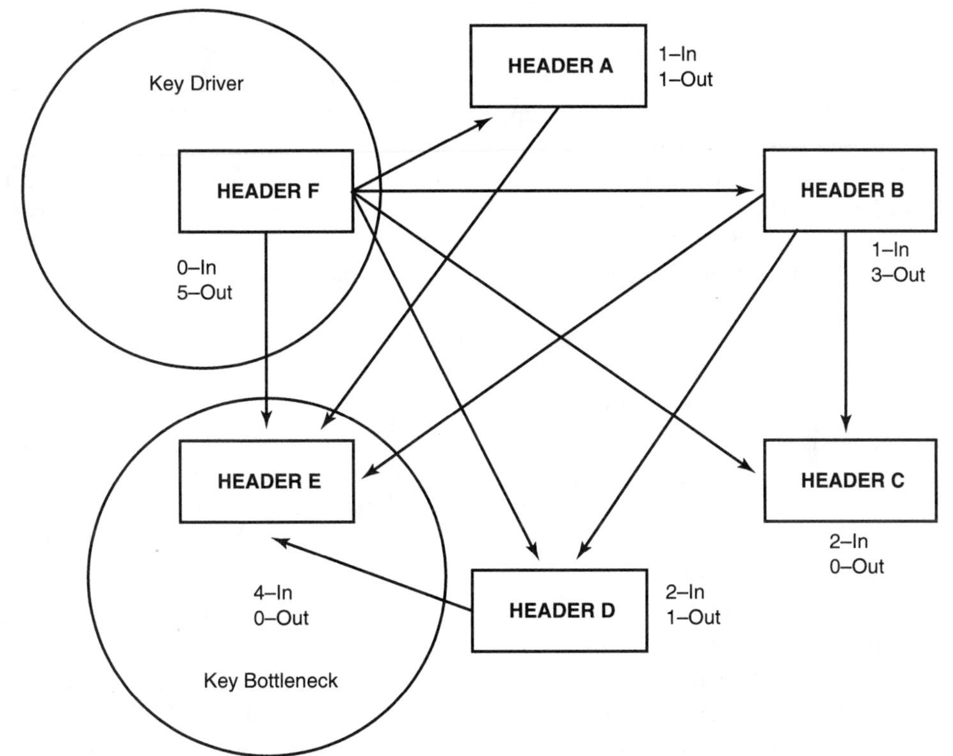

SELECTION WINDOW

A bit of wisdom from a book by Peter Drucker, *The Effective Executive,* taught that effectiveness comes not from doing things well but from "doing the right things." The selection window is a helpful vehicle for choosing the right thing to do. Apart from *The Toolbook,* the authors are unaware of any other sources for this tool. In his national best-seller, *The Seven Habits of Highly Effective People,* Stephen Covey describes a tool he calls "The Time Management Matrix." Using scales of importance and urgency, he teaches us to create the habit of putting first things first, or doing the right thing. The selection window uses a similar rationale but uses the scales of importance and effort. It is designed to integrate your resources and purposes and help you to decide what is the right thing to do.

The selection window is a simple technique to select the right things to do, integrating effort and importance with your purpose. It is a method for deciding when to use groups, as well as a way to evaluate and understand the importance and effort (resources) needed. It requires a clearly defined high-level purpose, a list of options or alternatives to accomplish the purpose, and the time to provide a careful consideration of each option. The selection window can keep you focused on your purpose and aid in short- and long-term projects.

To complete the selection window, begin by identifying your purpose. It helps to write your purpose where it can be a constant reminder. Generate a list of options, alternatives, or opportunities that can help you accomplish your purpose. One list that often benefits by this type of analysis is the "To Do" list.

Begin the selection window by drawing a square containing four equal boxes. The boxes must be large enough to write the opportunities inside. Mark the square with effort on the left and importance on the bottom. Use a numerical scale from a low of 1 to a high of 10. Evaluate each option against the criteria of effort and importance. Now review the selection window and take appropriate action.

Do Now. Items of high importance and low effort should be done immediately. These are the "right" things that you have the resources and time to do now. Each will have significant impact on achieving your purpose.

To Do. Items of low importance and low effort should be placed on a "To Do" list. Use these items as fillers. Although they are of low importance (we did not say no importance), they are possibly important enough to justify a small expenditure of resources. Be careful! It may seem unimportant to determine priorities, but these areas can dominate our time to the exclusion of our most important items.

Forget. Items of low importance and high effort do not justify the expenditure of the high level of resources required to complete them.

Groups. Items of high importance and high effort should be the focus of groups. They are important enough to deserve the attention that only a skilled group of people working together effectively can supply. They will determine whether or not you accomplish your purpose.

Figure 19.5 shows a completed selection window on things that could be done to satisfy a customer in a small office supply company.

TREE DIAGRAM

The concept of using a *tree* or subdividing a subject like branches of a tree is not new. We have all seen tree-type diagrams used to portray the structure and relationships within an organization. The traditional organization chart is a vertical tree. Saaty points out in *Decision Making for Leaders,* that hierarchies or trees are the mechanism the brain uses to structure and store complex information.

In *The 7 New QC Tools,* Mizuno introduces the systematic diagram with the alternate name of *dendrogram* from the Greek word for tree. The dendrogram is used "to find the most appropriate option." Mizuno then goes on to describe the wide variety of uses for the tree diagram, including:

- Functional analysis (from value engineering)
- Correlation tree

FIGURE 19.5 *Selection window using card sort headers*

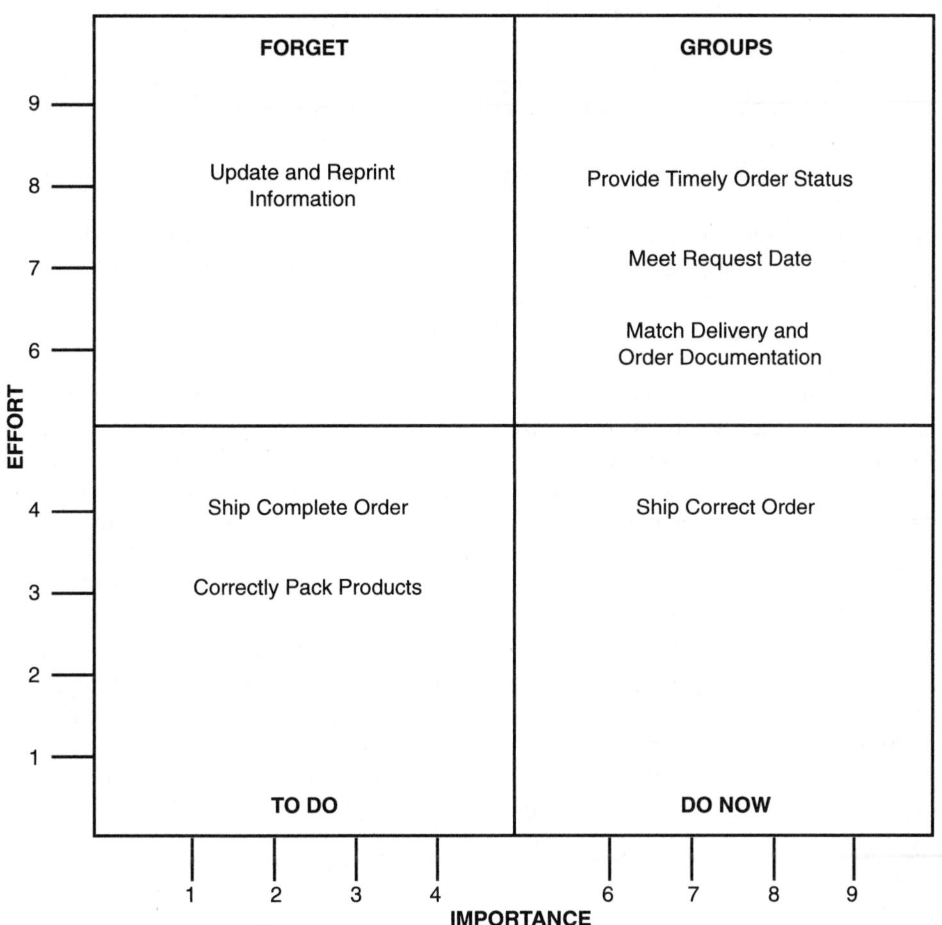

- Reverse PERT chart
- Decision tree
- Fault tree analysis
- YS technique (Yabiki Seiichiro)

The tree diagram is designed to expand a purpose into the tasks required to accomplish it. In this form it is also called an *outline diagram*. The tree diagram starts with a stated purpose and enables you to view the full range of details required to accomplish your purpose. It is also a method to expand your purpose into tasks to be performed. It can be used by individuals or a group of people focused on the purpose. The tree diagram is one method for viewing a complete hierarchy of tasks and their linkages. It provides the structure to ensure a complete plan.

Begin the tree diagram by reviewing your purpose to be accomplished. Be sure everyone in the group clearly understands the purpose. A review of your criteria for success at this point can further clarify planning. Write the purpose at the top or the left of your work area. The tree diagram can be expanded in any direction, but the left-to-right format lends itself to using other tools after completing the tree diagram.

The diagram will be easy to read if you enclose the purpose and the other elements of the tree diagram in boxes. Using cards or Post-it® notes can make it easier to reorganize the tree if it grows in an unexpected direction. You cannot predict the number of branches that will be formed, or the number of divisions for each branch.

Generate all the high-level tasks, or "targets" that must be completed to accomplish the purpose. Targets are those things that combined together accomplish the purpose and can be developed by applying brainstorming to the purpose. Another method is to use the headers or idea cards developed in a card sort performed on the purpose. A tree diagram cannot be completed by simply turning a card sort on its side.

Place each of the targets in a box, lined up to the right of the purpose. Leave plenty of space between each target to allow for growth of the tree diagram. Connect the targets to the purpose to form the first branches of the tree diagram. Expand each target to define the subordinate tasks that are necessary to accomplish each target. Use group dialogue, or any creative process, to define tasks. When the subordinate tasks have been defined and recorded for each target, draw the lines that will connect them to the target.

Each subordinate task should then be subdivided into further levels of subtasks until the final level is achievable. Each subtask should be broken down until it can be given to a person or group to be completed. This expansion may add more levels to your tree. Levels of detail may be added unevenly, causing one branch to grow larger than others.

The final step in making a tree diagram is to test the validity of the work. This is done by reviewing each task and level on the tree diagram to see if it logically connects to the tasks above and below it. You might consider expanding to a larger group that includes the people who will actually perform the tasks. Their knowledge and experience may help you see gaps or unnecessary tasks. When this is complete, review each subtask to ensure its necessity to the completion of the task. Expect this questioning process to cause change in the tree diagram. A tree diagram is shown in Figure 19.6.

FORCE FIELD ANALYSIS

Stephen R. Covey mentions the force field analysis in his book *The Seven Habits of Highly Effective People,* Simon and Schuster, (1989). He credits sociologist Kurt

FIGURE 19.6 ***Tree diagram using card sort headers and ideas***

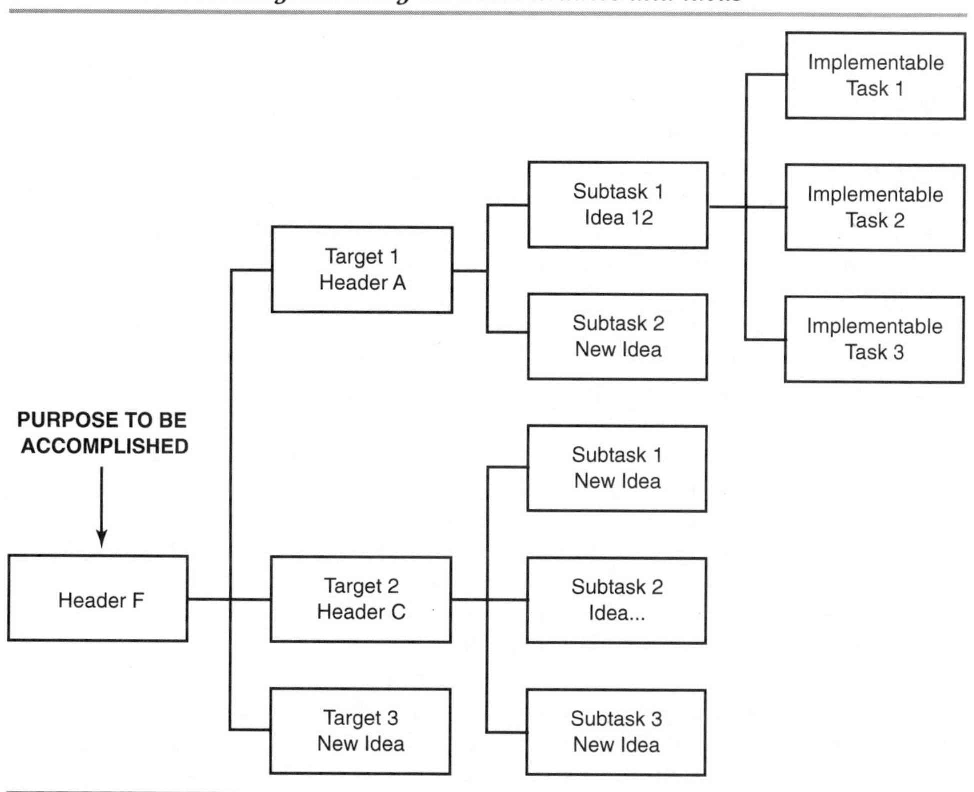

Lewin as the developer of this model that shows the driving forces as rising and restraining forces as pushing down. Lewin's focus on the dynamics at work in any change process began over 40 years ago. During World War II, our government tried to change the beef-buying habits of housewives to expand use of internal organs and to limit the use of muscle cuts to aid the war effort. Women were unwilling to change at first because they did not know enough about selecting and preparing the recommended meats. However, when the president's wife got involved in the problem and began to understand the benefits, change began to happen. Lewin learned:

> When people become involved in a problem, they become significantly and sincerely committed to coming up with solutions to the problem.

Moran, Talbot, and Benson in *A Guide to Graphical Problem-Solving Processes* (1990) described the procedural steps for the force field analysis as it is more typically shown and used.

The force field analysis is a technique to visually identify the forces affecting accomplishment of your purpose. It is a way to show supporting and resisting forces. Force field analysis can help you analyze the depths of your resources to overcome the resistance by providing a clear picture of the situation to share with others. It can be completed by one person, but it is most effective when applied by a diverse group with a clearly defined purpose and a method to accomplish it.

Begin by drawing vertical and horizontal lines. Make the spaces large enough that there is plenty of room to write. At the extreme right, under the horizontal line, print your purpose. This is to provide focus for the generation of supporting and resisting forces. It may further help to add an arrow to the horizontal line to indicate the direction of positive accomplishment. Further clarity can be added by marking the left side as driving forces and those on the right as resisting.

List the forces driving toward your purpose on the left side of the vertical line and those resisting your efforts on the right. These lists could be created by using brainstorming or simply by carefully examining your initial plan. When each list is complete, go over the lists again and assign a strength to each force. A scale from high to low provides a good initial view of the situation. Now draw an arrow under each force pointing to the vertical line. The arrow's length indicates the strength of the force.

Evaluate the results. Force field analysis provides a clear visualization of the forces with which you are dealing. Examine both the driving and resisting forces for opportunities for improvement. Your goals are first to seek ways to reduce or eliminate resisting forces. This action serves to conserve resources and reduce the effort required to accomplish your goal. If necessary, you should seek additional resources to aid in overcoming the resisting forces.

A completed force field analysis is shown in Figure 19.7. As shown, there is not always a resisting force for every driving force. By adding the strength of the force, it is easier to see which driving forces can be added to and which resisting forces can be decreased.

MATRICES

The matrix format of rows and columns has long been used to guide the gathering and organization of large amounts of information. Matrices are created manually or through a variety of semiautomated and automated vehicles including the computer spreadsheet. The number of rows varies widely, based on the application. The number and width of the columns varies based on the size and type of the data contained. The value of a matrix is defined by its contents. Two major types of matrices are the most common. The first type contains information and the second contains correlations between two sets of variables. Examples of both types of matrices follow.

S.M.A.R.T. plan

The S.M.A.R.T. plan is defined by the information it contains. This matrix provides the key information that is necessary to build a successful plan. The S.M.A.R.T.

FIGURE 19.7 ***Force field analysis on implementable task from tree diagram***

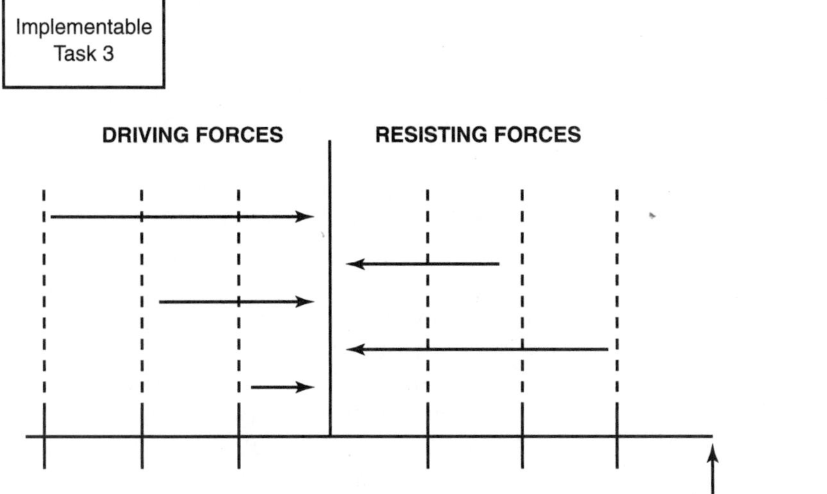

plan requires a set of tasks to accomplish your purpose. It can be a vehicle for guiding a group in the development of a working plan that defines clear accountability and goals. It is a technique for structuring task details, which includes a measure of completion, assignment of responsibility, resources required, time to complete, and predecessor tasks. It is a way to plan the implementation of the tasks necessary to accomplish your purpose.

Like all decision making and planning tools, the S.M.A.R.T. plan begins with a clearly defined purpose. Write this purpose at the top of your work area. List the tasks or specifics necessary to accomplish your purpose. These can be created as part of the process of building the S.M.A.R.T. plan, or they may be transferred from a completed tree diagram. The process of selecting the implementation details of each specific provides an additional test of the work performed in a tree diagram. If you find a specific or task is not sufficiently detailed, do not hesitate to return to the tree and modify it before continuing.

Now that the S.M.A.R.T. plan is set up, the work of defining the implementation details begins by identifying the measure of completion for each specific. A measure is a clearly visible indicator that the specific is complete. Measures can include dates, quantities, or performance levels. There must be no doubt when the measure has been reached. A good measure can also show progress. Measures are agreed upon by consensus.

Each specific must be assigned to a person or a group to assure its completion. Assignment is one of the keys to success in any plan. Assignment provides accountability. It must be very specific. In addition, it must provide opportunity for participation. No assignment should ever be made without at least the agreement of the assignee. The ideal situation is one in that qualified groups or group members have sufficient motivation or interest to volunteer.

Completion of each specific requires the availability of resources. Resources include time sufficient to create quality results as well as capital, capital equipment, raw materials, and supplies. Personnel with appropriate skill, knowledge, experience, and commitment is also essential.

Any form of planning requires an understanding of a desired endpoint. In more advanced planning techniques, the duration of each task is also included. The S.M.A.R.T. plan assumes that the group has considered project time as one of the resources. Timing provides a target for task or specific completion, a guide for planning the details of task implementation and acquiring resources, and an early start date for any task dependent on, or succeeding, this task.

Putting the proper priority and sequence on specifics requires an understanding of the linkages between them. A predecessor defines what must be done before this task can be accomplished. Predecessors provide an outline of the order in which tasks must be done as a guide for planning the implementation details and utilization of resources. A specific may have one, many, or even no predecessors.

For short specific lists, write the specific in the predecessor column. For longer lists, number the list of specifics and use the number of the predecessor. Figure 19.8 shows a S.M.A.R.T. plan type of matrix.

Correlation matrix

The second type of matrix is a correlation matrix. In this form of matrix, one list of variables is compared to a second list of variables. They are often compared with numbers or symbols. The most common symbols are ◎ for a strong relationship, ○ for a medium relationship, and △ for a weak relationship. The number 9 is often substituted for the strong relationship symbol, the number 3 for the medium, and the number 1 for the weak. These numbers are based on experience and are not numerically valid. The reason for the multiple is that it surfaces the most important items. These symbols come from the Japanese symbols for win, place, and show at the horse racetrack. The first translations contained these sym-

FIGURE 19.8 ***S.M.A.R.T plan matrix on implementable task from tree diagram***

SPECIFIC	MEASURABLE	ASSIGNMENT	RESOURCES	TIME	PREDECESSORS
Implementable Task 3	Deliverable	GH	8 Person Hours	1 Week	Target 1 Subtask 2 Implementable 4

bols, and they have become common in U.S. quality documentation. An example of a correlation matrix is shown in Figure 19.9.

PROBLEM PREVENTION PLAN (CONTINGENCY PLAN, PDPC)

What could go wrong? This question is an essential part of planning. Unfortunately, we often do little other than worry. The problem prevention plan is a method for planning around contingencies and creating alternatives or solutions for every foreseeable contingency.

The earliest reference to a contingency planning method that formulates the same questions is the process decision program chart (PDPC) described in *The 7 New QC Tools* by Shigeru Mizuno. This tool structures the implementation steps of a plan, and then asks "what if?" and prompts for possible countermeasures.

The two common methods used to implement the PDPC often cause confusion. The first is a modified tree diagram where each level of questioning is exploded downward. The second is a "book" outline format where process steps, their contingencies, and possible countermeasures are related by outline numbers like the chapters in a book.

The problem prevention plan is a much easier, more thorough method of contingency planning. It is also easier to understand. It is an enhanced implementation more closely related to the potential problem analysis used by J. D. James in the quality leadership process. In addition to defining the "what ifs?," now called *potential problems,* the tool defines potential causes to allow a more specific focus

FIGURE 19.9 ***Correlation matrix***

	Process 1	Process 2		Total
Customer Need 1		◎		9
Customer Need 2	△			1

on feasible countermeasures, or preventions. The last enhancement is the ranking of the levels of the plan based on achievement of the goal.

The problem prevention plan is a technique to determine what can go wrong with your plan before it does. It is a method for rating the seriousness and likelihood of potential problems, a vehicle for investigating the causes of potential problems, a way to identify actions that can prevent problems from occurring, and a tool to trigger implementation of preventive action. The power in this tool is the structured "worrying" process that yields precise actions to keep our plans on track and helps us accomplish our purposes.

The problem prevention plan requires a purpose to be accomplished and a plan to accomplish it. It can be especially valuable when uncertainty exists or risk is high because it provides a comprehensive strategy before a major plan is implemented. This type of planning can help you identify and remove roadblocks to your success.

Begin the problem prevention plan by defining a list of what could go wrong with your plan. Write the purpose to be accomplished at the top of the page, board, or chart pad. Consider using a creative tool, such as brainstorming, to develop the list. Look for potential problems that could get in the way (perhaps from a force field analysis). A potential problem is something that can prevent a plan or process step from occurring or producing the planned output. It can alter the quality of the resulting output or cause delays.

To construct the problem prevention plan, place the list to the left of a board or sheet of paper and create columns for probability and seriousness. For each of the potential problems, rank both the probability of its occurrence and the seriousness. Probability is the likelihood that the potential problem will happen. Seriousness is the impact on the accomplishment of the purpose if it does happen, ranked high to low.

Identify the potential problem with the highest probability of occurrence and of a most serious nature, marking them for further analysis. For each identified potential problem (high probability and seriousness), develop a list of potential causes. List the potential problem at the top of a page. Search for potential causes using dialogue, brainstorming, or some other creative process. Rate the probability of occurrence of each of the potential causes on a scale ranked high to low. Select the potential causes that are most likely to happen. Further analyze them to attempt to prevent them from happening.

For the highest probability, discuss and select actions that can prevent a future problem. List the potential cause at the top. Search for preventions using dialogue, brainstorming, or some other creative process. For each prevention, define a trigger that will signal the beginning of the prevention. A trigger can be an event, a time, or a measure.

In this planning stage, solutions are changes in our plans to prevent the possibility of a problem. Alternatives are actions that can be taken to minimize or eliminate the problem if it occurs. Figure 19.10 shows a problem prevention plan on matching delivery and order documentation.

FIGURE 19.10 *Problem prevention plan*

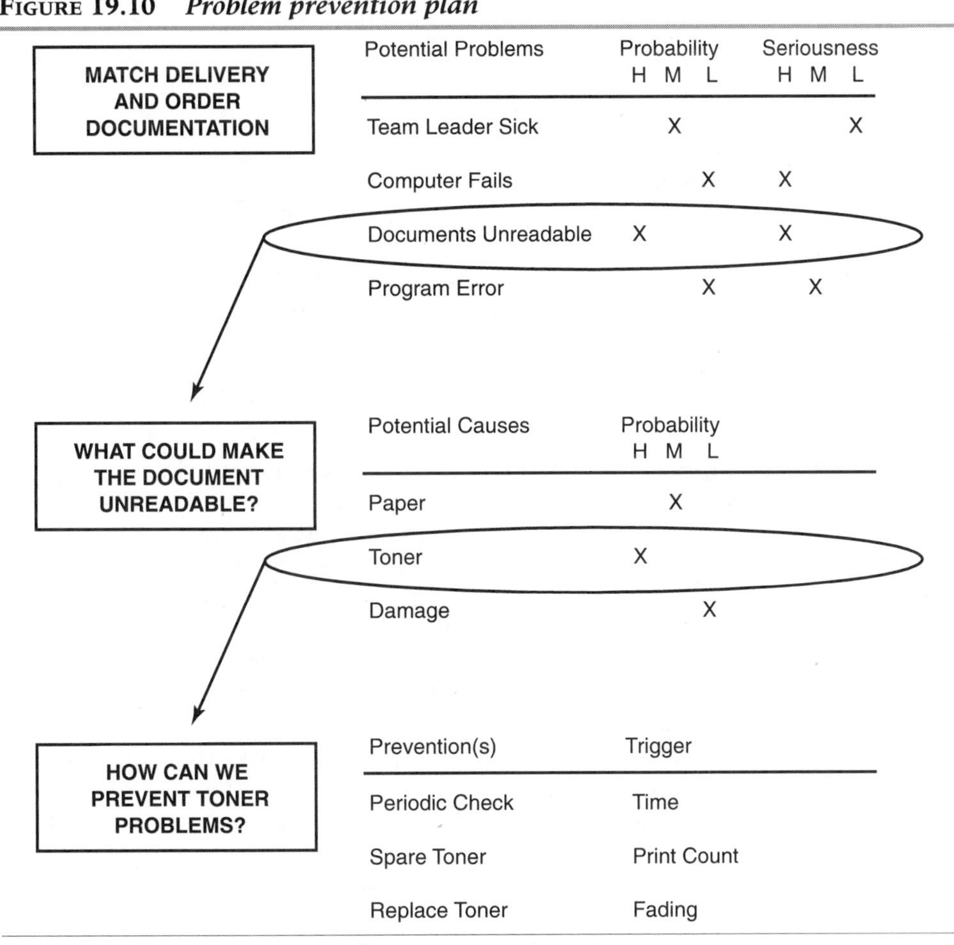

PERT CHART (CPM, ARROW DIAGRAM)

Some useful project planning and tracking methods have come from the work of Henry Gantt. The best known of these is PERT, or **p**rogram **e**valuation and **r**eview **t**echnique, and the PERT planning method.

A PERT chart is also called an *activity network diagram. Project Management with CPM, PERT and Precedence Diagramming* by Moder, Phillips and Davis, Van Nostrand Reinhold (1983) places the origin of the PERT chart in the work of a Polish scientist, Karol Adamiecki, in the early 1930s. Adamiecki created the "Harmony Graph" matrix with a time scale on the vertical axis and activities on the horizontal axis. Movable strips under each activity indicated the duration of the activity, and the horizontal axis contained a reference to inter-task dependencies.

The PERT Planning Method as we know it today was formed in 1958 by a research team from Lockheed Aircraft Corporation, the Navy Special Projects Office, and Booz, Allen, and Hamilton in their plan to develop the Polaris Missile System. The critical path method (CPM) was created concurrently by a team from DuPont and Remington Rand Univac. Their method identified the shortest, or critical, path through a project.

Today's PERT planning method has three variations based on the display and duration of activities. These include activity on arrow, activity on node, and precedence diagram. The full PERT planning method is extremely complex and can be confusing. The PERT chart contained in this article is a simplified activity on node diagram that includes the identification of a critical path. It is our goal to provide the benefits of PERT planning through a simplified charting technique designed to be used following the tree diagram and S.M.A.R.T. plan.

The PERT chart is a technique to organize tasks or activities into a schedule, a visual method for identifying predecessor activities, and a means of identifying the minimum time required to complete the project. It can identify gaps or missing tasks in your project plan, show the critical path through your project plan, and track your project to completion. The PERT chart requires a clear understanding of your purpose to be accomplished and a knowledge of the tasks or activities necessary to accomplish the purpose. Most often, computer planning programs are used to facilitate completing and updating PERT charts.

As with any decision-making or planning tool, the most important place to start is with a clear understanding of the purpose to be accomplished. A concise purpose statement can improve substantially your ability to plan. Once you have defined your purpose, establish a list of the tasks that must be performed. The PERT chart depends on other tools, such as the card sort, a tree diagram, or a S.M.A.R.T. plan, to define the tasks necessary to accomplish your purpose.

Record the predecessors for each task. These are the tasks that must be completed before the current task can be started. This information from the S.M.A.R.T. plan is recorded in the first blank column. For each task, define the task duration. This is the total time required to perform the task with the assigned resources. Use the same unit of time for each task, that is, hours or days. Assigning duration requires knowledge of the manner in which the work will be performed. The assistance of those who will perform the work can be invaluable. If the task is not sufficiently detailed, you will have difficulty. This can be an indication that the task needs to be subdivided.

The second key to defining duration is a knowledge of the resources available. Often an unacceptable duration can be shortened through the application of more resources. Warning: There are some operations that by their nature are sequential and cannot be done in parallel. Ensure that the availability of additional resources will help and not hinder or waste.

The PERT planning method works backward from the purpose to be accomplished to build a linked, time-driven plan that identifies each task and its starting point in order to meet a desired completion date. The reality of PERT is that it is often worked both ways several times to gain understanding and to help all the tasks fit together in the best possible manner.

The original PERT did not have the array of judgmental tools that we have today, nor was it assisted by today's computer technology. With the use of other judgmental tools, such as the S.M.A.R.T. plan and the tree diagram, it becomes possible to work forward from the earliest possible start to determine the actual completion of the purpose.

To use a PERT chart, create a temporary calendar scale that covers the time from a starting time to the date when it should be complete. Working forward or backward requires an initial calendar scale to facilitate the location of tasks on the chart. The final calendar scale is defined by the creation of the PERT diagram on the chart and can be placed only after the diagram is completed.

Working from the first task to be accomplished, place the tasks to be completed on the chart. Each task should be enclosed in a circle or ellipse with its required completion date written clearly above or below it. Remember this comes from the S.M.A.R.T. plan. Add the task number to the task. On large or complex charts, the task number will be vital to maintaining order and conserving space. Draw an arrow from the task to the next task to be accomplished. For the last task to be done, the arrow is drawn to the purpose. Place the task duration, or time required to complete the task, on the arrow as shown in Figure 19.11.

The completed PERT chart will provide a network of tasks that must be completed to accomplish your purpose. The total time to get from the start to a completed purpose will depend on how many tasks can be accomplished in parallel. The more things you can do at the same time, the sooner you will be done, but

FIGURE 19.11 ***PERT chart on implementable tasks from S.M.A.R.T plan***

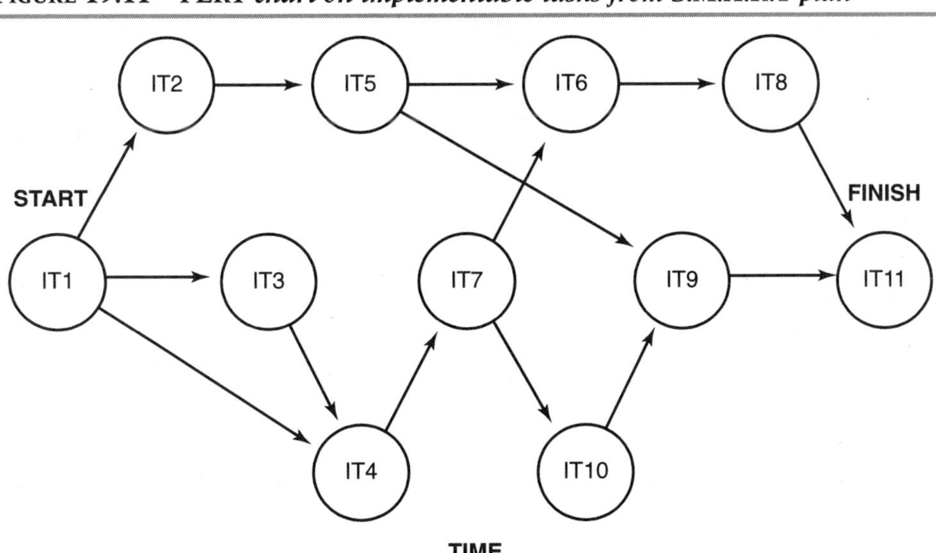

there is a limit. That limit is the critical path through your network of tasks. The critical path is the longest path of predecessor/successor tasks in the network. It is discovered by adding the duration of tasks together for each of the possible paths through the network. The path with the longest duration defines the minimum time required to accomplish your purpose. Clearly mark the critical path with double lines or color for all to see. The critical path will also determine the time or length of your calendar scale. At this point, redraw the calendar scale and PERT network to assure harmony between the network and scale and to ensure coherency of task placement.

Considerable development work has been performed on the PERT chart since it was created. Entire courses exist to teach the PERT/CPM (critical path method) planning method. There are also a number of computer programs on the market that implement this process. In a more intensive study, you will encounter some of the following terms:

Activity	The task to be done (or specific).
Node	The circle or ellipse in which the task to be done is written (or event).
Predecessor	A task that must be completed before the current task can be started.
Successor	A task that cannot be started until the current task is completed.
Duration	The time required to complete a task.
Early start	The soonest a task can be started.
Late start	The latest a task can be started and still stay on schedule.
Early finish	The soonest or most optimistic time a task can be finished.
Late finish	The latest a task can be finished and still not delay the following tasks.
Slack	The difference between the time a task should start and when it must start.

When used on a PERT, these terms are often abbreviated, such as EF for early finish and LS for late start. Figure 19.11 shows a completed PERT chart.

Reading 20

Reengineering: Process Redesign

By Terence T. Burton

Process redesign is the first element of a reengineering framework. The objective of process redesign is to reinvent, reposition, restructure, and de-departmentalize critical business processes in a manner that creates a renewed focus on customer need, not business as usual with a few added enhancements. Process redesign demands that we abandon the parochial rules about business and adopt a start-over mind-set.

Ultimately, our goal is to reengineer what is typically a homogeneous business into several stand-alone focused value centers. This is typically accomplished by a complete overhaul of the company's infrastructure, including such processes as:

- Physical
- Business
- Technical
- Information
- People

Some of the activities characteristic of process redesign include:

- Linking business processes together to decrease product and informational movement, defective business process queues, work-in-process, material or information handling, time, complexity, and associated costs.
- Reducing cycle times by overlapping business process activities, such as processing a customer order, developing a new product, purchasing raw materials, or preparing compliance documentation.

Source: Selected text and illustrations from *The Reengineering Toolbox* by The Center for Excellence in Operations, Inc. (CEO), Nashua, New Hampshire, Terence T. Burton, President. Reprinted by permission.

- Creating the conditions for an immediate exposure and solution to business process problems and opportunities achieved by the entire workforce.
- Providing real-time feedback mechanisms to business process and subprocess owners. This supports the creation of self-management, self-measurement, and self-adjustment.
- Process redesign has focused traditionally on making the "as-is" incrementally better. Reengineering causes individuals to work from a much broader definition of process redesign than occurs with traditional continuous improvement methods. Process redesign in a reengineering sense depends largely upon an organization's distance from its desired, or "ultimate," state.

In our implementation experiences, we have found that process redesign evolves to a new level of breakthrough improvement. Every organization performs at different levels, from excellent to poor, depending on the process and goal. Therefore, it is logical that the next generation of process redesign include concurrent activities focused on the following analyses:

1. Some business processes currently meet or exceed customer needs, and the proper activity to support process redesign is reinforcement of current practices. This usually includes the soft aspects of traditional continuous improvement, such as team building and improving facilitation and leadership skills.
2. Other business processes fall short of meeting customer needs and require small, incremental improvements. The proper activity to support process redesign is continuous improvement of the "as-is." This usually includes the soft aspects of continuous improvement as previously described, plus the traditional TQM problem solving tools (for example, The 7 Old Tools, The 7 New Tools, SPC, charting and measurement techniques, and so on).
3. Every organization has business processes that, no matter how much reinforcement or incremental improvement is pursued, will never meet the customer's need within the customer's time window. These are the candidates to be reinvented or rediscovered. One of the largest causes of reengineering failures has been the lack of tools to deal with reinvention needs.

Unfortunately, many reengineering initiatives are nothing more than slash and burn downsizing efforts, recycled TQM or continuous improvement activities, in vogue movements, or a new list of MIS projects. The major causes of reengineering failure include overreliance on technology as a solution and application of old tools that focus on continuous improvements of the "as-is." *Old* tools focus on competencies (for example, how to make current conditions better). *Reengineering* tools focus on antecedents (for example, what needs to be done) and encourage entrepreneurial thinking and invention of new business processes. Anything else results in what actually is downsizing, TQM, continuous improvement, created activities, or a new list of MIS projects.

CEO's Breakthrough! Reengineering framework addresses the full spectrum of inventing, managing, and implementing breakthrough improvement. The purpose of *The Reengineering Toolbox* is to share our implementation methodology and "out-of-box" tools because we feel these are critical to achieving real breakthrough results. Successful implementation makes the difference with reengineering separate organizations that "wish" or "think" things will automatically change simply because they have launched a reengineering initiative.

The Breakthrough! Reengineering BPR tools presented in this article are from CEO's book, *The Reengineering Toolbox*. These tools are much more difficult to apply in real life than, for example, the seven standard TQM tools because they must be applied by entrepreneurial process redesigners. We have learned from our implementation experiences that there are many reasons for this fact. The most pronounced difference in reengineering is that in many situations, the process forces you to start in the abstract to create a new reality. There may not be a process because it may not yet exist. Additionally, many of these tools are applied to knowledge-based activities, in which definitions of customers, products, processes, quality, performance, and success are often unclear.

Applying Pareto charts, run diagrams, and check sheets to real-life situations on the shop floor is a structured, linear problem-solving process. The operator typically is provided with quality and workmanship standards, process/routing, work instructions, set-up sheets, quality measurement criteria, and tooling/gauges. The operator has the benefit of a defined product and process and can measure physical results against a predetermined standard. Imagine how much success this operator would have if he or she were sent to an empty space to apply these tools! This is the challenge of reengineering. Application of these new reengineering tools for process redesign requires a totally new thinking process characterized by out-of-box thinking and business as unusual.

PROCESS REDESIGN

Ten P Business Reengineering Checklist

The 10 P Business Reengineering Checklist (Figure 20.1) is used in conjunction with business process mapping. The 10 P checklist adds dimensional value for each activity that is a business, technical, or administrative process. It also helps in rationalizing the real needs of a business process and to remove any unnecessary activities.

Business processes in most organizations have evolved over decades. As a consequence, many of the activities that are routinely performed in organizations do not stand up to the test of the 10 P checklist. Often, activities are identified that produce an unnecessary or incorrect product or have no customer. In practice, it is not unusual to find that some of the 10 P checklist items have no answer.

FIGURE 20.1 *Ten P Business Reengineering Checklist*

Process Description: Date:

Category	Answer	Answer Rating			Data Collection				
		Complete	Partial	Missing	Source	Data	Required	Who	When
Purpose									
Procedure									
Practice									
Participants									
Pace									
Place									
Period Frequency									
Product									
Purchaser									
Performance									
	Total Check Marks								

BPR methodology:

1. Decide and describe the business segment or process to be analyzed.
2. For each of the checklist categories, fill in the answer to the category in as much detail as possible.
3. For each answer provided, check off whether it is a complete, partial, or missing answer.
4. Total the number of check marks in each of the rating columns.
5. If you have 80 percent or more of the check marks in the "complete" rating column, you understand your business segment or process very well. Experience has shown that most organizations usually have most of the check marks in the partial or missing columns, indicating that much work is required.
6. Identify the data required to complete the answers to the categories, determine the data sources, and decide who will obtain the data and when.
7. Collect the data.

BPR results:

- Clear understanding of a business segment or reason for a process's existence.
- Compelling reason to eliminate the business segment or process where no clear answer can be found.

Business process mapping

Business process mapping (Figure 20.2) is a scoping tool used to document and diagnose the standard internal business processes that deliver products and/or services to the customer. This tool helps the enterprise understand the sequence of activities, relationships, process element cycle times, resources consumed, process cost, information and physical activity flows, and process participants.

Business process mapping is a flexible process that can be adapted to the preferences of the organization. Business process mapping can be accomplished through Post-it® notes, brown paper analysis, computer-generated flowcharts, freehand drawings, flip charts, and the like. The approach we choose is not as important as the purpose and results achieved.

FIGURE 20.2 ***Business process mapping***

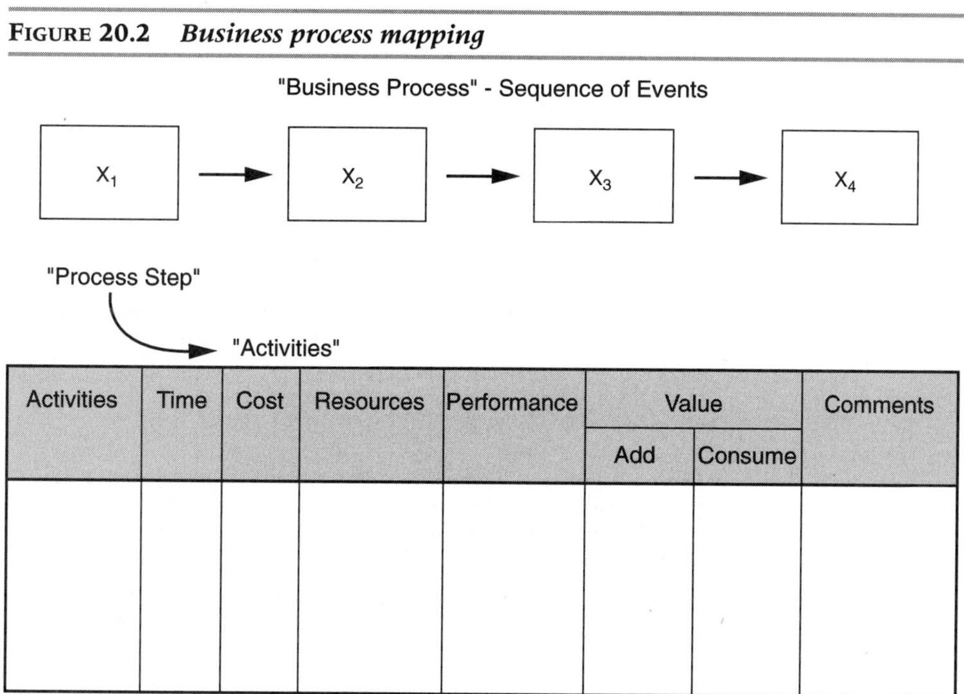

BPR methodology:

1. Chart the major cross-functional process steps and the sequence of events in a business process.
2. Document the specific activities and elements of each process step.
3. Determine critical descriptive data to analyze and assess the activities that are required to complete each process step.
4. Apply the 10 P Business Reengineering Checklist to each activity in the process.
5. Segment value-adding and value-consuming efforts in the process and begin identifying opportunities to eliminate, combine, or streamline process activities.

BPR results:

- Cross-functional business process maps.
- Process dynamics, redundancies, disconnects, waste.
- A solid foundation for breakthrough change.

Throw It Away (TIA) Analysis

Throw It Away Analysis (Figure 20.3) is a tool designed to stimulate innovation and reinvention. Throw It Away Analysis is conducted as a structured small group exercise made up of process participants and those who might be helpful who come from outside the business process. These forward-thinking individuals usually ask tough questions, such as "Why is this done and is it necessary?" The objective of this exercise is to get the process owners to think out-of-box and raise possibilities that may seem crazy, unthinkable, impossible, and ridiculous. Be aware that some of the results of Throw It Away Analysis may well be impossible or ridiculous but often one leads to the creation of a process breakthrough.

BPR methodology:

1. Assemble a small team of six to eight process and non-process owners.
2. List out the sequential steps on a flip chart using Post-it® notes.
3. Have the participants explore what would happen if one of the process steps were removed. The facilitator removes the process step Post-it® note from the flip chart so it is viewed as being thrown away. The facilitator should remove one Post-it® note at a time and encourage the team to rearrange the process flow without that step.
4. Record the results of the exploration on the Throw It Away Matrix.
5. Stop the exercise after each of the process steps has been subjected to the Throw It Away Analysis.

FIGURE 20.3 ***Throw It Away Analysis***

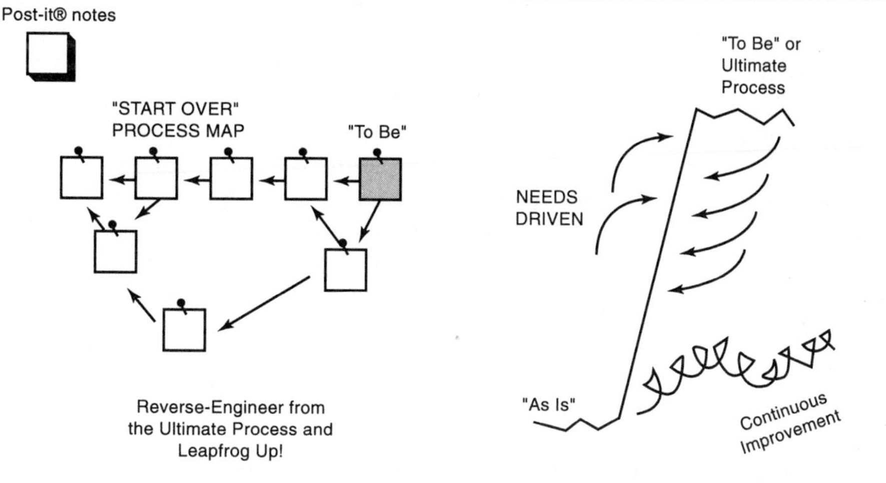

Business Segment of Process: ________________ Date: ________

Sequential Process Steps	Throw It Away or Rearrange It	What Could Happen	Potential Impact	Potential New Process Flow

BPR results:

- A detailed analysis of each process step's worth and contribution.
- A potentially new flow or simplified one.
- Development of an attitude favorable to change.

Touch versus Elapsed Analysis

Touch versus Elapsed Analysis (Figure 20.4) is an opportunity identification tool designed to define the ultimate potential improvement in an "As-is" business process. This tool compares the elapsed time documented from the business process mapping with the cumulative actual work time. This comparison is made through a pilot exercise where a subassembly, product, or document is walked through each of the process elements without any delays. Process participants are made aware that this exercise will happen and must give their immediate attention to it. They are instructed to drop whatever they are doing and complete their aspect of the business process as fast as possible. Once the exercise is completed, each participant is asked to analyze what is preventing him/her from continuous processing all of the time.

BPR methodology:

1. Record the sequential process steps from the business process mapping tool and the documented elapsed time.
2. Inform all those involved in the pilot exercise of their roles and responsibilities.
3. Run the pilot exercise and record the actual work time.
4. Calculate the Reengineering Improvement Ratio.
5. Identify the process steps for reengineering or elimination.

BPR results:

- A calculated ratio of actual work to total elapsed time.
- Targets of process reinvention to greatly reduce cycle time.

TOTAL ENTERPRISE QUALITY MANAGEMENT

ADAPT problem-solving network

ADAPT (Figure 20.5) is an analytical network to support reengineering that is similar to the PDCA cycle for TQM. Solving business problems via the reengineering ideology requires out-of-box thinking. This type of problem solving is unstructured, nonlinear, and random in nature. The ADAPT network is used to encourage entrepreneurial behavior and risk.

PDCA is a repetitive sequential process, and ADAPT is a network of conceptual activities connected by tightropes. Imagine the spatial masses moving on and off the page on a Z-axis. You might be in the Deploy space and determine that the next step is Plan. However, because of real circumstances (for example, the tightropes intersect and lead you on a new course of action), there is not enough

FIGURE 20.4 ***Touch versus Elapsed Analysis***

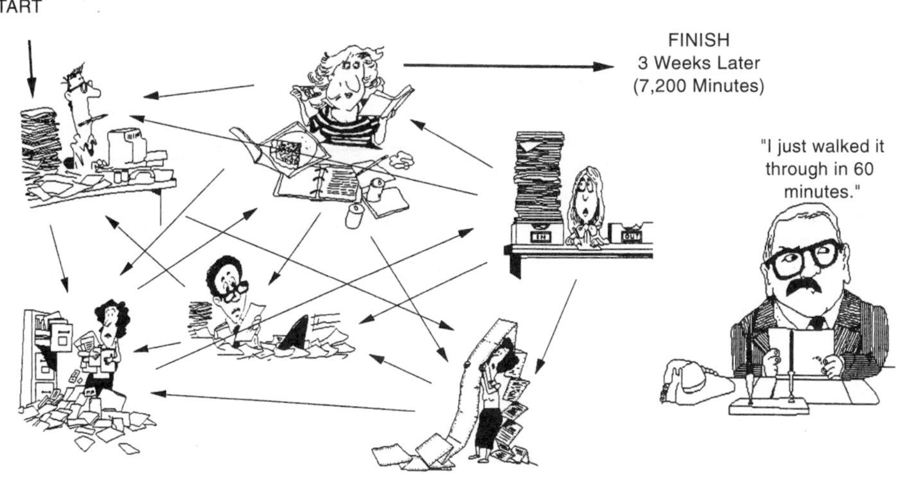

EE:AA = 7200:60
= 120:1

Business Segment of Process: ____________ Date: ____________

Sequential Process Steps	Documented Elapsed Time	Actual Work Time	Reengineering Improvement Ratio	Focus of the Reengineering Effort
Total			Elapsed / Actual, Expressed as an EE: AA Ratio (for example, 100:1)	

FIGURE 20.5 *ADAPT™ (out-of-box PDCA)*

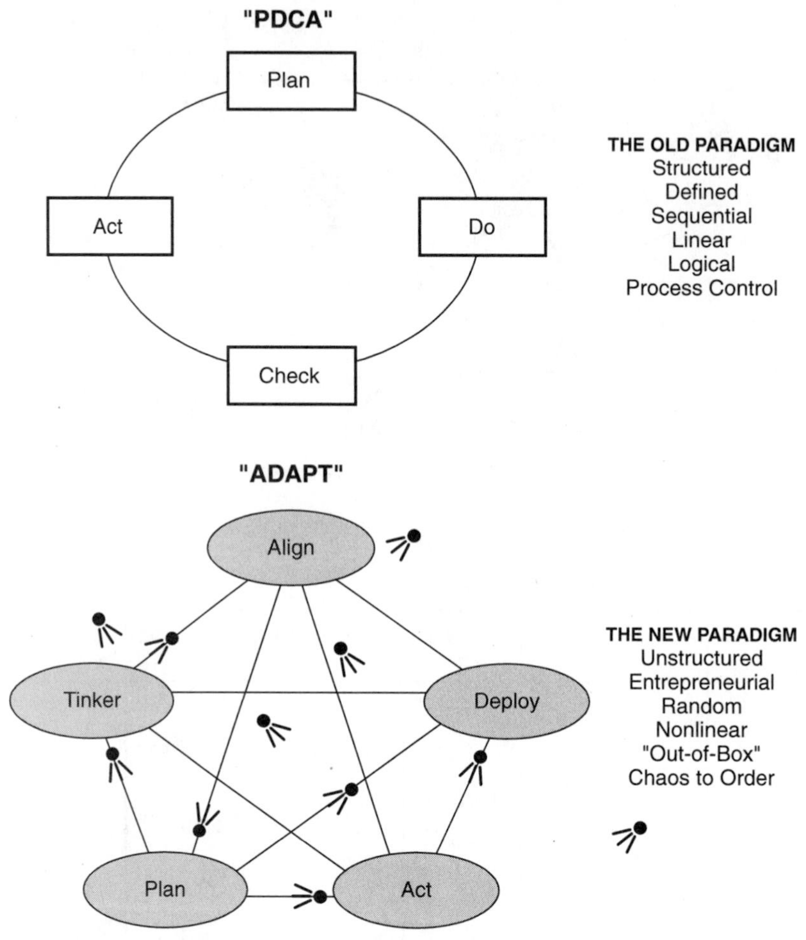

time for planning. The importance of ADAPT is to help us to recognize which space we are in, to determine the next space of the reengineering process, and to adjust if you land in a different destination. Reengineering is forced (but well managed) chaos and disequilibrium followed by order at a higher performance level.

BPR methodology:

1. *Align* resources toward a common set of reengineering goals and objectives that will generate new organizational orders, such as agility, seamlessness, self-management, and the best possible performance.
2. *Deploy* resources to work toward the achievement of reengineering goals.
3. *Act* or try something new. Keep in mind that with reengineering it is difficult to plan until you take action first (that is, unplug the existing PC-based 3 week quotation system and start from scratch).

4. *Plan* the next set of actions and the definitions of success.
5. *Tinker* or check and adjust your progress based on the latest information.

BPR results:

- A new awareness of managed chaos and development of individual thinking capabilities.

SUPPLY CHAIN MANAGEMENT

Supply Chain Activity Network (SCAN)

SCAN (Figure 20.6) is a method for diagramming the elements of a company's supply chain. This tool provides a generic framework for baselining the "as-is" supply chain, its execution steps and cycle times, and its performance criteria. SCAN also provides the foundation for out-of-box process redesign to eliminate or simplify the supply chain.

BPR methodology:

1. Expand the framework of SCAN to reflect the specific operational elements of the company's supply chain (that is, create the detailed supply chain map of your company).
2. Detail other descriptive elements of the supply chain, such as process elements, cycle times, methods deployed, and so on. Note: Detailing can be accomplished through the use of other tools such as Purpose and Process Mapping, Touch versus Walk-through, 10 P, Journeys between Charting, Bill of Resources, and the like.
3. Analyze the completed SCAN of your company for redundancies, duplicate efforts, waste, or non-value-added activities.
4. Brainstorm, discussing how to break the homogeneous SCAN into multiple purpose value centers with fault tolerant logistics characteristics.
5. Reengineer and simplify the SCAN. Define the implementation steps, resources, and organizational implications of the SCAN after reengineering.

BPR results:

- An "as-is" SCAN.
- A "to-be" SCAN.

Service Cost Value Matrix

The Service Cost Value Matrix (Figure 20.7) is based on activity-based costing and management approaches. Its objective is to analyze a business process in terms of values added versus values consumed.

FIGURE 20.6 *Supply Chain Activity Network*

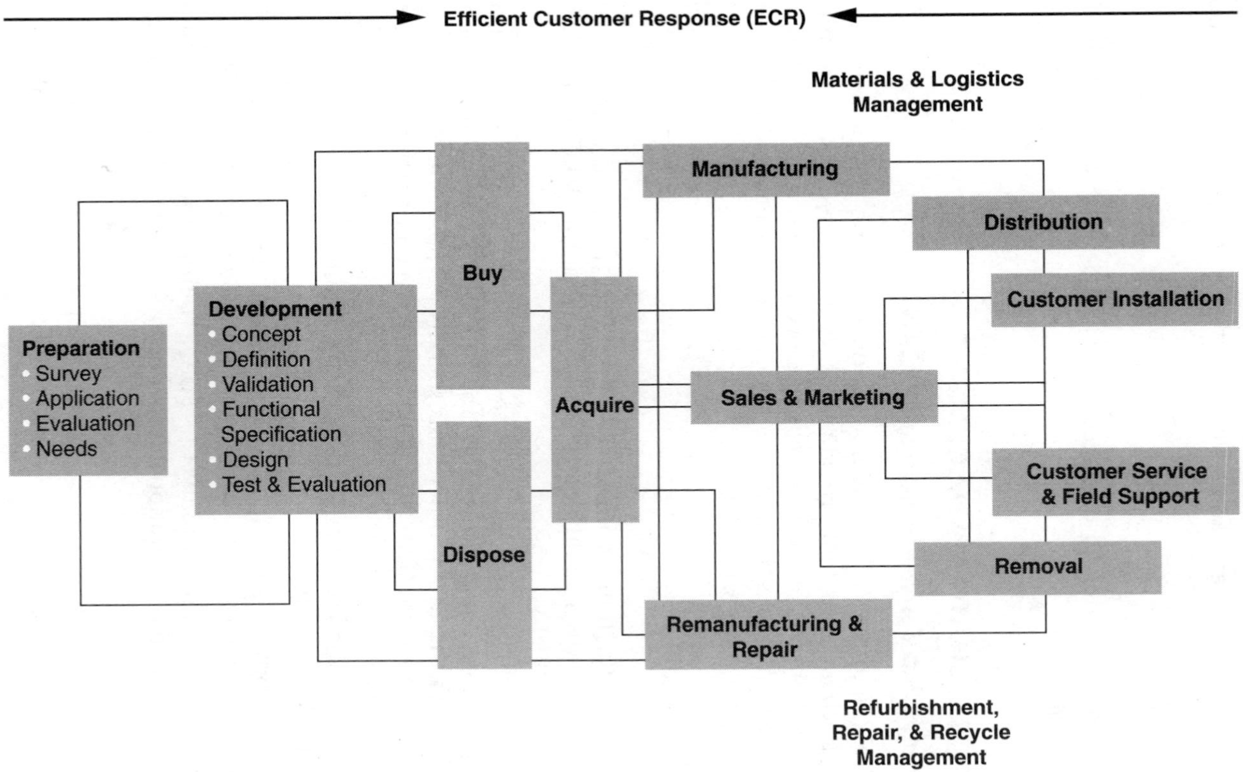

FIGURE 20.7 ***Service Cost Value Matrix***

Product/Service	% of Resource Consumption	Cost of Product/Service	Value of Product/Service

BPR methodology:

1. Define the services provided to the organization and the level of resources consumed to provide these services.
2. Identify an individual chart of account costs directly related to the business process and accumulate costs into a business process cost bucket.
3. Calculate ratios of total resource consumption based on services provided by the business process (this is used as the statistical base for allocating costs).
4. Allocate total costs to services provided based on the level of resource consumption.
5. Compare the value added with the value consumed and determine activities any future reengineering or continuous improvement efforts will focus on.

BPR results:

- An analysis of value of service versus cost of service for major elements of a business process.
- Definition of cost drivers.

ORGANIZATIONAL ROBUSTNESS

Organizational Involvement Mapping

The Organizational Involvement Mapping tool (Figure 20.8) is a process to understand better the core business or technical processes that deliver a valued product or service to your customer. Most organizations have between five to eight core business or technical processes that should not be confused with business functions. A few parts of many business functions are included in a business process.

FIGURE 20.8 ***Organizational Involvement Mapping***

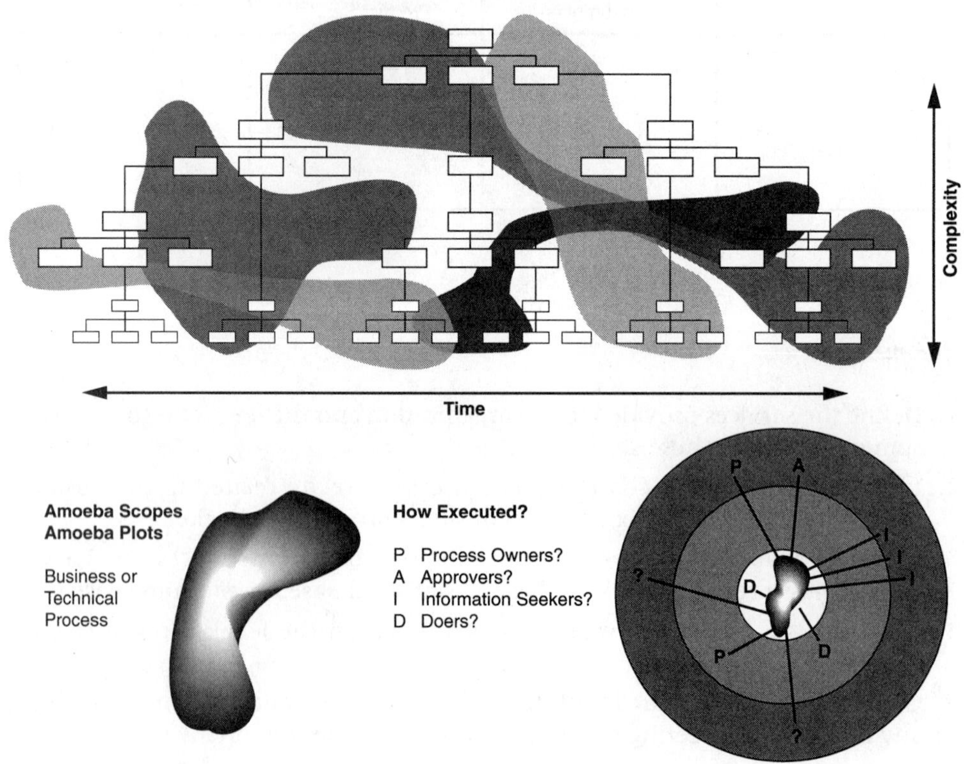

Organizations are arranged in a vertical hierarchy, but business processes flow in horizontal and diagonal directions and do not necessarily follow the formal structure. Organizational Involvement Mapping depicts visually the business and technical process flows, and who is involved in their execution.

BPR methodology:

1. Construct a detailed organization chart of the company or division under study.
2. Develop a listing of the core business or technical processes that deliver a valued product or service to the customer. Most organizations have between five to eight core business or technical processes.
3. Plot on the organization chart how each of the business or technical processes is accomplished. Connect the plotted points with a freehand amoeba figure that embodies all functions that make this process a reality.
4. Develop an execution plot that shows the level of involvement of each person who is identified in a function that contributes to this process. Identify each person as either a doer, a process owner, an approver, or an information seeker.
5. Determine if any of the work being performed in the rings can be eliminated or transferred to the doer ring. Most of the outer rings cause the majority of delays that the doer ring experiences.

BPR results:

- Identified core business or technical processes.
- Visualization of how these business or technical processes interact and are accomplished.
- Classification of those involved in these processes.
- Identification of work that can be moved to doers or eliminated.

SPEED-TO-CUSTOMER

Development Process Mapping

Development Process Mapping (Figure 20.9) is a reengineering tool used to define the structured, logical steps and the elapsed cycle times an organization deploys to develop new products. This tool can be used in conjunction with other reengineering tools (that is, touch development time versus elapsed development time, Development Process Capability, 10 P Checklist, Journeys between Charting, Organizational Involvement Mapping, and so on). This tool pinpoints areas and practices of the existing product development process that can be examined to reduce cycle times and improve development product and process quality. It can

FIGURE 20.9 *Development Process Mapping*

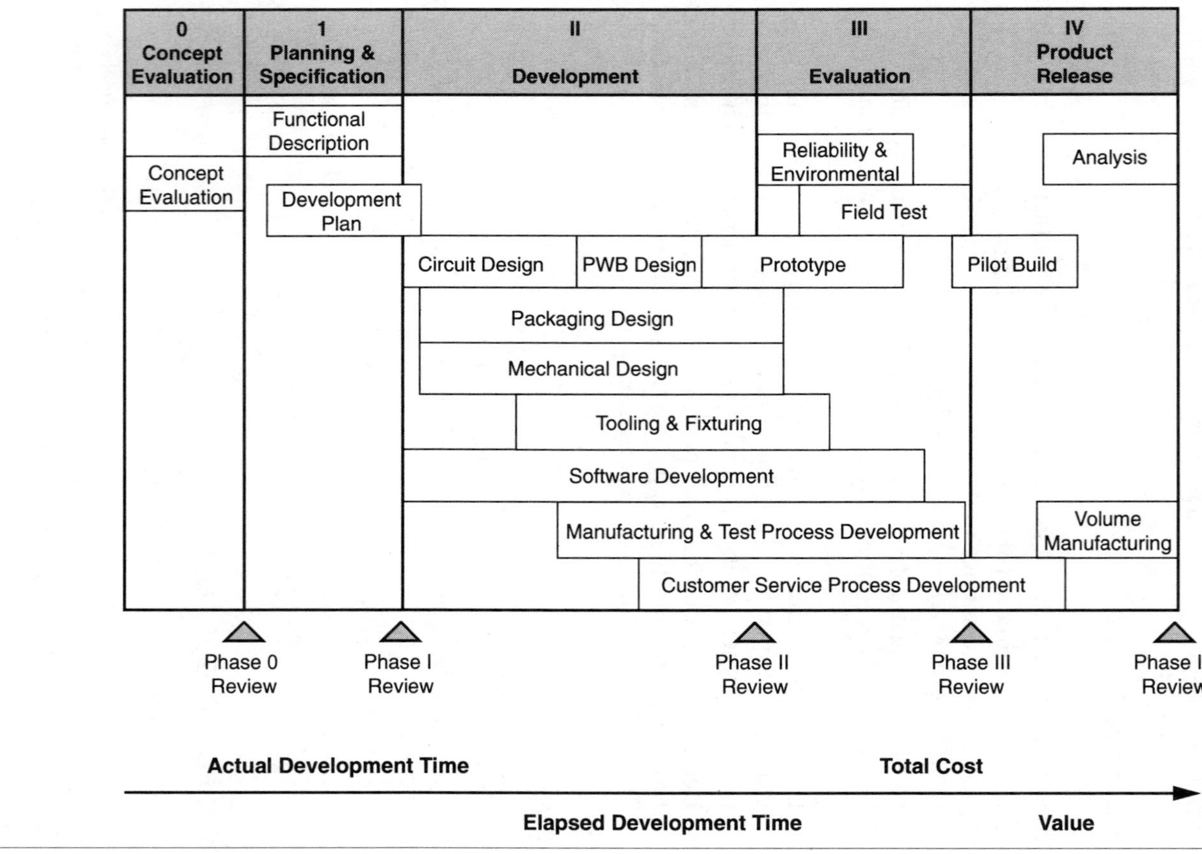

also be used as a basis for developing "fast lane" development rules that bypass normal development practices for certain exceptional situations.

BPR methodology:

1. Define the current product development phases, guidelines, check sheet items, and formal approval requirements.
2. Determine organizations, functions, departments, and specific activity skills involved in the current development process.
3. Develop "as-is" Development Process Maps for those new product development efforts that are known (for products currently being developed, or for products already released for commercialization).
4. Supplement Development Process Maps with descriptive or performance information, such as cycle times, development costs, time-to-market performance, organizational involvement, budgets, and so on.
5. Develop "to-be" Development Process Maps based on questions, such as, "How would you develop this new product all over again knowing what we know today? What would you have done differently? How could we have saved 50 percent of the time? How could we have reduced product cost by 20 percent? What changes will produce breakthroughs in product development?" Note: These maps can be developed in focus groups or brainstorming sessions.
6. Reengineer the Product Development Process, including Phase Definitions, Roles and Responsibilities, Phase Review and Gatekeeping, Design Review Procedures, Project/Resource Management Methodologies, and Success Measurement.

BPR results:

- Directions and requirements for developing a flexible, agile, rapid-response development process.

Development Project Mapping

Development Project Mapping (Figure 20.10) is a reengineering tool used to take an inventory of development projects-in-process. This tool can be used in conjunction with MVP Filtering to reconcile product/technology strategy and product development. In the majority of cases, organizations can "purge" their open development projects and thus regain focus and resource capacity for programs that are strategically important.

Development Project Mapping is typically an emotional and political exercise similar to reducing work-in-process on the plant floor. The philosophy is to avoid being caught up in developing faster processes to execute what you should not be doing in the first place.

FIGURE 20.10 Development Project Mapping

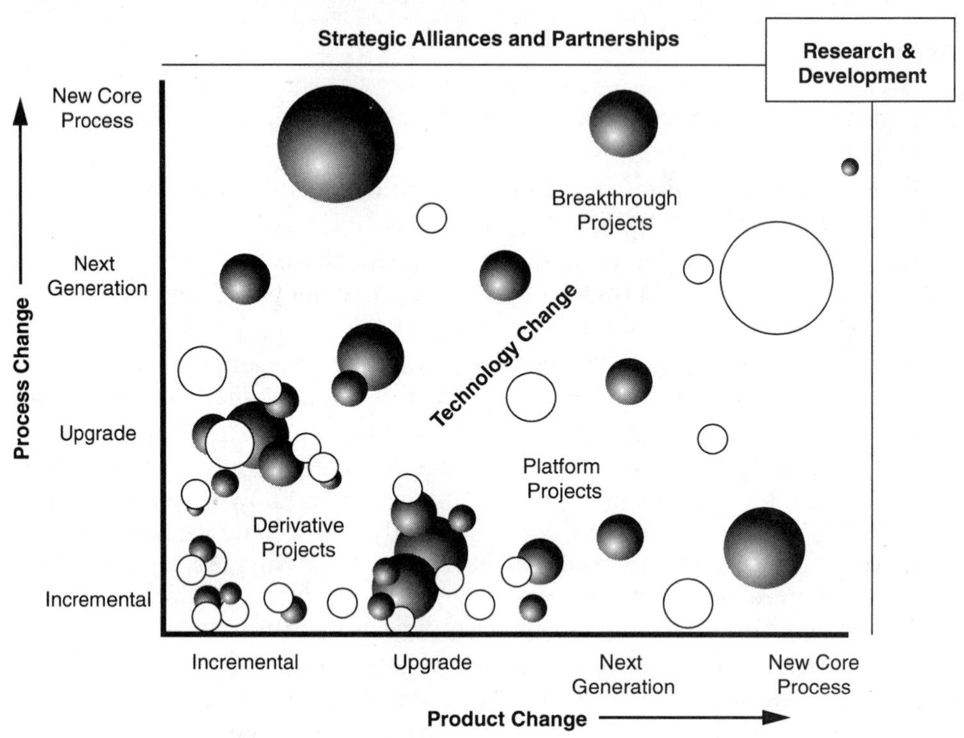

PROBLEMS
Too Many Projects (50%–75%)
Wrong Mix of Projects
Incorrect Execution Sequence
Misuse of Resources
Loss of Focus
Missed Market Windows
Products without Customers
Technologies without Markets

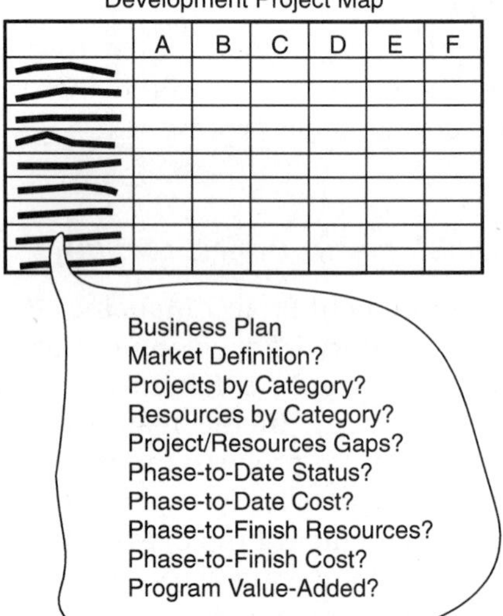

BPR methodology:

1. Create an inventory of Product Development Efforts based on the following classifications:
   - *Derivatives:* Projects that are cost-reduced versions or enhancements of existing products.
   - *Platforms:* Fundamental improvements in cost, quality, functionality, or performance over previous generations.
   - *Breakthroughs:* Significant developments to existing products and processes.
   - *Research and Development:* Creation of new technologies that eventually translate into commercial development.
   - *Strategic Alliances:* Activities outside the boundaries of the map that fit one of the categories previously mentioned.
2. Develop a descriptive profile for each project (for example, resources, costs, priorities, market potential, risk, and so on).
3. Determine Phase-To-Date and Phase-To-Finish facts, such as cost, cycle time, financial impact, resource constraints, trade-offs, and so on.
4. Purge the development workload based on short-term criteria and particular time-to-market needs.
5. Repeat the process monthly to manage development resources, program work flows, resource gaps, budget overruns, and development velocity.

BPR results:

- An effective Product Development Management tool to prevent overload conditions.

part

4

Total Quality Management Processes

This section of the book introduces some of most widely used TQM processes, which make extensive use of team-based problem solving and planning, and the tools presented in Part 3.

Among the most widely used TQM processes are:

Daily Management: a systematic approach to document, control, and continuously improve critical processes.

Statistical Process Control: a system design to keep continuous production processes under control and separate special from common causes.

Hoshin Planning: an integrated planning system that deploys breakthrough objectives throughout the entire organization.

Quality Function Deployment: a system that translates customer requirements into design and manufacturing specifications.

Basic TQM training involves the learning of the tools presented in Part 3, generally in the context of problem-solving models for the purposes of daily management applications. Advanced TQM training usually focuses on the other processes described in this section of the book.

As in the case of the tools, the implementation of TQM processes requires a particular set of teamwork-related skills. Experience suggests that the processes can be significantly enhanced if an experienced facilitator is involved in the planning and implementation stages.

Reading 21

Leading the Organization to Perfection through Daily Management

By John W. Moran, Jr.

Daily management can help American businesses capitalize on their human assets in the 1990s. This article explains how an organization can begin a process of continuous improvement involving everyone in the organization through daily management supplemented with a customer/supplier mapping process.

The continuous improvement of our daily work processes daily management is the foundation of any Total Quality Management effort. If all members of an organization constantly work to improve their process elements in a systematic and focused manner, they will lead the organization closer and closer toward perfection. The cumulative efforts of these daily management efforts will help an organization increase its market share and develop loyal and satisfied customers, contented employees, and satisfied shareholders. The most intensive part of the TQM process involving the greatest number of people in a given organization, daily management enables all employees to realize their impact and importance within an organization by measuring and controlling their daily work processes.

THE WHO, WHAT, AND HOW OF DAILY MANAGEMENT

Everyone in an organization—from top to bottom—must be involved in daily management for it to be successful. Daily management cannot work where managers say things like, "I support it; now you do it." Managers must lead by example. Their subordinates should see that this example improves their process and shows consistent and sustained improvements focused on customer satisfaction.

Source: Reprinted from Summer 1991 article in *National Productivity Review* with the permission of the author.

If an organization is to prosper and grow in the 1990s, it must become totally customer-focused. To be customer-focused, an organization must

- Involve all its members.
- Have strong top-level commitment.
- Link its incentive system to customer satisfaction ratings.
- Empower employees to solve customer problems on the spot.
- Remain in touch with the customer base through ongoing surveys.

It is not easy to change an organization's orientation from being quantity-driven to being customer-focused. Doing so requires changing the corporate culture and teaching every employee to be customer-focused.

The first step in reorienting an organization toward its customers is to have all employees view the work they do as a series of processes. The goal of each process must be total customer satisfaction. Everyone in the organization is responsible for establishing a system to define and assess the critical processes that make their job run smoothly. Once employees understand the critical processes, they embark on a never-ending journey of process standardization, continuous improvement, and restandardization of improvements in the process. Each process has three distinct phases of improvement:

Maintenance and Standardization. This is how we hold the current gains. If a process gives you a desired output, you must standardize the way you are doing the operation to hold the gains. This is the SDCA cycle (Standardize, Do, Check, and Act) and is shown in Figure 21.1.

Continuous Improvement. This is how you change direction when the process output slips or customer needs or expectations change. You then use the PDCA cycle (Plan, Do, Check, and Act), shown in Figure 21.2, to make a plan to change the process, do it, check it, and act if further corrections are needed.

FIGURE 21.1

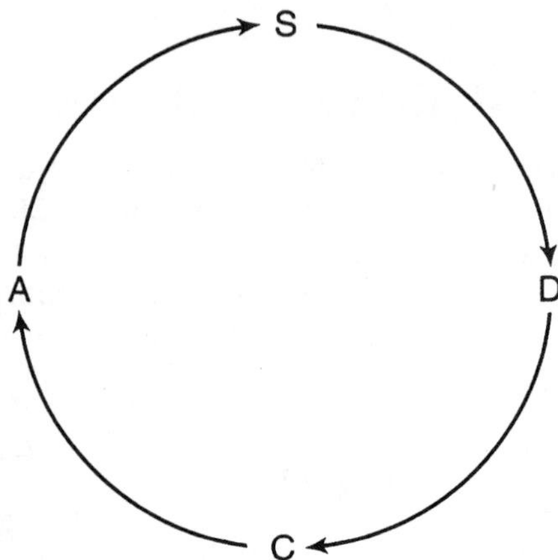

FIGURE 21.2

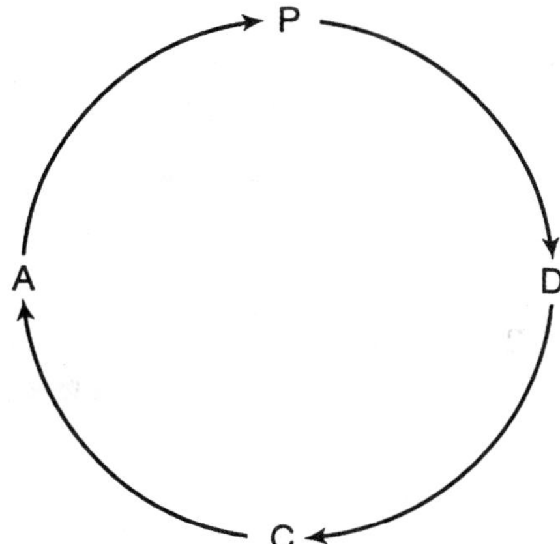

Once you have made a successful change, you standardize it with the SDCA cycle to hold onto the gains (see Figure 21.3).

Innovation and Breakthrough. In this phase you develop new approaches to increase the quality level of your process.

THE TOOLS OF DAILY MANAGEMENT

Assessing a process that identifies the critical elements that affect customer satisfaction requires that individuals or teams use some or all of the following tools of daily management. Training in these seven tools is a must.

FIGURE 21.3

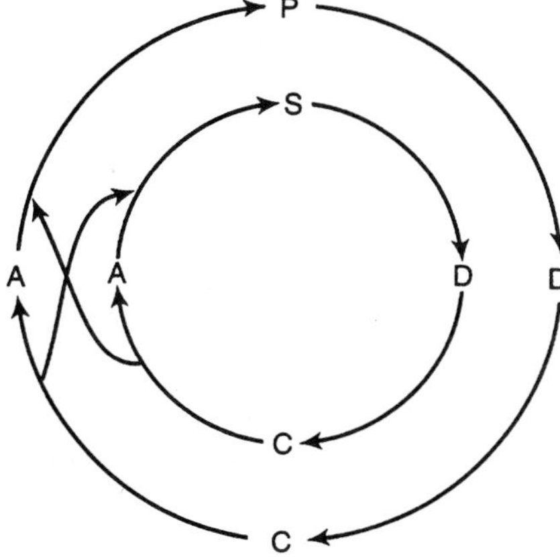

Cause-and-Effect Diagram. A graphic depiction showing the relationship between cause and effect. This is an investigative tool, as it organizes randomly connected causes.

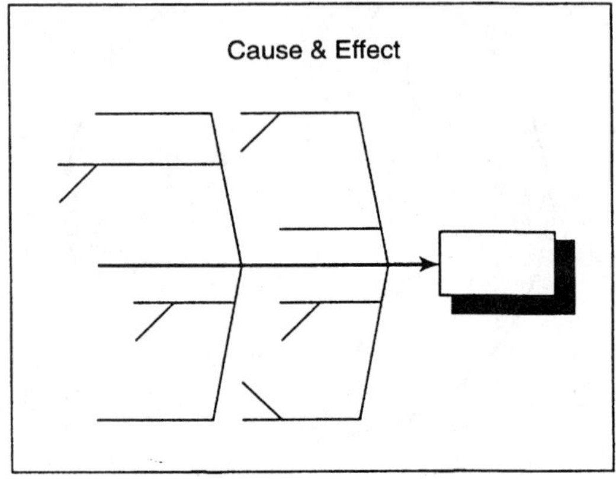

Flow Chart. A visual representation of all the steps in a process under study. This tool develops a clear and common group vision of all the elements in a process.

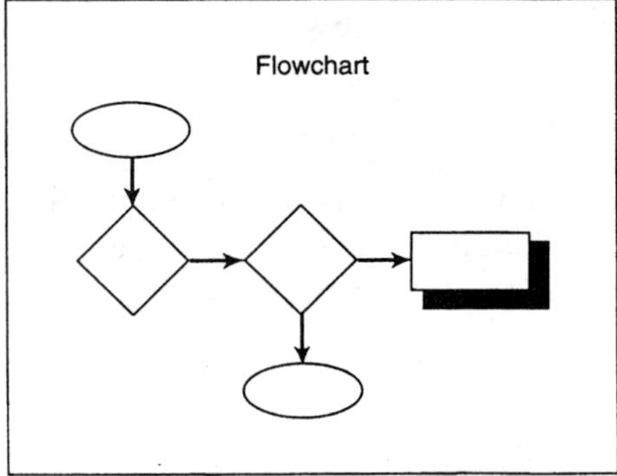

Pareto Chart. A graph showing in descending order the major contributors to a problem. It separates the vital few from the trivial many. This tool directs the team

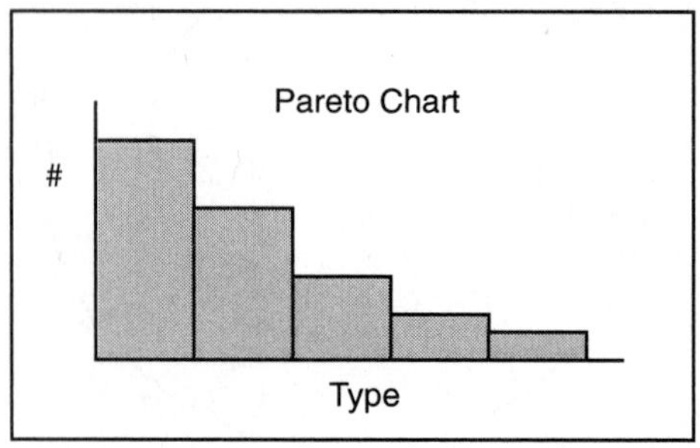

to the factors that are the major contributors to the issue being analyzed.

Run Chart. A graph of how a parameter of a process is behaving over time. This time is useful in highlighting trends, shifts, and possible cycles.

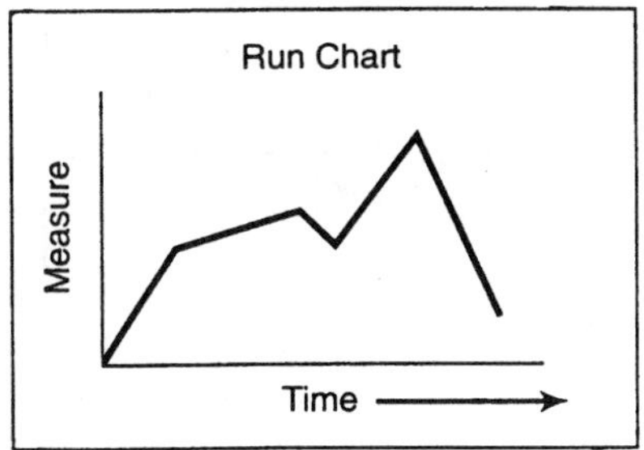

Histogram. A bar graph showing the frequency of occurrence of a measured characteristic of a process.

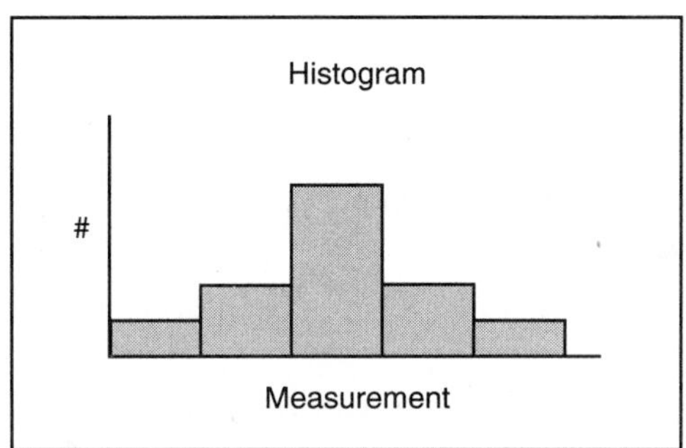

Control Chart. A graph of a process characteristic that is used to determine how much process variability is due to random variations and how much is due to unique events. The chart has control limits that point out events that require

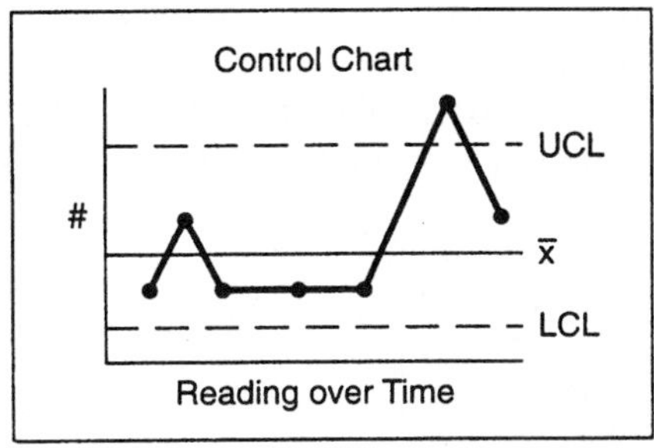

investigation and correction to aid in achieving and maintaining statistical control.

Scatter Diagram. A graphical analysis of the relationship between one variable and another. This tool can be used to screen for possible cause-and-effect relationships.

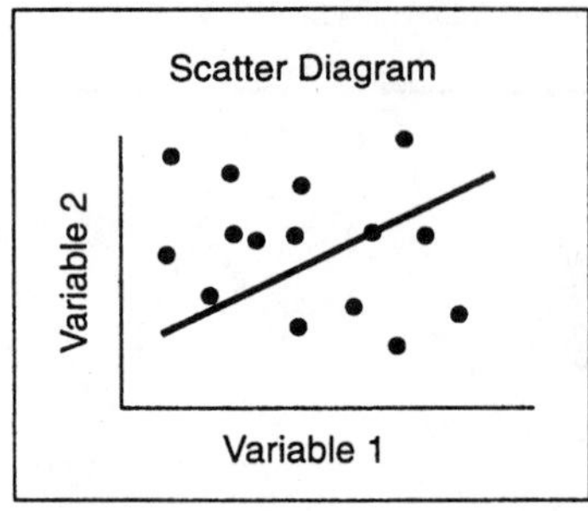

IDENTIFYING CUSTOMERS' AND SUPPLIERS' NEEDS AND EXPECTATIONS

To be effective at daily management, all members of the organization must understand

- Their work process
- Who their customers are
- What their customers' needs and expectations are
- Who their suppliers are
- How to communicate their needs and expectations to their suppliers

The customer/supplier map (1990 Moran, Collett, Cote, and Goal/QPC) is a vehicle that clearly displays these items and shows how they interact to produce a product or service for an internal or external customer. As shown in Figure 21.4, the customer/supplier map is a five-part process to help an individual or work team focus on customer-supplier relationships. During this mapping process, an individual or work team must reflect, itemize, and quantify how well they are meeting or exceeding their customer needs and how well their suppliers are meeting theirs.

***Step 1:** Process Flow Diagram* In the center of the map is a flow process diagram completed for the process under consideration. During this step, process elements or sequences of tasks that lead to a particular end are identified. Everyone must recognize that everything they do is a process. Here are some examples of processes:

- Typing a letter
- Producing a part or product
- Registering a hotel guest

FIGURE 21.4

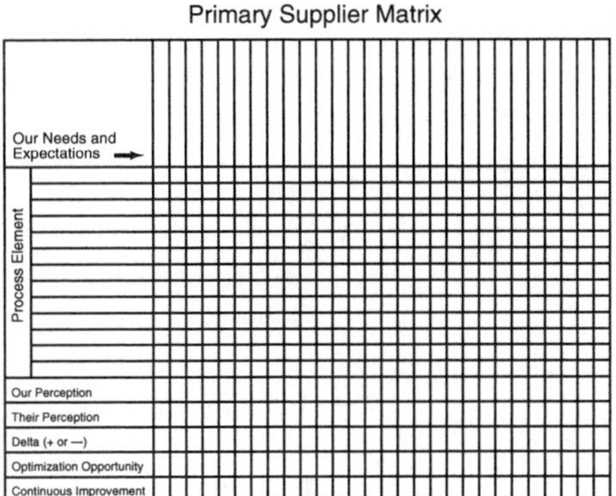

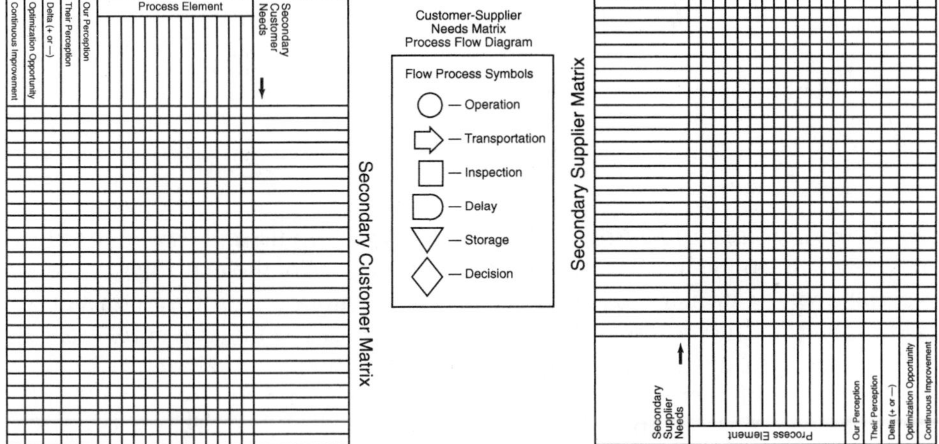

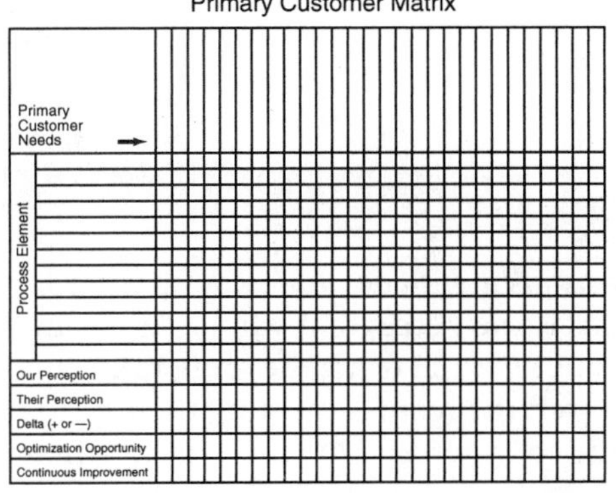

Blank — Not Applicable

1 Does not meet customer needs

3 Acceptable — meets customer needs

5 Exceeds customer needs

- Training a new employee
- Driving a car
- Investigating a crime

All these examples have a sequence of tasks that lead to a particular end. Everything we do is a process.

The team graphs out its process, using the following flow process symbols:

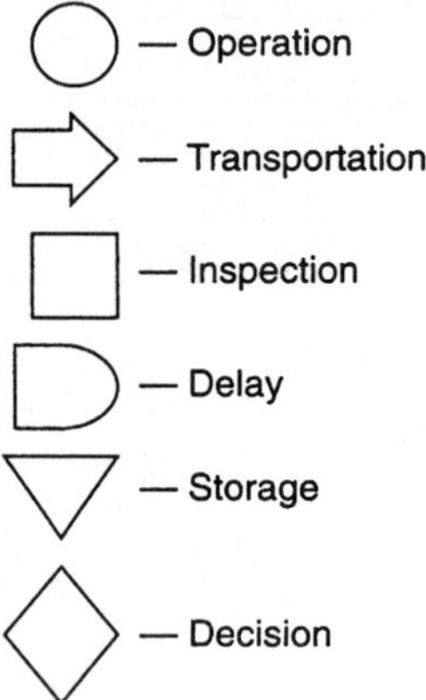

Step 2: *Primary Customer Matrix* Once the inputs, outputs, and flow of the process are known, the individual or team needs to develop a list of their customer needs and expectations. The primary customer of a process is whoever gets the product or service directly from the process. This primary customer can be internal or external.

The team fills out the primary customer matrix (bottom of Figure 21.4) by listing the process elements on the left vertical side and the primary customer needs across the top of the matrix. The next step is to compare each process element against each customer need and attach a score to each comparison as follows:

Blank	**Not applicable**
1	Does Not Meet Customer Needs
3	Acceptable—Meets Customer Needs
5	Exceeds Customer Needs

Once all the comparisons are made, you sum up the columns and divide by the number of entries. This is the perception value. The team then has the customer rate the primary customer matrix, using the same rating scale, and fill in their perception value of how well the team is meeting their needs and expectations. The team then subtracts the "our perception value" from "their perception value" and notes whether there is a plus (+) or minus (−) difference under each column.

The plus values are optimization opportunities and should be standardized and improved continuously because they keep customers satisfied. At this point, the SDCA cycle should be used to hold the gains on these customer satisfiers. Too often companies let the satisfiers turn into dissatisfiers through neglect. These satisfiers have to be monitored and improved continuously.

The negative values indicate items that are dissatisfiers. These need to be subjected to the PDCA cycle to identify the continuous improvement opportunities on which the team can work. Continuous improvement plans should be communicated to the customer. The customer needs to be aware of the fact that improvements are taking place and that these positive changes for improvement are a direct result of the shared communication between the customer and the supplier. The team should develop realistic time frames for these improvements. There is nothing worse than to build up the customer's expectations and then not deliver.

Step 3: *Secondary Customer Matrix* The process of Step 2 is repeated for any secondary customers using the secondary customer matrix (left side of Figure 21.4). A secondary customer is one who receives your output from your primary customer. This step helps you understand how your primary customer uses your output to satisfy their customer. This step leads to an understanding of further continuous improvement and continuous optimization opportunities.

Step 4: *Primary Supplier Matrix* The primary supplier matrix (top of Figure 21.4) forces the team to examine its relationship with its primary supplier, whether it be internal or external. It is the source from which your process directly receives its inputs. This step forces the team to switch roles and be a customer instead of a supplier, requiring a change in mind-set.

Step 5: *Secondary Supplier Matrix* This is a repeat of Step 4 and the reverse process of the Primary/Secondary Customer Matrix. This matrix is on the right side of Figure 21.4. Use of a daily management project activity plan sheet, as shown in Figure 21.5, will clarify the sequence that has to happen and determine who is responsible for each activity for successful implementation. This process helps an organization improve its relationship with a secondary or minor supplier.

THE BENEFITS OF CUSTOMER/SUPPLIER MAPPING AND DAILY MANAGEMENT

The customer/supplier map incorporates a series of matrices to empower employees to act on information and take action. Through it, an organization can develop

- Clear understandings of needs and expectations
- A process to communicate them
- Fact-driven teams

FIGURE 21.5 ***Daily Management Project Activity Plan***

Daily Management Project: ____________________ Team Name: ______ Date: ______

Activity	Primary Responsibility	Secondary Responsibility	PDCA Category	Month											
				Week	1	2	3	4	5	1	2	3	4	5	S

Once a work team or individual becomes skilled in the customer/supplier mapping process, they begin to understand their pockets of excellence, job functions, areas for immediate improvement, and metrics to track progress, and know how to set a time frame for improvements.

Customer/supplier mapping can be used to move a work team out of management-by-crisis mode and into management by fact. The team will appreciate that the customer's needs and expectations are dynamic and must be monitored continuously; thus, the team will meet changes in these needs and expectations proactively—not after the fact. Once the work team has identified continuous optimization and improvement opportunities, it can use daily management tools to discover the root causes of these identified opportunities and plan improvements. The work team can delineate its activities on a daily management project activities plan worksheet (Figure 21.5), which allows them to understand who is responsible for implementing the desired change and the time it will take to complete the change. The last column on the worksheet is marked "S" for standardization. The team checks off this category once the activity element is incorporated and standardized as part of the ongoing work process.

This intensive process involves everyone in the organization and helps develop a mind-set of continuous improvement that requires everyone to fully understand, measure, control, standardize, and constantly improve their work processes. The benefits to be reaped from it include more streamlined and efficient operations, bolstered by heightened employee and customer satisfaction.

Additional resources

King, R. *Hoshin Planning: The Developmental Approach.* Methuen, Mass.: Goal/QPC, 1989.

The Memory Jogger. Methuen, Mass.: Goal/QPC, 1988.

Moran, J., R. Talbot, and R. Benson. *A Guide to Graphical Problem-Solving Processes.* Milwaukee, Wis.: Quality Press, 1990.

Reading 22

Statistical Process Control: Sophisticated but Simple

BY ELLEN DOMB

Statistical Process Control (SPC) has been evolving over the last seventy years from a mathematical tool of specialists to a family of accessible methodologies to a hierarchy of tools used throughout the manufacturing process by operations workers, industrial engineers, quality specialists, statisticians and managers for process control, process analysis, and process improvement. The understanding gained through this evolution is now being applied to the challenges of quality in the service industries.

The sophistication of SPC has been very well documented (see accompanying reading list for some personal favorites). Detailed presentations are available at any level of mathematical complexity to explain how to collect process data, how to calculate all the SPC parameters, how to plot many kinds of charts, and how to interpret the charts in terms of process control and process improvement opportunities.

The simplicity of SPC is less frequently addressed—why use SPC? The answer: so that "how to" knowledge is applied in an environment for success in continuously improving the quality of what is delivered to the customer.

The intuitive appeal of SPC emerges at many levels depending on each user's experience and knowledge. For example:

Inspection is an inadequate method of assuring product or service quality.

Inspection never adds value. At best, it causes rejection of products that don't meet specification before they reach the customer. Since services are created at the time the customer needs them, inspection is even less effective for services, since it only finds problems after the customer has been affected.

SOURCE: 1993 report reprinted with the permission of the author.

Inspection never detects all defects. Inspection is a process like any other, with inherent variation.

Analysis of the causes of defects occurs after inspection detects them, which is frequently a considerable time after the defective product was created. Feedback to analyze the process and correct it if appropriate occurs after there has been an opportunity to create many more defective products or deliver more poor service.

The two concepts that move a process from the realm of quality assurance by inspection to quality creation are

Control

Capability

To appreciate both concepts, we need to appreciate the concept of

Variation

A process that is under control is consistent and predictable. Since it may consistently, predictably produce some results that are undesirable, inspection may still be needed after control is established.

Process capability is a measure of how well the control of the process causes its output to match the needs of the customer. A highly capable process produces services or products that consistently, predictably meet the customers' needs.

The objective of SPC is first to get processes under control, next to maintain the control, and then to improve them to increase capability.

Figure 22.1 is a pictorial view of moving a process from chaos, to control, to continuous improvement. The curves represent the frequency distribution of a process parameter, such as

Number of occasions a customer had to wait (vertical axis) versus length of wait (horizontal axis)

Number of items with a particular diameter versus diameter

Number of times a particular percentage of defects occurred versus percentage of defects

The uncontrolled process can be one where the distribution is constant in time but the mean shifts, where the mean is stable but the distribution shifts, or a combination of symptoms (Figure 22.1a, 1b, 1c). Figure 1d represents achieving control.

Why do processes have variation? After all, if we're talking about quality, a thing is either done right or it's not done right! Process variation results from the accumulation of activities that are not controlled or not well understood that influence any process. Examples range from vibration to humidity to wearing of a tool to "the computer is down" to use of many suppliers whose products all meet specification but differ in areas that weren't specified to whether the manager or the employee or the customer had a good breakfast that morning.

FIGURE 22.1 *From chaos to control. Time sequence of frequency distributions for a process*

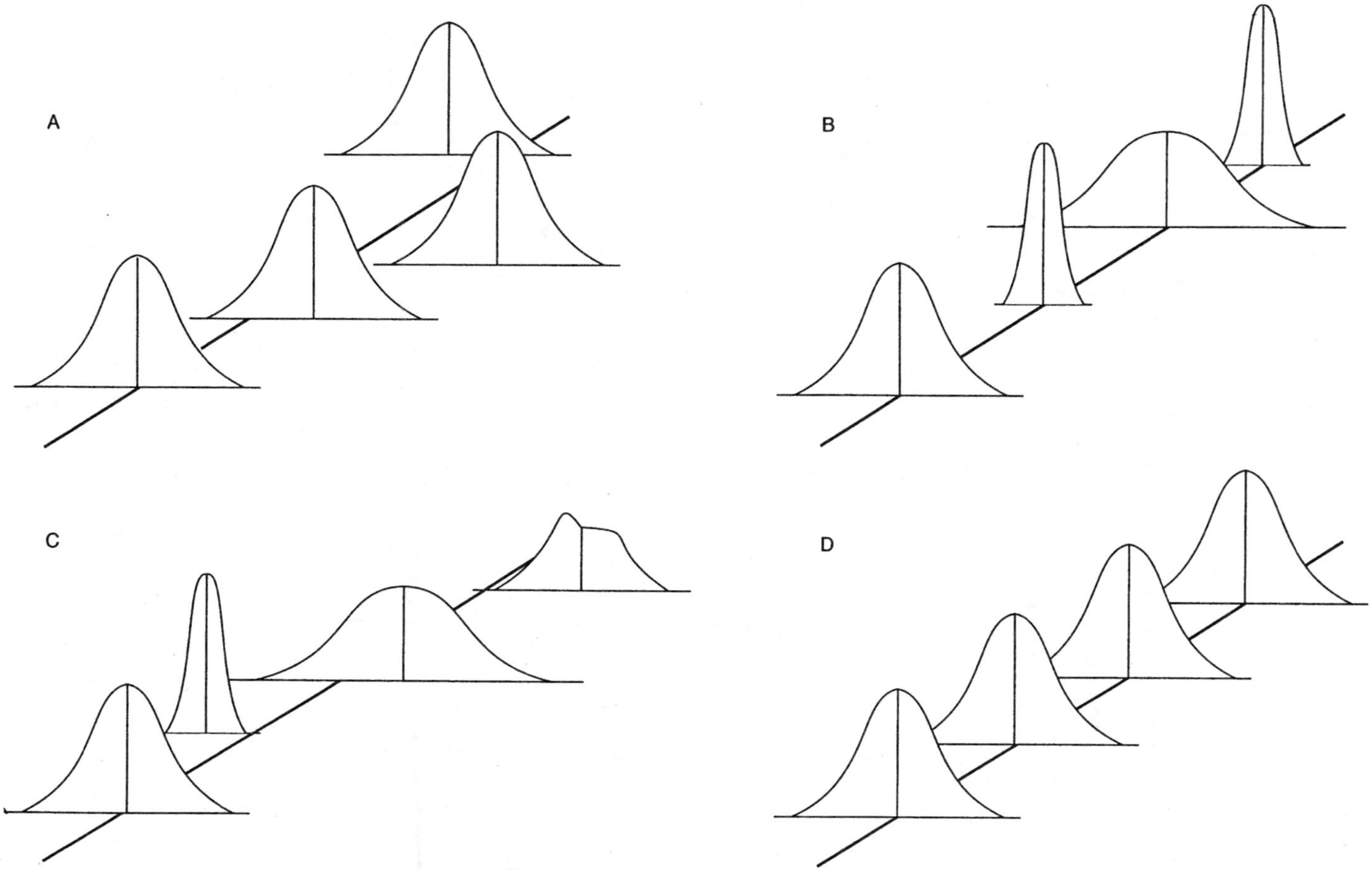

A

B

C

D

SPC identifies two categories of reasons for variation, called special causes and common causes. Special causes are attributable to specific changes from the normal process. Examples include trying to work with broken tools, a new employee told to "try your best" but not given training, new suppliers, and changes in the measuring technique or tools.

Common causes are present every time the process is performed, but combine randomly to create variation in the final result. Work originally done by Shewhart and expanded by Deming and others demonstrates that attempts to identify special causes and common causes are difficult but that the most expensive mistake is to assume that all causes of variation are either special or common. It is best to know that both can be present—and to be wrong part of the time—than to ignore the existence of the two categories.

The most common tool for monitoring process control and for identifying occurrences of special causes is the control chart, Figure 22.2. There are control charts that deal with variables (length, width, diameter, color intensity, voltage, waiting time, etc.) and those that deal with attributes (number of defects, pass/fail, go/no-go situations.) A simple variable chart is shown.

Significant features of the control chart are

Vertical axis, the value of the variable;

Horizontal axis, time or sample number;

Upper and lower control limits.

The upper and lower control limits are calculated values based on the results of running the process without interference or adjustment. The calculated values are an estimate of three standard deviations from the process mean (see Figure 22.3). In other words, there is a 99.73 percent probability that the measured variable will fall inside the control limits, if the process is under control.

In practical terms, companies using SPC usually teach their workers to gather data, make the charts, and stop the process if a measurement is out of control, or if any of several patterns appear in the data that indicate that the process is no

FIGURE 22.2 ***A typical variable control chart***

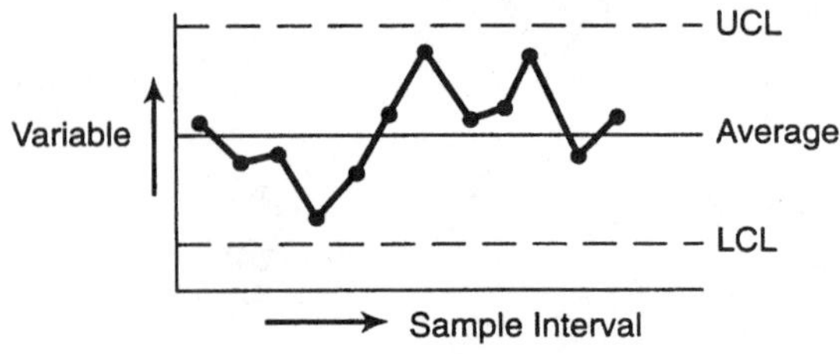

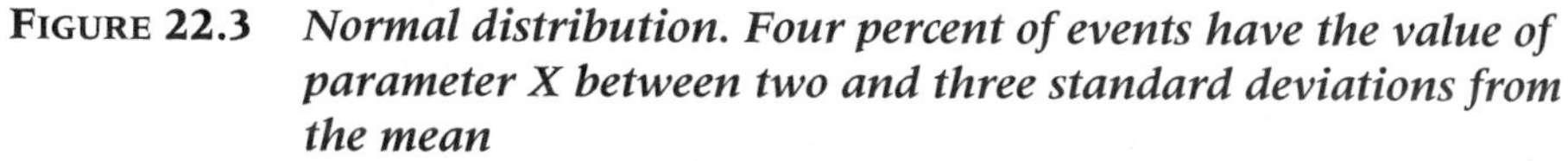

FIGURE 22.3 ***Normal distribution. Four percent of events have the value of parameter X between two and three standard deviations from the mean***

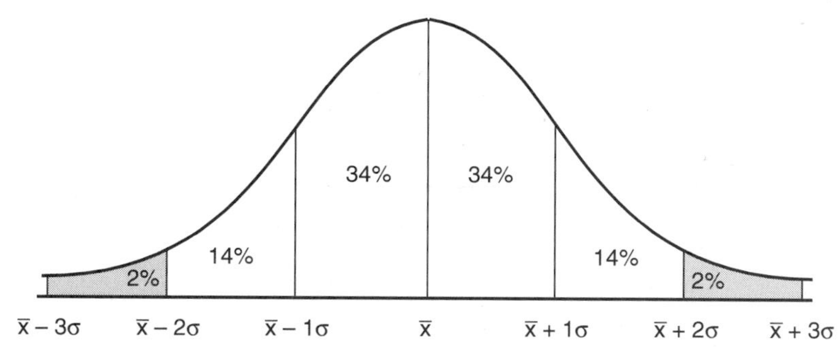

longer functioning normally. This prevents continuation of work when special causes are causing increases in variability. In many companies, the same workers, alone or with a team of colleagues, then diagnose and fix the problems, and resume work, monitoring the process control. In other situations and other company cultures, the worker identifies the situation, but diagnosis, cure, and startup are handled by supervisors, quality engineers, or other specialists.

Throughout this discussion of control, we have not mentioned customer satisfaction. The process can be under control statistically, and still not satisfy the customer. Figure 22.4 shows two situations:

> Fig. 22.4A. The specification limits (customer requirements) are wider than the control limits. In this case, the process is considered "capable" since staying in control statistically predicts a high probability of satisfying the customer.
>
> Fig. 22.4B. The specification limits are narrower than the control limits. The process is considered not "capable" since it can be in control and still produce a substantial number of out-of-specification results. Both cases shown here feature symmetrical normal distributions. If distribution is not symmetrical or not normal, the process may be not capable, even if the specification limit width is less than the control limit width.

The use of three standard deviations and the control limits as the defining parameters for capability is based on historical precedent. Organizations that have worked in quality transformation throughout the 1980s and 1990s are setting their own goals at six standard deviations (3.4 defects/million) and even higher.

Once the process is both under control and capable, i.e., predictable and meeting customer requirements predictably, why should you invest in continuing to improve?

FIGURE 22.4A ***Capable process***

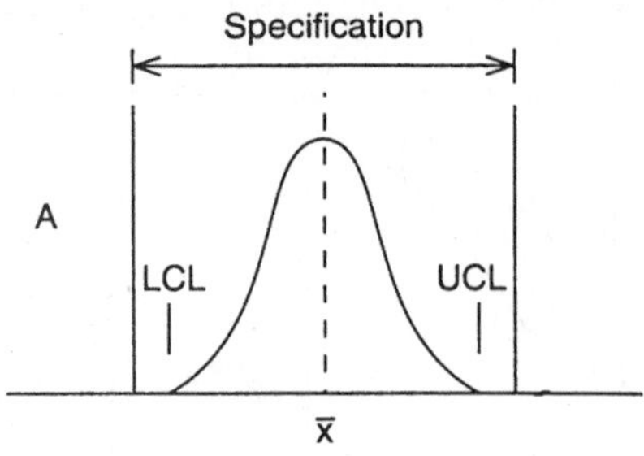

FIGURE 22.4B ***Not capable. Shaded areas are measurements in control but not producing usable results***

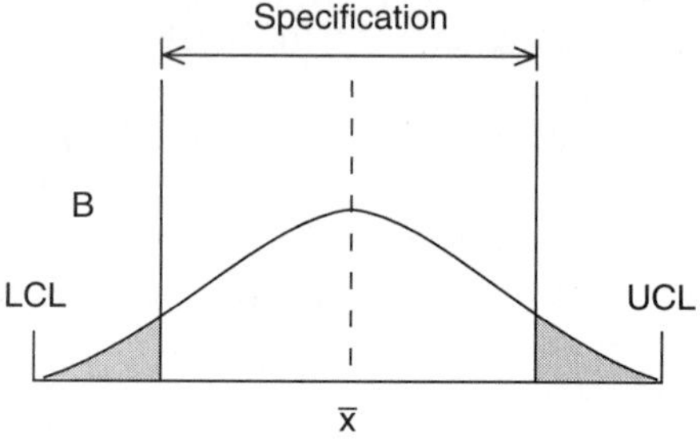

Specifications are frequently not set to optimize the usefulness of the service or product! They are set by tradition, by convenience, by known tooling parameters, or through a combination of perceptions of customer needs. A new view of the loss suffered by the user of high variability products is shown in Figure 22.5.

Conceptually, the closer the distribution is to the specification limit, the higher the probability that it will not be suitable for use. This is in marked contrast to the earlier view that any result was OK if it was within specification limits. The value to the customer is increased if variation is reduced. In manufacturing, many organizations are now taking steps beyond SPC to create processes that are insensitive to variation in intermediate process steps. These concepts are collectively called robust design or design for producibility. Equivalent concepts apply in service delivery, but are not yet widely known.

Statistical Process Control is the route to continuous improvement for many organizations. The journey from chaos to control to improvement is a learning

FIGURE 22.5 *Benefits of increasing capability*

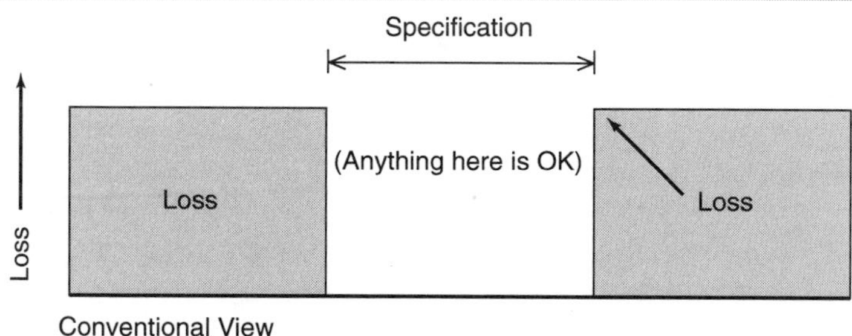

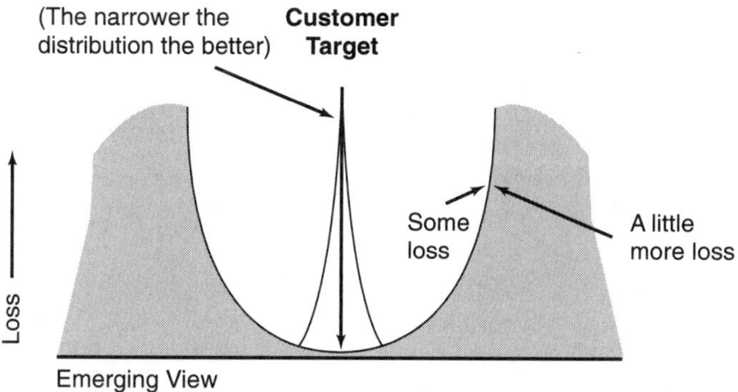

experience for all participants and rewards those who have the discipline to apply its lessons.

References

Amsden, R. T., H. E. Butler, and D. M. Amsden. *SPC Simplified: Practical Steps to Quality.* White Plains, NY: Quality Resources, 1989.

Deming, W. E. *Out of the Crisis.* MIT Center for Engineering, Cambridge, MA, 1986.

Hosotani, K. *Japanese Quality Concepts: An Overview.* English Translation 1992. Quality Resources, White Plains, NY.

Scherkenbach, W. W. *The Deming Route to Quality and Productivity: Road Maps and Roadblocks.* Washington, DC: CEEPress Books, 1986.

Wheeler, D. J., and D. S. Chambers. *Understanding Statistical Process Control.* Knoxville, TN: SPC Press, 1986.

Reading 23

Quality Function Deployment: A Process for Translating Customers' Needs into a Better Product and Profit

GOAL QPC Research Report

This report is a product of the Quality Function Deployment Team.

Prepared by:

Doug Daetz	Hewlett-Packard
Thomas K. Flaherty	Rockwell International
Mary Lou Kotecki	Deere & Company
Glen Mazur	Japanese Business Consultants
Stan Marsh	GOAL/QPC
Jack Moran	Polaroid Corporation
Jack B. ReVelle	Hughes Aircraft Company

Abstract

Quality Function Deployment was first introduced in the United States in an article by Dr. Yoji Akao in the October 1983 issue of *Quality Progress*, a monthly publication of the American Society for Quality Control. In November 1983 the Cambridge Corporation of Tokyo, under the leadership of Masaaki Imai, conducted a Total Quality Control (TQC) and Quality Function Deployment (QFD) workshop in Chicago.

Source: Excerpt from *GOAL/QPC Research Report* #89-10-02. Contributed by Copyright © GOAL/QPC, 13 Branch Street, Methuen, MA 01844-1953.

Quality Function Deployment is a structured process that provides a means to identify and carry the customer's voice through each stage of product and service development and implementation. QFD is achieved by cross-functional teams which collect, interpret, document, and prioritize customer requirements. Through the use of charts and matrices, quality responsibilities are effectively deployed to any needed activity within a company to ensure that appropriate quality is achieved.

QFD relies on easy to understand techniques supported by analytical tools. QFD, though structured, is a flexible planning tool which allows organizations to react quickly in developing or improving products and services and which also allows for creative and innovative thinking.

Application of QFD is growing at a rapid rate as product and service industries have begun to understand the need for customer-driven management and systems to continuously improve their competitive position.

INTRODUCTION

The evolution of a quality philosophy in Japan began with the visits of Dr. W. Edwards Deming and Dr. Joseph Juran from 1950 through 1954. The influence of these two individuals resulted in quality becoming the distinguishing characteristic that led to Japan's significant market successes. In the 1960s employee involvement at all levels within a Japanese organization became standard procedure. This quality philosophy and participative environment evolved in the 1970s into what is now called Total Quality Management.

Total Quality Management (TQM) begins with listening to the voice of the customer. TQM threads this voice throughout the product and service development process. As illustrated in Figure 23.1, the TQM concept can be represented by a wheel containing various supporting elements.

The hub of the wheel is the Customer-Driven Master Plan. This central plan describes fundamental improvements that an organization needs to make and how the improvements will be accomplished. The second level of detail in the TQM Wheel includes cross-functional management, which focuses on the horizontal activities in an organization. Quality Function Deployment is a subset of this element. QFD is a system for understanding what the customer wants and for assigning the responsibility of achieving appropriate quality to all the parts of an organization.

QFD, as a formalized approach, started in 1972 at the Kobe Shipyard, a division of Mitsubishi, with the introduction of product planning using a matrix. Dr. Yoji Akao expanded the basic concept from the Kobe exercise into a coordinated set of matrices and charts that looked into planning, cost, reliability, new technology, and production. This activity developed into many of the basic QFD approaches that are in use today.

In June 1987, *Business Week* stated that the typical American factory spends 20 percent to 50 percent of its operating budget to find and fix mistakes and that as

FIGURE 23.1 *The TQM wheel*

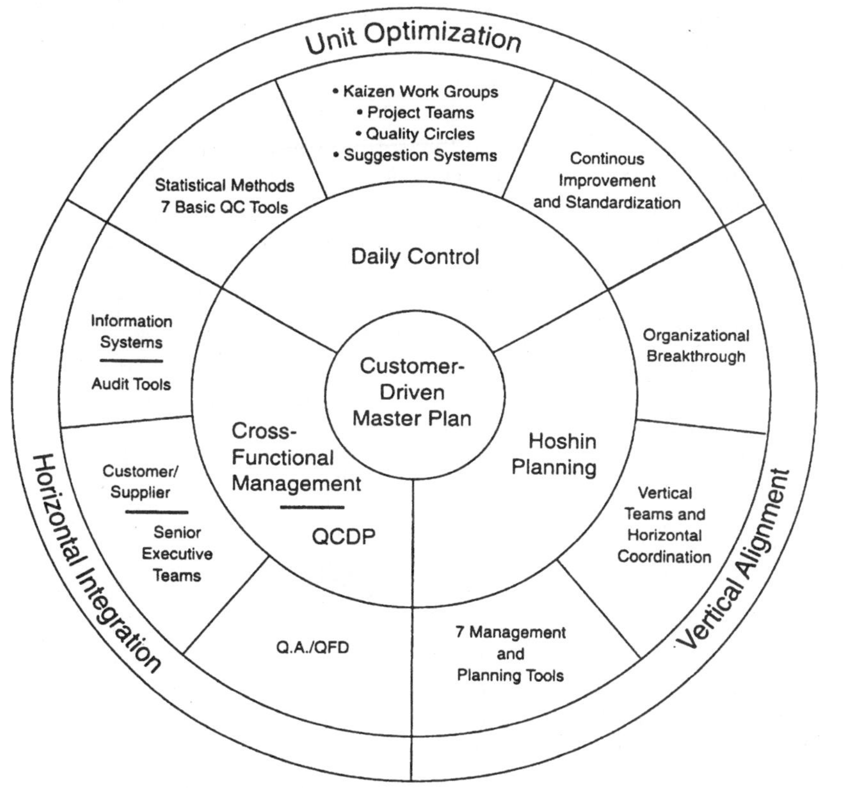

many as 25 percent of factory employees do not produce anything. These people rework things that were not done right the first time. The same article stated some 80 percent of quality related problems occur during the design phase of product development or during out-sourcing as the result of purchasing policies that value low price over the quality of purchased parts and materials. All of these behaviors add cost and ultimately affect a product's market position.

Many major companies have decided that if they are to remain competitive in the global marketplace, they must listen to their customers and develop products and services that satisfy customer needs. The October 1988 issue of *Quality Progress* reinforced that position with a set of articles written by top executives from prestigious companies. Colby H. Chandler, Chairman and CEO of Eastman Kodak Company, expressed his view by saying, "We must take quality beyond customer satisfaction to customer delight. Customer delight is the delivery of products and services that exceed expectations." Roberto C. Goizueta, Chairman of the Coca-Cola Company, reemphasized the thought with, "Make the consumer someone special to you, and your products will become something special to him or her." In the current economic environment, *listening to the customer* is a necessity if companies aspire to satisfy or exceed customer needs.

Quality Function Deployment is a planning tool and a process for translating customer requirements into products or services. It enables prioritization of needs, innovative responses to those needs, and coordinates implementation for maximum effect. When instituted, QFD leads to process or product efforts that enable a company to exceed the expectations of the customer. QFD works best within a company when there is organizational commitment and a disciplined approach to implementation. Fundamental changes in company culture may also be required.

Quality Function Deployment encompasses every phase of development and delivery of products and services. QFD involves the functions of marketing, research, design, manufacturing, quality, purchasing, sales, and service. The QFD discipline provides both a framework and a structured process to enhance an organization's ability to communicate, document, analyze, and prioritize. The documentation and analysis steps lead to breakthroughs which illuminate understanding and enhance competitiveness.

QFD AND THE VOICE OF THE CUSTOMER

Obtaining and clarifying the voice of the customer is an important task. Sources of customer input are market surveys, focus groups, warranty claims, and interviews. Regardless of the methods chosen, it is imperative to obtain the voice of the customer. Figure 23.2 is a cause and effect diagram which illustrates the complexity involved in capturing customer wants and needs.

It is unlikely that customers will define all of their preferences even with a very efficient method of gathering customer data. Through a graphical model, Dr. Noriaki Kano, a Japanese professor and consultant, clarified why customer input can be insufficient. This model shows relationships between product and service attributes and customer satisfaction. (See Figure 23.3.)

The arrow in the middle of the diagram labeled "one dimensional quality" illustrates instances where customers express what they want and where their satisfaction depends on product/service conformance to the expressed requirement. The arrow on the bottom represents details that customers expect. Because these characteristics are taken for granted, customers are less likely to mention them. Safety features are an example of this category. Products are expected to be safe. If they are not safe, customers are unhappy.

The arrow on the top represents "exciting" quality. Features which fall into this category can provide customer satisfaction, but not dissatisfaction. The customers do not know about them in advance and do not expect them. As a result, customers will not ask for them in an open-ended focus group. This category includes items that the producer or service provider often develop themselves. Generally, they result from talent resident within the producer or service organization and can represent significant competitive opportunities.

FIGURE 23.2 *Voice of the customer*

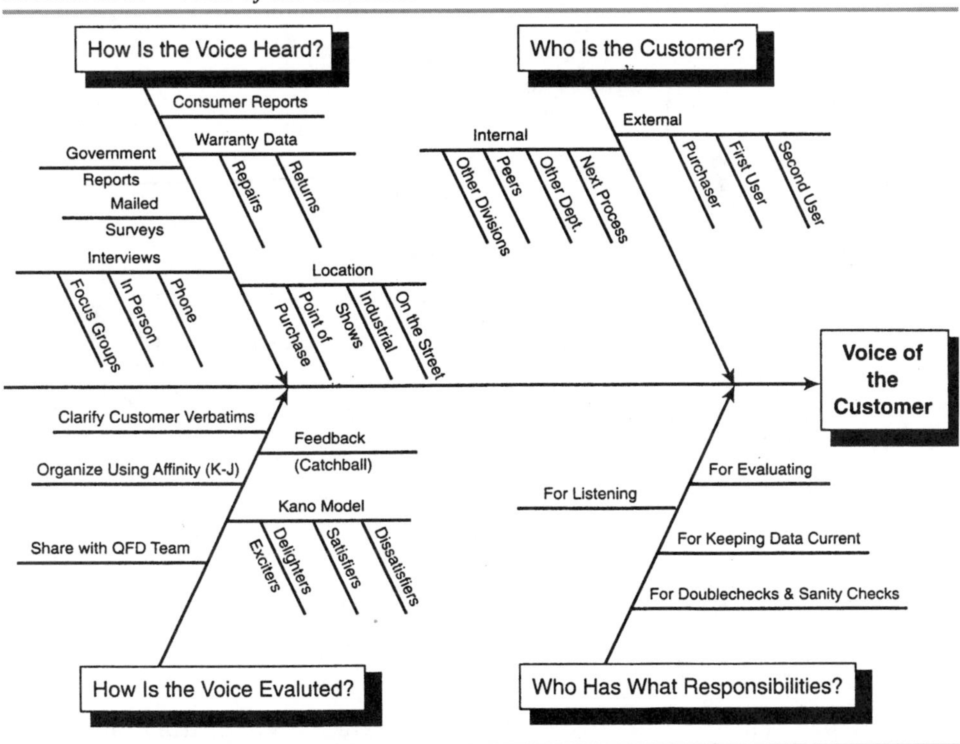

Features which contribute to exciting quality do not stay in this category very long. As customers become accustomed to them, the attraction level of the features moves toward the bottom and to the right on the Kano model. Eventually, customers will view these features as one dimensional or expected.

QFD IMPLEMENTATION

Implementation of QFD should be considered in terms of four phases:

1. ***Organization Phase:*** Management selects the product or service to be improved, the appropriate cross-functional team, and defines the scope of the QFD study. Initial QFD projects should address improvement on products or services that already exist and are well understood. This makes it possible to concentrate on the QFD techniques. Later projects can focus on new product or service introductions.
2. ***Descriptive Phase:*** The selected team defines the products/services from several viewpoints: customer demands, quality characteristics, functions, new

FIGURE 23.3 ***Kano model of customer satisfaction***

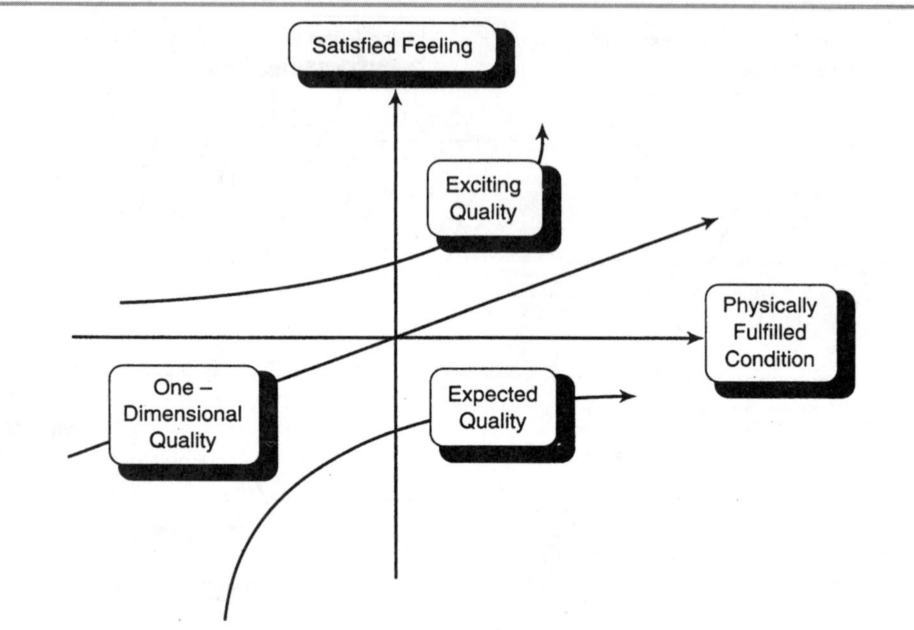

technology, reliability, and cost. QFD uses a matrix system to array the various viewpoints, to assess current and competitive positions, and to establish and plan for target values. QFD matrices are often shown in literature as illustrated in Figures 23.4 and 23.5.

3. ***Breakthrough Phase:*** The team selects areas for improvement and competitive advantage through investigation of technology, new concepts, better reliability, and cost reduction and monitors the bottleneck engineering process.
4. ***Implementation Phase:*** The team defines the product or service and how it will be produced. Using QFD, the team carries the development of the product or service through preparation for production, delivery, and confirmation of customer satisfaction.

USERS OF QFD

In 1986 Dr. Yoji Akao, past chairman of the QFD research committee of the Japan Society for Quality Control (JSQC), conducted a survey of QFD usage among the larger member companies of the Union of Japanese Scientists and Engineers (JUSE). The study showed that although QFD was not being used in some Japanese companies, it had grown significantly and was used with great success at many Japanese companies. (See Figure 23.6.)

FIGURE 23.4 ***Basic house of quality***

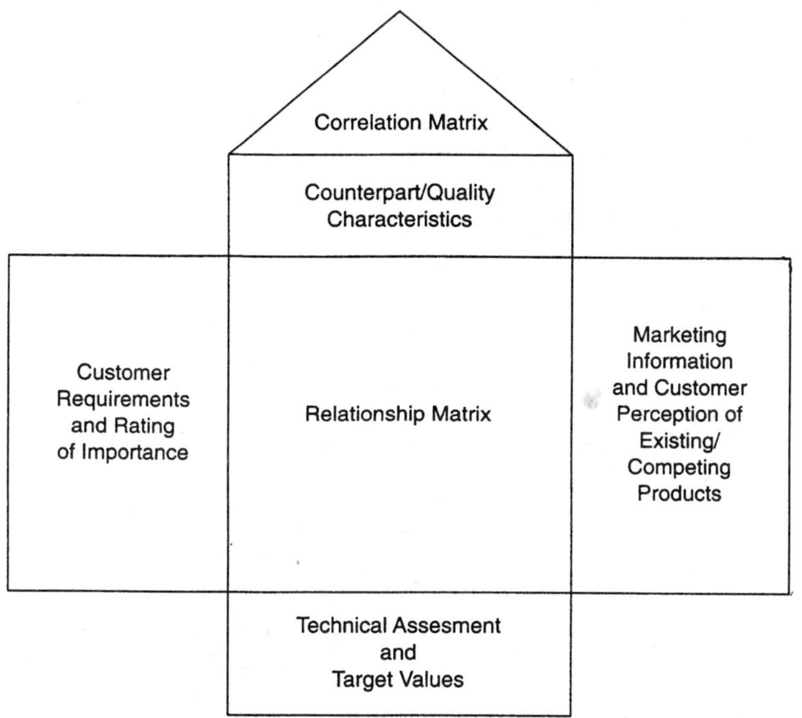

Currently, many U.S. companies are using QFD. In the automotive industry, Ford, Chrysler, and General Motors, users of QFD themselves, are involving their supplier bases in QFD studies. In the electronics field, Digital Equipment Corporation and Texas Instruments have been QFD pioneers. Numerous other companies use QFD including: Procter & Gamble, Deere and Company, The Kendall Company, Polaroid, Rockwell International, Hughes Aircraft, and Hewlett-Packard.

Because use of QFD in the United States is so recent, there are few documented success stories for a wide variety of industries. A further difficulty in obtaining detailed case studies which describe successes lies in the reluctance of companies that have had major successes to broadcast those activities to their competition.

THE BENEFITS OF QFD

The results of the 1986 JSQC survey conducted by Dr. Yoji Akao and others were published with details on the status of QFD in Japanese companies. Companies which used QFD reported the following benefits:

FIGURE 23.5 *QFD requirements carry through the development process*

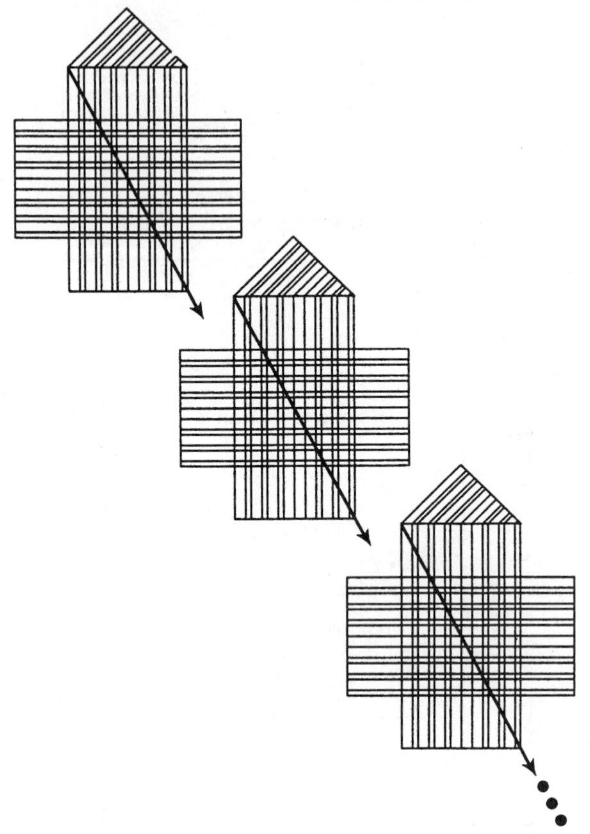

- Decreased start-up problems
- Competitive analysis became possible
- Control points clarified
- Effective communications between divisions
- Design intent carried through to manufacturing

Additional information gathered from translations of Japanese reports as well as U.S. company presentations and publications highlights other benefits:

- Better communication
- Fewer product/service changes
- Better reliability of key elements
- Improved market research

FIGURE 23.6 *Results of JSQC question: Do you use QFD?*

Industry / Answer	Electronics	Precision Machines	Transportation	Process Industry	Metal/steel	Construction	Other Manufacturing	Service	Total
Yes	24	14	13	10	1	9	2	7	80
No	14	7	2	15	2	2	11	15	68
Number of replies	38	21	15	25	3	11	13	22	148

- Quality is built in "upstream"
- Reduced product/service development time
- Lower start-up costs
- Increased understanding of complex relationships
- Greater clarity of organizational and program priorities
- Better designs
- Identification and resolution of conflicting requirements

Quality Function Deployment provides a tracking system for development efforts and preserves knowledge for future reference. QFD helps companies determine where to invest time and money, ensure that cost-oriented quality is achieved, and differentiate their products/services from those of the competition. QFD ensures that each phase of the development cycle is rooted in customer needs and, within the development process, serves to facilitate the use of other tools, techniques, and in-house expertise at the appropriate time.

CONCLUSION

Each year various conferences bring together speakers to describe a wide variety of continuous improvement tools that will enable companies to achieve "*world class*" status. These tools are important and certainly have their place in the quality improvement process. The tools alone, however, cannot provide a solution to needed quality improvement. Fundamental changes to planning and listening to customers must occur if a company is to become a strong competitor.

This paper has presented one of the TQM planning tools—Quality Function Deployment. QFD provides activities that bring together all required disciplines to work and plan the product or service development efforts in a highly disciplined, communicative, and effective manner. QFD's focus on the voice of the customer contributes to a company's ability to attain quality levels that provide a cost competitive position in the world marketplace.

Reading 24

Hoshin Planning: A Planning System for Implementing Total Quality Management

GOAL QPC RESEARCH REPORT

TQC Education Levels/Functions
Hoshin Planning/Management by Policy
Quality Function Deployment
Strategy: TQC Master Plan

Researched and edited by GOAL/QPC Research Committee. MBP/Hoshin Planning Team:

Donald Andrews	Dow Chemical/Canada
Michael Brassard	GOAL/QPC
Jack Brown	Procter & Gamble
James Cuddy	Spectra Incorporated
Lois Gold	Hewlett-Packard
David Lord	Procter & Gamble
Alberto Pardo	Apollo Division of Hewlett-Packard
James Riley	IBM

HOSHIN PLANNING RESEARCH TEAM

WHAT IS TOTAL QUALITY MANAGEMENT (TQM)?

TQM (used interchangeably with the Japanese term TQC) is a *system* for meeting and exceeding customer needs through company-wide continuous improvement based upon the implementation of the Plan-Do-Check-Act Cycle supporting *processes, organization,* and *tools* by every manager and employee.

Note that TQM is simply a *system* to better serve the customer. TQM is just a means to an end. Unless this view is maintained, it is very easy to focus more on the "what" of TQM (Models and Methods) rather than on the "why" of TQM.

WHAT IS HOSHIN PLANNING?

As in the case of TQM, Hoshin Planning is a system. It is a component of the TQM system that allows an organization to plan and execute strategic organizational breakthrough.

Its key elements are:

- A planning and implementation process that is continuously improved throughout the year (P-D-C-A)
- Focus on key systems that need to be improved to achieve strategic objectives
- Participation and coordination by all levels and departments as appropriate in the planning, development, and deployment of yearly objectives and means
- Planning and execution based upon facts
- Goals and action plans which cascade through the organization based upon the true capability of the organization

HOW DOES HOSHIN PLANNING INTEGRATE WITH TQM?

When all is said and done, TQM is a system to achieve the following organizational objectives:

Daily Control can be viewed as the application of Plan-Do-Check-Act (PDCA) to daily *incremental* continuous improvement. Hoshin Planning is simply PDCA applied to the planning and execution of a few critical (strategic) organization objectives. Cross-functional management concerns the systems by which functions and departments work together to achieve common organizational targets such as quality, cost, and delivery/productivity. Hoshin Planning is related to daily control and cross-functional management as follows:

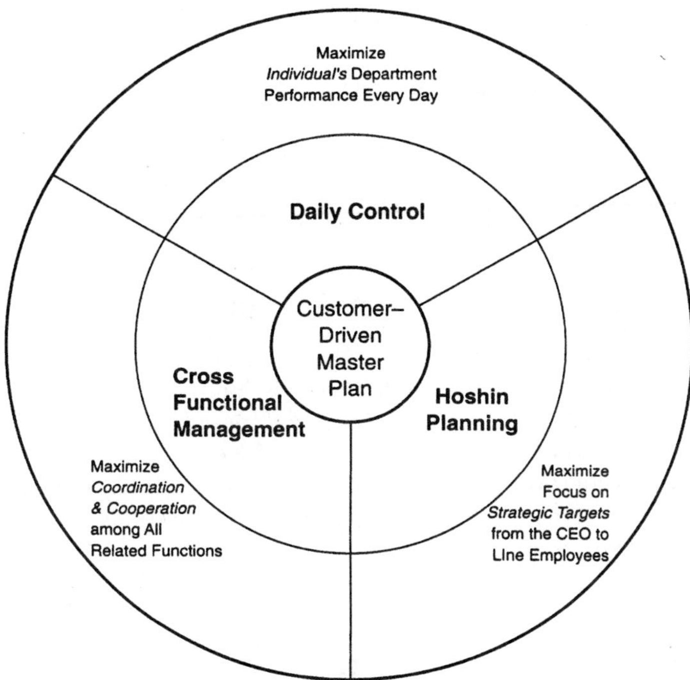

1. **Daily Control**

   (a) Hoshin Planning draws information from the ongoing data collection and analysis of the Daily Control process to identify broad system problems in which breakthrough is needed.

   (b) Once breakthroughs have occurred they can then become the focus of daily continuous improvement.

2. **Cross-Functional Management**

   (a) Quality Function Deployment (QFD), a key system for listening to and incorporating the "voice of the customer," can identify areas for planning breakthrough.

   (b) The Hoshin Planning process often requires cooperation across functions as well as vertical alignment.

WHAT ARE THE BENEFITS OF HOSHIN PLANNING?

- Creates an Established Process to Execute Breakthrough Year after Year
- Creates Commitment to Both the Direction and Implementation Paths Chosen
- Increases Interdepartmental Cooperation
- Draws upon and Reinforces the Plan-Do-Check-Act Cycle (PDCA) in Monthly Progress Reviews

- Creates a Planning and Implementation System that is Responsive, Flexible, Yet Disciplined
- Gives Leadership a Mechanism to Understand the Key Problem Areas in a Company
- Creates Quicker and More Accurate Feedback Loops
- Provides a Common Focus throughout the Organization

HOW DOES THE HOSHIN PLANNING PROCESS WORK?

In TQM *how* a process is implemented is as important as *what* that process includes. It is not enough to have a defined, disciplined set of process steps. TQM depends on predictable implementation. Traditional management approaches accept the fact that some managers will execute well and others will not. Hoshin Planning provides methods that eliminate at least some of the natural manager to manager variability. This combination of process and methods can be summarized in the following equation:

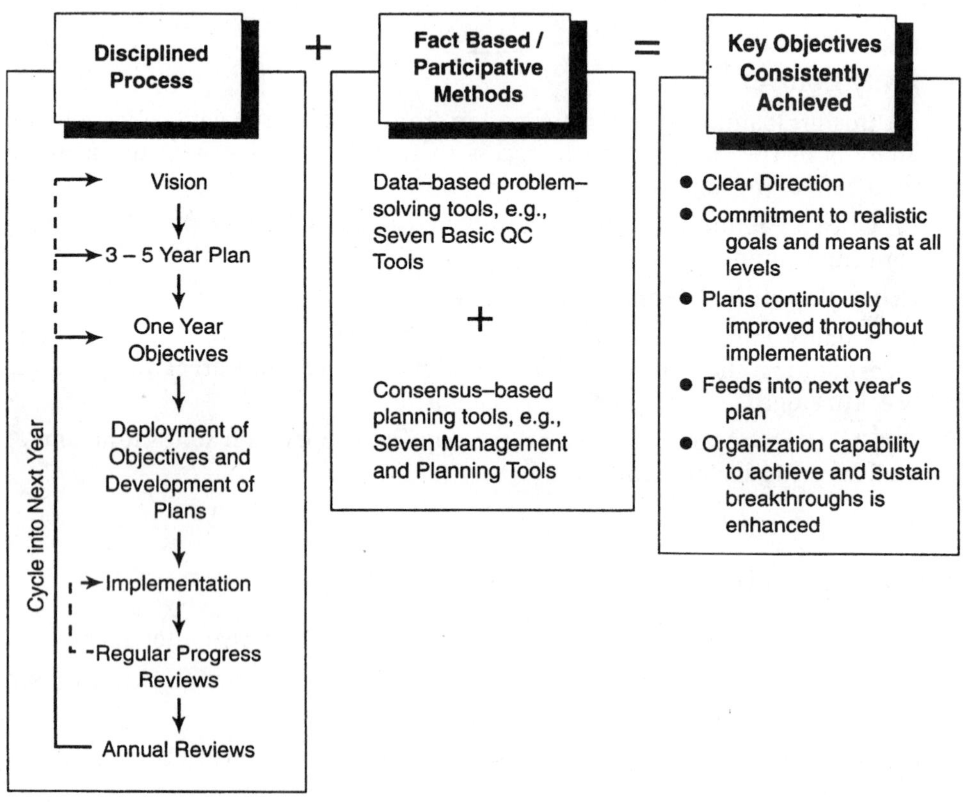

THE HOSHIN PLANNING PROCESS

The steps in the previous graphic describe the evolution of achievable objectives and plans that flow from any organization's long term vision. The vision results from a complete understanding of the outside world and how the organization plans to fit into it long term. The 3–5 year plan is based on an analysis of the broad areas for improvement that will block the attainment of the vision. The one year plan refines these broad areas into *a few key objectives* that must be achieved *this* year. The *key* departments/functions are then identified and involved in the development of sub-objectives and plans to achieve the one year plan. Each appropriate level within these departments/functions identifies areas of improvement that would help achieve the objective. These plans are then implemented. Each level reviews its own performance regularly (monthly or quarterly) and makes necessary changes to the plan. The overall progress for the year is reviewed 9–10 months into the fiscal year to determine whether the plans will be achieved and should be replaced with new objectives for next year or continued into the next year.

THE HOSHIN PLANNING METHODS

The process above is simply a *procedure* for planning and implementation. In order to ensure that the execution of this process is consistent with TQM, there are two sets of methods which participants utilize*:

7 basic QC tools	7 management and planning tools
• Check Sheet	• Affinity Diagram
• Pareto Chart	• Interrelationship Digraph
• Run Chart	• Tree Diagram
• Cause and Effect Diagram	• Prioritization Matrices
• Scatter Diagram	• Matrix Diagram
• Histogram	• Process Decision Program Chart (PDPC)
• Control Chart	• Activity Network Diagram

WHAT IS THE STATE OF DEVELOPMENT OF HOSHIN PLANNING IN THE UNITED STATES?

Even though Hoshin Planning (under the name Hoshin Kanri, Policy Deployment, or Management By Policy) has been developed and refined in Japanese

*These tools are indispensable in surfacing breakthrough ideas out of chaos and converting them into implementable plans. This closely resembles the core of Hoshin Planning. More information is available in *The Memory Jogger Plus,* GOAL/QPC, © 1989.

companies for nearly 25 years, it is still in its infancy in the United States. The most mature application dates back to 1984, but widespread interest has only occurred in the last two years. Although there is a handful of companies that are truly serious about Hoshin Planning implementation, Florida Power and Light and Hewlett-Packard are the most visible U.S. examples. Both have initiated and customized their own Hoshin Planning models. FP&L, using the term Policy Deployment, incorporated it in their Total Quality model that allowed them to win the coveted Deming Prize in Japan. They are the first non-Japanese company to win the Prize. Hewlett-Packard *has* initiated Hoshin Planning in most of its 50+ operating divisions.

The results in this country have been very encouraging but it remains to be seen whether Hoshin has the needed staying power. One fact should be highlighted, however. Hoshin Planning is the one element of TQM that is most consistently *applied* in Japanese companies of all sizes and in all industries.

CONCLUSION

It's difficult to predict the future of Hoshin Planning in the United States based upon the limited sample of implementations thus far. One thing does appear clear. If U.S. companies are serious about adapting and adopting a TQM model that works, a key ingredient is the ability to consistently identify, plan for, and achieve strategic objectives. It is not enough to have everyone doing better everyday in every way.

There is only one remaining question that must be answered by each American CEO: Are you satisfied with your present ability to consistently achieve strategic objectives? If not, then Hoshin Planning deserves serious consideration as an alternate implementation system.

HOSHIN PLANNING OVERVIEW

HISTORY OF HOSHIN PLANNING IN JAPAN

The modern quality movement began in Japan with Dr. W. Edwards Deming teaching statistical values and tools in 1950 and Juran teaching management of quality in 1954. The quality movement has progressed steadily ever since.

1965 The Japanese company Komatsu developed the flag system, an elementary form of Hoshin Planning, to speed the transition from Statistical Quality Control to Total Quality Control.

WHAT SHOULD BE IN PLACE TO MAKE HOSHIN PLANNING WORK?

Hoshin planning prerequisites

Knowledge and experience	Manager's role	Motivation	Organization
• Widespread understanding of the basics of TQM including where Hoshin Planning fits • Understanding of PDCA model • Widespread knowledge and use of the Seven Basic QC Tools • Some specialized knowledge of the appropriate Seven Tools for Management and Planning	• Set direction —Provide a clean focus —Establish priorities —Communicate it to everyone • Support for people's efforts —Provide resources —Create horizontal coordination —Remove system barriers —Teach and coach	• Clear and compelling answer to the question "Why do Hoshin Planning?" (Find a burning issue) • Desire on management's part to narrow and/or coordinate the focus	• Leadership demand from the top • Develop steering teams at different levels of deployment to coordinate problem solving • Facilitators (preferably bosses) in place • Champion/sponsor in a highly visible, influential management slot
• Widespread understanding of Daily Management/ Control	• Provide a focus on the process —Practice PDCA —Demand data • Reinforce and recognize employees' efforts		• A coordinating mechanism (team, committee, or individual) to integrate plans across functions and departments • A system for making Daily Management/ Control work

1970s Yoji Akao of Tamagawa University improved this system by introducing the target/means matrix as a way of clarifying measures, control items, and control points.

1980s Nayatani expanded the use of the system by enhancing it with the Seven New Tools for Management and Planning. In Japan during the 1970s and 1980s, MBO was replaced by Hoshin Planning because of Hoshin Planning's flexibility in dealing with quickly changing economic situations.

In its most recent study mission in Japan (October 1988), GOAL/QPC found that Hoshin Planning has become one of the most widely recognized and implemented TQM/TQC systems (along with well established systems such as Quality Circles and the Basic Quality Control (QC) tools, e.g., check sheet, pareto chart).

Hoshin Planning is known by various names: Hoshin Kanri (in Japan), Policy Deployment, Management by Policy, Hoshin, and Management by Planning (MBP).

IN THE UNITED STATES

Hewlett-Packard

In 1983 John Young, the CEO of Hewlett-Packard, announced a set of ambitious company-wide improvement targets: In 10 years Hewlett-Packard would increase its quality measures ten fold. Within five years they had made dramatic strides, but it was clear that the company was not "on the curve" to make the projected time line. They turned for guidance to Yokagawa Hewlett-Packard, a Japanese jointly owned subsidiary that won the Deming Prize in 1982. One of the primary components of YHP's success was its Policy Deployment/Hoshin Planning system. Hewlett-Packard learned from this and has been refining the version (referred to simply as "Hoshin") in a number of operating and service divisions.

Florida Power and Light

FP&L has been on its TQM journey since 1981. In 1986 it introduced Policy Deployment (Hoshin Planning). Under the guidance of Dr. Noriaki Kano of Tokyo Science University and the Japanese Union of Scientists and Engineers (JUSE), FP&L developed a system which now is the primary means by which the top management (chairman, CEO, and vice presidents) develops its improvement focus for the year. This is the core activity of an intensive three week annual executive planning process. In addition, the system presently involves about 20–25 percent of all FP&L managers and employees in the targeted breakthrough areas.

Other U.S. users

Other well-known companies that are involved in Hoshin Planning are Procter & Gamble, 3M Corporation, and Omark Corporation.

WHAT IS HOSHIN PLANNING?

Hoshin Planning is a system. It is a component of the TQM system that allows an organization to plan and execute strategic organizational breakthrough. According to Dr. Kano, "It is a marriage between the strengths of the East and the West: The strong leadership exercised by Western top management with the organization-wide consensus of traditional Japanese organizations." Therefore, in Hoshin Planning, *direction/focus flows down while organizational capability/commitment flows up*. (See Figure 24.1.)

Notice that the "bubble-up" has a direct effect on the direction that is then moved down through the organization. Hoshin Planning also involves coordination of all plans across departments and functions to prevent counterproductive and misdirected individual activities. Figure 24.2 shows how Kenzo Sasaoka, the President of Yokogawa Hewlett-Packard (YHP), graphically depicts this coordination.

Figure 24.2 also illustrates "catchball," which is the Japanese term describing the process of give and take across levels of management. Catchball includes:

1. What top management proposes as the key areas of the Hoshin Planning focus for the next year.
2. Identification by managers at various lower levels of other key areas upon which the organization should focus.
3. What these departments/functions could do about the areas that both top management and lower levels have identified.

Mr. Sasaoka admits that during the first year of YHP's Hoshin Planning implementation, what was sent down through the organization came back intact (nothing changed or added). He estimates that today, 60 percent of what is implemented is proposed by management. The remainder has been added or modified by lower level management input.

FIGURE 24.1

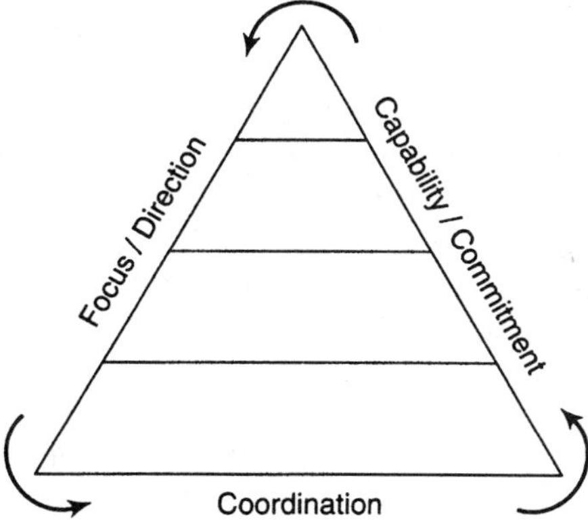

FIGURE 24.2 ***The YHP Hoshin Planning cycle***

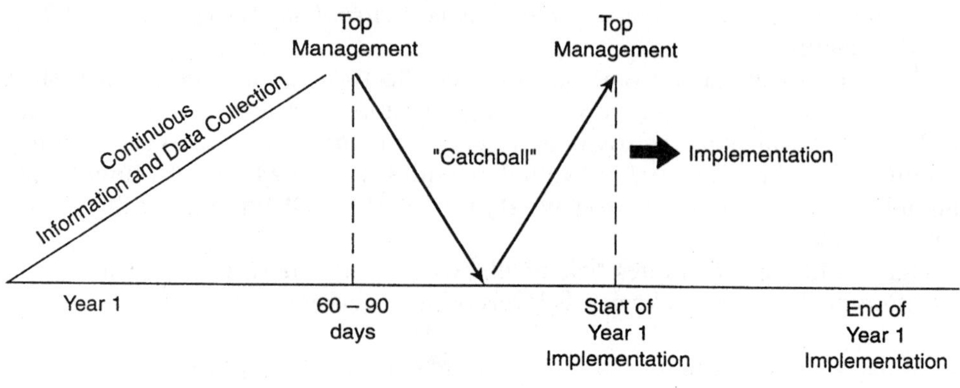

WHAT IS THE "BEST" METHOD?

In trying to find the "best" process model, the Research Committee considered a half dozen different models that detailed specific process steps. It was decided that rather than detail the pros and cons of each process model, the Committee's job was to find the common features of each model that fit U.S. applications. Actually this wasn't that difficult even when comparing U.S. and Japanese models. The Japanese models tended to be more elaborate, but the core remained surprisingly consistent. The Committee integrated the Seven Management and Planning Tools with each of the models considered. These tools, indispensable in surfacing breakthrough ideas out of chaos and converting them into implementable plans, closely resemble the core of Japanese Hoshin Planning. More information is available in *The Memory Jogger Plus*, GOAL/QPC, 1989.

The one key difference that we consistently found in the Japanese models was a stronger ongoing link between Hoshin Planning and performance data generated through Daily Control. Daily Control is the day-to-day process by which incremental improvement happens in TQM. It generates constant data that pinpoints performance strengths and weaknesses. The Japanese feed this into the Hoshin Planning priorities. (A detailed explanation of Daily Control is beyond the scope of this paper.)

The following diagram represents the Committee's summary of the Hoshin Planning process. Also identified on the following pages are the key steps, elements, and tools necessary to make Hoshin Planning work. This is intended as a

The core Hoshin Planning process

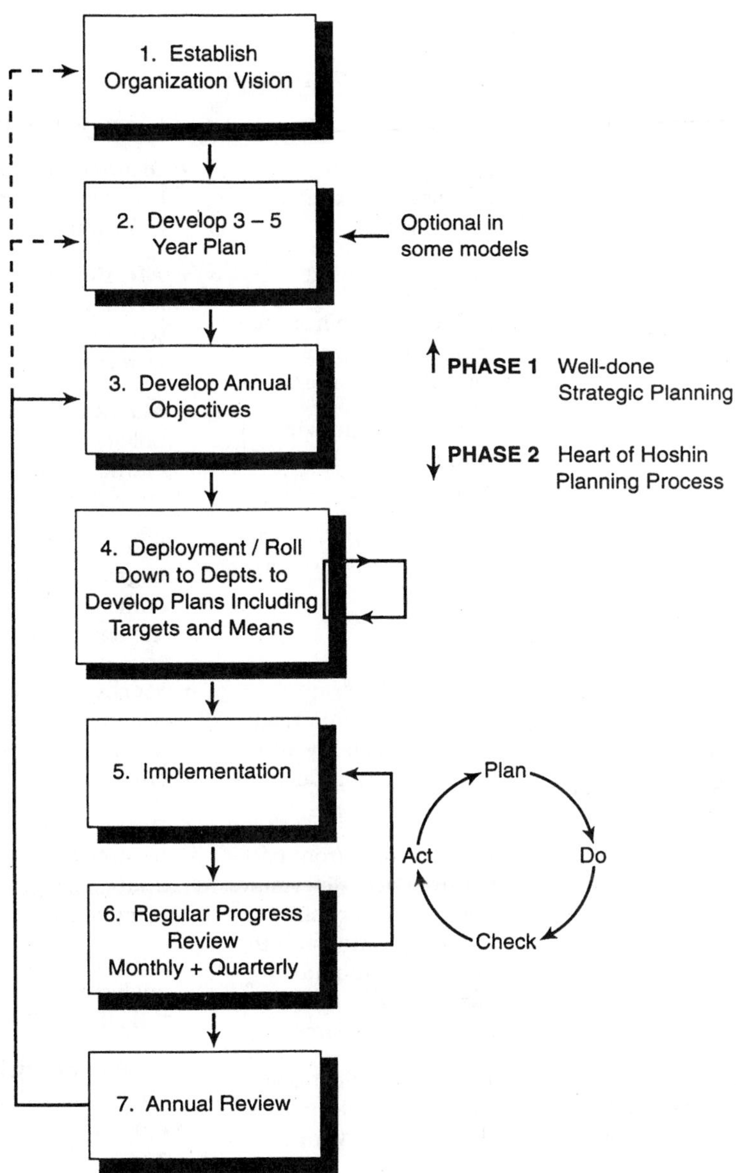

generic model against which any company can benchmark or compare its present planning process.

Hoshin Planning process

Step	Key elements	Key tools
1. Establish Organization Vision	• Data input from internal and external performance • Customer focused • Includes all environmental factors, e.g., social, regulatory, economic • Draft of vision reviewed with the organization for reality check • Finalized vision communicated clearly to everyone at all levels	• **Brainstorming** around issues in the external environment • **Affinity Diagram** to identify patterns among seemingly unrelated factors • **Market research** technology to obtain data on the external environment • **Interrelationship Digraph** to identify bottle neck factors in the environment
2. Develop three to five year objectives* *In some models this step is eliminated with the process shifting to a one year focus immediately	• Focus on the "gap" between present organizational capability and required performance to reach the vision • Accurate data from past performances determines the present capability of the organization and the means that should be pursued over the next three to five years • Three to five year objectives communicated clearly to everyone at all levels	• **Market research technology** to gather data in order to identify midterm environmental issues • **Broad internal performance reports and analysis,** e.g., customer complaints, market share • Data collection and analysis using the **7 Basic QC Tools** • **Interrelationship Digraph** to identify the most serious problem areas • **Matrix Diagram** to compare potential action plans with vision statement and criteria

Hoshin Planning process (continued)

Step	Key elements	Key tools
3. Develop annual objectives	• Completely integrated with three to five year objectives and vision • Small number of focus points, "Fewer more important efforts vs. more, more, more . . . " • Accurate data, minimally filtered is the basis for selecting the one year objective • "Reason for Improvement" must be compelling; convincing case must be made to work on any selected objective rather than on something else • Use data to identify broad patterns among problem areas. Identify the truly "broken" systems	• **Market research technology** to identify key short term external environmental factors • **Data collection and analysis** to identify broad internal performance problems, e.g., customer complaints, profit center information • **Seven Basic QC Tools** to analyze and summarize key problem areas. In a mature TQM organization, these would be in use everywhere. • **Tree Diagram** to explore all of the possible means to address key problem areas • **Matrix** of all of the possible means with the broad target areas for the year to choose the best means to pursue
4. Deployment/Roll down to departments to develop plans (including targets and means)	• Clear, disciplined action plans with direction of improvement, what is to be measured, and the process that is to be improved • Continuous give and take (catchball) between levels around the chosen targets and the organization's capabilities • Emphasizes the plans of departments/units vs. just individuals	• **Matrix Diagram** to match key departments/functions with chosen objectives and means • **Seven Basic QC Tools** and problem solving models at all involved levels to identify more specific problem areas to address • **Tree Diagram** to identify all the possible actions at all involved levels

Hoshin Planning process (continued)

Step	Key elements	Key tools
	• A team coordinates plans across departments • Responsibilities clearly designated • A team also ensures that the sum of the plans really reaches the target	• **Matrix Diagram** to match possible actions with the overall objectives in order to choose the best options
5. Implementation	• Disciplined data collection and measurement system implemented "in-process," not after the fact • Visible process (targets and means) allows for recognition and reinforcement in "real time" • Standardized methods reduce some manager to manager variability in outcomes • Problems visible, therefore management can put support where needed	• **Seven Basic QC Tools** in use to collect data as the year's plan progresses • **Process Decision Program Chart (PDPC)** to anticipate likely implementation problems and prepare reasonable means to prevent them • **Arrow Diagram** to create an implementation timetable against which to monitor results
6. Progress Review (Monthly and Quarterly)	• Strong emphasis on self diagnosis of targets and process • Standardized review format and language • Simple analysis emphasized • Builds Plan-Do-Check-Act continuously into the process • Problems are seen as opportunities to be surfaced, not skeletons to be buried	• **Seven Basic QC Tools** to define why a target and plan were not met. Emphasize the Cause and Effect Diagram, Run, and Pareto Charts • Simple **documents** to record any changes to the plan • **Tree Diagram** to develop revised plans with complete implementation detail

Hoshin Planning process (continued)

Step	Key elements	Key tools
	• Emphasizes recognition, support, and corrective action, not punishment • System problems not directly related to plan have a place to surface	
7. Annual Review	• Data collection and review done all year providing accurate and relevant diagnosis of missed targets and poor processes • Examine plans even when the target is hit, in order to show correlation. The emphasis must be on understanding which plans led to the achievement of which targets so that the resulting process can be standardized • Review Hoshin Process itself, aiming to improve it for the next year	• **Seven Basic QC Tools** as the format used to summarize the results of all of the plans for the entire year. The emphasis is on answering the question: Why did we miss any of our targets or plans? • **Affinity Diagram** to help identify all of the reasons for success or failure and any pattern which may emerge that can improve next year's planning

FOCUS POINTS AMONG LEADING JAPANESE HOSHIN PLANNING EXPERTS

Kano

- Don't spend too much time on the vision step
- Keep vision flexible and responsive to the market
- Don't over-formalize Hoshin Planning—becomes paper system
- Incomplete policies from the previous year may not roll over into following year's activities—must compete
- Focused deployment—not everyone needs to be involved in every policy

- Must prioritize department contribution to policy success—therefore deploy accordingly
- Presidential reviews (not audits) should occur throughout the year, not just one year
- Emphasize "synthesis" of results—examine all policies thoroughly even when target is achieved
- Stresses very strong top management leadership in medium to long term policy setting
- Strong emphasis on Daily Control (PDCA in daily job tasks) as needed in addition to Hoshin Planning
- Stresses using basic QC concepts (e.g., Q I Story) as means to establish and implement policies

Akao

- Can "bubble up" over 1½ to 2½ years
- Ultimate goal is company-wide involvement in policies
- Stresses importance of "catchball" at the medium term policy and vision steps
- Formal analysis of critical factors that caused organization to miss targets from the previous year
- Formal "stages" of development criteria for each Hoshin Planning effort

Nayatani

- Very close to Akao except:
  1. Emphasizes even more strongly the need for all departments to be involved in the formulation of all policies (including the work of the Quality Circles)
  2. Stresses the use of the Seven Tools for Management and Planning at every step of the MBP process

part

5

Reengineering and ISO 9000

The readings in Part 5 provide an overview of two of the most influential new approaches to quality improvement and process redesign: ISO 9000 and reengineering. The papers in this section introduce the key concepts related to reengineering and ISO 9000 and their relationship to TQM and also provide an analysis of how these models have developed over time. Of particular use to such understanding is the inclusion of the first and second edition of ISO 9001 in a comparative manner. ISO 9001 (the most comprehensive standard in the 9000 series) was first published in 1987. The second edition of the standard appeared in 1994.

It is tempting to focus exclusively on the differences among reengineering, ISO 9000, and TQM. This has been done extensively. However, it may be at least as rewarding to study the underlying similarities among the main models and strategies for quality improvement. What emerges from such a study is an understanding of the lasting contributions of the quality movement. These include a focus on quality through continuous process improvement and redesign, a respect for customers, and teamwork.

It is strongly recommended that students, working in teams, do a comparative analysis of different quality improvement models. This may include a synthesis of the concepts introduced by leading thinkers in the field in parts 1, 2, and 5 of this book. Further, students can download the current guidelines for the Baldrige Award and the European Quality Award (URLs are provided in the appendix), the two most influential, comprehensive, strategic models for quality improvement and organizational change worldwide.

Once similarities and differences among the different models for quality have been established and discussed, the focus of the analysis could shift to the question: "Under what conditions and in which environments may one or another model or strategy for quality improvement be most effective?"

Reading 25

The New Industrial Engineering: Information Technology and Business Process Redesign

By Thomas H. Davenport and James E. Short

Those aspiring to improve the way work is done must begin to apply the capabilities of information technology to redesign business processes. Business process design and information technology are natural partners, yet industrial engineers have never fully exploited their relationship. The authors argue, in fact, that it has barely been exploited at all. But the organizations that *have* used IT to redesign boundary-crossing, customer-driven processes have benefited enormously. This article explains why.

At the turn of the century, Frederick Taylor revolutionized the workplace with his ideas on work organization, task decomposition, and job measurement. Taylor's basic aim was to increase organizational productivity by applying to human labor the same engineering principles that had proven so successful in solving the technical problems in the work environment. The same approaches that had transformed mechanical activity could also be used to structure jobs performed by people. Taylor came to symbolize the practical realizations in industry that we now call industrial engineering (IE), or the scientific school of management.[1] In fact, though work design remains a contemporary IE concern, no subsequent concept or tool has rivaled the power of Taylor's mechanizing vision.

Source: Reprinted from "The New Industrial Engineering: Information Technology and Business Process Redesign" by Thomas H. Davenport and James E. Short. *Sloan Management Review,* Summer 1990, pp. 11–27, by permission of the publisher.

As we enter the 1990s, however, two newer tools are transforming organiztions to the degree that Taylorism once did. These are *information technology*—the capabilities offered by computers, software applications, and telecommunications—and *business process redesign*—the analysis and design of work flows and processes within and between organizations. Working together, these tools have the potential to create a new type of industrial engineering, changing the way the discipline is practiced and the skills necessary to practice it.

This article explores the relationship between information technology (IT) and business process redesign (BPR). We report on research conducted at MIT, Harvard, and several consulting organizations on nineteen companies, including detailed studies of five firms engaged in substantial process redesign. After defining business processes, we extract from the experience of the companies studied a generic five-step approach to redesigning processes with IT. We then define the major types of processes, along with the primary role of IT in each type of process. Finally, we consider management issues that arise when IT is used to redesign business processes.

IT IN BUSINESS PROCESS REDESIGN

The importance of both information technology and business process redesign is well known to industrial engineers, albeit as largely separate tools for use in specific, limited environments.[2] IT is used in industrial engineering as an analysis and modeling tool, and IEs have often taken the lead in applying information technology to manufacturing environments. Well-known uses of IT in manufacturing include process modeling, production scheduling and control, materials management, information systems, and logistics. In most cases where IT has been used to redesign work, the redesign has most likely been in the manufacturing function, and industrial engineers are the most likely individuals to have carried it out.

IEs have begun to analyze work activities in nonmanufacturing environments, but their penetration into offices has been far less than in factories. IT has certainly penetrated the office and services environments—in 1987 *Business Week* reported that almost 40 percent of all U.S. capital spending went to information systems, some $97 billion a year—but IT has been used in most cases to hasten office work rather than to transform it.[3] With few exceptions, IT's role in the redesign of nonmanufacturing work has been disappointing; few firms have achieved major productivity gains.[4] Aggregate productivity figures for the United States have shown no increase since 1973.[5]

Given the growing dominance of service industries and office work in the Western economies, this type of work is as much in need of analysis and redesign as the manufacturing environments to which IT has already been applied. Many firms have found that this analysis requires taking a broader view of both IT and business activity, and of the relationships between them. Information technology should be viewed as more than an automating or mechanizing force; it can fundamentally reshape the way business is done. Business activities should be viewed as more than a collection of individual or even functional tasks; they should be broken down into processes that can be designed for maximum effectiveness, in both manufacturing and service environments.

Our research suggests that IT can be more than a useful tool in business process redesign. In leading edge practice, information technology and BPR have a recursive relationship, as Figure 25.1 illustrates. Each is the key to thinking about the other. Thinking about information technology should be in terms of how it supports new or redesigned business processes, rather than business functions or other organizational entities. And business processes and process improvements should be considered in terms of the capabilities information technology can provide. *We refer to this broadened, recursive view of IT and BPR as the new industrial engineering.*

Taylor could focus on workplace rationalization and individual task efficiency because he confronted a largely stable business environment; today's corporations do not have the luxury of such stability.[6] Individual tasks and jobs change faster than they can be redesigned. Today, responsibility for an outcome is more often spread over a group, rather than assigned to an individual as in the past. Companies increasingly find it necessary to develop more flexible, team-oriented, coordinative, and communication-based work capability. In short, rather than maximizing the performance of particular individuals or business functions, companies must maximize interdependent activities within and across the entire organization. Such business processes are a new approach to coordination across the firm; information technology's promise—and perhaps its ultimate impact—is

FIGURE 25.1 ***The recursive relationship between IT capabilities and business process redesign***

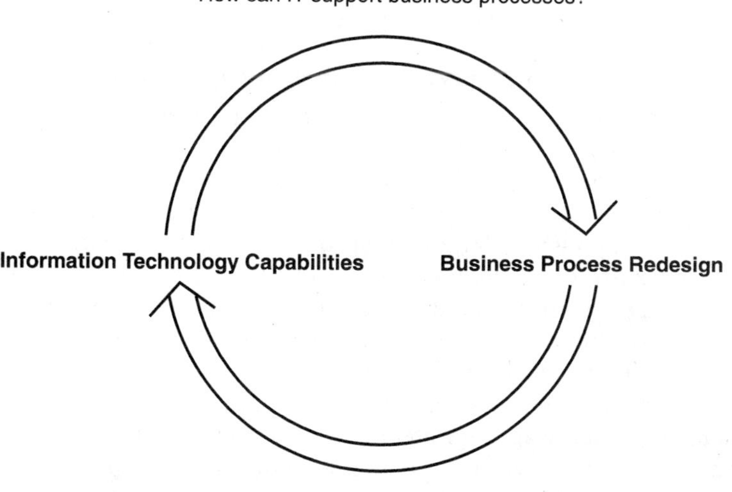

to be the most powerful tool in the twentieth century for reducing the costs of this coordination.[7]

WHAT ARE BUSINESS PROCESSES?

We define business processes as a set of logically related tasks performed to achieve a defined business outcome. This definition is similar to Pall's: "The logical organization of people, materials, energy, equipment, and procedures into work activities designed to produce a specified end result (work product)."[8]

A set of processes forms a business system—the way in which a business unit, or a collection of units, carries out its business. Processes have two important characteristics:

- They have customers; that is, processes have defined business outcomes, and there are recipients of the outcomes. Customers may be either internal or external to the firm.
- They cross organizational boundaries; that is, they normally occur across or between organizational subunits. Processes are generally independent of formal organizational structure.

Common examples of processes meeting these criteria include:

- developing a new product;
- ordering goods from a supplier;
- creating a marketing plan;
- processing and paying an insurance claim; and
- writing a proposal for a government contract.

Ordering goods from a supplier, for example, typically involves multiple organizations and functions. The end user, purchasing, receiving, accounts payable, etc., and the supplier organization are all participants. The user could be viewed as the process's customer. The process outcome could be either the creation of the order, or, perhaps more usefully, the actual receipt of the goods by the user.

Our examples so far are of large-scale processes that affect whole organizations or groups. There are more detailed processes that meet the definitional criteria above. These might include installing a windshield in an automobile factory, or completing a monthly departmental expense report. IT-driven process redesign can be applied to these processes, but the implications of redesigning them may be important only in the aggregate. In many of the firms studied, analyzing processes in great detail was highly appropriate for some purposes, for example, the detailed design of an information system or data model to support a specific work process. However, the firms that were truly beginning to redesign their business functions took a broader view of processes.

A BRIEF HISTORY OF PROCESS THINKING

Process thinking has become widespread in recent years, due largely to the quality movement. Industrial engineers and others who wish to improve the quality of operations are urged to look at an entire process, rather than a particular task or business function. At IBM, for example, "process management will be the principal IBM quality focus in the coming years."[9] But process discussions in the quality movement's literature rarely mention information technology. Rather, the focus is usually on improving process control systems in a manufacturing context; when IT is discussed, it is in the context of factory floor automation. Recent IE literature also borders on process thinking when advocating cross-functional analysis,[10] although, as we will discuss, cross-functional processes are only one possible type of process.

Other than quality-oriented manufacturing process redesign, most processes in major corporations have not been subject to rigorous analysis and redesign. Indeed, many of our current processes result from a series of ad hoc decisions made by functional units, with little attention to effectiveness across the entire process. Many processes have never even been measured. In one manufacturing company studied, for example, no one had ever analyzed the elapsed time from a customer's order to delivery. Each department (sales, credit checking, shipping, and so on) felt that it had optimized its own performance, but in fact the overall process was quite lengthy and unwieldy.

Even fewer business processes have been analyzed with the capabilities of IT in mind. Most business processes were developed before modern computers and communications even existed. When technology has been applied, it is usually to automate or speed up isolated components of an existing process. This creates communication problems within processes and impediments to process redesign and enhancement. For example, in a second manufacturing firm studied, the procurement process involved a vendor database, a materials management planning system, and accounts payable and receivable systems, all running on different hardware platforms with different data structures. Again, each organizational subunit within the process had optimized its own IT application, but no single subunit had looked at (or was responsible for) the entire process. We believe the problems this firm experienced are very common.

REDESIGNING BUSINESS PROCESSES WITH IT: FIVE STEPS

Assuming that a company has decided its processes are inefficient or ineffective, and therefore in need of redesign, how should it proceed? This is a straightforward activity, but five major steps are involved: develop the business vision and process objectives, identify the processes to be redesigned, understand and measure the existing process, identify IT levers, and design and build a prototype of the new process (see Figure 25.2). We observed most or all of these steps being performed in companies that were succeeding with BPR. Each step is described in greater detail on the next few pages.

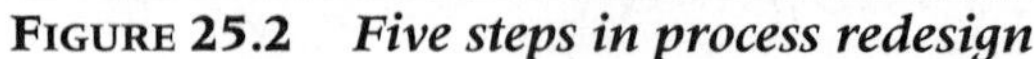

FIGURE 25.2 *Five steps in process redesign*

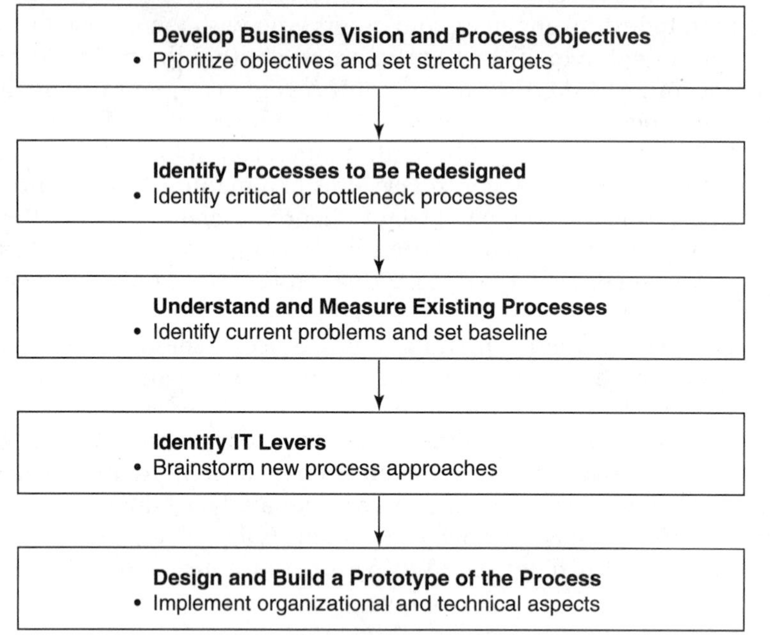

Develop business vision and process objectives

In the past, process redesign was typically intended simply to "rationalize" the process, in other words, to eliminate obvious bottlenecks and inefficiencies. It did not involve any particular business vision or context. This was the approach of the "work simplification" aspect of industrial engineering, an important legacy of Taylorism. An example of the rationalization approach appears in a 1961 "Reference Note on Work Simplification" from the Harvard Business School:

> A good manager asks himself *why* things are done as they are, extending his inquiry to every aspect of the job and the surroundings in which it is performed, from the flow of paper work to the daily functioning of his subordinates. . . . He is expected to supply the stimulus and show that job improvement or simplification of work is not only important but also is based on common-sense questioning aimed at uncovering the easiest, most economical way of performing a job.[11]

Our research suggests strongly that rationalization is not an end in itself, and is thus insufficient as a process redesign objective. Furthermore, rationalization of highly decomposed tasks may lead to a less efficient overall process. Instead of task rationalization, redesign of entire processes should be undertaken with a specific business vision and related objectives in mind.

In most successful redesign examples we studied, the company's senior management had developed a broad strategic vision into which the process redesign activity fit.[12] At Xerox, for example, this vision involved taking the perspective of the customer and developing systems rather than stand-alone products; both required cross-functional integration. At Westinghouse, the vision consisted largely of improving product quality. Ford's involved adopting the best practices of Japanese automobile manufacturers, including those of Mazda, of which it is a partial owner.

Each of these visions implied specific objectives for process redesign. The most likely objectives are the following:

- **Cost Reduction.** This objective was implicit in the "rationalization" approach. Cost is an important redesign objective in combination with others, but insufficient in itself. Excessive attention to cost reduction results in tradeoffs that are usually unacceptable to process stakeholders. While optimizing on other objectives seems to bring costs into line, optimizing on cost rarely brings about other objectives.
- **Time Reduction.** Time reduction has been only a secondary objective of traditional industrial engineering. Increasing numbers of companies, however, are beginning to compete on the basis of time.[13] Processes, as we have defined them, are the ideal unit for a focused time reduction analysis. One common approach to cutting time from product design is to make the steps begin simultaneously, rather than sequentially, using IT to coordinate design directions among the various functional participants. This approach has been taken in the design of computers, telephone equipment, automobiles, and copiers (by Digital Equipment, AT&T Bell Labs, Ford, and Xerox, respectively).
- **Output Quality.** AU processes have outputs, be they physical—such as in manufacturing a tangible product—or informational—such as in adding data to a customer file. Output quality is frequently the focus of process improvement in manufacturing environments; it is just as important in service industries. The specific measure of output quality may be uniformity, variability, or freedom from defects; this should be defined by the customer of the process.
- **Quality of Worklife (QWL)/Learning/Empowerment.** IT can lead either to greater empowerment of individuals, or to greater control over their output. Zuboff points out that IT-intensive processes are often simply automated, and that the "informating" or learning potential of IT in processes is often ignored.[14] Moreover, Schein notes that organizations often do not provide a supportive context for individuals to introduce or innovate with IT.[15] Of course, it is rarely possible to optimize all objectives simultaneously, and in most firms, the strongest pressures are to produce tangible benefits. Yet managers who ignore this dimension risk failure of redesigned processes for organizational and motivational factors.

Some firms have been able to achieve multiple objectives in redesigning processes with IT. American Express, for example, set out to improve the cost, time, and quality of its credit authorization process by embedding the knowledge of its best authorizers in an "Authorizer's Assistant" expert system. This successful redesign led to a $7 million annual reduction in costs due to credit losses, a 25 percent reduction in the average time for each authorization, and a 30 percent reduction in improper credit denials.

Finally, all firms found it was important to set specific objectives, even to the point of quantification. Though it is difficult to know how much improvement is possible in advance of a redesign, "reach should exceed grasp." Setting goals that will stretch the organization will also provide inspiration and stimulate creative thinking. For example, a company might decide to reduce the time to bring new products to market by 80 percent. In the accounts payable process at Ford, the "stretch" goal was to eliminate invoices—to pay suppliers upon receipt of their products or services. This goal has been achieved with help from an information system to confirm expected deliveries at the loading dock. As a result, Ford has eliminated three-quarters of the jobs in accounts payable.

Identify processes to be redesigned

Most organizations could benefit from IT-enabled redesign of critical (if not *all*) business processes. However, the amount of effort involved creates practical limitations. Even when total redesign was the ultimate objective, the companies we studied selected a few key processes for initial efforts. Moreover, when there was insufficient commitment to total redesign, a few successful examples of IT-enhanced processes became a powerful selling tool.

The means by which processes to be redesigned are identified and prioritized is a key issue. This is often difficult because most managers do not think about their business operations in terms of processes. There are two major approaches. The *exhaustive* approach attempts to identify all processes within an organization and then prioritize them in order of redesign urgency. The *high-impact* approach attempts to identify only the most important processes or those most in conflict with the business vision and process objectives.

The exhaustive approach is often associated with "information engineering" (developed by James Martin in the early 1980s), in which an organization's use of data dictates the processes to be redesigned.[16] For example, one information engineering method, employed at several divisions of Xerox, involves identifying business activities and the data they require using a data-activity matrix. The clusters of data activity interactions in the cells of the matrix are the organization's major business processes. Once processes are identified, Xerox managers prioritize them in the order in which new IT applications support should be provided. Although process identification in some Xerox divisions has taken as little as three months, many companies find this approach very time consuming.

The alternative is to focus quickly on high-impact processes. Most organizations have some sense of which business areas or processes are most crucial to their success, and those most "broken" or inconsistent with the business vision. If not, these can normally be identified using senior management workshops, or through extensive interviewing.[17] At IBM, the salesforce was surveyed to determine the relative importance of various customer support processes; the generation of special bids emerged as the highest priority and was the first process to be redesigned.

Companies that employed the high-impact approach generally considered it sufficient. Companies taking the exhaustive approach, on the other hand, have not had the resources to address all the identified processes; why identify them if they cannot be addressed? As a rough rule of thumb, most companies we studied were unable to redesign and support more than ten to fifteen major processes per year (i.e., one to three per major business unit); there was simply not enough management attention to do more. And some organizations have abandoned the exhaustive approach.[18]

Whichever approach is used, companies have found it useful to classify each redesigned process in terms of beginning and end points, interfaces, and organization units (functions or departments) involved, particularly including the customer unit. Thinking in these terms usually broadens the perceived scope of the process. For example, a sales manager may be aware that there are inefficiencies in customer order entry. A skilled process consultant might decide that the whole process—negotiating, receiving, and fulfilling orders—needs to be redesigned. Whether the problem is broken down into three processes or viewed as one is not important; expanding the *scope* of the process analysis is the key issue.

High-impact processes should also have owners.[19] In virtually all the process redesigns we studied, an important step was getting owners to buy in to both the idea and the scope of process redesign at an early stage. In several companies, managers felt that the process owner's job should be either above the level of the functions and units involved, or, if on the same level, that the owner should be willing—and able—to change the status quo. The difficulty, however, is that some processes only come together at the CEO level. In this situation, the CEO should designate a senior manager as owner and invest him or her with full authority. Processes that are fully contained within a single function or department can normally be owned by the manager of that area.

Understand and measure existing processes

There are two primary reasons for understanding and measuring processes before redesigning them. First, problems must be understood so that they are not repeated. Second, accurate measurement can serve as a baseline for future improvements. If the objective is to cut time and cost, the time and cost consumed by the untouched process must be measured accurately. Westinghouse Productivity and Quality Center consultants found that simply graphing the incremental cost and time consumed by process tasks can often suggest initial areas for redesign. These graphs look like "step functions" showing the incremental contribution of each major task.

This step can easily be overemphasized, however. In several firms, the "stretch" goal was less to eliminate problems or bottlenecks than to create radical improvements. Designers should be informed by past process problems and errors, but they should work with a clean slate. Similarly, the process should not be measured for measurement's sake. Only the specific objectives of the redesign should be measured. As with the high-impact process identification approach, an 80–20 philosophy is usually appropriate.

Identify IT levers

Until recently, even the most sophisticated industrial engineering approaches did not consider IT capabilities until after a process had been designed. The conventional wisdom in IT usage has always been to first determine the business requirements of a function, process, or other business entity, and then to develop a system. The problem is that an awareness of IT capabilities can—and should—influence process design. Knowing that product development teams can exchange computer-aided designs over large distances, for example, might affect the structure of a product development process. The role of IT in a process should be considered in the early stages of its redesign.[20]

Several firms accomplished this using brainstorming sessions, with the process redesign objectives and existing process measures in hand. It was also useful to have a list of IT's generic capabilities in improving business processes. In the broadest sense, *all* of IT's capabilities involve improving coordination and information access across organizational units, thereby allowing for more effective management of task interdependence. More specifically, however, it is useful to think about IT capabilities and their organizational impacts in eight different ways (see Table 25.1).

There are undoubtedly other important IT capabilities that can reshape processes. Organizations may want to develop their own lists of capabilities that are specific to the types of processes they employ. The point is twofold: IT is so powerful a tool that it deserves its own step in process redesign, and IT can actually create new process design options, rather than simply support them.

Design and build a prototype of the process

For most firms, the final step is to design the process. This is usually done by the same team that performed the previous steps, getting input from constituencies and using brainstorming workshops. A key point is that the actual design is not the end of the process. Rather, it should be viewed as a prototype, with successive iterations expected and managed. Key factors and tactics to consider in process design and prototype creation include using IT as a design tool, understanding generic design criteria, and creating organizational prototypes.

- **IT as a Design Tool.** Designing a business process is largely a matter of diligence and creativity. Emerging IT technologies, however, are beginning to facil-

TABLE 25.1 ***IT capabilities and their organizational impacts***

Capability	Organizational impact/benefit
Transactional	IT can transform unstructured processes into routinized transactions
Geographical	IT can transfer information with rapidity and ease across large distances, making processes independent of geography
Automational	IT can replace or reduce human labor in a process
Analytical	IT can bring complex analytical methods to bear on a process
Informational	IT can bring vast amounts of detailed information into a process
Sequential	IT can enable changes in the sequence of tasks in a process, often allowing multiple tasks to be worked on simultaneously
Knowledge Management	IT allows the capture and dissemination of knowledge and expertise to improve the process
Tracking	IT allows the detailed tracking of task status, inputs, and outputs
Disintermediation	IT can be used to connect two parties within a process that would otherwise communicate through an intermediary (internal or external)

itate the "process" of process design. Some computer-aided systems engineering (CASE) products are designed primarily to draw process models. The ability to draw models rapidly and make changes suggested by process owners speeds redesign and facilitates owner buy-in. Some CASE products can actually generate computer code for the information systems application that will support a modeled business process.

Several Xerox divisions, for example, are moving directly from process modeling to automated generation of computer code for high-priority processes. They report improved productivity and high user satisfaction with the resulting systems. A further benefit is that when the business process changes, the IS organization can rapidly modify the affected system. Use of code generation products generally presumes that process designers will use the exhaustive approach to process identification.

- **Generic Design Criteria.** Companies used various criteria for evaluating alternative designs. Most important, of course, is the likelihood that a design will satisfy the chosen design objectives. Others mentioned in interviews included the simplicity of the design, the lack of buffers or intermediaries, the degree of control by a single individual or department (or an effective, decentralized coordinative mechanism), the balance of process resources, and the generalization of process tasks (so that they can be performed by more than one person).

- **Organizational Prototypes.** Mutual Benefit Life's (MBL) redesign of its individual life insurance underwriting process illustrates a final, important point about process design. At MBL, underwriting a life insurance policy involved 40 steps with over 100 people in 12 functional areas and 80 separate jobs. To streamline this lengthy and complex process, MBL undertook a pilot project with the goal of improving productivity by 40 percent. To integrate the process, MBL created a new role, the case manager. This role was designed to perform and coordinate all underwriting tasks centrally, utilizing a workstation-based computer system capable of pulling data from all over the company. After a brief start-up period, the firm learned that two additional roles were necessary on some underwriting cases: specialists such as lawyers or medical directors in knowledge-intensive fields, and clerical assistance. With the new role and redesigned process, senior managers at MBL are confident of reaching the 40 percent goal in a few months. This example illustrates the value of creating organizational prototypes in IT-driven process redesign.

Creating prototypes of IT applications has already gained widespread acceptance. Advocates argue that building a prototype of an IT change usually achieves results faster than conventional "life cycle" development, and, more important, that the result is much more likely to satisfy the customer. Building prototypes of business process changes and organizational redesign initiatives can yield similar benefits.[21] The implications of this extension are that process designs, after agreement by owners and stakeholders, would be implemented on a pilot basis (perhaps in parallel with existing processes), examined regularly for problems and objective achievement, and modified as necessary. As the process approached final acceptance, it would be phased into full implementation.

DEFINING PROCESS TYPES

The five steps described above are sufficiently general to apply to most organizations and processes. Yet the specifics of redesign vary considerably according to the type of process under examination. Different types require different levels of management attention and ownership, need different forms of IT support, and have different business consequences. In this section, we present three different dimensions within which processes vary.

Understanding and classifying the different types of processes is important because an organization can appear to be a seamless web of interconnected processes. With various process *types* in mind, a manager can begin to isolate particular processes for analysis and redesign, including activities that, without process thinking, might otherwise be overlooked.

Three major dimensions can be used to define processes (see Figure 25.3). These are the organizational entities or subunits involved in the process, the type of objects manipulated, and the type of activities taking place. We describe each dimension and resulting process type on the following pages.

FIGURE 25.3 ***Types of processes***

Process Dimension and Type	Typical Example	Typical IT Role
Entities		
Interorganizational	Order from a supplier	Lower transaction costs; eliminate intermediaries
Interfunctional	Develop a new product	Work across geography; greater simultaneity
Interpersonal	Approve a bank loan	Role and task integration
Objects		
Physical	Manufacture a product	Increased outcome flexibility; process control
Informational	Create a proposal	Routinizing complex decisions
Activities		
Operational	Fill a customer order	Reduce time and costs; increase output quality
Managerial	Develop a budget	Improve analysis; increase participation

Defining process entities

Processes take place between types of organizational entities. Each type has different implications for IT benefits.

Interorganizational processes are those taking place between two or more business organizations. Increasingly, companies are concerned with coordinating activities that extend into the next (or previous) company along the value-added chain.[22] Several U.S. retail, apparel, and textile companies, for example, have linked their business processes to speed up reordering of apparel. When Dillard's (department store) inventory of a particular pants style falls below a specified level, Haggar (apparel manufacturer) is notified electronically. If Haggar does not have the cloth to manufacture the pants, Burlington Industries (textile manufacturer) is notified electronically. As this example of electronic data interchange (EDI) illustrates, information technology is the major vehicle by which this interorganizational linkage is executed.

For most companies, simple market relationships are the most common source of interorganizational processes. All the tasks involved in a selling-buying transaction form a critical process for sellers, and an increasingly important one for buyers seeking higher quality, cost efficiency, and responsiveness. Yet much of the focus has been on a simple transaction level, rather than on an interorganizational business process level. Again, how EDI is used illustrates this point.

Buyers and sellers have used EDI largely to speed up routine purchasing transactions, such as invoices or bills of materials. Few companies have attempted to redesign the broader procurement process—from the awareness that a product is needed, to the development of approved vendor lists, or even to the delivery and use of the purchased product. In the future, sellers will need to look at all buyer processes in which their products are involved.

Moreover, many firms will need to help the buyer improve those processes. DuPont's concept of "effectiveness in use" as the major criterion of customer satisfaction is one leading approach to measuring the effectiveness of interorganizational processes. DuPont is motivated not simply to sell a product, but to link its internal processes for creating value in a product, to its customer's processes for using the product. This concept led DuPont to furnish EDI-provided Material Safety Data Sheets along with the chemicals it sells to its customers to ensure their safe use.

Westinghouse used an interorganizational process approach in dealing with Portland General Electric (PGE), a major customer of power generation equipment. PGE managers called upon Westinghouse's Productivity and Quality Center, a national leader in process improvement, to help them implement EDI, but the Westinghouse team asked if it could analyze the entire process by which PGE procured equipment from Westinghouse and other suppliers. They found that, while implementing EDI could yield efficiencies on the order of 10 percent, changing the overall procurement process, including using EDI and bypassing the purchasing department altogether for most routine purchase orders, could lead to much greater savings. In one case, the time to execute a standard purchase order, for example, could be reduced from fifteen days to half a day; the cost could be reduced from almost $90 to $10.

A second major type of business process is *interfunctional*. These processes exist within the organization, but cross several functional or divisional boundaries. Interfunctional processes achieve major operational objectives, such as new product realization, asset management, or production scheduling. Most management processes—for example, planning, budgeting, and human resource management—are interfunctional.

Many manufacturing companies that focused on quality improvement found that producing quality products and services required addressing difficult interfunctional issues. Yet most firms have never even listed their key interactional processes, let alone analyzed or redesigned them, with or without the aid of IT.

Two companies that recently analyzed their key interfunctional business processes are Baxter Healthcare Corporation and US Sprint Communications Company. Baxter's 1985 merger with American Hospital Supply provided the context for a major analysis of key business strategies, and the alignment of the IT infrastructure with those strategies.[23] As part of a seven-month IT planning effort, the company defined twenty-nine major interfunctional processes and analyzed the current and future role of IT in supporting them. For example, in the distribution area, the company identified order entry, inventory, warehouse management, purchasing, transportation, and equipment tracking as key processes. The success of this IT planning effort led Baxter to incorporate the process definition approach into its annual corporate planning process.

At US Sprint, well-publicized problems with the customer billing system prompted the company's IT function to develop a model of information flows for the entire business as part of a comprehensive systems improvement program. This model defined the critical information and key interfunctional processes necessary to run the business. Sprint is now assigning ownership to key processes and continuing to identify improvements—and ways to measure them—in each process. The systems improvement program raised the IT organization's composite internal quality index by more than 50 percent in one year.[24]

A major problem in redesigning interfunctional processes is that most information systems of the past were built to automate specific functional areas or parts of functions. Few third-party application software packages have been developed to support a full business process. Very few organizations have modeled existing interfunctional processes or redesigned them, and companies will run into substantial problems in building interfunctional systems without such models.

Interpersonal processes involve tasks within and across small work groups, typically within a function or department. Examples include a commercial loan group approving a loan, or an airline flight crew preparing for takeoff. This type of process is becoming more important as companies shift to self-managing teams as the lowest unit of organization. Information technology is increasingly capable of supporting interpersonal processes; hardware and communications companies have developed new networking-oriented products, and software companies have begun to flesh out the concept of "groupware" (e.g., local area network-based mail, conferencing, and brainstorming tools).[25]

Several companies, including GM's Electronic Data Systems (EDS), are exploring tools to facilitate the effectiveness of meetings and small group interactions. At EDS, the primary focus is on enhancing the interpersonal processes involved in automobile product development. The company's Center for Machine Intelligence has developed a computer-supported meeting room, and is studying its implications for group decision making and cooperative work.[26]

We should point out that IT can make it possible for employees scattered around the world to work as a team. As an example, Ford now creates new car designs using teams that have members in Europe, Central America, and the United States. Because Ford has standardized computer-aided design systems and created common data structures for the design process, engineers can share complex three-dimensional designs across the Atlantic. Similarly, a small team at Digital Equipment used the company's electronic mail and conferencing capabilities to build the core of a new systems integration business. The team was scattered around the United States and Europe and only rarely met in person.

Defining process objects

Processes can also be categorized by the types of objects manipulated. The two primary object types are physical and informational. In physical object processes, real, tangible things are either created or manipulated; manufacturing is the obvious example. Informational object processes create or manipulate information. Processes for making a decision, preparing a marketing plan, or designing a new product are examples.

Many processes involve the combination of physical and informational objects. Indeed, adding information to a physical object as it moves through a process is a common way of adding value. Most logistical activities, for example, combine the movement of physical objects with the manipulation of information concerning their whereabouts. Success in the logistics industry is often dependent on the close integration of physical and informational outcomes; both UPS and Federal Express, for example, track package movement closely.

The potential for using IT to improve physical processes is well known. It allows greater flexibility and variety of outcomes, more precise control of the process itself, reductions in throughput time, and elimination of human labor. These benefits have been pursued for the past three decades. Still, manufacturing process flows are often the result of historical circumstance and should usually be redesigned before further automation is applied. This is particularly true in low volume, job shop manufacturing environments.[27] Redesigners of physical processes should also consider the role of IT in providing information to improve processes; Shoshana Zuboff has described this "informating" effect in detail for the paper industry.[28]

Strangely, the proportion of informational processes already transformed by IT is probably lower than that of physical processes. True, legions of clerks have become unemployed because of computers. But the majority of information processes to which IT has been applied are those involving high volume and low complexity. Now that these processes are well known even if not fully conquered, the emphasis needs to shift to processes that incorporate semistructured and unstructured tasks and are performed by high-skill knowledge workers. Relevant IT capabilities include the storage and retrieval of unstructured and multimedia information, the capturing and routinizing of decision logic, and the application of far-flung and complex data resources. A computer vendor's advertising videotape, for example, illustrates how artificial intelligence and "hypertext," or mixed-media databases, combine to lead a manager through the process of developing a departmental budget. The IT capabilities in the video are available today, but they are rarely applied to such information-intensive yet unstructured processes.

Defining process activities

Our examples of business processes have involved two types of activities: operational and managerial. Operational processes involve the day-to-day carrying out of the organization's basic business purpose. Managerial processes help to control, plan, or provide resources for operational processes. Past uses of IT to improve processes, limited as they are, have been largely operational. We will therefore focus almost entirely on managerial processes in this section.[29]

Applying IT to management *tasks* is not a new idea. The potential of decision support systems, executive support systems, and other managerial tools has been discussed for over twenty years. We believe, however, that the benefits have not been realized because of the absence of systematic process thinking. Few companies have rigorously analyzed managerial activities as processes subject to redesign. Even the notion of managerial activities involving defined outcomes (a central aspect of our definition of business processes) is somewhat foreign. How

IT-driven process redesign at Rank Xerox U.K.

Rank Xerox U.K. (RXUK), a national operating company of Xerox Corporation, has undertaken the most comprehensive IT-driven process redesign we have studied. The process was led by David O'Brien, the division's managing director, who arrived at the company in 1985. O'Brien quickly came to two realizations: First, the company needed to focus on marketing office systems in addition to its traditional reprographics products; and second, the company's strong functional culture and inefficient business processes would greatly inhibit its growth. He began to see his own organization as a place to test integrated office systems that support integrated business processes; if successful, he could use RXUK as a model for customers.

The company began to redesign its business in 1987. In a series of offsite meetings, the senior management team reappraised its external environment and mission, then identified the key business processes needed if the company was to achieve its mission. The group began to restructure the organization around cross-functional processes, identifying high-level objectives and creating task forces to define information and other resource requirements for each process. It created career systems revolving around facilitation skills and cross-functional management, rather than hierarchical authority. O'Brien decided to keep a somewhat functional formal structure, because functional skills would still be needed in a process organization and because the level of organizational change might have been too great with a wholly new structure.

The level of change was still very high. Several senior managers departed because they could not or would not manage in the new environment. Two new cross-functional senior positions, called "facilitating directors," were created, one for

IT-driven process redesign at Rank Xerox U.K. ***(continued)***
organizational and business development, the other for process management, information systems, and quality. O'Brien took great advantage of the honeymoon period accorded to new CEOs, but managing the change still required intense personal attention:

> Of course this new thinking was in sharp contrast to some of the skills and attitudes of the company. We were introducing a change in management philosophy in a company that, in many ways, was very skillful and effective, but in a different product-market environment. We faced all the issues of attitudinal change and retraining that any such change implies. We were moving to a much more integrated view of the world and had to encourage a major shift in many patterns of the existing culture. This meant a very hard, tough program of selling the new ideas within the organization as well as an extensive and personal effort to get the new messages and thinking to our potential customers.*

As the key processes were identified and their objectives determined, the company began to think about how information technology (its own and from other providers) could enable and support the processes. The facilitating director of processes and systems, Paul Chapman, decided that the firm needed a new approach to developing information systems around processes. His organization used the information engineering approach discussed earlier and worked with an external consultant to refine and confirm process identification. They uncovered 18 "macro" business processes (e.g., logistics) and 145 "micro" processes (e.g., fleet management).

The senior management team reconvened to prioritize the identified processes and decided that seven macro processes had particular importance: customer order life cycle, customer satisfaction, installed equipment management, integrated planning, logistics, financial management, and personnel management. It selected personnel management as the first process to be redesigned because this was viewed as relatively easy to attack and because personnel systems were crucial in tracking the development of new skills. The personnel system has now been successfully redesigned, using automated code generation capabilities, in substantially less time than if normal methods had been used.

RXUK's financial situation began to improve as it redesigned its business processes. The company emerged from a long period of stagnation into a period of 20 percent revenue

IT-driven process redesign at Rank Xerox U.K. ***(continued)***
growth. Jobs not directly involved with customer contact were reduced from 1,100 to 800. Order delivery time was, on average, reduced from thirty-three days to six days. Though many other market factors were changing during this time, O'Brien credits the process redesign for much of the improvement.

Other Xerox divisions heard of RXUK's success with process redesign and began efforts of their own. Xerox's U.S. product development and marketing divisions now have major cross-functional teams performing process redesign. Paul Chapman has been loaned to Xerox corporate headquarters, where he is heading a cross-functional team looking at corporate business processes. Commitment to IT-driven process redesign by Xerox senior corporate management is also growing.

---

*David O'Brien, quoted in B. Denning and B. Taylor, "Rank Xerox U.K., Office Systems Strategy (C): Developing the Systems Strategy," (Henley on Thames, England: Henley—The Management College case study, September 1988). Other Rank Xerox U.K. information comes from personal interviews.

would such managerial processes as deciding on an acquisition or developing the agenda for the quarterly board meeting be improved if they were treated as processes—in other words, measured, brainstormed, and redesigned with IT capabilities?

The generic capabilities of IT for reshaping management processes include improving analytic accuracy, enabling broader management participation across wider geographical boundaries, generating feedback on actions taken (the managerial version of "informating" a process), and streamlining the time and resources a specific process consumes. Texas Instruments and Xerox's corporate headquarters provide excellent examples.

Texas Instruments has developed an expert system to facilitate the capital budgeting process. Managers in a fast-growing and capital-intensive TI division were concerned that the time and experience necessary to prepare capital budget request packages would become an obstacle to the division's growth. The packages were very complex and time consuming, and few employees had the requisite knowledge to complete them accurately. The expert system was developed by two industrial engineers with expertise in both the technology and the budget process.

TI's system has radically improved the capital budget request process. Requests prepared with the system require far less time than the manual approach and conform better to the company's guidelines. One experienced employee reported a reduction in package preparation time from nine hours to forty minutes; of the first fifty packages prepared with the system, only three did not conform to guidelines, compared to an average of ten using a manual approach.[30]

At Xerox Corporation headquarters, IT has been used to improve the review of division strategic plans. Prior to the development of the company's Executive Information System (EIS), the planning process was somewhat haphazard; each division prepared its planning documents in a different format and furnished different types of information to corporate headquarters. Plans often came in too late for the corporate management committee to review them before the quarterly or annual review meeting. The EIS was developed to include standard information formats and a user friendly graphical interface enabling fast comprehension. Divisional plans are now developed on the EIS and delivered instantaneously over Xerox's network to all corporate management committee members. These members can now read and discuss the plans beforehand and can move directly to decisions at the review meetings. The workstations are even used in the meetings themselves, allowing revisions to be made and agreed upon before adjournment. As one manager put it, " . . . [the system] lets us communicate at higher speed and in greater depth."[31]

MANAGEMENT ISSUES IN IT-ENABLED REDESIGN

Companies have found that once a process has been redesigned, several key issues remain. These include the management role in redesigned activity, implications for organization structure, new skill requirements, creating a function to perform IT-enabled BPR, the proper direction for the IT infrastructure, and the need for continuous process improvement. We discuss each below.

Management roles

Perhaps the greatest difficulty in IT-driven redesign is getting and keeping management commitment. Because processes cut across various parts of the organization, a process redesign effort driven by a single business function or unit will probably encounter resistance from other parts of the organization. Both high-level and broad support for change are necessary.

To perform the five redesign steps described above, several companies created a cross-functional task force headed by a senior executive. These task forces included representatives from key staff and line groups likely to be affected by the changes, including IT and human resources. It was particularly important that the customer of the process be represented on the team, even when the customer was external. The team composition was ideal if some members had some record of process or operations innovation involving IT.

As the redesign teams selected processes and developed objectives, they needed to work closely with the managers and staff of the affected units. Managing process change is similar to managing other types of change, except that its cross-functional nature increases the number of stakeholders, thereby increasing the complexity of the effort.

It was also important to have strong, visible commitment from senior management. Employees throughout the organization needed to understand that redesign was critical, that differences of opinion would be resolved in favor of the customer of a process, and that IT would play an important role. In many cases, the CEO communicated any structural implications of the redesign effort.

An example of the importance of the CEO's role is found at GUS Home Shopping, the largest home shopping company in Europe. GUS undertook a $90 million project to redesign its logistical processes with IT. Redesign objectives involved both cost and time: to be able to sell a product within five minutes of its arrival on the loading dock, and to be able to deliver a product to the customer's door at an average cost of sixty cents. The company's managing director commented on his role in meeting these objectives:

> To change our business to the degree we have [done] demands integration. How involved should the managing director get in designing computer systems? My view is totally, because he's the one who can integrate across the entire organization.[32]

Process redesign and organizational structure

A second key issue is the relationship between process orientation and organizational structure. Certainly someone must be in charge of implementing a process change, and of managing the redesigned process thereafter. But process responsibilities are likely to cut across existing organizational structures. How can process organization and traditional functional organization be reconciled?

One possible solution is to create a new organization structure along process lines, in effect abandoning altogether other structural dimensions, such as function, product, or geography. This approach presents risks, however; as business needs change, new processes will be created that cut across the previous process-based organization. This does not mean that a process-based structure cannot be useful, but only that it will have to be changed frequently.

While no firm we studied has converted wholly to a process-based structure, a few organizations have moved in this direction. For example, Apple Computer recently moved away from a functional structure to what executives describe as an IT-oriented, process-based, customer satisfaction-driven structure called "New Enterprise." The company relishes its lack of formal hierarchy; Apple managers describe their roles as highly diffuse, and team and project based.

A more conservative approach would be to create a matrix of functional and process responsibilities. However, because of the cross-functional nature of most processes, the functional manager who should have responsibility for a given process is not always easy to identify. The company may also wish to avoid traditional functional thinking in assigning process responsibilities. For example, it may be wiser to give responsibility for redesigning supplies acquisition to a manager who uses those supplies (i.e., the customer of the process), rather than to the head of purchasing.

New skill requirements

For process management to succeed, managers must develop facilitation and influence skills. Traditional sources of authority may be of little use when process changes cut across organizational units. Managers will find themselves trying to change the behavior of employees who do not work for them. In these cases, they must learn to persuade rather than to instruct, to convince rather than to dictate. Of course, these recommendations are consistent with many other organizational maxims of the past several years; they just happen to be useful in process management as well.[33]

Several organizations that are moving toward IT-driven process management are conducting programs intended to develop facilitation skills. These programs encourage less reliance on hierarchy, more cross-functional communication and cooperation, and more decision making by middle- and lower-level managers. Such a program at American Airlines is being used to build an organizational infrastructure at the same time a new IT infrastructure is being built.

An ongoing organization

Organizations that redesign key processes must oversee continuing redesign and organizational "tuning," as well as ensure that information systems support process flows. In most companies, the appropriate analytical skills are most likely to be found in the IT function. However, these individuals will also require a high degree of interpersonal skills to be successful as the "new industrial engineers." The ideal group would represent multiple functional areas, for example, information systems, industrial engineering, quality, process control, finance, and human resources.

There are already some examples of such process change groups. Silicon Graphics has created a specific process consulting group for ongoing process management; it is headed by a director-level manager. At United Parcel Service, process redesign is traditionally concentrated in the industrial engineering function. The UPS group is incorporating IT skills in the IE function at a rapid rate, and creating task forces with IT and IE representation for process redesign projects. Federal Express has gone even further, renaming its IE organization the "Strategic Integrated Systems Group," placing it within the Information Systems function, and giving it responsibility for designing and implementing major IT-driven business changes.

Process redesign and the IT organization

Just as information technology is a powerful force in redesigning business processes, process thinking has important implications for the IT organization and for the technology infrastructure it builds. Though few IT groups have the power and influence to spearhead process redesign, they can play several important roles. First of all, the IT group may need to play a behind-the-scenes advocacy role, convincing senior management of the power offered by information technology and process redesign. Second, as demand builds for process redesign expertise, the IT group can begin to incorporate the IE-oriented skills of process measurement, analysis, and redesign, perhaps merging with the IE function if there is one. It can also develop an approach or methodology for IT-enabled redesign, perhaps using the five steps described above as a starting point.

What must the information systems function do technologically to prepare for process redesign? IT professionals must recognize that they will have to build most systems needed to support (or enable) processes, rather than buy them from software package vendors, because most application packages are designed with particular functions in mind. IT professionals will need to build robust technology platforms on which process-specific applications can be quickly constructed. This implies a standardized architecture with extensive communications capability between computing nodes, and the development of shared databases. However, like the organizational strategies for process management described above, these are appropriate technology strategies for most companies, whether or not they are redesigning processes with IT.

Continuous process improvement

The concept of process improvement, which developed in the quality movement, requires first that the existing process be stabilized. It then becomes predictable, and its capabilities become accessible to analysis and improvement.[34] Continuous process improvement occurs when the cycle of stabilizing, assessing, and improving a given process becomes institutionalized.

IT-enabled business process redesign must generally be dynamic. Those responsible for a process should constantly investigate whether new information technologies make it possible to carry out a process in new ways. IT is continuing to evolve, and forthcoming technologies will have a substantial impact on the processes of the next decade. The IT infrastructure must be robust enough to support the new applications appropriate to a particular process.

SUMMARY

We believe that the industrial engineers of the future, regardless of their formal title or the organizational unit that employs them, will focus increasingly on IT-enabled redesign of business processes. We have only begun to explore the implications and implementation of this concept, and only a few companies have ventured into the area. Many companies that have used IT to redesign particular business processes have done so without any conscious approach or philosophy. In short, the actual experience base with IT-enabled process redesign is limited.

Yet managing by customer-driven processes that cross organizational boundaries is an intuitively appealing idea that has worked well in the companies that have experimented with it. And few would question that information technology is a powerful tool for reshaping business processes. The individuals and companies that can master redesigning processes around IT will be well equipped to succeed in the new decade—and the new century.

Notes

The authors wish to acknowledge the support of the Center for Information Systems Research at the MIT Sloan School, Harvard Business School's Division of Research, and McKinsey & Company. They are also grateful for the comments of Lynda Applegate, James Cash, Warren McFarlan, John Rockart, Edgar Schein, and Michael S. Scott Morton.

1. L. Gulick, "Notes on the Theory of Organization," in L. Gulick and L. Urwick, eds., *Papers on the Science of Administration* (New York: Institute of Public Administration, 1937), p. 9.
2. S. Sakamoto, "Process Design Concept: A New Approach to IE," *Industrial Engineering*, March 1989, p. 31.
3. "Office Automation: Making It Pay Off," *Business Week*, 12 October 1987, pp. 134–146. For an alternative perspective, see R.E. Kraut, ed., *Technology and the Transformation of White-Collar Work* (Hillsdale, New Jersey: Lawrence Erlbaum Associates, 1987).
4. G. W. Loveman, "An Assessment of the Productivity Impact of Information Technologies" (Cambridge, Massachusetts: MIT Sloan School of Management, Management in the 1990s, Working Paper 90s:88-054, July 1988). Loveman studied microeconomic data from manufacturing firms to estimate econometrically the productivity impact of IT in the late 1970s and early 1980s. In finding no significant positive productivity impact from IT, he argues that his findings in manufacturing raise serious questions about impacts in nonmanufacturing firms as well. Baily and Chakrabarti (1988) studied white-collar productivity and IT as one part of a broader inquiry into poor productivity growth. They found no evidence of significant productivity gain. See M. N. Baily and A. Chakrabarti, *Innovation and the Productivity Crisis* (Washington, D.C.: Brookings Institution, 1988).
5. Loveman (1988); Baily and Chakrabarti (1988). See also L. C. Thurow, "Toward a High-Wage, High-Productivity Service Sector" (Washington, D.C.: Economic Policy Institute, 1989).
6. Robert Horton, who became chairman and chief executive of British Petroleum in March 1990, argues that his major concern in setting BP's course in the next decade is "managing surprise." Horton's belief is that the external business environment is so unpredictable that surprise, rather than managed change, is inevitable. See R. Horton, "Future Challenges to Management," *MIT Management*, Winter 1989, pp. 3–6.
7. T. Malone, "What is Coordination Theory?" (Cambridge, Massachusetts: MIT Sloan School of Management, Center for Coordination Science, Working Paper No. 2051-88, February 1988); K. Crowston and T. Malone, "Information Technology and Work Organization" (Cambridge, Massachusetts: MIT Sloan School of Management, Center for Information Systems Research, Working Paper No. 165, December 1987).

8. G. A. Pall, *Quality Process Management* (Englewood Cliffs, New Jersey: Prentice-Hall, 1987). Our definition also complements that of Schein, who focuses on human processes in organizations—e.g., building and maintaining groups, group problem solving and decision making, leading and influencing, etc. See E. H. Schein, *Process Consultation: Its Role in Organization Development,* Vol. 1, 2d ed. (Reading, Massachusetts: Addison-Wesley, 1988).
9. E. J. Kane, "IBM's Total Quality Improvement System" (Purchase, New York: IBM Corporation, unpublished manuscript), p. 5.
10. See, for example, M. F. Morris and G. W. Vining "The IE's Future Role in Improving Knowledge Worker Productivity," *Industrial Engineering,* July 1987, p. 28.
11. "Reference Note on Work Simplification" (Boston: Harvard Business School, HBS Case Services #9-609-0601961, 1961).
12. The relationship between business vision and IT has been explored by several researchers under the auspices of the MIT Sloan School's five-year "Management in the 1990s" research program. An overview volume is scheduled for publication by Oxford University Press in August 1990.
13. See, for example, G. Stalk, Jr., "Time—The Next Source of Strategic Advantage," *Harvard Business Review,* July–August 1988, pp. 41–51.
14. S. Zuboff, *In the Age of the Smart Machine* (New York: Basic Books, 1988).
15. E. H. Schein, "Innovative Cultures and Organizations" (Cambridge, Massachusetts: MIT Sloan School of Management, Management in the 1990s, Working Paper 90s:88-064, November 1988).
16. Information engineering and other redesign approaches based on data modeling are necessarily limited in scope. More than data is exchanged in many process relationships. Note too that many companies have used information engineering methods *without* a specific process orientation.
17. Examples of IT planning approaches where high-impact objectives and/or goals are defined include critical success factors (CSFs) and business systems planning (BSP). See J. F. Rockart, "Chief Executives Define Their Own Data Needs," *Harvard Business Review,* March–April 1979, pp. 81–93; and IBM, *Information Systems Planning Guide,* 3d ed. (Business Systems Planning Report No. GE20-05527-2, July 1981).
18. D. Goodhue, J. Quillard, and J. Rockart, "Managing the Data Resource: A Contingency Perspective" (Cambridge, Massachusetts: MIT Sloan School of Management, Center for Information Systems Research, Working Paper No. 150, January 1987).
19. J. F Rockart, "The Line Takes the Leadership—IS Management in a Wired Society," *Sloan Management Review,* Summer 1988, pp. 57–64.
20. J. C. Henderson and N. Venkatraman, "Strategic Alignment: A Process Model for Integrating Information Technology and Business Strategies" (Cambridge, Massachusetts: MIT Sloan School of Management, Center for Information Systems Research, Working Paper No. 196, October 1989).
21. Dorothy Leonard-Barton introduced the concept of organizational prototyping with regard to the implementation of new information technologies. See D. Leonard-Barton, "The Case for Integrative Innovation: An Expert System at Digital," *Sloan Management Review,* Fall 1987, pp. 7–19.

22. R. Johnston and P. R. Lawrence, "Beyond Vertical Integration—The Rise of the Value-Adding Partnership," *Harvard Business Review,* July–August 1988, pp. 94–101. See also N. Venkatraman, "IT-Induced Business Reconfiguration: The New Strategic Management Challenge" (Cambridge, Massachusetts: Paper presented at the annual conference of the MIT Center for Information Systems Research, June 1989).

23. T. J. Main and J. E. Short, "Managing the Merger: Building Partnership through IT Planning at the New Baxter," *Management Information Systems Quarterly,* December 1989, pp. 469–486.

24. C. R. Hall, M. E. Friesen, and J. E. Short, "The Turnaround at US Sprint: The Role of Improved Partnership between Business and Information Management," in progress.

25. R. R. Johansen, *Groupware: Computer Support for Business Teams* (New York: The Free Press, 1988). Also see C. V. Bullen and R. R. Johansen, "Groupware: A Key to Managing Business Teams?" (Cambridge, Massachusetts: MIT Sloan School of Management, Center for Information Systems Research, Working Paper No. 169, May 1988).

26. See L. M. Applegate, "The Center for Machine Intelligence: Computer Support for Cooperative Work" (Boston: Harvard Business School Case Study No. 189-135, 1988, rev. 1989).

27. J. E. Ashton and F. X. Cook, "Time to Reform Job Shop Manufacturing," *Harvard Business Review,* March–April 1989, pp. 106–111.

28. See cases on "Tiger Creek," "Piney Wood," and "Cedar Bluff" in S. Zuboff (1988); other industries discussed by Zuboff primarily involve informational processes.

29. One might consider managerial processes synonymous with informational processes. Certainly the vast majority of managerial processes, such as budgeting, planning, and human resource development, involve informational objects. Yet it is important to remember that informational processes can be either operational or managerial, so we believe that this separate dimension of process types is warranted.

30. A case study describes the process and the creation of the expert system. See "Texas Instruments Capital Investment Expert System" (Boston: Harvard Business School Case Study No. 188-050, 1988).

31. Some aspects of this process improvement are described in L. M. Applegate and C. S. Osborne, "Xerox Corporation: Executive Support Systems" (Boston: Harvard Business School Case Study No. 189-134, 1988, rev. 1989).

32. R. H. C. Pugh, address to McKinsey & Co. information technology practice leaders, Munich, Germany, June 1989.

33. See, for example, A. R. Cohen and D. L. Bradford, "Influence without Authority: The Use of Alliances, Reciprocity, and Exchange to Accomplish Work," *Organizational Dynamics,* Winter 1989, pp. 4–17.

34. See G. A. Pall (1987).

Reading 26

Chimera or Culture? Business Process Reengineering for Total Quality Management

BY KEN W. GADD AND JOHN S. OAKLAND

This article reviews the literature on business process reengineering (BPR) and explores its linkages with total quality management (TQM). The history of the development, ideals, beliefs, values, knowledge, means of implementation, and techniques involved have demonstrated many similarities in these two approaches. The early successes in BPR were in organizations with strongly evolving TQM cultures, and it is identified that the cultural change involved in maintaining the results of process redesign is the most difficult part of the BPR process.

TQM programs are claimed to have failed because they do not produce large enough gains quickly enough, but the cultural ideology of TQM in several organizations has provided the environment necessary to sustain the new and radical process redesigns, while BPR has provided the broader process perspectives described by many authors. This, in turn, has facilitated the realignment of business processes to achieve radical change in strategic direction.

BPR and TQM would appear to be part of an evolving culture of process orientation that started in the quality movement(s) of the 1980s, and has a commitment to continuous process improvement in the 1990s.

Key words: business process redesign, continuous improvement, discontinuous change, information technology, process improvement.

THE PROCESS REVOLUTION AND DISCONTINUOUS CHANGE

Discontinuous improvement

In 1990, the concept of business process reengineering (BPR) was introduced to the world via two articles that described the radical changes to business processes being performed by a handful of western businesses. These were among the first to embark on TQM initiatives in the quality revolution of the 1980s. Organizations included Xerox, Ford, AT&T, Baxter Healthcare, and Hewlett-Packard (Hammer 1990; Davenport and Short 1990).

Many companies adopted TQM initiatives in the 1980s hoping to win back business lost to Japanese competition. When Ford benchmarked Mazda's accounts payable department, Ford discovered a business process being run by five people, compared to Ford's 500. Given the difference in scale of the two companies, this still demonstrated the relative inefficiency of Ford's accounts payable process (Hammer 1990). At Xerox, taking a customer's perspective of the company identified the need to develop systems rather than stand-alone products, which highlighted Xerox's own inefficient office systems (Davenport and Short 1990). Both Ford and Xerox realized that incremental improvement alone was not enough. They had developed high infrastructure costs and bureaucracies that made them relatively unresponsive to customer service. Focusing on internal customer-supplier interfaces improved quality, but preserved the current process structure, and could not hope to achieve in a few years what had taken the Japanese 30 years. To achieve the necessary improvements required a radical rethinking and redesign of these processes.

Twenty-five years ago, Drucker said that organizations should expect many traditional approaches to be challenged, and that many assumptions held then would no longer apply in what he heralded as the "Age of Discontinuity" (Drucker 1969). Charles Handy referred to the "Age of Unreason," when traditional ways of perceiving things need to be replaced by discontinuous thinking. The slow and incremental change that has always been here has become rapid and discontinuous; not only in business, but also in the world in general (Handy 1989).

What was being applied by organizations such as Ford and Xerox was discontinuous improvement. In order to respond to the competitive threats of Canon and Honda, Xerox and Ford needed TQM to catch up; but to get ahead required radical breakthroughs in performance (Earl and Khan 1994). Central to these breakthrough improvements was information technology (IT).

The information technologists

The introduction of Sun Microsystems' workstation innovation changed history for computer manufacturers (Hammer and Champy 1993). Computer networks, open systems, client-server architecture, groupware, and electronic data interchange (EDI) have opened up the possibilities for the integrated automation of business processes. Neural networks, enterprise analyzer approaches, computer-assisted software engineering, and object-oriented programming now facilitate systems design around office processes (Baets 1993; Davenport and Short 1990; Dennis et al. 1994; Petrozzo and Stepper 1994; Swatman, Swatman, and Fowler 1994; Taylor and Williams 1994; Venkatraman 1994). The pace of change in IT has been enormous.

IT systems unavailable in the early 1980s have enabled sweeping changes in business process improvement, particularly in office systems. Just as statistical process control (SPC) enabled manufacturing processes to be improved by controlling variation and improving efficiency, so IT is enabling nonmanufacturing processes to be fundamentally restructured.

IT in itself, however, did not offer all the answers, automation frequently being claimed not to produce the gains expected. The IT-intensive financial services industry, widely reported to be going through many major BPR exercises, has been shown to be making very little use of new IT solutions (Watkins 1994). Many companies putting in major new computer systems have achieved only the automation of existing processes. Others have not overhauled their existing IT hardware, expecting new systems to integrate with the old (Watkins, Skinner, and Pearson 1993). Davenport (1994) warned that IT systems need to match the requirements of the people using them. Many managers do not rely on computer-based information to make decisions, and merely changing an IT system will not change a company's information culture.

Frequently, different functions within the same organization have systems that are incompatible with each other. Locked into traditional functional structures, managers have spent small fortunes on IT systems that have not been used cross-functionally. Yet it is in this cross-functional area that the big improvement gains through IT are to be made (Duffy 1994). Once a process view is taken to designing and installing an IT system, it becomes possible to automate cross-functional, cross-divisional, even cross-company processes (Davenport and Short 1990; Venkatraman 1991, 1994; Coyle 1992; Short and Venkatraman 1992; Dennis et al. 1994; Taylor and Williams 1994).

IT, processes, and organizational change

IT provided the means to achieve the breakthrough in performance required. The inspiration, however, came from understanding both the current and potential processes. This required a more holistic view than that taken in traditional quality programs (Chang 1994; Petrozzo and Stepper 1994). The changes documented by Hammer, Davenport, Short, and Venkatraman involved wholesale redesigns of the processes concerned.

Both Deming (1993) and Senge (1993) wrote about *systems thinking*. In any system, events will occur that have an effect elsewhere in the system. In order to have a full understanding of the effects of what is being done, it is necessary to understand the whole process and how it fits into the organizational system.

Ford estimated a 20 percent reduction in head count if it automated the existing processes in accounts payable. Taking an overall process perspective, Ford achieved a 75 percent reduction in one department (Hammer 1990). At Xerox, managing director David O'Brien took an organizational view and concentrated on cross-functional processes (Davenport and Short 1990). Baxter Healthcare's adoption of EDI allowed a cross-organizational process to be reengineered, radically changing the relationship between supplier and external customer (Short and Venkatraman 1992).

Clearly, the larger the scope of the process, the greater and farther reaching are the consequences of the redesign. At a macro level, turning raw materials into a product used by a delighted customer is a process made up of subsets of individual processes. The aim of the overall process is to add value to those raw materials. Taking a holistic view of the process makes it possible to identify non-value-adding elements and remove them. It enables people to question why things are done, and to determine what should be done.

Some of the reengineering literature advises starting with a blank sheet of paper and redesigning the process anew. The problems inherent in this approach are (1) the danger of designing another inefficient system, and (2) not appreciating the scope of the problem (Petrozzo and Stepper 1994). Therefore, many authorities recommend a thorough understanding of current processes before embarking on a reengineering project.

Current processes can be understood and documented by flowcharting and process mapping. As processes are documented, their interrelationships become clear and a map of the organization emerges. Figure 26.1 shows a much simplified process map. The aim of BPR is to make discontinuous, major improvements. This invariably means organizational change, the extent of which depends on the scope of the process reengineered.

Taking the organization depicted in Figure 26.1 as an example, if the decision is made to redesign the processes in finance, the effect may be that in Figure 26.2a. Eight individual processes have become three. There has been no organizational effect on the processes in the other functions, but finance has been completely restructured. In Figure 26.2b, a chain of processes, crossing all the functions, has been reengineered. The effect has been the loss of redundant processes and possibly many heads, but much of the organization has been unaffected. Figure 26.2c

FIGURE 26.1 ***Simplified process map***

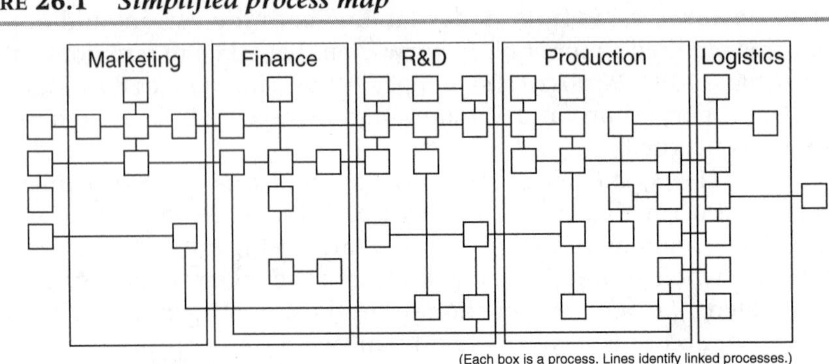

FIGURE 26.2a *Process redesign in finance*

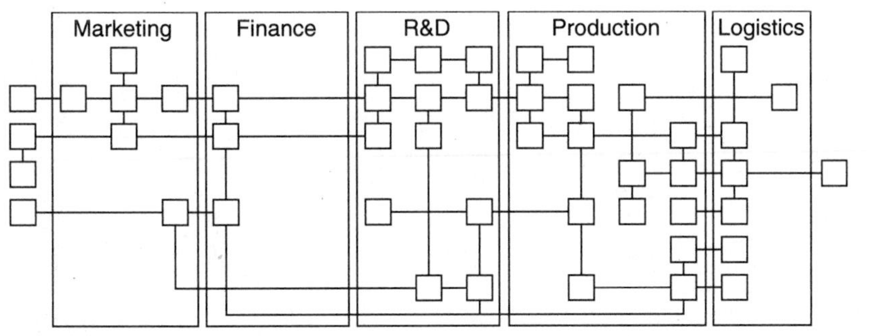

FIGURE 26.2b *Cross-functional process redesign*

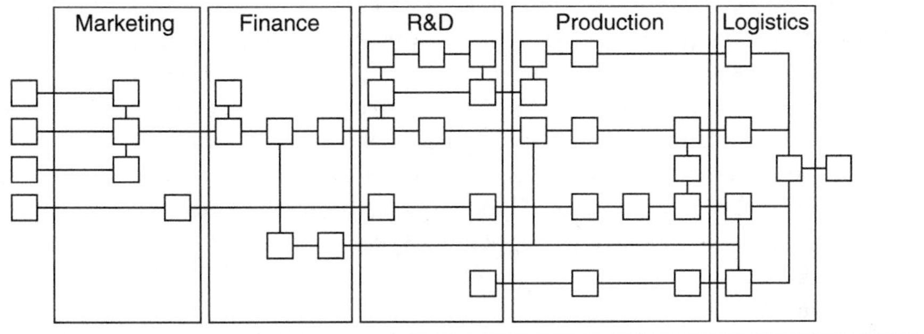

FIGURE 26.2c *Organizational process redesign*

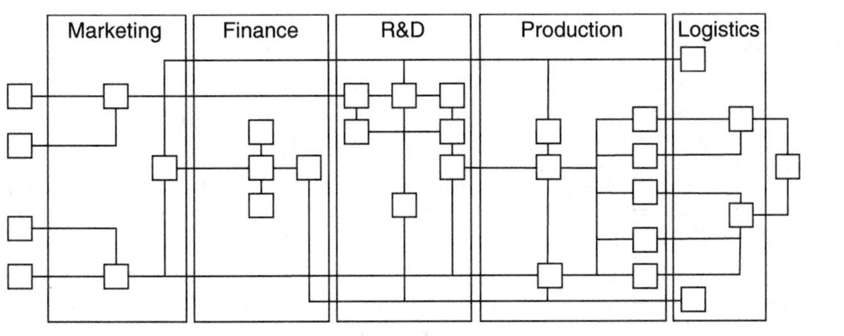

FIGURE 26.3 Process organization

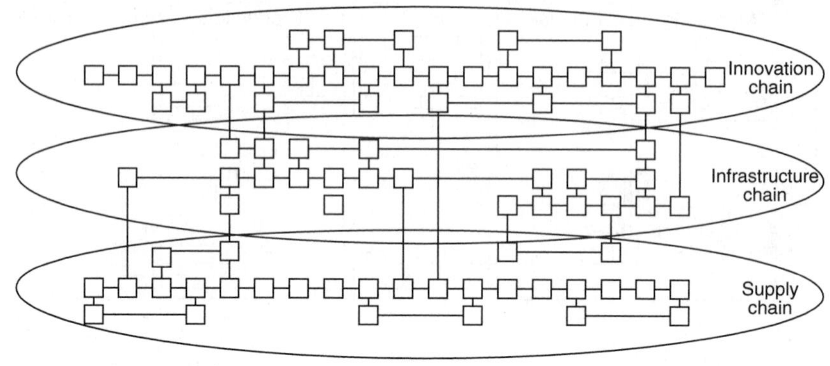

shows the organization after a thorough reengineering of all its processes. Some elements may remain the same, but the effect is organizationwide.

Whatever the scope of the redesign, head count is not the only change. When work processes are altered, the way people work alters. Figures 26.1 and 26.2 show an organization's functional departments with processes running through them. As these cross-functional processes are reengineered to improve added-value output and efficiency, many organizations are now questioning the need or even the relevance of traditional functional structures, and are beginning to organize around core processes. These are the handful of processes that make up what an organization does (see Figure 26.3) (Kaplan and Murdoch 1991).

DEFINITIONS OF BUSINESS PROCESS REENGINEERING

When businesses were making radical improvements in the late 1980s, the term BPR did not exist. Its application after the fact has led to much confusion as to what actually constitutes BPR.

BPR has been defined as

> The analysis and design of work flows and processes within and between organizations. (Davenport and Short 1990).
>
> The fundamental rethinking and radical redesign of business processes to achieve dramatic improvements in critical, contemporary measures of performance, such as cost, quality, service, and speed (Hammer and Champy 1993).
>
> To rethink, restructure, and streamline the business structures, processes, methods of working, management systems, and external relationships through which we create and deliver value (Talwar 1993).
>
> The concurrent redesign of processes, organizations, and their supporting information systems to achieve radical improvement in time, cost, quality, and customers' regard for the company's products and services (Petrozzo and Stepper 1994).

> The fundamental rethinking and redesign of operating processes and organizational structure, focused on the organization's core competencies, to achieve dramatic improvements in organizational performance (Lowenthal 1994).

Although the definition by Davenport and Short seems to have less range than the others quoted here, their description of the concept is every bit as far-reaching.

Talwar's (1993) categorization of process reengineering on the one hand, and business reengineering on the other, is an interesting and important one, but it is beyond the scope of this article. In practice, both TQM and BPR have focused on the definition and operation of business processes to produce products and services within a defined scope of business. Neither have focused on strategic business direction setting or planning, nor on reinventing business or industry.

None of these definitions refer to IT. BPR is not necessarily dependent on IT solutions. While there is general agreement that IT can be a powerful enabler, the radical improvements sought are a function of organizational process redesign rather than IT implementation per se. While IT specialists insist that new systems are central to BPR, the challenge is increasingly one of the implementation of organizational change and the visioning involved in that (Wastell, White, and Kawalek 1994). Where there is confusion, therefore, is in both the interpretation and the scope of the concept. Hammer referred to business process *reengineering;* Davenport and Short to business process *redesign.* The literature is filled with many variations on these terms, all referring to process changes large and small. For example,

- Business process improvement (Harrington 1991)
- Core process redesign (Kaplan and Murdoch 1991)
- Process innovation (Davenport 1992)
- Business process transformation (Burke and Peppard 1993)
- Breakpoint business process redesign (Johanssen et al. 1993)
- Organizational reengineering (Lowenthal 1994)
- Business process management (Duffy 1994)
- Business scope redefinition (Venkatraman 1994)

While some terms are clearly referring to a generic business process "improvement," albeit on a grand scale, some authors are attempting to differentiate between different *levels* of reengineering (Talwar 1993; Lowenthal 1994; Drucker 1993; Watkins, Skinner, and Pearson 1993; Earl and Khan 1994).

George Stalk, of the Boston Consulting Group, warned that reengineering the wrong processes will not achieve dramatic results. Although Ford's reengineered accounts payable process yielded large percentage improvements in costs, time, and quality, it had little effect on overall performance, because it was not a core process central to the strategy of the company (Thackray 1993).

Put into a strategic context, BPI becomes a means of aligning work processes with customer requirements in a dynamic way, in order to achieve long-term corporate objectives. This requires systems thinking (Senge 1993; Deming 1993), involving customers, suppliers, and the future. Gulden and Reck (1991) showed that the secrets to designing a process lie not so much in intimately understanding the way it is performed today but rather in thinking about how to reshape it for the future. This was also stressed in Robert Cole's (1994) excellent essay on Hammer and Champy's book.

BUSINESS PROCESS AND ORGANIZATIONAL REDESIGN

Outcomes, measurement, and competitive advantage

BPR is not intended to preserve the status quo, but to fundamentally and radically change what is done; it is *dynamic*. Therefore, it is essential for a BPR effort to focus on outcomes rather than tasks, and the required outcome will determine the scope of the BPR exercise. A simple requirement may be a 30 percent reduction in costs or a reduction in delivery time of two days. These would imply projects with relatively narrow scope, which are essentially inwardly focused and probably involve only one department; for example, the finance department in Figure 26.2a.

When Wal-Mart focused on satisfying customer needs as an outcome, it started a redesign that not only totally changed the way it replenished inventory, but also made this the centerpiece of its competitive strategy. The system put in place was radical, and required tremendous vision. In 10 years, Wal-Mart has grown from being a small niche retailer to the largest and most profitable retailer in the world (Stalk, Evans, and Shulman 1992).

Schaffer and Thomson (1992) highlighted how focusing on results rather than just activities makes the difference between success and failure in change programs. The measures used, however, are crucial. At every level of reengineering, a focus on outcome gives direction and measurability; whether it be cost reduction, head count reduction, increase in efficiency, customer focus, identification of core processes and non-value-adding components, or strategic alignment of business processes. Benchmarking is a powerful tool for BPR and is the trigger for many BPR projects, as in Ford's accounts payable process. The value of benchmarking does not lie in what can be copied, but in its ability to identify goals (Richman and Koontz 1993; Earl and Khan 1994). If used well, benchmarking can shape strategy and identify potential competitive advantage (Zairi 1994).

In a series of three articles, Hamel and Prahalad (1989, 1990, 1991) discussed establishing strategic direction via intent rather than portfolio analysis; identifying an organization's core competencies; and developing the skills required to achieve that intent via expeditionary marketing. Establishing its core processes focuses a company on what it does, how it does it, and how it should do it. Core process redesign can channel an organization's competencies into an outcome that gives it strategic competitive advantage (Kaplan and Murdoch 1991). The key element is visioning that outcome (Goss, Pascale, and Athos 1993).

The redesign process

Central to BPR is an objective overview of the processes to be redesigned. Whereas information needs to be obtained from the people directly involved in those processes, it is never initiated by them. Even at its lowest level, BPR has a top-down approach (Hammer and Champy 1993; Petrozzo and Stepper 1994). Therefore, most BPR efforts take the form of a project (Earl and Khan 1994). There are numerous methodologies being proposed, but all share common elements. Typically, the project takes the form of several discrete phases (based on Petrozzo and Stepper 1994).

- *Discover*
  Identify a problem or unacceptable outcome.
  Determine desired outcome—business assessment.
  Determine the process(es) involved—establish scope.
  Establish redesign team.
- *Hunt and gather*
  Analyze and document process(es).
  Acquire supporting information, such as benchmarking and IT possibilities.
- *Innovate and build*
  Rethink and redesign the new process using iterative approach.
  Establish new process design.
- *Reorganize, retrain, retool*
  Implement new process structure.
  Train for new technology and roles.

It is worth noting that these methods, as they are executed by the leading practitioners, are not capable of addressing outcomes that are beyond the scope of the defined business purpose of an enterprise. In many organizations there is a considerable gap between intention and reality. People need to be equipped to assess, reengineer, and support—with the appropriate technology—the key processes that contribute to customer satisfaction and corporate objectives (Coulson-Thomas 1993). Therefore, BPR efforts can involve substantial investment (Petrozzo and Stepper 1994), but they also require considerable top management support and commitment.

Critical to the success of the redesign is the make-up of the reengineering team. Most authors suggest that the team should comprise the following:

- Senior manager as sponsor
- Steering committee of senior managers to oversee overall reengineering strategy

- Process owner
- Team leader
- Redesign team

This structure varies depending on the author. For example, Harrington (1991) referred to executive improvement teams and process improvement teams rather than steering committees and reengineering teams. Champions (team leaders) and czars (sponsors) were also referred to, and, depending on the scope of the reengineering effort, the sponsor, process owner, and leader may be one or more people (Hammer and Champy 1993). The process owner is someone given the responsibility for the overall reengineering of a specific process.

It is generally recommended that the redesign team have between 5 and 10 people; represent the scope of the process (that is, if the process to be reengineered is cross-functional, so is the team); only work on one redesign at a time; and is made up of both insiders and outsiders. Insiders are people currently working within the process concerned who help gain credibility with coworkers. Outsiders are people from outside the organization who bring objectivity and can ask the searching questions necessary for the creative aspects of the redesign. Many companies use consultants for this purpose, although others employ specific individuals to do the job.

Continuous improvement or continuous redesign?

The project approach to BPR suggests a one-off approach. When the project is over, the team is disbanded, and business returns to normal, albeit a radically different normal. It is generally recommended that an organization not attempt to reengineer more than one major process at a time, because of the disruption and stress caused. Therefore, in major reengineering efforts of more than one process, as one team is disbanded, another is formed to redesign yet another process. Considering that Ford took five years to redesign its accounts payable process (Davenport 1993), BPR on a large scale is a long-term commitment. In a rapidly changing business environment, it is becoming more likely that companies will reengineer one process after another. Competitive advantage is a dynamic goal—one that does not stand still.

Once a process has been redesigned, most authors call for continuous improvement of the new process by the team of people working in the process.

Horizontal organizations

Once an organization has effectively redesigned cross-functional processes and has set up cross-functional teams to reengineer those processes, it has challenged the very nature of the functional organization. The process revolution has challenged the industrial era's basic premise of breaking work up into its component parts (Smith 1776) and has started to reorganize work around processes once again.

The dissemination of information via IT empowers people to make decisions and inevitably results in a delayering of management structures. Organizing work around processes is team forming. As the people involved in a particular process interact, they better understand the implications of, and take increasing responsibility for, what they do.

Elida Fabergé and the National and Provincial Building Society are two organizations that have totally restructured around processes. After mapping its existing processes, Elida Fabergé undertook a program of core process redesign. It identified the core processes necessary to reach its strategic objectives and redesigned its entire organization around these processes (Mitchell 1994). Elida Fabergé no longer has individual departments, such as marketing, and is organized as shown in Figure 26.4.

The functional specialisms have not disappeared, but are no longer managed as functions. Thus, there are marketing managers in brand development, supply chain development, and customer management development. Work is managed around the processes.

Following on from his work with Xerox, David O'Brien, as chief executive in 1990, led the National and Provincial Building Society through a fundamental organizational redesign, to what he called the Building Society's "team of teams" environment (O'Brien and Wainwright 1993; Adebayo 1993). He felt that "The design of an organization can be the main barrier to change, and it may therefore be necessary to implement a fundamental redesign before an organization can even start to handle the continuous challenge in today's environments (Coulson-Thomas and Coe 1991, 11). All processes, subprocesses, activities, and tasks were identified and mapped. People's roles within the organization were then determined by the processes. The evolutionary systems development approach based on continuing process redesign aimed for a completely flexible organization, and reusable process components allowed new processes to be created from stock. Any particular process component could be part of several different processes. The

FIGURE 26.4 ***Elida Fabergé organizational chart***

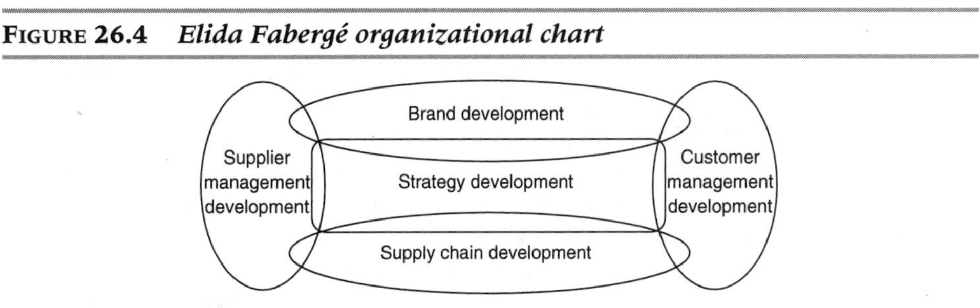

SOURCE: Elida Fabergé

FIGURE 26.5 ***National and Provincial Building Society organizational structure***

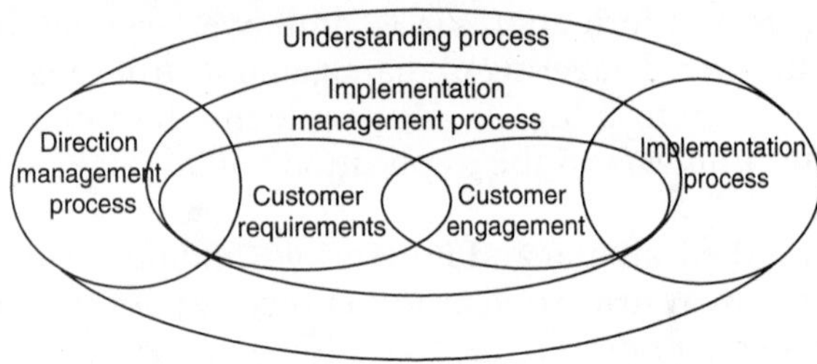

overall management structure had three layers and four core process levels (see Figure 26.5), and the understanding process linked the other three.

A key element in the approaches taken by organizations as diverse as Elida Fabergé and the N&P Building Society has been their focus on the customer. Building a customer focus into the business process redesign is a recurrent theme in all the literature on BPR.

PARTICULAR THEMES IN BUSINESS PROCESS REENGINEERING

BPR operates on several levels, both operational and managerial. At its simplest, it is a modern version of operations and management (O&M), though usually incorporating a new IT solution. A group of processes is selected for redesign on a once-and-for-all, project basis. A project team is established to identify areas for improvement, redesign the process, and implement the changes. More far-reaching are redesigns of major cross-functional processes, which are also typically project based, with the redesign team being cross-functional. At this level, major improvements are possible, as many of the problems involved in cross-functional handoffs can be solved. Bigger projects are the redesign of core processes involving wholesale organizational change. This level offers the opportunity of aligning business processes with the long-term strategy of the organization. External consultants have been used extensively in BPR projects of every level, both as a source of external input and for advice on implementation and technical issues. Once the redesign is in place, the project teams are usually disbanded.

Many companies see change as being continuous, and BPR as ongoing. There is a case then for repeating BPR; a continuous aligning and realigning of business processes to meet the changing strategic needs of the organization. This scenario is similar to that at the National and Provincial Building Society; that is, by mapping all of an organization's processes, it becomes possible to redesign and realign them on a continuous basis, priority being given to those of greatest strategic significance. In order to achieve this, the N&P have a permanent redesign team made up of in-company *reengineers.* They have built BPR into their organizational culture. It is important, of course, to reconcile the disruption and stress issue with the continual nature of the effort that is emphasized in this approach. The lack of attention to this aspect in some organizations may explain the success ratio. From the available data, this is about one in three projects.

TQM AND BPR

The linkages

Organizations and the literature have demonstrated clear linkages between TQM and BPR.

1. Both originated from disciplines outside conventional management theory. The practical application of SPC theory to manufacturing processes led to TQM (Deming 1993; Drucker 1992; Grant, Shani, and Krishnan 1994). Developments in IT brought about the advent of BPR.
2. Just as SPC enabled the organizational changes central to TQM, the effects of IT-enabled BPR have been largely organizational (Watkins, Skinner, and Pearson 1993). Both SPC and IT have empowered operators by putting information in the hands of those who can act upon it (Drucker 1992; Earl and Khan 1994).
3. Both TQM and BPR have evolved in organizations rather than in business schools, reflecting real-world change and challenging previous schools of management theory. TQM, through the work of Conway (1981) and others, has bridged the divide between Taylor's scientific management and the human relations approach (Drucker 1992; Grant, Shani, and Krishnan 1994; Taylor 1911). BPR has called for a rethinking of Adam Smith's principles (Smith 1776; Ackoff 1974). Both of these challenges have had their critics, claiming that BPR is O&M, work study, and design repackaged for the 1990s, and that TQM promotes Taylorism via a brainwashing effect. It has been said that stable processes, quality policies, and continuous improvement are a way of controlling employees to produce (Boje and Winsor 1993). These opinions conflict with the observations that SPC and IT have empowered both individuals and teams, thus changing management styles from controlling to coaching.
4. TQM and BPR have resulted in flat organizational structures. Redesign of business processes has enabled the empowerment of frontline individuals, with fewer supervisors and fewer layers of management.
5. Both have focused on process thinking, on continuous improvement in the quality of processes, and on the redesign of processes. The latter has required a holistic, systems approach, as advocated by Juran and Deming. Both approaches have made use of flow-charting, SPC, and process modeling techniques.

6. TQM and BPR have both been long-term strategies. Although the well-documented Ford case took five years to complete, BPR has achieved quick wins, dependent on the *scope* of the process change (Hall, Rosenthal, and Wade 1993).
7. Both have emphasized the importance of a team culture. Internal customer-supplier chains (processes) have led to cross-functional quality improvement teams. BPR has made use of cross-functional process teams in the assessment and redesign stages, and has advocated continuous improvement teams on implementation.
8. Both have required a fundamental change in organizational culture.
9. Both have challenged conventional measurement systems. Conventional accounting methods have not highlighted quality issues or areas for process improvement, nor have they pinpointed problems associated with internal, cross-functional, or cross-organizational processes. It has been suggested that activity-based costing provides an accounting system that fits the process view of both TQM and BPR (Bellis-Jones and Develin 1992; Armitage and Grant 1993; Letza and Gadd 1994), thus highlighting their similarities. Performance measurement of teams, especially cross-functional teams, has also required new measures (Katzenbach and Smith 1993a, 1993b; Meyer 1994).
10. Lack of senior management commitment has frequently been cited as a major reason for TQM failure. Senior management commitment has also been claimed to be a prerequisite of BPR (Hall, Rosenthal, and Wade 1993). TQM has been claimed to be a bottom-up approach because of its emphasis on continuous improvement, but also a cultural philosophy involving widespread organizational change, requiring senior management leadership (Juran 1989; Oakland 1993).
11. TQM's quality-driven focus has been based on satisfying customer requirements. The literature on BPR has repeatedly called for building a customer focus into the process redesign. Some authors have suggested that customers should be involved in process evaluation teams (Harrington 1991; Hammer and Champy 1993).
12. Taguchi's work on design of experiments linked research and development and manufacturing in a cross-functional process (Taguchi 1978). Shingo's single minute exchange of die, or SMED, technique at Toyota involved the redesign of a process to incorporate reusable setup components (Shingo 1986). This has parallels with the N&P's approach to reusable process components in its redesigns.
13. Benchmarking has been a key feature of both TQM and BPR (Zairi and Leonard 1994).
14. TQM has sought to reduce the number of suppliers and has developed practices such as just-in-time and *kanban*, radically improving the supply process. Interorganizational redesign using EDI has sought to radically improve the supplier-customer network.

15. Implementation of both TQM and BPR have shared similar characteristics. Figure 26.6 describes how a hierarchy of teams has linked senior management to deployment. Both TQM and business process improvement advocate continuous improvement teams, operating within functioning processes. By contrast, BPR ends when a newly redesigned process is established. The literature on BPR has frequently called for continuous improvement programs once the new process is in place.
16. Both approaches have required substantial vision and leadership.

The differences

Although fewer in number, there are some significant differences in the approaches and outcomes of TQM and BPR.

1. BPR has encouraged a holistic view of process improvement and has sought to make massive performance gains. Although Deming and Juran have argued for a systems view, companies focusing on continuous, incremental improvement within functions and departments have generally not achieved the same scale of improvement.
2. TQM has been demonstrated to be a long-term investment for future gain. While BPR has also been shown to be long term in both outlook and the time taken to achieve radical change, it has achieved quick wins, dependent on the scope of the process redesign.
3. TQM has enabled functional hierarchies to remain intact, focusing as it does on individual internal customer-supplier interactions. BPR has forced organizations to take a process view and to fundamentally rethink cross-functional processes.

BUSINESS PROCESS REENGINEERING FOR TOTAL QUALITY MANAGEMENT

TQM implementation

Lack of senior management commitment and the need for short-term results have frequently been cited as reasons for the failure of TQM initiatives (Wilkinson and Witcher 1991; Glover 1992; Mallinger 1993; Miller and Cangemi 1993; Zairi, Oakland, and Letza 1994). The commonality of implementation methods (see Figure 26.6) would suggest that BPR could be used as part of a TQM implementation program, with quality improvement teams being a logical extension of process redesign teams. A key factor in this scenario would be process scoping. By focusing on quick-win scenarios, BPR could, in theory, deliver the results necessary for continued senior management support of a TQM initiative.

FIGURE 26.6 ***Implementation through teams (TQM, BPI, and BPR)***

Total quality management (Oakland 1993)	Business process improvement (Harrington 1991)	Business process reengineering (Hammer and Champy 1993)	Management level
Quality council	Executive improvement team	Steering committee	Senior
Process quality teams	Process improvement team	Reengineering teams	Senior, multidisciplined
Quality improvement teams	Department improvement team	Continuous improvement	Process level
Individuals	Task teams		Employee

SOURCE: Oakland 1993; Hammer and Champy 1993; Harrington 1991

Dynamic stability

The issue that TQM seeks stable, controllable processes while BPR seeks dynamic change has made the two seem incompatible to many observers, who have felt that the drive to stabilize processes stamps out innovation. Others have claimed that TQM emphasizes dynamic performance improvement. Juran (1964) talked of achieving breakthrough performance through "a dynamic, decisive movement to new, higher levels of performance." This conflict can be partially resolved by the concept of dynamic stability (see Figure 26.7).

The dynamic stability model, developed with 1994 European Quality Award winner D2D, the manufacturing subsidiary of ICL, demonstrates the relationship between products/services and processes. In a controlled and stable environment, stable processes yield stable products/services. Producing dynamic products/services from stable processes is less likely; D2D would say it is impossible. First, the processes need to be made dynamic, which may take years. Dynamic processes yielding dynamic products/services take a long time to be stabilized in order to produce stable products/services. Being fast and responsive to changing customer requirements requires dynamic processes. Therefore, what is required are processes made up of stable elements, ensuring consistency of quality, with dynamic components that allow rapid response and innovation, that is, *dynamic stability.*

The N&P is moving toward the dynamic realignment of stable process elements by extensive use of process software. At Elida Fabergé a requirement for rapid introduction of innovative products led to a separation of stable and innovative processes. New product development processes are incorporated in the brand

FIGURE 26.7 *Dynamic stability model*

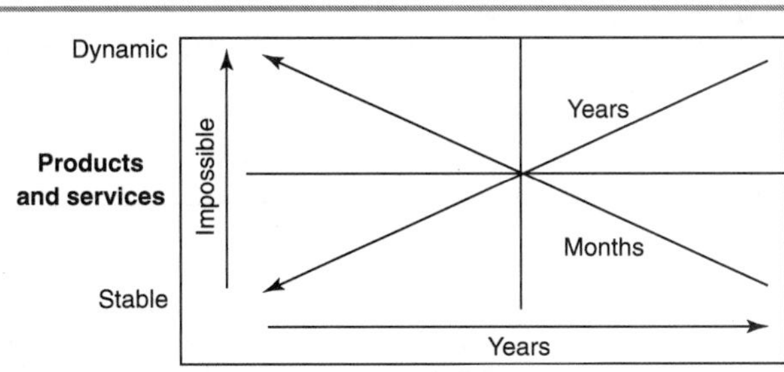

SOURCE: D. Goodsell, quality manager at D2D Ltd., 1994

development process chain. Stable processes producing established products are managed in the supply chain (see Figure 26.4).

The dynamic nature of BPR has been used to destabilize processes in order to achieve breakthrough improvement; stability and continuous improvement are restored once the redesign is in place. Dynamic and stable processes can and do coexist, however. In recent years, D2D has moved into contract manufacture, necessitating a rapid response to individual customer requirements. The surface mount lines installed at D2D have employed a stable element that is controllable and a dynamic element that has allowed breakthrough improvements in setup and changeover (Gadd and Oakland 1995).

CHIMERA OR CULTURE?

According to the *Concise Oxford Dictionary,* chimera is "a thing of hybrid character." And according to the *Collins English Dictionary, culture* is "the total of the inherited ideas, beliefs, values and knowledge which constitute the shared values of social action."

A question of chimera

There has been an increasing number of articles calling for the need for both continuous and discontinuous improvement. For example, Hammer (1991) suggested that they should both fit under the umbrella of process management, and Duffy (1994) has described the business process management method used by Motorola. These and others (Chang 1994; Furey 1993; Stewart 1993; Taylor 1993) described programs that integrate TQM and BPR as management tools. Hammer (1991) described sequential performance improvements using the two techniques (see Figure 26.8) and warned against using the two approaches concurrently (Hammer and Champy 1993). Looked at in this way, TQM and BPR are a chimera: two

FIGURE 26.8 *Process improvement implementation models: TQM implementation framework*

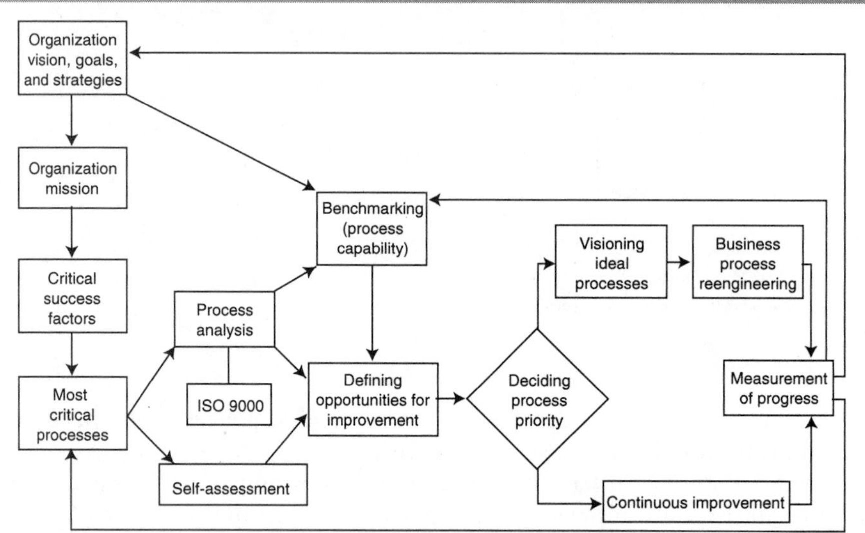

distinct and different approaches capable of coexisting in the same organization, but used at different times to achieve different levels of performance improvement.

A question of culture

The companies originally cited by Davenport and Short (1990) and Hammer (1990) had established TQM programs already in place. Their BPR efforts evolved out of a TQM environment, and once the redesigns were complete, kaizen teams continuously improved and adapted those processes. The current literature on BPR has emphasized the potential gains to be made from its use; however, less well publicized have been the comments, especially from IT specialists, that the most difficult aspect of BPR is not the redesign but the cultural and organizational change involved. Hammer stressed this point in his business diamond model describing the interplay of four forces (Hammer 1991). The fundamental assumption has been that changing business processes, and therefore people's jobs, changes the culture. Frequently, however, the literature has identified that it is in the area of cultural change where the problems arise.

There is no evidence in the literature to suggest that BPR has established a continuing process culture of its own, and its advocates have suggested continuous improvement to maintain redesigned processes. TQM and BPR have both had similar patterns of implementation, but while BPR projects have ended once the redesign of the new processes has been accomplished, TQM has continued as a long-term culture of empowered teams with a process perspective—the very things required for tong-term continuous improvement of redesigned business processes. (Hammer and Champy 1993).

Business process reengineering for Total Quality Management

Hammer and Champy (1993) claimed that TQM works with existing processes, while reengineering discards what exists and creates new processes that are simpler and more effective thus leading organizations to the major breakthroughs that are impossible with the quality management approach. Cole (1994), Hill and Wilkinson (1995), and others have pointed out, however, that despite the initial popularity of this diagnosis among shareholders, management consultants, and journalists, disillusionment with what BPR achieves set in less than three years after the publication of Hammer and Champy's book (Cole 1994; Hall, Rosenthal, and Wade 1993; Willmott 1994).

One of the core principles of TQM is the improvement of processes, and process reengineering is one of the standard improvement tools. Process improvements may be both incremental and transformational, and incremental improvements can accumulate into transformational or quantum shifts (Green 1995). Ten years ago Imai (1986) characterized kaizen (improvement) as both innovation (new ways of doing things) and maintenance (maintaining standards). While improvements usually happen through small steps, the continuous accumulation of these can lead to radical breakthroughs (Kano 1993), and quality improvement teams can move directly to major innovations of a "breakthrough" kind (Juran 1964). Green (1995) argued that the "breakthrough" and "leap innovation" components of the policy deployment approach to quality encompass such concepts. Green also quoted the earliest written evidence of large-scale process reengineering within total quality as the 1963 document from Matsushita Electrical Industrial Company, which won the Deming Prize for quality.

Hill and Wilkinson (1995) have also made clear that, while the BPR critique misunderstands the nature of TQM, it is possible that the practice of TQM in many organizations may have contributed to the misperception; some practitioners use its procedures mainly to generate incremental improvements and have a partial form of TQM that operates primarily among low-level employees, where small-scale incrementalism is likely. In this case BPR proponents have criticized the practice of organizations with partial quality management, rather than TQM itself. This may render more acceptable the failure of Hammer and Champy and others to come to grips with TQM. There is a paradox, according to Hall, Rosenthal, and Wade (1993), that BPR initiatives have tended to be too narrow or partial because they take place within functions and departments rather than across the organization, because they lack effective leadership from the top, and because they are not integrated with other changes (Hill and Wilkinson 1995).

It would appear then that business process reengineering is less likely to succeed outside TQM since it uses the methods, process, and customer orientations of TQM to deliver step changes. If it does so on an ad hoc basis, without the training, experience, and organizational infrastructure that TQM takes for granted, it might be anticipated that organizational resistance would be greater than in a culture where planned quality change is taken more for granted.

Cole's (1994) conclusions in his well-argued and supported essay on Hammer and Champy's book are that an extraordinary amount of overlap exists between the quality and reengineering movements and that the two initiatives complement each other. He believes that each component of the "quality house" is a building block onto which each subsequent effort should build. In a similar vein, Thomas (1994) writes about the "aesthetic of manufacturing" that simultaneously achieves mastery over current processes, promotes continuous improvement in those processes, and prepares for transformational change. As all these writers argue, if business process reengineering helps focus attention on transformational change, without damaging the first two elements, it can effectively contribute in the total quality implementation framework (see Figure 26.9).

BPR, then, has provided techniques with which total quality companies could redesign and realign business processes. Process modeling and benchmarking have been used to identify areas for process improvement, and BPR has allowed fundamental, radical improvement of inefficient or redundant processes. So-called continuous improvement has maintained stable, efficient processes in a continuing spiral of incremental productivity gains. Which techniques have been employed at which time has depended on required outcomes.

Continuous improvement and business process reengineering have both been used for effective process management within the TQM environment, at D2D for example, where stable, controlled processes have been continuously improved, and processes identified as inefficient have been redesigned. New processes have been incorporated that have necessitated realignment of existing processes amidst

FIGURE 26.9 ***Combining reengineering and quality***

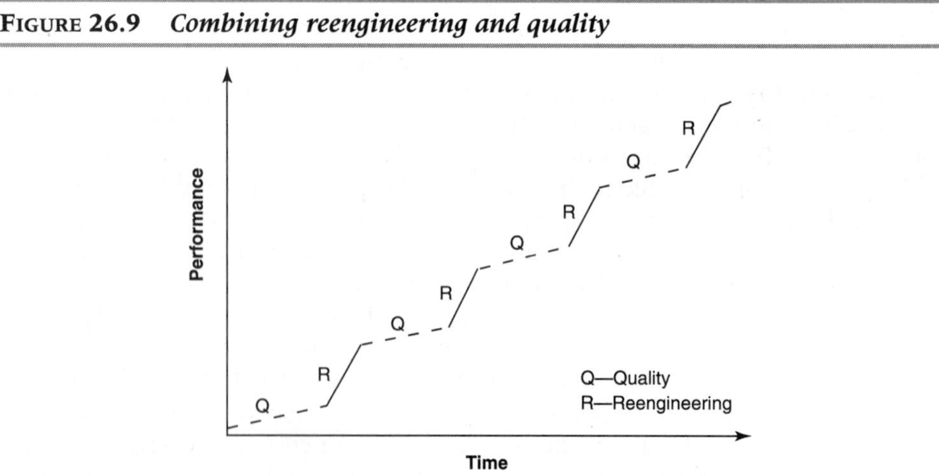

SOURCE: Hammer 1991

an ethos of continuous improvement that culminated in D2D winning the European Quality Award in 1994. Most senior managers interviewed at D2D regard their reengineering efforts as having been part of continuous improvement (Gadd and Oakland 1995).

The linkages identified suggest that TOM and BPR have many shared ideals, beliefs, values, and knowledge. The cultural ideology of TQM at D2D has provided the environment necessary to sustain new and radical process, and BPR has provided the broad process perspective described by Juran and Deming. In many successful organizations, BPR has been an integral part of the culture—a process-driven culture dedicated to the ideals and concepts of TQM.

References

Ackoff, R. H. "The Systems Age." In *Circular planning.* New York: John Wiley & Sons, 1974.

Adebayo, J. L. S. "Business Process Reengineering: The Case of the National and Provincial Building Society." Master's thesis, University of Bradford, 1993.

Armitage, H., and R. Grant. "Activity-Based Management Information: TQM's Missing Link." *CMA Magazine,* March 1993, p. 7.

Baets, W. "IT for Organizational Learning: Beyond Business Process Engineering." B*usiness Change and Reengineering* 2, 1993, no. 2, pp. 32–40.

Bellis-Jones, R., and N. Develin. "Activity-Based Cost Management." *Accountants' Digest,* Spring 1992, pp. 1–36.

Boje, D. M., and R. D. Winsor. "The Resurrection of Taylorism: Total Quality Management's Hidden Agenda." *Journal of Organizational Change Management* 6, 1993, no. 4, pp. 57–70.

Burke, G., and J. Peppard. "Business Process Redesign: Research Directions." *Business Change and Reengineering* 1, 1993, no. 1, pp. 43–47.

Chang, R. Y. "Improve Processes, Reengineer Them, or Both?" *Training and Development,* March, 1994, pp. 54–58.

Cole, R. "Reengineering the Corporation: A Review Essay." *Quality Management Journal,* July 1994, pp. 77–85.

Conway, W. Nashua Corporation paper. Rio de Janeiro: Nashua Corporation, March 1981.

Coulson-Thomas, C. J. "Corporate Transformation and Business Process Reengineering." *Executive Development* 6, 1993, no. 1, pp. 14–20.

Coulson-Thomas, C. J. and T. Coe. *The Flat Organization: Philosophy and Practice.* British Institute of Management Report, 1991.

Coyle, N. S. "IT-Enabled Business Process Reengineering." Master's thesis, University of Bradford, 1992.

Davenport, T. H. *Process Innovation: Reengineering Work through Information Technology.* Boston: Harvard Business Press, 1992.

———. *Process Innovation.* Boston: Harvard Business Press, 1993.

———. "Saving IT's Soul: Human-Centred Information Management." *Harvard Business Review* March–April 1994, pp. 119–131.

Davenport, T. H., and J. E. Short. "The New Industrial Engineering: Information Technology and Business Process Redesign." *Sloan Management Review,* Summer 1990, pp. 11–27.

Deming, W. E. *The New Economics: For Industry, Government, Education.* Cambridge, Mass.: MIT Center for Advanced Engineering Study, 1993.

Dennis, A. R., R. M. Daniels, G. Hayes, and J. F. Nunamaker Jr. "Methodology-Driven Use of Automated Support in Business Process Reengineering." *Journal of Management Information Systems* 10, 1994, no. 3, pp. 117–138.

Drucker, P. F. *Age of Discontinuity: Guidelines to Our Changing Society.* Oxford, England: Heinemann, 1969.

———. *Managing for the Future: The 1990s and Beyond.* Oxford, England: Butterworth Heinemann, 1992.

———. *Post-Capitalist Society.* New York: HarperBusiness, 1993.

Duffy, D. "Managing the White Space (Cross-Functional Processes)." *Management,* April 1994, pp. 35–36.

Earl, M., and B. Khan. "How New Is Business Process Redesign?" *European Management Journal* 12, 1994, no. 1, pp. 20–30.

Furey, T. R. "A Six-Step Guide to Process Reengineering." *Planning Review,* March/April 1993, pp. 20–23.

Gadd, K. W., and J. S. Oakland. "Discontinuous Change in a Total Quality Environment." D2D Ltd: A case study. *Business Process Reengineering and Management Journal* 7, 1995, no. 2.

Glover, J. "Achieving the Organizational Change Necessary for Successful TQM." *International Journal of Quality and Reliability* 10, 1992, no. 6, pp. 47–64.

Goss, T., R. Pascale, and A. Athos. "The Reinvention Roller Coaster: Risking the Present for a Powerful Future." *Harvard Business Review,* November–December 1993, pp. 97–108.

Grant, R. M., R. Shani, and R. Krishnan. "TQM's Challenge to Management Theory and Practice." *Sloan Management Review,* Winter 1994, pp. 25–35.

Green, R. *Competent Reengineering: Advice, Warnings, and Recipes from Eye Witnesses.* New York: Addison Wesley, 1995.

Gulden, G. K., and R. H. Reck. "Combining Quality and Reengineering for Operational Superiority." *Perspectives on the Management of Information Technology* 8, 1991, no. 1, pp. 1–12.

Hall, G., J. Rosenthal, and J. Wade. "How to Make Reengineering Really Work." *Harvard Business Review,* November–December 1993, pp. 119–131.

Hamel, G., and C. K. Prahalad. "Strategic Intent." *Harvard Business Review,* May–June 1989, pp. 63–76.

———. "The Core Competence of the Corporation." *Harvard Business Review,* May–June 1990, pp. 70–91.

———. "Corporate Imagination and Expeditionary Marketing." *Harvard Business Review,* July–August 1991, pp. 81–92.

Hammer, M. "Reengineering Work: Don't Automate, Obliterate." *Harvard Business Review,* July–August 1990, pp. 104–112.

———. "Why We Need Both Continuous and Discontinuous Improvement." *Perspectives on the Management of Information Technology* 8, 1991, no. 1, pp. 6–7.

Hammer, M., and J. Champy. *Reengineering the Corporation: A Manifesto for Business Revolution.* New York: HarperBusiness, 1993.

Handy, C. *The Age of Unreason.* London: Century Business, 1989.

Harrington, H. J. *Business Process Improvement.* New York: McGraw-Hill, 1991.

Hill, S., and A. Wilkinson. "In Search of TQM." *Employee Relations* 17, 1995, no. 3, pp. 8–20.

Imai, M. *Kaizen, the Key to Japan's Competitive Success.* New York: McGraw-Hill, 1986.

Johanssen, H. J., P. McHugh, J. Pendlebury, and W. A. Wheeler III. *Business Process Reengineering: Breakpoint Strategies for Market Dominance.* New York: John Wiley & Sons, 1993.

Juran, J. M. *Managerial Breakthrough.* New York: McGraw-Hill, 1964.

———. *Juran on Leadership for Quality: An Executive Handbook.* New York: Free Press, 1989.

Kano, N. "A Perspective on Quality Activities in American Firms." *California Management Review,* Spring 1993, pp. 12–31.

Kaplan, R. S., and L. Murdoch. "Core Process Redesign." *The McKinsey Quarterly,* 1991, no. 2, pp. 27–43.

Katzenbach, J. R., and D. K. Smith. "The Discipline of Teams." *Harvard Business Review,* September–October 1993, pp. 134–142.

———. *The Wisdom of Teams: Creating the High-Performance Organization.* Boston: Harvard Business School Press, 1993.

Letza, S. L., and K. W. Gadd. "Should Activity-Based Costing Be Considered as the Costing Method of Choice for Total Quality Organizations?" *The TQM Magazine* 6, 1994, no. 5, pp. 57–63.

Lowenthal, J. N. *Reengineering the Organization: A Step-by-Step Approach to Corporate Revitalization.* Milwaukee: ASQC Quality Press, 1994.

Mallinger, M. "Ambush along the TQM Trail." *Journal of Organizational Change Management* 6, 1993, no. 4, pp. 30–42.

Meyer, C. "How the Right Measures Help Teams Excel." *Harvard Business Review,* May–June 1994, pp. 95–103.

Miller, R. L., and J. P. Cangemi. "Why Total Quality Management Fails: Perspective of Top Management." *Journal of Management Development* 12, 1993, no. 7, pp. 40–50.

Mitchell, A. "Marketing's New Model Army." *Management Today,* March 1994, pp. 42–49.

O'Brien, D. O., and J. Wainwright. "Winning as a Team of Teams: Transforming the Mindset of the Organization at National and Provincial Building Society." *Business Change and Reengineering* 1, 1993, no. 3, pp. 19–25.

Oakland, J. S. *Total Quality Management.* Oxford, England: Butterworth Heinemann, 1993.

Oakland, J. S., and L. J. Porter. *Cases in Total Quality Management.* Oxford, England: Butterworth Heinemann, 1994.

Petrozzo, D. P., and J. C. Stepper. *Successful Reengineering.* New York: Van Nostrand Reinhold, 1994.

Richman, T., and C. Koontz. "How Benchmarking Can Improve Business Process Reengineering." *Planning Review* 21, 1993, no. 6, pp. 26–27.

Schaffer, R. H., and H. A. Thomson. "Successful Change Programs Begin with Results." *Harvard Business Review,* January–February 1992, pp. 80–89.

Senge, P. M. *The Fifth Discipline.* London: Century Business, 1993.

Shingo, S. *Zero Quality Control: Source Inspection and the Poke-Yoke System* (Translation). Cambridge, Mass.: Productivity Press, 1986.

Short, J. E., and N. Venkatraman. "Beyond Business Process Redesign: Redefining Baxter's Business Network." *Sloan Management Review,* Fall 1992, pp. 7–21.

Smith, A. *An Enquiry into the Nature and Causes of the Wealth of Nations,* 1776.

Smith, H. *Social and Rational Behavior in a Social Setting.* New York: John Wiley, 1957.

Stalk, G., P. Evans, and L. E. Shulman. "Competing on Capabilities: The New Rules of Corporate Strategy." *Harvard Business Review,* March–April 1992, pp. 57–69.

Stewart, T. A. "Reengineering: The Hot New Management Tool." *Fortune,* August 1993, pp. 33–37.

Swatman, P. M. C., P. Swatman, and D. C. Fowler. "A Model of EDI Integration and Strategic Business Reengineering. *Journal of Strategic Information Systems* 3, 1994, no. 1, pp. 41–60.

Taguchi, G. *Systems of Experimental Design.* New York: Unipub/Kraus International Publications and American Supplier Institute, 1978.

Talwar, R. "Business Reengineering—A Strategy-Driven Approach." *Long Range Planning* 26, 1993, no. 6, pp. 22–40.

Taylor, F. *The Principles of Scientific Management.* New York: Harper & Row, 1911.

Taylor, S. "Eastman Chemical Strives for Better Than World Class." *Industrial Engineering,* November 1993, pp. 28–34.

Taylor, J. A., and H. Williams. "The 'Transformation Game': Information Systems and Process Innovation in Organizations." *New Technology, Work and Employment* 9, 1994, no. 1, pp. 54–65.

Thackray, J. "Fads, Fixes and Fictions." *Management Today,* June 1993, pp. 40–42.

Thomas, R. *What Machines Can't Do.* Berkeley: University of California Press, 1994.

Venkatraman, N. "IT-Induced Business Reconfiguration." In *The Corporation of the 1990s: Information Technology and Organizational Transformation,* edited by Scott M. Morton. Oxford, England: Oxford University Press, 1991.

———. "IT-Enabled Business Transformation: From Automation to Business Scope Redefinition." *Sloan Management Review,* Winter 1994, pp. 73–87.

Wastell, D. G., P. White, and P. Kawalek. "A Methodology for Business Process Redesign: Experiences and Issues." *Journal of Strategic Information Systems* 3, 1994, no. 1, pp. 23–40.

Watkins, J. "Business Process Redesign in the UK Retail Financial Services Sector." *Business Change and Reengineering* 1, 1994, no. 4, pp. 38–48.

Watkins, J., C. Skinner, and J. Pearson. "Business Process Reengineering: Hype, Hazard or Heaven." *Business Change and Reengineering* 1, 1993, no. 2, pp. 41–46.

Wilkinson, A., and B. Witcher. "Fitness for Use? Barriers to Full TQM in the UK." *Management Decision* 29, 1991, no. 8, pp. 46–51.

Willmott, H. C. "Business Process Reengineering and Human Resource Management." *Personnel Review* 23, 1994, no. 3, pp. 34–36.

Zairi, M. *Measuring Performance for Business Results.* London: Chapman and Hall, 1994.

Zairi, M. and P. Leonard. *Practical Benchmarking: The Complete Guide.* London: Chapman and Hall, 1994.

Zairi, M., J. S. Oakland, and S. L. Letza. *TQM: Its Impact on Bottom Line Results.* Hertfordshire, England: Technical Communications Publishing, 1994.

Reading 27

A Focused Review of the Reengineering Literature: Expert Frequently Asked Questions

By Mark E. Nissen

Business process reengineering (BPR) is said to be entering its second phase. In its first phase, many disparate methodologies for process redesign were developed and employed, and BPR became a pervasive and important phenomenon in the fast-paced global economy. The second phase promises to be more challenging than the first, particularly as the reengineering phenomenon continues to have negligible theoretical basis. As organizations progress to take on the challenges of reengineering's second phase, it is important for the academic and practitioner communities to learn from the lessons of the first phase. Toward this end, this article includes a focused review of the reengineering literature, with the purpose of circumscribing the best practices and integrating the lessons learned. Drawing primarily from expert reengineering methodologies, the key lessons learned in the first phase are presented in terms of frequently asked questions (FAQs). These FAQs provide the basis of some integrating themes, from which an outline of a number of future research directions is drawn.

Key words: change management, process modeling, reengineering methodology, total quality management.

THE SECOND PHASE OF REENGINEERING

Business process reengineering (BPR) is said to be entering its second phase (Cypress 1994). Through the approximate half-decade of its first phase, many disparate methodologies for process redesign were developed and employed, and a multitude of reengineering books (such as Davenport 1993; Hammer and Champy 1993) were published in the management press and widely read. During this time, nearly all large U.S. corporations engaged in major reengineering projects, and more than half of the annual reports to stockholders by *FORTUNE* 500 companies addressed BPR activities in 1994 (Hamscher 1994).

In this first phase, the rise and fall of BPR in the trade press occurred, as the topic progressed from a state of perennial hype during the early 1990s (Anderson 1991; Currid 1994; Manager's Notebook 1994). Now, BPR has been superseded by today's focus on topics such as the Internet, "Intranets," Java, and the like (Wilder 1995; Wilder, Bull, and Gillooly 1995; Marshall and Rodriguez 1995). A number of academic investigations were conducted to study the reengineering phenomenon (Stoddard and Jarvenpaa 1995), which exposed a number of "myths" (Davenport and Stoddard 1994) in addition to outlining many "preconditions for success" (Bashein, Markus, and Riley 1994).

The second phase promises to be more challenging than the first, particularly as the reengineering phenomenon continues to have negligible theoretical basis (Saharia et al. 1994). Described in terms of a shift from "customer value chain" analysis to a paradigm of "wealth creation and consumption" (Cypress 1994), the second phase will require more knowledge, better understanding, and more context-sensitive methodologies (Nissen 1996) in order to avoid the same magnitude (50 percent to 75 percent) of failure rates (Caron, Jarvenpaa, and Stoddard 1994; Hammer and Champy 1993) ascribed to the first phase.

As organizations progress to take on the challenges of reengineering's second phase, it seems important for the academic and practitioner communities to learn from the lessons of the first phase. Despite the dearth of theoretical work on BPR, many practical lessons have been reported in the reengineering literature (Hammer and Stanton 1995), which can provide a basis for documenting current understanding of this field. Toward this end, this article includes a focused review of the reengineering literature, with the purpose of circumscribing the best practices and integrating the lessons learned. The article draws primarily from a segment of this literature described as the expert reengineering methodologies, which probably represents the best, clearly articulated accounting of the BPR phenomenon.

This article begins with a literary framework to help organize the key reengineering publications, and then the key lessons learned in the first phase are presented in terms of frequently asked questions (FAQs), which provide the basis of some integrating themes. The article closes with some conclusions and future research directions to help prepare for the second phase of reengineering.

REENGINEERING LITERARY FRAMEWORK

Frameworks can be very helpful in terms of organization. Provided that the underlying dimensions are informative, a reengineering framework should be able to impose order on the unruly body of reengineering literature and create a classification scheme that can be used, modified, and extended by other researchers. The reengineering literary framework described in this section provides a step toward these goals and represents an extension of the scheme proposed by Nissen (1995).

The central dimension of this framework is referred to as *knowledge content,* which is the amount of substantive knowledge conveyed by a publication. Knowledge content can be crudely operationalized in terms of the kinds of questions that can be answered through such knowledge (Bacharach 1989). With this, the reengineering literature can be categorized, in increasing order, according to five classes.

1. Trade press
2. Redesign cases
3. Expert reengineering methodologies
4. Academic investigations
5. Theory-building works

This framework is summarized in Table 27.1.

The trade press follows contemporary phenomena and technologies (Middlebrook 1994), more often through hyperbole and speculation than knowledge and fact (McPartlin 1993). Indeed, many would question inclusion of publications in this class as "literature," as many articles do little more than alert readers to the existence, prominence, or importance of a topic (for example, Champy 1990). Such articles might be described in terms of answering the question *huh?* They are generally very shallow in coverage of a topic, and the content contributes very

TABLE 27.1 ***Reengineering literary framework***

CLASS OF PUBLICATION
Trade press answers the question *huh?*
Redesign cases describe *who* and *which*
Expert reengineering methodologies motivate *whether* and prescribe *what*
Academic investigations describe *how*
Theory-building works explain *why* and predict *when*

little in terms of specific knowledge; hence the placement at the low end of the knowledge-content continuum.

A number of process redesign cases have been reported by various sources. Many such cases are used for educational purposes (such as Goldstein 1986; King and Konsynski 1990; Stoddard and Meadows 1992), while others serve as exemplars of effective reengineering techniques and technologies (such as Hammer and Champy 1993, 36–46; Hammer and Stanton 1995, 187–289). Cases of process redesign provide information to answer questions such as *who* is reengineering? and *which* processes are involved? Because cases are generally of a purely descriptive nature, little is gained in the way of knowledge beyond an increased understanding of a particular instance of process redesign.

Alternatively, the expert reengineering methodologies reflect a synthesis of many process redesign endeavors, and are generally developed by BPR consultants who are widely acknowledged as the most knowledgeable experts in the field. Admittedly, some of these "methodologies" (for example, Hammer and Champy 1993) appear to accomplish little more than motivating the case for BPR (Cole 1994) and are shown to have substantial room for improved analysis (Hansen 1994). In essence they answer the question of *whether* or not to reengineer. Others (for example, Davenport 1993), however, provide a start-to-finish guide to undertaking process improvement, answering questions such as *what* steps need to be taken and in which order. As noted, the expert reengineering methodologies from this class provide the basis for the expert FAQs discussed in the following section.

Because knowledge creation represents a fundamental objective of academic investigation, and academics are trained in the methods of defensible, extensible, and replicable research, publications in this class are positioned near the high end of the reengineering literary framework. In many ways, academic investigations build upon the kind of knowledge available through expert reengineering methodologies: for example, contributing knowledge in terms of frameworks (Davidson 1993; Guha, Kettinger, and Teng 1994) and guidelines (Henderson and Venkatraman 1993; Klein 1994) that begin to answer operationalized questions such as *how* to accomplish the redesign steps.

In this article, academic investigations that contribute to theory building are listed at the extreme along this dimension. The corresponding explanatory and predictive knowledge can be used to answer the most difficult questions, such as *why* a given enabling technology was successful in a certain instance, and *when* a particular redesign intervention can be expected to be effective for a specific organizational process. Unfortunately, the list of publications belonging to this class is very short.

EXPERT BPR FAQS

From its very likely beginning in the computer software industry, the FAQ file has become commonplace in both business and academic settings as an efficient method of knowledge transfer. Whether one is interested in learning about new software (for example, Java 1996), technology (for example, PowerBrowser 1996), or emerging phenomena such as electronic commerce (E-Commerce 1996), FAQ files are readily available and represent an excellent source of information with which to begin an investigation. That is the primary purpose of this article.

The questions themselves that are addressed by the FAQs that follow are determined primarily through participation in a number of reengineering and quality newsgroups, and summarized in part through an informal poll of colleagues. Although in no way intended to be comprehensive, the "answers" in the following sections should serve to address many of the common questions pertaining to the phenomenon of BPR. Moreover, by drawing from the reengineering literature, these answers take on a variety of perspectives and represent the knowledge and practice articulated by some of the best recognized authorities on process redesign.

FAQ 1: What are the key terms and concepts?

The reengineering literature represents an important source of terms and concepts. The term *reengineering* itself has been defined by Hammer and Champy (1993) as "the *fundamental* rethinking and *radical* redesign of business *processes* to achieve *dramatic* improvements in critical, contemporary *measures* such as cost, quality, service, and speed [emphasis added]" (p. 32). The fundamental nature of reengineering relates to questioning assumptions; that is, taking nothing about a business or organization as fixed or given, and challenging the appropriateness and existence of every aspect of business organization and operation. This is closely related to the accounting notion of zero-base budgeting (Cheek 1977), which was popular in the 1970s.

Radical redesign refers to transforming even the most enduring, stable, and central aspects of a process design configuration, and envisioning new redesign alternatives without limitations or constraints associated with a current design. Dramatic improvement implies that the level of performance can increase by severalfold (for example, 2×, 5×), as opposed to marginal improvements that are generally measured in percentages (for example, 5 percent, 20 percent).

The measures are associated with outputs, in terms of performance, as opposed to inputs to a business or organization. One issue relates to the fact that many outputs appear to be closely aligned, while others are surely oblique and orthogonal. For example, cost and cycle time (that is, speed) appear to be closely related (Stalk and Hout 1990), since a reduction in cycle time corresponds to a decrease in allocated fixed or period costs, which can also enable an increase in throughput or production. The relationship between cost (and cycle time) and quality or service is, however, less clear.

For example, a common TQM precept suggests that improvements in quality correspond to reductions in cost through the reduction of rework, returns, service, and so on. Alternatively, higher-quality output often requires the use of more expensive labor, materials, and technology, which clearly correspond to higher costs. Further, superior quality and service represent techniques used for a strategy based on differentiation (Wiseman 1988), which is not generally associated with a cost-based strategy (Porter 1980). It seems clear that the success of a reengineering project will necessarily depend on both the strategy being pursued and the output being measured.

Finally, from this definition, the process represents the central unit of analysis. The term *process* has been loosely defined by Hammer and Champy (1993) as "a collection of activities that takes one or more kinds of input and creates an output that is of value to the customer" (p. 35). From this definition, activities, outputs, customers, and measures represent key concepts associated with processes. A similar definition appears in Davenport (1993): "In definitional terms, a process is simply a structured, measured set of activities designed to produce a specified output for a particular customer or market" (p. 5). A related definition is found on page 2: "A process is thus a specific ordering of work activities across time and place, with a beginning, an end, and clearly identified inputs and outputs: a structure for action." This latter definition helps to identify additional key concepts, including ordering of work, time, space, beginning, ending, inputs, outputs, structure, and action. These concepts are useful for building knowledge. Table 27.2 provides a summary of the key reengineering concepts identified in this section.

FAQ 2: How does BPR differ from TQM?

Based on this review of the literature, probably the most distinguishing feature between BPR and TQM is a matter of degree. This view is largely consistent with that expressed in Cole (1994), in which an "extraordinarily large number of similarities between quality and reengineering" is asserted (p. 81). From the key terms and concepts, the emphasis of the former is on singular and dramatic performance improvement through radical process redesign (Barnett 1994; Scherr 1993; Ward 1993), whereas more continuous and incremental gains are generally expected through the latter (Flood 1993; Hoffherr, Moran, and Nadler 1994; Stein 1993). This view is echoed in Hammer and Champy (1993): Whereas "quality programs and reengineering share a number of common themes" on the one hand, these authors also state that "the two programs differ fundamentally" and contrast the continuous, incremental nature of TQM with discrete, quantum effects of BPR (p. 49).

The foundations of BPR are clearly set in TQM according to Harrington (1991), and, in building on this work, organizations are advised to "combine process improvement and process innovation in an ongoing quality program" (Davenport 1993, 14). Alternatively, this same author describes the "pace of change" as much more dramatic in a reengineering project. A similar contrast also exists in Andrews and Stalick (1994), but their eight-step reengineering approach concludes with the transition to a continuous process improvement (CPI) environment.

TABLE 27.2 ***Key reengineering concepts***

Topic	Concept
Reengineering	Fundamental rethinking Radical redesign Process Dramatic improvement Measures Return Risk
Process	Activities Customers Measures Work ordering Time Space Beginning Ending Inputs Outputs Structure Action Baseline
Redesign	Process configuration Design flaws Process transformation Redesign alternatives

There appears, however, to be nothing in these expert reengineering methodologies that would prevent the gains achievable through CPI from becoming dramatic (that is, of the same order as those sought through BPR). Neither would radical process redesign appear to ensure that improvements will exceed incremental levels (that is, as BPR authors generally attribute to TQM), or even be positive for that matter. Analogous to the well-known, risk-return relationship captured in the Capital Asset Pricing Model (Sharpe and Alexander 1990), organizations are cautioned by Davenport that "the risks of process innovation are at least proportional to the rewards" (p. 15). From the high BPR failure rates noted, this suggests that reengineering represents a more aggressive, but riskier, performance improvement endeavor than TQM.

The focus of measurement also differs in terms of emphasis between the BPR and TQM literatures. TQM publications, with their emphasis on CPI (Lynch and Cross 1991; Steeples 1993) and activity-based costing (Brimson 1991; O'Guin 1991), appear to reflect a relatively straightforward extension of traditional industrial engineering works, such as Bailey (1982) and Barnes (1980). Some experts draw a contrast between this and "the new industrial engineering" (Davenport and Short 1990), in which the enabling power of information technology (IT) is stressed. The role of IT in reengineering represents the subject of FAQ 5 below, but ex-ante process modeling (Curtis, Kellner, and Over 1992; Housel, Morris, and Westland 1993), complexity assessment (Albrecht and Gaffney 1983; Dreger 1989; Kanevsky and Housel 1994), and performance evaluation (Grady 1992; Nissen 1994) take on key importance in BPR.

To reiterate, differences between BPR and TQM may be best characterized in terms of degree (for example, singular versus continuous activity; dramatic versus incremental improvement objectives; radical versus fine-tuning process redesign, and so on). It would also appear that researchers in each area may have much to gain from their counterparts in the other. This point highlights one of the intended contributions of this article: to capture and organize a major segment of the reengineering literature for the benefit of researchers in BPR, TQM, and other relevant disciplines (such as information systems).

FAQ 3: Why reengineer organizational processes?

"The Crisis That Will Not Go Away" is the title of chapter 1 in Hammer and Champy (1993), in which the authors describe three forces that are driving companies to reengineer organizational processes: (1) customers taking charge, (2) competition intensifying globally, and (3) change perpetuating and increasing in pace. In addition to these external forces behind reengineering, the authors also highlight a problem internal to business processes themselves (p. 11).

> Most companies today—no matter what business they are in, how technologically sophisticated their product or service, or what their national origin—can trace their work styles and organizational roots back to the prototypical pin factory that Adam Smith described in *The Wealth of Nations,* published in 1776.

Despite the common usage of the term *reengineering,* such work styles and organizational roots do not appear to have been *engineered* to begin with; rather, this suggests that organizational processes are merely continuations of their predecessors, having evolved slowly and, in many cases, changed little through the decades (and centuries). Even if business processes had been engineered to begin with, say only 10 or 20 years ago, a strong case could still be made for their reengineering, particularly in light of "the tool that has changed business most over the past three decades—information technology" (Davenport 1993, 5). Not unlike the advent of electrical power near the turn of the century, IT can enable entirely new methods of performing work.

Further, as noted in the first section, reengineering has become very pervasive and important in business. The fact that nearly all U.S. corporations are undertaking major reengineering projects implies that a given company, which fails to reengineer, may fall behind simply by standing still. Management is adduced to simplify and streamline processes, and to employ "breakthrough strategies" to effect error-free and world-class levels of process performance (Harrington 1991,

206). Management is also exhorted to strive for "breakpoint strategies" for renewed competitiveness and competitive dominance (Johansson et al. 1993). Here, the authors define a *breakpoint* as "the achievement of excellence in one or more value metrics where the marketplace clearly recognizes the advantage, and where the ensuing result is a disproportionate and sustained increase in the supplier's market share" (p. 113). In terms of the Competitive Forces Model (Porter 1985), not only does reengineering represent a threat from rival firms in a competitive arena, but BPR can also be characterized as an approach to the attainment of sustainable competitive advantage. Indeed, there is evidence that a number of companies view reengineering itself among their essential core competencies. Such companies include Cigna (Caron, Jarvenpaa, and Stoddard 1994) and Taco Bell (Karlgaard 1994).

FAQ 4: What reengineering steps are required?

Each of the expert reengineering methodologies is comprised of a somewhat different sequence of redesign activities or steps, which reflects differing emphases across the various methods. For example, one of the earliest of these (Rummler and Brache 1991) includes an analytical technique that helps to focus on who (that is, what organizational role) is responsible for what (that is, which process activities). Specifically, it involves a two-dimensional technique for process mapping, which builds upon the standard, one-dimensional flowcharting approach employed in most methodologies. With this, the typical flowchart sequencing of tasks and activities is extended to incorporate the second dimension of organizational role; that is, it explicitly links process activities to the organizations and roles responsible for their execution.

As noted, another early expert reengineering methodology (Harrington 1991) has its focus on process simplification and streamlining. It involves five steps: (1) organize for improvement; (2) understand the process; (3) streamline; (4) measure and control; and (5) continuous improvement (p. 21). As should be apparent from steps 2 and 4, this methodology places considerable emphasis on the understanding and measurement of an existing process baseline, to which some refer as the "as-is" condition or configuration. A similar emphasis on the baseline process configuration is found in the later methodology of Davenport (1993). It outlines a sequence of five high-level activities, which are listed in Table 27.3, and highlights the importance of information pertaining to an existing process through step 4.

This emphasis provides a stark contrast with the methodology of Hammer and Champy (1993), the latter of which involves "starting all over, starting from scratch" (p. 2). Indeed, in this methodology, analysis of an existing process baseline configuration is purposefully excluded, including instead only a high-level understanding of "the what and the why, not the how, of the process" (p. 131). In a related work (Hammer and Stanton 1995), the rationale provided is that "the how is going to change anyway as a result of reengineering" (p. 19). The authors refer to this reengineering approach as "redesign with a blank sheet of paper"

(p. 131) and "the proverbial clean slate" (p. 4). The importance of baseline process analysis represents a major issue of division between the expert reengineering methodologies.

Returning to the methodology of Davenport (1993), each of the five high-level reengineering activities can be decomposed into a set of lower-level activities. For example, focusing on the elements of process redesign, steps 4 and 5 detail the requisite reengineering activities. Table 27.4 contains a listing of the second-level

TABLE 27.3 ***High-level reengineering activities***

1. Identifying processes for innovation
2. Identifying change levers
   (that is, enabling or transformation technologies)
3. Developing process visions
4. Understanding and improving existing processes
5. Designing and prototyping the new process

SOURCE: Adapted from Davenport (1993), p. 25.

TABLE 27.4 ***Critical redesign activities***

STEP 4—UNDERSTANDING AND IMPROVING EXISTING PROCESSES

1. Describe the current process flow.
2. Measure the process in terms of the new process objectives.
3. Assess the process in terms of the new process attributes.
4. Identify problems with, or shortcoming of, the process.
5. Identify short-term improvements in the process.
6. Assess current information technology and organization.

STEP 5—DESIGNING AND PROTOTYPING A NEW PROCESS

1. Brainstorm design alternatives.
2. Assess feasibility, risk, and benefit of design alternatives.
3. Select the preferred process design.
4. Prototype the new process design.
5. Develop a migration strategy.
6. Implement new organizational structures and systems.

SOURCE: Adapted from Davenport (1993), pp. 139 and 154.

activities corresponding to steps 4 and 5. Through its inclusion of baseline process analysis and measurement, this methodology effectively subsumes that of Harrington (1991), and it is quite comprehensive. Although this present framework effectively prescribes *what* reengineering activities to perform, and in which order they should be accomplished, it fails to describe *how* to perform them; that is, it is not operationalized. This represents a common theme that pervades the expert reengineering methodologies, a theme that was explicitly incorporated into the reengineering literary framework previously described.

A subsequent methodology (Andrews and Stalick 1994) also outlines a multi-step sequence of reengineering activities. Unlike its counterparts, greater emphasis is placed on implementation, as opposed to redesign. Implementation represents a key stage of activities in the reengineering life cycle (Guha, Kettinger, and Teng 1994) and represents a major area of risk in terms of BPR success. The eight steps are listed in Table 27.5. As noted, this methodology calls for transition to a CPI environment. Such institutionalization of process improvement is also noted as important in Davenport (1993): "Lest it slide back down the slippery slope of process degradation, a firm should then pursue a program of continuous improvement for the post-innovation process" (p. 14). Again, the consensus among reengineering experts suggests that BPR and TQM are both compatible and complementary.

FAQ 5: What is the role of information technology?

As noted, IT has had a profound effect on business. For a number of years researchers investigated the role of IT in BPR (Smith and McKeen 1993; Teng, Kettinger, and Guha 1992), employed IT-based analytical techniques (Daniels et al. 1991; Dennis, Daniels, and Nunamaker 1993), and developed frameworks to characterize reengineering in terms of how IT is strategically employed (Ives, Jarvenpaa, and Mason 1993; Venkatraman 1994). In the expert reengineering

TABLE 27.5 ***Eight-step approach***

1. Frame the project.
2. Create vision, values, and goals.
3. Redesign business operations.
4. Conduct proof of concept.
5. Plan implementation.
6. Get implementation approval.
7. Implement redesign.
8. Transition to CPI environment.

SOURCE: Adapted from Andrews and Stalick (1994), p. 93.

methodologies, IT is consistently described as the *central* enabling technology for process redesign.

For example, Hammer and Champy (1993) call IT the "essential enabler" in reengineering (p. 83), and management is urged to "think inductively" (p. 84) about how IT can be employed for process redesign. Such inductive thinking begins with known (information) technologies, such as those listed in Table 27.6, which managers use to identify problems that the technologies can help to solve. Although the authors caution against an overreliance on IT in reengineering—colorful terms such as "automating the mess" and "paving the cowpaths" have been used (Hammer 1990) to describe this situation—it is clearly central to their methodology.

IT also plays a key role in the methodology espoused in Davenport (1993): "Information technology [is] . . . the most powerful tool for changing business to emerge in the twentieth century." This author, however, also acknowledges the importance of other enabling or transformation technologies, which he refers to as "human and organizational development approaches" (p. 13). This mirrors a key concept from information systems that dates back to the early introduction of IT in business: The Leavitt Diamond (Leavitt 1965) indicates that management cannot simply introduce IT into a process; rather, people, tasks, structure, and technology must all be changed, or at least considered. Indeed, Davenport (1993) proceeds to state that "information technology is rarely effective without simultaneous human innovations" (p. 13).

Another view of IT's role in process redesign is provided by Davenport (1993), in terms of the nine effects that can be produced through IT: (1) automational, (2) informational, (3) sequential, (4) tracking, (5) analytical, (6) geographical, (7) integrative, (8) intellectual, and (9) disintermediating (p. 51). As an example, from the emerging phenomenon of electronic commerce, IT is now employed to enable consumers to book airline flights directly (that is, without the services of a

TABLE 27.6 ***IT enablers***

1. Shared databases
2. Expert systems
3. Telecommunications networks
4. Decision support tools
5. Wireless data communication and portable computers
6. Interactive videodisk
7. Automatic identification and tracking technology
8. High-performance computing

SOURCE: Adapted from Hammer and Champy (1993), pp. 91–101.

travel agent) through the Internet's World Wide Web (Southwest Airlines 1996). Thus, one effect of Web technology has been to disintermediate the airline flight-booking process. This latter view serves to extend the simple approach of "thinking inductively:" Whereas the inductive idea was to begin with certain technologies and try to identify problems that they could help to solve, this latter idea begins with the effects of information technologies, which pertain to different ways in which processes can be transformed through redesign. Clearly, consideration of IT effects on process performance brings one a substantial step closer to solving a redesign problem than simply considering the IT itself.

BPR FAQs summary

The five BPR FAQs are listed in Table 27.7. To briefly summarize, FAQ 1 provides the key terms and concepts associated with the phenomenon of reengineering. Central among these is the process as the fundamental unit of analysis in BPR, and the focus on dramatic performance improvement through radical process redesign. FAQ 2 addresses the similarities and differences between BPR and TQM. Despite differences in terms of scale, scope, and risk, BPR and TQM vary predominately in degree and represent both compatible and complementary endeavors.

FAQ 3 follows directly from FAQ 2, in much the same manner that the BPR phenomenon of the 1990s followed the TQM movement that originated in the 1980s; that is, by asking the question: If an organization has TQM, why reengineer its processes? The myriad perspectives circle around the issue of competitiveness. Firms reengineer either to keep up with performance improvements effected at rival firms that are reengineering, or in an attempt to attain competitive advantages of their own.

FAQ 4 outlines the key steps from a number of expert reengineering methodologies, from which a divisive issue pertains to the analysis of an existing process baseline configuration. Some experts note the importance of information that can be obtained through baseline analysis, whereas others exhort management to skip this step and pursue a "clean slate" or "blank sheet of paper" approach. Of the methodologies that stress baseline process analysis, measurement is assigned a very important role; however, the nature of measurement in IT-enabled process redesign has a different emphasis from previous measurement focuses in TQM.

Table 27.7 ***BPR FAQ summary***

FAQ 1. Key terms and concepts?
FAQ 2. BPR and TQM differences?
FAQ 3. Why reengineer?
FAQ 4. Reengineering steps?
FAQ 5. IT role?

Finally, FAQ 5 addresses the role of IT in process redesign. Although IT is heralded as the central enabling technology for reengineering, the experts caution against the sole or excessive reliance on this transformation technology, and other enablers of process innovation, such as human and organizational interventions, are adduced. Drawing from the Leavitt Diamond Model, readers are reminded that IT cannot simply be introduced into a process with the kind of dramatic performance improvements sought through reengineering expected. The colorful characterizations "automating the mess" and "paving the cowpaths" provide vivid reminders of this expert advice.

PREPARING FOR THE SECOND PHASE

As noted, the second phase of reengineering promises to be more challenging than the first. A key objective of this article is to provide a summary of the BPR lessons learned from the first phase. The BPR FAQs have been developed by drawing primarily from the class of expert reengineering methodologies. Together with the references, this article should serve as a useful review of BPR, helping both the academic and practitioner to focus his or her search through the reengineering literature. From the reengineering literary framework developed, however, this present focus on the expert reengineering methodologies clearly ignores the other classes of BPR publications. Because of the greater knowledge content inherent in academic investigations, preparations for the second phase of reengineering should also include a review of this class of the BPR literature.

As noted, the list of publications in the theory-building class of the literary framework was very short. Indeed, depending on interpretation, there may be no publications in this class. Although a number of propositions have been made regarding *how* to develop theory in the reengineering domain, for example, using sociotechnical systems design theory (Saharia et al. 1994), the *actual development* of such theory represents an open area of current research. Work along this theory-building line offers great potential to help prepare for the second phase of reengineering, due particularly to the high knowledge content of any publications forthcoming from this class.

Advances in the practice of process redesign also merit attention. Leading BPR proponents assert that reengineering has now progressed from mysterious art to become a learnable craft (Hammer and Stanton 1995). As a learnable craft, presumably the techniques for effective process redesign can be formalized and taught, not only by mystics and gurus, but also on a systematic basis through the educational system, such as MBA and executive programs. Such course work can help to educate this and the next generation of managers to prepare for the second phase of reengineering.

Moreover, to the extent that these techniques for effective process redesign can be formalized in a manner that integrates with computer-based inference, a good opportunity exists to capture and distribute expert reengineering knowledge through the methods of artificial intelligence (AI). Some preliminary measurement-based work along these lines has produced promising results (Nissen 1996), but a substantial amount of research is required to develop, test, and implement effective, operational, and industrial-strength knowledge-based systems (KBS) for redesign support. This represents another promising area of current research, as a huge amount of reengineering knowledge has been articulated, and available AI methods and technologies appear to be more than adequate for the job. The clearest beneficiaries of such redesign KBS will be the business practitioners, perhaps replacing the current dependence on the $2 billion external reengineering consulting industry (Caldwell 1994). Alternatively, such an "intelligent" redesign system may also provide BPR consultants with a source of competitive advantage. In either case, reengineering capabilities should improve, which can help to prepare for the second phase of reengineering.

Acknowledgments

I would like to thank George Easton and the anonymous referees for their very helpful comments and suggestions on an earlier draft of this article.

References

Albrecht, A., and J. Gaffney. "Software Function, Source Lines of Code, and Development Effort Prediction." *IEEE Transactions on Software Engineering* SE-9, 1983, no. 6, pp. 639–647.

Anderson, H. "The Open Corporation: Reengineering for the Client/Server Revolution." *Forbes* 148, 1991, no. 10, pp. 131–140.

Andrews, D. C., and S. K. Stalick. *Business reengineering: The Survival Guide.* New York: Yourdon Press Computing Series, 1994.

Bacharach, S. B. "Organizational Theories: Some Criteria for Evaluation." *Academy of Management Review* 14, 1989, no. 4, pp. 496–515.

Bailey, R. W. *Human Performance Engineering: A Guide for System Designers.* Englewood Cliffs, N.J.: Prentice-Hall, 1982.

Barnes, R. M. *Motion and Time Study: Design and Measurement of Work.* New York: John Wiley & Sons, 1980.

Barnett, J. L. "Process Visualization: Getting the Vision Right Is Key." *Information Systems Management,* Spring 1994, pp. 14–23.

Bashein, B. J., M. L. Markus, and P. Riley. "Preconditions for BPR Success: And How to Prevent Failures." *Information Systems Management,* Spring 1994, pp. 7–13.

Brimson, J. A. *Activity Accounting: An Activity-Based Costing Approach.* New York: John Wiley & Sons, 1991.

Caldwell, B. "Missteps, Miscues." *InformationWeek,* June 20, 1994, pp. 50–60.

Caron, J. R., S. L. Jarvenpaa, and D. B. Stoddard. "Business Reengineering at CIGNA Corporation: Experiences and Lessons Learned from the First Five Years." *MIS Quarterly,* September 1994, pp. 233–250.

Champy, J. "Organizational Revisionism." *CIO,* December 1990, p. 20.

Cheek, L. M. *Zero-Base Budgeting Comes of Age: What It Is and What It Takes to Make It Work.* New York: AMACOM, 1977.

Cole, R. E. "Reengineering the Corporation: A Review Essay." *Quality Management Journal* 1, 1994, no. 4, pp. 77–85.

Currid, C. "Have You Taken a Ride on the Reengineering Roller Coaster?" *Windows Magazine,* April 1, 1994, p. 51.

Curtis, B., M. I. Kellner, and J. Over. "Process Modeling." *Communications of the ACM* 35, 1992, no. 9, pp. 75–90.

Cypress, H. L. "Reengineering—MS/OR Imperative: Make Second Generation of Business Process Improvement Mode Work." *OR/MS Today,* February 1994, pp. 18–29.

Daniels, R. M., Jr., A. R. Dennis, G. S. Hayes, J. F. Nunamaker Jr., and J. S. Valacich. "Enterprise Analyzer: Electronic Support for Group Requirements Elicitation." In *Proceedings of the Twenty-fourth Annual Hawaii International Conference on System Sciences.* New York: IEEE Computer Society Press, 1991.

Davenport, T. H. *Process Innovation: Reengineering Work through Information Technology.* Boston: Harvard Business School Press, 1993.

Davenport, T. H., and J. E. Short. "The New Industrial Engineering: Information Technology and Business Process Redesign." *Sloan Management Review,* Summer 1990, pp. 11–27.

Davenport, T. H., and D. B. Stoddard. "Reengineering: Business Change of Mythic Proportions?" *MIS Quarterly,* June 1994, pp. 121–127.

Davidson, W. H. "Beyond Reengineering: The Three Phases of Business Transformation." *IBM Systems Journal* 32, 1993, no. 1, pp. 65–79.

Dennis, A. R., R. M. Daniels Jr., and J. F. Nunamaker Jr. "Automated Support for Business Process Reengineering: A Case Study at IBM." In *Proceedings of the Twenty-sixth Annual Hawaii International Conference on System Sciences.* Los Alamitos, Calif.: IEEE Computer Society Press, 1993.

Dreger, J. *Function Point Analysis.* Englewood Cliffs, N.J.: Prentice-Hall, 1989.

E-Commerce. 1996. Questions. Internet World Wide Web address http://www.kivex.com/doc3.htm.

Flood, R. L. *Beyond TQM.* New York: John Wiley & Sons, 1993.

Furey, T. R. "A Six-Step Guide to Process Reengineering." *Planning Review* 21, 1993, no. 2, pp. 20–23.

Goldstein, D. K. Hallmark Cards. Harvard Business School case no. 9-186-044, July 1986.

Grady, R. B. *Practical Software Metrics for Project Management and Process Improvement.* Englewood Cliffs, N.J.: Prentice-Hall, 1992.

Guha, S., W. J. Kettinger, and J. T. C. Teng. "Business Process Reengineering: Building a Comprehensive Methodology." *Information Systems Management,* Spring 1994, pp. 13–22.

Hammer, M. "Reengineering Work: Don't Automate, Obliterate." *Harvard Business Review,* July/August 1990, pp. 104–112.

Hammer, M., and J. Champy. *Reengineering the Corporation: A Manifesto for Business Revolution.* New York: HarperBusiness, 1993.

Hammer, M., and S. A. Stanton. *The Reengineering Revolution: A Handbook.* New York: HarperBusiness, 1995.

Hamscher, W. "AI in Business-Process Reengineering: A Report on the 1994 Workshop." *AI Magazine* 15, 1994, no. 4, pp. 71–72.

Hansen, G. "A Complex Process: The Case for Automated Assistance in Business Process Reengineering." *OR/MS Today,* August 1994, pp. 34–41.

Harrington, H. J. *Business Process Improvement: The Breakthrough Strategy for Total Quality, Productivity, and Competitiveness.* New York: McGraw-Hill, 1991.

Henderson, J. C., and N. Venkatraman. "Strategic Alignment: Leveraging Information Technology for Transforming Organizations." *IBM Systems Journal* 32, 1993, no. 1, pp. 4–16.

Hoffherr, G. D., J. D. Moran, and G. Nadler. *Breakthrough Thinking in Total Quality Management.* Englewood Cliffs, N.J.: Prentice-Hall, 1994.

Housel, T. J., C. J. Morris, and C. Westland. "Business Process Reengineering at Pacific Bell." *Planning Review,* May/June 1993, pp. 28–33.

Ives, B., S. L. Jarvenpaa, and R. O. Mason. "Global Business Drivers: Aligning Information Technology to Global Business Strategy." *IBM Systems Journal* 32, 1993 no. 1, pp. 143–161.

Java. 1996. Java FAQ archives. Internet World Wide Web address http://204.156.148.241/java/faq/.

Johansson, H. J., P. McHugh, A. J. Pendlebury, and W. A. Wheeler III. *Business Process Reengineering: Breakpoint Strategies for Market Dominance.* Chichester, U.K.: John Wiley & Sons, 1993.

Kanevsky, V., and T. J. Housel. "Value-Based Business Process Reengineering: An Objective Approach to Value Added." Pacific Bell Working Paper #96, 1994.

Karlgaard, R. "ASAP Interview: Susan Cramm and John Martin." *Forbes ASAP,* August 29, 1994, pp. 67–70.

King, J. L., and B. Konsynski. "Singapore Tradenet: A Tale of One City." Harvard Business School Case No. 9-191-009.

Klein, M. M. "Reengineering Methodologies and Tools: A Prescription for Enhancing Success." *Information Systems Management,* Spring 1994, pp. 30–35.

Leavitt, H. J. "Applying Organizational Change in Industry: Structural, Technological and Humanistic Approaches." In *Handbook of Organizations,* edited by J. March. Chicago: Rand McNally, 1965.

Lynch, R. L., and K. F. Cross. *Measuring Up! Yardsticks for Continuous Improvement.* Cambridge, Mass.: Blackwell, 1991.

Manager's Notebook. "Top Exec Initiatives." *InformationWeek,* December 19, 1994, p. 44.

Marshall, M., and K. Rodriguez. "Industry Lines Up for Java-Vendors Set Stage for Dynamic Web Apps." *CommunicationWeek,* December 11, 1995, p. 1.

McPartlin, J. P. "Just Chasing Rainbows? Critics Brand Much of the Reengineering Clamor as Sheer Marketing Hype." *InformationWeek,* February 1, 1993, p. 55.

Middlebrook, W. D. "Reengineering the Procurement Process: Reducing Cycle Time through EDI and Various Automation Techniques." *EDI World,* May 1994, pp. 46–48.

Nissen, M. E. "Valuing IT through Virtual Process Measurement." In *Proceedings of the Fifteenth International Conference on Information Systems,* 1994.

———. "Knowledge-Based Organizational Process Redesign: Using Process Flow Measures to Transform Procurement." Doctoral dissertation, University of Southern California School of Business Administration, 1995.

———. "Knowledge-Based Reengineering of Military Procurement: From Mysterious Art to Learnable Craft." Fisher Center for Information Technology and Management Working Paper no. CITM-96-WP-1012 (February 1996).

O'Guin, M. C. *The Complete Guide to Activity-Based Costing.* Englewood Cliffs, N.J.: Prentice-Hall, 1991.

Porter, M. E. *Competitive Strategy: Techniques for Analyzing Industries and Competitors.* New York: Free Press, 1980.

———. *Competitive Advantage: Creating and Sustaining Superior Performance.* New York: Free Press, 1985.

PowerBrowser. 1996. Frequently asked questions. Internet World Wide Web address http://www.oracle.com/products/websystem/powerbrowser/html/faq.html.

Rummler, G. A., and A. P. Brache. *Improving Performance: How to Manage the White Space on the Organization Chart.* San Francisco, Calif.: Jossey-Bass, 1991.

Saharia, A. N., T. M. Barron, T. J. Davenport, J. K. Ho, and H. Mendelson. "Is There a Theory of Reengineering?" In *Proceedings of the Fifteenth International Conference on Information Systems,* 1994.

Scherr, A. L. "A New Approach to Business Processes. *IBM Systems Journal* 32, 1993, no. 1, pp. 80–98.

Sharpe, W. F., and G. J. Alexander. *Investments.* 4th ed. Englewood Cliffs, N.J.: Prentice Hall, 1990.

Smith, H. A., and J. D. McKeen. "Reengineering the Corporation: Where Does I.S. Fit In?" In *Proceedings of the Twenty-sixth Annual Hawaii International Conference on System Sciences.* Los Alamitos, Calif: IEEE Computer Society Press, 1993.

Southwest Airlines. 1996. Southwest Airlines home gate. Internet World Wide Web address http://www.iflyswa.com/.

Stalk, G. Jr., and T. M. Hout. *Competing against Time: How Time-Based Competition is Reshaping Global Markets.* New York: Free Press, 1990.

Steeples, M. M. *The Corporate Guide to the Malcolm Baldrige National Quality Award: Proven Strategies for Building Quality into Your Organization.* 2d ed. Milwaukee: ASQC Quality Press, 1993.

Stein, R. E. *The Next Phase of Total Quality Management: TQM II and the Focus on Profitability.* New York: Dekker, 1993.

Stoddard, D. B., and S. L. Jarvenpaa. "Business Process Redesign: Tactics for Managing Radical Change. *Journal of Management Information Systems*" 12, 1995, no. 1:81–107.

Stoddard, D. B., and C. J. Meadows. "Capital Holding Corporation—Reengineering the Direct Response Group." Harvard Business School Case No. 9-192-001, 1992.

Teng, J. T. C., W. J. Kettinger, and S. Guha. "Business Process Redesign and Information Architecture: Establishing the Missing Links." In *Proceedings of the Thirteenth International Conference on Information Systems,* 1992.

Venkatraman, N. "IT-Enabled Business Transformation: From Automation to Business Scope Redefinition." *Sloan Management Review,* Winter 1994, pp. 73–87.

Ward, A. "TQM vs. Business Process Innovation." Paper presented at USC COMER Roundtable XVIII Seminar on Business Process Reengineering, 1993.

Wilder, C. "The Internet Pioneers—The Emergence of the World Wide Web and Mosaic Has Convinced Early Corporate Adopters of the Viability of Doing Business Online." *InformationWeek,* January 9, 1995, p. 38.

Wilder, C., K. Bull, and C. Gillooly. 1995. "Intranet Tools—Corporations Seek Internal Web Applications and Major Vendors Are Happy to Help." *InformationWeek,* November 6, 1995, p. 14.

Wiseman, C. *Strategic Information Systems.* Homewood, Ill.: Irwin, 1988.

Reading 28

ISO 9000—The Foundation for Change

By Philip Dargie

Today, management is faced with unique challenges requiring quick response and the ability to cope with rapid change in all aspects of business. We have entered the information age where the focus is shifting from physical tasks to service and knowledge work. We are in an age of paradigm shifts, reengineering, agile manufacturing, and a host of other change-driven concepts.

In this environment, where is the case to be made for ISO 9000 implementation, with its focus on documenting a planned and structured quality assurance system? When human resources need to be allocated to cope with continuous change, how can a company find the time to document a standardized system without neglecting urgent issues with which it is faced?

Isn't the standardization approach contrary to systemic thinking, which focuses on constant change? Are we not at odds with the objectives of other organizational quality and productivity initiatives when we focus resources on standardization while still addressing the overriding elements of change?

How does ISO relate to the models for organizational redesign and the strategic systems thinking that must be employed to address change? How does ISO 9000 relate to Total Quality Management and the subsequent changes fostered by Total Quality Management?

To discuss the relationships between ISO 9000 and successful management of change, we must first understand the fundamental concepts underlying ISO 9000 and their relationship to the overall structure of the organization and the quality systems. Specifically, we must understand how ISO fits into the Total Quality Management approach to implementing organizational change.

Source: Reprinted with the permission of the author.

HISTORY OF ISO 9000

In order to discuss ISO 9000 as the foundation for Total Quality Management, we need a full understanding of ISO 9000, its history and requirements. First, we need to be aware that "ISO" is not an acronym for "The International Organization for Standardization" which developed the ISO 9000 Standards for Quality Systems. "ISO" (eye-so) is derived from the Greek *isos,* meaning *equal* (isometric, isobars, etc.). The word "ISO" is used to denote that organizations using the ISO standard for quality systems will have basic systems that are comparable to each other. (Note: It is acceptable to refer to The International Organization for Standardization as ISO for lack of an appropriate acronym).

The International Organization for Standardization (ISO) was founded in Geneva, Switzerland, by 25 countries in 1947. Today, there are 124 member countries, each represented by a standardization body from that country. The United States is represented by the American National Standards Institute, a private sector organization, which develops standards for products and systems in the United States. Together with the International Electrotechnical Commission (IEC), which has the responsibility for developing standards for electrical and electronic engineering, ISO and IEC are recognized as the standards organizations for the entire world.

ISO's mission is to promote the development of standardization and related activities around the world, thus facilitating the international exchange of goods and services. Since its inception, ISO has published more than 11,000 voluntary international standards and guides covering a wide variety of needs and benefiting both producers and consumers.

ISO has subcommittees that work to develop the standards and guidelines. After the standards are developed, they are voted upon by the members and adopted for voluntary use if 75 percent vote in the affirmative.

The ISO 9000 series of standards consist of three contractual standards to which a company's quality system can be audited for compliance. These are ISO 9001, 9002, and 9003. ISO 9001 is used as a model for companies that design and develop as well as manufacture or service. ISO 9002 is used where companies do not have design responsibility but manufacture or service only. ISO 9003 is used for companies that do final inspection or testing only. The remainder of the ISO 9000 series are guidelines only, used to help interpret and implement the contractual standards.

ISO has also reserved the 10000 series of numbers for additional quality guidelines to augment the 9000 series. These include, as an example: ISO 10011—Guidelines for Auditing Quality Systems, ISO 10012—Quality Assurance Requirements for Measuring Equipment, and ISO 10013—Guidelines for Developing Quality Manuals.

The ISO 9000 model for quality assurance has achieved worldwide acceptance and is used by organizations to provide their customers or potential customers with proof that their quality system meets the quality assurance requirements of the standard. To provide the proof, companies that have implemented an ISO 9000 quality assurance system hire an independent third-party ISO 9000 assessment entity (registrar) to audit their system to determine if it meets the requirements of the standard. When the registrar determines that the system is adequate, a certificate is issued to the company. The company may use the certificate and the logo of the registrar to publicize its certification (or registration; either of the two terms may be used).

The registrar then performs periodic "surveillance" audits to ensure that the company continues to meet the requirements.

TOTAL QUALITY MANAGEMENT AND ISO 9000

TQM advocates sometimes criticize ISO 9000 since they perceive that the standards do not emphasize key TQM principles such as empowerment, Hoshin planning, quality function deployment, and others. Also, the detractors of ISO 9000 are concerned that fully documented systems may generate mountains of paperwork and impose a certain rigidity that can represent a barrier to continuous improvement and organizational change.

Frequently it is not understood that ISO 9000 is an integral part of TQM; it provides the platform for what is known in the TQM literature as daily management, i.e., the existence of "documented processes under control."

Frequently, TQM is described as a "customer driven master plan" encompassing three basic activities:

1. Daily Management
2. Hoshin Planning
3. Cross Functional Management

DAILY MANAGEMENT AND ISO 9000

ISO 9000, in the TQM scheme of management, is a documented daily management system. The first part of ISO 9000 implementation relates to the "Do (document), Check (adequate to meet requirements of the ISO standard), Act (audit), Standardize" (DCAS) cycle as depicted in Figure 28.1.

In this first stage (the standardization stage) of ISO 9000 implementation, the first step is the documentation of the quality assurance procedures as they actually exist. The second step is to determine if the documented procedures are adequate to meet the requirements of the standard. This is accomplished by reviewing the entire documented system to determine if all the requirements of the standard have been addressed (all the *shall* requirements of the standard). This presupposes that individuals performing the review (internal and/or external) have an adequate understanding of the standard and can adequately interpret it. The third

FIGURE 28.1 *DCAS cycle*

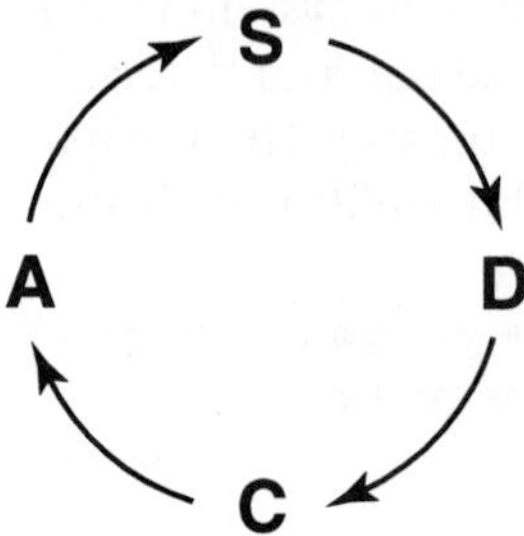

step involves auditing the system to ensure that the system is being complied with as documented.

The second stage of ISO 9000 (the continuous improvement stage) focuses on continuous improvement of the standardized system. This is accomplished primarily through internal auditing (soliciting from all associates ways to make their jobs easier and how to improve safety and quality), corrective action (eliminating the root causes of nonconformity), and preventive action (identifying opportunities to eliminate potential causes of nonconformity). ISO 9000 provides the framework for incorporating continuous improvement into the documented quality system. If one looks at the inputs from internal audits, corrective action, and preventive action as all part of the "Plan, Do, Check, Act (PDCA)" cycle (Figure 28.2), one can realize how ISO 9000 provides the platform for continuous improvement of the Daily Management part of TQM.

The standardization phase and the continuous improvement phase work together to ensure that the improvements are captured by the system and become a part of the standardized system. (See Figure 28.3.)

ISO provides the basic tools to establish the initial standardization upon which to improve. The "Plan-Do-Check-Act" cycle that problem solving teams utilize must be followed up with the "Plan-Do-Check-Standardize" cycle, if the solved problems are to remain solved.

HOSHIN PLANNING AND ISO 9000

Hoshin planning is that component of the TQM system that allows an organization to plan and execute strategic organizational breakthroughs, and ISO 9000 daily management is that component of TQM that maximizes individual and departmental performance every day.

Hoshin planning draws information from the ongoing data collection and analysis of the ISO 9000 process to identify broad system problems in which breakthrough is needed.

FIGURE 28.2 *PDCA cycle*

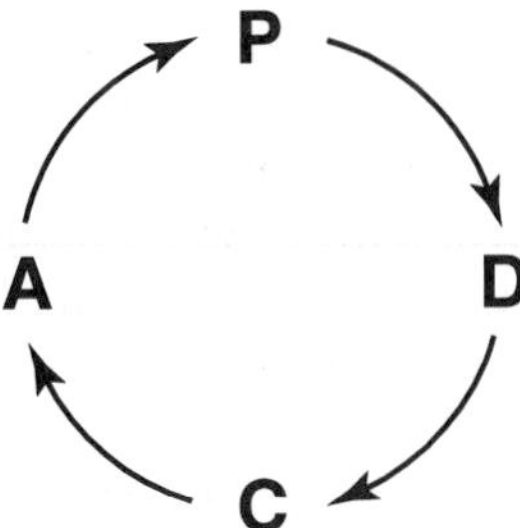

FIGURE 28.3 *The continuous improvement and standardization cycles*

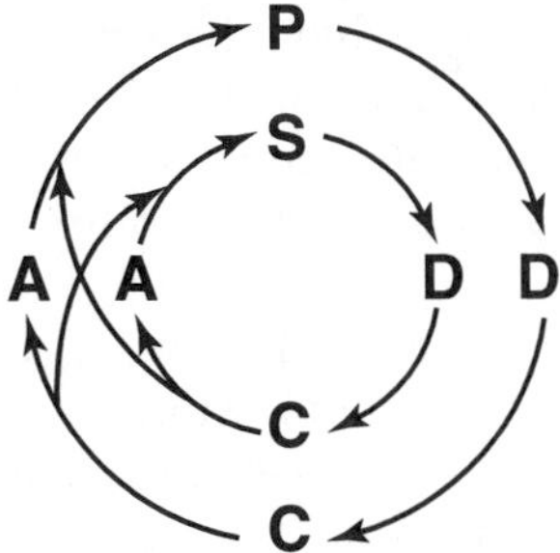

Once breakthroughs have occurred they then become part of the system by the Plan-Do-Check-Standardize cycle and are reflected in the maintained ISO 9000 quality assurance system.

CROSS-FUNCTIONAL MANAGEMENT AND ISO 9000

Cross-functional management is that component of TQM that focuses on all aspects of the quality system and ensures deployment of the quality function.

Cross-functional management draws on inputs from customers, suppliers, Hoshin planning, and ISO 9000 to focus the entire organization on the customer driven master plan for the organization. Routine management reviews, mandated by ISO 9000, require that the quality system be reviewed at defined intervals sufficient to ensure continuing suitability and effectiveness of the system and the meeting of the company's stated quality policy and objectives.

WHY SHOULD A COMPANY START WITH STANDARDIZATION (ISO 9000) AS THE FIRST STEP IN IMPLEMENTING TQM?

Simply stated, it's difficult to improve or change something if you don't know what you've got to begin with. It is not uncommon for companies to attempt to modify the quality culture of the company by instructing all associates in the company in team-oriented problem solving in an attempt to "get everyone involved." The downside to taking this as the initial approach is that as solutions to problems are developed there is no way to capture the solutions and ensure that they become an integral part of the way things are done in the future. There is no way to ensure that the solutions are practiced routinely by those involved. ISO 9000 provides the vehicle to accomplish this.

ISO 9000—COMPANY DRIVEN OR CUSTOMER DRIVEN

There probably are companies that have become certified to ISO 9000 only to have a perceived marketing advantage or to meet the demands of the European market and/or a customer's mandate. However, even these companies will profit from having done so, much as the suppliers to the automotive industry profited from the mandates placed on them in the 1980s to meet the requirements of similar quality systems. Companies that attained ratings of "preferred supplier" to the "Big Three," Chrysler, Ford, and General Motors, for instance, benefited significantly from their achievements. Undeniably, Chrysler, Ford, and General Motors have had a profound impact on the quality culture of the multitude of suppliers to the automotive industry.

And many, if not most, of the automotive industry preferred suppliers have long since built companywide quality systems in every aspect of their business and are well on their way to establishing a TQM environment in their companies, using the initial quality system requirements imposed on them by the Big Three.[1]

Those companies that have not been fortunate enough to have had customer-mandated quality systems or have not seen the wisdom in implementing ISO 9000 will have a decided disadvantage in coping with change in the immediate future. They are faced with the dual challenge of defining their current systems while addressing the daily aspects of change.

CHANGES: STRATEGIC QUALITY MANAGEMENT AND ISO 9000

Strategic quality management is the development of strategic quality goals for the organization, deploying them to all of the daily management aspects of the organization and reviewing the progress of meeting the goals. Strategic quality management develops three kinds of goals:

Quality goals	related to resource utilization
Quality effectiveness goals	related to customer commitment and satisfaction
Quality agility goals	related to responsiveness to change

Before goals can be set, there must be a clear understanding of the current state of the system. ISO provides the tools for an organization to effectively communicate the current state (documented system) and to evaluate where resources can best be allocated for improvement (corrective action, internal audits, management reviews).

As quality agility goals are addressed, the results in achieving the goals can be readily incorporated into the structured documented system such that the changes are immediately deployed throughout the organization.

The discipline imposed by the ISO requirements provides the vehicle to ensure that change is recognized, faced, and effectively deployed.

ISO 9000 AND ITS RELATIONSHIP TO QUALITY

The quality movement has gone through four basic stages:

Stage	Activity
First	Inspection
Second	Quality Control
Third	Quality Assurance
Fourth	Total Quality Management

The ISO 9000 Standard for Quality Systems is the foundation for the third stage. It focuses on prevention rather than correction and provides the tools to provide assurance that quality systems are functional and in a state of continuous improvement.

ISO provides for continuous improvement and change by requiring:

- The documentation of the activities that are necessary to make a quality product or provide a quality service.
- The maintenance of records of those activities primary to daily management.
- A focus on prevention of nonconformance in contract, design, manufacturing, and delivery of product.
- The internal auditing of the system frequently enough to ensure its continued functioning and effectiveness.
- The modification of the system to incorporate improvements to ensure that the improvements become an ongoing part of the organization's operation.

FIGURE 28.4 Customer-driven master plan

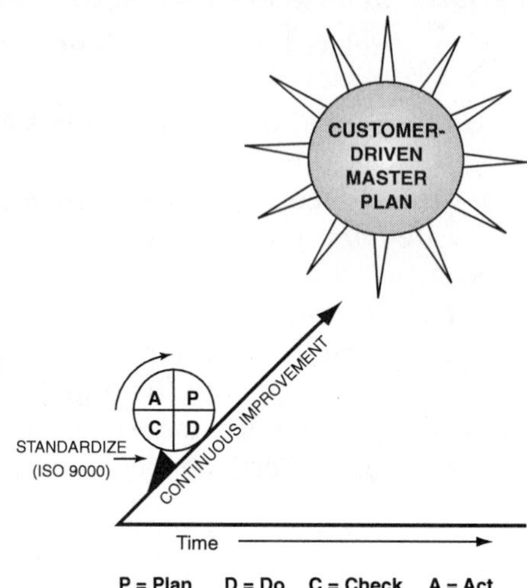

The Plan, Do, Check, Act (PDCA) cycle provides continuous feedback to the system and ISO provides the foundation upon which to incorporate improvements into the operation. The PDCA cycle feeds into the Plan, Do, Check, Standardize (PDCS) cycle upon which ISO is based. (See Figure 28.4.)

MEASURABLES/METRICS TO ASSESS CONTINUOUS IMPROVEMENT AND CHANGE

With continuous improvement, reengineering, agile manufacturing, and other change-driven concepts all being addressed at the same time, how does a company assess how each contributes to quality, productivity, and customer satisfaction?

Obviously, we are not wanting to make change for change's sake, and if we are making improvements/changes, metrics should be identified to measure the effect of the changes. Primary considerations are quality, productivity, efficiency, organizational effectiveness, costs, and profits.

Typically, companies measure the effects of change with trend charts of measurables some of which can be:

- Reduction in variability.
- Percent on time delivery.
- Reduction in customer concerns/complaints.

- Reduction in noncompliance and waste.
- Specific measurements related to a specific improvement project or change.

The trends in data and information are compared with progress toward overall business objectives with the intent of developing priorities as input to subsequent decision making and longer-term planning. The trends evaluate the progress that is being made relative to the goals established in the strategic quality management system.

It is not uncommon for companies to find, to their surprise, that as few as 10 to 15 trend charts are adequate to evaluate the effects of change and assess the effectiveness of the strategic quality management system.

TQM LONG-RANGE PLANNING AND INCORPORATING ISO 9000 INTO THE PLAN

From the beginning, companies should look upon the implementation of ISO 9000 within the framework of TQM. ISO defines Total Quality Management (TQM) in *"ISO 8402—Vocabulary"* as: "A management approach of an organization, centered on quality, based on the participation of all of its members and aiming at long term success through customer satisfaction, and benefits to the members of the organization and to society."

There are other definitions of TQM, but they all include the concept of the "participation of all of its members," viz: "involvement" and "empowerment."

In implementing ISO 9000, a company will obtain the maximum benefits if all employees are involved with the implementation from the start. Each employee should be involved with the development of the flow charts and procedures used for the standardization of the systems. Also, it would be a mistake if all functions in the company are not included in the standardization process. Companies that do just enough to satisfy the requirements of the ISO standard will not be utilizing the process to build a firm foundation for TQM.

To sum up, this paper discusses how ISO 9000 can be used as the first step to build a TQM culture, a perspective the developers of the standard clearly had in mind as the standards were developed.

Notes

1. The Big Three have since replaced each of their own quality system requirements with a new set of mutually agreed upon requirements based on ISO 9000, with additional requirements superimposed on the ISO standard to meet the specific needs of the automotive industry (QS 9000).

Reading 29

The Evolution of the ISO 9000 Series of Quality Standards

BY PHILIP DARGIE

In 1979, the International Organization for Standardization (ISO), a Geneva-based worldwide federation of quality organizations, formed Technical Committee ISO/TC 176 on quality management and quality assurance to develop a generic series of quality system standards. ISO/TC 176 then extensively researched existing national standards from ISO member countries including Great Britain's BS 5750 and BS 4891; France's AFNOR Z 50-110; Germany's DIN 55-355; the Netherlands' NEN 2646; Canada's Z-299; and the USA's ANSI/ASQC Z-1.15, MIL-Q-9858 A, ANSI/ASQC C-1, and ANSI/ASME NQA-1 to develop the ISO 9000 series.

The ISO 9000 series of standards was published in 1987 and revised in 1994 (the current valid international standard). The standard is evolving, and its evolution is a reflection of the international quality movement. Therefore, highlighting the changes from the first to the second edition of the standard can serve to illustrate how our general understanding of quality systems implementation has evolved.

SOURCE: Reprinted with the permission of the author.

ISO 9001
A COMPARISON OF: ISO 9001/1987 and ISO 9001/1994

Quality systems—Model for quality assurance in design, development, production, installation, and servicing
[Revision of first edition (ISO 9001: 1987)]

CODE: ~~Crossed out text has been deleted or replaced in the revised DIS version of ISO 9001.~~
Bold, italicized text has been added to the new revised 1994 version of ISO 9001.

0 Introduction

This International Standard is one of ~~a series of~~ three International Standards dealing with quality system ***requirements*** that can be used for external quality assurance purposes. The ~~alternative~~ quality assurance models, set out in the three International Standards listed below, represent three distinct forms of ~~"functional or organizational capability" suitable for two party contractual purposes:~~ ***quality system suitable for the purpose of a supplier demonstrating its capability, and for the assessment of such supplier capability by external parties.***

—ISO 9001 Quality systems—Model for quality assurance in design, development, production, installation, and servicing.

For use when conformance to specified requirements is to be assured by the supplier during design, development, production, installation, and servicing.

—ISO 9002 Quality systems—Model for quality assurance in production, ~~and~~ installation, ***and servicing.***

For use when conformance to specified requirements is to be assured by the supplier during production, ~~and~~ installation, ***and servicing.***

—ISO 9003 Quality systems—Model for quality assurance in final inspection and test.

For use when conformance to specified requirements is to be assured by the supplier solely at final inspection and test.

It is emphasized that the quality system requirements specified in this International Standard, ISO 9002, and ISO 9003 are complementary (not alternative) to the technical (product) specified requirements. ***They specify requirements which determine what elements quality systems have to encompass but it is not the purpose of these International Standards to enforce uniformity of quality systems. They are generic, independent of any specific industry or economic sector. The design and implementation of a quality system has to necessarily be influenced by the varying needs of an organization, its particular objectives, the products and services supplied, and the processes and specific practices employed.***

It is intended that these International Standards will normally be adopted in their present form, but on occasions they may need to be tailored ~~for specific contractual situations.~~ by adding or deleting certain quality system requirements for specific contractual situations. ~~ISO 9000~~ ***ISO 9000–1*** provides guidance on such tailoring as well as selection of the appropriate quality assurance model, viz ISO 9001, ISO 9002, or ISO 9003.

1 Scope

~~1.1 Scope~~

This International Standard specifies quality system requirements for use where a ~~contract between two parties requires the demonstration of a supplier's capability to design and supply product~~ ***supplier's capability to design and supply conforming product needs to be demonstrated.***

The requirements specified ~~in this International Standard~~ are aimed primarily at ***achieving customer satisfaction by*** preventing nonconformity at all stages from design ***through*** to servicing.

~~1.2 Field of application~~

This International Standard is applicable in ~~contractual~~ situations when:

a) ~~the contract specifically requires design effort~~ ***design is required*** and the product requirements are stated principally in performance terms or they need to be established;

b) confidence in product conformance can be attained by adequate demonstration of ~~certain~~ ***a*** supplier's capabilities in design, development, production, installation, and servicing.

2 ~~References~~ *Normative references*

~~ISO 8402, Quality—Vocabulary.~~

~~ISO 900, Quality management and quality assurance standards—Guidelines for selection and use.~~

The following Standards contain provisions which, through reference in this text, constitute provisions of this International Standard. At the time of

publication, the editions indicated were valid. All Standards are subject to revision, and parties to agreements based on this International Standard are encouraged to investigate the possibility of applying the most recent editions of the standards indicated below. Members of IEC and ISO maintain registers of currently valid International Standards.

ISO 8402: 1993[1]—Quality management and quality assurance—Vocabulary

NOTE—For informative references, see annex A.

3 Definitions

~~For the purposes of this International Standard, the definitions given in ISO 8402 apply.~~

~~NOTE—For the purposes of this International Standard, the term "product" is also used to denote "service", as appropriate.~~

3.1 General

For the purpose of this International Standard, the definitions given in ISO 8402 apply except for the following definition.

3.2 product: The result of activities or processes; product includes "hardware," "software," "processed material," and "service" or a combination thereof and shall apply to "intended product" only.

4 Quality System Requirements

4.1 Management responsibility

4.1.1 Quality policy

The supplier's management ***with executive responsibility for quality*** shall define and document its policy ***for quality including*** objectives for ***quality,*** and commitment to quality. ***The quality policy shall be relevant to the supplier's organizational goals and the expectations and needs of its customers.*** The supplier shall ensure that this policy is understood, implemented, and maintained at all levels in the organization.

4.1.2 Organization

4.1.2.1 Responsibility and authority

The responsibility, authority, and the interrelation of all personnel who manage, perform, and verify work affecting quality shall be defined ***and documented,*** particularly for personnel who need the organizational freedom and authority to:

[1]Currently in preparation.

a) initiate action to prevent the occurrence of ~~product~~ ***any*** nonconformities ***relating to product, process, and quality system;***
b) identify and record any product, ***process, and quality system*** ~~quality~~ problems;
c) initiate, recommend, or provide solutions through designated channels;
d) verify the implementation of solutions;
e) control further processing, delivery, or installation of nonconforming product until the deficiency or unsatisfactory condition has been corrected.

4.1.2.2 ~~Verification resources and personnel~~ *Resources*

The supplier shall identify ~~in-house verification~~ ***resource*** requirements, provide adequate resources, and assign trained personnel ***(see 4.18) for management, performance of work, and*** *verification activities* ***including internal quality audits.***

~~Verification activities shall include inspection, test and monitoring of the design, production, installation and servicing processes and/or product; design reviews and audits of the quality system, processes and/or product shall be carried out by personnel independent of those having direct responsibility for the work being performed.~~

4.1.2.3 Management representative

The supplier***'s management with executive responsibility for quality,*** shall appoint a ***member of its own*** management ~~representative~~ who, irrespective of other responsibilities, shall have defined authority ~~and responsibility~~ for:

a) ensuring that ***quality system requirements are established, implemented, and maintained in accordance with this International Standard;*** ~~the requirements of this International Standard are implemented and maintained.~~

b) reporting on the performance of the quality system to the supplier's management for review and as a basis for improvement of the quality system.

NOTE—The responsibility of a management representative may also include liaison with external bodies on matters relating to the supplier's quality system.

4.1.3 Management review

~~The quality system adopted to satisfy the requirements of this International Standard shall be reviewed at appropriate intervals by the supplier's management to ensure its continuing suitability and effectiveness.~~ ***The supplier's management with executive responsibility for quality shall review the quality system at defined intervals sufficient to ensure its continuing suitability and effectiveness in satisfying the requirements of this International Standard and the supplier's stated quality policy and objectives. (See 4.1.1).*** Records of such reviews shall be maintained (see 4.16).

~~Note Management reviews normally include assessment of the results of internal quality audits, but are carried out by, or on behalf of, the supplier's management, viz management personnel having direct responsibility for the system. (See 4.1.7.)~~

4.2 Quality System

4.2.1 General

The supplier shall establish and maintain a documented quality system as a means of ensuring that product conforms to specified requirements. ~~This shall include:~~

~~a) the preparation of documented quality system procedures and instructions in accordance with the requirements of this International Standard:~~

~~b) the effective implementation of the documented quality system procedures and instructions:~~ ***The outline structure of the documentation covering the quality system requirements of this International Standard shall be defined in a quality manual. The quality manual shall include or reference the documented procedures that form part of the quality system.***

NOTE—Guidance on quality manuals is given in ISO 10013.

~~Note In meeting specified requirements, timely consideration needs to be given to the following activities.~~

~~a) the preparation of quality plans and a quality manual in accordance with the specified requirements:~~

~~b) the identification and acquisition of any controls, processes, inspection equipment, fixtures, total production resources and skills that may be needed to achieve the required quality:~~

~~c) the updating, as necessary, of quality control, inspection and testing techniques, including the development of new instrumentation;~~

~~d) the identification of any measurement requirement involving capability that exceeds the known state of the art in sufficient time for the needed capability to be developed;~~

~~e) the clarification of standards of acceptability for all features and requirements, including those which contain a subject element;~~

~~f) the compatibility of the design, the production process, installation, inspection and test procedures and the applicable documentation;~~

~~g) the identification and preparation of quality records (see 4.16).~~

4.2.2 Quality system procedures

The supplier shall:

a) prepare documented procedures consistent with the requirements of this International Standard and the suppliers stated quality policy,

b) effectively implement the documented procedures and the quality system.

For the purposes of this International Standard the degree of documentation required for the procedures that form part of the quality system shall be dependent upon the methods used, skills needed, and the training acquired by personnel involved in carrying out the activity.

4.2.3 Quality planning

The supplier shall define and document how the requirements for quality will be met. Quality planning shall be consistent with all other requirements of the supplier's quality system and shall be documented in a format to suit the supplier's method of operation. The supplier shall give timely consideration to the following activities, as appropriate, in meeting the specified requirements for products, projects, or contracts:

a) the preparation of quality plans;

b) the identification and acquisition of any controls, processes, inspection equipment, fixtures, total production resources, and skills that may be needed to achieve the required quality;

c) ensuring the compatibility of the design, the production process, installation, servicing, inspection, and test procedures and the applicable documentation;

d) the updating as necessary of quality control, inspection, and testing techniques, including development of new instrumentation;

e) the identification of any measurement requirement involving capability that exceeds the known state of the art in sufficient time for the needed capability to be developed;

f) the identification of suitable verification at appropriate stages in the product realization;

g) the clarification of standards of acceptability of all features and requirements, including those which contain a subjective element;

h) the identification and preparation of quality records (see 4.16).

NOTE—the quality plans referred to (see 4.2.3a) may be in the form of a reference to the appropriate documented procedures that form an integral part of the supplier's quality system.

4.3 Contract review

4.3.1 General

The supplier shall establish and maintain ***documented*** procedures for contract review and for the coordination of these activities.

4.3.2 Review

Each ***accepted tender,*** contract, ***and order (statement of requirement)*** shall be reviewed by the supplier to ensure that:

a) the requirements are adequately defined and documented. ***Where no written statement of requirement is available for an order received by verbal means, the supplier shall ensure that the order requirements are agreed before their acceptance;***

b) any ***contract or accepted order*** requirements differing from those in their tender are resolved;

c) the supplier has the capability to meet contractual ***or accepted order*** requirements.

4.3.3 Amendment to contract

The supplier shall identify how amendment to a contract is made and correctly transferred to functions concerned within the supplier's organization.

4.3.4 Records

Records of such contract reviews shall be maintained (see 4.16).

~~Note The contract review activities, interfaces and communication within the supplier's organization should be coordinated with the purchaser's organization, as appropriate.~~

NOTE 1—Channels for communication and interface with the customer's organization in these contract matters should be established.

NOTE 2—For the purposes of this International Standard, the terms "contract" or "accepted order" are defined as "agreed requirements between a supplier and customer transmitted by any means."

4.4 Design control

4.4.1 General

The supplier shall establish and maintain ***documented*** procedures to control and verify the design of the product in order to ensure that the specified requirements are met.

4.4.2 Design and development planning

~~The supplier shall draw up plans that identify the responsibility for each design and development activity. The plans shall describe or reference these activities and shall be updated as the design evolves.~~

The supplier shall prepare plans for each design and development activity, including defined responsibility, and describe or reference these activities. The design and development activities shall be assigned to qualified personnel equipped with adequate resources. The plans shall be updated, as the design evolves.

~~4.4.2.1 Activity assignment~~

~~The design and verification activities shall be planned and assigned to qualified personnel equipped with adequate resources.~~

~~4.4.2.2~~ *4.4.3* Organizational and technical interfaces

Organizational and technical interfaces between different groups ***which input to the design process*** shall be ~~identified~~ ***defined*** and the necessary information documented, transmitted, and regularly reviewed.

~~4.4.3~~ *4.4.4* Design input

Design*ed* input requirements relating to the product ***including applicable statutory and regulatory requirements*** shall be identified, documented, and their selection reviewed by the supplier for adequacy. Incomplete, ambiguous, or conflicting requirements shall be resolved with those responsible for ~~drawing up~~ ***imposing*** these requirements.

Design input shall take into consideration the results of any contract review activities.

4.4.5 Design review

At appropriate stages of design, formal documented reviews of the design results shall be planned and conducted. Participants at each design review shall include representatives of all functions concerned with the design stage being reviewed as well as other specialist personnel, as required. Records of such reviews shall be maintained (see 4.16).

~~4.4.4~~ *4.4.6* Design output

Design output shall be documented and expressed in terms of requirements ~~calculations and analyses.~~ ***that can be verified.***

Design output shall:

a) meet the design input requirements;

b) contain or reference acceptance criteria;

c) ~~conform to appropriate regulatory requirements whether or not these have been stated in the input information~~ ***identify those characteristics of the design***

that are crucial to the safe and proper functioning of the product, (such as, operating, storage, handling, maintenance, and disposal requirements);

d) ~~identify those characteristics of the design that are crucial to the safe and proper functioning of the product.~~ ***include a review of design output documents before release.***

~~4.4.5~~ *4.4.7* Design verification

~~The supplier shall plan, establish, document and assign to competent personnel functions for verifying the design.~~

~~Design verification shall establish that design output meets the design input requirements (see 4.4.4) by means of design control measures such as:~~

At appropriate stages of design, design verification shall be performed to ensure that the design stage output meets the design stage input requirements. The design verification measures shall be recorded (see 4.16).

NOTE—In addition to conducting design reviews, design verification may include activities such as the following:

~~a) holding and recording design reviews (see 4.16);~~

~~b) undertaking qualification tests and demonstrations;~~

~~c) carrying out alternative calculations:~~

~~d) comparing the new design with a similar proven design, if available.~~

a) performing alternative calculations;

b) comparing the new design with a similar proven design, if available;

c) undertaking tests and demonstrations;

d) reviewing the design stage documents before release.

4.4.8 Design validation

Design validation shall be performed to ensure that product conforms to defined user needs and/or requirements.

NOTE 1—Design validation follows successful design verification (see 4.4.7).

NOTE 2—Validation is normally performed on the final product under defined operating conditions. It may be necessary in earlier stages. Multiple validations may be performed if there are different intended uses.

~~4.4.6~~ *4.4.9* Design changes

~~The supplier shall establish and maintain procedures for the identification, documentation and appropriate review and approval of all changes and modifications.~~

All design changes and modifications shall be identified, documented, reviewed, and approved by authorized personnel before their realization.

4.5 Document *and data* control

4.5.1 General

The supplier shall establish and maintain ***documented*** procedures to control all documents and data that relate to the requirements of the International Standard ***including, to the extent applicable, documents of external origin such as standards and customer drawings.***

NOTE—Documents and data can be in the form of hard copy media, or they can be in electronic or other media.

~~4.5.1~~ *4.5.2* Document approval and issue

~~The supplier shall establish and maintain procedures to control all documents and data that relate to the requirements of this International Standard. These~~ ***The*** documents ***and data*** shall be reviewed and approved for adequacy by authorized personnel prior to issue. ***A master list or equivalent document control procedure identifying the current revision status of documents shall be established and be readily available to preclude the use of invalid and/or obsolete documents.***

~~This~~ *C*ontrol*s* shall ***also*** ensure that:

a) the pertinent issues of appropriate documents are available at all locations where operations essential to the effective functioning of the quality system are performed;
b) ***invalid and/or*** obsolete documents are promptly removed from all points of issue or use, ***or otherwise assured against unintended use;***
c) any obsolete documents retained for legal and/or knowledge preservation purposes are suitably identified.

~~4.5.2~~ *4.5.3* Document changes/~~modifications~~

Changes to documents shall be reviewed and approved by the same functions/organizations that performed the original review and approval unless specifically designated otherwise. The designated ***functions***/organizations shall have access to pertinent background information upon which to base their review and approval.

Where practicable, the nature of the change shall be identified in the document or the appropriate attachments.

~~A master list or equivalent document control procedure shall be established to identify the current revision of documents in order to preclude the use of non-applicable documents.~~

~~Documents shall be re-issued after a practical number of changes have been made.~~

4.6 Purchasing

4.6.1 General

The supplier shall ***establish and maintain document procedure to*** ensure that purchased product ***(see 3.1)*** conforms to specified requirements.

4.6.2 ~~Assessment~~ *Evaluation* of sub-contractors

~~The supplier shall select sub-contractors on the basis of their ability to meet sub-contract requirements, including quality requirements. The supplier shall establish and maintain records of acceptable sub-contractors (see 4.16).~~

~~The selection of sub-contractors, and the type and extent of control exercised by the supplier, shall be dependent upon the type of product and, where appropriate, on records of sub-contractor's previously demonstrated capability and performance.~~

~~The supplier shall ensure that quality system controls are effective.~~

The supplier shall:

a) evaluate and select subcontractors on the basis of their ability to meet sub-contract requirements including quality system and quality assurance requirements;

b) define the type and extent of control exercised by a supplier over sub-contractors. This shall be dependent upon the type of product, the impact of sub-contracted product on the quality of the final product, and, where applicable, on the quality audit reports and/or quality records of sub-contractors' previously demonstrated capability and performance;

c) establish and maintain quality records of acceptable sub-contractors (see 4.16).

4.6.3 Purchasing data

Purchasing documents shall contain data clearly describing the product ordered, including, where applicable,

a) the type, class, ~~style,~~ grade, or other precise identification;

b) the title or other positive identification, and applicable issue of specifications, drawings, process requirements, inspection instructions, and other relevant technical data, including requirements for approval or qualification of product, procedures, process equipment, and personnel;

c) the title, number, and issue of the quality system ~~International~~ Standard to be applied ~~to the product.~~

The supplier shall review and approve purchasing documents for adequacy of specified requirements prior to release.

4.6.4 Verification of purchased product

~~Where specified in the contract, the purchaser or his representative shall be afforded the right to verify at source or upon receipt that purchased product conforms to specified requirements. Verification by the purchaser shall not absolve the supplier of the responsibility to provide acceptable product nor shall it preclude subsequent rejection.~~

~~When the purchaser of his representative elects to carry out verification at the sub-contractor's plant, such verification shall not be used by the suppliers as evidence of effective control of quality by the sub-contractor.~~

4.6.4.1 Supplier verification at sub-contractors

Where the supplier verifies purchased product at the sub-contractor's premises, the supplier shall specify verification arrangements and the method of product release in the purchasing documents.

4.6.4.2 Customer verification of sub-contracted product

Where specified in the contract, the ~~purchaser or his representative~~ ***supplier's customer or representative*** shall be afforded the right to verify at the ***sub-contractor premises and the supplier's premises that the sub-contracted*** product conforms to specified requirements. ***Such verification shall not be used by the supplier as evidence of effective control of quality by the sub-contractor.***

~~Such~~ ***V***erification by the ~~purchaser~~ ***customer*** shall not absolve the supplier of the responsibility to provide acceptable product nor shall it preclude subsequent rejection ***by the customer.***

4.7 *Control of customer* ~~Purchaser~~ supplied product

The supplier shall establish and maintain ***documented*** procedures for verification, storage, and maintenance of ~~purchaser~~ ***customer*** supplied product provided for incorporation into the supplies. Any such product that is lost, damaged, or is otherwise unsuitable for use shall be recorded and reported to the ~~purchaser~~ ***customer*** (see 4.16).

Note—Verification by the supplier does not absolve the ~~purchaser~~ ***customer*** of the responsibility to provide acceptable product.

4.8 Product identification and traceability

Where appropriate, the supplier shall establish and maintain ***documented*** procedures for identifying the product ***by suitable means*** from ~~applicable drawings,~~

~~specifications or other documents,~~ ***receipt and*** during all stages of production, delivery, and installation.

Where, and to the extent that, traceability is a specified requirement, ***the supplier shall establish and maintain documented procedures for unique identification*** of individual product or batches. ~~shall have a unique identification.~~ This identification shall be recorded (see 4.16).

4.9 Process control

4.9.1 General

The supplier shall identify and plan the production and, where applicable, installation, ***and servicing*** processes which directly affect quality and shall ensure that these processes are carried out under controlled conditions. Controlled conditions shall include the following:

a) documented ~~work instructions~~ ***procedures*** defining the manner of production, ~~and~~ installation, ***and servicing,*** where the absence of such instructions would adversely affect quality;

b) use of suitable production, ~~and~~ installation, ***and servicing*** equipment, suitable working environment;

c) compliance with reference standards/codes, ~~and~~ quality plans, ***quality plans, and/or documented procedures;***

~~b~~)d) monitoring and control of suitable process ***parameters*** and product characteristics during production, ~~and~~ installation, ***and servicing;***

~~c~~)e) the approval of processes and equipment, as appropriate;

~~d~~)f) criteria for workmanship which shall be stipulated, ~~to the greatest practicable extent~~ in ***the clearest practical manner e.g.,*** ~~in~~ written standards, ~~or by means of~~ representative samples ***or illustrations;***

g) suitable maintenance of equipment to ensure continuing process capability.

~~4.9.2 Special processes~~ [This subheading deleted]

~~These are~~ ***P***rocesses, the results of which cannot be fully verified by subsequent inspection and testing of the product and where, for example, processing deficiencies may become apparent only after the product is in use ***shall be carried out by qualified operators and/or require continuous monitoring and control of process parameters to ensure that the specified requirements are met.*** ~~Accordingly, continuous monitoring and or compliance with documented procedures is required to ensure that the specified requirements are met. These processes shall be qualified and shall also comply with the requirements of 4.9.1.~~

NOTE—Such processes requiring pre-qualification of their process capability are frequently referred to as special processes.

The requirements for any qualification of process operations including associated equipment and personnel (see 4.18) shall be specified.

Records shall be maintained for qualified processes, equipment, and personnel, as appropriate.

4.10 Inspection and testing

4.10.1 General

The supplier shall establish and maintain documented procedures for inspection and testing activities in order to verify that the specified requirements for product are met. The required inspection and testing, and the records to be established, shall be documented in the quality plan or documented procedures.

~~4.10.1~~ *4.10.2* Receiving inspection and testing

~~4.10.1.1~~ ***4.10.2.1*** The supplier shall ensure that incoming product is not used or processed (except in the circumstances described in ~~4.10.1.2~~

4.10.2.3) until it has been inspected or otherwise verified as conforming to specified requirements. Verification ***of the specified requirements*** shall be in accordance with the quality plan ***and***/or documented procedures.

4.10.2.2 In determining the amount and nature of receiving inspection, consideration shall be given to the amount of control exercised at the sub-contractor's premises and the recorded evidence of conformance provided.

~~4.10.1.2~~ ***4.10.2.3*** Where incoming product is released for urgent production purposes ***prior to verification,*** it shall be positively identified and recorded (see 4.16) in order to permit immediate recall and replacement in the event of nonconformance to specified requirements.

~~**NOTE** In determining the amount and nature of receiving inspection, consideration shall be given to the control exercised at source and documented evidence of quality conformance provided.~~

~~4.10.2~~ *4.10.3* In-process inspection and testing

The supplier shall

a) inspect, test, and identify product as required by the quality plan ***and***/or documented procedures;

~~b) establish product conformance to specified requirements by use of process monitoring and control methods;~~

~~c~~ ***b)*** hold product until the required inspection and tests have been completed or necessary reports have been received and verified except when product is released under positive recall procedures (see ~~4.10.1~~ ***4.10.2.3)***. Release under positive recall procedures shall not preclude the activities outlined in ~~4.10.2~~ ***4.10.3a).***

~~d) identify nonconforming product.~~

~~4.10.3~~ *4.10.4* Final inspection and testing

This paragraph and the next have swapped places.

The supplier shall carry out all final inspection and testing in accordance with the quality plan ***and***/or documented procedures to complete the evidence of conformance of the finished product to the specified requirements.

The quality plan ***and***/or documented procedures for final inspection and testing shall require that all specified inspection and tests, including those specified either on receipt of product or in-process, have been carried out and that the data meets specified requirements.

No product shall be dispatched until all the activities specified in the quality plan ***and***/or documented procedures have been satisfactorily completed and the associated data and documentation is available and authorized.

~~4.10.4~~ *4.10.5* Inspection and test records

The supplier shall establish and maintain records which ~~give evidence that the product has passed inspection and/or test with defined acceptance criteria (see 4.16).~~ ***provide evidence that the product has been inspected and/or tested. These records shall show clearly whether the product passed or failed the inspections and/or tests according to defined acceptance criteria. Where the product fails to pass any inspection and/or test, the procedures for control of non-conforming product shall apply (See 4.13).***

Records shall identify the inspection authority responsible for the release of product (See 4.16.)

4.11 *Control of* inspection, measuring and test equipment

4.11.1 General

The supplier shall ***establish and maintain documented procedures to*** control, calibrate, and maintain inspection, measuring, and test equipment ***(including test software) used by the supplier,*** ~~whether owned by the supplier, on loan, or provided by the purchaser,~~ to demonstrate the conformance of product to the specified requirements. ***Inspection, measuring, and test e***quipment shall be used in a manner which ensures that measurement uncertainty is known and is consistent with the required measurement capability.

Where test software or comparative references such as test hardware is used as suitable forms of inspection they shall be checked, to prove that they are capable of verifying the acceptability of product, prior to release for use during production, installation, or servicing and shall be re-checked at prescribed intervals. The

supplier shall establish the extent and frequency of such checks and shall maintain records as evidence of control (See 4.16).

Where and to the extent that the availability of technical data pertaining to the measurement devices is a specified requirement, such data shall be made available, when required by the customer or customer's representative, for verification that the devices are functionally adequate.

This section is replaced by that which follows: ~~— The supplier shall~~

~~a) identify the measurements to be made, the accuracy required and select the appropriate inspection, measuring and test equipment;~~

~~b) identify, calibrate and adjust all inspection, measuring and test equipment and devices that can affect product quality at prescribed intervals, or prior to use against certified equipment having a known valid relationship to nationally recognized standards where no such standards exist, the basis used for calibration shall be documented;~~

~~c) establish, document and maintain calibration procedures, including details of equipment type, identification number, location frequency of checks, check method, acceptance criteria and the action to be taken when results are unsatisfactory;~~

~~d) ensure that the inspection, measuring and test equipment is capable of the accuracy and precision necessary;~~

~~e) identify inspection, measuring and test equipment with a suitable indicator or approved identification record to show the calibration status;~~

~~f) maintain calibration records for inspection, measuring and test equipment (see 4.16);~~

~~g) assess and document the validity of previous inspection and test results when inspection, measuring and test equipment is found to be out of calibration;~~

~~h) ensure that the environmental conditions are suitable for the calibrations, inspections, measurements and tests being carried out;~~

~~i) ensure that the handling, preservation and storage of inspection, measuring and test equipment is such that the accuracy and fitness for use is maintained;~~

~~j) safeguard inspection, measuring and test facilities, including both test hardware and test software, from adjustments which would invalidate the calibration setting.~~

~~Where test hardware (e.g. jigs, fixtures, templates, patterns) or test software is used as suitable forms of inspection, they shall be checked to prove that they are capable of verifying the acceptability of product prior to release for use during production and installation and shall be rechecked at prescribed intervals. The supplier shall establish the extent and frequency of such checks and shall maintain records as evidence of control (see 4.16). Measurement design data shall be made available, when required by the purchaser or his representative, for verification that it is functionally adequate.~~

4.11.2 Control procedure

The supplier shall:

a) ***determine the measurements to be made, the accuracy required, and select the appropriate inspection, measuring, and test equipment that is capable of the accuracy and precision necessary;***

b) ***identify all inspection, measuring, and test equipment including measurement devices that can affect product quality and calibrate and adjust them at prescribed intervals, or prior to use, against certified equipment having a known valid relationship to internationally or nationally recognized Standards. Where no such Standards exist, the basis used for calibration shall be documented;***

c) ***define the process employed for the calibration of inspection, test, and measuring equipment including details of equipment type, unique identification, location, frequency of checks, check method, acceptance criteria, and the action to be taken when the results are unsatisfactory;***

d) ***identify inspection, measuring, and test equipment with a suitable indicator or approved identification record to show the calibration status;***

e) ***maintain calibration records for inspection, measuring, and test equipment (see 4.16);***

f) ***assess and document the validity of previous inspection and test results when inspection, measuring, and test equipment is found to be out of calibration;***

g) ***ensure that the environmental conditions are suitable for the calibration, inspections, measurements, and tests being carried out;***

h) ***ensure that handling, preservation, and storage of inspection, measuring, and test equipment is such that accuracy and fitness for use is maintained;***

i) ***safeguard inspection, measuring, and test facilities, including both the test hardware and test software, from adjustments which should invalidate the calibration setting.***

NOTE—The quality assurance requirements for measuring equipment given in ISO 10012 may be used for guidance.

4.12 Inspection and test status

The inspection and test status of product shall be identified by ~~using markings, authorized stamps, tags, labels, routing cards, inspection records, test software, physical location or other~~ suitable means, which indicates the conformance or nonconformance of product with regard to inspection and tests performed. The identification of inspection and test status shall be maintained, as ~~necessary~~ ***defined in the quality plan and/or documented procedures,*** throughout production, ~~and~~ installation, ***and servicing*** of the product to ensure that only product that has passed the required inspections and tests ***(or released under an authorized concession (see 4.13.2)*** is dispatched, used, or installed.

~~Records shall identify the inspection authority responsible for the release of conforming product (see 4.16).~~

4.13 Control of nonconforming product

4.13.1 General

The supplier shall establish and maintain ***documented*** procedures to ensure that product that does not conform to specified requirements is prevented from ~~inadvertent~~ ***unintended*** use or installation. Control shall provide for identification, documentation, evaluation, segregation (when practical), disposition of nonconforming product, and for notification to the functions concerned.

4.13.1 Nonconformity review and disposition

The responsibility for review and authority for the disposition of nonconforming product shall be defined. Nonconforming product shall be reviewed in accordance with documented procedures. It may be

a) reworked to meet the specified requirements, or
b) accepted with or without repair by concession, or
c) re-graded for alternative applications, or
d) rejected or scrapped

Where required by the contract, the proposed use or repair of product [see ~~4.13~~ ***4.13.2***b)] which does not conform to specified requirements shall be reported for concession to the ~~purchaser or his~~ ***customer or customer's*** representative. The description of nonconformity that has been accepted, and of repairs, shall be recorded to denote the actual condition (see 4.16).

Repaired and***/or*** reworked product shall be re-inspected in accordance with ***the quality plan and/or*** documented procedures requirements.

4.14 Corrective *and preventive* action

This section is replaced by that which follows: ~~The supplier shall establish, document and maintain procedures for:~~

~~a) investigating the cause of nonconforming product and the corrective action needed of prevent recurrence;~~

~~b) analyzing all processes, work operations, concessions, quality records, service reports and customer complaints to detect and eliminate potential causes of nonconforming product;~~

~~c) initiating preventative actions to deal with problems to a level corresponding to the risks encountered;~~

~~d) applying controls to ensure that corrective actions are taken and that they are effective;~~

~~e) implementing and recording changes in procedures resulting from corrective action;~~

4.14.1 General

The supplier shall establish and maintain documented procedures for implementing corrective and preventive action.

Any corrective or preventive action taken to eliminate the causes of actual or potential nonconformities shall be to a degree appropriate to the magnitude of problems and commensurate to the risks encountered.

The supplier shall implement and record any changes to the documented procedures resulting from corrective and preventive action.

4.14.2 Corrective action

The procedures for corrective action shall include:

a) the effective handling of customer complaints and reports of product nonconformities;

b) investigating the cause of nonconformities relating to product, process, and quality system and recording the results of the investigation (see 4.16).

c) determining the corrective action needed to eliminate the cause of nonconformities;

d) applying controls to ensure that corrective action is taken and that it is effective.

4.14.3 Preventive action

The procedures for preventive action shall include:

a) the use of appropriate sources of information such as processes and work operations which affect product quality, concessions, audit results, quality records, service reports, and customer complaints to detect, analyze, and eliminate potential causes of nonconformities;

b) determining the steps needed to deal with any problems requiring preventive action;

c) initiating preventive action and applying controls to ensure that it is effective;

d) ensuring that relevant information on actions taken including changes to procedures is submitted for management review (see 4.1.3).

4.15 Handling, storage, packaging, *preservation*, and delivery

4.15.1 General

The supplier shall establish, ~~document~~ and maintain ***documented*** procedures for handling, storage, packaging, ***preservation,*** and delivery of product.

4.15.2 Handling

The supplier shall provide methods ~~and means~~ of handling ***product*** that prevent damage or deterioration.

4.15.3 Storage

The supplier shall ~~provide secure~~ ***use designated*** storage areas or stock rooms to prevent damage or deterioration of product, pending use or delivery. Appropriate methods for authorizing receipt and the dispatch to and from such areas shall be stipulated.

In order to detect deterioration, the condition of product in stock shall be assessed at appropriate intervals.

4.15.4 Packaging

The supplier shall control packing, packaging, and marking processes (including materials used) to the extent necessary to ensure conformance to specified requirements. ~~and shall identify, preserve and segregate all product from the time of receipt until the supplier's responsibility ceases.~~

4.15.5 Preservation

Appropriate methods for preservation and segregation of product shall be applied when such product is under the supplier's control.

~~4.15.5~~ *4.15.6* Delivery

The supplier shall arrange for the protection of the quality of product after final inspection and test. Where contractually specified, this protection shall be extended to include delivery to destination.

4.16 *Control of* Quality *records*

The supplier shall establish and maintain ***documented*** procedures for identification, collection, indexing, access, filing, storage, maintenance, and disposition of quality records.

Quality records shall be maintained to demonstrate ~~achievement of the required quality~~ ***conformance to specified requirements*** and the effective operation of the quality system. Pertinent sub-contractor quality records shall be an element of these data.

All quality records shall be legible and ~~identifiable to the product involved. Quality records~~ shall be stored and ~~maintained~~ ***retained*** in such a way that they are readily retrievable in facilities that provide a suitable environment to minimize deterioration or damage and to prevent loss. Retention times of quality records shall be established and recorded. Where agreed contractually, quality records shall be made available for evaluation by the ~~purchaser~~ ***customer*** or his representative for an agreed period.

NOTE—Records can be in the form of hard copy media, or they can be in electronic or other media.

4.17 Internal quality audits

~~The supplier shall carry out a comprehensive system of planned and documented internal quality audits to verify whether quality activities comply with planned arrangements and to determine the effectiveness of the quality system.~~

The supplier shall establish and maintain documented procedures for planning and implementing internal quality audits to verify whether quality activities and related results comply with planned arrangements and to determine the effectiveness of the quality system.

Internal quality audits shall be scheduled on the basis of the status and importance of the activity ***to be audited and shall be carried out by personnel independent of those having direct responsibility for the activity being audited.***

~~The audits and follow-up actions shall be carried out in accordance with documented procedures.~~

The results of the audits shall be ~~documented~~ ***recorded (see 4.16)*** and brought to the attention of the personnel having responsibility in the area audited. The management personnel responsible for the area shall take time corrective action on the deficiencies found during the audit ~~(see 4.1.3)~~.

Follow-up activities shall record the implementation and effectiveness of the corrective action taken (see 4.16).

NOTE 1—The results of internal quality audits form an integral part of management review activities (see 4.1.3).

NOTE 2—Guidance on quality system audits is given in ISO 10011.

4.18 Training

The supplier shall establish and maintain ***documented*** procedures for identifying ~~the~~ training needs and provide for the training of all personnel performing activities affecting quality. Personnel performing specific assigned tasks shall be qualified on the basis of appropriate education, training and/or experience, as required. Appropriate records of training shall be maintained (see 4.16).

4.19 Servicing

Where servicing is ~~specified in the contract~~ ***a specified requirement,*** the supplier shall establish and maintain ***documented*** procedures for performing ***these services and for reporting*** and verifying that ~~servicing~~ ***such services*** meet ~~the specified~~ ***these*** requirements.

4.20 Statistical techniques

~~Where appropriate, the supplier shall establish procedures for identifying adequate statistical techniques required for verifying the acceptability of process capability and product characteristics.~~

4.20.1 Identification of need

The supplier shall identify the need for statistical techniques required for establishing, controlling, and verifying process capability and product characteristics.

4.20.2 Procedures

The supplier shall establish and maintain documented procedures to implement and control the application of statistical techniques identified in 4.20.1.

Annex A (informative)

References

ISO 9000-1: 1993(1)	***Quality Management and quality assurance standards*** ***Part 1: Guidelines for selection and use***
ISO 9002: 1993(1)	***Quality systems—Model for quality assurance in production, installation and servicing***
ISO 9003: 1993(1)	***Quality systems—Model for quality assurance in final inspection and test***
ISO 10011-1: 1990	***Guidelines for auditing quality systems*** ***Part 1: Auditing***
ISO 10011-2: 1991	***Guidelines for auditing quality systems*** ***Part 2: Qualification criteria for quality system auditors***

ISO 10011-3: 1991	***Guidelines for auditing quality systems*** ***Part 3: Management of audit programs***
ISO 10012-1: 1992	***Quality assurance requirements for measuring equipment*** ***Part 1: Metrological qualification system for measuring equipment***
ISO 10013: 1993(1)	***Guidelines for developing quality manuals***

(1) Currently in preparation.

part

6

TQM-Related Frameworks and Implementation Issues

Readings in this section address diverse implementation issues and TQM-related issues and frameworks like the assessment of the cost of quality and concurrent engineering. One of the papers also focuses on techniques for increased "customer sensitivity," one of the key tenets of the quality movement and a critical linkage with the marketing function.

During the fifties, American pioneers like Deming, Juran, and Feigenbaum profoundly influenced the quality movement, and delineated systems that were widely implemented in Japanese industry. During the '60s, '70s, and '80s, the quality movement became strongly influenced by Japanese thinking and experience, and the so-called Japanese management style, which is based on participative decision-making. One of the readings focuses on the historic origins of Japanese practices like lifelong employment and management-labor cooperation. The author addresses the question of whether these practices are contemporary post-WWII developments or deeply rooted in Japanese culture. This question is key to the problem of cross-cultural transfer of management experience.

Reading 30

Becoming Customer Oriented

By Mary Lou Roberts

In the late 1960s and early 1970s American automobile makers ignored the desire of their customers for economical, reliable cars and thus triggered a decades-long decline in market share.

Mass-market retailers including Sears and Montgomery Ward ignored changing consumer demographics, lifestyles, and tastes and opened the way for the success of new entrants such as Kmart and later Wal-Mart.

Federal Express created a new industry by offering customers guaranteed overnight delivery of small packages even though the founder was assured that this business concept was not viable.

McDonald's revolutionized the fast food industry by promising that customers would always receive "Quality, Service, Cleanliness, and Value" beneath the golden arches.

These and many other examples highlight the importance of being attuned to not only what the customer demands of today's products and services but also what the customer will want and need in the marketplace of tomorrow. Meeting customer wants and needs is one of the cornerstones of the quality approach. Simple as this may sound, it is difficult to do on a consistent basis. The larger the company becomes, and the further management is removed from direct customer contact, the harder it is. Becoming—and remaining—customer oriented requires effort and discipline just like any other aspect of TQM. In this chapter we will discuss both the philosophy and the techniques required to be truly customer oriented.

Source: 1992 report reprinted with the permission of the author.

A FEW WORDS ABOUT TERMINOLOGY

Before we look at a formal definition of the concept of "customer orientation," it is important to clarify the meaning of a number of terms that will be used in the chapter. Many of them are used inconsistently in the literature of marketing and quality, and confusion results.

In this chapter the term *customer* is used in its broadest sense. It encompasses both internal and external, consumer and industrial, product and service, purchaser and user, intermediary and final. Or to put it another way, everyone who produces any kind of economic good has customers who either add value and pass the good on to the next customer or who are final consumers or users of the good. By the same reasoning, virtually all workers are suppliers to one or more customers, either internal or external. In this chapter we will focus primarily on the external customer, but virtually everything that we say also applies to understanding and satisfying internal customers.

In discussions of marketing and quality there is some controversy over whether the terms *customer orientation* and *market orientation* are the same, or whether *market orientation* has a broader meaning. In this chapter we will use them synonymously.

The term *product* can be another source of confusion. Here again we will use the broadest interpretation. Unless otherwise specified, *product* will be used to mean both tangible goods and intangible services. In this context, it is irrelevant whether the goods and services are produced by for-profit or not-for-profit organizations.

Another term that we will use broadly in this chapter is *research.* In a business setting the term *research* usually implies a formal process with an outcome that is frequently expressed in quantitative terms, although qualitative research is recognized as appropriate in many circumstances. In discussions of quality we frequently hear the term *listening to the customer.* While there is no formal definition of this term, it is often inclusive of formal research, both quantitative and qualitative, and of a variety of less formal techniques for obtaining customer feedback. Consequently, it is really the preferred term, but it can lead to some very awkward sentences. In this chapter, we use the word *research* to include any method of obtaining feedback from the customer.

With these issues of terminology in mind, let's begin by looking at what it means to be customer oriented.

WHAT IS "CUSTOMER ORIENTED"?

For many years marketers have been exhorting businesses to base their activities on a thorough understanding of the wants and needs of their customers. Levitt (1960, 1975) was among the first. He faulted businesses for unjustified reliance on the belief that constantly increasing population or decreased costs achieved through cost-cutting and economies of scale or lack of substitute products would assure continuous growth and profits. He argued that an industry is "a customer-satisfying process, not a goods-producing process" (1975, p. 174).

More recently the consulting firm McKinsey and Company set out to study the strategies and management practices of successful firms. According to Peters and Waterman,

> When we started our survey, we expected to find the excellent companies putting stress on cost or technology or markets or niches. In other words, we felt some would have strategies oriented to one thing, and some to another, but we weren't expecting any particular bias. But that is not what we found. While there are differences among industries, we did find a striking commonality: The excellent companies tend to be more driven by close-to-the-customer attributes than by either technology or cost (p. 186).

Being customer oriented is critical to the success of any business in any industry at any time. While technology or fad may seem to take precedence at some points in time, over the long term the business must create products and services and market them in a way that satisfies their customers.

Customer orientation plays an additional role in a firm that is actively engaged in a TQM program. Improving internal processes is a critical part of TQM. It can all too easily become the central focus of the program. A genuine customer focus, one that has become institutionalized within the organization, continually draws attention back to the customer's wants and needs. Without the constant pressure to meet marketplace needs, businesses are in danger of improving a product or process that no one wants!

Granted then, customer orientation is critical. A formal definition is still needed. A recent definition by Kohli and Jaworski seems to capture the essence, even though they use the term *market orientation*. They describe it as:

> The organization-wide **generation** of market intelligence pertaining to current and future customer needs, **dissemination** of the intelligence across departments, and organization-wide **responsiveness** to it (p. 6).

This definition has three key aspects that cause it to tie in very well with TQM practices. First, it speaks of **market intelligence,** a broad term that includes not only data from formal research but also a variety of less formal techniques for listening to the customer that will be discussed in the third section of this chapter. Second, it highlights the importance of **dissemination** of intelligence findings throughout the organization. A necessary prerequisite for TQM success is that information be shared widely within the organization, not hoarded by one person or department. Third, this definition requires organizational **responsiveness** to information about customer wants and needs. Information is not produced for its own sake. Research reports are not written to gather dust on some office shelf. Customer views are not solicited and then ignored as the firm continues doing what it prefers to do. Instead, the customer and the market environment are the focal point of organizational decision making.

For this to be accomplished most firms must make two changes in the way they have typically operated. First, the monitoring of the customer and the market environment must be **continuous.** Most firms view formal marketing research from a project perspective. A project is specified, executed, and a report is made to management. Management acts or doesn't act, but the project is completed. Perhaps it is followed up with another project in a few months. Perhaps it is even repeated (or in research terms replicated) at a later time to see what has changed. However frequently or infrequently research is conducted, the basic orientation is that of discrete projects.

The market intelligence that drives the quality process must be viewed differently. It must be a continuous process of listening, documenting, analyzing, sharing, and acting. It must be an integral part of the manner in which the firm operates. It must be considered a necessity, not a postponable discretionary item or a luxury.

Second, the customer-oriented firm must make decisions cross-functionally in a spirit of cooperation, not competitiveness (Shapiro, 1988). Integrated decision making allows various viewpoints and types of expertise to be incorporated into the decision. It goes a long way toward achieving buy-in on the part of all persons and departments that have a stake in the decision outcome. It also accomplishes something else that is increasingly important in today's globally competitive economy. Cross-functional decision making is necessary to speed products and services to market. It helps to avoid redesign, rework, and more generally the NIH (Not Invented Here) syndrome that can make the introduction of new products and processes agonizingly slow. In an age of ever-shorter product life cycles the organizational disunity that stems from narrow functional perspectives cannot be tolerated.

Before looking at, first, the process of becoming customer oriented and then research and listening techniques that are necessary to achieve and maintain customer orientation, it is important to recognize the danger of becoming bogged down in technique. **Customer orientation is first and foremost a business philosophy**—a way of looking at the world. It requires focusing outward, not inward. It requires always keeping customer wants and needs at the center of decision-making activities. It demands a genuine commitment to satisfying the customer no matter how much effort is required. Without this kind of outlook, focus—and perhaps even obsession—a firm cannot be customer oriented, no matter what techniques it employs.

THE PROCESS OF BECOMING CUSTOMER ORIENTED

Few businesses are really customer oriented. Therefore, the assumption is that we must take an existing firm and transform it. At the same time we make this assumption, it is important to point out that these same principles apply to starting a business that is customer oriented from the beginning. This is one of the few areas in which the entrepreneur has an easier task than the manager in an existing business. It is easier to create a new organization than to turn around an existing culture. However, most of us are faced with the job of instilling customer orientation where it does not now exist. We need to recognize this task as a process of organizational change, one that requires great thought and effort and that will undoubtedly encounter resistance along the way from people who simply do not want to change the way in which they are accustomed to doing things. A planned process, not an overnight transformation, must be undertaken.

Figure 30.1 is a fishbone model that specifies the steps that are necessary to drive the process of becoming customer oriented. This process begins with management commitment, requires training and customer research, continues by establishing standards and benchmarks, empowers employees, provides technology if necessary, and gives rewards and recognition in order to achieve a customer oriented organization. Let's take a brief look at each step in the process.

Management commitment and actions

Being customer oriented is not easy. It isn't always neat and structured because it introduces people with their hopes, fears, and aspirations into the business equation.

FIGURE 30.1 *The process of becoming customer oriented*

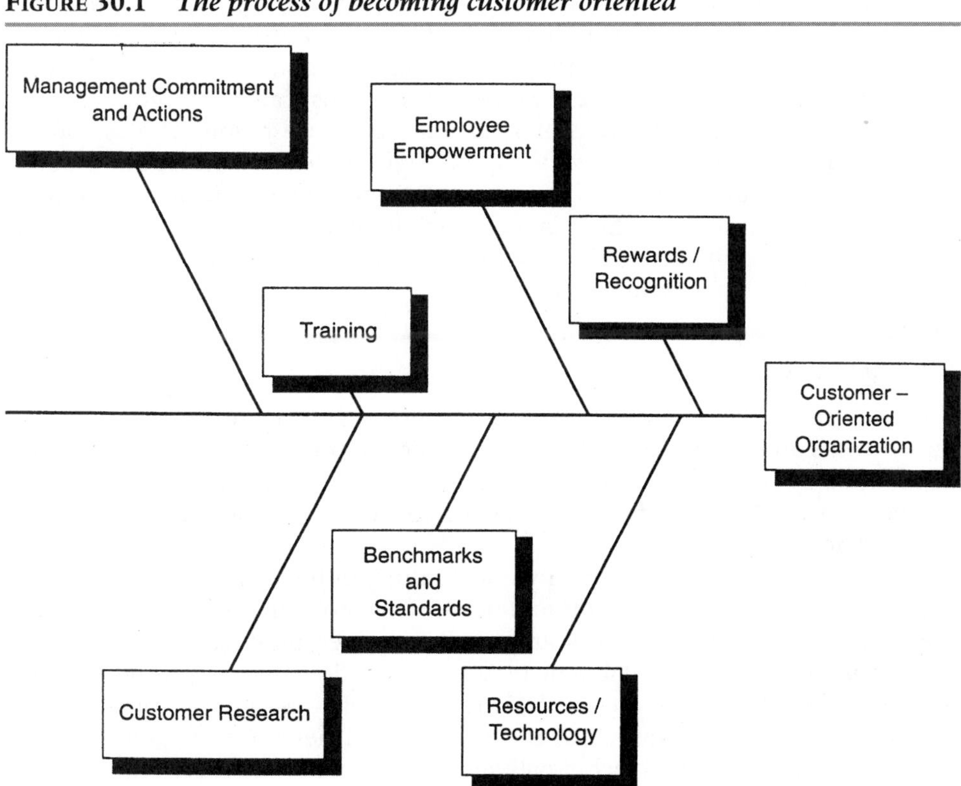

Perhaps most important of all, it is often in conflict with the training and preferred modes of behavior of people educated in narrow technical specializations in management, engineering, and the sciences. To overcome all these barriers strong and persistent support from management, especially those at the very top, is essential.

As in all aspects of the TQM process, management must be genuinely committed and must demonstrate its commitment by actions, not by words alone. In the next section you should recognize that there are a number of the "research" activities in which management can be actively involved. Managers can take a turn on customer service telephone lines and can, and should, participate in customer visits. When formal research is involved, upper management can demonstrate concern by attending presentations. Most important of all, however, managers from top to bottom must see that information about customers is available and used in all decision making. No amount of customer data can take the place of constant pressure from management to make satisfaction of customer wants and needs the primary criterion for all decisions.

Training

Training in all aspects of TQM is a vital part of the process. In addition to training in group dynamics and problem-solving techniques, most groups of employees need training in customer research techniques. Again, it should be clear from the wide variety of techniques described in the third section that some techniques require more training than others. Some of the sophisticated techniques such as quantitative research or analysis of a customer database require the use of specialists. Many of the others, however, require lower levels of skills and training and can be made available to all employees. It is desirable for front-line employees to collect as much customer data as possible themselves. Not only does that data have great credibility to these same front-line personnel but it is also more likely to be available in a timely fashion.

Customer research

Customer research must begin early in the process. It seems obvious that customer wants and needs cannot be satisfied if decision makers do not have a clear understanding of what they are. Continuous data is required, however, to keep decisions focused on *real* wants and needs, not what decision-makers *think* customers want and need.

A perplexing problem, to which we will return in the third section, is how to anticipate customer's *future* wants and needs. This problem is compounded when the satisfaction of future wants and needs involves products or technologies which may not yet be available or may not be understood by prospective customers. Conventional research techniques, especially quantitative ones, are not particularly helpful in illuminating the future in sufficient detail to guide decision making. Insight-generating techniques and creative applications are required. This is another good reason to engage as many minds as possible—including those of front-line personnel—in the search for the successful products and services of the future.

Benchmarks and standards

The activity of benchmarking is a commonly accepted part of TQM. It involves locating the best practices in the industry or in performing a particular business function and measuring performance against them. Benchmarking against the best is a powerful stimulus to improved performance. Benchmarks can range from length of time required to produce a specific product to number of acceptable rings before a telephone call is answered. They are useful operational measures, but some have little direct impact on the satisfaction of customer wants and needs. Production cycle time is invisible to many customers. Number of telephone rings may be only a minor point; more important is whether the person who answers can deal with the caller's issue.

Standards are objectives that are set by the firm on the basis of customer expectations and behavior. They come into play in two instances. One is when the firm cannot find best practices that are similar enough to use as benchmarks or when competitors will not release the data. The second is when the issue is more closely related to customer expectations than to operational feasibility. It is theoretically possible to answer all telephone calls on the first ring. It is almost certain, first, that answering all calls on the first ring would be prohibitively expensive and, second, that it would not make much difference in overall customer satisfaction. The answers to questions like "how many rings are too many" and "how long are customers willing to wait for the shipment of a particular product" can be obtained, although often not by a single direct question. When customer expectations are measured, they can be used to establish standards. It then becomes a business decision as to whether setting standards that simply satisfy customer expectations is sufficient or whether it is worthwhile to exceed expectations and thereby delight the customer.

Employee empowerment

In the last few years empowerment has become a fashionable term, one that is often used loosely. Yet, we should not let this trendiness mask the potential of the concept. Empowerment implies pushing decision making down to the lowest possible level. More specifically it means giving teams or individual employees power to make customer-satisfying decisions. In a production setting this can mean giving every employee on the assembly line the authority to stop the line if quality is outside acceptable boundaries. In a service setting, it can mean giving frontline personnel the authority to satisfy most customer requests or solve problems on the spot without recourse to a supervisor.

It has become a truism that employees "on the line" have ready answers to many problems that elude management because they deal with those problems on a daily basis and often are frustrated by their lack of resolution. Giving the people who know best the power to resolve problems, again, sounds rather easy. In practice it is incredibly difficult. It means that managers and supervisors must relinquish decision-making power, which previously has been their prerogative. To say that managers and supervisors are often reluctant to do this is a gross understatement.

TECHNOLOGY AND OTHER ORGANIZATIONAL RESOURCES

Empowered employees must also have the resources they need to perform their tasks effectively. Many of the resources that lead directly to the satisfaction of customer wants and needs do involve use of the latest technology. Production workers may need automated equipment or on-line access to computerized information at their own work stations. Customer service workers often require direct access to multiple databases of customer and product information. This may call for large up-front investments in technology. Sometimes the technology is unproven. Often its payback is difficult to quantify. Even so, thoughtful investments in technology can make workers more productive and can provide customer-pleasing products and levels of customer service that are difficult for competitors to duplicate.

At the same time, management should not overlook the possibility that decidedly low-tech resources may better meet requirements. There is no substitute for a trained, empowered, and genuinely concerned human being to help customers identify and solve problems. Anyone who has become entangled in an endless web of automated telephone instructions with no human intervention in sight can attest to the fact that technology, though it is vital in many applications, is not always an unmixed blessing. The greatest customer frustrations occur when technology is mindlessly substituted for human concern and judgment.

Rewards and recognition

Rewards and recognition of both individuals and teams are also standard operating procedures in TQM. They should be used to acknowledge increased productivity and also to acknowledge "softer," less easily measurable successes in achieving satisfied customers. Quality planning should deal with two issues; what to reward and what kinds of rewards to bestow.

It is wise to begin with the premise that everyone who participates in the quality process should be recognized in some manner. This is easy to do in the beginning; as time goes on and numbers grow it may take a little more effort. The approach here is to celebrate the firm's quality progress and to thank all who have contributed. It presents an excellent opportunity to gather people together and to involve top management in not only celebrating achievements but also reinforcing the vision and the momentum of the quality process. While there should be a definite social aspect to this gathering, there should also be a clear linkage to the quality process. Many firms use the occasion to present awards to teams or individuals and to have presentations based on award-winning efforts.

Very different from the celebratory approach is the increasingly frequent practice of encouraging employees at all levels to acquire stock in the firm and take a proprietary attitude toward its success. Employees in firms from Wal-Mart to Polaroid to Avis have significant ownership stakes. Avis has used this in advertising to give credibility to their claims of excellent customer service. The merits of this approach seem obvious, but by itself employee ownership may not be sufficient to motivate excellent performance. In addition, many organizations do not have the ability to provide for employee ownership. Many, in fact, complain that they have little in the way of tangible (translate that monetary) awards to give.

All organizations can, however, recognize excellence. The recognition can be a certificate, a reserved parking space, a letter of commendation, time off, being singled out for additional training, or something more creative. If the tribute is genuine and sincere, it will be effective. Quality planning must treat reward and recognition as an important strategic issue, no matter how large or how small the pool of resources devoted to it.

These, then, are the activities necessary to create a customer-oriented firm. Each may receive more or less emphasis at various times but they are all essential. Again, however, their focus will be inappropriate if the customer is not always at the center of both planning and execution. We must, then, provide an overview of the techniques that will help accomplish that customer centrality.

RESEARCH APPROACHES

In deciding what kind of research activity is best to meet a particular need, quality planners should use several criteria. These include the cost and time required by the techniques under consideration and the expertise required to collect the data, analyze it, and prepare a presentation. Whether team members are doing the research themselves or whether they can use staff members or external service bureaus to conduct the research is also important. These considerations can become complex and are clearly beyond the scope of this chapter, but the references provided at the end will be helpful to the neophyte. In this chapter we will approach the subject of research only from the perspective of how it can contribute to the quality process.

Figure 30.2 presents a comprehensive listing of research techniques that are useful in the context of TQM. They are loosely grouped into three categories that reflect the timeliness of the data gathered by each technique. It is also worth remembering that the more complex the technique the longer it may take to analyze the data and therefore the greater the time before it can be incorporated into the decision-making process.

Early signals and in-depth understanding of the customer

The first category has been labeled "insight generating." The techniques in this group can produce useful ideas or insights. These ideas or insights are rarely quantified, at

FIGURE 30.2 *Overview of customer research approaches*

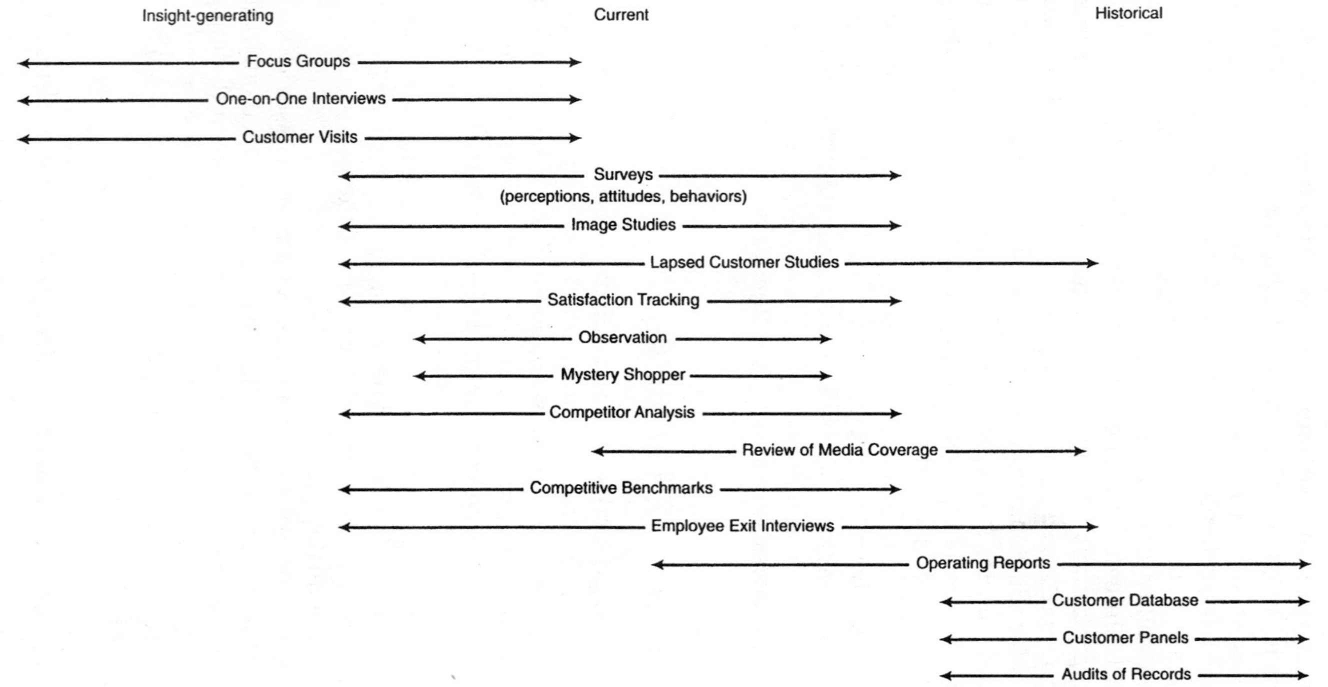

least at this point. They are sometimes vague and in need of refinement through further data gathering and analysis. However, the insights produced by this set of techniques probably would not be achieved by the exclusive use of approaches in the other two categories.

It is extremely important to recognize that these "insights" are a type of leading indicator. They may provide a warning of looming customer dissatisfaction or competitive activity long before marketplace indicators such as market share or other research techniques would uncover them. They may also alert the firm to potential opportunities in time to achieve a head start over competitors. Their importance cannot be overstated even though they are open to criticism for lack of methodological rigor. These techniques often provide signals that warrant action by the firm. They are also frequently used as input to large-scale quantitative research.

The three research approaches that fall completely into this category are focus groups, one-on-one interviews, and customer visits. Focus groups and one-on-one interviews are the qualitative techniques of conventional marketing research. Much has been written about their ability, when professionally conducted, to probe for deeply held but not easily verbalized customer attitudes and perceptions (see, for example, Goldman and McDonald, 1987). Focus groups are especially highly regarded for the effect of group interaction in encouraging customers to reveal thoughts and feelings that they might otherwise keep to themselves. Recent research, however, suggests that one-on-one interviews may be even better for specific uses such as eliciting ideas for new products (Griffin and Hauser, 1992).

Customer visits, on the other hand, have only recently been recognized as a research technique (McQuarrie, 1991). Their value, however, is well known to "close to the customer" firms such as Hewlett-Packard and DuPont. Customer visits should not be delegated to research suppliers or considered a by-product of sales activities. Instead they should be viewed as an opportunity to involve top managers and cross-functional teams directly with customers. They are not just a "fishing expedition"; they should be carefully planned and executed (McQuarrie and McIntyre, 1992).

Other techniques sometimes produce important insights or early signals. Customer surveys of many types and competitor analyses can generate useful ideas. Surveys of lapsed customers and employee exit interviews can be especially important for obtaining early indications of dissatisfaction.

All these techniques, whether purely qualitative or whether relying for insight on the interpretation of quantitative data, are dependent on thoughtful questioning and careful, nonbiased analysis to produce valid indicators of marketplace sentiment. Even then, their sample sizes are usually too small to permit generalizing their results to nonstudied populations.

Obtaining data about the current state of affairs

The second category is labeled "current." It includes techniques that provide descriptions of the current status of many indicators and that can provide diagnostics or "reasons why" these conditions exist. They provide opportunities to study the customer's verbalizations of thoughts, feelings, and behaviors. There are also techniques that focus on competitors and the competitive marketplace. Many of the techniques in this group are readily quantifiable. Some lend themselves to sophisticated quantitative analysis. They are invaluable current indicators, but few of them have much to offer in the way of generating insights about future wants and needs.

The applications of traditional survey research fall into this category. Almost by definition, a survey is conducted at one point in time and is often likened to a snapshot of conditions at that time. When repeated, or replicated, it can illuminate trends. This is often referred to as a tracking study. Surveys, whether of customer attitudes, images, or satisfaction with a particular product, are very good at answering "what" types of questions. They also can be designed to get at "whys" although they are usually open to criticism of the depth of response to "reasons why" questions. Surveys of lapsed customers can be especially revealing, but it is important to remember that these customers have already been lost, and the best research can do is to prevent further damage.

Surveys of all kinds lend themselves to carefully chosen samples. If sufficient funds are available, these samples can be large enough to permit statistically valid generalization of results to the population from which the sample was drawn. In addition, large and carefully constructed samples permit the analysis of data by segment.

Observational research techniques also fall squarely into the current category because, by definition, a researcher can only observe current behavior. Simple observation, in the hands of knowledgeable collectors and users of data, can be very powerful. Potential customers' reactions to both exterior features and the interior design of automobiles are carefully observed during the design process. Small children cannot effectively verbalize their reaction to toys, but observation of their play activities is very revealing. The "mystery shopper" is an old retailing technique revived by quality personnel to obtain first-hand, and therefore difficult to refute, data about how customers are treated.

Analyses of secondary data generally fall into the current category but lean toward the historical. Just how far they learn depends on the age of the data. Activities like competitor analysis and documented reviews of media coverage add another, potentially important, dimension to a firm's assessment of its current standing in the broad marketplace.

Competitive benchmarks can be thought of as a type of secondary data that is unique to TQM activities. It is true that for years trade associations have been disseminating to their members many industry-specific operating statistics such as sales per square foot for a certain type of retail store or percent of scrap in a particular operating process. However, these are usually aggregate figures, made up of both the best and the worst. Quality experts argue that using these measures causes firms to set objectives that are lower than excellence demands. Competitive benchmarks are preferred. Benchmarks, however, tend to deal with operating parameters which may or may not have a direct relationship to customer satisfaction.

The final technique that has been placed in this category is the employee exit interview. Relatively few firms do exit interviews on a regular basis, and that is an unfortunate oversight. Many things can be learned as employees exit the firm. Simple structured surveys can shed light on major problems. Open-ended questions administered by skilled interviewers can uncover more subtle but potentially more revealing issues.

This group of research techniques can be very powerful. Alone, however, they are rarely sufficient to provide all the data required for effective TQM planning and implementation.

Records of actions and activities

The third category is called "historical." The techniques in this group are primarily reports of customer actions or internal operations of the firm. This data is often captured on line, for example, by the computerized cash registers in a retail store or as the by-product of computerized sales activities or service requests. It has the advantages of being very detailed and complete; i.e., not for just a sample of customers or activities but for all of them. On the other hand, by its very nature this data reports on behaviors or activities that have already occurred—on mistakes that have been made or on customers that have been left unsatisfied. This category might be thought of as containing lagging indicators, ones that are only available after the fact. This can be dangerously late when customer satisfaction is at stake. The customer may have already been lost by the time the data becomes available.

Operating reports on any relevant activity of the firm seem to fall into this category. In many firms they do, because reports reach decision makers so slowly that they are of only historical interest. However, by using appropriate information technology these data can be collected on-line and transmitted immediately to the relevant users. When this is done operating results become much more than historical artifacts.

Databases that contain records of sales and service plus descriptive information about the household or business firm can be a rich source of data about the firm's entire customer base. Customer panels can add data about product and media use but usually only for a sample of customers.

Finally, audits of internal records such as warranty repairs or customer complaints can yield important information. Such audits can be immensely valuable in the early stages of TQM when the organization is looking for the 20 percent of the activities that typically generate 80 percent of the problems. Properly used, internal records then become an important way of tracking progress toward resolving these problems.

These measures of past activity should not be overlooked or undervalued. They contain vital information. They should also be readily available, and some have little incremental cost from a TQM perspective because they are necessary to everyday operations. These data are important, but they are not sufficient. They rarely reveal the "whys" behind the "whats" they report. They do not generally lead to insights about how the customer might be delighted in the present or what he or she might want and need in the future. Data about past actions and activities can only be one part of the critical base of customer information in an effective TQM environment.

SUMMARY

The overall theme of this chapter has been that a customer orientation is critical to the success of TQM. The overriding objective of all businesses must be to at least meet—and preferably to exceed—customer wants, needs, and expectations. Without this focus on the customer, firms are likely to spend a great deal of time and effort improving internal processes that make only marginal differences in customer satisfaction.

This chapter has described customer orientation in two ways. First, it is a business philosophy that puts customer wants and needs at the center of all decision making activities. Second, it is a process, like TQM itself, that requires committed top managers, empowered employees, and data on which to base customer-centered decisions.

There are many techniques that can be used to collect data for the TQM process. The appropriate technique depends on many factors including the type of data required, the speed with which it is needed, and the resources available for collection, analysis, and reporting.

Above all, this chapter has stressed that becoming—and remaining—customer oriented requires an organization-wide commitment. The entire organization, from top management to front-line personnel, must recognize the importance of keeping customer satisfaction as its central focus. Even more important, *actions* of personnel from top to bottom of the organizational ladder must consistently put customer satisfaction first. Then the organization can consider itself truly customer oriented.

References

Customer orientation

Howe, Roger J., Dee Baekkert, and Maynard A. Howe. *Quality on Trial* (St. Paul, MN: West Publishing Company, 1992).

Kohil, Ajay K., and Bernard J. Jaworski. "Market Orientation: The Construct, Research Propositions, and Managerial Implications," *Journal of Marketing,* April 1990, pp. 1–18.

Levitt, Theodore. "Marketing Myopia," *Harvard Business Review,* July/August 1960, pp. 45–56; September/October 1975, pp. 26–44, 173, 181.

Narver, John C., and Stanley F. Slater. "The Effect of a Market Orientation on Business Profitability," *Journal of Marketing,* October 1990, pp. 20–35.

———. *Becoming More Market Oriented: An Exploratory Study of the Programmatic and Market-Back Approaches* (Cambridge, MA: Marketing Science Institute Report No. 91-128, October 1991).

Peters, Thomas J., and Robert H. Waterman, Jr. *In Search of Excellence: Lessons from America's Best-Run Companies* (New York: Warner Books, Inc., 1982).

Shapiro, Benson, P. "What the Hell Is 'Market Oriented'?" *Harvard Business Review,* November/December 1988, pp. 119–125.

Slater, Stanley F., and John C. Narver. *Market Orientation, Performance, and the Moderating Influence of Competitive Environment* (Cambridge, MA: Marketing Science Institute Report No. 92-118, July 1992).

Whiteley, Richard C. *The Customer Driven Company: Moving from Talk to Action* (Reading, MA: Addison-Wesley Publishing Company, 1991).

Customer research techniques

Bitner, Mary Jo, Bernard H. Booms, and Mary Stanfield Tetreault. "The Service Encounter: Diagnosing Favorable and Unfavorable Incidents," *Journal of Marketing,* January 1990, pp. 71–84.

Blankenship, A. B., and George Edward Breen. *State-of-the-Art Marketing Research* (Lincolnwood, IL: NTC Business Books, 1993).

Eccles, Robert G. "The Performance Measurement Manifesto," *Harvard Business Review,* January/February 1991, pp. 131–137.

Goldman, Alfred E., and Susan Schwartz McDonald. *The Group Depth Interview* (Englewood Cliffs, NJ: Prentice-Hall, 1987).

McQuarrie, Edward F., "The Customer Visit: Qualitative Research for Business-to-Business Marketers," *Marketing Research,* March 1991, pp. 15–28.

——— and Shelby H. McIntyre. *The Customer Visit: An Emerging Practice in Business-to-Business Marketing* (Cambridge, MA: Marketing Science Institute Report No. 92-114, May 1992).

Griffin, Abbie, and John R. Hauser. *The Voice of the Customer* (Cambridge MA: Marketing Science Institute Report No. 92-106, March 1992).

Parasuraman, A., Leonard L. Berry, and Valarie A. Zeithaml. "Guidelines for Conducting Service Quality Research," *Marketing Research,* December 1990, pp. 34–44.

———, Valarie A. Zeithaml, and Leonard L. Berry. "SERVQUAL: A Multiple-Item Scale for Measuring Consumer Perceptions of Service Quality," *Journal of Retailing,* Spring 1988, pp. 12–40.

Smith, Daniel C., Jonlee Andrews, and Timothy R. Blevins, "The Role of Competitive Analysis in Implementing a Market Orientation," *The Journal of Services Marketing,* Winter 1992, 23–36.

Smith, R. P. "Research and Other Data in the Monitoring of Product Quality," *Journal of the Market Research Society,* July, 1979, pp. 189–205.

Urban, Glen L., and John R. Hauser. *Design and Marketing of New Products* (Englewood Cliffs, NJ: Prentice-Hall, 1980).

Westbrook, Robert A. "A Rating Scale for Measuring Product/Service Satisfaction," *Journal of Marketing,* Fall 1980, pp. 68–72.

Reading 31

Historical Sources of Japanese Management Practices

By Jan C. Knakal

INTRODUCTION

The goal of this paper is to present the historical events and the cultural traditions that according to our belief have shaped the current Japanese management practices. We will accomplish this by first identifying some distinctive attributes of Japanese management, using *The Art of Japanese Management* from Pascale and Athos as our guide.[1] We will turn next to the historical events which other authors credit with helping to create these distinctive management practices. Then, we will examine ancient Japanese cultural traditions which may also be at work in contemporary management techniques. Our last step will be to bring all these ideas together and draw some conclusions.

In their work, *The Art of Japanese Management*, Pascale and Athos note the emphasis managers place on so-called soft factors. These include: *staff* (a focus on personnel), *skills* ("things which the organization and its key personnel do particularly well") and *style* ("patterns of behavior of the top executive and the senior management team").[2]

Drawing a distinction between American and Japanese management practices, the two authors say the Japanese approach allows great corporations to "successfully persist in harmony with their culture's deepest values."[3]

Because Japanese managers take the "*whole* of human needs"[4] into account when dealing with their workers, according to Pascale and Athos, Japanese behavior and performance in the work place closely reflects their ideals and values.

Again making a comparison with the West, Pascale and Athos point to the Matsushita company, whose founder "fundamentally believes that people can be

Source: 1992 report reprinted with the permission of the author.

trusted." One high-level manager at Matsushita said this faith turns the "individual" into the "drive" of the system.[5]

"The Japanese," say Pascale and Athos, "see each individual as having economic, social, psychological, and spiritual needs, much as we do when we step back and think about it. But Japanese executives assume it is *their* task to attend to much more of the whole of the person, and not leave so much to other institutions (such as government, family, or religious ones). And they believe it is only when the individual's needs are well met within the subculture of a corporation that they can largely be freed for productive work that is in a larger part outstanding."[6]

Crediting the Japanese for doing a better job in human resource development, they add that "the essence of Japanese success in these areas is rooted in assumptions that are rather fundamental to life."[7]

We will explore this connection between Japanese management and traditional values in more detail later. Our purpose at this point is only to establish the link the Japanese themselves see between management and their system of values.

Another student of the Japanese character in the corporate environment is William Ouchi, author of "Theory Z." He defines the key to successful Japanese management as: trust, subtlety, and intimacy.[8] He says these are at the core of corporate interactions. Thus, Japanese in the work place relate as whole human beings and do not overly concentrate on each other's "productive" or "business" functions.

The father of the Total Quality Management concept, Dr. Kaoru Ishikawa, insists that "all the employees participate in its implementation."[9] Through his work and others which we will refer to later, there emerges a pattern of strong involvement between the Japanese employee and his company. Workers and companies seem linked both in terms of giving and receiving. These ties of dedication and expectation—for example, life-time employment—take place in the unique context described by Pascale and Athos in the aforementioned book.

According to Pascale and Athos, Japan has not made many of the mistakes of the Occident because their nation has not separated the social or spiritual being from the "productive" being. Unlike the West, the Japanese have not decided "one's spiritual and social life should reside *outside* the workplace."[10] They have not been overly influenced by the separation of Church and State or Machiavelli's belief that management is separate from moral law.[11]

REBORN FROM THE ASHES

Now we will explore the historical aspects of this issue and consider the special development of Japanese industry in the aftermath of World War II, according to the author Kenichi Ohmae.[12]

Ohmae, a management consultant, contends that much of the interpretation of Japanese business practices is "mystifying and misleading,"[13] discarding the theoretical elements as real factors.

Ohmae says much of Japanese management has its roots in the poverty and turmoil which followed World War II. He writes:

> Nearly everyone was jobless. Virtually all factories had been burned to ashes. Money had become nearly worthless, with inflation exceeding 100 percent per annum. The capitalists—the Big Five as well as many smaller companies—were broken up by zaibatsu kaitai, because General MacArthur was convinced that some sort of military-industrial complex had pushed Japan into war.
>
> There was virtually nothing there with which to start a corporation. Fortunately, the technology that had been devoted to the creation of tanks, airplanes, and ships was preserved in the heads of trained engineers, and some of these got together with a handful of managers from the prewar *zaibatsu* companies to start small factories producing rice cookers, clothing, and other necessities. These enterprises welcomed skilled labor but lacked money to pay wages, and so most of them paid in food, which in those days was more important than money.[14]

Thus, it was out of necessity, says Ohmae, that Japanese firms became more like communes than corporations. He notes, "People shared their lives, hardships, and toil. If anyone tried—and some did—to organize and run a company in the old way, seeking to exploit the hungry laborers, strikes would break out."[15]

Born of hardship, this spirit would have shaped future Japanese management practices, creating special ties more like a family bond than a society getting together for a common economical end. According to Ohmae, the hard circumstances were the ones that generated the special "esprit de corps" in Japanese companies.

Other Japanese historical analysts consider traditional values to have had an important role in the shaping of management styles and social behavior in general. The author of the book *Why Japan Has "Succeeded"* Michio Morishima[16] describes what he sees as a strong national ethos combining religious, social, and technological influences, at the core of this success.

Morishima says that Japan had her own special way to assimilate the influence of China: "Chinese Confucianism is, at all events, humanistic, whereas Japanese Confucianism is remarkably nationalistic."[17]

He adds that "Japan has perpetually been in the position where she has felt herself under pressure from a strong world empire and has, as a result, perhaps become excessively defensive. She has instinctively perceived that to continue to exist in her corner of East Asia she has to be both frugal and courageous."[18]

Morishima describes the process of how the values rooted in the Samurai class spread to the rest of the society during the Meiji revolution (1867–1868): "In the process of 'taking off,' a most important part was played by the secularization of Confucianism and Japanese chivalry. This began in the closing of the Tokugawa Shogunate and accelerated as the Meiji government spread Confucianism, which had not yet become generally popular among ordinary people in the Tokugawa era, by means of compulsory education."[19] In the process of modernization—he says—the old spirit was conserved as expressed in the slogan of the post Meiji revolution period: "Wa-kon Yo-sai" (Japanese spirit with Western ability) as an inspiring principle in importing occidental technology.[20]

As an economist and lecturer at Cambridge University, Morishima offers later a more complete explanation of how the Code of Chivalry got into the general population: "In those days (Tokugawa period, 1603–1867) samurai were expected to excel in the moral virtues of loyalty, righteousness, and propriety; they gained honor as the ruling class because of their moral training. But their material lives were poor, sometimes miserably so, especially those of the lower samurai. The populace, on the other hand, were despised because they did not need to practice Confucian ethics. . . . Farmers and tradesmen were also called upon to be loyal to their bosses and faithful to their friends and customers. It should be noted that in the mid-Tokugawa period large landowners and large-scale shops emerged, while many people became tenant farmers, shop boys, and servants. They were soon taught that they should devote themselves to their masters in the same way as the samurai did to their lords. The 'secularization' of *bushido* (that is, samurai ethics) had started."[21]

In regard to the strong influence of the Shinto religion to "maintain" the social system, Morishima says: "Because of the influence of Shintoism and Confucianism, the Japanese people set much value on ancestor worship, self-sacrifice for the benefit of one's master, and concord with other members of society."[22]

Morishima also contends that part of the strength of the Japanese people stems from their feeling toward their land, grounded on religious, mainly Shinto, values: Japan is the land where "the gods settled, the land of the gods."

He also says that "the growth of the 'land of the gods' doctrine resulted in a corresponding increase in the emphasis on the deity of the Emperor."[23]

SOURCES

Let us look at some traditional sources in order to explore more fully those ideas and values. In describing the Ancient Japanese character of the samurai, Inazo Nitobe, author of the book *Bushido, the Soul of Japan*,[24] states that the Bushido, the ethical code of the warrior class, indeed became a common spirit for the whole nation, reaching beyond the limits of this group. He says that this spirit, being deeply rooted in the people, permeated the centuries.

> Nitobe speaks also about the ancient feudal lord's concept of authority: A feudal prince, although unmindful of owing reciprocal obligations to his vassals, felt a higher sense of responsibility to his ancestors and to Heaven. He was the father to his subjects, whom Heaven entrusted to his care. According to the ancient Chinese *Book of Poetry*, 'Until the house of Yin lost the hearts of the people, they could appear before heaven.' And Confucius in his *Great Learning* taught: 'When the prince loves what the people love and hates what the people hate, then he is what is called the parent of the people.'[25]

The sense of commitment has often been mentioned by different scholars as something essential in explaining the behavior of Japanese employees. This approach to their work is almost "sacred," as shown in Pascale's explanation that the separation between the spiritual and productive life did not take place in Japan.

In A. L. Sadler's translation of the work of the samurai Daidoji Yuzai, published as *The Code of the Samurai*,[26] it explains the commitment of the samurai as being based upon the consideration of life as temporal and the soul as eternal:

> For existence is impermanent as the dew of evening, and the hoarfrost of morning, and particularly uncertain is the life of the warrior, and if he thinks he can console himself with the idea of eternal service to his lord or an unending devotion to his relatives, something may well happen to make him neglect his duty to his lord and forget what he owes to his family. But if he determines simply to live for today and take no thought for the morrow, so that when he stands before his lord to receive his commands he thinks of it as his last appearance and when he looks on the faces of his relatives he feels that he will never see them again, then will his duty and regard for both of them be completely sincere, while his mind will be in accord with the path of loyalty and filial duty.[27]

This idea of life as a service to others for a samurai implied the understanding that the most important thing in his life was his mission. This sense of mission is reinforced by Ohmae when he writes that after setting a strategy, it has to be executed with a sense of mission.

This dedicated attitude arises from the myth of the origins of Japan as being the "Land of the Gods." It says that the gods Izanami and Izanaghi chose the beautiful island of Awasi to live and procreate beautiful children that would play in the nice valleys. But, when the children began to grow up, sadness fell over the parents.

> The divine couple could not ignore that everything that lives on the earth will sooner or later die. And the sweet Izanami trembled in imagining that she would have to close the eyes of their children and to keep enjoying immortality. Indeed, she would prefer to go down with them to the grave. Izanaghi resolved to put an end to the situation and persuaded his companion to go up to the heavenly dwelling before the spectacle of death would sadden his domestic happiness. 'Truly,' he said to his wife, 'our children cannot follow us to the mansion of the immutable happiness, but in abandoning them I will sweeten the separation by leaving for them a legacy that will enable them to approach us as nearly as their mortal condition will allow.'[28]

That is the origin of one of the most important symbols and great inspirations for Japan: That "legacy," "left by the gods," is symbolized in the mirror that stands in the shinto shrines, the most ancient creed of Japan. In that mirror they are told they should look upon themselves and remember their divine origin. . . . As the moon reflects the sun, so the mirror reflects what is behind the eyes, the soul, albeit, imperfectly.

As we will see later, the "know thyself" is present as a central and key element in the Japanese tradition and religion. In looking at that mirror they are supposed to see the painful effects of the earthly life upon their faces and to imagine the harmony of the heavenly life of their ancestors. That is what Izanaghi said in the ancient shinto myth when he left the mirror. Their legacy, though painful, is with them.

"Shinto theology," says Nitobe, "has no place for the dogma of 'original sin.' On the contrary, it believes in the innate goodness and God-like purity of the human soul, adoring it as the adytum from which divine oracles are proclaimed. Everybody has observed that the Shinto shrines are conspicuously devoid of objects and instruments of worship, and that a plain mirror hung in the sanctuary forms the essential part of its furnishing. The presence of this article is easy to explain: it typifies the human heart, which, when perfectly placid and clear, reflects the very image of the Deity. When you stand, therefore, in front of the shrine to worship, you see your own image reflected on its shining surface, and the act of worship is tantamount to the old Delphic injunction, 'Know Thyself.'"[29]

To Know Thyself in this way enabled the worshipers to "recognize" themselves as sons of the gods, to increase their virtues by seeing them in the image of their ancestors. Also in contemplating the mirror, the 'human sons of the gods' could perfect themselves by becoming aware of their passions and managing them, thus, some day, to join their divine parents again.

So, a special sense of loyalty is related to keeping a certain attitude and harmony as something owed to their ancestors. That implies a path of achievement, as a gradual realizing of that harmony that has to be discovered.

THREE SOURCES

Inazo Nitobe speaks about three main sources of the Bushido: Buddhism, Shinto, and the teachings of Confucious. They shaped from ancient times the "Soul of Japan." Buddhism furnished a "sense of calm trust in Fate, a quiet submission to the inevitable, that stoic composure in the sight of danger or calamity, that disdain of life and friendliness with death."

The author continues: "A foremost teacher of swordsmanship, when he saw his pupil master the utmost of his art, told him, 'Beyond this, my instruction must give way to Zen teaching.' 'Zen' is the Japanese equivalent for the Dhyâna, which 'represents human effort to reach through meditation zones of thought beyond the range of verbal expression.' Its method is contemplation, and its purport, so far as I understand it, is to be convinced of the principle that underlies all phenomena, and, if it can, of the Absolute itself, and thus to put oneself in harmony with this Absolute. Thus defined, the teaching was more than the dogma of a sect, and whoever attains to the perception of the Absolute raises himself above mundane things and awakes 'to a new Heaven and a new Earth.'"[30]

The Shinto, explains Nitobe, inculcated into the Japanese people the sense of family and strong ties between the different classes of the society, especially toward the emperor, whose image was a sort of cornerstone of the social system.[31]

Also, in regard to the social ties and commitments, the Chinese philosopher Confucius was a great influence. Nitobe says: "As to strictly ethical doctrines, the teachings of Confucius were the most prolific source of Bushido. His enunciation of the five moral relations between master and servant (the governing and the governed), father and son, husband and wife, older and younger brother, and between friend and friend, was but a confirmation of what the race instinct has recognized before his writings were introduced from China. The calm, benignant, and worldly-wise character of his politico-ethical precepts was particularly well suited to the samurai, who formed the ruling class."[32]

Nitobe states that the writings of Confucius and Mencius were the principal textbooks for youth and the highest authority in discussions among the old. A common proverb ridicules a person that possesses an intellectual knowledge but doesn't act accordingly. To be studious is not to be wise. Another saying points out: "A man who has read little smells a little pedantic, and a man who has read much smells yet more so; both are alike unpleasant." The writer meant thereby that knowledge becomes really such only when it is assimilated in the mind of the learner and shows in his character. The doctrine is summarized by the Chinese philosopher Wan Yang Min: "To know and to act are one and the same."[33]

Work ethics and commitment to performance appears to be as something with very deep roots. These teachings combined with the experiences and special circumstances shaped the special character of the Japanese work force. A very traditional symbol, the sword of katana, symbolizing the power of the will, is of tantamount influence upon the Japanese. The Japanese character is pragmatic in that it insists upon applying what has been learned.

Nitobe later explains that "whatever the sources, the essential principles that *Bushido* imbibed from them and assimilated to itself, were few and simple."[34]

Life, then becomes a work of art. Through daily practice, one gets nearer to the achievement of that harmony that reflects itself in beauty. This is symbolized in the Tea Ceremony or Cha-No-Yu.

CONCLUSIONS

To support our thesis about the important role of the traditional elements in the Japanese management, recall the comments of Pascale and Athos.

The authors explain the importance in management of the capacity to deal with human nature—the complexities of human reactions—and to be able to reach to other human beings by going beyond our own uniqueness and overcoming the differences of views.

They point out the necessity to overcome the routine and mechanical patterns of behavior. They present concepts that help us to reach further into the subtlety and richness of human nature via attitudes related to those of old.

The Japanese believe, say Pascale and Athos, that by removing yourself from the picture you gain greater insight into what is truly there. We are blinded by our own egos from seeing the full possibilities of life. If we discipline ourselves to adopt periodically a 'no-ego' state, we can perceptively drink in the full meaning of a situation without imposing ourselves upon it.[35]

In talking about this capacity of mastering psychological states, they mention Zen Buddhism and its insistence upon "emptying ourselves" before looking into something in order to fully appreciate it. That concept of emptying ourselves is related to the way that they conceive of the universe. In it the "emptiness" has a great value, because as seen in the philosophy of Lao Tse, the emptiness is much more than just that. It becomes a kind of metaphysical source of everything, like a sort of mythological mother goddess, containing everything essential within her.

The space in-between things, the undefined, is what gives meaning to and unites the defined things. Pascale and Athos explain the importance of seeing the big picture in management. Thus going beyond the personal vision of the manager, of being able to integrate the complexities of human relationships. In this way, the manager should not always be "assertive," and defined in his opinions. Rather he should, within the context of his strategy and vision, be flexible and open enough to deal with complex situations. These require understanding of the various factors involved before taking a stand. They mention the need of ambiguity as a management skill and the necessity to sometimes "decide" to "proceed": "As proceeding yields further information, the best course may be to move toward the goal through a sequence of tentative steps rather than by bold stroke actions."[36]

Well, that's very much what Lao Tse meant when he spoke in an even more obscure language. He said that the "weak wins over the strong and the small is more than the big, and from the emptiness is where things really can be managed" such as in the "eye of the storm." What makes a cup of coffee useful? The emptiness inside it.[37] (*Note:* As Morishima explains, the teachings of the Chinese philosopher Lao Tse became part of the Shinto religion. This integrated new form served as a rational and social bond for all the people.)

So, we find an approach that enables us to experience the following concepts; in the tides of life, the interaction of the "Yin and Yang"; the positive and negative, active and passive. This approach then leads us to the identification with the "Tao," the ultimate wholeness that is beyond those tides. Thus, an understanding would be created in us that helps us to deal with the uniqueness of others.[38]

There are many examples that we could use if space would allow. We definitely suggest the work of Pascale and Athos as a reference in this aspect. They present many concrete examples that we cannot enumerate here and show useful attitudes in daily management which are definitely rooted to those characteristic of the Japanese of old. They are drawn from vital and metaphysical sources, integrated with technical aspects.

In Japan many people attend and draw inspiration equally from Shinto, Buddhist, and Confucian services and rituals. This practice helps the people at large to participate more deeply in their work. This process of inner transformation becomes a kind of art form that was highly developed by the samurais. Actually a samurai was supposed to read and hopefully even write poetry.

As we stated at the beginning of this work, it is not the philosophical elements alone, but the way in which they were combined that finally shaped the Japan that we admire today. To more fully understand the historical development, such as the Meiji period of reform in the VI c., the slogan "occidental technology and Japanese spirit" and the "secularization of the samurai" processes, we recommend to the reader the quoted work of *Why Japan Has "Succeeded."*

We would state that, according to traditional thought, they believe that their performance is a part of their spiritual development and not something separate.

There were and will be other countries destroyed by war. There are others, some of which are islands, that lack natural resources. Many countries were also rebuilt with the help and the technological aid from the United States, but there is only one country of the rising sun.

Without doubt, what we see operating in Japan is unique. The historical forces that have shaped her are complex. We do not pretend to explain it here. It is, however, our wish to give the reader some "appetizers" to rouse his further interest in those ancient sources of inspiration that, although they have been changed, adapted, and mutated, still remain basically entrenched in modern Japan. The samurai of old and current Matsushita are different in many ways, yet they have much in common as well. The same light of the legendary Amateratsu, the goddess of the sun, shines forth from the soul of each, though in different manners and degrees. Equally present is the mythical hero SusunaHo, who re-instated the rituals that link man to the sacred, and thus returning the meaning to music and the arts.

In Japan today, the sun may not be rising as it once did. However, the same intrinsic elements that were present in antiquity are also found to some degree in the Japanese management. Some of these elements are the sense of family, the concept of a nation as a large integrated family, commitment to the land, and the need to have a motivating and unifying bond that is higher and far broader than a monetary profit.

Due to the fact that these same social values exist in other cultures around the world, we may speculate that they constitute a forgotten legacy of Mankind. A Mankind which is currently falling into diversification, self-absorption, and has lost the ability to see the "whole picture." We can indeed learn much from the example set by Japan by understanding and appreciating its ancient and current history. Perhaps, it may inspire us as a nation to achieve more, to unite as a people, and to become better human beings and in this way to be more competitive in business. So, let's look for and develop in ourselves values that would enable us to embrace the whole spectrum of human needs. And that is not "Japanese"; or is it?

Notes

1. Richard Tanner Pascale and Anthony G. Athos, *The Art of Japanese Management* (New York: A Warner Comm. Co., 1979).
2. Ibid., p. 124.
3. Ibid., p. 129.
4. Ibid., p. 31.
5. Ibid., p. 59.
6. Ibid., p. 132.
7. Ibid., p. 135.
8. William G. Ouchi, *Theory Z* (New York: 1981).

9. Dr. Kaoru Ishikawa, "Total Quality Management."
10. Richard Tanner Pascale and Anthony G. Athos, *The Art of Japanese Management* (New York: A Warner Comm. Co., 1979) p. 29.
11. Ibid., p. 28.
12. Kenichi Ohmae, *The Mind of the Strategist* (New York: Penguin Group, 1982).
13. Ibid., p. 217.
14. Ibid., p. 217.
15. Ibid., p. 217.
16. Michio Morishima, *Why Japan Has "Succeeded"* (Cambridge University Press, 1982).
17. Ibid., p. 15.
18. Ibid., pp. 15, 16.
19. Ibid., p. 17.
20. Ibid., p. 23.
21. Ibid., pp. 49, 50.
22. Ibid., p. 51.
23. Ibid., p. 63.
24. Inazo Nitobe, *The Soul of Japan* (Tokyo: Tuttle Co., 1969).
25. Ibid., pp. 38, 39.
26. Daidoji Yuzan (by A. L. Sadler translator), *The Code of the Samurai* (Tokyo: Tuttle Co., 1988).
27. Ibid., pp. 15, 16.
28. *Ankh* magazine, (Madrid: Nueva Acropolis, 1991).
29. Inazo Nitobe, *The Soul of Japan* (Tokyo: Tuttle Co., 1969) pp. 12, 13.
30. Ibid., pp. 11, 12.
31. Ibid., p. 12.
32. Ibid., pp. 15, 16.
33. Ibid., pp. 17, 18.
34. Ibid., p. 20.
35. Richard Tanner Pascale and Anthony G. Athos, *The Art of Japanese Management* (New York: A Warner Comm. Co., 1979) p. 143.
36. Ibid., pp. 144, 145.
37. Lao Tzu Tao Teh Ching (Boston: Shambhala Pub., Inc., 1989) p. 23.
38. Ibid., pp. 9, 25, 33, 87, 89.

Reading 32

Models for Assessing the Cost of Quality—Theory and Practice in the United States

BY Y. S. CHANG

What is the cost of quality in your organization? What savings have you realized in your cost of quality? What are your objectives in measuring the cost of quality? What refinements have you made to your cost of quality since you started measuring it? How well is your cost of quality meeting the initial objectives?

These are some of the questions that we posed to a group of oil and petrochemical companies. This chapter begins with a brief overview of the methodology of measuring cost of quality. Early examples reported from all industries show the need to expand on the understated portion of cost of quality from lost sales and lost customers. The 1–10–100 rule is reviewed as well as the cost of customer defection, and these elements have been added to improve the methodology of measuring cost of quality.

Using the refined methodology as the interview guide, this chapter summarizes the state-of-the-art practices of how some of the best managed oil and petrochemical companies have customized cost of quality measures and used it to generate some added energy in their quality improvement efforts.

BACKGROUND

The methodology advocated by the American Society of Quality Control Handbook and defined in the British Standard: BS 6143 Guide to the Economics of Quality, Part 2, is that the cost of quality (or rather the cost of poor quality)

SOURCE: Reprinted with the permission of the author.

comprises four components. They are internal failure costs, external failure costs, appraisal costs, and prevention costs.

Internal failure costs "are costs associated with defects that are found prior to transfer of the product to the customer; they are costs that would disappear if no defects existed in the product before shipment".[1] Products that are produced that are beyond repair or the cost associated with repairing a product before shipment are classic examples of this type of quality cost. External failure costs "are associated with defects that are found after a product is shipped to the customer".[1] Likewise, these costs would be eliminated if no defects were made originally. Classic examples of this are warranty costs and returned merchandise costs. The third category of appraisal costs "are costs incurred to determine the degree of conformance to quality requirements".[1] A company's quality standards must be adhered to and thus there must be a way to ensure that these standards are being met. Inspection costs for examining raw material, work-in-process material, and end-product are all appraisal costs. Prevention costs "keep failure costs and appraisal costs to a minimum".[2] A company must train its employees in order to produce defect-free products, perform periodic quality evaluations of its suppliers, and devise a plan for achieving high quality.

According to Philip Crosby, the cost of quality can be divided into two components. The first is the cost of non-conformance or the price of not doing things the right way the first time. This includes reworking products, repairing products covered under warranty, etc. Crosby states, in his book titled *Quality Without Tears,* that the price of non-conformance can represent 20 percent or more of the sales in manufacturing companies and 35 percent of operating costs in service companies.[3] The second part of the cost of quality is the cost of conformance. These are the costs incurred in order to make products turn out defect free the first time. Sources of these costs can be quality education programs and inspection processes.

The recently published Part 1 of British Standard BS 6143 describes the process cost model for assessing cost of quality. This formalizes cost of conformance and cost of non-conformance as integral parts of managing business processes.

In summary, the cost of quality is measured in two different ways by two leading quality gurus, Crosby and Juran. Crosby states that the cost of quality is the cost of conformance and the cost of non-conformance while Juran advocates measuring internal failure, external failure, appraisal, and prevention costs. Cost of quality helped to make Total Quality Management into the critical management issue in the early 1980s because the magnitude of the cost was such that it was a 'wake up call' for senior management. This raised the awareness about quality and the need to use quality for improvement.

Example 3A: measurement of the cost of quality

In early 1981, the Willimantic Division of Rogers Corporation realized they were having problems with higher than normal scrap yields. The company decided to measure the cost of quality as a part of their quality improvement effort in May 1981 in the belief that "a total different approach to quality in manufacturing" would help not only reduce the cyclical up and down nature of their yields but also the overall quality of their products. By following a Total Quality Control (TQC) process which emphasized top management commitment, organization-wide understanding of TQC, initial training, project teams, and further training, Rogers, Corp. was able to realize a marked improvement in their cost of quality. As seen in Figure 32.1, Rogers customized their measurement of the cost of quality into three broad categories: scrap, appraisal and prevention, and returns and reworks. The result was a decrease in the cost of quality from 18.9 percent to 10.9 percent of total manufacturing cost, which represented 42.3 percent reduction over 2 years.

At Texas Instruments, the decision to measure the cost of quality in financial terms was made in 1981. TI's Materials and Control Group started out with an initial list of 77 items which they felt needed to be measured in order to capture the cost of quality. By eventually grouping the costs into four categories of either prevention, appraisal, internal failure, and external failure, the Materials and Control Group had reduced the initial list down to 17 key variables, which were grouped under the four categories (Table 32.1).

As seen in Table 32.2, the tracking of these measurements has allowed the Materials and Control Group of TI to go from a 1982 cost of quality of 10.7 percent of net sales to a 1987 cost of quality of 7.8 percent.

The two examples, Rogers and TI, seem to extol the virtues and the benefits of cost of quality. However, we believe that the point to be made by exampling these companies is that these two, and probably many others in industry, are in fact grossly underestimating the true magnitude of the cost of external failures. The numbers that these companies derived for their cost of external failure, Rogers of 0.3 percent and Texas Instrument of 0.4 percent, merely include the cost of repair and probably overlook the hidden costs of an external failure such as lost revenue and bad reputation. When including lost customers' revenues due to failure of products plus the actual cost to repair the defective product, the true hidden cost can be 100 times more than the cost of prevention and appraisal.

FIGURE 32.1 ***Cost of quality as a percentage of total manufacturing cost, Willimantic Division of Rogers Corp.***

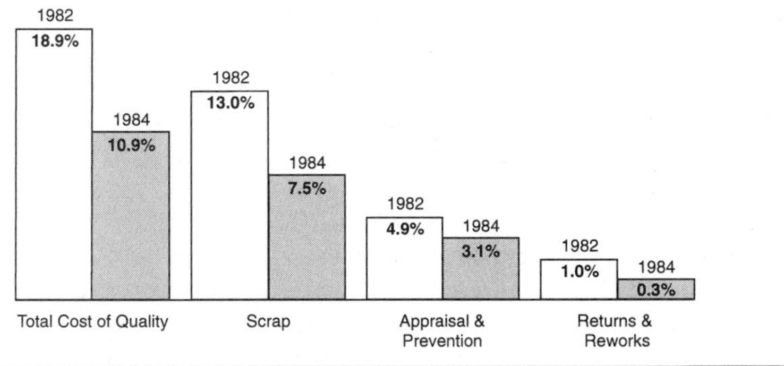

TABLE 32.1 ***Texas Instruments: Materials & Controls Group: 17 variables measured in the cost of quality***

Prevention	Internal failure
Quality Engineering	Quality Scrap
Receiving Inspection	Rework
Equipment Repair/Maintenance	Manufacturing/Process Engineering
Manufacturing Engineering	
Design Engineering	
Quality Training	
Appraisal	**External failure**
Quality Testing Laboratory	Return Merchandise Cost
Design Analysis	Marketing
Product Acceptance	Manufacturing/Process Engineering
Manufacturing Inspection	Repair

SOURCE: Harvard Business Case: 9–189–029, pp. 16–17.

TABLE 32.2 ***Texas Instruments Materials & Controls Group: cost of quality as a percentage of net sales billed***

	1982	1983	1984	1985	1986	1987
Prevention	2.3	2.0	2.0	2.1	2.3	2.3
Appraisal	2.2	1.9	1.7	1.9	1.9	1.8
Internal Failure	5.3	4.8	4.5	4.2	3.6	3.3
External Failure	0.9	0.7	0.6	0.4	0.4	0.4
Total Cost of Quality	10.7	9.4	8.8	8.6	8.2	7.8

SOURCE: Harvard Business Case: 9–189–029, p. 23.

THE COST OF NON-CONFORMANCE: 1–10–100 RULE

In general, industries vastly underestimate the true value of not conforming to quality standards. In order to show this, we introduced the concept of 1–10–100 in 1987.[4] In essence for every dollar your company might spend on preventing a quality problem, you will spend ten dollars to inspect and correct the mistake after it occurs. Furthermore, if a quality failure or problem goes unchecked or unnoticed until after your customer takes delivery, you may end up paying approximately one hundred times what you could have paid to prevent it from happening at all. One of the reasons why the failure in the customers' hands is so high is due to a poorly served customer acting as an "Ill Will Ambassador" to spread the tale of failure to many other customers. For this reason, most companies should consider themselves very fortunate when a customer complains of a defective product or service. Research indicates that 96 percent of your dissatisfied customers will never tell you about their quality complaint, and therefore never give you the chance to fix the defective product. However, most customers will take the opportunity to advise your other potential customers not to select your products or services. These "Ill Will Ambassadors" can easily tarnish your reputation, reduce the effectiveness of your sales force, and help your competition take away valuable business.[4]

Some industry people think that the one hundred portion of the "1–10–100 rule" may grossly underestimate the true magnitude of a field failure. Various critics think the cost of a field failure could be as high as one thousand times the cost of prevention. Moreover, there are people who insist that even one thousand times the cost of prevention is a conservative view of the full impact of the true cost of non-conformance.

Example 3B: the 1–10–100 rule

IBM Rochester, Minnesota is responsible for manufacturing the AS/400 computer system and hard disk storage device. This division, when applying for the Baldrige Award, decided to measure the cost in hours of preventing a defect in the early stages of design and to compare it to the cost incurred when a defect had to be repaired during the manufacturing process and/or after customer installation. As seen in Figure 32.2, IBM found the cost of non-conformance in hours to adhere to a 1–13–92[5] rule, which approximates to 1–10–100.

First Chicago Corp. is another company that tracks the cost of non-conformance. They found that when a wire transfer was executed, the average cost was $10. However, if the wire transfer was sent in error or for the wrong amount, the average cost to correct the mistake was $400.[6] As the amount of the wire transfer increases so does the cost of correcting an error associated with it. A wrong wire transfer for several million dollars can result in Federal Reserve penalties, large operational error correction costs, and also the potential loss of that client's income generating business.

FIGURE 32.2 *Cost of non-conformance: 1–10–100. IBM Rochester, Minnesota.*

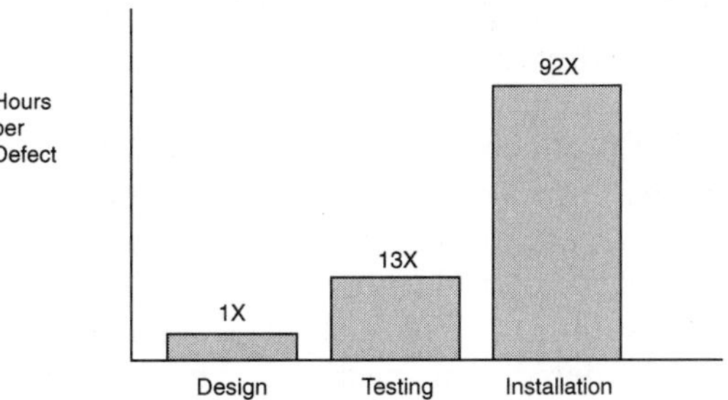

SOURCE: IBM 1990 Baldrige Award summary.

Similarly, Corning Glass found that the cost of correcting an external failure or a defective product which had already reached the customer to be significantly higher than the cost associated with fixing an error at the pre-cutting stage. Corning states that "at each step of the process, a drafting error became increasingly expensive to correct—$250 if it was caught before the tool makers cut the tools, $20,000 if it was discovered before the assembly line started running, and as much as $100,000 after the pressings reached the customer."[7] Instead of a more conservative estimate of 1–10–100, Corning sees the relationship of the cost of conformance versus the cost of non-conformance to be $250–$20,000–$100,000 or 1–80–400.

In yet another example in the oil industry, Ken Hall, the plant manager at the Port Arthur refinery for Star Enterprise (Texaco), is a firm believer in the 1–10–100 rule. Mr. Hall states that "we do random testing on the octane level of gas stored at 5000 gallon underground tanks at the service stations. If the stored gas does not meet the octane standard, the cost of upgrading to a better grade gasoline to fix the problem is 100. If the variation is discovered at the wholesale terminal, the cost of fixing the problem is 10. At the plant level, the variation can be very simply corrected as a part of our routine adjustment. Thus, at this point the cost of correction is 1."[8]

THE COST OF CUSTOMER DEFECTION

Another way to measure the cost of an external or field failure is the industry specific methodology introduced by Reichheld and Sasser.[9] The cost of defection of a customer that a company has had for only one year, although significant, barely compares to the loss sustained when a long time customer defects to the competition. A first time customer usually buys cautiously while looking for any reason to change sides. As time progresses and a relationship of trust, confidence, and quality service and product are built, a customer tends to purchase more. For example, Figure 32.3 shows that the cost of losing a 5th year customer in the credit card industry is 1.8 times the cost of the loss of a first year customer. In the auto service industry, this number jumps to 3.5 and to 3.7 in the industrial distribution.

It is clear that the cost of defection is expensive not only for new customers but also for old customers. Thus, the damage sustained to a company's revenue (not to mention profitability) when a long time customer leaves can have devastating consequences.

"Companies can boost profits by almost 100 percent by retaining just 5 percent more of their customers."[9] An interesting and true statement. Figure 32.4 shows that with a 5 percent decrease in the defection rate, profits in various industries rise 25 percent to 85 percent. By reducing defections by 5 percent, the credit card, branch deposits, and insurance industry showed an increase in profit of 75 percent, 85 percent, and 50 percent, respectively. The result is that Reichheld and Sasser[9] have developed a methodology for assigning a monetary cost to the cost of external failures and the cost of non-conformance.

FIGURE 32.3 ***Customer generated profit over 5 years. (a) Credit Card Industry; (b) Auto Servicing; (c) Industrial Distribution; (d) Industrial Laundry***

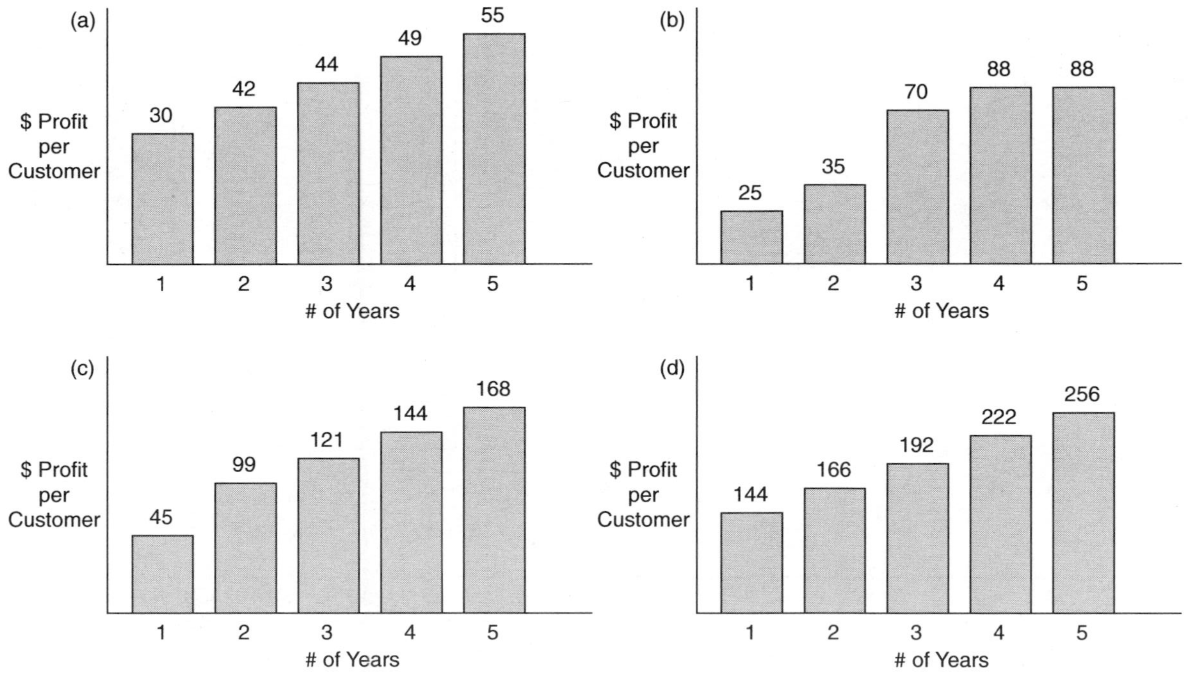

FIGURE 32.4 ***Reducing defections 5% boosts profits 25% to 85%***

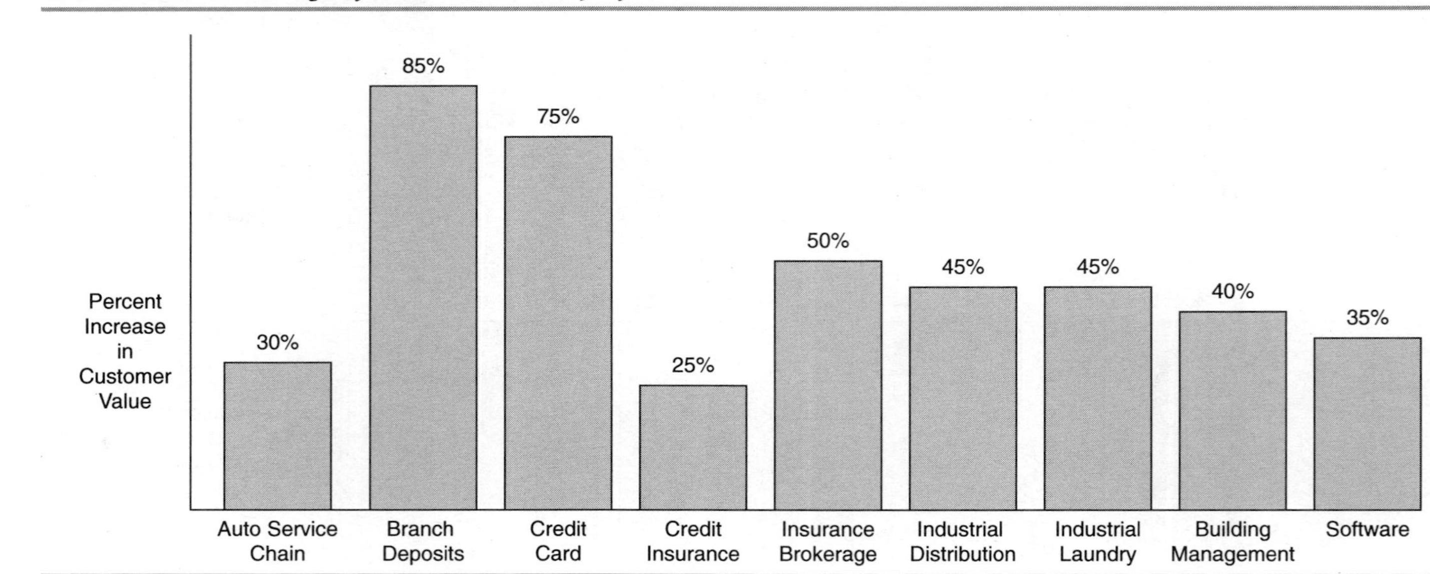

SOURCE: Ref. 9.

TABLE 32.3 ***Xerox cost of quality definitions***

1. Cost of Conformance
   - Prevention: Cost to Avoid Failure, e.g. Training and Communications
   - Inspection/Appraisal: Cost to Check Work, e.g. Incoming Inspection, Pre-installs, and Auditing
2. Cost of Non-conformance
   - Failure to Meet Customer Expectations: Cost of redoing work, waste, and remakes e.g. Aborted Installs and Machine Replacement
   - Exceeding Customer Requirements: Cost of unnecessary extras, e.g. Response Time in Excess of Requirements and Overly Elaborate Presentations
3. Lost Opportunities
   - Customer Defection: Profits not earned owing to lost customers and reduction in revenue because of non-conformance, e.g. Cancellation Due to Poor Service

SOURCE: *Sloan Management Review,* Summer 1992, p. 73.

The general methodology we found to be useful, which combines 1–10–100, the cost of defection, and traditional measurements, is found in the Xerox model. In 1987, the U.S. marketing group of Xerox decided that it was time that they joined the quality movement that was already in full swing throughout most of Xerox. The U.S. marketing group modified the traditional definitions of the cost of quality into three major groups and then into five subgroups. Table 32.3 details how the U.S. marketing group defines its cost of quality. Xerox has explicitly tried to measure lost opportunities from customer defection. For example, cancellation due to poor service, such as delayed shipments, inaccurate billings, and unresponsive customer service will be expressed in terms of dollars and cents. In addition, the cost of conformance will include the cost of unnecessary extras such as response time in excess of requirements and overly elaborate presentation which exceed customers' requirements. In using this broadened definition, the U.S. marketing group of Xerox estimated the cost of quality at $1.05 billion or approximately 25 percent of the group's sales revenue. The group targeted 11 top quality problems, having a total cost of $250 million, and was able to save $53 million in 1 year by improving the quality of the products associated with these areas. In Figure 32.5, we can see that in 1989, the cost of quality was reduced by 21.2 percent for all 11 areas and, more specifically, by 61.8 percent for equipment obsolescence, 58.0 percent for airfreight, and 100 percent for third part financing.

OIL INDUSTRY SURVEY

By using the definitions of the cost of quality as shown by Xerox in Table 32.3, we were able to develop the basis for our survey (see Appendix A). By contacting fifteen of the largest oil and petrochemical companies in North America and interviewing directors and managers of quality of these companies by phone, we were

FIGURE 32.5 ***Cost of quality in 11 quality problem areas, U.S. marketing group at Xerox (figures in $000,000)***

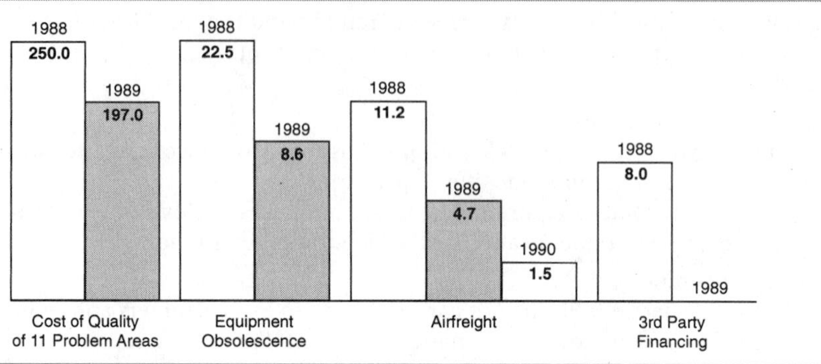

SOURCE: *Sloan Management Review* Summer (1992) 75.

able to talk with seven firms and have six completed interviews. The detailed results of these interviews can be found in Appendices B–G. In analyzing these responses, we were able to identify five main issues that seem to be common to these companies.

The first finding of our survey is that all six companies interviewed are tracking the cost of quality measure. Poor cost of quality of the respondents ranged from 20 percent to 30.5 percent of their annual sales. In another case, the company gave us the dollar value of $152 million as its cost of quality. In all of these cases, the magnitude of the number indicated, even after a number of years of quality improvement, must still be viewed as critical. One more company we were able to contact told us that they had not yet undertaken the measurement of the cost of quality.

The second theme we found was that the companies were focusing their major efforts of measurement on the cost of non-conformance rather than on the cost of conformance. Two out of six companies in fact do not track the cost of conformance. The reason being that either it is not a significant number, or in one case, the cost of conformance was viewed as a negative signal within the organization. Even though the respondents focused on tracking the cost of non-conformances, many of them admitted that what they measure does not cover the full impact of a customer experiencing a poor product or service. For example, one company guessed that the true opportunity cost of a lost customer was probably twice the cost of their non-conformance, which was currently at 20 percent of sales. Another company stated that their cost of failure was 8–10 percent of sales, whereas a more accurate prediction of their cost of failure is probably 25 percent of sales. Furthermore, a different company believed that in comparing the cost of conformance to the cost of non-conformance the 1–10–100 rule should be more near a relationship of 1–10–150, and another believed that 1–10–1000 was an even better ratio.

Our third finding was that some companies had a portion of their cost of quality attributed to exceeding customer specifications and quality requirements. For example, one company said that this cost, which was estimated to be approximately 1 percent of sales, was a marginal loss due to using premium raw materials. Several companies acknowledged that exceeding customer specifications and quality requirements was a factor in their cost of quality numbers but that the number was either too small to track or that they had not progressed to a stage in their quality initiative to have these numbers available.

One of the strongest themes conveyed to us by our survey respondents was that the cost of quality is in fact an "evolutionary management process." Each company started out by measuring and tracking the cost of quality as defined in its most basic and traditional sense. However, as time progressed, each company found that the measurement of the cost of quality could be refined and customized. For example, one company had classified their measurement into the three categories of ongoing savings, one time savings, and avoided costs. While avoided costs dealt with opportunity cost saved, ongoing savings measured annual savings in cash flow for the company. In other words, this company required that all ongoing savings be factored into the next budget cycle so that the cost of quality savings flowed permanently into the bottom line result of the company. This is a case where the cost of quality has been customized to reflect the more conservative nature of the accounting practices at this company and thus reducing the debate of the accuracy of the measures that had existed at the plants. The evolution at another company took the cost of quality measurement for a specific set of processes and problems for the whole plant and eventually expanded it to the whole company.

Finally, as an extension of this evolutionary nature, every respondent had a future desire or plan for improving their measurement further. In general, they have expressed their hope to improve the accuracy as well as the relevancy of their measures. For example, one company had explicitly mentioned that they are moving towards an activity based cost approach for their cost of quality. In fact, almost all of the respondents were looking for some way to quantify data more precisely and accurately and were trying to assign a value to the opportunity cost of possibly losing customers. A number of other companies were trying to focus cost of quality on specific issues and processes so that improvement activities could be launched.

CONCLUSION

In conclusion, the oil and petrochemical industries are becoming more specific in how they are measuring the cost of quality, especially in how they are using the cost of quality. In short, cost of quality has long passed its primary function for awakening organizations to the need for improvement, and is now serving more as an operational cost benefit metric for ongoing improvement activities. When the cost of quality is used to generate improvement activities and objectively measure the resulting benefit from these improvements, management will continue to demand cost of quality measures as a part of metrics to monitor improvement efforts in their organization.

ACKNOWLEDGEMENT

I am happy to acknowledge the assistance provided by Alan R. Richardson, a Research Assistant at the Asian Management Center, Boston University.

Appendix A

Cost of quality survey

1. Do you measure the cost of quality? When did you start and why?
2. What are your objectives (what do you hope to achieve) in measuring the cost of quality?
3. What is your cost of conformance (prevention and appraisal) as a percentage of sales?
4. What is your cost of non-conformance (internal and external failure) as a percentage of sales?
5. What is the extra cost you incur in order to exceed customer demand (exceeding 6 sigma requirements, etc.)?
6. If you include lost sales, deterioration of goodwill, what do you think the true magnitude of non-conformance versus conformance is?
7. If a customer experiences a poor product, what is the chance that they will defect to another company's product?
8. If you do lose a customer, what is the economic impact or value or penalty of losing that customer in terms of real dollar loss?
9. If you do lose a customer, how many additional customers are you likely to lose because of that lost customer (chain effect)?

Overall

10. What prevents you from measuring the true magnitude of the Cost of Quality?
11. Overall, what refinements have you made to your Cost of Quality program since you started it? (Changes in tracking of costs)
12. Are you meeting your objectives as stated previously (Question 2)?

Appendix B

Company 1

This company started the cost of quality in 1986 based on a quarter to quarter measurement. However, as time progressed, the quality manager realized that people inferred too much information from the numbers. This led this company to the conclusion that, in their minds, the cost of quality is more of a negative report. Managers are relying on the integrity, skill, and wisdom of the reporting people. Too many times, numbers were being changed to represent a more favorable cost of quality.

Consequently, the reporting system was changed to one that focused on "demonstrated improvements" only. Only actual accomplishments were merited and only legitimate numbers were used.

In the last 5 years, the cost of quality has become a positive report. Accomplishments were published in a weekly *Wall Street Journal* format that averaged 12 pages of point form listing corrective action accomplishments.

In 1992, a decision was made to revamp the existing measurement system. Teams decided to look at three categories of cost: (1) ongoing savings; (2) one time savings; and (3) general avoided costs. In 1992, the costs of these categories were as follows:

1. Ongoing Savings: $93 million
2. One time Savings: $9 million
3. Avoided Costs: $50 million

   Total: $152 million

The company requires that all ongoing cost savings be factored into the budget. This is a benefit since people must be committed to ensuring the maintenance of achieved cost savings.

In the future, they will look more closely at the Baldrige categories and hope to use corrective action teams, process improvement teams, and benchmarking teams.

Appendix C

Company 2

The Cost of Quality at this firm is tracked by projects on an individual basis. This allows for a more precise indication of the actual meaning of the numbers achieved. This company does track quality company wide. The cost of conformance is estimated at 0.5 percent of sales. The tracking of the cost of conformance has increased the overall sales of the company by 2 percent. The cost of non-conformance amounts to 20 percent of sales but this figure is only for reworks. Thus, when the company factors in hidden costs of non-conforming, a true magnitude of the cost of non-conformance may be around 30 percent of sales.

If this manager could assign new numbers to the 1–10–100 rule, they would be nearer 1–10–150.

This company believes that if a customer experiences a poor product, the chance of defection is 65 percent. In addition, the economic impact of a defection can be broken down into four categories. The loss associated with each category is estimated as follows:

- Small: $1,000
- Medium: $30,000
- Large: $100,000
- Mega: $10,000,000

As a result of a poor product or service, this company believes that the "Ill Will Ambassador" chain effect will result in one dissatisfied customer telling 10–12 companies.

Appendix D

Company 3

Measurement of the cost of quality began in 1983. This was the firm's single largest cost improvement effort. The process was continued once gains were achieved in order to maintain these gains.

The following data were made available by this company:

- Cost of Quality: 30% of sales
- Cost of Failure as a percentage of sales: 8–10%
- Cost of Appraisal as a percentage of sales: 1–1.5% ("too small to track")
- Cost of Prevention as a percentage of sales: 2–3%

Chances of Defection were given as follows:

- Early problem resolution: 0%
- Problem exists for 1 year: 50–75%
- If commodity product: 100%
- If unique product: <50%

There is recognition that the Cost of Defection is an extremely important issue. However, no ongoing system is in place to track this cost. The justification is because the event is highly rare.

This firm did spend more in order to exceed customer's requirements and specifications. There is a marginal loss due to buying premium materials in order to surpass customer's requirements and expectations. This amounts to approximately 1 percent of sales.

What are you doing now? Trying to determine the hidden opportunity costs? Trying to identify and quantify these costs?

Appendix E

Company 4

Cost of quality was first measured in 1986. The purpose was to highlight the cost of non-conformance associated specifically with a set of processes and problems. Beginning in 1989, the cost of non-conformance was expanded to cover the whole plant, yielding $200 million, representing 10 percent of sales. The purpose was to focus business planning to reduce the cost.

This company does not measure the cost of conformance.

Opportunity cost of lost sales or lost customers is estimated to be twice the cost of non-conformance (20 percent). The bulk of the opportunity cost is in the probable loss of growth in sales or product due to not having exactly the right mix and inputs so that the plant cannot produce optimum mix of outputs that would maximize revenue or profit. It is too difficult to estimate the true magnitude of this opportunity loss.

The additional cost of exceeding cutter requirements is incurred when the plant is delivering products which exceed the specifications or octane for which the customers are unwilling to pay extra (sometimes because they do not recognize the quality difference). Difficult to estimate how much of the margin loss is incurred.

As for future improvement, they would like to move more towards activity based costing that will pinpoint critical business processes to be improved in order to prevent rather than react. They know intuitively which critical areas to attack, but are unable to prove with objective cost measure.

Appendix F

Company 5

Cost of quality was measured in 1990. The reason was to identify how much room there was to improve and to hopefully attract management's attention to the importance of the cost of quality. The objectives also included prioritizing duties and improvement initiatives.

Cost of conformance was tracked but not available and the cost of non-conformance was also tracked but not available.

Cost of exceeding customer requirements will be done eventually but is not tracked now, as they are not at the stage where they can track this.

True magnitude of 1–10–100 (probably 1–10–100 to 1–10–1000, or somewhere in between).

No refinements made as yet to the way in which they measure the cost of quality. However, they anticipate that they will refine the tracking of the numbers and make the numbers more precise indicators of the cost they are suppose to be tracking.

Poor products:

- chance of defection: around industry number;
- economic impact of lost customer: small customer, few hundred $$$; mega customer, few million $$.
- chain effect: same as industry.

Appendix G

Company 6

The cost of quality at this firm, which is engaged in exploration and production of crude oil, is measured in a different perspective. Their effort is focused on getting the product out faster and cheaper than its competitors. After a major internal reorganization, inspection teams were almost entirely eliminated from the company.

This company does the bulk of its business through contractual agreements. Thus, very rarely does the company ever exceed customers' specifications. However, every once in a while, the product may not meet a customer's specifications. A penalty may be imposed. The cost of fixing these external failures is less than $40,000.

Internal product failures are not present at this firm. The meaning behind this statement is that since they produce crude, which is governed by mother nature, they have no control over the product that they receive. However, they do have an internal production cost of failure. This would be the cost associated with well failures, machinery malfunctions, etc. Hence, their cost of internal production failure is 20–25 percent of sales, with sales being roughly estimated at $250 million.

Customers are rarely affected by a well failure due to the magnitude of the number of wells producing crude. A major wide scale breakdown would have to occur and the chances of this occurring are so rare as to be considered a non-existent chance.

In terms of cost of prevention, the company does use chemicals and equipment redesigns to prevent well failures. The cost associated with the chemicals used for prevention maintenance is 10–15 percent of sales.

The company stated that they are constantly refining their metrics in order to better use the data that they are able to obtain.

References

1. J.M. Juran, *Quality Control Handbook,* McGraw-Hill, New York, 1974, p. 4.5.
2. J.M. Juran, *Quality Control Handbook,* McGraw-Hill, New York, 1974, p. 4.6.
3. P.B. Crosby, *Quality Without Tears,* McGraw-Hill, New York, 1984, pp. 85–86.
4. G.H. Labovitz, and Y.S. Chang. *Quality Costs: The Good, The Bad and The Ugly,* Organizational Dynamics Inc., 1987, pp. 1–3.
5. Report issued by IBM Rochester, Malcolm Baldrige Office, Rochester, MN, 1990.
6. R.L. Thomas, "Bank on Quality," *Quality Progress,* February (1987) p. 29.
7. R. Henkoff, "Make Your Office More Productive," *Fortune* 123 (4) (1991) p. 78.
8. Survey results from telephone interview with Mr. Ken Hall, plant manager of Port Arthur Refinery of Star Enterprises.
9. F.F. Reichheld and W.E. Sasser, Jr. "Zero Defections: Quality Comes to Services," *Harvard Business Review* (1990) p. 105.

Reading 33

Organizational Impact of Introducing Concurrent Engineering

BY ELLEN R. DOMB, ROBERT C. CULVER, AND RICHARD H. RAWCLIFFE

ABSTRACT

The introduction of concurrent engineering as the primary method of new product development stimulates organizational change. An existing model is examined which integrates all elements of the organization, not just the structure and strategy. This "7-S" model draws attention to the issues which must be addressed effectively to institutionalize the formal tools of concurrent engineering. Key formal methods include Quality Function Deployment (QFD) to help the planning for a quality product; Robust Design, including Taguchi methods, to desensitize the product to manufacturing and user environments; and Statistical Process Control (SPC) to help manufacture the quality product. Products that combine hardware, software, and field support elements present particular challenges but demonstrate significant benefits from the concurrent engineering approach.

INTRODUCTION

The benefits of concurrent engineering in both the commercial and the government contracting environments have been demonstrated repeatedly.[1,2] New products and improvements to old ones are conceived, developed, produced, and in the customers' hands 25 to 45 percent faster than with conventional serial product development. Successful pilot projects have shifted the emphasis in many

---

SOURCE: Reprinted with the permission of the authors.

companies from the question, "Will concurrent engineering work for us?" to, "How do we make concurrent engineering our only way of doing business?"

Multifunctional product development teams are the most common first approach, as documented by Ancona and Caldwell,[3] and recommended in the widespread concurrent engineering courses given by the GOAL/QPC, the American Supplier Institute, and the Juran Institute.[4,5,6] Teams attempt to replace the serial structured communication of the conventional product development process ("toss it over the wall") with continuous communication among team members from many specialty fields. Teams are formed to overcome the communication and coordination problems of serial product development. Techniques for communication in concurrent engineering teams range from informal, ad hoc techniques through the highly structured use of quality function deployment (QFD).

Typical cross-functional teams include people from marketing, program management, systems engineering, design engineering, production, distribution, and field support, and may include suppliers and customers. The team may also draw on a larger pool of specialists in reliability, quality assurance, contracts, human factors, process design, packaging, finance, etc. Just making the list demonstrates why simply forming the team will not solve the problems of communication; the complexity of product development requires the application of many kinds of knowledge, while the pressure to get better products to market faster requires something much more difficult: that all these specialists understand each other.

Reorganization is the trite solution to changing communication patterns. Frequently the new organizational structure is derived from the old, or is designed to overcome perceived weaknesses and preserve perceived strengths of the previous structure. The new structure may be no more effective than the old, but because of resistance to the stress of further change, or the failure to measure the effectiveness before and after the change, or the considerable time it takes for new communication patterns to be established, the first new structure tried may become the only new structure tried. The progress of concurrent engineering from the occasional pilot project stage to organization-wide acceptance as the normal way of business will then be set back by the perception that the organization's management is not committed to concurrent engineering, to Total Quality Management, and to customer service since it is not providing structural support to the product development teams.

It is necessary to find a model for organizational change that will enhance the probability of success for the concurrent engineering teams, a model that is flexible enough to deal with existing and new products, and that can be a vehicle for continuous improvement so that the organizational structure itself is seen as part of the TQM process. One useful model for alignment of structure with strategy and a full network of support is the set of organizational factors described by Waterman, Peters, and Phillips in their "7-S" model[7,8] (Fig. 33.1).

To demonstrate the application of the 7-S paradigm to concurrent engineering, we will step through the elements of the 7-S model, showing how each of the "S" elements supports the others and supports the effectiveness of the emerging concurrent engineering organization. The concentric wheel model of concurrent

FIGURE 33.1 ***The 7-S Framework for Effective Organizational Change***

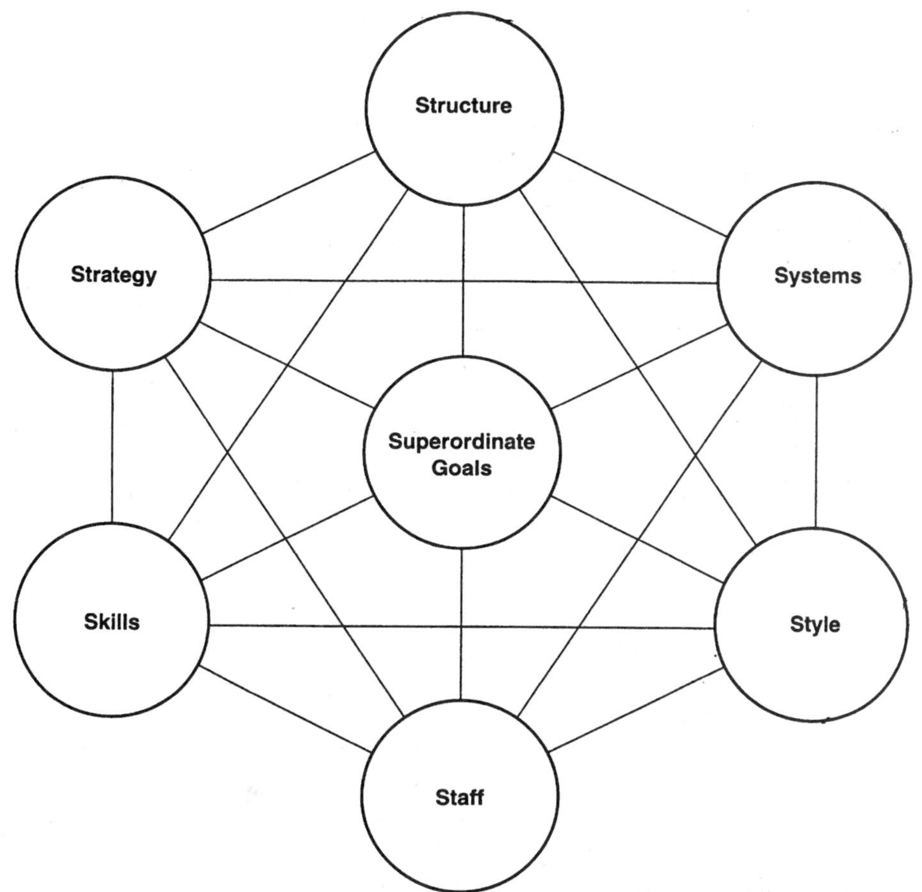

SOURCE: Reprinted from *Business Horizons,* June 1980. Copyright 1980 by the Foundation for the School of Business at Indiana University. Used with permission.

engineering (Fig. 33.2), derived by Rawcliffe from the work of Winner,[1,4] will be used as a general catalog of concurrent engineering attributes that require support.

APPLYING THE 7-S MODEL

Structure

Organizations have formal structures in order to divide tasks and coordinate effort. As businesses have grown, functional organizations have largely been abandoned in favor of decentralized structures. The linear increase in the number of people or activities drives a geometric increase in the number of interactions;

FIGURE 33.2 ***The Concentric Wheel Model of Concurrent Engineering***

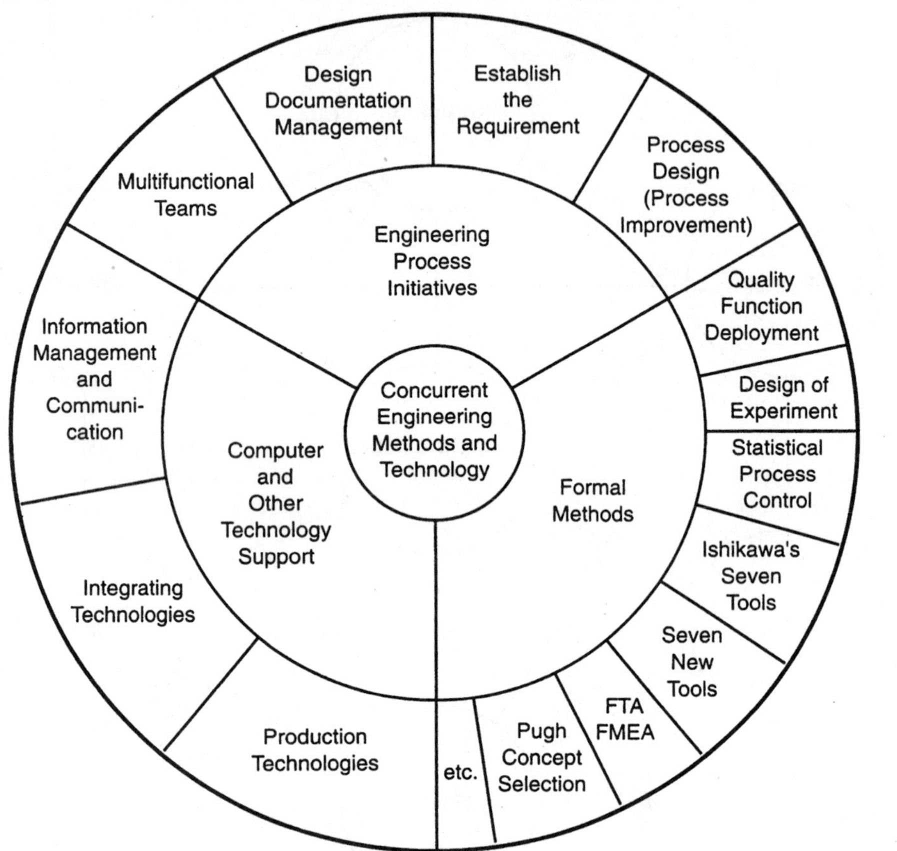

SOURCE: Reprinted from *Business Horizons,* June 1980. Copyright 1980 by the Foundation for the School of Business at Indiana University. Used with permission.

beyond some threshold of size and complexity, centralized functions must give way to decentralized operations to reduce the number of interactions to a manageable level. Matrix organizations are frequently the next step in evolution, to keep some central control while minimizing the coordination complexity. In the aerospace/defense community, matrix organizations have been used since the mid-1950s, and have developed new vocabulary to describe their evolution, ranging from the "strong" (program management oriented) to the "weak" (functional organization dominated) to the "balanced" matrix.

The product development teams which implement concurrent engineering have either "strong" or "balanced" matrix forms. A team can be flexible in membership, depending on the skills needed at each stage of product development, and can use the resources of the matrix to respond quickly to changing customer environments. The functional organizations provide the basis of standards and tools, and of education and training, for team members. On the concentric wheel, a team uses all the elements of the outer ring at various times in the development process, while the functional organization maintains and improves the processes, methods, and technologies. Companies as diverse as Hewlett-Packard, Boeing, General Motors, and Aerojet use a combination of central standards organization and flexible product development teams as the practical solution to the problems of complexity and speed.

Strategy

Strategy is what a company does in response to or in anticipation of changes in its external environment—its customers, its competitors, or its regulatory agencies. Strategy is the company's concept for providing unique value to its customers. Many companies articulate clear strategies but they fail to implement them; the flaw may not be in the strategy or the structure, but in other elements of the organizational design. The decision to implement concurrent engineering is a strategy to provide customer satisfaction through quality services and products delivered quickly to market; actually implementing this strategy needs the full use of the other five elements of the 7-S model.

Systems

Systems are the procedures and processes, both formal and informal, that are the foundation of how the work in the organization gets done. Extensive systems development is required to support the evolution of concurrent engineering. Many companies find it necessary to change the system of design documentation and design release, since the design is now shared by people from many specialties, and from supplier and customer organizations. A large industry of CAD/CAE/CAM/CIM has developed to provide tools to automate these information exchange processes. A strong theme at many recent conferences on TQM and concurrent engineering[9,10] has been the need to simplify processes before you automate them, to get the maximum advantage of speed and simplicity. The supporting systems of the organization—particularly planning and budgeting systems—must be brought into the conversion to concurrent engineering, to be sure that they help to keep the product development teams flexible and responsive while retaining the financial controls needed to protect the business.

Style

Management style is, to many people in changing organizations, like pornography—"I can't define it, but I know it when I see it." The patterns of management's actions are the manifestations of a management style, and are used to convey a manager's values to the organization.

One key element of a manager's style is choosing among all the issues that demand his or her time. If quality improvement is the last item on management's agenda and is frequently dropped for lack of time, all the motivational efforts in the catalog won't be effective in developing quality awareness.

If management solicits employee involvement in policy development but implements few of the policies, the response to future involvement invitations will be small.[11,12] Many organizations have top management TQM Councils, or Quality Planning Councils, as a way of using a visible style to convey the message that quality is the management's concern.[6,11]

In the early stages of implementing concurrent engineering, management must educate itself to use the communication tools of the product development teams, and must develop the styles that support those teams. For example, if QFD and design of experiments (robust design, Taguchi methods) are primary tools of product development, management must cultivate the style of conducting reviews based on the vocabulary and mathematical structures of these tools. The style then shows that the managers know the difficulty of learning new communication and design modalities, but also appreciate the benefits enough to take the time to learn the techniques themselves, and make the effort to combine traditional management techniques with the new philosophies.[13]

Popular catch phrases express the importance of style in delivering the messages of change:

> "Don't talk the talk unless you walk the walk."
> "Watch their feet, not their lips."
> "If you always do what you always did, you'll always get what you always got."

Staff

In the 7-S model, "staff" encompasses all the "people" issues, especially those that involve preparing people for future leadership in the company. In the context of introducing concurrent engineering, the staff issues include systems issues, such as the development of performance evaluation and career planning assistance, pay and promotion policies that reward both team and individual contributions and skills, and training and education in use of new skills and new communication methods. In virtually all concurrent engineering introductions, formal training programs are needed as well as on-the-job training (frequently provided by team facilitators).

A company's style greatly influences the way it handles staff issues under the stress of a new strategy like concurrent engineering, but successful implementations have been observed in both very rigid and very loose cultures.[1,3,7]

Skills

We characterize companies by what they do best. The dominating attributes, or capabilities, are the "skills" of the 7-S model, and range from financial control to marketing, to technological innovation. To implement a new strategy, it may be necessary for a company to develop new skills. The classic success story of the past decade has been the "Baby Bell" companies developing speed, flexibility, and marketing skills after the AT&T divestiture. Skills can drive strategy several ways; both Xerox and Hewlett-Packard realized that their strong skills in field service had developed in response to low product reliability, and with different techniques developed quality strategies to reduce the need for field service.

The attributes of a company that has successfully deployed concurrent engineering are visibly different from those of competitors which have not. These company skills depend on integrating the technical and management skills of people throughout the company with the company's technical resources, to support the customer-oriented organization. The customers' appreciation of new skills can be there ahead of the company's own deployment schedule. At Aerojet, our Air Force Space Systems Division customer appreciated the benefits of concurrent engineering in improved system requirements development after exposure to our first pilot project, and asked for our help teaching their staff the techniques of QFD, and providing facilitators for their staff on other new projects.

A challenge to any organization developing new skills is weeding out old skills and the systems, structures, and styles that support them. If we try to implement concurrent engineering while maintaining all our old product development methods, the contradictions will stall the system, and neither the old nor the new methods will work.

Superordinate Goals

The values, aspirations, and guiding concepts of an organization are the fundamental ideas around which the business is built. They are the broad concepts of future direction and present activity. A technical paradigm for superordinate goals is that they are the postulates of the system. They are not logically derived from anything, but if they are not logically consistent the system, structure, skills, staff, strategy, and style will not work as a coherent whole. The recognition in many TQM processes that the organization's vision and mission must be stated clearly so that all can work on making it a reality reflects the importance of superordinate goals. The rewards to the companies that have persevered in defining their superordinate goals and fully integrating their actions with their goals have been documented extensively, at this conference and throughout the literature of TQM.[7,9]

CONCLUSION

Implementing Total Quality Management challenges all seven "S" attributes of any company (Table 33.1). Because concurrent engineering requires the simultaneous implementation of new skills and new support mechanisms in many areas, it challenges severely an organization's ability to deal with change.

The networked nature of the 7-S model invites continuous iteration and continuous improvement. For companies implementing concurrent engineering, it can be an excellent tool to balance all the elements of company organization.

TABLE 33.1 ***Organizational Factors in Introducing Concurrent Engineering***

"S" factor	Concurrent engineering manifestation
Structure	The TQM team structure can be either a "strong" or a "balanced" matrix, drawing on the strengths of functional organizations.
Strategy	The *decision* to implement concurrent engineering is a strategy.
Systems	Systems must change to support concurrent engineering communication, planning, budgeting, and "traditional" product development systems, such as configuration management, information sharing, design reviews, and production reviews.
Style	When management does take concurrent engineering seriously, it shows in their style and the company follows.
Staff	Introducing concurrent engineering requires training, and affects compensation and evaluation policies.
Skills	Concurrent engineering may require building new skills, and unlearning old ones.
Superordinate Goals	Concurrent engineering must be introduced in a way that keeps it consistent with the company's vision and mission.

References

1. R. I. Winner, J. P. Pennell, H. E. Bertrand, and M. M. C. Slusarczuk, "The Role of Concurrent Engineering in Weapons System Acquisition," Institute for Defense Analysis (IDA) Report R-338, December 1988.
2. R. H. Rawcliffe and R. L. Randall, "Concurrent Engineering Applied to an SDIO Technology Program," *AIAA/ADPA/NSIA First National TQM Symposium,* 89-3191, November 1989.
3. D. G. Ancona and D. Caldwell, "Improving the Performance of New Product Teams," *Research Technology Management,* March–April 1990, 25–29.
4. R. King, *Better Designs in Half the Time,* GOAL/QPC, Massachusetts, 1987.
5. American Supplier Institute (ASI), "Quality Function Deployment Workshop," Michigan, 1987.
6. Juran Institute, Inc., "Juran on Quality Planning," Connecticut, 1988.
7. R. H. Waterman, Jr., *The Renewal Factor,* Bantam Books, New York, 1988.
8. R. H. Waterman, Jr., T. J. Peters, and J. R. Phillips, "Structure Is Not Organization," *Business Horizons,* 484-017, June 1980, 1–13.
9. AIAA, Second National Total Quality Management Symposium, Maryland, November 1990.
10. D. Clausing, "Concurrent Engineering," Presented at the Concurrent Engineering Design Clinic Sponsored by the Society of Manufacturing Engineers (June 1990).
11. R. King, *Hoshin Planning,* GOAL/QPC, Massachusetts, 1989.

12. A. R. Shores, *Survival of the Fittest,* ASQC Quality Press, Wisconsin, 1988.

13. R. L. Randall, "Results of Quality Function Deployment as Applied to Focal Plane Arrays," to be presented at 1991 Conference on the Producibility of Infrared Focal Plane Array Assemblies, sponsored by the Environmental Research Institute of Michigan (February 1991).

part 7

People and Teams as a Source of Competitive Advantage

This section addresses the most important principles of TQM: *respect for people and cooperation.* In TQM literature, cooperation translates into concepts and applications such as teamwork, the development of a shared corporate mission and vision with input from all levels of the organization, and labor-management cooperation.

In a knowledge-driven, post-capitalist society it should become evident that people are the only sustainable source of competitive advantage, argues Pfeffer. People are "the" capital in knowledge intensive industries, a fact often overlooked in discussions of the role of technology as an agent for change.

The use of teams for continuous improvement of processes and problem solving was seen during the late seventies and early eighties as the key to Japanese industrial success. Consequently, many U.S. companies formed quality circles with varying degrees of autonomy.

Quality circles fell into disrepute over time, as much time and effort was seen as wasted in endless meetings and efforts to solve often trivial problems. However, the problem did not lay in the use of teams for problem solving but in the prevalent interpretation of what Japanese quality efforts were all about.

Recent research suggests that quality circles in Japan work under the banner of coordinated, focused efforts of problem-solving throughout the organization. These teams are never totally independent in their selection of issues to focus on but work under supervision and in coordination with other quality efforts.

Today, other forms of teams have emerged in organizations. Quality circles have largely been replaced by quality improvement teams (QITs), also known as process improvement teams (PITs), which usually work on predetermined, clearly focused issues. In the last decade, thousands of companies have organized front-line employees into self-directed teams (SDTs), which plan, implement, and improve the daily work of the organization. Drawing on the experience with autonomous work groups in the field of sociotechnical systems, these SDTs are empowered to make many decisions without any direct supervision.

Reading 34

Sources of Sustained Success

BY JEFFREY PFEFFER
Stanford University Graduate School of Business

Suppose that in 1972, someone asked you to pick the five companies that would provide the greatest return to stockholders over the next 20 years. And suppose that you had access to books on competitive success that were not even written. How would you approach your assignment? In order to earn tremendous economic returns, the companies you picked should have some sustainable competitive advantage, something that 1) distinguishes them from their competitors, 2) provides positive economic benefits, and 3) is not readily duplicated.

Conventional wisdom then (and even now) would have you begin by selecting the right industries. After all, "not all industries offer equal opportunity for sustained profitability, and the inherent profitability of its industry is one essential ingredient in determining the profitability of a firm."[1] According to Michael Porter's now famous framework, the five fundamental competitive forces that determine the ability of firms in an industry to earn above-normal returns are "the entry of new competitors, the threat of substitutes, the bargaining power of buyers, the bargaining power of suppliers, and the rivalry among existing competitors."[2] You should find industries with barriers to entry, low supplier and buyer bargaining power, few ready substitutes, and a limited threat of new entrants to compete away economic returns. Within such industries, other conventional analyses would urge you to select firms with the largest market share, which can realize the cost benefits of economies of scale. In short, you would probably look to industries in which patent protection of important product or service technology could be achieved and select the dominant firms in those industries.

You would have been very successful in selecting the five top-performing firms from 1972 to 1992 if you took this conventional wisdom and turned it on its head.

The top five stocks, and their percentage returns, were (in reverse order): Plenum Publishing (with a return of 15,689 percent), Circuit City (a video and appliance retailer; 16,410 percent), Tyson Foods (a poultry producer; 18,118 percent), Wal-Mart (a discount chain; 19,807 percent), and Southwest Airlines (21,775 percent).[3] Yet during this period, these industries (retailing, airlines, publishing, and food processing) were characterized by massive competition and horrendous losses, widespread bankruptcy, virtually no barriers to entry (for airlines after 1978), little unique or proprietary technology, and many substitute products or services. And in 1972, none of these firms was (and some still are not) the market-share leader, enjoying economies of scale from moving down the learning curve.

The point here is not to throw out conventional strategic analysis based on industrial economics but simply to note that the source of competitive advantage has always shifted over time. What these five successful firms tend to have in common is that for their sustained advantage, they rely not on technology, patents, or strategic position, but on how they manage their workforce. Our first task is to explore how and why some sources of competitive success that were important in the past are less so now and why the workforce, and how it is organized and managed, is an increasingly important source of competitive advantage. This is the topic of this chapter. The chapter also considers how achieving competitive advantage through the workforce affects the development of some human resource policies and practices.

The very factors that made Southwest Airlines, Wal-Mart, Plenum, and other organizations such as Nordstrom, Lincoln Electric, and the New United Motor plant of the Toyota–GM joint venture so successful are things that are difficult to imitate. That is what provides such competitive leverage, the ability to almost literally make gold out of lead—exceptional economic returns in highly competitive, almost mundane industries. The paradox of this book, and of courses and seminars in how to manage the workforce, is that even if we succeed in changing what we do, the basis of sustained competitive success will alter again. At the moment, however, we are a long way from having to worry about that problem.

THE CHANGING BASIS OF COMPETITIVE SUCCESS

People and how we manage them are becoming more important because many other sources of competitive success are less powerful than they once were. Recognizing that the basis for competitive advantage has changed is essential to develop a different frame of reference for considering issues of management and strategy. Traditional sources of success—product and process technology, protected or regulated markets, access to financial resources, and economies of scale—can still provide competitive leverage, but to a lesser degree now than in the past, leaving organizational culture and capabilities, derived from how people are managed, as comparatively more vital.

Product and process technology

One important source of competitive advantage was product technology, protected by patents or other proprietary know-how. In 1959, Xerox developed and prepared to introduce its first plain-paper copier. Some 13 years later, in 1972, it enjoyed a market share of more than 90 percent with machines that, although improved, still relied, fundamentally, on the same technological foundation. How many companies, industries, or products today could retain more than 90 percent of the market on the basis of 13-year-old technology? A quote from the annual report of Sun Microsystems, a computer workstation manufacturer, makes the point: "Sun's avowed intention [is] doubling the performance of its high-end workstations about every 18 months, on average."[4]

Since product life cycles are shortening and new-product introductions are coming much more rapidly, relying on a static product technology for success is increasingly problematic:

> Research has shown that new product introductions are vital to most manufacturing firms' growth and prosperity. A Booz, Allen and Hamilton study of over 700 *Fortune* 1000 companies estimated that new products would provide over 30 percent of these firms' profits during a five-year period from 1981–1986. . . . The same study suggested that the number of new products introduced by these firms was expected to double compared to the previous five-year period.[5]

The rapid development of computer-aided design (CAD), computer-aided manufacture (CAM), the linking of design and manufacture in CAD/CAM systems, and a myriad of other innovations that facilitate product design and introduction all erode how long one can achieve competitive success solely through proprietary product or service technology. George Stalk and Thomas Hout argue that the growing rate of product obsolescence makes the ability to rapidly innovate increasingly important.[6] They found that market share, profits, and costs are all related to the speed with which companies can accomplish things. Peter Thigpen, former senior vice president of manufacturing at Levi Strauss, noted that, assuming a 20 percent annual growth rate in the market, a 12 percent annual price erosion, and a five-year product life, a 50 percent development cost overrun results in a 3.5 percent reduction in after-tax profits; production costs that are 9 percent too high result in a 22 percent reduction in profits; but being just six months late in shipping the product costs a full one-third of the after-tax profit potential.[7]

The increasing pace of product change means that a technical edge, even once achieved, will erode quickly and must be renewed. The need for continuous innovation and rapid response to market and technological changes virtually requires a workforce that delivers superior performance.

Not only is the length of product life cycles diminishing, there is an erosion in the protection provided by patents because of competitors' ability to imitate product innovations. One of the most comprehensive studies of this question examined 48 product innovations of firms in the chemical, drug, electronics, and machinery industries.[8] The study found that, on average, the imitation cost to innovation cost ratio was approximately .65, and the ratio of imitation time to innovation time was about .70.[9] Although patents provided some protection, particularly in pharmaceuticals, the protection was less than one might think. "Contrary to popular opinion, patent protection does not make entry impossible, or even unlikely. Within 4 years of their introduction, 60 percent of the patented successful innovations . . . were imitated."[10]

Firms sought competitive advantage not only in their product technology but also in the process technology used to produce the product or service. General Motors was perhaps the archetype of this approach, investing heavily in technology to automate its factories in the 1980s. The company spent some $40 billion for modernization and new facilities, in the process substituting fixed costs for variable costs.[11] In fact, GM spent enough money on capital equipment to have purchased both Honda and Nissan.[12] Unfortunately, it did not get much for that investment.

There are several problems with seeking competitive advantage through investments in process technology. First, little of that technology is proprietary—the people who sell you robots or point-of-sale terminals or software to analyze production or service delivery will sell the robots, terminals, and software to your competitors. Your ability to obtain the benefits of, let alone get any advantage from, this technology—which is often widely available and readily understood—depends on your ability to implement it more rapidly and more effectively. This almost inevitably involves the skill and motivation of the workforce.

Second, investment in specialized technology is not a substitute for skill in managing the workforce; it actually makes the workforce even more crucial for success. This is because more skill may be required to operate the more sophisticated and advanced equipment, and with a higher level of investment per employee, interruptions in the process are increasingly expensive. This means that the ability to effectively operate, maintain, and repair equipment—tasks all done by first-line employees—becomes even more critical.

Paul Adler noted that "in banks, a fully on-line system integrating numerous branches meant that people at the extremities . . . would have to be absolutely reliable, since any data they entered . . . would be fed instantaneously into all the bank's accounts and corresponding funds transferred instantaneously."[13] He also noted that in the case of numerically controlled machine tools, in spite of manufacturers' promises, the skill requirements of machinists have remained constant or increased. They often required expanded training and higher levels of responsibility, even with the more technologically sophisticated machines.

When the Shenandoah Life Insurance Company spent some $2 million to computerize its processing and claims operations in the early 1980s, it found that it got almost nothing for its expenditure—it still required 27 working days and 32 clerks in three departments to handle a policy conversion.[14] Only after the company changed how it organized and managed its workforce—relying on semiautonomous teams of 5 to 7 people, upgrading training and skills, and paying more for the more responsible and more skilled workers—did case-handling time drop and service complaints virtually disappear. "By 1986, Shenandoah was processing 50 percent more applications and queries with 10 percent fewer employees than it did in 1980."[15]

Finally, investments in process technology provide only limited competitive advantage because, as the senior manufacturing executive in the paper-making division of a large forest products company said, "Machines don't make things, people do." Commenting on the tremendous investment in advanced computer technology to automate factory processes, one writer perceptively noted: "[I]t is rather ironic that the application of artificial intelligence to manufacturing is becoming a popular topic. If intelligence is so helpful to manufacturing in its artificial form, then why have the benefits of the real intelligence been overlooked so far."[16]

Protected and regulated markets

Another way in which firms achieved competitive success was by avoiding competition through protected or regulated domestic markets. Some years ago while visiting Italy, I noticed that there were many Fiats and almost no Japanese cars—indeed, only about 2,000 Japanese cars per year were sold in Italy during the mid-1980s. This sales level did not reflect the relative prices and product qualities or consumer tastes, but resulted from a limit on the imports of Japanese cars. Fearful of the power and success of Fiat after World War II, Japan struck a bargain in which the Japanese automobile market would be protected from Fiat while the Italian market would be protected from Japanese automakers.

With the growing importance of free-trade areas in Europe, North America, and elsewhere, and with the increasing investment in manufacturing facilities all over the world (e.g., the building of Japanese automobile plants in the United States and Europe), the ability to sustain competitive success by foreclosing markets is disappearing. The changing role of foreign trade in the United States and the world economies over the past few decades has been truly remarkable—and the growth of both exports and imports means that firms are now competing not only domestically but globally: "In 1950 real exports and imports of goods and services were under 5 percent of real GNP . . . [B]y 1980 real exports and imports were 12.2 percent and 10.4 percent of real GNP, respectively. In 1988 exports were 13.1 percent and imports 15 percent of GNP."[17] Thus, between 1950 and 1990, foreign trade grew from less than 5 percent to almost 30 percent of the U.S. gross national product.

The automobile industry nicely illustrates the move toward the internationalization of markets and its consequences. The share of imports in the U.S. passenger car market soared from 7.3 percent in 1966 to 14.8 percent 10 years later and to 29.3 percent by 1982.[18] Similar increases were occurring elsewhere as well—from 1966 to 1982, imports of passenger cars in France rose from 13.9 percent to 21.7 percent; in Germany from 13.7 percent to 24.9 percent; and in the United Kingdom from just 5 percent to 57.7 percent. As markets opened to foreign competition, production of motor vehicles shifted. In 1950, companies in the United States produced some 75.4 percent of the total world output of motor vehicles (trucks, buses, and automobiles), with Europe producing 19.8 percent and Japan essentially none.[19] Thirty years later, motor vehicle production located in Europe was 37.6 percent, 28.6 percent in Japan, and only 20.8 percent in the United States. The globalization of competition has occurred in telecommunications equipment and financial services as well. For instance, 31 percent of the business loans, 21 percent of the assets, and 14 percent of the total deposits in the United States are now controlled by foreign or foreign-owned banks.[20]

Regulation can limit competition by setting prices and by restricting entry.[21] In the United States, for many years entry into transportation industries such as airlines and trucking was strictly controlled. MCI's success as a provider of long-distance telephone service came only after the company won a protracted struggle to even be permitted to operate. The wave of deregulation sweeping the United States and the rest of the world, however, has eliminated many protected markets. Moreover, there is some evidence that once deregulated and opened to competition, markets are difficult to close or reregulate. Thus, these trends seem to be irreversible.

Access to financial resources

Another traditional source of competitive advantage was access to financial resources. With less efficient capital markets, a firm's ability to finance itself through substantial financial resources afforded protection from competitors less able to acquire the resources necessary to mount a serious challenge. This source of competitive advantage has eroded in the face of increasingly efficient financial markets in which capital moves worldwide on an unprecedented scale. The venture capital industry is now international, so that if U.S. investors, for instance, are unwilling to bear the risk of financing leading-edge technologies in pharmaceuticals, semiconductors, and equipment, foreign investors will pick up the slack. Table 34.1 is a partial listing of the extent of direct foreign investment in important California leading-edge companies and technologies in the 1980s.

As one author noted:

> The growth of international direct investment by multinational corporations has outpaced the growth of the world economy and world trade in the 1980s. . . . Not only do United States multinational corporations face stronger competition from foreign multinationals in international markets, but affiliates of foreign firms—often with new production technologies and different management techniques—have become more active in the United States.[22]

Between 1967 and 1987, worldwide outward direct investment increased from $112 billion to $1.023 trillion, an average annual growth rate of 12.4 percent. The U.S. share of this outward direct investment declined from 50 percent to 31 percent. Meanwhile, direct foreign investment in the United States grew dramatically, from $9.9 billion in 1967 to $272 billion in 1987, a growth rate of some 17.8 percent per year.[23] Capital is now less important as a source of competitive advantage because the money to finance a good idea, or strong management, is increasingly available to all attractive projects.

TABLE 34.1 ***Selected examples of direct foreign investment in California, 1981–1990***

Firm	Investor	Country	Percentage Holding
Biotechnology			
Genentech	Roche	Switzerland	60
Mycogen	Kubota	Japan	9.6
Chiron	CIBA-Geigy	Switzerland	6.2
Genencor	Cultor Oy/Kodak	Finland/U.S.	100
Cetus	Roche	Switzerland	3.5
Cytel	Sandoz	Switzerland	100
Semiconductors and Equipment			
Zymos	Daewoo	South Korea	35
Siltec	Mitsubishi	Japan	33
Varian's Tube Division	Thorn EMI	United Kingdom	100
Siscan Systems	Mitsubishi	Japan	11.5
Computer Hardware and Peripherals			
NeXT	Canon	Japan	17
Poquet Computer	Fujitsu	Japan	38
MIPS Computer	Kubota	Japan	25
Ardent Computer	Kubota	Japan	44
Wyse	Private investors	Taiwan	100
System Integrators	Birmingham	United Kingdom	100
Fortune Systems	French government	France	100

SOURCE: David J. Teece, "Foreign Investment and Technological Development in Silicon Valley," Copyright 1992 by The Regents of the University of California. Reprinted from the *California Management Review,* Vol. 34, No. 2. By permission of The Regents.

Economies of scale

Yet another source of competitive advantage that is now less significant than it used to be is economies of scale. The famous Boston Consulting Group experience curve postulated that a firm that entered a market early and achieved large production volumes would face significantly lower costs as it achieved the benefits of learning as well as more traditional scale economies. Although there is some evidence for the economic benefits of large market share,[24] there is much evidence that this source of competitive advantage is diminishing in importance. The trend toward more fragmented markets, with the need to cater to the specialized tastes of particular subsegments of the population, has been described in detail by Piore and Sabel in their book about flexible specialization.[25] In general, the same computer-aided design and manufacturing technologies that make imitation easier also make it possible to more economically design and manufacture a more differentiated product line.

Several examples help make the point. Consider first so-called natural monopolies, such as telecommunications and electric power generation. Even here, evolving technology makes it possible for smaller competitors to effectively exploit market segments. In downtown Chicago, an independent company laid its own fiber-optic cable and provides telephone service to a set of commercial clients in that densely populated area. Stanford University has its own telephone system to handle both data and voice communications on the campus. Electric utilities compete with industrial clients that now dispose of their wastes in co-generation facilities, which produce power from the heat. In the steel industry, the so-called minimills are a well-known phenomenon, in many instances more profitable and cost-competitive than their larger competitors. The ability of the Japanese to make car models profitably, even when they sell fewer than 100,000 units per year, has given firms with that capability a tremendous competitive advantage. And finally, the textile industry, particularly suppliers of men's clothing, traditionally competed on the basis of price and did so by making large lots of standard products. With major retailers now wanting to stock leaner inventories and be more responsive to shifting customer tastes and what actually sells, the basis of success has shifted to the ability to deliver the product quickly. "Rather than allowing order response times of one month or more, the lean retailer currently requires 13 days for order fulfillment. In two years, the response time will decrease to 6 days."[26]

Without debating whether scale economies and market share ever provided the advantages that some claimed, it is clear that whatever those advantages, they are smaller now than they once were and will probably be even smaller in the future.

The importance of the workforce and how it is managed

As other sources of competitive success have become less important, what remains as a crucial, differentiating factor is the organization, its employees, and how they work. Consider, for instance, Southwest Airlines, whose stock had the best return from 1972 to 1992. It certainly did not achieve that success from economies of scale. In 1992, Southwest had revenues of $1.31 billion and a mere 2.6 percent of the U.S. passenger market.[27] People Express, by contrast, achieved $1 billion in revenues after only 3 years of operation, not the almost 20 it took Southwest. Southwest exists not because of regulated or protected markets but in spite of them. "During the first three years of its history, no Southwest planes were flown."[28] Southwest waged a battle for its very existence with competitors that sought to keep it from flying at all and, failing that, made sure it did not fly out of the newly constructed Dallas–Fort Worth international airport. Instead, it was restricted to operating out of the close-in Love Field, and thus was born its first advertising slogan, "Make Love, Not War." Southwest became the "love" airline out of necessity, not choice.

In 1978, competitors sought to bar flights from Love Field to anywhere outside of Texas. The compromise Southwest wrangled permitted it to fly from Love to the four states contiguous to Texas.[29] Its competitive strategy of short-haul, point-to-point flights to close-in airports (it now flies into Chicago's Midway and

Houston's Hobby airports) was more a product of its need to adapt to what it was being permitted to do than a conscious, planned move—altbough, in retrospect, the strategy has succeeded brilliantly. Nor has Southwest succeeded because it has had more access to lower-cost capital—indeed, it is one of the least leveraged airlines in the United States. Southwest's planes, Boeing 737s, are obviously available to all its competitors. It isn't a member of any of the big computerized reservation systems; it uses no unique process technology and sells essentially a commodity product—low-cost, low-frills airline service at prices its competitors have difficulty matching.

Much of its cost advantage comes from its very productive, very motivated, and by the way, unionized workforce. Compared to the U.S. airline industry, according to 1991 statistics, Southwest has fewer employees per aircraft (79 versus 131), flies more passengers per employee (2,318 versus 848), and has more available seat miles per employee (1,891,082 versus 1,339,995).[30] It turns around some 80 percent of its flights in 15 minutes or less, while other airlines on average need 45 minutes, giving it an enormous productivity advantage in terms of equipment utilization.[31] It also provides an exceptional level of passenger service. Southwest has won the airlines' so-called triple crown (best on-time performance, fewest lost bags, and fewest passenger complaints—in the same month) *nine* times. No competitor has achieved that even once.[32]

I will give numerous examples of achieving competitive success through people in this book. What is important to recognize now is why success, such as that achieved at Southwest, can be sustained and can not readily be imitated by competitors. There are two fundamental reasons. First, the success that comes from managing people effectively is often not as visible or transparent as to its source. We can see a computerized information system, a particular semiconductor, a numerically controlled machine tool. The culture and practices that enable Southwest to achieve its success are less obvious. Even when they are described, as they have been in numerous newspaper articles and even a segment on *60 Minutes,* they are difficult to really understand. Culture, how people are managed, and the effects of this on their behavior and skills are sometimes seen as the "soft" side of business, occasionally dismissed. Even when they are not dismissed, it is often hard to comprehend the dynamics of a particular company and how it operates because the way people are managed often fits together in a system. It is easy to copy one thing but much more difficult to copy numerous things. This is because the change needs to be more comprehensive and also because the ability to understand the system of management practices is hindered by its very extensiveness.

Thus, for example, Nordstrom, the department store chain, has enjoyed substantial success both in customer service and in sales and profitability growth over the years. Nordstrom compensates its employees in part with commissions. Not surprisingly, many of its competitors, after finally acknowledging Nordstrom's success, and the fact that it was attributable to the behaviors of its employees, instituted commission systems. By itself, changing the compensation system did not fully capture what Nordstrom had done, nor did it provide many benefits to the competition. Indeed, in some cases, changing the compensation system produced employee grievances and attempts to unionize when the new system was viewed as unfair or arbitrary.

Achieving competitive success through people involves fundamentally altering how we think about the workforce and the employment relationship. It means achieving success by working *with* people, not by replacing them or limiting the scope of their activities. It entails seeing the workforce as a source of strategic advantage, not just as a cost to be minimized or avoided. Firms that take this different perspective are often able to successfully outmaneuver and outperform their rivals. In the remainder of this chapter, I address two issues—training and the use of contingent workforce—to show how viewing people as a source of success changes the formulation of both public policy and managerial strategy.

TRAINING AND SKILL DEVELOPMENT

If competitive success is achieved through people, then the skills of those people are critical. Consequently, one of the most obvious implications of the changing basis of competitive success is the growing importance of having a workforce with adequate skills. Historical studies show that between 1929 and 1982, education prior to work accounted for 26 percent of the growth in the productive capacity of the United States, with learning on the job contributing to an additional 55 percent. It seems clear that "learning in school and learning on the job are by far the most important factors behind American economic growth and productivity in this century, and will determine the nation's economic prospects in the next."[33] The evidence, however, is that skill problems in the U.S. workforce are widespread and growing. Moreover, there is little evidence that U.S. employers, for the most part, are doing what is required to address this problem.

Regarding the first point, the skill problem, an overview of training and preparation for work concluded, "As we approach the end of this century, it becomes ever more apparent that the demand for more skilled workers is on a collision course with the quantity and quality of the labor supply."[34] In an article reporting the declining position of the United States in world trade in telecommunications equipment, the New York Telephone Company reported that "it tested 57,000 job applicants in 1987 and found that 54,900, or 96.3 percent, lacked basic skills in math, reading, and reasoning."[35] A human resource planning document prepared at the Bank of America in 1990 reported that "Chemical Bank in New York must interview 40 applicants to find one who can be successfully trained as a teller";[36] "at Pacific Bell in Los Angeles, 95 percent of the 3,500 people who recently took a competency test for entry-level jobs not requiring a high school education failed"; and "at Motorola, 80 percent of its applicants cannot pass a simple 7th grade English comprehension or 5th grade math test. At Bell South in Atlanta, fewer than 1 in 10 applicants meet all qualification standards."[37]

A U.S. Department of Education report covering document, prose, and quantitative literacy summarized the findings of a study mandated by Congress because of its concern about skill deficiencies in the workplace and came to equally grim conclusions.[38] For instance, in 1986, only about 50 percent of all high school graduates achieved literacy at a level that would enable them to follow directions to travel from one location to another using a map, and only 10 percent of the graduates could use a bus schedule to select the appropriate bus for given departures and arrivals.[39] Only 3 percent of high school graduates could orally interpret distinctions between types of employee benefits, and just 4.5 percent could estimate cost using grocery unit-price labels.[40] Assessments of mathematical proficiency are also distressing.[41] Almost one-quarter of high school seniors could not accurately determine the cost of a simple meal from a short menu of items and prices,[42] and fewer than half "demonstrated a consistent grasp of decimals, percents, fractions, and simple algebra."[43]

The response to the skills deficit, and to the growing recognition that competitive success will depend on a firm's employees, has been less than overwhelming. For instance, "though 73 percent of employers polled by placement consultant Right Associates expect a skilled-labor shortage, three fourths don't have a plan to keep most-needed workers."[44] A follow-up to the famous Workforce 2000 report undertaken by the Hudson Institute and the consulting firm Towers Perrin

> reports pressing shortages of technical, professional and secretarial workers at many companies. . . . But managers aren't responding to the changes quickly enough, the study suggests. It cites a lack of "leading-edge" recruitment and training strategies. . . . Companies . . . have been slow to make a strong commitment to training the workers they do hire. Two-thirds of the surveyed firms spend less than $2,000 for classroom and other on-the-job education for first-year workers.[45]

Training tends to go to those already fairly well trained, most often in the management or professional ranks. Much less is done to upgrade the skills of front-line employees. The Bank of America's human resource planning document noted that "nation-wide companies are three to four times more likely to offer workshops on stress-management or how to run meetings than to train laborers seeking to upgrade their positions."[46] Another study reported that while 17 percent of executive, administrative, and managerial personnel received training provided by their employers in a given year, the comparable figure for machine operators was 4 percent.[47]

There are several reasons why many organizations provide less training than is optimal. First, unlike many other countries, the United States presently has no specific public policy designed to encourage training. Although such expenditures are obviously tax-deductible, in many countries there is a requirement that 1 percent or so of payroll (wages) be spent on training. If less than the prescribed amount is spent, the difference goes to the government as a tax. Also, unlike many other countries, there is little coordination from the government, industry associations, or other collective organizations to formulate training policy and standards and to facilitate the training enterprise. For instance, in New Zealand, legislation has established coordinating bodies for training in various industries, and these bodies tend to be active in setting standards, developing curricula, implementing certification, and so forth.

Second, the costs of training funded by the company are clear and immediate, but the benefits are often long term and may, in fact, accrue to other organizations. If I train someone and the person leaves to work for another employer, then the other organization obtains the benefits of my organization's expenditures. Economic theory, consequently, suggests that general training, of use in numerous jobs, be funded by the trainee, who, after all, stands to reap the benefits. Firm-specific training, for skills that are of use primarily to a particular organization, should be funded by that organization. Of course, what constitutes general or firm-specific training is likely to be very much open to question, and firms will therefore have a tendency to underinvest in skill development.

Third, training's benefits are inherently long term. Under the pressure of short-term budget or profit pressure, training, particularly in the United States, is often the first thing to be cut. Every dollar saved on skill building this year flows immediately to pretax profit, and the loss of competitive position that may be caused is less clearly visible and, in any event, will probably occur only sometime in the future.

This, however, does mean that organizations that choose to do so can use training, and the skills developed thereby, as a competitive weapon. As one example, consider the New United Motor automobile assembly plant in Fremont, California, a joint venture of Toyota and General Motors. Under the agreement establishing the joint venture, a certain proportion of the production was to go to Toyota and a portion to GM. When the Nova was being produced for GM at the plant, and sales weren't sufficient to keep the plant busy, rather than laying off workers, the company gave them other tasks such as painting and repair, and trained them extensively in statistical process control (SPC), how to work in groups, how to analyze jobs and the work process, and so forth. The plant manager at the time remarked that in the 1990s, having a skilled and committed workforce would be the key to success in the automobile industry and wanted to ensure that this facility would be competitive with the best in the world. Indeed, many of the Japanese transplant automobile assembly facilities surprised people with the extensive training they provided workers. Often, selected workers were sent to Japan prior to the start-up, and workers were routinely given as much as four times the amount of initial training that was customary in the U.S. automobile industry. This training obviously costs money, but the Japanese believed that it would produce a workforce with the skills to provide a competitive advantage in an industry facing excess manufacturing capacity.

Using training to gain a competitive edge is diffusing to U.S. automakers as well. When General Motors opened a new truck plant in Fort Wayne, Indiana, that relied not only on new technology but also on team-based production, both workers and management went through intensive training in group problem solving and interpersonal dynamics.[48] The 3,000 employees at the factory received 1.9 million hours of training, or about 633 hours per worker, to learn the new technology and develop skills in working in teams.

At Advanced Micro Devices' submicron development center, a state-of-the-art development and manufacturing facility producing wafers with circuits of less than 1 micron in width, the company spends over 40,000 hours and $1 million per year on training for its approximately 400 employees in the facility. The firm believes that this training, and other innovative practices, are the only way to benefit from a capital investment in plant and advanced manufacturing equipment in excess of $300 million.

In a world in which your competitors treat training as a luxury, don't know how to organize and deliver it, and don't link it tightly to the strategic objectives of the business, your organization's ability to maintain appropriate training can produce real competitive advantage. Moreover, public policies that facilitate, encourage, or enable training enhance the competitiveness of those who are subject to those policies.

THE "EXTERNALIZATION" OF EMPLOYMENT

If competitive success is achieved through people—if the workforce is, indeed, an increasingly important source of competitive advantage—then it is important to build a workforce that has the ability to achieve competitive success and that cannot be readily duplicated by others. Somewhat ironically, the recent trend toward using temporary help, part-time employees, and contract workers, particularly when such people are used in core activities, flies in the face of the changing basis of competitive success. This raises the questions of why these practices seem to be growing, what effects they have on the ability to achieve advantage through people, and what the implications are for organizations that might follow a different strategy.

At the most fundamental level, it is obvious that, at the limit, if all employees are temps or contract workers, or even if they are part-timers, they cannot serve as a basis of distinction. As is the case with technological equipment, the temporary agencies will furnish staff to all customers. Outside contractors will work for anyone, and part-timers, many of whom are in that status involuntarily, have insufficient attachment or commitment to a particular organization to provide it with some comparative advantage. Consider the case of professional services, such as law, accounting, or management consulting. Why use McKinsey, the consulting firm, or Jones, Day, the large law firm, or KPMG Peat Marwick, the accounting firm, and pay a premium price to do so, if these companies simply hired contract or temporary workers? The distinctive competence of a professional services firm is the skill of its staff and if those people can be obtained just as readily elsewhere, and if they have no attachment to a particular firm, then the competitive position of the organization is diminished. This is why many well-managed professional services firms emphasize recruitment, selection, and building strong cultures to retain the skilled employees who constitute the basis for their success. To the extent that people are a source of competitive success for firms other than those in professional services, the same logic applies.

Nevertheless, taking employees out of the organization or diminishing their attachment to it is a growing trend.[49] For instance, between 1970 and 1984, the temp industry outgrew the GNP by almost 2 to 1 and grew 21 percent faster than even the computing equipment industry over that same time period. A study of flexible employment in California reported that the number of temps grew 800 percent from 1972 to 1985, more than seven times the rate of employment growth in nonagricultural industries.[50] Contracting for services has made business services industry growth outstrip even the growth of services provided to consumers—with employment doubling between 1974 and 1984.[51] Part-time work has also increased in prominence. As the nonagricultural workforce grew 54 percent between 1970 and 1990, the number of people involuntarily employed part time increased more than 120 percent,[52] so that by 1985, part-time work constituted almost a quarter of total employment in the state of California.[53]

The reasons behind this growth are many. It is often much quicker to staff using these sources of labor. Hiring a so-called permanent employee requires possibly posting the job, collecting applications, screening, and making a final selection. Getting a temporary requires a phone call, and the person can often be there within an hour. Speed in filling the position is a mixed blessing, however. On the one hand, you get someone quickly. On the other hand, the absence of the formal process may mean you have people who would not meet the regular requirements. In a study at Apple Computer, managers were asked whether they would be willing to hire the contingent employees on a regular basis. In about 80 percent of the cases, the response was that the person did not meet Apple's hiring standards. These same people, however, performed almost 25 percent of the corporation's jobs in the mid-1980s, working on everything from hardware to software development and quality control.

A second reason for using contract or temporary workers is that the unit may not have authorization to hire. Many organizations manage head count much more stringently than they manage monetary budgets. This permits them to trumpet figures like sales per employee or, in the case of government, for political leaders to announce that they have reduced the size of government. However, if all one has done is replace regular employees with outsiders or temporaries, the presumed savings may be illusory or worse. For example, during the Reagan administration's drive to cut the size of government, the Department of Energy went from 21,208 employees in 1980 to 16,103 in 1989. But outside contracts increased 56 percent just between 1986 and 1990, and a study by the General Accounting Office "found that most of the department's $522 million in support service contracts in the fiscal year 1990 were . . . signed because the agency 'lacked sufficient resources' to properly perform the activities."[54]

Third, the use of contingent employees is a buffer to absorb fluctuations in demand while avoiding the morale problems that layoffs engender. The traumatic 1985 layoffs at Apple, an organization with a strong culture, caused many managers to want to avoid a repeat of the situation. One way was to use very lean staffing levels and contingent workers to do the additional work. A study of 442 private firms observed that both the seasonality and cyclicality of demand affected the use of temporaries. However, neither factor affected the extent of contracting out.[55] The use of contingent employment to buffer a set of critical, core employees is one that is compatible with achieving competitive advantage through the workforce.

Finally, one of the most important reasons why organizations use contingent employees is that they cost less. The issue of cost is complex, as there are many costs (and possibly offsetting benefits) that need to be accounted for. In many organizations, as at Apple, a facilities charge is levied for permanent employees, since they need work space, but not for contingent workers. Of course, this cost saving is illusory if one has temporary workers who actually occupy space continuously.

Temporary and contract employees may also cost less because they are paid less and do not receive the benefits—particularly health insurance, retirement, and vacation—of regular employees. Katherine Abraham reported that "the average wages for less-skilled workers . . . employed in the business service sector are from 15 to 30 percent lower than average wages for workers holding similar jobs in manufacturing,"[56] and a study of contract workers in petrochemical facilities found that such workers earned less even after numerous characteristics were statistically controlled.[57] Wages, however, are often the same or even higher for contingent workers in high-skilled occupations. The evidence is that benefits are not offered on a pro rata basis to part-time employees[58] and are less likely to be offered to low-skilled workers in business services compared to the same jobs in manufacturing.[59] The desire to save on benefits costs is so strong that "Federal civil service regulations were changed in June 1985 to permit the federal Office of Personnel Management to hire temporary workers for up to 4 years without providing fringe benefits."[60]

Many of the benefits of using contingent employees are immediate and measurable. The disadvantages or costs are more likely to accrue over time and occur in ways that make them less readily captured by traditional accounting systems. Consequently, there is a tendency for organizations, particularly those under immediate financial pressure, to overuse these arrangements and thereby lose the opportunity to achieve some market advantage through their workforce.

The biggest disadvantage of contingent employment arrangements is the difficulty in obtaining loyalty, dedication, or willingness to expend extra effort on behalf of the organization. One Hewlett-Packard executive commented, "They don't tend to be dedicated to the corporate ideal. . . . They're here to make money, not to fulfill the corporate vision."[61] Sometimes it is even difficult to get them to do their jobs:

> Shortly after Carroon & Black Corp. hired a temporary worker to stuff 80,000 insurance certificates into envelopes . . . the company found thousands of documents dumped in a freight elevator. The "temp" had become bored working alone and thought nobody would notice if she cut her work load.[62]

The costs of reduced productivity, diminished motivation, and less commitment to the organization can be "large and sometimes subtle."[63]

The use of contingent workers also affects the likelihood of the organization's obtaining strategic advantage through training and the development of a skilled workforce. Contingent work arrangements preclude the organization's capturing the benefits of any firm-specific knowledge or capabilities that the employees may develop. More important, the work arrangements themselves discourage training and development—hiring temporaries or outside contractors is, after all, sometimes done to enable the organization to change its skill set or avoid taking the time and incurring the cost to develop its own people.

A contingent, poorly trained workforce can be a dangerous one in the wrong setting. In the chemical industry, maintenance and repair tasks are often contracted out, with contract employees performing about a third of that work during regular operations and half of the work in upgrading or repairing equipment.[64] These less educated, experienced, and trained workers are associated with the growing number of serious accidents in petrochemicals. From January to June 1991, "of the 11 workplace accidents known to involve explosions, fires, and spills in the United States petrochemical industry . . . nine were reported to involve contract employees."[65] In nursing, the use of temporary agencies to solve staffing shortages had two adverse effects. With a short-term palliative, the orga-nizations seldom addressed their fundamental problems. Quality control was a major problem. Temp nurses were used in positions for which they were not qualified; they worked excessive hours for several different clients; and the poor performers were simply reassigned to a different hospital until the performance deficiencies were again noticed.[66]

The appropriate use of a contingent workforce involves first understanding the real sources of success in one's business and then ensuring that key activities are performed by people with enough connection to the organization that they are likely to do a good job and to receive the necessary training and skill development, either through on-the-job learning or through more formal programs. Wal-Mart, although a discount chain, uses fewer part-timers and temporary-help employees than virtually any of its competitors. Wal-Mart sees an important component of its success coming from customer service and from the ability to tap into localized knowledge of customer wants and needs. Seeking advantage in part through its workforce, the company staffs itself to have the opportunity to obtain a more dedicated and skilled set of employees.

By contrast, People Express, a low-cost airline begun in the first wave of deregulation, staffed its reservation agent positions with temporary workers. Travel agents tended not to sell People's tickets, so for most customers, the first point of contact was the reservation agent. Feeling left out of the company culture, with no career mobility prospects, these individuals did not provide an initial point of customer contact that was consistent with the service the airline sought to offer.

The allure of the immediate cost and benefit savings may be seductive, but the costs of contingent employees can be high. The critical decision involves determining whether people will be a source of distinct competitive advantage and, if so, in what activities they are the most critical. Contingent employees should be used with great caution in such activities.

Considering the issues of training and contracting out provides two concrete illustrations of how thinking about the extent to which sustainable competitive advantage originates from the workforce helps us make sound decisions about policies and practices related to managing the workforce. It is by making the right choices about managing people that firms such as Nordstrom, New United Motor, Wal-Mart, Lincoln Electric, and Southwest Airlines achieved their well-known success.

Notes

1. Michael E. Porter, *Competitive Advantage* (New York: Free Press, 1985), 1.
2. Ibid., 4.
3. "Investment Winners and Losers," *Money,* October 1992, 133.
4. George Stalk, Jr., and Thomas M. Hout, *Competing against Time* (New York: Free Press, 1990), 141.
5. Billie Jo Zirger and Modesto A. Maidique, "A Model of New Product Development: An Empirical Test," *Management Science* 36 (1990), 867.
6. Stalk and Hout, *Competing against Time.*
7. Presentation by Peter Thigpen at Stanford Graduate School of Business, February 26, 1991.
8. Edwin Mansfield, Mark Schwartz, and Samuel Wagner, "Imitation Costs and Patents: An Empirical Study," *The Economic Journal* 91 (1981), 907–918.
9. Ibid., 909.
10. Ibid., 913.
11. Maryann Keller, *Rude Awakening: The Rise, Fall, and Struggle for Recovery of General Motors* (New York: William Morrow, 1989), 213.
12. Richard Pascale, *Managing on the Edge* (New York: Simon & Schuster, 1990), 73.
13. Paul Adler, "New Technologies, New Skills," *California Management Review* 29 (1986), 10.
14. "Management Discovers the Human Side of Automation," *Business Week,* September 29, 1986, 70.
15. Ibid.
16. M. Hossein Safizadeh, "The Case of Workgroups in Manufacturing Operations," *California Management Review* 33 (1991), 61.
17. Allen Unsworth and Barbara N. McLennan, "Exports and the U.S. Economic Outlook," *U.S. Industrial Outlook 1990,* 16.
18. Stephen Woolcock, Jeffrey Hart, and Hans Van Der Ven, *Interdependence in the Post-Multilateral Era* (Cambridge, MA: Center for International Affairs, Harvard University, 1985), 73.
19. Ibid., 71.
20. Kenneth H. Bacon, "Foreign Banks Seek Help as Congress Begins Writing Some Checks on Them," *The Wall Street Journal,* June 6, 1991, A18.
21. George J. Stigler, "The Theory of Economic Regulation," *Bell Journal of Economics and Management Science* 2 (1971), 3–21.

22. John W. Rutter, "Recent Trends in International Direct Investment and the Implications for U.S. Business," *U.S. Industrial Outlook 1990,* 6.

23. Ibid., 7.

24. Robert Buzzell and Bradley T. Gale, *The PIMS Principles: Linking Strategy to Performance* (New York: Free Press, 1987).

25. Michael J. Piore and Charles E. Sabel, *The Second Industrial Divide* (New York: Basic Books, 1984).

26. John T. Dunlop and David Weil, "Human Resource Innovations in the Apparel Industry: An Industrial Relations System Perspective," unpublished ms. (Cambridge, MA: Harvard University, 1992).

27. Bridget O'Brian, "Southwest Airlines Is a Rare Air Carrier: It Still Makes Money," *The Wall Street Journal,* October 26, 1992, A1.

28. James Campbell Quick, "Crafting an Organizational Culture: Herb's Hand at Southwest Airlines," *Organizational Dynamics* 21 (Autumn 1992), 47.

29. O'Brian, "Southwest Airlines," A7.

30. Quick, "Crafting an Organizational Culture," 50.

31. O'Brian, "Southwest Airlines," A1.

32. Ibid., A7.

33. Anthony P. Carnevale and Harold Goldstein, "Schooling and Training for Work in America: An Overview," in Louis A. Ferman, Michele Hoyman, Joel Cutcher-Gershenfeld, and Ernest J. Savoie (eds.), *New Developments in Worker Training: A Legacy for the 1990s* (Madison, WI: Industrial Relations Research Association, 1990), 30.

34. Ibid., 27.

35. Keith Bradsher, "U.S. Lag in Phone Trade Seen," *New York Times,* August 17, 1990, C3.

36. Bank of America, "Human Resource Planning," *Perspectives* 11 (Winter 1990), 40.

37. Ibid., 43.

38. Paul E. Barton and Irwin S. Kirsch, *Workplace Competencies,* Policy Perspective Series (Washington, DC: Office of Educational Research and Development, U.S. Department of Education, 1990).

39. Ibid., 9.

40. Ibid., 8, 10.

41. Ina V. S. Mullis, John A. Dossey, Eugene H. Owens, and Gary W. Phillips, *The State of Mathematics Achievement* (Washington, DC: National Center for Education Statistics, U.S. Department of Education, 1991).

42. Ibid., 9.

43. Ibid., 7.

44. "Labor Letter," *The Wall Street Journal,* July 31, 1990, A1.

45. Gilbert Fuchsberg, "Many Businesses Responding Too Slowly to Rapid Work Force Shifts, Study Says," *The Wall Street Journal,* July 20, 1990, B1.

46. Bank of America, "Human Resource Planning," 49.

47. Carnevale and Goldstein, "Schooling and Training," 33.

48. "Where the Jobs Are Is Where the Skills Aren't," *Business Week,* September 19, 1988, 106.

49. Jeffrey Pfeffer and James N. Baron, "Taking the Workers Back Out: Recent Trends in the Structuring of Employment," in Barry M. Staw and L. L. Cummings (eds.), *Research in Organizational Behavior,* vol. 10 (Greenwich, CT: JAI Press, 1988), 257–303.
50. Rodger L. Dillon, "The Changing Labor Market: Contingent Workers and the Self-Employed in California," Special Report to Senator Dan McCorquodale and Senator Bill Greene, Office of Senate Research (Sacramento: Senate of California, 1987), 46.
51. Wayne J. Howe, "The Business Services Industry Sets Pace in Employment Growth," *Monthly Labor Review* 110 (1986), 29–36.
52. Peter T. Kilborn, "Part-Time Hirings Bring Deep Changes in U.S. Workplaces," *New York Times,* June 17, 1991, A1.
53. Dillon, "The Changing Labor Market," 33.
54. "Congressional Study Challenges Federal Use of Private Contractors," *New York Times,* September 16, 1991, A8.
55. Katherine C. Abraham, "Restructuring the Employment Relationship: The Growth of Market-Mediated Work Arrangements," in Katherine C. Abraham and Robert B. McKersie (eds.), *New Developments in the Labor Market* (Cambridge, MA: MIT Press, 1990), 106.
56. Ibid., 101–102.
57. James B. Rebitzer, "Short-Term Employment Relations and Labor Market Outcomes: Contract Workers in the U.S. Petrochemical Industry," unpublished ms. (Cambridge, MA: Sloan School of Management, MIT, 1991).
58. S. D. Nollen and V. H. Martin, *Alternative Work Schedules, Part 2: Permanent Part-Time Employment* (New York: Amacom, 1978).
59. Abraham, "Restructuring the Employment Relationship," 102.
60. Dillon, "The Changing Labor Market," 26.
61. L. Reibstein, "More Companies Use Free-Lancers to Avoid Cost, Trauma of Layoffs," *The Wall Street Journal,* April 18, 1986, 21.
62. Michael J. McCarthy, "Managers Face Dilemma with 'Temps,'" *The Wall Street Journal,* April 5, 1988, 31.
63. Ibid.
64. Keith Schneider, "Study Finds Link between Chemical Plant Accidents and Contract Workers," *New York Times,* July 30, 1991, A10.
65. Rebitzer, "Short-Term Employment Relations and Labor Market Outcomes," 3.
66. Walt Bogdanich, "Danger in White: The Shadowy World of 'Temp' Nurses," *The Wall Street Journal,* November 1, 1991, B1, B6.

Reading 35

There's Three Kinds of Teams

By Peter Drucker

"Team-building" has become a buzzword in American business. The results are not overly impressive.

Ford Motor Company began more than ten years ago to build teams to design its new models. It now reports "serious problems," and the gap in development time between Ford and its Japanese competitors has hardly narrowed. General Motors' Saturn Division was going to replace the traditional assembly line with teamwork in its "factory of the future." But the plant has been steadily moving back toward the Detroit-style assembly line. Procter and Gamble launched a team-building campaign with great fanfare several years ago. Now P&G is moving back to individual accountability for developing and marketing new products.

One reason—perhaps the major one—for these near-failures is the all-but-universal belief among executives that there is just one kind of team. There actually are three—each different in its structure, in the behavior it demands from its members, in its strengths, its vulnerabilities, its limitations, its requirements, but above all, in what it can do and should be used for.

The first kind of team is the baseball team. The surgical team that performs an open-heart operation and Henry Ford's assembly line are both "baseball teams." So is the team Detroit traditionally sets up to design a new car.

The players play *on* the team; they do not play *as* a team. They have fixed positions they never leave. The second baseman never runs to assist the pitcher; the anesthesiologist never comes to the aid of the surgical nurse. "Up at bat, you are totally alone," is an old baseball saying. In the traditional Detroit design team, marketing people rarely saw designers and were never consulted by them. Designers did their work and passed it on to the development engineers, who in turn did their work and passed it on to manufacturing, which in turn did its work and passed it on to marketing.

The second kind of team is the football team. The hospital unit that rallies around a patient who goes into shock at 3 A.M. is a "football team," as are

Japanese automakers' design teams. The players on the football team like those on the baseball team have fixed positions. But on the football team, players play as a team. The Japanese automakers' design teams, which Detroit and P&G rushed to imitate, are football-type teams. To use engineering terms, the designers, engineers, manufacturing people, and marketing people work "in parallel." The traditional Detroit team worked "in series."

Third, there is the tennis doubles team—the kind Saturn management hoped would replace the traditional assembly line. It is also the sort of team that plays in a jazz combo, the team of senior executives who form the "president's office" in big companies, or the team that is most likely to produce a genuine innovation like the personal computer fifteen years ago.

On the doubles team, players have a primary rather than a fixed position. They are supposed to "cover" their teammates, adjusting to their teammates' strengths and weaknesses and to the changing demands of the "game."

Business executives and the management literature have little good to say these days about the baseball-style team, whether in the office or on the factory floor. There is even a failure to recognize such teams as teams at all. But this kind of team has enormous strengths. Each member can be evaluated separately, can have clear and specific goals, can be held accountable, can be measured—as witness the statistics a true aficionado reels off about every major-leaguer in baseball history. Each member can be trained and developed to the fullest extent of the individual's strengths. And because the members do not have to adjust to anybody else on the team, every position can be staffed with a "star," no matter how temperamental, jealous, or limelight-hogging each of them might be.

But the baseball team is inflexible. It works well when the game has been played many times and when the sequence of its actions is thoroughly understood by everyone. That is what made this kind of team right for Detroit in the past.

As recently as twenty years ago, to be fast and flexible in automotive design was the last thing Detroit needed or wanted. Traditional mass production required long runs with minimum changes. And since the resale value of the "good used car"—one less than three years old—was a key factor for the new-car buyer, it was a serious mistake to bring out a new design (which would depreciate the old car) more than every five years. Sales and market share took a dip on several occasions when Chrysler prematurely introduced a new, brilliant design.

The Japanese did not invent "flexible mass production"; IBM was probably the first to use it, around 1960. But when the Japanese auto industry adopted it, it made possible the introduction of a new car model in parallel with a successful old one. And then the baseball team did indeed become the wrong team for Detroit, and for mass-production industry as a whole. The design process then had to be restructured as a football team.

The football team does have the flexibility Detroit now needs. But it has far more stringent requirements than the baseball team. It needs a "score"—such as the play the coach signals to the huddle on the field. The specifications with which the Japanese begin their design of a new car model—or a new consumer-electronics product—are far more stringent and detailed than anything Detroit is used to in respect to style, technology, performance, weight, price, and so on. And they are far more closely adhered to.

In the traditional "baseball" design team, every position—engineering, manufacturing, marketing—does its job its own way. In the football team there is no such permissiveness. The word of the coach is law. Players are beholden to this one boss alone for their orders, their rewards, their appraisals, their promotions.

The individual engineer on the Japanese design team is a member of his company's engineering department. But he is on the design team because the team's leader has asked for him—not because the chief engineer sent him there. He can consult engineering and get advice. But his orders come from the design-team chief, who also appraises his performance. If there are stars on these teams, they are featured only if the team leader entrusts them with a "solo." Otherwise, they subordinate themselves to the team.

Even more stringent are the requirements of the doubles team—the kind that GM's Saturn Division hoped to develop in its "flexible-manufacturing" plant, and a flexible plant does indeed need such a team. The team must be quite small, with five to seven members at most. The members have to be trained together and must work together for quite some time before they fully function as a team. There must be one clear goal for the entire team yet considerable flexibility with respect to the individual member's work and performance. And in this kind of team only the team "performs"; individual members "contribute."

All three of these kinds of teams are true teams. But they are so different—in the behavior they require, in what they do best, and in what they cannot do at all—that they cannot be hybrids. One kind of team can play only one way. And it is very difficult to change from one kind of team to another.

Gradual change cannot work. There has to be a total break with the past, however traumatic it may be. This means that people cannot report to both their old boss and to the new coach, or team leader. And their rewards, their compensation, their appraisals, and their promotions must be totally dependent on their performance in their new roles on their new teams. But this is so unpopular that the temptation to compromise is always great.

At Ford, for instance, the financial people have been left under the control of the financial staff and report to it rather than to the new design teams. GM's Saturn Division has tried to maintain the authority of the traditional bosses—the first-line supervisors and the shop stewards—rather than hand decision-making power over to the work teams. This, however, is like playing baseball and a tennis doubles match with the same people, on the same field, and at the same time. It can only result in frustration and nonperformance. And a similar confusion seems to have prevailed at P&G.

Teams, in other words, are tools. As such, each team design has its own uses, its own characteristics, its own requirements, its own limitations. Teamwork is neither "good" nor "desirable"—it is a fact. Wherever people work together or play together they do so as a team. Which team to use for what purpose is a crucial, difficult, and risky decision that is even harder to unmake. Managements have yet to learn how to make it.

Reading 36

Implementing TQM with Self-Directed Teams

By Michael J. Brower

Abstract

Teams are highly useful, probably essential, vehicles for implementing TQM. Most companies developing TQM have used temporary project teams, also called process improvement teams (PITs) or process action teams (PATs) to study and recommend improvements in critical processes. More recently a large and rapidly growing number of organizations are removing and retraining their first line supervisors, flattening their hierarchies, and building self-directed teams (SDTs) at the base, the frontline, of their organizations. These SDTs serve as the main building block of the organization; they plan, carry out, and improve the daily work of the organization. And they become the main vehicle for implementing TQM in the day to day operations—all without traditional direct supervision. But SDTs are not simple or easy to create, develop, and support. For significant and lasting success, SDTs must be empowered, which means they must have authority, ableness, accountability, and alignment. In addition, empowered teams depend upon reinforcing support from around and above them, on leadership, at four levels, and on everyone's understanding that this is an evolutionary process.

INTRODUCTION AND OVERVIEW

Total Quality Management, or TQM, has many different meanings. The definition I choose to work with is the one developed and refined by the research committee of GOAL/QPC. TQM is "a structured system for creating organization-wide

Source: 1992 article reprinted with the permission of the author.

participation in planning and implementing a continuous improvement process to meet and exceed customer needs."

Fundamental to this definition of TQM, and most others, are the purposes of meeting and exceeding customer needs, a focus on processes, a commitment to continuous improvement, and the importance of involving the whole organization, all employees, in this effort and system.

The most common way of involving employees in most approaches to TQM is through the use of project teams, also called, in various organizations, quality improvement teams, process improvement teams, or process action teams. These teams may be formed within a particular function or department. Usually they are cross-functional, involving employees from all of the departments and functions that own a part of the process targeted for improvement. Normally these teams focus only on that single specific topic or issue or process needing improvement. Usually they are temporary, finishing their work in a few weeks or months and disbanding. Often they are led by an appointed team leader, typically a manager. In every case their members are representatives of their respective functions and do not include all the employees in any single department.

In some organizations, supervisors are encouraged and trained to form teams of all their employees to work on improving processes. These teams may be more permanent, they may work on many process improvement ideas, and they may involve all employees in a given work area. By definition, they are supervisor led and the traditional role of the supervisor is unchanged.

However, going beyond these common approaches to TQM, a rapidly growing number of organizations are turning to a different kind of team, the self-directed team (SDT), or self-directed work team, as the basic building block of their organizations for doing and managing the daily work, and as the fundamental group for implementing TQM at the base and on the front line.

SELF-DIRECTED TEAMS: DEFINITIONS, DESCRIPTIONS, AND DIFFERENCES FROM OTHER TEAMS/QUALITY CIRCLES

Self-Directed Teams are:

> On-going teams that plan, perform, and improve their own value-adding work and develop the ableness to do this, all without traditional direct supervision. They also determine their own Direction in interdependence and alignment with customers and other teams and with the Direction of the organizational levels above. They are composed of all the people who work in a given work area.

A typical self-directed team will have anywhere from 5–20 members, including all of the people who work in a given work area. If there are too many people for one team, two or more teams will be formed, with each team taking accountability for a complete value-adding transform process or set of processes. These teams typically will have the authority to plan and schedule their work, to assign work among team members, to schedule their own vacations, to hold regular meetings daily or weekly or both, and to call special meetings as needed. They solve problems and improve processes. But in addition, they manage themselves—all day long, every day—without traditional supervision. They manage their equipment and may even repair it themselves when they have the necessary know-how. They manage their own material inputs and they are responsible for their own quality. They have no supervisor. SDTs are thus different from quality circles and employee involvement groups and similar teams popular a few years ago that typically had little or no authority, that had volunteer membership, and that made very few fundamental changes in how work was structured and managed.

Self-directed teams are also different from the project teams, or process improvement teams, widely used today for developing process improvements under TQM. These project teams may or may not have any clear authority, they have a specific focus and a limited life. They are usually made up of representatives of several departments or functions. These differences are illustrated below.

Some differences between self-directed teams and project teams

Project teams	Self-directed teams
Temporary	Permanent
Cross-functional/cross-departmental/ Cross unit	Within one department or function or unit
Representatives of different departments	Everybody in the department or unit is on the team
Focus on a single process improvement	Team plans, does, improves all their work; focus on customers
Led by appointed manager, supervisor, or sometimes, hourly employee	Led by elected, or sometimes in the beginning appointed, team leader
Team finishes its project and disbands	Team does the daily work, works on many improvement projects; never disbands
Team makes recommendations to upper management or a steering committee; usually given little decision authority	Team empowered to make decisions; as scope and depth of ableness grows, team given more and more authority
Employees still have supervisor	As team develops readiness, supervisor is phased out

THE HISTORY AND BENEFITS OF SELF-DIRECTED TEAMS

SDTs are not new. Although they are only now reaching widespread use as an ideal vehicle for creating continuous improvement at the front line under TQM, their existence in some U.S. companies goes back long before anyone started talking about and implementing TQM in this country.

Those whose national pride is bothered by all of the TQM techniques and tools imported from Japan might be pleased to learn that SDTs were not invented in Japan or imported here from Japan. They were born in England in the late 1940s

(Trist, 1981) and gained some footholds in Norway, Sweden, India, and Australia in the next couple of decades—usually under the title of Autonomous Work Groups, or Semi-Autonomous Work Groups. In this country several companies were already building new plants based on SDTs in the late 1960s, under the name of Technician Systems (Procter and Gamble) and Intact Work Groups or High Performance Teams in General Foods and other companies. Based on the early very impressive results, Procter and Gamble today has many plants with SDTs, and several hundred of our largest and many hundreds more not-so-large companies have at least one plant or office area organized this way.

The roster of U.S. SDT users includes: A. O. Smith, Aid Association for Lutherans, AT&T Credit, Bridgestone, Coors Brewery, Corning, Cummins Engine, Diebold, Inc., DuPont, Frito-Lay, General Foods, General Motors, Harley Davidson, Hewlett-Packard, Honda America, Johnsonville Foods, Loyola University Medical Center, Motorola, Northern Telecom, Alliant Health Care Systems, Rohm & Haas, Saturn Corporation, Skippy Peanut Butter, Tektronix, the Town of Windsor, Connecticut, Xerox, General Electric, Texas Instruments, Quad Graphics, Masland Industries, and many, many more.

Why have so many companies, and the number is expanding very rapidly now, decided to implement SDTs? Because the benefits are enormous when these teams are well designed, established, and supported. There are many documented quantifiable benefits in terms of improved quality, increased productivity and reduced costs, and improved service to customers. In manufacturing, these SDTs balance the production line by smoothly shifting cross trained team members up and down the line as needed. In any organization, they adapt quickly to replace absent employees with the most qualified possible temporary replacements. In the design world these teams contribute to creating better product and service designs in greatly reduced time.

Major cost savings come not only from increased frontline worker productivity, but also from reduced levels of hierarchy, of bureaucracy, since one level, or even several levels of supervisors or managers are taken out. These flatter organizations, compared to a traditional hierarchical organization, save a great deal of money now being spent on middle managers' salaries, benefits, offices, support staffs, and other perks. This also reduces the time required for decision making. And it improves the quality of decisions, because those with frontline information are making many more decisions themselves, based on real unadulterated information. In traditional hierarchies, the quality of information decreases (decreased signal to noise ratio in technical language) as information is moved across several boundaries upward in a traditional hierarchy (and sometimes across) to the level authorized to make a decision, and again when the decision is moved back down to those on the front lines who will implement it.

Other related benefits of empowered SDTs are improved flexibility and responsiveness to customer requirements—a greater ability to "turn on a dime" and give a situation specific appropriate response, quickly, to individual customers. For the employees, there are benefits of increasing skills and knowledge, and greater understanding of the whole, of how their work fits into and contributes to the ultimate end user of the product or service. This enhances state of being and self-worth, and increases employees' ableness to work in teams, interdependently. Overall, this brings a greater meaning to work, and a greater ownership of the work. All of this, in turn leads to reduced turnover and absenteeism from employment. Finally, it probably leads to improved mental and physical health, although on this I have anecdotal but not published scientific evidence.

THE REQUIREMENTS FOR SELF-DIRECTED TEAMS TO BECOME EMPOWERED AND TO SUCCEED

One does not make changes this significant in the structures and operations of large organizations, and one does not reap such deep and widespread benefits quickly, easily, or cheaply. Establishing and developing self-directed teams, and creating the required organizational support above and around them, is a complex and difficult process.

After years of working with teams, both empowered and not-so-empowered, I have developed a definitional model of team empowerment. Put simply, empowerment requires that teams have the four A's and that they receive reinforcement, leadership, and understanding that this is a process of *evolution* over time. So:

Empowerment means *Authority* delegated to the teams,
Accountability accepted by the teams,
Alignment of the teams' direction, and
Ableness development of the teams.

In addition, for empowerment to succeed over time, these teams need

Reinforcement from around and above the teams,
Leadership within, of, and above the teams, and
Evolution over time.

The remaining sections of this chapter examine these seven requirements in more detail.

AUTHORITY DELEGATION TO THE TEAMS AND ACCOUNTABILITY ACCEPTANCE BY SDTs

Authority to make decisions without checking with "the boss," or his boss above, is what most people think of first when they talk about empowerment. It is basic. If a team can make decisions on its own, without getting specific permission from someone above them in the hierarchy, then they have at least some authority. If the team, or individuals within it, can spend up to a certain amount of money on their own decision, then they have that degree of authority.

Authority is therefore not seamless; it is not "all or nothing," although organizations and managers sometimes make the mistake of acting as though it is. Teams can be, and should be, given specific degrees of authority for specific realms of decision making, with the degree and number of realms or arenas of authority growing as the teams developing ableness and demonstrated accountability justifies it.

Here is a generic list of the kinds of decision authority that many self-directed teams have been delegated, in some degree or other, in a wide range of manufacturing and service organizations.

Planning their work; scheduling their work; team member assignment; material input control; quality; equipment management; equipment maintenance; vacation scheduling; dealing with team member absenteeism and tardiness; balancing the production line; writing and upgrading process descriptions; problem solving; process improvement; safety; housekeeping; budgeting; environmental control; expenditure control; service recovery; team ableness development through training and other means; screening, selecting, and hiring new members; peer review on knowledge and skills for pay increases; disciplining team members; and firing. (These last two are often specifically *not* taken on by teams in their first few years, except for informal forms of peer pressure and discipline.)

Accountability is the other side of the authority coin. Accountability means: "I, or we, accept accountability for designated activities, for designated responsibilities, for managing and improving designated processes, and/or for creating designated outcomes." In short, it means: "You can count on me to . . . " People in our society often say they want authority. Some are less eager to accept accountability. It is "where the rubber meets the road," and "where the buck stops." Yet without accountability, authority delegation won't last; it will be pulled back as a result of performance failures. So authority delegation and accountability acceptance must march forward, in parallel, hand-in-hand.

Here is a specific example of this kind of accountability acceptance. For public training workshops we need to have workbooks prepared, printed, and inserted into three-ring binders, with copies ready for each participant at 8:00 A.M. on the opening morning. As the trainer, I am accountable for preparing the master copy of the workbook and turning it in to production people with enough lead time for them to get it ready. Even if I do this, the print shop may be backed up and deliver the copied material late in the afternoon before the workshop to the person who is to assemble the workbook into 25 three-ring binders. He then goes to the stock room and finds only 7 of the correct size binder. It is almost 5:00 P.M. What does he do? If he is a "normal," "unempowered" employee who has not accepted accountability, he (1) blasts the print shop for taking so long; (2) curses (under his breath) the person who let the supply of three ring binders run down so low; (3) packs the few that are available; (4) maybe notifies his supervisor, if she is still around, that she has a problem to solve; and (5) goes home at 5:00 P.M. as always.

But if he is a person who has accepted accountability for his piece, his role, in this value adding stream, as I have defined accountability, he does something like the following, all without having to ask permission, or be told or asked to do this by a supervisor. He: (1) checks around the stock room and the offices to see if anybody has stashed away somewhere enough empty binders. Finding none, he: (2) telephones around to find an office supply store that is open late and that has enough acceptable binders, and he telephones home to warn that he will be late; (3) drives his own car, or gets a friend to drive him or takes a taxi if no car is available; (4) buys the binders with his own cash, check, or credit card; (5) stays late to pack all the necessary binders; (6) checks his work carefully; (7) places one workbook at each person's place in the training room; and (8) scans the room to see if there is anything else missing or to be done (not his job of course); before (9) going home very late. The next day he submits his costs for reimbursement. He also goes to the appropriate team or manager to suggest that a team go to work on improving the critical processes of maintaining adequate stocks of binders and of getting printing orders ready, to the print shop in time, and out of the print shop in time, for he and others to have adequate time for assembling materials into binders and checking their work.

Another example. A hotel employee took a telephone call, receiving a message for an elderly guest who was not in her room. The message was that she should call home and prepare to return home immediately because a close relative was gravely ill. In addition the caller expressed grave concern because the guest was very elderly, was traveling with a tour group on a set ticket, was perhaps too frail to travel alone without the help of her group from the hotel to the plane, and might not have enough money or credit available to buy the special ticket. The hotel employee reassured the worried caller that he would handle everything for the elderly guest, and "not to worry," and that he would report back.

The hotel employee then: (1) found the elderly guest, and in the kindest way he could think of, notified her of the family member's grave illness; (2) reassured the guest that he would handle her airline reservation and get her to the airport and onto the plane; (3) called the airline, reserved a seat, paid for it on his own credit card, and asked the airline to have a flight attendant ready to watch over the passenger and to have a wheelchair available for her at the other end; (4) arranged for hotel personnel to back him up during his time away (because they worked in effective teams this was not difficult); (5) assisted the woman to check out and get her bags down to his car; (6) drove her to the airport and personally escorted her onto the plane; (7) verified with the flight attendant that the message had come through and that the passenger would be taken care of on the flight and at the destination; (8) telephoned back to the relative who had made the initial call and told her of the arrangements and arrival time; and (9) learned how he would be reimbursed for the cost of the ticket.

Sound unlikely? Exaggerated? Utopian? Well, it actually happened. This is the kind of accountability that empowered employees are accepting and demonstrating in those companies that have moved into, or are in transit towards providing world-class quality of product and service.

ABLENESS DEVELOPMENT IN SDTs

Self-directed teams require all of the ableness to plan and do their basic work; to chart, study, control, and improve their processes; to plan and lead effective meetings, to reconcile conflict, and to accept the authority and perform the roles and processes formerly in the job description of the supervisor. This is not simple or easy to accomplish. It is in fact a tall order, and requires a long and difficult and sometimes expensive process of individual and team development.

Ableness is not a common term; it needs defining. Ableness is the state of being able to perform well in a given role, or in a set or mixture of roles. This includes being capable of handling certain tasks, which means having the knowledge and skills necessary to perform these tasks. Being able to perform also requires a certain state of being, a level of mental energy, a sense of self-worth and self-esteem. Without these, a person, even with all the necessary knowledge and skills, may still not be able to perform the roles. Finally, ableness requires that there be sufficient affirming and receptive will in the person or team to take on the roles and perform them well. In street language, motivation or determination are terms we use for affirming will. Being a good listener and being open to change are common terms for receptive will.

Back to our SDT. As a whole the team will need to have, or develop, a wide range of job skills plus coordinating, decision making, communicating, and conflict resolution capabilities, plus the whole kit bag of TQM/SPC problem solving and process improvement capabilities. In addition, the team will need to develop its own identity, its own culture, or norms and values and state of being. Furthermore, the team will, to be successful, have to develop its own mission and vision, and to hold and live out a strong set of values which will serve to pull forth the will and effort of its individual members.

But the team of course is made up of individual members. Those SDTs which have survived the longest and been most effective are those that have done the best job of respecting, nurturing, developing, and utilizing the individual ableness, the self-identity, of its members. In short it is not team development *or* individual development; it is team development *and* individual development. It is not team identity *or* individual identity; it is team identity *and* individual identity that are required.

Call it ableness, as I do here, or capability, or whatever, SDTs both depend upon, and serve to create, a wide range of knowledge and skill development, a strong and healthy state of being/identity, and a high degree of will or motivation, in its members and itself. The organization embarking on the establishment of self-directed teams, either to support TQM or for whatever other reasons, had best recognize up front that a major investment in training and coaching will be required. Or they might as well not start.

ALIGNMENT OF DIRECTION WITH SDTs

Highly successful SDTs have their own mission or purpose, and they have a vision, whether written or not, that guides and pulls its members together and forward. They develop their own set of guiding principles, either as written principles or as unwritten norms of behavior, that help individual members make difficult decisions on behalf of the team, customers, and the overall business.

This combination of mission, vision, and principles is what I call direction. Do SDTs set their own direction? Yes. But not in isolation. We are talking about teams that exist within, and carry out, the basic work of large organizations. So they cannot be totally self-directed, to the exclusion of taking account the needs, requirements, and expectations of other stakeholders. If every SDT, or for that matter every team of any kind, or every work department or functional unit in a modern organization set its own direction, and optimized its own performance, in isolation from the others, the result would be sub-optimization of the whole at best, and chaos and anarchy at worst.

The way we reconcile this is to acknowledge, and insist, that self-directed teams determine their own direction in *interdependence and alignment with* customers and other teams, and with the direction of organizational levels above. It is important that each SDT develop its own mission. And it is important that this mission be aligned with the corporate mission. It is also important that this not be a one way street. If the corporation, or other large organization, wants its work to be done, improved, and managed by SDTs, then the organization must also learn how to align its mission, vision, and principles with those of its SDTs and with the general requirements for successful SDTs.

But we are left with a bit of unease about terminology. The problem is the same as that facing those SDT ancestors which were called "autonomous work groups." Critics said these work groups or teams were not really autonomous, since they were part of, and interdependent with, larger organizations. So in some companies these came to be called "semi-autonomous work groups." OK. It satisfied truth in labeling requirements. But it doesn't exactly roll easily off your tongue. So we don't hear so much about them anymore. So what should we call self-directed teams? One organization, I've been told, calls them shared-directed work teams. More nearly correct, but clumsy. So I will continue to call SDTs self-directed teams, and will continue to try to help all parties understand that we live in an interdependent world and work in interdependent teams, and that directions must be set interdependently.

REINFORCEMENT AND SUPPORT FOR SDTs FROM AROUND AND ABOVE

There are at least half a dozen different kinds of support that SDTs require from their larger organizations.

1. There need to be several or many SDTs starting at once. If only a couple of SDTs are launched initially, there is a high probability that failure of the one or two will result in cancellation of the whole idea. "Don't put all your eggs in one basket." So one form of reinforcement that the initial SDTs need is that of numbers, to have enough started at once so that even if one or two fail or limp along, the others will still survive.

2. The initial SDTs should not be set up as "pilots" in an "experiment" to decide whether to cancel the whole idea of SDTs, or to expand the concept into additional departments and teams. If SDTs are seen as an experiment, which may be cancelled if the initial teams don't do so well, then those who feel threatened by them will find ways, subtle or not-so-subtle, to sabotage the pilots and make sure the experiment fails. The support these initial SDTs need is that they be viewed not as a pilot to decide whether or not to go forward, but rather as pilots from which to learn what leadership, training, and other support will be required to ensure success of present and future SDTs. The decision to go forward with SDTs should have already been made, up front.
3. Support Functions. SDTs are often, although not always, initially set up in production or other operations departments and groups. If so, they will need reinforcement and support from the other functions and departments. For example, production SDTs cannot succeed without a lot of help from maintenance people, since so many line improvements they will think of will require maintenance help in rebuilding equipment, moving equipment, adding or moving controls, and a thousand other ways to improve the production process. Production teams also are greatly dependent upon the purchasing and materials control people, who can make or break a production team by succeeding in supplying the quality and quantity of parts and other inputs which the production team depends upon. Other support functions are from time to time equally important to SDTs—HRD, engineering, accounting, payroll, and information systems, among others. Many of these departments, in traditional large organizations, will refuse telephone calls and requests for information from hourly people. They will ask them over and over "who are you?" and tell them "you are not authorized to file a maintenance (engineering, training, purchase order) request" and instruct them to "have your supervisor call us." To succeed, SDTs will need a whole revolution in mind set in these support functions, so that they shift from suspicion and hostility to truly being *support* functions—even to these new, dangerous looking SDTs!
4. Systems. SDTs are based on new paradigm assumptions about people, trust, human development, the importance of processes, and so on. Most of the systems in a large organization were created at various times, for various purposes, and based on various sets of assumptions about people, human nature, the purpose of the organization, etc. Although SDTs can survive and even thrive in an organization with outdated systems, eventually it will become very important to review and revise as necessary all of the important systems of the organization. These include the management information systems, the absenteeism and tardiness control systems, the discipline systems, the pay and promotion systems, the performance review system, the purchasing systems, and the materials control system.
5. Mistakes. Empowerment and Growth require experimentation, taking risks, pushing boundaries, and therefore, inevitably, making mistakes. If we are not making mistakes, we are being too cautious, not taking any risks, not

stretching ourselves at all. SDTs will make mistakes, must make mistakes. What will be the attitude and behavior of upper and middle management when the SDTs make their mistakes? Will they scold, or worse, at the team and member that made the mistake? Once or twice is all it will take before risk taking, and empowerment, will be driven out. Or will managers leave the teams alone as they make mistakes, or encourage them to learn from the mistake, and reinforce the expectation that empowered people take risks and occasionally make mistakes?

6. Celebrating Successes. Positive reinforcement means SDTs celebrating their successes, and having lots of management support for, and participation in this.

LEADERSHIP OF AND ABOVE SDTs, AT FOUR LEVELS

Four levels of leadership are required for successful empowered teams: (1) the team leader (leader *of* the team); (2) distributed leadership within the team (leaders *in* the team); (3) the leader *above* the team; and (4) executive leadership of the organization.

Team Leader

The first level of leadership is that of team leader, the one person (or in some cases two persons) who are selected or elected to be *the* team leader. Some people argue that a team doesn't need one single designated leader. They say that leadership can float around the team, that the leadership that is needed in any situation will simply come forth as needed, or that the "natural leader" of the team will emerge. No doubt these alternatives can and sometimes do happen. A group of friends who play jazz together for fun and an occasional paid gig certainly don't have to designate one of their members as the leader if they don't want to. And they may play, and work, very well together. Even inside an organization the same thing *can* happen. Especially with very stable, mature, and experienced teams. But the *probability* of a team succeeding, I believe, is greatly reduced if there is no one designated leader. So those of us guiding and leading the conversion of organizations to self-directed teams have some obligation, I think, to strongly recommend that, to increase the probability of success, every team should have one person as the leader.

Now, having said all that, four other related questions must be addressed. One, should this team leader be permanent, or rotating. Here the benefits of rotation seem very strong. It reduces the probability of turning a team leader into just an old-fashioned supervisor with a different title. It gives several, and eventually perhaps all, team members an opportunity to grow into and step up to the requirements of leadership.

The second question is: How often should leaders be rotated? My recommendation, in most cases, is that the rotation be fairly slow, such as every six to twelve months. This is enough to allow a significant amount of learning and ableness development by the team leader during her/his term in office before it is passed on to another. However, SDTs in the real world are rotating their leaders every day, every week, every month or six weeks, and all the way up to once a year—or not at all.

The third question to be addressed is whether the team leader should be elected by the team, or selected by management. On the face of it, the answer should be obvious: a team, if it is empowered, will have the authority to elect its own leader. So long as the team leader is appointed by management that is one aspect of authority, of empowerment that has been withheld from the team. However, management, especially in the initial period of transition from a traditional supervisory culture to an empowered team, is often reluctant to let go of the myth that management knows best when it comes to leadership. There is, of course, the legitimate concern that the team, any team, might turn the leadership election into a popularity contest, electing the member most popular but not most qualified to be leader. To reduce this risk I encourage teams, and coach internal facilitators to do the same, to think about and record on a flipchart what characteristics they are looking for in their leader, what qualities of character are important in leadership. This should take place a week or two before there are any actual nominations or election for leader. Managers observing this process are sometimes surprised that very similar qualities of leadership emerge from this process, regardless of whether the team is highly educated professionals or high school dropouts in low-skilled jobs.

Sometimes management still insists on appointing the team leader(s), even after being offered this process, and even after accepting the undeniable argument that election increases the leaders' legitimacy with the rest of the team, compared to an appointed leader. Management clings to the security of a more traditional approach in which they exercise their right (i.e. power) and allegedly superior judgment to appoint the team leader. In such cases I strongly recommend that management appoint *only* the first leader, and only for a fixed term of 3 to 6 or 8 or 9 months, that is called a transition period for team formation and development, after which the team will elect its own leaders.

Another question emerges in the case of management appointed team leadership. Should management appoint the existing supervisor to be team leader? Pros: It solves the problem, at least temporarily, of where to place the existing supervisor. It retains the work knowledge and skills of the supervisor in that area which otherwise might be lost. It allows for a transition period that may be less disruptive than if the supervisor were pulled out with very short notice. Cons: Very little may change. The supervisor may—in fact is very likely to—continue to act in the same old way with a new title of team leader. Team members may come out more cynical than ever; if the organization is making no real change in authority/empowerment, it is better not to make claims (propaganda?) that something is changing.

Reconciliation: If management decides to appoint the existing supervisor, they should make sure that the following six things also happen simultaneously:

1. The supervisor, and team, are told that this is temporary, for a known period of time.
2. A commitment is made that in *x* months the team will elect its own leader.
3. The supervisor is given, well in advance, a new and different future role in the organization.
4. The supervisor is told, repeatedly, that his/her present temporary assignment is to lead the team, not direct and control it in the old paradigm, and to develop the team's ableness, so that in *x* time the team will no longer need the experience, knowledge, skills, etc. of the supervisor. The performance rating system is changed, and the supervisor is fully informed about this change, to reflect this new transitional role of the supervisor. Her/his next performance review will in large part depend upon how well s/he prepared the team during this transition period.
5. The supervisor is given lots of training and coaching, up front, and on-going, in mind-set and skills, overall ableness actually, to be a leader-coach instead of the former boss-manager.
6. The manager above the supervisor (see below) not only monitors this process, and steps in to facilitate any needed adjustments; she also learns how to be a leader-coach herself and thereby is able to be a role model. S/he "walks the talk" and "educates by example."

Distributed leadership within the team

Even if a company moves, immediately or after a transition period, from appointing a team leader to enabling the team to elect its own leader, there remains a considerable risk of the team relying too much on the judgment and decision making of that one person. The result can be, even with an elected team leader, that the team comes to function very little differently than it did under a more traditional supervisor. One answer is distributed leadership within the team. Not instead of, but in addition to, an elected team leader.

This is usually accomplished by having the team define, with help from an experienced facilitator, the main or key processes that it needs to manage well, or have someone manage well for it, to enable it to create and deliver high quality products/services to its customers. This is the parallel, at the level of an SDT, of a whole organization determining its critical processes under a TQM implementation model. The facilitator then puts to the team questions such as these: Under our prior system, who was responsible for ensuring that these processes, essential for our team success, were managed well? (The typical answer that comes back is: "the supervisor.") Second question: Under our new system, with a single elected team leader, who are we likely to expect will handle all these processes? (Usual answer: "the team leader"). This can lead into a full discussion of what empowerment really means and requires, of the risks of putting too much on the shoulders of one person, and of the importance of all members taking some accountability.

This then leads to the idea of distributed leadership, under which various team members each take accountability for being a coordinator for one of these key processes for a given limited time period such as six months.

The actual processes which need to be managed or coordinated are often grouped around a visual structural model, such as a five pointed star, which helps ensure completeness and distinctiveness in describing the requirements for a successful ongoing entity such as a team. The star, used first in Procter and Gamble and DuPont team-based plants, originally had the following five general categories, derived by consultant Charles Krone from general systems theory: managing or leading processes, site processes, operations processes, personnel processes, and auditing processes. Today, after many adaptations and copies of copies there are dozens of different versions of this star in use, and in the literature on SDTs.

There are many benefits of having some, or if possible all, team members accepting accountability for one of these processes for a time, and then later for others. These benefits include:

1. It focuses accountability for each key process with a single person (or in very large teams it is sometimes one coordinator and an assistant coordinator, or back-up coordinator, or coordinator in training).
2. It avoids overloading accountability, authority, and work on one single person—the team leader.
3. It enhances participation in team planning and decision making.
4. It provides personal growth and development "stretch" opportunities for many or all team members. I like to call SDTs with distributed leadership, "schools of leadership."
5. Overall, it results in enhanced team synergy and in the team becoming a "learning organization."

The leader above the team

Self-directed teams, by definition, do not have a supervisor. But, except in the most advanced, dynamic, free-form and experimental organizations, SDTs do still fit within a hierarchy and are responsible (accountable) to a manager above them. This manager may have three or four or as many as eight or ten SDTs in the organization chart "under" her/him. This manager may in the past have operated very much like a traditional boss-manager. Job description, written or informal: direct and control people. Make decisions. Tell supervisors what to do. Hold them accountable. Reward the good supervisors, reform or drive out the weak ones, etc., etc. If this manager continues to operate out of this old mind set, the SDTs below will not thrive nor even survive for long. Such a manager, with no first line supervisors between him and the teams, will be frequently tempted to move into the area of one SDT after another and start behaving like the traditional supervisor would have in the old days. The manager will be tempted into trying to be a substitute himself for the removed supervisors. Of course with several teams, and up to 100 individual employees in those teams, the new span-of-control is so wide that these efforts will inevitably fail. Nobody can give direct supervision, or succeed at directly managing, so many people. That is the virtue of such an extended span-of-control: it makes it evident to all that traditional efforts to manage other people can't work and must be replaced with something better—empowerment. The something better is leading and coaching. Space does not allow for a full discussion of the beliefs, styles, and processes used by leader-coaches. In short the leader-coach creates with others a compelling mission and vision, operates from principle rather than from self-interest or whim, delegates, listens and ask questions a great deal, invests time and effort in evoking and enabling the development of others, and is constantly observing and managing his/her own thoughts, actions and state.

Perhaps one real example will serve to illuminate this significant shift from manager to leader-coach. A manager that I was working with once had been a traditional "direct and control" manager and was then put in charge of starting up a new product line composed of three new SDTs. This manager, who became a friend, asked me one day for advice. He said:

> I really feel unsure of myself in this new role. I'm never sure whether or not I'm dealing with employees in the right way. For example, this morning a member of one of our teams came up to me, explained a problem he was having, and asked me what to do. In the old days I would have told him. But this morning, I caught myself before answering, and instead I started asking him a series of questions. What do you think might work? Have you had a similar situation come up in the past? How did you handle that one? Did it work? What are some alternatives that you might consider? This seemed to work, because he eventually came up with a couple of ideas he wanted to check out. But did I do the right thing? It certainly took longer that just telling him what to do.

I reassured my friend that I thought he had done very well and that I admired two things. First, the way he handled the situation, turning it into an opportunity for the employee's continued growth in ableness. And I also admired the way he was observing himself, reflecting on what he did, and seeking advice and help in assessing and improving himself. I told him I thought he was right on track, and serving as an excellent role model for other managers, ex-supervisors, and team leaders.

Other questions he might have asked the employee include: Who else on your team have you consulted with about this? Who might you go to? Does your team have a formally designated coordinator for an area or process that includes this situation? Or is there a team member who would be particularly knowledgeable (or creative) about this kind of problem? Did you check this out with your team leader? What did he say? Etc., etc.

Executive leadership

SDTs are sometimes established at the base of an organization, and succeed for a time, to some degree, without top executives' strong support. But rarely. And not for long. For SDTs to be established in more than an isolated department or two, and for them to reach their full evolution and potential, they depend in many ways on top executive strong support. Someone must lead in the creation of a vision of a new style organization based upon SDTs, and in the creation of a clear and compelling overall Mission that SDTs can align with. Someone must find new roles for present supervisors. Someone must insist that middle managers shift or evolve from being boss-managers into being leaders-coaches, and must be role models themselves from this process. Someone must allocate the resources—time and money—for the very significant amounts of training and meeting time required. Someone must make the decision to start sharing information, in understandable formats, about the competitive situation and economic health of the business all the way to the bottom, to the SDTs. Often this is information that until now has not even been shared with middle managers.

In short, establishing and developing SDTs in a way that leads to long term success requires major systemic changes in the whole organization. These changes must be led, can only be led, by top managers.

IT IS AN EVOLUTIONARY PROCESS

All involved should understand this. Three of the most important implications of this are:

1. Time. It takes many years to fully empower a team of employees who have been managed, and limited, in a traditional organization.
2. Development. Individual and team ableness can evolve over time, if it is planned and supported and the PDCA cycle, or some equivalent structured model or approach, is used.
3. Persistence. Setbacks and difficulties are to be expected. All should be seen as, and turned into, learning opportunities. Teams must be allowed, even encouraged, to take risks. Taking risks means making mistakes, even failing. An evolutionary process is not straight and smooth. There will be failures along the way. Leadership must understand this, take it in stride, learn from it, and process with, in the words of Dr. Deming's First Point: Constancy of Purpose.

Bibliography

Articles

Alster, Norm. "What Flexible Workers Can Do," *Fortune,* February 13, 1989.

Blache, Klaus, M., et al. "Process Control and People at General Motors Delta Engine Plant," *IE,* March, 1988.

Brown, Tom. "Why Teams Go 'Bust,'" *Industry Week,* March 2, 1992.

Dumaine, Brian. "Who Needs a Boss?" *Fortune,* May 7, 1990.

Geber, B. "From Manager into Coach," *Training,* February 1992.

Hammer, Michael. "Reengineering Work: Don't Automate, Obliterate," *Harvard Business Review,* July–August 1990.

Hoerr, John. "The Cultural Revolution at A. O. Smith," *Business Week,* May 29, 1989.

Hoerr, John. "The Payoff from Teamwork," *Business Week,* July 10, 1989.

Holpp, Lawrence. "Making Choices: Self-Directed Teams or Total Quality Management," *Training,* May 1992.

Hughes, B. "25 Stepping Stones for Self-Directed Teams," *Training,* December 1991.

Reid, Peter C. "How Harley Beat Back the Japanese," *Fortune,* September 25, 1989.

Schelder, J. "Productivity," *Personnel Journal,* February 1992.

Semler, Ricardo. "Managing Without Managers," *Harvard Business Review,* September–October 1989.

Zenger, J. H., E. Musselwhite, K. Herson, and C. Perring. "Leadership in a Team Environment," *Training and Development,* December 1991.

Books

Barker, Joel Arthur. *Discovering the Future: The Business of Paradigms,* St. Paul: ILI Press, 1989.

Bothwell, Lin. *The Art of Leadership,* New York: Prentice-Hall, 1983.

Byham, William C. *Zapp! The Lightening of Empowerment,* Pittsburgh: Development Dimensions International Press, 1989.

Cohen, M. H. *The Power of Self-Management,* Oak Park, IL: Canoe Press, 1992.

Covey, Stephen R. *The 7 Habits of Highly Effective People,* New York: Simon & Schuster, 1989.

DePree, Max. *Leadership Is an Art,* New York: Bantam, Doubleday, Dell, 1989.

Emery, Fred E. *Systems Thinking,* Baltimore: Penguin Books, 1969.

Goodman, Paul S. & Associates. *Designing Effective Work Groups,* San Francisco: Jossey-Bass, 1986.

Hackman, J. Richard, Ed. *Groups That Work (and Those That Don't),* San Francisco: Jossey-Bass, 1990.

Harper, Bob, and Ann Harper. *Skill-Building for Self-Directed Team Members,* Croton-on-Hudson: MW Corporation, 1989.

Harper, Bob, and Ann Harper. *Succeeding as a Self-Directed Work Team,* Croton-on-Hudson: MW Corporation, 1989.

Hicks, R. F., and D. Bone. *Self-Managing Teams: Creating and Maintaining Self-Managed Work Groups,* Los Altos, CA: Crisp Publications, Inc., 1990.

Johnsonville Sausage Co., Harvard Business School, Case Study Number 9-387-103, Revised 6/27/90.

Kelly, Mark. *The Adventures of a Self-Managing Team,* Raleigh, NC: Mark Kelly Books, 1992.

Ketchum, Lyman D., and Eric Trist. *All Teams Are Not Created Equal: How Employee Empowerment Really Works,* Newbury Park, CA: Sage Publications, Inc., 1992.

Lawler, Edward E., III. High-Involvement Management, San Francisco: Jossey-Bass, 1986.

Miller, Lawrence M., and Jennifer Howard. *Managing Quality through Teams,* Atlanta: The Miller Consulting Group, 1991.

Orsburn, Jack D., Linda Moran, Ed Musselwhite, and John H. Zenger. *Self-Directed Work*

Teams, Homewood, IL 60430: Business One Irwin, 1991.

Peters, Tom. *Thriving on Chaos,* New York: Knopf, 1987.

Scholtes, Peter R. *The Team Handbook,* Madison, Joiner Associates Consulting Group, 1988.

Scott, C. D., and D. T. Jaffe. *Empowerment: A Practice Guide for Success,* Los Altos, CA: Crisp Publications, 1991.

Senge, Peter M. *The Fifth Discipline: The Art & Practice of the Learning Organization,* New York: Doubleday, 1990.

Trist, Eric. *The Evolution of Socio-Technical Systems,* Toronto, Ontario: Quality of Working Life Centre, 1981. Reprinted in Andy Van de Ven and William Joyce, Eds., Perspectives on Organizational Design and Behavior, Wiley Interscience, 1981.

Weisbord, Marvin R. *Productive Workplaces,* San Francisco: Jossey-Bass, 1990.

Wellins, Richard S., William C. Byham, and Jeanne M. Wilson. *Empowered Teams,* San Francisco, CA: Jossey-Bass, Inc., 1991.

part

8

TQM in Higher Education

Readings in this section illustrate efforts to implement TQM principles and processes in higher education. These applications are of general interest since colleges and universities are complex organizations with many stakeholders ranging from society at large to local governments, parents, students, faculty, and staff. In other words, a multiorganization institution is responsible for addressing simultaneously a myriad of needs, wants, and claims.

Early efforts to bring TQM to higher education settings have focused on administrative processes, which are largely similar to those of any large service organization. Under increasing cost containment pressures, higher education administrative units have to do more with less, and process improvement becomes an overriding priority.

Implementation of TQM principles and processes in the classroom is trickier and requires fundamental paradigm shifts. The shift of the role of the instructor from provider of knowledge to that of facilitator, the shared responsibility in course design and delivery, and the decrease of importance of grades, require new attitudes and skills from both faculty and students. In other words a radical change in organizational culture is required to build learning environments where fear is eliminated (one of Deming's essential requirements for true organizational change) and responsibility shared. It is yet to be seen to what extent such lofty goals will become a reality.

Reading 37

Quality in Education

BY HARRY COSTIN

This paper intends to clarify some of the key issues surrounding the discussion of quality improvement in education, which affects all of us in our multiple roles as students, teachers, parents, and citizens concerned about the efficient use of our tax money. It is because we all care about education, and it affects us in so many ways that the public discourse on quality improvement in education has become so politicized and confusing.

The quality movement has addressed quality improvement in education since its early developments, and some of the *founding fathers* of the quality movement, like Ishikawa, went so far as to say that *quality begins and ends with education.* Deming also had a particular interest in learning, which for him defined to a large extent what the human experience is about. Further, Deming's Plan-Do-Check/Study-Act model for quality improvement and his fourteen points have been influential in the systematic introduction of quality processes in schools and colleges. Senge linked his *organizational learning* model directly to Deming's idea that human growth relates closely to learning rather than cutthroat competition, an idea we can trace back to Aristotle.

Building upon its strengths and experiences, the quality movement has interpreted the concept of *quality in education* as *learning from experience* (the fundamental notion underlying the P-D-C/S-A model) and *process improvement.* In other words, quality improvement in education can be achieved by improving critical processes of the educational system such as training of teachers, student learning, and planning. It is difficult to argue against these basic ideas. However, they may be more difficult to operationalize than what is commonly thought, and they may just represent "one" perspective on quality in education, one among various others discussed below.

A BASIC MODEL OF THE EDUCATIONAL PROCESS

A highly simplified, linear model of the educational process is shown in Table 37.1 below.

In this model education is defined as the system in which inputs (students, teachers, classrooms, educational materials, etc.), through the mediation of critical processes (learning and teaching), become outcomes (students with specific skills, measurable knowledge, etc.) and more broadly defined outcomes (an educated, productive workforce).

This model encompasses only a limited aspect of the educational process. Nevertheless, it is useful to illustrate the difficulties inherent to the general discourse on quality improvement in education. From this model we can develop four different sets of definitions of quality in education:

Inputs

Educational inputs are seen as fundamental to quality in education. In other words, trained teachers, appropriately equipped classrooms, good educational materials, and motivated students all contribute greatly to learning. This definition of quality is often implicitly used in the public discourse on education, and a relationship is established between the level of resources spent on education (measured at the national level as a percentage of GNP) and the perceived quality of education. It can be said that quality of education understood as quality of inputs dominates the educational policy discourse.

Processes

The greatest strength of the quality movement lies in applied notions of process improvement. In other words, from this perspective *quality improvement is equivalent to process improvement.* In theoretical terms it is difficult to argue against this definition. In practice, many contributions of quality practitioners to the improvement of quality in education have been full of lofty intentions but based on naive conceptions of educational processes. It can be said that processes are *industry specific,* and critical educational processes such as learning and teaching are particularly complex, since an important part of these processes is invisible and unmeasurable (we are referring for example to the process of cognition). As *The Little Prince* would say: *The important is invisible to the eye.*

The most important contributions of quality practitioners to quality of education have been in the areas of planning and resource allocation. Therefore, it is no wonder that most *success stories* focus on improvements in administrative and service areas.

TABLE 37.1: *The Educational Process*

Inputs ⟶ Processes ⟶ Outputs ⟶ Outcomes

Outputs

Quality in education from the perspective of outputs refers to familiar notions such as educational standards, skills, and cognitive development. One of the reasons defining quality of education in terms of outputs seems appealing is that *outputs can often be measured.* However, what is frequently forgotten is that the achievement of certain educational standards (commonly measured through use of standardized tests, which for the sake of this discussion we will assume to be able to measure what they intend to measure) is not equivalent to *learning.*

Strictly speaking, learning (understood here as an output, not as a process) refers to a ratio between an initial state and a later state. Simplifying the process, we can conceive a student who knows X in the beginning and Y at the end. (E.g., a student does not know Russian when she begins taking private lessons and becomes fluent after two years. A talented student!) Learning would be defined as the ratio between Y and X:

$$Y/X = L \text{ or Learning}$$

It may also be useful to define R as the level of resources or inputs needed to bring about L (number of lessons, time spent studying, cost of the lessons). Under this conception of quality we will attempt to maximize L as a function of R; i.e., bring about maximum learning for a given level of resources.

$$L = \mathrm{f}(R) \quad \text{and} \quad \text{maximum efficiency is achieved at max. } \mathrm{f}(R)$$

Using this framework, quality in education is equivalent to *the achievement of educational goals with maximum efficiency,* i.e., with the minimal investment of resources.

When it comes to education the main difficulty in using this definition of quality exclusively is that some of the inputs (resources) are difficult to measure in order to define efficiency levels. The main reason is that not all inputs are standardized (students may have different natural abilities and additional resources such as a supporting home environment).

The policy implications of this apparently simple notion of *quality of education as learning* are significant:

- Some so-called very good schools may not be so good when measured in terms of learning as defined above. With optimal resources or inputs such as smart students who come from a highly supporting family environment, trained teachers, good learning materials, and a high entry level into the system (X in our equation; i.e., the knowledge students have when they begin the formal learning process), it may be easy to achieve high standards. However, the achievement of high educational standards is not equivalent to *high efficiency,* or maximum learning as a function of resources. Higher learning may take place in poor schools where students come from challenging environments.

- The argument above (to be tested on a case-by-case basis) may provide support to one of the key policy goals of large education systems, *equity.* Commonly, it is believed that equity can only be achieved at the expense of *quality.* However, it may be useful to test the hypothesis that these two concepts are largely what the statistician would call *orthogonal,* or unrelated. In other words, higher equity does not necessarily imply lower quality. There may even be cases when higher equity (decreasing the variance of level of resources available throughout the system) leads to higher efficiency of resource utilization, one of the key ways to define quality in education.
- Although it may be tempting to define quality as the attainment of specific educational outputs (standards), it may not be the most efficient alternative, and *if* the achievement of certain standards is the key goal (e.g., a certain level of math competence for 8th graders) *then* an unequal resource allocation (even under the assumption of constant efficiency throughout the system) will be necessary to compensate for unequal levels of inputs.

It can be argued that in our function for learning (L) maximum efficiency can be achieved as a function of inputs or resources (R) available and the entry level of the students (X). This may not represent the greatest practical challenge to quality in education defined as learning, as long as expectations for Y (what students should know at the end of a course). Our own experience suggests that we also have to examine the variance of R and X as a function of each individual student. In plain English this means that it is very difficult to work simultaneously with a significant number of students at very different entry levels (X), and who have access to very unequal resources (most learning takes place outside the classroom, and classroom time represents a small percentage of time on task). A certain degree of variance among the student body can be enriching (diversity), but beyond a certain point, the system becomes unmanageable, as public school teachers can attest.

Private schools not only benefit from higher entry levels into the system (X), and a higher level of in- and out-of-class educational resources, but also have a control over the variance of X, which in my opinion is the most challenging contributor to quality in education conceived as learning.

Our intention with the discussion above has not been to arouse controversy, but to highlight the fact that most of the ongoing public discourse on quality of education does not elaborate upon underlying assumptions and is, therefore, muddled and often of little practical use.

Outcomes

Outcomes refer to a societal perspective of the value of education. There is a difference between a student who has developed specific skills or mastered a given body of knowledge (educational outputs) and the notion of a *responsible citizen* or a *productive workforce.* Most of society cares about the latter, but the educational system should concentrate on the former.

What is often forgotten is that different societies may have different values and, therefore, place different emphasis upon specific outcomes. For example, in traditional societies the integration of the children into the existing social setting was and still is considered to be a more important outcome than practical, economic goals.

QUALITY IN EDUCATION

From the simplified model introduced at the beginning of this paper (which often implicitly underlies educational policy discussions), we can derive different definitions of *quality in education*. Some examples are:

Inputs

- Quality of education is equivalent to quality of inputs such as trained teachers, safe and well-equipped schools, and students who have prerequisite skills and knowledge and are eager to learn.
- Good students mean good education (the Ivy League model).

Processes

- The quality of education depends fundamentally on *how* we do things, and improvement comes about by changing the way we do things based upon our experience. We can do more with the same resources.
- Quality of teaching and learning bring about the best quality of education.

Outputs

- Quality means achieving specific standards of excellence.
- Learning is the true measure of the quality and efficiency of education.

Outcomes

- A quality education should develop a sense of responsible citizenship in individuals.
- A productive workforce is the true measure of a quality system.

It should be noted that most of the definitions of quality in education discussed above are not mutually exclusive. Nevertheless, depending upon which set we choose, educational priorities and practices will vary. What should be evident is that unless we specify what we mean by quality in education any discourse on the topic will be a highly frustrating and a futile experience.

THE EDUCATIONAL SYSTEM

Using the simplified, generic model presented above we will now briefly discuss some of the particular characteristics of the educational system, which, until now has been largely assumed to be homogenous and united.

It may be useful to differentiate stakeholders, levels of analysis, and institutions, segmented according to their focus upon specific priorities and developmental levels.

Stakeholders

Everybody is a stakeholder of the educational system, which explains the controversy surrounding the issue of quality in education. Further, many are stakeholders playing different, sometimes contradictory, roles.

Stakeholders include taxpayers, concerned about level of taxes and efficient resource utilization; parents, who want the *best* education for their children, which commonly is interpreted as quality of inputs; students, increasingly concerned about outcomes that tie to their future employment opportunities as they progress through the system; teachers, concerned about learning as a process and as an output; lawmakers, concerned about cost of inputs, standards, and outcomes; administrators, concerned about resource maximization and optimization and the achievement of standards.

We can easily imagine a man pulled in different directions by four horses when we begin to closely examine the pressures placed upon the educational system.

Understanding the diversity of stakeholders of the educational system is critical to understanding the relationship between quality and planning in educational settings.

Quality and planning

One of the most important perspectives for quality in education relates to planning. The role of planning is highlighted throughout the quality literature as a starting point for a continuous improvement process. For example, the best-known model for quality improvement, the Shewhart cycle, best-known as PDCA (Plan-Do-Check-Act), and popularized by Deming, begins with planning.

Implicit in the concept of planning, as understood in the quality literature, is the assumption that there are *goals and means to achieve these goals*. This basic concept can be *wishful thinking* in the field of education. Some of the reasons are as follows. A goals/means perspective of planning is based upon a linear, rational thinking model of human behavior; i.e., that given the right information and professional training, an individual or team will be able to define goals and appropriate means to accomplish these goals. However, when the focus shifts to the process of planning in environments with a multitude of stakeholders, political and bureaucratic models of planning can have a higher descriptive value.

To begin with, when there are many stakeholders, which is the case for educational planning at the school, district, and national levels, consensus on goals cannot be taken for granted. Commonly, there are many conflicting or complementary goals, whether they are acknowledged or not. One way to deal with such conflict is to be vague about goals, which may create the illusion of consensus. However, vague goals cannot be translated into means, since there may be as many descriptions of what those goals are as there are stakeholders in the system. It is sad but true that one of these vague goals for educational systems is "quality in education," since there is such a wide range of possible notions of what "quality" means in the context of education.

From the discussion above it should be clear that the first condition for quality in educational planning is a fundamental level of *consensus on goals, goal congruence* (to have goals that do not contradict or undermine each other), and *clarity of goals.* The second condition relates to the relationship between many, potentially even complementary goals, to be reached with limited resources. In other words, *goals need to be attainable* with existing resources, which in practice means that they need to be *prioritized,* a new source of potential conflict among stakeholders.

It should be noted that *resource-driven planning and goal definition* (what can we achieve with the resources we have?) runs the risk of circular thinking (we cannot accomplish anything because of lack of resources) and lack of search for creative solutions to resource constraints. Commonly, *vision-driven planning* has been advocated, which forces us to break cognitive and practical boundaries. These two approaches to planning are not necessarily mutually exclusive, since vision-driven planning is strongest for long-range planning, and resource-driven planning is best for short- and, in some cases, medium-term planning.

Taking planning as an outcome (a set of clearly defined, congruent, and realistic goals and means to achieve them), it can be said that *quality, from the perspective of planning, can be defined as the achievement of clearly defined goals.* This is the notion behind the PDCA model. We define goals and means (Plan), implement the means (Do), verify the results of implementation (Check), and, based upon empirical experience, make improvements (Act).

LEVELS OF ANALYSIS

Until now we have treated the educational system as if it were a unitary entity with many stakeholders. This is evidently an oversimplification, and we will now address two potential perspectives on differentiation within the educational system: levels of analysis and institutional differentiation.

Levels of analysis of the educational system

There are several levels of analysis of the educational system, grouped into two categories, that do not exhaust the possibilities of classification:

By level of education

- Preschool
- Elementary education (which is mandatory in most countries)

- Secondary education
- Higher education
- Adult education
- Continuing professional education

Micro and macro analysis

- School
- School district
- State
- National level
- Regional level (for example, member countries of the European Union)

One of the potential sources of confusion surrounding the discussion of quality in education is due to a lack of clarity and differentiation between these different levels. It is evident that goals will vary widely according to the level of analysis. For example, common goals for primary education are *universal access* and the development of reading and writing skills. By contrast, specialized higher education institutions such as professional schools (e.g., medical or law schools) may focus on the development of highly specialized skills. In a similar vein, concerns about the quality of education will differ among schools, school districts, and states. Some states, for example, will be concerned about equity, others about the achievement of educational standards, and others about the development of model, showcase educational institutions.

Institutional differentiation

In the quality literature there is a higher degree of clarity when it comes to addressing institutional differences. One of the key concepts of both the literature on quality and on planning, which provides a guideline to understanding institutional differentiation, is *institutional mission*.

Mission represents the top of the planning pyramid and limits the institutional goals and practices that are acceptable for a specific educational organization. It also represents a form of control for external stakeholders, which, through diverse means such as allocation of resources (e.g., by the state legislature to public higher education institutions) and legal action, can hold an institution accountable for its actions. A further benefit of a clear definition of institutional mission is to limit the potential conflict among the stakeholders of a specific educational institution.

In general it can be said that from this perspective quality of education at the institutional level can be defined as the *implementation of a clearly defined institutional mission*. Further, in a rapidly changing environment, the *institutional mission* needs to be reevaluated periodically and tied to the *institutional vision*, an image of how the institution sees itself in the future.

CONCLUSION

This paper has attempted to show that any discussion on quality in education needs to be based on a common understanding of the concept of quality. Using a simplified, linear model of the educational system, it can be shown that conceptions of quality can relate to educational inputs, processes, outputs, and outcomes. Further, definitions of quality will vary greatly depending upon the level of analysis of the system, a macro or micro analysis perspective, and also for each institution, since quality goals should be closely tied to the institutional mission. Without such clarification, the discourse on quality in education, which affects all of us directly or indirectly, will remain muddled and confusing.

The quality literature has made important contributions to the discussion of quality in education, such as the understanding of quality improvement as process improvement, and the emphasis placed upon the importance of quality goals formulation within the context of institutional mission. At the same time these significant contributions need to be recognized, a note of caution is warranted. Quality professionals, for the most part, work in organizations and are familiar with processes that are extremely different from those encountered in most educational institutions. The lack of understanding of practices common in education has often led to a "preachy" attitude on the part of the quality professionals attempting to influence education, a deep sense of frustration about goal formulation and implementation in educational institutions (which can be more easily understood using political organizational models, rather than rational planning ones), and naive suggestions for the improvement of complex educational processes, such as learning and teaching.

Reading 38

TQM Reaches the Academy

By Ted Marchese

Total Quality Management . . . an American set of ideas, engine behind the Japanese economic miracle, agent for the dramatic turnabouts at Ford and Motorola . . . suddenly it's at work in more than half the Fortune 1000 firms . . . it's the "preferred management style" of the federal government . . . you'll find it in hotels, city government, your local hospital . . . *it's in the air* . . . can the academy be next?

In fact, TQM has *already* arrived in higher education, in dozens of institutions, notably research universities and community colleges. TQM's collegiate practitioners, their zeal and worries on full display, already have networks in place and a literature at hand; their quality-improvement message dominated last spring's AACSB conference of business schools and this month's ABET meeting of engineering educators; next April 5–8, TQM debuts as a major theme of AAHE's National Conference on Higher Education in Chicago.

What's going on here? How relevant can TQM be to the special work of a college or university? Are we about to be shelled again by the latest fad in corporate management?

To get answers to these questions, last July I traveled to Los Angeles for the Second Annual Symposium on the Role of Academia in National Competitiveness and Total Quality Management, hosted by the University of Southern California. A hundred colleges had representatives among the 300 people on hand. Afterwards I met with two dozen of TQM's lead practitioners in higher education; since then, through interviews and document collection, I've pieced together a picture of the movement's first days on campus. This is what I found.

Source: AAHE, 1991. Reprinted with the permission of the publisher from the November 1991 issue of *AAHE Bulletin*, a publication of the American Association of Higher Education, Washington, D.C.

THE TQM STORY

The saga is triumphal: W. Edwards Deming, an American statistician whose ideas about quality find little response at home, lectures in 1950 to Japan. He excoriates his hosts for their cheap, shoddy goods; he tells them that an emphasis on quality will reap lasting benefits in market share and profitability; he lays out principles—eventually fourteen in number—for making quality a "strategic advantage." They listen to him. They listen also, in 1954, to Joseph Juran ("management for quality"); they devour Armand Feigenbaum's 1951 classic, *Total Quality Control,* and later the writing of Philip Crosby (*Quality Is Free*). They struggle, adapt, develop their own gurus (Ishikawa, Imai), pursue the quality ideal relentlessly. . . . The rest, as they say, is history.

In the early and mid-1980s, hard-pressed American firms take up the message: at Motorola (1982) and Ford (1984), quality becomes "everybody's job" and "Job 1." Soon Xerox, Federal Express, IBM, Westinghouse, Disney, Corning, Hewlett-Packard, and the Hospital Corporation of America are on board; the books, workshops, and consultants multiply; the U.S. Navy coins the phrase "Total Quality Management." In 1987, Congress sets up a Malcolm Baldrige National Quality Award; its seven criteria become a consensus statement of TQM values. In 1988, the Department of Defense mandates TQM for itself and all contractors; a Federal Quality Institute starts to implement TQM across all departments and agencies. Surveys show that buyers—nine of ten in 1990 versus three in ten in 1980—now place a first value on quality (above price and styling); studies demonstrate that quality-oriented firms in fact do better in market share and profits.

In banking and airlines, in manufacturing and services, from microchips to pet food, the word is out: Consumers value *products* that work and last, *service* that's prompt, courteous, and dependable, and *TQM* is the way to deliver it.

With all that, I wondered aloud in Los Angeles why *all* firms hadn't given themselves over totally to the concept. "They haven't," an executive from McDonnell Douglas told me, "because not many companies have felt as hard-pressed as Ford and Motorola did ten years ago. Firms claim to be into TQM, but their implementation is spotty. It's too great a change to make without a big need at your backside."

WHAT IS IT?

What is TQM, this "too great a change"? At one level, it's an approach to management and a set of tools, a coalescing of new and old ideas—from systems thinking and statistical process control, from theories of human behavior, leadership, and planning, plus lessons from earlier, less-than-successful attempts at quality improvement (such as quality circles)—all these brought together in a new orthodoxy.

But at another level, and looking at TQM as a phenomenon, it is a call to leadership for the reform of American enterprise. Its advocates want more than a change in management practice; they want an entirely new organization, one whose culture is quality-driven, customer-oriented, marked by teamwork, and avid about improvement . . . "corporate revolution" and "paradigm shift" are the words one hears. Armand Feigenbaum, now an international consultant, told the Los Angeles conference that American corporate philosophy has been to "make it quick and cheaper, finance it cleverly, and sell it hard. The value of 'making it better' was left out. Firms have to march to an entirely new drumbeat: quality."

From among the many strands of thought and prior experience feeding into TQM, I've teased out a dozen themes that seem at its core (see pages 572–574).

The Baldrige Award

Secretary of Commerce Malcolm Baldrige, a quality advocate, died in a rodeo accident in 1987. Shortly thereafter, Congress authorized a "National Quality Award" in his name, a public-private endeavor administered from the Commerce Department. A distinguished group of quality experts was empaneled to write criteria for the award; the panel's ultimate scheme, derived from TQM, quickly became the accepted template for judging corporate quality-improvement efforts.

The Baldrige criteria categories and their relative values (on a 1,000-point scale) are as follows:

Leadership. The senior management's success in creating and sustaining a quality culture. (100 points)

Information and analysis. The effectiveness of the company's collection and analysis of information for quality improvement and planning. (70)

Planning. The effectiveness of integrating quality requirements into the company's business plans. (60)

Human resource utilization. The success of the company's efforts to utilize the full potential of the workforce for quality. (150)

Quality assurance. The effectiveness of the company's systems for ensuring quality control of all operations. (140)

Quality results. The company's results in quality achievement and quality improvement, demonstrated through quantitative measures. (180)

Customer satisfaction. The effectiveness of the company's systems to determine customer requirements and demonstrated success in meeting them. (300)

The Baldrige application is detailed: The seven categories are broken down into thirty-two subcategories with ninety-nine "areas to address." The award's key values are self-described as customer-driven quality, leadership, continuous improvement,

The Baldrige Award ***(continued)***

fast response, actions based on facts, and participation by all employees. The criteria ask about results but especially focus on the conditions and processes that led to them.

The guidelines themselves constitute a self-study exercise for applicants, a corporate "examination" (with an accompanying "scoring system") in quality commitment; firms that apply get feedback from the Baldrige judging panels. Because of these diagnostic features (and low entry fees), many companies apply just for the self-study exercise . . . Ford, Motorola, and IBM even make their suppliers go through the process. Last year, 200,000 copies of the guidelines were distributed; in a poll, 86 percent of business executives claimed to know the criteria; 6 percent of all firms actually applied. This year's winners were announced October 29th from the White House.

In the September/October *Change,* SHEEO director James Mingle proposed that regional accrediting bodies mount a Baldrige Aware competition for higher education. His colleague Peter Ewell, of NCHEMS, doubts the idea would work just now ("It assumes a process within colleges that isn't there yet."); but the idea is alive, with several parties in the country now trying to cook up "higher-ed versions" of the criteria. At the Los Angeles conference, Baldrige director Curt Reimann acknowledged that "if such an award could make a contribution, and educators expressed interest, the Secretary would welcome the suggestion."

1. ***A focus on quality***. The alpha and omega of TQM is its singular focus on quality as the defining characteristic of an organization. Quality in this view is not just an attribute of products or services; it is a mindset, the soul of the company itself, an all-pervasive drive of such intensity that it defines the corporate culture. Just as geneticist Barbara McClintock's breakthroughs came when she was able to "think like corn," TQM enjoins managers to "imbibe" quality; the corporation that lives for quality, that takes quality as its strategic advantage, is promised long-run gains in market share and return on investment.
2. ***Customer-driven.*** What is quality? To Juran, it's "fitness for use" by the consumer; to Deming, it's that which "surpasses customer needs and expectations." In TQM companies, a keen sense of customer needs governs all activities. The cardinal rule is to identify explicitly who your customers are, know their needs systematically, and commit to meeting those needs. Why? Because in a competitive environment the customer—not executives, engineers, or inspectors—defines quality. If you don't satisfy the customer, someone else will.

3. ***Continuous improvement.*** An American adage says, "If it ain't broke, don't fix it." TQM responds, "Wrong!" Customers, markets, technologies change every day; what's good enough now will be suicide tomorrow. Deming preaches "constancy of purpose" on behalf of continuous adaptation and improvement; he and Juran describe quality as a "journey." Education undersecretary David Kearns, former Xerox CEO and a quality champion, proclaims, "In the race for quality, there is no finish line."
4. ***Making processes work better.*** Every organization is a network of processes. These range from the "single-purpose" (discharging a patient from a hospital) to the "cross-functional" (Federal Express's hub-and-spoke delivery system). The aim is to identify those processes; enable the people who work in them to understand that work in relation to customer needs (Are we doing the right thing? How well?); and set in motion, through problem-solving teams, process improvements.
5. ***Extending the mindset.*** In the old paradigm, attention to quality began and ended on the shop floor; it was a matter to be "controlled" or "inspected in." In the new, quality concerns reach in all directions. An "absence of defects" isn't enough; goods are followed "out the door," where their quality is judged by how well they fit or exceed customer expectations in actual use. Quality, too, is a function of good, up-front product and process design. And it reaches backward from the shop floor: No longer will it do for automakers to say, "We know our cars aren't very good, but our lowest-bid suppliers sent us so-so goods." With quality precedent to price, TQM companies attempt to develop stable relations with a small set of suppliers who agree to be partners in the quality-improvement process.
6. ***The discipline of information.*** TQM people always want to see the data, and they want it to be public data, up on the shop or office wall. If you're serious about improving quality, they say, everybody has to know how they're doing. Customers aren't just bowed to; they're systematically surveyed, interviewed, poked, prodded, and begged for suggestions. Process-improvement teams are taught to track meticulously every fault, complaint, breakdown, accident, or shortage that comes their way; "Every process," Wisconsin's George Box teaches, "generates the data to improve it." A variety of statistical tools—ingenious diagrams, charts, matrices, graphs, and checksheets—are deployed in what the Japanese call *Kaizen* (continuous improvement) methods of process control.
7. ***Eliminate rework.*** An aim of all this attention to work processes is to ferret out the "scrap, waste, and complexity" (Deming) from a system . . . simplify, standardize, get it right the first time. The time spent fixing earlier mistakes (rework), in useless work that has to be done over (scrap), and in extra steps that add no value to a product or service (complexity) can equal 20 percent of all costs, say "findings" in the Baldrige legislation. Service organizations can have an even greater problem: Crosby concludes they spend "35 percent or more of their operating costs doing things wrong and then doing them over."

8. ***Teamwork.*** From top management to the shop floor, within units and across functions, quality issues are attacked in teams. "Teams" are *not* your familiar committees; they are "self-directed work groups" with their own required competencies and protocols. Unlike committees, teams aren't "representative": they bring together most or all of the people who work in a process to work on its improvement—no others need apply. TQM wants all persons to share responsibility for the processes they work in and for the whole; it believes in the superiority of collaborative work that achieves "team learning."
9. ***Empowering people.*** In Deming's view, 85 percent of all problems are traceable to the process itself, just 15 percent to the people in them. Stop attacking people, he admonishes managers, look to your systems: "Drive out fear from the workplace!" Patrick Townsend says management must "believe that its personnel department has been in the habit of hiring adults"; TQM "empowers" people "by trusting all employees . . . to act responsibly and giving them appropriate authority." People *want* to do the right and better thing, TQM urges, they *want* pride in their work; the task of managers is to remove the system barriers that prevent people from doing so. Who, in TQM, reviews work processes? Again, not distant managers or external evaluators but the people closest to the processes, those who do the work itself.
10. ***Training and recognition.*** So that all employees can understand the corporate vision of quality, have the skills of teamwork and problem solving they need, and relate more effectively to customers, TQM firms invest heavily in human resource development. Across its various units, Motorola spends 2 to 6 percent of its salary budgets on training; IBM-Rochester invests 5 percent across the board. Personnel systems in TQM companies rely less on incentives and rewards directed at the individual than on team-oriented "recognition, honors, and celebration."
11. ***Vision.*** The TQM world wants stripped-down, plain-English statements of the organization's core values, and it wants these "vision statements" a clear part of every employee's work. A story is told: When Tylenol was recalled a few years back, it wasn't an act of J&J's top management . . . a third-line manager learned of the peril and, with specific reference to J&J's values statement, recalled the product on his own authority. Unlike the lofty piffle of "mission" statements, TQM urges compelling, down-to-earth language that gets all parties focused on the right thing to do.
12. ***Leadership.*** To achieve all the above, TQM partisans want fewer managers, at least of the old type—powerful figures in sole command of vertical authority structures. Instead, they want leaders, and of a new type—vision-givers, listeners, team-workers, committed to quality and customer needs, avid but patient, for long-term ends, orchestrators and enablers of people-driven improvement. Lehigh University president Peter Likins puts this change more simply: ". . . we'll need to talk to each other more and control one another less."

The book I found TQM practitioners reading last summer was Peter Senge's *The Fifth Discipline* (Doubleday, 1990). In it, Senge (of MIT) describes the "ensemble of disciplines" that lie behind an organizational capacity for innovation: systems thinking, personal mastery, mental models, shared vision, and team learning. Senge barely mentions TQM, even as his "disciplines" capture the movement's values.

STILL NOT SURE?

Did I return from Los Angeles a convert? Not exactly. But I heard on reflection, a lot of good answers to the objections I came with.

"Students aren't customers!" A "student as a customer" analogy, for sure, falls well short of full description; students are important agents for their own learning, indeed the creators of it. All that said, the customer analogy—taken as an attempt to understand the experience of college from a student point of view—should hardly be taken as alien; it provides a useful lens for introspection and improvement. Want to improve registration or a chemistry major or library services? Why not talk with students?

TQM, importantly, does not imply pandering to student satisfaction or every short-term expression of needs. Faculties do well to weigh student views alongside their own professional judgment about the requirements of learning, of society, of future employers, and of a student's own longer-term interests. Some TQM educators entertain a responsibilities-oriented "student as worker" theme.

"We already talk with our students." Let us hope. The objection misses, however, what TQM wants: systematic, across-the-board listening, based on notions of customer importance. But as Kansas business professor Larry Sherr told an AIR audience recently, ". . . very few of our institutions have any idea even of who their customers are."

Customer analysis is one of TQM's fresh ideas, and it doesn't begin or end with students. Indeed, the prime "customer" of most administrative offices turns out to be . . . other administrative offices. While the end-point customer counts (a lot), more often the customer at hand is the in-house individual or unit to whom you supply products, a service, or information; the goal is for the work of each office to meet or exceed the expectations of its internal customers. Thinking in such terms tends to raise a host of new questions for collegiate TQM project teams.

It follows also that each person and unit has *suppliers,* most of them internal, on whom it relies for its work. "How can we be partners in quality-improvement work?" TQM would have teams ask one another.

"Oh, that language!" There are, let it be said, more-technical versions of TQM than I've recounted here; an engineer or statistician's view of the thing would whip you quickly into an exotic work of Pareto charts, cause-and-effect ("fishbone") diagrams, and "Plan, Do, Check, Act" schemes. Initial presentations of TQM to faculty-staff audiences at Wisconsin and Maryland faltered when just such versions were

paraded forth . . . reminding one of assessment's rocky road to faculty understanding when first versions of it were presented by psychometricians.

But, just as with assessment, there are plain-English, larger-picture versions of TQM that can make sense to academic ears. Viewed broadly, TQM is a call to quality and a mindset about improvement; it values data, teams, and process; for the many faculty and staff of an institution, it offers respect and a voice. As for its special tools and vocabularies, they come second and are for adaptive use.

"It's okay for corporations but. . . . " In a recent TQM newsletter, Ellen Chaffee described her interview in Tokyo with Prof. Masao Kogure, a revered leader in the application of quality improvement to the service sector. Kogure told her that every time TQM came to a new industry in Japan it encountered resistance: "We're not like the industry that is already using it."

Pondering Kogure's words, then higher education's special history and character, I came to wonder how different many of our functions really were from those in business—generating a bill, advising a student or client . . . if hospital TQM programs can teach doctors to introduce themselves to patients and listen to their questions, might there not be *something* here for us? Rutgers biologist Lion Gardner phoned in October to tell me of his own new interest in the topic: "We have to do something with the hard, alienating structures of the university," he told me; "TQM is relevant for its humanistic thrust."

"It's okay for administrators, but . . . " Most faculty members wouldn't mind at all if their institution's administrators used TQM (or anything else) to get a better act together. Indeed, we've all seen and come to appreciate the new customer orientation and service ethic in certain hotel chains, department stores, car-rental companies, and so on, and no doubt wondered why these new standards for service stopped at the campus gate. TQM, its early practitioners have found, finds many targets of opportunity in collegiate administration.

In that sense, its academic applications are, well, academic; let TQM be for administrators. Faculty have their own, more apt set of questions in assessment (which also is about quality, listening to students, and continuous improvement). Winona's Darrell Krueger, for years a national leader in the uses of assessment for academic improvement, is enthusiastic about TQM's arrival on the administrative side: "It brings the whole rest of the university into the quality quest."

Does TQM, though, have anything to contribute on the academic side? I think it might, especially to improving aspects of a department's services and to helping it to a keener sense of who its customers and suppliers are. Also, though most of the early collegiate adopters of TQM have left the academic side alone, a few have used the emphasis to encourage faculty to try the assessment-like techniques of Classroom Research—certainly a plus.

Does TQM have anything to add to assessment itself? Again I think it might. Pat Hutchings and Peter Ewell three years ago taught assessors the importance of getting "behind outcomes," of understanding the crucial processes of learning that contribute to outcomes . . . the process-analysis approaches of TQM are more than a bit suggestive here. Also suggestive is the TQM concept of "benchmarking," which insists that an organization intent on improving quality compare its per-

Hoshin Planning

TQM far from ignores "outcomes" (recall "fitness for use") or "inputs" (good design, work with suppliers); but its distinctive contributions center or organizational processes. It's not that process is more important than input or outcome, simply a judgment about where new effort should best be focused. "The crux of the thing is that it forces us to pay attention to a lot of daily processes we've typically ignored," Carnegie Mellon's Richard Cyert told the Los Angeles conference.

What about planning, then? TQM practitioners in Japan evolved their own version of what Americans know as strategic planning, called *Hoshin,* or "breakthrough," Planning. It starts, as you'd expect, with a "vision statement," typically for the next five years. This is followed by goals (which have a customer orientation), work plans (for specific critical processes), deployment and execution, followed by monthly "audits" to monitor progress toward the vision. An important feature in Hoshin is the identification of no more than four "breakthroughs" (fundamental quality improvements), items that all units in the organization will specially pursue in a given time frame.

Hoshin practitioners have developed their own set of planning tools (the matrix and affinity diagrams, for example). They're also prone to put value statements in plans, as a reminder that how things are done can be as important as their direction. In American higher education, at least two institutions—Oregon State and Delaware County C.C.—have used Hoshin Planning.

formance not with industrywide averages but with a corporate "best of class." In educational testing, for example, this might imply comparing student performance not against local norms but against "high, international standards" (as the new National Education Goals will do).

"None of this is new . . . it's just good management." A quick way to dismiss TQM—business professors do this—is to resort to the above, a truism. Indeed, as mentioned earlier, TQM itself is an amalgam of ideas and tools, many of which have been around for quite some time—which is not to say they've been much used. And on most campuses, let it be noted, one will find offices and departments that seem perfectly well managed without the grace of TQM. But there are plenty more that aren't, that could sorely use the bursts of insight and energy TQM seems to bring.

"Here we go with another fad." Those of us who've been around long enough have sharp memories of earlier management nostrums—MBO, zero-based budgeting, endless planning schemes. Typically these arrive at higher education's

doorstep five years after their trial in business, often just as corporations are discarding them. Let the record note here that first grumblings about TQM have started to appear in the business press, and that one of TQM's star companies—Florida Power and Light, a winner of Japan's Deming Prize, no less—has taken recent steps to deemphasize it.

It's easy to cry "fad," though, and miss the real article—as we saw with assessment. Two management "fads," in my memory, proved valuable and stuck: marketing in the late 1970s, strategic planning in the mid-1980s. They stuck, Michigan's Marvin Peterson reminded me, because they seemed to speak to an environmental need, they found their guru (Kotler, Keller), and they proved adaptable. TQM has yet to find its collegiate guru, but the first and third of the conditions do apply. Given the doldrums many college administrations find themselves in today, maybe it's time for the next "fad" to step up and find its uses.

THE EARLY ADAPTERS

At and since Los Angeles, I've tried to keep track of TQM's campus parties of interest. My best sense is that the number of individuals devoted to the topic runs well up in the hundreds, the number of institutions trying TQM in particular offices might be near one hundred, the number of those that have committed to TQM on an institutionwide basis stands at two dozen, of which the number with deeper experience constitutes a mere handful.

An intriguing observation is that most of the early innovators are from just two institutional types: either prominent research universities or *un*prominent (up to now) community colleges. Among the former are Oregon State, Wisconsin, Penn, and Colorado State, followed by Harvard, Carnegie Mellon, Maryland, Lehigh, Chicago, Minnesota, Wyoming, Clemson, Georgia Tech, and Miami. Interestingly, the TQM initiator in many universities has been the president—several of these presidents have technical or business backgrounds, so they can't help knowing of TQM. Sometimes pressure for TQM adoption comes from community or alumni friends; Ford's Donald Peterson happens to be Oregon State's best-known alum, as Lee Iacocca is Lehigh's. The Lehigh Valley area, not incidentally, is a hotbed of TQM interest; so is the city of Madison, a fact not unrelated to Wisconsin's decision to hire that city's TQM manager as its own in-house facilitator.

Among the two-year colleges, community relatedness and expectation have also clearly played a role in spurring TQM adoption. Within the sector, Fox Valley Technical College (WI) and Delaware County C.C. (PA) are the leaders, having each been at this since 1985; Houston (TX), Jackson (MI), and Lamar (CO) are among the recent adopters. Fox Valley has an especially beguiling story to tell: As it drove TQM concepts deeper and deeper into the institution, it began to reap high, measurable returns in morale, cost reduction, student attainment, and community approbation. As a result, it has become a Mecca of sorts for TQM initiates, the Alverno of the movement, with eighty colleges visiting last year and a new Quality Institute offering publications, training materials, consultation, and workshops.

Books, brains, and bucks

A huge literature has sprung up around TQM, as you'll see in the business section of any good bookstore. Many authors have their peculiar slant on the thing; more than a few **TQM books** are given over to exhortation and self-help. None of the masters—Deming, Juran, Crosby, Feigenbaum—has on the shelves today a "must read" book for TQM newcomers. Several practitioners recommend starting with journalist Mary Walton's *The Deming Management Method* (Putnam, 1986) or her *Deming Management at Work* (Putnam, 1990). I find in bibliographies at least five published papers on Deming's fourteen points applied to higher education; Tennessee's Trudy Banta heads a **FIPSE project** that will scrutinize corporate quality-improvement ideas for relevance to the academy.

On November 22, ACE/Macmillan releases the first book-length treatment of **TQM in the academy,** *On Q: Causing Quality in Higher Education,* by Daniel Seymour, a contributor to this *Bulletin* ($27.95; for a credit card order, phone 1-800-323-7445). Last month, the Jossey-Bass New Directions for Institutional Research series brought out *Total Quality Management in Higher Education,* edited by Lawrence Sherr and Deborah Teeter, seven good essays plus an annotated bibliography; order it for $13.95. The American Society for Quality Control (310 West Wisconsin Ave., Milwaukee, WI 53203) has a publishing and sales arm called Quality Press Publications that stocks most of the field's essential books, training materials, and so forth; write for a catalogue.

For a free copy of the **Baldrige Award application** guidelines, phone (301) 975-2036.

Notably absent from TQM rosters are liberal arts colleges (Samford, Belmont, and Pepperdine come to mind as exceptions) and the regional publics (Winona, Towson, Northwest Missouri, Central Connecticut, and Arkansas Tech are active). North Dakota's board of higher education two years ago mandated TQM for the state's public colleges; last year, the Minnesota state university system adopted a TQM-derived "Q-7" program; both initiatives look to an enhancement of public confidence. Samford, a small Baptist university in Alabama, has built its interest in TQM on thoughtfully developed notions of Christian stewardship and collaboration.

Abroad, TQM is knocking at the door of higher institutions in the Netherlands and Australia; it's been a non-starter in Japan; in Britain, it's swept the polytechnic sector—Liverpool Polytechnic, for example, is as far along as Fox Valley.

Books, brains, and bucks *(continued)*

Most of the colleges and universities mentioned in this article have moved into TQM with a **corporate partner**—Winona State with IBM-Rochester, Oregon State with training from Hewlett-Packard, Fox Valley with Nashua Paper, and so on. Typically the consultation comes at little or no cost—TQM companies want to spread the gospel. Colleges warn not to rely on corporate people to sell a TQM vision internally; it's better to call them in to learn specific things like team building, statistical tools, or Hoshin.

Within the **consulting world,** a stand-out is the nonprofit GOAL/QPC of Methuen, Mass. Its early research focused on corporate implementation; later came work with hospitals and state and local governments; it now targets help for educators. It has useful publications, notably a 1989 research report (No. 89-10-03) on *Hoshin Planning: A Planning System for Implementing Total Quality Management* ($11.95 each). For information or publications, call (508) 685-3900.

TQM practitioners find one another at the "Role of Academia" conference described in this article, with the next scheduled for July at Lehigh; at the annual GOAL/QPC meeting in Boston, this November 11–13; at meetings of SCUP and AIR; and soon at AAHE **meetings,** including our National Conference next April 5–8 in Chicago and our Assessment Conference next June 21–24 in Miami Beach. People are also linked through a **newsletter,** with lists maintained by W.A. Golomski and Associates, 59 E. Van Buren St., Chicago, IL 60605-1220.

IBM announced October 1st a **major grants program** to promote TQM in colleges and universities—to teach, use, and do research on it. Eight $1 million awards will be made. For guidelines, write Director, Market-Driven Quality Management Systems, IBM Corporation, 208 Harbor Dr., Room 2C-09, Stamford, CT 06904-2501, or call (203) 973-7397.

IMPLEMENTATION STRATEGIES

Anything as comprehensive as TQM, so sweeping in its reach (and claims), raises daunting prospects for the adopter. Deming was once asked how to implement his fourteen points. "What!" he huffed, "You want me to do your work for you?"

Nothing but admiration should go to the handful of institutions that have dug in and confronted the full TQM agenda—Fox Valley, Delaware County, and

Samford, led by their presidents, have pursued nothing less than institutional transformation.

But many TQM advocates—administrative or faculty champions of the concept—confront difficult situations, which they were candid about in Los Angeles. Obstacle one is often the president—he's a loner, she doesn't trust teams, he relies on intuition (his own) over data, she could never be a provider of vision, and so on. Most administrative cabinets and staff are unpracticed at team work; powerful individuals and offices resist from sheer inertia. Very importantly, there's often no perceived external pressure to take up TQM or the concerns it addresses.

In the circumstance, some converts have set out first to educate colleagues and build a critical mass of support for TQM; they've brought in speakers, engaged consultants, staged retreats. Oregon State began this way, in 1989, then was quickly able to implement a whole array of process improvement projects, ten pilot teams at first, now fifty (the OSU work enjoys full presidential support and has a vice-presidential champion, the energetic Ed Coate). Other TQM advocates, however, have basically decided to ignore for now their president, the faculty, and other offices, to try TQM in their own units and attract attention through results.

Much of the early implementation of TQM falls in this latter category—that is, it is within-unit, addresses single functions, uses TQM techniques selectively, and begs (for now) larger change agendas. The Penn story is a good one here. Activity proceeded within the domain of a single (senior) vice president; a trainer was engaged (from the Juran Institute); criteria were developed for choice of projects; four were run in 1990–91, three of them successfully. One of the latter entailed reducing the cost of trash removal; another sought ways to ensure timely recovery of sponsored research funding. (Participants in the process uncovered, as they went along, lots of make-work, confusing forms, loose ends in existing procedures, *and* $1.7 million in billable charges!)

This sort of adaptive use of TQM, while it won't please the purists, seems the near-term future of the thing in most institutions. The stories here are compelling: the time spent in generating a student work-study check reduced from sixteen days to three (Kansas); the percentage of faculty grades handed in on time up from 30 percent to 98 percent (Connecticut College—which doesn't use TQM language); transcript request time cut from ninety days to five (Samford); registration and course-availability "greatly improved" (Fordham's business school).

At Oregon State, Coate has already identified 250 internal processes potentially amenable to TQM analysis. Where do you start? According to Coate, "You look first for a screwed up process that's fixable, important to customers, and that can save you money." Penn's Quality Council looked for projects that were of manageable size, had campuswide visibility and impact, and that promised savings. "But if a unit is sick," Coate observes, "TQM can't cure it. In fact, it won't work. You'll need other remedies."

Is TQM a way to cut costs and save money? The party line is *no;* TQM is about quality and putting customers first, *after* which come the market and financial returns. But Coate's university faces major losses in state support; he feels forced to include in the process a hard look for cost savings, including personnel slots (captured by attrition).

Doubtless other institutions will skip Oregon State's careful groundwork and turn directly to TQM as a retrenchment tool, which would seem a mistake. "TQM is not instant pudding!" snorts Deming. Larry Sherr observes, "If resources are being used unwisely, they can't be found on the day you have to retrench." Fordham's Sylvia Westerman, a former NBC News executive, observes that "TQM absolutely can achieve efficiencies, raise morale, show good stewardship of funds, and win public trust. . . . but it's hard to make claims for cost-savings."

The Japanese experience and U.S. research show that it is only when firms attack cross-cutting functions (enrollment management, for example) that they realize major gains in effectiveness and cost-savings. But such functions prove very difficult to address, especially in a collegiate ethos of semi-autonomous units. Samford and UM-Duluth both report disappointment with first attempts at cross-functional projects; Delaware County, on the other hand, brought off a full-blown TQM review of its general-education program. TQM advisors with the Hospital Corporation of America recommend several years of work and learning with single-function projects (which Delaware County indeed had) before pursuing more ambitious targets.

REFLECTION

TQM doesn't speak to some of higher education's toughest problems (like working through the implications of multiculturalism); it is probably less profound a development than assessment (which speaks to the difficult, central issues of student learning); it won't rescue sagging public support or inept administrations; it might not save us any big sums of money.

It's unlikely, too, that TQM will sweep through our full 3,614 campuses soon—many just won't feel the customer or competitive pressure to undertake its difficult tasks. What I'd anticipate is the spread of TQM concepts, selectively deployed, across hundreds of institutions in the years ahead, with many of the resultant benefits and pitfalls described here.

The Chinese have an expression for "fad" that translates as "a gust of wind." It's been several years now since we've had a good gust of fresh ideas for college and university administration; TQM seems poised to provide just that. If TQM people will talk us into a greater interest in quality, customers, teamwork, and getting things right the first time, I'm ready to listen.

Reading 39

Total Quality Management in Higher Education Institutions

BY HARRY COSTIN

Over the last decade, Total Quality Management has moved from manufacturing and service sector applications into the public sector, especially into education. Many institutions have implemented pilot TQM programs with the intention of translating TQM principles, such as advocacy for shared decision making or customer focus, into practical applications. The results of such efforts have been mixed and, as yet, not well documented.

In the nineties, with increasing pressure on higher education institutions to decrease costs and increase efficiency, the interest in potential applications of programs such as TQM or reengineering has grown. However, there is confusion regarding what TQM is and its feasible applications in higher education institutions.

MAPPING TOTAL QUALITY MANAGEMENT

Any application of TQM to higher education implies a basic consensus among experts regarding what TQM is. A fully documented attempt to answer this question can be found in the first sections of this book. A brief illustration of several possible approaches to address this question may serve as an introduction and a summary:

Historical evolution of the quality movement

Garvin (Reading 2) shows how quality concepts moved from inspection to quality control, to quality assurance, and finally to a strategic view of quality. A further development can be found in Senge (Reading 4), who sees TQM as a step toward building learning organizations.

TQM principles, processes, and tools

I found it useful to distinguish the following three concepts in trying to address the question, "What is TQM?"

Principles These are core values such as "the customer is first" or the need for "shared decision making." They can be found in the writings of the leading writers of the field and in the most important TQM models.

Processes These are some specific implementation approaches for diverse needs at different levels of the organization:

- Quality improvement teams
- Self-directed teams
- Daily management
- Quality function deployment
- Hoshin planning
- Statistical process control
- Experimental design

Other related processes useful for quality improvement efforts are benchmarking and reengineering.

Tools The tools are used by teams in the context of the processes mentioned above. They integrate creative (e.g., brainstorming) and analytical (e.g., Fishbone) approaches to problem solving. The best-known TQM tools are the seven quality control tools and the seven management and planning tools. Some tools are known under different names (e.g., Fishbone or Ishikawa diagram) and have been adapted from more complex applications (e.g., PERT analysis used in engineering applications such as project management).

The 14 TQM tools mentioned above are complemented by other tools, such as the force field diagram and brainstorming. A description of the tools can be found in Part 4 of this book. It is to be noted that there are many more tools commonly used in team-based problem solving. Jack Moran and Glenn Hofherr have counted over one hundred!

Total Quality Management models

These models provide a good conceptual framework for implementation of TQM.

The best-known models are:

1. *The PDCA model* This model, also known as the Shewhart cycle, was taught by Deming in Japan and became the cornerstone of Japanese TQM. It is a continuous improvement cycle based on systematic learning from experience.

2. *The Deming Prize* The Deming Prize represents the benchmark for organizational excellence in Japan; in contrast to the Baldrige Award, it is not based on a point system.
3. *The Baldrige Award model* The Baldrige Award has become the most important benchmark for organizational excellence in the United States. Together with Deming's 14 points and the PDCA cycle, it is used as a point of reference to define and implement some basics of TQM. The Baldrige Award now also includes a category for educational institutions.
4. *The European model for Total Quality Management* The model is related to the European Award for Quality, the European equivalent of the Deming and Baldrige Awards. The award has been given since 1992.

TQM as a strategy for organizational change

I have found it useful to interpret TQM as a systemic approach to organizational change. In highly competitive environments, (even in higher education institutions), change has become a way of life. TQM offers a series of processes that can bring about change through participation at all levels of the organization.

TQM IN EDUCATION: A NOTE OF CAUTION

TQM can be of benefit at many levels of the educational process; however, it is certainly unrealistic to see such efforts as *the* solution to the severe educational crisis we are now experiencing. If TQM is about learning and building upon specific experiences, then we need to focus on documenting and evaluating the many different pilot experiences that are now occurring. Consistent with TQM principles, even a failure represents a step in the right direction as long as we learn from it.

During my personal interactions with educators, many have expressed a strong interest in learning what TQM is and how it could be applied to education. Some have also raised a justified concern that many so-called "TQM experts" are suggesting changes in the structure and processes of educational systems in ways that only reflect their ignorance of a complex field. If we are to influence education, let us first learn from professional educators. Otherwise, we will simply become proponents of a fad that will soon prove to be deeply unsatisfactory.

TQM IMPLEMENTATION EFFORTS IN HIGHER EDUCATION INSTITUTIONS

The following examples are intended to be descriptive rather than normative and reflect the experiences of many colleges and universities. Some of the most important applications of TQM principles, processes, and tools in higher education institutions are:

To use process improvement teams and models in administrative units

Administrative processes in academic institutions are similar to those of other service organizations; therefore, it is not surprising that early TQM implementation efforts in higher education institutions have started in administrative units, such as admissions, the registrar's office, or accounting, where the implementation experience of other service organizations could be applied.

To use TQM processes such as Hoshin Kanri for strategic planning

One key TQM principle is the need to connect the mission and vision of an institution with short-, medium-, and long-term objectives and implementation plans. This may seem to be an obvious requirement in any planning effort, and not a particular contribution of TQM. However, the congruence of objectives and means is difficult to achieve in practice when the PDCA model (the key model of process improvement) has not been institutionalized. Vision and mission statements tend to be somewhat abstract, and, therefore, difficult to translate into achievable objectives. Within the context provided by the institutional mission and vision, TQM processes (such as Hoshin planning) provide a framework that develops coherence between clearly stated objectives and specific implementation plans to achieve such objectives in a stated amount of time.

Recently, accrediting institutions such as the AACSB (American Assembly for Collegiate Schools of Business) have begun to change their accrediting guidelines, from semirigid program content requirements (specific courses for certain programs) to a mandate for greater consistency between the declared mission of an institution and its deployment through academic and community outreach programs and other implementation efforts. In other words, a small regional business college no longer needs to emulate large research institutions to have its programs accredited by the AACSB.

To use TQM processes in academic units

With few exceptions, attempts to introduce TQM processes into academic units have stalled. Existing processes such as tenure, or values and principles such as academic freedom, have largely been blamed for these failures. However, an overlooked and equally important cause of failure is the disparity of academic units with traditional service organizations.

To introduce TQM in academic units with any hope for success, the first step is to examine which values would relate to TQM, and, secondly, which objectives would be appropriate for academic functions. Are the standards by which faculty performance is evaluated something that is functional within a "TQM" framework?

TQM advocates have often criticized academics, protected by tenure, for engaging in useless research activities (research that has no practical applications), thereby neglecting the prime function of an academic institution—teaching.

What is often forgotten is that academics clearly owe a double allegiance—to their academic institutions and to their own professional organizations and standards as educators and researchers. If career advancement is largely a measure of their "intellectual contributions," measured as publications in peer-reviewed academic journals, it is not surprising that major efforts are devoted to publishable research, largely unrelated with teaching. Papers published in journals affect academics directly through the tenure-evaluation process.

Tenure is a process based on values such as "academic freedom," rooted in widely held societal beliefs such as the need to encourage independent intellectual inquiry and reflection. Academics are supposed to be able to freely voice their opinions without fear of retaliation by the administration. Higher education institutions are held to be areas in which diverse opinions can be freely expressed, rather than "one-party" organizations with singular ideological and political agendas.

It is inappropriate to engage in a discussion regarding values such as academic freedom with concepts such as efficiency. Values provide a fundamental framework upon which organizations are built, and cannot be directly measured for "efficiency." Efficiency can only be measured against clearly defined strategic objectives, and values precede strategy. Therefore, if academic freedom is an essential value, it cannot be judged by concerns with efficiency. Thus, a more direct "framing" question is whether tenure is the best process to ensure academic freedom, and, from a pragmatic perspective, it is unlikely that tenure will be abolished in the short- or medium-term since it is an important part of a system rooted in tradition and experience.

Still, the difficulty of implementing TQM in academic units remains. An organizational analysis of academic institutions might provide some answers. Higher education institutions are essentially "loosely coupled systems" in which committees and subsystems (each class or course) have a high degree of autonomy. This is the fundamental operational basis of a "college" or "department" in which each member is seen as a specialist in his/her field.

It is likely that TQM experiences related to the development of teams formed by professionals (as in QFD applications) may be relevant for academic environments. Also, consistency between mutually agreed-upon objectives and specific implementation efforts can be sought. However, any efforts to bring about a major power shift under the guise of efficiency concerns is likely to fail. Centralization of power proposed by the administrators of academic units will be fought against by the members of institutions with a clear collegiate tradition.

To use TQM processes for the development of new academic programs

Processes such as quality function deployment allow us, as planners, to take into account the interests and needs of diverse constituencies in the development of new products and services. This approach may be particularly well suited to the development of new academic programs in professional schools, i.e., those programs in which the skills required by employers should play an important role in program design.

The business community has severely criticized business and engineering programs that produce graduates lacking essential skills, such as the ability to work in teams and communicate effectively. Customer-focused design processes may provide some insights regarding ways to integrate the needs of employers into curriculum development. At the same time, it should not be forgotten that the educational process is much more than a list of skills to be instilled or developed, this being a fact implicitly acknowledged by employers in most fields who increasingly require "soft" skills from recent graduates.

To foster the development of partnerships among communities, business, and educational institutions

Many such efforts are currently underway in the United States, Western Europe, Latin America, and elsewhere. With dwindling federal resources allocated to education, such partnerships are increasingly considered a viable alternative to provide financial and nonfinancial resources. One example is a recent IBM initiative to sponsor eight one-million-dollar projects by ten universities to introduce TQM into curriculum and institutional development. As part of the grants, local partnerships with IBM sites were established and executives were "loaned" to the participating institutions.

A further example of such partnerships can be found at Lehigh Valley, PA, where communities, businesses, and higher education (including Lehigh University and several community colleges) are collaborating in diverse academic and nonacademic projects.

To introduce TQM principles and values into mainstream educational thought

Some of the founders of the quality movement, such as Deming, Juran, and Feigenbaum, have written about fundamental changes they consider necessary in educational practices. Deming went as far as advocating the abolition of the grading system, which, in his view, fosters senseless competition and stifles the basic human instinct to learn for the sake of learning.

Educational institutions have also become interested in potential contributions of TQM to K–12, technical, and higher education. As an example, David Kearns, former CEO of Xerox, was invited to teach a course at the Harvard Graduate School of Education.

To introduce TQM curricula into professional programs, such as engineering and business

TQM modules Modules describing particular TQM processes, such as team-based problem solving or statistical process control (SPC), increasingly are part of business and engineering core courses such as organizational behavior or operations management. Engineering curricula had integrated SPC long before the quality movement acquired high visibility.

Courses with TQM content Such courses are becoming commonplace as elective undergraduate and graduate, engineering and business seminars. They usually focus on the "soft" skills (such as team-building), and/or the "hard" skills (statistical process control) needed for TQM implementation.

TOM courses using TOM principles and processes to run the class A fully documented experience by the author of this paper is included in the companion instructor's manual of this book, but a few comments may be useful at this point:

1. *You will need to define TQM and select specific TQM principles and processes* There is no "one" interpretation of TQM, as can be inferred from the readings included in this book. You may wish to select a particular approach such as Deming's 14 points (which he would not have wanted to be known as "TQM gospel"), since they already have been applied to educational systems. You may also use the guidelines of the Baldrige model or the writings of other TQM gurus. Any approach may be useful as long as the principles and processes you select are internally consistent, and you are clear about your choices and the resulting outcomes.
2. *You will need to take into account the needs of different "customers" or stakeholders* The "customers" include your academic unit, which may have defined grading standards and some core curriculum content, your students, employers, and yourself. Problems arise when the needs of an important group of customers are not taken into account, or when conflicting needs require a compromise.
3. *You will have to face confusion and/or distrust from your students as they grasp the philosophy and methods of TQM applications in college courses* Too many times students have met "nice" teachers and been unpleasantly surprised at the time of exams and final grades. Your particular approach to teaching will probably be quite different from the experiences your students have had in other classes. In other words, a clash of expectations is almost inevitable.
4. *Your learning experience will be very valuable, but neither yourself nor your students may necessarily feel fully satisfied at the end of the course* You are entering new, unknown territory, and everybody will have to learn new norms and behaviors.

Reading 40

Implementing Total Quality Management in a University Setting

By L. Edwin Coate

INTRODUCTION

Leadership is not so much the exercise of power itself as the empowerment of others.
Warren Bennis

Total Quality Management (TQM) is a commitment to excellence by everyone in an organization—excellence achieved by teamwork and a process of continuous improvement. TQM means dedication to being the best, to delivering high quality services which meet or exceed the expectations of customers.

As with any significant cultural change, TQM requires strong leadership at all levels. Inspiring people to do things differently takes leaders who can communicate what needs to be done and why. It takes leaders who have a clear goal or vision, can impart that vision to others, and then demonstrate through action how to make the vision a reality.

Most of all, TQM requires leadership that empowers people to work toward achieving their shared vision. No single company or university has successfully implemented and maintained progress in the concepts of Total Quality Management without that leadership by top management.[1]

At Oregon State University, our President, Dr. John V. Byrne, committed himself to lead OSU into a Total Quality Management program. We began about one year ago. Our goal was simple: to implement TQM throughout the university by 1994. This paper is designed to tell the story of that process.

Source: 1990 article reprinted with the permission of the author.

A LITTLE HISTORY

The quality gurus

W. Edwards Deming was first, the pioneer, the American who believed: "Improve quality and you automatically improve productivity. You capture the market with lower prices and better quality. You stay in business and you produce jobs. It's so simple."[2] Deming was the American who took his message to Japan, in 1950, and was instrumental in turning Japanese industry into an economic world power.

Juran arrived in Japan a few years after Deming and built an equally impressive record around quality planning, quality control, and quality improvement. Crosby became the third "quality guru" in 1979. The message of all three is basically the same:

- Commit to quality improvement throughout your organization.
- Attack the processes, not the employees.
- Strip down the process to find and eliminate problems that diminish quality.
- Identify your customers and satisfy their requirements.
- Instill teamwork and create an atmosphere for innovation and permanent quality improvement.[3]

The quest for quality in the United States

The quest for quality took 30 years to catch on in the United States. Organizations such as Ford Motor Company, Hewlett-Packard, Xerox, and Motorola have led the quality movement in the industry.

Ask almost anyone in industry today and they either have or are planning to implement TQM or another quality program. A recent survey by GOAL/QPC of Massachusetts found that about 50 percent of the "1000" *Business Week* top companies had initiated some form of quality improvement.[4] As each major company implements Total Quality Management, it requires its "vendors" to implement a similar program: hence, the movement is growing logarithmically.

WHY USE TQM?

The major underlying principle of the quality movement in industry has been survival. Lost sales and declining profits have forced companies to try anything—even total quality management—to survive. Although public sector problems have not been that severe, across the country, belt tightening is now the rule in the public sector as the growth rate of tax revenues drops and services are shifted from the federal government to state and local levels. States, cities, and universities all hear the same cry: "Do more with less." They are asked to maintain or even increase productivity in spite of budget and staff cuts. (Stanford University recently faced a 20 percent across-the-board cut of administrative staff.)

How can we cope with this pressure? One answer may lie in the total quality management movement. Deming and Juran both say that with TQM we can achieve savings of up to 30 percent, and this has been validated by industry.

TQM in the public sector

Several attempts have been made to adapt Total Quality Management to the public sector. Two that have been particularly well documented are Florida Power and Light and the city of Madison, Wisconsin. Several hospitals and states are also implementing TQM. However, comparatively few attempts are under way in the education sector. (See Figure 40.1 for a partial listing.)

Delaware County Community College and Fox Valley Technical College began their work in TQM in 1986 using the Crosby model. Both started by providing training to business and industry and then expanded the concept to their own service areas. Both are now working to introduce TQM on the academic side.

TQM in higher education

In a telephone survey, we contacted 25 colleges and universities who are involved in some way with the TQM process. We found that 17 institutions are implementing a TQM focus in some part of the graduate or undergraduate curriculum, usually in business- or industry-related courses. In Florida, TQM is being implemented in the post-secondary vocational school system with the aim of producing well-trained graduates for industries that follow Total Quality principles and want to meet the criteria that will soon be required by the European common market.

We found that half of the institutions surveyed have significantly implemented TQM, using the process to the point of forming study teams. In five, TQM is used only for instruction or research. Of the 25 schools, 15 have significant efforts going on the service side and 10 have efforts going on the academic side. The most significant work in the academic area appears to be in two-year institutions. (See Figure 40.1)

The big questions

The big question is: How adaptable are the methods of Deming, Juran, and Crosby to the education industry? Manufacturing processes are far more predictable and controllable than the learning process. However, the service areas of the institution—facilities, billing, registration, security, etc.—all have counterparts in industry and should easily lend themselves to training in precision performance. This side of the educational enterprise can become the beginning point for TQM.

In addition, we do know a great deal about educational processes. Measurements of student achievement, curriculum, and instruction may yield more widely variable

FIGURE 40.1 ***Status of TQM in 25 U.S. institutions of higher education***

Institution \ Status of TQM	1 Used in administrative areas	2 Used in academic areas	3 Used in instruction	4 Doing research on TQM	5 Doing TQM consultation	6 Number of TQM teams operating	7 Use external consultants/trainers	8 Have TQM coordinator	9 Have TQM "champion"	10 Use "Guru" model	11 Use other models	12 Have TQM models	13 Have TQM publications	14 Have had training
Carnegie-Mellon U			X									X		
Chicago, Univ of	X		X	X					X			X		
Colorado State U	X		X			50	X	X	X	X	X	X	X	
Columbia U			X											
Delaware Co CC	X	X	X		X	@15	X	X	X	X			X	
Florida State U				X			X		X			X	X	
Fox Valley Tech	X	X	X	X	X	45	X	X	X	X		X	X	
Harvard U			X	X	X	3		X		X	X	X	X	
Hawkeye Inst of Tech	X	X	X			8	X	X	X		X	X	X	
Illinois Inst of Tech			X	X	X									
Jackson CC				X	X	3					X		X	
Lamar CC	X	X					X	X	X					
Michigan, Univ of				X										
Milwaukee Sch of Engin	X	X	X			15-20			X	X	X			
Minnesota, Univ of	X	X	X				X							
North Carolina, Univ of			X											
N D University System	X	X			X	2	X		X			X	X	
Northwestern U			X											
Oregon State U	X					15	X		X		X	X	X	
Palm Beach CC	X		X		X	3	X	X	X		X	X	X	
Pepperdine U	X	X	X		X				X		X	X		
Pittsburgh, Univ of			X							X				
St. Augustine Tech Cent	X	X	X			4	X	X		X	X		X	
Wisconsin, Univ of	X	X		X	X	5	X	X	X	X			X	
Wyoming, Univ of	X					9	X		X	X			X	

results than measurements on an assembly line. Nevertheless, using the principles and techniques of quality improvement, we can learn much.

We must not, however, apply TQM principles without research, adaptation, training, and pilot testing in the actual university setting. Educators will need to be trained to collect and interpret data on program effectiveness and pupil achievement and to identify patterns that develop over a period of time. When a pattern is having a negative effect on the educational process, changes must be made. The quality improvement tools of TQM are available to do this.

The purpose of this paper

The purpose of this paper is to document Oregon State University's attempt to implement TQM throughout its structure, focusing on what we have learned to date in OSU's quest for improved quality. Particular attention will focus on documents developed, lessons learned from mistakes, structural changes, e.g., a reward system, that evolved from the program, and on changes in the behavior and attitudes of the participants.

Methodology

The matrix was derived from an informal telephone survey conducted during June 1990. Twenty-four institutions of higher education known to be involved in some form of Total Quality Management were contacted (Oregon State University is the 25th). Information was supplied by one or more persons knowledgeable about the status of TQM at the institution. A list of the institutions contacted, with their locations, is in Appendix D. The matrix does not represent all U.S. institutions of higher education involved in TQM. The survey was developed with assistance from Samford University, Birmingham, AL, and Fox Valley Technical College, Appleton, WI.

WHAT IS TOTAL QUALITY MANAGEMENT?

Total Quality Management is a system that combines the quality control theory, systems, tools, and organizational models developed over the last 40 years both in the United States and Japan. It is a logical evolution of management by objectives (MBO). Strategic Planning, Quality Circles (QC), Quality Assurance (QA), and many other systems. It builds on the successful components of each and discards the failures.

TQM is a structural system for creating organization-wide participation in planning and implementing a continuous improvement process that **exceeds** the expectations of the customer/client. It is built on the assumption that 90 percent of our problems are process problems, not employee problems.

TQM has three major components:

1. **Breakthrough Planning,** sometimes called Hoshin Planning. (Figure 40.2 diagrams the full planning process.) The purpose is to:
   - Clarify a vision of where the organization wants to go in the next five or ten years;
   - Identify goals and objectives that move the organization toward its vision;

FIGURE 40.2 ***Full planning process***

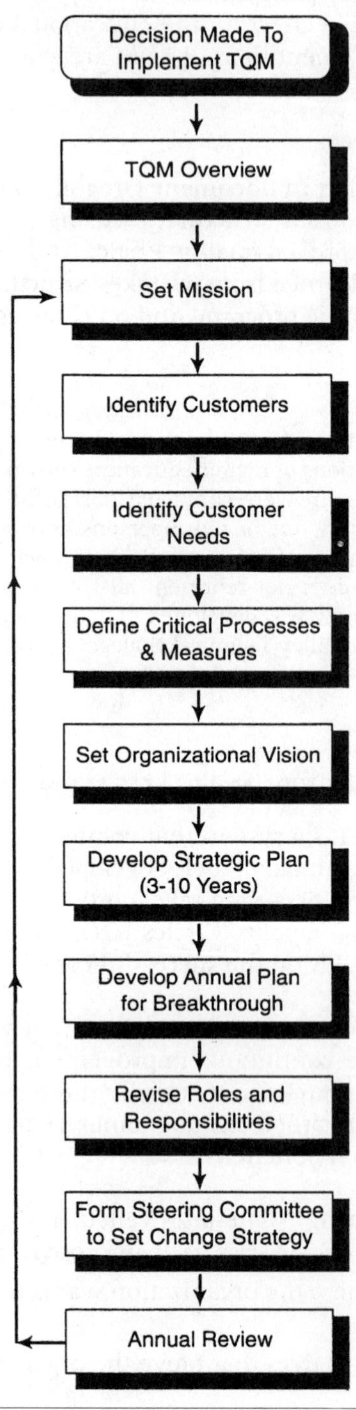

- Identify critical processes that must deliver the services provided to clients in a way that exceeds their expectations;
- Select a few (no more than 4) breakthrough items that can help the organization reach its vision quickly;
- Communicate this vision and the methods by which it will be met to all employees;
- Provide a structure for monitoring progress toward the vision.

Vision planning allows the organization to identify and focus on key areas of service, and it ensures full development of the methods and pathways by which "breakthroughs," major, fundamental quality improvements, can be implemented. All vertical levels of the organization then participate in the planning, development, and deployment of the identified strategic breakthroughs (see Figure 40.2).

Breakthrough planning is an evolution of strategic planning which adds value statements, reminding us that "how we got here" is just as important as where we are going.

2. **Daily Management.** This system shows people what they personally must do, and what they must measure and control, to keep the organization running smoothly. It helps them define and understand the processes they use in producing services to meet customers' needs and expectations. Once these processes are understood, individuals and departments can continuously improve them, then standardize the improvements to ensure that gains are maintained.

   This continuous improvement is achieved by problem-solving teams who engage in identifying customer problems, finding solutions, and then providing ongoing control of the improved process. Use of several basic quality control tests and statistical methods helps people manage with facts, not opinions, and solve the real problems, not just the symptoms. Problem solving requires the collective efforts of everyone in the organization, working in study teams with the 10-step process shown in Figure 40.5 on page 614.

   Daily Management is the most revolutionary of the three components of TQM. It empowers employees at all levels of the organization and focuses management improvement efforts on process problems.

3. **Cross-Functional Management.** This is the integration of team activities across divisions/departments to achieve organizational goals. It is the vehicle for breaking down departmental/divisional barriers. Through cross-functional management, top level managers can ensure that all groups in the university—faculty, staff, etc.—are working together for the good of the institution.

   This system leads the institution to listen to the "voice of the customer," identify customer needs, and incorporate those needs into every phase of the university operation.

IMPLEMENTING TQM

In TQM, how a process is implemented is as important as what the process includes. Many organizations still labor under the remnants of a departmentalized Taylor approach in which some employees plan improvements, others carry out the work, and still others inspect to see if procedures and results are correct. In TQM, all employees, every day, commit to improving the quality of their service so that customers' needs are not only met but exceeded.

At OSU, we found the growing TQM literature inundated with techniques, prescriptions, admonitions, and anecdotes. But little attention was devoted to how firms have implemented TQM, the hurdles they encountered, and how they responded and adapted TQM principles to their existing cultures.

Furthermore, the lack of agreement among the TQM gurus produces contradictions and inconsistent prescriptions that are puzzling to would-be users. Deming says "eliminate slogans," while Crosby uses the slogan of "zero defects." Deming says "drive out fear," while Juran says "fear can bring out the best in people." Deming's process starts at the top and works down, while Juran starts with middle management and works both ways.

A nonprofit TQM research company in Massachusetts, GOAL/QPC, found that six implementation models are currently being used.[5]

1. **The TQM Element Approach.** This approach, used in the early eighties, employs elements of quality improvement programs such as Quality Circles, Statistical Process Control, Quality Functional Deployment, etc., rather than full implementation of TQM.
2. **The Guru Approach.** This approach uses writing of a guru such as Deming, Juran, or Crosby, as a benchmark to determine what the organization lacks, then uses the guru's systems to make changes. Use of Deming's 14-point model is an example.
3. **The Japanese Model Approach.** Organizations using this method focused on study of the Japanese "Deming Prize Winners" as a way to develop an implementation master plan. This approach was used by Florida Power and Light.
4. **The Industrial Company Model Approach.** In this approach, people visit a U.S. industrial company using TQM, identify its successes, and integrate this information with their own ideas to create a customized approach. This method was used in the late 1980s by many of the Baldrige National Quality Award winners.
5. **The Hoshin Planning Approach.** This approach, developed by a Japanese firm, Bridgestone, was used successfully by Hewlett-Packard. It focuses on successful planning, deployment, execution, and monthly diagnosis.
6. **The Baldrige Award Criteria Approach.** In this model, an organization uses criteria for the Malcolm Baldrige National Quality Award to identify areas of improvement. The criteria cover seven key components of TQM. As the 1990s begin, this approach is being used by hundreds of industrial companies.

All of these approaches work. At OSU, we developed a model most closely associated with the Hoshin Planning Model used by Hewlett-Packard, and we used the Baldrige Award Criteria to help develop our five-year plan. Figure 40.3 shows OSU's model.

IMPLEMENTING TQM AT OREGON STATE

Implementation of Total Quality Management at OSU moved through the following phases.

FIGURE 40.3 ***The OSU Total Quality Management implementation model***

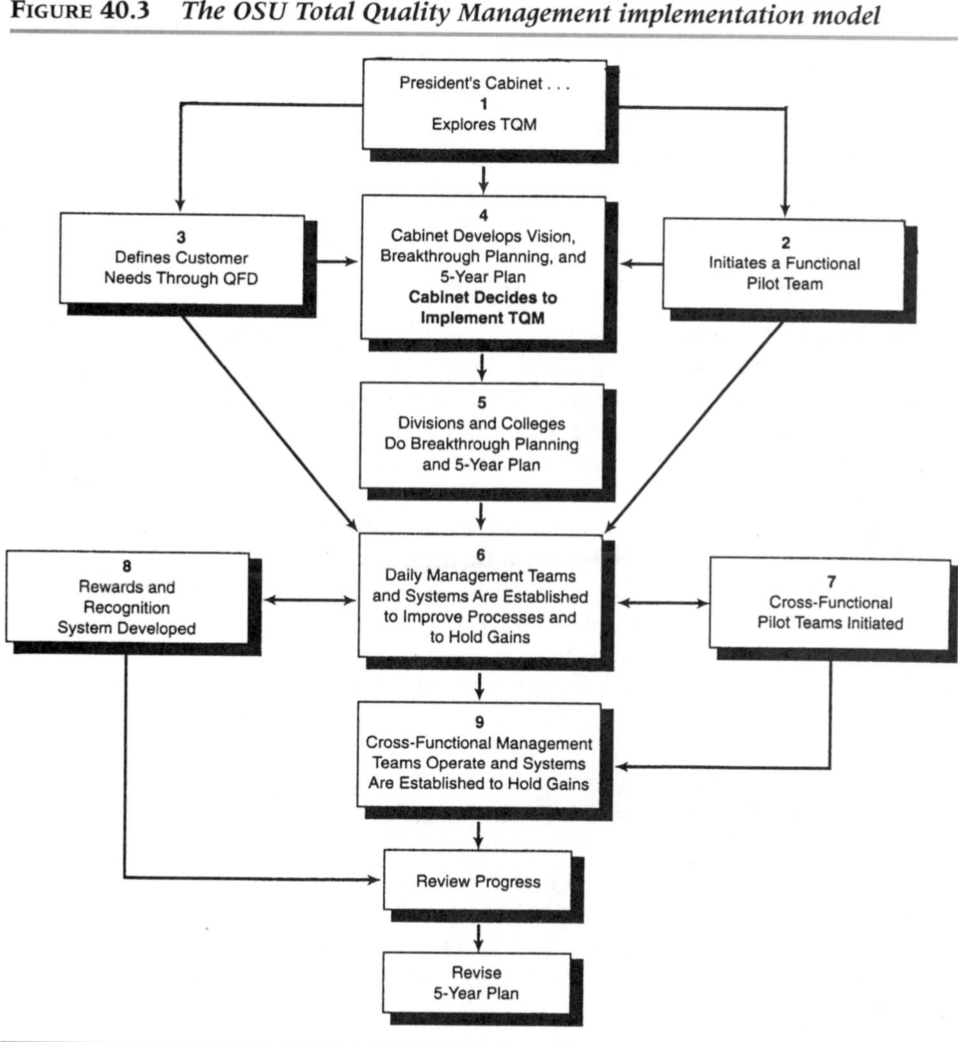

Phase one: exploring Total Quality Management

Our purpose in exploring TQM was to provide a "critical mass" of top management people who would understand what TQM is and why it might be of use to the university, and who would be willing to try a pilot to test the concept in our culture. This step was initiated because of the positive potential of the quality vision and in response to major challenges such as unhappy customers, lack of resources, and low employee morale.

Activities carried out during Phase One:

- Visited excellent companies with TQM programs, including Ford, Hewlett-Packard, and Dow, whose CEOs were alumni.
- Invited Dr. Deming to visit our university and explain TQM. (OSU awarded him an honorary doctorate in June 1989.)
- Read key books and articles on TQM (see Bibliography).
- The president, two other top managers, the staff development officer, and I attended an OSU continuing education class taught by Hewlett-Packard TQM staff on the seven TQM tools.
- Reviewed Baldrige Award criteria.

What we learned

At the conclusion of Phase One, the president and cabinet were enthusiastic about the potential of TQM. However, as word of these activities began to circulate, we perceived skepticism about TQM on the academic side of the university. TQM was seen as the "latest fad" in management style, and there was a severe "language barrier." Faculty members objected to terms like "total quality" and "management," feeling that they might lose control of important academic processes.

Title change. At this point we made the mistake of attempting to change the TQM title to something we felt would be more palatable—System Improvement Process. However, this simply generated suspicion and reinforced the idea that, by any name, this was just another management fad.

Faculty concerns. At a deeper level, faculty members see themselves as emphasizing diversity. To them, the idea of "quality control" suggests uniformity—trying to bring everything to the same level. In addition, faculty members are often accustomed to working alone, to competing, in fact, for limited resources such as grant money. Gaining acceptance for the idea of working together in teams to change processes may be a challenge on the academic side.

"Qualified approval." Some members of the academic community, however, began to give qualified approval to TQM. One said that "the great value I see in this concept is changing our orientation to seeing students as customers. This will require a turnaround in our culture." In fact, we were later able to establish TQM teams in two academic service-oriented areas: international education and continuing education.

Begin with service areas. For many reasons, then, we decided to proceed slowly on the academic side. We realized that our service areas would be the place to begin, as there are many parallels with industry in such areas as physical plant, computing, and business services. Our next step was the initiation of a pilot project in the Physical Plant Department.

Phase two: initial pilot study team

In order to apply what we had learned about TQM and to learn more, we formed a TQM study team in the physical plant. We asked them to address a specific, high-priority issue that:

- Had a high probability of success,
- Management agreed was important,
- No one was working on, and
- Was very important to the customer.

Initial situation

When the TQM study team was formed, OSU's Physical Plant Department was characterized by poor internal communication and low worker morale. The department's image among many of its customers was extremely negative. Its services were seen to be slow, expensive, and delivered with little concern for customers' needs or desires.

The TQM process

The pilot study team included managers and front-line workers, a team leader, and a training officer/facilitator, for a total of 12. The issue the team developed for study was "To decrease turnaround time in the remodeling process." As they moved through the TQM process, the team opened communication with the entire department, briefing other employees on progress, publishing team minutes, and posting their "process flow diagram" on the office wall for comments and suggestions.

The team found overlaps, time delays, and unnecessary paper flow in the remodeling process. They came to realize that their issue, though solvable, required study of too many facets. (The process flow chart, if laid out in a straight line, would be 17 feet long.) The team also found that a key area, engineering, needed more representation on the team.

To solve these problems, the team leader formed two sub-teams: engineering design, and construction. These groups identified problems in their processes, brainstormed causes, and proposed solutions to the team.

The result: change

Solutions implemented through TQM changed the basic structure of the physical plant and shortened the remodeling process by 10 percent, a percentage that continues to increase. Process changes affected worker attitudes and behaviors and delighted many customers. Among the changes were these:

- A new Customer Service Center was formed. Work requests and questions had formerly come to a secretary, who then sought information from several people in different places who were responsible for work scheduling, control, and follow-up. Now these people form a common unit that customers can call to find out what they need to know. The new unit is meeting with tremendous customer satisfaction, improving both project scheduling and the image of Physical Plant.
- To improve communication with customers, the team recommended and management established the position of project manager. Shop supervisors report work progress to the manager, and customers can talk about their needs with one person, face-to-face. The team recommended elements of the position description, criteria for measuring the position's effectiveness, and plans for customer and internal surveys to assess communication improvements.
- Four time-saving changes suggested by subteams are being implemented:
  - A free initial consultation with customers, using a brochure explaining the project process;
  - Hand-carrying of design and project authorization forms to the customer for consultation and completion;
  - Identification of equipment and materials that can be purchased during the design process;
  - A "shop participation walk-through" at the beginning of design to get input from the shops and identify possible problems.

Employee attitudes

Formation of TQM teams in the physical plant has brought tremendous changes in work relationships and attitudes. The process showed top managers internal problems they had not recognized before and exposed workers to problems managers face in day-to-day operations. The result is cooperation.

Because team members came from all levels of the organization, they were able to improve internal communication. Shortly after the team was formed, word filtered out to the shops that things were changing for the better. Shops began talking with each other, and coordinating projects became much easier.

Physical Plant has become a much better place to work, employees say. Networks are spreading across the whole workforce. Spirits are high. Workers are making many suggestions for improvements. With worker cooperation, areas that have had too many or too few employees are being reorganized.

One factor that is not measurable, the TQM team leader says, is a change in the work ethic. People are conscious of possibilities for improvement. They are doing a better job. Even beyond the teams and the TQM process, the result has been more trusting relationships between workers and happier customers.

Customer satisfaction

A survey of customers showed that, even when the time to completion of a project has not decreased, they are more satisfied and more understanding of delays. Customers see that the Physical Plant Department is concerned and working on its problems. Customers feel that they are important because they've been listened to and are getting more personalized service.

Phase three: defining customer needs through quality function deployment

Quality Function Deployment (QFD) is an organized system to identify and prioritize customer needs and translate them into university priorities. QFD is also a strategic tool in which customer needs and the characteristics of a service system are pulled into a matrix and compared.

We began QFD by identifying our customers and placing them in major groupings. They included:

Tools such as customer surveys, focus groups, complaints/feedbacks, etc., helped us to identify customer needs. These data sources were pulled together to form a set of customer views that is as accurate and complete as possible. This information helped executive management to understand where the university is and where it should be in its customers' eyes. It also highlighted points where data on customer needs and expectations is incomplete or non-existent.

About our customers

Three customer surveys conducted in 1989–90 provided the following data about OSU's customers.

The OSU Image Survey evaluated the perceived images of Oregon State University in the minds of six important customer groups: the general public, college-bound Oregon high school students, OSU alumni living in Oregon, OSU undergraduate students, classified staff, and faculty. Some findings:

- About one-third of the general public, one-sixth of the prospective students, and nearly one half of the alumni are not knowledgeable about OSU, its programs and activities.
- Physical attractiveness of OSU received the highest ratings, and while most groups perceived a friendly atmosphere, students, alumni, staff, and faculty gave low ratings to the concern of the OSU administration in dealing with their needs.
- Customers in the general public gave OSU good ratings in areas of providing service to the state, such as preparing graduates to be useful employees, listening to Oregonians, and helping them solve their problems.
- In general, OSU's academic reputation was rated as average, with recruitment of top students and matters of rigor and requirements rated low.

The Admitted Students Survey gave us additional information about student customers, those who did and did not enroll at OSU. Respondents compared OSU with other institutions they considered. In the basic area of information provided about OSU, they gave lowest marks to financial aid communications, college-sponsored meetings, contact with faculty, and contact with coaches. Contact with students and campus visits were rated highest. The images of OSU most frequently cited were friendly, social, comfortable, and fun.

The 1990 Faculty Survey provided this information about the university's internal academic customers:

- Their highest professional goal is to be good teachers, and their undergraduate teaching goal is to develop students' ability to think clearly.
- Their highest priority issues for the university are promoting intellectual development and conducting basic applied research.
- Job satisfaction centers mainly on having autonomy and independence; time pressures are the greatest source of stress.
- The primary funding priority is salaries, with support services, including facilities repair and library, second.

A survey of classified staff is currently being conducted.

What we learned

Universities have traditionally shied away from marketing. The idea of designing classes/courses to fit the "market" has been foreign to our university's way of think-

Customer Survey

Name ______ Date ______

1.
2.
3.

3-12-90

ing. Faculty know what students need, not the other way around! To begin to deal with this, we created a marketing committee to look at OSU's image and the products we deliver, a first step in beginning to realign classes offered with classes needed.

The marketing committee will become one of our first cross-functional teams. Training will help them to better understand TQM concepts and carry out Quality Functional Deployment activities. Because of the lack of non-industry examples (most QFD "house of quality" matrix examples focus on automobile designs) we are still having problems fully utilizing this concept. Total commitment to developing "customer-driven" systems will not come easily.

Phase four: top management breakthrough planning (Hoshin planning)

There are five major steps in the breakthrough planning process (see Figure 40.2):

- Mission;
- Customers;
- Critical Processes;
- Vision; and
- Breakthrough.

Step 1: Mission. All universities have a mission of teaching: because we are a land grant and sea grant university, we also have a mission of research and service. Hence:

> **OSU's mission as a land grant university is to serve the people of Oregon, the nation, and the world through education, research, and service.**

Step 2: Customers. Customers are becoming increasingly more value conscious. If we are to be a leader in the future educational marketplace, we at OSU need to firmly establish ourselves as the highest value supplier, most responsive to our customers' expectations.

This means evaluating everything we do in terms of the value it brings to our external customers. It means asking our customers what their expectations are and taking action to meet those expectations. It also means continually surveying our customers for feedback on how we're doing.

Step 3: Critical Processes. Identifying the critical processes of the president of the university builds the foundation for the TQM processes. To do this, we identified the president's principal customers and the services we provide to each customer group. We then identified the key critical processes for these groups. The 12 processes and their performance measures are shown in the box below.

Step 4: Vision. OSU's vision began to take shape with the creation of an affinity diagram.

This chart is a TQM tool which collects attributes of the ideal university and organizes them into sets of related information. Discussions around the reasons why senior managers may differ in the desired characteristics of their future university highlighted the uniqueness of our university and its mission. OSU's vision statement was built on the university's mission and values statements (Appendix A).

> "It is OSU's vision to be recognized as a premier international university. We want each student to have at least one additional language, to have at least one quarter's

OSU's 12 critical processes

Process	Performance Measure
1. Admissions	concordance with enrollment management plan
2. Curriculum Development	peer acceptance
3. Teaching	student teaching evaluation
4. International Development	number of students going overseas
5. Research	number of publications
6. Service Delivery (Extension)	% of community participation
7. Community Relations	number of complaints
8. Information Services	computer-student ratio
9. Long-Range Planning	% objectives met
10. Workforce Hiring and Development	% first choice hires
11. Facilities Development	% of value to money for repairs
12. Funding Development	$ obtained/$ requested

We also integrated the university's goals with our critical processes (see Figure 40.4). OSU's goals and objectives are listed in Appendix B.

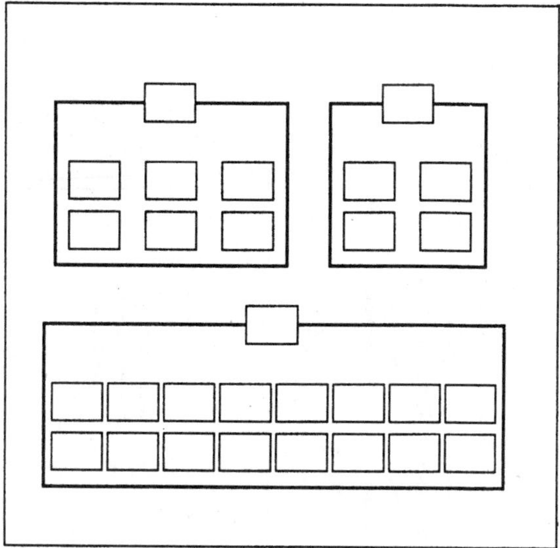

experience in a foreign country, and to be computer literate. We want our faculty to have international experience and to increase our international research programs by 100 percent (from 26 countries now to 52). We want to increase foreign undergraduates from 10 to 15 percent of the student body.

"We also want our university to be the best university in which to study and work. We want to be a university that knows what its clients will want ten years from now and what it will do to exceed all expectations. We want to be a university whose employees understand not only how to do their jobs but also how to significantly improve their jobs on a regular basis; where problems and challenges are met by a team of the most appropriate people, regardless of their level or jobs in the university."

After completing the vision statement, attention shifted to identifying barriers to achieving it. Using the affinity chart process again, we explored characteristics of the barriers, then used another TQM tool, the spider chart, to prioritize them. The purpose was to develop actions to deal with the barriers that might keep us from reaching our vision.

Spider Diagram

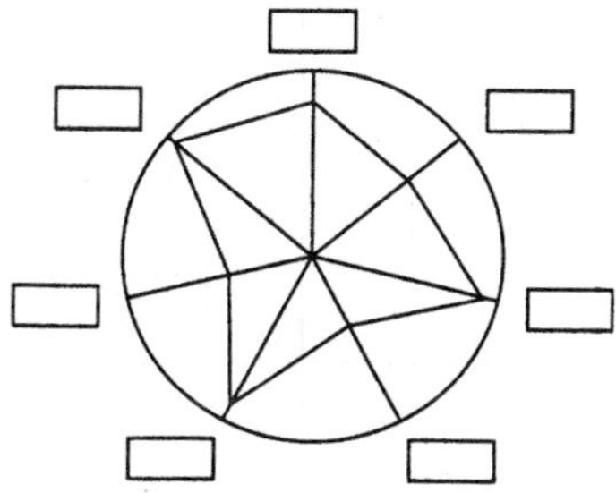

FIGURE 40.4 *OSU critical processes: finance and administration detail*

PRESIDENT: CRITICAL PROCESSES AND RELATED OSU GOALS

Admissions	Curriculum Development	Teaching	International Development	Research	Service Delivery (Extension)	Community Relations	Information Services	Long-Range Planning	Workforce Hiring & Development	Facilities Development	Funding Development
Goal 6	Goal 2	Goal 1	Goals 2,7	Goals 1,3	Goal 1	Goal 10	Goal 9	Goals 1–10	Goals 3,4,5	Goal 8	

VICE PRESIDENT FOR FINANCE AND ADMINISTRATION: CRITICAL PROCESSES AND RELATED OSU OBJECTIVES

Fiscal Services	Information Services	Workforce Hiring & Development	Long-Range Planning	Budgeting	Community Relations	Facilities Management	Law Enforcement	Safety
7.4, 9.4	9.3, 9.4, 9.5 9.7, 9.8	3.1, 4.4, 4.5, 4.7 4.8, 5.1, 5.2, 5.4, 5.5, 5.6, 5.8	10.1, 10.3, 10.4	1.4, 4.1, 8.4	10.2, 10.5	3.2, 4.2, 5.4, 8.1, 8.2, 8.3, 8.5, 8.6, 9.2		

Business Affairs
Accounting
Property Control
Travel & Transport
Fiscal Services
Telecommunications
Purchasing
Contracting
Risk Management
4.2, 4.4, 7.4, 9.4, 9.5, 9.8

Computing Services
Maintaining Hardware
Computer Purchasing
Networking
Training
Developing Standards
9.3, 9.4, 9.5, 9.7, 9.8

Printing & Mailing
Accounting
Printing
Quick Copy
U.S. Mailing Services
Blank Paper Sales
4.4, 7.4

Human Resources
Hiring
Labor Relations
Staff Development
Position Classification
Personnel Reporting
Benefits Administration
Workers' Comp. Claims Management
3.1, 4.4, 4.5, 4.7, 4.8, 5.1, 5.2, 5.4, 5.5, 5.6, 5.8

Radiation Center
Teaching
Research
Technical Services
1.2, 1.3, 1.7, 3.2, 3.3, 3.5

Budgets and Planning
Long-Range Planning
Archiving/Records Management
Data Analysis
Budgeting
Policy Communication
1.4, 4.1, 4.2, 4.4, 8.4

Institutional Research and Planning
Information Gathering
Information Dissemination
Long-Range Planning
10.1, 10.3, 10.4

FIGURE 40.4 *OSU critical processes: finance and administration detail (continued)*

ASSISTANT VICE PRESIDENT

Community Relations	Law Enforcement	Facilities Management	Security	Environmental Health and Safety

Facilities	**Facilities Planning**	**University Police**	**Security**	**Environmental Health and Safety**
Maintenance & Repair Remodeling & Construction Delivery Service 3.2, 4.2, 5.4, 8.1, 8.2, 8.3, 8.5	Campus Planning Facilities Allocation Capital Construction 3.2, 4.2, 5.4, 8.1, 8.2, 8.3, 8.5, 8.6, 9.2	Criminal Law Enforcement Traffic Law Enforcement 4.4	Security Parking 4.4	Information Dissemination Compliance Monitoring Technical Services 4.4

Barriers identified for OSU included:

- Deteriorating physical infrastructure,
- Increasing costs of doing research,
- Deteriorating public image,
- Deteriorating staff morale, and
- Inadequate information systems (computing, library, telecommunications).

Step 5: Identifying Priority Breakthrough Items. Using our vision statement, our goals and objectives (Appendix B), and the barriers identified in Step 4, the process led us to focus on key breakthrough areas of service. We concluded that TQM's breakthrough planning does not replace the university's strategic plan, but supplements it by:

- Ensuring that employees at all levels understand their role in achieving the vision;
- Deploying the plan to the department level and ensuring that each academic or support department develops targets and strategies for reaching the vision;
- Providing detailed plans for support and measurement of progress toward the vision;
- Providing more operations detail than most traditional plans.

Results. As a result of these activities, three priority breakthrough items were identified:

- Increase computing capability in the university,
- Increase internationalization of the university, and
- Increase administrative efficiency by implementing TQM.

We then developed a preliminary 5-year plan (Appendix C) based upon the assessment and selection of priority breakthrough items and the Baldrige Award Criteria.

What we learned

Breakthrough Planning is a logical extension of strategic planning, and we found that the planning process went very smoothly. We held four 4-hour sessions with the president and his cabinet. Originally, we had hoped to use 8-hour sessions on Saturdays, but we found that four hours was the maximum time we could work effectively. We also found that the president's attendance at all sessions was critical.

We realized that all products of planning must be considered "first cut." They are continually modified as the process cascades down. For example, after we developed our critical processes at the vice president's level, we found that we needed to expand the president's critical processes from ten to twelve. We had missed two critical areas.

We also realized that it would take at least five years to implement TQM in all facets of university life. This was a surprise to our president and required him to make a significant, long-term commitment.

(Figure 40.2 details breakthrough planning process OSU followed.)

Phase five: divisions do breakthrough planning

The vice president and the division directors of finance and administration followed the process used by the cabinet to create a vision statement, revise their unit's mission statement, and identify nine critical processes for finance and administration. Directors also identified the critical processes within their divisions.

The goals and objectives previously developed as part of OSU's Management by Objectives process were then distributed among the division directors as shown in Figure 40.4. Our major breakthrough item was to implement TQM throughout finance and administration.

Phase six: form daily management teams

Teams are at the very heart of TQM. Better solutions emerge when everyone is given a chance to work on process problems. Just as importantly, solutions are implemented faster and last longer because the people affected have helped to develop them.

Study teams are composed of people who normally work together on the process being reviewed. They are led by someone from the natural work group, typically the supervisor. They usually work on processes that can be improved with resources they control. Teams are kept small (no more than ten) and each has a sponsor, usually the group's division director. The sponsor ensures that the team's work is linked to the critical processes and moves the university toward its vision.

Team roles

If teamwork is to be successful, roles must be clearly identified and communicated at the outset.

The team leader is responsible for planning meetings, establishes constraints, distributes agendas in advance, keeps minutes, communicates with the sponsor, and ensures that the team completes its action plans.

The facilitator makes problem-solving suggestions, helps the team stay focused, provides "just-in-time" training on the problem-solving process, and ensures that everyone has a chance to participate.

The team member attends all meetings, contributes ideas, collects data, recommends solutions, and helps to implement them.

10-step problem solving process

How do teams make improvements? They do it by using the 10-step problem solving process (Figure 40.5). The process is designed to provide a common technique and language for process improvement. It begins with the customer, focuses on root causes/barriers to improvement, and ensures that decisions and actions are based on real data.

ONE. At the "sponsor" level, identify and select the most important opportunities for improvement. We started with our critical processes, especially those that support our goals, objectives, and breakthrough items. Select team members and empower them to make improvements.

TWO. Determine the key customers of the processes and the services we provide them. Then survey the customers, using a standard format, and analyze the survey data using check sheets, Pareto diagrams, etc.

THREE. Select the most important issue and write a clear issue statement.

FOUR. Identify and flow chart the key process or processes. This enables the team to more clearly recognize opportunities for improvement.

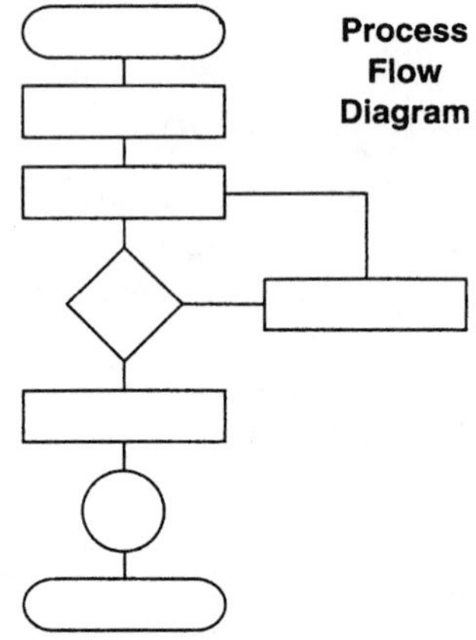

FIVE. Agree on which aspects of your performance you want to measure and, with your customers, set goals for continuous improvement in meeting or exceeding their expectations. To do this, the team must realistically evaluate current performance and set obtainable goals for improvement.

SIX. Begin to explore probable causes of the problems and barriers to improvement. A fishbone diagram tool is used in this step.

SEVEN. Gather data on the probable causes. The information collected gives the team a benchmark against which to measure its future progress.

EIGHT. Evaluate the data and show it in "pictures"—charts and graphs.

NINE. Brainstorm and develop permanent solutions. Implement solutions; monitor their performance; adopt them if they work.

TEN. If the problem is solved, standardize the fixes as normal operating procedures.

Fishbone Diagram

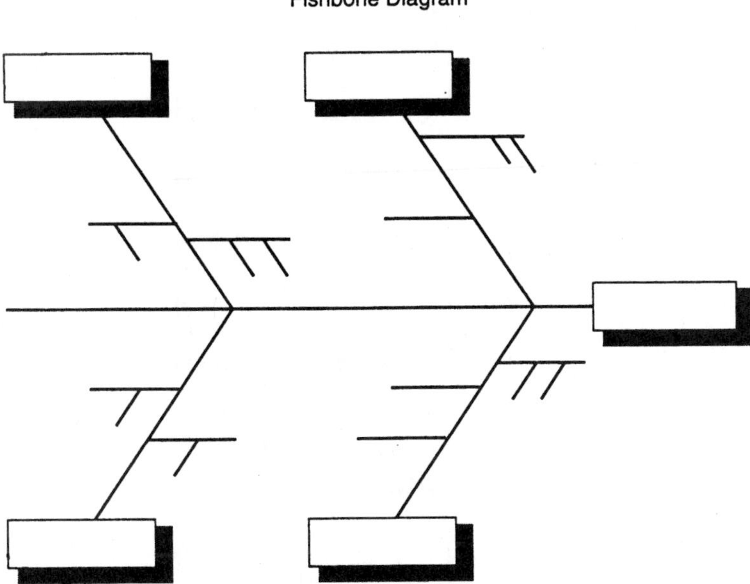

New teams being formed

We are now forming study teams in areas outside the finance and administration area in international education, continuing education, housing, and development. We have formed a steering committee to begin implementation in the academic area. Ultimately, all OSU employees will have the experience of being on a team. About 400 teams will be required.

What we learned

In evaluating the finance and administration TQM study teams, participants said they liked the fact that teams were formed at all levels of the organization. They believed they had seen process improvements that impact their own and other departments.

Survey, flow chart. The parts of the problem-solving process members found most valuable were the customer survey and the flow chart. Surveys helped them get to know their customers as people. The flow chart often helped them visualize their process for the first time. Teams used a standard computer software package called "Easy Flow" to create their diagrams.

Issues. We found that although all ten teams began with the issue/problem suggested by their sponsor, through customer surveys, every team discovered the issue to be different than the sponsor had perceived. All changed their issue

FIGURE 40.5 *Step problem solving process*

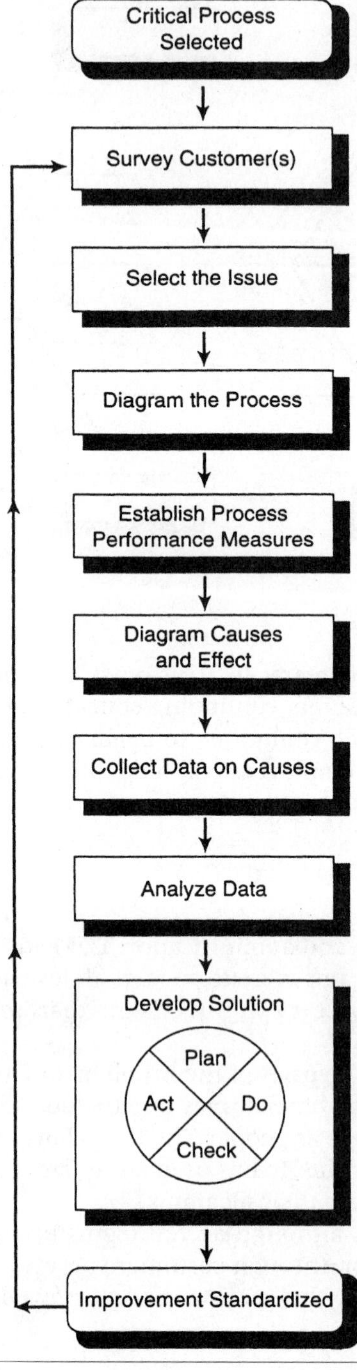

TQM teams in finance and administration

In finance and administration, we formed teams in each division around one of the division's critical processes, if possible, a process that dealt with a university objective. The first ten teams, their processes and issue statements, are shown below.

Team	Division	Critical process	Issue Statement
1A	Physical Plant	Facilities Management	Reduce the amount of time it takes to complete the remodeling process.
1B	Physical Plant	Facilities Management	Improve servicing of fixed equipment.
2	Printing	Information Services	Reduce the amount of time in the pre-press stage of the printing process.
3	Budgets and Planning	Budgeting	Increase the timeliness of the Budget-Status-at-a-Glance report development process.
4	Computing Services	Information Services	Increase the timeliness and consistent delivery of network information.
5A	Business Affairs	Fiscal Services	Increase the availability of information provided by Business Affairs for the monitoring of 050 income and expense projections.
5B	Business Affairs	Fiscal Services	Reduce the time expended in processing grant and contract documents within Business Affairs.
6	Public Safety	Safety	Decrease response time for requests for service.
7	Radiation Center	(President's critical processes: teaching, research, service delivery	Increase customer demand for the Center's products and streamline response process.
8	Human Resources	Workforce Hiring & Development	Increase the speed of initial response in the information dissemination process.

statements before moving on. Many teams said they would rather choose their own issues than have one assigned.

Team diversity. Each team used the tools of the TQM process in the way that best fitted their situation. Some moved rapidly, others more cautiously. Some teams felt pushed by their sponsor, leader, and facilitator. They wanted more time to do the process and less pressure to succeed. Other teams felt they were moving too slowly and wanted to rush ahead. We learned that sponsors and other managers needed to accept the uniqueness of each group's functioning, not expecting everyone to reach the same point at the same time.

Time. Many team members said that taking time away from their regular tasks for team meetings and study assignments was a problem. Some felt that they should be released from some duties. Sponsors need to show their commitment to TQM by supporting the team members as they deal with time and job pressures.

Training. The quality of training was an issue, especially for facilitators and team leaders. As consultants gradually withdrew from the process, some facilitators felt unprepared for their role. Some teams asked for more training as well, with a focus on the specific procedures teams need to use.

Phase seven: cross-functional pilot projects

Frequently, difficult problems and opportunities lie across several functional areas. The purpose of cross-functional teams is to provide advanced skill development within the university, to target team efforts on key projects that cross functional lines, and to evaluate and improve the work of ongoing study teams. Cross-functional teams can integrate study across division lines, often improving systems at the policy level.

Cross-functional teams can also select projects aligned with the priority breakthrough items. These well-educated team members can use their knowledge in selecting study problems and evaluating results.

At OSU, our pilot cross-functional team was composed of finance and administration division directors. They selected the issue of improving the study team process.

This team has completed a survey of its customers—the other study team members, sponsors, and facilitators—and is in the process of refining their issue statement. As early evaluations by team members showed ("What We Learned," page 613) time required by TQM work and the content of training are problems the cross-functional team will need to address as they continue through the TQM problem-solving steps.

Phase eight: cross-functional management

The cross-functional pilot project is still under way and results are not yet in. However, we can already see many excellent applications of this process. Universities operate with many committees, most of them composed of faculty, staff, and students.

As the vice president for finance and administration, I have 15 committees advising me in such areas as parking, safety, handicapped access, university computing, etc. Most of these committees have cross-functional responsibility and, with the necessary training, are naturals for implementing TQM at a cross-functional level. Within the next year, we plan to convert these committees to cross-functional study teams.

Phase nine: reporting, recognition, and awards

Reporting Each division director reports monthly to the vice president for finance and administration. These monthly reports focus on the performance measures of each division director's critical processes. Each year, the vice president reviews improvements made in each critical process with each division director and sets the goals for the director for the next year. These performance evaluations are also tied to salary setting, with salary increases reflecting improvements.

As study teams finish their efforts on a particular issue, the vice president and the division directors meet as a review committee and hear the team's presentation of their solutions. The team sponsor reports on progress in implementation of the solutions.

Teams also report to the president and his cabinet. These presentations demonstrate senior management interest in TQM and provide immediate recognition. However, team members have identified implementation of their solutions as the best reward possible, and implementation tracking is an important part of our reporting and recognition program.

Awards We are also developing an awards program for outstanding team or individual performance based on savings (time and money), uniqueness of solutions, and importance to the university. Three categories of awards will be presented.

Each category is open to any employee; any employee can make nominations; and we are developing specific criteria and a selection process for each award.

- **Quality Award.** This award recognizes employees who have participated in an activity (problem-solving task) that, either through teamwork or outstanding individual effort, has made a significant, measurable impact on the university. The activity must have reached its objectives, have measurable results, and have a daily management plan established.

  One or more Quality Awards are presented once a year during University Day and include a personalized plaque, a monetary award, recognition in the staff newsletter, and engraving of the name on a Quality Award Winners plaque that is displayed in the administration building.
- **Beaver Award.** This award, named for OSU's mascot, recognizes and shows appreciation for employees or teams who have sustained continuous

high-quality work performance that goes beyond expectations. For instance, recipients will have completed special projects while maintaining high efficiency in regular duties; repeatedly accepted added responsibilities; continually accomplished major job objectives above expected levels; and shown innovation and initiative.

Beaver Awards may be given twice a year to any number of recipients and include a pin and certificate and a Beaver Balloon as well as recognition in the staff newsletter and at University Day.

- **Great Performance Award.** This award is used to spontaneously recognize and show appreciation to employees who have exceeded expectations in the performance of a specific activity or action, either unique or routine, showing at least one of the following: initiative, competence, customer service, flexibility, communication, cooperation, or tenacity. Examples: showing good judgment in handling a crisis; developing a procedure, identifying an ineffective system, or correcting an omission that saves money; receiving commendations from customers.

  The Great Performance Award is given at any time, within one month of the employee's action. It can include a small gift, a Great Performance balloon or certificate, and includes recognition in the staff newsletter.

Lessons learned

Recognition is very important, and presentations to the president are critical. Team sponsors have also participated in the recognition process by purchasing team hats, coffee cups, etc. Everything helps. We are also exploring the possibility of financial awards based solely on savings; awards of up to ten percent of the savings are allowed by state government. In the early going, we found that simply being on a team is a form of recognition, giving the team member special status.

CONCLUSIONS AND RECOMMENDATIONS

In creating Oregon State's vision statement, we identified Total Quality Management as vital, not only for the realization of our vision, but also for OSU's continued survival in the university's world marketplace. Quality is what our customers tell us it is, not what we say it is. Both internal and external customers want to receive the same high-quality service at all times, with no surprises. Progress can only be determined and improved by measurement.

While Total Quality Management is a relatively simple concept, putting it to work in a university was more challenging than many of us realized at first. The language was foreign to us (universities do use different words than industry). The teamwork approach to problem solving was unfamiliar to most of our mid-level managers. But so far, we consider TQM a real success at OSU. We now have 15 teams operating and the results have been spectacular. Time has been saved, costs have been reduced, people have been empowered at all levels, and morale has skyrocketed.

Managers must lead the TQM process. Each manager's job is to continuously demonstrate in both words and action that TQM is a top priority. This means regularly using study teams, reviewing progress in staff meetings, providing training to everyone, and recognizing and rewarding those who use the process.

Six key points . . .

Let me conclude by suggesting six key points in the successful implementation of TQM in a college or university:

- **Support from the top.** It is essential to have a firm commitment from the president or chief operating officer of the university. Deming found this to be the single most important step in implementing TQM.
- **Just do it!** Don't study it to death. Learn about the steps the teams go through and get one started. Only then will you understand what TQM is all about and whether it will fit into your culture.
- **The teams are everything!** Focusing teams on process improvement is what it is all about. Make sure they have adequate training before they begin. Then stick to the process. The Hawthorn effect is prevalent at first, but the TQM process will see that solutions get implemented. Team building is almost as important as process improvement.
- **You need a champion.** Implementation of TQM takes a long commitment (five years), a lot of time (up to 20 percent), and costs money (at least 60K/year). Someone has to be the champion to get it going, keep it going, and make sure solutions are implemented.
- **Breakthrough planning helps.** Not all TQM programs include breakthrough planning. But it helps in vertical alignment, integration of strategic planning processes already under way, and in focusing efforts on processes that can really make a difference.
- **Try the service side first!** In a university setting, the service sector is an easier place to start than the academic side. Start with a unit that is having trouble; they know they need help and will appreciate being helped. You need early success to get momentum going.

An invitation . . .

As we look toward the future, a future of increasing international competition, TQM will be more important than ever. Implemented properly, it can make the difference between success and failure. Is it a fad? Who knows? But I believe it can make a real difference and that it **can** be implemented in a university setting.

If you are considering a TQM program at your institution and want more information, please call me at Oregon State University. I'll be glad to help!

Appendix A

OSU's mission, values, and guiding principles

Oregon State University is among the leading comprehensive teaching and research universities in the nation. Our mission as a land grant university is to serve the people of Oregon, the nation, and the world through education, research, and service. Through our dedicated teaching, through the pursuit of knowledge, and through our extended relationships to the broader society, we seek continually to improve our contributions to the general welfare.

Values

How we accomplish our mission is as important as the mission itself. The following values are fundamental to our success:

People. Our people—students, faculty, staff, and alumni—are our strength. They are the source of our creativity, they determine our reputation, and they provide our vitality.

Respect. All our people are important contributors. Respect, humanity, and integrity are required in our treatment of each other.

Openness. In the classrooms, laboratories, studios, and field stations, our efforts are open to challenge and debate.

Truth and Truths. We seek truths in our pursuit of knowledge. But we know that there is no such thing as "the truth." Understandings in the sciences, arts, and humanities change. We challenge dogma when we encounter it in our classrooms, in our laboratories and studios, and in our role of serving the broader society.

Guiding Principles

Students are our most important clients. The quality and completeness of their education is our top priority.

We have a responsibility to society to contribute to its social, aesthetic, and economic well-being.

Our social responsibility extends to offering informed criticism even when that criticism may not be well received. We maintain an internal environment that will nurture this important contribution.

Flexibility, change, and constant improvement are essential to our continued success.

In instruction, research, and service activities, we honor and impart principles of academic honesty, freedom, and integrity.

Diversity is a key to our success. Not only are our doors open to men and women alike without regard to race, ethnicity, personal belief, disability, age, or sexual preference, but we also have a moral obligation to open the doors wider for any groups that are underrepresented or that have suffered from discrimination.

Appendix B

Oregon State University's strategic plan goals and objectives

GOAL 1 Serve people through instruction, research, and extension.

1.1 Promote and recognize good teaching.

1.2 Adequately staff and support academic programs essential to the university's mission.

1.3 Adequately support essential programs of research and artistic creativity.

1.4 Periodically review programs to shift resources to areas of need.

1.5 Use evening, weekend classes, and Oregon's Ed-Net to make degree programs available to nontraditional students.

1.6 In developing criteria, procedures for assignment of rank, evaluation, and promotion and tenure, continue to recognize the varied roles of faculty in programs.

1.7 Involve faculty and staff in extension programming and cooperation with other agencies to help Oregonians solve problems, develop leadership, and manage resources.

GOAL 2 Help students to achieve their full potential.

2.1 Improve recognition for teaching, academic advising, and student-faculty interaction.

2.2 Improve students' experiences in living groups, orientation, peer relationships, academic learning/assistance centers.

2.3 Streamline and personalize support service rules, procedures.

2.4 Provide child care for children of students.

2.5 Encourage awareness and understanding of cultural diversity by developing international programs and campus interaction between students of different cultures.

2.6 Improve analysis and evaluation of student achievement, advising, academic support services, and overall university experience.

2.7 Regularly review undergraduate curricula not subject to special accreditation.

GOAL 3 Expand research and artistic creativity.

3.1 Recruit and support faculty, staff, and students of high research, artistic capability.

3.2 Improve research facilities and equipment.

3.3 Encourage interdisciplinary studies and research.

3.4 Enable scholarly and creative productivity of faculty in humanities, social sciences, arts, and education.

3.5 Promote, coordinate, and publicize research and artistic achievement.

GOAL 4 Attract, develop, retain excellent faculty and staff.

4.1 Bring faculty salaries to competitive levels.

4.2 Expand facilities and program support as required for a major teaching and research university.

4.3 Strengthen programs and rewards that promote good teaching.

4.4 Provide a work environment that builds cooperation, mutual respect, and high morale.

4.5 Expand programs that promote faculty and staff professional development.

4.6 Establish university day-care services for faculty and staff.

4.7 Promote upward mobility for staff positions.

4.8 Improve faculty/staff recruiting procedures.

GOAL 5 Expand opportunities for minorities, females, disadvantaged, and disabled.

5.1 Intensify recruitment of women and people of color to faculty positions in which they are under-represented.

5.2 Evaluate classified employment processes to increase personnel from under-represented groups; seek external policy change where necessary.

5.3 Improve recruitment of students from under-represented or disadvantaged groups.

5.4 Remove physical barriers for persons with disabilities and increase their representation at management and senior levels.

5.5 Promote retention of students, faculty, and staff from under-represented groups.

5.6 Sustain a campus climate sensitive to the needs of under-represented groups and help to make the Corvallis community more attractive to people of color.

5.7 Diversify curriculum to include courses and materials relevant to the culture and experiences of women and people of color.

5.8 Ensure pay equity for women and people of color.

GOAL 6 Increase enrollments of outstanding students.

6.1 Improve the quality and rigor of academic programs.

6.2 Raise undergraduate admission standards.

6.3 Strengthen the Honors Program and other academic enrichment programs for outstanding students;

6.4 Actively market the highest quality academic programs.

6.5 Expand resources for merit scholarships, awards, and research stipends.

6.6 Target recruitment of outstanding applicants.

6.7 Improve instructional support services.

6.8 Develop a policy on the makeup of the OSU student body.

GOAL 7 Sharpen the university's international focus.

7.1 Strengthen the international dimensions of the curriculum.

7.2 Expand the international perspective of faculty.

7.3 Increase students' global awareness and interest in international educational experiences.

7.4 Support international activities.

7.5 Strengthen liaison with international constituents.

7.6 Support international programs and services in higher education in Oregon.

GOAL 8 Improve facilities and equipment.

8.1 Give fund-raising priority first to library expansion, second to visual and performing arts instructional facilities, third to computer science facilities.

8.2 Upgrade instructional laboratory facilities and equipment.

8.3 Upgrade classroom facilities and equipment and provide more large classrooms.

8.4 Increase funding for facilities repair and remodeling.

8.5 Improve and maintain research facilities and equipment.

8.6 Promote joint use of facilities and equipment.

GOAL 9 Improve library and computing services.

9.1 Qualify for membership in the Association of Research Libraries.

9.2 Review information support services needs and fund a major library facilities expansion to meet them.

9.3 Provide computing services consistent with the university's research and instructional mission.

9.4 Implement the Student Information System and Financial Information System.

9.5 Continue to expand student access to computing facilities.

9.6 Improve print and non-print collection to meet needs.

9.7 Coordinate decision-making for computing management.

9.8 For library and computing services, expand networking access on campus, statewide, nationally, and internationally and keep pace with new technologies.

9.9 Coordinate collection development, resource sharing, and automated access with other libraries.

GOAL 10 Improve the university's relationships with its constituencies.

10.1 Create and maintain a clear OSU image to emphasize quality of students, instruction, research, and service.

10.2 Motivate OSU's constituencies to increase their support.

10.3 Improve responsiveness of faculty, staff, administrators to their clients.

10.4 Maintain programs to evaluate OSU's effectiveness in meeting constituency needs.

10.5 Maintain close, productive relationships with community citizens and leaders.

Note: Some objectives have been abbreviated for the purposes of this paper.

Appendix C

Oregon State University Total Quality Management

	Aim	Jul	Aug	Sept	Oct	Nov	Dec	Jan	Feb	Mar	Apr	May	Jun
	Items to Accomplish This Year.						F&A Pilot projects						
					Strategic, daily mgmt systems established, deployed								
					Executive consensus on TQM direction			Announce TQM to staff					
				Steering Comm established									
System Changes	Daily Management	Top mgmt team establishes mission, critical processes & measures, vision, strategic plan framework.						Deploy ⟶					
				F&A mgmt team establishes mission, critical processes, and vision.							Review plans		
	Hoshin Planning		Top mgmt team selects Year 1 breakthrough objective and review dates. ⟶								Review plans		
				F&A team selects and plans breakthrough objectives in keeping with top mgmt plans. ⟶									
	Cross-functional Management			Top mgmt team establishes plans to support daily mgmt ⟶ and Hoshin plans.							Review plans		
	Training and Teams	Top mgmt attends TQM class.			Ten teams, one in each unit of F&A, trained in philosophy, tools of TQM.					Ten teams in units other than F&A trained in TQM.			
				Quarterly executive briefings: a. Steering committee b. F&A mgmt team						Two teams started in cross-functional processes			

	Aim	Year 2: 1990–91	Year 3: 1991–92
	Items to Accomplish This Year.	Pilot project evaluation; annual review of plans; expand pilot areas and planning systems. Pilot "Presidential Review."	Expand TQ to all areas; establish "Presidential Review" in all areas. (6.1) Plans now based on customer competitive and past performance data.
System Changes	Daily Management	All managers using daily management methods of planning and process control. (5.7) Educate employees on customer/supplier issues.	(5.5) Document TQ systems in Quality manual. (5.7) (7.1) Improve understanding of customer/supplier needs. Daily management system improved and standardized. (7.2) Measure trends in customer data.
	Hoshin Planning	(7.1) (3.2) (2.1) (2.2) Customer, competitive data gathered and fed into plans. (Quality Function Deployment)	All managers trained in planning tools. All managers using breakthrough planning system. Conduct Baldrige Award review.
	Cross-functional Management	(5.6) (5.7) (6.2) Results of QFD shared with all managers. University-wide standing committee established on Quality.	QFD results aid planning processes. University-wide standing committee established on cost.
	Training Teams	(6.3) Require use of QC story to record team results. (4.1) Daily management and Hoshin systems include employee education and involvement in TQ.	Interdepartment TQ results sharing/seminars. (4.2) All employees trained in TQ. (4.4) Employee recognition system developed.

	Aim	Year 4: 1992–93	Year 5: 1993–94
	Items to Accomplish This Year.	Hoshin, daily management system based on data and well-established. (5.3) (2.3) Systems standardized and prevention-oriented.	WIN BALDRIGE AWARD.
System Changes	Daily Management	Daily management plan based on data; now a continuous system (year-to-year) with small shifts. (7.3) Monitor macro-trends in customer data, "wins - losses."	
	Hoshin Planning	Address Baldrige Award deficits. (5.1) Vision, strategic plan and breakthrough objective based on data; continuous process with small shifts.	
	Cross-functional Management	(5.2) Standing cross-functional teams. Team results shared cross-functionally.	
	Training Teams	University-wide team seminars. Results well-documented. (4.5) Total Quality includes Quality of Worklife issues.	(1.4) Teams share with other universities.

Appendix D

TQM survey: institutions contacted

Four-Year Institutions

Carnegie-Mellon University, Pittsburgh, PA

Colorado State University, Fort Collins, CO

Columbia University, New York, NY

Florida State University, Tallahassee, FL

Harvard University, Cambridge, MA

Illinois Institute of Technology, Chicago, IL

Milwaukee School of Engineering, Milwaukee, WI

Northwestern University, Evanston, IL

Oregon State University, Corvallis, OR

Pepperdine University, Malibu, CA

University of Chicago, Chicago, IL

University of Michigan, Ann Arbor, MI

University of Minnesota, Minneapolis, MN

University of North Carolina, Chapel Hill, NC

University of Pittsburgh, Pittsburgh, PA

University of Wisconsin, Madison, WI

University of Wyoming, Laramie, WY

Two-Year Institutions

Delaware County Community College, Media, PA

Fox Valley Technical College, Appleton, WI

Hawkeye Institute of Technology, Waterloo, IA

Jackson Community College, Jackson, MI

Lamar Community College, Lamar, CO

Palm Beach Community College, Lake Worth, FL

St. Augustine Technical Center, St. Augustine, FL

Other:

North Dakota University System, Bismarck, ND

Notes

1. W. Edwards Deming, *Out of the Crisis* (Cambridge: Massachusetts Institute of Technology Center for Advanced Engineering Study, 1986): Chapter Two.
2. Joseph Oberle, "Quality Gurus, the Men and Their Message," *Training Magazine* (January 1990): 47.
3. Oberle: 48.

4. *Vision 2000, America's Top 1,000 Companies' Quality Progress,* 1990 Research Report (GOAL/QPC, Methuen, MA).

5. *Competitive Times,* Volume I, 1990 (GOAL/QPC, Methuen, MA).

Bibliography

Aubrey, Charles A., III, and Patricia K. Felkins. *Teamwork: Involving People in Quality and Productivity Improvement.* Milwaukee: Quality Press, 1988.

Block, Peter. *The Empowered Manager.* San Francisco: Jossey-Bass Publishers, 1989.

Bone, Diane, and Rick Griggs. *Quality at Work.* Los Altos: Crisp Publications.

Bowsher, Jack E. *Educating America.* New York: John Wiley & Sons, Inc., 1989.

Byham, William C., Ph.D., with Jeff Cox. *Zapp! The Lightning of Empowerment.* DDI Press.

Crosby, Philip B. *The Eternally Successful Organization.* New York: McGraw-Hill, 1988.

Crosby, Philip B. *Quality Is Free. The Art of Making Quality Certain.* New York: McGraw-Hill, 1979.

Crosby, Philip B. *Quality Without Tears.* New York: McGraw-Hill, 1984.

Davis, Stanley M. *Future Perfect.* New York: Addison-Wesley Publishing Co., 1989.

Deal, Terrence E., and Allen A. Kennedy. *Corporate Cultures, the Rites and Rituals of Corporate Life.* New York: Addison-Wesley Publishing Co., 1982.

Deming, W. Edwards. *Out of the Crisis.* Cambridge: Massachusetts Institute of Technology Center for Advanced Engineering Study, 1986.

Goldzimer, Linda Silverman. *'I'm First.' Your Customer's Message to You.* New York: Rawson Assoc., MacMillan, 1989.

Hart, Marilyn K. and Robert F. *Quantitative Methods for Quality and Productivity Improvement.* Milwaukee: ASQC Quality Press, 1989.

Imai, Masaaki. *Kaizen, The Key to Japan's Competitive Success.* New York: Random House Business Division, 1986.

Ishikawa, Kaoru. *What Is Total Quality Control? The Japanese Way.* New York: Prentice Hall, 1986.

Joiner Associates, Inc. *A Practical Approach to Quality (Selected Readings in Quality Improvement).* Madison, 1985.

Juran, J. M. *Juran on Leadership for Quality, An Executive Handbook.* New York: The Free Press, Macmillan.

Kume, Hitoshi. *Statistical Methods for Quality Improvement.* Tokyo: The Association for Overseas Technical Scholarships (AOTS), 1985.

McLean, Gary N., and Susan H. DeVogel. *Role of Organization Development in Quality Management and Productivity Improvement.* Minneapolis: University of Minnesota & ASTD.

Miller, William C. *The Creative Edge, Fostering Innovation Where You Work.* New York: Addison-Wesley Publishing Co., 1987.

Ray, Michael, and Rochelle Myers. *Creativity in Business.* New York: Doubleday, 1989.

Reddy, W. Brendan, and Kaleel Jamison, eds. *Team Building, Blueprints for Productivity and Satisfaction.* NTL Institute for Applied Behavioral Science & University Associates, Inc.,

1988.

Rosander, A. C. *Applications of Quality Control in the Service Industries.* Milwaukee: ASQC Quality Press.

Rosander, A. C. *The Quest for Quality in Services.* Milwaukee: Quality Press, 1989.

Schwarz, Robert A. *Midland City, Recovering Prosperity Through Quality.* Milwaukee: ASQC Quality Press, 1989.

Townsend, Patrick L., with Joan E. Gebhardt. *Commit to Quality.* New York: John Wiley & Sons, 1990.

Tucker, Allan. *Chairing the Academic Department.* 2nd ed. New York: Macmillan, 1984.

Walton, Mary. *The Deming Management Method.* New York: Putnam, 1986.

Reading 41

TQM Contributions to Academic Processes in Higher Education

By Harry Costin

Concern about *quality of teaching* and *quality of learning* in higher education is widespread. In the United States, criticism of the current level of accountability of public higher education institutions has led to the introduction of mandatory evaluation instruments in many states. Internationally, similar concerns are echoed, and a recent World Bank policy paper examining the state of higher education in developing countries also calls for "introducing policies designed to give priority to quality" as a critical direction for reform (1994, 4).

The alleged success of Total Quality Management (TQM) principles and processes in the revitalization of manufacturing and service delivery institutions worldwide has led to a growing interest in the potential applications of TQM principles and processes to education at the K–12 and higher levels. Unfortunately, most suggestions offered to date in the literature are out of context. They do not take into account the particular structural and governance characteristics of higher education institutions.

In my opinion, the strongest potential contributions of the quality movement to academic applications in higher education are:

1. The literature offers many useful ways to conceive and *operationalize* the notion of quality.
2. Quality models, such as the PDCA, provide a *structure* that allows for the integration of specific quality improvement efforts. The overall aim is continuous improvement, achieved through systematic, documented learning from experience.

   I refer to a structure for continuous improvement efforts, such as the one provided by the PDCA model, as a main contribution of the literature. I do not consider the systemic models, such as the Baldrige model, or Senge's learning organization, to be among the most important contributions. The main reason is that Senge's model is a useful conceptual framework, but difficult to operationalize; also, the Baldrige model reflects lofty but unrealistic expectations for most higher education institutions.

3. A third major contribution of TQM is *focus.* Improvement in quality is said to result systematically from focusing on improving specific critical processes.

The discussion in this article focuses on providing examples of quality definitions and a continuous improvement model (PDCA) useful to the improvement of teaching and learning, considered as two critical academic processes in higher education.

QUALITY IN THE ACADEMIC PROCESS

Murgatroyd and Morgan (1993) provided a useful set of definitions of quality drawn from the literature, which can be translated to educational applications:

The first approach is *quality assurance,* which "refers to the determination of standards, appropriate methods and quality requirements by an expert body, accompanied by a process of inspection and evaluation that examines the extent to which practice meets these standards." (45).

From this perspective, clearly defined standards provide a benchmark and a measure of progress. Commonly applied in professional fields in which ongoing certification is required, this approach is far from obsolete. On the contrary, it is likely that quality assurance norms such as ISO 9000 may be increasingly a requirement for higher education institutions, considered "federal contractors." ISO 9000 places an emphasis on conformance of actual practices to self-defined, documented processes, rather than to absolute standards.

The second approach is *contract conformance,* "where some quality standard has been specified during the negotiation of forming a contract." (45) In academic practices this definition may translate into meeting specific contractual obligations by both the teacher and the students. Homework assignments provide a useful example of conformance:

> Conformance is assessed by the teacher in terms of on-time performance (meeting deadlines) by the student and an assessment of the student's ability to meet the requirements of the task. Conformance is assessed by the student in terms of the teacher's on-time performance in returning the assignment (marked and commented upon) and on the teacher's reliability in marking from student to another. Quality means meeting agreed deadlines in appropriate ways. (48)

The importance of contracting in the classroom has been highlighted by Christensen et al. (1991) in their model for classroom discussion, which emphasizes the need for the instructor to focus both on the content and process of learning. This model, referred to by some as the case method, is one of the most consistent with principles advocated in the quality literature. The similarities between both approaches stem from the emphasis on managing processes and on shared responsibilities for teaching and learning on the part of both the instructor and the students.

The third approach is *customer-driven quality,* the "notion of quality in which those who are to receive a product or service make explicit their expectations for this product or service and this quality is defined in terms of meeting or exceeding the expectations of customers." (46)

This definition of quality has met widespread criticism when translated to educational applications. Some have argued that students are unable to define their educational needs and the processes to achieve them. Interpreted this way, customer-driven quality can not be translated to academic applications. However, a broader understanding of the concept of *customer,* and the inclusion of the concept of *need,* may provide a definition consistent with both TQM principles **and** academic applications.

Students are not the only *customers* who receive the benefits provided by educational services. Among the key customers are also employers (who require graduates with certain skills), parents (who finance the education of their children) and the state (which subsidizes public education). These diverse customers are entitled to both high-quality educational processes and measurable learning outcomes.

Further, students' *needs,* rather than simply expectations, include measurable outcomes such as skills required by employers. Thus, the definition of customer-driven quality can be fully compatible with current concerns about measurable learning outcomes.

The final area of alleged incompatibility between the concept of customer-driven quality and current academic thinking relates to the goals of a broadly based liberal arts education, which may not translate immediately into learning outcomes valued by most employers. This incompatibility may be more apparent than real, since a high-quality liberal arts education translates into higher-level cognitive skills, which are increasingly valued in knowledge-intensive, state-of-the-art industries. Further, skills such as high-level writing ability and critical thinking are highly valued even in specialized technical fields.

The fourth approach to quality, which lies at the core of TQM principles and should be added to the other three, is the notion that quality of outcomes is directly related to quality of processes and quality of inputs. The Baldrige guidelines state that only those outcomes that directly relate to specific, improvable processes should be measured.

PDCA IN THE CLASSROOM

A second example of potential contributions of TQM to academic processes in higher education is the PDCA model, which provides a structure for continuous improvement efforts. As defined in the Baldrige guidelines, continuous improvement refers to both incremental and breakthrough improvement. PDCA can be broadly translated as a systematic approach to learning from experience and acting upon what has been learned. This simple notion should be a guideline to all learning, since it is simply common sense in operation.

Specific suggestions to apply PDCA to the delivery of courses, in order to improve the quality of teaching and learning, are the following:

P: Planning

Planning under TQM, and its application to course delivery in higher education settings, includes two critical notions:

1. *Previous learning and experiences should influence the new plans* Unless a course is offered several times by the same instructor, systematic learning from past experiences is the exception rather than the norm in the development of syllabi for courses.
2. *All relevant constituencies should participate directly or indirectly in the planning phase* Course design is commonly decided unilaterally by the instructor, who may or may not follow broad curricular guidelines in designing core courses. Uniformity or standardization of course content is fundamentally a function of content uniformity of textbooks used in higher education.

In my opinion, current course design practice violates a basic TQM principle—shared decision making. It is evident that the instructor needs to unilaterally make some decisions before the semester begins, such as textbook choice; however, other decisions (such as specific course delivery methods, and type and due date of projects) may easily be made jointly. Currently there is an unwarranted degree of rigidity in course design. Every process should relate to specific course objectives rather than to the preferences of an individual instructor.

Potential implementation guidelines for the planning phase in a manner consistent with PDCA include:

- Review syllabi, written feedback and any other relevant documentation if the course has been offered before.
- Review the current learning objectives and prescribed content for the course as stated in the official course catalogue.
- Define your (instructor's) objectives for the course. Do not confuse your objectives with the operationalization of them.
- Discuss the course objectives, defined in the catalogue and approved by the curriculum committee, and your own objectives with the course participants. Have the participants define "their" objectives.

Implementation (materials and pedagogy used) should be a function of the three sets of objectives (official curriculum, instructor, and participants).

D: Doing

The doing or implementation of the plan should be a direct function of the objectives set for the course. The instructor and students may have available a variety of possible approaches or pedagogies to achieve specific learning objectives. Learning style considerations may provide additional criteria for the selection of particular *processes* to achieve the chosen learning objectives.

Suggested guidelines for classroom implementation:

- Define alternative teaching methods and instructional materials which relate directly to the objectives of the course (lectures, videos, cases, student presentations, group projects, etc.).
- Consider learning styles in the final selection of learning processes.
- Emphasize teamwork.

There is a rich literature that evaluates diverse *teaching and learning processes* conducive to *active learning*. Guidelines such as *The Seven Principles for Good Practice in Undergraduate Education* and collaborative learning approaches represent innovative choices and a starting point for the design of new learning processes.

C: Checking (Learning)

The results of implementation need to be evaluated, since they represent a critical tool for improvement. Evaluation focuses on unambiguous "vital signs" that measure performance of specific process steps against clearly defined benchmarks.

The literature offers rich insights into the potential use of assessment as a learning process in its own right (as in the use of portfolios as a tool for self-reflection for students). In my opinion, the usefulness of assessment models has been hampered by two factors: first, the apparent contradiction between assessment and evaluation, understood as measurement against absolute standards. The use of one approach does not preclude the other. The second handicap is the lack of willingness to assign sufficient resources to systematic assessment and evaluation. This could change if a structured approach to improvement, such as the PDCA model, were applied at the course, departmental, or institutional level (institutional accountability).

A: Adjusting

The last step in the PDCA model is the one missing most frequently in academic processes in higher education: the information collected is not used as a tool for systematic improvement, for several reasons:

- The course is only taught once, or is taught again by somebody else, who redesigns it to fit his/her own preferences. In the best of cases, syllabi or comments about pedagogical tools, such as instructional materials, may be shared.

- Assessment or evaluation instruments are used either to grade students or because they are mandatory (state laws demanding accountability of public universities). The information does not include the instructor (except for often ill-designed student evaluations) and is not seen as an important tool to improve teaching and learning.
- Teaching performance remains of low priority in the tenure process.

In brief, if action is not taken, as results of lessons learned from experience gained systematically, there will be no improvement. Most of the discussion related to the improvement of academic processes in higher education has focused on quality of inputs (better students, better teachers, more pedagogical aids). The missing link has been to learn systematically from each instructor's experience and to translate the lessons into improved processes.

The main problem with focusing the discussion of quality in academic processes on quality of inputs is that lack of resources is often a convenient excuse for lack of improvement. This is simply unacceptable. Better teaching and better learning result from focusing on improving specific, critical academic processes, based on the lessons learned from experience.

Bibliography

Christensen, Roland, David Garvin and Ann Sweet. *Education for Judgment: The Artistry of Discussion Leadership.* Harvard Business School, Cambridge, 1991.

Murgatroyd, Stephen and Colin Morgan. *Total Quality Management and the School.* Open University Press, Bristol, 1993.

The World Bank. *Higher Education: The Lessons of Experience.* Washington, D.C., 1994.

Reading 42

The Paradigm Shifts Required to Apply TQM and Teams in Higher Education

By Michael J. Brower

Abstract

From manufacturing, where it got its major start in this country, TQM has spread recently and rapidly into many service industries, including hospitals and health care organizations. Finally, in the last few years, some institutions of higher educations have begun to study and apply TQM, in one or more of three forms. The largest number are applying TQM philosophy, principles, and tools to improve their supporting services and functions that are most like those in industry, such as student registration, housing, financial services, housekeeping, buildings and grounds, etc. Another very large group has approached TQM as new subject matter to be taught, as content, for courses in Business, Engineering, and other departments and schools. On the other hand, only a small handful of colleges and universities are now beginning to apply TQM to their heart and core: the education of students. This essay deals with nine of the fundamental concepts used in TQM, and with the shifts in mind set, in mental models or paradigms, that are required if TQM and Teams are to be seriously applied to the core educational processes of colleges and universities. These nine concepts: the customer, the product, the producer, the process, teams, the source of quality, the role of management, continuous improvement, and benchmarking.

Source: 1992 article reprinted with the permission of the author.

INTRODUCTION AND OVERVIEW

Total Quality Management (TQM) and Teams are rapidly becoming the preferred fundamental ways of organizing, planning, and leading for competitiveness in manufacturing. They are spreading now rapidly in dozens of service industries, including financial institutions, hospitals, and other health care institutions. Institutions of post-secondary education are also, finally, getting involved with TQM and the use of teams. (This essay applies to all such institutions, including two and four year colleges and universities, public and private. However for simplicity in writing, I will hereafter use the single word universities to apply to any and all institutions of post-secondary or higher education.) There are three general arenas in which universities are applying TQM. First, of the couple of hundred institutions that are known to be interested in and acting in some way on TQM, the vast majority are applying it to their administrative, service, and support functions, such as buildings and grounds, student registration and housing, food service, and financial administration (Axland, Marchese, Seymour & Collett). These support activities are most similar to those in private business, they are easiest to start with, and they are least threatening to the traditional power and paradigms of the faculty. The other arena in which TQM is showing up at large numbers of universities is in the curriculum. Faculty in business schools and in engineering and other departments are beginning to teach courses *about* TQM, as though this is just another business or manufacturing topic to be included in the course curriculum (Axland).

Finally, a far smaller number of universities, perhaps a dozen or two at most, are actually beginning to *apply* TQM and teams to the core mission of the university, the educational process itself, which is the focus of this essay. The leaders in this process may be Samford University in Birmingham, Delaware County Community College in Media, PA and Fox Valley Technical College in Appleton, Wisconsin. Also on the path are Terra Technical College in Fremont, Ohio, Lakeshore Technical College in Cleveland, Wisconsin, the University of Rhode Island, and the Deming Scholars MBA Program at the Fordham University Graduate School of Business. There are of course in addition many hundreds and probably thousands of individual faculty who are experimenting with applying various of these ideas and concepts on their own, within the limits allowed by the requirements of their universities. Some of these individuals that I am aware of include David Porter at the Air Force Academy, Mark Borzi at the University of Hartford, the editor of this book at the University of Massachusetts in Dartmouth, and Merlin Ricklefs during his 1991–92 year as a visiting professor at the University of Minnesota—Duluth.

Of course this is not new. Carl Rogers includes some very interesting well-documented examples in his 1983 book, *Freedom to Learn.* Back then we did not use the terminology of TQM, but many of these concepts and approaches have been around a long time, although not part of a comprehensive disciplined system.

I myself was one of those individually experimenting faculty almost thirty years ago. Teaching at the M.I.T. Sloan School of Management during the early 1960s,

I was a very traditional lecturer. My lectures were over-prepared, and I was young and insecure and thoughtless about any possible differences between teaching and learning. So I lectured the complete class period, barely tolerating the first student question and almost literally "chopping off the head" of the second student to raise his hand and ask a question. The reasons? I still had too much lecture material prepared *and* I was scared to death that I might not know the answer to the next question. Sometime in my early years as a high speed lecturer I was up all night with sick children and could only prepare half a dozen topic ideas instead of a full lecture. The next morning I walked out of the classroom exhausted and exhilarated. I was the worst prepared I had been in my short academic career, and I had clearly just conducted my best class! Since I couldn't fill the hour with lecturing I was "forced" to ask the students questions, engage their minds, and support full class participation. Surely there was something here I was supposed to learn!

Within a couple of years I had transformed my teaching process into a guiding/coaching, facilitating process and was using small student teaching teams. Typically, I would teach about the first third of the semester, using that time to lay out some theory and concepts and to lead the organizing process for the remainder of the semester. The students talked about and prioritized what they wanted to learn in the course. Then we used a decision matrix (although I didn't know then what it was called) in which we put down the side the students' top priorities for learning in the class, and then put across the top of the matrix what they wanted to teach. We used the matrix to make sure we had a high correlation. No student taught alone; they were always required to prepare and lead the class in small, two 4-person teams. No team taught any topic that had not been identified by the class as a high priority topic. Most teams used a more creative, comprehensive, interesting, and multimedia teaching approach than I had ever thought of on my own. In the early 1970s I adapted this process to a wide variety of courses first at the Brandeis University Heller Graduate School and later at the University of Massachusetts—Boston, with blue collar working and commuting students. At all three institutions the students learned more content, learned more about learning, and about teaching, and came out with enhanced self-esteem, than if they had sat through my lectures. No, I cannot document that with solid research, but many, many students demonstrated that and reported that to me.

There are many definitions of TQM, many gurus, a few "absolutes" (or none, depending on who you listen to or read), many steps, recipes, or components, etc. In the discussion that follows, I do not attempt to be all inclusive. Rather, I have taken nine of the most fundamental concepts of TQM and Teams, and for each I attempt to show the contrast between the "old paradigm" or traditional mindset in higher education, and the new thinking required if higher education is to learn from how industry is thinking about and applying TQM and Teams. The nine concepts are: the customer; the product; the producer; the process; teams; the source of quality; the role of management; continuous improvement; and benchmarking. On each concept, to fully embrace the teachings and learnings of TQM and use of Teams, faculty will have to accept a major shift in perceptions and in mindsets so massive that they truly add up to a whole Paradigm Shift for faculty.

THE CUSTOMER: IDENTIFYING, UNDERSTANDING, AND DELIGHTING YOUR CUSTOMERS

TQM calls for us to be customer focused, led, driven. If universities are to adopt, learn from, and apply Total Quality Management, they too will have to determine who are their customers, and they will have to develop ways of listening to their customers and meeting and exceeding their requirements. Who are the customers of universities?

If we define our customers as those who receive our products, or as those who benefit from our existence, or as those who pay for our services, then universities have many customers—a bewildering variety of customers. Let us list some of the more obvious groups of customers, as seen through the eyes of university administration and/or faculty.

Faculty may be seen as internal to a university, as its employees, or its heart and soul. But faculty are often highly mobile. They move around a lot. So educational institutions compete for attracting and holding faculty, which makes them customers to be sought after and catered to. And faculty themselves often identify less with the university that is providing their temporary home and more with the peers, journals, and organizations of their separate professions that provide periodic peer review, plaudits, and mobility.

Some universities see their primary mission as developing new knowledge, and many others see this as at least a secondary mission. They compete to attract research funding from *foundations and federal government agencies,* and provide them in return with basic or applied research and a share in the resulting status. So these groups too are seen as customers.

Businesses hire the graduates and make donations with an eagerness roughly proportional to how they rank a college's quality, so they too must be seen as customers.

Other universities accept graduates for advanced and professional degree programs based in part on *their perception* of the quality of the undergraduate output. So they are also customers.

Accrediting agencies must be constantly thought about, understood, and periodically provided with evidence on whatever standards of excellence they use, in order to ensure that programs, departments, and schools within the university continue to earn the official stamp of approval.

Alumni receive an ongoing stream of status from their alma mater. In exchange they recruit new students and give and raise money. Their effort is proportional to how they feel about good old U. So good old U. must work constantly to impress alumni and those whose opinions the alumni respect.

Public universities provide graduates, research, football and other sports for local pride, and, in general, status to the citizens of their city, state, or region. In return they receive financing, and expectations, from their *citizens and governments,* which are also therefore customers.

Finally, for at least some faculty, the future of society, or the ideal of a good society, or serving the timeless quest for art, beauty, and truth is the customer (god) they cherish.

Hold on! Where and when do the students come in? Aren't they customers too? Certainly the answer is yes, or should be. But have we really come very far since the 1960s when an underground classic pamphlet described student's lack of status and influence in university affairs under the title "The Student as Nigger"? On the whole the student is still taken for granted, and is told what classes to attend, what to study, and what to learn, and in what sequence. The student is even told how to learn: listening to lectures, taking notes, reading, and by boring, repetitive study, alone, not in teams. At the end of each course, semester, and year the student is also told whether or not she or he had "learned" (actually memorized) enough information to have passed inspection (examination) with sufficient marks to be allowed to continue. In short, the student is seen, and treated, as anything *but* an important customer.

In the new paradigm, the student is seen as the primary customer of the institution. But many faculty in many universities today still choke on even thinking of the student as one customer among many. On the other hand, the institution that has adopted the new paradigm treats the students with the respect due its most important customers. It is constantly seeking to understand them and their requirements. And, as is happening now in industry, the university and its faculty will seek to build a partnership with the student—a partnership in discovery and learning. This is already the model in our best graduate schools; it is coming in our colleges more slowly. One of the many results of this shift to a partnership is that the role of evaluation shifts from the institution evaluating students to a continuing improvement partnership in which each joins in developing processes for evaluating themselves, the other, and their joint process.

THE PRODUCT

The product of education is a person empowered to educate herself or himself—an "educating person," not an "educated person." What is the product of education? And how can we specify it with sufficient clarity to give guidance to the processes chosen to produce that product? In the old paradigm the student's growing body of knowledge is seen as the product of education. In the worst cases, this is simply how much knowledge, clearly defined, broken up, isolated into chunks, even atomized, can the student memorize and retain just long enough to pass the exams. (As this is written the newspapers are carrying reports on a National Science Foundation study that is said to show how destructive this process of studying for tests has been to the real education of our people.)

In the best of cases there still is an assumption that the product of higher education is "an educated man or woman." Let's listen in, for example, at the Harvard commencement. Every spring the president of Harvard University tells the graduates at commencement, if memory serves and this hasn't been modernized, that he "takes great pride in admitting you into *the company of educated men and women.*" There you have it. Until the moment of graduation they were uneducated. Then, after four years at Harvard, they are finally educated. Complete. Finished. Now they are educated men and women and can get on with the rest of their lives.

Perhaps you think this is merely a leftover legacy of ancient Harvard. Consider the following recent news from Dartmouth:

> Dartmouth College, in the first revision of its curriculum in 70 years, is replacing required courses in traditional subjects with mandated study of a series of 'intellectual fields' such as social analysis, and is formalizing a multicultural requirement. The curriculum overhaul, which also includes an interdisciplinary requirement and a required senior-year project, was approved by the Dartmouth faculty Monday night. The effort is an attempt to redefine what it is *to be an 'educated person,'* said Dartmouth president James O. Freedman. (Flint. Emphasis added.)

Now the old paradigm of the product of education being "an educated person" was probably appropriate in former times, when change was slow, when the function of higher education was to help create and certify a leadership elite, and when a hard working reasonably bright person could learn some meaningful fraction of all the scientific and cultural knowledge then available in the world—or at least in the Western world, which was all that mattered to most Western elites.

What has changed in this picture? Everything! Change is continuous—and accelerating. The relevant world is not every culture, every nook and cranny of the planet, in every period of time—and every interpretation of the universe. The total amount of knowledge available is so vast, and increasing so rapidly, that no student in any four-year program could possibly learn even a tiny, tiny fraction of 1 percent of the total. And whatever the knowledge content the student learns in these four years is inevitably going to be outdated within a few years—or even a few months!

Thus, a person cannot possibly be "educated" in four years—or any other given period of time. For the modern world a person is never truly educated. So we need a new concept, a new paradigm, to clarify what our best faculty have long been practicing, which is that the product of higher education is a person "empowered to continue their own education for the rest of their life." Not an *educated* person, but an *educating* person. Not developed, but developing. Put bluntly, if education is completed, or thought to be completed, in four years, it is a failure. Put another way, the *product* of education is not a product at all; it is a *process* of never ending education. To be empowered in this way requires that the student gain from education:

- Knowledge of how to continue learning and developing for the rest of her/his life,
- Skills in continuing to learn and develop,
- A state of mind and being that enables lifelong learning, that sees and feels self-guided learning to be natural, doable, and fun, and
- A strong drive, a will, to continue learning and developing her/himself.

WHO IS THE PRODUCER OF EDUCATION?

This question is not so often raised and addressed in TQM, mostly because the answer is usually clear and obvious. But in education this question is crucial. In the old paradigm, teachers, the faculty, are seen as the producers of education. It is something that they "do to" the student, whenever the student cooperates by paying attention and doing what she is told. In the new paradigm, if the *product* is to be a person enabled, empowered to be a continuously learning, self-developing person, then the *producer* of that education must be, can only be, the *student herself.* This basic truth has been known for thousands of years by our greatest educators and philosophers, and has been equally forgotten and ignored in thousands of universities and schools to this day. Education takes place within a person, not on the outside or the periphery. So it is beyond the direct reach of any outsider and can only be produced by the insider, the person himself. Complete education involves the development of the whole person, of all parts of the person, of the mind, the emotions, the values, and the spirit. This can, and should, be undertaken by the person herself. You and I produce our own education—no one else can do it for us or to us.

THE PROCESS OF EDUCATION

A fundamental concept of TQM is that we must focus our attention as much or more on the process as on the product. We must visualize that process, draw it, understand it thoroughly. Then we can find out whether or not it is under control, producing predictable results, and whether or not it is capable of meeting the customers' requirements. And then we can, and must, work on developing continuous improvement of that process.

In the old paradigm, there is little in-depth attention to, thinking about, or understanding of educational process. It is mostly taken for granted, since all the attention is on "getting the content across." There is almost no concern for, and attention to, the process of learning. All the attention is on the process of something called "teaching." The best analogy for our actual old paradigm process of education may be the auto assembly line. The student and his knowledge content play the part of the slowly growing auto body. He is moved slowly and boringly down the four-year "assembly line of education." As the student moves down the long line of teachers, each of them tries to pour in or to attach some fragments and pieces of disconnected knowledge to the student. Periodically he is tested and either held back for another try or passed on to the hands of the next classroom and teacher. The student is mostly passive. The quality of the student's knowledge "assembly" is always suspect, so we inspect (examine) it frequently. And a high proportion of students are tossed aside as they fail along the way and at the end. Many are not even eligible to be reworked in the repair bay, which is what a mediocre auto assembly line does. Instead, they are tossed out of the institution and onto the scrap heap of life with less caring than we show to our machinery mistakes.

In the new paradigm, we start by specifying that the student is simultaneously the customer, the product, *and the producer* of her own educator. We further specify that quality of learning and development is the primary objective, not quantity, and that if students are *not* producing their own education/learning/development now, and throughout the remainder of their life, the system has failed.

THE ROLE OF TEAMS IN HIGHER EDUCATION

TQM relies on teams and teamwork. Project teams work within each department and function to study, plan, carry out, monitor, and learn from improvement efforts. Cross functional teams work on special projects that cut across departmental lines to improve a given critical process, and on continuous cross departmental cooperative efforts to improve quality, cost, and customer service. A rapidly growing number of organizations are redesigning and restructuring themselves around self-directed teams that plan, perform, and improve the basic work of the organization at the base and the front lines, without direct supervision.

In the old paradigm in higher education students work in isolation, or in one-to-one interaction with the professor, or more likely, in the larger universities, with a teaching assistant. There is little or no room for teams and teamwork. In fact when this happens, it is usually called cheating. The honor system at many universities includes: "I will neither give nor receive help." Yet industry, and life, require skills and attitudes that support working teams. In a study of 20 year alumni of three dozen colleges and universities, Georgetown vice president Joe Petit found that over 80 percent reported that "work in groups to accomplish goals" is an important current need, but only 20 percent said their college had helped them learn it (Marchese, 1990 as cited in Porter, "Total Quality Learning" (1991).

In the new paradigm, students are encouraged to study in groups and teams, or are actively organized into learning teams. The Second Report of the Harvard Assessment Seminars came up with the "surprise" finding that "students who get the most out of college, who grow the most academically, and who are happiest *organize their time to include interpersonal activities with faculty members, or with fellow students, built around substantive work.*" The author, Professor Light, points out that for many students this is difficult. He makes the specific point that it is different from studying alone. Based on research reports by, and input from, many students, he recommends to faculty that they create study groups in large classes and that they have several students share their papers each week, in advance of class, with other members (Light, p. 21). He further recommends that advisors encourage their students to create or join a study group outside of their classes (p. 53). And he adds that these small study groups are especially important for students in the sciences (p. 56).

Have there been any scientific controlled experiments? David Porter reports on one:

> A study at the Air Force Academy compared the performance and satisfaction of students enrolled in classes employing group-oriented projects and grades to those receiving traditional instruction. The 53 students in the group-oriented classes (in sections taught by four different instructors) performed significantly better on four different, common, objective tests than students in the control group. Students' self reports of participation and effort were also significantly higher. The most interesting finding, however, was the extent to which students in the experimental sections attributed their learning to one another rather than to their teacher. Student 'testimonials' from previous similar experiments illustrate this: 'I noticed an attitude developing in the class I'd

never seen anywhere else. Everyone had prepared for the quiz but not just for themselves . . . for each other.

THE SOURCE OF QUALITY

In the old paradigm, a small percentage of students produce really high quality learning. Another large block produce lower, but still acceptable, quality. And another significant number produce unacceptable quality and are failed. How do we know who is in which group? Examinations. We use them to weed out the low quality learning and hold it back or refuse to certify it. Examinations are in higher education what traditional inspection is in industry. A final attempt, in the hands of non-producers, to screen out the errors caused by the system, before they get to the outside world (customers). In fact, in higher education it is even worse; a second purpose of examinations, or at least an unfortunate by-product, is to inculcate and maintain fear in the "workforce" (students).

Many corporations, thanks to TQM, have learned that final inspection: (1) does not catch all the mistakes of the system, and lets some, sometimes many, slip through to the customer; (2) takes responsibility for quality out of the hands, and therefore out of the minds, of the producers; (3) does nothing to raise, and actually lowers, the ableness of the system to produce consistently high quality, since it does nothing to improve the average or reduce the variability; and (4) is very expensive, since it requires a lot of people and time, is not value adding, and actually encourages waste. As a result, industry is rapidly switching (but education is not) to the new paradigm, which includes: specifying the product, studying the process, getting the process under control, improving the process average and variability, improving all the surrounding systems that enable or undermine quality, educating the producers (workforce) on what high quality and acceptable quality are, according to measurements, and what they look like (and in some cases sound, feel, smell, taste like). Then, along with all of this, the workforce is given the authority, and the accountability is accepted by them, for the quality of the output they are producing. In this process, the old uses of inspection, and the old separate inspector roles, are eliminated. Instead, everyone inspects the product as they receive it, as they work on it, and before it leaves their hands or work area.

The parallels to higher education are massive and obvious, if extremely questionable and unpleasant to those "educators" locked in the old paradigm. Students, or student-faculty partnerships together, must develop baseline and milestone measures for how the student's ableness for self-development is progressing and for helping the student, or the partnership, discover what would be helpful and logical paths and next steps for improvement.

THE ROLE OF MANAGEMENT

Under TQM in industry, and especially where on-going empowered teams are in use, the role of managers is dramatically changing. In higher education, the equivalent of the manager is the teacher, although most teachers will reject this. For TQM to work, the teachers' role must also change dramatically.

As we have said, in the old paradigm, teachers see their role as, and act as though they are, the producers of education. They design curriculum, decide on content within each course and module, decide the teaching process (not usually asking whether it is or is not identical to a learning process), then they teach, and finally they examine. Of course, they are still learning this method.

But for the new paradigm, we have said that the students themselves are the producers of their own learning, and that, in fact, they are the only players on the learning stage who can actually produce learning.

What then is the role of teachers in the new paradigm? To become what many great and good teachers have always been doing. Try on the roles below, described in terms of action verbs, and see if they don't sound more like what is needed for the new paradigm than do the older terms of professor (one who professes?), instructor (one who instructs), and teacher (one who teaches). The new paradigm faculty may do some or all of the following:

- Lead
- Inspire
- Coach
- Facilitate
- Create a vision
- Question
- Enable
- Empower
- Evoke
- Support
- Share a vision
- Listen
- Call forth (educate)
- Resource
- Guide
- Encourage
- Role model
- Create context

It is perhaps relevant that many of these are exactly the same new roles that thousands of middle managers are being asked to learn and take on, and are taking on, in industry today. It is difficult, but not impossible, for traditionally trained managers to learn these new roles. Could teachers do the same?

CONTINUOUS IMPROVEMENT

In the old paradigm, continuous improvement is only partially in the faculty mindset. With respect to students, the faculty expects to see improvement of some kind in their ability to take tests and write papers. With respect to themselves, faculty expect to increase their knowledge and skills in their own specialized academic field. But until recently there has been little systemic thinking about, or application of, the idea of continuous improvement of processes, either for the teacher's own development, or for that of the student. (Under the new accreditation guidelines of the American Assembly for Collegiate Schools of Business this may be changing.)

In the new paradigm, the concept of continuous improvement, and the Shewhart-Deming PDCA model is applied to every process, great and small, in the organization, starting with the core educational processes. In Japan and many U.S. companies this model is called the Deming model because they learned it from W. Edwards Deming. But Dr. Deming calls it the Shewhart model, since he learned it from his teacher, Walter Shewhart. Plan something, Do it, Check or Audit what we did (Study it, Deming now says), then Act on what was learned. That is what the model says.

Applied to higher education, the teachers and students Plan some educational process together. They then Do it, carry it out. During the process, and at the end, they audit, or Check on their process. Are we following the plan? Are we accomplishing our objectives? What is working? What needs to be modified? Mid-course corrections are made, so that the Check can result in some immediate process improvements. At the end of the process, a more thorough Check or audit is performed. Student evaluations, both quantitative and qualitative are gathered. Hard data is obtained as much as possible and is carefully analyzed. Nonquantitative information is also obtained and studied.

Then, after all the auditing is completed, the teachers and students step back and carefully evaluate. What did we learn from that effort? What part of the process worked well and is worth using again, worth building on in future learning efforts? How will we save the best of what we just did, institutionalize it, "hold the gain"? What part of our process did not work so well? Why didn't it? What can we learn from that? How will we modify future planning and doing to avoid those mistakes and do better next time? These and dozens of similar questions are asked in the fourth, evaluation, quadrant, which perhaps should be called

Shewhart-Deming PDCA model

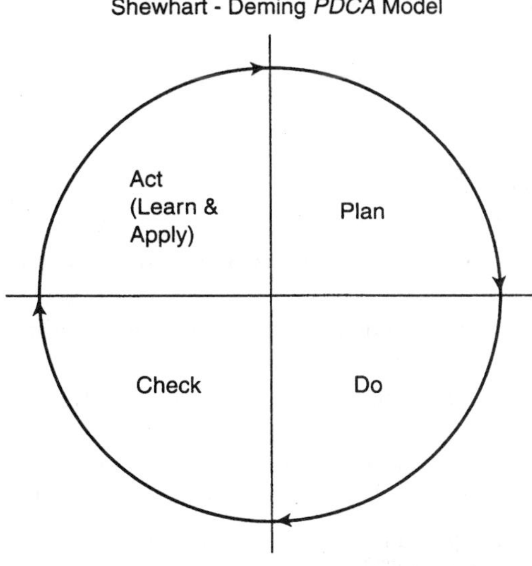

evaluation, or learn and apply, which seems to be nearer the authors' original intent. And then new Acts of learning are planned, based on this evaluation.

In this way every process is planned, done, checked on, learned from, and the learnings are fed into another round of planning, doing, checking and learning. Can you think of a better way to build in continuous improvement?

BENCHMARKING

In the old paradigm, faculty see no reason to learn from others about how to "teach" (or about how students learn). In fact, at its worse, the concept might be called: "You stay out of my classroom and I'll stay out of yours." This changed years ago in schools of education, and is certainly changing in some schools and departments now.

In the new paradigm, since continuous improvement is a fundamental value and goal and since the faculty are not teachers, they, together with the students in partnership, are constantly seeking the best examples, the best methods, the best processes, for learning and development of ableness to learn from. They seek, as does industry today, to learn from any organization, in any industry, in any part of the world, that is doing something well that we might learn from.

With the growing national attention to our national and international deficits and the growing awareness of the relationship of education to quality and productivity, there does seem to be a growing interest in benchmarking as a foundation for continuous improvement. Hopefully faculty everywhere will come to see that different students learn differently, that different courses need different approaches, and that involving the students in designing their own educational processes will pay off doubly: in improved processes now and in students more empowered to continue their own education for the rest of their lives.

Bibliography

Articles and Speeches

Axland, Suzanne. "Looking for a Quality Education?" *Quality Progress,* October 1991.

Flint, Anthony. "At Dartmouth, 'Educated Person' Redefined," *The Boston Globe,* April 8, 1992, pp. 21, 25.

Marchese, Ted. "A New Conversation about Undergraduate Teaching," *American Association of Higher Education Bulletin,* 1990.

Marchese, Ted. "TQM Reaches the Academy," *American Association of Higher Education Bulletin,* November 1991.

Porter, David B. "Course Critiques: What Students Can Tell Us about Educational Efficacy," *Proceedings of the Human Factors Society, 32nd Annual Meeting, 1988.*

Porter, David B. "Educating from a Group Perspective," *Proceedings of the Human Factors Society, 33rd Annual Meeting, 1989.*

Porter, David B., Megan E. Bird, and Arthur Wunder. "Competition, Cooperation, Satisfaction, and the Performance of Complex Tasks among Air Force Cadets," *Current Psychology: Research & Reviews,* Winter 1990–91, Vol. 9, No. 4, 347–354.

Porter, David B. "Total Quality Leadership," Chapter 11 in K. D. Lam, Frank D. Watson, and Steven D. Schmidt, *Total Quality: A Textbook of Strategic Quality Leadership and Planning,* Colorado Springs: Air Academy Press, 1991.

Porter, David B. "A Perspective on College Learning," *Journal of College Reading and Learning,* Vol. XXIV, Number 1, 1991.

Ricklefs, Merlin. "Total Quality Management in the Academic & Business Life of a University," Presentation at Lehigh University, Third Symposium on Quality in Action in Academe, July 29, 1992.

Books

Baugher, Kathy. *Learn: The Student Quality Team Process for Improving Teaching and Learning,* Birmingham: Samford University, 1992.

Glasser, William. *The Quality School,* New York: Harper and Row, 1990.

John W. Harris and J. Mark Baggett, eds. *Quality Quest in the Academic Process,* Birmingham: Samford University, and Methuen, MA: GOAL/QPC, 1992.

Light, Richard J. *The Harvard Assessment Seminars, Second Report,* Cambridge: Harvard University, 1992.

Ritter, Diane. *Education and Total Quality Management . . . A Resource Guide,* Methuen, MA: GOAL/QPC, November 1991.

Rogers, Carl, *Freedom to Learn for the '80's,* New York: Macmillan, 1983.

Seymour, Daniel T. *On Q: Causing Quality in Higher Education,* New York: Macmillan, 1992.

Seymour, Daniel and Casey Collett, *Total Quality Management in Higher Education: A Critical Assessment,* Methuen, MA: GOAL/QPC, 1991.

Appendix

Researching Quality Improvement Topics

By Kate Randall Haley and Harry Costin

The research process, like any process, is one that requires strategic preparation, careful execution, and revision based on feedback from results (not unlike the implementation of a total quality management program.)

Total quality management as a concept dates back to the early 1950s and was introduced as "total quality control." TQM, as a true subject heading utilized in indexes and abstracts to literature, did not emerge until the early 1980s. It was frequently used as an "identifier" or an unofficial subject heading in the 1970s. Many print indexes still required the researcher to look under "quality control" or for quality or process control as a part of a particular industry, such as aerospace or automotive. Now, however, TQM is ubiquitous, and the researcher must take care to look for quality initiatives once again in relationship to a particular industry or service area.

A recent glance at **ABI/Inform** listed nearly 500 entries under "total quality" in the descriptor field from January of 1997 alone, while **IAC SearchBank's General BusinessFile** listed 668 articles available from 1995 onward on "total quality management." This list could go ever onward, without even beginning to look at Internet resources!

If the researcher wishes to refine research strategies to manage optimally information retrieval, there are some key methods to follow. Clearly, the information is available, and it becomes a question of focusing on specific subtopics linked with total quality in order to improve your search results. The researcher must define the area in which he or she wishes to discover the use of total quality management processes as a tool within a particular industry or service area. For example, total quality initiatives have been in place successfully in the U.S. military, various hospital systems, and certain companies in the automotive industry for some time. TQM in higher education has become a major focus of many academic communities, and a number of Internet resources are devoted to this area alone.

Frequently, the researcher might also incorporate other terms, such as "benchmarking," or "business process engineering" or "reengineering" with TQM or total quality, in order to further refine a search strategy regardless of industry or service area.

A researcher may begin within the indexes and abstracts of business literature to look for applications of TQM principles in all possible industry and service areas. Some of the most useful of these indexes/abstracts are **ABI/Inform,** which is delivered within **ProQuest Direct,** and **Business Periodicals Index** and **IAC SearchBank's General BusinessFile,** all of which currently offer a significant proportion of full-text articles in addition to abstracts. These resources are available in print, CD-ROM, and electronically either via an Internet interface or through online services such as **DIALOG** or **WILSONLINE. DIALOG** also offers the capability of simultaneously searching many management-oriented databases, such as Management Contents, ABI/Inform, PAIS International, Harvard Business Review, Delphes European Business, and Economist Intelligence Unit (EIU): Business International. This is a boon to researchers, especially from an international perspective. It is not, however, free of charge. While many libraries will typically hold many CD-ROM databases that are generally available to the public, online access rarely is, and is usually on a fee-for-service basis. Always consult your local public or academic library professional for the types and costs of resources available.

Business literature is not the only place to search, however. Researchers should consider subject-specific databases, indexes, and abstracts, or CD-ROM or other electronic files in the various areas where they would like to find applications of total quality management principles. For example, the Cumulative Index to Nursing and Allied Health Literature (CINAHL) is available both in print and electronically, and both the Health Periodicals Database and MEDLINE database are available via the Internet and **DIALOG,** among many other medicine-related files. These resources would offer access to articles or books detailing TQM implementation in hospitals, nursing homes, and so on.

Another excellent source of information on quality in many areas is the **Anbar Management of Quality Abstracts,** available in print and on CD-ROM, accompanied by an electronic update service. It deals specifically with quality management issues, and includes regular references to quality sites on the Internet.

Many publishers specialize in certain areas of quality issues, among them the American Society for Quality (P.O. Box 3005, Milwaukee, WI 53201, 800-952-6587); Business One Irwin (1818 Ridge Rd., Homewood, IL 60430, 800-634-3961); Chapman & Hall (29 W. 35th St., New York, NY 10001, 212-244-3336); GOAL/QPC (13 Branch St., Methuen, MA 01844, 800-643-4316); Productivity Press (P.O. Box 13390, Portland, OR 97213, 800-394-6868); and John Wiley & Sons (605 Third Ave., New York, NY 10158, 800-225-5945.) This list is not exclusive, merely representative of publishers currently producing numerous titles related to total quality management. Catalogues are readily available from publishers (these days not only in print but also online) so that one can keep abreast of the most recent trends and purchase volumes directly if so desired.

The Internet is a rich source of information on total quality. In addition to numerous library online catalogs that may be searched for their holdings on quality topics, there are numerous Web sites devoted to quality management. Some which are notable are reproduced below.

If you are familiar with the previous edition of this book (entitled *Readings in Total Quality Management* in the first edition) you will have realized that the appendix on quality awards has been eliminated. The reason is that since the first edition Internet-based resources have become widely available. The following sites include all the information that was previously available in printed form, as well as many more, continuously updated resources.

American National Standards Institute
"The American National Standards Institute (ANSI) has served in its capacity as administrator and coordinator of the United States private sector voluntary standardization system for 80 years. Founded in 1918 by five engineering societies and three government agencies, the Institute remains a private, nonprofit membership organization supported by a diverse constituency of private and public sector organizations."

http://www.ansi.org

American Society for Quality (ASQ, previously ASQC)
ASQ is the leading U.S. quality organization and administers the Baldrige Award for the Department of Commerce and NIST. The site includes a wealth of useful information on quality related issues and standards, such as ISO 9000 and ISO 14000.

http://www.asq.org

National Institute for Standards and Technology (NIST)
NIST is the U.S. government institution that controls the Baldrige Award. Their Web site includes the award guidelines for several years (a useful feature to research the evolution of the quality movement), profiles of all previous Baldrige Award winners (some of which were included in the previous edition), and links to company sites of the Award winners.

http://www.quality.nist.gov

International Standards Organization (ISO)
ISO, the leading worldwide organization for standardization, is based in Switzerland. Their information-rich Web site includes a description of how international standards, such as the well-known 9000 series, are developed.

http://www.iso.ch

Free Online Publications

Quality Digest http://www.qualitydigest.com

Other TQM, ISO 9000, and Related Resources on the Internet
TQM Web pages, TQM tools, ISO standards and resources—an excellent collection.

http://fiat.gslis.utexas.edu/~rpollock/tqm.html

A collection of downloadable articles by well-known quality gurus can be found at:

http://curiouscat.com/guides/library.htm

Links to a long list of downloadable articles on a variety of quality topics can be found at the Department of Industrial Engineering at Clemson University.

http://deming.eng.clemson.edu/

Center for Organizational Learning at MIT
The site includes excellent articles by leaders in the field of organizational learning (among them, articles by Senge and Schein).

http://learning.mit.edu/res/wp/

European Quality Online

http://www.european-quality.co.uk

European Foundation for Quality Management (EFQM)
EFQM administers the European Quality Award, the European equivalent of the Baldrige Award. Their Web site describes the guidelines for the Award and includes other related useful information.

http://www.efqm.org

European Organization for Quality (EOQ)
The efforts of EFQM are complemented by EOQ. Their Web site describes European efforts for quality improvement. The site also includes useful links to other quality organizations in Europe, Japan (JUSE, the Union of Japanese Scientists and Engineers), and the U.S.

http://www.eoq.org

Other Resources

Other pathways on the Internet, using search engines such as Yahoo or Alta Vista, lead the researcher to files detailing books, articles, projects, and a variety of other items on total quality. Researchers now have a wealth of information available to them. As is often the case, an information professional can be the best guide through the forest to the specific trees that will yield the information the researcher is seeking. Always check with your business or other subject-specialist librarian for the sources that can give you the best results.

Index

A

B

D

H

I

N

O

P

Q

T

U

V

W

X

Y

Z

Reckoning with the Past

Historical Essays on American Evangelicalism from the Institute for the Study of American Evangelicals

Edited by D. G. Hart

A Division of Baker Book House Co
Grand Rapids, Michigan 49516

To David E. Johnston,
friend and supporter of the ISAE

Published by Baker Books,
a division of Baker Book House Company
P.O. Box 6287
Grand Rapids, MI 49516-6287

Printed in the United States of America

Library of Congress Cataloging-in-Publication Data

Reckoning with the past : historical essays on American evangelicalism from the Institute for the Study of American Evangelicals / edited by D. G. Hart
p. cm.
Includes bibliographical references and index.
ISBN 0-8010-4397-2
1. Evangelicalism—United States—History. 2. United States—Church history. I. Hart, D. G. (Darryl G.) II. Institute for the Study of American Evangelicals (Wheaton, Ill.)
BR1642.U5R43 1994
277.3—dc20 94-36916

Contents

Foreword

In the autumn of 1985 I drove from Ann Arbor, Michigan, through landscapes that lend imperious force to the Midwest's otherwise unmerited reputation for dullness, to South Bend, Indiana. The sky was damp, gray, featureless: it began halfheartedly to drizzle, too bored to rain.

I was making the trip to attend a seminar at the University of Notre Dame, under the aegis of its Cushwa Center for the Study of American Catholicism. In this setting, amid discussion of a book on religious unbelief, I met my first members of the passel of scholars associated with the Institute for the Study of American Evangelicals. Other historians of American religion were (with sometimes uncertain smiles) already coming to call them "the evangelical mafia." Precisely which *mafiosi* were present at the seminar my memory cannot at this distance in time establish. Surely Nathan Hatch, on the faculty at Notre Dame? Probably Mark Noll and Joel Carpenter, from nearby Wheaton College? What I do remember clearly is the contrast between the sky and these new acquaintances. All the effort nature poured into drabness was helpless to dull the edgy energy with which my colleagues pursued ideas—and vivisected them once captured.

As a rule, my penchant for plucking yellowed scraps of memory from the wastebasket of time is scrupulously repressed in print. I inflict it on you now, hapless reader, because this minor-league reminiscence suggests the salience of the authors and essays you, too, are about to encounter. I do not mean only their ever present élan, though that is to the point. More to the point, however, is a quality *absent* on that gray Indiana morning. Imagine us seated around a table in the University of Notre Dame, the intellectual citadel of Roman Catholicism in the United States. We are deep in discussion of a book that attempts sympathetically to explain the good reasons why many American intellectuals rejected Christianity. Neither context is one in which, a generation earlier, evangelical Protestants would have been apt to appear. Even today, they might not be expected to feel entirely at home. Yet *these* evangelicals clearly do. They exude not a whiff of cognitive dissonance.

This fact is key to the extraordinary influence of the authors represented in this volume. They are full, respected, and often admired members of the large, diverse, and mostly secular-minded guild of American professional historians; they put no metaphorical asterisk beside their names. The emphases of their numerous publications vary. The quality, naturally, varies also (though they have achieved an impressively high average). What does not change is commitment to the standards of contemporary historical scholarship—insistence on speaking in an ordinary professional voice to the entire community of historians.

Yet, in so speaking, these evangelical scholars have had something distinctive to say. This in large part is because they are not simply standard-issue historians. As believing Christians they understand the gravity of religious belief in everyday human lives. They take theological ideas seriously. They refuse to reduce faith to an epiphenomenon of social forces or material circumstances. Thus, while following secular-minded historians in exploring how everyday life shapes religious belief, how theological ideas reflect the culture that produces them, how social forces and material circumstances condition the expressions of faith, the ISAE historians have taught the rest of us sensitivity to the religious side of these dyads: appreciation that religion is a force in history in its own right.

Specifically, of course, American evangelical religion; for that species has remained the perduring object of their scrutiny. As a result of their efforts, those of us who cultivate that particular historical vineyard—or just stray into it occasionally—have seen its vines trimmed, its weeds cleared away, its walls rebuilt, its entire appearance very largely altered over the past two decades. I cite only three examples from the many and influential books and essays of Rawlyk, Wacker, and the rest. Hatch has placed a radically different cast of characters in the spotlight of the Second Great Awakening; Noll has mapped the largely unexplored relations of evangelical Christianity to late eighteenth- and nineteenth-century American intellectual life; Marsden has opened up the first really comprehensive view of the modernist-fundamentalist split that destroyed the old nineteenth-century evangelical establishment. Were a historian from 1973 to awake in 1993, the history of evangelicalism as it appears today would startle him out of his socks.

Yet it is not only the story of American evangelicalism that these historians are telling, but larger stories of American history—seen in new depth, heard with new resonances, in consequence of the evangelical perspective. To recur, conveniently, only to the three scholars just mentioned, none is merely telling us about evangelicalism. Hatch is also explaining the political culture of American republicanism; Noll is tracing the rise and fall of the Scottish Enlightenment as the hegemonic influence in American intellectual life; Marsden has recently turned to showing the consequences for higher education and academic knowledge of the secularization of American minds. The same point, *mutatis mutandis,* could be made about the other contributors to this collection.

All are uncovering the buried and ill-understood past of evangelicalism; all, in doing so, are revealing the centrality of evangelicalism in the wider American past. They have not soldiered alone on this historical project; but they have in many ways commanded it. So successful have these efforts proved that other historians of American religion are beginning to wonder—especially in relation to the nineteenth century—whether the repressed has returned so forcefully as itself to become the repressor; whether the once-marginalized have now marginalized the others; whether, in short, historians have made evangelicalism *too* central in our national story. Twenty years ago that claim would have appeared bizarre beyond belief. I note it now, not to enter a judgment of its accuracy, but only as evidence of a revolution worked within the last generation of professional historians.

If the Lenins and Trotskys of this revolution have been the writers of the essays before us, then the Bolshevik Party has had its headquarters at Wheaton College in Illinois. On that leafy suburban campus, at the Institute for the Study of American Evangelicals, the soviets and party congresses have held their sessions; the agitprop machinery has poured out its posters and leaflets. Under the successive directorships of three of the authors here represented—Carpenter, Hart, and now Blumhofer—the ISAE has established itself as the intellectual and organizational center of the New Evangelical History.

I can think of no other center for American historical scholarship in my professional lifetime that has worked quite the influence of the ISAE. Its methods (and here the Bolshevik trope collapses) have been unremarkable, simple, straightforward, and persistent. Perhaps ironically, few institutions bent on promoting a particular brand of history have shown less inclination to revivalist techniques or mentality than the ISAE (or perhaps aptly, since few institutions know better where revivalism is appropriate and where not). Modest but accurately targeted subventions have supported basic research. A strong publication program has kept the results of research before the community of historians. Possibly most effectively, a long and various series of conferences has brought together evangelical and other scholars, historians of evangelicalism and other historians, to share ideas on a wide range of historical problems. Secular and sober though they have been, these conferences have produced (metaphorically) the effect of a revival: they have converted a lot of scholars to the historical importance of evangelical Protestantism.

The essays before you go a long way toward explaining why.

James Turner
Professor of History
University of Michigan

Contributors

Edith Blumhofer, director, Institute for the Study of American Evangelicals, Wheaton College, Wheaton, Illinois.

Joel A. Carpenter, former director, Institute for the Study of American Evangelicals, and program director for religion, The Pew Charitable Trusts, Philadelphia, Pennsylvania.

Michael S. Hamilton, coordinator, Pew Evangelical Scholars Program, University of Notre Dame, Notre Dame, Indiana.

D. G. Hart, former director, Institute for the Study of American Evangelicals, and librarian and associate professor of church history and theological bibliography, Westminster Theological Seminary, Philadelphia, Pennsylvania.

Nathan O. Hatch, advisor, Institute for the Study of American Evangelicals, and vice president for graduate studies and research, University of Notre Dame, Notre Dame, Indiana.

George M. Marsden, advisor, Institute for the Study of American Evangelicals, and McAneney Professor of History, University of Notre Dame, Notre Dame, Indiana.

Mark A. Noll, senior advisor, Institute for the Study of American Evangelicals, and McManis Professor of Christian Thought, Wheaton College, Wheaton, Illinois.

George A. Rawlyk, advisor, Institute for the Study of American Evangelicals, and professor of history, Queen's University, Kingston, Ontario.

Harry S. Stout, advisor, Institute for the Study of American Evangelicals, and Jonathan Edwards Professor of American Christianity, Yale University, New Haven, Connecticut.

Grant Wacker, advisor, Institute for the Study of American Evangelicals, and professor of the history of Christianity, The Divinity School, Duke University, Durham, North Carolina.

Introduction

In a survey of works on American religion published in 1982, Martin Marty lamented the "paucity of good research" on evangelicalism and the absence of "more vitality in historical fields surrounding it."[1] The spate of informative and provocative writings on the evangelical tradition in America published within the last ten years suggests that historians and sociologists have taken Marty's complaint as a challenge. Bibliographies on American religion alone reveal that evangelicalism, once neglected by the academy, has become a live concern among scholars. For instance, in Ernest R. Sandeen's and Frederick Hale's 1976 bibliography, *American Religion and Philosophy,* the compilers chose not to use "evangelicalism" as a category in their subject index, an omission that implies that evangelicalism was not then a readily identifiable area of research. In contrast, two bibliographies have recently appeared that are dedicated exclusively to evangelicalism: *Twentieth-Century Evangelicalism: A Guide to the Sources,* edited by Edith L. Blumhofer and Joel A. Carpenter (Garland); and *American Evangelicalism: An Annotated Bibliography,* edited by Norris A. Magnuson and William G. Travis (Locust Hill). Even if one factors in the many primary works that these bibliographies include, the appearance of these volumes is indicative of the growing scholarly interest in American evangelicalism.

One obvious explanation for the burgeoning literature on American evangelicalism has been the resurgence of the movement itself since World War II. Journalists were quicker than historians and sociologists to note the mounting influence of evangelicals in American public life. Indeed, even since 1976, "the year of the evangelical" according to *Time,* evangelicalism has been perceived to be an increasingly important factor in electoral politics, whether through the candidacies of evangelicals such as Pat Robertson, evangelical lobby groups such as the Moral Majority, or through specific issues such as abortion. To be sure, assessing evangelicalism as a political phenomenon has produced some superficial literature from both the movement's advocates and critics. Yet, the resurgence of evangelicalism as a cultural force has prompted many scholars to take another look at a religious tradition that had been written off as unimportant.

1. Marty, "The Editor's Bookshelf: American Religious History," *The Journal of Religion* 62 (1982): 102.

Still another reason for the surge of scholarship on evangelicalism is that these books and articles have in many cases been written by evangelicals or by scholars from evangelical backgrounds. In his book on evangelical biblical scholarship Mark Noll observed that not since the turn of the twentieth century "have evangelicals participated in the larger scholarly community as they have during the last two decades."[2] Noll's description of evangelical biblical scholars is equally valid for evangelical historians and for the evangelical academy in general. Forty years ago, as George Marsden has written, there were almost no accomplished scholars in the evangelical community.[3] Those who were, such as Harold Ockenga, Carl Henry, and Edward Carnell, were engaged almost exclusively in theology. Today, self-conscious evangelicals can be found throughout the academy, doing competent work in a variety of disciplines. No doubt, the growth of evangelicals entering the historical profession accounts for much of the recent boom in historical studies of American evangelicalism.

The emergence of a significant number of evangelicals pursuing advanced training at the leading American graduate schools and conducting informed scholarship is certainly one of the remarkable features of evangelical history since World War II. Few observers or students of fundamentalism would have predicted that the heirs of what many thought to be an anti-intellectual movement would walk so confidently in the halls of mainstream academic institutions. In some ways, the creation of an evangelical academy was precisely what so-called progressive fundamentalists in the 1940s had in mind. Tired of the militant separatism and convinced that the movement needed an intelligent defense of the faith, evangelical leaders such as Ockenga, Henry, and Carnell pursued doctoral studies at so-called liberal institutions and promoted a vision for Christian scholarship that would change minds along the way to winning souls. Yet, the emergence of an evangelical academy cannot be explained strictly by the ideas of a few important individuals. Evangelicals, like most Americans, benefited from the dramatic expansion of opportunities in higher education during the post-World War II era. Likewise, evangelical intellectual achievement depended on the growing wealth and resources that American society provided for its middle class. As federal and state governments increased support for higher education, evangelical families sent more students off to college with higher professional expectations. Cynicism might suggest that the neo-evangelical rapprochement with the world of American learning was merely a rationalization

2. *Between Faith and Criticism* (San Francisco, 1986), 129.

3. Marsden, "The State of Evangelical Scholarship," *Christian Scholar's Review* 27 (1988): 348–52.

for the rising affluence of evangelicals. Still, any explanation for the dramatic increase of evangelicals involved in higher education must take into account the changing social base of the movement.

Another important factor in the flowering of historical literature on evangelicalism has been a historiographical shift that has transformed the academic study of religious history. Prior to 1965, the dominant approach to the history of religion in the United States was through the history of the Christian church (mainly Protestant). Indeed, American historiography throughout much of the twentieth century focused on the development of the dominant religious bodies and traditions, namely, the denominations that constituted mainstream Protestantism. Furthermore, the leading historians of religion taught for the most part at divinity schools and seminaries affiliated with the Protestant establishment. To be sure, historians working outside those institutions, such as Perry Miller, Ralph H. Gabriel, and Arthur O. Lovejoy made significant contributions. But even they were exploring movements, groups, and ideas that were central to uncovering the development of mainstream Protestantism.

During the 1960s, however, *religious* history began to replace *church* history. In part, this change was theoretical in nature. Historians who studied American religion abandoned the old style of historiography that was grounded in a theological or confessional understanding of the church for a methodology that was informed by the university world and explored religion as just one more phenomenon of human experience. This transformation was also closely attuned to the important cultural changes that the decade witnessed. The civil rights movement, protests against the Vietnam War, and the demands of modern feminists demonstrated to many that American ideals of freedom and equality did not extend to all segments of the United States. In an atmosphere that reveled in the diversity of American culture and questioned the dominance of any single cultural group, writing the history of American religion from the perspective of the history of mainline Protestantism became increasingly problematic.

It was not accidental, then, that the history of American evangelicalism gained considerable momentum during the last twenty years. Even though mainline Protestants and evangelicals share a similar heritage, evangelicalism, because of its association with fundamentalism, has been regarded commonly as a dissenting or outsider tradition. The shift within the discipline of religious history toward rediscovering the variety of American religion thus created an opening for scholars pursing the history of evangelicalism. Furthermore, mounting suspicions about the superiority of just one world view and the ensuing pluralism of the academy have permitted evangelical historians to be more open about their own convictions while striving to understand a neglected aspect of American religious history. Consequently, and somewhat ironically, at the same time that the study of non-mainstream traditions in American religion has taken root and blossomed so has the history of evangelicalism, a tradition with the same cultural roots as mainstream Protestantism.

Thus, the recent outburst of scholarship on evangelicalism is related directly to the growing numbers of evangelicals who are pursuing advanced degrees in history and religious studies. The Institute for the Study of American Evangelicals at Wheaton College is just one manifestation of these larger trends. The idea for the Institute arose most directly from a successful academic conference in 1979 on the Bible in American history, sponsored by Wheaton College and the Lilly Endowment. That meeting, and the resulting volume of essays, *The Bible in America: Essays in Cultural History* edited by Mark Noll and Nathan Hatch (Oxford, 1982), was just one facet of the growing interest among historians in the role of evangelicalism in American culture. Founded in 1982 by Noll and Hatch, the ISAE has continued to sponsor through the good graces of the Lilly Endowment and The Pew Charitable Trusts a number of programs to encourage the study of evangelical Christianity in America. Through its conferences it has drawn upon many of the scholars responsible for the recent interest in evangelicalism specifically and American religious history more generally. The ISAE has also nurtured close cooperation and fellowship among a handful of evangelical historians working in the field. It has, then, created a forum for developing a perspective on the history of American evangelicalism that is at once sympathetic with and critical of the movement.

This volume brings together a number of articles previously published by advisors and administrators of the ISAE that span the history of evangelical Christianity in America. It is intended, in one sense, to commemorate the tenth anniversary of the Institute. By collecting and making available these essays which were originally published in a number of scholarly journals dealing with American religious history, this book samples the wide range of topics, from seventeenth-century Puritanism to post-World War II neo-evangelicalism, upon which the recent flourishing of evangelical history has shed light. And by covering the span of American evangelical history, these articles provide a fairly coherent perspective on the development of this particular religious tradition. This is not to suggest that this volume deals with American evangelicalism in all of its variety, nor is our intent the imperialistic one of limiting the evangelical tradition only to the particular events, individuals, groups, and institutions mentioned in the following pages. Perhaps only readers will be able to determine whether this book represents the kind of "observer-participant" history that shows, as Leonard Sweet has written, that "the nature of genuine scholarship is critical engagement" and "interested love."[4] Whatever the assessment, our hope is that this book will provide a handy overview of evangelical history in the United States that taps the contributions made by some of the evangelical historians who have been closely associated with the Institute for the Study of American Evangelicals.

Reckoning with the Past is arranged chronologically, and its contents cover a variety of topics and issues within the history of American evangelicals. The essays in the first section by George Marsden and Harry Stout explore Puritanism in seventeenth-century New England. Marsden assesses one of Puritanism's foremost interpreters, Perry Miller, and Stout examines the social implications of the Puritans' theological convictions. The second section deals with the relationship between evangelicalism and the American Revolution. In his second essay in the volume, Stout traces the social dynamics of eighteenth-century revivals and their effects upon America's quest for independence. Nathan O. Hatch argues for the Puritan influence upon millennial expectations voiced by Protestant clergy during the war for independence. Mark Noll, in contrast, discusses the effects of revolutionary politics and philosophy upon evangelical religious thought. In the third section Hatch, Noll, and I demonstrate the growing diversity of American evangelicalism in the antebellum period. Hatch spells out the development of evangelicalism as a popular and democratic movement while Noll in two essays and I look at the impact of philosophical developments upon evangelical theology. The fourth section covers different aspects of evangelical experience in the late nineteenth century. Marsden considers the displacement of evangelicals within the academy. Grant Wacker notes the common evangelical roots of the theologies that diverged into fundamentalism and liberal Protestantism. In a similar fashion, Edith Blumhofer uncovers the influence of evangelicals with Reformed backgrounds upon Pentecostalism. The final section surveys some significant twentieth-century developments. George Rawlyk examines the origins of the fundamentalist controversy among Baptists in Canada and the effects of that struggle on higher education on both sides of the U.S.–Canada border. Marsden's essay on fundamentalism compares conservative Protestantism in America with its British counterpart. Joel Carpenter explores the surprising vitality and growth of fundamentalism during the 1940s in the emergence of neo-evangelicalism. And Wacker turns a perceptive eye to the emergence of Southern leaders within fundamentalism since World War II. The book concludes with an epilogue by Hatch (with assistance from Mike Hamilton) which

4. Sweet, "Wise as Serpents, Innocent as Doves: the New Evangelical Historiography," *Journal of the American Academy of Religion* 56 (1988): 413.

assesses the strengths and weaknesses of evangelicalism in the Billy Graham era.

Those readers who desire a ready and handy definition of evangelicalism will be disappointed by this volume. Considerable effort in recent years has been devoted to the problem of defining the term *evangelical.* Interpretations tend to stress either the theological convictions that unite evangelicals or the dynamics of evangelicalism as a social movement. Some have thought that the historians associated with the ISAE have tended toward a theological definition. Yet as the essays in this book make clear, the Institute has long recognized the diversity within evangelicalism. To be sure, the book is weighted toward Congregationalist and Presbyterian elites in the northeastern United States, but not to the exclusion of the Wesleyan/Holiness tradition (Blumhofer and Wacker's first essay), the populist impulse with evangelicalism (Stout's second essay, Hatch's second essay, Rawlyk, and Carpenter) or the contribution of Southern evangelicals (Wacker's second essay) and Canadians (Rawlyk). Yet the slant of this book toward evangelicals in Presbyterian and Reformed traditions is not without historical justification. As Grant Wacker has written of another ISAE publication, "If the Reformed tradition claims the lion's share of the entries in this volume, it may be because . . . Reformed evangelicals have proved themselves by far the most culturally aggressive members of the evangelical family."[5]

While this book avoids defining evangelicalism as either a social movement or a theological paradigm, it does highlight the tension within evangelicalism between theologians who speak for a certain intellectual tradition and lay believers for whom evangelicalism is a religion of the people. As Stout's and Hatch's chapters in the second section suggest, cultural elites who criticized the First and Second Great Awakenings would find it difficult to agree that evangelicalism should be defined as an intellectual tradition. Indeed, the heart and soul of evangelicalism have been the revival, and historically the methods and ideology of the revival have been directed against traditions of learning and social conventions. What was true for eighteenth-century revivals and Disciples of Christ in the antebel-

5. Wacker, "Twentieth-Century Evangelicalism: A Guide to the Sources," *Evangelical Studies Bulletin* 7, 2 (fall 1990): 8. On the historiographical debate surrounding evangelicalism, see Donald W. Dayton and Robert K. Johnston, eds., *The Variety of Evangelicalism* (Knoxville, 1991); Douglas A. Sweeney, "The Essential Evangelicalism Dialectic: The Historiography of the Early Neo-Evangelical Movement and the Observer-Participant Dilemma," *Church History* 60 (1991): 70–84; George M. Marsden, "The Evangelical Denomination," in *Evangelicalism in America,* ed. Marsden (Grand Rapids, 1984), vii–xix; Donald W. Dayton, *Discovering An Evangelical Heritage* (San Francisco, 1976); and Timothy L. Smith, "The Evangelical Kaleidoscope and the Call to Christian Unity," *Christian Scholar's Review* 15 (1986): 125–40.

lum era was also true, according to Wacker in his first essay, Rawlyk, and Carpenter, for the Holiness and fundamentalist movements in the late nineteenth and early twentieth centuries. A recurring impulse within evangelicalism has been a suspicion of formalism and tradition in religion and society. For this reason, the lay orientation of evangelicalism has been well adapted to the American environment where individualism and egalitarianism are valued so highly. Indeed, evangelicalism has often functioned as a vehicle for popular protest against religious hierarchies and by implication social privilege. Yet, as Wacker and Blumhofer also note, these popular expressions of evangelicalism have often constructed intellectual edifices of remarkable complexity. While Pentecostalism and higher-life theology (dispensationalism could also be added) appealed to people of limited economic means, those believers did not lack for theological controversy and intellectual debate.

A number of the essays that follow treat the theologians and ministers that gave shape to the evangelical intellectual tradition. Marsden's opening piece and Hatch's first essay show how important Puritan convictions were for later evangelicals. Indeed, the Bible, systematic doctrine, and Christ have been characteristic themes in American evangelical theology. Yet, evangelical religious thought has not been simply warmed-over Puritanism. As Noll's three pieces, Marsden's other essay on the evangelical academy, and my chapter make clear, Enlightenment philosophy has given evangelical theology its particular texture and hue. Specifically, the Scottish philosophy of common-sense realism not only prompted evangelical theologians to talk of the scientific character of their work, but also informed their moral reasoning and political and social views. Yet evangelical theologians clung to this philosophical outlook and so failed to adapt to many of the intellectual changes that would transform American higher education.

The readiness of evangelical theologians to appropriate Enlightenment philosophy underscores another theme, namely, that evangelicalism is at once repelled by and addicted to modernity. Evangelical intellectual life is just one example. Evangelicals have been remarkably open to some very modern ideas and at other times, for seemingly inexplicable reasons, adamantly opposed to the values of modern society. This characteristic has been especially prominent in recent evangelical history, as the essays in the last section reveal. Fundamentalism emerged in opposition to efforts that proposed to accommodate Christianity to modern intellectual developments. Yet for all of their hostility toward theological modernism, fundamentalists were busy spreading the faith with techniques and technologies of the most recent vintage. This pattern has repeated itself in the resurgence of the New Christian Right, as the epilogue demonstrates. Leaders of this movement hail from the South and lament the effects of modernization on their families, schools, and communities. At the same time they spread this message with all the glitz and savvy that modern technology and marketing strategies can muster. Stout's selection on the First Great Awakening and Hatch's second essay go a long way to solving this riddle by showing how evangelicalism from its inception relied upon the popular appeal of its messengers to express the discontent of ordinary believers.

Together, then, these essays demonstrate the diversity within American evangelicalism while also highlighting some common historical themes. Rather than settling definitional debates or invoking a pristine evangelical tradition, these essays will reveal the historical complexity of evangelicalism. The purpose of this book, then, is not unlike the aim of the Institute for the Study of American Evangelicals, which is to help evangelicals develop a mature understanding of their own heritage and to inform others about evangelicals' historical significance and contemporary role.

Part 1

Puritanism

1

Perry Miller's Rehabilitation of the Puritans: A Critique

George M. Marsden

Reprinted with permission from *Church History* 39 (March 1970): 91–105.

In the era between the Civil War and the Depression the mythical character called the "American Mind" was troubled. All was well during the day when prosperity and success faced him at every turn, but at night he would sometimes dream of his childhood and awake feeling strangely uneasy. His analyst explained that this tension was the product of latent guilt feelings and suggested for therapy that he read himself to sleep with recent studies of the oppressive effects of Puritanism on young national minds. Turning to these works, the "American Mind" found that the analyst had been quite right. The source of the guilt feelings, he discovered, was an irrational phase of his development called the Reformation. This phase had been dominant when he lived in New England (he since had moved to the Midwest), but he was assured that the latest scholarship had discovered its influence to be harsh, grotesque, superstitious, narrowminded, il-liberal, and worst of all intolerant.[1] The problem was, one expert informed him, that this era "was unleavened by

1. See, for example, Brooks Adams, *The Emancipation of Massachusetts* (Boston: Houghton, Mifflin, 1887), 42; James Truslow Adams, *The Founding of New England* (Boston: Atlantic Monthly Press, 1921), 174; and Vernon Parrington, *The Colonial Mind 1620–1800* (New York: Harcourt, Brace and Co., 1927), 15, 29.

the spirit of the Renaissance."[2] Another observed that the Reformation attitudes were a "subtle poison" flowing through the veins of the entire social organism.[3] Still another implied that the "splendor of the Renaissance" had been delayed three hundred years by Reformation intolerance.[4] Convinced that the openmindedness of the Renaissance was healthier than the irrational bigotry of the Reformation, the "American Mind" of this era began to feel easier about his past. He resolved to tolerate everyone, except of course his more conservative enemies whom he damned as "Puritan."

By the 1930s, however, Puritan baiting was becoming less and less entertaining. Living Puritans were becoming scarce, and the novelty of abusing Puritans of the past was wearing off. Then while American intellectuals, led by historians Samuel Eliot Morison and Kenneth Murdock, were cautiously considering allowing dead Puritans back into their club, Perry Miller confronted them in 1939 with the evidence that the Puritans were the most respectable of charter members. In *The New England Mind: The Seventeenth Century* he presented the startling assertion "that the reason later generations ceased marching to the Puritan beat was simply that they could no longer stand the pace."[5] In one stroke the last had been made first in American intellectual history. Paradise was regained.

Perry Miller's restoration of the Puritans is now so thoroughly accepted that it may be evaluated critically without seriously endangering the reputation of either the Puritans or of Miller himself. Almost without a doubt Miller was the greatest American intellectual historian of our era; yet no historian is immune from the prejudices of his age. As Carl Becker has observed, "All historical writing, even the most honest, is unconsciously subjective, since every age is bound, in spite of itself, to make the dead perform whatever tricks it finds necessary for its own peace of mind."[6] It is possible, therefore, to discover in Miller's portrait of the Puritans aspects which reflect the values of twentieth-century America as much as those of seventeenth-century New England.

In his most comprehensive work, *The New England Mind*, Miller begins his rehabilitation of the Puritan image by emphasizing Puritan piety.

2. Parrington, *op. cit.*, 5.
3. J. T. Adams, *op. cit.*, 66.
4. Brooks Adams, *op. cit.*, 1–2.
5. Perry Miller, *The New England Mind: The Seventeenth Century* (Boston: Beacon, 1939), 59 (hereafter cited as NEM). References in the text to *The New England Mind* all refer to this volume and not to the admirable sequel, *The New England Mind: From Colony to Province* (Boston, 1953).
6. Carl Becker, *The Heavenly City of the Eighteenth-Century Philosophers* (New Haven: Yale University Press, 1932), 44.

Critics prior to Miller had usually been most impressed by the rigor of Puritan *action* and had played the trick of evaluating the Puritans in terms of their acts in the spheres of politics, economics, and personal morality. Miller, on the other hand, observes that the action was only secondary in the Puritan scheme of things, and was worthless to the Puritan without the profound piety which was its source. Puritan piety, he says, was "one more instance of a recurrent spiritual answer to interrogations eternally posed by human existence." New England's founders were (perhaps like Kierkegaard or Kafka, it seems suggested) confronted with "an urgent sense of man's predicament." Their piety was not so much "Calvinist" (a term of opprobrium in twentieth-century America) as "Augustinian" (a term of approbation).[7]

Though Miller's portrayal of "The Augustinian Strain of Piety" in *The New England Mind* is itself impressive, it is overshadowed by his extensive and penetrating analysis of the Puritan intellect. By restoring the respectability of Puritan thought Miller answers the earlier critics most effectively, destroying their caricatures of the Puritans as narrow-minded obscurantists who made careers out of retarding the Renaissance. In Miller's works it is always clear that the Puritans were "spokesmen for what we call the Renaissance."[8] The inhabitants of seventeenth-century New England were not "as they are often pictured, merely dogmatic Calvinists," but rather "disciples of Erasmus and Colet."[9] Far from being irrational bigots, they were rationalists who precipitated a modification of Calvinism by gradually escalating the estimate of the capabilities natural to man. They were humanists who championed the latest intellectual fashion. "The fundamental fact concerning the intellectual life of the New Englanders is that they ranged themselves definitely under the banner of the Ramists." The "method" of Petrus Ramus "is a testimony to the importance of logic for the Renaissance mind."[10] It is a "typically Renaissance product" which "cleared away the rubbish of scholasticism." It is "the logic of a *Humanist.*"[11]

Such emphases on previously neglected aspects of the quality of Puritan intellect and piety have much that legitimately commends them to a twentieth-century audience. Yet when Miller deals with the *content* of Puritan religion his otherwise excellent account involves a subtle trick played on the Puritans themselves in order to win sympathy for them in

7. NEM, 4.
8. NEM, ix. Cf. Perry Miller and Thomas H. Johnson, eds., *The Puritans* (New York: Harper Torchbooks, 1963), 1:19 (from Miller's introduction).
9. *Puritans,* 24, 21.
10. NEM, 116.
11. *Puritans,* 30, 36.

the mid-twentieth century. In the foreward to *The New England Mind,* while attempting "to advertise his impartiality," he acknowledges his own point of view. "I wholeheartedly admire the integrity and profundity of the Puritan character," he writes, "but . . . I am far from sharing in its code or from finding delight in its every aspect."[12] Unquestionably both Miller and many twentieth-century readers find little delight in certain aspects of Puritan belief, and although Miller seldom presents any aspect of Puritanism inaccurately, he consistently weights his presentations in slight ways that will minimize such unattractive aspects of Puritan religion. To illustrate how these subtle modifications misrepresent the actual character of Puritanism, this study will consider the types of modifications that Miller consistently makes in four areas, Puritan biblicism, doctrinal formulations, emphasis on the place of Christ, and their Calvinism, and then illustrate how the modifications in each of these four areas contribute to a basic distortion of one of the most crucial of Puritan concerns, their doctrine of the covenant.

One aspect of Puritan thought which Miller seems to find particularly uninviting is its biblicism. Although he clearly states that the most basic source of Puritan ideas was the Bible,[13] he also goes out of his way to avoid suggesting the stereotyped conclusion that their biblicism amounted to "a brutal authoritarianism."[14] Accordingly, Miller almost never acknowledges the direct scriptural antecedents of specific Puritan concepts. The biblical arguments which were at the heart of nearly every Puritan statement are simply ignored. The result of these omissions is the occasionally quite misleading impression that the Puritans invented concepts which in fact they took directly from Scripture. In one of Miller's characteristic arguments that the Puritans were "carrying the frontiers of reason to the very boundaries of faith," he states, "Here was indeed a triumph in the justifying of God's way to man! Natural knowledge, such as all men can attain, cannot make a man holy, but it can at least render him inexcusable, and God is exculpated from the charge of injustice for his condemnation."[15] He neglects to mention, however, that this ingenious doctrine is precisely one of the arguments of Paul in Romans 1 and 2. The same applies to several references to the law as "schoolmaster." Miller suggests that the Puritans devised this idea in order to soften the demands of the law, viewing God "not so much as a mail-clad seigneur as a skillful

12. NEM, viii.

13. As, for example, NEM, x, 20; *Puritans,* 43–44.

14. NEM, 65.

15. "The Marrow of Puritan Divinity," *Errand into the Wilderness* (New York: Harper Torchbooks, 1964), 78; cf. 82. This essay was originally published in *The Publications of the Colonial Society of Massachusetts* for February 1935 (hereafter cited as "Marrow").

teacher."[16] Yet it turns out that both the phrase (schoolmaster) and its application are borrowed directly from Galatians 3.[17]

Granted that the biblical source of Puritan ideas is a commonplace observation and that Miller's exposition of extrabiblical influences is a valuable counterbalance to previous accounts; it is nonetheless not entirely accurate to write the intellectual history of the Puritans with only passing mention of the most important source of their ideas. The men who created the New England mind insisted on the principle of *Scriptura sola.* They were painstakingly scrupulous to avoid reading their own ideas into Scripture. Unquestionably, they did not always succeed; but doubtless also, they did succeed in a great many instances. Yet Miller seems to assume the Puritans were very seldom strictly guided by biblical precedents. He betrays this assumption, for instance, when he says, "For the content of their belief, for the meanings which they read into Scripture or the principles they deduced from it, the Puritans both in England and New England drew freely upon the stores of knowledge and the methods of thinking which were then available to educated men."[18] His implication is that Puritans normally either read meanings into Scripture or derived from its principles that were controlled by current intellectual fashion. Accordingly, readers of *The New England Mind* are likely to come away with the impression that the most important characteristics of the Puritan intellect were reverence for reason and particularly Ramist logic.[19] While it is certainly important to recognize that New Englanders "read the Word of God in the light of Ramus,"[20] it is very unlikely that the cautious Puritan exegetes would *characteristically* have allowed the lamp of Ramist logic (which after all was primarily a common-sense method of arranging arguments)[21] to observe the light of revelation.

A second aspect of Puritan thought with which Miller and most mid-twentieth-century readers have little patience is that of doctrinal formulations. Although Miller observes that systematic organization was an "obsession" with the Puritans,[22] he seldom presents the precise theolog-

16. NEM, 397, 384; "Marrow," 69, 82.

17. For other examples see NEM, 384, where Miller gives no hint that the concept of man's "debt to the law" is taken from Galatians 5:3; NEM, 40, where Genesis 1:28, the source of the "cultural mandate" (a standard Calvinist concept) is not mentioned; and the discussion on the covenant, below.

18. NEM, 89.

19. Miller does present a convincing argument for the case that Puritan confidence in reason had the *potential* for undermining the biblical norm. See, for example, NEM, 73.

20. NEM, 124.

21. Cf. Miller's own statement to this effect, *Puritans,* 29.

22. NEM, 95.

ical formulas which strictly defined the limits of their inquiries. Never does he deal with their creeds at any length (compare, for example, Williston Walker's *Creeds and Platforms of Congregationalism*). While he does discuss at some length such basic concepts as God, sin, regeneration, and especially the covenant of grace, he fails to define clearly other standard Puritan doctrines such as unconditional election, limited atonement, effectual calling, adoption, justification, sanctification, union with Christ, and perseverance of the saints. There is, of course, some merit in sparing modern readers the burden of mastering these concepts and their intricate interrelationships. Miller intentionally avoids "dealing with the verbal propositions through which the ideas were embodied in the technical handbooks," seeking rather "to understand the connotations behind these beliefs "without resorting to sanctimonious and hackneyed phrases."[23] The result is commendable. He reads far more between the lines than anyone previously had imagined, and with rare exceptions his insights are astute. Nonetheless, the drawbacks of this neglect of systematic doctrine must be acknowledged as well.[24] Most significantly, a detailed account of the Puritan mind with little regard for the detail of their finished theological system seems to suggest that their methods were more important than their results.

The lack of emphasis on the place of Scripture and doctrine suggests that Miller realized that the Puritans could not be rehabilitated in the mid-twentieth century unless they were dissociated as far as possible from their exclusively Christian emphases. This suspicion receives further confirmation when we realize that Miller all but ignores the most crucial aspect of any Christian system—that of the person and work of Christ. Other than in quotations from the sources, Christ is seldom mentioned except incidentally in relation to other teachings. At least, one hardly comes away from any of Miller's accounts with the feeling that Christ was even theoretically central in the Puritan system. Yet Miller makes no apologies for this omission. He even goes so far as to suggest that the Reformation was perhaps more engrossing to the Puritan mind than was the appearance of Christ.[25] Admittedly the Puritans were deeply engrossed in

23. NEM, 10.

24. Occasionally, it simply obscures the precision of Puritan thought. On 54, NEM, for instance, Miller invents the term *imperfect regeneration* to describe what is clearly the process of sanctification. In another place he virtually denies that the Puritans held to the dual character of the transmission of original sin as *both* inherited depravity and judicial imputation of guilt ("Marrow," 81). Cf. the "Savoy Declaration," 6. 2. 3, where this distinction is scrupulously maintained, Williston Walker, *Creeds and Platforms of Congregationalism* (New York: Charles Scribner's Sons, 1893), 367ff.

25. NEM, 467; cf. 45, where he claims that they "minimized the role of the Savior in their glorification of the Father." It is, of course, true that the sovereignty of God played

the intellectual battles of the Reformation; but if the doctrine of Christ was not often a subject of their disputations, it is only an indication that here was one area of almost universal agreement. Puritan sermons, the heart of their intellectual activity, abound with so many references to Christ that their sincere evangelical emphasis on the love of Christ is unmistakable.[26] Perhaps for this reason the importance of Christ to the Puritans is so patent that it requires only passing mention. Yet it is difficult to present a balanced portrait of the Puritan mind with little regard for the author and finisher of their faith.

By minimizing Scripture, systematic doctrine, and the role of Christ, Miller in effect seems to be engaging in a kind of demythologizing, or more properly "de-Christianizing," of Puritanism. This process is not by any means a fully developed thesis, but it is an undeniable subtle tendency.

Far more explicit, thoroughgoing, and misleading is Miller's attempt to dissociate the Puritans from a currently much less reputable aspect of their heritage—their Calvinism. Earlier historical critics had given John Calvin a very bad press. Miller, in response, attempted to place the Puritans in a more favorable light by asserting that "Simon-pure Calvinism is a much more dogmatic anti-rational creed than that of the Congregational parsons of Massachusetts."[27] As David Hall of Yale has recently pointed out, Miller simply accepted his predecessor's characterizations of Calvin's God as an arbitrary despot and then presented the Puritans as though they had lessened the severity of Calvin's system. Hall shows further that this provided a means of dramatizing the development of the Puritan intellect by suggesting that their most original contributions were efforts to make Calvin's "unpredictable deity" rational and comprehensible.[28] Miller claims that Calvin demanded that his disciples "contemplate, with steady, unblinking resolution, the absolute, incomprehensible, and transcendent sovereignty of God; he required men to stare fixedly and without relief into the very center of the blazing sun of glory."[29] On the other hand, the Puritans, while retaining some essential affinities to Calvin, reputedly transformed God into "a kindly and solic-

---

a major role in their thinking, but it does not follow therefore that they "minimized" the doctrine of Christ.

26. Cf. H. Richard Niebuhr, *The Kingdom of God in America* (New York: Harper Torchbooks, 1959), 94.

27. *Puritans,* 57.

28. David D. Hall, "The Puritans versus John Calvin: A Critique of Perry Miller, *The New England Mind,*" unpublished paper delivered at the Meeting of the American Historical Association, 30 December 1967. I am indebted to David Hall for furnishing me with a copy of this fine paper and for some useful advice and encouragement.

29. "Marrow," 51.

itous being."[30] "The God of the whirlwind" was changed to "the gentle father sorrowing for his lost children."[31] Miller is correct in maintaining that the Puritans viewed God (as Scripture does also) in many roles, not only as the hidden deity or mail-clad seigneur, but also as the benevolent father or skillful teacher. He is simply wrong, however, in supposing that Calvin did not view God in all these same ways.[32]

The fact of the matter seems to be that although Miller apparently read and comprehended nearly everything the Puritans wrote, he either knew or cared very little about Calvin. This may be illustrated in an astonishing way by examining his references to Calvin in "The Marrow of Puritan Divinity" and *The New England Mind.* In more cases than not his notes on Calvin are substantial misrepresentations.[33] In emphasizing the Puritan doctrine of judicial imputation of Adam's sin, for instance, Miller notes, "There is no suspicion of the legal imputation theory in Calvin (see *Institutes,* II, i, 7–8)."[34] When we do see the *Institutes* we find that, although Calvin does not describe imputation in precisely the same terms as do the Puritan "federal" theologians, he clearly both suggests and maintains that the transmission of sin is judicial as well as a natural inheritance. "Christ himself, the heavenly judge," says Calvin, "declares, in the most unequivocal terms, that all are born in a state of depravity and corruption." And the "sin of Adam renders us obnoxious to the Divine judgment."[35] Miller in another case, in explaining the Puritan doctrine (from Romans 1 and 2) that the light of nature makes man "inexcusable for a neglect of God's laws," asserts that the entire "direction" of this argument "had been condemned in Calvin in so many words."[36] The passage cited (from the *Institutes* 2. 2. 4), however, turns out to have nothing to do with the doctrine of inexcusability (which Calvin elsewhere explicitly defends), but rather is an attack on Pelagianism—a doctrine that was anathema to every self-respecting Puritan.[37] In a similar instance Miller

30. Ibid., 64; cf. 93.

31. NEM, 397.

32. See, for instance, John Calvin, *Institutes of the Christian Religion,* trans. Henry Beveridge, 2 vols. (Grand Rapids: Eerdmans, 1957), 3. 20. 36–40 on the fatherhood of God; 2. 7.11 and 2. 9. 5 on God's skill as a teacher; and cf. Calvin's denial that God acts with the "caprice of a tyrant," 3. 23. 2. (Hereafter Beveridge translation will be cited unless otherwise indicated.)

33. Discounting duplications, Miller cites Calvin's work ten times in these studies. Of these, eight misrepresent Calvin in some substantial way. The only one of Calvin's work ever cited is the *Institutes.*

34. "Marrow," 81n.

35. *Institutes*, 2. 1. 6, and 2. 1. 8; cf. 2. 1. 5.

36. "Marrow," 82 and 82n.

37. Here again the confusion on this point is created by Miller's speaking of a *potential* of Puritan doctrine as though it were an actuality. His misleading observations on the im-

makes the remarkable suggestion that John Preston's view of natural man's remaining rational abilities was closer to that of the deist Lord Herbert of Cherbury than to Calvin. "Calvin," says Miller, "is arguing for the utter incapacity of nature, relieved by occasional grants of power bestowed at the mere pleasure of an arbitrary sovereign."[38] Even in the passage noted *(Institutes,* 2. 2. 12–17), however, Calvin makes it perfectly clear that the depraved mind is not devoid of reason. "The human mind, however much fallen and perverted from its original integrity, is still adorned and invested with admirable gifts from its Creator," he says. Moreover, "it appears that one of the essential properties of our nature is reason, which distinguishes us from the lower animals."[39] An even clearer case of distortion is Miller's argument that men in 1600 demanded greater assurance of salvation than did men in 1550. "Calvin," he says, "had wisely advised caution in promising positive assurance, since predestination takes place in the inmost recesses of divine wisdom. . . ."[40] He then quotes a statement from Calvin which refers solely to the doctrine of election in general and not to the question of assurance, even though in the very same section Calvin states that *only* in the doctrine of election do we find "any sure ground of confidence" in our salvation.[41] On the same subject, while describing Calvin's supposed unblinking acceptance of predestination and his condemnation of speculations on the question, Miller cites a passage where Calvin is merely warning against such inquiries *going beyond Scripture* and is himself introducing a fifty-page exposition of the doctrine.[42] Similarly, Miller supports his claim that Calvin simply left it a mystery why men should do good works if grace is irrespective of works, by referring to a section of the *Institutes* on man's depravity;[43] he neglects to mention, however, two

---

plications of inexcusability seem all the more strange in the light of his mention in a previous note that inexcusability "is a good Calvinist doctrine" ("Marrow," 78n). Even in this previous note, however, Miller claims incorrectly that in Calvin, natural man's knowledge of natural law had "no validity for any further regulation of life" (i.e., further than showing their inexcusability), whereas Calvin says, "Nothing, indeed, is more common, than for man to be sufficiently instructed in a right course of conduct by natural law," *Institutes,* 2. 2. 22.

38. "Marrow," 75, 75n; cf. NEM, 186–87.

39. *Institutes,* 2. 2. 15, and 2. 2. 17. In each of the above instances Miller does sense differences in nuances between Calvin and the Puritans. The present analysis is not intended to deny that there were such differences. It does, however, point out that Miller exaggerates them to the point of distortion.

40. NEM, 370.

41. *Institutes,* 3. 21. 1. In this, as in the example that follows, Calvin warns only against speculations into the divine mysteries that go *beyond* Scripture. Cf. 3. 24. 4, for a more complete statement on election as the primary ground of assurance.

42. "Marrow," 51; cf. *Institutes,* 3. 21–25.

43. *Institutes,* 2. 2. 1; cited in NEM, 367 and in "Marrow," 54.

other passages where Calvin explains the very issue at length.[44] In all these cases it is clear that the trick Miller plays in the interest of refurbishing the Puritan image is not on the Puritans themselves, but on the most influential of their immediate predecessors.

The extent to which each of the foregoing aspects of the rehabilitation process controls Perry Miller's account of the New England mind can best be demonstrated by a consideration of his treatment of the covenant of grace, a concept that he correctly maintains played a crucial role in Puritan thought.

The covenant of grace, according to Miller, was the Puritan divines' most ingenious stratagem for resolving the dilemma of maintaining human responsibility in a deterministic system, and hence the major component in their "revision of Calvinism."[45] Miller therefore repeatedly presents the covenant as though it were part of a conscious plot by Puritan ministers to promote morality. "The divines," he says, "had to discover some more explicit grounds on which to plead the necessity of works." The covenant was "an extremely subtle . . . device within the framework of predestination for arousing human activity." It was "a juridical relationship slyly substituted for the divine decree."[46]

In fact, however, it seems that Miller has slyly substituted his plot for the actual development of the covenant doctrine. First of all, he minimizes the extent to which the concept of the covenant of grace was derived directly from Scripture.[47] He does acknowledge, but only in the appendix to *The New England Mind,* that the covenant "is found in the Old Testament in a sense not too remote from that in which they took it."[48] Nonetheless Miller clearly considers such a biblical precedent almost incidental to the Puritans' motives for accepting the covenant teaching. It is of course possible that he is correct in suggesting that the covenant became popular in the sixteenth and seventeenth centuries because of the appeal of contractualism to the spirit of the age and because of its usefulness in explaining man's responsibilities to a sovereign God. The simpler

44. *Institutes,* 2. 5. 1–7; 3. 23. 9–14.

45. NEM, 396.

46. NEM, 368; NEM, 394; "Marrow," 73.

47. With regard to the social covenant Miller acknowledges the scriptural origins more prominently (NEM, 399). Here his contention that this was designed primarily to encourage obedience to the government is more satisfactory than is the same argument with regard to the covenant of grace, since in the social covenant the complicating feature of the gracious work of Christ is removed. The development of the Congregationalist church covenant, for which there is less biblical precedent, presents the best case for showing that the Puritans simply made a logical (probably Ramist) extension of the concept to another sphere.

48. NEM, 502. Cf. "Marrow," 61, where Miller describes how the covenant was given to Abraham.

explanation, and the one the Puritans themselves would have given, however, seems far more probable. The covenant doctrine was emphasized primarily because it was discovered to be a central biblical concept. It was emphasized in the sixteenth and seventeenth centuries (rather than in some previous era) because the Protestant Reformers studied the whole Scripture intensively and demanded that it all be taken seriously and, whenever possible, literally. This was particularly important with regard to the Old Testament, which since the time of Augustine had been frequently allegorized and seldom studied systematically and where the idea of covenant *(berith)* appears hundreds of times. It is hardly surprising, therefore, that the Puritan interpretation (which, incidentally, included the New Testament explanations as well) resembled the biblical interpretation. The development of the covenant doctrine was basically one more instance of the Protestant recovery of biblical teaching. That this is the case is supported by the fact that the covenant doctrine began to appear in numerous places almost as soon as the Reformation had begun. Zwingli, Oecolampadius, Bullinger, Bucer, Tyndale, and several lesser figures developed early formulations of the concept.[49] The connections among these as well as their connections with the Puritans are not entirely clear. But a major part of the explanation is most likely that they all read the same source.

Miller's second offense in his treatment of the covenant of grace is that in the course of his argument he inadvertently demolishes the precision of Puritan systematic theology. Anxious to dramatize the Puritan pastors' zeal to prevent moral laxity, Miller claims that "the final outcome in all New England preaching of the covenant theory was a shamelessly pragmatic injunction. It permitted the ministers to inform their congregations that if any of them could fulfill the Covenant, they were elected."[50] Such statements, he contends, were designed to promote morality because faith was impossible without performance, and the performance required was stated in the moral law.[51] His implication is that New England ministers were informing their congregations that if they tried to fulfill the moral law they would contribute something to their salvation. But this would be the exact opposite of what the Puritans actually said about the covenant of grace. The covenant was of *grace* precisely because it could not be *fulfilled* by good works. There had been a "covenant of works"

49. Leonard J. Trinterud, "The Origins of Puritanism," *Church History* 20 (1951): 39–41; Jens G. Moeller, "The Beginnings of Puritan Covenant Theology," *Journal of Ecclesiastical History* 14 (1963): 46–54; and Everett H. Emerson, "Calvin and Covenant Theology," *Church History* 25 (1956): 136–37.

50. NEM, 395, and "Marrow," 88.

51. NEM, 396.

with Adam; but when Adam fell this was replaced by the covenant of grace. Repeatedly the Puritans maintained that faith (which is not a work but a gift of grace) is the only requirement of this new covenant, and that man can do no work to *fulfill* its terms.[52] True, they did say that there is no faith without good works. But to say that works proceed from faith or that faith without works is dead is hardly new with the Puritans.

The ambiguity Miller permits regarding Puritan covenant doctrine is closely related to his minimization of the place of Christ in their thinking. If we are to believe the Puritans' own statements, the gracious work of Christ is central for understanding the covenant of grace; yet Miller mentions this aspect only in passing.[53] According to the Puritans, the covenant of grace was fulfilled by Christ alone. Though the requirements of the moral law were an integral part of the covenant, no man after Adam's fall could hope to keep those requirements. Christ, however, by his perfect obedience and sacrifice had perfectly kept the law and thus satisfied God's justice.[54] Seen in this light, the covenant adds relatively little as a means of urging good works. It is a contract which God graciously offers to men, and it does demand obedience. But since man cannot fulfill his side of the contract, it augments the incentive to obey God only slightly. The only incentive provided derives from the relation of the covenant concept to the idea that the works of regenerated men will be graciously accepted and rewarded despite their manifold imperfections.[55] Nevertheless, man's duty to keep God's law as well as God's condescending love in accepting men's unprofitable works can be (and often has been) preached just as effectively without any explicit reference to the covenantal relationship.[56]

Miller's mistreatment of the Puritan emphases concerning the covenant seems relatively slight compared to his abuse of Calvin's doctrine.

52. See, for instance, Walker, *Creeds and Platforms of Congregationalism,* the "Savoy Declaration," 8. 3: ". . . the covenant of grace; wherein he freely offereth unto sinners life and salvation by Jesus Christ, requiring of them faith in him, that they may be saved. . . ." And 16. 5: "We cannot by our best works merit pardon of sin, or eternal life. . . ." Notice also that men's "ability to do good works is not at all of themselves, but wholly from the Spirit of Christ. . . ." 16. 3.

On faith as a gift of grace, see "Savoy Declaration," 14. 1. Miller neglects this aspect when he suggests that the covenant is "a *quid pro quo,* an 'if I believe' necessitating a 'you have to save me,'" rather than involving "irresistable grace, unexpected and undeserved." "Marrow," 71, cf. NEM, 389.

53. NEM, 377, 383, for example.

54. "Savoy Declaration," 8. 5.

55. "Savoy Declaration," 14. 5, 6; cf. 7. 1. Miller does mention this aspect (NEM, 387), but he does not follow its implications in his subsequent analysis (e.g., NEM, 395).

56. In the "Savoy Declaration," for instance, the covenant is never mentioned in the chapter on "Good Works," and the primary ground for urging obedience is simply that God demands it.

In this historical trick Calvin is clearly the straight man. Calvin, who reputedly "made hardly any mention of the covenant," is said to "turn in his grave" as the Puritan theologians made the covenant "the foundation for the whole history and structure of Christian theology."[57] "The horrified ghost of Calvin shuddered" as he beheld "his theology twisted into a spiritual commercialism."[58] Though picturesque, this portrait of Calvin is an inaccurate caricature. We can quickly see how remarkably inaccurate it is by comparing Calvin's own statements on the covenant to the supposed Puritan modifications of Calvinism. From several recent studies of Calvin's doctrine it can be shown not only that Calvin knew much of the covenant but that he developed its implications concerning the unity of Scripture, God's sovereignty, and man's responsibility in very nearly the same ways as did the Puritans.

Though the covenant is not prominent in the *Institutes,* it does appear and plays an important role in the defense of the continuity of the administration of grace in the Old and the New Testaments and in the corollary argument for infant baptism (based on continuity of circumcision and baptism as covenantal signs).[59] Calvin says, for instance, "The covenant of all the fathers is so far from differing substantially from ours, that it is the very same; it only varies in its administration."[60] Thus when Miller pictures the Reformer turning in his grave as Williams Ames announces that since Abraham there has been one covenant, "yet the manner . . . of administering this new Covenant, hath not alwayes beene one and the same . . . ," Miller is failing to recognize that in this very instance, "Ames is merely quoting Calvin, as every Calvinist theologian did."[61]

Calvin's fullest exposition of the implications of the covenant of grace for understanding God's sovereignty and man's responsibility is found in his sermons on Deuteronomy, preached in 1555 and 1556. These sermons leave no doubt that Perry Miller was mistaken in supposing that the Puritans contrived the covenant concept in order to circumscribe the sovereignty of Calvin's God or to transform "the hitherto stern Deity" into a "condescending," "kindly and solicitous being." In support of this ar-

57. "Marrow," 60.

58. NEM, 389.

59. See the excellent treatment of these subjects by Anthony Hoekema of Calvin Theological Seminary, "The Covenant of Grace in Calvin's Teaching," *Calvin Theological Journal* 2 (1967). Hoekema argues that "for Calvin the covenant idea is the thread which ties salvation history together," and provides documentation for this from seven separate sections of the *Institutes*; 136–39.

60. *Institutes,* 2. 10. 2 (John Allen translation).

61. Moeller, "Puritan Covenant Theology," 49n; "Marrow," 69. Miller claims incorrectly that "The beginnings of this conception are to be found in Ames, and it was probably his chief contribution to the system."

gument Miller quotes from John Preston, "how great a mercie it is, that the glorious God of Heaven and . . . he the Creator, and we but the creatures; and yet he is willing to enter into Covenant, which implyes a kinde of equality between us."[62] But compare Calvin:

> The creatures do see that the living God abases himself so far as to be willing to enter into treaty with them, as if he should say, Come, let us see at what point we are: indeed there is an infinite distance between you and me. I might command you what seems good to me without having anything further to do with you . . . yet . . . I am willing to govern you, and you shall be as my little family. . . . I am here ready to enter into covenant with you, and to bind myself to you.[63]

The mutuality of this covenant is likewise clear in Calvin's sermons. He says, for instance, "There must be this mutual bond between us, that since God binds himself so to us, we must also submit ourselves wholly to him."[64] Miller presents an almost identical passage from John Preston's comments on Genesis 17, claiming that such condescension of God, amounting to "mutual obligation," is another Puritan invention. Here Miller's note reads, "The innovation of this theology upon the theology of Calvin becomes apparent when its interpretation of Biblical texts is compared with him. Calvin, for instance, finds no such proposal in Genesis, XVII. . . ."[65] Had he turned to the more obvious source than the *Institutes,* he would have found that Calvin in his *Commentary* on Genesis 17 represents God as saying, "whereas I owe thee nothing, I condescend graciously to engage thee in a mutual covenant."[66]

Calvin also used the covenant of grace to urge man's moral responsibilities in a way almost identical with that which Miller attributes to Puritan ingenuity. Miller claims that Calvin "simply disregarded" the problems in motivation implicit in *unconditional* election, whereas the great achievement of the Puritans was their resolution of such problems by developing a "conditional covenant."[67] However, as Anthony Hoekema in his fine study of Calvin's covenant teaching observes, "Calvin did not

62. "Marrow," 64.

63. Quoted in Hoekema, "Covenant . . . in Calvin," 142, from *Corpus Reformatorum,* 26. 242, trans. Arthur Golding, *Sermons of Master John Calvin upon the Fifth Book of Moses called Deuteronomie* (London, 1583), 179–80.

64. Quoted in Hoekema, "Covenant . . . in Calvin," 145 from Golding, *op. cit.,* 913b. See Hoekema, 140–44, for further examples of Calvin's teachings on the above points.

65. "Marrow," 61n.

66. *Commentary on Genesis,* Calvin Translation Society edition (Edinburgh, 1847), 444; cf. Moeller, "Puritan Covenant Theology," 49, and Hoekema, "Covenant . . . in Calvin," 143.

67. NEM, 395; cf. "Marrow," 88.

hesitate to speak of conditions of the covenant."[68] Already in the *Institutes* Calvin, speaking of God's rejection of some men, says, "For the condition had been laid down that they should faithfully keep God's covenant which they faithlessly violated."[69] In his sermons on Deuteronomy he elaborates on such moral obligations regarding the elect:

> For this reason we must be aroused and spurred on by his promises to serve him. Thus we see how the conditional promises shall not be in vain in respect to us, namely, when they are referred to the freely bestowed goodness of God, where he receives us though we are not worthy to be so received. . . .[70]

Surely this is precisely the emphasis which Miller thought was so novel with the Puritans. Moreover, it makes clear what was clear also to the Puritans (but not consistently so in Miller's account of them), that God accepts the good works of the elect not because they fulfill the conditions of the covenant, but in spite of the fact that they do not. The conditions of the covenant "are real, but not meritorious."[71] Only with this balance, which the Puritans following Calvin maintained, could they avoid the Arminian implications which Miller reads into the covenant of grace.

It must be admitted, of course, that Calvin was not a covenant theologian in the sense that Ames or Preston was. The covenant doctrine is not conspicuous in much of his work. Furthermore, he did not extend the terminology to concepts such as the "covenant of works," the "covenant of creation," the "covenant of nature," or the "church covenant."[72] Nevertheless, there is sufficient evidence to support Hoekema's contention that, although the covenant of grace was not the one all-controlling principle in Calvin's theology, it was (at least by the time of the Deuteronomy sermons) "the key to Calvin's understanding of the God–man relationship."[73]

The question of whether the Puritans received their basic notions of the covenant directly from Calvin or from somewhere else remains, despite several competent studies of the subject,[74] a moot point. One reason may be that by the Puritan era the covenant idea was already so generally dis-

68. Hoekema, "Covenant . . . in Calvin," 155. Hoekema's study makes no reference to Miller.

69. *Institutes*, 3. 21. 6 (Battles translation).

70. Quoted in Hoekema, "Covenant . . . in Calvin," 147, from Golding, *op. cit.*, 923–24. See Hoekema, 144, 155–61 for numerous other examples of how Calvin developed this doctrine, together with a valuable exposition.

71. Hoekema, "Covenant . . . in Calvin," 155.

72. Cf. Trinterud, "Origins of Puritanism," 48.

73. Hoekema, "Covenant . . . in Calvin," 140; cf. 134.

74. See especially, Trinterud, "Origins of Puritanism"; Moeller, "Puritan Covenant Theology"; and Emerson, "Calvin and Covenant Theology."

seminated that it could have been found almost anywhere. A further explanation suggests itself as well. Since Calvin developed the implications of the covenant doctrine in his Deuteronomy sermons preached during 1555 and 1556, and since this was the very time that a considerable number of the Marian exiles were in Geneva, is it not possible that some of those Englishmen tutored in covenant doctrine from Calvin's pulpit carried the teaching, nearly full grown, back to Elizabethan England?[75]

Whether or not the covenant doctrine was derived directly from Calvin, it is abundantly clear that with regard to the covenant of grace and its uses the teachings of New England's Puritans were consistent with those of the Genevan reformer.

At the end of these critical remarks it is important to point out that the vast majority of what Miller says about the Puritan mind still stands. *The New England Mind* remains one of the great masterpieces in American intellectual history. Its flaws are few and, except for those concerning Calvinism and the covenant of grace, are matters of emphasis that add as much as they detract. In almost every case Miller at least *mentions* those aspects of Puritanism that do not fit the main themes of the drama he is portraying. Miller's excellence resided in his ability to read between the lines and then to translate seventeenth-century statements into twentieth-century meanings. The result is a shift in balance. When Miller dwells extensively on what is between the lines, the contents of the lines themselves often become buried in the middle of paragraphs. When he interprets Puritan thought for his contemporary audience, concepts which the Puritans themselves considered most essential are lost among the riches of the comments of the twentieth-century observer.

The quality of Miller's rehabilitation of the Puritan image should not be taken lightly either. His work was a revision, and like all revisions errs somewhat in the other extreme. Certainly Miller played fewer historical tricks on the Puritans than did his American predecessors. His contribution to both understanding and appreciating Puritanism is invaluable. He does, however, restore the Puritan image at the expense of important aspects of Puritan theology and religion. When we remember, as Miller has demonstrated, that the Puritans were tough-minded men of the Renaissance, let us recall also that they were uncompromising Christians and (in the twentieth-century view) bigoted Calvinists. As for the thesis that the covenant of grace represented a revision of Calvinism, Miller has created a myth that has been so elegantly presented and widely repeated that it will be difficult to destroy.

75. This suggestion would be supported by Moeller's evidence of the influence of the Genevan Bible of 1560 in disseminating covenant views in England; "Puritan Covenant Theology," 57.

2

Word and Order in Colonial New England

Harry S. Stout

Many scholars see in American Puritanism the first statement of America's self-consciousness as a divinely appointed "redeemer nation." Most recently, and in greatest detail, Sacvan Bercovitch describes how the Puritans' enduring sense of millennial expectancy and special calling came to represent a national "ritual of consensus" that helped to bring the new nation together around a common messianic identity.[1] The role of the Bible for personal faith and social order is central to such understanding of the Puritans' identity. Whether as the "covenanted society," "theocracy," "Bibliocracy," "new Israel," or "Bible Commonwealth," the Puritan experiment depended on the Bible. It was the Puritans' commitment to reading and comprehending the Bible, after all, that wrought in New England an educational system that made Yankees, on the eve of the American Revolution, one of the most literate peoples in the world.[2]

1. Sacvan Bercovitch, *The American Jeremiad* (Madison, Wis., 1978).
2. Kenneth A. Lockridge has argued that male literacy in eighteenth-century Anglo-America hovered around 60 percent, except in Scotland and New England, where, by the end of the century, rates approached universal male literacy. Apparently the only force suf-

It is surprising then, that with all of the attention to Puritan biblicism, the actual translation used in New England has not come under very close scrutiny. Entire histories of Puritanism in Old and New England have been written which do not even consider the possibility that a crucial element may have been the particular translation employed. And this failure is symptomatic of an even greater omission that skims over the Bible generally in accounting for the rise of Puritanism and moves directly to landmark theological statements circulated among the civil and ecclesiastical hierarchy.[3] To the extent that students of English and American Puritanism ignore this most basic of all texts in reconstructing the popular wellsprings of the movement they overlook the basic life work of an entire people whose *sole* reading habit was the vernacular Bible. In this essay we shall see that Puritanism was actually the product of two Bible translations, each of which dominated at different stages in the movement's history, and each of which served different needs and purposes. In its infant stage, English Puritanism was organized around the Genevan translation of 1560. As the movement grew in power and influence, clerical loyalties switched to the Authorized or "King James" version of 1611. This later version furnished the primary text on which New England's Bible Commonwealth would rest.[4]

The roots of the earlier Genevan translation go back to the age of religious persecution under the reign of Mary Tudor (1553–58), when a group of committed Protestants fled the homeland eventually to settle in Geneva.[5] By 1556, two of these exiles, the Hebrew scholar Anthony Gilby

ficient to generate a significant change in literacy in this period was the intense biblicism and associated schools of these Calvinists. See Lockridge, *Literacy in Colonial New England: An Enquiry into the Social Context of Literacy in the Early Modern West* (New York, 1974), 72–101.

3. George M. Marsden has suggested that Perry Miller underestimated the extent to which the Puritan thought was biblically oriented. See Marsden, "Perry Miller's Rehabilitation of the Puritans: A Critique," *Church History* 39 (1970): 91–105.

4. The use of the Authorized Version in New England printed sermons is well known. In addition I have discovered that unpublished sermon manuscripts throughout the colonial period rely upon the Authorized Version or free renderings of Greek and Hebrew texts. At the same time, sufficient numbers of Genevan Bible translations survive in historical archives to indicate continued popular usage of the Geneva Bible in New England. I am indebted to Rebecca Guild for cataloguing the Bible holdings of the following archives: Harvard University Libraries, Episcopal Theological Seminary Library, Massachusetts Historical Society, and the Congregational Historical Society. The condition of colonial Bibles reflects the lack of attention given them in historical research. For the most part they are haphazardly maintained and poorly indexed.

5. The Genevan exiles who would prepare the English translation of the Bible were a splinter group from the English community in Frankfurt. For a contemporary account of the differences that led to the Genevan removal, see William Whittingham, *A Brief Discourse of the Troubles at Frankfurt 1554–1558 AD* (privately printed, London, 1907).

and William Whittingham, later Dean of Durham, conceived a plan to publish a new translation of the English Bible that would be aimed primarily at a common lay audience.[6] At that time vernacular Bibles were still in their infancy, and ordinary people had no ready access to the Word of God in an intelligible and affordable edition. Until that need was met, the Reformation ideal of *sola Scriptura* would remain just that: an ideal with no realistic prospect of implementation in a living society. The exiles' proposed translation, then, represented the necessary precondition for a biblically-based culture organized solely on God's ordinances.

The exiled translators could not have been better situated for their ambitious undertaking. In addition to the earlier translations of Martin Luther's German edition (the prototype of all vernacular Bibles), and the earlier English translations of William Tyndale (1494–1536) and Myles Coverdale's "Great Bible" (1550 edition), they had direct access to the cultural milieu of Geneva, then the leading center of print and biblical scholarship in the Reformed Protestant world.[7] Under the theological leadership of John Calvin, the textual criticism of Theodore Beza, particularly his Latin translation of the New Testament (1556), and the printing presses of Robert Estienne, vernacular translations of the Bible were simultaneously undertaken in French, Italian, Spanish, and English. Diverse scholars willingly collaborated on the various translations and shared textual explanations, woodcuts, maps, and commentaries that could be included in each translation.[8] By means of "suche diversities of translations in diverse tongues," the English translators were able to incorporate innumerable improvements in their translation, making it one of the finest vernacular editions of its day.

The "great and wonderful worke" was completed in 1560 and copies were available in England almost immediately. Despite the fact that the "Bishop's Bible" was sanctioned by ecclesiastical authority for use in public worship, the Geneva Bible circumvented official channels and found its way into common dwellings throughout the realm. Within a generation it had outstripped all other versions in circulation and came to stand as the unchallenged emblem of popular piety in the English

6. Others thought to be involved in the translation at various stages include John Knox, Myles Coverdale, Christopher Goodman, Thomas Sampson, John Bodley, and William Cole.

7. Lewis Lupton, *A History of the Geneva Bible,* 7 vols. (London, 1966), 1:67.

8. For descriptions of the textual and exegetical aspects of the Genevan translation see Lewis Lupton, *A History of the Geneva Bible;* Brooke Foss Westcott, *A General View of the History of the English Bible,* 3d ed. (reprinted New York, 1972), 90–95; Basil Hall, *The Genevan Version of the English Bible* (London, 1957); S. L. Greenslade, ed., *The Cambridge History of the Bible,* 3 vols. (Cambridge, 1963), 3:155–59; and F. F. Bruce, *The English Bible: A History of Translations* (New York, 1970), 86–92.

realm.[9] Biblical scholar F. F. Bruce points out that the Genevan version "became the household Bible of English-speaking Protestants . . . its excellence as a translation was acknowledged even by those who disagreed with the theology of the translators."[10] When presented with their own copies of the Geneva Bible, common English readers encountered a document that was directed to their convenience and comprehension in every way. Physically, the work was issued in a relatively inexpensive single volume, Roman type edition that was conveniently organized into sentence units of "verses" and "chapters." Substantively, they enjoyed a "plainly rendered" translation expressed in the language of their own idiomatic speech. As the Bible's preface to the reader made plain, the translation was not aimed at learned scholars but at common readers throughout the realm. Textual decisions were governed by the needs of "simple readers" to understand the "hard places" of Scripture. Like the "plain style" sermons that flowed from it, the translation was devoid of circumlocutions and Latinisms which would only distract the reader from a text "which is the light to our paths, the keye of the kingdome of heaven, our comfort in affliction, our shielde and sworde against Satan, the schoole of all wisdome, the glasse wherein we beholde God's face, the testimonie of his favour, and the only food and nourishment of our soules." The Geneva Bible was, in brief, the first English translation that could legitimately be characterized as a people's Bible.

To enhance the Bible's popular intelligibility the translators included a massive body of marginal commentary, which was drawn largely from Olivetan's French translation revised and commented on by Calvin and published in Geneva in 1558.[11] In all, the commentary exceeded three hundred thousand words in length and constituted, in effect, a self-contained theological library for common readers. The marginal notes immediately excited comment from friends and foes alike, and they have continued to intrigue historians. It would be difficult to overstate their influence in molding lay perceptions of godly living and Christian faith. Aside from the Bible itself, the Genevan commentary was the only literary product all people shared in common and it exerted a far more direct influence on the popular religious imagination than the less widely circulated sermons, devotionals, and spiritual autobiographies.[12] The physical

9. Between 1560 and 1640 the Geneva Bible went through more than 160 editions from presses in Geneva, London, and Amsterdam. See Charles Eason, *The Genevan Bible: Notes on Its Production and Distribution* (Dublin, 1937).

10. Bruce, *The English Bible,* 91.

11. Greenslade, ed., *Cambridge History,* 3:158–59.

12. The only rival of the Geneva Bible in popularity was John Foxe's *Book of Martyrs.* See William Haller, *The Elect Nation: The Meaning and Relevance of Foxe's Book of Martyrs* (New York, 1963).

linkage of text and commentary on every page gave added weight to the notes and gave them the appearance of a direct extension of sacred writ. When we view the contents of these notes we are observing the symbolic universe of popular piety at its most direct and formative level.

The inclusion of theological commentary was not original with the Geneva Bible. Martin Luther's German translation included it, as did Calvin's French. Indeed, what would have been novel in the sixteenth century would have been the preparation of a popular translation *without* comment. Protestant churchmen believed they were already taking risks simply in making Bibles available to the masses and encouraging their active use. Such an endeavor was unprecedented and its effects were unpredictable. To provide this Word raw, with no interpretive guidance, would be socially and spiritually reprehensible. It would encourage readers to think they were also their own interpreters of Scripture when, in fact, they lacked the linguistic tools necessary to interpret the "real" Scriptures preserved in the original tongues and ancient manuscripts.[13] While the people could and must read their Bibles, they could not interpret them independent of ministerial guidance. The commentary, together with the sermon, was responsible for leading Bible readers into true spiritual awareness.

Like its Lutheran and Calvinist prototypes, the Geneva Bible's commentary largely ignored peripheral theological issues of interest to the specialist, and concentrated instead on the central meaning of Scripture as recently articulated by Martin Luther. Both in time and circumstance the Geneva Bible was a *popular* Reformation document. It ignored technical disputes common among English and Continental churchmen and focused singlemindedly on the signal rediscovery of justification by faith in Christ alone. At every point in the commentary the reader's attention is focused unblinkingly on the person and work of Jesus Christ. This was particularly evident in the Old Testament marginal notes in which, as Luther insisted, Christ must be the sole object of contemplation. If he is not explicitly mentioned in texts then the reader must go beyond the "grammar" or literal meaning, to the inner spiritual meaning visible only through the eyes of faith. In Luther's words, "Grammar is necessary for declension, conjuga-

13. See W. Schwarz, *Principles and Problems of Biblical Translation: Some Reformation Controversies and Their Background* (Cambridge, 1955), 211–12: "Like the humanists, [Luther] believed that only the original could be used for the interpretation of Holy Writ, for no human endeavor could produce a translation which would replace God's Word. Yet he wanted the Bible to be read by the public in the vernacular German. The resolution of the apparent logical contradiction between these two views is of some delicacy, since of necessity it creates Bibles of different values; the original for the learned theologian who is able to interpret the text, and the translation for the congregation, who cannot arrive at an exegesis without the help of the theologian."

tion and construction of sentences, but in speech the [Christocentric] meaning and subject matter must be considered[,] not the grammar, for the grammar shall not rule over the meaning."[14] Throughout their commentary the Genevan translators retained this perspective. There is, they repeatedly insisted, "no joye no consolacion, no peace or quietnes, no felicitie nor salvation, but in Jesus Christ, who is the very substance of the Gospel, and in whome all the promises are yea and amen."[15]

The single term which recurred most frequently in the marginal notes and best captures their central interpretive thrust, is *promise.*[16] Phrases such as "the faithful keeping of his promises," or the "just performances of his promise," saturate the commentary. All competing themes were subordinated to the proclamation of a deliverance freely promised and freely bestowed upon an undeserving humanity. The emphasis was on personal salvation and eternal life. The meaning of Old Testament laws, rituals, objects, and historical covenants was to be sought uniformly as precursors, representations, and "types" of the deliverance fully manifest in the cross and the open sepulcher. There was not one preface to an Old Testament book that did not explicitly focus on the life and person of Christ. Indeed, so conscious were the translators of the actual presence of Christ in the Old Testament that references to the "Angel of the Lord" were routinely identified as the preexistent Christ who lay at the core of both Old and New Testament.[17] In this interpretive framework, the Old Testament language of national covenant, judicial laws, or temporal rewards and punishments was uniformly spiritualized and interpreted as "signs" or "figures" of the Messiah.

The spiritualized quality of the commentary and popular faith did not keep pace with the main body of Puritan thought emanating from the universities at Cambridge and Oxford. Here the primary issues came to be centered on "covenant theology" and the related exegetical question of "national election." Not surprisingly, covenant themes dominate the

14. Quoted in Schwarz, *Principles and Problems of Biblical Translation,* 211.

15. Lloyd E. Berry, ed., *The Geneva Bible: A Facsimile of the 1560 Edition* (Madison, Wis., 1969), New Testament, 2. All references to the Geneva Bible will be to the Berry edition.

16. This too reflects a Reformation perspective. Jaroslav Pelikan observes in *Luther the Expositor: Introduction to the Reformer's Exegetical Writings* (St. Louis, 1954), 59, that "Luther often equated the Old Testament term 'Word of God' with 'promise'; for when God spoke His redemptive Word to Israel, the redemption which the Word wrought and brought was the redemption ultimately accomplished in Christ. By this profound insight Luther was able to go beyond the 'Messianic prophecies' *of* the Old Testament to a recognition of the Word of God *in* the Old Testament even in the passages where the Messiah was not mentioned." The theme of promise is developed more fully in James S. Preus, *From Shadow to Promise: Old Testament Interpretation from Augustine to the Young Luther* (Cambridge, 1969).

17. See, for example, *The Geneva Bible,* Old Testament, 15, 23, 111, 115.

intellectual history of the period.[18] But they were not representative of the popular piety centered on the Geneva Bible and its notes. Contained within the marginalia was a structure of symbols that stood outside of the issues raised by most intellectual historians. It was a world severely circumscribed in literary range and theological implication. This is most apparent when we examine the treatment given to covenant in the Genevan commentary. There was no effort to elevate the term to unifying theological significance. Where the term appeared in the biblical text it was seldom elaborated on except to point out that the "ark of the covenant" was a type of Christ. Where explicit references to covenant appeared in the Bible text they were identified solely with the "covenant of grace" which, in the translators' usage, stood as a synonym or metaphor for God's redemptive promises to his people completed in Christ. There was no extension of this individual and personal covenant of grace to a national ("federal") covenant between God and an entire people (including both saved and unsaved) which, as with Israel of old, would be premised on mutual obligations and temporal rewards and punishments. Indeed the commentary did not even refer to the nation of Israel, but instead to the "people of God" or the "heirs of the promise," or the "true seed of Abraham," who always constituted a redeemed minority within the larger nation. Israel itself was a type of the invisible church of Christ. Lest the reader be misled by the Old Testament language of covenant and duty into thinking that it implied some sort of literal "conditions" or works that might "prepare" the way to personal salvation or national preeminence, the translators insisted that the covenant was personal and "grounded upon [God's] free grace: therefore in recompensing their obedience he hath respect to his mercie and not to their merites."

Signal events and personalities in the history of Israel were appreciated less for their national, historical significance, than for the gospel truths they prefigured. Israel, Canaan, or Jerusalem were all understood as "temporal" signs of the invisible "kingdom of Christ." Thus, for example, in explaining Psalm 49:36 the commentators pointed out that "under the temporal promises of the land of Canaan he comprehendeth the promises of life everlasting to the faithful and their posterity." Important personages were similarly spiritualized as Christ-types. Readers learned that Joshua was important to them not as a conquering soldier of the Lord but because he "doth represent Jesus Christ the true Joshua, who leadeth us into eternal felicitie, which is signified unto us by this land of Canaan."

18. On the development of covenant theology, see Jens G. Møller, "The Beginnings of Puritan Covenant Theology," *Journal of Ecclesiastical History* 14 (1963): 46–67; and J. Wayne Baker, *Heinrich Bullinger and the Covenant: The Other Reformed Tradition* (Athens, Ohio, 1980).

Place and personality frequently came together in Christic unity as in the commentary on Isaiah 11:1 where the readers learned that "because the captivitie of Babylon was a figure of the spiritual captivitie under sinne, he sheweth that our true deliverance must come by Christ for as David came out of Ishai a man without dignitie: so Christ shulde come of a poore carpenters house. . . ." Throughout, the effect was never to deny the historicity of the Old Testament nation of Israel, but rather to subordinate that history to the fuller spiritual meaning embodied in the gospel.

Given the strong identification of the Genevan translation with the rise of Puritan preaching and popular piety, scholars have hypothesized that the translation—particularly the commentary—constituted an implicit political or economic manifesto compatible with the new social ethic of middle-class Puritanism.[19] This view unfortunately will not do. It takes isolated statements of social teaching and expands them into full-blown interpretive themes.[20] Social commentary appears, of course, but only in grammatical explanations where it is explicitly mentioned in the text. In fact, what made the Geneva Bible distinctive was not its radical social commentary, but rather the very *absence* of any particular social or political platform. The detached, apolitical vantage point of the commentators grew naturally from the Bible's origins in exile and abandonment. The translators assumed no official social or political responsibility in the home country and were free to fashion a translation which was not responsible for upholding social order. They could concentrate with single-minded attention on the spiritual claims of the Bible, leaving concrete social applications to others. In tracing the history of the English Bible, the nineteenth-century churchman Brooke Foss Westcott pointed out, rightly, that "the Genevan revision was the work of exiles whose action was unfettered by considerations of national policy. A work was comparatively easy for them which was not possible in the English Church."[21]

19. On the identification of the Geneva Bible with nonconformity see Paul Christianson, *Reformers and Babylon: English Apocalyptic Visions from the Reformation to the Eve of the Civil War* (Toronto, 1978), 36–39; Christopher Hill, *Society and Puritanism in Pre-Revolutionary England* (London, 1964), 32–49; and Patrick Collinson, *The Elizabethan Puritan Movement* (Berkeley, 1967), 175. Explicit identifications of the Geneva Bible as a radical document can be found in Harding Craig, "The Geneva Bible as a Political Document," *Pacific Historical Review* 7 (1938): 40–49; Richard Greaves, "Traditionalism and the Seeds of Revolution in the Social Principles of the Geneva Bible," *Sixteenth Century Journal* 7 (1976): 94–109; and Christopher Hill, *The World Turned Upside Down: Radical Ideas During the English Revolution* (New York, 1972), 129–30.

20. It is significant that, in an age known for its censorship and suppression of the press, neither Elizabeth nor the Star Chamber prohibited the publication and sale of the Genevan translation. Most editions of the Geneva Bible were issued by the queen's printer, Christopher Barker.

21. Westcott, *A General View*, 95.

As the Puritan movement continued to grow, and as the prospect of New World settlement began to dawn, questions of national policy and social order increasingly received attention from the learned divines. Taking seriously their own insistence that Scripture speaks to all of life completely and infallibly, the ministers found it increasingly necessary to apply biblical doctrines to questions of a temporal and political nature. The changed social situation together with numerous advances in biblical scholarship since 1560 convinced many of the need for a new vernacular edition of the Bible better suited to the needs of the new century. The resultant Authorized Version of 1611 was soon adopted by most Puritan clergymen and inaugurated a new era in Puritan history. Unlike the earlier Genevan translation, the Authorized Version lacked marginal comment and was, in every sense, an establishment Bible of impeccable social and intellectual credentials. The forty-seven translators included the finest Anglican and Puritan scholars in the realm and were supported by royal and ecclesiastical preferment.[22] The new version of the Bible coincided with a period of new beginnings for the Puritan clergy. Now that the people had been indoctrinated in the truths of Holy Writ, it was possible to begin moving to the second, and more ambitious, phase of building an entire social order according to scriptural blueprint.

Where the Geneva Bible and its marginalia served well the purpose of an embattled religious minority with thoughts fixed firmly on martyrdom and the world to come, it was less useful in fashioning binding principles of social organization and order in this world. It is not coincidental that the Puritan leaders' preference for the Authorized Version grew in direct proportion to their growth in numbers and influence. Before the New World settlement English Puritans had gradually moved beyond the Reformation emphases of the Geneva Bible and spoke increasingly of a special national covenant that existed alongside of a personal covenant of grace. In a study of the changes wrought in seventeenth-century Puritanism Leonard Trinterud points out that

> As early as 1572 [Thomas] Cartwright had noted that disinterest in the Geneva Bible was growing. A federalist Puritan, John Reynolds, at the Hampden Court conference had urged the preparation of a new translation of the Bible, and the edition of 1611 had been due to his suggestion.

22. The instructions to the translators can be found in Westcott, *A General View,* 115–16. One significant effort to base a new translation on the Genevan text rather than the Bishop's Bible was undertaken by the Hebraist, Hugh Broughton. Broughton died before bringing his work to completion, but of the Authorized Version he had the following comments: "The cockles of the sea shores and the leaves of the forest, and the grains of the poppy, may as well be numbered as the gross errors of this Bible. . . ." Quoted in Bruce, *The English Bible,* 107.

> Although numerous editions of Calvin's works had been issued during the Elizabethan era, it is significant that from 1603 to 1700 only eight printings of any and all of Calvin's works were made in England and Scotland combined. Moreover, even before the Civil War well-known Puritans were cool toward, and quite independent of, Calvin's theology. The covenant theology had won its brief struggle for supremacy with the Geneva Bible and Calvin's theology.[23]

Nowhere was the movement beyond the Geneva Bible more evident than in the Puritan-sponsored migration to Massachusetts Bay in 1630. This migration had as its overarching mission nothing less than the carving out of a new world order solely according to biblical precept. Theirs would be a society governed in every detail according to the Word of God as interpreted by his ministers. Elements of the population could, and no doubt did, demur from this official policy privately, but they could not introduce their grievances publicly. In public settings, the only allowable voice was the Word of God as channeled through his personal ambassadors, the clergy.

Other New World colonies and cultures, of course, had their own regenerative hopes for the New World, but only in New England were messianic themes and biblical texts fused with an official public mission that bound an entire populace to its terms. William Penn, the Quaker, for example, was certainly no less biblical when he dreamed of planting a "Holy Experiment" yet he came to despair of ever seeing his vision of brotherly love widely shared or deeply held by Pennsylvania's citizens. For one thing, the Quakers placed the Bible in a secondary role, lest it supplant the initiative of God's Spirit and the need of obeying the Light within. "Friends conceded that the Bible was authoritative," Hugh Barbour has written, "and then talked about the Spirit."[24] In addition, the Quakers refused to ordain a regular clergy to ensure a definitive interpretation of Scripture, failed to pursue comprehensive education as a religious mission, and welcomed rather than resisted religious dissent and ethnic pluralism.[25]

23. Leonard J. Trinterud, "The Origins of Puritanism," *Church History* 20 (1951): 50. On the shift away from Calvin toward a "conditional" or "Preparationist" covenant theology see also Møller, "The Beginnings of Puritan Covenant Theology," 64; John von Rohr, "Covenant and Assurance in Early English Puritanism," *Church History* 34 (1965): 195–203; Everett H. Emerson, "Calvin and Covenant Theology," *Church History* 25 (1956): 134–44; and Perry Miller, *Errand into the Wilderness* (New York, 1956).

24. Barbour, *The Quakers in Puritan England* (New Haven, 1964), 158.

25. The Keithian Schism, early Pennsylvania's most volatile crisis, concerned, ironically, the attempt of the dissenter George Keith to place more emphasis on the Bible and less on "the Light within." The Quaker majority, however, developed no mechanism for expelling such malcontents and thus could only learn to put up with antagonistic factions.

The result was a surprisingly unstable mix of antiauthoritarianism, ethnic tension, and factionalism—a world of competing visions over which no single one could claim hegemony. As this pluralism intensified during the eighteenth century, the Quakers lost all hope of subduing the province they had created. Withdrawing from politics entirely, they moved toward purity rather than providence and nourished modest aims rather than cosmic errands. The vision of a redeemer nation, which the American republic would in time come to own, was the manifestation of a sense of history that had its primary roots in Puritan Boston rather than Quaker Philadelphia.[26]

The Puritans' new order was given classic formulation in the first New World sermon of their governor John Winthrop, preached while still on board the flagship *Arbella*. In words familiar to pastors, school children, song writers, and civic leaders since, he proceeded to inform his fellow travelers that they were different from all other peoples on earth; not because of their own righteousness, but because God had singled them out, like Israel of old, to be the instruments of his redemptive plan for mankind. Other colonists could worry about profit and worldly advancement; the business of New England would be the carrying out of a divine "commission" from God to establish his Word in the midst of a professing, "peculiar" people.[27] Borrowing a metaphor from Christ's Sermon on the Mount he informed the people that they would be as a "City upon a Hill" entrusted with enacting a "modell of Christian charity" that would flow from their special covenant with God. The stakes were high: "soe that if wee shall deale falsely with our God in this worke wee have undertaken and soe cause him to withdrawe his present helpe from us, wee shall be made a story and a by-word through the world . . . wee [shall] be consumed out of the good land whether wee are goeing."

It is important to remember that in delivering his platform Winthrop was not simply expressing a private opinion which he would *like* to see implemented. He was articulating the official, public ideology of the land. Henceforth New England society would go on public record as a

For excellent discussions of this religious and political instability, see Gary B. Nash, *Quakers and Politics: Pennsylvania, 1681–1726* (Princeton, 1968), 127–80; and Jon Butler, "Gospel Order Improved: The Keithian Schism and the Exercise of Quaker Ministerial Authority in Pennsylvania," *William and Mary Quarterly*, 3d ser. 31 (1974): 430–52.

26. For two provocative statements about the contrasting cultural legacies of Pennsylvania and New England, see Daniel T. Rodgers, "Democracy, Mediocrity, and the Spirit of Max Weber," *Reviews in American History* 8 (1980): 465–70; and Mary Maples Dunn, "Saints and Sisters: Congregational and Quaker Women in the Early Colonial Period," *American Quarterly* 30 (1978): 582–601.

27. Quotations from Winthrop's sermon are taken from Michael McGiffert, ed., *Puritanism and the American Experience* (Reading, Mass., 1969).

special covenant people who would be regulated in every regard by Scripture. The vernacular Word, particularly the Old Testament, provided them with the "articles of our Covenant with him." Along with the performance of those articles or "duties" came an eternal promise: if they performed them in a proper spirit of humility and dependence they would be blessed, and if they failed to perform them, then as surely as Israel met its Babylon, even so would he "make us knowe the price of the breache of such a Covenant." Everything would hinge on the faithful proclamation and application of the Word in every community throughout the land.

Winthrop's sermon vividly illustrates how Scripture was bound indissolubly to the New England way. The platform was delivered in the form of a sermon rather than a constitution and scriptural citations underscored every point. The citations themselves were drawn, deliberately or not, from both Genevan and Authorized translations and indicate how the Puritan leaders fused the original concern with personal salvation to the novel task of model society building.[28] For Winthrop and his clerical peers the interpretive framework of the Geneva Bible was not so much wrong as it was anachronistic. It continued to speak authoritatively to questions of justification, and was even used in some regular preaching. But two generations of Christians nourished on the vernacular Word now faced more ambitious challenges which placed new demands on scriptural interpretation. The New World realities of community formation, social containment, and survival shifted the interpretive concerns from personal to corporate piety, and from the saint's progress to heaven to his life on earth.

For the model Bible Commonwealth to survive in the "howling wilderness" of the New World and not splinter off in a hundred different directions, the highest sanctions would have to be invoked. The populace had to be convinced that their personal salvation depended in some measure on their collective behavior in the New World. As Winthrop had warned, they would have to "be knitt together in this worke as one man . . . alwayes having before our eyes our Commission and Community." Questions of personal and corporate regeneration could not be separated and the leaders could ignore questions of corporate duty and national covenant only at the expense of undermining all social order. For the first time Puritan leaders experienced the responsibility of power. And this responsibility placed them on the horns of a dilemma they would never entirely escape.[29] Their personal faith rested firmly on the doctrine of *sola fides,*

28. I am indebted to Professor McGiffert for pointing out Winthrop's variant Bible usage to me in private correspondence.

29. The Puritan dilemmas of power in the New World are treated from a slightly different perspective in Edmund Morgan's *The Puritan Dilemma: The Story of John Winthrop* (Boston, 1958).

while their social doctrine was modeled directly after the Old Testament theocracy. The Puritans' separatist "Pilgrim" neighbors avoided the dilemma by retaining the original message of free grace uncontaminated by notions of special errand or national covenant. Not surprisingly, the Geneva Bible remained the preferred version in Plymouth Colony.[30] But as Plymouth itself revealed, such doctrinal purity provided no cultural glue for a world-redeeming mission. It was a view that led ultimately to withdrawal and separation from the world.

As Perry Miller first demonstrated, the more culturally aggressive Puritans responded to the dilemma by affirming *both* an absolute and a conditional covenant.[31] This was articulated in the vocabulary of a national covenant involving both personal and historical redemption. The individual could not earn his salvation, but he could "prepare" for it by attending to the preaching of the Word and by being a loyal citizen in the society. He could find assurance in the realization that New England was God's chosen nation. If the leaders could not resolve the dilemma, they could hold it in balance by simultaneously affirming a personal salvation dependent solely upon free grace and a collective covenant premised on works and duties.

With respect to biblical interpretation, the revamped and expanded covenant theology meant that the leaders must read the Old Testament with a closer eye to historical and literal implementation. The only historical model directly relevant to their enterprise was ancient Israel. Of all the peoples who preceded them, only Israel stood as they in a special redemptive covenant with God. For that reason, the "Jewish Commonwealth" enjoyed a normative status even greater than that ascribed to classical Greece and Rome. The spiritualization of the Old Testament which dominated the Geneva Bible must now accommodate an increasing literalization or actualization of Old Testament practices, including the judicial law. Because the American Puritans identified themselves as a peculiar people, historical covenants stated in the conditional language of corporate duties, mutual obligations, and temporal rewards and punishments were reactivated. If presented in the form of a syllogism, the American Puritans' reasoning would go something like this:

> Major premise: God's promises of blessing and judgment recorded in Scripture apply to professing peoples as well as to individuals.

30. Berry, ed., *The Geneva Bible,* introduction, 22. Samuel Eliot Morison described the use of the Geneva Bible in Plymouth in his edition of William Bradford's *Of Plymouth Plantation 1620–1647* (New York, 1963).

31. See especially "The Marrow of Puritan Divinity," reprinted in *Errand into the Wilderness,* 48–98; and *The New England Mind: The Seventeenth Century* (New York, 1939), 4:365–492.

Minor Premise: New England is a professing people bound in public submission to the Word of God.
Conclusion: Therefore New England is a peculiar people of God.

As we have already seen, a precondition of the minor premise was that a prospective people of God actually have access to the Word, together with the requisite literacy skills to understand it, and a faithful ministry to apply it in local settings. On all counts the New England Puritans believed themselves uniquely fitted to the work at hand. They had at least one and often two university-trained ministers in every community throughout the land. Bibles existed in virtually every household, and the regional literacy rates were perhaps the highest in the world.[32] When all of these factors were read into biblical exegesis, the simple and irresistible conclusion was that the meaning of America could be found *specifically* in biblical prophecies. Bercovitch describes the new exegesis in the following words:

> Unmistakably the New World, like Canaan of old, belonged wholly to the history of salvation. Other peoples, the colonists explained, had their land by providence; *they* had it by promise. Others must seek their national origins in secular records and chronicles; the story of America was enclosed in the scriptures, its past postdated and its future antedated in prophecy.[33]

The identification of America with the New Israel was understood by the leaders not as a repudiation of the earlier evangelical message of free grace, but as its culmination. The new exegesis was engrafted onto the existing message of free grace and Puritan ministers would preach unconditional individual election and conditional corporate rewards and punishments at the same time and with equal enthusiasm. In local contexts Puritan preaching included some of the most searching, heartfelt evangelical sentiments in all of Protestant history.[34] At the same time, the official printed literature of the colonies reflectively scrutinized colonial settlements from the standpoint of a people collectively bound in a special covenant with God.[35] Although formal syllogisms seldom appeared in printed sermons, they were ubiquitous in abbreviated form and invariably pressed home the point that New England was a special people. In

32. See Lockridge, *Literacy in Colonial New England.*

33. Sacvan Bercovitch, ed., *The American Puritan Imagination: Essays in Revaluation* (Cambridge, 1974), 9.

34. See especially the collected sermons of Thomas Shepard, Richard Mather, and John Cotton.

35. The classic formulation was Peter Bulkeley's *The Gospel-Covenant: or The Covenant of Grace Opened* (London, 1646).

his Election Sermon of 1673 Urian Oakes, president of Harvard College, reiterated the ancient litany of special mission:

> You have been as a City upon a hill (though in a remote and obscure Wilderness) as a Candle in the Candlestick that gives light to the whole House. You have, to a considerable Degree, enlightened the whole House (world I mean) as to the pattern of God's House; the Form and Fashion and Outgoings and Incomings thereof: convinced and helped many, and left others, that shut their eyes against the Light of your Profession and Practice, without excuse. God hath been doing (in my Apprehension) the same thing for the substance of it here, that shall be done more universally and gloriously, when *Israel shall blossom and bud and fill the face of the world with fruit:* Isaiah 27:6. You have been though a handfull of people separated from the greatest part of the Christian World (as it prophesied of Jacobs remnant that it should be in the midst of many people. Mic. 5:7) *as a Dew from the Lord, and as the flowers upon the grass.* God hath priviledged and honoured you greatly in this respect.[36]

In sermon after sermon the point was pressed home that New England's covenant people were God's special instruments and stood in a unique relationship to church history and revelation.

Although the synthesis of absolute and conditional covenant was largely the creation of the Puritan ministers, many common people such as the Woburn joiner and militia captain Edward Johnson embraced the new orthodoxy as a harbinger of the millennium. In his manuscript history of the first-generation settlers he extolled the Bible Commonwealth and its covenant theology as nothing less than a "new Heaven, and a new Earth in, New Churches, and a new Commonwealth." In words that would resound through the following decades he issued the following challenge to posterity: "Then judge all you . . . whether these poore New England People, be not the forerunners of Christ's Army."[37]

Others however were less certain and were unwilling to grant the major premise that God's promises extended to nations as well as individuals. Their spiritual consciousness and reading world continued to be informed by the otherworldly perspective of the Geneva Bible commentary, where they could find no justification for a conditional covenant in personal or national terms. Believing that the national covenant had ended with Christ, they could only understand New England's public corporate identity as a "covenant of works" that jeopardized one's personal relationship with Christ. We do not know how many people

36. Urian Oakes, *New England Pleaded With* (Cambridge, 1673), 9.

37. J. Franklin Jameson, ed., *Johnson's Wonder-Working Providence 1628–1651* (New York, 1910), 25, 60.

throughout the colonies shared misgivings about the new orthodoxy. We do know they were particularly strong in Boston where, under the "prophesyings" of Anne Hutchinson and her brother-in-law the Reverend John Wheelwright, a dissenting party emerged in opposition to the official ideology of the Bay colony.[38] The complex theological issues which surrounded the ensuing "Antinomian crisis" have tended to obscure the fact that the two sides of the controversy drew their inspiration and proofs from different translations of Scripture. The Hutchinsonian party spoke from the Geneva Bible, while the leaders accused them from the Authorized. At stake in the controversy was who could speak for God in public settings. For the New England way to survive intact there could be only one official voice of God articulated by his prophet, the settled minister. Alternative interpretations and applications of Scripture threatened an exegetical anarchy where everyone became his or her own interpreter of Scripture. If competing voices such as Anne Hutchinson's were allowed public expression, they would rend the fabric of colonial society and jettison the special status and mission of the land.[39]

The first skirmish in the battle for public authority took place in 1637 when Wheelwright preached an inflammatory Fast Day sermon from the Genevan translation of Matthew 9:15.[40] From start to finish the sermon was characteristically Christocentric in theme and disdainful of all efforts to impute adherence to corporate duty as a preparation for personal salvation. Wheelwright responded to the covenant theology by saying, "No, no, this is a covenant of works, for in the covenant of grace, nothing is revealed but Christ for our righteousness . . . not by the works of righteousness, they are layd aside, and the Lord revealeth only to them the righteousness of himselfe given freely to the soul. . . ."[41] In the precarious New World settlements such a sentiment threatened to undermine the credibility of the entire society. In spite of popular protest, Wheelwright was convicted of sedition and banished from the colony.

38. The fullest account of the Antinomian crisis is found in Emery Battis, *Saints and Sectaries: Anne Hutchinson and the Antinomian Controversy in the Massachusetts Bay Colony* (Chapel Hill, N.C., 1962).

39. For an interpretation which discusses Antinomianism in feminist terms, see Lyle Koehler, "The Case of the American Jezebels: Anne Hutchinson and Female Agitation During the Years of Antinomian Turmoil, 1636–1640," *William and Mary Quarterly,* 3d ser. 31 (1974): 55–78. Mary Maples Dunn also discusses Hutchinson's biblical defenses of her rights as a woman in "Saints and Sisters: Congregational and Quaker Women in the Early Colonial Period," *American Quarterly* 30 (1978): 582–601.

40. Wheelwright's sermon is reprinted in David D. Hall, ed., *The Antinomian Controversy, 1636–1638: A Documentary History* (Middletown, Conn., 1968), 152–72. Throughout the sermon biblical references are to the Genevan version.

41. Ibid., 269.

Wheelwright's battle was continued on a more sophisticated level by Anne Hutchinson who, in the course of her trial, evidenced a nearly verbatim memory of long portions of the Geneva Bible.[42] Throughout her defense she focused singlemindedly on the person of Christ and the actual moment of spiritual union when the soul is infused with divine grace. Her scriptural supports were drawn particularly from the Epistle to the Galatians which, according to Governor Winthrop's account, she termed "the rule of the new creature. . . ."[43] Something of the flavor of the Genevan gloss on Galatians can be captured from the commentary on Galatians 1:7 which posits an unbridgeable gulf between grace and works, free promise and conditional covenant: "For what is more contrarie to our fre[e] justification by faith, then the justification by the Law, of our workes? Therefore to joyne these two together, is to joyne light with darkness, death with life, and doeth utterly overthrow the Gospel."

Anne Hutchinson never fully comprehended the new mission of American Puritan orthodoxy and its eschatological vision. Nor could she accept its conditional terms and unique construction of biblical prophecies in national terms. She and her followers came from an older language and, like foreigners, spoke past their clerical opponents. The language issue was settled abruptly and decisively in favor of the new orthodoxy and its world-redeeming vocabulary. In March 1637 Anne was excommunicated from the Boston Church and one month later banished to Rhode Island. Other exiles from the Puritan experiment would join her there, dissenters such as the Baptist John Clarke, who founded Newport in 1639. Clarke's Bible, one is not surprised to learn, was a 1608 edition of the Geneva Bible—a book that survives today in the possession of the Rhode Island Historical Society.[44]

With the removal of Anne Hutchinson the issue of who spoke for God was settled finally and irrevocably, and the Puritan clergy proceeded to construct their own unique meaning of America on the foundation of their own interpretation of Scripture. Throughout the colonial period the vernacular Bible interpreted by a learned ministry remained the mainstay of New England culture. Amidst disappointments, defeats, and periodic failures of nerve, the faith in God's promise of ultimate triumph for his covenant people remained fixed and unchanged. As with Israel of old, failures and judgments were incentives for renewal, and defeats

42. See Patricia Caldwell, "The Antinomian Language Controversy," *Harvard Theological Review* 69 (1976): 345–67.

43. Quoted in Hall, ed., *The Antinomian Controversy*, 269.

44. Edwin S. Gaustad has suggested that Baptists in early New England were most familiar with the Geneva Bible. See Gaustad, ed., *Baptist Piety: The Last Will and Testimony of Obadiah Holmes* (Grand Rapids, 1978), 113, 158.

merely temporary reverses on a larger battlefield in which victory was ultimately assured. Despite division between the people and their ministers and, in the Great Awakening, divisions among the clergy themselves, all shared in an unbroken allegiance to the Bible as the inspired Word of God and infallible rule for all issues of life. The terms *liberal* and *evangelical* taken to distinguish the eighteenth-century clergy did not extend to differences over the authority and sufficiency of Scripture. This remained a common legacy.

When revolution came in 1776 it was greeted with the same unswerving faith in scriptural promises that had animated the first-generation founders. As Winthrop's sermon marked the beginning of one epoch in 1630 so did the Reverend Samuel West inaugurate a new beginning for the ages in his Election Sermon of 1776.[45] The two sermons were separated by more than 150 years of social change and adaptation to the realities of New World settlement. No longer did ministers alone speak for God (that right was now bestowed on the people as a whole), and New England's special status was now extended to include America. But the biblically-based sermon remained the primary ritual of social order and the institution entrusted with interpreting life's meaning to God's special New World inhabitants. That meaning, as West made plain, had not changed. Repeating words that had been internalized over six generations, he observed that God had "planted a vine in this American wilderness which he has caused to take deep root, and it has filled the land, and will never be plucked up or destroyed." The bedrock of West's doctrine of resistance and revolution remained the Bible. To underscore its importance to the American cause, he devoted no less than eleven pages of his sermon text to an exegesis of the apostle Paul's injunction in Romans 13:1–6 to "be subject to the higher powers." This command, he makes plain, applies only to legitimate rulers and not to tyrants who subvert the purposes and ends of government and good order. Indeed, from scriptural warrant, he concludes that it is a sin *not* to resist tyranny. Rebellion against false leaders who jeopardized Americans' special relationship with God was not merely a right but "a duty so sacred that it cannot justly be dispensed with for the sake of our secular concerns."

Like Winthrop, West concluded that the success of the American cause "depends upon our being firmly united together in the bonds of love to one another. . . ." If such love and obedience to divine authority is maintained then by the terms of God's covenant Americans can lay hold of his promise of both temporal and spiritual deliverance: "he will not forsake

45. Samuel West, *A Sermon Preached* . . . (Boston, 1776). Quotations are from a reprinting of this sermon in John Wingate Thornton, ed., *The Pulpit of the American Revolution* (New York, 1970; orig. 1860), 267–322.

us if we do not forsake him. Our cause is so just and good that nothing can prevent our success but only our sins . . . I cannot help hoping, and even believing, that Providence has designed this continent for to be the asylum of liberty and true religion. . . ."

Other colonists might celebrate "the rights of man," and justify their rebellion solely with reference to the libertarian thought of the age. But New England people bred on the Word could never accept such a man-centered, optimistic ideological platform. Their world, like that of their fathers before them, was entirely suffused with the Word of God. It furnished the terms and vocabulary with which they instinctively confronted life's meaning, and interpreted the significance of their collective presence in the New World. As ministers never tired of pointing out, there was not one week nor one town in the colony's history in which the Word was not faithfully proclaimed. And on that basis of direct dependence on divine Providence, they would march forth to war strong in the conviction that they remained God's special Bible-believing people. And if God was for them, then who could be against them?

Part 2

From the Great Awakening to the Revolution

3

The Ideological Origins of the American Revolution

Harry S. Stout

Reprinted by permission from *William and Mary Quarterly* 34 (1977): 519–41.

> . . . I saw before me a Cloud or fogg rising; I first thought it came from the great River, but as I came nearer the Road, I heard a noise something like a low rumbling thunder and presently found it was the noise of Horses feet coming down the Road and this Cloud was a Cloud of dust made by the Horses feet; it arose some Rods into the air over the tops of Hills and trees and when I came within about 20 rods of the Road, I could see men and horses Sliping along in the Cloud like shadows and as I drew nearer it seemed like a steady Stream of horses and their riders, scarcely a horse more than his length behind another, all of a Lather and foam with sweat, their breath rolling out of their nostrils every Jump; every horse seemed to go with all his might to carry his rider to hear news from heaven for the saving of Souls, it made me tremble to see the Sight. . . .

Nathan Cole's description of George Whitefield's appearance before four thousand avid listeners in Middletown, Connecticut, in 1740 captures our attention at least partly because Cole's voice is one that is rare in early American literature.[1] The crude spelling and syntax signal a ver-

1. Michael J. Crawford, ed., "The Spiritual Travels of Nathan Cole," *William and Mary Quarterly,* 3d ser. 33 (1976): 93. The crowd estimate at Middletown is taken from *George Whitefield's Journals* (Philadelphia, 1960), 479.

nacular prose composed by an ordinary man, whose purpose is less to analyze the theological issues of the revival than to describe an exhilarating event. Lacking the literary refinements of a classical education, Cole portrayed his experience in the form of a "realistic narrative" framed against a concrete social background.[2] Although common in setting, the passage is hardly trivial, for it brings to life the impassioned world of the common people and conveys, in their own words, a sense of the irrepressible spontaneity that marked the revivals throughout the colonies. Thunderous noise, clouds of dust, horses in a lather, and unrecognizable shadowy figures dominate a vocabulary that manages to express, as no official account could possibly do, the powerful emotions evoked by the Great Awakening.

With Whitefield's celebrated speaking tours of the colonies there appeared an innovative style of communications that redefined the social context in which public address took place. The sheer size and heterogeneity of the audience exceeded anything in the annals of colonial popular assembly. To organize the mass meetings, both speaker and audience altered the roles and language they customarily adopted in public worship. In the process, a new model of social organization and public address developed—a model which could be applied to a broad range of social, political, and religious contexts.

Contemporary and historical accounts agree that the Awakening was the most momentous intercolonial popular movement before the Revolution. Indeed, the parallel between the popular engagement and "enthusiasm" evidenced alike in the revivals and the rebellion merits close attention. Unfortunately, however, attempts to explain the meaning those two movements had for their participants must confront the fact that the documentary evidence originates overwhelmingly from an elitist "rhetorical world" that excluded the common people from the presumed audience.[3] Although the informed writings of the Founding Fathers provide the official Revolutionary vocabulary, they do not render in a realistic

2. Hans W. Frei distinguishes a "realistic narrative" in the following terms: "Realistic narrative is that kind in which subject and social setting belong together, and characters and external circumstances fitly render each other. . . . [R]ealistic narrative, if it is really seriously undertaken and not merely a pleasurable or hortatory exercise, is a sort in which in style as well as content in the setting forth of didactic material, and in the depiction of characters and action, the sublime or at least serious effect mingles inextricably with the quality of what is casual, random, ordinary, and everyday" (*The Eclipse of Biblical Narrative: A Study in Eighteenth and Nineteenth Century Hermeneutics* [New Haven, Conn., 1974], 13–14).

3. The term *rhetorical world* is taken from Gordon S. Wood, "The Democratization of Mind in the American Revolution," in *Leadership in the American Revolution*, Library of Congress Symposia (Washington, D.C., 1974), 72.

narrative form the ideological arousal of the common people, who, by the very rhetoric of those documents, were excluded from the message. How were Revolutionary sentiments communicated with ideological force to an audience unversed in the rhetorical forms of the literature? And, conversely, how did the active popular self-consciousness manifested in the popular movement energize a republican vocabulary and push it in egalitarian directions the leaders had never intended? The documents are of little help here. More to the point, they actually create the problem of interpretation.

Cole's description of the popular enthusiasm of the revival suggests a different approach to the problem of popular culture and republican ideology. If *what* was communicated is qualified by the restrictive rhetoric through which the ideas were intended to be transmitted, it may help to ask instead *how* communications were conducted and how they changed during the second half of the eighteenth century? There could be no egalitarian culture as we know it today without an ideological predisposition toward the idea that the vulgar masses ought to be reached directly. By examining the changing style of communications in the revivals it is possible to gain insights into the nature of an egalitarian rhetoric through which, and only through which, republican ideas could be conveyed to an unlettered audience.

David Ramsay, a noted participant in and historian of the Revolution, recognized that, to understand the meaning of the Revolution, "forms and habits" must be regarded.[4] Before a republican vocabulary could communicate radical social meanings, a new rhetoric had to appear in which familiar terms were used to express unfamiliar thoughts. And this, it is argued here, is precisely what happened in the mass assemblies inaugurated by preachers like Whitefield. Despite the differences in intellectual substance between the revivals and the rebellion, those movements exhibited a close rhetorical affinity that infused religious and political ideas with powerful social significance and ideological urgency.

The point of departure for this article is Alan Heimert's study of *Religion and the American Mind.*[5] Published in 1966, the book had a generally cool reception. Critical essays by Edmund S. Morgan and Sidney E. Mead pointed out conceptual shortcomings in the work but failed to recognize its value in suggesting a method of historical analysis that focuses

4. David Ramsay, *The History of the American Revolution* (1789), in Edmund S. Morgan, ed., *The American Revolution: Two Centuries of Interpretation* (Englewood Cliffs, N.J., 1965), 8.

5. Alan Heimert, *Religion and the American Mind: From the Great Awakening to the Revolution* (Cambridge, Mass., 1966).

on the context of communications.[6] This failure had the unfortunate effect of foreclosing a line of inquiry into the subject of religion and the ideological origins of the Revolution.

Heimert's foreword states his central thesis: religious "Liberalism was profoundly conservative, politically as well as socially, and . . . its leaders, insofar as they did in fact embrace the Revolution, were the most reluctant of rebels. Conversely, 'evangelical' religion, which had as its most notable formal expression the 'Calvinism' of Jonathan Edwards, was not the retrograde philosophy that many historians rejoice to see confounded in America's Age of Reason. Rather Calvinism, and Edwards, provided pre-Revolutionary America with a radical, even democratic, social and political ideology, and evangelical religion embodied, and inspired, a thrust toward American nationalism."[7] This assertion diverged dramatically from the conventional wisdom regarding the relations of religion and the Revolution. In demonstrating his thesis Heimert contended, in now notorious words, that it was necessary to read the sources "not between the lines, but, as it were, through and beyond them."[8] Only by doing this would it be possible to cut through the immediate idiom of political discourse that dominated the official Revolutionary debates and discover the underlying "relationship of ideology and political commitment to modes of persuasion."[9] In Heimert's view, these "modes of persuasion" were derived from the evangelical rather than the liberal tradition.

Against this thesis, and the method upon which it rests, Morgan and Mead launched an impressive assault. The conceptual framework they impose on early America, and their way of reading historical documents, were molded largely by Perry Miller, and it was as an extension of Miller's work that they interpreted Heimert.[10] To them, Heimert's tactic

6. Edmund S. Morgan's review in *WMQ*, 3d ser. 24 (1967): 454–59, and Sidney E. Mead, "Through and beyond the Lines," *Journal of Religion* 47 (1968): 274–88. The prominent exception to the negativity of the reviews is William G. McLoughlin's "The American Revolution as a Religious Revival: 'The Millennium in One Country,'" *New England Quarterly* 40 (1967): 99–110.

7. Heimert, *Religion and the American Mind,* viii.

8. Ibid., 11. Heimert's terminology is not meant to imply that one reads beyond the documents by ignoring documentation (as nearly two thousand footnotes fully attest). Rather, it is the recognition, recently articulated by Gene Wise, that to get at the meaning of verbal statements "one would have to go beyond the documents to the original experience they came out of" (*American Historical Explanations: A Strategy for Grounded Inquiry* [Homewood, Ill., 1973], 73).

9. Heimert, *Religion and the American Mind,* vii.

10. Mead is most explicit here in the opening comments of his review: "Essentially Mr. Heimert's work seems to me to be a 639-page expansion, with massive footnoting of some suggestions imaginatively adumbrated in 1961 by Perry Miller. . . . The voice seems to be

of reading "beyond" the content of the documents to the styles they expressed smacked, in Morgan's word, of "fantasy."[11] They contended that the method not only detached the historian from the security of objective reference (that is, the content of the documents) but also ignored social and intellectual connections between revivalism and republicanism that were neither as sharp nor as consistent as Heimert supposed.

Influential as these criticisms have been in stifling consideration of *Religion and the American Mind,* we must ask whether in fact Heimert wrote the book the critics reviewed. If Heimert's study is simply an extension of Miller, then the problems with the book become insurmountable because, as the critics demonstrate, there is no clear and consistent link between revivalism and republicanism at the level of ideas. But if the book is viewed in a different context altogether—if Heimert was not seeking to establish direct intellectual links between religious thought and political rebellion—then the entire effort needs to be reevaluated.

Perry Miller's fullest statement on religion and the ideological origins of the Revolution appeared in his essay "From the Covenant to the Revival," published in 1961.[12] Addressing the role of "Calvinistic" Protestantism (a term he applied indiscriminately to liberals and evangelicals) in the Revolution, Miller insisted that, with the exception of a few hopelessly optimistic Anglicans, the American people shared a religious tradition articulated in the Reformed vocabulary of "federal" theology.[13] Under the influence of this austere covenantal tradition the colonists could never be moved by self-congratulatory appeals to natural rights and enlightened self-interest. Rather, the dynamic for revolution issued from a deep sense of moral corruption and degradation that found a target in English oppression but, more important, spoke to the sins of colonial society itself. For generations of colonists schooled in the language of covenant, judgment, and collective accountability, the jeremiad functioned as the "form of discourse" capable of driving them to a moral revolution. Considered as an intellectual movement, the Revolution represented a spiritual purge administered to a corrupt established order in the interest of restoring a pure order that would both free the colonists from a decadent oppressor and cleanse their own society. The Revolution was

---

that of Jacob, but the hand that tapped the typewriter was that of Esau" ("Through and beyond the Lines," 274).

11. Morgan states in his review: "The world he offers us has been constructed by reading beyond the lines of what men said; and what he finds beyond the lines is so far beyond, so wrenched from the context, and so at odds with empirical evidence, that his world, to this reviewer at least, partakes more of fantasy than of history," 459.

12. In James Ward Smith and A. Leland Jamison, eds., *The Shaping of American Religion* (Princeton, N.J., 1961), 322–68.

13. Ibid., 325.

inspired by this highly unstable compound of pious contrition and political rebellion, moral reformation and patriotic resistance.

Miller's essay came to exert an enormous influence on assessments of the role of religion in the Revolution.[14] Yet nowhere did it reflect a recognition of the social dislocations and divisions which we now know proliferated in eighteenth-century America.[15] Miller's framework fails to show how Americans sharing the "Puritan Ethic" could have been so sharply divided over the issue of independence or why, among the patriots, such confusion and contradiction raged over the question of what the Revolution was all about.[16] Finally, it is impossible in Miller's terms to account for receptivity to rebellion on the part of a populace of limited literacy.[17] To focus solely on the ideas set forth in surviving documents as the source of ideological change is to confuse a deep cultural transformation with its subsequent manifestation in a self-conscious, theoretical vocabulary.

In opposition to Miller, Heimert describes two clearly separate and distinctive revolutionary styles in eighteenth-century America, each originating in opposing "rhetorical strategies" that crystallized after the mass revivals.[18] On the one hand, there was the rebellion itself—the movement

14. See, in particular, Edmund S. Morgan, "The Puritan Ethic and the American Revolution," *WMQ*, 3d ser. 24 (1967): 3–43, and Bernard Bailyn, *The Ideological Origins of the American Revolution* (Cambridge, Mass., 1967), 7, 32, 140, 193, 250. It is instructive to note exactly where Miller's "From the Covenant to the Revival" fits in Heimert's work. In *Religion and the American Mind* the essay is cited only three times, and never expanded on. Even more revealing, in his introductory essay to the volume of Great Awakening documents jointly edited with Miller (*The Great Awakening: Documents Illustrating the Crisis and Its Consequences* [Indianapolis, Ind., 1967], Heimert includes Miller in every historiographical citation, but not one of those citations is to "From the Covenant to the Revival."

15. See Kenneth A. Lockridge, "Social Change and the Meaning of the American Revolution," *Journal of Social History* 6 (1973): 403–39, and Jack P. Greene, "The Social Origins of the American Revolution: An Evaluation and Interpretation," *Political Science Quarterly* 88 (1973): 1–22.

16. See John R. Howe, Jr., "Republican Thought and the Political Violence of the 1790s," *American Quarterly* 19 (1967): 147–65.

17. Drawing upon a sampling of colonial will signatures, Kenneth A. Lockridge concludes that "the literacy of that American generation which took the colonies into the Revolution was less than perfect. It seems probable that one-quarter of the generation born around 1730 . . . was totally illiterate. Including New England in the total would not much alter the level of enduring illiteracy since two-thirds of the population lived outside of New England" (*Literacy in Colonial New England: An Enquiry into the Social Context of Literacy in the Early Modern West* [New York, 1974], 87).

18. I use the term *mass revival* here intentionally to distinguish multicommunity meetings addressed by itinerating preachers, who were often uneducated and of low social origins, from local revivals conducted by a settled pastor. Heimert's concentration on Jonathan Edwards and the established New England ministry tends, I believe, to work at cross-interests to his point concerning the stylistic innovation of the revivals. Historians

for independence from England, which Heimert concedes may well have proceeded from liberal assumptions. On the other hand, there emerged with the rebellion an egalitarian impulse that pointed toward the creation of a society fundamentally incompatible with traditional conceptions of order, hierarchy, and deference.[19]

Approaching the problem of popular receptivity and concentrating on the verbal forms through which ideas were presented, Heimert locates the sources of this animating egalitarianism in the Great Awakening but concludes that it can be understood only by reading beyond the religious content of evangelical ideas to the new forms of public address established in the revivals. At some point prior to the popular reception of a revolutionary vocabulary, a new rhetoric must appear in which familiar terms can be used to mean something different—and this change in the *form*, as distinguished from the *content*, of communications marks the moment of a fundamental transformation of popular consciousness. Any revolution in world view requires a new rhetoric. The most conspicuous and revolutionary product of the revivals was not to be found in doctrine, in the creation of new ecclesiastical or academic institutions, or even in resistance to the tyranny of established religion or monarchy. Evangelicalism's enduring legacy was a new rhetoric, a new mode of persuasion that would redefine the norms of social order. In Heimert's words, "quite apart from the question of Revolution, the contrasts between Liberal and Calvinist social thought were possibly of less ultimate significance than the remarkable differences between their oratorical strategies and rhetorical practices."[20]

Heimert's recognition of the revolutionary potentialities of the revivals suggests a closer look at evangelical oratory, particularly in relation to the forms of public worship that prevailed before the revivals. Despite differences in style and substance between Puritanism and southern Anglican-

---

would do better to concentrate on Whitefield and the awakening he inspired through his public addresses to unprecedented thousands of auditors. The fundamental problem raised by the revivals was not Edward's treatises but the itinerants' practices.

19. Heimert, *Religion and the American Mind*, 14, 532. To avoid terminological confusion I will use the term *rebellion* to refer to independence from England and *revolution* to describe the radical internal impulse to reorder American society in an egalitarian direction. Similarly, the classical (deferential) theory of republicanism richly described in Gordon S. Wood, *The Creation of the American Republic, 1776–1787* (Chapel Hill, N.C., 1969), 3–124, and J. G. A. Pocock, "The Classical Theory of Deference," *American Historical Review* 81 (1976): 516–23, must be distinguished from the more radical egalitarian "republicanism" that ultimately came to mean, in Wood's terms, "nothing less than a reordering of eighteenth-century society and politics as they had known and despised them . . ." (*Creation of the American Republic*, 48).

20. Heimert, *Religion and the American Mind,* 18.

ism, all churchmen believed traditionally with Samuel Willard that God did "Ordain Orders of Superiority and Inferiority among men."[21] This hierarchical world view presupposed a society of face-to-face personal relationships in which people identified themselves with reference to those around them and acted according to their rank in the community. Forms of attire, the "seating" of public meetings, and patterns of speech were among the more conspicuous indications of a pervasive social stratification that separated the leaders from the rank and file. As Stephen Foster observes, "Mutuality, subordination, and public service constituted a kind of sacred trinity of all respectable societies, Puritan or otherwise."[22]

The social institutions of colonial America were designed to sustain this prevailing perception of proper social organization. In this traditional social ethic, itinerancy was inconceivable because, in Increase Mather's words, "to say that a Wandering Levite who has no flock is a Pastor, is as good sense as to say, that he that has no children is a Father."[23] What made a pastor was not simply the preaching of the Word but also a direct, authoritarian identification with a specific flock. To ignore the personal and deferential relationships of a minister with his congregation would be to threaten the organic, hierarchical principles upon which both family and social order rested.

That ministers be "settled" was no idle proposition but rather an insistence carrying with it responsibility for the whole social order. An institution as critically important as the church could deny the forms of social hierarchy only at the peril of undermining the entire organization of social authority. In terms of communications this meant that speaker and audience were steadily reminded of their *personal* place in the community; in no context were they strangers to one another, for no public gatherings took place outside of traditional associations based upon personal acquaintance and social rank.[24]

21. Perry Miller and Thomas H. Johnson, eds., *The Puritans* (New York, 1938), 251. For a discussion of the inherited social ethic which the revivals challenged see especially William G. McLoughlin, *Isaac Backus and the American Pietistic Tradition* (Boston, 1967), 1–22; Rhys Isaac, "Religion and Authority: Problems of the Anglican Establishment in Virginia in the Era of the Great Awakening and the Parsons' Cause," *WMQ*, 3d ser. 30 (1973): 3–36; and Isaac, "Evangelical Revolt: The Nature of the Baptists' Challenge to the Traditional Order in Virginia, 1765 to 1775," *WMQ* 31 (1974): 345–68.

22. Stephen Foster, *Their Solitary Way: The Puritan Social Ethic in the First Century of Settlement in New England* (New Haven, Conn., 1971), 18.

23. Quoted in Cedric B. Cowing, *The Great Awakening and the American Revolution: Colonial Thought in the Eighteenth Century* (Chicago, 1971), 23.

24. On the cultural implications of a face-to-face traditional society see Rhys Isaac, "Dramatizing the Ideology of Revolution: Popular Mobilization in Virginia, 1774 to 1776," *WMQ*, 3d ser. 33 (1976): 364–67. I am indebted to Professor Isaac for sharing his article with me prior to its publication and for clarifying many of the points raised in this essay.

Within this world of public address liberals and evangelicals alike realized that something dramatically different was appearing in the revivalists' preaching performances. The problem raised by the revivals was not their message of the new birth. Indeed, it was the familiar message of regeneration that lulled leaders into an early acceptance and even endorsement of the revivals. The problem, it soon became clear, was the revolutionary setting in which the good news was proclaimed. The secret of Whitefield's success and that of other evangelists (no less than of Patrick Henry in the 1770s) was not simply a booming voice or a charismatic presence. It was a new style: a rhetoric of persuasion that was strange to the American ear. The revivalists sought to transcend both the rational manner of polite liberal preaching and the plain style of orthodox preaching in order to speak directly to the people at large.[25] Repudiating both the conventions of the jeremiad and the ecclesiastical formalities, they assaulted the old preaching style no less devastatingly than they attacked the doctrines of covenant theology. Their technique of mass address to a voluntary audience forced a dialogue between speaker and hearer that disregarded social position and local setting.

Immensely significant were the separation of the revivalists from local ministerial rule and their unfamiliarity with the audience. Until then, preachers, like political leaders, had to know whom they were addressing. Because the very act of public speaking signified social authority, they were expected to communicate through the existing institutional forms. When public speakers in positions of authority communicated outside of the customary forms, they set themselves, by that act itself, in opposition to the established social order. The eighteenth-century leaders' obsession with demagogy and "enthusiasm" can be understood only in the context of a deferential world view in which public speakers who were not attached to the local hierarchy created alternative settings that represented a threat to social stability. The frenzy raised by the itinerants was not born of madness but was derived from the self-initiated associations of the people meeting outside of regularly constituted religious or political meetings and, in so doing, creating new models of organization and authority. As the Harvard faculty clearly recognized in their censure of Whitefield, the "natural effect" of his preaching was that "the People have been thence ready to despise their own Ministers."[26]

25. Although Puritan rhetoric rejected the ornamental tropes and "witty" figures common to classical (Ciceronian) rhetoric, the New England plain style remained a literate rhetoric born in the schools and designed to instruct a reading public. The plain style was not intended to persuade essentially illiterate audiences unused to the logic of rational discourse. See Walter J. Ong, *Ramus: Method, and the Decay of Dialogue* (Cambridge, Mass., 1958), 212–13.

26. Heimert and Miller, eds., *Great Awakening,* 352.

In gathering their large and unfamiliar audiences the revivalists utilized the only form of address that could be sure to impress all hearers: the spoken word proclaimed extemporaneously in everyday language. As historians immersed in printed documents, we scarcely recognize the dominance of speech and oratory in aural cultures—an orality that, by definition, never survives in the written record. Alphabetic writing and print emerged, after all, as an *imitation* of spoken words, and so they have remained ever since. Recognition of the powerful social and psychological imperatives of direct oral address has led Walter Ong to observe that "writing commits the words to space. But to do so, it makes words less real, pretends they are something they are not: quiescent marks."[27] Print and typographic culture create highly visual, sequential, and analytic patterns of thought which aural cultures, attuned to easily remembered forms of speech, cannot readily comprehend.[28] Unlike print, which is essentially passive, reflective, and learned, sound is active, immediate, and spontaneously compelling in its demand for a response. Speech remains in the deepest sense an event or psychological encounter rather than an inert record—an event that is neither detached from personal presence nor analyzed, but is intrinsically engaged and calculated to persuade. Print cannot match the persuasive power of the spoken word whose potential audience includes everyone who can understand the language. It is no wonder that literate elites have feared persuasive orators from Plato condemning the sophists to Charles Chauncy damning the demagogues of the revival. Once orators are allowed the opportunity to address the people, there is, in Chauncy's words, "no knowing how high it [their influence] may rise, nor what it may end in."[29]

To portray the word as event, as a vital indwelling principle, the revivalists employed what Miller termed a "rhetoric of sensation"[30]—a new rhetoric that, through its recognition of the singular power of the spoken word delivered to a mass audience, differed fundamentally from the Old Light or rational preaching which was written out like a lecture and was more concerned, in the revivalists' words, with "ornament" than with the

27. Walter J. Ong, *Why Talk? A Conversation about Language* (San Francisco, 1973), 17.

28. On the relationship of literacy and analytical thought see Jack Goody and Ian Watt, "The Consequences of Literacy," *Comparative Studies in Society and History* 5 (1963): 304–45, and Jack Goody, "Evolution and communication: the domestication of the savage mind," *British Journal of Sociology* 24 (1973): 1–12.

29. Heimert and Miller, eds., *Great Awakening*, 256.

30. Perry Miller, *Errand into the Wilderness* (Cambridge, Mass., 1956), 167–83. Heimert brilliantly develops this theme in his chapter on "The Danger of an Unconverted Ministry," which he singles out as the "principal hinge" of his study (*Religion and the American Mind*, 159–236).

"affections." The animadversions of liberals against what they called the revivalists' "mighty noise," which not only stimulated enthusiasm but also challenged the social order, were certainly justified from their perspective.[31] Ong makes the important point that "script, and particularly the alphabet, provides a heightened experience of order. The world of thought is itself a beautifully intricate world, and the world of words is likewise impressively, if mysteriously, organized. . . . To attack the printed word would be to attack *the* symbol of order."[32]

Looking to the New Testament as their model, the revivalist rediscovered the effectiveness of extemporaneous address in their struggle against the standing order. Recent analyses of New Testament rhetoric demonstrate the prevailing orality of the gospel. Amos Wilder, for example, notes that "Jesus never wrote a word. . . . In secular terms we could say that Jesus spoke as the birds sing, oblivious of any concern for transcription. Less romantically we can say that Jesus' use of the spoken word alone has its own theological significance."[33] Throughout the Gospels the Word is the oral word, and the Good News is uttered through ordinary speech. In his classic study of the Western literary tradition Eric Auerbach pointed out that "in the last analysis the differences in style between the writers of antiquity and early Christianity are conditioned by the fact that they were composed from a different point of view and for different people."[34]

Returning not only to the social doctrine of the gospel but to its rhetoric as well, the evangelists excited the people to action by "calling them out" and exhorting them to experimental Christianity. Radical attacks on an "unconverted ministry" that acted more like "Letter-learned . . . Pharisees" than preachers of the Word take on additional meaning in the social context of eighteenth-century established religion.[35] The danger that the liberals sensed in the revivals was rhetorical as well as doctrinal. The Anglican commissary Alexander Garden correctly, and sarcastically, identified this threat: "*What went you out,* my Brethren, *to see,* or rather

31. John Caldwell, *The Nature, Folly, and Evil of rash and uncharitable Judging. A Sermon Preached at the French Meeting-House in Boston . . .* (1742), in Richard L. Bushman, ed., *The Great Awakening: Documents on the Revival of Religion, 1740–1745* (New York, 1969), 159.

32. Walter J. Ong, *The Presence of the Word: Some Prolegomena for Cultural and Religious History* (New Haven, Conn., 1967), 136.

33. Amos N. Wilder, *Early Christian Rhetoric: The Language of the Gospel* (Cambridge, Mass., 1971), 13.

34. Eric Auerbach, *Mimesis: The Representation of Reality in Western Literature,* trans. Willard R. Trask (Princeton, N.J., 1953), 46.

35. Gilbert Tennent, *The Danger of an Unconverted Ministry, Considered in a Sermon on Mark VI.34* (1741), in Heimert and Miller, eds., *Great Awakening,* 73.

to *hear*? Any *new* Gospel, or message from Heaven? Why, no? but the *old* one explained and taught in a *new* and better Manner."[36] Pointing to the spirit of this new manner, one opponent of the revivals observed that "it abhors Reason, and is always for putting out her Eyes; but loves to reign Tyrant over the Passions, which it manages by Sounds and Nonsense."[37] The identification of sight with reason, and of sound with the passions, is here obvious and comes very near to the center of the raging controversy surrounding the itinerants. At stake was nothing less than the rules and conventions governing public address and social authority.

The revivalists' repudiation of polite style and their preference for extemporaneous mass address cut to the very core of colonial culture by attacking the habit of deference to the written word and to the gentlemen who mastered it. Evangelical rhetoric performed a dual function: it proclaimed the power of the spoken word directly to every individual who would hear, and it confirmed a shift in authority by organizing voluntary popular meetings and justifying them in the religious vocabulary of the day. Partly through doctrine, but even more through the rhetorical strategy necessitated by that doctrine, the popular style of the revivals challenged the assumption of hierarchy and pointed to a substitute basis for authority and order in an open voluntary system.

The popular rhetoric of the evangelists contrasted sharply with the much more formal modes of address preferred by upholders of established authority. Nowhere were the social divisions of American society more clearly reflected than in the leaders' utilization of a printed form of discourse that separated the literati from the common people. Throughout the eighteenth century, public communications were not only increasingly printed but were tuned to a genteel European literary style governed by canons of correct usage. As George Philip Krapp observed in his seminal history of the English language, "pronunciation, grammar and spelling were not then tests of respectability [in the seventeenth century] . . . in the degree to which they have since become. What seems now like illiterate speech, the speech of persons who do not reflect how they speak, was then merely the normal speech of the community."[38] With no printed dictionaries to provide authority for correct spelling and usage, seventeenth-century vernacular literature exhibited a high degree of variability. As the spread of printing in the eighteenth century gave increased importance to writing, however, there emerged a concomitant movement

36. Alexander Garden, *Regeneration, and the Testimony of the Spirit. Being the Substance of Two Sermons* . . . (1740), ibid., 58.

37. *A true and genuine Account of a WANDERING SPIRIT, raised of late* . . . . , ibid., 149.

38. George Philip Krapp, *The English Language in America* (New York, 1925), 1:ix.

toward standardization of spelling and usage. Following the appearance of Samuel Johnson's dictionary in 1755, language came to be thought of as written rather than spoken, and educated elites on both sides of the ocean adopted a written style intended to communicate with their literate peers.[39] Linguistic divisions between the well-bred and the vulgar became increasingly clear to both sectors of the colonial society. One revealing example of a distinctive lower-class style is a radical essay, *The Key of Libberty,* written (though never accepted for publication) in 1797 by James Manning, an untutored Massachusetts farmer who "neaver had the advantage of six months schooling in my life." In organization, spelling, and grammar the essay stands in stark contrast to the polished style of the Whig patriots. It was, as Manning recognized, "not in the language and stile of the Larned for I am not able."[40]

Linguistic uniformity conspired with classical education to establish a learned discourse that effectively separated the literate elite from the common folk. Hugh Blair, whose handbook, *Lectures on Rhetoric and Belles Lettres,* came to epitomize the style for aspiring gentlemen, averred that the educated class "is now so much accustomed to a correct and ornamental style, that no writer can, with safety, neglect the study of it."[41] To encourage such a style Blair pointed to the patrician cultures of classical Greece and Rome, and urged his fellow literati "to render ourselves well acquainted with the style of the best authors. This is requisite, both in order to form a just taste in style, and to supply us with a full stock of words on every subject."[42] The classical heritage provided a vocabulary and mode of discourse which leaders had to learn if they were to communicate through the proper forms.[43]

39. See, for example, H. L. Mencken, *The American Language: An Inquiry into the Development of English in the United States,* 4th ed. (New York, 1936), 380, and James Root Hulbert, *Dictionaries: British and American,* rev. ed. (London, 1968), 10.

40. Samuel Eliot Morison, ed., "William Manning's *The Key of Libberty,*" *WMQ*, 3d ser. 13 (1956): 202–54.

41. Hugh Blair, *Lectures on Rhetoric and Belles Lettres* (Philadelphia, 1862), 1:215. Blair's lectures and essays were gathered together for publication in 1783.

42. Ibid., 214.

43. Ong observes in "Latin and the Social Fabric," that "using Latin was like playing a game whose rules could never be changed. . . . Latin was not merely one subject among many or even among several. . . . Latin effected the transit from ignorance to tribal or communal wisdom. . . . Youngsters were given to understand that the treasures of all understanding were stored in the ancient tongues" (*The Barbarian Within* [New York, 1962], 206, 215). For descriptions of the classical grounding of colonial thought and education see Richard M. Gummere, *The American Colonial Mind and the Classical Tradition* (Cambridge, Mass., 1963); Robert Middlekauff, "A Persistent Tradition: The Classical Curriculum in Eighteenth-Century New England," *WMQ,* 3d ser. 18 (1961): 54–67; Meyer Reinhold, ed., *The Classick Pages: Classical Reading of Eighteenth-Century Americans* (University Park, Penn., 1975); and Wood, *Creation of the American Republic,* 48–53.

Classical learning inculcated a set of social and cultural attitudes about the nature of speaker and audience that went far beyond the content of literature. A formal, analytical style conveyed social as well as literary prerogatives. For centuries, masters of print and the written word enjoyed social power and prestige partly because the people were awed by a sequential form of communications they could not understand. The eighteenth-century rise in learned treatises, tightly argued pamphlets, and belletristic writing reflected an effort, in Mather Byles's words, to "cultivate *polite* Writing, and form and embellish the Style of our ingenious Countrymen.—"[44] But Byles's "ingenious Countrymen" did not include the common folk.

The eighteenth-century shift in the direction of print and polite style was reflected in the growing appeal of rational religion among the educated elite. Cotton Mather typified this shift as early as 1726 in his *Manuductio ad Ministerium,* which, as Miller recognized, "in its catholicity of taste and urbanity suggests the spirit of current periodical essays rather than the utilitarian aim of a preaching manual."[45] Followers of deism, which carried the liberal print-centered rationalism to an extreme, tended, in Ong's words, "to think of God himself as no longer a communicator, one who speaks to man, but as a Great Architect . . . , a manipulator of objects in visual-tactile space."[46] Treating communications as written rather than spoken, and locking words in printed space, rational Protestantism was incapable of penetrating the soul of an aural society; its ideas set forth in printed sermons and treatises could never inform a popular mentality attuned to the spoken word.

Attached to the elitist typographic culture were social imperatives. As long as social identities depended on a traditional social order for context and location within a finely graded hierarchy, communications had to be transacted through an elitist rhetoric. Power became so closely tied to print that advanced literacy and a classical education were virtually prerequisite to authority, and a college education guaranteed rapid advance

44. Miller and Johnson, eds., *The Puritans,* 689. For a description of the increasingly high incidence of colonial borrowing from polite British culture see T. H. Breen, *The Character of the Good Ruler: A Study of Puritan Political Ideas in New England, 1630–1730* (New Haven, Conn., 1970), 203–39; and Jack P. Greene, "Search for Identity: An Interpretation of the Meaning of Selected Patterns of Social Response in Eighteenth-Century America," *Journal of Sociological History* 3 (1970): 189–200.

45. Miller and Johnson, eds., *The Puritans,* 669. See also Johnson's discussion of Puritan rhetoric, ibid., 64–79.

46. Ong, *Presence of the Word,* 73. The same print-centered ("visual") mode of perception is apparent in the Lockean epistemology that underlay liberal assumptions in both religious and political contexts. See Ernest Tuveson, "Locke and the 'Dissolution of the Ego,'" *Modern Philology* 52 (1955): 164–65.

in the social hierarchy.[47] By 1776 there were nearly three thousand college graduates in the colonies who, through the remarkable improvements in post and press, were able to communicate with one another on a scale and with a frequency unimaginable in the seventeenth century.[48] The cosmopolitan "better sort" formed a close-knit community that provided both authors and audience for the wave of printed literature that began to surge in the late eighteenth century. Pamphlets written by educated gentlemen, primarily lawyers, merchants, ministers, and planters, were addressed to their peers.[49] The common people were not included in the audience, but it was assumed that they would continue to defer to the leaders. There was no recognition that the pamphleteers' impassioned celebration of republicanism would require a new rhetoric of communications reflecting a profound shift in the nature of social authority—a rhetoric, in brief, that threatened to undermine the exclusive world in which the pamphlets were originally conceived.

With the coming of independence the American leadership could congratulate itself on the creation of a unique republican world view through their publications. At the same time, however, these leaders could neither anticipate nor appreciate an egalitarian rhetoric that would soon compel them to relinquish their traditional claims to power and authority in the new republic. As a model of society, the neoclassical world of the colonial gentlemen was essentially stable; their exclusion of the common people meant that their writings could not reflect a changing self-consciousness initiated from below. The very outlook that created a learned and articulate "Republic of Letters" served, at the same time, to limit the writers' historical consciousness. Quite simply, the people were neither heard nor understood in their own terms.

47. On the social meaning and political significance of a classical education in the colonies see James Axtell, *The School upon a Hill: Education and Society in Colonial New England* (New Haven, Conn., 1974), 201–44; James J. Walsh, *Education of the Founding Fathers of the Republic: Scholasticism in the Colonial Colleges. . .* (New York, 1935); and Robert M. Zemsky, "Power, Influence, and Status: Leadership Patterns in the Massachusetts Assembly, 1740–1755," *WMQ*, 3d. ser. 36 (1969): 511–12.

48. Axtell, *School upon a Hill*, 213. For classic descriptions of the expanding networks of communications in 18th-century America see Frank Luther Mott, *American Journalism: A History of Newspapers in the United States Through 250 Years, 1690–1940* (New York, 1941), 3–110; and Wesley Everett Rich, *The History of the United States Post Office to the Year 1829* (Cambridge, Mass., 1924), 3–67.

49. Gordon S. Wood observes that "even more indicative of the limited elitist conception of the audience was the extraordinary reliance on personal correspondence for the circulation of ideas. It is often difficult to distinguish between the private correspondence and the public writings of the Revolutionaries, so much alike are they" ("Democratization of Mind," *Leadership in the American Revolution*, 67–72).

The creation of an egalitarian rhetoric owed nothing to the classical heritage. If we are to understand the cultural significance of the Revolution, we must move beyond the rhetorical world of informed publications to the social world of popular assembly. We must *listen* as the "inarticulate" would have listened and determine to what extent religious and political meetings had a common rhetorical denominator that reached a revolutionary crescendo in the movement for independence.[50] For Philip Davidson, whose work continues to stand as the best general description of communications in the Revolutionary period, there was an unmistakably oral orientation to patriot "propaganda."[51] Throughout the colonies there existed a broad range of dramatic and oral communications in which, in William Eddis's words, "the busy voice of preparation echoes through every settlement."[52] The mobilization of the people was accomplished through extra-institutional mass meetings which, Merrill Jensen recognizes, were "of even greater long-range importance than mob action."[53]

The Founding Fathers were reluctant, for obvious reasons, to dwell on the oral dynamic unleashed in the course of rebellion; the same cannot be said of the loyalist opposition. Jonathan Sewall recognized both the evangelical and oral connections with republicanism: "there is an Enthusiasm in politics, like that which religious notions inspire, that drives Men on

50. That the revivals did, in fact, continue to grow is most clearly reflected in the rapid growth of the dissenter movements in the colonies. Thomas Jefferson, for example, observed that by the time of the Revolution "two-thirds of the people [of Virginia] had become dissenters" (*Notes on the State of Virginia,* ed. William Peden [Chapel Hill, N.C., 1955], 158). More generally, Isaac Backus noted that, by 1795, the number of Separate Baptist preachers had grown to 1,125 (*A History of New England with Particular Reference to the Baptists,* ed. David Weston, 2d ed. [Newton, Mass., 1871], 401).

51. Philip Davidson, *Propaganda and the American Revolution, 1763–1783* (Chapel Hill, N.C., 1941). Despite his penetrating description of Revolutionary communications, Davidson failed to recognize that the sort of mass society in which a manipulative propaganda could flourish did not exist in pre-Revolutionary America. What made the pamphlets significant was not the writers' intent to hoodwink the people but rather their exclusion of the people from the presumed audience. Both the term and the practice of mass propaganda originated after the Revolution. See David Hackett Fischer, *The Revolution of American Conservatism: The Federalist Party in the Era of Jeffersonian Democracy* (New York, 1965), 144–49.

52. William Eddis, *Letters from America,* ed. Aubrey C. Land (Cambridge, Mass., 1969), 100.

53. Merrill Jensen, "The American People and the American Revolution," *Journal of American History* 57 (1970): 15. For suggestive descriptions of how these "mass meetings" aroused "popular enthusiasm" for independence see Davidson, *Propaganda and the American Revolution,* 173–208; Isaac, "Dramatizing the Ideology of Revolution," *WMQ,* 3d ser. 33 (1976): 357–85; and Robert Middlekauff, "The Ritualization of the American Revolution," in Stanley Coben and Lorman Ratner, eds., *The Development of an American Culture* (Englewood Cliffs, N.J., 1970), 31–43.

with an unusual Impetuosity, that baffles and confounds all Calculation grounded upon rational principles. Liberty, among Englishmen, is a Word, whose very Sound carries a fascinating charm."[54] Loyalist literature is replete with complaints that American towns were increasingly "filled with mock orations and songs, which for composition and sentiment would disgrace the most stupid and abandoned. . . ."[55]

Whigs and loyalists used against one another the same arguments from constitution, law, and natural rights, but the charge of demagogic orality was a one-way criticism. The loyalist opposition never mustered a counterattack until after 1773; and when it finally appeared, it was almost exclusively printed. Like earlier liberal rhetoric, that of the loyalists disdained the "wild uproars" of the Whigs which culminated in nothing less than a "Yell of Rebellion," and concentrated instead on pen and press.[56] In Davidson's words, "the Tory appeal was a written appeal; the dearth of oral, dramatic, and pictorial suggestions is striking."[57]

Insofar as the Whig gentlemen favored traditional modes of public address, they failed to plumb the depths of a popular revolutionary spirit that was oral and egalitarian rather than printed and elitist. Bernard Bailyn, who has examined the ideological origins from the Revolution more deeply than any other scholar, relies almost exclusively on printed sources as a sufficient explanation for the development of a Revolutionary mentality. It was "the opposition press, as much as any single influence," Bailyn argues, "that shaped the political awareness of eighteenth-century Americans."[58] Although this is true for the informed populace,

54. "A Letter from Jonathan Sewall to General Frederick Haldimand," May 30, 1775, in Jack P. Greene, ed., *Colonies to Nation, 1763–1789: A Documentary History of the American Revolution* (New York, 1975), 267.

55. Margaret Wheeler Willard, ed., *Letters on the American Revolution* (New York, 1925), 81. See also Ramsay, *History of the American Revolution,* 16–17.

56. Daniel Leonard, "To the Inhabitants of the Province of the Massachusetts-Bay," (1775), in Leslie F. S. Upton, ed., *Revolutionary Versus Loyalist: The First American Civil War, 1774–1784* (Waltham, Mass., 1968), 39.

57. Davidson, *Propaganda and the American Revolution,* 298, 301.

58. Bernard Bailyn, *The Origins of American Politics* (New York, 1967), 38–39. Bailyn attributes many of the ideas presented in the "opposition press" to the English "real Whig" tradition. This is of some importance because, like the American Whigs, the English libertarian persuasion was almost exclusively print-centered. As Caroline Robbins observes, "the Real whigs, the liberals, seem to have been associated in certain areas and institutions around a few persuasive men. They were related by a bewildering series of marriages. . . . They relied on conversation, on letters among themselves or occasionally in the public press, on the dissemination of the printed word. . . . [T]hey followed a hit-and-miss method, consistent only in their determined faith in the printed tracts and treatises continually produced by them" (*The Eighteenth-Century Commonwealthman: Studies in the Transmission, Development and Circumstance of English Liberal Thought from the Restoration of Charles II until the War with the Thirteen Colonies* [Cambridge, Mass., 1959], 381, 382, 383).

the link between print culture and the people, between pamphlets and popular ideology, is assumed, not demonstrated. Despite the rhetorical incompatibility of a popular culture and tightly reasoned pamphlets, the existence of a distinctive popular ideology is denied.[59] But as Patrick Henry pointed out, "the middle and lower ranks of people have not those illumined ideas which the well-born are so happily possessed of—they cannot so readily perceive latent objects."[60] Henry's refusal to enter into "the labyrinths of syllogistic [Latin] argumentative deductions" in his public address may well account for the power of his oratory, which more than one commentator has likened to that of the revivalists in style and impact.[61]

The problem with Bailyn's analysis is not that it is wrong in the way it portrays ideology; indeed, it represents a brilliant plea for the late eighteenth century as an "age of ideology." The problem is pamphlets: although central to the rebellion and to the articulation of classical republican theory in the colonies, they are not sufficient to explain the process of an egalitarian cultural transformation. Bailyn concentrates on the pamphlets and the "real Whig" country ideology as the formative sources of the rebellion. Having set the ideological background for rebellion, he describes some of the manifestations of the "transforming radicalism" unleashed by the Revolution.[62] But the instances of transforming radicalism which Bailyn isolates are described far more effectively than they are explained in terms of their cultural sources. Pamphlets could never represent the primary source of radical republicanism, any more than the revivals could have issued from printed sermons or the loyalist critique of the rebellion organize itself through oral popular appeals.

59. Bernard Bailyn argues that "the outbreak of the Revolution was not the result of social discontent. . . . Nor was there a transformation of mob behavior or of the lives of the 'inarticulate' in the pre-Revolutionary years that accounts for the disruption of Anglo-American politics" ("The Central Themes of the American Revolution: An Interpretation," in Stephen G. Kurtz and James H. Hutson, eds., *Essays on the American Revolution* [Chapel Hill, N.C., 1973], 12).

60. William Wirt Henry, ed., *Patrick Henry: Life, Correspondence and Speeches* (New York, 1891), 3:462.

61. Heimert, *Religion and the American Mind,* 232, 233; Rhys Isaac, "Preachers and Patriots: Popular Culture and the Revolution in Virginia," in Alfred F. Young, ed., *The American Revolution: Explorations in the History of American Radicalism* (DeKalb, Ill., 1976), 152–54.

62. Bailyn states that "the radicalism the Americans conveyed to the world in 1776 was a transformed as well as a transforming force. . . . Institutions were brought into question and condemned that appeared to have little if any direct bearing on the immediate issues of the Anglo-American struggle" (*Ideological Origins of the American Revolution,* 161, 232).

Recognizing the failure of pamphlets to capture the growing revolutionary sentiment in America, a writer for the *Pennsylvania Packet* argued in 1776 that "our cause will never appear to advantage in a pamphlet. . . . When you write a pamphlet you are expected to say the best, if not all that can be said on the subject, and if it contains [only] a few weighty arguments the author is despised and the subject suffers."[63] The writer was referring, of course, to pamphlets generally. Not every pamphlet was limited by the rhetorical constraints of a classical style. What made Thomas Paine's *Common Sense* so unlike the prevailing pamphlet literature of the day was its scorn for the best literary canons and its repudiation of the language and forms of classical discourse. Coming from a lower-class Quaker background, Paine lacked the formal Latin education common to other pamphleteers; in its place he managed to establish a new style that anticipated the wave of nineteenth-century literature intended for the people generally.[64]

Another major atypical pamphlet to appear in the colonies before independence was *An Oration on the Beauties of Liberty,* published in 1773 by the Baptist minister and linen-draper John Allen. Like Paine, Allen was a recent arrival from England at the time *An Oration* was printed, and, like *Common Sense*, the tract enjoyed immense popularity in the colonies.[65] In style it bears repeated resemblances to the "enraged" language which scholars have found throughout *Common Sense.*[66] Also, as in *Common Sense,* the references and quotations are not drawn, as in the other pamphlets, from classical republicanism or British constitutional theory, but rather from the Bible. There is not one page of *An Oration* that does not supply biblical precedent or injunction for the assault on privilege and tyranny. Ahab, the golden calf, Zedekiah, Cain, Abel, and Rehoboam constituted a familiar vocabulary that was "opened up" and explained repeatedly in colonial sermons. To liken a ruler to Ahab or a social order to Babylon was to call for a revolution.

Perhaps the most important aspect of *An Oration* is that it was obvi-

63. Quoted in Thomas R. Adams, *American Independence, the Growth of an Idea: A Bibliographic Study of the American Political Pamphlets Printed Between 1764 and 1776. . . .* (Providence, R.I., 1965), xiv–xv.

64. This point is effectively developed in Eric Foner, *Tom Paine and Revolutionary America* (New York, 1976), xv–xvi, 80–87.

65. *An Oration Upon the Beauties of Union* (Boston, 1773) was exceeded in separate editions by only two pamphlets including the "runaway best seller" *Common Sense.* For tabulations see Adams, *American Independence,* xi–xii.

66. See, for example, Bernard Bailyn, "Common Sense," in *Fundamental Testaments of the American Revolution,* Library of Congress Symposia (Washington, D.C., 1973), 7–22.

ously meant to be heard as well as read.[67] Its full impact can be felt only when one *listens* to the rhetoric. Addressing the common people, Allen repeatedly relied on a coarse prose, rather than on logical syllogisms or authorities from a printed past. Reminding the people that rulers and ministers were "servants" who must "hear" a free and "affectionate" people, Allen demanded, "Has not the voice of your father's blood cry'd yet loud enough in your ears, in your hearts? . . . Have you not heard the voice of blood in your own streets. . . ?"[68] In striking contrast to virtually all the other pamphleteers, but like Paine later, Allen aimed his rhetoric beyond the literate elite to the rank and file.

If action proceeds from a cultural perception of public events in terms of symbolic forms, then analyses of the mobilization of ideas into ideology and action must recognize, at least in part, the cultural preconditions for receptivity, particularly on the popular level. A discontinuous ("revolutionary") cultural change could, by definition, never emerge from a continuing intellectual tradition; there must be a break somewhere. Where are the sources of such a radical ideology to be discovered?

Without denying the influence of typographic culture on the leaders of the rebellion and in the formation of the new governments, it might be helpful to think of republicanism in a pluralistic context as absorbing both traditional and egalitarian perceptions of social order. The theoretical work of J. G. A. Pocock builds upon an understanding of the unavoidable "multivalency" of language that derives from the different experiences of speakers and hearers.[69] Recognizing the truism that words do not necessarily mean what either the speaker or the historian believe they mean, Pocock does not examine language and ideas as fixed entities, but rather insists that language and communications not be separated from the circumstances and comprehension of their individual users. When "conceptual and social worlds" are placed in conjunction, no singular "constellation of ideas" or "climate of opinion" appears to have embodied an identical meaning for all social ranks.[70] To get at the popular meaning of republican ideology requires moving beyond the verbal content of the documents themselves to the social world in which they were transmitted.

Pocock's insights, placed in the context of the American Revolution, reveal that not one but two ideological explosions propelled the colonies

67. John M. Bumsted and Charles E. Clark, "New England's Tom Paine: John Allen and the Spirit of Liberty," *WMQ*, 3d ser. 21 (1964): 570.

68. Allen, *An Oration on the Beauties of Liberty*, 19, 27.

69. See, especially, J. G. A. Pocock, *Politics, Language and Time: Essays on Political Thought and History* (New York, 1971), 3–41.

70. Ibid., 15.

into a new nation. Both leaders and followers were possessed of an extraordinarily powerful ideology that at points converged on common antagonists and a common vocabulary, and at other points diverged dramatically. No ideology that is pieced together solely from the literate world of print can fully comprehend the radical dynamic of the Revolution. It is incapable of accounting for the enormously creative power of *vox populi* to organize a social order bound together in voluntary associations based on discussion and public address. Resisting John Adams and others who located the Revolution's *raison d'être* among the classical world view of the elite, Benjamin Rush issued the following advice to historians: "I hope with the history of this folly, some historian will convey to future generations, that many of the most active and useful characters in accomplishing this revolution, were strangers to the formalities of a Latin and Greek education."[71]

The social conditions that allowed for the popular upsurge in the revivals and rebellion did not permit unstructured public address to degenerate into "anarchy" and mass rebellion, as the standing order had always feared. Perhaps the enduring legacy of the Revolution lay in its demonstration that distinctive ideologies *could* work in concert. The typographic ideology of the real Whig tradition was, as Bailyn and others demonstrate, an "inner accelerator" of a transforming radicalism, but only in the sense that the aroused elite were compelled by the logic of their argument for rebellion to create, in law and politics, an egalitarian vocabulary, and, in communications, the secular equivalents of the revival in voluntary political parties and free presses.[72] Beneath that impulse, however, we must also recognize typographic ideology and the rebellion as accelerating a movement *already in progress,* a movement that originated among the lower rather than the upper strata of colonial society, and that, combined with profound social strains which increased throughout the eighteenth century, opened the way for the "enchanting sound" of mass public address.[73]

While the Whig justification of the rebellion pointed to an "invisible government" of ministers, cliques, and venal officials, another conspiracy, recognized as early as 1773 by the loyalist Boucher, was equally "invisible" and far more powerful. Attacking the foundations of traditional social order, this conspiracy derived its "invisibility" from its essentially extemporaneous nature. In Boucher's words: "as though there were

71. Quoted in Meyer Reinhold, "Opponents of Classical Learning in America during the Revolutionary Period," American Philosophical Society, *Proceedings* 112 (1968): 230.

72. Bailyn, *Ideological Origins of the American Revolution,* 95.

73. Garden, *Regeneration, and the Testimony of the Spirit,* in Heimert and Miller, eds., *Great Awakening,* 47.

some irrefutable charm in all extemporaneous speaking, however rude, the orators of our committees and sub-committees, like those in higher spheres, *prevail with their tongues.* To public speakers alone is the government of our country now completely committed. . . . An empire is thus completely established within an empire; and a new system of government of great power erected, even before the old one is formally abolished."[74] An empire premised on talk, wholly lacking in the formal coercive structure that kings, churches, aristocracies, standing armies, and mercantile controls provided, did indeed represent a revolutionary departure in the principles of government and social order. Voluntaryism, the very linchpin of social, religious, and political organization in the new republic, was perhaps the clearest manifestation of this revolutionary system of authority.[75] Of course, public address did not replace print, nor was the populace hostile to print and literacy *per se,* but only to a print culture that was elitist and hierarchical. Still, it is no accident that early republicanism represented the "Golden Age of Oratory," because mass address was, for a time, the most effective means of reaching the new audience and utilizing the egalitarian style seized upon by republican orators and revivalists as the creative force within the popular ideology.[76]

The rhetorical transformation in the revivals signified an emerging popular culture asserting itself against a paternalistic social ethic. In the course of the Revolution, the social order prefigured in evangelical assemblies was suffused with secular and political meanings articulated in the world view of republicanism. This new order, in Michael Kammen's description, was not so much a "seamless web" as an "unstable plural-

74. Jonathan Boucher, *A View of the Causes and Consequences of the American Revolution in Thirteen Discourses. . . .* (New York, 1967 [orig. publ. London, 1797]), 320, 321. See David Ammerman's discussion of "government by committee," in *In the Common Cause: American Response to the Coercive Acts of 1774* (Charlottesville, Va., 1974), 103–24 and Wood, *Creation of the American Republic,* 319–28.

75. On the frontier the essentially oral, voluntary association was most clearly manifested in the revivals which, as Donald G. Matthews suggests, represented a critical "organizing process" in the new nation. See Matthews, "The Second Great Awakening as an Organizing Process, 1780–1830," *American Quarterly* 11 (1969): 23–43. Similarly, Leonard L. Richards points out how, in the voluntary reform efforts of the "evangelical crusade," evangelical abolitionists effectively utilized the "revolution in communications and the creation of mass media" to bypass traditional social channels and organize voluntary associations within "impersonal, large-scale organizations" (*"Gentlemen of Property and Standing": Anti-Abolition Mobs in Jacksonian America* [New York, 1970], 167).

76. Wood points this out in *Creation of the American Republic,* 621–22, and "Democratization of Mind," in *Leadership in the American Revolution,* 78–82. Perhaps not sufficiently emphasized in studies of early American literature is the abrupt decline in public significance of pamphlets, letters, treatises, and printed sermons after the Revolution.

ism" defying reduction to any one ideology or social system.[77] The rhetorical division resulting from the revivals played a major role in generating subsequent tensions and conflicts in American society. These tensions, moreover, reflected not so much opposing ideas with conflicting literary traditions as entirely different social outlooks and attitudes toward social authority, all deriving legitimacy from the individualism implicit in a mass democratic society. Evangelical attacks on a settled and educated ministry may have expressed a pristine "anti-intellectualism" in the colonies,[78] but it was an anti-intellectualism that was positive and creative—indeed, revolutionary. Without it there would have been no creation of an egalitarian American republic.

The oral explosion and egalitarian style evidenced in the revivals were not limited to religion, nor was the articulation of a radical ideology the conscious objective of itinerant evangelists. The primary concern of the revivals was the saving of souls, and the rhetorical innovations that lent force to the movement were not fully perceived or verbalized for what they could come to represent: a revolutionary shift in world view. As a movement initiated from below, the social experience of the revivals existed in fact before the emergence of a literate rationale. This does not mean that the experience proceeded from irrational impulses but, rather, that the terms necessary for rational comprehension and formal legitimation had to be invented. What opponents of the revivals termed a "spirit of superstition" was, for Jonathan Edwards, a new "sense" that could not easily be rendered into the existing forms of speech: "Some Things that they are sensible of are altogether new to them, their Ideas and inward Sensations are new, and what they therefore knew not how to accommodate Language to, or to find Words to express."[79] Edwards's concern was to fit the new social experience of the revivals to its proper spiritual vocabulary, while acknowledging that no language could fully express the essence of religious faith.

What Edwards and other churchmen failed to recognize was that the "spirit of liberty" manifest in the revivals would not be contained in religious categories. In the movement for independence both leaders and followers adopted a political vocabulary that expressed the egalitarian im-

77. Michael Kammen, *People of Paradox: An Inquiry Concerning the Origins of American Civilization* (New York, 1972), 89–96. The social ramifications of this cultural pluralism are treated in Robert H. Wiebe, *The Segmented Society: An Introduction to the Meaning of America* (New York, 1975).

78. Richard Hofstadter, *Anti-Intellectualism in American Life* (New York, 1962).

79. Jonathan Edwards, *The Distinguishing Marks of a Work of the Spirit of God . . .* (1741), in Bushman, ed., *Great Awakening,* 123. On Edwards's use of language see Harold P. Simonson, *Jonathan Edwards: Theologian of the Heart* (Grand Rapids, 1974), 91–118.

pulse in the secular language of republicanism. This vocabulary was largely provided, as Bailyn and Caroline Robbins demonstrate, through the Commonwealth tradition. But the ethos and ideological fervor of republicanism did not derive so much from the injection of Commonwealth vocabulary into colonial pamphlets as from the translation of the evangelical experience into a secular theoretical vocabulary that more adequately embodied, for some, the revolutionary thrust first widely experienced in the revivals. Words that were abstracted from their restrictive, deferential context came to mean something else. In Tocqueville's observation, Americans had a penchant for abstract words because only by using a vocabulary lacking specificity could they communicate radical ideas that destroyed a conventional style. "An abstract word," Tocqueville noted, "is like a box with a false bottom; you may put in it what ideas you please and take them out again unobserved."[80] The "country" publicists did not provide the textbook of revolution, so much as a lexicon of revolution, the meaning of which could be grasped only within a persuasion that celebrated the sovereignty of the new political audience.

80. Alexis de Tocqueville, *Democracy in America,* eds. J. P. Mayer and Max Lerner (New York, 1966), 482. See also Robert E. Shalhope, "Toward a Republican Synthesis: The Emergence of an Understanding of Republicanism in American Historiography," *WMQ* 29 (1972): 72–73.

4

The Origins of Civil Millennialism in America

Nathan O. Hatch

Reprinted by permission from *William and Mary Quarterly* 31 (1974): 407–30.

No doubts clouded the Reverend Samuel Sherwood's assessment of the impending war between Great Britain and the American colonies. "God Almighty, with all the powers of heaven, are on our side," he declared to his Connecticut audience early in 1776. "Great numbers of angels, no doubt, are encamping round our coast, for our defence and protection. Michael stands ready, with all the artillery of heaven, to encounter the dragon, and to vanquish this black host." With a confidence almost prophetic, Sherwood announced the coming defeat of the "antichristian tyranny" which the British government represented; because the king's chief ministers had sipped the golden cup of fornication with "the old mother of harlots," they faced the imminent doom reserved for the wicked, persecuting tyrants of the earth. In building the climax of his address, which translated the conflict into a struggle of cosmic significance, Sherwood predicted that the British attack on America was one "of the last efforts, and dying struggles of the man of sin." From this apocalyptic point of view America's victory would initiate Christ's millennial kingdom.[1]

1. Samuel Sherwood, *The Church's Flight into the Wilderness: An Address on the Times* (New York, 1776), 39–49, quotations on 46, 15, 49.

Sherwood was by no means the only American minister whose millennial hopes were fired by the Revolutionary struggle. The cosmic interpretation of the conflict—God's elect versus Antichrist—appeared as a significant pattern in the intricate tapestry of ideas used by New England clergymen to explain the war's purpose. Moreover, by the time American victory seemed assured, the rhetoric of New England sermons was brimming with euphoric images of America's role in hastening the kingdom. The prospects for this blessed age had not seemed so bright since the founding of New England. "Vice and immorality shall yet here, become . . . banished," proclaimed George Duffield, chaplain to the Continental Congress, "and the wilderness blossom as the rose."[2]

Certainly the most striking feature of this millennial language in the Revolutionary era is the way it adapted the framework of apocalyptic history to commonly held political ideas. Sermons during the war stressed repeatedly that American liberty was God's cause, that British tyranny was Antichrist's, and that sin was failure to fight the British. With the coming of peace many ministers envisioned Christ's thousand-year reign on earth as an extension of the civil and religious liberty established in America.[3] This amalgam of traditional Puritan apocalyptic rhetoric and eighteenth-century political discourse I have chosen to call "civil millennialism," a term warranted by the extent to which these themes were directed by the society's political consciousness. Under the aegis of civil millennialism ministers of varying theological persuasions came to do homage at the same shrine, that of liberty, and expressed their allegiance in projections about the future which were as novel as they were pervasive.[4]

2. George Duffield, *A Sermon Preached in the Third Presbyterian Church* . . . (Philadelphia, 1784), 17.

3. For sermons that interpret the Revolution as the struggle of the elect versus Antichrist see Abraham Keteltas, *God Arising and Pleading His People's Cause* . . . (Newburyport, Mass., 1777), and Samuel West, *A Sermon Preached before the Honorable Council* . . . (Boston, 1776). For good examples of ministers whose millennial hopes were aroused by American victory see Ezra Stiles, *The United States elevated to Glory and Honor* . . . (New Haven, Conn., 1783), and Benjamin Trumbull, *God is to be praised for the Glory of his Majesty* . . . (New Haven, Conn., 1784).

4. I have described this apocalyptic orientation as "civil" rather than "civic" or "political" because this was the adjective most frequently used by ministers to define those privileges of citizenship which increasingly occupied their attention. Several scholars who have written about millennial interpretations of the Revolution have recognized a fundamental change from earlier apocalyptic understanding. See Ernest Lee Tuveson, *Redeemer Nation: The Idea of America's Millennial Role* (Chicago, 1968), 24; John G. Buchanan, "Puritan Philosophy of History from Restoration to Revolution," *Essex Institute Historical Collections* 104 (1968): 342–43; and J. F. Maclear, "The Republic and the Millennium," in Elwyn A. Smith, ed., *The Religion of the Republic* (Philadelphia, 1971), 183–94.

The language of civil millennialism has a strange ring to an ear accustomed to that of Puritan apocalyptic thought, but not because the political dimension of millennialism was itself a novelty. Englishmen since the Reformation had often been willing to oppose civil governments deemed to be under the control of antichristian power. They assumed that the frustration of French and Spanish hegemony abroad and Catholic political influence at home played a major role in realizing the day when swords would be beaten into plowshares. Across the Atlantic, New Englanders for a century also had watched political developments for signs of the coming times. What *does* give civil millennialism its distinctive quality is the new configuration of civil and religious priorities in the minds of the clergy. In a subtle but profound shift in emphasis the religious values that traditionally defined the ultimate goal of apocalyptic hope—the conversion of all nations to Christianity—became diluted with, and often subordinate to, the commitment to America as a new seat of liberty. Although its rhetoric was conventional, this new form of millennialism, channeled in the direction of prevailing political values, stood in marked contrast to traditional New England apocalyptic hopes.

Nothing makes this point clearer than the differences between civil millennialism and the apocalyptic expectations of the Great Awakening. Jonathan Edwards may have resembled Sherwood or Duffield in the application of apocalyptic ideas to his own times and in his postmillennial view of the future, but such similarities are less significant than the fundamental contrasts between the two perspectives. The New Light confidence in the progressive course of history was based on the spread of vital piety; Christ's kingdom advanced toward its completion by the effusion of God's spirit in widespread revivals. The Revolutionary millennialist, on the other hand, based his apocalyptic hopes on the civil and religious liberty that American victory over Britain would insure. His vision of the future inspired him to attempt to thwart the precipitate advance of power rather than to advocate the conversion of sinners. Edwards saw the Concert of Prayer as the primary institution for promoting the kingdom; praying bands of pious saints were the avant-garde who would drive back the forces of darkness. In contrast, ministers such as Abraham Keteltas or Samuel Langdon welcomed to the cause of God anyone who would take up the sword against the antichrist of British tyranny. The spontaneous defense of liberty in America encouraged them to interpret existing American society as the model upon which the millennial kingdom would be based. Inspired by the complex of ideas here called civil millennialism, New England ministers of the Revolutionary era resisted tyranny in God's name, hailed liberty as the virtue of the "New American Israel," and proclaimed that in sharing these values with all mankind America would become the principal seat of Christ's earthly rule.[5]

In view of the substantial differences between these two interpretations of prophecy it is necessary to reexamine the origins and development of civil millennialism in order to explain more adequately how it became so ingrained in the minds of New England ministers. Put another way, the intention is to rethink the assumption common in recent literature that the origins of civil millennialism can be traced directly to the piety of the Great Awakening. According to this interpretation, the revivals of the 1740s aroused a new, potent sense of American destiny—expressed by the millennialism of such New Lights as Edwards—which flowered into the intense religious patriotism of the young republic. In his massive study of the mind of eighteenth-century New England Alan Heimert attributes the fervor of the Revolutionary clergy to an excited millennial expectancy that flowed from the Awakening.[6] Heimert recognizes certain characteristics of civil millennialism but sees them only as modifications of the dynamic postmillennialism of New Light ministers. In emphasizing the dominant imprint of the Awakening on the intellectual activity of the mid-eighteenth century, he not only dismisses the heritage of pre-Awakening Puritanism but also jumps quickly from the Awakening to the Revolution, assuming that the imperial wars of the period were "incidental, even irrelevant" to the clergy's definition of New England identity. Within this framework the ideas that developed before and after the Awakening had little bearing on the shifting patterns of religious patriotism. Edwards and his successors rekindled the torch of American mission and destiny lit by the founders of the "city on a hill" and passed it directly to the patriots who fought for a new republic.[7] Although not all scholars would accept Heimert's stress on the New Light origins of the Revolution, few would doubt that the piety of the Awak-

5. For an excellent example of the striking contrast between the millennium of Edwards and that of the Revolution cf. Edwards, *Some Thoughts Concerning the Revival of Religion in New England* . . . in C. C. Goen, ed., *The Works of Jonathan Edwards,* 4 (New Haven, Conn., 1972), 348–70, with the sermon by Ebenezer Baldwin, *The Duty of Rejoicing under Calamities and Afflictions* . . . (New York, 1776).

6. Alan Heimert, *Religion and the American Mind: From the Great Awakening to the Revolution* (Cambridge, Mass., 1966), 59, 413–509.

7. According to Heimert, the Awakening shattered "the social assumptions inherited from the seventeenth century [and] allowed the evangelical ministry to offer the American people new commitments, political as well as ethical." After 1740 little of intellectual significance remained outside of the issues posed by the "two parties" formed in the Awakening. Ibid., 14, 3. For Heimert's discussion of the insignificance of developments between the Great Awakening and the Revolution, particularly the Anglo-French wars, see ibid., 84–85.

ening was the main source of the civil millennialism of the Revolutionary period.[8]

This interpretation is open to serious question. In the first place, if the roots of civil millennialism are to be found primarily in New Light enthusiasm, it is strange that its rhetoric was employed by Old Lights such as Langdon, Jeremy Belknap, and Samuel West, as well as the rationalist John Adams. The prevalence of this way of thinking among men of contrasting theologies can hardly be explained simply by reference to the New Light intellectual tradition.[9] Secondly, while recent scholarship has focused on the exultant hopes that characterized the Awakening, it has conspicuously avoided the same careful analysis of New Light thought in the years of the revival's demise. There has been little effort to examine the influence of an increasingly secular society upon the millennial perspective derived from the Awakening. Scholars have not adequately considered the significance of the decline of apocalyptic hope in the later 1740s, when Americans concentrated on concerns other than vital religion.[10] The third and most basic flaw is the almost total neglect of the apocalyptic categories used by the clergy to explain their intense interest in the Anglo-French wars. Assuming that after the Awakening the clergy's sense of history included a moral distinction between the Old World and America—an incipient American nationalism—many scholars slight the importance of the conflict with France for New England thought. Looking only for signposts pointing in the direction of Ameri-

8. A complete historiographical essay could be written to explain the current scholarly paradigm of tracing the origins of American patriotism and nationalism primarily to the Great Awakening. See Sacvan Bercovitch, "Horologicals to Chronometricals: The Rhetoric of the Jeremiad," in Eric Rothstein, ed., *Literary Monographs,* 3 (Madison, Wis., 1970), 81; Darrett B. Rutman, ed., *The Great Awakening: Event and Exegesis* (New York, 1970), 4–5, 70; Conrad Cherry, ed., *God's New Israel: Religious Interpretations of American Destiny* (Englewood Cliffs, N.J., 1971), 29–30; and Cedric B. Cowing, *The Great Awakening and the American Revolution: Colonial Thought in the 18th Century* (Chicago, 1971), 203.

9. When numerous opposers of enthusiastic religion discuss the Revolution using a millennial paradigm, how can scholars assume that the Great Awakening was their common source? It would seem far more reasonable that a viewpoint prevalent among both Old and New Lights would have its intellectual origins in their shared heritage and experience rather than in the source of their theological division.

10. Few authors who discuss religion and its relation to the Revolution fathom the profound intellectual shift that Edmund S. Morgan has captured so poignantly in one sentence: "In 1740 America's leading intellectuals were clergymen and thought about theology; in 1790 they were statesmen and thought about politics." It is necessary to reconsider what happens to New Light millennial confidence when society at large substitutes politics for religion "as the most challenging area of human thought and endeavor." "The American Revolution Considered as an Intellectual Movement," in Arthur M. Schlesinger, Jr., and Morton White, eds., *Paths of American Thought* (Boston, 1963), 2.

canization, they have made an easy detour around many issues, significantly imperial in character and scope, which profoundly influenced New England ministers in the two decades before the Stamp Act.[11]

In 1742 Edwards anticipated with excitement the dawning of the millennium. In his defense of the Great Awakening, *Some Thoughts Concerning the Revival of Religion,* he suggested that this "very great and wonderful, and exceeding glorious work" surpassed any that had ever been seen in New England or in other lands. The great increase in seriousness, the new conviction of the truth of the gospel, and the unusual changes in young people throughout New England were convincing signs that God would soon transform the world into the "Latter-day Glory." Edwards was so encouraged by the progress of piety that he announced that the millennium would probably begin in America.[12]

Edwards did not stand alone in interpreting the renewal of vital religion as a foretaste of Christ's kingdom. *The Christian History,* published by Thomas Prince and his son to propagate the Awakening, reflected widespread assurance that the kingdom was making significant advances. Typical was the report of Peter Thacher, pastor at Middleborough, Massachusetts: "I desire to rejoice to hear that the Lord Christ is carrying on his own Word with such a mighty Arm in so many Places.... If it be the Dawn of the glorious Gospel-Day; I trust the whole earth shall soon be filled with the Knowledge of the *Saviour.*"[13] In the summer of 1743 almost seventy New England ministers signed *The Testimony and Advice of an Assembly of Pastors,* supporting the revivals and declaring that these effusions of the Spirit confirmed the expectations "of such as are *waiting for the Kingdom of God,* and the coming on of the . . . latter Days."[14]

These New Lights saw the millennium as a culmination of processes at work in the revival. They pictured the imminent age of peace in images

11. For Heimert nothing can be of real intellectual significance in eighteenth-century New England unless it encouraged Americanization. The Awakening was "in a vital respect an American declaration of independence from Europe." The "guiding light" of subsequent Calvinism was "a delight in the New World itself." Thus New Lights found little to interest them in the conflict with France because the drama of history no longer included foreign characters. *Religion and the American Mind,* 14, 86–87, 98, 267–69. For a conflicting interpretation that sees New England intensely caught up in the French wars "as another battle to make the world safe for Protestantism and purified of popery," see Kerry A. Trask, "In the Pursuit of Shadows: A Study of Collective Hope and Despair in Provincial Massachusetts during the Era of the Seven Years War, 1748 to 1764" (Ph.D. diss., University of Minnesota, 1971), 223–86.

12. Edwards, *Some Thoughts Concerning the Revival,* in Goen, ed., *Works,* 4:343–44, 353.

13. Thomas Prince, Jr., ed., *The Christian History* (Boston, 1743–1745), 2:95.

14. Ibid., 1:158, 163–64, 182.

that expressed the realization of revival hope. It would be a time of vital religion, when holiness of life rather than empty profession would prevail. Confident that these ends would be accomplished by a "wonderful *revival and propagation* of religion," Edwards identified the Awakening as "the earnest," "the dawning," "the prelude," "the forerunner" of that blissful age which was swiftly approaching.[15] In *The Christian History* Daniel Putnam made the connection between vital religion and the millennium even more explicit when he encouraged his fellow clergymen to pray for revival in order that "the *Kingdoms of this World* may become the *Kingdom* of OUR BLESSED LORD AND SAVIOUR JESUS CHRIST."[16]

For Edwards the revival impulse greatly overshadowed any political means of overthrowing Antichrist and initiating the thousand years of peace. "The authority of princes" could never accomplish the goal of the Spirit, nor could political and military activities in themselves sound the knell for Satan's empire. This could only be done by "multitudes flocking to Christ."[17] Later, during the French wars, Edwards was often encouraged by God's providential defeat of the enemy, who fought on the side of Antichrist, but these defeats he interpreted as "temporal mercies," incentives to the more important works of repentance and revival. Even in the political realm Edwards's primary vision was of the day when "vital religion shall then take possession of kings palaces and thrones; and those who are in highest advancement shall be holy men."[18]

To their dismay Edwards and the other revivalists did not see their dreams fulfilled in the immediate dawning of the new age. As early as the summer of 1743 indications began to appear in *The Christian History* that all was not well with the revival. While the pastors explained with a touch of nostalgia the earlier spiritual movings in their churches, they wondered unhappily why the Spirit had withdrawn. "*Manna* grows tasteless and insipid after a Year or two's Enjoyment," one minister lamented, "and too many are for making a Captain, and returning to

15. Jonathan Edwards, *The Works of President Edwards* (reprint ed., New York, 1968 [orig. publ. London, 1871]), 5:239; Edwards, *Some Thoughts Concerning the Revival,* in Goen, ed., *Works,* 4:353–58.

16. *The Christian History,* 1:182.

17. Edwards, *Works,* 5:239, 241.

18. Ibid., 2:480; 5:253. In a letter to William M'Culloch, Sept. 23, 1747, Edwards reconfirmed his subordination of political and military affairs to the issue of vital religion: "New-England has had many other surprising deliverances from the French and Indians. . . . These deliverances are very wonderful . . . but there are no such effects of these mercies upon us that are the subjects of them, as God requires, and most justly expects. The mercies are acknowledged in words, but we are not led to repentance by them; there appears no such thing as any reformation or Revival of religion in the land." S. E. Dwight, *The Light of President Edwards* . . . (New York, 1830), 243–44.

Egypt."[19] Throughout 1744 the clergy's dejection deepened. While not a single minister reported a fresh revival, many expressed anxiety at the "melancholy abatements" of divine grace. A letter signed by ten ministers in eastern Connecticut depicted the situation with imagery drawn not from the hopeful visions of Saint John's Apocalypse but from the humble prayer of Isaiah that in the midst of wrath God would remember mercy.[20] Even Edwards had to confess that "the work is put to a stop every where, and it is a day of the Enemy's triumph."[21]

If the Great Awakening was the catalyst that transformed postmillennialism into a dynamic paradigm to explain current events, what happened when the fires of the revival flickered and went out? How did the New Lights respond to the increasingly difficult problem of relating millennial hope to historical reality? By the spring of 1745 this problem had become acute. *The Christian History* collapsed early that year for at least the obvious reason that there were simply no revivals to report. As New Englanders challenged the French at Louisbourg later that spring, their attention was further distracted from the concerns of vital piety. A new tour by George Whitefield went almost unnoticed amid the frenzied activity inspired by the "mad scheme" to seize Cape Breton Island.[22]

Several options, all rather unpleasant, faced the minister who had anticipated that the Awakening would issue directly into the millennium. The fact that the kingdom's advance was checked, at least temporarily, led to deferred hope among some and outright pessimism among others. The writings of Edwards, Aaron Burr, and Joseph Bellamy expressed three different responses to the pressing need to forge new links between an optimistic tradition of providential history and the discouraging facts of day-to-day experience in a society increasingly unsympathetic to the millennial message.

One solution was to take celebrational note of revivals wherever they might be found. The decline of piety in New England had no necessary counterpart in Europe or in other parts of the British Empire. In this context we can understand Edwards's increasing involvement in transatlantic affairs after 1745. His extensive correspondence with Scottish ministers reflected an interest in the success of awakened Protestantism that went far beyond any provincial commitment to New England or America. Never again did he assert that America would have a special role in

19. *The Christian History,* 1:259.
20. Ibid., 2:114, 168, 311–12.
21. Dwight, *Life of Edwards,* 212.
22. John E. Van de Wetering, "The *Christian History* of the Great Awakening," *Journal of Presbyterian History* 44 (1966): 129; Edwin Scott Gaustad, *The Great Awakening in New England* (New York, 1957), 79.

the coming of the millennium. Thus in his *Humble Attempt* of 1747, written in response to a proposal by Scottish ministers for extensive networks of Christians who would pray regularly for new revivals, Edwards showed no inclination to draw a moral distinction between the Old World and the New. In lamenting the spiritual decadence of the whole British Empire he manifested a pessimism about America no less pronounced than for the British Isles.[23] On other occasions, in numerous letters to friends in Scotland, he contrasted the woeful decay of religion in America—"at present very sorrowful and dark"—with comforting evidences of divine activity elsewhere in the Empire. In one of these letters he expressed the hope that recent news from Britain would excite New Englanders to seek God's face, if they were not too far "buried in ignorance, or under the power of a lethargic stupor." Edwards could no longer find signs of the coming millennium exclusively in America; the decline of experimental religion there forced him to look beyond the Atlantic to see God at work.[24]

Edwards's solution to the problem of relating history to millennial theory was at best a holding action that avoided the major question: How could one anticipate the millennium in a society unaffected by revivalism? What happened, for instance, when revival fires were extinguished not only in New England but also throughout the Empire? This was the problem that Edwards's son-in-law, Aaron Burr, faced in the 1750s. Finding that both England and America were afflicted by irreligion and infidelity, and fearing the spiritual destruction of the whole British people,[25] Burr maintained Edwards's postmillennialism but reshuffled his categories to develop a millennial vision that can only be called pessimistic.[26] Thus in his sermon *The Watchman's Answer*, Burr developed a view of history and the apocalypse that Edwards would hardly have recognized. According to Burr, the course of history since the Reformation had not progressed in a millennial direction. Not only had the initial break with Rome fallen far short of the hopes it had raised, but in more

23. Edwards, *Works,* 2:476.

24. Dwight, *Life of Edwards,* 262, 278, 287, 412.

25. Aaron Burr, *A Discourse Delivered at New-Ark* . . . (New York, 1755), 23, 28. In his interpretation of this sermon Heimert singles out Burr's denunciations of Great Britain as an indication of the increasing American dissatisfaction with Old World Protestantism. Apparently he overlooks the fact that Burr directed this criticism as much to America as to England. *Religion and the American Mind,* 85–86.

26. James W. Davidson has made the excellent point that postmillennialism was not a constant "which affected the behavior of people in different times and situations in any consistent manner." He effectively demonstrates that a postmillennial framework did not necessarily imply an imminent millennium, an unclouded optimism, or an intense activism to bring on the kingdom. "Searching for the Millennium: Problems for the 1790s and the 1970s," *New England Quarterly* 45 (1972): 241–61, esp. 250–55, quotation on 255.

recent times the night of antichristian domination had continued and even deepened. Burr climaxed this pessimistic argument by disagreeing explicitly with Edwards's interpretation of the slaying of the witnesses in Revelation 11. Whereas for Edwards this worst time of persecution for the church had already taken place, Burr confessed his belief that the "sorest Calamity and Distress" were yet to come. The church should prepare itself to suffer cheerfully in an era of "Heresy and Wickedness, Tumults and Corruptions." Instead of sounding a trumpet of hope, Burr issued an exhortation to endurance; instead of projecting a vision of progress, he renewed the jeremiad theme.[27] He saw the millennium as the ultimate extrication of the church from its plight of "Midnight Security." Like Cotton Mather, whose chiliasm envisioned no interruption of the downward course of the church until God supernaturally intervened, Burr articulated a postmillennialism in which only a cosmic reordering would defeat the evil forces rampant among men.[28]

Both Edwards and Burr related their apocalyptic hopes to the events of contemporary history. The failure of the Awakening thus left them no choice but to alter their views of the future. Edwards maintained his optimism by broadening his vision to include the Empire; for Burr even that panorama failed to inspire hope. In contrast to both, another New Light leader, Joseph Bellamy, maintained his millennial expectations by disassociating the millennial future from contemporary history. He was thus able to speak optimistically of Christ's eventual kingdom without regard to its current record of success or lack thereof. His 1758 sermon *The Millennium*, without mentioning a single contemporary event, either religious or political, offered Christians only the timeless hope that someday Christ would prevail.[29]

The New Light millennial vision could never have provided the intellectual foundation for the historical optimism prevalent among ministers of the Revolutionary era. Based on the success of awakened piety, it could not sustain the interest of a generation whose infatuation with revivalism faded as quickly as it had flowered. When society ceased to march to the

27. Aaron Burr, *The Watchman's Answer*... (Boston, 1757), 19–22, 34–40, quotations on 22, 39.

28. For Cotton Mather's views on the second coming of Christ see Robert Middlekauff, *The Mathers: Three Generations of Puritan Intellectuals, 1596–1728* (New York, 1971), 320–49, esp. 335.

29. Joseph Bellamy, *The Millennium,* in Alan Heimert and Perry Miller, eds., *The Great Awakening: Documents Illustrating the Crisis and Its Consequences* (Indianapolis, Ind., 1967), 609–35. In other sermons Bellamy displays the same exclusively religious and apolitical concern. See *A Blow at the Root of the refined Antinomianism of the present Age* (Boston, 1763); *An Essay on the Nature and Glory of the Gospel of Jesus Christ*... (Boston, 1763); and *The Half-Way-Covenant* (New Haven, Conn., 1769).

revival's cadence, the New Light drummers faced the necessity of developing a more compelling beat. The Anglo-French conflicts that claimed New England's attention after 1745 provided just such an opportunity. In the wars with France the New England clergy found a broader basis for a millennial hope that could encompass all of society.

In July 1745 the New England press reported what must have been for its readers the most astounding news story in memory: the French fortress of Louisbourg had been captured by New England arms! In reactions that were almost ecstatic, newspapers, firsthand accounts, and sermons told how four thousand undisciplined "Land-Men unused to War" had sailed to Cape Breton Island in a makeshift fleet without British naval support or heavy artillery and there had besieged and reduced the most awesome military bastion in North America. Poetic descriptions compared the feat to the greatest victories of Marlborough, and ministers were inspired to proclaim that God had "triumphed gloriously over his and our antichristian enemies." This mighty blow to the man of sin evoked numerous expressions of millennial hope from the clergy and pointed to the new concerns that would preoccupy them in the subsequent years of imperial war.[30]

In the years between the "crusade" against Louisbourg in 1745 and the signing of the Peace of Paris in 1763 the conflict with France gripped New England society with an overriding intensity. Villages had to be defended against unpredictable attack and forces marshaled for offensive engagements. The urgency of other public affairs faded for those who experienced the anxiety of battle, the despair of defeat, the joy of victory.[31] New Englanders in general, and clergymen in particular, perceived the "Gallic peril" as a massive, insidious threat to their religion and liberties. John Mellen warned his countrymen in 1756: "Our enemies may yet triumph over us, and the gospel taken from us, instead of being by us transmitted to other nations. It is possible, our land may be given to the beast, the inhabitants to the sword, the righteous to the fire of martyrdom, our wives to ravishment, and our sons and our daughters to death and torture!"[32] Similarly, Ebenezer Pemberton declared that "the fires of *Smith-*

30. Thomas Prince, *Extraordinary Events the Doings of God* . . . (Boston, 1745), 20; *Joseph Sewall, The Lamb Slain* . . . (Boston, 1745), 29. There is no adequate analysis of the psychological impact on the Louisbourg campaign upon New Englanders. Francis Parkman, *A Half-Century of Conflict,* 2 (Boston, 1892), is as helpful as anyone.

31. For discussions of New England's intense involvement in the French wars see John M. Murrin, "Anglicizing an American Colony: The Transformation of Provincial Massachusetts" (Ph.D. diss., Yale University, 1966), 118–19, and Trask, "In the Pursuit of Shadows," 13, 223–86.

32. John Mellen, *The Duty of all to be ready for future impending Events* (Boston, 1756), 19–20.

field, which burnt with such *unrelenting* fury in the days of *Queen Mary*," should remind New England of the "*inhuman* barbarities" and the "methods of *torture* and *violence*" that characterized French rule.[33] Mellen and Pemberton joined a host of their colleagues who vented their anxiety by picturing the grim consequences of French victory. Images of enslavement, prisons, galleys, and horrible tortures expressed the clergy's fear that life under the yoke of France would be "lingering Death." To French tyranny, Solomon Williams preferred that New England be destroyed by an earthquake.[34]

The ministers' rhetoric associated France inseparably with "the merciless Rage of *Popish* power" and evoked images of the inquisition, the fury of Queen Mary, the schemes of the Stuarts, and the more recent suppression of Protestants in France. Roman Catholicism represented for New Englanders not only their ancestors' most hated foe but also an immediate conspiracy against the liberties of all mankind.[35] Typical of this mood was the fear expressed by Prince that "our inveterate and *popish* Enemies both without and within the Kingdom, are restless to enslave and ruin us." If France won the struggle, "Cruel *Papists* would quickly fill the *British Colonies*, seize our Estates, abuse our Wives and Daughters, and barbarously murder us; as they have done the like in *France* and *Ireland*."[36]

These perceptions of a massive French-Catholic conspiracy were linked directly to an apocalyptic interpretation of history in which the French were accomplices in Satan's designs to subjugate God's elect in New England. According to John Burt, the conduct of the French "bespeaks them the Offspring of that *Scarlet Whore, that Mother of Harlots,* who is justly *the Abomination of the Earth*."[37] In the years of the French wars the ministers' constant use of such highly charged images as "the Man of Sin," "the North American Babylon," "the Mother of Harlots," and "the Romish Antichristian Power" expressed their sense of the cos-

33. Ebenezer Pemberton, *A Sermon Delivered at the Presbyterian Church in New-York, July 31, 1746* (New York, 1746), 19.

34. Gad Hitchcock, *A Sermon Preached in the 2d Precinct in Pembroke* . . . (Boston, 1757), 19; Solomon Williams, *The Duty of Christian Soldiers* . . . (New London, Conn., 1755), 33–34; Isaac Stiles, *The Character and Duty of Soldiers* . . . (New Haven, Conn., 1755), 2.

35. William McClenachan, *The Christian Warrior* (Boston, 1745), 5; Thomas More Brown, "The Image of the Beast: Anti-Papal Rhetoric in Colonial America," in Richard O. Curry and Thomas More Brown, eds., *Conspiracy: The Fear of Subversion in American History* (New York, 1972), 1–20; Sister Mary Augustina Ray, *American Opinion of Roman Catholicism in the Eighteenth Century* (New York, 1936).

36. Thomas Prince, *A Sermon Delivered At the South Church in Boston* . . . (Boston, 1746), 12, 18.

37. John Burt, *The Mercy of God to his People* . . . (Newport, R.I., 1759), 4.

mic significance of the conflict and showed that the traditional apocalyptic view of history retained great power.[38]

In delineating this moral dichotomy between themselves and the French, New Englanders altered the patterns of apocalyptic thought. Turning from spiritual introspection, they began to underscore their collective role in the last decisive struggle with Satan. Rather than becoming "indifferent to and weary with" this interpretation of history, clergymen at mid-century manifested an intensity of interest in Antichrist's overthrow unknown since the time of John Cotton and Edward Johnson.[39] Vivid perceptions of an external foe confirmed their sense of identity as God's elect people living in the end times and linked their lives to the cosmic war between good and evil. In the minds of Old Lights images of Antichrist shifted from "enthusiasm" to the French menace, and New Lights ceased to be preoccupied with the dangers of an unconverted ministry. More concerned with the common struggle than with divisive questions relating to the spread of vital piety, the clergy found remarkable solidarity in a renewed sense of apocalyptic history.[40]

The response of New England ministers to French defeat reveals the power of this apocalyptic perspective. Had the clergy, burdened by the anxiety of war, used the imagery of prophetic Scripture as mere rhetoric to stir their countrymen to fight, one would expect this form of discourse to have ended with the cessation of conflict. Yet British victories, far from signaling the demise of the apocalyptic vision, gave rise to an unprecedented outpouring of hope that Christ's kingdom was imminent. When Louisbourg fell, ministers overcame their theological differences to join in a harmonious chorus of millennial rejoicing. Not only would

38. Nathaniel Appleton, *A Sermon Preached October 9 . . .* (Boston, 1760), 36; Williams, *Duty of Christian Soldiers,* 26; Sewall, *The Lamb Slain,* 34.

39. Heimert, *Religion and the American Mind,* 85. For a concise discussion of New England's collective introspection in the late seventeenth and early eighteenth centuries see Perry Miller, "Errand into the Wilderness," in his *Errand into the Wilderness* (Cambridge, Mass., 1956), 1–15. This literature of the jeremiad stands in marked contrast to the European orientation of both New England's first settlers and that generation which after 1745 was preoccupied with imperial conflict. Aletha Joy Gilsdorf discusses the important role that Antichrist played in the thought of early New Englanders in "The Puritan Apocalypse: New England Eschatology in the Seventeenth Century" (Ph.D. diss., Yale University, 1965).

40. The intensity of Old Light hatred of factionalism can be seen in Charles Chauncy, *Seasonable Thoughts on the State of Religion in New-England* (Boston, 1743), 175, and Isaac Stiles, *A Prospect of the City of Jerusalem . . .* (New London, Conn., 1742), 45. There was remarkable unanimity, for instance, in the Old and New Light reactions to the Louisbourg campaign. Cf. the thanksgiving sermons given on the same day by Prince, *Extraordinary Events,* and Charles Chauncy, *Marvellous Things done by the right Hand and holy Arm of God . . .* (Boston, 1745).

the man of sin no longer rule as vice-regent in the area of Cape Breton, but the conquest of Louisbourg was a sign that the day was not far off when it would be proclaimed that "Babylon the Great is fallen."[41] Less than a year later the defeat of the Pretender at Culloden evoked even greater displays of millennial expectancy.[42] Not since the rousing times of the Awakening had the ministers been so sure that the new age was about to dawn.

For the duration of the French wars the apocalyptic dimensions of the conflict became even more pronounced in the minds of the clergy. By the mid-1750s references associating France with Antichrist had increased significantly.[43] Nor was this perspective limited to New England. For the Virginian Samuel Davies the contest of an all-Catholic French alliance with the all-Protestant British coalition suggested nothing less than "the commencement of this grand decisive conflict between the Lamb and the beast." Without qualification he pictured the consequence of French victory as the slaying of the witnesses when Antichrist would establish his reign. French defeat, on the other hand, would introduce the most significant revolution in history, namely, "*a new heaven and a new earth.*"[44]

When the long-awaited news of French downfall in Canada reached New England millennial optimism knew no limits. In sermon after sermon ministers celebrated the removal of the last and greatest obstruction to the coming kingdom. Typical was the thanksgiving sermon of Nathaniel Appleton, who delighted in God's judgment upon the French—"A Vial of his Wrath [poured] upon this Part of Antichrist"—and anticipated the "greater and more marvellous Works" that God was about to accomplish. Samuel Langdon anticipated the "final ruin of that spiritual tyranny and *mystery of iniquity.*" The time was at hand for the shout of general joy: "*Babylon the great is fallen, is fallen!*"[45] Jonathan Mayhew, reversing his pessimistic estimation of the course of history prompted by the earthquake of 1755, expressed elation that God was re-

41. Sewall, *The Lamb Slain,* 34; Chauncy, *Marvellous Things,* 21.

42. Hull Abbot, *The Duty of God's People to pray for the Peace of Jerusalem . . .* (Boston, 1746), 25–26; Prince, *Sermon Delivered At the South Church,* 37.

43. Trask notes that there were more publications with eschatological themes during the 1750s than in any other decade of the colonial period. "In the Pursuit of Shadows," 199.

44. Davies presented this apocalyptic interpretation of the war in a fast sermon at Hanover, Va., in Oct. 1756. See Samuel Davies, *The Crisis: or, the Uncertain Doom of Kingdoms at Particular Times,* in his *Sermons on Important Subjects,* 5 (Philadelphia, 1818), 239–66, quotations on 257, 258.

45. Appleton, *Sermon Preached October 9,* 1–6, 26, 36; Samuel Langdon, *Joy and Gratitude to God . . .* (Portsmouth, N.H., 1760), 42–43. See also Andrew Eliot, *A Sermon Preached October 25th 1759 . . .* (Boston, 1759), 42.

vealing his purpose to destroy the Beast; in confounding the antichristian forces by a succession of judgments he would initiate "a most signal revolution in the civil and religious state of things in this world; and all the kingdoms thereof are to become the kingdoms of our Lord."[46] Only such acts of divine intervention as the Reformation, the defeat of the Armada, the overthrow of the Stuarts, the founding of New England, and the accession of the Hanoverians could be compared with the remarkable conquest of Canada, a victory that Solomon Williams declared to be "of more Importance than has ever been made by the *English*, since *England* was a Nation."[47]

In light of this rhetoric the suggestion that New England ministers had disengaged from the French and Indian War or saw it as "incidental, even irrelevant, to the central theme of history" seems as unbelievable as eighteenth-century Harvard College requesting the pope to give the Dudleian Lecture. Far from withdrawing from the imperial conflict, New Englanders translated it into genuinely cosmic categories. Fighting the French became the cause of God; marching to battle hastened the destruction of Antichrist; victory proclaimed a "Salvation, a Deliverance, by far superior to any—nay to all that *New-England* ever experienced."[48] If there were still some clergymen who in 1760 could not discern the progress of providential history in the French defeat and who still found their spirits uplifted solely by the Concert of Prayer, they were few and insignificant. With rare exceptions the clergy saw the war's end as unequivocal evidence that the kingdom of darkness could no longer restrain the latter-day glory. "What a Scene of Wonder opens to our View!" exclaimed Mather Byles, almost breathless with anticipation. "Good God! what an astonishing Scene of Wonders! Methinks, a universal Transport animates every Countenance, and sparkles in every Eye."[49]

By 1760 New England clergymen appear to have lost a clear distinction between the kingdom of God and the goals of their own political community. Military victories of Protestants over Catholics, which for earlier New Englanders had been means to the end of worldwide revival, now pointed toward a different end. The idea of a millennium of liberty both civil and religious had captured the clergy's imagination. During the

46. Jonathan Mayhew, *Two Discourses Delivered October 25th. 1759* . . . (Boston, 1759), 49, 61.

47. Solomon Williams, *The Relations of God's People to him* . . . (New London, Conn., 1760), 19. See also Thomas Barnard, *A Sermon Preached before his Excellency Francis Bernard* . . . (Boston, 1763), 36–44.

48. Heimert, *Religion and the American Mind,* 85; Eli Forbes, *God the Strength and Salvation of his People* . . . (Boston, 1761), 9.

49. Mather Byles, *A Sermon, Delivered March 6th 1760* . . . (New London, Conn., 1760), 13.

two decades of war with France ministers had continued the long-established practice of aligning their own cause with that of God, but these years had worked a reordering of the clergy's values and priorities. Yet because the French wars were not the only cause of this pervasive shift, one must trace other, no less crucial intellectual changes by which Antichrist became much more a symbol of tyranny than of heresy and the millennium much more an age of liberty than of piety.

Rarely did New Englanders tire of building myths about the heroic acts of the founders of "the city on a hill." For the historian these myths are important because they reflect their authors' values and were used by them to express their concerns.[50] In analyzing the rhetoric of the jeremiad Perry Miller has shown how second- and third-generation New England ministers reproached their contemporaries by constructing exalted myths of the early settlers. Similarly, by tracing the formulation of myths during the two decades after 1740 we can more easily grasp the changing values and interests of the eighteenth-century ministers who created them.[51]

Although the Great Awakening shattered the traditional language of the jeremiad, it did not replace it with an alternative paradigm by which ministers interpreted the mission of early New England. Rather, it bisected the earlier myth so that each side in the dispute over enthusiastic religion inherited a facet of the older interpretation. In contrasting the exemplary first generation with the declension of their own age, both Old and New Lights focused on the particular characteristics of the founders that confirmed their own points of view. While New Lights exalted the "Power of Religion among the primitive Planters" and lamented its subsequent decay, Old Lights dwelt upon the love and unity of the first settlers and bemoaned the "Unscriptural Separations and Disorderly Practices" that disturbed their own day.[52] Most important, neither of these myths about early New England differed in substance from the interpretation that characterized the traditional jeremiad. Both the New Light emphasis on vital religion and the Old Light stress on unity and charity

50. Wesley Frank Craven, *The Legend of the Founding Fathers* (New York, 1956), 1–65; Carl Bridenbaugh, *Mitre and Sceptre: Transatlantic Faiths, Ideas, Personalities, and Politics, 1689–1775* (New York, 1962), 171–206.

51. Perry Miller, *The New England Mind: From Colony to Province* (Cambridge, Mass., 1953), 27–39.

52. *The Christian History*, 1:37; Stiles, *Prospect of Jerusalem*, 46. For New Light statements that idealized the power of vital religion among the first generation see *The Christian History*, 1:1, 72, 98, 106. Old Light jeremiads, which emphasized the unity of New England's founders, are seen in William Worthington, *The Duty of Rulers and Teachers in Unitedly Leading God's People . . .* (New London, Conn., 1744), 23–24, and Nathaniel Appleton, *The Great Blessing of Good Rulers . . .* (Boston, 1742), 42.

were fragments of the same earlier myth that had honored the forefathers for both their piety and their harmony.[53]

During the French wars this religious mythology underwent a massive change. As early as 1736 Prince pointed in the new direction when he called for imitation of the "worthy Fathers" not only for their vital and pure Christianity, but also for their "LIBERTY both *Civil* and *Ecclesiastical*."[54] Reflecting the increasing concern of New Englanders for the privileges confirmed to them by the Glorious Revolution and the Massachusetts Charter of 1691, this new emphasis began to appear in numerous sermons on the nature of good government, but it was only after the Awakening that the myth of the forefathers as stalwarts of liberty became a dominant theme, revealing the clergy's changing concerns.

In 1754 Mayhew articulated the form of this myth, which would become standard for the following generation. "Our ancestors," he declared, "tho' not perfect and infallible in all respects, were a religious, brave and vertuous set of men, whose love of liberty, civil and religious, brought them from their native land, into the American deserts."[55] By the end of the French and Indian War this grafting of Whig political values into the traditional conceptions of New England's collective identity was virtually complete. In his thanksgiving sermon for the victory at Quebec Samuel Cooper reflected on New England's history and surmised that his progenitors had transplanted themselves into the wilds of America because they were "smitten with a Love of Liberty, and possessed with an uncommon Reverence to the Dictates of Conscience."[56] In repeating this interpretation of the myth New England ministers did not argue for a more secular interpretation of their own origins. Instead, they incorporated certain prevailing political values into a framework that still idealized the religious motivations of their ancestors. It was not piety alone but also the sacred cause of liberty that had inspired migration to the New World.[57]

The new terms of this myth indicate the evolution of the clergy's definition of their society's meaning and purpose as with greater frequency

53. Both of these themes are evident in such earlier jeremiads as that of Samuel Danforth, *A Brief Recognition of New Englands Errand into the Wilderness* (1671), in A. W. Plumstead, ed., *The Wall and the Garden: Selected Massachusetts Election Sermons 1670–1772* (Minneapolis, Minn., 1968), 65–67.

54. Thomas Prince, *A Chronological History of New England* (Boston, 1736), 1, "Dedication," 2.

55. Jonathan Mayhew, *A Sermon Preach'd in the Audience of His Excellency William Shirley* . . . (Boston, 1754), 28.

56. Samuel Cooper, *A Sermon Preached before His Excellency Thomas Pownall* . . . (Boston, 1759), 28.

57. Eliot, *Sermon Preached October 25th*, 17.

and intensity they attributed religious significance to commonly held political values. This quest for "civil and religious liberty" became the social ideal of clergymen who in many cases made a virtual identification of piety and whiggery. Benjamin Stevens expressed the sentiment of a growing number of ministers when he proposed that "liberty both civil and religious is the spirit and genius of the sacred writings."[58]

This new pattern of identity found expression in distinctly apocalyptic categories. The civil and religious liberty of British Protestants became the divine standard against the antichristian foe of French popery and slavery. In a sermon to soldiers in 1757 James Cogswell indicated the civil priorities that had come to evoke a religious reaction: "I would entreat you to see to it that *you engage in so noble a Cause for right Ends*. Let your principal Motives be the Honor of God, and the Defence of your Country. Fight for Liberty and against Slavery. Endeavour to stand the Guardians of the Religion and Liberties of *America*; to oppose Antichrist, and prevent the barbarous Butchering of your fellow Country-men." Cogswell urged the troops to be "inspired with an unconquerable Aversion to Popery and Slavery and an ardent Love to Religion and Liberty." In this new eschatology the French were identified with cosmic evil as much for their civil tyranny as for any other reason, and, as Samuel Davies admitted, "the Art of War becomes a Part of our Religion."[59]

As the ministers more closely identified religion and liberty, it was not uncommon for them to attribute to Antichrist a plot between "the *scepter* and the *surplice* for enslaving both the *bodies* and *souls* of men."[60] The civil dimension of Satan's designs became a major theme both in the development of myths about the past and in the depiction of the French threat. In this way New Englanders moved in the direction of equating the war of the dragon against the woman with the threat of "slavery" common to Whig ideology.[61] Thus when John Adams in 1765 pictured the course of history as a progressive, if embattled, advance of civil and religious liberty against the tyranny of Antichrist represented in the

58. Benjamin Stevens, *A Sermon Preached at Boston . . . May 27, 1761 . . .* (Boston, 1761), 8.

59. James Cogswell, *God, the pious Soldier's Strength and Instructor . . .* (Boston, 1757), 26, 2; Samuel Davies, *The Curse of Cowardice . . .* (Woodbridge, N.J., 1759), 2, 304. See also John Ballantine, *The Importance of God's Presence with an Army . . .* (Boston, 1756), 18–19.

60. Jonathan Mayhew to Experience Mayhew, Oct. 1, 1747, Jonathan Mayhew Papers, Boston University Library, Boston.

61. Charles W. Akers, *Called unto Liberty: A Life of Jonathan Mayhew, 1720–1766* (Cambridge, Mass., 1964), 81–97.

canon and feudal law, he was expressing a pattern of thought that was prevalent among New England intellectuals.[62]

Perceiving that popery and slavery had struck a bargain for their destruction, New Englanders grounded their collective identity solidly in the ideals of British Protestantism and the British constitution. Far from developing in the twenty years before the Stamp Act a sense of America's moral superiority to England, the clergy identified Great Britain as the bastion of freedom and the bulwark against Antichrist. For most ministers the corollary of abhorring the superstition and idolatry of popish religion was "Loyalty to the Crown . . . Attachment to the Protestant Succession in the illustrious House of *Hanover* . . . and . . . Establishment in Protestant Principles."[63] New Englanders had never been more proud of their birthright as British subjects because increasingly the liberties they most valued were perceived as those of freeborn Britons. By the end of the French wars the preachers often referred to God's British Israel and included Britons among God's covenanted people.[64]

The clearest indication of the clergy's anglicization is the new dimension of their myth-building. During the two decades after the Great Awakening they not only altered the purposes for which their ancestors settled New England but enlarged their myths to include Great Britain. It is fair to say, in fact, that during the French wars New England ministers gave far more time to creating a usable British past than to formulating myths about the New World. Tracing providential history as the continuous battle of liberty versus tyranny, they centered their attention on the British constitution—"the admiration and Envy of the World."[65] In sermon after sermon they lifted up the standard of British liberty against the aggressive tyranny of Roman Catholicism. Assuming that popery and slavery were inseparably connected, they discovered that all Britain's past evils were attributable to Catholicism and France.[66] According to Thomas Prince, King Charles I "married a *French Papist*, Sister of King *Lewis* XIII of *France*, which was the pernicious Fountain of almost all the Miseries of the *British* Nations ever since." Similarly, the arbitrary government of James II could be linked to his "popish and despotic Principles," as could the futile designs of Charles the Pretender, whose outlook

62. John Adams, *A Dissertation on the Canon and Feudal Law*, in Charles Francis Adams, ed., *The Works of John Adams . . .*, 3 (Boston, 1851), 447–52.

63. Abbot, *Duty of God's People*, 17–18.

64. Thomas Foxcroft, *Grateful Reflections on the signal Appearances of Divine Providence . . .* (Boston, 1760), 10, 12; *Langdon, Joy and Gratitude*, 23–24.

65. Barnard, *Sermon Preached before Bernard*, 37.

66. Charles Chauncy, *The Counsel of two confederate Kings . . .* (Boston, 1746), 26; Foxcroft, *Grateful Reflections*, 12–20.

was characterized by "*Popish* Tyranny, Superstition, Bigotry, and cruel Principles."[67]

Although the ministers did include the founding of New England among the great acts by which providence had secured their rights as free men, they focused their myth-making on the Glorious Revolution and the accession of the Hanoverians. It was King William, "the Deliverer of the Nation, and the Shield of its Liberty," who more than anyone else protected succeeding generations from popish enslavement. Ministers repeatedly exalted the Glorious Revolution as the fountainhead of the privileges enjoyed by eighteenth-century Britons.[68] In similar fashion the standard myth portrayed the Hanoverians as preservers of liberty and Protestantism. According to Thomas Foxcroft, if George I had not come to the throne, events "might have involved *Britain*, and these Colonies with it, in Blood and Ruin, and might have entail'd Chains and Misery on the latest Posterity."[69] In another sermon Foxcroft summed up this myth of the British past:

> Now to single out a few very memorable Times, and not go back beyond the Memory of many yet alive:—Never to be forgotten is that glorious *Year* 1688, signalis'd as a *Year of the Right Hand of the most High,* by that most seasonable Interposition of Divine Providence in the wonderful REVOLUTION; delivering us from the Perils we were in of *Popery* and *Slavery*, two of the most comprehensive Mischiefs, and securing to us our invaluable Laws and Liberties, the Rights of Conscience, and the Religion of Protestants—Again, Never to be forgotten is that glorious Year 1714, signalis'd as a *Year of the Right Hand of the most High,* by the happy and most seasonable *Accession* of the illustrious House of HANOVER to the *British* throne; Preventing that imminent Danger the *Protestant Succession* (in the Fate of which all our valuable Interests must be involv'd) was in at that Juncture, when deep-laid Plots of Papal Enemies and false Brethren threatened to subvert it.[70]

This idealization of British liberty, both civil and religious, came to maturity in the 1740s and 1750s. Although the Anglo-French wars were by no means the single determinant of this development, the conflict brought into the forefront of religious thinking certain Whig political ideals which since the seventeenth century had been latent in New England thought. Against the onslaught of popery and slavery the sacred cause of

67. Prince, *Sermon Delivered At the South Church,* 8, 12.

68. Foxcroft, *Grateful Reflections,* 20. See also Chauncy, *Counsel of two confederate Kings,* 26, and Barnard, *Sermon Preached before Bernard,* 38.

69. Foxcroft, *Grateful Reflections,* 23.

70. Thomas Foxcroft, *A Seasonable Memento for New Year's Day* (Boston, 1747), 70.

liberty became the banner under which New Englanders rallied. The clergy expressed this new feeling of identity in the themes that reflected their sense of the past and view of the future. Not only had the course of providential history followed the rise of liberty, but the triumph of liberty would be realized in the coming of the millennium. Just as New Lights in the 1740s had seen the past and future in terms of the concerns of vital piety, so clergymen at war with France expressed their allegiance to liberty in the framework of civil millennialism.

Understandably exhilarated by the expulsion of France from North America, New Englanders anticipated the total destruction of the power of Antichrist. They had scarcely savored victory, however, when the grasping hand of tyranny reappeared in a new and dangerous form. What is remarkable about the ministers' response both to the Stamp Act and to the attempt to create an American bishopric is their application of the compelling ideology of civil millennialism to these unexpected challenges.[71] Although the threats now came from England, they represented a continuation of the man of sin's assault on liberty. Thus when Sherwood attributed the Quebec Act to "the flood of the dragon that has been poured forth . . . for the establishment of popery," or when Langdon suspected that British taxation originated in popish religion, they were speaking from the same perspective of providential history that had fired New England's opposition to French tyranny.[72] Attempting to identify the Image of the Beast (Rev. 13), Sherwood in the mid-1770s gave an illuminating demonstration of how civil millennialism could be mobilized against the British:

> Whether that persecuting power be intended, that has in years past, been so cruelly and barbarously exercised in France, and other popish countries, against the humble followers of Christ, to the massacre and destruction of

71. In his thanksgiving sermon on the repeal of the Stamp Act Joseph Emerson viewed this taxation in the same historical framework in which New Englanders had seen the threat of French oppression. It was another in a long succession of attempts by popery and slavery to subvert liberty. The purpose of the taxation was "to support the pride and vanity of diocesan Bishops, and it may be by and by making us tributary to the See of Rome." Emerson feared that the conflict between England and the American colonies would weaken both so that the French or the House of Stuart might come to power. *A Thanksgiving Sermon, Preach'd at Pepperrell* . . . (Boston, 1760), 11–21. In similar fashion William Patten suggested that the sponsors of the Stamp Act were "perhaps no enemies to France, and not very friendly to Christian liberty," while Stephen Johnson feared the tyranny of "a corrupt, Frenchified party in the nation." *A Discourse Delivered at Hallifax* . . . (Boston, 1766), 21. See also Stephen Johnson, *Some Important Observations* . . . (Newport, R.I., 1766), 15.

72. Sherwood, *The Church's Flight,* 33; Samuel Langdon, *Government Corrupted By Vice* (Boston, 1775), 28–29.

> so many thousands of protestants; or whether there be a reference to the corrupt system of tyranny and oppression, that has of late been fabricated and adopted by the ministry and parliament of Great-Britain, which appears so favourable to popery and the Roman catholic interest, aiming at the extension and establishment of it, and so awfully threatens the civil and religious liberties of all sound protestants; I cannot positively determine. But since the prophesies represent this wicked scheme of anti-christian tyranny, as having such an extensive and universal spread over the earth . . . it need not appear strange or shocking to us, to find that our own nation has been, in some degree, infected and corrupted therewith.[73]

The civil millennialism of the Revolutionary era, expressed by rationalists as well as pietists, grew directly out of the politicizing of Puritan millennial history in the two decades before the Stamp Act crisis. In marked contrast to the apolitical millennial hopes of Jonathan Edwards, which had been based on the success of the revival, civil millennialism advanced freedom as the cause of God, defined the primary enemy as the antichrist of civil oppression rather than that of formal religion, traced the myths of its past through political developments rather than through the vital religion of the forefathers, and turned its vision toward the privileges of Britons rather than to a heritage exclusive to New England.

During the Revolutionary crisis, when ministers once again emphasized the moral distinction between the Old World and the New, ironically they did so because in the previous years their own identity had become shaped in the image of British culture.[74] The sacred cause of liberty of which the patriot clergy were so enamored was not the flowering of an incipient American nationalism planted by the Awakening, nor did the initial volley of American muskets transform the millennialism of Edwards into that of Sherwood or Langdon. Instead, the religious patriotism that animated the Revolution had intellectual roots far more British than American. In the early 1770s, however, the intellectual and emotional force of civil millennialism, incorporating Whig political values, was brought to bear against England itself, as ministers linked apocalyptic vision to the cause of American liberty, identified the "fixed plan to enslave the colonies" with Satan's continuing conspiracy against God's people, and detected in the growth of arbitrary power, the corruption of placemen, and the ominous threat of standing armies the unabated malice of the man of sin. It was this redefinition of the terms of providential history that constituted the distinctive contribution of the New England

73. Sherwood, *The Church's Flight,* 14–15.

74. For a full description of the British orientation of eighteenth-century American culture see Murrin, "Anglicizing an American Colony."

clergy to Revolutionary ideology. In picturing the struggle of liberty versus tyranny as nothing less than the conflict between heaven and hell, the clergy found their political commitments energized with the force of a divine imperative and their political goals translated into the very principles which would initiate the kingdom of God on earth.[75]

75. An adequate understanding of the clergy's role in the Revolution awaits a thorough analysis of the relationship between traditional ideas of providential history and the prevailing mood of "country" ideology. The most helpful work in this direction is Bernard Baily, "Religion and Revolution: Three Biographical Studies," *Perspectives in American History* 4 (1970): 85–169.

5

The Reconciliation of Politics and Religion in Revolutionary New Jersey

Mark A. Noll

Reprinted by permission from *Journal of Presbyterian History* 54 (1976): 217–37.

Fresh from his unexpected victories over the British at Trenton (25 December 1776) and Princeton (3 January 1777), George Washington took his heartened but still beleaguered troops into winter headquarters at Morristown, New Jersey. Among the patriots of Morris County who rendered aid and comfort to the Continental Army that winter few were more active than the Presbyterian minister of nearby Hanover. Not only did the Reverend Jacob Green open his home to some fourteen of Washington's junior officers, but he also assisted with the inoculation of soldiers and the local citizenry against smallpox, and he offered his church as a hospital for those soldiers for whom the smallpox inoculation came too late.[1] The significance of Jacob Green for a proper

1. General accounts of Green's life are provided by Clifford K. Shipton, *Sibley's Harvard Graduates* (vols. 4–14; Boston: Massachusetts Historical Society, 1933–1968), 11:405–16; and Joseph F. Tuttle, "Rev. Jacob Green, of Hanover, N.J., as an Author, Statesman and Patriot," *Proceedings of the New Jersey Historical Society,* 2d ser. 12 (1892–1893): 189–241. The most important primary source for Green's life is his autobiography which his son, Ashbel Green, edited, amplified, and published in *The Christian*

understanding of Revolutionary America is, however, far greater than his patriotic service of 1777 indicates, for Green had played an active role in the politics of rebellion during 1775 and 1776 both in New Jersey and in a wider colonial context. Green is of particular importance for an understanding of the relationship between political ideology and religious thought in Revolutionary America because of the way he fulfilled his responsibilities as a pastor.

A study of Green's life sheds rewarding light on the current discussion of relationships among religious thought, political ideology, and social reform in the Revolutionary period. His career suggests that the most attractive interpretations of the religious-political connection may not be entirely adequate. Some have argued that the predominant political and social stances of the 1770s can properly be understood only as products of the opposing religious positions of the Great Awakening earlier in the century. In this view, the theology of the revival came to be translated into an egalitarian, millennial, and nationalistic political ideology, while the world view of the Awakening's opponents grew into the political and cultural conservatism of the Revolutionary period.[2] Against this interpretation, Green's career suggests that the application of the theology of the Awakening to American society was not primarily in explicitly political form.

Others argue that no systematic connection existed between religious points of view and political allegiance; it was not New Light religion but the political thought of the radical Whigs which supplied the Revolutionary ideology for individuals from all parts of the theological spectrum.[3] Green's career does not call into question this conclusion concerning the origins of Revolutionary politics, but it does suggest that there was a connection between religious convictions and the way in which the basic Whig viewpoint was manipulated. In particular, the nature of Green's

---

Advocate 9 (August–December 1831): 408–12, 465–68, 522–25, 578–81, 633–37; 10 (January–May 1832), 11ff., 51–55, 99–102, 145–48, 194–99. I will henceforth refer to this as "Autobiography" and indicate whether statements taken from it are by Jacob Green himself or by Ashbel Green acting as editor and amplifier. For Green's activities during the winter of 1777, see Ashbel Green, ed., "Autobiography," 9, 522n.; Shipton, *op. cit.*, 412; and Ashbel Green, *The Life of Ashbel Green, V.D.M.*, ed. Joseph H. Jones (New York: Robert Carter and Brothers, 1849), 92 (hereafter referred to as *Life*).

2. Cf. Alan Heimert, *Religion and the American Mind from the Great Awakening to the Revolution* (Cambridge: Harvard University Press, 1966), vii and elsewhere; and Cedric B. Cowing, *The Great Awakening and the American Revolution: Colonial Thought in the Eighteenth Century* (Chicago: Rand McNally, 1971), 178ff.

3. Cf. Bernard Bailyn, "Religion and Revolution: Three Biographical Studies," *Perspectives in American History* 4 (1970): 85; and Nathan O. Hatch, "The Sacred Cause of Liberty: Political Religion in New England from the First to the Second Great Awakening" (Ph.D. diss., Washington University, St. Louis, 1974), vii–ix.

dedication to social reform argues against Bernard Bailyn's hypothesis concerning "the contagion of liberty" in Revolutionary America. Bailyn contends in his *Ideological Origins of the American Revolution* that the political arguments used by the patriots to justify independence from Great Britain created, by the mere outworking of their internal logic, strong pressures for reform in American social life.[4] For Jacob Green, however, it appears that the theology of Jonathan Edwards had more to do with the effort to reform American society than did the ideology of real Whig politics. A biographical study of Jacob Green will not by itself call forth a radically new interpretation of the religious-political connection in Revolutionary America, but it will indicate that more refined historical reconstructions are required than have to date appeared.

Jacob Green was born in Malden, Massachusetts, on 22 January 1722. Despite an early bent toward books and learning, he was put out to learn a trade when he was fourteen years old. After he made several unsuccessful attempts to find a suitable vocation, a concerned brother-in-law urged him to prepare for college. Green took this advice gladly, and after a year and a half in a Latin grammar school, he entered Harvard College in the summer of 1740. Throughout his early life he had felt periodic religious stirrings, but he had not been able to come to a settled conviction concerning his place before God. The Congregationalism of his native New England was the mold in which his ecclesiastical thinking was shaped. In spite of his later service as a Presbyterian minister, Green seems never entirely to have forsaken the Congregationalist disposition of his early years.

Green's arrival in Cambridge preceded George Whitefield's tumultuous entry into Boston by only a few months. When Whitefield spoke at Harvard in September 1740, Green, in his own words, "heard him with wonder and affection, and approved highly of his preaching and conduct." It was, however, not until January of the next year when Gilbert Tennent arrived in the Boston area that Green experienced the first pangs of the conversion which would determine the course of his later life. While at a sermon by Tennent on "false hope," preached on Saturday, 24 January 1741, Green received "a new and dreadful sense" of his wickedness, and of "God's holiness and justice—especially of his justice and equity in damning sinners for their sins; and I saw myself altogether defiled." For some time thereafter Green labored under a deep impression of his own sinfulness even as he granted the justice in God's condemna-

4. Bernard Bailyn, *The Ideological Origins of the American Revolution* (Cambridge: Harvard University Press, 1967), chap. 6, "The Contagion of Liberty."

tion of sinners such as he. Soon, however, Green began to sense the other side of the gospel:

> About two months after the great shock by Mr. Tennent's preaching, I began to get views of Christ's atonement for sin, and that God could glorify himself in pardoning a sinner through Jesus Christ. . . . I was much taken up with the fulness, sufficiency, and suitableness of Jesus Christ, to illustrate the divine perfections in our salvation.[5]

As a result of his religious experiences in 1740 and 1741, Green found within himself "a remarkable desire for the good of others . . . a strong, longing desire for the good of souls." At the same time Green did not feel called to the ministry both because he distrusted his own spiritual worthiness and because he feared he was not fluent enough in the things of religion. Hence, when Green graduated he determined "to be at God's disposal and to follow the calls of Providence." Providence led Green to teach school for one year and then provided a more unusual opportunity. It was then the early summer of 1745, and George Whitefield had returned for another preaching tour of New England. Green's friends introduced him to Whitefield and apprised the evangelist of Green's pious character. As a result Whitefield invited Green to accompany him to Bethseda, Georgia, and there to oversee Whitefield's orphanage. Green was at first unnerved by this proposal, but he eventually consented. He told Whitefield that it would take about a month for him to settle his affairs in New England, after which he would join the evangelist as the latter "went on in his circuitous preaching southward."[6]

When Green caught up with Whitefield in Elizabethtown, New Jersey, at the home of the Reverend Jonathan Dickinson, disappointing news awaited him. Whitefield had received word from Georgia that an expected source of funds had dried up and that he would be able to offer Green employment for no more than six months. In the rapid sequence of events which followed, Green overcame his reluctance to enter the ministry, exchanged New England for New Jersey as his place of service, and set aside his native Congregationalism for a Presbyterian vocation. In his autobiography Green related these crucial events with charming succinctness:

> I consulted Mr. Dickinson . . . and he advised me to stop; and he, with Mr. [Aaron] Burr of Newark, prevailed with me to stay, and be licensed and preach here, and not return to New England. I had a great regard for Mr.

5. Jacob Green, "Autobiography," 9:523f., 580.
6. Ibid., 9:634; 10:12f.

> Dickinson and Mr. Burr—their advice swayed me. Accordingly, I was licensed in September, 1745, at Elizabethtown, and the first place that invited me to preach, was Hanover, in Morris county, New Jersey . . . thus following the calls of Providence I was led to Hanover. Here I preached one year on probation, was called to settle, and was ordained in November, 1746.[7]

Green's nearly forty-five years in Hanover were sometimes difficult, but they were also years of productive service. Soon after his ordination he was forced to sources outside the ministry in order to support his growing family. Green married Anna Strong in June 1747 and had four children by his first wife, who died in 1756. By his second wife, Elizabeth Pierson, who survived him by twenty years, he had several more children, including the future president of Princeton College, Ashbel Green. Throughout the course of his pastorate Green served the Hanover area as a physician, legal advisor, and schoolmaster; he built and ran a grist mill, a brick kiln, and a distillery; and he bought and sold real estate.[8] His lifelong interest in education was manifested locally in the grammar school which he maintained for his own and neighboring children and in a wider sphere by his service to Princeton College. Green was a charter member of the Trustees of the College of New Jersey and served in this capacity from 1748 to 1764. After the untimely death of Jonathan Edwards in March 1758, Green acted as the temporary head of the college until the appointment of Samuel Davies as president in May 1759.[9] Green's involvement in Revolutionary developments will be discussed at greater length shortly, but the range of his interest in public affairs is also indicated by three contributions to *The New Jersey Journal* in 1780 and 1782 on the subjects of taxation and the payment of the public debt. In these articles Green proposed that the government redeem its paper debts on a sliding scale determined by their approximate market value at their date of issue. Whether or not the Confederation Congress took the suggestion from Green, it was his plan which the Congress followed in meeting its fiscal obligations.[10]

The burden of Green's lifelong concern was not, however, his part-time employments or his activity in public affairs, but his ministry as a preacher of the gospel. His autobiography contains repeated reflection on his own religious condition, as this recital of the high and low moments of his spiritual experience:

7. Ibid., 9:13.
8. Ibid., 9:52; Shipton, *op. cit.*, 408; Tuttle, *op. cit.*, 194f.
9. Tuttle, *op. cit.*, 195f.; Shipton, *op. cit.*, 409.
10. *The New Jersey Journal*, 5 April 1780, 1; 26 April 1780, 1; 19 June 1782, 1. On the Confederation Congress' adoption of Green's proposal, see Ashbel Green, *Life*, 73; and Ashbel Green, ed., "Autobiography," 10:196f.

> As to myself, through the whole of my ministry I had many elevations and depressions—times of great fear, darkness and discouragement, and other times of more light, hope and courage. Besides what was common, there were three or four times, when I met with something more than ordinary.[11]

His ministry at Hanover was graced by three "special appearances of religion among the people of my charge," during the last of which in 1790 Green contracted influenza and died. Although he did not itinerate to any great extent, he was a proponent of Edwardsean-style awakenings. His most popular publication, *A Vision of Hell,* was directed at the revival of religious sensibilities in America.[12] By recording the dialogue among inhabitants of hell, it sought to inform the inhabitants of the country of their need to turn to Christ without delay.[13]

The theological underpinnings of Green's religious aspirations and activities passed through a series of modifications. The zealous Calvinism which he had acquired in "the *New Light* time" had cooled somewhat by the time of his ordination. Under the influence of Dickinson and Burr, Green adopted a Stoddardean position on the sacraments and church membership. And in the early years of his ministry he was, as he put it, "inclined to some notions that were Arminian, or that bordered upon Arminianism; especially as to the power of the creature, the freedom of the will, the origin of action, etc." As Green goes on to say, however, "I continued not long in these notions." Of particular aid in bringing him "off from all the notions that bordered on Arminianism" were "Watt's *Terms of Communion;* Edwards's *Inquiry concerning Qualifications for Sacraments,* and his book on *the Will.*"[14] Green's return to Edwardseanism was proclaimed to the world in a sermon published in 1767, *Sinners Faultiness, and Spiritual Inability,* in which he proposed to show: "How it appears that Sinners are altogether faulty and condemnable for continuing in Sin and Unbelief, when there is in them a spiritual inability to do otherwise."[15]

It was thus as a man of broad public concerns, a dedicated local minister, and a revivalistically-inclined Edwardsean that Jacob Green re-

11. Jacob Green, "Autobiography," 10:53.

12. *A Vision of Hell, And a Discovery of some of the Consultations and Devices there In the Year 1767.* This tract, published under the name of Theodorus Van Sherman, was printed many times in many places; for its publishing history, see Shipton, *op. cit.,* 415f.

13. Another example of Green's skillful use of irony in the service of an evangelical appeal appeared in *The New Jersey Journal,* 25 April 1781, 1–2. In a "Letter on training of youth" Green, tongue well fixed in cheek, urged parents to give their children absolutely free rein and to indulge their dissipations as a way to bring them up successfully.

14. Jacob Green, "Autobiography," 10:147.

15. *Sinners Faultiness, and Spiritual Inability, considered in a Sermon* (New York: Hugh Gaine, 1767), 10.

sponded to the increasingly ominous evidences of British designs upon the colonies in the early 1770s.

In the lengthy roll call of Presbyterians who worked energetically against British encroachments upon colonial freedom during the Revolutionary period, Green deserves a prominent place.[16] His adopted colony of residence, New Jersey, was the scene of his most practical service on behalf of an independent United States. As a result of a widely-circulated appeal for American independence that we will examine more closely in due course, he was elected in May 1776 to the fourth assembly of the New Jersey Provincial Legislature.[17] In response to a request issued that same month by the Continental Congress in Philadelphia, this New Jersey assembly set about the process of creating a new instrument of state government to replace the royal charter of 1702. On 21 June 1776, the New Jersey assembly voted overwhelmingly to establish a new government, and it named a committee to prepare the state constitution. To chair this committee the legislature appointed Jacob Green. Green's constitutional committee reported on Wednesday, 26 June, and on the following Tuesday, 2 July 1776, the assembly approved the document that had been produced by the committee. New Jersey thus became the fourth colony to establish an independent state government.[18]

The New Jersey constitution itself was a typical product of the general Whig thought lying behind the Revolutionary movement. Its preamble bears striking resemblance to the document which the Continental Congress was contemplating almost simultaneously in Philadelphia as an intercolonial declaration of independence:

16. On Presbyterian politics in the Revolutionary era, see Leonard J. Kramer, "Presbyterians Approach the American Revolution," *Journal of the Presbyterian Historical Society* 31 (June 1953): 71–86, and (September 1953): 167–80; Kramer, "Muskets in the Pulpit: 1776–1783," ibid. 31 (December 1953): 229–44, and 32 (March 1954): 37–51; "Presbyterians and the American Revolution: A Documentary Account," *Journal of Presbyterian History* 52 (winter 1974), and "Presbyterians and the American Revolution: An Interpretive Account," ibid. 54 (spring 1976).

17. The course of this assembly and Green's role in it are described by Charles R. Erdman, Jr., *The New Jersey Constitution of 1776* (Princeton: Princeton University Press, 1929).

18. Green's exact role in the authorship of this document is not clear. Modern students of Revolutionary New Jersey, while recognizing Green's capabilities, lean toward Jonathan D. Sergeant, a Princeton lawyer and friend of President Witherspoon, as the author. Witherspoon himself was a member of the Provincial Congress but had been sent as a delegate to the Continental Congress on 16 June. Cf. Tuttle, "Jacob Green," 213ff.; Erdman, *New Jersey Constitution,* 34–37; and Larry Gerlach, "Revolution or Independence? New Jersey 1760–1776" (unpublished Ph.D. diss., Rutgers University, 1968), 700.

> Whereas all the constitutional authority ever possessed by the Kings of Great Britain over these Colonies . . . was, by compact, derived from the people . . . ; allegiance and protection are, in the nature of things, reciprocal ties. . . . And whereas George the Third, King of Great Britain, has refused protection to the good people of these Colonies . . . and has also made war upon them, in the most cruel and unnatural manner, for no other cause, than asserting their just rights—all civil authority under him is necessarily at an end.[19]

The body of the constitution created a virtual "legislative omnipotence" in that the assembly itself exercised not only legislative authority but also considerable sway in executive and judicial procedures.[20] The governor, who was to be elected yearly, had a very restricted role in the running of government, and in general the document does not exhibit the sensitivity to balances of power which the United States Constitution would later evidence. Very obviously the fear of wanton executive power was uppermost in the minds of the provincial legislators as they framed this instrument of government. On balance, however, it is not a radical document. A recent historian of Revolutionary New Jersey, Larry Gerlach, has put the constitution into perspective by noting that although the new government was "more democratic and representative" than colonial charters, "it is unlikely that either traditional voting patterns or the practice of deference politics was significantly altered. . . . [The 1776 constitution] was not a document for the ages. Rather, it was a codification of custom, time-honored practices, and innovations mandated by the exigencies of rebellion."[21] Although we have inexact knowledge concerning Green's role in the formation of this document, his chairmanship of the committee in which it was drafted is indicative of his concern to defend the liberties which patriots considered to be under such dire attack.

Green's behavior after the assembly's approval of the constitution offers a revealing insight into his personal attitude toward the intermingling of religious and political spheres. Immediately after the acceptance of the constitution by the New Jersey legislature, Green left the assembly and returned to Hanover. According to Green's son, Ashbel, Green "was so far from seeking to obtain a seat in that Congress, that he did all he could to avoid it, short of absolutely refusing to serve." Green left the assembly as abruptly as he did,

19. Erdman, *op. cit.*, 145.
20. Ibid., 69.
21. Larry Gerlach, "Revolution or Independence? New Jersey 1760–1776" (Ph.D. diss., Rutgers University, 1968), 703.

> not because he regretted what he had already done, but because he held that only on some very extraordinary occasion, such as that to which he had yielded, was it lawful for a minister of the gospel, who had a parochial charge, to leave his flock and the full discharge of his spiritual duties, for any civil and secular station or employment whatsoever.[22]

Green had far fewer qualms about rendering other forms of service to the patriotic effort. We have already mentioned his labors during the winter of 1777. Later in the war Green opened his home to a dozen colonials who had just been released from a British prisoner of war camp. Green and his family undertook to nurse these individuals, who were in a pitiable condition, back to health.[23] On another occasion during the war Green is said to have justified depredations by colonial troops upon his poultry stock. To his wife's lament at the loss of a prize turkey to marauding colonials, Green justified the action by quoting Proverbs 6:30—"Men do not despise a thief, if he steal to satisfy his soul when he is hungry."[24]

Green provided his most notable services to the patriotic effort by convincing American public opinion of the justice of the cause and by pushing it toward acceptance of the idea of independence from Great Britain. Early in 1776 as public reluctance to make the final break with Britain continued, Green published a tract arguing against rapprochement, *Observations: On the Reconciliation of Great-Britain and the Colonies*.[25] Green also took to the public press with two letters on liberty in the difficult days of the war to encourage those grown weary in the struggle.[26] And he explored other dimensions of the conflict in his fast day sermon of April 1778, a sermon which he sent to the Continental Congress for its consideration.[27]

Green's conception of the conflict shared the standard Whig world view with its picture of British corruption, its exaltation of God-given liberty and natural rights, its fear of governmental conspiracies leading to tyrannical slavery, and its conjunction of civil and religious liberty.[28] In the words of his son, Green "although a clergyman, was a whig of the first

22. Ashbel Green, *Life,* 60.
23. Ibid., 87.
24. Ashbel Green, ed., "Autobiography," 10:198.
25. Philadelphia: Robert Bell, 1776.
26. *The New Jersey Journal,* 3 May 1780, 1; 10 May 1780, 1.
27. *A Sermon Delivered at Hanover, (in New-Jersey) April 22d, 1778, Being the Day of public Fasting and Prayer throughout the United States of America* (Chatham, N.J.: Shepard Kollock, 1779). Important sections from this sermon have been excerpted in "Presbyterians and the American Revolution . . . ," *Journal of Presbyterian History* 52 (winter 1974): 449–54. Ashbel Green, ed., "Autobiography," 10:198, relates that Green sent the sermon to the Continental Congress.
28. Bailyn, *Ideological Origins,* 34–93.

water."[29] His *Observations on Reconciliation* scored British corruption and announced that Britain's vicious acts against the colonies constituted a *prima facie* abrogation of colonial dependence. On the positive side, a new independent American government would be "the most equitable, rational, natural mode of civil government; most adapted to answer the end of government, according to the word of God"; it would end "tyranny and oppression"; it would not, as royal governments were wont to do, countenance, "incroachments upon our natural rights"; and its concern for liberty would foster successes in all areas of life.[30] Larry Gerlach has praised this tract as an unusually effective presentation of the Revolutionary argument: "Instead of railing against the British government with abusive and emotive language, he coupled a remarkably detached discussion of the arguments on both sides of the issue with a scholarly, albeit plainly-worded, discourse on the nature of civil authority, the contract theory of government, and the right of revolution."[31] It was primarily due to the respect accorded to this publication that Green was elected to the New Jersey assembly in 1776.[32] Green also did not hesitate to bring his political viewpoint into his religious discourses. In his fast day sermon, for example, he described "our cause" as "just" and "glorious."[33]

Green's first newspaper article on freedom sang the praises of "the glorious cause of *Liberty*" and "the natural rights of mankind," defied the British design to reduce the colonies "to a state of mean and abject slavery," and proclaimed that "Liberty is given us by God."[34] In good Whig fashion the second article on liberty warned that "vice is the general, radical cause of" the loss of liberty. This essay's penultimate phrases called on the colonists to give thanks to God's blessings on the patriotic effort by maintaining "the practice of virtue" and using "all proper means to preserve our freedom."[35]

In contrast to Alan Heimert's contention, there is no directly apparent connection between Green's religious beliefs and his conception of the political conflict. Heimert has argued that "Green's *Observations on the Reconciliation of Great-Britain and the Colonies* was a point-by-point application of Calvinist doctrines to political affairs."[36] To the contrary,

29. Ashbel Green, *Life,* 33.

30. *Observation on Reconciliation,* 7, 12, 19f., 22, 24, 28f.

31. Gerlach, *op. cit.,* 684. Shipton, *op. cit.,* 411, calls the tract "brilliant and influential"; this is high praise from an author who usually looked askance at the Whig efforts to justify independence.

32. On the details of Green's election, see Tuttle, *op. cit.,* 205–8.

33. *Sermon of public Fasting,* 4.

34. *The New Jersey Journal,* 3 May 1780, 1.

35. *The New Jersey Journal,* 10 May 1780, 1.

36. Heimert, *op. cit.,* 478.

it is only in the fast day sermon and in certain hints in the letters on liberty printed by *The New Jersey Journal* that any mixing by Green of religious and political ideology can be glimpsed. Writing in August 1777, Green describes how during an illness in mid-1776 he had come to see a clear gulf between spiritual and political realities.

> In this sickness I had remarkable views of the difference between the church and the world, and how much Christ regards his church, or true believers, above all and everything in the world beside. That Christ's kingdom is not of this world, and that he cares little how things go in the kingdoms of the world, compared with his regard to what they are in his church; and I had clear and strong views of the duty of ministers of the gospel to be wholly engaged to promote the kingdom of Christ, or true religion, in the hearts and practice of men.[37]

Rather than a translation of religious beliefs into political points of view, Green's politics expressed the received Whig ideology that patriots of all theological persuasions espoused. When Green described the conflict with England, he did so in the terms that Bernard Bailyn has identified as common to clerical patriots across the theological spectrum: the corruption of governmental power, the necessity for virtue in good government, the need for checks on the exercise of power, and the value of the natural and God-given liberties threatened by arbitrary power.[38]

Yet before deprecating Heimert's analysis of the religious-political connection too strongly or acceding too precipitously to Bailyn's interpretation, it must be noted that Green's attitude toward the Revolution was systematically colored by his religious beliefs. It was, however, not in a translation of religious into political views that his theology played a central role but rather in an application of his Christian beliefs themselves to social problems in the colonies.

Green's politics may have been standard fare, but his willingness to criticize aspects of traditional ecclesiastical or social life in the colonies was most definitely not. Other Presbyterian clergymen, it is true, also invited the colonists to inspect their own lives in the light of divine standards and to repent accordingly. But these efforts were directed primarily toward commonplace sins of drinking, cursing, infidelity, a general contempt for religion, and the particularly Revolutionary sins of selfishness and individualism. And they proposed no more specific solution than, in

37. Jacob Green, "Autobiography," 10:55.
38. Bailyn, "Religion and Revolution," 85.

Leonard Trinterud's words, "repentance, renewal, and godly living."[39] These exhortations for repentance and reform, furthermore, often assumed a one-sided character. The perception of the struggle against Great Britain which, in its extreme form, saw "the cause of America [as] the cause of Christ" was not particularly sensitive to flaws in American life.[40]

Green's suggestions for reform were, by contrast, both more specific and less partisan. He did denounce in general terms the "greedy grasping" of war profiteers, and he did call ritualistically for a revival of religion,[41] but his critique of the colonial order was also made up of quite detailed concerns. On the ecclesiastical front his struggles against what he considered the oppressive and unscriptural control wielded by the Synod of New York and Philadelphia led to the formation of the "associated Presbytery" of Morris County in 1780.[42] Green argued at length that rigorous educational requirements for clergymen handicapped the Presbyterians in their competition with Baptists on the frontier. He also thought that such requirements violated the liberty of properly equipped ministerial candidates by forcing them to acquire the veneer of culture before entering into active ministry.[43]

The focus of Green's denunciation of colonial society during the Revolutionary period was, however, the practice of Negro slavery. He devoted a lengthy footnote to this topic in his *Observations on Reconciliation,* developed it extensively in the second half of his fast day sermon, and also treated it in essays sent to *The New Jersey Journal.* His attack, although it drew heavily on Whig arguments, possessed a solid religious foundation. Slavery, a "most cruel, inhuman, unnatural sin" was indicted

39. Leonard Trinterud, *The Forming of an American Tradition: A Reexamination of Colonial Presbyterianism* (Philadelphia: Westminster, 1949), 254, also 253, and Kramer, "Muskets in the Pulpit," 32:37.

40. Robert Smith, *The Obligations of the Confederate States of North America to Praise God . . . for the various interpositions of his providence in their favour, during their contests with Great Britain . . .* (Philadelphia: Francis Bailey, 1782), 33.

41. *Sermon of public Fasting,* 11, 9.

42. The influence of Green's Congregational heritage is readily apparent in the document which sets out the reasons for the formation of the "Associated Presbytery": *A View of A Christian Church, and Church Government; Containing many interesting Matters; With an Address to our Congregations, and an Appendix, Representing the Case and Circumstances of the associated Presbytery of Morris County. To which is subjoined, A Letter, Relative to the same Subject* (Chatham: Shepard Kollock, 1781). On Green's ecclesiology—"I am for Presbyterian ordination, and Independent church government" is the way he put it—see Jacob Green, "Autobiography," 10:146, and Ashbel Green's notes on the same page. The rise of the "Associated Presbytery" is discussed by Trinterud, *op. cit.,* 280f.; and at greater length by E. H. Gillett, *History of the Presbyterian Church in the United States of America,* 2 vols. (Philadelphia: Presbyterian Publications Committee, 1864), 1:207–12.

43. Shipton, *op. cit.,* 414.

on four counts: (1) it violated God's command to love one's neighbor as one's self; (2) it unjustly placed people in bondage who had never forfeited their right to freedom; (3) it interdicted the natural and inalienable right to freedom; and (4) it was condemned by the apostle Paul when he classified man-stealing with murder.[44] Slavery thus fell under the judgment of both the law of God and the finest of human wisdom. Green noted with pointed irony the juxtaposition of colonial opposition to Great Britain and colonial support of slavery: "What a dreadful absurdity! What a shocking consideration, that people who are so strenuously contending for liberty, should at the same time encourage and promote slavery!"[45] Furthermore: "What foreign nation can believe that we who so loudly complain of Britain's attempts to oppress and enslave us, are, at the same time, voluntarily holding multitudes of fellow creatures in abject slavery; and that while we are abundantly declaring that we esteem liberty the greatest of all earthly blessings."[46] Green feared that the hand of divine wrath would remain on America if slavery were not abolished.[47] He thought that the colonies would probably succeed in gaining independence from Britain, for even the evil of slavery could not efface the vile conduct of Britain toward its American possessions. He also thought that the colonies might prosper in a material way after the war because of their great resources. Nevertheless, the stain of slavery would be a blot and a mark of shame upon the new nation: "However we may be free from British oppression, I venture to say, we shall have inward convulsions, contentions, oppressions, and various calamities, so that our liberty will be uncomfortable, till we wash our hands from the guilt of negro slavery."[48]

Early in the 1780s Green's distaste for slavery found overt public expression. His second letter on liberty of 10 May 1780, concluded by urging patriots to respond virtuously to God's blessings upon the war effort. The last thing Green asked of his readers was to "cast an eye of pity on the negro slaves among us, who are groaning under a bondage which we think worse than death."[49] In January of the next year he ingeniously proved in a newspaper submission that slaveowners were "tories of the worst sort": "It is demonstrable that . . . slave holders are friends to sla-

44. *Sermon of public Fasting,* 14. See also 18, where slavery is denounced as incompatible with the nature of freedom, as criminal, and as something which jeopardizes the slaver in God's final judgment.

45. *Observations on Reconciliation,* 29n.

46. *Sermon of public Fasting,* 12.

47. Ibid., 15: "I am persuaded these united American States must, and will groan under the afflicting hand of God, till we reform in this matter."

48. Ibid., 16.

49. *The New Jersey Journal,* 10 May 1780, 1.

very, ergo are enemies to liberty, ergo are enemies to our present struggle for liberty, ergo are enemies to these United States."[50] When vigorous exception was taken to this sentiment in the next issue of the *Journal,* Green produced a more straightforward attack on slavery as anti-Christian and as violating the principles of the Revolution.[51]

Later that same year Green's church took a forthright stand against the admission of slaveholders to ecclesiastical fellowship. (Slaveholding in New Jersey was not abolished until 1820.) The tenth "article of agreement" approved by the Hanover Presbyterian Church late in 1781 stated:

> As we look upon the slavery of human creatures who are naturally free to be an unnatural evil and one of the greatest injuries that can be done to human nature, we cannot admit into our Church any that hold persons in slavery as slaves during life, unless in some particular cases, where the Church shall judge it agreeable to humanity and Christianity; and when aged slaves ought to be taken care of and supported during life; or in similar cases.[52]

For his pains in opposition to slavery Green suffered public rebuke and private threats. Ashbel Green relates an incident which probably took place some time in 1781 as a reaction to Green's vigorous attacks upon slavery in the newspapers:

> For a publication . . . against African slavery, he did suffer a personal insult—so far as language could insult him—in his own house, by a company of slave holders, who paid him a domiciliary visit. He made them no irritating reply, but endeavoured to reason with them mildly, and requested them when about to leave his house, to pledge him in a mug of cider—but they were too angry to consent.[53]

As Green's active opposition to slavery attests, he was able to distinguish between the justice of the colonial case against Great Britain and of colonial society itself. As righteous as he considered the patriot political cause, he was not dissuaded from subjecting the patriots to rigorous moral scrutiny. His confidence in the righteousness of the colonial cause was tempered by a perception of serious indigenous evil: "I cannot help animating you from the consideration that we are engaged in a glorious

50. [Letter on Slavery], ibid., 10 January 1781, 1.

51. Green announced his intention to publish a more comprehensive letter on slavery, ibid., 24 January 1781, 4. The longer attack appeared 31 January 1781, but I have not been able as yet to locate a copy of that issue of the *New Jersey Journal.*

52. In Tuttle, *op. cit.,* 224.

53. Ashbel Green, ed., "Autobiography," 10:197.

cause. In this cause I would have you encouraged and emboldened, though I must lead your thoughts to some disagreeable subjects. There are sins among us. God is angry and contending with us."[54] The way that Green pictured and attacked these "sins among us" set him apart from his patriotic colleagues, for his radical attack on British oppression did not, as was the case with many patriotic clergymen, resolve itself into a conservative defense of the institutions and practices of colonial society.[55]

Bernard Bailyn has proposed an attractive hypothesis in his *Ideological Origins of the American Revolution* to account for this ability to urge significant social reform during the Revolutionary period. Referring specifically to the attack on slavery at the time of the Revolution, Bailyn argues that it came about as the result of individuals "following out the logic of Revolutionary thought."[56] That is, the discussion of natural rights, tyranny, and slavery in the context of British-colonial relations could not be restricted to the political sphere but came, willy-nilly, to be focused on the problem of slavery as well. Bailyn has called this process, which he sees working not only against slavery, but also against religious establishments, antidemocratical processes of government, and the general hierarchical structure of late-colonial society, "the contagion of liberty." In Bailyn's estimation, the works of two New Light ministers from New England, Samuel Hopkins and Levi Hart, provided the clearest expression of this "contagion of liberty" in the area of slavery. In 1775 and 1776 they presented "a broad range of antislavery arguments explicitly associated with Revolutionary ideology and centered on the key doctrines of neo-Puritan theology."[57] While recognizing the contribution of "neo-Puritan theology" (i.e., Edwardsean New Divinity) to the attack on slavery, Bailyn does not dwell on this aspect but instead stresses the telling effectiveness with which Hopkins and Hart turned Whig arguments against the institution of chattel slavery. He closes his section on antislavery during the Revolution by pointing again to the central role played by "the extension of Revolutionary ideas" in the attack.[58]

54. *Sermon of public Fasting*, 5.

55. For perceptive comments on Presbyterian conservatism on the home front, see James H. Smylie, "Presbyterian Clergy and Problems of 'Dominion' in the Revolutionary Generation," *Journal of Presbyterian History* 48 (fall 1970): 168f. I have described the way in which one New England clergyman combined political liberalism in the struggle against Great Britain with cultural and social conservatism at home in "Ebenezer Devotion, Religion and Society in Revolutionary Connecticut," *Church History* (forthcoming).

56. Bailyn, *Ideological Origins*, 232.

57. Ibid., 242.

58. Ibid., 246.

Bailyn's account is compelling, particularly in light of the logical connection, so apparent from a twentieth-century perspective, between arguments against the tyranny of taxation without representation and against the bondage of chattel slavery. That Hopkins, Hart, and Jacob Green attacked slavery because they were following out the logic of *libertarian* ideas is, however, less evident than the internal logic of Whig thought might lead us to believe. Bailyn's account provides no clue why the internal logic of libertarianism led Hopkins but not Whigs in general to attack slavery. To account for just this phenomenon, David S. Lovejoy has argued that it was the logic of Hopkins's *religious* commitments which was extrapolated into an attack on slavery. Lovejoy contends that Hopkins did not derive his attack on slavery from libertarianism but merely used that ideology to drive home points determined by prior theological commitments. In Lovejoy's words:

> Hopkins did not find the origin of his reform in the Revolutionary philosophy or even in the equalitarian principle imbedded in the Declaration of Independence. Rather, he exploited the Declaration and the Revolution to *support* a conviction about equality already arrived at on other grounds. These grounds were religious, and they stemmed from the Great Awakening of the 1740's.[59]

It was Hopkins who attacked slavery not because of his particularly profound grasp of libertarian thought, but because of the structure of his theology.[60] In like manner, it can be argued that Jacob Green, although he understood Whig thought and adopted it as the basis for his political position, was able to "exploit" that Whig thought precisely because his ultimate allegiance had been pledged to the ideology of the New Light.

Green, as has been noted, adhered to an Edwardsean theology.[61] With Edwards and Hopkins, Green laid great stress on supernatural activity as the key to theology and Christian behavior. In his social ethics Green accepted the Edwardsean categories of "disinterested benevolence" and "love to Being in General" along with the practical mandate to treat all

59. David S. Lovejoy, "Samuel Hopkins: Religion, Slavery, and the Revolution," *The New England Quarterly* 40 (June 1967): 227.

60. It is noteworthy that of Bailyn's two primary examples of the fullest expression of the contagion of liberty against slavery, one was Samuel Hopkins and the other was Levi Hart, student and son-in-law of Joseph Bellamy, who with Hopkins constituted the leadership of the New Divinity. On the connection between Hart and Bellamy, see Glenn Paul Anderson, "Joseph Bellamy (1719–1790): The Man and his Work" (Ph.D. diss., Boston University, 1971), 418ff.

61. See Gillett, *op. cit.,* 1:208n: "He is the first minister in the country—so far as I am aware—who publicly declared himself an 'Edwardian.'"

things in accordance with their nature. Since slaves were also human beings made in the image of God, they were not to be treated as if they were beasts of the field. If Green did not propound the specifics of Edwardsean ethics as thoroughly as did Hopkins, he did articulate the Edwardsean position in a closely related area—standards for church membership.

Green's thought in this area provides a better way of accounting for his social views than does the concept of a contagious Whig liberty. Edwardsean ecclesiology, no less than Edwardsean ethics, went into the process which ultimately enabled Green, Hopkins, and other followers of the New Light to criticize aspects of colonial society while yet remaining loyal to that society during the struggle against Great Britain.

Jonathan Edwards's ecclesiology made the kind of sharp division between church and world which American Puritanism had tended to obscure since the time of the Half-Way Covenant. The Edwards whose soteriology had no place for the "good" man who was not truly regenerate—"There are two competitors for the kingdom of this world, *Christ* and *Satan*"—proposed an ecclesiology in which "none ought to be admitted as members of the visible church of Christ but visible and professing saints."[62] By seeking to reserve the Lord's Supper for the professedly regenerate and baptism for the children of just these same individuals, Edwards had no place in the church for the "good" man in order to emphasize its true character as the society of the children of God. His concern was not with the Puritan social covenant but with the covenant of grace, strictly defined. Edwards's rejection of half-way and Stoddardean practices of church membership eventually cost him his Northampton pulpit,[63] but it also bequeathed to his followers a means to escape the tribalistic chauvinism which beset American Puritanism and which came to characterize American nationalism during the course of the eighteenth century.[64]

62. Jonathan Edwards, *Misrepresentations Corrected, and Truth Vindicated . . .* (1752), *Works of President Edwards* (New York: Burt Franklin, 1968 [London, 1817]), 8:215; *An Humble Inquiry into the Rules of the Word of God, concerning the Qualifications Requisite to a Complete Standing and Full Communion in the Visible Christian Church* (1749), *Works of President Edwards,* 8:11f.

63. George Leon Walker, "Jonathan Edwards and the Half-Way Covenant," *The New Englander,* n.s. 7 (September 1884): 601–14.

64. The dangers of such a tribalism are described well by Edmund S. Morgan, *The Puritan Family* (rev. and enlarged ed.; New York: Harper Torchbook, 1966), 161–86. Nathan O. Hatch has provided an excellent description of the way in which expectations and attitudes concerning the Puritan spiritual community were transferred at the time of the last French and Indian War to general colonial society in "The Origins of Civil Millennialism in America: New England Clergymen, War with France, and the Revolution," *The William and Mary Quarterly,* 3rd ser. 31 (July 1974): 417–20.

Well before Green's overt participation in patriotic activities, his own commitment to the Edwardsean ecclesiology had been tested under fire. In 1766 he published a sermon on *Christian Baptism* which called for a reservation of this initiatory sacrament for the children of the regenerate.[65] A more substantial work, published in 1768, discussed *The Constitution and Discipline of the Jewish Church,* and sought to bring Old Testament history to bear on the controversy over church membership.[66] When in 1769 the Reverend George Beckwith replied from Connecticut with a tract defending Stoddardeanism, entitled *Visible Saints lawful Right to Communion in Christian Sacraments,* Green replied that Beckwith's position was inconsistent with a truly Reformed faith.[67]

Green's argument against half-way and Stoddardean church membership was grounded in an Edwardsean perception of the gospel and the church.[68] Since baptism was a seal of the gracious work of God in a heart, a profession of true religion was a requirement both for taking the Lord's Supper and for bringing children to baptism.[69] Even in Old Testament times, God required true belief for participation in the Jewish ordinances in spite of the fact that the Israelites repeatedly prostituted these divine standards through the substitution of human norms. As circumcision was to reflect true belief in the Old Testament period, so baptism was in New Testament times.[70] With Edwards, Green also argued that, when considering candidates for admission, it was not more difficult to judge a person's profession of true holiness than his moral sincerity or doctrinal knowledge, requirements still in force under the half-way and Stoddardean systems.[71] In order to defend the practice of strict membership, the practice which he desired to inaugurate in his churches in New Jersey, Green thus expounded many of the themes set out by Edwards in 1749 and 1750 and later developed at great length by Joseph Bellamy in a subsequent phase of the church membership controversy.[72] Green reflected

65. *Christian Baptism. A Sermon Delivered at Hanover, in New-Jersey, November 4, 1764* (Woodbridge, N.J.: Samuel F. Parker, 1766).

66. *An Inquiry into The Constitution and Discipline of the Jewish Church; In order to cast some Light on the Controversy, concerning Qualifications for the Sacraments of the New Testament* (New York: Hugh Gaine, 1768).

67. George Beckwith, *Visible Saints lawful Right to Communion in Christian Sacraments, Vindicated (In Way of Answer to . . . Jacob Green) . . .* (New London: Timothy Green, 1769); Green, *A Reply to the Reverend Mr. George Beckwith's Answer, To Mr. Green's Sermon . . .* (New Haven: Thomas and Samuel Green [1769]).

68. Green quotes Edwards directly in his *Christian Baptism,* 12, and *Jewish Church,* 22.

69. *Christian Baptism,* 4, 8, 10, 18, 22.

70. *Jewish Church,* 15, 37, 44, 56, 69.

71. *Reply to Beckwith's Answer,* 4, 6, 19.

72. Green announced in *Christian Baptism,* 22–26, that he intended to begin the practice. Of this action, Shipton, *op. cit.,* 409f., has written: Green "became the first American

the Edwardsean concern for the purity of ecclesiastical communion when he described the damage done to the church, the visible manifestation of God's holiness on earth, by a loose plan of church membership: "The Principles I oppose have a bad Tendency, in that they open the Church to the World of ungodly Men, so as greatly to profane gospel Ordinances: And take in so many carnal Ones, as to interrupt, if not to destroy, Brotherly Love and Christian Communion."[73] In reflecting on his early life Green regretted the damage that had been done to his own spiritual development when he was admitted into full church membership before he had reasonable assurance of his conversion.[74]

Green's opinions on church membership become important for a proper understanding of his social and political views, for it is in his discussion of ecclesiology that his conception of the distinction between the church and the world appears most clearly. Green could make no sense of an "external covenant" which allowed individuals to consider themselves "visible saints, where there [was] nothing in their character, not so much as in their profession, that [made] them appear, out of the character of the unregenerate." He simply could not fathom how people could be "visible saints, and visibly unregenerate, at the same time."[75] To allow this kind of fuzzy thought and these deceiving practices to function in the church amounted to much more than minor ecclesiastical deviance. Rather, it cut to the heart of the gospel as it had been restored at the Reformation and preserved in classic Calvinism:

> In my Opinion, the whole Controversy concerning the Sacraments, depends upon the following Principles or Sentiments, *viz.* That many unregenerate Persons have some good Principles, mean well, and have some sincere Regard for, and liking to God in his proper Character . . . and that God in degree approves of them and their Duties. These are *Arminian* tenets, very agreeable to natural Men. On the contrary, thorough *Calvinists* maintain that fallen Man is totally depraved . . . and while unregenerate does nothing from better Principles than selfish Idolatry.[76]

Presbyterian to take the stand that only those who were hopefully pious should be received into the membership of the church." For the essential bibliography on the controversy over church membership from 1769 to 1772 in which Bellamy was the focal point, see Williston Walker, *The Creeds and Platforms of Congregationalism* (Boston: Pilgrim, 1960 [1893]), 241–44. Mark A. Noll, "Church Membership and the American Revolution: An Aspect of Religion and Society in New England from the Revival to the War for Independence" (Ph.D. diss., Vanderbilt University, 1975), discusses in some detail the possible range of connections between ecclesiological and political points of view.

73. *Jewish Church,* ix.
74. Jacob Green, "Autobiography," 9:522f.
75. *Reply to Beckwith's Answer,* 23.
76. *Jewish Church,* viin–viiin.

Other ministers who adopted the concept of an "external covenant" were much more prone to see colonial society as a divine entity enjoying the privileges of a church at large.[77]

The implications of Green's Edwardsean ecclesiology, however, posed a serious challenge to the notion that colonial society in the aggregate was under God's special care. In Green's first treatise on the membership issue he argued that the church reflects a higher reality than colonial society and should not be equated with it. Hence, "the door of the church is not to be opened to take in all the world, while persons evidently appear to be of the world: The church and the world are distinct things according to scripture; nor is it baptism merely that will distinguish them."[78] Again:

> In fine, I know of no middle way between opening the church doors too wide, and admitting those only who come into full communion. There is no *medium* between right and wrong. . . . I can see no reason, that in this world there should be a sort of community erected by *protestants,* that belongs neither to the visible kingdom of Christ, nor to the visible kingdom of satan.[79]

And we have noted that in the very heat of the Revolution itself, when so many Christians joined their religious and political concerns, Green drew a strict distinction between areas of spiritual and social significance.[80]

Baptism and church membership were to be signs clearly setting the believer apart from the world. Baptism was not to be administered indiscriminately to all and sundry who desired it, for such baptismal practice broke down the rightful barriers separating church and world. Loose standards of membership also cast a false aura of holiness over society at large by bestowing the sanction of Christian sacraments where there was no Christian substance.

Green took his theological bearings from Jonathan Edwards. As a result, his theology stressed the fact that salvation was not a social process involving an "external" covenant but a personal experience marked by an internal covenant with God. As had Edwards, Green applied this theological insight to the church. The church, the special object of God's interest, must be preserved as something distinct from society, even the society of a colonial America that had been hallowed by the godly heritage of Puritanism. Precisely because Green made such a sharp distinction be-

77. The process by which an advocacy of loose standards of church membership led to a perception of colonial society itself as God's special object of affection has been discussed in Noll, "Church Membership and the American Revolution," 259–63 and *passim.*

78. *Christian Baptism,* 5.

79. Ibid., 27.

80. See above, 131.

tween the church and the world, he was able to bring religious judgments to bear on a society that other Christians, who had not made such a distinction, regarded during the Revolution as the faultless embodiment of God's concern.

In light of the issues which engaged Green's attention for a decade before he turned to political matters, it is probable that the thrust of his religious views exercised a greater influence in the formation of his criticism of colonial society than did the contagion of Whig liberty. Green's perception of the distinction between the church and the world is the key to understanding the nature of his participation in Revolutionary events. The thinking which distinguished church and world in his ecclesiology enabled him, while contending most ardently for an independent United States, to upbraid colonial society for religious and moral shortcomings. Green did take the Whig view of the Revolutionary crisis seriously, but he was also able to transcend libertarian categories and to call American society to account by a higher law to which he owed first allegiance. Green's case, therefore, militates against Bailyn's conclusions concerning the source of moral reform in Revolutionary America. Green's criticism of slavery did not proceed primarily from a libertarian perspective but from a religious orientation derived from Edwardsean theology. The colonies did have the better of the political argument with Great Britain. Colonial society was not, however, to be confused with the church nor exempted from the demands for social righteousness which Green's Edwardsean theology had defined long before Whig thought became popular in the public arena.

In this struggle against Great Britain, Green was not merely concerned with defending the established orders of colonial society against British encroachments but was rather dedicated to implementing righteousness in society. In this respect Green's career supports those who see a consistent relationship between religious and sociopolitical commitments. But here again, it was Green's religious conviction itself rather than its translation into political or social ideology which defined his concept of social righteousness. The righteousness Green desired did have a political flavor which would have seemed foreign to the New Lights in 1740, but its essence sprang from the religious principles of the Great Awakening as these had been refined by Jonathan Edwards.

Part 3

Evangelicalism before the Civil War

6

The Irony of the Enlightenment for Presbyterians in the Early Republic

Mark A. Noll

Reprinted by permission from *Journal of the Early Republic* 5 (1985): 150–75.

The heroic age of American religious thought came to an end on 22 March 1758, when Jonathan Edwards died. It is hardly an exaggeration to say that in the next fifty years the total contribution from all American religious thinkers failed to match in spiritual discernment the work of Thomas Hooker, in energetic versatility the labors of Cotton Mather, or in philosophical acumen the books of Edwards or even Samuel Johnson.[1] Specifically religious thought revived in America only after the turn of the century when the Second Great Awakening called forth the same kind of theological explications, attacks, and defenses that had followed in the wake of the First. Hard on the heels of the revival came also professional schools for ministers—at Andover in 1808, at Prince-

1. An excellent brief account of the eclipse of theology in the revolutionary period is provided by Edmund S. Morgan, "The American Revolution Considered as an Intellectual Movement," in *Paths of American Thought,* ed. Arthur M. Schlesinger, Jr., and Morton White (Boston, 1963), 11–33.

ton, Yale, Harvard, and elsewhere shortly thereafter—which provided a renewed environment for formal religious thought. When, however, theology reappeared in the early national period, it looked quite different from its form in the age of Edwards. American religious thought was no longer uniformly Calvinistic or Trinitarian. Before too many years had passed, some of the best religious thinking in American was no longer even Christian in a traditional sense.[2] But most importantly for the purposes of this chapter, the religious thought of the early national period was everywhere at peace with the Enlightenment.

In America the Enlightenment which mattered most for religious thinkers was that "didactic" form characterized by Henry May as the effort to preserve "the intelligible universe, clear and certain moral judgments, and progress" from skeptical and revolutionary *éclaircissement.* It was an Enlightenment smitten by Newton and guided by the philosophers of the Scottish Renaissance. It was also an Enlightenment that reflected the pervasive influence of those republican values that had provided the ideological basis for the American Revolution and the guiding vision for the new nation.[3]

During the half-century from Edwards's death to the founding of Andover Seminary, American religious thinkers gradually accommodated theology to the demands of science, reason, and law. This development was especially important for the Presbyterians clustered around the educational establishments in Princeton.

For their less orthodox contemporaries—whether Deists, Unitarians,

2. For the importance of non-Calvinist or non-Christian thought in this period, see Timothy L. Smith, *Revivalism and Social Reform: American Protestantism on the Eve of the Civil War* (Nashville, 1957), 15–33; Conrad Wright, *The Beginnings of Unitarianism in America* (Boston, 1955); Sydney E. Ahlstrom, *A Religious History of the American People* (New Haven, 1972), 599–609; and Perry Miller, "From Edwards to Emerson," in *Errand into the Wilderness* (Cambridge, Mass., 1956), 184–203.

3. Henry May, *The Enlightenment in America* (New York, 1976), xiv, for definitions, and 307–62 for exposition concerning the "didactic" Enlightenment. Donald H. Meyer, *The Democratic Enlightenment* (New York, 1976) is also a reliable guide to the combination of continental ideas and British republicanism that constituted the Enlightenment in America. Gordon Wood, "Evangelical America and Early Mormonism," *New York History* 61 (October 1980): 359–86, and Nathan O. Hatch, "The Christian Movement and the Demand for a Theology of the People," *Journal of American History* 67 (December 1980): 545–67, explore the ramifications of revolutionary thinking for religious life. For specific consideration of these matters among the Presbyterians, see Theodore Dwight Bozeman, *Protestants in an Age of Science: The Baconian Ideal and Antebellum American Religious Thought* (Chapel Hill, N.C., 1977); George M. Marsden, *The Evangelical Mind and the New School Presbyterian Experience: A Case Study of Thought and Theology in Nineteenth-Century America* (New Haven, Conn., 1970); and John C. Vander Stelt, *Philosophy and Scripture: A Study in Old Princeton and Westminster Theology* (Marlton, N.J., 1978), 65–200.

or Jeffersonians—it had become intuitively fitting to express fundamental religious convictions in the language of Enlightenment. There is thus little irony to the way in which these self-consciously Enlightenment thinkers developed their religious convictions amid the contingencies of antebellum life, whatever irony may have attended their beliefs about race or their hopes for the Union. On the other hand, it is not self-evident why an intellectual tendency that moved in secular, antitraditional, and naturalistic directions should have had such an appeal for the orthodox Presbyterians. Nonetheless, these Presbyterians joined other American intellectuals in taking for themselves an English moderate commitment to cosmic predictability and a Scottish didactic belief in benevolent common sense.[4] From these sources the Presbyterians adopted convictions—that science and reason were as persuasive as tradition and revelation, that a natural moral sense could light the path to social virtue, and that intuition provided a reliable foundation for arguments about God and the world—by which they thought to refurbish their Calvinistic heritage. So armed, they advanced to demonstrate conclusively the truthfulness of Christianity, to establish an ideology for social order, and to rebuff skeptics and revolutionaries who prostituted the heroic efforts of Bacon, Newton, and Locke. From first to last—adoption, expectations, and consequences—this Presbyterian embrace of the Enlightenment was filled with irony. It was an irony that began with the rejection of Jonathan Edwards and that ended in confusion, with Presbyterians maintaining an enthusiastic theoretical support for the didactic Enlightenment while repudiating it in practice.

The beginning of this story is the Presbyterian volte-face on Jonathan Edwards who, by the mid-eighteenth century, had become the most influential figure among colonial Calvinists. His importance for the New Divinity of Samuel Hopkins and Joseph Bellamy is well known.[5] Yet he carried only slightly less influence among the New Side Presbyterians of the middle and Southern colonies. Samuel Davies sought unsuccessfully to secure a Virginia pulpit for Edwards when he left Northampton in 1750. The Presbyterians of New York City tried for years to call Edwards's student, Joseph Bellamy, as their pastor. Trustees of the College of New Jersey were elated when Edwards accepted the presidency of their school in 1757. And

4. May, *Enlightenment in America,* 59–64, 337–50. Nicholas Phillipson, "The Scottish Enlightenment," in *The Enlightenment in National Context,* ed. Roy Porter and Mikulas Teich (Cambridge, 1981), is a good summary of the Scottish achievement.

5. For overviews, consult Frank Hugh Foster, *A Genetic History of the New England Theology* (Chicago, 1907), and Conrad Cherry, *Nature and Religious Imagination from Edwards to Bushnell* (Philadelphia, 1980), 66–84.

even ten years later many of those same trustees were eager to give Samuel Hopkins, also a close friend of Edwards, a chance at the same position.[6]

Edwards, however, was more than just an influential Calvinistic minister. By mid-century he had also become the most searching American foe of the Enlightenment. Although Edwards probably understood Locke and Newton nearly as well as anyone in the colonies, the corpus of his work amounted to a significant rejection of Enlightenment verities.[7] His examinations of free will and original sin restated an Augustinian dependence upon God where the Enlightenment would appeal, in Kant's famous phrase, to "man's emergence from his self-imposed nonage."[8] His *Treatise Concerning Religious Affections* denied that a mechanistic psychology could adequately explain either conversion or the religious life when all around physicians of the soul were attempting to turn "the Newtonian trick" on these very subjects.[9] Edwards's discussion of *The Nature of True Virtue* attacked sharply the idea that a natural moral sense was an adequate basis for more than commonplace virtue at precisely the time when thinkers in Scotland, Europe's most advanced center of learning, were estimating its value much more highly.[10]

When Edwards died in 1758 his reputation rode a crest among the Presbyterians. Yet within little more than a decade Presbyterians had turned from him completely. While the history of Edwards's displacement among the orthodox of New England is a lengthy, and somewhat tedious tale, that same history among the Presbyterians is sharp, swift, and dramatic. It is, from one perspective, a simple account of John Witherspoon's whirlwind descent upon America and his effectiveness, as president of the College of New Jersey and as moving spirit of Revolutionary Presbyterianism, in spreading the principles of the Scottish Enlightenment. From another, it is a complex story of Witherspoon's own

6. Leonard J. Trinterud, *The Forming of an American Tradition: A Reexamination of Colonial Presbyterianism* (Philadelphia, 1949), 138, 212–13; Thomas Jefferson Wertenbaker, *Princeton, 1746–1896* (Princeton, 1946), 42.

7. Wallace E. Anderson, ed., *The Works of Jonathan Edwards: Scientific and Philosophical Writings* (New Haven, Conn., 1980), 97, 133; and, more generally, Norman Fiering, *Jonathan Edwards's Moral Thought and Its British Context* (Chapel Hill, N.C., 1981), 322–61.

8. Jonathan Edwards, *Freedom of the Will,* ed. Paul Ramsey (New Haven, Conn., 1957), and *Original Sin,* ed. Clyde A. Holbrook (New Haven, Conn., 1970). Immanuel Kant, "What Is Enlightenment?" in Peter Gay, ed., *The Enlightenment: A Comprehensive Anthology* (New York, 1973), 384.

9. Jonathan Edwards, *Religous Affections,* ed. John E. Smith (New Haven, Conn., 1959). For the phrase *Newtonian trick,* see Charles Beard, "Written History as an Act of Faith," *American Historical Review* 39 (January 1934): 223.

10. Edwards, *The Nature of True Virtue,* ed. William K. Frankena (Ann Arbor, 1960), 27–107; Gladys Bryson, *Man and Society: The Scottish Inquiry of the Eighteenth Century* (Princeton, 1945); Phillipson, "The Scottish Enlightenment," 29.

tangled allegiances and the even more tangled allegiances of Presbyterian religious thought in the century after Witherspoon.

John Witherspoon, in spite of a rough and ready character, remains an enigma. The Scottish clergyman who read Joseph Bellamy with delight, who urged ministers not to meddle in politics, who denounced Francis Hutcheson, who opposed ecclesiastical patronage as tyrannical, and who mobilized troops against the Rebellion of '45, was also the American college president who banned Bellamy's works from his campus, who joined legislative assemblies, who modeled his collegiate instruction on Hutcheson, who supported a moderate establishment of religion, and who championed the Rebellion of '76.[11] Upon his arrival at Princeton in 1768 Witherspoon immediately set instruction in order and also rescued the college from the institutional uncertainty that had prevailed after the death of yet another president, Samuel Finley, in 1766.

One of Witherspoon's most important early actions had great consequences for the future direction of American Presbyterian thought. When he arrived he was chagrined to find that some of the tutors were teaching philosophical idealism. In published accounts of Witherspoon's earliest days at the College of New Jersey, Bishop George Berkeley's name appears as the primary authority for this position. Yet in light of the fact that four of the five junior faculty at Princeton in 1768, including Jonathan Edwards, Jr., had strong ties to New England's revivalistic Congregationalism, it is probable that the Princeton idealism reflected Edwards's thought as well.[12]

In the face of the teaching that prevailed at Princeton, Witherspoon mounted a general attack on idealism and a specific assault on Berkeley, whose "immaterialism takes away the distinction between truth and falsehood." In addition, Witherspoon linked the errors of Berkeley to the even more pernicious errors of David Hume, "a man of extensive learning and an excellent historian, but of damna(ble) [*sic*] principles."[13] To

11. Biographical details are from Varnum Lansing Collins, *President Witherspoon* (Princeton, 1925). The best short study of Witherspoon is "The Scottish Enlightenment Comes to Princeton: John Witherspoon," in Douglas Sloan, *The Scottish Enlightenment and the American College Ideal* (New York, 1971), 104–45. Briefer perceptive accounts are in May, *Enlightenment in America,* 62–65, 346–47, and Meyer, *Democratic Enlightenment,* 186–98.

12. See the biographical essays on James Thomson (class of 1761), Joseph Periam (1762), Jonathan Edwards, Jr. (1765), and Ebenezer Pemberton (1765) in James McLachlan, *Princetonians, 1748–1768: A Biographical Dictionary* (Princeton, 1976).

13. John Witherspoon, "Lectures on Moral Philosophy," in *The Works of the Rev. John Witherspoon,* 4 vols. (Philadelphia, 1802), 2:377, for comments on "immaterialism." Witherspoon's words on Hume are from Ashbel Green, *The Life of the Revd John Witherspoon,* ed. Henry Lyttleton Savage (Princeton, 1973), 274. Witherspoon attacked Hume directly in his "Lectures on Moral Philosophy," *Works,* 3:395.

counteract these errors Witherspoon turned, almost as if by reflex, to the work of his countryman, Francis Hutcheson, who had systematically advanced the teaching of the third Earl of Shaftesbury on the natural capacities of the moral sense and who, by encouraging a strictly empirical study of human nature, had hastened the liberation of Scottish thought from the Kirk's traditional deference to revelation.[14]

In Scotland, Witherspoon, champion of the evangelical party, had attacked Hutcheson, soul of the moderates, for infidelity.[15] But at Princeton, Hutcheson's *Short Introduction to Moral Philosophy* became Witherspoon's guide, especially its depiction of ethics as a *natural* human *science.* With Hutcheson, Witherspoon expressed great confidence in the ability of unreconstructed human feelings to uncover the truth about human nature and the powers of virtue: "The principles of duty and obligation," he said early in his lectures on moral philosophy, "must be drawn from the nature of man." An examination of human nature discloses that individuals have an internal sense for virtue and beauty very much analogous to the external senses that communicate the reality of the physical world. According to Witherspoon, this "internal sensation," what Hutcheson "calls the finer powers of perception," constitutes "a sense of moral good and evil" or "conscience." When humans cultivate this internal moral sense, which is common to all humanity, they are able to discern the nature of duty. And when people are able to do "what is dictated by moral sense," they experience "a sense of moral excellence." Furthermore, Witherspoon shared Hutcheson's great faith, and the faith of the Enlightenment generally, in an empirical approach to ethics. If moral philosophers faithfully study their own natures, he felt, contradictions would even out, and "a time may come when men, treating moral philosophy as Newton and his successors have done natural, may arrive at greater precision."[16]

These convictions placed Witherspoon at an advanced stage in the development of what Norman Fiering has called "the new moral philosophy," an approach to truth that grew in part out of Puritan piety but which in larger measure represented a rejection of the older practical theology stretching back from Edwards through William Ames and John Calvin to Augustine.[17] With Hutcheson and most other eighteenth-

14. For context and examples of Hutcheson's work, see Jane Rendall, *The Origins of the Scottish Enlightenment* (New York, 1978). Sloan, *Scottish Enlightenment,* 123–45, and Jack Scott, ed., *An Annotated Edition of "Lectures on Moral Philosophy" by John Witherspoon* (Newark, Del., 1982), 26–28, 35–37, and 42–43, learnedly discuss Witherspoon's dependence upon Hutcheson.

15. For example, Witherspoon, "Ecclesiastical Characteristics" (1753), in *Works,* 3:229, 231, 232.

16. Witherspoon, "Lectures on Moral Philosophy," *Works,* 3:369, 379, 381, 470.

17. Fiering, *Jonathan Edward's Moral Thought,* 4–12, and Fiering, *Moral Philosophy at Seventeenth-Century Harvard* (Chapel Hill, N.C., 1981).

century moral philosophers except Edwards, Witherspoon, at least in his lectures, set aside an Augustinian distrust of human nature; he denied, in practice, that original sin harmed the ability to cultivate natural virtue; and he came to speak of the achievements of science as triumphs of empirical inquiry rather than as manifestations of God's glory.[18]

Witherspoon's philosophical allegiance, regarded in this light, was no minor matter. It not only united him with his erstwhile theological opponents, Scottish moderates and Old Side Presbyterians, but also divided him philosophically from his putative theological allies, the New Side/New Light American Calvinists.[19] When Witherspoon allowed principles from the Scottish Enlightenment to govern instruction at Princeton, it forced him to sacrifice earlier Presbyterian convictions about ethics, epistemology, and the relationship between revelation and reason. In particular his commitment to a Scottish version of the Enlightenment meant that there was no longer any room at Princeton, and soon among the Presbyterians, for the thought of Jonathan Edwards.

To be sure, the College of New Jersey had never been a thoroughly Edwardsean place, in spite of its manifold connections with New England's New Light. Yet the presidents and trustees of early Princeton had generally aligned themselves with Edwards's combination of Calvinistic revivalism and theistic learning. They held implicitly, as Edwards held explicitly, that the world was not primarily matter in motion, that knowledge did not begin with a human *tabula rasa,* that ethics was not a value-free science, that Christian virtue was altogether different from the natural expressions of the moral sense, and that God's providence and Christian revelation provided the indispensable framework for education.[20]

18. Fiering, *Moral Philosophy at Seventeenth-Century Harvard,* 43, points out that Witherspoon spoke of the virtues of "moral philosophy" in nearly the same terms as Cotton Mather had earlier spoken of "piety."

19. Hutcheson's teaching first came to America through Francis Alison, an Old Side Presbyterian who strongly opposed the New Side emphases of the College of New Jersey, and who feared Witherspoon for his evangelical reputation, at least before joining him in support of the revolution. See also L. H. Butterfield, *John Witherspoon Comes to America* (Princeton, 1953), 12, 34, and *passim;* David Fate Norton, "Francis Hutcheson in America," *Studies on Voltaire and the Eighteenth Century* 154 (1976): 1547–68; James L. McAllister, Jr., "Francis Alison and John Witherspoon: Political Philosophers and Revolutionaries," *Journal of Presbyterian History* 54 (spring 1976): 33–60; and Caroline Robbins, "'When It Is That Colonies May Turn Independent': An Analysis of the Environment and Politics of Francis Hutcheson (1694–1746)," *William and Mary Quarterly* 11 (April 1954): 214–51.

20. For material revealing basic similarities between Edwards and the Princeton officials, see Trustees of the College, *A General Account of the Rise and State of the College, Lately Established in the Province of New-Jersey* (New York, 1752), 5–6; Samuel Davies, *Little Children Invited to Jesus Christ . . . With an Account of the late . . . Religious Impressions among the Students in the College of New-Jersey* (Boston, 1765), 22–23; and

With Witherspoon, who yet shared the Calvinistic theology of his predecessors, all of this changed. In practice he began theoretical inquiry with Descartes's denial of inherited authority and with Locke's assumption that matter in motion grounded knowledge of the external world. Under Hutcheson's influence, and in spite of his manifest religious sincerity, Witherspoon sharply divided the testimony of the moral sense and the testimony of revelation. Moral philosophy itself, Witherspoon contended in the first paragraph of his lectures, is worthy of the name "*Philosophy*, because it is an enquiry into the nature and grounds of moral obligation by reason, as distinct from revelation." Witherspoon paused often to assert the truthfulness of special revelation, but this display of orthodoxy did not prevent him from also asserting that "we derive either the nature or obligation of duty from [human nature]."[21]

As if conscious of the direction in which he was taking instruction at Princeton, Witherspoon paused at the outset of his lectures to note that "An author of New-England, says, moral philosophy is just reducing infidelity to a system." That author was Cotton Mather, whose views on moral philosophy expressed in crude form what Jonathan Edwards would refine in *The Nature of True Virtue,* where the entire drift of eighteenth-century moral philosophy is criticized for its equation of natural and regenerate virtue. Edwards had honored the natural moral sense, but he denied that its cultivation yielded true virtue, for this came only from God's grace. Witherspoon, however, dismissed such objections with a shrug: "But however specious the objections, they will be found at bottom not solid."[22] In sum, Witherspoon exalted a value-free science of ethics to the place in morality that Edwards had reserved for divine activity, and he thought to demonstrate the truthfulness of revelation through reason and science instead of presupposing revelation as the foundation for science and reason.

The nearly incomprehensible feature of Witherspoon's sea change was the casualness with which it occurred. There was no great debate. There was no apparent recognition of the importance of the transformation. There was only a bluff and hardy realist flourishing common sense to

---

Wertenbaker, *Princeton,* 3–46. Unlike the apologetics of Witherspoon, Aaron Burr's focused mostly on a proper understanding of the Bible rather than on demonstrations of the Bible's truthfulness; see Burr, *The Supreme Deity of our Lord Jesus Christ, maintained . . .* (Boston, 1757).

21. Witherspoon, *Works,* 3:367, 380; and on special revelation, ibid., 3:369, 386–90, 398, 471.

22. Ibid., 3:367; Scott, *Annotated Lectures by Witherspoon,* 64, 68, with citation to Cotton Mather, *Manuductio ad Ministerium* (Boston, 1726), 37; and Fiering, *Jonathan Edwards's Moral Thought,* 129–38, 322–61.

rout a febrile immaterialism. This, at least, is the picture that Ashbel Green left in the only direct account of Witherspoon's immediate intellectual impact on Princeton: "The Berklean system of Metaphysics was in repute in the college when he entered on his office. The tutors were zealous believers in it, and waited on the President, with some expectation of either confounding him, or making him a proselite. They had mistaken their man. He first reasoned against the System, and then ridiculed it, till he drove it out of the college."[23] The fact that Witherspoon was so obviously a person of sincere religion made for continuity with the Presbyterian past. But that underneath a common commitment to broadly Calvinistic theology a profound shift was taking place—from idealism, metaphysics, and conversion toward realism, ethics, and morality; from Edwards to the Enlightenment—constituted one of the most important developments in the history of American religious thought.

Remarkable as Witherspoon's exorcism of Edwards was, even more remarkable was the rapid acceptance of his point of view by the intellectual elite of the Presbyterians.[24] There was hardly a major figure among them in the half century after the revolution, especially at the college and seminary in Princeton, who did not imitate Witherspoon's approach. The College of New Jersey, which remained the dominant source of Presbyterian learning through the first decade of the nineteenth century, continued to cultivate moderate Enlightenment thought and confessional Calvinism in an uneasy alliance. Samuel Stanhope Smith, Witherspoon's successor as president from 1795 to 1812, drifted toward more consistently Enlightenment positions.[25] In youthful debate with James Madison he had argued an anti-Edwardsean position on the will. He grounded his own apologetical use of science "on the evidence of facts" derived exclusively from nature "independently of the authority of divine revelation." He offended pious students by his enthusiastic recommendation for the "grossly Arminian" Thomas Reid. And he defined "faith" intellectually

23. Green, *Life of Witherspoon,* 132. Sketchy details from contemporary accounts of students at Princeton when Witherspoon arrived and from modern studies of the tutors who were promoting Berkeley's ideas only confirm these details. [Frederick Beasley], "An Account of the Life and Writings of the Rev. Samuell Stanhope Smith," *The Analectic Magazine,* new ser. 1 (1820): 447–50; McLachlan, *Princetonians, 1748–1768,* 399–402.

24. Witherspoon's position at the College of New Jersey played a major role. In 1789 at the first General Assembly of the Presbyterian church, which Witherspoon had helped to establish, the denomination reported 188 ministers; of these 97 were graduates of Princeton and 52 were students of Witherspoon. Elwyn A. Smith, *The Presbyterian Ministry in American Culture: A Study in Changing Concepts, 1700–1900* (Philadelphia, 1962), 92.

25. Wesley Frank Craven, "Samuel Stanhope Smith," in Richard A. Harrison, *Princetonians, 1769–1775: A Biographical Dictionary* (Princeton, 1980), 42–51, is a good general sketch.

as "a rational offering to truth and reason."[26] Yet Smith never relinquished a Calvinist piety, which seeped through especially in his occasional sermons.[27] Smith's successor, Ashbel Green, came to distrust Smith's views, and he turned the college more consciously to piety. Yet Green was also a fervent admirer of Witherspoon, whose pupil he had been. His reform of Princeton's educational practices amounted to little more than a substitution of Witherspoon's *Moral Philosophy* and the works of William Paley for Smith's own textbooks, a change which, in spite of Green's pious intentions, only solidified the Enlightenment character of a Princeton education.[28]

By the time Green became president of the College of New Jersey in 1812, he had also played a major role in the founding of Princeton Theological Seminary, the institution that rapidly became the intellectual mainstay for the self-consciously orthodox Presbyterians. Piety and Calvinist confessionalism loomed larger at Princeton Seminary than they had at Princeton College under Smith, but the leaders of the seminary still approached religious thought along lines suggested by Witherspoon.[29] Archibald Alexander, the first professor, had learned philosophy from William Graham, one of Witherspoon's most ardent disciples. Alexander, for all his piety, still relied heavily on Enlightenment models, revealed especially by his extensive demonstrations for the truthfulness of

26. Smith to Madison, ca. November 1777 to August 1778; and Smith to Madison, 15 September 1778, *The Papers of James Madison*, vol. 1: *16 March 1751–16 December 1779*, ed. William T. Hutchinson and William M. E. Rachal (Chicago, 1962), 194–212, 253–58; Smith, *An Essay on the Causes of the Variety of Complexion and Figure in the Human Species*, 2d ed. (1810), ed. Winthrop D. Jordan (Cambridge, Mass. 1965), 3, 7; William Weeks to Ebenezer Weeks, 11 April 1808, Weeks Papers (Sheldon Art Museum, Middlebury, Vt.); Smith, *Lectures on the Evidences of the Christian Religion* (Philadelphia, 1809), 3.

27. As examples, Smith, "On Death—the Uncertainty of that Interesting Event, and the Proper Improvement of it," in *Sermons* (Newark, 1799), and Smith, "The Promised Seed of the Woman: Or, the Power of Evil Destroyed by Jesus Christ," and "The Excuses for not entering at Present on a Religious Life, Vain and Absurd," from *Sermons of Samuel Stanhope Smith* . . . (Philadelphia, 1821).

28. A good modern sketch is James McLachlan, "Ashbel Green," in Richard A. Harrison, ed., *Princetonians, 1776–1783: A Biographical Dictionary* (Princeton, 1981), 404–20. On his educational reforms, see Green, *Discourses, Delivered in the College of New Jersey . . . including a historical sketch of the college . . .* (Philadelphia, 1822), 290; and *The Life of Ashbel Green, V.D.M.*, ed. Joseph H. Jones (New York, 1849), 20–21.

29. Lefferts A. Loetscher, *Facing the Enlightenment and Pietism: Archibald Alexander and the Founding of Princeton Theological Seminary* (Westport, Conn., 1983), 109–38; Raleigh Don Scovel, "Orthodoxy in Princeton: A Social and Intellectual History of Princeton Theological Seminary, 1812–1860" (Ph.D. diss., University of California, Berkeley, 1970), 32–62; Vander Stelt, *Philosophy and Scripture*, 90–147; and Mark A. Noll, "The Founding of Princeton Seminary," *Westminster Theological Journal* 42 (fall 1979): 72–110. All of these accounts show how Witherspoon's intellectual point of view remained dominant at the seminary.

Christianity.[30] The seminary's second professor, Samuel Miller, though not a student of Witherspoon, was an equally ardent proponent of philosophical common sense.[31] Its third, Charles Hodge, had imbibed Witherspoon's commitment to disinterested inquiry and the illuminating function of the natural moral sense from Ashbel Green, his pastor and, later, instructor in college, and from Alexander and Miller, his professors at the seminary.[32] The intellectual stance of Princeton Seminary was not merely its own, but exemplified views on the natural powers of reason and the moral sense that Presbyterian laymen and Old School Presbyterians north and south also espoused.[33] The relationship between the Enlightenment and Calvinism at Princeton Seminary was, however, especially piquant. Alexander, Miller, and particularly Hodge were sharper dialecticians than Witherspoon and Green, and hence more skilled in using the naturalistic tools of the Enlightenment to defend faith and social order. But they were also more obvious in their piety than Smith, and hence more insistent upon the supernatural character of God's actions in the world.

The Presbyterian successors of Witherspoon remained Calvinists, and they continued to speak of the irreducible need for special revelation, but the configuration of their thought was thoroughly of a piece with the Enlightenment. Discoveries of the natural moral sense constituted the standard for virtue against which to justify biblical morality; intuitive convic-

30. Wesley Frank Craven, "William Graham," in Harrison, *Princetonians, 1769–1775,* 289–94; Loetscher, *Archibald Alexander,* 189–212.

31. Bruce M. Stephens, "Samuel Miller (1769–1850): Apologist for Orthodoxy," *Princeton Seminary Bulletin* 67 (winter 1975): 33–47. Miller was a graduate of the University of Pennsylvania, but because of the legacy of Francis Alison at that institution, he received the same picture of the world that Witherspoon gave to his students. Miller's position is suggested by the fact that in his *Brief Retrospect of the Eighteenth Century,* 2 vols. (New York, 1803), he waxed nearly rhapsodic about "the stupendous mind of Newton, and the penetrating genius of Locke" (1:11), he described with great respect and at considerable length "the principles and reasonings of certain modern metaphysicians of North-Britain," at whose "head . . . stands Dr. Reid" (2:11), but his only mention of Edwards, whom he did call "our great countryman," was in connection with Edwards's work on "*Liberty and Necessity.*" Miller spoke of this work with respect, but not of the "extremes" to which Edwards's heirs had carried his ideas (2:30–31).

32. Vander Stelt, *Philosophy and Scripture,* 120–47, and Ralph J. Danhof, *Charles Hodge as Dogmatician* (Goes, The Netherlands, 1929), 176–85. For a discussion of Hodge's specific uneasiness with Edwards, see W. Andrew Hoffecker, *Piety and the Princeton Theologians* (Grand Rapids, 1981), 73–74.

33. For a lay example, see the work of Elias Boudinot, such as his refutation of Paine, *The Age of Revelation. Or the Age of Reason shewn to be an Age of Infidelity* (Philadelphia, 1801), esp. vi, ix. Excellent discussions of the rationalistic strands in Old School Presbyterian theology are found in Theodore Dwight Bozeman, *Protestants in an Age of Science,* and E. Brooks Holifield, *The Gentlemen Theologians: American Theology in Southern Culture, 1795–1860* (Durham, N.C., 1978), 72–100.

tions of common sense provided the foundation for demonstrating the truthfulness of special revelation; and an ability to show the eminently scientific character of the faith became the main reason for its commendation. Some of the great lights of the Presbyterians, like Samuel Stanhope Smith and William Graham, seemed oblivious to the possibility of tension between inherited Calvinism and the Enlightenment. Others, like Ashbel Green and Archibald Alexander, showed great practical attachment to piety. Yet all espoused the philosophical convictions of Witherspoon, as if an alternative, the anti-Enlightenment vision of Edwards, had never existed at all.

The Presbyterian abandonment of Edwards would be less of a puzzle if this action had produced the positive results that Calvinists anticipated. In fact it did not. To the extent that they offered justification at all, Presbyterians defended their rapprochement with the Enlightenment because of its usefulness in providing a public ideology for social order and in demonstrating the truth of traditional orthodoxy. Their great fear was that proponents of more radical forms of Enlightenment would destroy society and the faith together. Their great goal in the struggle against irreligion and disorder was, in Witherspoon's words, "to meet [infidels] upon their own ground, and to show them from reason itself, the fallacy of their principles."[34] Yet for both society and the arena of religious thought, when Presbyterians reached for Enlightenment principles to undergird their aspirations, instability and the reverse of their intentions were the results.

The political context for the Presbyterian embrace of the Enlightenment was the War for Independence and the subsequent efforts to establish a new nation. Whatever Puritan or explicitly biblical elements may have contributed to the ideology of the American Revolution, this ideology also shared fully the assumptions of Europe's moderate Enlightenment.[35] "Real" Whig thought was predicated upon a defense of nat-

34. Witherspoon, "Lectures on Moral Philosophy," *Works,* 3:368. For profession of similar intent, see Smith, *Essay on Variety in the Human Species,* 4, where Smith speaks of "cooperating, in some degree, with those who are defending religion's outworks, and carrying their attacks into the enemy's camp"; or Elias Boudinot, *Age of Revelation,* 30, which speaks of an effort to refute Paine by "the rules of *common sense.*"

35. See Henry Steele Commager, *The Empire of Reason: How Europe Imagined and America Realized the Enlightenment* (Garden City, N.Y., 1977), for the longest case concerning the Enlightenment character of the revolution; and Gordon S. Wood, "Conspiracy and the Paranoid Style: Causality and Deceit in the Eighteenth Century," *William and Mary Quarterly* 39 (July 1982): 401–41, for the sharpest. Specific discussion of how religious approaches to the revolution involved the adoption of Enlightenment assumptions is provided by George Marsden, "The American Revolution: Partisanship, 'Just Wars,' and Crusades," in *The Wars of America: Christian Views,* ed. Ronald A. Wells (Grand Rapids, 1981), 11–24; and Mark A. Noll, "The Bible in Revolutionary America," in *The Bible in American Law, Politics and Rhetoric,* ed. James T. Johnson (Philadelphia and Chico, Calif., 1985).

ural rights, sustained a continual optimism concerning capacities to create the world anew, and staked its future on an ability to discover a natural science of politics.[36] Realists like James Madison, Alexander Hamilton, and John Adams might temper in different ways some of the Enlightenment optimism concerning the new order, but they never doubted that the secret of the revolution's success lay in discovering the moral laws of human behavior and putting them to use in creating a new age, a process Gordon Wood has called "the consuming passion of the Enlightenment."[37]

In the charged days of the revolution, Presbyterians with great fervor also became republicans.[38] But they did so in a confused way, first by conceding the Enlightenment basis of republican principles, and then by elevating these natural principles into the realm of divine truth. Witherspoon's lectures on politics provide an illustration. It was a longstanding commonplace at Princeton, and most other centers of learning in the eighteenth century, that social welfare rested on the virtues of a population. The early Presbyterians at Princeton differed from the commonplace only in their insistence that social well-being was best served by a supernaturally infused virtue, by the regenerating grace of God. Witherspoon himself had expressed such an opinion in 1758 during a fast sermon in Scotland, when he took special pains to attack the idea that a merely natural morality could be the basis of social health:

> It is not, indeed, to be wondered at, that not only this nation, but the protestant states of Europe in general should be brought under the rod, as they have so shamefully departed from that purity of faith and strictness of morals which was the glory of the reformation. How many have of late been ashamed of the cross of Christ, and the doctrine of the grace of God? And what hath been substituted in their room? A pliant and fashionable scheme of religion, a fine theory of virtue and morality. . . . And hath it not, in this, as in every preceding age, in this, as in every other Christian country, whenever it gained any credit, been the fore-runner and brought fast at its heels a deluge of profaneness and immorality in practice?[39]

36. Bernard Bailyn, *The Ideological Origins of the American Revolution* (Cambridge, Mass., 1967), 184–89; Gordon S. Wood, *The Creation of the American Republic, 1776–1787* (Chapel Hill, N.C., 1969); Wood, "Conspiracy and the Paranoid Style"; and Doug lass Adair, "'That Politics May Be Reduced to a Science': David Hume, James Madison, and the Tenth Federalist," in *Fame and the Founding Fathers,* ed. Trevor Colbourn (New York, 1974), 93–106.

37. Wood, "Conspiracy and the Paranoid Style," 414.

38. Trinterud, *Forming of an American Tradition,* 242–57; Mark A. Noll, *Christians in the American Revolution* (Grand Rapids, 1977), 49–77.

39. Witherspoon, "Prayer for National Prosperity and for the Revival of Religion inseparably connected" (1758), *Works,* 2:463.

When Witherspoon addressed this same connection between personal virtue and social well-being in his lectures at Princeton, however, he sounded less like his predecessors, or his own 1758 sermon, and more like the moralists of human nature whom he had pilloried in Scotland. "Piety" was still the key to "making a virtuous and regular people." But in America Witherspoon's "piety" had become a product of nature rather than grace. The only deity necessary now was the Author of Nature:

> Promoting the public or general good seems to be so nearly connected with virtue, that we must necessarily suppose that universal virtue could be of universal utility. . . . From reason, contemplation, sentiment and tradition, the Being and infinite perfection and excellence of God may be deduced; and therefore what he is, and commands is virtue and duty. Whatever he has implanted in uncorrupted nature as a principle is to be received as his will. . . . The result of the whole is, that we ought to take the rule of duty from conscience enlightened by reason, experience, and every way by which we can be supposed to learn the will of our Maker, and his intentions in creating us such as we are.[40]

Most Presbyterians agreed with Witherspoon that the new nation arose from this kind of piety and that it deserved their highest allegiance.

Presbyterian thinkers were not usually as explicit as Witherspoon in their political theory, but as a body they seem almost never to have questioned the Enlightenment assumptions that grounded hope for the future in the natural capacities of the population. Even more, they transformed these general Whig assumptions about social well-being into a special loyalty to the new United States, and then made the fate of the country a matter of ultimate religious concern. So completely did the results of the revolution come to stand for the future of religion that an erstwhile Edwardsean, the father of Samuel Stanhope Smith, could proclaim in a sermon of 1781 that "the cause of America is the cause of Christ."[41] Once such a transformation had been made, republicanism, itself a product of largely natural reasoning, even became a schoolmaster for the children of grace, as in this injunction from Ashbel Green's father, also in 1781, to his fellow Presbyterians: "The plan of church government which we have chosen, and we think derived from scripture, is a plan for liberty; the land we live in is a land of liberty; the time we live in is, especially a time of liberty; and we cannot but desire . . . that many others . . . will revise their

40. Witherspoon's discussion of "virtue and piety," "Lectures on Moral Philosophy," *Works,* 3:447–48, refers the reader back to the material quoted here, ibid., 3:387–88.

41. Robert Smith, *The Obligations of the Confederate States of North America to Praise God . . . for the Various Interpositions of His Providence in Their Favour* (Philadelphia, 1782), 33.

ecclesiastical principles, and see if they do not want something to make them fully consistent with Christian liberty."[42] In similar ways, republican visions of liberty and of the future decisively influenced, if they did not altogether overpower, the way in which Presbyterians used the Bible on public occasions and the way in which they speculated on God's designs for the future.[43]

By the 1790s, however, Presbyterians had cause to question their attachment to revolutionary republicanism and its underlying Enlightenment disposition. They were scandalized when Tom Paine, apostle of republican liberty, stepped forth as a publicist for libertarian Deism.[44] They professed horror as a wanton republicanism spread violence in France and democracy at home, and as the tentacles of a shadowy Enlightenment conspiracy stretched across America. New England Calvinists like Timothy Dwight and Jedidiah Morse led the way in decrying the social carnage of republican infidelity, but Presbyterians were not far behind.[45]

The Presbyterian General Assembly of 1798, with Samuel Stanhope Smith's brother, John Blair Smith, in the chair as moderator, spoke of prospects for America in terms no less alarming than Presbyterian Whigs of a generation before had used to decry the tyranny of Parliament: unprecedented political wrangling between forces of order and self-proclaimed champions "of the people," combined with manifest social confusion, resulted in a crisis that paralleled Europe's "scenes of devastation and bloodshed, unexampled in the history of modern nations" and that portended a "bursting storm which threatens to sweep before it the religious principles, institutions, and morals of our people."[46] From his central position in Princeton, Stanhope Smith repeated the same message in

42. Jacob Green, *A View of a Christian Church, and Church Government* (Chatham, N.J., 1781), 56.

43. Mark A. Noll, "The Image of the United States as a Biblical Nation, 1776–1865," in *The Bible in America: Essays in Cultural History,* ed. Nathan O. Hatch and Mark A. Noll (New York, 1982), 41–45; Fred J. Hood, *Reformed America: The Middle and Southern States, 1783–1837* (University, Ala., 1980), chap. 4, "The Millennium: Scenario for an American Theocracy."

44. Gary B. Nash, "The American Clergy and the French Revolution," *William and Mary Quarterly* 22 (July 1965): 402–4; and James H. Smylie, "Clerical Perspectives on Deism: Paine's *The Age of Reason* in Virginia," *Eighteenth-Century Studies* 6 (winter 1972–73): 203–20.

45. On ramifications of democracy that upset the Calvinists, see Gordon S. Wood, "The Democratization of Mind in the American Revolution," in *Leadership in the American Revolution* (Washington, D.C., 1974); and May, *Enlightenment in America,* 252–77.

46. *Minutes of the General Assembly of the Presbyterian Church in the United States of America from its Organization A.D. 1789 to A.D. 1820 inclusive* (Philadelphia, 1847), 152–53. For a similar view from an influential clergyman, see Ashbel Green, *Obedience to the Laws of God, the sure and indispensable Defence of Nations . . .* (Philadelphia, 1798).

a wide correspondence. In 1799 he bewailed to Jedidiah Morse "the torrent of infidelity & immorality that is overspreading the country." In December 1801 he subjected Jefferson's congressional message to severe criticism since its general "complexion" was "calculated merely to amuse & flatter a shortsighted & misjudging populace; the sure fore-runner of turbulance & anarchy in all republics." And after a fire had destroyed the college's main building in 1802, he concluded in no uncertain terms: "It is not doubted . . . by those who are best acquainted with the whole state of opinion here that [the fire] is one effect of those irreligious and demoralizing principles which are tearing the bands of society asunder, & threatening in the end to overturn our country."[47]

As these catastrophes rolled over their heads, Presbyterians, with other Federalists, defended the revolution by arguing that "jacobins," Jeffersonians, and democrats generally were destroying a good thing through excess. Unlike secular Federalists, however, Presbyterians began to inch back toward a belief that something supernatural was required to ground social well-being. Pietists like Ashbel Green placed increased emphasis on revival as a way to stabilize both small societies like Princeton College and larger ones like the nation. And, with almost none of the uneasiness which their Old School party would later display, Presbyterians in the early nineteenth century began to advocate voluntary societies and evangelistic campaigns rather than the new nation's political structures as the religiously inspired means to preserve American society.[48] As Fred J. Hood has recently demonstrated, Presbyterians in the years immediately following the revolution had tended to believe that governmental structures, whether official or unofficial, could best serve true religion and the good of the country.[49] Very soon, however, Presbyterian leaders began to turn toward voluntary societies as the institutional framework for encouraging virtue, controlling the culture, preserving the faith, saving the nation, and bringing in the millennium. Sometime after 1800, moreover, Presbyterians also began to look toward more strictly spiritual revival in order to achieve their religious and social goals. In the end, Presbyterian reliance upon benevolent societies and revivals almost entirely replaced their earlier confidence in the ability of the new American government to establish social well-being.

47. Smith to Jedidiah Morse, 24 Feburary 1799; to Jonathan Dayton, 22 December 1801; and to Morse, 10 March 1802, Samuel Stanhope Smith Collection (Manuscripts Division, Princeton University Library).

48. Clifford S. Griffin, *Their Brothers' Keepers: Moral Stewardship in the United States, 1800–1865* (New Brunswick, 1960); and, as a corrective, Lois W. Banner, "Religious Benevolence as Social Control: A Critique of an Interpretation," *Journal of American History* 60 (June 1973): 23–41.

49. Hood, *Reformed America*, 48–67.

Presbyterians, as it turned out, were not quite as active in the great confluence of revival and benevolent reform as members of other denominations. But Presbyterian leaders nonetheless hailed the accomplishments of the Second Great Awakening and were pleased to indicate when they had played their own part in them.[50] They, like more recent historians, were aware that "means of grace"—evangelistic revival and voluntaristic benevolence—had achieved a measure of success. Considerable order emerged from their efforts. An "evangelical empire" came into existence. And righteousness and hope flourished in some corners of the land.[51]

Although this social equilibrium was achieved as much through religious actions as through political inspiration, Presbyterians never questioned whether their earlier belief in the efficacy of American political systems has been misguided. The United States, portrayed everywhere as the embodiment of republicanism, had proven to be, by their own reading of events, anything but virtuous and harmonious. Yet even as Presbyterians turned more overtly to religion to achieve their social goals, even as a social order emerged that owed at least as much to the grace of the Second Awakening as to the Enlightenment of the revolution, they continued to revere the principles upon which the nation was founded and to assume that the health of the faith was dependent upon the political health of the country. This measure of social stability had been achieved only when Presbyterian and other religious leaders turned away from the revolution's Enlightenment programs to more strictly religious strategies. Yet all of this occurred without shaking the intellectual hegemony of the republican-Enlightenment synthesis. The result was intellectual confusion: Presbyterians mingled indiscriminately a vision of nature's nation and God's new Israel. They continued to venerate self-evident truths that in their own best judgment had failed.

50. As examples, Ashbel Green, *Glad Tidings, Or An Account of the State of Religion, within the bounds of the General Assembly . . . and in other parts of the world* (Philadelphia, 1804); Green, *A Report to the Trustees of the College of New Jersey: relative to a revival of religion among the students . . .* (Philadelphia, 1815); and Samuel Miller, *A Sermon . . . before the New York Missionary Society . . . [with] the annual report of the directors and other papers relating to American Missions* (New York, 1802).

51. Donald G. Mathews, "The Second Great Awakening as an Organizing Process, 1780–1830: An Hypothesis," *American Quarterly* 21 (spring 1969): 23–43; Martin E. Marty, *Righteous Empire: The Protestant Experience in America* (New York, 1970); Timothy L. Smith, "Righteousness and Hope: Christian Holiness and the Millennial Vision in America, 1800–1900," *American Quarterly* 31 (spring 1979): 21–45; and Martha Tomhave Blauvelt, "Society, Religion, and Revivalism: The Second Great Awakening in New Jersey, 1780–1830" (revision of Ph.D. diss., Princeton University, 1974), esp. chap. 6, "Life After Conversion: Visible Sainthood in the Early Republic."

An even more enduring result of the Presbyterians' acceptance of the Enlightenment involved their characteristic attitude toward the defense of the Christian faith. Presbyterian apologetics rested on one Enlightenment assumption and two Enlightenment procedures. The assumption was that disputants could maintain intellectual neutrality when confronting arguments of fundamental religious significance. In 1836 John Henry Newman questioned just such an assumption, with special reference to William Paley's *View of the Evidences of Christianity* (1794), a work of great popularity among Presbyterians during the early national period. "Nothing is so common . . . as for young men to approach serious subjects as judges—to study them as mere sciences. . . . The study of the Evidences as now popular (such as Paley's) encourages this evil frame of mind—the learner is supposed external to the system."[52] Newman, as did also a few Americans, eventually fled from Protestant scientism to Catholic authoritarianism. Jonathan Edwards, especially in his reasoning on free will and true virtue, had made the same objections, only in favor of a Protestant conception of the Holy Spirit.[53] But between the First Great Awakening and the Oxford Movement, almost no one in American Presbyterian circles seems to have appreciated the positions represented by Newman and Edwards.

The two Enlightenment procedures which the Presbyterians worked assiduously, were scientific demonstration and common-sense intuition, the first a memorial to Newton and Bacon, the second to the Scottish Renaissance. Together they provided the foundation for a mighty apologetical effort which seemed for a while to have preserved the keep, but which eventually left orthodoxy itself in ruins.

Examples of a scientifically rational defense of the faith abound in the early national period. The Presbyterians especially excelled at what T. D. Bozeman has called a "Baconian" approach to the faith. In divinity, rigorous empiricism became the standard for justifying belief in God, revelation, and the trinity. In moral philosophy, it marked out the royal road to ethical certainty. It also provided a key for using physical science itself

52. Newman went on, in words with an Edwardsean tone: "In all these cases the student is supposed to look upon the system from without, and to have to choose it by an act of reason before he submits to it—whereas the great lesson of the gospel is faith, an obeying prior to reason, and *proving* its reasonableness by making experiment of it. . . ."; Newman to Arthur Percival, 11 January 1836, as quoted in Marvin R. O'Connell, *The Oxford Conspirators: A History of the Oxford Movement, 1833–1845* (New York, 1969), 178–79. On Paley's popularity in America, see Wilson Smith, "William Paley's Theological Utilitarianism in America," *William and Mary Quarterly* 11 (July 1954): 402–24; David Lundberg and Henry F. May, "The Enlightened Reader in America," *American Quarterly* 28 (summer 1976), the 20th and 21st pages (not numbered) following 271; and Cherry, *Nature and Religious Imagination,* 92–99.

53. For example, Edwards, *The Nature of True Virtue,* 12, where the relish of virtue depends upon having the necessary "temper" in oneself to be able to appreciate it.

as a demonstration of religious truths.[54] In every case the appeal was, as Stanhope Smith put it, "to the evidence of facts, and to conclusions resulting from these facts which . . . every genuine disciple of nature will acknowledge to be legitimately drawn from her own fountain."[55] This approach guided responses to Paine's *Age of Reason* in the 1790s, and to other infidels thereafter. It also was useful for counteracting the impious use of science, by making possible the harmonization of first revelation and astronomy, and then the Bible and geology.[56]

Presbyterians seem not to have realized, as they leaned so heavily on inductive science to mount a tradition-free defense of traditional orthodoxy, that the prop could give way. Some Presbyterians sensed the fragility of a faith resting on the whims of scientific fashion. Most, however, considered this phase of the battle won, and so were hardly prepared for the staggering blows which, beginning with the *Origins of Species,* rapidly knocked away the old Baconian props.[57]

Closely related to the orthodox reliance upon scientific reason was dependence upon intuitive common sense, for common sense was everywhere considered the basis for reliable knowledge of the external world and trustworthy employment of logic. Yet the way in which appeals to common sense rested frankly on intuition, and an intuition which affirmed far more than the mere knowability of the universe, meant that the orthodox had staked a very great deal on the clear and distinct deliverances of the mind.[58]

54. For examples in divinity, Witherspoon, "Lectures on Divinity," *Works,* 4:22–75; Samuel Stanhope Smith, *Lectures on the Evidences of the Christian Religion, and a Comprehensive View of the Leading and Most Important Principles of Natural and Revealed Religion* (New Brunswick, 1815); and Archibald Alexander, *A Brief Outline of the Evidences of the Christian Religion* (Princeton, 1825). Besides Witherspoon's "Moral Philosophy," Stanhope Smith and Alexander also wrote widely used lectures on the same subject. Smith's *Essay on Variety in the Human Species* is the best early example of Calvinistic uses of science for apologetical purposes, but see Bozeman, *Protestants in an Age of Science,* 71–159, and Herbert Hovenkamp, *Science and Religion in America, 1800–1860* (Philadelphia, 1978), for many later examples.

55. Smith, *Essay on Variety in the Human Species,* 3.

56. Ronald L. Numbers, *Creation by Natural Law: Laplace's Nebular Hypothesis in American Thought* (Seattle, 1977), 55–56; Bozeman, *Protestants in an Age of Science,* 96–97; Hovenkamp, *Science and Religion in America,* 119–46.

57. Good discussions of the effects of Darwinism on this intellectual construct are provided by Bozeman, *Protestants in an Age of Science,* 167–69, and George Marsden, "Everyone One's Own Interpreter? The Bible, Science, and Authority in Mid-Nineteenth-Century America," in Hatch and Noll, eds., *Bible in America,* 94–95.

58. On the importance of Scottish Common Sense Realism for American religious thinkers in this period, see Sydney E. Ahlstrom, "The Scottish Philosophy and American Theology," *Church History* 24 (September 1955): 257–72, and Elizabeth Flower and Murray G. Murphey, *A History of Philosophy in America,* 2 vols. (New York, 1977), 1:203–361.

Witherspoon again paved the way for Presbyterians by observing early in his philosophy lectures "that there are certain first principles or dictates of common sense, which are either simple perceptions, or seen with intuitive evidence."[59] These both grounded theoretical inquiry and established the need for religion. "The truth of christianity . . . ," according to Stanhope Smith, "rests on such evidences as every man of a sound mind, who honestly applies his understanding to the subject, is capable to judge of; evidences which propose themselves directly to the senses, or arise out of the known and immutable laws of human nature."[60] Archibald Alexander, who criticized Smith for laxity at the college, told much the same thing to his seminarians: "To prove that our faculties are not so constituted as to misguide us, some have had recourse to the *goodness* and *truth of God,* our creator, but this argument is unnecessary. We are as certain of these intuitive truths as we can be. . . . Besides we must be sure that we exist, and that the world exists, before we can be certain that there is a God, for it is from these *data* that we prove his existence."[61] The orthodox phalanx had no doubts about its ability to use intuition and the data it provided to prove God's existence and to demonstrate the need for biblical revelation. But it was not as simple as that.

Calvinistic reliance upon Enlightenment views of science portended difficulties mostly for the future. Their turn inward to moral and common sense began to have unfavorable consequences much earlier.[62] If the orthodox could look to the intuitively known structures of common humanity to silence Hume, others could go to the same place to silence them. Arminianism, of which Charles Grandison Finney offered the most conspicuous example, made the Presbyterian defenders of Calvinistic orthodoxy cringe. Yet Finney's convictions, as he rejoiced in pointing out, rested on the same irrefragable dictates of human nature that

59. Witherspoon, "Lectures on Moral Philosophy," *Works,* 3:395.

60. Smith, *Lectures on the Evidences of the Christian Religion,* 34.

61. Alexander, "Nature and Evidence of Truth," ms. lecture (1812), Speer Library, Princeton Theological Seminary, in Mark A. Noll, ed., *The Princeton Theology, 1812–1921: Scripture, Science, and Theological Method From Archibald Alexander to B. B. Warfield* (Grand Rapids, 1983), 65.

62. Sydney Ahlstrom saw this clearly when he described the way in which the common-sense emphasis on "selfconsciousness" could become an "oracle for religious truth." Ahlstrom, "Scottish Philosophy and American Theology," 269. Others who have described the path from common sense to nonorthodox forms of intuitionism or romanticism include Morton White, *Science and Sentiment in America: Philosophical Thought from Jonathan Edwards to John Dewey* (New York, 1972), 86–96; Walter Jackson Bate, *From Classic to Romantic: Premises of Taste in Eighteenth-Century England* (New York, 1961; orig. publ. 1946), 133–36; May, *Enlightenment in America,* 356; and Holifield, *Gentlemen Theologians,* 138.

Witherspoon, Smith, and Alexander had used to buttress their faith.[63] Unitarians also knew well what to do with the dictates of a common moral sense.[64] And Horace Bushnell brought consternation to Princeton polemicists as he too relied on what his moral faculty revealed about the human heart and the nature of things. It was no accident, even if theologians at Princeton could not see the connection, that Bushnell derived great early inspiration for his work from Victor Cousin, a Frenchman who had championed Thomas Reid's ideas on the continent.[65] Even the Transcendentalists, entirely beyond the pale, showed great skills at using "intuitive perception," "intuitive reason," and "consciousness" to identify, in Anne Rose's words, "an original source of truth in the heart." If Ralph Waldo Emerson could move easily from Dugald Stewart's "moral sense" to Coleridge's "reason," it was obvious that the Presbyterians were getting more from intuitional common sense than they had bargained for.[66]

In reaction to the promiscuous use of common sense, Presbyterians made a confused response. On the one hand, they turned away from intuition to sources of religious authority that were beyond the reach of infidels. Charles Hodge, his modern reputation as a thoroughgoing theologian of common sense to the contrary notwithstanding, did in fact lead Old School Presbyterians part way back to the Reformed confessions and the inward testimony of the Holy Spirit.[67] The disillusioned "Puritan," John Williamson Nevin, found in the Heidelberg Catechism, as

63. As examples, Finney, *Lectures on Systematic Theology* (Minneapolis, 1976; orig. publ. 1878), 23, 479–500, and *passim.* Finney's colleague at Oberlin, Asa Mahan, also made frequent use of innate categories of reason and logic in his religious thought, as in his rebuttal of Edwards on the will. Mahan, *Doctrine of the Will* (New York, 1846), 228–31. For a general account of the Oberlin intuitionism, see Edward H. Madden, "Oberlin's First Philosopher [Asa Mahan]," *Journal of the History of Philosophy* 6 (January 1968): 57–66.

64. Daniel Walker Howe, *The Unitarian Conscience: Harvard Moral Philosophy, 1806–1861* (Cambridge, Mass., 1970), 27–40 and *passim.*

65. For Bushnell's use of Cousin, see his essay, "Christian Comprehensiveness" (1848), in *Horace Bushnell,* ed. H. Shelton Smith (New York, 1965), 110, and Smith's introduction to this volume, 27–29.

66. The quotations are from George Ripley as cited by Anne C. Rose, *Transcendentalism as a Social Movement, 1830–1850* (New Haven, Conn., 1981), 42–43. On the passage from Dugald Stewart to Emerson, see Merrell R. Davis, "Emerson's 'Reason' and the Scottish Philosophers," *New England Quarterly* 17 (June 1944): 209–28.

67. Although Hodge's work regularly reflects themes paralleling Archibald Alexander's rationalism, it just as often relies upon an almost Edwardsean belief in the immediate activity of the Spirit, as in "Lecture, Addressed to the Students of the Theological Seminary," *Biblical Repertory and Princeton Review* 1 (January 1829): 90–98; "The Latest Form of Infidelity," ibid. 12 (January 1840): 33; or "Beecher's Great Conflict," ibid. 26 (January 1854): 138. For a well-rounded discussion, see Hoffecker, *Piety and the Princeton Theologians,* 55–94.

Hodge found in the Westminster Confession, an antidote to democratic intuition.[68]

On the other hand, the orthodox also continued to rely on an Enlightenment kind of intuition as if virtually nothing had happened. Archibald Alexander's *Outlines of Moral Science,* published a year after his death in 1851, still proclaimed that a moral sense, or conscience, communicated fully formed conceptions of virtue and vice that proved the existence and goodness of his Calvinistic God. Charles Hodge began his massive *Systematic Theology* in 1872 with the same naively Baconian proclamations that Witherspoon had championed in his lectures nearly a century earlier. And the same note was still to be heard from Presbyterians among the fundamentalists who reacted to modernism at the end of the century.[69]

Presbyterian promotion of intuition had been intended to solidify the authority of Scripture and of traditional doctrine. Others found it a convenient way to escape these very restraints. Yet Presbyterian conservatives retreated hardly at all from their reliance on that innate sense, which they discovered in the Moderate Enlightenment of the eighteenth century, and which—in practice, but never consciously—they found it necessary to forsake in order to preserve their faith.

When Presbyterian religious thinkers of the early national period resorted to the Enlightenment, the result, sooner or later, was the opposite of what they had intended. Still, the embrace of the Enlightenment did not lead them, as it did other Americans, to break cleanly with traditional Christianity. Neither, however, did the failure of the Enlightenment to accomplish for the faith what they had hoped lead them to abandon the Enlightenment. And so the Enlightenment and Presbyterian orthodoxy continued to travel side by side through the nineteenth century. The result in some cases was gradual liberalization, a modification of the old faith as intuition led to romanticism and beyond, and as science pushed past Darwinism to pragmatism or positivism.[70] Yet many Presbyterians remained steadfast in their orthodoxy.[71] As they did so, however, their

68. James Hastings Nichols, *Romanticism in American Theology: Nevin and Schaff at Mercersburg* (Chicago, 1961), 48–49, 285–86, and *passim.*

69. Alexander, *Outlines of Moral Science* (New York, 1852), discussed ably in D. H. Meyer, *The Instructed Conscience: The Shaping of the American National Ethic* (Philadelphia, 1972), 21; George M. Marsden, *Fundamentalism and American Culture: The Shaping of Twentieth-Century Evangelicalism, 1870–1925* (New York, 1980), 219–20; Hodge, *Systematic Theology,* 3 vols. (New York, 1872–73), 1:9–15.

70. Lefferts A. Loetscher, *The Broadening Church: A Study of Theological Issues in the Presbyterian Church Since 1869* (Philadelphia, 1957), 39–68.

71. The importance of a continuing Calvinism at Princeton Seminary is suggested by the fact that when that institution celebrated its centennial in 1912, the total of its students

thinking preserved the ambiguities of the early national period. It furthered a muddled Christian nationalism which, for all its ability to preserve a moral tone to thoughts about America, frustrated both Christian self-understanding and the possibility of a truly neutral public policy. It also fostered a confused approach to epistemology and ethics which, for all its benefits to Victorian public decency, foreclosed the possibility of consistent Christian thinking and hamstrung explorations in science and philosophy. American Presbyterians enjoyed many respectable intellects in the nineteenth century, but no Tertullian, no Augustine, no Luther, Calvin, or Pascal, no Ames or Edwards. And especially because none of the Presbyterians missed Jonathan Edwards, or sensed how valiantly he had struggled with the "deeper spirit" of the Enlightenment,[72] none of them felt the need for a successor who, perhaps with as yet unimaginable genius, could have appropriated both Enlightenment and Calvinism without doing violence to either.

(over six thousand) was more than one thousand greater than the number of students who had attended any other institution of graduate study in the United States. In 1912 the seminary's fourth professor specializing in theology, B. B. Warfield (in succession Alexander, Charles Hodge, and A. A. Hodge) was continuing to offer approximately the same theological and philosophical perspectives that Alexander had first enunciated in 1812. Noll, *Princeton Theology, 1812–1921,* 13–45.

72. This phrase and a fine discussion of "deeper" and more "superficial" appropriations of eighteenth-century science in American religious thought, with special consideration of Edwards, may be found in James Ward Smith, "Religion and Science in American Philosophy," in *The Shaping of American Religion,* ed. James Ward Smith and A. Leland Jamison (Princeton, 1961), 402–42.

7

The Christian Movement and the Demand for a Theology of the People

Nathan O. Hatch

Reprinted by permission from *Journal of American History* 67 (December 1980): 545–67.

In 1776, John Adams posed the question that would preoccupy his generation of American citizens and their children. "It is certain, in theory," he said, "that the only moral foundation of government is, the consent of the people. But to what extent shall we carry this principle?" The Revolution brought an accent of reality to a new self-evident truth, the sovereignty of the people, which Edmund Morgan has recently described as a "political fiction." For the Founding Fathers the fiction of popular sovereignty held some resemblance to the facts, but they fully expected the governed and the governors to "join in a benign conspiracy to suspend disbelief" in the new fiction, in other words, to believe it rhetorically rather than literally. The people were not so kind, however, and the shrill and unending debate that characterized American history from Adams to Andrew Jackson concerned how seriously this fiction should be taken.[1]

A number of scholars have recently explored the dimensions of this cultural ferment over the meaning of freedom. In the wake of their own

1. Charles Francis Adams, ed., *The Works of John Adams, Second President of the United States,* 10 vols. (Boston, 1850–56), 9:375; Edmund S. Morgan, "The Great Political Fiction," *New York Review of Books* 25 (9 March 1978), 13–18.

and the French Revolution, Americans witnessed the rapid growth of voluntary organizations and popular newspapers, the formation of organized political parties amid heated and increasingly popular political debate, the armed protest of unprotected economic groups, sharp attacks upon elite professions and upon slavery, and new ideas of citizenship and representation, of old age and women's identity.[2] Eugene Genovese has even argued that a revolutionary ideology of liberty and equality transformed the character of slave resistance in North America and in the Caribbean.[3] Lamenting the awakening to political consciousness of the common man, Harrison Gray Otis gave to a Harvard audience in 1836 his view of what had happened since the Revolution. "Everywhere the disposition is found among those who live in the valleys, to ask those who live on the hills, 'How came we here and you there?' accompanied with intelligible demonstrations of a purpose in the former, to partake of the benefits of the mountain air."[4]

What became of American religion in these years—roughly 1780 to 1820—when traditional values were being turned upside down by what Gordon S. Wood has called a "democratization of mind"?[5] Despite a

2. James A. Henretta, *The Evolution of American Society, 1700–1815* (Lexington, Mass., 1973); Richard D. Brown, *Modernization: The Transformation of American Life, 1600–1865* (New York, 1976); Richard D. Brown, "The Emergence of Voluntary Associations in Massachusetts, 1760–1830," *Journal of Voluntary Action Research* 2 (April 1973): 64–73; Jackson Turner Main, "Government by the People: The American Revolution and the Democratization of the Legislatures," *William and Mary Quarterly* 23 (July 1966): 391–407; Bernard Bailyn, *The Ideological Origins of the American Revolution* (Cambridge, 1967); Richard E. Ellis, *The Jeffersonian Crisis: Courts and Politics in the Young Republic* (New York, 1971); David Brion Davis, *The Problem of Slavery in the Age of Revolution, 1770–1823* (Ithaca, 1975); David Hackett Fischer, *Growing Old in America* (New York, 1977); Robert A. Gross, *The Minutemen and Their World* (New York, 1976); and Mary Beth Norton, *The Revolutionary Experience of American Women, 1750–1800* (Boston, 1980).

3. Eugene D. Genovese, *From Rebellion to Revolution: Afro-American Slave Revolts in the Making of the Modern World* (Baton Rouge, 1979).

4. Harrison Gray Otis, who had delivered the English oration at Harvard when he graduated in 1783, was asked to give the primary address at Harvard's bicentennial celebration in 1836. His speech is the lament of an old man who had witnessed the "fiery furnace of democracy" destroy much of what he held dear. While he had hoped that the Revolution had been "completed by the establishment of independence," he lived to see a "new school" take charge that "would identify revolution with perpetual motion. They would put all ancient institutions, laws, customs, courts, colleges, and schools upon wheels, and keep them whirling for ever with the steam of their own eloquence." Josiah Quincy, *The History of Harvard University*, 2 vols. (Cambridge, 1840), 2:662–70.

5. Gordon S. Wood, "The Democratization of Mind in the American Revolution," *Leadership in the American Revolution* (Washington, 1974), 63–89; and Gordon S. Wood, "Social Radicalism and Equality in the American Revolution," *The B. K. Smith Lectures in History* (Houston, 1976), 5–14.

wealth of recent scholarship on the role of religion in the coming of the American Revolution, surprisingly little work has been done on the changing nature of popular religion after the Revolution. This imbalance stems in part from the conventional division between the era of the republic's founding and that of the middle period, but it also reflects the simple fact that a quickened interest in religion as a cultural force has emerged within a broader historiographical tendency to downplay the social impact of the Revolution. The result has been that while historians have noted many links between the Great Awakening and the Revolution, they have not followed through to ask how rapid social change in the young republic affected structures of religious belief and organization.[6] What happened when people began to call for a strenuous application of popular sovereignty to the church? What did Christian freedom come to mean for people ready to question any source of authority that did not begin with an act of individual choice?

To explore these questions, this essay will focus on the cultural roots of a movement that assumed the name *Christian* or *Disciples of Christ.* Between 1790 and 1815 this loose network of religious radicals demanded, in light of the American and French revolutions, a new dispensation set free from the trammels of history, a new kind of institutional church premised on the self-evident principles of republicanism, and a new form of biblical authority calling for the inalienable right of common people to interpret the New Testament for themselves. The central figures in the reform movement—Elias Smith in New England, James O'Kelly in Virginia, Barton Stone in Kentucky, and Alexander Campbell in Pennsylvania—were a motley crew with few common characteristics, but they all moved independently to similar conclusions within a fifteen-year span. A

6. On the new scholarly interest in religion, see Henry F. May, "The Recovery of American Religious History," *American Historical Review* 70 (October 1964): 79–92. The broader trend to dismiss the social repercussions of the Revolution is evident in Frederick B. Tolles, "The American Revolution Considered as a Social Movement: A Re-Evaluation," *American Historical Review* 60 (October 1954): 1–12. Studies of the Second Great Awakening in New England and the Great Revival in the Southwest have generally not addressed the question of how cultural ferment might have altered religion; they have focused, rather, on how traditional religion championed the revival technique in order to impose social order upon a disordered and secularized society. See Perry Miller, "From Covenant to Revival," in *The Shaping of American Religion,* ed. J. W. Smith and A. L. Jamison (Princeton, 1961), 350; Lois W. Banner, "Religious Benevolence as Social Control: A Critique of an Interpretation," *Journal of American History* 60 (June 1973): 23–41; and John B. Boles, *The Great Revival, 1787–1805: The Origins of the Southern Evangelical Mind* (Lexington, Ky., 1972). More sensitive to the ongoing impact of the Revolution in religious affairs is Donald G. Mathews, "The Second Great Awakening as an Organizing Process, 1780–1830: An Hypothesis," *American Quarterly* 21 (spring 1969): 23–43.

Calvinist Baptist, a Methodist, and two Presbyterians all found traditional sources of authority anachronistic and found themselves groping toward similar definitions of egalitarian religion.[7] In a culture that increasingly balked at vested interests, symbols of hierarchy, and timeless authorities, a remarkable number of people would wake up one morning to find it self-evident that the priesthood of all believers meant just that—religion of, by, and for the people.

At the dawn of the nineteenth century, the Federalist citadel of Essex County, Massachusetts, witnessed a major assault on its well-bred and high-toned culture. Religious enthusiasm had taken hold among common people and its rude challenge to authority dismayed even the tolerant Jeffersonian diarist William Bentley of Salem. As late as 1803, Bentley had confided smugly that Essex County remained virtually free of sects. During the next five years, he watched with dismay the lower orders of his community championing "religious convulsions," "domestic fanaticism," and "Meeting-Mania." In chronicling the parade of sects that won attention—Baptist, Freewill Baptist, Methodist, Universalist, and Christian—Bentley noted the first field meeting in the county since George Whitefield, preaching by blacks and illiterate sailors, and servants angering their employers by frequenting night lectures "as in Mother Hutchinson's time." What Bentley found most appalling was that "the rabble" not only noised abroad strange doctrine but actually went beyond what they were told, attempting "to explain, condemn and reveal" religious matters. The people, he groaned, were doing theology for themselves.[8]

Bentley saved his sharpest barbs for an itinerant preacher, the "notorious" Smith who regularly barnstormed through Essex County, preaching in the open air, singing in the streets, and accosting people to question their spiritual state. If this was not enough to discomfit the respectable citizens of Salem, Smith kept the pot boiling by leaving behind bundles of his tracts and pamphlets.[9]

7. Luther P. Gerlach and Virginia H. Hine define a social "movement" as "a group of people who are organized for, ideologically motivated by, and committed to a purpose which implements some form of personal or social change; who are actively engaged in the recruitment of others; and whose influence is spreading in opposition to the established order within which it originated." Luther P. Gerlach and Virginia H. Hine, *People, Power, Change: Movements of Social Transformation* (Indianapolis, 1970), xiv. The Christians, like the movements of which Gerlach and Hine speak, were decentralized and segmented, their web-like structures without clear lines of authority and often dependent upon shared publications. Their unity stemmed from little more than common ideology and perceived opposition from religious and political elites.

8. William Bentley, *The Diary of William Bentley, D.D.,* 4 vols. (Salem, Mass., 1911), 3:65, 503, 515, 271.

9. In May 1805 William Bentley commented about Elias Smith that "the press has lately vomited out many nauseaus things from this writer." Ibid., 157, 370, 291.

For all its parallels with the dissent of a Whitefield or an Isaac Backus, Smith's gospel for the people did have one different twist. It was laced with the language of politics and reflected the experience of a man whose radical pilgrimage began with a political conversion. Until 1800 Smith filled the pulpit of the respectable Baptist Church in Woburn, Massachusetts, and gave little attention to political questions of the day. During the election of 1800, however, he fell under the influence of the radical Jeffersonian publicist Benjamin Austin, Jr., who wrote regularly for the *Boston Independent Chronicle*. Smith quickly imbibed Austin's heady wine, which made much of the right of common people to think and act for themselves. Resigning from his church—as a manifesto of his own liberty—and denouncing formal religion of every kind, Smith began to translate the sovereignty of the people to the sphere of religion.[10] "Let us be republicans indeed," he declared in 1809. "Many are *republicans* as to *government,* and yet are but half republicans, being in matters of religion still bound to a catechism, creed, covenant or a superstitious priest. Venture to be as independent in things of religion, as those which respect the government in which you live."[11] From Portsmouth, New Hampshire, Smith launched the first religious newspaper in the United States, a fortnightly *Herald of Gospel Liberty,* which he edited from 1808 to 1818. From that forum and in scores of pamphlets and sermons, he and a band of fifty or so itinerants, who called themselves merely Christians, carried on a blistering attack upon Baptists, Congregationalists, Methodists, and Federalists of any religious persuasion. The *Herald of Gospel Liberty,* which by 1815 had fourteen hundred subscribers and over fifty agents around the country, became a vehicle of communication for other individuals who were moving independently to the same conclusions as Smith.[12]

10. Elias Smith, *The Life, Conversion, Preaching, Travels and Sufferings of Elias Smith* (Portsmouth, N.Y., 1816), 341–42.

11. Elias Smith, *The Lovingkindness of God Displayed in the Triumph of Republicanism in America: Being a Discourse Delivered at Taunton (Mass.) July Fourth, 1809; at the Celebration of American Independence* (n.p., 1809), 32. Smith's colleague Abner Jones also experienced what he called a "disintegration" of his Calvinist beliefs and was quick to note the theological implications of demands for social equality. "In giving the reader an account of my birth and parentage," Jones wrote in 1807, "I shall not (like the celebrated Franklin and others,) strive to prove that I arose from a family of eminence; believing that all men are born equal, and that every man shall die for his own iniquity." Abner Jones, *Memoirs of the Life and Experience, Travels and Preaching of Abner Jones* (Exeter, N.H., 1807), 3.

12. For a brief sketch of Smith's life, see William G. McLoughlin, *New England Dissent, 1630–1883: The Baptists and the Separation of Church and State,* 2 vols. (Cambridge, 1971), 2:745–49. Otherwise, no one has undertaken a serious study of Smith, despite his prominence as a religious and political radical in New England from 1800 to 1820, his scores of publications addressed to a popular audience, his newspaper that ran for a decade, and his fascinating memoir. The number of his itinerant followers is taken

From Virginia came word of O'Kelly's Republican Methodists, founded in 1794 to undo the "ecclesiastical monarchy" in the Methodist church. A prime mover among early Virginia Methodists, O'Kelly could not abide the bishopric of Francis Asbury and withdrew with over thirty ministers to form a connection which had as many as twenty thousand members when it merged with Smith's forces, under the name *Christian*, in 1809.[13] "Episcopacy makes a bad appearance in our republican world," O'Kelly argued in 1798. "Francis was born and nurtured in the land of Bishops and Kings and what is bred in the bone, is hard to get out of the flesh."[14] O'Kelly, who had taken up arms in the Revolution and served a brief stint as a British captive, argued that he was "too sensible of the sweets of liberty, to be content any longer under British chains. . . . As a son of America, and a Christian," he challenged Asbury, "I shall oppose your political measures and contend for the Saviour's government. I contend for Bible government, Christian equality, and the Christian name."[15]

Stone was an equally interesting figure who had ventured upon much the same pilgrimage prior to the appearance of the *Herald of Gospel Liberty*. In 1802, in the wake of the Cane Ridge Revival in Kentucky, Stone decided he could no longer live under Presbyterian doctrine or church organization. A year later, he and five other ministers pushed this idea to its logical extreme and proclaimed that it was not just the Presbyterians who were wrong: all church structures were suspect. Signing "The Last Will and Testament of Springfield Presbytery," these men vowed to follow nothing but the Christian name and the New Testament.[16]

---

from one of his Congregational assailants. Thomas Andros, *The Scriptures Liable to be Wrested to Men's Own Destruction, and an Instance of This Found, in the Writings of Elias Smith* (Taunton, Mass., 1817), 18. A list of agents for Smith's newspaper is found in *Herald of Gospel Liberty,* 18 August 1809, 104. For the number of subscribers, see ibid., 29 September 1815, 720. On Smith's movement, which became known as the Christian Connection, see Thomas H. Olbricht, "Christian Connection and Unitarian Relations," *Restoration Quarterly* 9 (September 1966): 160–86.

13. The best treatment of James O'Kelly is Charles Franklin Kilgore, *The James O'Kelly Schism in the Methodist Episcopal Church* (Mexico City, 1963). See also Edward J. Drinkhouse, *History of Methodist Reform,* 2 vols. (Baltimore, 1899), 1; and Milo T. Morrill, *A History of the Christian Denomination in America* (Dayton, 1912). O'Kelly's primary works are James O'Kelly, *The Author's Apology for Protesting against the Methodist Episcopal Government* (Richmond, 1798); and James O'Kelly, *A Vindication of the Author's Apology* (Raleigh, 1801).

14. O'Kelly, *Author's Apology,* 4, 21.

15. O'Kelly, *Vindication,* 60–61.

16. "The Last Will and Testament of Springfield Presbytery," in John Rogers, *The Biography of Elder B. Warren Stone* (New York, 1972), 51–53. For other primary accounts of this movement, see Barton W. Stone, *An Apology for Renouncing the Jurisdiction of the Synod of Kentucky* (Lexington, Ky., 1804); [Richard McNemar], *Observations on Church*

Scholars have generally viewed Stone's beliefs as the product of the rough-and-tumble context of the frontier and of the rampant emotionalism of the Great Revival.[17] Stone was a rawboned character, no doubt, but he also spent his formative years during the Revolution, and his theology of "gospel-liberty" reflected this early experience. "From my earliest recollection I drank deeply into the spirit of liberty," he confessed late in life, "and was so warmed by the soul-inspiring draughts, that I could not hear the name of British, or tories without feeling a rush of blood through the whole system. . . . I confess their magic influence to this advanced day of my life." It was not without deep connotation that Stone characterized his break with the Presbyterians as the "declaration of our independence."[18]

The final member of the quartet whose democratic theology this essay analyzes is the Scottish immigrant Alexander Campbell—the only college graduate among the four and the only one not to participate in the American Revolution.[19] Whatever Alexander Campbell may have brought to America of his Scottish and Presbyterian heritage, he found much of it convenient to discard for an explicitly American theology. Writing to his uncle back in Scotland in 1815, he described his seven years in the United States: "During this period of years my mind and circumstances have undergone many revolutions . . . I have . . . renounced much of the traditions and errors of my early education." He described the change elsewhere in these words: "My mind was, for a time, set loose from all its former moorings. It was not a simple change: but a new commencement.

Government, by the Presbytery of Springfield (Cincinnati, 1807); Robert Marshall and James Thompson, *A Brief Historical Account of Sundry Things in the Doctrines and State of the Christian, or, as It Is Commonly Called, the Newlight Church* (Cincinnati, 1811); Levi Purviance, *The Biography of Elder David Purviance* (Dayton, 1848); and Robert H. Bishop, *An Outline of the History of the Church in the State of Kentucky, during a Period of Forty Years: Containing the Memoirs of Rev. David Rice* (Lexington, Ky., 1824).

17. There is a considerable body of uncritical denominational literature on Barton W. Stone by the Disciples of Christ. See William Garrett West, *Barton Warren Stone: Early American Advocate of Christian Unity* (Nashville, 1954). For emphasis on Stone's contribution to the revivalist heritage of the South, see Boles, *Great Revival.* For appreciation of Stone in his full cultural context, see Ralph Morrow, "The Great Revival, the West, and the Crisis of the Church," in *The Frontier Re-examined,* ed. John F. McDermott (Urbana, 1967), 65–78.

18. Rogers, *Biography of Elder B. Warren Stone,* 3, 47.

19. For discussions of the origins of the Campbellites, see David Edwin Harrell, Jr., *Quest for a Christian America: The Disciples of Christ and American Society to 1866* (Nashville, 1966); Robert Frederick West, *Alexander Campbell and Natural Religion* (New Haven, Conn., 1948); Lester G. McAllister, *Thomas Campbell: Man of the Book* (St. Louis, 1954); and Errett Gates, *The Early Relation and Separation of Baptists and Disciples* (Chicago, 1904). In addition, see the extensive memoirs of father and son: Alexander Campbell, *Memoirs of Elder Thomas Campbell* (Cincinnati, 1861); and Robert Richardson, *Memoirs of Alexander Campbell,* 2 vols. (Cincinnati, 1913).

. . . the whole landscape of Christianity presented itself to my mind in a new attitude and position."[20] By 1830 Alexander Campbell's quest for primitive Christianity led his movement, the Disciples of Christ, into union with Stone's Christians. By 1860 their denomination claimed about two hundred thousand adherents, the fifth largest Protestant body in the United States.[21] More important, for our purposes, his theology fell into an unmistakable pattern that was emerging in the early republic. Smith, O'Kelly, and Stone all knew what Campbell meant when he proclaimed that 4 July 1776 was "a day to be remembered as was the Jewish Passover. . . . This revolution, taken in all its influences, will make men free indeed."[22]

In many ways the message of the Christians built upon the kind of radical piety that Americans had known since the Great Awakening of the 1740s. These new reformers hammered relentlessly at the simple themes of sin, grace, and conversion; they organized fellowships that resisted social distinctions and welcomed spontaneous experience; and they denounced any religion that smacked of being bookish, cold, and formal. What sets the Christians apart from earlier revivalists is the extent to which they wrestled self-consciously with the loss of traditional sources of authority and found in democratic political culture a cornerstone for new foundations. Taking seriously the mandate of liberty and equality, the Christians espoused reform in three areas. First, they called for a revolution within the church that would place laity and clergy on an equal footing and would exalt the conscience of the individual over the collective will of any congregation or church organization. Second, they rejected the traditions of learned theology altogether and called for a new view of history that welcomed inquiry and innovation. Finally, they called for a populist hermeneutic premised on the inalienable right of every person to understand the New Testament for themselves.

A zeal to dismantle mediating elites within the church, more than anything else, triggered the Christians' revolt against tradition. O'Kelly broke with Asbury when the Methodist bishop refused to put up with

20. Richardson, *Memoirs of Alexander Campbell,* 1:465–66, 438. Many scholars have assumed that Thomas and Alexander Campbell applied to an American context beliefs that they had learned under the influence of Scottish reformers such as Robert Haldane and James Alexander Haldane. See, for example, Sydney E. Ahlstrom, *A Religious History of the American People* (New Haven, Conn., 1972), 448–49. The early documents of the Campbellite movement, however, manifest a keen awareness that the issues to be faced were, in their intensity at least, peculiarly American and demanded new solutions. See, for example, Thomas Campbell, *The Declaration and Address of the Christian Association of Washington* (Washington, Penn., 1809).

21. Lester G. McAllister and William E. Tucker, *Journey in Faith: A History of the Christian Church (Disciples of Christ)* (St. Louis, 1975), 154–55.

22. Alexander Campbell, "An Oration in Honor of the Fourth of July, 1830," *Popular Lectures and Addresses* (Philadelphia, 1863), 374–75.

representative government in the church. Smith bade farewell to Backus and the Warren Association after influential colleagues criticized his plain dress and suggested that the respectable parishioners of Woburn, Massachusetts, deserved more decorum. Both Stone and Thomas Campbell—Alexander's father, who had preceded him to America—withdrew from the Presbyterians when their orthodox colleagues began to clamp down on their freedom of inquiry concerning Presbyterian standards. Before their respective separations, each of these men in his own way had offered stern opposition to received tradition, yet their dissent was contained within taken-for-granted cultural boundaries. Once they had severed organizational ties, however, mild questions reappeared as seething hostility, and suggestions for reform turned to ecclesiastical defiance.

The Christians excelled at popular communication. They ferreted out converts with an unremitting itineracy and cranked out an avalanche of pamphlet and newspaper copy, which, in its form and content, conspired against social distinction.[23] Smith was aware of his innovative role when he began the first religious newspaper in the United States; he confessed on its opening page that the utility of such a paper had been suggested to him by the explosion of popular print all around. "In a short and cheap way," he asserted, "a general knowledge of our affairs is diffused through the whole." While his paper did include accounts of revivals of religion throughout the world, its overall strategy showed little resemblance to previous revival periodicals such as the *Christian History* of the Great Awakening, largely an intramural communication among the clergy. By promoting in common language the idea that *"right is equal among all,"* Smith knew that he would incur the judgment that he was "stirring up the people to revolt" and "turning the world upside down."[24] Just as he expected, the established clergy found his "vulgar stories and malicious sarcasm" totally beneath them, but they could hardly ignore the popularity of his "poisoned arrows of ridicule and reproach."[25]

The style of Smith's communication is well illustrated in one of his early pamphlets, *The Clergyman's Looking-Glass,* a stinging attack on men of the cloth that went through at least a dozen printings. Smith juxtaposed passages of the New Testament with satirical jibes at the contemporary clergy in mock-scripture style. After quoting from 1 Peter the in-

23. "Elias Smith was here last week, distributing his books & pamphlets, & preached a lecture last week without sparing any of the hirelings as he calls them." Bentley, *Diary,* 3:338.

24. *Herald of Gospel Liberty,* 1 September 1808, 1.

25. Stephen Porter, a Presbyterian clergyman, attempted to ward off the influence of Smith and his lieutenants among his congregation. Stephen Porter, *A Discourse, in Two Parts, Addressed to the Presbyterian Congregation in Ballston* (Ballston Spa, N.Y., 1814), 42–44.

structions that elders were to serve God's flock "not for filthy lucre . . . neither as being lords over God's heritage," Smith gave his Petrine rendition of the modern clergy:

> The reverend clergy who are with me I advise, who am also a clergyman, and a D.D. a member of that respectable body, who are numerous, and 'who seek honor one of another;' and a partaker of the benefit of it; feed yourselves upon the church and parish, over which we have settled you for life, and who are obliged to support you, whether they like you or not; taking the command by constraint, for filthy lucre, not of a ready mind, as lords over men's souls, not as ensamples to them, and when commencement day shall appear, you shall receive some honorary title, which shall make you appear very respectable among the reverend clergy.[26]

In a similar vein, Alexander Campbell used his first newspaper, the *Christian Baptist,* to mock the pretensions of the clergy. In a burlesque "Third Epistle of Peter," a document reportedly discovered by a monk, he instructed preachers to live well, wear the best clothes, adorn themselves with high-sounding titles, drink costly wine, and fleece the people.[27] Evangelicals in the past had often questioned the spiritual state of individual clergymen; the Christians now took the liberty to slander the entire profession as money-grubbing tyrants.

This kind of billingsgate journalism employed two very powerful appeals. In the first place, it portrayed society as horizontally polarized: the people were arrayed against elites of all kind, military, legal, civic, and religious. In an early edition of the *Herald of Gospel Liberty,* Smith sketched a most revealing dialogue between the people and the privileged class. "The picture, is this: two companies standing in sight of each other, one large, the other small. The large containing every profession useful to society, the other small, wearing marks of distinction, appearing as though they did no labour, yet in rich attire, glittering with gold and silver, while their plump and ruddy countenances, prove them persons of leisure and riches." Seething with resentment, the people of Smith's dialogue happened to overhear what the privileged were saying to each other: "To mix and place ourselves on a level with the *common people,* would be beyond all measure degrading and vilifying. What! are they not born to serve us? and are we not men of a totally distinct blood and superior pedigree?" In response, the people insisted that they were going "to take the management of our affairs into

26. Elias Smith, *The Clergyman's Looking-Glass: Being a History of the Birth, Life, and Death of Anti-Christ* (Portsmouth, N.H., 1803), 11. For examples of Smith's sensitivity to elitist codes of all sorts, even while he was still a Baptist, see Smith, *Life,* 279–80.

27. *Christian Baptist,* 4 July 1823, 280.

our own hands. . . . When the people declare themselves free, such *privileged classes* will be as useles[s] as candles at noonday."[28]

Abel M. Sargent, another radical figure associated with the Christians, used his paper, the *Halcyon Itinerary and True Millennium Messenger,* to present a virtual class analysis of society. Writing in 1807 to extol Thomas Jefferson as the forerunner of a new millennial age, Sargent demanded that life, liberty, and happiness be extended to "the oppressed who have been deprived of them." His images of society bristle with the ongoing conflict between the powerful and the oppressed: "How often do we see it the case in earthly courts, under the dominion of the beast, that the power and influence of money and false Agency over-balance equity and right; so that the poor have but a dull chance to obtain Justice in carnal courts; and again, how often is the poor industrious and honest labourer, reduced to the absolute necessity of yielding up his rights and falling a prey to cruelty and injustice, merely for want of money enough to discharge the fees of those whose interest and livings (like the wolf and raven) depend on the ruin and destruction of others."[29]

For all its innovation, however, this bombast against the privileged also employed a second appeal. It appropriated the rhetoric of civil and religious liberty that the respectable clergy had made popular during the Revolution and marshaled it for an entirely new purpose, to topple its very architects. The Christians exploited to the hilt the potent themes of tyranny, slavery, and Antichrist; they delighted in regaling their audiences with the latest chapter in the saga of the beast and the whore of Babylon. Simply put, Antichrist now worked his evil machinations through elites of all kind, particularly the clergy. In a splendid example of the multivalency of language, rhetoric that had seemed benign when used by respectable clergymen during the Revolution came to have radical connotations when abstracted from a restricted context and transferred to people who had reason to lash out at vested interests.[30]

28. *Herald of Gospel Liberty,* 8 December 1808, 29–30.

29. Abel M. Sargent founded a radical sect in Marietta, Ohio, where he published six issues of *Halcyon Itinerary and True Millennium Messenger.* The quotation is found in *Halcyon Itinerary and True Millennium Messenger* (December 1807), 147–48. For a letter from Sargent to Smith, see *Herald of Gospel Liberty,* 16 August 1811, 310. On Sargent, see John W. Simpson, *A Century of Church Life* (Marietta, 1896), 31.

30. Christians assailed the clergy as "tyrannical oppressors," "the mystery of iniquity," "friends of monarchy religion," "old tories," "an *aristocratical body of uniform nobility,*" and "hireling priests"; people who would submit to such tyrants they labeled priest-ridden, slavishly dependent, passively obedient. See Smith, *Life,* 384, 402–3; *Herald of Gospel Liberty,* 13 October 1809, 117; O'Kelly, *Vindication,* 47. In 1815 Smith claimed that most people in New England from forty to seventy years old could remember the respectable clergy emphasizing apocalyptic themes such as "*Anti-Christ, mystery Babylon,* the *great whore* that sitteth on many waters, the *beast* with seven heads and ten

But what end did the Christians have in view when decrying ecclesiastical authority? What positive implications did they wring out of the notion of religious liberty? Smith came right to the point in an early issue of the *Herald of Gospel Liberty* when he contrasted the mere separation of church and state with "being wholly free to examine for ourselves, what is truth." He argued that every last Christian had the "unalienable right" to follow "the scripture wherever it leads him, even an equal right with the Bishops and Pastors of the churches . . . even though his principles may, in many things, be contrary to what the Reverend D. D.'s call Orthodoxy."[31] Using the same language, Alexander Campbell pressed for "the inalienable right of all laymen to examine the sacred writings for themselves." Brimming with conspiratorial notions of how clergymen of every stripe had "hood-winked" the people, this logic eventually led each of these Christian leaders to demand that the traditional distinction between clergy and laity be abolished and that any leadership in the local church function according to new rules: "liberty is no where safe in any hands excepting those of the people themselves."[32] With demands for this sort of liberation afoot, it is little wonder that Congregational and Presbyterian clergymen came to view the Christians as but another tentacle of the Bavarian Illuminati's conspiracy to overthrow authority in church and state.[33]

The Christian idea of religious liberty stands in marked contrast to the eighteenth-century notion that religious liberty meant the civil right to choose or not to choose affiliation with a church. The religious dissent that had come out of the Great Awakening, despite its popular sources, had never begun to suggest that power should be surrendered to the people in this fashion. The Baptists in Virginia set themselves off from the culture of gentlemen by striving for more order, more discipline, and more social control within the local congregation.[34] In New England, as

---

horns, the *man of sin* &c." *Herald of Gospel Liberty,* 20 May 1815, 685. On the multivalency of language , see J. G. A. Pocock, *Politics, Language and Time: Essays on Political Thought and History* (New York, 1971), 3–41; and Harry S. Stout, "Religion, Communications, and the Ideological Origins of the American Revolution," *William and Mary Quarterly* 34 (October 1977): 538.

31. Smith, *Lovingkindness of God Displayed,* 26–27; Smith, *Life,* 352–53. See also *Herald of Gospel Liberty,* 14 April 1809, 67.

32. *Christian Baptist,* 2 January 1826, 209; Smith, *Life,* 402–3; *Herald of Gospel Liberty,* 15 September 1808, 6. See also Richardson, *Memoirs of Alexander Campbell,* 1:382–83.

33. See David Rice, *An Epistle to the Citizens of Kentucky, Professing Christianity* (Lexington, Ky., 1805), 11–12.

34. Rhys Isaac, "Evangelical Revolt: The Nature of the Baptists' Challenge to the Traditional Order in Virginia, 1765 to 1775," *William and Mary Quarterly* 31 (July 1974): 345–68.

well, Baptists and Separatists called for closed communion and a tighter discipline within the pure church. By the 1760s, they were educating their clergy, forming associations to regulate doctrine and local disputes, and, as their people began to drift away to other sects during the Revolution, actually imposing stiff creedal tests upon local churches. Backus did not long for some new order that leveled the clergy and exalted the laity; he reminisced, instead, about the pious fathers of early New England. He argued time and again that his Baptists agreed "with the most eminent fathers of New England, except in sprinkling infants upon the faith of their parents and calling it baptism."[35] The same point has been made about the Separatists of New England: "they were reformers, not rebels; . . . they wished to fulfill their history as Puritans, not repudiate it."[36]

In contrast, the Christians called for the abolition of organizational restraints of any kind. In the "Last Will and Testament of Springfield Presbytery," Stone and five colleagues dissolved their association, already a splinter group from the Presbyterian church. Only by renouncing all institutional forms could "the oppressed . . . go free, and taste the sweets of gospel liberty."[37] Alexander Campbell did not even want to hear the words *church government:* "We have no system of our own, or of others, to substitute in lieu of the reigning systems. We only aim at substituting the New Testament."[38] In a similar vein, Stone and his associates declared that the attempt "to impose any form of government upon the church . . . should be justly abandoned by every child of gospel liberty." They went on to say that any human form of government would be "like binding two or more dead bodies together" and coercing people "like parts of a machine."[39] The organization of Protestant churches, which in colonial culture had been seen as vibrant and alive—the very body of Christ—now smacked of being dead and mechanistic.

By their appeal to "Bible government," the Christians removed the issue of power and authority from any concrete application. They op-

35. Isaac Backus, *A History of New England with Particular Reference to the Denomination of Christians Called Baptists,* 2 vols. (Newton, Mass., 1871), 2:487. For evidence of the Baptist quest for respectability in the generation after the Great Awakening, see C. C. Goen, *Revivalism and Separatism in New England, 1740–1800* (New Haven, Conn., 1962). For the reaction of Baptists to the dissent spawned by the Revolution, see McLoughlin, *New England Dissent,* 2:710.

36. James Patrick Walsh, "The Pure Church in Eighteenth Century Connecticut" (Ph.D. diss., Columbia University, 1964), 143.

37. Rogers, *Biography of Elder B. Warren Stone,* 51–53.

38. *Christian Baptist,* 3 November 1823, 25; Richardson, *Memoirs of Alexander Campbell,* 2:63–64.

39. [McNemar], *Observations on Church Government,* 4, 9, 15. This pamphlet, the best-developed statement of Christian ecclesiology, rejects "external rules" and insists that all human organization spring from the deliberate and uncoerced choice of the individual.

posed all ecclesiastical names not found in the New Testament, advocated the right of the individual unilaterally to withdraw from church membership, and refused to adhere to creeds as tests of fellowship, to undergo theological examinations, or to offer a confession of faith upon joining a church. In short, no human organization could exist that did not spring from the uncoerced will of the individual. When pressed by Bishop Asbury to heed the scriptural injunction, "Obey them that have rule over you," O'Kelly responded: "Rule over, is no more than for the church to follow those guides who delivered unto them the Word of God." O'Kelly was suggesting that, by submitting to the New Testament, a Christian in 1800 never would have to doff his hat to any mere mortal.[40]

In a passing reference in *The American Revolution Considered as a Social Movement,* J. Franklin Jameson noted the growth in numbers and zeal of those religious bodies that were revolting against Calvinism—the Methodists, Universalists, Unitarians, and Freewill Baptists.[41] He might also have included the loose combination of mavericks who called themselves merely Christians. Except for O'Kelly, whose Methodist background made Calvinism a dead issue, the other primary figures in this movement—Smith, Stone, and Campbell—were all zealous Calvinists early in life and experienced a conversion to what they called gospel liberty.

On one level this revolt seems simple enough to understand. The heady concepts of liberty that had led to denunciations of institutional constraints also rendered meaningless such concepts as unconditional election and limited atonement. After great intellectual turmoil, each of these men came to the point of harmonizing theology with their social experience. As a Calvinist, Stone confessed that he was "embarrassed with many abstruse doctrines." "Scores of objections would continually roll across my mind." What he called the "labyrinth of Calvinism" left his mind "distressed," "perplexed," and "bewildered." He found relief from this dissonance of values only as he came to attack Calvinism as falsehood.[42]

The revolt against Calvinism, however, becomes somewhat harder to understand when placed in its full context. The Christians were venting their hostility not against Calvinism in some narrow sense, as if they might find their niche as Methodists or Freewill Baptists, but against an entire system. "We are not personally acquainted with the writings of

40. O'Kelly, *Vindication,* 49. For similar expressions of resistance to human mediation of divine authority by Alexander Campbell and Thomas Campbell, see *Christian Baptist,* 3 April 1826, 229, and Campbell, *Declaration and Address of the Christian Association,* 3. For the recurrence of this line of thought a generation later, see Lewis Perry, *Radical Abolitionism: Anarchy and the Government of God in Antislavery Thought* (Ithaca, 1973).

41. J. Franklin Jameson, *The American Revolution Considered as a Social Movement* (Princeton, 1926), 157.

42. Rogers, *Biography of Elder B. Warren Stone,* 14, 31, 33.

John Calvin," wrote Robert Marshall and John Thompson, two of Stone's colleagues, "nor are we certain how nearly we agree with his views of divine truth; neither do we care."[43]

This was no mere revolt against Calvinism but against theology itself. What was going on that gave Stone the audacity not only to reject the doctrine of the Trinity—Unitarians right and left were doing that—but also to maintain, "I have not spent, perhaps, an hour in ten years in thinking about the Trinity"? What made it credible for Smith, after seriously debating whether he would be a Calvinist or a Universalist, to remove the dilemma altogether by dropping them both? "I was now without a system," he confessed with obvious relief, "and felt ready to search the scriptures."[44] How could these men convince themselves, not to mention their followers, that the stage was set for a church without organization and a theology without theory?

Whatever else the Christians demanded, the rallying cry of their theological revolution was a new view of history. They called for a new dispensation of gospel liberty, radically discontinuous with the past. They advocated new theological ground rules that dismissed everything since the New Testament as irrelevant, if not destructive. What led Americans in the finest evangelical tradition of Jonathan Edwards, John Witherspoon, Backus, and Asbury to repudiate their heritage? Furthermore, what gave credence to the idea that they were standing on the brink of a new age?

One cannot understand the Christians apart from their deep conviction that they had witnessed in the American and French revolutions the most momentous historical events in two millennia—a *novus ordo seclorum.* The opening line of the *Herald of Gospel Liberty* proclaimed that "the age in which we live may certainly be distinguished from others in the history of Man," and Smith was quick to point out that it was the struggle for liberty and the rights of mankind that set it apart. According to Smith, the foundations of Christ's millennial kingdom were laid in the American and French revolutions. "The time will come," he said, "when there will not be a *crowned head* on earth. Every attempt which is made to keep up a Kingly government, and to pull down a Republican one, will . . . serve to destroy monarchy. . . . Every small piece, or plan, of Monarchy which is a part of the *image* [of Antichrist] will be wholly dissolved, when *the people* are resolved to 'live free or die.'"[45]

43. Marshall and Thompson, *Brief Historical Account,* 3–4.

44. Elias Smith, *Sermons, Containing an Illustration of the Prophecies* (Exeter, N.H., 1808), vi.

45. *Herald of Gospel Liberty,* 1 September 1808, 1; Elias Smith, *A Discourse Delivered at Jefferson Hall, Thanksgiving Day, November 25, 1802; and Redelivered (by Request) the Wednesday Evening Following, at the Same Place: The Subject, Nebuchadnezzar's Dream* (Portsmouth, N.H., 1803), 30–32. The sociologist Guy E. Swanson has

The following year in Washington, Pennsylvania, Thomas Campbell published the first salvo of their movement and pointed to the same state of revolutionary and apocalyptic affairs: "Do ye not discern the signs of the times? Have not the two witnesses arisen from their state of political death, from under the long proscription of ages? . . . Who amongst us has not heard the report of these things—of these lightnings and thunderings, and voices, of this tremendous earthquake and great hail; of these awful convulsions and revolutions that have dashed and are dashing to pieces the nations like a potter's vessel?" In their view, such political convulsions spoke as the voice of providence "loudly and expressly calling us to repentance and reformation. . . . Resume that precious, that dear bought liberty, wherewith Christ has made his people free; a liberty from subjection to any authority but his own, in matters of religion. Call no man father. . . ." Alexander Campbell argued that the War for Independence unveiled a new epoch that would deliver men from "the melancholy thraldom of relentless systems." America's "political regeneration" gave her the responsibility to lead a comparable "ecclesiastical renovation."[46] An expectancy and overt respect for novelty characterized the Christians, as Stone's two associates confessed: "We confidently thought that the Millennium was just at hand, and that a glorious church would soon be formed; we thought, also, that we had found the very plan for its formation and growth." Opponents of these men agreed, moreover, that a sense of apocalyptic urgency had fueled the movement from the start.[47]

If the age of democratic revolutions gave the Christians good reason to sever ties with the past, it also suggested egalitarian models for a new age. In describing the true gospel that would revolutionize the world, Alexander Campbell called it "the declaration of independence of the kingdom of Jesus." Smith and Stone chose the same term to describe their withdrawal from the Baptists and Presbyterians, respectively. Similarly, O'Kelly claimed that he broke with the Methodists because they left him no option but "unlimited submission" or separation.[48] The lengths to which they allowed political idioms to color their thinking are sometimes

---

argued that the political forms under which a people live significantly color their theological perceptions, particularly in times of rapid change. See Guy E. Swanson, *Religion and Regime: A Sociological Account of the Reformation* (Ann Arbor, 1967), 231.

46. Campbell, *Declaration and Address of the Christian Association,* 14; Campbell, "Oration in Honor of the Fourth of July," 374; *Christian Baptist,* 6 February 1826, 213.

47. Marshall and Thompson, *Brief Historical Account,* 255. Presbyterian David Rice complained in 1805 about Stone and his followers: "Another thing that prepared the minds of many for the reception of error, was their high expectation of the speedy approach of the Millennium." Rice, *Epistle to the Citizens of Kentucky,* 13.

48. Campbell, "Oration in Honor of the Fourth of July," 377; Smith, *Life,* 292; Rogers, *Biography of Elder B. Warren Stone,* 47; O'Kelly, *Author's Apology,* 52.

difficult to comprehend: for example, they referred to the early church as a republican society with a New Testament constitution. In 1807, however, one maverick Christian in Marietta, Ohio, outdid them all, claiming that "the great potentate of the world, in principle, is the most *genuine* REPUBLICAN that ever existed."[49]

From a modern viewpoint, it may seem odd that men so committed to the separation of church and state held up a given political structure as a model for the church. They endowed the republic with the same divine authority as did defenders of the standing order such as Timothy Dwight and Noah Webster, but for opposite reasons. The republic became a new city on a hill not because it kept faith with Puritan tradition, but because it sounded the death knell for corporate and hierarchic conceptions of the social order. For these radical sectarians, the constitutional guarantees of separation of church and state laid the groundwork for a new age. In sum, a government so enlightened as to tell the churches to go their own way must have also had prophetic power to tell them which way to go.[50]

Millennialism, then served different functions for the Christians from those that it had during the Great Awakening. Revivals of the 1740s drew upon millennial themes to challenge traditionalists in the name of a greater commitment to traditional values.[51] This sense of eschatological drama, furthermore, served to define an evangelical identity over against political culture. By contrast, the democratic ferment experienced by the Christians convinced them that, in thinking about the future, they should work to erase the memory of the past and should learn from political culture whatever they could about a gospel of equality.

The Christians expressed their revolt against history most clearly in the radical way they chose to read the Bible. Amid unraveling cultural norms, they clung tenaciously to one final, unassailable authority, the *ipse dixit* of the New Testament. The direct propositions of Scripture became the only ground of certainty. In a letter to the *Herald of Gospel Liberty* in 1809, seventeen Christian ministers spelled out this central plank of the Christian platform: "In consequence of your receiving Christ as only

49. Abel Sargent, *Halcyon Itinerary and True Millennium Messenger* 5 (December 1807), 146.

50. Smith devoted a sermon of over 120 pages to the subject of how republican values should be applied to the church. See Elias Smith, *The Whole World Governed by a Jew; or the Government of the Second Adam, as King and Priest* (Exeter, N.H., 1805). On the standing order's conservative use of millennial themes, see Nathan O. Hatch, *The Sacred Cause of Liberty: Republican Thought and the Millennium in Revolutionary New England* (New Haven, Conn., 1977), 97–138. See also Richard M. Rollins, *The Long Journey of Noah Webster* (Philadelphia, 1980).

51. James West Davidson, *The Logic of Millennial Thought: Eighteenth-Century New England* (New Haven, Conn., 1977), 122–41.

head, and ruler of his church, it necessarily follows, *that his law as contained in the New Testament,* should be received without any addition, abridgment, alterations, or embellishments, to the exclusion of all articles of religion, confessions of faith, creeds, &c. &c. &c. composed by men." "The New Testament has been as the law once was, *among the rubbish,*" proclaimed Smith. "Now we have found it, let us read it to the people from morning till evening."[52] These were fighting words, no doubt, to the genteel clergy, men accustomed to covenants being the linchpin of society and to thinking of America as the new Israel. But even more radical than dismissing the Old Testament as a priestly rag used to hoodwink the people was the approach that Christians used to interpret Scripture. "I have endeavored to read the scriptures as though no one had read them before me," claimed Alexander Campbell, "and I am as much on my guard against reading them to-day, through the medium of my own views yesterday, or a week ago, as I am against being influenced by any foreign name, authority, or system whatever." Protestants had always argued for *sola Scriptura,* but this kind of radical individualism set the Bible against the entire history of biblical interpretation. In this hermeneutic, no human authority, contemporary or historical, had the right to advise the individual in his spiritual quest. In order to ward off any systematic theology, these men insisted that religious discussion be limited to Bible language, as Smith put it, "to prove every particular from plain declarations recorded in the Bible."[53]

This fresh hermeneutic had considerable appeal because it spoke to three pressing issues. First, it proclaimed a new ground of certainty for a generation perplexed that it could no longer hear the voice of God above the din of sectarian confusion. If people would only abandon the husks of theological abstraction, the truth would be plain for all to see. Second, this approach to Scripture dared the common man to open the Bible and think for himself. All theological abstractions—such as the Trinity, foreordination, and original sin—were abandoned, and all that was necessary to establish a given point was to string together texts from the King James Bible. Any Christian using New Testament words could fend off the most brilliant theological argument by the simple retort that he was using God's word against human opinion. All the weight of church history could not begin to tip the scale against the Christian's simple declaration, say, that the New Testament did not contain the word *trinity.*

52. *Herald of Gospel Liberty,* 23 June 1809, 87, 2 February 1809, 47. The Christians repeatedly suggested that Americans accord the New Testament the same kind of exclusive authority that they did constitutions in civil affairs. See Smith, *World Governed by a Jew,* 114; and Campbell, *Declaration and Address of the Christian Association,* 16.

53. *Christian Baptist,* 3 April 1826, 229; Smith, *Life,* 292.

This approach had a third appeal—obvious success in befuddling the respectable clergy. Smith, O'Kelly, Stone, and Alexander Campbell were to a man brilliant theological debaters, but they refused to abide by the etiquette of the opposition. Their coarse language, earthy humor, biting sarcasm, and commonsense reasoning appealed to the uneducated but left the professional clergy without a ready defense. In a pamphlet written in 1817 to combat Smith's influence in Massachusetts, the Congregationalist Thomas Andros recognized the new tactics:

> Ridicule, sneer, malignant sarcasm and reproach, are the armor in which he goes forth. On this ground, and not on sober argumentation, he knows the success of his cause depends. . . . If he knows the doctrine of original sin is not true, let him sit down and write a manly and candid answer to President Edward's great work on that subject. . . . Were he a dignified, candid, and intelligent controversalist, there would be enough to answer him, but who would wish to attack a windmill? Who can refute a sneer?

Andros also recognized that popularity rather than virtue was the clarion call of the movement: "They measure the progress of religion by the numbers, who flock to their standard; not by the prevalence of faith, and piety, justice and charity, and the public virtues in society in general."[54]

Other Congregationalists and Presbyterians, less sensitive to the new measures, continued to use the language of orthodoxy to lambaste the Christians as a new form of the threadbare heresies of Arius, Pelagius, and Socinius.[55] The Christians merely sidestepped these attacks by putting the disputed points before their followers and letting them choose between the language of Scripture and that of metaphysical subtlety. This democratic revolution in theology wrenched the queen of the sciences from the learned speculations of Harvard, Yale, and Princeton men and encouraged the blacksmith, cooper, and tiller of the soil not only to experience salvation but also to explain the process. Its genius was to allow common people to feel, for a fleeting moment at least, that they were beholden to no one and masters of their own fate.

How does one explain the theology of the people that came to be championed between 1790 and 1815? What kind of cultural context gave rise to similar movements in New England, the South, and the Midwest? Many historians have imagined that these radical pietists simply continued a tradition of dissent that had rippled through American culture since the 1740s. Others have viewed the Christians as prophets of the American frontier, men who developed notions in keeping with the self-

54. Andros, *Scriptures Liable to be Wrested to Men's Own Destruction,* 21, 6.
55. Porter, *Discourse in Two Parts,* 14; Rice, *Epistle to the Citizens of Kentucky,* 9–12.

sufficient characters that pushed into the hill country of New England and made their way across the Appalachians. This was religion following the frontier par excellence. Still other scholars have linked the Christian movement to the general revolt against Calvinism that followed the American Revolution. Rigid notions of depravity and predestination simply could not stir a generation that had witnessed at home and abroad the electrifying effects of liberty and natural rights. All of these—the ongoing tradition of evangelical dissent, the surge westward after the Revolution, and the disdain for Calvinistic explanations of the world—figure importantly in any explanation of the Christian movement.[56]

Yet these points of reference fail to locate the most intimate link between the Christians and American culture at the turn of the eighteenth century: a pervasive collapse of certainty within popular culture. From the debate over the Constitution to the election of Jefferson, a new and explicitly democratic revolution united many who were suspicious of power and many who were powerless in a common effort to pull down the cultural hegemony of a gentlemanly few. In a complex cultural process that historians have just begun to unravel, people on a number of fronts began to speak, write, and organize against the authority of mediating elites, of social distinctions, and of any human tie that did not spring from volitional allegiance.[57]

This crisis of confidence in a hierarchical, ordered society led to demands for fundamental reform in politics, law, and religion. In each of these areas, radical Jeffersonians, seizing upon issues close to the hearts of the people, resurrected "the spirit of 1776" to protest the control of elites and the force of tradition. Rhetoric that had once unified people across the social spectrum now drove a powerful wedge between rich and poor, elite and commoner, privileged classes and the people. Federalists, members of the bar, and the professional clergy heard the wisdom of the ages ridiculed as mere connivances of the powerful to maintain the status quo.

56. William G. McLoughlin views the later wave of dissent as but an extension of the revivalism of the Great Awakening. McLoughlin, *New England Dissent,* 2:697–750. William Warren Sweet described the Christians as "a new denomination which arose directly out of the soil of the west." William Warren Sweet, *Religion in the Development of American Culture, 1765–1840* (New York, 1952), 221; and Winifred Ernest Garrison, *Religion Follows the Frontier: A History of the Disciples of Christ* (New York, 1931). Sweet also links the Christians to the broader revolt against Calvinism.

57. For the importance of the idea of volitional allegiance in this period, see James H. Kettner, *The Development of American Citizenship, 1608–1870* (Chapel Hill, N.C., 1978), 173–209. See also Gordon S. Wood, *The Creation of the American Republic, 1776–1787* (Chapel Hill, N.C., 1969), 483–99; Alfred F. Young, *The Democratic Republicans of New York: The Origins, 1763–1797* (Chapel Hill, N.C., 1967); and Edmund S. Morgan, *The Challenge of the American Revolution* (New York, 1976), 211–18.

The violence of politics from 1780 to 1800, more than anything else, gave sharp definition to egalitarian impulses in American society. From the Revolution onwards, republican equality became a rallying cry for people seeking to challenge all sorts of political authority. Incidents in South Carolina, Massachusetts, and New York illustrate how thoroughly the "virtue" of subjection and deference was giving way to an itching, smarting, writhing awareness of inferiority. In 1784, the South Carolina legislature threatened William Thompson, a tavern keeper, with banishment from the state for insulting the eminent John Rutledge. Thompson responded with a newspaper article that blasted the claims of "self-exalted" characters like Rutledge who had "conceived me his inferior." Thompson refused to "comprehend the *inferiority*" and denied the right of a conspicuous few to speak for the people.[58] During the debate over the Constitution, Antifederalists turned repeatedly to such arguments. At the Massachusetts ratification convention, for example, the self-taught Worcester County farmer Amos Singletary denounced the Constitution as a plot to consolidate the influence of the great: "these lawyers and men of learning, and moneyed men . . . talk so finely, and gloss over matters so smoothly, to make us poor illiterate people swallow down the pill. . . . They expect to be the managers of this Constitution, and get all the power and all the money into their own hands. And then they will swallow up us little fellows, like the great Leviathan."[59]

A decade later the urban democratic leader William Keteltas was able to shake Federalist control of New York City by a shrewd media campaign depicting politics as a clash between rich and poor. Ketaltas made into a cause celèbre the case of two Irish-born ferrymen whom Federalist magistrates punished summarily for reportedly insulting one of their number. Ketaltas dramatized the issue in the popular press and eventually came to attack the New York assembly for not impeaching the responsible magistrates. This led to his own arrest by the Federalist legislature on a charge of breach of privilege. When Keteltas appeared before the assembly, a crowd of several thousand gathered in protest. His release from a brief prison sentence prompted a grand celebration in which the people pulled Keteltas through the streets in a carriage decked with American and French flags, a cap of liberty, and a picture of a man being whipped with the inscription, "What you rascal, insult your superiors?" By championing the cause of the ferrymen—what Keteltas called "the most flagrant abuse of [the people's] rights' since Independence"—he ef-

58. Wood, *Creation of the American Republic,* 482–83.

59. Jonathan Elliot, *The Debates, Resolutions, and Other Proceedings, in Convention on the Adoption of the Federal Constitution,* 4 vols. (Washington, D.C., 1827–30), 1:112.

fectively mobilized the common people of New York to challenge Federalist domination.[60]

Such repeated attacks on the capacity of a conspicuous few to speak for the whole of society struck at the root of traditional conceptions of society.[61] Extending the logic of Antifederalists, radical Jeffersonians came to ridicule the assumption that society was an organic hierarchy of ranks and degrees; they argued, rather, that it was a heterogeneous mixture of many different classes, orders, interest groups, and occupations. In such a society the elites could no longer claim to be adequate spokesmen for people in general. In this climate, it took little creativity for some to begin to reexamine the social function of the clergy and to question the right of any order of men to claim authority to interpret God's Word. If opinions about politics and society were no longer the monopoly of the few, why could not anyone and everyone begin to think for themselves in matters of religion?

The 1790s also witnessed fundamental challenges to the legal profession and the common law. Richard E. Ellis has documented the strident attacks against the legal system that surfaced in the popular press and in serious political movements to reform the law in Kentucky, Pennsylvania, and Massachusetts.[62] Radical republicans such as Boston's Austin denounced the legal profession for needlessly confusing court cases in order to charge high fees, deliberately making the law inaccessible to laymen, bartering justice to those who could afford to pay, and monopolizing legislative and judicial posts.

Those who called for radical legal reform addressed three primary issues. First, they demanded a simplified and easily accessible legal process, "a system of laws of our own, dictated by the genuine principles of Republicanism, and made easy to be understood to every individual in the community."[63] Second, they attempted to replace the common law—authority by precedent—with fresh legal codes designed for the new republic. For many of these radicals, the common law conjured up images of complexity, mystery, intolerance, and bias in favor of the elite: "Shall we be directed by reason, equity, and a few simple and plain laws, promptly executed, or shall we be ruled by volumes of statutes and cases decided by the

60. Young, *Democratic Republicans of New York,* 468–95.

61. Wood, *Creation of the American Republic,* 483–99. One of the clearest calls that common people should resist the traditional distinction between gentlemen and commoners came from the pen of the uneducated Massachusetts farmer William Manning in 1798. Samuel Eliot Morrison, ed., "William Manning's *The Key of Libberty,*" *William and Mary Quarterly* 13 (April 1956): 202–54.

62. Ellis, *Jeffersonian Crisis.*

63. Benjamin Austin, Jr., "Observations on the Pernicious Practice of the Law" (1786), in *American Journal of Legal History* 13 (July 1969): 258.

ignorance and intolerance of former times?"[64] Third, having jettisoned the "monkist priesthood" of lawyers and the "absurdity of the common law," those who sought root-and-branch reform exhibited great faith in the ability of ordinary citizens to ascertain and dispense justice before the law. "Any person of common abilities," said Austin, "can easily distinguish between right and wrong" and "more especially when the parties are admitted to give a plain story, without any puzzle from lawyers."[65]

In retrospect, this faith in democratic, personalized, and simplified law appears hopelessly naive and utopian. Yet it reflects a moment of historical optimism, a time when many in politics, law, and religion, flushed with the promise of the American Revolution, found it reasonable to take literally the meaning of *novus ordo seclorum* and to declare a decisive expatriation from the past.[66]

That Smith came to jettison orthodox Calvinism through reading Austin's articles in the *Independent Chronicle* in 1799 and 1800 underscores the correlation between the Christian movement and reform efforts in politics and law.[67] In method, substance, and style, Smith championed the cause to which radical Jeffersonians were committed: an appeal to class as the fundamental problem of society, a refusal to recognize the cultural authority of elites, a disdain for the supposed lessons of history and tradition, a call for reform using the rhetoric of the Revolution, a commitment to turn the press into a sword of democracy, and an ardent faith in the future of the American republic. Smith's primary interest, of course, was the spread of evangelical religion; yet he could never divorce that message from the egalitarian principles that the frantic pace of the 1790s had made self-evident.

That other individuals came to advocate virtually identical reform is further evidence that questions were raging in popular culture that popular religion simply could not avoid. While other claims to truth also flourished in this atmosphere, the Christian movement stands out as an attempt to bring some harmony between denominational traditions and egalitarian values. In lashing out at the tyranny of the clergy, the foolishness of abstract theology, and the bondage of church discipline, the Christians fulfilled a mandate for reform that was widespread in popular culture. In exalting the idea that every man was his own interpreter, they

64. "Decius," *Independent Chronicle*, 30 January 1804, 1.

65. Ellis, *Jeffersonian Crisis*, 171, 177; Austin, "Observations on the Pernicious Practice of the Law," 264.

66. For the importance in Thomas Jefferson's thought of breaking the grip of custom and precedent, see Edmund S. Morgan, *The Meaning of Independence: John Adams, George Washington, Thomas Jefferson* (Charlottesville, 1976), 71–79; and Daniel J. Boorstin, *The Lost World of Thomas Jefferson* (Boston, 1948).

67. Smith, *Lovingkindness of God Displayed*, 32.

brought a measure of certainty to people committed to the principle that all values, rights, and duties originate in the individual—the principle that Alexis de Tocqueville later called individualism.[68]

The legacy of the Christian movement is riddled with irony. Instead of taking America by storm, the Christian connection under Smith and O'Kelly vanished into insignificance, while the Disciples in the West grew into a major denomination only by practicing the kind of organization they had once hoped to stamp out. Instead of calming sectarian strife and restoring edenic harmony, the Christians engendered controversy at every step and had to put up with chronic factionalism within their own ranks.[69] Instead of offering a new foundation for certainty, the Christian approach to knowledge, which made no man the judge of another's conscience, had little holding power and sent many early advocates scrambling for surer footing.[70] Instead of erecting a primitive church free from theological tradition and authoritarian control, the Christians came to advocate their own sectarian theology and to defer to the influence and persuasion of a dominant few. These ironies suggest that the real significance of the Christian movement is not to be found in its institutional development or in the direct influence of Smith, O'Kelly, Stone, and Alexander Campbell. What the movement does illustrate graphically is a moment of wrenching change in American culture that had great import for popular religion. Many followed the path even if they did not know its trailblazers.

The Christian movement illustrates, in the first place, the intensity of religious ferment at work in a period of chaos and originality unmatched, perhaps, since the religious turbulence of seventeenth-century England.[71] As in England a century and a half before, common folk in America at the dawn of the nineteenth century came to scorn tradition, relish novelty and experimentation, grope for fresh sources of authority, and champion

68. Alexis de Tocqueville, *Democracy in America,* trans. Henry Reeve, 2 vols. (New York, 1959), 1:104–5.

69. For an excellent example of the potential for factionalism within a local Christian church, see Don Harrison Doyle, *The Social Order of a Frontier Community: Jacksonville, Illinois, 1825–70* (Urbana, 1978), 157–60.

70. Smith himself left the Christian Connection in 1818 to join the Universalists, and two of his colleagues, Joshua V. Himes and Joseph Marsh, became early advocates of William Miller. David L. Rowe, "A New Perspective on the Burned-Over District: The Millerites in Upstate New York," *Church History* 47 (December 1978): 408–20. Of five men who signed the "Last Will and Testament of Springfield Presbytery," two returned to the Presbyterians, two became Shakers, and only Stone retained his identity as a Christian. Alexander Campbell, similarly, saw his best preacher, Sidney Rigdon, defect to the Mormons. Mario S. De Pillis, "The Quest for Religious Authority and the Rise of Mormonism," *Dialogue: A Journal of Mormon Thought* 1 (spring 1966): 68–88.

71. Christopher Hill, *The World Turned Upside Down: Radical Ideas during the English Revolution* (New York, 1972).

an array of millennial schemes, each in its own way dethroning hierarchy and static religious forms.[72] The resulting popular culture pulsated with the claims of supremely heterodox religious groups, with people veering from one sect to another, with the unbridled wrangling of competitors in a "war of words."[73] Scholars have only begun to assess the fragmentation that beset American religion in the period generally referred to as the Second Great Awakening, which they have too often viewed as a conservative response to rapid social change. The Christian movement serves as a helpful corrective and invites fresh appraisals of the popular culture that nourished people like William Miller, John Humphrey Noyes, and Joseph Smith. Theirs was a religious environment that brought into question traditional authorities and exalted the right of the people to think for themselves. The result, quite simply, was a bewildering world of clashing opinion—to the sympathetic Smith, an "age of inquiry," to the distraught David Rice, a "hot bed of every extravagance of opinion and practice." Another erstwhile pilgrim, the Presbyterian-turned-Christian-turned-Shaker Richard McNemar, took up verse to capture the spirit of his times:

> Ten thousand Reformers like so many moles
> Have plowed all the Bible and cut it [in] holes
> And each has his church at the end of his trace
> Built up as he thinks of the subjects of grace.[74]

The Christians also illustrate the exaltation of public opinion as a primary religious authority. They called for common folk to read the New Testament as if mortal man had never seen it before. People were expected to discover the self-evident message of the Bible without any mediation from creeds, theologians, or clergymen not of their own choosing. This explicit faith that biblical authority could emerge from below, from the will of the people, was the most enduring legacy of the Christian movement. By the 1840s one analyst of American Protestantism concluded, after surveying fifty-three American sects, that the principle "No

72. J. F. C. Harrison, *The Second Coming: Popular Millenarianism, 1780–1850* (New Brunswick, 1979), 163–206.

73. The phrase is that of Joseph Smith, who reacted strongly to the sectarian competition he knew as a young man. Joseph Smith, *The Pearl of Great Price* (Salt Lake City, 1891), 56–70. In this period evangelicals were preoccupied with a sense of the transforming power of the printed word. See Joan Jacobs Brumberg, *Mission for Life: The Story of the Family of Adoniram Judson* (New York, 1980), 44–78.

74. Elias Smith, *The Age of Enquiry* (Exeter, N.H., 1807); David Rice, "A Second Epistle to the Citizens of Kentucky, Professing the Christian Religion," in *An Outline of the History of the Church in the State of Kentucky*, ed. Robert Bishop (Lexington, Ky., 1824), 354; Richard McNemar, "The Mole's Little Pathways" as quoted in De Pillis, "Quest for Religious Authority," 75.

creed but the Bible" was the distinctive feature of American religion. John W. Nevin surmised that this emphasis grew out of a popular demand for "private judgment" and was "tacitly if not openly conditioned always by the assumption that every man is authorized and bound to get at this authority in a direct way for himself, through the medium simply of his own single mind."[75] Many felt the exhilarating hope that democracy had opened an immediate access to biblical truth for all persons of good will. What was difficult for Americans to realize was that a commitment to private judgment could drive people apart even as it raised beyond measure their hopes for unity.

The Christian movement also demonstrates the process by which popular culture became christianized in the early republic. One reason that evangelical churches and sects grew so rapidly during these years was that they proclaimed value systems that endowed common people with dignity and responsibility. People gladly accepted a theology that addressed them without condescension, balked at vested interest, and reinforced ideas of volitional allegiance and self-reliance. While such egalitarian strains were deeply rooted in the Great Awakening and subsequent revivals, historians have failed to appreciate the ways in which the founding of the American republic wrought, in Devereux Jarratt's words, "a vast alteration" in American religion. A staunch evangelical minister in Virginia prior to the Revolution, Jarratt by the 1790s had come to fear the volatile mix of things evangelical and egalitarian. Bemoaning the "levelling" spirit in "our high republican times," Jarrett recoiled from a religion "under the supreme controul of tinkers and taylors, weavers, shoemakers, and country mechanics of all kinds."[76] The theology that emerged between 1790 and 1815 to empower just these kinds of people certainly helps to clarify a process by which an America that had been largely Presbyterian, Congregational, Anglican, and Calvinist Baptist became a cauldron of Methodists, Disciples, Freewill, Free-Communion, and Primitive Baptists, Universalists, Mormons, and Millerites—to name a few. This new religious culture, which sanctioned the right of the individual to go his own way, would have been unthinkable apart from the crisis of authority in popular culture that accompanied the birth of the American republic.

75. John Williamson Nevin, "Antichrist and the Sect," in *The Mercersburg Theology*, ed. James Hastings Nichols (New York, 1966), 93–119, 98–99.

76. Devereux Jarratt, *The Life of the Reverend Devereux Jarratt* (Baltimore, 1806), 14–15, 181.

8

The Critical Period for Protestant Thought in America

D. G. Hart

Reprinted by permission from *Journal of Ecclesiastical History* 38 (1987): 254–70.

In 1854, Philip Schaff, professor of church history at Mercersburg Theological Seminary and minister of the German Reformed Church, reported to his denomination on the state of Christianity in America. Although the American church had many shortcomings, according to Schaff the United States was "by far the most religious and Christian country in the world."[1] Many Protestant leaders, however, took a dimmer view of Christianity's prospects. In the middle decades of the nineteenth century, a nagging sense prevailed that traditional theology was no longer capable of integrating religion and culture, or piety and intelligence. Bela Bates Edwards, a conservative New England divine, complained of the prevalent opinion "that an intellectual clergyman is deficient in piety and that an eminently pious minister is deficient in intellect."[2] Edwards was not merely lamenting the unpopularity of Calvinism. A Unitarian writer also noted a burgeoning "clerical skepticism." Intelligent and well-trained men who wished to defend and preach the

1. Perry Miller, ed., *America: A Sketch of Its Political, Social and Religious Character* (Cambridge, 1961), 11.
2. "Influence of Eminent Piety on the Intellectual Powers," in B. B. Edwards, *Writings* (Boston, 1853), ii, 472.

gospel, he wrote, "find themselves struggling within the fetters of a creed by which they have pledged themselves."[3] An 1853 Memorial to the Bishops of the Protestant Episcopal Church summed up the doubts of Protestant clergymen when it asked whether the church's traditional theology and ministry were "competent to the work of preaching and dispensing the Gospel to all sorts and conditions of men, and so adequate to do the work of the Lord in this land and in this age."[4]

The crisis of the 1850s was in some ways a variation on the tension between faith and reason found throughout the history of Christian thought. But the response to clerical doubts introduced an approach to the problem of religious authority that drove a wedge between the leaders of the Protestant establishment in America. A number of clergymen found a solution in the romantic epistemology that Samuel Taylor Coleridge offered in his popular work, *Aids to Reflection.* Despite the criticism of conservative theologians, Coleridge's followers hoped that, by granting the emotions a greater role in apprehending religious truths, the breach between religion and culture could be resolved while maintaining the authority of Christianity.[5]

Between 1848 and 1852, the problems that romantic ideas raised for Christianity initiated a debate in America that had no real parallel in England.[6] The chief participants were America's four leading Protestant thinkers, Horace Bushnell, Charles Hodge, Henry B. Smith, and Edwards A. Park. In the course of this debate, these men assumed opposing positions, stressing either the objective or subjective essentials of Christian faith. Bushnell (1802–76), a Congregational minister from Hartford, and Hodge (1797–1878), professor of theology at Princeton Theological Seminary, took the most consistent and antithetical positions. Relying on romantic insights, Bushnell heralded the primacy of religious experience for genuine faith while Hodge insisted on the rational character of faith. Smith (1815–77), professor of philosophy at Amherst and later the New School Presbyterian Church's premier theologian at

3. George E. Ellis, "The New Theology," *The Christian Examiner* 27 (1857), 339.

4. Quoted in Charles C. Tiffany, *A History of the Protestant Episcopal Church in the U.S.A.* (New York, 1895), vii, 486.

5. See William R. Hutchison, *The Modernist Impulse in American Protestantism* (Cambridge, 1976), 21–30, 41–48; Sydney E. Ahlstrom, "Theology in America: A Historical Survey," in James Ward Smith and A. Leland Jamison, eds., *The Shaping of American Religion* (Princeton, 1961), 285–88; and Philip F. Gura, *The Wisdom of Words* (Middletown, 1981), 35–74. German idealist philosophy actually had little direct influence on American thought until after the Civil War. In mid-nineteenth-century America, the ideas of Immanuel Kant and Friedrich Wilhelm von Schelling were mediated through the English channels of Coleridge and Carlyle. See Perry Miller's introduction to *American Thought: Civil War to World War I* (San Francisco, 1954), xi.

6. Cf. Owen Chadwick, *The Victorian Church, I, 1829–1859* (London, 1966), 544–58.

Union Seminary, and Park (1808–1900), the leading theologian at Andover Seminary, took mediating positions in this debate. Sharing Hodge's concern for a rational faith, Smith looked to the Christocentric theology of Germany for a proper synthesis of the objective and subjective elements of faith. In contrast, Park used Bushnell's insights to develop a theological method that would harmonize New England's competing theologies and would also enhance piety as well as intelligence.

Until recently the work of these theologians has been largely ignored. Assuming their work to be superficial and without influence, many religious historians have failed to evaluate America's nineteenth-century theology with any seriousness.[7] But even recent discussions have overlooked the significance of the mid-nineteenth century's theological debates for the subsequent history of American Protestantism.[8] Consequently, the impression continues that the late nineteenth and early twentieth centuries were the critical period for Protestants in America. Because of doubts stemming from Darwinism, biblical criticism, and the study of world religions, according to some historians, Protestant liberals and conservatives argued fiercely over accommodations to science and of the nature of Christian revelation.[9]

The seeds of the division between liberals and conservatives, however, were planted during the debate between Bushnell, Hodge, Park, and Smith, which provides the focus of this chapter. Not only was this debate indicative of the clergy's dissatisfaction with traditional formulae of Reformed theology and of a turn to German philosophy to meet the need, but it was decisive for the spiritual crisis of the Gilded Age. What eventually polarized Protestants was not the theory of Darwin or biblical crit-

7. See Sidney E. Mead, *The Lively Experiment* (New York, 1963), 54; and Winthrop S. Hudson, *American Protestantism* (Chicago, 1961), 131–34. Both criticize nineteenth-century theology for its obscurity and superficiality.

8. See Bruce Kuklick, *Churchmen and Philosophers: from Jonathan Edwards to John Dewey* (New Haven, Conn., 1985); Lewis Perry, *Intellectual Life in America: A History* (New York, 1984), 229–35; and Ann Douglas, *The Feminization of American Culture* (New York 1978), 143–96. Kuklick, whose treatment is the most judicious, is concerned primarily with the status of theology in relation to philosophy. Consequently, he regards the crisis at mid-century as the point at which philosophy and theology went their separate ways; see 209–14. Conversely, Douglas and Perry argue that the ideas of Park and Bushnell demonstrate the triumph of emotionalism and sentimentalism within theological circles.

9. Arthur M. Schlesinger, Sr., "A Critical Period in American Protestantism, 1875–1900," *Massachusetts Historical Society Proceedings* 64 (1932): 523–48; Paul A. Carter, *The Spiritual Crisis of the Gilded Age* (Dekalb, Ill., 1971); William G. McLoughlin, *The Meaning of Henry Ward Beecher* (New York, 1970); Donald H. Meyer, "American Intellectuals and the Victorian Crisis of Faith," in Daniel Walker Howe, ed., *Victorian America* (Philadelphia, 1976), 59–77; Ferenc Morton Szasz, *The Divided Mind of Protestant America, 1880–1930* (1982).

icism but rather the way in which these new findings were appropriated. The debate studied here laid the groundwork for the ways in which the next generation of Protestant thinkers would reconcile the sometimes contradictory claims of Christianity and learning.

In 1848, Andover Seminary invited Horace Bushnell to speak before its Porter Rhetorical Society. Entitled "Dogma and Spirit," Bushnell's address specified his solutions to "the mournfully low state of religion, the growth of worldliness, the want of godliness, the decay of ministerial force, and the afflicting signs of a delicate and earthly spirit of the ministry." What the church needed was not another revival or a more rigorous theology. Instead, to lift it out of its doldrums, the church needed to re-experience "Christian truth as spirit and life" through a combination of faith and "right feelings."[10] Although Bushnell's proposal would draw fire from conservative Congregationalists for its resemblance to Transcendentalism, "Dogma and Spirit" actually represented the culmination of tensions within the Hartford preacher's career.

As a Yale undergraduate in 1823, Bushnell first recognized the disparity between piety and learning. New Haven society was considerably more sophisticated than Bushnell's rural home, New Preston, Connecticut, and the "great folk" of the college made him conscious of his awkward manners. He categorized his roommate, who regularly attended the town's social functions, as "profane and dissipated." The pious students, however, "were men, without any refinement either of manners or of feeling—fresh from the country." Whether owing to peer pressure or a change in his own taste, Bushnell improved his status in the college. Upon graduation he tried his hand at journalism in New York and eventually returned to Yale to study law in 1829. But as his social position improved, his faith atrophied to the point that, when he finally chose a ministerial career in 1831, his decision was made in response to the expectations of his mother and pious friends rather than personal conviction.[11] Some may suggest that Bushnell's doubts merely reflected his sense of social inferiority. Although he did experience a tension between social status and piety, this ambivalence was bound up with his intellectual struggles which prohibited him from entering the ministry with full confidence. Too much of traditional theology, he confessed, could be shattered "all to pieces" by logic. But in those times of doubt, Bushnell

10. "Dogma and Spirit," in H. Shelton Smith, ed., *Horace Bushnell* (New York, 1965), 54.

11. This is suggested by Mary Bushnell Cheyney in *Life and Letters of Horace Bushnell* (New York, 1880), 32. On Bushnell's struggles at Yale, see Barbara Cross, *Horace Bushnell; Minister to a Changing America* (Chicago, 1958), 4–11; and Theodore T. Munger, *Horace Bushnell: Preacher and Theologian* (Boston, 1889), 19–29.

turned inwards, for it was only in the act of faith that he could accept the traditional tenets of Christian dogma.[12]

Bushnell's studies at Yale Divinity School and the problems that confronted him in his Hartford parish reinforced his suspicions of New England orthodoxy. At Yale he trained under Nathaniel W. Taylor whose system of New Divinity continued New England's controversies over free will and original sin.[13] Bushnell respected Taylor but he blamed an exceedingly rational method, the heart of his professor's theology, for the lifeless character of Congregationalism. Later, when he assumed pastoral charge of Hartford's North Church in 1833, Bushnell witnessed first-hand the adverse effects of New England's theology. The congregation was divided along partisan theological lines. To avoid the logic chopping of both sides, Bushnell preached the benefits of Christian experience.[14]

Even though Bushnell's methods met with little opposition, his intellectual doubts persisted.[15] Then on one cold February morning, he finally discovered what he had been preaching to his church. All of Bushnell's admirers stress the importance of this intuitive experience for his theology.[16] Not only did the experience resolve Bushnell's doubts, it also confirmed his convictions about the nature of religious knowledge. Since his undergraduate days he had read with delight the writings of Samuel Taylor Coleridge and Victor Cousin. Both Coleridge and Cousin offered a version of German idealism that defined the faculty of reason so that knowledge received intuitively was made superior to knowledge yielded by observation or reflection. To Bushnell, this romantic epistemology provided a surer foundation for Christian faith than rational assent,[17] and he combined it with his theory of language to undercut further the preoccupation with reason among New England theologians. Relying on the work of Josiah Willard Gibbs the elder, language professor at Yale, Bushnell posited that all language is in some sense metaphorical.[18] Words that denote objects in the physical world came closest to a literal meaning, he said, but those that represent ideas were at best figurative. And because religious language, whether creed or Scripture, was primarily fig-

12. Munger, *op. cit.,* 25.

13. For a brief summary of Taylor's theology, see Ahlstrom, "Theology in America," 254–60.

14. Munger, *Horace Bushnell,* 53.

15. Horace Bushnell, *Twentieth Anniversary: A Commemorative Discourse, Delivered in the North Church, of Hartford, May 22, 1853* (Hartford, 1853), 8–9.

16. Cheyney, *Life and Letters,* 191–92; Smith, *Horace Bushnell,* 25–26; and Munger, *op. cit.,* 113–15.

17. Gura, *Wisdom of Words,* 51–55; Smith, *op. cit.,* 25–29; and Cross, *Horace Bushnell,* 21–30.

18. For Gibb's influence on Bushnell, see Smith, *op. cit.,* 36–37, 80–81.

urative, Bushnell regarded theological discourse as an expression of religious intuition.[19]

In his address, "Dogma and Spirit," Bushnell drew upon his theories of language and religious knowledge, as well as on his own recent religious experience to propose a wholesale re-evaluation of the relationship between piety and theology. He declared that the low state of New England Christianity resulted from its concern for dogma at the expense of spirituality. "We suppose that learning and debate can master Christian truths and handle them as it can questions of grammar and archaeology." The situation in New England, however, was not unique. Throughout the church's history, whenever theologians regarded Christianity as a set of "propositions and articles" rather than as life-giving faith, the church always descended into darkness. For a "true reviving of religion," the church needed to rediscover that "Christian truth can be *in* our soul only as it is of it, begotten there by the indwelling of Christ, and the private rehearsal of the Spirit."[20]

Some historians have found similarities between Bushnell's religion of the heart and Jonathan Edwards's ideas on religious affections. According to H. Shelton Smith, Bushnell's insistence that Christian truth be felt in the soul was a revival of the evangelical strain in Puritan thought. Although formal similarities exist between Bushnell and his New England predecessors' emphasis on the subjective nature of genuine faith, Bushnell broke with the Reformed tradition of Congregationalism over the rational ground of faith. Edwards and most Reformed theologians averred that rational assent to doctrinal truths was essential for true faith because doctrine described the objective basis of Christianity. Bushnell's theory of language and his romantic conception of theology put him at odds with the Puritan tradition because he denied that any system could express adequately the truths of Christianity.[21] By revising the role of dogma in faith, Bushnell hoped to reconcile religion and culture in a way that would give Christianity a greater hearing in the marketplace of ideas. Confident in Christianity's superior method of knowledge, Bushnell believed that

19. On Bushnell's theory of language, see Cross, *op. cit.*, 93–115; Gura, *op. cit.*, 58–71; and Charles Fiedelson, *Symbolism in American Literature* (Chicago, 1972), 151–57.

20. Bushnell, "Dogma and Spirit," 63.

21. Smith, *Horace Bushnell*, 29–34. On the importance of sound doctrine in the conversion experience, see Jonathan Edwards, *The Works of Jonathan Edwards*, 2: *Religious Affections*, ed. John Smith (New Haven, Conn., 1959). H. Shelton Smith supports his argument by citing Bushnell's 1872 sermon, "The Immediate Knowledge of God," where Bushnell says that rational knowledge is presupposed in all faith, *Sermons on Living Subjects* (New York, 1910), 114–28. Bushnell's position in this sermon seems to contradict his earlier ideas on religious knowledge and language and may explain why Cross asserts that Bushnell abandoned his semantic theory in his later writings, *Horace Bushnell*, 113.

Christians had little to fear from other kinds of knowledge. "Whatever truth there is in the universe belongs to the Lord of Christianity and holds a real consistency, both with him and it." Yet the nature of faith, Bushnell believed, should also yield humility because, as the range of human knowledge grows, "Christianity will better know her place, her office and her nature." Consequently, even though Bushnell still maintained the unity of truth, he allowed that this unity could not always be accomplished on Christian terms but instead would require concessions.[22]

Although the rapprochement made possible by Bushnell's religious epistemology encouraged some, it boded ill for the systematic theologian. If theology were only poetic expression and if it required constant revision according to the latest scholarship, the theologian's traditional task of constructing systems was jeopardized. But Bushnell believed that there was still plenty of work for the theologian, and he continued to write on such traditional topics as the incarnation, the atonement, and the trinity in *Christ in Theology* (1851), *Nature and the Supernatural* (1858), and *The Vicarious Sacrifice* (1867). Bushnell gave several reasons for pursuing theological subjects. One was to bring Christianity into harmony with all other knowledge. A second was to defend it against unbelief. A third was to recast doctrine in language that "stimulates the soul in reaching after God."[23] The most important reason, however, was to create a "comprehensive theology." Assuming that all dogmatic formulae communicate only partial truth, Bushnell strove to synthesize all contradictory doctrinal systems by clarifying and combining their different insights.[24] He believed that the result would be a theology "so convoluted with spirit, and so mixed with faith that it will be as much a life, a holy breath and catholicity of spirit, as a theory." And it would be, he hoped, "as far from possible representation in any of the niggard forms of abstract science or the debated articles of school divinity, as can be conceived."[25]

To professors of divinity, Bushnell's reasons for pursuing theology were not good enough. Not only did his theory of language render "school divinity" useless, but his conception of faith seemed to challenge the necessity of doctrine altogether . When Bushnell said that many of the "humblest babes of faith . . . really knew more and have a truer science of God, than some who are most distinguished among the Christian doctors," the three most formidable Reformed theologians of mid-nineteenth-century America, Smith, Park and Hodge, took notice.[26]

22. Bushnell, "Dogma and Spirit," 66–67.
23. Ibid.
24. H. Bushnell, "Christian Comprehensiveness," *New Englander* 6 (1848), 84.
25. Bushnell, "Dogma and Spirit," 63.
26. Ibid., 62–63.

Henry B. Smith was the first to respond in detail to the issues that Bushnell raised regarding the relationship between faith and learning. Reared in a Unitarian home in Portsmouth, Maine, Smith attended Bowdoin College where he converted to Trinitarian Christianity in his senior year. Of his conversion he said, "I know nothing but that Christ is my redeemer and has atoned for my sins."[27] Christology was thereafter central in his theology. His aim, even at the age of twenty-one, was "to make and harmonize a system" that would "make Christ the central point of all religious truth."[28] Smith's theological studies, continually interrupted by bouts of illness, took him to Andover Seminary, Maine's Bangor Seminary, and eventually to Germany. At the University of Halle, Friedrich August Gottreu Tholuck reinforced Smith's Christocentrism. Tholuck was the leader of Germany's "mediating theology," a broad movement that drew together Pietists as well as followers of Friedrich Schleiermacher. Tholuck sought to integrate traditional theology with German philosophical and scientific thought through the mediating principle of the incarnation.[29] Smith's study in Germany also exposed him to that country's philosophical and historical scholarship. From Halle, he went on to study in Berlin with Leopold von Ranke and the Hegelian scholar Adolf Trendelenburg. On his return to America in 1840, the Andover faculty and the Boston Transcendentalists greeted him eagerly because of his German education. But it was not until 1847 that Amherst College offered him a job teaching philosophy.

Smith's career took a significant turn in 1849 when the Porter Rhetorical Society invited him to give the annual address. In response to Bushnell's "Dogma and Spirit" given to the same audience only a year before, Smith chose as his topic "The Relations between Faith and Philosophy." He started tactfully by agreeing with Bushnell's overall assessment that the intellectual currents of the day were running against Christianity. Not just Calvinism, but Christian belief itself appeared to be inferior to modern ethical, social, and metaphysical systems. But instead of appealing to the figurative and poetic aspects of creeds as Bushnell seemed to advocate, Smith sought to reconcile theology and philosophy on rational grounds. In his estimation, the antagonism between faith and philosophy resulted from the existence of "two diverse human activities." Philosophy pertains to the knowledge of things, "the knowing them in their causes, their relations and their ends; the knowing them in the harmony and completeness

27. Mrs. Henry Boynton Smith, ed., *Henry Boynton Smith: His Life and Work* (New York, 1881), 15.

28. Ibid., 32.

29. William K. B. Stoever, "Henry Boynton Smith and the German Theology of History," *Union Seminary Quarterly Review* 24 (1968): 70–71.

of a system."[30] Conversely, faith is an act of trust. "It rests upon authority. . . . It is content with miracles, and it accepts mysteries." The antagonism between faith and philosophy at this level is merely the opposing claims of two different epistemologies, rationalism and mysticism.[31]

For Smith, however, the conflict between faith and philosophy ran deeper than the one between trust and reason. Hegelian Idealism, which Smith referred to as pantheism, was waging a subtle and almost condescending war on the tenets of Christian theology. It regarded Christianity as "the highest possible form of man's religious nature," thereby rendering it nothing more than the unfolding of the immanent Spirit. This assimilation of Christianity, Smith conceded, "seduces many," but in reality it was an assault of "most daring" proportions, for it produced "the great alternative of our times . . . the choice between Christ or Spinoza," between faith or philosophy.[32] From the perspective of this antagonism between faith and Germany philosophy, Smith's conception of faith included more than just an experience of trust. Faith "is always trust in something external . . . an historical revelation, a revelation recorded in a volume which claims to be inspired."[33] Here is where Smith's definition of faith went beyond Bushnell's and where he took issue with the Hartford preacher's proposed reconciliation of faith and reason. Any harmonization of faith and philosophy would have to include the objective elements of Christian faith, not only the subjective act. Consequently, Smith proposed that systematic theology was the best synthesis of faith and philosophy. "Systematic theology is the combined result of philosophy and faith, and it is its high office to present the two in their most intimate conjunction and inherent harmony." This process of putting Christian truth into propositional forms reconciles faith and reason by requiring both piety and a sound "philosophic intellect." It also harmonizes Christianity with philosophy because it demonstrates that theology answers the most profound questions which philosophy can pose, questions about God, man, providence, and human destiny.[34]

Smith's defense of theology, however, provided no excuse to maintain the status quo. His concerns were definitely traditional and orthodox, but Christianity's conflict with German philosophy required that traditional dogma be recast in updated forms. The old questions of New England orthodoxy—those of divine sovereignty and free agency—had lost

30. "The Relations of Faith and Philosophy," in H. B. Smith, *Faith and Philosophy* (New York, 1877), 3.

31. Ibid., 4.

32. Ibid., 11.

33. Ibid., 19.

34. Ibid., 18. See also Smith, "The Idea of Christian Theology as a System," in *Faith and Philosophy,* 125–66.

their relevance. Instead, the age's paramount question was "what is the real nature of Christianity; what are its essential characteristics?"[35] Smith found the answer in Germany's Christocentric theology. The incarnation because it united God and man, divinity and humanity, answered the fundamental queries of theology and philosophy. It also satisfied rational and emotional needs because Christ was central in Scripture and in Christian experience. In sum, Germany's mediating theology reconciled philosophy with theology and the head with the heart. Moreover, it corrected the subjective tendencies of Bushnell's thought by supplying Christian experience with an objective knowledge of Christ.[36] By orthodox standards, Smith's address was a well-conceived synthesis of German thought and Christian theology. It rescued Christianity from the perils of mysticism by emphasising the rational components of faith. But Smith also showed his moderation by expressing appreciation for Schleiermacher. Even though he criticized Schleiermacher's extreme positions, he praised the German theologian for stressing that Christ is the foundation for theology. Smith suffered no adverse criticism in the religious press and in fact was offered a teaching post at New York's Union Theological Seminary because of his well-argued ideas.[37]

However, the leading doctor of New England divinity, Edwards A. Park, was not satisfied by Smith's reconciliation of faith and reason, perhaps because it rested on a German solution for New England's problems. Park revelled in the New England theological tradition. His Christian name reflected his parents' hopes for him. At the age of ten he possessed "a great reverence for Dr. Emmons and Dr. Hopkins," two prominent disciples of Jonathan Edwards.[38] Park produced two full-scale memoirs of these men and would become one of the century's most prolific and authoritative historians of the New England theology.[39] Ac-

35. "Relations of Faith and Philosophy," 33.

36. Ibid., 35–37. For Smith's orthodox concerns, see William S. Karr, ed., *Introduction to Christian Theology* (New York, 1883).

37. George M. Marsden, *The Evangelical Mind and the New School Presbyterian Experience* (New Haven, Conn., 1970), 162–63.

38. Anthony C. Cecil, Jr., *The Theological Development of Edwards Amasa Park: Last of the "Consistent Calvinists"* (Missoula, 1974), 3. Samuel Hopkins (1721–1803), who studied with Jonathan Edwards, and Nathaniel Emmons (1745–1827), who studied with Hopkins, were both New England pastors and trained many other ministers in the "Edwardsian" tradition. Both claimed to be the direct theological heirs of Edwards, but both made Arminian concessions regarding the extent of human ability. For different perspectives on Edwards's followers, see Joseph Haroutunian, *Piety versus Moralism: The Passing of the New England Theology* (New York, 1932); and Frank Hugh Foster, *A Genetic History of the New England Theology* (Chicago, 1907).

39. *Memoir of Nathaniel Emmons, with Sketches of His Friends and Pupils* (Boston, 1861); "Memoir of the Life and Character of Samuel Hopkins," in *The Works of Samuel*

cording to Park, New England theology was largely a footnote to Edwards's Calvinism, providing only minor improvements on the nature of original sin and free will.[40] In fact, however, New England theology after Edwards had never been as monolithic or as Calvinist as Park imagined it. After graduating from Brown, his own studies with Leonard Woods at Andover and Nathaniel W. Taylor at Yale nurtured ideas that were antithetical to those of Edwards. Park's deference to Hopkins and Emmons allowed him to retain the Calvinist notion of the sovereignty of grace, yet he was content to term his departure from Edwards "Consistent Calvinism."[41]

Like Smith, Park also studied in Germany with Tholuck, but his studies there only confirmed his historical interests.[42] The organic Christianity of German theology seemed to offer few insights into the problems of divine sovereignty and human responsibility in New England. Contrary to Smith's observation that these problems were no longer relevant, Park was convinced that New England's ecclesiastical divisions could be rectified on Yankee terms. In a sermon entitled "The Theology of the Intellect and That of the Feelings," delivered before the convention of Congregational ministers of Massachusetts on 30 May 1850, Park offered a way of reconciling New England's competing systems of divinity. In Park's scheme, the theology of the intellect is a product of the mind's reasoning faculties; it is concerned with propositional and literal truth. In contrast, the theology of the feelings is produced by the emotions and expresses itself in figurative expressions and tangible images. Park made this distinction in order to achieve a higher synthesis. Both theologies express the same truths, one in a rational form and the other in aesthetic terms. According to this view, New England's controversies were actually caused by taking figurative statements literally or vice versa. Park reasoned that unity might prevail once theologians recognized that they were essentially arguing the same points in different terms.[43]

The problem for Park was how to decide which systems of theology belonged to the intellect and which to the feelings. More often than not,

---

Hopkins, D.D. (Boston, 1852). Park also contributed countless entries to the *Schaff-Herzog Encyclopedia of Religious Knowledge*. For a complete list of his historical works, see Cecil, *Theological Development*, 297–303.

40. "New England Theology," *Bibliotheca Sacra* (hereinafter cited as *BS*) 9 (1852): 173–80.

41. Although Hopkins and Emmons modified Edwards's view of the nature of the will, their position was still far more Calvinist than that of Nathaniel W. Taylor's New Divinity, Haroutunian, *Piety versus Moralism*, 254.

42. Cecil, *op. cit.*, 75–77.

43. E. A. Park, "The Theology of the Intellect and That of the Feelings," *BS* 7 (1850): 534–40.

he placed the harsher doctrines of Calvinism in the category of figurative expression, while arguing that "Consistent Calvinism" was literally true.[44] To a great extent, Park had appropriated Bushnell's insights. He, too, considered theological sophistication detrimental to piety. He had been professor of rhetoric at Andover and gave his full approval to revival preaching, recognizing that sermons filled with doctrine rarely moved lost souls. But he thought Bushnell had gone too far. As both professor of theology and historian of New England divinity, Park knew the importance of sound doctrine. He maintained that in the experience of faith, feelings always followed the common sense of the intellect. Since only a theology that persuaded the head could reach the heart, New England needed a theology that was reasonable. "Consistent Calvinism" was the solution. It accommodated the ethical and moral systems of the day, and it harmonized God's sovereignty with human responsibility. Park also believed that this system, even though a theology of the intellect, could appeal also to the heart.[45] There was, however, an ambiguity in Park's sermon. He relied on Bushnell's religious epistemology only to soften the harsher side of orthodoxy but did not accept the priority of the feelings in faith. As Bushnell would later complain, Park had missed the argument of "Dogma and Spirit." Bushnell believed that to accept the theology of the feelings, Park would have to reject the literal meaning of all doctrinal statements, even his "Consistent Calvinism."[46]

In reaction to Park's sermon, Charles Hodge, the Old School Presbyterian divine, thrust himself into the debate. His role throughout was that of naysayer. Most commonly known to historians for his curmudgeonly resistance to Transcendentalism and Darwinism, Hodge provided an aphoristic expression of his conservatism when he said "a new idea never originated at Princeton Seminary."[47] Connotations of this remark not-

44. Park took exception to the Calvinist doctrines of original sin, the immediate imputation of Adam's sin and the substitutionary atonement and called them expressions of the feelings, while New Divinity distinctions—such as all sin consists in sinning; the power to the contrary is essential to free agency; and ability limits responsibility—he attributed to the intellect, ibid., 535–38. For the evolution of these doctrines in New England, see H. Shelton Smith, *Changing Conception of Original Sin: A Study in American Theology Since 1750* (New York, 1953).

45. Park, "Theology of the Intellect," 540–48.

46. H. Bushnell, "Our Gospel a Gift to the Imagination," *Hours at Home* 10 (1869): 164.

47. Quotation from Archibald Alexander Hodge, *Life of Charles Hodge* (New York, 1880), 521. Hodge's views on Transcendentalism, "The Latest Form of Infidelity," are included in Perry Miller's *The Transcendentalists: An Anthology* (Cambridge, 1950), 233–34. For the complete text see C. Hodge's *Essays and Reviews* (New York, 1856), 87–128. His *What Is Darwinism?* (New York, 1874), has been regarded as a proto-fundamentalist reaction to evolution by Theodore Dwight Bozeman, *Protestants in an Age of Science: The*

withstanding, Hodge's defence of Old School positions was usually perceptive and well informed.[48]

Hodge was born and reared in Philadelphia where his family attended Ashbel Green's Second Presbyterian Church. Green, one of the founders of Princeton Seminary, influenced Hodge to attend the College of New Jersey and then Princeton Seminary where Archibald Alexander, Princeton's first professor of theology, became the young man's mentor. After Hodge's graduation in 1822, Alexander secured for him a post as professor of biblical languages, and, except for a two-year leave of absence to study in Germany, Hodge taught at Princeton until his death. The seminary adhered strictly to the Westminster Confession of Faith, allowing little room for creative thought. The best ideas that a Princeton theologian could generate were those that defended the tenets of Calvinism. In this tradition, Hodge established himself and the seminary as nineteenth-century America's foremost apologists for Calvinism.

Hodge was severely critical of Park's departure from Edwards's Calvinism, and his remarks prompted a war of words that lasted for two years.[49] What concerned Hodge more than Park's teaching was the Andover theologian's use of a German epistemology. From Hodge's perspective, Park's method for reconciling contradictory theologies resembled Schleiermacher's efforts to ground Christianity in religious feelings.[50] Park denied Hodge's charge and with seemingly good justification, since he still affirmed the literal meaning of Andover theology.

Baconian Ideal and Antebellum American Religious Thought (Chapel Hill, N.C., 1977), 174ff. For a different assessment, see James R. Moore, *The Post-Darwinian Controversies: A Study of the Protestant Struggle to Come to Terms with Darwin in Great Britain and America, 1870–1900* (Cambridge, 1979), 204.

48. Ahlstrom, "Theology in America," 266.

49. The controversy ran as follows: (1) Park, "The Theology of the Intellect and That of the Feelings," *BS* 7 (1850): 533–69; (2) Hodge, "The Theology of the Intellect and That of the Feelings," *Biblical Repertory and Princeton Review* (hereinafter cited as *BRPR*) 22 (1850): 642–74; (3) Park, "Remarks on the Princeton Review," *BS* 8 (1851): 135–80; (4) Hodge, "Prof. Park's Remarks on the Princeton Review," *BRPR* 23 (1851): 306–47; (5) Park, "Unity and Diversities of Belief even on Imputed and Involuntary Sin; with Comments on a Second Article in the Princeton Review," *BS* 8 (1851): 594–97; (6) Hodge, "Prof. Park and the Princeton Review," *BRPR* 23 (1851): 674–95; (7) Park, "New England Theology," *BS* 9 (1852): 170–220.

This long-winded debate merged into one that had never been resolved in the 1830s on the nature of original sin, the imputation of Adam's sin, and free will. For a brief summary of that controversy, see Raleigh Don Scovel, *Orthodoxy in Princeton: A Social and Intellectual History of Princeton Theological Seminary, 1812–1860* (Ann Arbor, 1971), 182–215.

50. C. Hodge, "The Theology of the Intellect and That of the Feelings, Article I," *Essays and Reviews*, 540–43.

But Hodge perceptively noted the inconsistency of Park's sermon. The German ideas implicit in that sermon were rooted in its appropriation of Bushnell, but they were not necessarily derivative because the common sense philosophical tradition on which Park was reared contained elements of the romantic sensibility. As others have argued with regard to Transcendentalism, it required little effort to harmonize the Scottish intuitive epistemology with that of Coleridge or Cousin.[51] Park's sermon may provide further evidence of the role that Scottish philosophy played in the transition from the Enlightenment to Romanticism in America.

Hodge objected to German thought on almost every level, although he recognized the superiority of Germany's historical scholarship. What was particularly reprehensible about German philosophy was its implicit pantheism. It merged God in the universe, the infinite in the finite, or the absolute in human history. For Hodge the consequences of this idealism when applied to Christianity were devastating. It denied the personality and real existence of God, history and creation were stripped of their God-given meaning and man and the universe were elevated to the status of constituting the consciousness of God. Furthermore, such basic distinctions as those between God and man, sin and holiness and salvation and damnation were virtually denied. Hodge believed that any theology that tried to accommodate German idealism would be entirely different from the faith once delivered to the saints. Even though he appreciated Schleiermacher's pietism and stress on Christ, the "mediating theology's" organic Christianity was quite different from Hodge's judicial version. Hodge's orthodoxy relied on precise notions about legal imputation and justification by faith. He feared that these ideas would become irrelevant in a system that made the incarnation merely a union of divinity with "generic humanity" and spoke of salvation in corporate and organic, rather than individual and legal, terms.[52]

Hodge was most concerned, however, with Schleiermacher's attempt to base faith on right feeling, and this is where he thought Bushnell and Park were furthest from the straight and narrow. Although Hodge labeled both Park and Bushnell's theology "Arminian," he went beyond doctrinal specification to what he regarded as the root of the problem. He found their celebration of the feelings to be the "creedal chemistry" behind their departure from Calvinism. If Christianity were merely a "life in the soul" then "all creeds are ultimately alike" as the expressions of that life, and

51. See Merrell R. Davis, "Emerson's 'Reason' and the Scottish Philosophers," *New England Quarterly* 17 (1944): 209–28; and Edgelley Woodman Todd, "Philosophical Ideas at Harvard College, 1817–37," *New England Quarterly* 16 (1943): 63–90.

52. See "The Latest Form of Infidelity"; "What Is Christianity?" *BRPR* 32 (1860): 118–61; and "The Princeton Review and Cousin's Philosophy," *BRPR* 28 (1856): 331–87.

Scripture and doctrine are no more than "a poem or picture." So Hodge argued for the orthodox understanding of religious knowledge. It is a unified experience, involving both the affections and the intellect. It is, then, not only an intuition or a feeling of trust but also a rational assent to the objective truths taught in Scripture. At times Hodge equivocated on the priority of the feelings or the intellect, but he always insisted that faith involved human reason.[53] By emphasizing the rational nature of faith Hodge's concerns in this debate were made similar to those of Smith. All of the participants assumed that an individual's salvation depended on a change of heart rather than on an ability to memorize creeds. But doctrine was still important because salvation also depended on historical facts revealed in Scripture: it was the theologian's task to make dogma the "scientific" exposition of the data. Both Hodge and Smith believed that Bushnell's ideas and Park's use of them threatened the scientific nature of theology and the rational foundations of faith.[54]

In the religious press most conservative observers regarded Bushnell and Park as providing striking evidence of New England's faltering orthodoxy. In New England, conservative Congregationalists singled out Park for most of their criticism. Andover was the main source for Congregational pulpits, and Park's Arminianism threatened to poison the supply. Bushnell's address also provoked some testy reviews. But in both cases the critics reacted to Bushnell's and Park's unorthodox positions rather than responding to their underlying notions about religious knowledge.[55] David A. Wallace was representative of this line of attack when he reminded the church of its duty to "maintain and propagate" the gospel of the Puritans and "to regard as traitors" those who abandon the truth.[56] Outside New England, critics used the Bushnell and Park affair to boost their respective denominations at the expense of Congregationalism. A Southern Presbyterian writer suggested that the moral taught by the New England tale was that "polity of the Presbyterian church is wiser, safer, and better adapted to guard and maintain truth and Godliness" than that of the Congregationalists.[57] Anglicans also took heart

53. For a good summary of this tension in Princeton theology, see W. Andrew Hoffecker, *Piety and the Princeton Theologians* (Phillipsburg, 1981).

54. Hodge, "Bushnell's Discourses," *BRPR* 21 (1849): 295–96; Smith, "The Relations of Faith and Philosophy," 42–43.

55. See David N. Lord, "Review of Prof. Park's Theologies of the Intellect and of the Feelings," *Theological and Literary Journal* 3 (1850): 177–234; David A. Wallace, *The Theology of New England* (intro. Daniel Dana) (Boston, 1856); Enoch Pond, *Review of Dr. Bushnell's "God in Christ"* (Bangor, 1849); and Chauncey A. Goodrich, *What Does Dr. Bushnell Mean?* (Hartford, 1849).

56. Wallace, *Theology of New England,* 56.

57. "Orthodoxy in New England," *Southern Presbyterian Review* 7 (1853): 58.

from this episode for, as one Episcopalian wrote, apostolic succession was essential to ensure ecclesiastical purity.[58]

Perhaps the most unbiased and astute account of the affair came from the Unitarian George E. Ellis. According to Ellis, the "New Theology" of Bushnell and Park was really a ploy that retained the form of orthodoxy while rejecting its Calvinist meaning in order to gain a wider hearing for Christianity. Ellis admired the efforts of Bushnell and Park and admitted that Unitarianism could well benefit from such earnest Christians. But in the end, Ellis agreed with Hodge and confessed that the "rebellion" of the New Theology carried it "far beyond the lawful limit of explanation," and made it "treacherous to the creed with whose fair, honest, well understood teachings orthodoxy stands or falls."[59] Ellis's comments were almost as prophetic as they were perceptive for, as the nineteenth century progressed, American Protestants would divide into camps much like those sketched in the Unitarian's observations. Through students attending Andover, Union, and Princeton seminaries, the positions of Hodge, Bushnell, Smith, and Park were transmitted to the Reformed denominations. Eventually, as liberals and conservatives formed more self-conscious groups, arguments began to be heard that sounded much like those articulated during the decade before the Civil War.

The contributions of Hodge and Bushnell were the most influential, perhaps because their arguments made it easier to avoid ambiguity and contradiction. The influence of Hodge is understandable since by 1912 Princeton Seminary had trained over one thousand more students than any other seminary, and Hodge himself had taught over two thousand students during his fifty years in the classroom.[60] What is surprising is the influence of Bushnell without an institutional base like that of Hodge. But Andover Seminary was eventually to serve as the platform for Bushnell's ideas. Andover liberals, who looked to Bushnell as their seminal and inspiring leader, transformed the school into one of the most important sources of Protestant liberalism in America.[61] Bushnell's religious epistemology proved to be a resilient one that could weather the storms of Darwinism and biblical criticism. But the priority of religious experience was not meant to be merely a method of defense. It also had the potential to

58. "New England Theology," *Church Review and Ecclesiastical Register* 9 (1852): 357.

59. Ellis, "The New Theology," 336–37.

60. Mark A. Noll, ed., *The Princeton Theology, Scripture, Science, and Theological Method from Archibald Alexander to Benjamin Warfield, 1812–1921* (Grand Rapids, 1983), 19.

61. See Hutchison, *The Modernist Impulse,* 43, 77–80; Kuklick, *Churchmen and Philosophers,* 216–21; and Daniel Day Williams, *The Andover Liberals: A Study in American Theology* (New York, 1941).

accommodate scientific discoveries so that there would be consistency between Christianity and "all other truth." Consequently Bushnell maintained that Christianity "must open its bosom . . . and gather to its poles all particles of knowledge and science as the loadstone gathers the particles of iron."[62] Bushnell's theory of religious knowledge was crucial for adapting religion to culture, a significant trait of liberal theology.[63]

The younger generation of liberals acknowledged readily the groundwork laid by Bushnell. Theodore Munger spoke for most when he wrote: "It is no exaggeration to say that had it not been for the relief [Bushnell] brought to them on theological questions, many of the ablest young men in Congregational pulpits could not or would not have remained in them."[64] But perhaps the greatest tribute to Bushnell was the extensive use of his ideas by the next generation. To take but one example, William Newton Clarke's *An Outline of Christian Theology,* one of the first widely used American texts in liberal theology, relied heavily on Bushnell's insights. Rather than starting with Scripture as the basis for theology, Clarke took "the religious sentiment" as his point of reference. He then echoed Bushnell by asserting that all faiths or theologies are merely the expressions of religious feeling, differing in form rather than substance, for "any given theology must be at best a partial presentation of truth."[65] By conceding that other religions besides Christianity contained elements of religious truth, Clarke had certainly gone beyond Bushnell's liberal evangelicalism. But the continuities between Clarke and Bushnell are still unmistakable.

Hodge resisted resolutely the subjective tendencies of Bushnell and clung to orthodox notions about the objectivity of faith. For him, real faith could not be separated from correct doctrine, and the task that he set for Princeton theology was to demonstrate that Christianity was a "proposition" and not just a "life," or, in Bushnell's terms, that it was "dogma" and not just "spirit."[66] Princeton theologians built upon Hodge in two ways. First, they defended the propositional nature of Scripture. Biblical scholars like Benjamin B. Warfield and William Henry Green defended the Calvinist interpretations in the light of contemporary criticism.[67] Secondly, Princeton theologians argued for the primacy of doctrine itself. During the modernist-fundamentalist controversy, J. Gresham Machen summed up this line of argument in *Christianity and*

62. Bushnell, "Dogma and Spirit," 76–77.
63. Hutchison, *op. cit.,* 101–5.
64. Munger, *Horace Bushnell,* 372.
65. W. C. Clark, *An Outline of Christian Theology* (New York, 1898), 4.
66. Hodge, "What Is Christianity?" 161.
67. B. B. Warfield, *The Inspiration and Authority of the Bible* (Phillipsburg, 1948); W. H. Green, *The Higher Criticism of the Pentateuch* (New York, 1902).

Liberalism, where he insisted upon a clear choice between orthodox Christianity and an entirely different religion.[68]

Owing either to inconsistency or incomprehensibility, Smith and Park left ambiguous legacies. Park almost immediately recanted the liberal implications of his concessions to Bushnell. In 1866, at a National Council of the Congregational Church, Park fought to retain Calvinism as the official designation of that denomination. In the 1870s, Park became embroiled in a bitter controversy at Andover. He opposed the appointment to the faculty of several liberals. When he finally won his point, two of the contested professors resigned rather than subscribe to the school's conservative creed. Park, however, lost the struggle to appoint a conservative successor when he retired in 1881. He looked on with disappointment as Andover assumed a position of leadership of liberalism in New England. Sadly, he was unable to complete his biography of Edwards before his death, but passed into history as the last of the Edwardsians.[69]

A few years after Park's death, George A. Gordon, a liberal Congregational pastor in Boston, recalled the importance of Park's convention sermon of 1850. Gordon mused that if only Park had allowed that discourse's principles to control all of his thought, he would have "stood for the dawn of a new day in America."[70] A more recent historian of Andover liberalism also regarded Park's sermon as a forerunner of the theology that later characterized the school.[71] Park's subsequent career indicates that he would have rejected these interpretations, but the tensions in his thought stand out clearly. Why Park shied away from the implications of his sermon or why he did not see them before delivering it is difficult to say. Whatever the reason, these inconsistencies prevented him from harmonizing piety and learning in a way that would satisfy either liberals or conservatives of the next generation.

The influence of Smith's thought is also difficult to determine. Isaak A. Dorner, a German theologian who influenced many American liberals, considered Smith the greatest theologian of his day.[72] American historian George Bancroft, who was among the first Americans to study in Germany, thought that Smith was the one most qualified to write the history of America's religious and philosophical ideas.[73] No doubt Smith's reliance on German theological and historical methods earned him such high praise. And his cordial use of German thought in his lectures at Union

68. J. Gresham Machen, *Christianity and Liberalism* (New York, 1924).
69. Cecil, *Edwards Amasa Park,* 155–205.
70. "The Achilles in Our Camp: An Acute and Inspiring Characterization of the Late Dr. Edwards A. Park," *The Congregationalist* 88 (1903): 840.
71. Williams, *The Andover Liberals* (New York, 1941), 19–21.
72. Stoever, "Henry Boynton Smith," 86.
73. Ibid.

Seminary must have been a factor in that institution's eventual shift to liberalism. After Smith's death in 1877, Union became a home for higher criticism and was forced to break its official Presbyterian ties early in the twentieth century.[74] Yet Smith's theology was sufficiently orthodox to pass Hodge's scrutiny and to facilitate the reunion of the Old and New School branches in 1869. Moreover, Smith's conservative views on Scripture required his sympathetic, though liberal biographer, to apologize for his rigidness.[75] Overall, Smith was both more orthodox and more indebted to German thought than Park. Perhaps his synthesis of faith and reason could have been a refuge for younger conservatives when German ideas pervaded the mainline denominational seminaries in the late nineteenth century. Smith's fate, however, was similar to Park's; his thought remained enigmatic to his followers.

As the repercussions of this debate show, the German ideas that many had hoped would harmonize competing theologies and end religious controversy actually left American Protestantism completely divided. After the Civil War, Bushnell's romantic Christianity made it possible to be both religious and well informed, while Hodge's orthodoxy maintained the distinctions of Calvinism no matter what the latest discovery. In the wake of Darwinism and biblical criticism, which polarized the religious community, the extreme positions of Hodge and Bushnell appeared to be the only viable alternatives while the mediating positions of Smith and Park passed into oblivion. Consequently, the debate signaled a major realignment within American Protestantism. Increasingly, Protestants were forced to choose between Christian experience and traditional theology as the ground for Christian unity, and attitudes about the priority of dogma or spirit usually influenced that decision.[76]

74. Lefferts A. Loetscher, *The Broadening Church: A Study of the Theological Issues in the Presbyterian Church since 1869* (Philadelphia, 1957), 97.

75. Lewis F. Stearns, *Henry Boynton Smith* (Boston, 1892), 198–99.

76. See Hutchison, *The Modernist Impulse;* and George M. Marsden, *Fundamentalism and American Culture: The Shaping of Twentieth-Century Evangelicalism: 1870–1925* (New York, 1980).

9

The Contested Legacy of Jonathan Edwards in Antebellum Calvinism

Mark A. Noll

Reprinted by permission from *Canadian Review of American Studies* 19 (1988): 149–64.

For some time, historians of American culture have realized that there are at least two stories for intellectual life in the antebellum period. One is the "American Renaissance" of Emerson, Thoreau, Margaret Fuller, the Transcendentalists, Hawthorne, Melville, and Whitman, a story of marginal national consequence before the Civil War, but of great significance for twentieth-century commentary.[1] More recently, historians with a feel for the intellectual terrain south of Boston and west of the Hudson have been telling a second story, in which religion is far more central. The study of post-Revolutionary, precritical theologians is still in its early stages, but it has advanced far enough to reveal an interesting account.[2] A few of these largely neglected ministers and professors were

1. For a succinct description of how limited the popular appeal of these writers was in the 1850s, see F. O. Matthiessen, *American Renaissance: Art and Expression in the Age of Emerson and Whitman* (New York, 1941), x–xi.

2. See especially George M. Marsden, *The Evangelical Mind and the New School Presbyterian Experience* (New Haven, Conn., 1970); T. D. Bozeman, *Protestants in an Age of Science: The Baconian Ideal and American Religious Thought* (Chapel Hill, N.C., 1977); E. Brooks Holifield, *The Gentlemen Theologians: American Theology in Southern Culture*

men of unusual critical acumen. Many more were consequential, if not exactly brilliant, casuists, less ignorant about European matters and less naïve about their own intellectual activity than once was thought by the likes of Oliver Wendell Holmes or Vernon Louis Parrington.

Study of these antebellum figures also brings into sharper focus the significance of Jonathan Edwards, America's most important pre-Revolutionary thinker, for his ghost was a full participant in some of the most interesting antebellum intellectual controversies.[3] Theologians who battled over conflicting conceptions of the self and its powers, over divergent applications of science, over contrasting pictures of true religion, true virtue and the meaning of human nature, regularly went out of their way to enlist Edwards as an ally. Or if they felt that Edwards was aligned with the wrong side in their battles, he often loomed so large that it was necessary to silence him before turning to the errors of contemporaries. And so it was that in the decades between the Revolution and the Civil War, Edwards was called upon to both justify and denounce the revivalistic "new measures" associated with Charles Finney;[4] his treatises on original sin and true virtue were upbraided by Presbyterians as the source of doctrinal heresy and ethical folly;[5] and he was repeatedly, if usually respectfully, castigated for his fearsome teaching on the will.[6]

The longest-lived and most consequential controversy over Edwards took place between the Old School Presbyterians and the New England Congregationalists who during the middle third of the nineteenth century were locked in a great struggle over the destiny of Calvinism. This debate involved the three leading graduate schools in the country—Andover, Yale, and Princeton[7]—and many of the nation's finest intellects, includ-

---

1795–1860 (Durham, 1978); Fred J. Hood, *Reformed America: The Middle and Southern States, 1783–1837* (University, Ala., 1980); and Bruce Kuklick, *Churchmen and Philosophers from Jonathan Edwards to John Dewey* (New Haven, Conn., 1985).

3. Discussion of Edwards's place in antebellum thought is greatly assisted by M. X. Lesser, *Jonathan Edwards: A Reference Guide* (Boston, 1981).

4. For example, Charles G. Finney, *Lectures on Revivals of Religion,* 2d ed. (New York, 1835), 241–42; versus Albert Dod, "Finney's Lectures," *Princeton Review* 7 (1835): 656–58.

5. For example, Samuel Baird, "Edwards and the Theology of New England," *Southern Presbyterian Review* 10 (1858): 581–90; and Baird, *The First Adam and the Second: The Elohim Revealed in the Creation and Redemption of Man* (Philadelphia, 1860), 161.

6. Among the best of the many refutations were Henry Philip Tappan, *A Review of Edwards's "Inquiry into the Freedom of the Will"* (New York, 1839); and Asa Mahan, *Doctrine of the Will* (New York, 1845).

7. In 1840, Andover had 153 students and 5 faculty, Yale 72 students and 4 faculty, Princeton 110 students and 4 faculty. The only other graduate schools of comparable size were the New School Presbyterian Seminary in New York City (90 students, 5 faculty) and the General Theological Seminary of the Episcopal Church, also in New York (74 stu-

ing Nathaniel William Taylor and Noah Porter at Yale, Edwards Amasa Park at Andover, and Princeton's Archibald Alexander and Charles Hodge.[8] In retrospect, the great controversy over who should be allowed to speak for Calvinism was an ironic one. While the leading lights of the Presbyterians and Congregationalists did battle with each other, Methodists, Baptists, and Catholics, who had little interest in the rarified subjects of this debate, were surpassing the older churches as the most numerous denominations in the country. By 1850 there were even more congregations of Disciples than of the ancient Congregationalists.[9] An even more important incongruity concerned the intellectual character of the discussion. At the same time that the Atlantic community had begun to contend with Kant, the idealism of Hegel, the historicism of Lessing, and a developmentalism soon to receive its champion in Darwin, the most prominent American theologians still pursued a debate whose terms had been set in the previous century by the epistemology of Hume, the psychology of Locke, the mechanics of Newton, and the ethics of Hutcheson.

Still, the Calvinistic theologians at Andover, Princeton, and Yale were neither anachronistic nor inconsiderable. Their debate represented the most comprehensive American discussion at mid-century of the great questions concerning God and the fate of civilization. The disputants were the self-conscious heirs of an imposing history: the honored traditions of Calvin, the weighty legacy of Puritanism, the domesticated Enlightenment of Scotland, and the visionary promise of the American Revolution. The thrust and parry of their exchange took place in the most consequential journals in the land.[10] And because they felt that Jonathan

---

dents, 5 faculty); figures from Robert Baird, *Religion in the United States of America* (New York, 1969; orig. 1844), 368–69. As a comparison, the Harvard Law School enjoyed a boom attendance of 140 students in 1845, but throughout the 1830s and 1840s attendance between 40 and 90 was more typical; Arthur E. Sutherland, *The Law at Harvard* (Cambridge, 1967), 100, 123.

8. Biographical information on the theologians may be found in Sidney Earl Mead, *Nathaniel William Taylor 1786–1858: A Connecticut Liberal* (Chicago, 1942); for Porter, Louise L. Stevenson, *Scholarly Means to Evangelical Ends: The New Haven Scholars and the Transformation of Higher Learning in America, 1830–1890* (Baltimore, 1986); Anthony C. Cecil, Jr., *The Theological Development of Edwards Amasa Park: Last of the "Consistent Calvinists"* (Missoula, Mont., 1974); Lefferts A. Loetscher, *Facing the Enlightenment and Pietism: Archibald Alexander and the Founding of Princeton Theological Seminary* (Westport, Conn., 1983); and Archibald Alexander Hodge, *The Life of Charles Hodge* (New York, 1881).

9. Timothy L. Smith, *Revivalism and Social Reform: American Protestantism on the Eve of the Civil War* (Nashville, 1957), 20–21; and E. S. Gaustad, *Historical Atlas of Religion in America,* rev. ed. (New York, 1976), 166–67.

10. Although this point is not made explicitly, it is an important conclusion from Frank Luther Mott, *A History of American Magazines: Volume 1: 1741–1850* and *Volume 2: 1850–1865* (Cambridge, 1930, 1938).

Edwards had played a determinative role in defining Calvinism, the Enlightenment, and the American character, the contention for his mantle was a significant part of their more general controversy.

The battle between New England and Princeton over Jonathan Edwards naturally involved complex theological issues worthy of extensive analysis in their own right. On such a level the central question concerns the ownership of Edwards: who succeeded in establishing a better claim to his convictions? At the same time, however, the clash between New England and Princeton illuminates broader matters involving the general history of thought in America. This chapter focuses on the points of substantive theological disagreement only briefly, in order to direct more attention at the general picture, for that broader view reveals how very much the antebellum combatants shared with each other, especially as proponents of common sense philosophy, and how that shared perspective set all of them apart from Edwards.

By mid-century, the more conservative Presbyterians and the mainstream New England Congregationalists had clearly diverged. No longer did they look like merely the Northern and mid-state variations of ancestral British Calvinism.[11] The Plan of Union of 1801, which had joined the two bodies for the Christianizing of the frontier, came unglued in 1837. In New England, the major theological challenge throughout the first half of the century was the religious innovations of Unitarians and then Transcendentalists. In the middle states and the South, Presbyterians were challenged as much by the absence of religion as by religious heterodoxy. In New England, Christianity seemed imperilled by the allure of sophistication; in Presbyterian regions, the greatest apparent danger was the disorder of the frontier. Congregationalists fretted over the intellectual leadership of Boston, Presbyterians over the perils of fanaticism. The institutions of New England Congregationalism, Andover and Yale, existed to defend the Christian faith against Unitarianism and to promote revival and reform. The institutions of the Presbyterians, Princeton Seminary and the College of New Jersey, existed to expound a creedal Calvinism and to promote a well-ordered piety. As the century wore on, it became clearer that a widening gap separated the earlier theological allies into a self-consciously orthodox party of Old School Presbyterians who brooked no innovations, over against several varieties of New England Congregationalists who were modifying the old faith in order to preserve its vitality in a changing intellectual world. At intermediate points between the two poles were the New School Presbyterians and some of the

11. For the general picture described in this paragraph, see Marsden, *The Evangelical Mind,* 7–87; Hood, *Reformed America,* 178–85; and Sydney E. Ahlstrom, *A Religious History of the American People* (New Haven, Conn., 1972), 456–69.

more conservative Congregationalists. This, in brief, describes the landscape where the battle for Edwards was joined.

Attitudes toward Edwards were well in place before the polemics began. To New England, Jonathan Edwards was a treasured possession. The Congregationalists uniformly held that he had established the course which they followed. Early in this century, Frank Hugh Foster summed up their attitude nicely: "To agree with Edwards was still the high ambition of them all; and when they consciously disagreed, as did [N.W.] Taylor, they thought they were only expressing better Edwards' true meaning."[12]

Old School Presbyterians did not possess this same intimacy with Edwards, although eventually they came to make much of the fact that he had once expressed a preference for presbyterian polity over congregational.[13] While the leaders of the Old School admired Edwards from afar, there was no questioning the depth of that admiration.

Although New England's bond to Edwards was closer than that of Princeton, it was nonetheless the Presbyterians who made the first contentious claims for his legacy. Much more than in New England, where Edwards was regarded as a fount of practical piety or philosophical theology, for the Presbyterians Edwards was an ecclesiastical issue. Their attention to Edwards and claims about his legacy arose with the Presbyterian division into Old and New School denominations in 1837 and did not subside until the reunion in the North of New and Old School in 1868. At issue was the extent to which general theological principles from New England and the specific ideas of Yale's N. W. Taylor had infected Presbyterians. In a word, Princeton abominated Taylor's New Haven theology and any other theology from which they caught the barest whiff of New Haven's errors. From Princeton, it seemed especially galling that misguided New Haven and other New England theologians continued to call themselves the descendents of Edwards who, the Old Schoolers felt, had propounded pretty much the same theology they did. Presbyterian attention to Edwards, therefore, was adventitious from the start. Holding him up as a standard of the old orthodoxy and documenting latter-day deviations from his views, they hoped to scotch the errors of New Englanders by appealing to the supposed font of their theology. Not unexpectedly, a number of able New Englanders objected.

With Edwards as ammunition, Princeton sniped away steadily at New England from the eve of the Presbyterian schism in 1837 throughout the

12. Frank Hugh Foster, *A Genetic History of the New England Theology* (Chicago, 1907), 369.

13. Samuel Miller, *The Life of Jonathan Edwards*, in *The Library of American Biography*, ed. Jared Sparks, *Volume 3: Lives of Jonathan Edwards and David Brainerd* (New York, 1849; orig. 1837), 118–19.

next decade. Then the battle raged from both sides for nearly twenty years, with ten blasts from Princeton and eleven from New England in the years 1851–1868. Most of the essays, books, and reviews in this battle did not deal with Edwards exclusively, but he was a part, sometimes extensive, of each one. After 1868 and the reunion of New and Old School Presbyterian bodies, the belligerence tailed off, but sporadic firing continued until the last full volley came from the pen of Princeton's B. B. Warfield in 1912.[14]

A struggle of such dimensions is capable of many interpretations. But without extensive exposition or nuance, here are the main theological results.

On the question of the freedom of the will, Princeton had no trouble demolishing the New England assertion that N. W. Taylor's formula of "power to the contrary" and its variations were consistent with the spirit and the letter of Edwards's great treatise on the subject.[15]

The Old School could also show, a trifle less conclusively, that it was largely a mistake to contend, as E. A. Park did at great length, that Edwards supported a governmental or moral influence view of the atonement (whereby Christ's death acted as an example to follow rather than as an actual vicarious reception of God's wrath).[16]

On the twin questions of Adam's connection to all humanity and the imputation of Adam's sin to later generations, however, the struggle was inconclusive. Try as they could, Princeton theologians could not twist Edwards into supporting their view of immediate imputation (the notion

14. Many of the essays from 1851–1868 are cited below. After 1868 the major statements were E. A. Park, "Jonathan Edwards," in *Cyclopedia of Biblical, Theological, and Ecclesiastical Literature,* eds. John McClintock and James Strong (New York, 1870), 3:63–67; L. H. Atwater, "The Great Awakening of 1740," *Presbyterian Quarterly and Princeton Review* 5 (1876): 676–89; G. P. Fisher, "The Philosophy of Jonathan Edwards," *North American Review* 128 (1879): 284–303; and B. B. Warfield, "Edwards and the New England Theology," in *Encyclopedia of Religion and Ethics,* ed. James Hastings (New York, 1912), 5:221–27.

15. Princeton claims to Edwards on the matter of the will were well secured by L. H. Atwater in four essays in the *Princeton Review,* "The Power of Contrary Choice," 12 (1840), 532–49, "Dr. Edwards's Works," 15 (1843), 57, 64; "Modern Explanations of the Doctrine of Inability," 26 (1854), 236–46; and "Whedon and Hazard on the Will," 36 (1864), 679–703. The weak case from New England is found in Edward Beecher, "The Works of Samuel Hopkins," *Bibliotheca Sacra* 10 (1853): 76–80; and E. A. Park, "New England Theology," *Bibliotheca Sacra* 9 (1852): 170–220.

16. Park advanced his claim that Edwards anticipated later New England beliefs in a lengthy introduction to his collection of New England writings on *The Atonement: Discourses and Treatises*, 3d ed. (Boston, 1863, orig. 1859), xi–xxxix. On this issue, the definitive Old School response came from a conservative Congregationalist, the Reverend Parsons Cook of Lynn, Massachusetts, "Edwards on the Atonement," *American Theological Review* 11 (1860): 97–120.

that God accounted all people guilty of sin because all were related to Adam by a covenant). New England, on the other hand, could not make him say that sin resided only in the sinning. Neither appreciated Edwards's opinion that all humanity existed in Adam through a kind of seminal Realism.[17]

New Englanders scored points by enlisting Edwards as a proponent of revival. They did not find it difficult to show that when Charles Hodge pictured Edwards as a positive influence, *except* for his support of the Great Awakening, Hodge was cutting the heart out of Edwards's most basic concern.[18]

Finally, New England as thoroughly routed Princeton on the significance of Edwards's *The Nature of True Virtue* as Princeton had routed New England on the will. Edward Beecher and other allies of E. A. Park easily disposed of the Old School assertion that this book and its concerns were unfortunate and irrelevant appendages to Edwards's genuine concerns.[19]

Tallying up the theological scorecard, we have something of a draw on substantive theological questions. Princeton prevailed on the will and the atonement, New England on revival and true virtue, and the two sides battled to a standstill on the imputation of Adam's sin. But to step back from the immediate conflict is to see that its most interesting feature may not be who won or lost in the use of Edwards, but how very different all of the combatants were from the very figure each wanted to enlist as its own.

17. On this issue, see, from Princeton, Miller, *Life of Edwards,* 236–37; L. H. Atwater, "Outlines of Moral Science, By Archibald Alexander," *Princeton Review* 25 (1853): 22; Anonymous, "Short Notices," *Princeton Review* 27 (1855): 702; and Atwater, "Jonathan Edwards and the Successive Forms of the New Divinity," *Princeton Review* 30 (1858): 589. From New England, see Park, *The Atonement.* A good overview of the complicated discussion of the atonement is provided by B. B. Warfield, "Imputation," in *New Schaff-Herzog Encyclopedia of Religious Knowledge* (New York, 1909), 5:465–67.

18. Hodge developed his reservations about Edwards and revival in *The Constitutional History of the Presbyterian Church in the United States of America, Part 2: 1741–1788* (Philadelphia, 1851; orig. 1840), 42–61. He was answered most competently by Edward Beecher, "The Works of Samuel Hopkins," *Bibliotheca Sacra* 10 (1853): 69; and Noah Porter, "The Princeton Review on Dr. Taylor, and the Edwardean Theology," *Bibliotheca Sacra* 18 (1860): 731–32.

19. Princeton misreadings of *The Nature of True Virtue* are found in Miller, *Life of Edwards,* 241–44; Archibald Alexander, *Outlines of Moral Science* (New York, 1852); L. H. Atwater, "Outlines of Moral Science, By Alexander," 19–23; and Charles Hodge, *Systematic Theology* (Grand Rapids, 1979; orig. 1872–73), 1:432–34. Convincing replies came in three articles from *Bibliotheca Sacra*: Edward Beecher, "The Works of Samuel Hopkins," 10 (1853), 77–78; Anonymous, "Dr. Alexander's Moral Science," 10 (1853), 390–414; and Anonymous, "President Edwards's Dissertation on the Nature of True Virtue," 10 (1853), 705–38.

Evidence for such a conclusion is found in the various debates, especially as the warriors commented on themselves in relation to Edwards while quoting him against their foes. As it turns out, these revealing statements also illuminate the basic theological positions since they occurred at critical junctures in the ongoing debate.

The first such statement came as the parting shot in one of the great theological controversies of the nineteenth century, the furious running battle between Park in the pages of Andover's *Bibliotheca Sacra* and Hodge in the pages of the *Princeton Review* over the interpretation of traditional Calvinistic formulas, a debate touched off by Horace Bushnell's "Preliminary Dissertation on Language."[20] Park felt that some traditional Christian doctrines, like the substitutionary atonement of Christ (pictured as the acceptance of God's anger intended for sinful humans), must be understood as metaphorical. Hodge considered such a suggestion anathema. In the penultimate round of this exchange, Hodge closed his polemic by charging Park with promoting an "anti-Augustinian system" directly at odds with Jonathan Edwards, and not only Edwards but also his immediate successors, like Joseph Bellamy and Timothy Dwight.[21]

Park's rejoinder was swift (appearing in January, 1852, as a response to Hodge's essay of October, 1851), lengthy, and contemptuous. Against Hodge, he contended that "the spirit and genius of the system" of theology taught in New England was unified from Edwards to his own day. In a very abridged summary of this long and quotation-packed essay, Park argued that New England from Edwards onward had always believed: (1) that there is, strictly speaking, no sinful nature lying behind individual acts of sin—all sinfulness arises from the acts of evil themselves; (2) that, as a consequence, no guilt or absolutely foreordained certainty of sinning passes down from Adam throughout the whole sinful race—guilt before God is not imputed from Adam but is each one's own responsibility; and (3) that by nature people have the power to do what God's law demands—there is no bondage of the will to the sinful inclinations of a sinful nature.[22]

Toward the end of his essay, Park defined the essence of the New England theology in a way that revealed his own significant differences with Edwards: "This scheme unites a high, but not an ultra Calvinism, on the

20. For a helpful recent overview of the more general situation, including Bushnell, see D. G. Hart, "Divided Between Heart and Mind: The Critical Period for Protestant Thought in America," *Journal of Ecclesiastical History* (1987): 254–70.

21. Hodge, "Professor Park and the Princeton Review," *Princeton Review* 23 (1851), as reprinted in Hodge, *Essays and Reviews* (New York, 1857), 631–32.

22. Park, "New England Theology," *Bibliotheca Sacra* 9 (1852): 170–220.

decrees and agency of God, with a philosophical, but not an Arminian theory, on the freedom and worth of the human soul. Its new element is seen in its harmonizing two great classes of truths; one relating to the untrammelled will of man, another relating to the supremacy of God."[23]

Park's key assertion was his acknowledgement that "a philosophical . . . theory, on the freedom and worth of the human soul" had entered New England thought after Edwards. To be sure, the New England "scheme" was rooted in Edwards. Yet its expression also benefited, as Park put it, from "the philosophy of Reid, Oswald, Campbell, Beattie, Stewart . . . *the philosophy of common sense.*" These Scottish philosophers had been able "to develop 'the fundamental laws of human belief.'" Their contribution "has aided our writers in shaping their faith according to those ethical axioms, which so many fathers in the church have undervalued." The result was that "the metaphysics of New England Theology . . . is the metaphysics of common sense." As a follower of this theology, Park could also take pride in the fact that "the New England system is not only scriptural, but is scriptural *science.*"[24] That is, it not only drew axioms from the moral sense, but also read the Bible with the aid of Baconian insights about the construction of theories. For Park, Edwards was so great that he could not be given up. Yet so powerful was Park's commitment to Scottish moral philosophy that his only course was to read Edwards through the lenses which it provided.

As Park closed his essay, he predicted the long life of the New England theology, rooted sturdily in Edwards and fructified by the improvements of Scottish thought. As Park put it, "the science of the world is in favor of it. The spirit and plain import of the Bible, are in favor of it. The moral instincts of the race are in favor of it."[25] And so he rested his defense.

Park, however, was not the only one putting the Scottish thinkers to use. Their works were also being studied at Princeton. For their part, the Presbyterians drew on the Scots for answers to different questions than those which troubled New Englanders. But the result was to distance them, as it had the Congregationalists, from Edwards.

The posthumous publication in 1852 of Archibald Alexander's *Outlines of Moral Science* was the occasion for a fresh outbreak of contention as well as for a revealing statement of Princeton's basic intellectual position over against Edwards. Alexander had taught ethics to the Princeton seminarians from his appointment as the institution's first professor in 1812 to his death in 1851. As it turns out, his ethics were also strongly indebted to the Scottish philosophy. Alexander held that a universal (or

23. Ibid., 212.
24. Ibid., 191–92, 210.
25. Ibid., 219.

common) moral sense provided a basis for ethical judgment in every creature. From "reason and experience," people discovered what were those "dictates of conscience," or "the law of nature, written on the hearts of all men." These "first principles or intuitive truths in morals" were "as certainly and as universally believed, as any mathematical axioms."[26] Furthermore, these universal intuitions revealed the moral qualities of actions in and of themselves, regardless of consequences. Alexander's convictions on these matters represented an extension of the moral philosophy which John Witherspoon had introduced at Princeton in the 1770s and which William Graham, a Witherspoon student, had passed on to Alexander in the 1780s. With these beliefs, Alexander looked with repugnance upon Edwards's proposals in *The Nature of True Virtue* about love to Being in General, and their expansion into theories of benevolence in the works of Hopkins, Dwight, and Taylor. Alexander interpreted Edwards as directing his primary attention to the happiness of humanity in the universe. He also thought Edwards proposed a thoroughgoing utilitarianism, that is, we should do good because it will increase the amount of moral happiness in the world.

In the exchange that followed the publication of Alexander's *Moral Science,* Lyman Atwater, a native of New Haven who had actually studied with Taylor before taking sides with the Presbyterians and eventually coming to teach at Princeton College, upheld the Old School position. Atwater extended Alexander's criticism of New England ethics, but also attempted to show that Edwards's mistakes in *The Nature of True Virtue* did not justify later New England errors on the will and human nature.[27] Two anonymous articles in *Bibliotheca Sacra,* by contrast, defended Edwards and argued that New England's ethical position originated in *The Nature of True Virtue.*[28] It was a confusing exchange, but certainly one in which the New Englanders triumphed. They showed clearly that Edwards's *True Virtue* was an integral part of his theology, and they were able to point to an antinomy in the Princeton position. How was it that the Old School Presbyterians, who insisted so unbendingly on an original sinfulness that rendered humans morally unwilling to seek salvation, postulated a universal moral sense as the foundation for virtue?[29]

26. Quoted from manuscripts of Alexander's lectures, in Loetscher, *Archibald Alexander,* 184.

27. Atwater, "Outlines of Moral Science, By Archibald Alexander," *Princeton Review* 25 (1853): 1–43.

28. Anonymous, "Dr. Alexander's Moral Science," *Bibliotheca Sacra* 10 (1853): 390–414; and "President Edwards's Dissertation on the Nature of True Virtue," *Bibliotheca Sacra* 10 (1853): 705–38.

29. See especially "President Edwards's Dissertation on the Nature of True Virtue," 728–29.

The Princeton answer to this question was revealing, precisely because it showed how much these Old School theologians, though claiming to present nothing but unvarnished classical Calvinism, were also children of their age. Lyman Atwater regarded Edwards's assertion "that all virtue is reducible to benevolence" as the source of a "disposition to reduce all religion to philanthropy." And that was "a dangerous vice of the times." One danger was directly doctrinal, since this line of thought provided an excuse, dignified by "the great and sacred name of the elder Edwards," for "a denial of the imputation of Adam's sin, and of Christ's righteousness, and to some important innovations upon the received doctrine of the atonement." Atwater held that *True Virtue* lay behind the error of "resolv[ing] all sin into selfishness." The New England extension of Edwards's ideas was also dangerous in practice because it "laid the foundation of virtue in mere utility or tendency to promote happiness."[30] To Atwater, Edwards's ruminations on virtue had led unwittingly to utilitarianism masquerading under the cloak of benevolence.

Atwater may have been partially correct in describing what later New Englanders made of Edwards. But his criticism did not come to grips with the burden of Edwards's work itself. Unlike Alexander, Atwater did recognize that *True Virtue* was thoroughly anti-utilitarian. What he did not see, however, was that Edwards had grounded his reasoning in the supernatural work of God among the elect. For Edwards, true virtue could only exist among the redeemed. To forget this basic fact was to confuse true virtue with its shadowy imitations.[31] For Alexander, Atwater, and Hodge this was the Achilles heel.[32] The Princeton theologians, though fervent Calvinist defenders of God's particular grace among the elect, were—on questions of ethics—philosophers of a universal moral sense. As Alexander put it, "Virtue is a peculiar quality of certain actions of a moral agent, which quality is perceived by the moral faculty with which *every man* is endued."[33] To Atwater, in fine Scottish phrase, "moral rectitude is as much a part of the nature of things, and as much an ultimate good, and a simple uncomprehended idea, as beauty, truth or happiness." Or again, "The power of perceiving what is . . . right or morally good, [God] has implanted in *all moral agents,* by ending them with conscience, or the moral faculty."[34] To Princeton, true virtue was embedded in universal human nature. On this basis, then, Edwards's conception

30. Atwater, "Outlines of Moral Science, By Alexander," 21, 23, 22, 23, 18.

31. Jonathan Edwards, *The Nature of True Virtue,* ed. William K. Frankena (Ann Arbor, 1960).

32. For Hodge, see Sydney E. Ahlstrom, "The Scottish Philosophy and American Theology," *Church History* 24 (1955): 266, 272 n. 50–51.

33. Alexander, *Outlines of Moral Science,* 184, italics added.

34. Atwater, "Outlines of Moral Science, By Alexander," 19, 25, italics added.

was faulty, even though Edwards had worked out his moral theory precisely to keep genuine virtue within the framework offered by the Calvinist doctrines of original sin and supernatural regeneration that Princeton otherwise supported. Edwards's opponents, like Scotland's Francis Hutcheson, were the ones who grounded virtue in the natural, rather than in the regenerate, powers of humanity as a whole.[35]

A century later, Edwards's would-be heirs in New England, whose views on human nature were similar to Hutcheson's, gleefully pointed out Princeton's inconsistency on this point. Princeton protested its desire to uphold the divine power of election that Edwards had also advocated, yet it based ethics on a system in which divine activity was superfluous. It was the oddest moment in the whole controversy. Princeton theologians rejected Edwards on virtue because they were committed to the same philosophy that New Englanders used to modify Edwards on the will in directions that Princeton considered heretical. "Axioms of the mind" and "moral intuition" were the hidden link between the antagonists.

An important variant on New England's claim to Edwards came in the late 1850s and involved a shift of scene. Yale replaced Andover on the stage, and different New England figures emerged. George Park Fisher, a student of both Taylor and Park who eventually became professor of ecclesiastical history at the Yale Divinity School, began this episode with a commemorative address in 1857 on the history of the Congregational church in Yale College. The spark that ignited a cannonade from Princeton's Lyman Atwater was Fisher's brief comment about the ways in which the successors of Edwards had "improved" his theology.[36] Atwater's rejoinder was, if nothing else, unambiguous: "We think it easy to show," he contended, "that the distinctive features of this New Divinity, in all its successive forms [from Hopkins through Taylor], are utterly abhorrent to his [Edwards's] entire system."[37]

At last the Princeton polemic seems to have made an impression, for when New England next reasserted its claim to Edwards, it did so with an approach quite different from Park's earlier effort. The occasion for this new reading of the Edwardsean heritage was yet another slashing attack by Lyman Atwater on the theology of his former mentor, N. W. Taylor. Taylor had died in 1858, but the publication the following year of his *Lectures on the Moral Government of God* provided an opportu-

35. On the tension in Alexander's thought over this issue, see D. H. Meyer, *The Instructed Conscience: The Shaping of the American National Ethic* (Philadelphia, 1972), 55–57.

36. G. P. Fisher, *A Discourse Commemorative of the History of the Church of Christ in Yale College* (New Haven, Conn., 1858), 7, 80–82.

37. Atwater, "Jonathan Edwards and the Successive Forms of New Divinity," 589.

nity for a full rehearsal of Old School complaints against the New Haven divine. Part of Atwater's massive assault on Taylor was a pointed reference to the changes after Edwards—"Orthodoxy in New England . . . undergoing transformations in the laboratories of successive metaphysical schools"—which had set the stage for Taylor's many errors.[38]

This time the response came from Noah Porter, professor of moral philosophy and metaphysics at Yale, a student of Taylor and also his son-in-law. Porter's aim was to vindicate Taylor and rout the Princetonians, tasks to which he devoted great energy and biting rhetoric. Unlike Park, however, Porter did not attempt to show that the *substance* of New England theology had been carefully preserved from generation to generation. Rather, he intended to show that Edwards's *spirit* had been the motivating force among the theologians who gathered under his name.

Porter's main point was that Princeton "overlooked those peculiarities in Edwards which have caused him to be properly regarded as the founder of a new school in theology; and again, that the later Edwardseans were not only properly his successors, but developed improvements that have been rightly judged to be of important service to Christian theology." The dogmaticians at Princeton failed to observe that the "leading peculiarity which distinguished Edwards as a theologian, was, that he was a philosopher as well as a divine." Edwards was not content with "servilely copying the compromising philosophy" of the Westminster divines, but rather aspired to show the "unphilosophical" errors of his contemporaries. "The secret of Edwards's influence" was his willingness to innovate, to contradict inherited authority, to strike out boldly for the truth.[39] To Porter, the enduring Edwards was an Edwards of innovation.

This new approach, so different from Park's, provided Porter with the grounds for defending N. W. Taylor as a proper descendent of Edwards. To Porter it was not important whether or not bits and pieces of Edwards's specific theology had been rearranged as time went by. Porter conceded that contemporary New Englanders held to propositions that differed from Edwards's—that people possess a moral freedom to choose God, that morality is a quality of action rather than underlying character, that all virtue consists in benevolence, that neither guilt nor righteousness can fairly be imputed from one person to another, and that Jesus' death was a demonstration of God's moral government rather than a placation of divine wrath.[40] But these matters were secondary. Taylor's predilec-

38. Atwater, "Taylor's Lectures on the Moral Government of God," *Princeton Review* 31 (1859): 492.

39. Noah Porter, "The Princeton Review on Dr. Taylor and the Edwardean Theology," *New Englander* 18 (1860): 736–37, 739.

40. Ibid., 742.

tion for bold and independent inquiry, for refined philosophical reflection, was the key that marked him as Edwards's true successor.

More specifically, Porter praised Taylor for continuing Edwards's efforts "to vindicate the gospel from the incumbrances with which a false metaphysic and foolish interpretations had loaded it."[41] This assessment then brought Porter to his central assertion about Taylor's achievement. Unlike Princeton, Taylor had been able to build a theological system logically from first principles of reason—"no teacher could possibly be more alive to the absolute necessity of intuitions, or more enforce the obligation to believe in and ascertain them as the necessary precondition of all logical deductions and all philosophy." The insignia of Scottish moral sense routed Princeton and proved Taylor's right to speak as an Edwardsean: "we adduce the earnestness with which he asserted as first moral truths that are self-evident . . . that no man ought to be punished or incur penal evil except for his own sin—that neither the sin nor the holiness of one can be imputed to another—that the cause or condition of sin cannot be sinful—that an act, in order to be morally good or evil involves 'the power to the contrary.'" Unlike the Old School Presbyterian, "who by shuffling statements and self-contradictory propositions and scholastic refinements and questionable interpretations, patched up a vindication of what he calls Orthodoxy," Taylor "used conscience and common sense to assail traditionary and fantastic speculations." The final result was an advance for the Christian cause that paralleled the advance under Edwards and that greatly benefited the church. The "progress" which Taylor brought about lay "in the conviction that the truths of the gospel ought to be interpreted and preached by forms of statement more free from scholastic metaphysics and more in accordance with the moral intuitions of the race, and that the scriptures can and ought to be interpreted so as to be commended to the conscience and common sense, and that the scriptures, when thus interpreted, and the gospel when thus vindicated, are invested with greater power to command the homage of man."[42]

In this reading of Edwards and New England theology, Porter shifted the grounds of debate. He conceded what Park was always reluctant to admit, that the later New England theologians differed significantly from Edwards on individual doctrines. But by remaining faithful to Edwards's "new method in theology," to his "principles in respect to philosophical theology," the New Englanders had demonstrated their right to the mantle of Edwards. Although the reigning philosophy was now the moral intuitionism of common sense instead of Edwards's theocentric idealism, the result was the same.

41. Ibid., 770–71.
42. Ibid., 743, 744, 772, 769.

The struggle for Edwards's mantle was a manifest testimony to his enduring significance. New Englanders and Princetonians differed in every particular of their appropriation of Edwards except in their desire to put him to use for partisan theological purposes. Yet perhaps the most striking feature of their exchange was not theological at all, but the way in which the debate testified to the nearly unremarked philosophical revolution in America. Princeton, Yale, and Andover had each in its own way become a center of common sense philosophy.[43] As such they accepted assumptions that were not only foreign to Edwards, but which he had largely opposed. To be sure, it made considerable difference which aspect of common sense prevailed at the various theological institutions in the nineteenth century. Princeton poured a thin broth of epistemological and ethical common sense into its traditional Calvinistic stew. Andover and Yale both were more creative in the philosophical kitchen, working self-consciously and comprehensively to develop the implications of common-sense moral intuitions while tincturing these commitments with a modest dash of Coleridgean romanticism.[44]

Princeton had the greatest difficulty in understanding Edwards where he most explicitly denied what later became the foundation of Princeton's ethical theory. From John Witherspoon and Archibald Alexander, Princeton inherited convictions about the moral sense which came originally from Francis Hutcheson, the very theorist whom Edwards had labored to refute in *The Nature of True Virtue*.[45] There Edwards taught that only the regenerate, because of a supernatural gift, could exercise genuine virtue. Princeton, on the other hand, was committed to the belief that a natural moral sense gave all humans the ability to perceive true virtue. In a similar fashion, Princeton's intellectualist picture of faith, which was related to the Baconianism that characterized common-sense thought in its American manifestation, made it difficult for its spokesmen to appreciate the affectional grounds of Edwards's piety. Yet in both cases, the Princeton commitments in moral philosophy, which were so different from Edwards's, did not materially alter the loci of their religious thought. The result was a theology with a deep inner tension, divided between belief in

43. On the prevalence of the Scottish philosophy in the early nineteenth century, see Ahlstrom, "The Scottish Philosophy and American Theology"; Daniel Walker Howe, *The Unitarian Conscience: Harvard Moral Philosophy, 1805–1861* (Cambridge, 1970); and the works cited in notes 2 and 51.

44. On differences between ethical, epistemological, and methodological appropriations of the Scottish philosophy in America, see Mark A. Noll, "Common Sense Traditions and American Evangelical Thought," *American Quarterly* 37 (1985): 216–38.

45. On Witherspoon's fulsome reliance on Hutcheson, see Jack Scott, ed., *An Annotated Edition of Lectures on Moral Philosophy by John Witherspoon* (Newark, Del., 1982).

God's special work among the elect and the universal human capacity to perceive true virtue. It is this central tension of the Princeton theology that explains both why Princeton could not understand Edwards on ethics and yet why it could remain so close to him on questions of the will.

New England's appropriation of common sense led the theology of Yale and Andover further away from Edwards's doctrines. However, especially with the creative Taylor and the more workmanlike Park, New England broke through the tension that characterized Princeton. These thinkers frankly accepted the fact that the new moral philosophy should play a primary role in theological reflection on the will and human salvation, as well as in ethics. The foundation of all thought, including theology, Taylor contended, came to us "in the very nature and structure of the mind—it is given to us in actual cognitions of the inner man, in the knowledge of ourselves; and therefore in a manner not less distinct nor less impressive than were it sent in thunder from . . . [God's] throne."[46] This position, which eventually made New England's intellectual stance more coherent than Princeton's, also, however, made it very different from Edwards's. For his part, Edwards eventually had come to hold that the moral intuitions of unredeemed humanity were ambiguous and often ironic. In Norman Fiering's fine phrase, "the deepest lesson he [Edwards] took from the Great Awakening may have been a renewed appreciation of the labyrinth of the human heart."[47] Later New Englanders lost sight of Edwards's whole-scale opposition to the idea that a natural moral capacity could ground religion or ethics. In fact, they made the natural moral capacity the basis of their entire enterprise. This is evident most clearly in Taylor, but anticipated also among Taylor's predecessors, where the old orthodoxy was modified repeatedly out of deference to what was assumed to be the common moral sense of the age—whether this was Joseph Bellamy on the extent of the atonement, Jonathan Edwards, Jr., on its nature, Samuel Hopkins on original sin, or Timothy Dwight on free choice and imputation.[48] In their eagerness to incorporate

46. Quoted in Kuklick, *Churchmen and Philosophers*, 99, in the context of a lucid discussion of Taylor's thought.

47. Norman Fiering, *Jonathan Edwards's Moral Thought and Its British Context* (Chapel Hill, N.C., 1981), 174.

48. For Bellamy, Foster, *Genetic History of New England Theology*, 113–17, and Glenn Paul Anderson, "Joseph Bellamy (1719–1790): The Man and His Work" (Ph.D. diss., Boston University, 1971), 737–47; Robert L. Ferm, *Jonathan Edwards the Younger 1745–1801* (Grand Rapids, 1976), 114–33; Joseph A. Conforti, *Samuel Hopkins and the New Divinity Movement* (Grand Rapids, 1981), 159–74; and John R. Fitzmier, "The Godly Federalism of Timothy Dwight, 1752–1817; Society, Decline, and Religion in the Life of New England's 'Moral Legislator'" (Ph.D. diss., Princeton University, 1986), 111–58.

the assured results of mental science into theology proper, New Englanders, as Princeton charged, had indeed left Edwards far behind. In sum, when Princeton and New England assumed that the common moral sense was ethically or spiritually efficacious, they in that measure abandoned Edwards.

It would be nice if such a conclusion were fresh and original, but in fact it merely echoes a judgment rendered as long ago as 1862 in an essay by the New School Presbyterian, Henry Boynton Smith. In one of the most perceptive accounts ever written on theology in New England, Smith recognized that "the whole state of the case was entirely altered, when Berkeleianism was supplanted by the Scotch philosophy, and the distinctions between the soul and its exercises, between tendencies and voluntary acts, between the heart and the will, were reinstated in their rational right. . . . [The theology] was cut loose from its Calvinistic moorings; it was divorced from the divine efficiency. The divine element was eliminated, and the human will, in the construction of the system, took the place of the divine will. . . . The same phrases may be used, but there is another sense; there may be, to outward seeming, the same eyeball, but another soul looks out; the hands feel like the hands of Jacob, but the voice is the voice of Esau."[49]

The only way to improve on this judgment at our late date is to take advantage of Edwards's philosophical writings that had not yet been published in Smith's day. Such material, as summarized by Wallace Anderson, shows even more clearly that "the main point of Edwards's response to materialism is that the 'very existence' of bodies depends immediately upon the divine Being, that bodies do not exist by themselves as substances at all. In taking this position [Anderson goes on], Edwards not only fashioned a rebuttal of materialism, but in doing so he undermined the assumptions of the metaphysical dualism of Descartes and the Newtonians,"[50] and, we might add, of Princeton and New Haven as well.

In the end, we have the irony that since Edwards was an idealist and none of his successors were, he really had no nineteenth-century followers at the points of his actual theological genius. This fact also helps explain why the arguments between New England and Princeton over Edwards could go on for as long as they did.

The importance of this recondite theological battle for American intellectual history is surprisingly large. Among other things, it points to the

49. H.B. Smith, "The Theological System of Emmons," in *Faith and Philosophy: Discourses and Essays* (Edinburgh, 1878), 243–44; see also the discussion of Smith's insight in Kuklick, *Churchmen and Philosophers*, 212.

50. Wallace Anderson, ed., *The Works of Jonathan Edwards: Scientific and Philosophical Writings* (New Haven, Conn., 1980), 59.

striking absence in our intellectual and cultural histories of plausible explanations accounting for this dramatic change in philosophical orientation, and even more to a surprising absence of historians' curiosity as to how such a change could have taken place while those who were its beneficiaries did not recognize either its importance or its extent. The transition from Edwards's idealism to the common-sense positions of Princeton and New England is, moreover, a cryptogram for the general intellectual shift which carried the most sophisticated expression of American thought from affectional Augustinian idealism in the mid-eighteenth century to a mingled intellectualist and romantic anti-Augustinian realism in the mid-nineteenth. Works by Edmund Morgan, Gordon Wood, Henry May, D. H. Meyer and a few others have begun to describe the complicated relation of cultural, political, intellectual, religious, and social contexts within which this change took place.[51] But good as these accounts are, they amount to no more than introductory efforts at explaining this important intellectual transition.

Edwards, the theologians of Princeton, and the New Englanders were all Protestant and evangelical in their insistence upon regeneration, their deference to Scripture, and their encouragement of active piety. But apart from this common heritage, the relationships are more complicated. Edwards was revivalistic and doctrinal, Princeton nonrevivalistic and doctrinal, New England revivalistic and intuitional. Edwards was biblical-speculative, Princeton biblical-nonspeculative, New England speculative-biblical. Edwards advocated an affectional Puritan Calvinism, Princeton an intellectualist Old Calvinism, and New England an intuitional Consistent Calvinism. Most importantly, Edwards was idealist, Princeton Baconian, New England Baconian-romantic. The discontinuities between the mid-eighteenth century and the mid-nineteenth century are, at the last, even more worthy of attention than the differences over Edwards among antebellum Calvinists.

51. E. S. Morgan, "The American Revolution Considered as an Intellectual Movement," in *Paths of American Thought,* eds. A. M. Schlesinger, Jr., and M. White (Boston, 1963); Gordon Wood, "Evangelical America and Early Mormonism," *New York History* 61 (1980): 359–86; Wood, "Conspiracy and the Paranoid Style: Causality and Deceit in the Eighteenth Century," *William and Mary Quarterly* 39 (1982): 401–41; Henry F. May, *The Enlightenment in America* (New York, 1976); and D. H. Meyer, *The Democratic Enlightenment* (New York, 1976).

Part 4

Evangelicalism in Victorian America

10

The Collapse of American Evangelical Academia

George M. Marsden

By the mid-twentieth century being evangelical and being a scholar were widely viewed as incompatible traits. Indeed, by 1950 the American evangelical scholarly community was in disarray. Scattered evangelical academic institutions boasting a few competent scholars survived, but only in ethnic, regional, and denominational pockets or in the intellectually suspect fundamentalist movement. Few outsiders took these institutions seriously or realized they existed. Some competent Christian scholars could be found in American universities, but evangelical thought would seldom have been counted as a part of American academic life.

Evangelical academia, if noticed at all, seemed from the prevailing liberal humanist perspective the vestiges of a lost civilization. Only seventy-five years earlier almost all of America's leading colleges and universities had borne the deep imprint of their evangelical connections.[1] Academic thought had been largely evangelical thought. In 1950, however, persistent ideas of intellectual progress encouraged the view that traditional re-

1. Mark A. Noll, "Christian Thinking and the Rise of the American University," *Christian Scholar's Review* 9 (1979): 3–16, presents a valuable summary of these developments.

ligious outlooks were declining irreversibly. Advanced scientific views were supposed to be replacing backward religions, superstitions, and prejudices throughout the world. The actual decline of evangelical academia during the past two generations lent credence to such hypotheses.

The particular issue I wish to address is, What was the intellectual component in this demise of evangelical academia and scholarship? Was the collapse significantly related to the intellectual stance characteristic of nineteenth-century American evangelicals? Today this question has renewed significance. Since 1950 American evangelicalism has begun to recover intellectually. This recovery has brought renewal of some thought patterns prominent in nineteenth-century evangelicalism. It is important to inquire, therefore, as to the extent these thought patterns were structural weaknesses that contributed to the original collapse. Does their renewal involve building similar weaknesses into evangelical thought today?

The answers will not be simple. The complexity of history precludes most single-cause explanations. American evangelical academia did not collapse simply because of an intellectual error. Comparable secularizing transformations occurred almost everywhere in the Protestant world during the nineteenth century. The positivist claims that modern science provides the only sure ground for certainty combined with the modern historical model of explanation in terms of origins seemed for a time a nearly irresistible intellectual combination. Only strongly institutionalized authority, as in the citadels of Roman Catholicism, was able to withstand such tendencies on a large scale, and then at the cost of sacrificing some academic respectability.

The new ideas gained popularity in Protestant lands such as America not simply by the force of argument but also because they provided explanations that fit many social trends toward secularization.[2] In America, for instance, the long dominance of evangelicals in the colleges was built directly on the ethnic dominance of "Anglo-Saxon" Protestants. Priority of settlement gave this group social and economic dominance and hence control over private (and even much of state) education. By the late nineteenth century, however, ethnic and religious heterogeneity was becoming an overwhelming reality in American culture, so that such dominance had to give way. Americans' professed democratic ideals in fact conflicted with the virtual control of higher education by one religious outlook. The new naturalistic and scientific explanations had the appeal not only of its arguments but of fitting a social need, offering a new and seem-

2. For example see Owen Chadwick, *The Secularization of the European Mind in the Nineteenth Century* (Cambridge, England, 1975). By "secularization" I mean here simply the decline of distinctly Christian influences.

ingly neutral basis for refashioning education. It also provided a compelling secular account of the dynamics of a civilization that in many areas was losing its religious orientation.

Another of the many social factors contributing to the triumph of the new views was the rise of professionalism. Whereas in 1800 someone like Thomas Jefferson could be an expert in virtually every field of knowledge, by the late decades of the century professional specialization was the key to success. The rise of the universities reflected this cultural trend. The Ph.D. thesis, a demonstration of technical expertise in an area accessible only by specialists, became the prerequisite for entry into academic life.[3] By contrast, nineteenth-century evangelical colleges had been havens for generalists, theologian-philosophers who provided the community with advice in economics, politics, morality, and often in natural science. The new specialists who were taking over by the end of the century could usually outclass the old-time teachers in any of the specialties.[4] Moreover their new concept of being "scientific" meant simultaneously to specialize and to eliminate religiously derived principles from their disciplines. The technical achievements of this new specialization thus reinforced prejudices against evangelicalism, which had been heavily committed to the older generalist approach.

Such factors, formidable as they were, do not seem quite to account for the displacement of the nineteenth-century evangelical outlook turning into such a total rout. One might imagine the revolution in American higher education having taken quite different forms. The rise of pluralism might not have driven out the old establishment so entirely. Excellent Christian colleges (say Oberlin or Wellesley) might have continued as both excellent and Christian even through the dim days for evangelicalism in the first half of the twentieth century. Moreover, evangelical Christian education might have made some adjustment to the university system as Catholic schools did. One of the most puzzling features of American academic life today is that even in these times of evangelical resurgence there is still not a full-fledged evangelical university in America. Why was the severance of evangelicalism from the main currents of American academic life so total?

With only social or cultural explanations the answers to these questions surely would remain incomplete. The specifically intellectual fac-

3. Burton J. Bledstein, *The Culture of Professionalism: The Middle Class and the Development of Higher Education in America* (New York, 1976). Cf. Noll, "Christian Thinking." A fine account of the impact of professionalism on philosophy is Bruce Kuklick, *The Rise of American Philosophy: Cambridge, Massachusetts, 1860–1930* (New Haven, 1977).

4. Noll, "Christian Thinking."

tors are, at least, essential aspects of the picture. Most obviously the academic revolution involved a remarkable change among intellectuals in their view of authority. For evangelicals the Bible stood beside the highest scientific and historical authorities whenever it spoke on such matters. Moreover, it also spoke definitively on many areas that science by itself could not reach. The new combination of scientific positivism and historicism, however, struck particularly hard at the Bible itself, questioning its accuracy at innumerable points and offering alternative naturalistic and seemingly scientific explanations for the rise of human religious beliefs. In simplest terms, the intellectual aspect of the revolution involved the replacement of the old authorities with the new in all but the obscure crannies of American academia.

In reality, of course, this intellectual revolution was much more complex. Battle lines were seldom neatly drawn between secular humanists who reverenced science and history and Bible-believing evangelicals who did not. Rather, a whole spectrum of middle positions attempted to reconcile Christian faith with modern intellectual trends. Some were frank expressions of humanist faith in mankind with a touch of Christian ethics thrown in. Others were modernist theologies, claiming a distinctly Christian heritage but insisting that God continued to reveal himself in the best of modern science and culture. Others were explicitly evangelical positions that attempted to ground Christian faith on truths of the heart or on moral sentiments insusceptible to scientific or historical attack. After 1930 neoorthodoxy provided Americans an alternative that preserved traditional Christian theology while keeping the core of sacred history in a transcendental realm likewise immune to scientific-historical criticism.

A peculiarity of these middle positions, however, is that they flourished in American academia almost solely in theological institutions. They generated few, if any, alternative nontheological educational institutions or even academic organizations. The reason for this striking absence is not hard to surmise. Every one of these middle positions endorses to some degree the historical and scientific canons of the day. They thus maintained cordial relations with American academia by conceding its virtual autonomy. Their solution to the crisis in authority was to grant the authority of the new science and history, but to emphasize that this authority was limited to certain secular domains. Picking up and vastly accentuating a theme present in the thought of their evangelical predecessors, indeed found in almost all Christian thought, they now rested the entire weight of their apologetic on the point that Christianity went far beyond that which mere scientific reason could reach. They differed from most of their predecessors, however, in suggesting that Christianity had to do only with the aspects of things wholly immune from scientific or historical inquiry. Secular institutions, accordingly, were the proper location for such inquiries.

More traditional evangelicals, however, are the focus of the present inquiry. During the twentieth century they did not concede that Christianity involved exclusively the aspects of things beyond scientific and historical inquiry. The Bible, they insisted, was an historical book in some ordinary ways, even if it was also God's revelation. Many of its claims were in principle susceptible to the same sorts of intellectual analysis as any other claims. Faith and scientific reason were not at odds.

Why was this view, once dominant in American higher education, so preemptively banished from most of American academia? Why did proponents of this view lose virtually all their institutional strongholds? Was there some defect in their defenses of biblically based Christianity and its proper relation to reason, especially scientific reason?

The most incisive analysis of this subject appeared in a 1961 essay by a Princeton philosopher, James Ward Smith, "Religion and Science in American Philosophy."[5] Smith pointed out that among American Protestants there was no crisis of science versus religion associated with the first, or Newtonian, scientific revolution. The American Puritans and their heirs, by and large, embraced the new science with enthusiasm. Their accommodation of Protestantism to science, however, was "superficial." With the notable exception of Jonathan Edwards, says Smith, their accommodation involved simply adding the corpus of modern scientific knowledge to the body of ideas they accepted. They saw these conclusions of modern sciences as additional evidence for the theistic argument from design. Such reconciliation of the new science with Christianity was superficial because they did not closely examine or challenge the speculative basis on which the modern scientific revolution was built. Rather than challenging modern science's first principles, they came to be among the chief defenders of these principles. They were entirely confident that objective scientific inquiry could only confirm Christian truth.

Despite Christians' struggles with Deism and Enlightenment skepticism, this reconciliation of Christianity and modern science by the method of addition generally worked well until the second scientific revolution, that associated with Darwin. Suddenly, rather than the prestige of modern science lending support to Christianity, the supposedly neutral scientific methodology turned its forces directly against Christian thought. Out of nowhere, it must have seemed, came an unprecedented scientific assault. The Christian community, having thoroughly trusted

5. In James Ward Smith and A. Leland Jamison, eds., *The Shaping of American Religion* (Princeton, 1961), 402–42.

science and the scientific method, had welcomed them, even parading them as their staunchest friends. So, according to Smith's thesis, this superficial accommodation left them with no defenses when the celebrated ally proved to be a heavily armed foe. No mere Trojan horse, we may add, had been imported into the Christian citadel. The very foundations of their defensive walls had been built by Greek philosophers and their modern scientific heirs and hid massive forces potentially hostile to the Christian religion.

Elaborating such themes briefly, we can see that rather than supporting the old argument from design, nineteenth-century science suddenly produced a series of alternative explanations for the apparent order and purpose in reality. The divisions of the intellectual armies of this revolution usually had two features in common. They claimed for themselves the full prestige of the positive scientific methodology. They also had adopted (as it turns out, quite paradoxically) later-nineteenth-century historical assumptions. That is, they viewed reality, not as essentially stable with fixed truths, but as essentially in process of development. The scientific methodology was applied to explaining that development, with the assumption that such developments could be understood best in terms of natural forces observable by scientific method itself. These assumptions, that life was best viewed as processes and these processes were susceptible to scientific analysis, were behind most of the major intellectual assaults offering alternatives to the Christian explanations of reality. Darwinism offered accounts of the origins of life, of design, and of human intelligence itself. Freudianism added naturalistic explanations for the human sense of meaning, of love and beauty, and of religion itself. Marxism, and similar social explanations, claimed to explain the meaning and apparent direction of history. They offered as well an alternative basis for social ethics. Biblical criticism turned the fire power of such scientific-historical explanation point-blank on the origins of Hebrew religion and the Bible itself. With awesome swiftness the edifice built by the method of addition that had worked so well for Christians in accommodating Christianity to the first scientific revolution had been demolished by the second.

Smith's basic thesis, here considerably elaborated—that the fault in repelling this assault, or even in sensing that it was coming, involved a defect in the American evangelical method of reconciling faith and science—warrants more detailed analysis. Particularly, we can look at how eighteenth- and nineteenth-century American Protestants characteristically viewed the issues concerning faith and reason. We can ask whether their approach was as essentially naive as in retrospect it might seem. And we can consider what we might learn, positively or negatively, from their approach and their experience.

The Background: Thomas Reid

Until after the Civil War almost all American evangelical theologians built their discussions of faith and reason on principles drawn, at least in part, from the Scottish "Common Sense" school of philosophy. The progenitor of this important school was Thomas Reid (1710–96).[6] Americans also studied Reid's followers, Dugald Stewart, James Beattie, Thomas Brown, and William Hamilton, some of whom (especially Hamilton) modified Reid's views considerably, but in general the Americans' views were readily identifiable as belonging to the Reidian school.[7]

One of the firmest commitments of Reid and his American followers was to the British inductive-empirical school of thought associated with Francis Bacon and Isaac Newton (and more generally with John Locke) concerned above all to establish a firm base for inductive scientific investigation. Reid himself was a great admirer of Bacon, the early seventeenth-century philosopher of science. The influence of "Lord Bacon" on Reid, Dugald Stewart observed approvingly, "may be traced on almost every page."[8] Bacon had taught Newton, said Reid in one of his encomiums, "to despise hypotheses as fictions of human fancy." Newton in turn demonstrated "that the true method of philosophizing is this: from real facts ascertained by observations and experiment, to collect by just induction the laws of nature." Such reasoning from "chaste induction" was a type of "probable" reasoning rather than demonstrative deduction, yet its firmest results were no less certain than those of mathematics. "Probable" evidence, said Reid, often involved many strands, like the twisted filaments of a rope, rather than one argument, yet "many things are certain for which we have only that kind of evidence which philosophers call probable." Evidence from induction, Reid emphasized, "is the only kind of evidence on which all the most important affairs of human life must rest."[9]

6. Some recent and generally favorable philosophical discussions of Reid are found in Stephen F. Barker and Tom L. Beauchamp, eds., *Thomas Reid: Critical Interpretations* (Philadelphia, 1976) and Elizabeth Flower and Murray G. Murphey, *A History of Philosophy in America* (New York, 1977).

7. This connection is well documented in many works. For instance, Flower and Murphey, *History of Philosophy in America;* Theodore Dwight Bozeman, *Protestants in an Age of Science: The Baconian Ideal and Antebellum American Religious Thought* (Chapel Hill, 1977); Herbert Hovenkamp, *Science and Religion in America, 1800–1860* (Philadelphia, 1978).

8. Quoted in Bozeman, *Protestants in the Age of Science,* 5. For more documentation of Reid's admiration for Bacon see Bozeman, 5–21 passim.

9. Thomas Reid, *Essays on the Intellectual Powers of Man,* ed. Baruch A. Brody (Cambridge, Mass., 1969 [1785]), II:8, 145, and VII:3, 737; Reid discusses "probable reasoning" in VII:3. "Probable reasoning" includes reasoning on evidence from human testi-

By Reid's time, however, the classical foundations on which such inductive scientific inquiry ultimately rested seemed to be crumbling. Classical foundationalism, as it is now sometimes called, was the ideal in the Western philosophical heritage since the time of the ancient Greeks, that a sure structure of knowledge could be built on the absolutely firm foundations of indubitable certitudes. Typically these foundational certitudes included our states of consciousness (such as, I am awake), self-evidently necessary truths (such as 1 + 2 equals 3), and perhaps those things evident to the senses (I am sure I see a tree over there). Such foundationalists typically maintained that these fundamental certitudes did not need to be held on the basis of any other beliefs that one held. They could be taken for granted without demonstration.[10] David Hume, however, an older contemporary of Reid, raised serious questions as to whether such certainty was possible in empirical scientific investigation. By the mid-eighteenth century John Locke's account of the mental operations involved in empirical knowledge had been widely accepted. External objects, said Locke, stimulate the senses in such a way as to imprint "ideas" of themselves on our minds (which prior to such imprintings were blank). Hume, however, took a skeptical stance toward this account. For instance, he questioned whether we can be certain that these ideas occurring in our minds correspond to anything outside the mind itself. Reason thus seemed to undermine the certainty of the immensely popular scientific empiricism.

Reid's reply to Hume's skepticism revealed his explicit intention to establish a new foundationalism on which inductive science could be based. "All knowledge got by reasoning," he says, "must be built on first principles." He adds that "This is as certain as that every house must have a foundation." Furthermore, some, though not all, of these first principles "yield conclusions that are certain."[11] Reid's account of these first principles arose from his subtle analysis of the psychological mechanisms by which people arrive at those beliefs they take to be self-evident or certain. The conclusion was inescapable, he argued, that our knowledge rests on first principles, or "basic beliefs" . . . , that rest on nothing other than the fact that we find ourselves compelled to hold them. Along with classical

---

mony, on reputable authority, or based on: the identity of things, some assumptions about human behavior, chances, or induction. The all-importance, even for savages, of inductively determining the "laws of nature" (fire burns, water drowns, etc.) is discussed on 736.

10. Descartes provided an alternative version of foundationalism by reducing the basic (or nondemonstrable) beliefs to the minimum—his consciousness that he was thinking—and attempted to derive the rest from that certitude. Reid thought Descartes and his ilk vastly overestimated the importance and the competence of demonstrative reasoning.

11. Reid, *Essays,* VI:4, 596–97.

foundationalists he said that such foundational principles "seldom admit to direct proof; nor do they need it." These are "the foundation of all reasoning, and of all science."[12]

Reid differed from the classical foundationalists principally in that his close look at those beliefs that people were in practice virtually compelled to hold yielded a considerably expanded set of first principles. Not only did he include states of consciousness, self-evidently necessary truths, and those things evident to our senses, he affirmed also that virtually all normal adults inevitably hold such basic beliefs as the connection between cause and effect, the general regularity in nature, the predictability of some human behavior, the relationship between past and present, the existence of other minds, the continuity of one's self and of others, the reliability of their clear and distinct memories, the trustworthiness of the testimony of others under certain conditions, and the difference between right and wrong. Reid even held that certain beliefs about beauty were compelled in all normal people, and hence universal ("I never heard of any man who thought it a beauty in a human face to want a nose.")[13] People seldom hold any of these beliefs on the basis of reasoning. Rather they are basic beliefs, beliefs not established by arguments, but caused immediately by "common sense," or the belief-producing faculties that underlie all reasoning.[14]

Reid's concern was to reestablish a basis for our certainty about our knowledge of the real world. His philosophy was in this sense a type of "realism," sometimes called "Common-Sense Realism." That there was surely a connection between our certain beliefs and the real world, external to our minds, was itself a dictate of common sense, not susceptible to rational demonstration. Only philosophers or crackpots, he was fond of pointing out, would construct theories that would cast doubt on these common-sense beliefs. Locke's theory of "ideas," for instance, suggested that the immediate (or most direct) objects of our knowledge are our *ideas* about reality. This speculative theory opened the door for the Humean objection that perhaps he had access *only* to our ideas. In fact, Reid insisted, all normal people find themselves compelled to believe that they directly and immediately experience the external world itself. As to the skeptical philosophers who claimed to doubt such things as the existence of the external world, even they ducked when they went through low doorways.

Notably, Reid does not include belief in God among the commonsense first principles. Though as far as I know he does not explain this omission

12. Ibid., I:2, 31.
13. Ibid., VI:6, 646.
14. Ibid. VI:2, 567.

directly, the reasons seem plain enough. For a principle to be a common-sense principle it had to be common to virtually all normal adults in all nations and ages. Of course, we do not believe these first principles *because* we find them to be universal; that would be believing them for a reason. We believe them because we are forced to by the constitution of our natures. Nonetheless, universality is a test for identifying common-sense principles. A negative test is that a person devoid of such beliefs would nearly everywhere be considered a lunatic. Reid says: "All men that have common understanding agree in such principles, and consider a man as lunatic, or destitute of common sense, who denies or calls them into question."[15] Belief in God does not meet this test.

Moreover, in asserting this universality of common-sense principles, Reid is eager to establish the basis for a universal science. Disagreements, he says, often terminate in appeals to common sense. Such disagreements could be avoided if "the decisions of common sense can be brought into a code, in which all reasonable men shall acquiesce." Such a universal code would be a great boon to logic. "And why," Reid adds, "should it be thought impossible that reasonable men should agree in things that are self-evident?"[16] Clearly, a matter so much disputed as belief in God would not qualify as a universally held common-sense foundation stone for such definitive science.

Reid, however, was a moderate Presbyterian, and belief in God played a significant, though often implicit, role in his philosophy. Reid held that the existence of a Supreme Being could be demonstrated by a simple, but irrefutable, process of reasoning. Starting characteristically with a common-sense principle "Which we get, neither by reasoning nor by experience," Reid made the major proposition of his argument "That design and intelligence in the cause, may with certainty be inferred from marks or signs of it in the effect." If then we accept as the minor proposition that "there are, in fact, the clearest marks of design and wisdom in the world of nature," then we must conclude that there is a wise and intelligent cause.[17]

This simple argument from design appears to play an incidental role in Reid's philosophy, but the "Creator," the "Almighty," and "the wise Author of our nature" are mentioned constantly in Reid's writings. The Creator has constituted nature and all beings in it with the relationships they have. "The laws of nature," he says with regard to scientific inquiry, "are the rules by which the Supreme Being governs the world."[18] All others be-

15. Ibid., I:2, 30–31.
16. Ibid., VI:2, 559–60.
17. Ibid., VI:6, 667–69.
18. Ibid., VII:3, 735.

ings "must depend upon the nature God has given them; the powers with which he has endowed them, and the situation in which he has placed them."[19] Reid is careful not to argue from the existence of a wise Creator to the reliability of common-sense first principles (which require no argument); nonetheless, when he speaks of beliefs determined by "the constitution of human nature,"[20] he certainly has in mind that these belief-mechanisms and the world that they encounter are constituted by the Creator.[21]

Reid's frequent mention of the Author of our natures reveals an important feature about his thought and that of his nineteenth-century American followers that distinguished their outlooks sharply from later discussions. Almost all philosophies since the later nineteenth century have assumed "the evolution of self-consciousness."[22] An implicit premise usually has been that our mental mechanisms arose simply from natural causes. Such accounts often make what humans call "truth," or at least a good portion of it, a matter of convention. Since our mechanisms for knowing about reality are evolving, "truth" changes with our cognitive development. Furthermore, cultural evolution, a major category of recent thought, often has been interpreted to suggest that "truth" is largely relative to time and place, almost wholly a matter of conditioning and custom.

The naturalistic and evolutionary assumptions on which such attitudes are based were totally foreign to Reid and his nineteenth-century American admirers. They took it for granted that the universe was packed with fixed laws placed there by intelligent design. Reid introduced the fact of evidence of design in the universe as a proposition in his argument for the deity with hardly an explanation. He did note that some ancients had thought "that there are not in the constitution of things such marks of wise contrivance as are sufficient to put the conclusion beyond doubt." Modern science, Reid asserted, in a characteristic eighteenth-century display of the faith in a fixed order that Newtonianism inspired, proved this view obviously fallacious. "The gradual advancement made in the knowledge of nature," Reid observed without elaboration, "has put this opinion quite out of countenance."[23]

19. Ibid., VI:5, 616.

20. Ibid., VII:3, 736.

21. The mottoes of Reid's first two books are "The inspiration of the Almighty giveth them understanding" and "Who hath put wisdom in the inward parts." S. A. Grave, *The Scottish Philosophy of Common Sense* (Oxford, 1960), 159.

22. This is the phrase of a key American transitional figure, Chauncey Wright (1830–75). See Bruce Kuklick, *The Rise of American Philosophy;* and Flower and Murphey, *A History of Philosophy in America,* vol. 2, for discussions of this transformation in America.

23. Reid, *Essays,* VI:6, 669.

The Background: Paley and Butler

Christians more directly concerned to defend the faith than was Reid himself took full advantage of the era's widely held belief that natural science had produced irrefutable confirmation of intelligent design in the universe. So the same large group of American apologists who used Reid as the unanswerable reply to general skepticism[24] readily employed William Paley's popular *Natural Theology* (1802) to demonstrate the necessity of theistic belief. Both in nineteenth-century England and America his volume was a widely used text, so that virtually every educated person was acquainted with his arguments.

Paley, like virtually every English-speaking thinker of the era, displayed an implicit trust in empiricism. He claimed that his arguments were built on no special philosophy except some generally accepted "principles of knowledge."[25] He observed also, as Reid and others often said, that an overwhelmingly probable empirical case was virtually as decisive as a logical demonstration. Starting with his famous example of finding a stone and a watch and concluding that the watch must have a designer, Paley built up his probabilistic case by multiplying examples of apparent design in nature, especially in humans themselves. The eye has as much evidence of a designer as the telescope. Moreover, nature reveals a designer with personality, great power, everywhere working on a unified design, present at "the beginning," and (when all was considered) benevolent.[26]

The popularity of Paley reveals an important aspect of the outlook of eighteenth-century Britain and nineteenth-century America. Though the argument from design might be useful to counter adolescent skepticism or the village atheist, for most practical purposes the dictates of natural theology were taken for granted as much by the opponents of Christianity as by its friends. In an age enamored of the order of the Newtonian universe, few doubted that the universe had an intelligent designer. For practical purposes the real debate was between the Deists and the Christians. So Christians and most non-Christians shared a great deal of common ground, especially on first principles. Both agreed that the universe was designed by a Creator who built into it law-structures that humans could discover through scientific procedures. The ghost of David Hume

24. For instance, James Beattie, *An Essay on the Nature and Immutability of Truth in Opposition to Sophistry and Scepticism* (1770), essentially a popularization of the philosophical arguments of Reid, was published in a series entitled *The Evidences of the Christian Religion* (London, 1816).

25. William Paley, *Natural Theology: Selections*, ed. Frederick Ferre (New York, 1963), chapter 6, 32.

26. Ibid., passim.

seemed safely enough laid to rest by the likes of Reid and Paley, so that the key question for the apologist was not natural religion, but revealed religion, that is, the Bible.

On this topic the immense popularity of another eighteenth-century figure suggests some of the characteristic assumptions of the nineteenth-century American apologists. Even more than Paley's work, Bishop Joseph Butler's *The Analogy of Religion, Natural and Revealed* (1736) (which in one American edition enjoyed over twenty printings)[27] left its mark on nineteenth-century American thought. Butler too endorsed empirical inductionism as the only safe avenue to the truth.[28] Moreover, as was commonplace, he emphasized that his arguments for Christianity were cumulative and only pointed toward a probability, and did not yield demonstrative proof or absolute knowledge. Nonetheless, he remarked in an often quoted statement, "Probability is the very guide to life."[29]

Butler's arguments provided some counterparts to those of Reid. Reid established on practical grounds, rather than on argument from evidence, the necessity of trusting in common-sense principles. Butler started at a similar point. Making observations about what we are obliged to believe about nature, he argued for Christianity not by presenting a proof, but by pointing out that virtually the same objections that might be lodged against biblically revealed religion could be made against that which we absolutely rely on as true in nature. Thomas Reid recognized this affinity.

> I know no author who has made a more just and happy use of analogical reasoning than Bishop Butler, in his "Analogy of Religion." In that excellent work, the author does not ground any of the truths of religion upon analogy as their proper evidence. He only makes use of analogy to answer objections against them. When objections are made against the truths of religion, which may be made with equal strength against *what we know to be true* in the course of nature, such objections can have no weight.[30]

Christian and Non-Christian Science

Reid, Paley, and Butler agreed among themselves and with most of the English-speaking opponents of Christianity on most of their first princi-

27. Bernard Ramm, *Varieties of Christian Apologetics* (Grand Rapids, 1962), 107.
28. Ibid., 112. For an affirmation by Butler of the Baconian ideal of reasoning from the "observation of facts" as opposed to "building a world upon hypothesis, like Des Cartes," see Joseph Butler, *The Analogy of Religion, Natural and Revealed to the Constitution and Course of Nature* (London, 1852) [1736]), 75–76.
29. Butler, *Analogy,* Malcom and Barnes edition, quoted in Ramm, *Varieties,* 117.
30. Quoted, Butler, *Analogy,* 79n.

ples. They were confident that the laws of the human mind were attuned to fixed laws of nature in such a way that careful empirical observation would yield truth. The empiricist tradition dominating much of English thought was gripped by the hopes for dramatic advances in knowledge promised by the scientific method described by Francis Bacon. Newton symbolized the spectacular fulfillments of such promises. For a time this vision of reality was so compelling and the possibility of human advance so promising that few would challenge it. In the early nineteenth century this vision persisted especially in America. "The Baconian philosophy," said Edward Everett in 1823, "has become synonymous with the true philosophy."[31] So great was the reverence in America among scientists, theologians, and most academics for this ideal that a recent historian's phrase, "the beatification of Bacon," seems aptly to describe it.[32]

This blanket endorsement of the Baconian-Newtonian scientific assumptions and method, shared by Christians and non-Christians, had the important implication that, outside of theology, Christians did not consider themselves to belong to any special school of thought. Science, built on firm foundations universally recognized, and proceeding to virtual certainty by careful Baconian principles of induction, would yield the same results to all inquirers. Christians, who had the advantage of trusting special revelation, had access to some facts that non-Christians refused to acknowledge. Nonetheless, since the Creator had built a definite set of laws into nature and provided laws of the human mind that guided our access to nature's laws, in almost all areas Christians and non-Christians stood on exactly the same footing. Thomas Jefferson, for instance, might be an infidel, but the Declaration of Independence spoke of rights of mankind "endowed by their creator" "self-evident" to all.[33] Such areas were in the domain of science and could be analyzed without recourse to any special Christian teachings.

These assumptions were extremely influential in shaping early American thought and in setting the course of much of American public policy—especially toward education. Their influence is evident, for instance, in virtually all the college texts prior to the Civil War. Francis Wayland, America's most successful college text writer of this era, provides an ex-

31. Quoted in Bozeman, *Protestants in the Age of Science,* 3.

32. This phrase is from Bozeman, ibid., 72. This theme is well documented also in George H. Daniels, *American Science in the Age of Jackson* (New York, 1968); E. Brooks Holifield, *The Gentlemen Theologians: American Theology in Southern Culture, 1795–1860* (Durham, 1978); and Hovenkamp, *Science and Religion in America.*

33. For the considerable influences of Scottish philosophy on Jefferson and the Declaration see Garry Wills, *Inventing America: Jefferson's Declaration of Independence* (New York, 1978). Wills, however, likely overestimates the centrality of these influences in Jefferson's thought.

cellent example for seeing this influence. Wayland, the president of Brown University, was an ordained Baptist minister and a thoroughgoing evangelical. Of his three major texts, *The Elements of Moral Science* (1835), *The Elements of Political Economy* (1837), and *The Elements of Intellectual Philosophy* (1854), the first deals most explicitly with questions of the relations of science to faith. Ethics, he holds, is as much a science as physics: specifically it is "the Science of Moral Law." Wayland was convinced that the laws of morality, essentially "sequences connected by our Creator" of rewards and punishments for various acts, could be discovered "to be just as invariable as an order of sequence in physics." These moral laws may be known by three means: by conscience, by natural religion, and by biblical revelation. These three are thoroughly complementary, differing only in their degrees of certainty and usefulness. Conscience, though certainly providing a universal sense that there is such a thing as right or wrong, does not clearly reveal some important moral laws (as obligations to universal forgiveness) and is often overcome by base passions. Additional moral laws can be discovered by the purely inductive scientific procedures of natural religion—by observing the rewards and punishments God has provided for various acts. Natural religion, however, is an imperfect moral guide also.[34]

Hence a further revelation is required. The moral precepts of revealed religion are "in perfect harmony" with those of natural religion. Revealed religion only goes beyond natural religion. It provides some facts (as about the Atonement or the afterlife) that we could not discover otherwise. The Bible also is "directing us to new lessons, taught us by nature." These clues point us to see how the moral laws observable in nature confirm the precepts taught in Scripture. "So complete is this coincidence, as to afford irrefragable proof that the Bible contains the moral laws of the universe; and, hence, that the Author of the universe—that is, of natural religion—is also the Author of the Scriptures."[35]

Wayland's method in *Moral Science* accordingly is to "derive these moral laws from natural or from revealed religion, or from both, as may be most convenient for our purpose." So, for instance, on Sabbath laws he starts with Scripture and confirms the laws from nature. On laws of property he starts with a mixture of principles from nature and from Scripture. "Everything we behold," he says, "is essentially the property of the Creator," and God reveals how he wants us to use our property. God's will, however, is in perfect accord with scientific analysis, or natural religion. For instance, God reveals that private ownership of property

34. Francis Wayland, *Elements of Moral Science*, ed. Joseph Angus (London, 1860 [1835]), 1, 3, 4, 100, 116–21.
35. Ibid., 219–20.

is proper, but this is well demonstrated by economic science which has shown the favorable consequences such an arrangement produces.[36]

A peculiar feature of this way of relating Christianity to the sciences shows up, however, when we look at Wayland's other texts. While the Christian might want to integrate his scientific work with biblical principles, by showing their mutual confirmations, he might just as legitimately deal with the issues as purely scientific ones, with no reference to explicitly Christian considerations. The assumption behind this thinking was that the law structures in creation that science discovers could in no way conflict with scriptural principles. God had created one set of laws. He had endowed us with various means of learning of these laws—including the firm principles of common sense.[37] One could therefore proceed purely on universally accepted principles of science with no fear of conflicting with the Bible.

So in *Elements of Political Economy* Wayland treats his subject as though it were a purely objective science. He acknowledges in his preface that almost every question in political economy could be discussed in moral philosophy. "He [Wayland writes of himself] has not, however, thought it proper in general, to intermingle them, but has argued economical questions on merely economical grounds." For with ethical questions, Wayland maintains, "Political Economy has nothing to do." Rather, questions of economics deal with whether an economical act is "wise," questions that can be settled on inductive grounds.[38]

Wayland's economics is essentially a defense of free enterprise, attempting to explicate the natural system of rewards and punishment (work is rewarded, idleness is punished) that controls economic activity and should not be interfered with. Certainly he thought these were no less God's laws because they could be discovered scientifically. Moreover, Wayland does not refrain from introducing Christianity by the back door. A demonstrable economic fact, he argues, is that the spread of Christianity leads to improvement in education, raising of moral standards, and increases in gross national product. "How much greater benefits does North America confer upon the world," he asks rhetorically, "than it would if it were peopled by its aboriginal inhabitants?"[39]

A number of twentieth-century commentators have suggested that

36. Ibid.

37. Wayland says: "God has created everything double; a world without us, and a correspondent world within us. He has made light without, and the eye within; beauty without, and taste within; moral qualities in actions, and conscience to judge of them; and so in every other case. By means of this correspondence, our communication with the external world exists." Ibid., 85.

38. Francis Wayland, *The Elements of Political Economy* (Boston, 1860 [1837]), iv.

39. Ibid., 132.

Wayland's approach was basically a species of secularization. Martin Marty, for instance, suggests that a characteristic form of secularization in nineteenth-century America was for Christians to acquiesce in a division of labor, separating the "religious realm" from the secular and the scientific.[40] Wayland's wholly scientific approach to *Political Economy* and *Intellectual Philosophy*,[41] for instance, then was inadvertently paving the way for the gradual fading away in the second half of the century of biblical confirmations or the idea of laws of God. Since technical texts in fields such as economics or philosophy did not make these issues explicit, later nineteenth-century thinkers could drop the implicit assumptions entirely with little struggle against Christian alternatives. William Graham Sumner, successor to Wayland as America's leading economist and originally trained for the ministry, remarked that early in his professional career he put his religious ideas in a drawer; years later he opened the drawer and found the beliefs gone.[42] Christian thinkers' encouragement of the independence of science certainly fostered such a quiet, but devastating, revolution in much of academia.

Similar tendencies appear in evangelicals' approaches to the natural sciences. On the one hand evangelical scientists in mid-nineteenth-century American colleges proclaimed themselves true Baconians, defenders of pure objective inquiry. On the other hand, since all laws were God's laws, inescapable evidence of benevolent design, their science was thoroughly "doxological"—never ceasing to lead us to praise the wisdom of the Creator.[43] They did not lack, then, zeal to relate Christianity to their science. Yet the way they did it was to grant scientific inquiry virtual independence, consistent with Baconian principles of objectivity. The only proviso was that whatever laws were discovered by this autonomous scientific method must be acknowledged as evidence of the wise design of the Creator. As several historians have pointed out, this amounted to a "rickety compromise" between piety and the ideal of absolutely free scientific inquiry.[44]

40. Martin Marty, *The Modern Schism: Three Paths to the Secular* (New York, 1969), 98.

41. Francis Wayland, *The Elements of Intellectual Philosophy* (New York, 1868 [1854]) is essentially a technical account of intellectual mechanisms and faculties in the tradition of common-sense philosophy.

42. Paul A. Carter, *The Spiritual Crisis of the Gilded Age* (DeKalb, Ill., 1971), 3–4; Richard Hofstadter, *Social Darwinism in American Life* (New York, 1955 [1944]), 51–66, describes Sumner's career.

43. This tendency is abundantly documented in Bozeman, *Protestants in the Age of Science;* George H. Daniels, *American Science in the Age of Jackson;* E. Brooks Holifield, *The Gentlemen Theologians: American Theology in Southern Culture, 1795–1860.*

44. This is the statement of Bozeman, *Protestants in an Age of Science,* 88, summarizing historian John C. Greene. Hovenkamp, *Science and Religion in America,* makes similar observations.

Natural science was an especially important building block in the edifice of evangelical thought. Far from incidental or peripheral, natural science was supposed to demonstrate design in the universe and hence, as Paley showed, provide important evidence for theism. Moreover, Bishop Butler's analogies suggested striking harmonies between natural and biblical revelation. Evangelicals placed a great deal of weight on the claim that these two sources of knowledge would never conflict. In fact, however, by the mid-nineteenth century such harmonies were being severely strained. Geology had forced admission that Genesis allowed much greater time periods than previously thought. Numerous other scientific theories in conflict with Scripture were in the air. In fact collapse was imminent.

Evangelical apologists, however, continued to rely on the argument from design with great displays of confidence.[45] Typical is "The Harmony of Revelation and Natural Science," delivered in 1850–51 as part of a series on evidences of Christianity at the University of Virginia (where once the enlightened thought of Jefferson had prevailed). The author, L. W. Green, president of Hampden-Sydney College, insists that "*The theology of natural science*, then, is in perfect harmony with *the theology of the Bible.*" Science "starts with *one instinctive principle, one intuitive conviction,* of the invariable connection between a CAUSE and its appropriate effect." Looking at nature with this intuitive principle, we inexorably are led to a "First Great Cause." At the same time we have an irresistible intuitive conviction of the "*relation between right and wrong,* that there is a moral element in man, and a moral law in the universe, that the *highest power and the highest right are at one, and both are* enthroned, supreme over all worlds." These two intuitions, then, an intuition of sufficient causes and a moral intuition (or, perhaps, a "moral government" intuition), secure human belief in a God of order, design, and benevolence. No amount of scientific evidence, thought Green, could dislodge the conclusions drawn from these intuitively based beliefs. Science could only add evidence of God's astonishing design. Astronomy could discover new worlds, geology might discover new ages, extinct races and species, and incalculable ages for the earth, "yet would the Christian welcome joyfully, and appropriate each successive revelation."[46]

45. Ibid., passim. For examples of nineteenth-century uses of the argument from design see Charles Hodge, *Systematic Theology* (New York, 1971), 1:215–33, and Robert L. Dabney, *Syllabus and Notes of the Course of Systematic and Polemic Theology* (Richmond, 1927 [1871]), 9.

46. L. W. Green, *Lectures on the Evidences of Christianity* (New York, 1854), 463–64. As some of the examples below indicate, evangelical apologists differed somewhat on what they considered intuitive beliefs. Most included, however, a sense of causality and/or moral order.

The Evidences of Christianity

In the meantime, so long as evangelicals were thoroughly convinced that science must support theism, natural theology was not so much their concern as was the defense of the authority of the Bible.[47] Indeed the Bible was the key issue. For American evangelicals prior to the era of Darwin the chief opponents were Deists and Transcendentalists. Each defended a form of theism known through nature. The real apologetic problem seemed to be, not whether nature pointed toward God, but whether the Bible pointed to the same God. This issue was of supreme importance for Protestants in the age of Enlightenment. America was in unique ways a Bible civilization, the land of *Scriptura sola.*[48] Major issues of the survival of Anglo-Saxon and Christian civilization seemed to rest on the question of the authority of the Bible. In a civilization where in practice the authority of science was seldom challenged, a crucial need seemed to be to demonstrate the congruence of the two authorities.

The evangelical views of the relationships between faith and reason appear most clearly in their arguments used to demonstrate that the Bible was indeed the revelation of the same God known in nature.

Mark Hopkins, famed evangelical teacher ("The ideal college is Mark Hopkins at one end of a log and a student on the other"), states as typically as anyone the case for Christianity as it stood at midcentury. "Truth is one," Hopkins insists. "If God has made a revelation in one mode, it must coincide with what he has revealed in another." Hopkins presumes, therefore, that we can proceed from what we know with certainty—that which nature reveals—to settle the matter in dispute—the claims of Christianity. Either Christianity harmonized with known truths or it did not. If it did, there was every reason to expect that a scientific inquiry could assemble an overwhelming accumulation of evidences of that harmony. "The Christian religion admits of certain proof," he declares accordingly. All that is required to see this proof is to approach the evidence, not with the prejudices of skeptics, but "in the position of an impartial jury." "This course alone," says Hopkins in Baconian tones,

---

Green's show of confidence is evident in his remarks on geology: "It furnishes by far the most conclusive of all arguments for the existence of God; explodes the atheistic theory of an infinite series of beings; and thus dispels the last remaining doubt that might otherwise have thrown its shadow over the soul of man," 62.

On the centrality of the themes of design, benevolence, and order, cf. Bozeman, *Age of Science,* 82.

47. An essay by "a society of clergymen" in *Bibliotheca Sacra* 3 (May 1846), "Natural Theology," lamented that "so noble a department of study should have fallen into unmerited neglect," 241–42.

48. See Nathan Hatch, "*Scriptura Sola and Novus Ordo Seclorum,*" in *The Bible in America,* ed. Nathan Hatch and Mark Noll (New York, 1982), 59–78.

"decides nothing on the grounds of previous hypothesis, but yields itself entirely to the guidance of facts properly authenticated."[49]

Common-Sense philosophy was the starting point of this inquiry. The dictates of common sense provide us with considerable knowledge about nature and human nature. So we should be able to test the congruence of Christian claims with this intuitive and indisputable knowledge. Hopkins agreed with the prevailing opinion that although we were not born with innate ideas, our minds were endowed with innate powers that inevitably led us to certain beliefs.[50] The commonality of these powers and beliefs throughout the race established the "common ground" from which philosophy and the proof of Christianity could proceed.[51] Humans, said Hopkins, were obliged to rely on the authority of their faculties, such as states of consciousness, sense perceptions, memory, testimony, and reasoning, each of which could, under the proper circumstances, yield virtual certainty. Moreover, Hopkins pointed out in typical common-sense fashion an equally firm basis for certainty is "reason" (to be distinguished from reasoning) by which one perceives "directly, intuitively, necessarily, and believes, with a conviction from which he can not free himself, certain fundamental truths, upon which all other truths, and all reasoning, properly so called, or deduction are conditioned."[52] These immediate, noninferential beliefs include much the same list as Reid had proposed, such as the existence of the self, the existence of other personal and rational beings, the existence of the material world, the relationship of cause and effect, the continuity of past and present, mathematical axioms, our sense of choosing, of freedom, and of obligations and responsibilities. "By Reid they were called principles of common-sense, and by Dugald Stewart fundamental laws of belief."[53]

49. Mark Hopkins, *Evidences of Christianity* (Boston, 1876 [1846]), 97–98 and 39.

50. Cf. Dabney, *Theology,* 83, and Francis Wayland, "The Philosophy of Analogy," in *American Philosophical Addresses 1700–1900,* ed. Joseph L. Blau (New York, 1946), 348, for similar statements.

51. Mark Hopkins, "Grounds of Knowledge and Rules for Belief," *Princeton Review* 57 (January 1881): 1.

52. Hopkins, *Evidences,* 24–27.

53. Hopkins, "Grounds of Knowledge," 4; cf. Hopkins, *Evidences,* passim. Some differences of opinion existed among evangelicals as to the relation of knowledge of God to these intuitive first principles. Charles Hodge held that some sort of general knowledge of God was indeed intuitive and universal. This, he said, the Bible taught. This knowledge was incomplete, so that further instruction was necessary "to give them any adequate knowledge of the nature of God, and of their relations to Him." Hodge, *Systematic Theology,* 1:199; cf. 191–203. Hodge thought, nonetheless, that it was perfectly legitimate to use the traditional proofs to confirm such intuitive knowledge, 202–3. The Southern Presbyterian theologian, Robert Dabney, criticized Hodge, saying that Hodge confused intuition with an elementary deduction of common sense (the deduction from an intuitive sense of obligation to an obligator). Dabney, *Theology,* 7. Mark Hopkins thought that the

With this common ground to work from, Hopkins could proceed with a major preliminary step in his defense of Christianity: showing that what the Bible reveals is fully consistent with what we already know through nature and natural revelation. "If," he says, "it can be shown that Christianity does not coincide with the well-authenticated teaching of natural religion, it will be conclusive against it." That biblical revelation passes this test establishes a presumption in its favor. On this point Hopkins' arguments are similar to Bishop Butler's in pointing out the many analogies between the two revelations, hence suggesting a single author. Each revelation, for instance, leaves us with incomplete knowledge, not forcing all its truths upon us, and hence leaving us some freedom of judgment and inquiry. The Bible may not be perfectly clear, but then neither is a great deal of what we trust completely in nature.[54]

More positively, Hopkins maintained that he could show that the Christian religion was ideally adapted to the human condition as revealed in nature. "There is a harmony of adaptation," he says, "and also of analogy. The key is adapted to the lock; the fin of the fish is analogous to the wing of the bird. Christianity, as I hope to show, is adapted to man." The human religious nature furnished considerable presumption in this direction. To suppose that the Creator would have created this virtually universal tendency toward religion in mankind and yet not have provided for him a proper object for it "is like supposing that he would create the eye without light." Since every theist (and Hopkins could assume that few in his audience would deny theism) agreed that God was a "moral Governor," they should also admit that such a good Creator probably would reveal himself to his creatures. Moreover, the glaring moral defects of the race made a revelation such as the Bible's seem even more likely. "If a rational being, capable of religion," says Hopkins, "had lost the moral image, and consequently the true knowledge of God and it should be the object of God to restore him, it could be done in no other way than by a direct revelation."[55]

The suitability of Christianity to the known character of humanity is evidenced especially clearly in the correspondence of its moral teachings to human moral needs. Nature revealed a system of morality, of rewards and punishments (as Wayland similarly argued). The Bible taught pre-

natural world was ambiguous in revealing God, and our natural sense of moral obligation might be blinded. So the knowledge of God (from the starry heavens above and moral law within) was not immediate or intuitive, even though it was a simple demonstration.

Dabney and Hopkins appear to be closer to Reid on this point, while Hodge tries to harmonize Common-Sense philosophy with Calvin's view.

54. Hopkins, *Evidences*, 98, 80–91.

55. Ibid., 75 and 48.

cisely the same system,[56] but only more precisely, fully, and explicitly. "In fact," says Hopkins,

> moral philosophy, and political economy, and the science of politics, . . . are, so far as they are sound, but experience and the structure of organized nature echoing back the teachings of Christianity. What principle of Christian ethics does moral philosophy now presume to call into question?[57]

Each of these considerations added a strand to the rope that was to form an unbreakable link between what was known from nature and what was claimed in Scripture. To establish Christian truth these Protestants, of course, considered it essential to establish the full authority of the Bible. Such authoritative claims, they held, should be susceptible to analysis. As in almost every other area of life, it should be possible to produce the evidence that would distinguish the genuine revelation from the pretenders. Such evidences might be an accumulation of considerations that, taken as a whole, would be compelling. It would be strange indeed if the true revelation lacked at least enough supporting evidence to establish a strong presumption in its favor.

The arguments for the Bible's authenticity as God's revelation appealed to two areas where human science had access. The moral and religious content of Scripture could, as we have seen, be tested against what was known about morality and religion by simply looking at nature and human nature. In addition, the historical claims of Scripture could be examined like any other historical statements. These two approaches converged in one of the strongest arguments for the Bible's authority. Natural religion and moral philosophy confirmed that the moral teachings of Scripture were unsurpassed. The presence of this exalted moral teaching helped confirm the honesty and integrity of the authors of Scripture in their other claims. "It is incredible and contradictory," says Hopkins, "contrary to all the known laws of mind, to suppose that men whose moral discrimination and susceptibilities were so acute—who could originate a system so pure, so elevated, so utterly opposed to all falsehood—would, without reason or motive that we can

56. Hopkins regarded the superiority of Christianity to other religions as needing little argument. Of the chief contender he says: "But I need not spend time in comparing, or rather contrasting, the religion of Mohammed, unsustained by miracles or prophecies, propagated by the sword, encouraging fatalism, and pride, and intolerance, sanctioning polygamy, offering a sensual heaven,—a religion whose force is already spent, which has no sympathy or congruity with the enlarged views and onward movements of these days, and which is fast passing into a hopeless imbecility,—with the pure, and humble and beneficent religion of Christ." Ibid., 66.

57. Ibid., 102–3.

see, deliberately attempt to deceive mankind concerning their highest interests."[58]

To this evidence of the integrity of the biblical writers could be added a host of other historical considerations. Prophecies had been fulfilled. The sixty-six books were marvelously unified. Ancient church authorities whose memories reached back to the first centuries affirmed the integrity of the writers and attested their complete trust by being willing to die for their beliefs. The New Testament writers showed similarly total confidence in their claims, and many became martyrs. Their theological claims were confirmed by miracles, to which these authors were eyewitnesses. No contemporary witnesses refuted these miracle claims, even though many thousands of people would have been in a position to do so had fraud been involved.[59] All these evidences confirmed that the biblical writers were witnesses of the highest integrity. We could rely on their testimony, including their claims to be reporting God's revelation, with complete confidence.

Hopkins and the other evangelical writers followed Thomas Reid closely in pointing out that such evidence is "probable" as opposed to demonstrative, "moral" as opposed to mathematical. Lyman Beecher explains this use of "moral": "The difference between demonstration and moral certainty is, that in one case the mind sees the objects of comparison and sees the result, which, of course, is knowledge; but in the other, derives its confidence from the perception of probabilities multiplying till

58. Ibid., 119. Hopkins is not especially concerned with the accuracy of detail of the biblical statements. He says, for instance, that the discrepancies among the gospels are evidence of their authenticity, since a fraud likely would have tried to make all the details match previous accounts, 204.

59. Hopkins, *Evidences,* passim. The impact of Christianity in changing the course of history, especially its demonstrably beneficial moral impact, helped support these claims.

Every evangelical author included a refutation of Hume's arguments on miracles and pointed out that only a prejudice against all miracles would lead one to rule out the authenticity of the biblical accounts. Hopkins, 28, says that he will review the well-known arguments refuting Hume because it is still the custom of those who defend Christianity to do so, just as it was "the custom of British ships to fire a gun on passing the port of Copenhagen, long after its power had been prostrated, and its influence had ceased to be felt."

Lyman Beecher, "The Bible a Revelation from God to Man," *Works* (Boston, 1852), 1:219, contrasts the public miracles of the Bible (those of Moses were witnessed by a whole nation that could have revolted against a fraud) to the private miracles of Mahomet and the Catholic Church.

George Fisher of Yale, *Essays on the Supernatural Origins of Christianity* (New York, 1890 [1866]), xxvii, expresses complete confidence in authenticating the miracle accounts: "That the narratives of miracles which are given in the Gospels are, in the main, a faithful record of facts which actually occurred, is the result of a sound, unbiassed historical criticism, and must, sooner or later, be generally acknowledged."

they produce confidence, or moral certainty."[60] Such certainty can become virtually as secure as in the case of mathematical demonstrations. Practically all the important affairs of life, in fact, depend on reliance on such accumulations of probable evidence. Particularly relevant to the case for Christianity is that many important human activities depend entirely on complete reliance on the "probable" evidence of testimony. Courts of law, and all our knowledge of historical figures, depend almost entirely on such testimony.[61] Every normal adult, of course, knows that testimony may deceive. But just as certainly, every society rests matters of life and death on the testimony of witnesses of demonstrated integrity. Reason, of course, often must be used to assemble the evidences of such integrity, but when it does so beyond a reasonable doubt, humans in all ages have accepted such testimony as a ground of certainty.[62] To present the evidences for Christianity, then, is no different than what one might do in other important affairs of life. "The proof of the authenticity of the Holy Scriptures," as Francis Wayland puts it, is "only a particular exemplification of the general laws of evidence."[63]

Faith and Reason

What view of faith and reason emerges from this evidentialist apologetic? On the face of it, it appears that these evidentialists thought that reason must play a very large role in support of faith. "Without reason," says Archibald Alexander of Princeton, "there can be no religion: for in every step which we take, in examining the evidences of revelation, in interpreting its meaning, or in assenting to its doctrines, the exercise of this faculty is indispensable."[64] "Reason is necessarily presupposed in every revelation," echoed his famous student, Charles Hodge.[65] Such statements appear more moderate, however, when we take into account their broad use of "reason." "Reason," as we saw in Hopkins, included reliance in all those common-sense faculties by which people might know things intuitively and directly. So Hodge used the term "reason" to include any capacities for understanding. "The first and indispensable office of reason, therefore," says Hodge, "in matters of faith, is the cognition, or intelligent apprehension of the truths proposed for our recep-

60. Beecher, *Works,* 1:54; Hopkins, *Evidences,* 22.

61. Cf. Reid, *Essays;* cf. Wayland, *Intellectual Philosophy,* 317–32.

62. Reid points out the necessity of the mutual aid of reason and testimony in *An Inquiry into the Human Mind* (Chicago, 1970), VI:24, 24.

63. Wayland, *Moral Science,* 203.

64. Archibald Alexander, *Evidences of the Authenticity, Inspiration, and Canonical Authority of the Holy Scriptures* (Philadelphia, 1848 [1836]), 9.

65. Hodge, *Systematic Theology,* 1:49.

tion." "Communication of truth," he explains, "supposes the capacity to receive it."[66]

When the evidentialists, then, spoke of the priority of "reason" in relation to faith, that did not mean at all that a Christian's faith needed to be based on reasoning or arguments. They all agreed emphatically on this point. "It is absurd," says Hodge, "to say that no man believes in God, who has not comprehended some philosophical argument for his existence, it is no less absurd to say that no man can rationally believe in Christ, who has not been instructed in the historical arguments which confirm his mission."[67] Since Christianity was both true and perfectly attuned to human needs, its truth might be recognized immediately. "It is very possible," says Hodge, "that the mind may see a thing to be true, without being able to prove its truth, or to make any satisfactory exhibition of the grounds of its belief."[68] Mark Hopkins explained the case as similar to that of the various disciples believing the evidence when they encountered the resurrected Christ. Some believed just by seeing him. Others had to hear him speak. Others, like Thomas, had to have more proofs and touch the actual marks of the crucifixion wounds.[69]

These observations help clarify the evidentialists' meaning of "evidence." As in the case of "reason," they use a broad meaning that does not necessarily have to do with producing arguments. So when the evangelical apologists make remarks like "man cannot believe, or be obligated to believe, without evidence" (Lyman Beecher)[70] or "faith without evidence is either irrational or impossible" (Charles Hodge),[71] they are not making radical proposals. By "evidence" they seem to mean simply those qualities of something (as an object or the truth of a statement) that can make it evident or apparent to us. Since many things have qualities that

66. Ibid.

67. Hodge, "Ground of Faith in the Scriptures," *Essays and Reviews* (New York, 1879), 191. First appeared in *Princeton Review* 17 (1845).

68. Ibid., 188.

69. Hopkins, *Evidences,* 353. Cf. Paley, who responds to the observation that most readers of his *Natural Theology* never doubted the truths he argues for: "Now, I answer that by *investigation* the following points are always gained in favor of doctrines even the most generally acknowledged, supposing them to be true, namely stability and impression. Occasions will arise to try the firmness of our most habitual opinions. And upon these occasions it is a matter of incalculable use to feel our foundation, to find a support in argument for what we have taken upon authority," 83. The evidentialists' motives in exhibiting the evidences and arguments in support of Christianity seem to be (1) to aid the doubter and (2) to keep strong the case for Christianity in the ongoing debates in the intellectual world as to which viewpoint is true: evidences of its truth must be available, and these assembled would constitute a stronger case than could be made for any false system.

70. Beecher, *Works,* 1:203.

71. Hodge, *Systematic Theology,* 1:53.

make the thing immediately apparent to us, seeing the evidence for something need not involve having any arguments about it.

Charles Hodge clearly explains the role of evidence and of immediate recognition of it in relation to belief in the authenticity of the Bible. The Bible contains sufficient evidence of its authenticity, as truly the Word of God. This evidence is of the sort that, like a truth of mathematics, when one properly apprehends it one simply finds oneself compelled to believe it. One finds that the Bible "is so holy, so true, so consonant to right reason and right feeling, that he cannot doubt its truth." These biblical truths are so compelling to those who see them aright because the account of human sinfulness and the provisions for holiness and atonement so exactly suit our condition and needs. "They are truths which have their foundation in our nature and in our relation to God." Whatever other evidences or whatever arguments one may or may not have, when he perceives these truths directly, he does so "on the highest possible evidence; the testimony of God himself with and by the truth to his own heart; making him see and feel that it is truth."[72] Seeing such evidence, then, is not at all dependent on being able to produce an argument or proof.[73]

People, however, may not recognize the evidence for even the plainest truths. This is especially the case with biblical truths. Human sinfulness and moral perversity make them refuse to use their native faculties for recognizing God's truth. So one's moral condition can stand in the way of recognizing even that which is self-evident (especially when the sinfulness that one loves so deeply is that which is being exposed and threatened). "Let a man who hears the forty-seventh proposition of Euclid announced for the first time," explains Mark Hopkins, "trace the steps of the demonstration, and he *must* believe it to be true; but let him know that, as soon as he does perceive the evidence of that proposition so as to believe it on that ground, he shall lose his right eye, and he will never trace the evidence." On the other hand, says Hopkins with regard to biblical truth, "Let 'the mists that steam up before the intellect from a corrupt heart be dispersed,' and truths, before obscure, shine out as the noonday."[74] Seeing such truths might, of course, be aided by arguments. Arguments, however, could not compel belief. What compelled belief is

72. Hodge, "Ground of Faith," 189–92.

73. Hodge compares our knowing of this sort of truth to knowing mathematical truths, recognizing beauty or genius and recognizing moral truths. Of the latter he says: "This is not a thing which, in the proper sense of the word, admits of proof. The only possible proof of the correctness of a moral doctrine, is to make us see its truth; its accordance with the law of God, the supreme standard, and with that law as written in our own hearts." Ibid., 189.

74. Hopkins, *Evidences*, 20–21.

just the seeing of the truth or, put another way, the proper seeing of the evidence.

The acceptance of these truths on God's authority is faith. "Faith," says Charles Hodge, "means belief of things not seen, on the ground of testimony."[75] One trusts what God says and assents to the truths he presents. The Holy Spirit supplies these truths to our hearts, so that the faith is not simply abstract belief, but saving faith.[76] "Faith is founded on testimony," says Hodge. "It is not founded on sense, reason, or feeling, but on the authority of him by whom it is authenticated."[77] Reason accordingly precedes faith, but only in the sense that normal understanding is necessary to apprehend the truth before one believes it. Reason is not the ground of faith, even though it is essential to it. Reason involves faculties necessary for us to see God and what is true; our faith is in God and his truth. Moreover, through faith, or trust in God's authority, we learn truths from the Bible that reason by itself could never teach.

Faith and reason can never conflict. This conviction is central to the entire evangelical outlook. God is the author of all things, so truth discovered in various ways will always harmonize. Faith in the irrational, says Hodge, is impossible. "It is impossible to believe that to be true which the mind sees to be false."[78] Philosophy and theology, he explains, occupy "common ground." "Both assume to teach what is true concerning God, man, the world, and the relation in which God stands to his creatures." Moreover,

> God is the author of our nature and the maker of heaven and earth, therefore nothing which the laws of our nature or the facts of the external world prove to be true, can contradict the teachings of God's Word. Neither can the Scriptures contradict the truths of philosophy or science.[79]

The Hidden Assumptions

We can return now to the central question of this essay. What, if anything, about this mid-nineteenth-century American evangelical apologetic made it particularly vulnerable to onslaughts of the scientific revolution associated with Darwinism? Was, as James Ward Smith maintains, this seemingly formidable intellectual edifice in fact built on a foundation of a superficial accommodation to the modern scientific revolution?

75. Hodge, *Systematic Theology,* 3:63.

76. Ibid., 3:68–70. Nineteenth-century evangelical writers, of course, differed on their definitions of faith. Hodge, however, is an important representative.

77. Ibid., 3:63.

78. Ibid., 3:83.

79. Ibid., 1:56.

The key to the answer to this question seems to have to do with the relation of one's assumptions to what one knows about reality. If careful thinkers find arguments absolutely compelling to themselves, but these arguments soon are widely regarded, even by many sympathetic observers, as specious, chances are that the arguments rested on some questionable hidden assumptions.

The evidentialist apologists were well enough aware of some of their basic assumptions. Charles Hodge, on whom we can concentrate as one of the strongest representatives of the outlook, noted that both the scientist and the theologian must start with "certain assumptions." First, "He assumes the trustworthiness of his sense perceptions." Second, "He must also assume the trustworthiness of his mental operations." Third, "He must also rely on the certainty of those truths which are not learned from experience, but which are given in the constitution of our nature," such as every effect must have a cause and the uniformity of effects from identical causes.[80]

None of these assumptions appears to be especially controversial. Few people would want seriously to challenge the first two, and although some might argue that belief in cause and effect is learned, everyone but a few philosophers and crackpots would agree that indeed we are obliged to assume such beliefs as true. If there is a weakness in this Common-Sense outlook, it does not seem to lie in these acknowledged and widely held assumptions.

Behind these, however, were several other assumptions that were not clearly recognized as such and which appear more controversial. Most striking from a twentieth-century view is the immense confidence they had in the possibility of establishing most of one's knowledge objectively. Starting with the certainties of common sense and following the careful inductive methods of Baconian science, they were confident one could reach sure conclusions, compelling to any unbiased observer, in almost every aspect of human inquiry. Hodge reveals this assumption by constantly speaking of intellectual inquiry as the discovery of "facts." By "facts" he seems to mean states of affairs about reality which are true independently of our knowing them. Once discovered, he insists, "Facts do not admit of denial." "To deny facts," he says in reference to scientific discoveries, "is to deny what God affirms to be true. This the Bible can not do."[81] What seems controversial is, not so much this concept of fact, but rather the wide application it is given. As we have seen, the evangelicals characteristically assumed that the Baconian method would yield indubitable facts in all areas: morality, political thought, economics, and

80. Ibid., 1:9.
81. Ibid., 1:57.

den

Hodge describes the Bible as a "store-house of facts." "The the theologian what nature is to the man of science."[82] Such ealed in God's Word, when properly understood, can be known certainty as "logical propositions."[83] "They are so set forth, that the meaning of the terms employed, and the sense of the propositions themselves, are understood, and understood in the same way by the renewed and the unrenewed."[84]

The evangelical apologists, of course, recognized bias. Bias, however, was something other people had. "Tell me what a man's philosophy is," said Hodge, "and I will ask him no questions about his theology."[85] They, on the other hand, considered themselves to hold no special philosophy. Their own views were simply open-minded, unbiased, candid, objective, and scientific.

This immense confidence rested on other hidden assumptions. The evangelical apologists' assurance of a high yield of objective certainty in intellectual inquiry rested on their assumptions about nature. Nature, they assumed, was ordered, intelligible, and meaningful. They saw in nature qualities that it would be likely to have only if it were created by a deity much like the God of the Bible—a benevolent Creator and Governor, interested in the welfare of his creatures. The existence of such a benevolent Creator and Governor, then, was in effect a tacit assumption of their outlook. Such a deity, they assumed further, would not systematically deceive his creatures by giving them faulty intellectual mechanisms. Rather, he would ensure that if they used their faculties responsibly, they would gain substantial knowledge about him and about the rest of creation.

The type of confidence they had in common sense also was influenced by this assumption concerning the design of nature. While their convictions about the reliability of common sense may formally have rested (as they did in the case of Reid) on just the fact that people find themselves obliged to trust common-sense faculties and principles, the implications drawn from such observations typically went far beyond what such ob-

82. Ibid., 1:10.

83. Hodge, "The Theology of Intellect and That of the Feelings," II, *Essays and Reviews* from the *Princeton Review* 22 (1851): 609. "Logical" here seems to have no special force, since he has just listed a number of biblical teachings like the Incarnation, that Christ died for our sins, and such. Hodge seems to mean that these beliefs are like the propositions used in logic.

84. Ibid. Hodge adds: "That the one class perceive in the truths thus revealed an excellence, and experience from them a power, of which the other class have no experience, does not alter the case."

85. Quoted in John C. Vander Stelt, *Philosophy and Scripture: A Study in Old Princeton and Westminster Theology* (Marlton, N.J., 1978), 147.

servations by themselves would sustain. As Hodge (following Reid) r marked in stating his assumptions, common-sense truths were "given ir the constitution of our nature." Having been so purposely designed, they could be relied on with perfect security. Moreover, the design of nature was assumed to involve the creation of a single universal human nature. Hence the presumption was that common-sense principles were universal and unalterable. So, as we have seen, Reid thought it possible to establish once for all a universal code of agreed-upon common-sense principles.

Such assumptions greatly abetted the idea that finding truth was essentially an objective process of discovering the "facts." As already observed, most recent twentieth-century ideas of "truth" have assumed an evolution of self-consciousness. With process rather than design as a basic category for thought, "truth" tends to become far more relative to the observer, his time and place. "Facts" commonly are regarded as not fixed, but as some combination of an objective reality and interpretation imposed by the observer.[86]

The weakness in the evidentialists' intellectual system, then, appears to be, not so much in that they started with common-sense assumptions and principles, but in their failure to recognize that a good many other assumptions were in fact functioning in their thought. The role of such assumptions concerning design and a benevolent Designer can be identified more clearly if we take their stated assumptions and add to them premises antithetical to their own, such as "there is no benevolent creator" or even "we do not know whether there is a benevolent creator." With these premises even the reliability of common-sense perceptions looks less secure. The phenomenon that people almost always find themselves trusting common-sense faculties and principles, and even that for the sake of argument they may be obliged to trust them, does not yield a strong presumption that these faculties and principles are especially reliable. Certainly it does not yield any presumption that these are universal throughout the race or unalterable, or that there is one set of assumptions that, in principle, everyone should agree to.

The critical role of the foundational assumptions concerning design in nature and a benevolent Designer became most acutely apparent in the debate over Darwinism. Darwinism was especially threatening to the entire evangelical edifice because it boldly removed the presumed intelligent design of nature and hence the benevolent Designer. Eighteenth- and early nineteenth-century evangelicals, and most of their contemporaries,

86. Cf. my discussion of this point with reference to the historical views of Carl Becker in "J. Gresham Machen, History, and Truth," *Westminster Theological Journal* 42 (fall 1979): 157–75.

took the intelligent design of nature to be indisputably a matter of common sense, confirmed by a good bit of reasoning. In fact, however, if one did not first presuppose a benevolent Creator, the intelligence and intentionality of the design was not nearly as evident as supposed. Darwin showed that with a premise such as "we do not know whether there is a benevolent creator" the apparent design and order could be explained at least plausibly on other grounds.

Charles Hodge saw this threat clearly in his famous essay *What Is Darwinism?* (1874), but he could only reassert the common sense of his own position. "The grand and fatal objection" to Darwinism, he said, was that Darwin's principle of natural selection excluded intelligent design. Hodge retorted:

> But in thus denying design in nature, these writers array against themselves the intuitive perceptions and irresistible convictions of all mankind, . . . a barrier which no man has ever been able to surmount.

Hodge bolsted this appeal to irresistible intuition with appeals to Paley and Butler. Paley had produced a "solid irrefragable argument" for a Designer, based on the inescapable evidence of design. "If a man denies that there is design in nature," Hodge argued by analogy, "he can with quite a good reason deny that there is any design in any or in all the works ever executed by man."[87]

The argument was futile as far as the Western intellectual community was concerned. Hodge could claim that the conviction of intelligent design in nature was irresistible and universal, but large parts of the next generations demonstrated that in fact the belief was quite resistible and far from universal. Common-Sense philosophy, claiming to be objective, claiming to rest on no prior assumptions, had no adequate response to such an attack on one of its fundamental principles. The supposed objectivism of the system suffered from a fatal flaw. Common sense could not settle a dispute over what was a matter of common sense.

Even more vulnerable in the evidentialists' defense of Christianity were the other central pillars in their arguments—the appeals to human religious and moral sentiments. Again, with the tacit assumption of one be-

87. Hodge, *What Is Darwinism?* (London, 1874), 169, 170, and 173. James R. Moore, *The Post-Darwinian Controversies: A Study of the Protestant Struggle to Come to Terms with Darwin in Great Britain and America, 1870–1900* (Cambridge, 1979), shows that a number of Christian thinkers, notably some conservative Calvinists, viewed Darwinism as compatible with design, pointing out that in principle it raised no new questions regarding the relationship of God's controlling providence and secondary natural means. No longer, however, could they claim with Paley et al. that an intelligent designer was the *only* plausible explanation.

nevolent Creator these phenomena seemed to point toward a confirmation of Christian claims. So, as we have seen, Mark Hopkins argues, "There is a harmony of adaptation, and also of analogy. The key is adapted to the lock; the fin of the fish is analogous to the wing of the bird. Christianity, as I hope to show, is adapted to man."[88] To first principles of morality, especially, followers of the Scottish philosophy characteristically assigned normative status parallel to the first principles of knowledge. In response to Darwinism, apologists such as Hopkins and Hodge continued to appeal to the supposedly normative principles. Darwinism, they said, could not adequately account for universal religious and moral sentiments.[89] The fact of the matter was, however, that Darwinism *could* account for these phenomena, at least as far as the logic of the case was concerned. Only if one already had a tacit premise that these religious and moral sentiments must have been designed for a purpose did it follow that they were clearly evidence for a Designer. Darwinism, starting with the premise that these phenomena arose naturally, found them to be survival mechanisms—primitive and prescientific ones at that. Such attacks left the evangelical apologetic in a shambles. Great weight had been placed on the analogies of biblical Christianity to what was known about nature. Darwin too saw the contrivances of nature and those of morality and religion as analogous; only in his view they were analogous means of survival with no further point or normative status.

The Claims and Limits of Science

In *What Is Darwinism?* Charles Hodge perceptively related the immediate issue to the larger questions of science and religion. "Science," said Hodge, was coming to have a new and more limited meaning. Etymologically "science" meant simply "knowledge." It has long had this broad meaning which Hodge himself employed. Recently, however, the meaning was becoming increasingly restricted. "Science" in this restricted sense was limited to "the ordered phenomena which we recognize through the senses." Such a definition gave scientists a disposition "to undervalue any other kind of evidence except that of the senses."[90]

This recent trend to limit the meaning of "science" reflected the philosophical tendencies of the day. Various popular versions of the Kantian distinction between the phenomena and the noumena were being widely circulated and adopted. Two of the most prominent defenders of Darwinism, Herbert Spencer in England and John Fiske in America, made

88. Hopkins, *Evidences*, 75.
89. Mark Hopkins, *The Scriptural Idea of Man* (New York, 1884), 25.
90. Hodge, *What Is Darwinism?* 127 and 129.

much of this point. The knowledge that we have access to scientifically is limited to the realm of the observable phenomena. We know that underlying these observable phenomena must be some essential qualities or noumena to which we do not have access. All we know about these is that they must exist and that they have effects in the phenomena we observe.[91] So Spencer and Fiske posited a great "Force" or "Power" behind the universe—"the noumenon of all phenomena," as Hodge tagged it.[92] T. H. Huxley, another of the prominent proponents of Darwinism, went further, coining the word "agnostic" to describe his view. "Agnostic" fit exactly the immensely influential intellectual trend growing from these philosophical developments. Positive science, dealing with phenomena, gave us knowledge. Other areas, such as religion or ultimate moral principles, were in the realm of the noumena or the unknowable.[93] So widely have such views of science and religion been adopted in Western culture that we can aptly designate the century after 1869, when Huxley invented the term, as the "age of agnosticism." If the metaphysical aspects of religion were to be discussed at all, they were to be relegated to a realm of "mystery" insusceptible to scientific inquiry.

Hodge recognized clearly enough the beginnings of this trend, but he had little way to counter it. His position was weakened for two related reasons. First, he had as high a view of the powers of pure scientific inquiry as did his most positivistic and secularistic contemporaries. Having had such an exalted view of the possibility of scientific certainty, he and his evangelical counterparts were hardly in a position to discount *prima facie* the extravagant claims of the new science.

The problem, however, went deeper into their basic philosophical stance. Hodge and his evidentialist counterparts claimed to start with a neutral objective epistemology that could be shared by all persons of common sense. Such a view worked well enough so long as there was a general consensus in the culture on certain metaphysical issues. Through the first half of the nineteenth century substantial elements of metaphys-

91. Spencer, in fact, got this idea directly from the nineteenth-century Scottish philosopher Sir William Hamilton (1788–1856). Hamilton's very influential philosophy combined elements of Reid and Kant. Hamilton held "that our knowledge of mind and of matter is relative and conditioned and that 'of existence absolutely and in itself, we know nothing'." We are, however, compelled to think of something absolute, unknown and unknowable by virtue of a "law of thought." Timothy J. Duggan, "William Hamilton," *The Encyclopedia of Philosophy,* ed. Paul Edwards (New York, 1967), 3:409. Spencer's relation to Hamilton is discussed in Flower and Murphey, *History of Philosophy in America,* 2:528–31. Hodge offered a long critique of this aspect of Hamilton in his *Systematic Theology.*

92. Hodge, *What Is Darwinism?* 19.

93. T. A. Goudge, "Thomas Henry Huxley," *Encyclopedia of Philosophy,* 4:101–3. Cf. Ronald W. Hepburn, "Agnosticism," 1:56–59.

ical assumptions of the Christian worldview survived. People generally assumed, for instance, that God, other spiritual beings, and normative moral principles were realities that were proper objects of human inquiry and knowledge. When this consensus disappeared, the proponents of a neutral and objective epistemology had little grounds for rebuttal. The question became, Were such areas proper areas for scientific inquiry and knowledge? But science itself could not settle a dispute over what was a proper area for scientific inquiry. This was a metaphysical question that had to be decided on some other grounds.

The evangelical apologists had conceded too much. In 1871, for instance, Hodge had boldly stated that the solution to the seeming conflicts of science and religion was simply "to let science take its course, assured that the Scriptures will accommodate themselves to all well-authenticated facts in time to come, as they have in the past."[94] But again the fatal flaw of such objectivism appears. Who was to settle a dispute over what "the facts" were? The new science was excluding whole realms of religion and morality from "the facts." It did not help to respond, as inductivists such as the evidentialists characteristically did, by saying "just look at the evidence." Who was to settle a question of what was "evidence" or of what was possible evidence for what? Hodge complained, in the passage quoted above, that the new science tended "to undervalue any other kind of evidence except that of the senses." But what principle would decide what should be valued as evidence? Common sense might be appealed to. But, as already observed, a neutral common sense cannot settle a dispute over what is neutral common sense.

Here is the point at which James Ward Smith appears to be right in his analysis and critique of the dominant school of American Protestant thought prior to Darwin. With the exception of Jonathan Edwards, evangelicals had developed no effective critique of the first principles on which scientific inquiry rested. They had failed to appropriate Edwards' insight that the prior questions are metaphysical. There is no wholly neutral epistemology that can settle disputes over what areas of human knowledge are neutral and objective. Rather, a Christian epistemology must frankly begin, more or less as does that of Edwards, not only with common sense but also with data derived from revelation. Our understanding of something of the full range of human knowledge is in important ways derived from our belief in a Creator who communicates to his creatures both in nature and Scripture. Commitment to such a view allows us to see in reality the evidences of spiritual things.[95] Lacking such commitment, the

94. Hodge, *Systematic Theology,* 1:57.

95. Discussion of Edwards' views has recently been advanced by Norman Fiering, *Jonathan Edwards's Moral Thought and Its British Context* (Chapel Hill, 1981).

modern agnostic sees the same phenomena but does not apprehend their spiritual aspects.

Two Kinds of People and Two Kinds of Science

The question of how these issues might have been worked out in the setting of late nineteenth-century science may be clarified by a comparison. The value of this comparison—with the response of Abraham Kuyper in The Netherlands—is suggested not only by the Dutch-American context in which this essay is written but also by the fact that the evidentialist and the Kuyperian traditions are two of the strongest influences on current American evangelical thought on faith and reason.

Of all the countries in the Western world The Netherlands is the one in which traditional and evangelical Protestantism suffered the least serious decline in numbers and in intellectual influence during the heyday of science and secularism through the first half of the twentieth century. Furthermore, the school of thought of which Abraham Kuyper was the best representative and which substantially influenced the Dutch Protestant community differed markedly from the characteristic stance of American evangelical evidentialists exactly at the point we have been considering. Kuyper himself was not only a theologian but also the founder of a university and the prime minister of The Netherlands from 1901 to 1905, so that his views were well represented in the culture, even though never dominant. Of course, to suggest that the influence of Kuyper's views accounts for the markedly differing degree of impact traditionalist Protestantism had on the culture and the intellectual community of Holland as compared to America would be to oversimplify vastly relations of causes and effects. As emphasized earlier in this paper, many factors help account for the relative intellectual and cultural strength of various religious movements. Nevertheless, just as the evangelical apologists articulated trends in relating Christianity to culture and science prevalent in nineteenth-century America, so Kuyper articulated tendencies in Dutch Reformed thinking that had deep roots. Thus a comparison of the intellectual outlooks, while not meant to reduce the explanation of the differing cultural developments to one of their intellectual components, may provide important clues for seeing how the challenges of the recent scientific age might have been met differently than they were in evangelical America.

Like his American counterparts, Abraham Kuyper believed that in our encounter with reality we are forced to start with the common-sense operations of our minds. The axioms of our thought (such as consciousness of our own self or trust in our senses) are not susceptible to proof, so that "Nothing remains, therefore, but to declare that these axioms are given with our self-consciousness itself; that they inhere in it; that they are inseparable from it; and that of themselves they bring their certainty with them."[96] These common-sense starting points, as the Americans sometimes said also,[97] rested on "faith," as opposed to any demonstration. "By faith," says Kuyper, "you are sure of all those things of which you have a *firm conviction,* but which conviction is *not* the outcome of observation or demonstration." Such faith produces beliefs that are just as certain as any knowledge built on scientific demonstration; indeed, all scientific demonstration rests on such beliefs derived from faith. "All scepticism," Kuyper moreover remarks somewhat extravagantly, "originates from the impression that our certainty depends upon the results of our scientific research."[98]

The point at which Kuyper was departing most radically from the American evidentialists was in insisting that spiritually derived knowledge of God had the same epistemic status and provided the same sort of immediate grounds for certainty as did everyday common-sense experience. Knowledge of God is founded, not upon something prior to itself, but rather on God himself breathing into the minds of humans. This inspiration, the work of the Holy Spirit in communicating from God through Scripture[99] to humans, provides its own certainty. "The sense of this," says Kuyper, "stands entirely in line with every other primordial sense, such as with the sense of our ego, of our existence, of our life, of our calling, of our continuance, of our laws of thought, etc." This sense of "inspiration of God into the mind of the sinner" differs from the general principles of our consciousness in that it is not shared by virtually all people. However, many other valuable inner impulses lack this quality of universality. "Think of the poet, the virtuoso, the hero, and the adventurer. The want of general consent is no proof of want of foundation, and often works the effect, that the conviction becomes the more firmly founded."[100]

With respect to the knowledge of God the crucial element making this immediate knowledge far less than universal is the presence of sin among

96. Abraham Kuyper, *Encyclopedia of Sacred Theology: Its Principles,* trans. J. Hendrik De Vries (New York, 1898 [1894]), 136.

97. Hopkins, *The Scriptural Idea of Man,* acknowledges that Sir William Hamilton shows that in a sense knowledge rests on "faith," but Hopkins complains that this is a different use of the word than when "faith" means Christian faith, 34–39. Benjamin B. Warfield, "On Faith in Its Psychological Aspects" (1911), *Studies in Theology* (New York, 1932), takes a more positive view of Hamilton's position and says it is also Augustine's. In a sense, says Warfield, reason rests on faith or trust in our understanding, though in another sense "reason underlies all acts of faith," 325.

98. Kuyper, *Encyclopedia,* 131 and 95.

99. Ibid., 361.

100. Ibid., 356 and 357.

humans. As much as anything, emphasis on the effects of sin separated Kuyper's thought from the evidentialist, or Common-Sense, theological tradition in America. Whereas in the views of the Common-Sense apologists sin was a factor that could prevent one from taking an objective look at the evidence for the truth of divine things, for Kuyper unacknowledged sinfulness inevitably blinded one from true knowledge of God. Although all people had an innate sense of God, this natural relation was so broken and injured by sin as to be of no use in its present state as a foundation for knowing God truly. Only if one recognized the brokenness of this relationship, that is, only if one recognized one's own sinfulness, could one recognize this sense of God for what it truly was. Such a recognition, however, was not fully possible without God's inspiring communication of special grace.[101]

True knowledge of God, then, could not be founded upon anything other than already having some true knowledge of God specially communicated to one's heart. Hence every effort to prove God to sinners who lack the essential foundation for such knowledge was bound to fail.[102] By contrast, whereas Kuyper thought unrecognized human sinfulness a preventative to true knowledge of God, the American Common-Sense apologists saw it only as an inhibitive. Sin indeed could stand in the way of an objective look at the facts, but the Americans remained confident in the possibility of an objective scientific knowledge available to all intelligent humans. Moreover, they saw no reason why knowledge of God could not be a species of such a knowledge.

Kuyper saw the problem as having to do with the concept of objectivity itself. Kuyper and the Common-Sense thinkers agreed that the nature of our consciousness forces us to believe in an organic harmony between subject and object. That is, we must believe that our subjective perceptions of reality can correspond to an actual reality external to ourselves. The Common-Sense thinkers took this correspondence as given, a dictate of common sense, needing no further justification. Kuyper did not quarrel on the immediate and common-sense status of this belief but observed that it was fraught with difficulties unless connected with another primal belief—belief in God as Creator.[103] Whatever necessity we might have to live by the belief in a subject/object correspondence, it could not by itself

101. Ibid., 359.

102. Kuyper sees a more general problem in any effort to get from subject to object without starting with knowledge of God. Cf. quotation below, note 103.

103. "We actually owe all our convictions of the reality of the object exclusively to faith. Without faith you can never go from your *ego* to the *non-ego*; there is no other bridge to be constructed from phenomena to noumena; and scientifically all the results of observation hang in air. The line from Kant to Fichte is the only line along which you may continue." Kuyper, *Encyclopedia*, 133.

stand up as a basis for objective science—that is, knowledge for the whole race, not just for individuals. Objective scientific knowledge would have to have the qualities of necessity and universality.[104] In fact, however, scientific thought is riddled with subjectivity. The English, Kuyper observed, were dropping the name "science" for all but the natural sciences, apparently as an admission of the speculative nature of other areas of inquiry. Even in natural science, as soon as they got beyond weighing and measuring, the subjectivity of the theorizing (as Darwinism showed) was becoming conspicuous.

Kuyper explained the reign of subjectivity in terms of the Fall of mankind. In an ideal state of innocence the *subject* of science would be "the universal ego in the universal human consciousness." The *object* would be the cosmos. In such a situation universality of scientific knowledge would be possible, because the relations between subject and subject and subject and object would be so organically constituted as to ensure agreement in knowledge. Sin and the Fall of mankind disrupted this harmonious relationship among subjects and between subjects and objects. So now subjectivism reigns. Each subject is inclined "to push other subjects aside, or to transform the object after itself." Under Satan's influence falsehood is rampant, which is devastating to reliance on personal communication for access to truth. Add to such problems mistakes, self-delusion, delusive imagination, and various ways for distortions in human understandings and relationships to reinforce other distortions and misunderstandings, and the dream of objectivity is obliterated by subjectivism and sin. Such problems are, of course, most devastating in the spiritual science, though they infect all areas of human knowledge where the ego plays an active role in interpretation.[105]

The common-sense starting point in the assumption of a harmonious correspondence between our subjective perceptions and objective reality, however necessary it is for us to rely on it, dies of a thousand such qualifications unless it has some other supposition to support it. And so says Kuyper:

> And however much we may speculate and ponder, no explanation can ever suggest itself to our sense, of the all-sufficient ground for this admirable correspondence and affinity between object and subject, on which the possibility and development of science wholly rests, until at the hand of Holy Scripture we confess that the Author of the cosmos created man in the cosmos as a microcosmos "after his image and likeness."[106]

104. Ibid., 90.
105. Ibid., 89, 90, 107, and 107–9.
106. Ibid., 83.

Though Kuyper is convinced that this is the only good solution to the human epistemic predicament, he presents it not so much as a proof as a confirmation. Human consciousness could be wholly deluded, of course, in supposing a subject-object correspondence, so the argument has a questionable premise. Moreover, no matter how strongly the case is made, many people will refuse to believe that their trust in subject-object correspondence necessitates belief in God. So Kuyper holds the view that God as revealed in Scriptures is known by us, not as a conclusion of an argument, but as a primary truth immediately apprehended as the result of spiritual communication to the human consciousness. People whose hearts and minds are closed to this spiritual communication will not be convinced by arguments. Nonetheless, it remains true that only if the basic truths that we learn immediately by being open to God's Word are added to our basic beliefs will we find adequate explanations to confirm such basic beliefs as our belief in the relationships of subject and object.

Science that includes the Creator of the harmonious correspondences between subject and object among its first principles will differ substantially from science, which includes no such principle. There are two kinds of people, says Kuyper, regenerate and unregenerate. Unregenerate do not at all clearly know the Creator. Hence there are two kinds of science. Not that everything that Christians and non-Christians know is different. "There is a very broad realm of investigation in which the difference between the two groups exerts *no* influence." Yet the differences in basic principles mean that the two sciences soon diverge, much as a branch of a fruit tree grafted beside the branch of a wild root. "Near the ground the tree of science is one for all. But no sooner has it reached a certain height, than two branches separate, in the same way as may be seen in a tree which is grafted on the right side, while on the left side there is allowed to grow a shoot from the wild root." Ultimately the goal and direction of these two sciences are at odds with each other, even though in some respects they are alike. Using another metaphor, Kuyper says, "We only affirm that formally both groups perform scientific labor, and that they recognize each other's scientific character, in the same way in which two armies facing each other are mutually able to appreciate military honor and military worth."[107]

Kuyper implemented his theories with the establishment of the Free University of Amsterdam in 1880, an institution in which the theme of the fundamental differences between Christian and non-Christian thought was strongly expressed through most of the twentieth century. Even the presence of this one institution separated the Dutch academic experience from that in the United States, where no major university

107. Ibid., 157, 168, and 156.

clearly articulated the conflict between Christian and non-Christian thought as arising at such a primal level. Even in America's surviving Christian colleges such a contrast between Christian and non-Christian thought has until recently not been widely taught. Kuyper's views do seem to offer the kind of critique of the first principles of modern science that James W. Smith said were lacking in American Protestant responses to the Darwinist revolution.

The issue, however, should not be settled so glibly. Kuyper, it seems, had taken into account an assumption in evaluating science that the Common-Sense apologists had neglected. Nevertheless, his alternative appears to rest Christian faith substantially on the mysterious and inaccessible foundation of the testimony of the Holy Spirit to one's heart. Parallel to the questions that plagued the objectivists (common sense does not well settle a dispute over what is common sense), Kuyper's view seems to have the troubling problem that further appeals to the Holy Spirit will not well settle a dispute over what is truly the voice of the Holy Spirit. Kuyper, in traditional Calvinist fashion, stresses that the Spirit works through Scripture and the body of believers, and these authorities are susceptible to some testing, at least for consistency.[108] Nevertheless, even with these sources of faith practically central, Kuyper emphasizes so much the lack of reasons in coming to faith that the charge of arbitrarily trusting authorities seems a natural one.

Such objections are well articulated by perhaps the greatest proponent of the Common-Sense-evidentialist apologetic, Princeton's Benjamin B. Warfield, in two brief comments on Kuyper's work. Warfield's position, which has had great influence in twentieth-century American evangelicalism, well represents the reasons why Kuyper's views have been unattractive to many American evangelicals.

Warfield professed to find Kuyper's views simply baffling. To him it seemed crucial that the Holy Spirit, though unquestionably primary in granting faith, always worked through means. "The Holy Spirit does not work a blind, an ungrounded faith in the heart." Rather the Holy Spirit granted "just a new ability of the heart to respond to the grounds of faith." So why not expect that there would be sufficient evidence for Christian faith if we only examined it carefully? Faith, said Warfield, is "a form of conviction and is, therefore, necessarily grounded in evidence." To the objection that his stance might seem to make faith dependent on arguments, Warfield retorted simply: "We do not believe in the existence of the sun without evidence because we are not learned in astronomical science." Whether individual believers needed to stop and analyze the evidence was to Warfield of little importance. The important

108. Ibid., 553–63.

point for Christian apologetics was that the evidence could be analyzed and the faith could be shown to be fully rational.[109]

Lying behind this difference in apologetic strategy was a fundamental disagreement with Kuyper's dictum that there were "two kinds of people" and hence "two kinds of science." Warfield agreed that the regenerate had some advantage over the unregenerate in doing science, but he emphasized that they were doing the same sort of work. Each was working on the same edifice of human scientific knowledge and benefited from the other's accomplishments. Regeneration, he said, made far less difference than Kuyper supposed, since regenerated people remained infected by sin. Moreover, and perhaps more importantly, even if there were sinless men, "Sinful and sinless men are, after all, both men; and being both men, are fundamentally alike and know fundamentally alike." If truth was on the side of the Christians, Warfield reasoned, then in an argument Christianity eventually would triumph. This conclusion rested on an assumption with deep roots in the Common-Sense tradition: "All minds are of the same essential structure; and the less illuminated will not be able permanently to resist or gainsay the determinations of the more illuminated."[110]

The whole argument between these two groups of Reformed Christians rested on differences concerning this question. Did the fact that all human minds were of the same essential structure imply that regenerate and unregenerate know essentially alike? Scripture and other basic Christian assumptions did not clearly settle this issue. Neither did philosophy. In part the difference turned on differing concepts of what is involved in achieving human knowledge. Kuyper, closer to the idealist tradition, while not denying that human minds had similar structures, viewed knowledge in terms of the overall relationships it involved—the organic relationships among Creator, cosmos, and knowing subjects. Doing science, he was convinced, presupposed a whole theory about the fundamental structures of the universe. Knowledge accordingly did not come in isolated packages but was understood by subjects in the context of other beliefs the subject held—beliefs determined either by the subjective urge to remake the universe in one's own image or by proper reverence for God. Warfield, on the other hand, viewed knowledge in an essentially inductionist, or Baconian, fashion. Knowledge was gained by considering evidence and drawing conclusions that that evidence would support. Whether one immediately drew the proper conclusion (as in the nonastronomer's knowledge of the sun) or reached it by carefully weigh-

109. Benjamin B. Warfield, *Selected Shorter Writings of Benjamin B. Warfield,* vol. 2, ed. John E. Meeter (Nutley, N.J.: 1973), 98–99, 99, 113, and 105. These comments were first published in 1903.

110. Ibid., 101 and 103.

ing evidence and making inferences, the basic idea was the same. Each item of knowledge could exist independently. Knowing depended essentially on looking at the evidence for the individual item. It did not depend substantially on what else one knew or on one's worldview. Once science establishes the evidence and conclusion, the item of knowledge becomes accessible to all rational people, virtually regardless of their other beliefs.

Warfield represented the grand Enlightenment ideal for science, which had deep roots in Western thought dating back to the Greeks. It has been an ideal especially appealing in the United States, a nation founded on principles drawn from Enlightenment thought. Kuyper, coming out of a Dutch "anti-Revolutionary" tradition that sharply criticized these Enlightenment categories, was much more ready to offer a critique of this ideal.

Since Warfield's view continues to have such wide appeal in American evangelicalism, it is worth commenting on this debate. Kuyper seems to have the better of the argument in explicitly relating his philosophy to its Christian assumptions, refusing to accept uncritically the Enlightenment ideal of one science for all humanity, and in providing a basis for building a Christian intellectual outlook that can withstand the claims both of modern science and modern subjectivism. Nevertheless, we should not leave this debate until we have considered why Warfield's views seem to many people so appealing and compelling, and Kuyper's so counter-intuitive.

Christianity involves many specific claims about history, morality, and the structure of relationships in the universe. Many of these claims appear to be of the sort that are commonly subjected to analysis when matters are in dispute. In disputed cases the natural thing for humans to do is to examine the evidence for and against the claims in question. Perhaps such an examination will not settle the issue, but at least we should see whether the preponderance of evidence is on one side or the other. To say that such examination of the evidence is irrelevant or of little importance to Christian belief appears to be an evasion. It seems to put Christian claims in a category immune from the tests that we normally use for our beliefs. It suggests to many people that we do not think there is very good evidence to support Christian belief. The evidentialist, on the other hand, is convinced that there ought to be some such evidence. For instance, nineteenth-century apologists made much of the point that if the same God who created the world and humanity also revealed the Bible, there ought to be some evidence of that common authorship. Similarly, if Christianity makes certain historical claims—if it is preeminently a *historical* religion based on God's entering history and becoming to some degree knowable by normal human standards—then there ought to be some evidence favoring the authenticity of those historical claims.

The principal point at which the arguments of the evidentialists failed was, not in supposing that there should be a preponderance of evidence favorable to Christian claims, but rather in supposing that such evidence and arguments constituted conclusive arguments for the truth of Christianity. As we have seen, the general arguments for Christianity do not stand up as logically compelling unless one already grants certain assumptions about reality that virtually presuppose a benevolent Creator. Otherwise alternative explanations can explain the phenomena as logically as can Christianity. Historical arguments are no better, since historical events are typically susceptible to more than one plausible interpretation. Furthermore, sinful people whose minds are adamantly closed to hearing God and his Word will be quick to point out the logical plausibility of the alternatives.

Nevertheless, arguments that are not compelling logically may have great psychological and even intellectual force, particularly for those who are wavering in their resolution to deny the presence of God and his Word. This should be especially true if in fact Christianity accurately describes human conditions and needs and God's saving acts. For instance, if humans indeed have certain moral and religious sensibilities and needs to which the Gospel best responds, then people might well be brought to some intuitive recognition of the suitability of Christianity to their conditions and needs. Compared with secularism, for instance, Christianity may be simply vastly superior in accounting for their actual sense of worth, of right and wrong, or of guilt and of need for redemption and new direction in their lives. This superiority will not appear in that Christianity will be the only hypothesis that can provide a good explanation of these phenomena; rather it may be the one that is the most attractive, given humans' actual needs and sensibilities.[111] How convincing such considerations will be depends of course on the psychological, intellectual, and spiritual condition of the person being addressed. Sin or commitments to other religions will blind many to any such considerations. For others the Holy Spirit may remove such blinders and allow them to see their conditions and needs for what they really are. Such a sight of the true contours of reality may be no more the result of arguments than is the recognition of the beauty of a symphony, but it may be just as much the result of considering the evidence. Once a person has such an insight, the other evidences for Christianity—for instance, that the claims of Scripture are based on testimony of people of apparently high integrity—

111. This seems to be the argument of Clark Pinnock's chapter on "pragmatic arguments" in *Reason Enough* (Downers Grove, Ill., 1980).

may add force to the Christian claims, even if not providing arguments to which there is no logical alternative. If people were consistent to their sinful and subjectivistic commitments, they would be, as Kuyper said, unable to be touched by such evidences and arguments. Nonetheless, the Gospel miraculously becomes convincing to sinners who seem to hold the denial of its claims as one of their most basic beliefs. Many are given the insight to see the truth of Christianity even without arguments—or with only a few very informal ones. Others are helped by the spelling out of the evidence. In either case the Holy Spirit helps sinners to see truths that the deepest impulses of their unregenerate natures would have them utterly deny.[112]

Perhaps a similar resolution of the differing approaches to the "two science" questions might be reached. Kuyper appears to say something that is almost essential for the survival of the Christian academic community in a secular setting—that science cannot be regarded as a sovereign domain that sets its own rules to which Christians and everyone else must conform if they are to retain their intellectual respectability. As philosophers of science now are also recognizing, science itself is controlled to substantial degrees by assumptions and commitments.[113] Christians, then, should be free frankly to state their metaphysical starting points and their assumptions and to introduce these into their scientific work in all areas of human inquiry; they should employ underlying control beliefs that differ widely from those of non-Christians.[114]

Nonetheless, despite the impulses to subjectivity, personal knowledge, and special interests that twentieth-century people have become so alerted to, Christians may affirm, as Kuyper and Warfield would have agreed, that "all minds are of the same essential structure." Hence much that common sense affirms is reliable. Among other things, common sense tells us that in fact we can communicate remarkably well even with

112. Kuyper likely would agree with most of this. Cf. his similar discussion, *Encyclopedia,* 558–63. He disagreed with the evidentialists over whether the truths of Christianity should be held on the basis of demonstrative arguments based on other premises. So he says of belief in Scripture: "Hence this principium, as such, can be no conclusion from other premises, but is itself the premise, from which all other conclusions are drawn. Aside from this question of demonstrative arguments, however, much of the debate between the two sides revolves around differing terminologies, since much of what evidentialists call belief on the basis of evidence (in their broad sense of that by which something evidences itself) Kuyper would regard as accepted on the basis of faith (i.e. 'becoming firmly convinced of a thing, and of making this conviction the starting-point of conduct, while for this conviction no empirical or demonstrative proof is offered or found.')." Ibid., 131.

113. I am indebted to my colleague in the Calvin Center for Christian Scholarship, Robert Manweiler, for his discussions of these points.

114. See Nicholas Wolterstorff, *Reason within the Bounds of Religion* (Grand Rapids, 1976).

many people who differ from us quite radically in some perceptions and basic assumptions. So theoretically there is a vast difference between Christian and non-Christian thought—that is, if each were always a logical system consistent with its premises. In reality, however, God has structured our thought so that it is not dominated by such logical categories. Most of what we know goes beyond what is susceptible to logical analysis. Hence radical differences in fundamental assumptions, which might seem to entail wholly incompatible thought systems, turn out to be surmountable in most practical affairs. Warfield is probably right that regeneration does not usually transform people and their thinking as radically as we might like and that our common humanity guarantees us considerable commonality of thought. Hence, the Christian psychologist and the secular behaviorist might find themselves easily able to work together on many psychological projects—to understand each other and to take each other's fundamental assumptions into account. Perhaps the mutual respect and understanding that is in fact possible is, as Kuyper suggested, like that between two contending armies. Nonetheless, through God's grace the relationships between Christians and non-Christians are perhaps more often those of peace than those of open war. Underneath there are warring principles, and these are part of a deeper cosmic contest between the forces of good and evil. Yet the captain in our warfare is the Prince of Peace, so we can rightfully live in peace with our epistemic enemies, even though at some fundamental intellectual levels we may be struggling against them.

In conclusion we can say that the demise of American evangelical academia involved a significant component of intellectual weakness. Specifically, the nineteenth-century evidentialists' overestimation of the prowess of the scientific method seems a serious error. So does the underestimation of the degree to which people's thought is of a whole (is made up of a complex and vital relationship among ideas), so that sinfully determined basic first beliefs and commitments can pervade the rest of one's intellectual activity. Nevertheless, despite such overestimations of the possibilities for objectivity, we can learn from the Common-Sense tradition. It emphasizes that many of our beliefs are not derived from other beliefs but arise out of the constitution of our nature. Moreover, regenerate and unregenerate live in the same world and share many of the same experiences. They can communicate with each other. Furthermore, evidences of God's care, power, and provision for salvation abound, and in fact people often see these evidences when presented. The Kuyperian insights qualify these observations by pointing out that such recognition is not founded simply on an appeal to beliefs shared by virtually all people. Rather, sin creates a widespread abnormality. Trust in God which ought to be a spontaneous act providing us with some intuitive first principles of knowledge is lacking in most people. Christians should not be embarrassed to say frankly that this is the issue. If one trusts in God, one will view some evidence differently than a person who basically denies God. If people trust in God, their science and knowledge should have some substantial traits that differ from the science and knowledge of those who basically deny God. Nonetheless, the appeal to trust in God is in a way an appeal to common sense, even though to a suppressed aspect of common sense. The American and the Dutch evangelical-Reformed traditions have offered differing insights on these issues. Evangelical academics in the late twentieth century might benefit by looking at the insights from both these traditions.

11

The Holy Spirit and the Spirit of the Age in American Protestantism, 1880–1910

Grant Wacker

Reprinted by permission from *Journal of American History* 72 (June 1985): 45–62.

In the winter of 1887, the Evangelical Alliance for the United States met in Washington, D.C., to assess the "perils and opportunities" of the age. Participants included some of the most distinguished scholars, editors, and college presidents in the nation. Afterward, everyone agreed that the meeting had been a sparkling success. Indeed, fifty years later a leading historian of American religion judged that it had been one of the three "most significant conferences ever held in the United States in the interests of social Christianity." Even so, from the perspective of the 1980s, the gathering seems curious in a number of ways.[1]

The devotional mood of the proceedings is a case in point. The first session opened with the hymn "Come Gracious Spirit, Heavenly Dove."

1. [Evangelical Alliance for the United States], *National Perils and Opportunities: The Discussions of the General Christian Conference Held in Washington, D.C., December 7th, 8th, and 9th, 1887* (New York, 1887), viix; Charles Howard Hopkins, *The Rise of the Social Gospel in American Protestantism, 1865–1915* (New Haven, Conn., 1940), 113–14.

The participants then read the second chapter of the Book of Acts. Those verses, which describe the Holy Spirit's activity in the early days of the church, effectively set the tone for the rest of the meetings. At the end of the week, William E. Dodge, president of the Evangelical Alliance, asked the delegates to search their hearts to see if they too were open to the Spirit's guidance. "Christ is waiting for us," he urged. "Are we ready?"[2]

The ideological diversity of the speakers is also surprising. At least three distinct groups can be discerned. The largest might be called mainstream conservatives. Their position is difficult to define, but it suffices to say that they were manifestly pious, sincere, and supportive of middle-class sensibilities. The second group embodied a growing liberal impulse widely known as the new theology. Representative speakers included Washington Gladden, pastor of the First Congregational Church of Columbus, Ohio, and Daniel Coit Gilman, first president of Johns Hopkins University. Persuaded that God is immanent in the processes of modern culture, individuals such as Gladden and Gilman were noted for their commitment to metaphysical idealism, biblical higher criticism, a progressive view of history, and the notion that contemporary science and philosophy are in some sense normative for Christian theology. The third group embodied an equally vigorous evangelical impulse that went by different names but probably was most commonly known as the higher-life theology. Speakers who reflected that concern included Arthur T. Pierson, incoming editor of the *Missionary Review of the World,* and Adoniram Judson Gordon, a leading Baptist minister in Boston and founder of what is now Gordon College and Gordon-Conwell Theological Seminary. Certain that the Lord's return was at hand, individuals such as Pierson and Adoniram Judson Gordon were noted for their support of urban revivalism, world missions, and the theology and practice of divine healing and, most of all, for a conviction that conversion ought to be regarded, not as the goal, but as the mere beginning of a triumphant Christian life.

The predominance of mainstream conservatives at the Evangelical Alliance is not particularly remarkable, for they were, after all, the backbone of the Protestant establishment and the mainstay of countless organizations of this sort. Rather, it is the mingling of new theologians and higher-life theologians that captures our attention, for their concerns seem to have been not only different but also clearly incompatible. Indeed, thirty years later their children would be pitted against each other as modernists and fundamentalists, and a generation after that their grandchildren would be (and still are) locked in a wary standoff as ecumenical liberals and evangelical fundamentalists.

2. [Evangelical Alliance for the United States], *National Perils and Opportunities,* 1, 378.

Yet to our eyes the most surprising feature of the conference may be something else, for it is at least arguable that it was not the liberal new theologians but the evangelical higher-life spokesmen, Pierson and Adoniram Judson Gordon, who offered the most trenchant analyses of contemporary social conditions. Pierson attributed the "estrangement of the masses" from the church to the "caste spirit" of modern Christianity. If to respectable churchgoers the poor seem unclean, he charged, it may be because overcrowding "makes impossible not only refinement, but even decency." If the poor seem "often tempted into the saloon," it may be because they seek to escape homes that are without "light, air, space, warmth." Pierson admonished the delegates to remember that the "pre-eminent duty and privilege" of the church was "to reach, and if necessary, re-construct, the pyramidal base of society." Adoniram Judson Gordon was even more blunt. He acknowledged that "impatient murmurings of communism" were one of the perils of the age but retorted that the cause of the murmurings was not difficult to find: "Money hoarded up in the hands of Protestant Christians." Reminding his audience of the "Christian communism" of the early church, he warned that "it is not an orthodox creed which repels the masses, but an orthodox greed."[3]

All in all, the 1887 meeting of the Evangelical Alliance seems quite incongruous. With new theologians championing the transformative power of the Holy Spirit and with higher-life theologians prodding the church toward social reconstruction, the scenario appears, in fact, more fantastic than real. One reason it does not ring true is that, after seventy years of unremitting acrimony between their liberal and evangelical descendants, there is little in living memory that would lead us to expect a working alliance between the two groups. But a more salient reason is that historians have persistently stereotyped the early history of both movements. This imprecision becomes evident when we look at the way that those traditions have been choreographed in survey textbooks and specialized studies of American religious history.

Typically, the new theology has been pictured as the creation of a small number of well-educated and exceptionally talented ministers and seminary professors who lived, for the most part, in or near New England and who did their most creative work in the sunset of the nineteenth century. It has been said that most came from denominations rooted in the Reformed (or Calvinist) side of the Protestant tradition—notably, Baptist, Congregational, Presbyterian, or Episcopal—but a few belonged to non-Reformed groups such as the Methodists and the Disciples of Christ. Although most accounts have acknowledged that the movement was indebted to an earlier and broader tradition of Protestant liberalism stem-

3. Ibid., 112–14, 380–83.

ming from the work of Friedrich Schleiermacher and of other German theologians in the early nineteenth century, they have traditionally depicted the new theology as a distinctively American achievement that synthesized the cardinal tenets of Reformed Protestant theology with the best insights of modern civilization. In the most recent studies, however, the new theology's debt to Roman Catholic as well as Protestant thinking in Britain, France, and Germany has been underscored. The newer works have made clear, moreover, that the enduring significance of the movement is not so much its contribution to technical theological discourse as its ability to express the highest aspirations of the age in the language of religious symbols.[4]

The historiography of higher-life theology has not fared so well. In most treatments of the period, its ideational scaffolding has been ignored, the story of its development has been chopped up and strewn through different parts of different chapters, and crucial social and cultural distinctions have been overlooked. Often the movement appears to have merited historical attention, not for its own sake—not, that is, for what it represented in the 1880s—but for what it became in the 1920s: the ideological backbone of fundamentalism. Even in self-consciously empathetic accounts, the higher-life theology has often emerged as picturesque folk belief or, more commonly, as a tool for demobilizing lower-class discontent. The scholarship on the higher-life movement is rapidly improving, however. One of the most important accomplishments of the recent literature is its refinement of the differences between the higher-life impulse, which (like the new theology) was predominantly rooted in the Reformed side of the Protestant tradition, and the similarly evangelical yet decidedly non-Reformed Wesleyan Holiness movement. Both higher-life and Wesleyan Holiness leaders were committed to the idea that conversion ought to be followed by another landmark religious experience, and they both called that experience the baptism of the Holy Spirit. But there were significant differences between them regarding the purpose of the baptism experience. The higher-life writers insisted that its main function was to empower believers to serve the church and to witness for Christ, whereas Wesleyan Holiness writers argued that its main function was to eradicate "inbred sin" and thereby to break the stranglehold of selfish desires. The former, in other words, emphasized

4. The best book-length study of the new theology is William R. Hutchison, *The Modernist Impulse in American Protestantism* (Cambridge, Mass., 1976), esp. 41–225. Others include Lloyd J. Averill, *American Theology in the Liberal Traditions* (Philadelphia, 1967); Kenneth Cauthen, *The Impact of American Religious Liberalism* (New York, 1962), esp. 3–143; and Daniel Day Williams, *The Andover Liberals; A Study in American Theology* (New York, 1941).

service, whereas the latter stressed purity. Besides that difference, recent scholarship has shown that the higher-life spokesmen were more interested than their Wesleyan rivals in eschatological speculations. They also were more interested in the theology and practice of divine healing for the body. To contemporary outsiders those distinctions undoubtedly seemed trivial, but much theological blood was spilled over them, and by the end of the 1880s those essentially evangelical movements were strenuously competitive.[5]

That, then, is a composite profile of the way that the new theology and the higher-life theology have been depicted in American religious-history textbooks and monographs. The literature is increasingly subtle, but two distortions are still discernible.

The first distortion is a tendency to portray the new theology as a fresh spiritual resource cascading across mainstream Protestantism and the higher-life theology as a residue of tradition and sectarian isolation. What this really means is that the former is treated in its own terms, as an ideational phenomenon, and a remarkably interesting and creative one at that, whereas the latter is explained in unvarnished sociological terms as a reaction to economic hard times or to cultural stress. The result is predictable. Because different methods are used to interpret comparable phenomena, the web of social and cultural relationships that linked the two movements is easily overlooked.

The second and more serious distortion is a tendency to pose those impulses as sharply contrasting forms of spirituality. To some extent it is one instance of a perennial temptation to read history backward—in this case, to organize the events of the 1880s and 1890s in adversarial categories derived from the 1920s and 1930s. But the real problem is knottier. To depict the movements in oppositional terms is to take their self-perceptions at face value. Thus creedal and denominational boundaries drawn by understandably partisan church historians have been allowed

5. For recent discussions of the higher-life movement, see Ernest R. Sandeen, *The Roots of Fundamentalism: British and American Millenarianism, 1800–1930* (Chicago, 1970), 132–87; George M. Marsden, *Fundamentalism and American Culture: The Shaping of Twentieth-Century Evangelicalism: 1870–1925* (New York, 1980), 72–101; and Donald Wilber Dayton, "Theological Roots of Pentecostalism" (Ph.D. diss., University of Chicago, 1983), 101–219. See also William W. Menzies, "The Non-Wesleyan Origins of the Pentecostal Movement," in *Aspects of Pentecostal-Charismatic Origins*, ed. Vinson Synan (Plainfield, 1975), 81–98; J. Edwin Orr, *The Flaming Tongue: The Impact of Twentieth Century Revivals* (Chicago, 1973), 65–100, 178–200; Bruce Shelley, "Sources of Pietistic Fundamentalism," *Fides et Historia* 5 (spring 1973): 68–78; Timothy L. Smith, "Righteousness and Hope: Christian Holiness and the Millennial Vision in America, 1800–1900," *American Quarterly* 31 (spring 1979): 21–45; and Edith Lydia Waldvogel, "'The Overcoming Life': A Study in the Reformed Evangelical Origins of Pentecostalism" (Ph.D. diss., Harvard University, 1977).

to set the terms of the discussion. The immediate result is to heighten the fences between the movements, making them more distinctive than they really were. The long-range result is to lose sight of the extent to which those liberal and evangelical stirrings were in fact similar responses to common problems.[6]

I am not suggesting that the historiographic terrain is, as Perry Miller once said of another era, "a parched land, crying for deliverance." Over the years historians have of course uncovered many of the ligaments that bound the movements together. But more often than not, their insights have been incidental to other lines of research, and thus the significance of their work has remained undeveloped.[7] The point is that we need a more systematic examination of the social relations and cultural assumptions shared by new theologians and higher-life leaders. The effort will reveal, I think, that both movements emerged from the same religious womb and, like biological twins, matured in formally comparable ways precisely because they inherited similar genetic blueprints. Understanding the extent of their genetic similarity might, in turn, help us to understand

6. William Warren Sweet, for example, typically described the new theology as performing a "great service to multitudes of people" and its representatives as the "most distinguished scholars" in the church. Higher-life sects, on the other hand, he depicted as "otherworldly in outlook" and "largely produced by hard times." Even in Sydney E. Ahlstrom's justly acclaimed survey of American religious history, the new theology is generously unfolded in a chapter titled "The Golden Age of Liberal Theology," whereas higher-life thought is briefly treated in a chapter titled, significantly, "Dissent and Reaction in Protestantism." Despite his manifest desire to be fair, Ahlstrom links the latter with "baseball and wild-west movies," "laymen who had almost no contact with the history of ideas," and "other radical conceptions." William Warren Sweet, *The Story of Religion in America* (New York, 1950), 343–44, 422; Sydney E. Ahlstrom, *A Religious History of the American People* (New Haven, 1972), 806, 818. For additional examples in the better textbooks, see Catherine L. Albanese, *America: Religions and Religion* (Belmont, 1981), 102–3, 105–6; Winthrop S. Hudson, *Religion in America: An Historical Account of the Development of American Religious Life* (New York, 1981), 271–76, 284–85, 343–47; Martin E. Marty, *Righteous Empire: The Protestant Experience in America* (New York, 1970), 178–87, 191–92, 216–17; H. Shelton Smith, Robert T. Handy, and Lefferts Loetscher, eds., *American Christianity: An Historical Interpretation with Representative Documents,* 2 vols. (New York, 1960), 2:256, 265, 312–15; and Peter W. Williams, *Popular Religion in America: Symbolic Change and the Modernization Process in Historical Perspective* (Englewood Cliffs, 1980), 135–41, 201.

7. Perry Miller, *The New England Mind: From Colony to Province* (Cambridge, Mass., 1953), 484–85; Winthrop S. Hudson, "Walter Rauschenbusch and the New Evangelism," *Religion in Life* 30 (summer 1961): 412–30; William G. McLoughlin, Jr., *Modern Revivalism: Charles Grandison Finney to Billy Graham* (New York, 1959), 360–65, 382–84; Richard Jensen, *The Winning of the Midwest: Social and Political Conflict, 1888–1896* (Chicago, 1971), 58–88, 318–19; Ernest R. Sandeen, "The 'Little Tradition' and the Form of Modern Millenarianism," *Annual Review of the Social Sciences of Religion* 4 (1980): 165–81.

why liberals and evangelicals in the 1980s still find each other the best of adversaries.

At the outset it is necessary to acknowledge that there is a measure of truth in the conventional view of the relation between these liberal and evangelical impulses, especially after 1910. When we look at the class position of the two groups just before World War I, it is evident that by that date the new theology was supported mainly by the middle and upper-middle classes, whereas the higher-life theology was supported mainly by the stable working and lower-middle classes. One indication of the disparity is that the new theology had gradually acquired a firm footing in the better-known colleges and seminaries, whereas the higher-life theology had largely retreated to struggling denominational schools and independent Bible institutes. In the eyes of the general public, moreover, the gap was even greater. Higher-life distinctives were commonly associated with seemingly bizarre sects such as John Alexander Dowie's Christian Catholic Apostolic Church in Zion City, Illinois, and Frank W. Sandford's Holy Ghost and Us Bible School in Durham, Maine—authoritarian theocracies devoted to ascetic living, divine healing, and preparation for the Lord's immediate return. Nor was the identification wholly groundless. Despite efforts by higher-life leaders to dissociate themselves from grass-roots stirrings of that sort, it is undeniable that their teachings were gradually appropriated by a motley assortment of visionaries, faith healers, skid-row preachers, and outright charlatans.[8]

The other part of the conventional portrait—the part that positions new theology and higher-life spokesmen at opposite ends of the theological battlefield, the former consorting with "scientific modernism" and the latter with "militant fundamentalism"—also contains a measure of truth. By 1910 higher-life leaders were uncritically lumping the new theology with Christian Science, Theosophy, and Romanism as heresies needing special rebuke. And it is true that individuals who were leaders

8. Walter E. W. Ellis, "Social and Religious Factors in the Fundamentalist-Modernist Schism among Baptists in North America, 1895–1934" (Ph.D. diss., University of Pittsburgh, 1974), 138–78, 211–34, 252–53; Gregory H. Singleton, "Fundamentalism and Urbanization: A Quantitative Critique of Impressionistic Interpretations," in *The New Urban History: Quantitative Explorations by American Historians,* ed. Leo F. Schnore (Princeton, 1975), 224; H. Paul Douglass and Edmund de S. Brunner, *The Protestant Church as a Social Institution* (New York, 1935), 291; Everett L. Perry, "The Role of Socio-Economic Factors in the Rise and Development of American Fundamentalism" (Ph.D. diss., University of Chicago, 1959), 132–34, 147–48; Virginia L. Brereton, "The Public Schools Are Not Enough: The Bible and Private Schools," in *The Bible in American Education: From Source Book to Textbook,* ed. David L. Barr and Nicholas Piediscalzi (Philadelphia, 1982), 52–58; Kirsopp Lake, *The Religion of Yesterday and To-Morrow* (London, 1925), 61–62; Robert Mapes Anderson, *Vision of the Disinherited: The Making of American Pentecostalism* (New York, 1979), 28–78, 137–52.

of, or closely associated with, the higher-life network of the 1880s and 1890s wrote most of the articles in a notable set of polemical booklets called *The Fundamentals* (1910–1915). Although the articles in *The Fundamentals* were not so hard-hitting as the volleys of the postwar years, it is clear that by 1910 disagreement between liberals and evangelicals about the deity, miracles, and the resurrection of Jesus Christ were deep and rapidly getting deeper. It is also clear that disagreements about this or that particular point in the creeds almost always reflected more basic philosophical and temperamental differences about the source of religious authority itself. As the years passed, polite debates turned into fratricidal brawls, and by the eve of World War I, thoughtful observers knew that a showdown was inevitable. They also knew that both sides would play for keeps.[9]

Nonetheless, it is precisely because there has been so much acrimony between liberals and evangelicals throughout most of the twentieth century that the commonalities of the 1880s and 1890s are so striking. When we look, for example, at the social composition of the two movements before the turn of the century, both impressionistic and quantitative data suggest that the social standing of congregations with liberal ministers was not appreciably different from that of congregations with evangelical ministers. And when we look at the ministers themselves, it is even clearer that the two groups occupied proximate positions in the social system.[10]

The career of Reuben A. Torrey (1856–1928), a major architect of higher-life theology, illustrates the general comparability of the two sides. Like many higher-life spokesmen, Torrey later became so entangled in the modernist-fundamentalist struggle that it is difficult to imagine him as anything but a pugilist for the Lord. But in the 1880s and 1890s, things were quite different. Torrey's father had been a New York City attorney who was prosperous and farsighted enough to put him through Yale College and Yale Divinity School. After additional theological study at Er-

9. For the underlying philosophical and temperamental differences, see Hutchison, *Modernist Impulse in American Protestantism,* 257–69; Marsden, *Fundamentalism and American Culture,* 55–62, 224–27; and Ferenc Morton Szasz, *The Divided Mind of Protestant America, 1880–1930* (University, Ala., 1982), 15–41, 68–83.

10. Ellis, "Social and Religious Factors in the Fundamentalist-Modernist Schism," 102, 116–17, 252–53; Clyde C. Griffen, "Rich Laymen and Early Social Christianity," *Church History* 36 (March 1967): 46; Richard James Anderson, "The Urban Revivalists, 1880–1910" (Ph.D. diss., University of Chicago, 1974), 87; William R. Hutchison, "Cultural Strain and Protestant Liberalism," *American Historical Review* 76 (April 1971): 406–11. For the social position of higher-life theologians, see notes 11 and 12. For indications of comparability as late as the 1930s, see Mark A. May, *The Education of American Ministers,* 4 vols. (New York, [1934]), 3:277–85, esp. 281.

langen and Leipzig, Torrey founded the (Congregational) Open Door Church in Minneapolis, an early "institutional church" designed to meet the medical, educational, recreational, and spiritual needs of the urban poor. He soon became superintendent of the Minneapolis Congregational Mission Society and, along with liberal or liberally inclined reformers such as Graham Taylor, Josiah Strong, and Jacob Riis, helped to organize the Convention of Christian Workers—an institution ranked by the historian Aaron Ignatius Abell as one of the two most influential social-reform groups of the era. Eventually, Torrey entered urban evangelism, and when Dwight L. Moody died in 1899, many believed Torrey would take Moody's place in the public eye. Always impeccably attired, Torrey earned a reputation for humorless, tediously exegetical sermons—a reputation well deserved if the unrelieved gravity of his forty-odd books is any indication. And although he is usually remembered for the contentiousness of his later years, it is often forgotten that his contentiousness was aimed at Pentecostals on his right as much as at theological modernists on his left.[11]

Torrey was not unique. Tokens of middle-class respectability marked the careers of most of the higher-life leaders. In the 1890s J. Wilbur Chapman was senior pastor of Bethany Presbyterian Church in Philadelphia, probably the largest Presbyterian church in the United States and one of the foremost "institutional churches" of the era. Henry Clay Trumbull, for many years owner and editor of the *Sunday School Times*, sent his son Charles Gallaudet Trumbull to Yale and moved in a social circle that included Horace Bushnell, Mark Hopkins, and Mark Twain. The extremely popular writer Hannah Whitall Smith, author of the devotional classic, *The Christian's Secret of a Happy Life*, educated her children at Radcliffe College and Oxford University and counted Walt Whitman, William James, and the young Bertrand Russell as family friends. Even A. C. Dixon, eventually deemed the impresario of fundamentalism, was pastor of the wealthy and progressive Ruggles Street Baptist Church in Roxbury, Massachusetts, in the early 1900s and preached the commencement sermon for his alma mater, the University of North Carolina, in 1903. If the financial ability to travel is considered, the mobility of higher-life leaders may be the most decisive indicator of their class standing. They crisscrossed the northeastern states and the North Atlantic with astonishing regularity. Pierson alone made twenty-nine

11. Marsden, *Fundamentalism and American Culture*, 73–83; McLoughlin, *Modern Revivalism*, 364–74; Robert Harkness, *Reuben Archer Torrey: The Man, His Message* (Chicago, 1929), 37–38, 69; Ed Reese, *The Life and Ministry of Reuben Torrey* (Glenwood, [1975]); Aaron Ignatius Abell, *The Urban Impact on American Protestantism, 1865–1900* (Cambridge, Mass., 1943), 89, 95–98.

trips to Europe and three to the Orient. Here, as in other mundane matters, they easily rivaled their liberal counterparts.[12]

Evidence of that sort could be extended indefinitely. There are, however, more direct indications that until the turn of the century the higher-life movement was closer to the mainstream than to the backwaters of American Protestantism. Year after year new theologians and higher-life speakers shared the platform at the great summer conferences hosted by Moody in Northfield, Massachusetts. Whether Moody exactly understood the differences between them is irrelevant. The important point is that liberal and evangelical leaders themselves were still quite willing to join forces in order to achieve larger aims. They all published in journals such as the *Sunday School Times*, the *Christian Herald*, the *Homiletic Review*, and the *Record of Christian Work*.[13] Together they plotted the evangelization of the world at conferences such as the New York Ecumenical Missionary Convention in 1900 and in organizations such as the Interseminary Missionary Alliance and the Student Volunteer Movement. They worked for progressive reforms at home and abroad through associations such as the Evangelical Alliance, the Convention of Christian Workers, the Lake Mohonk Peace Conference, and the Woman's

12. John C. Ramsey, *John Wilbur Chapman: The Man, His Methods, and His Message* (Boston, 1962), 39–46; Philip E. Howard, *The Life Story of Henry Clay Trumbell, Missionary, Army Chaplain, Editor, and Author* (Philadelphia, 1905), 255, 419, 469; Melvin E. Dieter, "The Smiths," *Asbury Seminarian* 38 (spring 1983): 7–47, esp. 24, 29–30; Helen C. A. Dixon, *A. C. Dixon: A Romance of Preaching* (New York, 1931), 146–49, 152; Brenda M. Sheehan, "A. C. Dixon: An Early Fundamentalist," *Foundations* 10 (January–March 1967): 51–53; Delavan L. Pierson, *Arthur T. Pierson: A Biography by His Son* (London, 1912), 300; Sandeen, *Roots of Fundamentalism*, 132–61; Ernest B. Gordon, *Adoniram Judson Gordon: A Biography with Letters and Illustrative Extracts Drawn from Unpublished or Uncollected Sermons and Addresses* (New York, 1896), 11–22, 122–23, 153–55, 165–67, 330; Charles Gallaudet Trumbull, *The Life Story of C. I. Scofield* (New York, 1920), esp. 11–25; A. W. Tozer, *Wingspread: Albert B. Simpson, a Study in Spiritual Altitude* (Harrisburg, 1943), 12–15, 32–37, 67–68; Frank S. Reader, *Moody and Sankey: An Authentic Account of Their Lives and Services* (New York, 1876), 43–55; John David Hannah, "James Martin Gray, 1851–1935: His Life and Work" (Th.D. diss., Dallas Theological Seminary, 1974).

13. James F. Findlay, Jr., *Dwight L. Moody: American Evangelist, 1837–1899* (Chicago, 1969), 411–12. See virtually any issue of those journals between 1880 and 1910, especially during the 1890s—for example, A. C. Dixon, "The Streets of the City," *Homiletic Review* 22 (November 1891): 431–34; George F. Pentecost, "Christian Unity in Diversity," ibid., 34 (September 1897): 234–37; L. W. Munhall, "The Advantages of Professional Evangelism," ibid., 35 (April 1898): 308–11; Lyman Abbott, "The Reason of Hope," ibid., 19 (May 1890): 432–35; George A. Gordon, "The Calf and Dancing," ibid., 30 (August 1895): 133–38; and Newman Smyth, "The Waiting Christ," ibid. (July 1895): 43. See also Marsden, *Fundamentalism and American Culture*, 84; and Norris Magnuson, *Salvation in the Slums: Evangelical Social Work, 1865–1920* (Metuchen, 1977), x, 25, 132, 136, 168.

Christian Temperance Union. They exchanged pulpits, labored together in union revivals, and wrote tolerant reviews of each other's books and activities.[14] Indeed, in the context of the times it is not particularly surprising that Walter Rauschenbusch, the prophet of the Social Gospel, translated the higher-life hymns of Fanny J. Crosby and Ira Sankey into German; nor that Phillips Brooks, the eloquent rector of Boston's Trinity Episcopal Church, preached in Moody's Boston revival in 1877; nor that higher-life evangelist George F. Pentecost addressed the World's Parliament of Religions in Chicago in 1893.[15]

The web of social connections was mirrored in a corresponding web of theological connections. In the 1850s, for example, Bushnell, the putative father of the new theology in the United States, was still insisting that contemporary accounts of divine healing and of speaking in tongues could be taken at face value as reports of genuine miracles. In the 1870s David

14. William Richey Hogg, *Ecumenical Foundations: A History of the International Missionary Council and Its Nineteenth-Century Background* (New York, 1952), 42, 46; [Lyman Abbott], "Meeting of Interseminary Missionary Alliance," *Outlook,* 28 November 1896, 986; C. Howard Hopkins, *John R. Mott, 1865–1955: A Biography* (Grand Rapids, 1979), 70, 104–10, 416–17; Robert T. Handy, ed., *Religion in the American Experience: The Pluralistic Style* (Columbia, S.C., 1972), 196–206, esp. 203; *Report of the First Annual Meeting of the Lake Mohonk Conference on International Arbitration, 1895* (Lake Mohonk, 1895), 84, 85; *Report of the Second Annual Meeting of the Lake Mohonk Conference on International Arbitration, 1896* (Lake Mohonk, 1896), 144–45; *Report of the Third Annual Meeting of the Lake Mohonk Conference on International Arbitration, 1897* (Lake Mohonk, 1897), 138–40; *Report of the Fourth Annual Meeting of the Lake Mohonk Conference on International Arbitration, 1898* (Lake Mohonk, 1898), 111–13; *Report of the Fifth Annual Meeting of the Lake Mohonk Conference on International Arbitration, 1899* (Lake Mohonk, 1899), 123–25; *Report of the Sixth Annual Meeting of the Lake Mohonk Conference on International Arbitration, 1900* (Lake Mohonk, 1900), 119–21; Pierson, *Arthur T. Pierson,* 203, 225; Gordon, *Adoniram Judson Gordon,* 122–23; P. C. Headley, *George F. Pentecost: Life, Labors, and Bible Studies* (Boston, 1880), 112, 152–54; A. E. Thompson, *The Life of A. B. Simpson* (New York, 1920), 96–97, 106, 110; McLoughlin, *Modern Revivalism,* 360, 379, 397–99; Jacob Henry Dorn, *Washington Gladden: Prophet of the Social Gospel* ([Columbus], 1966), 284, 318, 380–82; editor's introduction to Adolf Harnack, "Did Jesus Do Away with the Old Testament Law?" *Sunday School Times,* 15 January 1910, 35–36; G. Campbell Morgan, "The Holy Spirit as the Conservator of Orthodoxy," ibid., 29 September 1900, 610–11; "Moody's Meetings in New York," *Outlook,* 28 November 1896, 986; review of *The Acts of the Holy Spirit* by A. T. Pierson, ibid., 1 August 1896, 216. For a particularly striking illustration of liberal endorsement of higher-life endeavors, see Walter Rauschenbusch, "The Welsh Revival and Primitive Christianity," *Examiner,* 15 June 1905, 25–26.

15. Hudson, "Walter Rauschenbusch and the New Evangelism," 422; Alexander V. G. Allen, *Phillips Brooks, 1835–1893: Memories of His Life with Extracts from His Letters and Note-Books* (New York, 1907), 325–26; George F. Pentecost, "The Invincible Gospel," in *The World's Parliament of Religions: An Illustrated and Popular Story of the World's First Parliament of Religions, Held in Chicago in Connection with the Columbian Exposition of 1893,* 2 vols. (Chicago, 1893), 2:1166–72.

Swing, the subject of a nationally publicized Presbyterian heresy trial in Chicago, was still proclaiming the innate sinfulness of human beings, the necessity of personal conversion, and the final separation of the righteous and the wicked. In the 1890s Gladden was still advocating foreign missions as the "only sovereign remedy" for the woes of the unchristianized lands. In the early 1900s Charles Augustus Briggs, the eminent (and eminently controversial) Bible critic at Union Theological Seminary in New York, was still seeking a scriptural warrant for "future probation" for persons who die outside the Christian faith. And in the 1940s Harry Emerson Fosdick, a direct descendant of the new theologians, was still preaching at Riverside Baptist Church in New York about human sinfulness and God's grace in rolling phrases most evangelicals could warmly appreciate (especially if they heard him on the radio and did not know it was Fosdick).[16]

All of this is to say that the fabric of theological agreement between liberals and evangelicals, like the rapport at the practical level, took a long time to come unraveled. Yet these continuities are the most obvious and probably the least important aspect of their relationship. More significant is the extent to which they shared a common definition of social reality. When we cut through the differences of idiom, it becomes clear, I believe, that both discerned the inner nature and defined the most pressing needs of the age in remarkably similar ways. Succinctly stated, both exhibited a deep and enduring fascination with the work of God's Spirit. That led, in turn, to a fresh understanding of the meaning of religious experience and to a renewed conviction that history unfolds in a dialectic of divine judgment and promise.

Few would doubt that the central impulse of the higher-life movement was its determination to recover the theology and presence of the Holy Spirit. Indeed, the whole nineteenth-century evangelical movement, Wesleyan as well as Reformed, might well be defined as historic Protestant orthodoxy spiced with a tingling expectation that the power of the Holy Spirit, lost since the days of the apostles, was about to be restored. Thus in 1892 Adoniram Judson Gordon typically declared that the desideratum of the age was "*a more intelligent and conscious hold upon the living and most gracious personality of [the] Holy Spirit.*" By the end of the century, even C. I. Scofield, who was soon to acquire virtual immortality by editing the reference Bible that bears his name, was persuaded that the

16. Horace Bushnell, *Nature and the Supernatural, as Together Constituting the One System of God* (New York, 1858), 464–91; Committee of the Presbytery, eds., *The Trial of the Rev. David Swing, before the Presbytery of Chicago* (Chicago, 1874), 20; Washington Gladden, *The Christian Pastor and the Working Church* (New York, 1916), 364–65; Charles Augustus Briggs, *Church Unity: Studies of Its Most Important Problems* (New York, 1909), 360–63; Harry Emerson Fosdick, *The Living of These Days: An Autobiography* (New York, 1956), 221–26.

church was "in the midst of a marked revival of interest in the Person and work of the Holy Spirit." Scofield was a rationalist at heart and suspicious of any revival. Yet he approvingly observed that "within the last twenty years more has been written and said upon the doctrine of the Holy Spirit than in the preceding eighteen hundred years."[17]

There was more truth in Scofield's comment than he perhaps realized, for as the century drew to a close, the fascination with the work of God's Spirit became equally evident among liberals. The latter articulated their interests in a vocabulary more attuned to the modern world, but in the end they addressed the same issues in very much the same way.

Although the new theologians were acutely embarrassed by the two-story universe of traditional orthodoxy, they had no difficulty conceiving God as essentially immanent, and God in the modality of immanence, as God the Holy Spirit. The true significance of the day of Pentecost, urged William Newton Clarke, Baptist theologian at Colgate Seminary, was that from that day forward the church had been able "to identify the Holy Spirit as God himself indwelling." Evangelicals often complained that the new theologians tended to reduce the Holy Spirit to an impersonal force or, at best, a vaguely divine influence in human affairs. But Clarke tried to correct that misperception by insisting that the Holy Spirit "is no mere influence, derived, secondary, impersonal, and vanishing, but is no other than God himself, in vital contact and communication with . . . men." Indeed, many liberals perceived the Spirit as intimately personal. For example, Lewis French Stearns, Congregational theologian at Bangor Seminary, averred that "the reality and present power of things unseen and eternal" is disclosed by "the Holy Spirit [in whom] God comes near to us and dwells in us." Some liberals even argued that the Spirit was the very vehicle of God's grace. Alexander V. G. Allen, church historian at the Episcopal Divinity School, contended that grace is best understood as Christ's "own eternal life [in] contact with human souls," a contact made possible by the "infinite indwelling Spirit." Or as Theodore T. Munger, a widely respected Congregational minister in New Haven, memorably phrased it, when the soul "tastes the satisfactions of the Spirit . . . death is swallowed up [and] the eternal order takes the place of this shadowy and elusive order of nature."[18]

17. A. J. Gordon, *The Holy Spirit in Missions: Six Lectures* (New York, 1893), 206–7; C. I. Scofield, *Plain Papers on the Doctrine of the Holy Spirit* (New York, 1899), 9.

18. William Newton Clarke, *An Outline of Christian Theology* (Cambridge, Mass., 1894), 147, 331, 332–33; Lewis French Stearns, *Present Day Theology: A Popular Discussion of Leading Doctrines of the Christian Faith* (New York, 1893), 536, 541; Alexander V. G. Allen, *The Continuity of Christian Thought: A Study of Modern Theology in the Light of Its History* (Boston, 1884), 16–17; Theodore T. Munger, *The Freedom of Faith* (Boston, 1883), 69.

For liberals and evangelicals alike, the focus on the theology and presence of the Holy Spirit stirred a corresponding interest in the meaning of religious experience. It meant, for one thing, that both groups were energetically involved in the life and work of the church. Indeed, one historian has recently argued that in the eyes of European Protestants those American liberals and evangelicals often looked like identical twins precisely because they both seemed so inclined toward vigorous, if not frenetic, "activism."[19]

There is, however, a less obvious but more significant way in which the two movements exhibited a common concern for religious experience. Briefly stated, both insisted that the cognitive and affective cycles of the religious life are inseparable. Here we need to be especially careful, for over the years a great deal of nonsense has been written about the "sentimentalism" of the new theology and the "emotionalism" of higher-life revivalism. The plain truth is that neither set of leaders had much use for undisciplined feeling, religious or otherwise. What they shared, rather, was a determination to rethink and to reappropriate the biblical understanding of religious experience. It is undeniable that their approaches were quite different. The higher-life theologians regarded religious experience as essentially ahistorical and therefore knowable principally through illumination by the Holy Spirit. The new theologians regarded it as essentially historical and therefore knowable principally through the medium of human language. Yet underlying that difference was a common inclination, especially in the early years, to be impatient with questions of confessional regularity and to assume that abstract speculation must be anchored in and tested by the ebb and flow of daily experience.

For higher-life writers the fulcrum of all religious experience was, of course, conversion, or the new birth, but they also believed that conversion is incomplete until it is fulfilled by the baptism of the Holy Spirit, which initiates a believer into a "higher Christian life." The second experience is, as Torrey phrased it, "a work of the Holy Spirit separate and distinct from His regenerating work." In principle, higher-life spokesmen tested the validity of those and all other religious experiences by criteria clearly enunciated in the Bible; but more often than they admitted, religious experience acquired an authority of its own. A few leaders, such as the evangelist B. Fay Mills (who later became a Unitarian), virtually discounted the importance of correct doctrine in the first place. As he put it, anyone who "wills to do the will of God, knows the doctrine." Usually, however, the concern for doctrinal regularity was quietly but effectively overwhelmed by a consuming interest in the dynamics of the higher life.

19. William R. Hutchison, "Innocence Abroad: The 'American Religion' in Europe," *Church History* 51 (March 1982): 71–84.

Typical in that respect was Smith, who in 1898 observed that "the trouble with most of the religion of the day is its extreme complexity." But the higher-life, she pointed out, avoids "theological difficulties [and] doctrinal dilemmas. . . . No theological training *nor any especial theological views* are needed." Sooner or later most of these men and women adopted the theology and practice of divine healing, and many admitted that the experience had led to the doctrine, not the other way around. Adoniram Judson Gordon was quite candid about it: "Experience is the surest touchstone of truth. It is not always infallible [but] this is a kind of testimony which is not easily ruled out of court." Or as A. B. Simpson, the founder of the Christian and Missionary Alliance (and a man never known to be lax about doctrinal regularity), put it, "all caviling criticism [is silenced] before the logic of divine realities and tested facts."[20]

The higher-life theologians ordinarily construed religious experience as a succession of discrete events; the new theologians, on the other hand, characteristically understood it as a process, a dynamic appropriation of the divine life flowing through the veins of human history. Thus Munger averred that the new theology "finds its methods in the every-day processes of humanity, rather than in formal logic. It deals with human life as do the poets and dramatists: it views humanity by a direct light, looks straight at it, and into it, and across its whole breadth." Newman Smyth, the scholarly minister of the Center Church in New Haven, cut to the epistemic roots of the issue. Orthodox creedalism, he argued, is artificial because it is unnourished by the "higher power at the foundations of our moral religious consciousness." Carefully noting that that higher power is not, as some romantics had intimated, mere sentiment, Newman Smyth insisted that the divine life in human consciousness derives from the incarnation of Jesus Christ in history itself. "Therefore we say, we have more than a religion of ideas; ours is a better confession of faith than that we have a religion of what God has done for us; a religion of historical facts."[21]

Eschatology was a third area of substantial continuity between the two movements. Since growing awareness of the work of God's Spirit in his-

20. R. A. Torrey, *The Baptism with the Holy Spirit* (New York, 1895), 10, 12, 32; B. Fay Mills, *Victory through Surrender: Plain Suggestions concerning Entire Consecration* (Chicago, 1892), 17; Hannah Whitall Smith, "Introduction," in *The Practice of the Presence of God: The Best Rule of a Holy Life: Being Conversations and Letters of Nicholas Herman of Lorraine, Brother Lawrence* (New York, 1895), iii–iv [emphasis added]; A. J. Gordon, *The Ministry of Healing; or, Miracles of Cure in All Ages* (Brooklyn, 1882), 175; A. B. Simpson, ed., *A Cloud of Witnesses for Divine Healing* (New York, 1887), vii–viii.

21. Munger, *Freedom of Faith,* 8, 11, 28; Newman Smyth, *The Orthodox Theology of To-Day* (New York, 1881), 43–50.

tory was as much a way of thinking about the future as it was about the past, it is not surprising that evangelicals and liberals started to emphasize the "future tenses of the blessed life" and the "coming Kingdom of God" (as they respectively phrased it) at approximately the same time.

It is true that the higher-life view of the future was expressed in the rich symbolism of a doctrinal tradition technically known as dispensational premillennialism, and it is also true that the latter was filled with predictions of cataclysmic events soon to precede and to accompany the second coming. But the apocalyptic imagery of the movement's rhetoric camouflages the essential optimism of its message. For one thing, throughout the 1880s and 1890s, the higher-life leaders were discernibly enthralled by the moral and salvific meaning of the Lord's return. Adoniram Judson Gordon's confident declaration in 1895 that the rain of the Spirit would soon "fructify the earth for the final blessing of the age to come" illustrates the expansive and redemptive tone of their outlook. After the turn of the century, some writers were drawn into arcane numerological calculations, and many more became preoccupied with speculations about the political and military ramifications of Armageddon. But by then the movement was closer to the combative fundamentalism of the 1920s than to the robust evangelicalism of the 1880s. Another indication of the essential optimism of the higher-life outlook in the late nineteenth century is the zealousness of the movement's leaders to reclaim souls and to reform society at home and abroad. The sheer magnitude of their efforts is persuasive evidence that premillennialism was not an ideology of despair but an efficient instrument for mobilizing religious energies. When the premillennialist argued that the "perfect society of the millennium would be created only by the cataclysmic return of Christ," Ernest R. Sandeen perceptively noted years ago, "he was suggesting different means, not different ends."[22]

All in all, then, close scrutiny of the way that premillennialism actually worked suggests that it is best understood as a manifestation of the same surge of historical hopefulness that irradiated the new theology. Although the liberal vision of the future took a postmillennial form, it is, I think, a distinction without much of a difference, for evangelical and liberal leaders were equally convinced of the spiritual maturity of the age. Differently stated, both were certain that God's unfolding truth, richer and fuller than ever before, had rendered the time ripe for the Lord's harvesting.

22. F. B. Meyer, *The Future Tenses of the Blessed Life* (New York, 1892); A. J. Gordon, *The Ministry of the Spirit* (New York, 1894), 212; Ernest R. Sandeen, "Millennialism," in *The Rise of Adventism: Religion and Society in Mid-Nineteenth-Century America,* ed. Edwin S. Gaustad (New York, 1974), 115.

Among liberals that optimism was well represented in the work of Egbert C. Smyth, a Congregational theologian at Andover Seminary. "The church of today," he wrote in 1885, "has a fuller knowledge of the purpose of God [and] a better conception of the dispensation of the spirit . . . than it was possible to communicate to the early church." Indeed, "the fulfillments of prophecy" have yielded an "ampler knowledge" of God's ways than ever before. To doubt it, he warned, "is a symptom of unbelief." Oberlin College president Henry Churchill King similarly insisted that the time had come for a "reconstruction in theology," as his 1901 study is titled, not because of "a demand from without," but because of "a deepening of the Christian spirit itself." But perhaps the most eloquent articulation of that outlook came from a voice far to the left of Egbert C. Smyth and King. Octavius Brooks Frothingham, a Unitarian leader in the Free Religious Association and author of a widely read treatise significantly titled *The Religion of Humanity*, roundly proclaimed that "it is not ours to remould the age, to recast it, to regenerate it, to cross it or struggle with it, but to penetrate its meaning, enter into its temper [and] blend with its endeavors," for the "interior spirit of any age is the spirit of God." Feeling little tension between his own highest ideals and the highest ideals of the age, Frothingham urged the church simply to acknowledge that "the life of the time appoints the creed of the time."[23]

Convinced that they were living in an age throbbing with redemptive power, the new theologians found it easy to believe that the divine guidance of history was leading to the imminent realization of the kingdom of God on earth. Stearns spoke for a generation of liberals when he insisted that the coming kingdom would embrace "all human interests. The kingdom is to come in the regeneration of society, in all its institutions, in all its corporate interests, in its spirit and tone . . . in the redemption of the human body from disease and the dominion of death . . . in the deliverance of nature from the bondage of corruption." A more ringing assertion of the sovereignty of the coming Lord is difficult to imagine. And until the eve of World War I, liberals such as Stearns remained confident that God's governance of history was direct and continuous even though it was implemented through secondary causes. It is important to add that the liberal view of the future was not a secular doctrine of inevitable progress dressed up in pious terminology. Thoughtful spokesmen knew that suffering is embedded in the processes of history. But they also knew

23. Egbert C. Smyth, "Progressive Orthodoxy," in *Progressive Orthodoxy: A Contribution to the Christian Interpretation of Christian Doctrines,* ed. the editors of *Andover Review* (Boston, 1892), 8–9; Henry Churchill King, *Reconstruction in Theology* (New York, 1901), 29; O. B. Frothingham, *The Religion of Humanity* (New York, 1873), 7–8.

that the kingdom would triumph. Congregational writer George Harris of Andover Seminary articulated one of the new theologians' most cherished convictions when he insisted that in the end "the moral order, as observed in history, is a divine order, for it is above the purpose of this or that individual, above the purpose of any single generation." Eventually, Harris's words would sound as fantastic as the premillennialist scenarios of the higher-life leaders. But for a time both visions had the glow of a sunlit world that now seems forever lost.[24]

It would be misleading to suggest that in the final analysis the leaders of those rival and, later, antagonistic movements were only using different words to say the same thing. The point, rather, is that in the midst of rapid social change, new and higher-life theologians were genuine adversaries precisely because each was struggling to establish the dominance of one side of a common theological heritage. Differently stated, the relation between liberals and evangelicals in the 1880s and 1890s is best understood, not as a confrontation between aliens, but as a contest—albeit a deadly serious contest—between siblings who perceived and defined the issues in remarkably similar ways.

This interpretation gains plausibility, I think, when we recognize how entangled the roots and the destinies of the two movements really were. Historically, both experienced a false start in the 1850s, both reemerged in strength in the late 1870s, and both reached the meridian of their cultural influence just before World War I. Geographically, both grew most luxuriantly in the urban centers of the Northeast and the northern Midwest, and neither took root in the Deep South or Far West until the 1920s and 1930s. The geographic distribution is not surprising, for virtually all of the new theologians and a majority of the higher-life theologians had grown up in small or medium-sized towns of the Northeast or the northern Midwest.[25] The denominational distribution is equally significant. Although the new theology was better received among Episcopalians and

24. Stearns, *Present Day Theology,* 123–24; George Harris, *Moral Evolution* (Boston, 1896), 191.

25. Hutchison, *Modernist Impulse in American Protestantism,* 45, 76–77, 184; Marsden, *Fundamentalism and American Culture,* 75–80, 101; Leonard I. Sweet, "'A Nation Born Again': The Union Prayer Meeting Revival," in *In the Great Tradition: In Honor of Winthrop S. Hudson: Essays on Pluralism, Voluntarism and Revivalism,* ed. Joseph D. Ban and Paul R. DeKar (Valley Forge, 1982), 194, 209, 211–13; Hutchison, "Cultural Strain and Protestant Liberalism," 406–11; Sandeen, *Roots of Fundamentalism,* 151; Robert Elwood Wenger, "Social Thought in American Fundamentalism, 1918–1933" (Ph.D. diss., University of Nebraska, 1973), 57–62, appendix; Samuel S. Hill, Jr., *The South and the North in American Religion* (Athens, 1980), 110–11, 115, 120–25; Edwin Scott Gaustad, *Historical Atlas of Religion in America* (New York, 1962), 48–51; James R. Shortridge, "Patterns of Religion in the United States," *Geographical Review* 66 (October 1976), 424–28.

Congregationalists, and the higher-life theology among Baptists and Presbyterians, the more pertinent fact is that both were nourished in the common soil of the Reformed tradition. Moreover, in both movements most of the leaders remained loyal to the denominations of their youth; yet when they switched they almost always switched to other Reformed denominations. Even the failures look alike. Both sets of leaders had an ambivalent relationship with their liberal and evangelical counterparts in the Methodist Episcopal Church, both provoked the displeasure of Old School Presbyterians, and both failed to penetrate Lutheran or other self-consciously ethnic traditions until the mid-twentieth century.[26]

Even so, to see new and higher-life theologians as combative siblings is to see only the foreground of the family portrait. Always looming in the background was the father. And this is the critical point, for the movements were parallel and, to some extent, patricidal protests by brothers and sisters against a common father. The common father was, of course, mainstream conservatism—or, to put it more precisely, the broad Reformed current in the center of mainstream conservatism—now perceived as orthodox rationalism without life or heart. The perception may have been unfair, given the demonstrable vitality of the Edwardsean and Princeton traditions in many pulpits, but unfairness is beside the point. The plain fact is that the leaders of both movements had come to believe that encrusted scholasticism in the mainstream seminaries and formalism and lovelessness in the mainstream churches had made a new birth by the Spirit imperative. Yet there were important differences in the way that the two movements carried out the patricidal ritual.

The new theologians were prone to score the established churches for their preoccupation with sin, death, and judgment. In the typical church, Gladden remembered, the minister seemed to think that "the business of religion was to fill the hearts of men with fear." Fosdick similarly recalled that the "most wretched hours" of his youth grew from the "pettiness and obscurantism, the miserable legalism and terrifying appeals to fear

26. Hutchison, *Modernist Impulse in American Protestantism,* 3; Sandeen, *Roots of Fundamentalism,* 152–53; Marsden, *Fundamentalism and American Culture,* 80; Frederick A. Norwood, *The Story of American Methodism: A History of the United Methodists and Their Relations* (Nashville, 1974), 319–20, 323–24; Timothy L. Smith, *Called unto Holiness: The Story of the Nazarenes: The Formative Years* (Kansas City, 1962), 25, 38–47, 51–53; Lefferts A. Loetscher, *The Broadening Church: A Study of Theological Issues in the Presbyterian Church since 1869* (Philadelphia, 1954), 29–108; Benjamin Breckenridge Warfield, *Perfectionism,* ed. Samuel G. Craig (Philadelphia, 1974), esp. 349–99; Eugene L. Fevold, "Coming of Age, 1875–1900: The Theological Scene," in *The Lutherans in North America,* ed. E. Clifford Nelson (Philadelphia, 1975), 305–28; Milton L. Rudnick, *Fundamentalism and the Missouri Synod: A Historical Study of Their Interaction and Mutual Influence* (St. Louis, 1966), 69–74, 86–88, 103–4.

that were associated with the religion of the churches." William Adams Brown, a Presbyterian theologian at Union Theological Seminary in New York, wryly pointed out that in *Systematic Theology,* the work of Brown's teacher and predecessor, William G. T. Shedd, "four pages sufficed for his treatment of heaven, but sixty were needed for his chapter on hell." It is tempting to suspect that the liberals' critique of mainstream conservatism was in fact a rationalization of their own secularism and accommodation to wealth. And for some that may have been true. But for most of the leaders, or at least for the most articulate and thoughtful ones, the problem with the established churches was that their theological and spiritual offerings had grown too meagre rather than too abundant, too lean rather than too rich. In the words of George A. Gordon, the venerable minister of Boston's Old South Congregational Church, America's pulpits became filled with "noble men . . . heroic in a way, but without insight into . . . the Kingdom of God." They were conscientious pastors, yet without feeling for "a Christianity that streams through all of life as the sunshine streams through the clouds."[27]

For the higher-life leaders, on the other hand, the problem with mainstream conservatism was not so much its austerity as its impotence, its lack of a supernaturally imparted vitality, its inability to inspire and to empower believers for Christian service. Pierson charged that the established churches were more and more "leavened by sectarianism, sacramentalism, ritualism, Romanism, rationalism and . . . secularism." Simpson, like many liberals, felt emotionally starved by the severity of his Calvinist upbringing. But his deeper grievance was against the laxity and flaccidness of the typical church where, he charged, one is confronted by "the strange spectacle of a great, broad mass of professing Christians who know or want to know little of the power of the Holy Ghost." Adoniram Judson Gordon was similarly appalled by the "confessions of weakness our Protestant Churches are unconsciously putting forth on every hand"—"new organs and frescoings and furnishings and . . . strawberry festivals." Such complaints were not limited to American higher-life circles. The British higher-life leader F. B. Meyer lamented the churches' inability to pass from "the realm of shadows into that of realities." Or as the Cambridge University cricket star Charles T. Studd mem-

27. Washington Gladden, *Recollections* (Boston, 1909), 61; Fosdick, *Living of These Days,* 33; William Adams Brown, *A Teacher and His Times: A Story of Two Worlds* (New York, 1940), 76; George A. Gordon, *My Education and Religion: An Autobiography* (Boston, 1925), 234, 239. For an interpretation that links the erosion of Reformed orthodoxy to secularization and economic affluence, see Daniel Walker Howe, "The Decline of Calvinism: An Approach to Its Study," *Comparative Studies in Society and History* 14 (June 1972): 306–27.

orably phrased it, the Anglicanism of his youth was not "a religion that amounted to much. It was just like having a toothache."[28]

Much of the evidence, then, seems to indicate that the dry rot of mainstream conservatism, seen on one side as morbidness and on the other as powerlessness, helped to precipitate the religious ferment of the late nineteenth century. This is not to say that the emergence of the new and the higher-life theologies can be wholly explained as reactions to the real or perceived exhaustion of the Reformed tradition. For some individuals, nonreligious factors such as physical infirmity, personal misfortune, aptitude for abstract thought, and paternal dominance may have helped to make a new orientation conceptually plausible or emotionally congenial. Moreover, the movements were part of a larger pattern in which Wesleyans, Adventists, Mormons, and not a few Roman Catholics similarly evinced profound interest in the Spirit's work in contemporary history. Indeed, it is arguable that many Jews and some secular philosophers felt comparable stirrings. The desire for renewal was not, in short, a strictly religious (much less Protestant Reformed) phenomenon, but a widespread cultural impulse.[29] Nonetheless, the Reformed quest for renewal was particularly self-conscious and, as it turned out, particularly resilient. Few would doubt that from the 1880s to the present, Reformed liberalism and evangelicalism—embodied first in the new and the higher-life theologies, then in modernism and fundamentalism, and today in ecumenical liberalism and evangelical fundamentalism—have been the most articulate, conspicuous, and combative players on the American religious stage.

All of this is to say that the story of the new theology and its higher-life counterpart is an important part of the story of American culture in the late nineteenth century. Yet to be properly understood, it must be placed in a larger context. And that larger context is the murky realm, notoriously resistant to conventional historical analysis, where religious im-

28. Arthur T. Pierson, *Forward Movements of the Last Half Century* (New York, 1912), vii–viii; A. B. Simpson, *The Holy Spirit or Power from on High*, 2 vols. (Harrisburg, 1924), 1:287, 289; Gordon, *Ministry of Healing*, 10; F. B. Meyer, *The Way into the Holiest: Expositions of the Epistle to the Hebrews* (London, n.d.), 221–22; "The Personal Testimony of Charles T. Studd," in *The Fundamentals: A Testimony to the Truth*, 12 vols. (Chicago, 1910–1915), 3:119.

29. Hutchison, "Cultural Strain and Protestant Liberalism," esp. 394–404; May, *Education of American Ministers*, 2:38–51; Thomas A. Symington, *Religious Liberals and Conservatives: A Comparison of Those Who Are Liberal in Their Religious Thinking and Those Who Are Conservative* (New York, 1935), 40–49. For a striking illustration of the desire for cultural renewal through the Holy Spirit, see John Farina, *An American Experience of God: The Spirituality of Isaac Hecker* (New York, 1981), 150–56, 168–70. More generally, see the selections in Edwin S. Gaustad, ed., *A Documentary History of Religion in America since 1865* (Grand Rapids, 1983), 104–305.

pulses come into play. Whatever else it may have been, the decision to break rank and to march under the banner of a self-conscious liberalism or of an evangelicalism was prompted by a desire to flee ordinary religion in search of extraordinary religion. Both movements hoped to find the holy in the midst of the mundane. In the thought world of the early church, Shirley Jackson Case once remarked, the "sky hung low."[30] In the lengthening shadows of the nineteenth century, he might well have added, it seemed to many thoughtful men and women that the sky had grown cold and distant. In that setting the new and the higher-life theologies emerged as languages of aspiration, symbolizing a conviction that God's Spirit truly embraced the spirit of the age.

30. Ahlstrom, *Religious History of the American People*, 22.

12

The "Overcoming" Life: A Study in the Origins of Pentecostalism

Edith Blumhofer

Reprinted by permission from *Pnuema* 1 (1979): 7–19.

Early-twentieth-century American Pentecostalism has been perceived as part of a worldwide awakening which, in turn, became an international phenomenon.[1] More specifically, American Pentecostalism emerged in Topeka, Kansas, at the end of 1900 when a small, interdenominational group of evangelicals agreed among themselves that glossolalia was the scriptural evidence of an experience of baptism with the Holy Spirit.

There have been two traditional approaches to the study of American Pentecostalism. The first cites the Wesleyan Holiness revival as the movement's primary source: the second focuses on Pentecostalism's distinctive emphasis on glossolalia and therefore suggests the movement's continuity with an idealized and presumedly continuous stream of Christianity in which glossolalia consistently reappeared. Neither perspective takes into account the emergence during the late nineteenth century of a strongly doctrinal emphasis on the Holy Spirit among non-Wesleyan evangelicals and outside the context of the Holiness associations. One

1. J. Edwin Orr, *The Flaming Tongue* (Chicago, 1973), 178–85.

can do justice to Pentecostalism's multiple, involved relationships within American evangelicalism only if one recognizes that its heritage has both a broader base than the Holiness movement and a more mainstream theological context than continuity with the appearances of glossolalia in church history would imply.

The non-Wesleyan emphases in the quest for holiness and spiritual power differed significantly from those of the Holiness movement in at least three general areas. Most importantly, the context in which Reformed evangelicals expressed their teaching was strongly doctrinal and primarily premillennialist: the conviction that Christ might return at any time provided these believers with both a powerful incentive for holiness and an awareness of an urgent need for effectiveness in evangelism. Secondly, their emphasis on holiness and the Holy Spirit rejected the central Holiness concept of a "second blessing" and focused rather on an "overcoming" life. They further objected to the contemporary Wesleyan terminology which sometimes described the "second blessing" as Spirit baptism, claiming that the baptism with the Holy Spirit was not a cleansing experience but rather a special "enduement with power for service." Thirdly, they, more than their Wesleyan contemporaries, incorporated into their evangelical faith a practical emphasis on divine healing. They contributed most directly to the heritage of the largest Pentecostal denomination—the Assemblies of God.

Probably the most prominent among those whose premillennialist persuasion made them contemporary advocates of a "walk in the Spirit" and an experience of "enduement with power for service" was Dwight L. Moody. His interest in these subjects became important to the emerging interest in the Holy Spirit among certain of his premillennialist contemporaries who systematized his understanding of the relationship between the Holy Spirit and the believer.

Several prominent contemporaries with roots in the major Reformed denominations shared Moody's persuasion that evangelicals too often neglected to cultivate a relationship with the Holy Spirit—R. A. Torrey, a Congregationalist who became the first supervisor of Moody's Chicago Training Institute in 1889 and pastor of the Chicago Avenue Church in 1894; A. J. Gordon, Boston Baptist pastor; A. T. Pierson, a Presbyterian minister; and A. B. Simpson, who left the Presbyterian church to found the Christian and Missionary Alliance. Though these men did not function as a formal group or espouse a well-defined program, their remarkably similar spiritual odysseys formed a basis for a distinct understanding of the evangelical message: each ultimately accepted baptism by immersion, became convinced of Christ's premillennial advent, espoused divine healing and, for a time, "faith" living, became associated with foreign missionary efforts, and stressed the necessity of a close relationship between the believer and the Holy Spirit. The conservative evangelical doctrinal framework into which they incorporated their particular emphases was similar to that which would later characterize the Assemblies of God.

In direct response to Moody's urging, Torrey's ministry particularly emphasized the person and work of the Holy Spirit.[2] He claimed that the Christian could find the true source of spiritual power in a definite experience of baptism with the Holy Spirit. He regarded this baptism as distinct from the progressive experience of sanctification but closely related to it. The subject of sanctification became a focus of disharmony among those whose desire for holiness made them participants in the various contemporary quests for the "fulness" of salvation.

These evangelicals rejected two central tenets of the contemporary Holiness message: (1) they denied that sanctification was instantaneous, and (2) they contended that sanctification was not the baptism with the Holy Spirit. Torrey focused on the subjugation rather than on the eradication of the sinful nature: only as long as the believer consciously permitted the Holy Spirit to subdue his will could he be assured of constant inward victory over sin.[3] A. B. Simpson agreed: sanctification was not a "work of grace," but a "gift of faith": not "the extinction of evil" but "the putting off, the laying aside of evil."[4]

Among their fellow Reformed evangelicals, the principal objections to this emphasis on "overcoming" included rejection of the suggestion that the believer could either determine to any extent his participation in the process of sanctification or be conscious of its progress. The response to the concomitant proposition that believers should experience a definite, postconversion baptism with the Holy Spirit, moreover, demonstrated a potential for serious disunity on the subject within that tradition.

Like Moody, Torrey believed that the primary purpose of Spirit baptism was enduement with power for service.[5] In addition, Spirit baptism was the "short cut to holiness." The Holy Spirit revealed Christ, and the "quickest way of getting the world out," Moody admonished, was "to get Christ in."[6] Simpson—more fully than the others—stressed the "all sufficiency" of Christ as a truth the believer could only apprehend by the

2. R. A. Torrey, "D. L. Moody, the Unity of His Life," *Institute Tie* 1 (March 1901): 203; R. A. Torrey, *Why God Used D. L. Moody* (New York, 1923).

3. R. A. Torrey, *What the Bible Teaches* (Chicago, 1898), 249–50.

4. A. B. Simpson, *A Larger Christian Life* (Harrisburg, n.d.), 40; A. B. Simpson, *Wholly Sanctified* (Harrisburg, 1925), 14.

5. R. A. Torrey, *The Baptism with the Holy Spirit* (Chicago, 1895).

6. D. L. Moody, "Christ and the Holy Spirit," in *College Students at Northfield,* ed. T. J. Shanks (New York, 1888), 170ff.; D. L. Moody in E. M. Fitt's Scrapbook, Moodyana Collection, Moody Bible Institute, Chicago.

Holy Spirit's revelation. He noted that even in the special experience of "enduement with power" Christ figures prominently:

> Jesus only is our Power,
> His the gift of Pentecost;
> Jesus, breathe Thy power upon us;
> Fill us with the Holy Ghost.[7]

These evangelicals refused to specify any single uniform evidence of baptism with the Holy Spirit. "You shouldn't be looking for any token," Moody cautioned. "Just keep asking and waiting for power. And . . . if you get filled . . . it is no sign that you are going to have it always. The fact is, we are very leaky vessels. We need to keep right under the fountain all the time."[8] They believed the experience was essential to effective service: "If I *may* be baptized with the Holy Spirit," Torrey affirmed, "I *must* be."[9]

Reformed objections to these emphases appeared in reviews and articles. Talbot Chambers, reviewing Torrey's *The Baptism* with the Holy Spirit for the *Presbyterian and Reformed Review* maintained, for example, that the Pentecostal "upper room" experience should not be expected to recur.[10] Presbyterians noted erroneous implications in some of A. J. Gordon's writings on these subjects: they dismissed as "self-surrender fiction" the teaching of "constant victory over self," and claimed that there was little actual difference between his emphasis on holiness and "the most pronounced sinless perfection."[11] There was, furthermore, objection to the tendency to make premillennial teaching "the mountaintop from which the whole landscape of the gospel" was to be understood.[12]

Of the several conference ministries which these men used to present their emphasis, that which Moody sponsored at Northfield from 1880 became particularly important to the presentation of teaching on the Holy Spirit. From 1881 when Scottish Free Church leader Andrew Bonar served as the Northfield Conference's principal speaker, British visitors often addressed the gatherings. Simpson's independent conventions in Old Orchard Beach, Maine, from 1886 developed his own interpretation

7. A. B. Simpson, "Jesus Only," *Songs of the Spirit* (New York, 1920), 36.
8. D. L. Moody, "Question Drawer," in *Northfield*, ed. Shanks, 204–5.
9. Torrey, *Baptism*, 28.
10. Talbot W. Chambers, Review of R. A. Torrey, *The Baptism with the Holy Spirit, The Presbyterian and Reformed Review* 6 (October 1895): 789–90.
11. Review of A. J. Gordon, *The Ministry of the Spirit, The Presbyterian Quarterly* 9 (April 1895): 346.
12. D. N. McLauchlin, Review of A. J Gordon, *How Christ Came to Church, The Presbyterian Quarterly* 10 (October 1896): 530.

of related teaching and frequently featured the same speakers. During the 1890s, incorporating as they did the particular emphasis on the Holy Spirit which characterized their founders, Moody's Northfield Conferences and Simpson's Old Orchard Beach Conventions were influenced by a British conferences ministry, centered at Keswick, with roots in an earlier phase of American evangelicalism, that also stressed "overcoming" and "enduement." The last decade of the century was a period of increasingly frequent interchange between American and European evangelicals who shared these emphases in non-Wesleyan contexts.

The roots of the Keswick movement were diverse, but its most immediate source was the British ministry from 1873 to 1875 of two American "higher-life" exponents, William E. Boardman and R. Pearsall Smith. Their emphasis was simple, stressing constant cleansing: "Expect Jesus to save you moment by moment from your greatest enemy in all the universe—Satan. . . . Assume the conquering position—it is yours in Christ."[13]

Despite Boardman's seniority, Smith dominated their combined efforts. Early in June, 1875, his brief but impressive leadership terminated amid discrediting rumors of "dangerous doctrines" and immoral conduct. Smith returned to America, and his followers, to whom he had had little time to give permanent structure, faced strong opposition. Several weeks after Smith's departure, Thomas Harford-Battersby, Vicar of St. John's Keswick, convened a gathering at which some of those who had accepted Smith's message assembled.

Controversy surrounded their teaching. Opponents cited persistent reports that the Keswick meeting had endorsed a perfectionist doctrine of entire sanctification.[14] In fact the meetings concentrated on the "quality" of the believer's experience. The leaders conscientiously stressed the reign of Christ within the soul rather than the instantaneous eradication of the sinful nature. "A belief in sinless perfection is not only foreign to, but diametrically opposite of, faith in our Lord Jesus Christ as our deliverer from the dominion of sin, and sustainer in a practical walk with our God," they asserted.[15]

Theological debate over holiness and sanctification continued for months in the pages of the *Church Record*. The movement had its critics in America as well. Princeton's prolific Benjamin Warfield noted tendencies in the "higher-life" ideology that would continue to prove trouble-

13. *Account of the Union Meeting for the Promotion of Holiness* (London, 1874), 41.

14. "The Brighton Convention and Its Opponents," *The London Quarterly Review 45* (October 1875): 84–128; Thomas Smith, "Means and Measure of Holiness," *British and Foreign Evangelical Review 25* (April 1876): 251–80.

15. *The Christian's Pathway of Power* 3 (February 1876), 21.

some throughout its history. He found its source in the "dissolution" and "Pelagianizing" of hereditary Calvinism. Without denying the guilt of sin, he asserted, "higher-life" proponents detracted from the basic concept of sin by focusing attention on "the practice of sinning" rather than on sin itself. In addition, Warfield maintained that the terminology of the movement reflected a subtle emphasis on personal ease: "Men grow weary of serving the Lord; they do not wish to fight to win the prize; they prefer to be carried to the skies on flowery beds of ease."[16]

The premillennialism which motivated some of Moody's associates to stress "enduement with power for service" was not so prominent at Keswick: the Keswick message stressed aspects of the "overcoming" life which Moody thought would complement the practical American view.[17] After 1892, when Moody attended briefly part of the Keswick Convention, F. B. Meyer, Hanmer William Webb-Peploe, Evan Hopkins, Andrew Murray and others brought to Northfield the Keswick understanding of victorious Christian living.[18]

During the last quarter of the nineteenth century, some of those evangelicals whose biblical literalism motivated them to both premillennialism and a stress on "overcoming" and "enduement" incorporated into their evangelical faith a doctrine of physical healing which later became part of the Pentecostal heritage. Their concern over the unorthodox theologies and sensational aspects of various healing methods of their day reinforced their conviction that God healed not only through means but also by direct intervention. Gordon and Simpson articulated understandings of healing which summarized the basic teaching on the subject: healing was both "in the atonement," and related to the "fullness" of salvation. Their belief in healing was rooted in their biblical literalism and related to both their understanding of the "overcoming" life and their premillennialism.[19]

A shared emphasis on the Holy Spirit, on a specific enduement with power and on "overcoming" inward sin had fostered considerable harmony among those evangelicals who gathered at Northfield and Keswick during the 1890s and had motivated them to pray earnestly for revival. By 1904, their prayers seemed about to be answered. From 1902 until

16. Benjamin Warfield, *Perfectionism* (Philadelphia, 1958), 245, 264ff.

17. Moody had, one contemporary Northfield historian reported, determined to make Northfield "the American Keswick." Hamlin, "Evolution of Northfield," *Northfield Echoes 3* (1896): 23.

18. This unofficial but cordial relationship between the two conferences terminated soon after Moody's death in 1899 primarily because of changes in the administration at Northfield.

19. A. J. Gordon, *The Ministry of Healing* (New York, 1882); A. B. Simpson, *The Gospel of Healing* (New York, 1915).

1905, Torrey conducted evangelistic campaigns around the world. Keswick leaders supported his extensive ministry in Britain during 1904 and 1905, and in 1904, he addressed the Keswick Convention. During these years, a British observer noted, Torrey's "logical presentation" of Spirit baptism as an experience of enduement for service "did much to establish the doctrine."[20]

During Torrey's British ministry, a revival emerged in Wales which, in spite of an utter lack of promotion or program, seemed to contemporary observers to move across the country "with the order of an attacking force." Its slogan became "bend the church and save the world."[21]

To the extent that any individual led the revival, Evan Roberts, a young miner, was its recognized spokesman. Roberts expressed his conviction that the revival would spread from Wales around the world. It seemed to some that a pervasive "sense," which they described as "the spirit of expectation," increased.[22] "When that remarkable revival broke out in Wales," wrote one American, "our hearts, like those of all Christendom, were greatly stirred. The power of God working so mightily, the absence of human machinery, the tremendous results in the salvation of souls, made us very hungry to know God in His fulness."[23]

Among the foreigners who visited Wales to observe the revival was the pastor of the First Baptist Church in Los Angeles, Joseph Smale. On his return, Smale instituted daily prayer meetings for revival in the city. When opposition among his members prompted his resignation, he organized the First New Testament Church. Smale's firsthand reports from Wales and the circulation of a pamphlet by G. Campbell Morgan about the revival helped nourish the longing for revival that many local evangelicals, Wesleyan and non-Wesleyan, shared: "Businessmen's groups, Bible class groups, holiness groups and people from different churches met to pray. Denomination made little difference. Christian workers, laymen and ministers alike, felt a need for more spiritual power in their lives."[24]

Such unanimity was short-lived, however. In April 1906, the *Los Angeles Times* included a first-page account of strange phenomena that had appeared among a small Holiness group in the city:

> Breathing strange utterances and mouthing a creed which it would seem no sane mortal could understand, the newest religious sect has started in Los

20. Donald Gee, *The Pentecostal Movement* (London, 1941), 4–5.

21. Evan Hopkins, "The Teaching of the Revival," in *The Story of the Welsh Revival* (New York, 1905), 73.

22. "A Call to Prayer," Historical Collection, M.B.I.; Ethel Goss, *The Winds of God* (New York, 1958), 21–22.

23. E. V. Baker, "Chronicles of a Faith Life," *Trust* 15 (May–June, 1916): 3.

24. *A Historical Account of the Apostolic Faith* (Portland, Ore., 1965), 43.

> Angeles. Meetings are held in a tumbledown shack on Azusa Street, and the devotees of the weird doctrines practice the most fanatical rites, preach the wildest theories, and work themselves into a state of made excitement in their peculiar zeal.[25]

The Azusa Street meetings stressed glossolalia as the uniform initial evidence of Spirit baptism. This claim, derived from the teaching of an obscure, Midwestern Holiness evangelist, Charles Parham, would ultimately disrupt the measure of unity that a shared concern for revival had fostered among many local evangelicals.

The meetings on Azusa Street continued throughout the summer of 1906 under the general direction of a black Holiness preacher, William Seymour. By September, the reports that had reached other parts of the country had begun to draw visitors of various theological persuasions from a distance. Missionaries and ministers went out from Seymour's mission, convinced that the New Testament Pentecost had been restored. Several Holiness groups accepted the teaching that glossolalia was the biblical evidence of Spirit baptism and ultimately became Pentecostal fellowships. Many of those who were inspired by the Los Angeles meetings to a Pentecostal persuasion, however, were rejected by their former churches and gathered in homes and missions to worship. The congregations lacked organization and discipline, and the short history of the movement had already demonstrated many weaknesses. Before long, the theological differences that had seemed unimportant in the enthusiasm of the revival threatened the future of the spreading movement. The two major traditions which had contributed to the movement's emergence and growth made disagreement over the doctrine of a "second blessing" inevitable and also helped assure the persistence within the nascent movement of the recognition of the diversity of its evangelical heritage.

Florence Crawford was among the outspoken Pentecostal defenders of the Wesleyan doctrine of sanctification. She claimed to have received both sanctification and Spirit baptism under Seymour's ministry in Los Angeles in 1906 and later established an independent, loosely organized fellowship in Portland, Oregon. "Entire sanctification is the act of God's grace by which one is made holy," she maintained. "It is the *second, definite* work wrought by the Blood of Jesus through faith, and subsequent to salvation and regeneration."[26] The baptism with the Holy Spirit could only be experienced after one had received this "second work": it was "enduement with power" upon "the clean, sanctified life." In her zeal to protect the "purity" of the movement, Crawford launched a scathing at-

25. *Los Angeles Times*, 18 April 1906, 1.
26. *The Apostolic Faith*, 48.

tack on those within the Pentecostal groups who failed to stress the "second definite work of grace."

This faction was ably led by William H. Durham, pastor of the North Avenue Mission in Chicago. Whereas Holiness advocates insisted that two distinct "works of grace" were required to save and to cleanse, Durham maintained that God "dealt with the nature of sin" at conversion. The initial experience of salvation included the "crucifixion" of the "old nature": "We are not saved simply because we are forgiven our sins," he taught. "We are saved through out identification with our Savior Substitute, Jesus Christ."[27] Some Holiness Pentecostals went so far as to suggest that, unless one received the "second blessing," enough sin remained in him to damn him: this, Durham's followers claimed, "nullified the work of regeneration."[28]

This controversy not only began to define clear lines of separation among the small Pentecostal groups; it also identified them with major evangelical traditions and contributed to the emerging sense that some formal organization of the movement was desirable.

In April 1914 a loose association called "The General Council of the Assemblies of God" was organized to "recognize scriptural methods and rules of unity, fellowship, work, and business for God" and to disapprove all unscriptural methods and conduct."[29] Two years later, in response to serious theological disunity over the "oneness" of the Godhead, the Assemblies of God adopted a "Statement of Fundamental Truth."

The "Statement" is largely an expression of Reformed evangelical theology, affirming the verbal inspiration of Scripture; the triune Godhead; justification by faith; sanctification as a process to be "earnestly pursued by walking in obedience to God's Word (this was later restated to describe a process initiated by "identification with Christ in his death and resurrection" and accomplished by "reckoning daily upon the fact of that union"); divine healing; and the imminent premillennial return of Christ. In addition, it included two articles affirming that all believers "are entitled to, and should ardently expect, and earnestly seek" the baptism with the Holy Spirit. "The full consummation of the baptism of believers in the Holy Ghost and fire is indicated by the initial sign of speaking in tongues," it maintained.[30]

27. William Durham, "The Finished Work of Calvary," *Pentecostal Testimony* 2 (1912): 6.

28. *Way of Faith,* 4 December 1913; *Word and Witness* 9 (20 December 1913): 2.

29. "Minutes of the General Council of the Assemblies of God," 1914, 4.

30. "Minutes of the General Council of the Assemblies of God," 1916, 10–11. Assemblies of God leader W. I. Evans later explained sanctification in terms reminiscent of Torrey, Simpson, or Meyer in *This River Must Flow* (Springfield, Mo., 1954).

The most nearly unique feature of the Pentecostal movement, as far as outsiders were concerned, was this association of glossolalia with Spirit baptism. The reaction of both Wesleyan and non-Wesleyan evangelicals was generally hostile. Those in the non-Wesleyan tradition who had objected to Torrey's and Simpson's focus on the "walk in the Spirit" and Spirit baptism repudiated even more emphatically the Pentecostal claim of uniform initial evidence. More significantly, Torrey, Simpson, and others of their evangelical colleagues disassociated themselves from the movement.

Years before the formulation of the Pentecostal teaching, Torrey had decided against accepting glossolalia as the uniform initial evidence of Spirit baptism.[31] Torrey's specific objections to Pentecostalism focused on its concept and use of glossolalia which, Torrey maintained, were untenable: he concluded that "the 'Tongues Movement' is a movement upon which God has set the stamp of his disapproval in a most unmistakable way in his Word, and also in what He has permitted to develop in connection with it."[32]

Arthur Pierson shared Torrey's concern over an emphasis on glossolalia: in two articles in the *Missionary Review of the World,* he cautioned readers against unduly coveting this gift. Tongues speakers seemed to him to be too often unsuccessful in separating the genuine from the spurious. He noted a tendency among Christians to become too absorbed in "Holy Spirit manifestations," and warned that overemphasis on the Spirit might "hinder His revelation of Christ."[33]

Torrey and Pierson also shared reservations about tendencies they observed in some aspects of the Pentecostal proclamation of healing, particularly in the convening of healing rallies. Torrey noted with concern the subtle tendency toward a shift in emphasis from salvation to physical well-being that the healing movement reflected. He objected also to the "techniques" that he observed in some healing ministries—"the mes-

31. R. A. Torrey, *The Person and Work of the Holy Spirit* (Grand Rapids, 1974), 158.

32. R. A. Torrey, *Is the Present Tongues Movement of God?* (Los Angeles, 1913), 8. Torrey's opposition to Pentecostalism must be considered in the context of his insistence that it was essentially a tongues movement. It was precisely because Torrey and the leaders of the Assemblies of God regarded Pentecostalism so differently that the latter were ultimately able to assert their appreciation of Torrey's writings and ministry. After Torrey's death, some of his students tried to disassociate his teaching on Spirit baptism from Pentecostalism, claiming that he had been careless and inconsistent in his use of key terms. Mrs. Torrey denied such reports, claiming that his views on the subject had never changed despite his rejection of glossolalia as uniform initial evidence. Clara Torrey to Paul W. Sawtell, 4 January 1941, Moodyana Collection, M.B.I.; Ernest Wadsworth, "Did Torrey Mean Baptism or Filling?" Moodyana Collection, M.B.I.

33. Arthur T. Pierson, "Speaking with Tongues," *Missionary Review of the World* 20 (July 1907): 487–92, 682–84.

meric atmosphere . . . where there is skillfully planned, highly emotional music, and swaying of the body and passings of the hand and shouts of hallelujahs, that excite the imagination and thrill the body."[34]

In spite of their shared evangelical orthodoxy, their espousal of glossolalia and divine healing made Pentecostals particularly unwelcome in cooperative fundamentalist efforts. The sympathy of the Assemblies of God with the fundamentalist tenets and the stress on premillennialism and the Holy Spirit presented at Northfield and Keswick in the preceding generation was demonstrated not only in avowals of allegiance to the conservative faith but also by the enthusiastic recommendation of many books by Torrey, Gordon, Pierson, Simpson, Meyer, Murray, and their colleagues in the *Pentecostal Evangel.* Of the many evangelical authors editor Stanley Frodsham endorsed, he recommended none more highly than A. B. Simpson. Assemblies of God leaders considered that Simpson, probably more than any other single evangelical, had anticipated their movement. Simpson was unable to accept the doctrine of uniform initial evidence, however, and, although the Alliance officially adopted a policy of "seek not, forbid not" with regard to glossolalia, its leaders effectively excluded the Pentecostal stress from their churches.[35]

In order to understand opposition to the movement, one must recognize the fanaticism that accompanied its emergence. Distinctions made by Pentecostals between "authentic" and "counterfeit" operations of the Holy Spirit often seemed meaningless to outsiders but became crucial to the self-image of the movement. "There is a so-called 'Free Pentecost' over the country," wrote Assemblies of God leader J. R. Flower, "and you can find most any kind of doctrine or practice in the 'Free Pentecost' assemblies. There is also a well ordered Pentecostal Movement."[36]

From its inception in 1914, the Assemblies of God recognized the non-Wesleyan contributions to its heritage. The story of this late-nineteenth-century non-Wesleyan emphasis on the Holy Spirit, when combined with the related story of the Wesleyan Holiness revival, provides a neglected perspective on conservative evangelical interrelationships. The doctrinal perspective which distinguished the Reformed emphasis from the Wesleyan stress survived in Pentecostalism. And the continuity Assemblies of God leaders perceived between late-nineteenth-century evangelicalism and their own movement (at least as demonstrated by the books and articles recommended in early Pentecostal publications) focused on the ministries of Torrey, Gordon, Simpson, Meyer, Murray,

34. R. A. Torrey, *Divine Healing* (New York, 1925), 13.

35. William W. Menzies, *Anointed to Serve* (Springfield, Mo., 1971), 72.

36. J. R. Flower, "The Present Position of Pentecost," *Pentecostal Evangel,* 13 June 1925, 7.

G. Campbell Morgan and their non-Wesleyan colleagues. By 1941, when Pentecostals were invited to join the National Association of Evangelicals, the emphases within Reformed evangelicalism which had made it a contributor to the Pentecostal context were no longer so prominent: only Simpson had devised a formal framework in which to stress and to perpetuate systematically his own emphases. Much of the conception of the ministry of the Holy Spirit, with the emphasis on Spirit baptism, together with the practical understanding of the doctrine of divine healing which had been expressed in these non-Wesleyan as well as in Wesleyan-Holiness contexts at the end of the nineteenth century had become the province of the Pentecostals.

Part 5

From Fundamentalism to Evangelicalism

13

Fundamentalism as an American Phenomenon

George M. Marsden

Reprinted with permission from *Church History* 46:2 (June 1977): 215–32.

"Fundamentalism" is used in so many ways that a definition is the only place to begin. As I here use the term, "fundamentalism" refers to a twentieth-century movement closely tied to the revivalist tradition of mainstream evangelical Protestantism that militantly opposed modernist theology and the cultural change associated with it. Fundamentalism shares traits with many other movements to which it has been related (such as pietism, evangelicalism, revivalism, conservatism, confessionalism, millenarianism, and the Holiness and Pentecostal movements), but it has been distinguished most clearly from these by its militancy in opposition to modernism. This militancy has typically been expressed in terms of certain characteristic theological or intellectual emphases: whereas modernism or liberal theology tended to explain life and much of religion in terms of natural developments, fundamentalists stressed the supernatural. Accordingly their most distinctive doctrines (although not all have been held by everyone in the movement)[1] were the divinely guar-

1. Fundamentalism especially in the 1920s was a coalition of rather diverse cobelligerents. For helpful accounts of some varieties within the leadership see the essays of C. Allyn Russell, collected in *Voices of American Fundamentalism: Seven Biographical Studies* (Philadelphia, 1976).

anteed verbal inerrancy of Scripture, divine creation as opposed to biological evolution, and a dispensational-premillennial scheme that explained historical change in terms of divine control. In America, where fundamentalism originated, adherence to the first of these teachings became a test for the purity of denominations, the second a symbol for efforts to preserve the Christian character of the culture, and the third a basis for fellowship among fundamentalists themselves.

During the 1920s, fundamentalists in America engaged in furious and sensational battles to control the denominations and the wider culture. When these efforts failed they became increasingly separatist, often leaving major denominations and flourishing in independent churches and agencies.[2] They continued however to have an impact on large areas of American Protestantism and most of the pietistic or conservative movements with which they had contact took on some fundamentalist traits.

The phenomenon that I have defined as "fundamentalism" was overwhelmingly American in the sense that almost nowhere else did this type of Protestant response to modernity have such a conspicuous and pervasive role both in the churches and in the national culture.[3] An examination of fundamentalism should reveal some significant traits of American culture and, conversely, the American context will provide a key for understanding fundamentalism.

The crucial variables in the American environment can best be identified by comparing the American development of fundamentalism with its closest counterpart, English evangelicalism. The approach is particularly revealing since from the time of the Puritans down through the awakenings to the end of the nineteenth century British and American evangelicalism had been in many respects parts of a single transatlantic movement. Ernest R. Sandeen has even argued (although too simplistically) that on the basis of one of the many connections—millenarianism—the origins of

2. In "From Fundamentalism to Evangelicalism: An Historical Analysis," *The Evangelicals,* ed. David Wells and John Woodbridge (Nashville, 1975). I have discussed the changes in the character of fundamentalism since the 1920s. Among those close to the movement the meaning of the term *fundamentalist* has narrowed in recent decades to include almost solely doctrinally militant premillennialist revivalists. Cf. George W. Dollar, *A History of Fundamentalism in America* (Greenville, S.C., 1973).

3. Ulster appears to be an exception—one that would offer another illustration of the relationship of fundamentalism to relatively unique cultural experiences. Canada has some fundamentalism, although I have the United States primarily in mind in the "American" comparison. In many nations, confessionalists and churchly conservatives survived and in some, such as The Netherlands, they had considerable influence; but these lacked the revivalist ties and some of the intellectual emphases characteristic of fundamentalists. Evangelical or pietist revivalism, sometimes with genuinely fundamentalist traits, could be found throughout the world in the twentieth century, but even if vigorous, as scattered minorities often operating with an aspect of a religious underground.

fundamentalism were essentially British.[4] In any case, British-American ties were taken for granted even as late as the beginnings of the organized fundamentalist crusade; in *The Fundamentals,* published from 1910 to 1915, one-fourth of the authors were British.[5] Yet, strikingly, by the 1920s when the American fundamentalists were engaged in intense spiritual warfare, there were few on the English front willing to sound the battle cry.

As will be seen, a number of English evangelicals during the 1920s firmly resisted the almost overwhelming trend to accept liberal theology; yet, despite their similarity to American fundamentalism, most of their efforts lacked its aggressiveness and militancy and certainly had no comparable role in the culture and the churches. For Englishmen the Scopes trial, for instance, was totally foreign to their own experience and almost inconceivable. "Perhaps no recent event in America stands more in need of explanation . . ." wrote one British observer in 1925.[6] Even those who closely followed English church life saw no counterpart to militant fundamentalism. "Perhaps it was [his] greatest service," observed the *Times* of London in 1929 concerning A. S. Peake, a moderate British evangelical who had done much to introduce the public to biblical criticism, ". . . that he helped to save us from a fundamentalist controversy such as that which has devastated large sections of the church in America."[7]

There had been, of course, considerable controversy when the new evolutionary and higher critical views were first publicized in Great Britain, but it never grew to the proportions of the American reaction. In fact, one of the striking differences between the patterns of reactions is that, while in America the controversies intensified from the 1860s to the 1920s, in England the peak of popular furor had been reached already by the 1860s. Initial reactions in English churches to *Origin of Species* (1859), *Essays and Reviews* (1860), and the first volume of Bishop John Colenso's *The Pentateuch and Book of Joshua Critically Examined* (1862–79) were largely negative. Yet the sensational and emotional aspects of the controversies had already largely passed by the end of the

4. *The Roots of Fundamentalism: British and American Millenarianism 1800–1930* (Chicago, 1970). My criticisms are found in a review article, "Defining Fundamentalism," *Christian Scholar's Review* 1:2 (winter 1971): 141–51; see Sandeen's reply, 1, 3 (spring 1971): 227–33. See also LeRoy Moore, Jr., "Another Look at Fundamentalism: A Response to Ernest R. Sandeen," *Church History* 37 (June 1968): 195–202.

5. A number of the British authors, however, were no longer living.

6. S. K. Ratcliffe, "America and Fundamentalism," *Contemporary Review* 128 (September 1925); now in *Controversy in the Twenties: Fundamentalism, Modernism, and Evolution,* ed. Willard B. Gatewood, Jr., (Nashville, 1969), 414. Other British commentators seem to have agreed that fundamentalism was peculiarly American; see Gatewood in ibid., 409–12.

7. 20 August 1929, obituary of Dr. Arthur Samuel Peake, quoted in David G. Fountain, *E. J. Poole-Connor (1872–1962): "Contender for the Faith"* (London, 1966), 91.

1860s.[8] After that, biological evolution never became a divisive issue of nearly the proportions reached in America.[9] The question of the nature of Scripture was more difficult to resolve; but in general, once moderate historical-critical ideas were advanced by evangelicals known as reverent defenders of the faith, the new attitudes were accepted with remarkable swiftness. By the 1890s most of the clergy had abandoned traditional assumptions concerning the full historical accuracy of Scripture for some form of higher criticism.[10] Considerable numbers of church members still did not accept the newer ideas;[11] but most were at least familiar with the major issues so that there was little potential for an outbreak of public alarm after that time. In all, this rather peaceful development suggests that nineteenth-century British evangelical religion, like British politics, was closer in style to Edmund Burke than to Oliver Cromwell.

What accounts for the relatively smooth and rapid acceptance in England of the same views that caused so much turmoil in America? Both a strong tradition of theological latitude dating back to the Elizabethan settlement and a policy of toleration since at least the Act of Toleration of 1689 were major factors. These policies, however, were at least officially

8. This interpretation and that immediately below follow that of Willis B. Glover, *Evangelical Nonconformists and Higher Criticism in the Nineteenth Century* (London, 1954). Owen Chadwick, *The Victorian Church: Part II,* 2d ed. (London, 1972) provides a similar account of Anglican reactions to *Essays and Reviews* (75–90) and Colenso (90–97). A recent general account of British reaction to Darwinism in the 1860s is M. J. S. Hodge, "England," in *The Comparative Reception of Darwinism,* ed. Thomas F. Glick (Austin, Tex., 1972). See Edward J. Pfeifer's interesting essay, "United States," in ibid.

9. Chadwick, *op. cit.,* 23, says that evolution was fully accepted and respectable among clergymen by 1896. G. Stephen Spinks, "Victorian Background," in Spinks *et al., Religion in Britain since 1900* (London, 1952) remarks that it was easier for the British to come to terms with the new biology than with biblical criticism, 20.

10. Glover, *op. cit.,* 71–90, 109–10. On Anglican parallel see p. 9 and Chadwick, *op. cit.,* 1–111. Cf. H. D. McDonald, *Theories of Revelation: An Historical Study 1860–1960* (London, 1963), 101–18. By 1900, English champions of higher criticism thought "the battle was won" and that higher criticism had already "penetrated to the country clergymen" (116). McDonald, however, shows that at least the former of these statements was an overestimate since a few conservative attacks continued (118–36, 203–17). Already by the time of *Lux Mundi* (1889) which helped promote higher criticism among Anglicans, all the bishops except J. C. Ryle of Liverpool (a rather tolerant conservative) reportedly accepted the new ideas. See Marcus L. Loune, *John Charles Ryle 1816–1900: A Short Biography* (London, 1953), 47–48, 56–57. Anti-evolution does not seem to have been a major issue even for the most conservative twentieth-century English evangelicals cited below.

11. Chadwick, *op. cit.,* 24, says that "for a decade or two after 1896 some members of the Church of England, especially among the evangelicals . . . and most of the simple worshippers among the chapels of the poor, continued to know nothing of evolution or to refuse to accept it on religious grounds. . . ." This estimate would still place the general popular acceptance by World War I. Cf. Glover, *op. cit.,* 217, for a similar observation regarding acceptance of higher criticism.

parts of the American religious heritage, and in fact Americans since the Revolution had been proud of their country's unusual degree of religious liberty and tolerance. The fact that often in American religious life there was not the degree of toleration that the popular mythology proclaimed is in part the phenomenon that needs to be explained.

Given the generally greater tolerance among evangelicals in nineteenth-century England, other factors are still needed to explain why the revolutionary new views concerning higher criticism and evolution did not foment a long and major controversy in England. Clearly the English were prepared in some way for the new ideas, but the initially strong opposition of the 1860s indicates that this preparation was not one of direct familiarity. English theologians seem not to have had, for instance, a great deal more of sympathetic contact with the earlier German higher criticism than did their American counterparts. More basic than any specific preparation seems to have been a general intellectual climate—that is, the concepts of natural and historical development on which both Darwinism and higher criticism were based were closely akin to trends that had been developing in British thought for some time.[12] The whole English constitutional system (in contrast to America, where newness demanded written and traditional definition) reflects a sense of gradually developing tradition that appears characteristic of English thought generally. Regarding the acceptance of higher criticism in nineteenth-century England, Willis Glover in his careful study of the Nonconformists correctly makes much of this point. He says:

> But the most essential presuppositions of criticism, such as the unity and continuity of history, were a part of the general climate of opinion shared by traditionalists and critics alike. The historical sense of the century was so strong that the defenders of tradition found it extremely difficult to deny higher criticism in principle. In the last quarter of the century even those who upheld tradition against the critics on every count were often ready and even anxious to make it clear that they did not oppose the critical and historical study of the Bible but merely the conclusions of "rationalistic" critics.[13]

12. Darwinism quite evidently reflected tendencies developing in the British intellectual climate for some time. The sense of history as "a natural and organic development" was commonplace by the mid-nineteenth century. See, for example, the account in Walter E. Houghton, *The Victorian Frame of Mind: 1830–1870* (New Haven, Conn., 1957), 29–31, and *passim.* Romanticism, which had been a major force in England since before 1800, also encouraged emphasis on process rather than on fixed or static truth. (Cf. note 43, below).

13. Glover, *op. cit.,* 25. Cf. Chadwick, *op. cit.,* 59, who attributes the widespread agreement on new views of the Old Testament ". . . not only to German criticism and to English scholarship but to the general growth of historical consciousness. . . ." Cf. 462.

This estimate of Glover applies well, for instance, to the work of James Orr of Scotland, the leading British theological critic of liberalism around the turn of the century. Because of his reputation as a defender of the faith, Orr had close and cordial relations with the American revivalists who organized *The Fundamentals* and was a major contributor to that series. Yet unlike the American leaders of the emerging fundamentalist movement, Orr not only was amenable to limited forms of biological evolution but also accepted historical criticism of Scripture in principle, even while vigorously attacking most of its usual applications. The attempt to defend the faith on the basis of "inerrancy," said Orr, was simply "suicidal."[14]

While most British evangelicals in the twentieth century were moving much further than James Orr,[15] and few were doctrinally militant, some conserved traditional views chiefly through vigorous piety. Outstanding in this respect was the Keswick Convention, founded in 1875 in the wake of the Moody revivals. The Keswick summer conferences became the informal meetingplace for British conservative evangelicals and its emphases on Bible study, evangelism, missions, personal piety, and "victory over sin" had wide influence. Like Moody, Keswick teaching took for granted a conservative view of Scripture, yet explicitly avoided any controversy.

This noncontroversialist stance gave Keswick and much of the British conservative evangelicalism that it nourished an emphasis rather different from twentieth-century American fundamentalism. While many American fundamentalists adhered to Keswick teaching concerning the "victorious life," its irenic emphases were overshadowed in the early decades of the twentieth century by antiliberal militancy. By the 1920s Keswick was becoming suspect even to fundamentalist leaders. After a

14. Orr, *Revelation and Inspiration* (New York, 1910), 198; cf. 209–10, 214–15. Orr was critical of the emphasis of the Princeton theologians on inerrancy although he thought he had much in common with them regarding Scripture. On evolution see Orr, "Science and the Christian Faith," in *The Fundamentals: A Testimony to the Truth* (Chicago, 1910–15), 4:91–104. The inclusion of Orr's moderate statement on evolution in *The Fundamentals* indicates that the lines had not yet firmly hardened on this point among the American revivalists.

15. Even some evangelicals who protested against the more liberal trends were rather progressive themselves. Charles H. Vine, ed., *The Old Faith and the New Theology: A Series of Sermons and Essays on Some Truths Held by Evangelical Christians* (New York, 1907), being protests by British Congregationalists against the "new theology," and B. Herklots, *The Future of the Evangelical Party in the Church of England* (London, 1913) both parallel fundamentalist concerns over questions such as miracles yet assume a tolerance toward higher criticism not found among American fundamentalists. See, e.g., Vine, *op. cit.*, 225 and 227; Herklots, *op. cit.*, v, 57–68, 107, 113. Cf. general accounts by E. L. Allen, "The Acids of Modernity," in Spinks, *Religion in Britain*, 49–64 and John Kenneth Mozley, *Some Tendencies in British Theology from the Publication of* Lux Mundi *to the Present Day* (London, 1951), 24–46.

visit in 1928, William B. Riley, president of the World Christian Fundamentals Association, criticized Keswick for "carelessness" in tolerating doctrinal error and noted, no doubt in reference to himself, that "'a controversialist' could never be on its platform."[16]

While in England enthusiasm for controversy was hardly considered evidence of true faith, some British conservative evangelicals more or less in the Keswick tradition responded to the threats of liberalism by maintaining doctrinal purity and a degree of separateness.[17] Prominent among such efforts was the Inter-Varsity Fellowship organized in 1928 among university student groups that had been steering a course separate from the more liberal Student Christian Movement. The constitution of IVF affirmed "the fundamental truths of Christianity," including the infallibility of Scripture, and decreed its continued noncooperation with liberals. Despite these fundamentalist resemblances IVF placed far more emphasis on the personal piety and evangelism reminiscent of the Moody-Keswick era (when its progenitor the Cambridge Inter-Collegiate Christian Union had originated) than on the doctrinal militancy of the fundamentalist era.[18] Its

16. *The Christian Fundamentalist* 2 (1928): 7, 17. General accounts of Keswick are found in Bruce Shelley, "Sources in Pietistic Fundamentalism," *Fides et Historia* 5 (1973): 68–78 and Steven Barabas, *So Great Salvation: The History and Message of the Keswick Convention* (Westwood, N. J., 1952). At this same time Riley was engaged in an all-out attack on the well-known conservative-evangelical British preacher, G. Campbell Morgan, sometimes also associated with Keswick, and a contributor to *The Fundamentals.* Morgan, concluding a brief and stormy stay at the Bible Institute of Los Angeles, described as "frankly impossible" the attitude of fundamentalists. "They separate themselves, not only from those who accept evolutionary theory, but from those who deny the literal inerrancy of Scripture." Quoted from *The British Weekly* in *The Christian Fundamentalist* 2 (1928): 14.

17. I am very greatly indebted to Ian S. Rennie of Regent College, Vancouver, for pointing me toward much of the information used in the following sections on English evangelicalism. In two very extensive critiques of an earlier version of this essay he argues that there was "an identifiable movement known as English Fundamentalism" and that "its controversies were only different in the fact that England provided a somewhat different context." While I am impressed by the evidence used to support this conclusion, and hope that Professor Rennie will publish his own account of it, I nevertheless remain convinced that the English movement differed significantly from American fundamentalism. However, I do not object strongly to calling the British movement (as Rennie does) "fundamentalist," which I think is consistent with British parlance. With such a broader definition, my thesis would be that there is a qualitative difference between British and American fundamentalism as well as a difference in impact on the churches and the culture.

18. J. C. Pollock, *A Cambridge Movement* (London, 1953) gives a very complete account of the background and origins of I.V.F. His work may be supplemented by broader accounts in Frederick Donald Coggan, ed., *Christ and the Colleges: A History of the Inter-Varsity Fellowship of Evangelical Unions* (London, 1934), which contains the constitution, and Douglas Johnson, ed., *A Brief History of the International Fellowship of Evangelical Studies* (Lausanne, 1964).

ties to America were confined largely to the moderate variety of fundamentalism eventually known as "neo-evangelicalism."[19]

A similar development was the split in 1922 of the Church Missionary Society, the missions agency of the evangelical party in the Church of England. A rather distinguished group of conservatives, who made the historical trustworthiness of Scripture a doctrinal test, withdrew in protest over inclusivist tendencies and formed the Bible Churchmen's Missionary Society. This move closely paralleled American controversies concerning missions following World War I, yet it was effected without prolonged dispute;[20] questions of separation and independent action could readily be resolved within the wider spirit of Anglican comprehension. Within the Bible Churchmen's Missionary Society and in numerous older agencies[21] evangelicals felt free to operate without purging established ecclesiastical structures.

Although the foregoing examples illustrate that uncompromising conservative evangelicalism survived in England, the contrast to America becomes apparent when we consider the fragmentary scope of English attempts to organize something like a militant antiliberal crusade. The prototype of such efforts was the separation of Charles Haddon Spurgeon from the Baptist Union in the "Downgrade controversy" of 1887. This action near the end of the career of this illustrious London preacher seems to have had little wider impact.[22] It was not that no effort was made to carry

19. George W. Dollar in his militantly fundamentalist *A History of Fundamentalism in America* (Greenville, S.C., 1973) includes I.V.F. in "An Enemy Within: New Evangelicalism," 205; cf. 258. On the other hand more liberal critics in England called I.V.F. "fundamentalist" in the 1950s, e.g., Gabriel Hebert, *Fundamentalism and the Church of God* (London, 1957); cf. J. I. Packer's defense, *"Fundamentalism" and the Word of God* (London, 1958). The "fundamentalism" in these debates is more sophisticated, scholarly, and flexible than all but a very small portion of American fundamentalism.

20. Complementary accounts of this dispute are found in Gordon Hewitt, *The Problems of Success: A History of the Church Missionary Society 1910–1942* (London, 1971) and in G. W. Bromiley's sympathetic biography of the leader of the conservatives, *Daniel Henry Charles Bartlett: A Memoir* (Burnham-on-Sea, Somerset, Eng., 1959).

21. Rennie points out that there was a substantial infrastructure of such agencies. Among those he mentions are the Church Pastoral-Aid Society, the South American Missionary Society, the (now-named) Commonwealth and Continental Missionary Society, and the Church's Ministry to the Jews (all Anglican), the Scripture Union and Children's Special Service Mission, the Christian Alliance of Women and Girls (a secession in 1919 from the YWCA), the Bible League, and the Victoria Institute (a center for anti-evolution thought); among theological schools, Tyndale, Clifton, Oak Hill, and to some extent St. John's Highbury, a few Bible colleges, but no colleges at the universities; publications, *The Christian, The Life of Faith* and the annual *Keswick Week*. Correspondence with author.

22. Ian Murray, *The Forgotten Spurgeon* (London, 1966), whose title is revealing, documents a sympathetic account of Spurgeon's role as a controversialist in Downgrade, 145–206. Willis B. Glover, "English Baptists at the Time of the Downgrade Controversy,"

on his controversialist work, for A. C. Dixon, one of the editors of *The Fundamentals,* came from America in 1911 to serve as pastor of Spurgeon's Metropolitan Temple but departed again in 1919 without leaving any substantial fundamentalist organization behind him.[23] Slightly more successful in organizing a full-fledged controversialist fundamentalist movement in England[24] was E. J. Poole-Connor, who also thought he was carrying on Spurgeon's cause. Poole-Connor opposed any cooperation with or tolerance for theological liberalism, and in 1922 he founded the Fellowship of Independent Churches which he described in 1925 as having "a strongly fundamentalist credal basis."[25] The organization remained quite small (perhaps 100 to 150 congregations and six to seven thousand members in its first twenty years)[26] and Poole-Connor himself compared the nonmilitant stance of most conservative evangelicalism in England unfavorably to American fundamentalism.[27] The general extent of Poole-Connor's influence in English church life is revealed by the remark of his admiring biographer, "Truly he was a prophet 'without honour.'"[28]

Foundations 1 (1958): 46, goes so far as to conclude of Downgrade, "its chief interest is the fact that it has so few long-range effects."

23. Among the Baptists, however, a "Baptist Bible Union" was organized by the 1920s. See a report on its fundamentalist activities by its founder, John W. Thomas, "Modernism and Fundamentalism in Great Britain," *The King's Business* 14 (1923): 817–21. The impact, however, appears to have been slight. E. J. Poole-Connor, *Evangelicalism in England,* rev. ed. (London 1965 [1951]), 249, laments that modernism had triumphed almost completely among British Baptists by 1925. Arthur H. Carter, in "Modernism: the Outlook in Great Britain," *The King's Business* 15 (1924): 691, remarks: "But the saddest aspect of the situation lies in the fact that the entire body of English Nonconformity accepts their theological position, and, save in a few isolated cases, the whole body of the Free Churches has gone *holus bolus* over to the ranks of Modernism." No doubt more nonmilitant biblicism survived among Nonconformists than these estimates would allow. Yet contrast American fundamentalists at this time who often claimed to represent the majority of American church members, e.g., "A Divided House," *The King's Business* 15 (1925): 347.

24. Another Englishman who qualified as a full-fledged fundamentalist was W. H. Griffith Thomas (1861–1924). He was associated with *The Fundamentals,* Keswick, dispensationalism, and the founding of Dallas Theological Seminary. However, he left a position as principal at Wycliffe Hall, Oxford, in 1910 to become professor of Old Testament at Wycliffe College, Toronto, hence reducing his influence in England. C. G. Thorne, Jr., "William Henry Griffith Thomas," *The New International Dictionary of the Christian Church,* ed. J. D. Douglas (Grand Rapids, 1974), 972.

25. Quoted in Fountain, *E. J. Poole-Connor,* 126.

26. The statistics are approximations, Fountain, *Poole-Connor,* 18. Nearly three hundred congregations were claimed by the time of Poole-Connor's death in 1962, 211.

27. Fountain, *Poole-Connor,* 34, 44, 131–34. Fountain, 119, observes, "In the United States the conflict was sharper than in this country for two reasons. The Liberals were more extreme and the Evangelicals more faithful and more able."

28. Fountain, *Poole-Connor,* 134. Conservative evangelical scholarship also seems to have been at its nadir during the period between the wars. H. D. McDonald, *Theories of*

Paradoxically one factor contributing to this notable lack of success of such separatist fundamentalist efforts was the significant presence in England of the Plymouth Brethren. The Brethren had many of the same traits as American fundamentalists, and no doubt attracted some persons who in the American context might have become involved in wider denominational struggles. Between 1910 and 1960 the principal (Open) Brethren group increased in adherents by roughly half, reaching a total of perhaps ninety thousand.[29] However, by the nature of the case, Brethren separatism left them with little ecclesiastical influence outside their own circles. Even among other conservative evangelicals they were viewed with some suspicion and regarded as operating too much like a secret society.[30] In all, Brethren influence in England was much like a religious underground and did not gain the role in the churches and the culture that fundamentalism had in America.

In conclusion it appears that the English conservative evangelicals differed from their American counterparts in two major respects: (1) a lack of widespread militancy, but instead Keswick-type emphases on noncontroversialist piety; (2) a lack of general impact on the churches and the culture.[31]

America

Compared to the English, what in the American situation fostered militant fundamentalism as a major and sometimes influential religious

Revelation, in a very sympathetic account remarks nevertheless on this era that "There was, on the whole, however, no serious conflict, because, not only were other interests uppermost, but evangelicals were in the backwood as far as convincing Biblical scholarship was concerned," 208; cf. 280–82. The founding of the *Evangelical Quarterly* in 1929 signaled the reversal of this trend.

29. F. Roy Coad, *A History of the Brethren Movement* (London, 1968), 185. The figures are for the entire British Isles.

30. Ibid., 284. They included, nonetheless, notable elements from higher economic and social standing. Rennie correspondence with author.

With respect to the possibility of a more general social factor, Rennie, noting a variety of evidences, observes, "Thus a significant difference does appear—English Fundamentalism often seems upper middle class while its American counterpart is usually much more plebian."

31. These conclusions may be compared to those of William R. Hutchison, "The Americanness of the Social Gospel: An Inquiry in Comparative History," *Church History* 44 (1975): 367–81, who stresses the essential similarities between British and American Social Gospel. Hutchison does find American liberals to have been more optimistic in their humanism and affirmations of the present age than were their British counterparts. It might be added that by the 1920s liberalism appeared to have triumphed far more completely in British churches (cf. note 23 above).

force? The answers to this intriguing question inevitably will be rather speculative. The most significant factors on the American scene can be broken down conveniently into three interrelated categories, the social, the religious, and the intellectual.

Social Factors

Although a number of social factors might be explored, the most apparent involves the communication of ideas. Every observer has noticed, for instance, that fundamentalism sometimes flourished in isolated rural areas. Such cases suggest that in a very large, recently settled, and rapidly changing country, cultural pockets developed that were effectively insulated from the central intellectual life. The importance of this phenomenon can be seen more clearly by comparison with England. English intellectual and cultural life is relatively centralized. Ancient and well-established channels of communication made it difficult for an issue to be discussed in the universities, for instance, without soon being well-known throughout the parishes. Although there might have been a few "backward" areas,[32] the dissemination of new trends seemed to proceed at a relatively even pace.

In America there were great lags in communication. These resulted primarily from sociological, ethnic, and geographical factors, but were also reinforced by denominational differences. Congregationalists, Presbyterians, and Baptists, for instance, became familiar with the novel ideas at differing times. Within these groups, Northerners and Southerners, or Easterners and Westerners, might seriously encounter the ideas as much as generations apart.[33] Theological discussion could proceed in one section of the country, in one denomination, or among the educated elite while many people in other areas were virtually oblivious. In a period of rapid intellectual change, the potential for theological warfare once these diverse groups discovered each other was immense. In fact, the principal moment of discovery came just following World War I, when a general sense of cultural alarm heightened the intensity of fundamentalist reactions.

Although during the controversies of the 1920s fundamentalism appeared to many as primarily a social phenomenon, especially related to rural-urban tensions, such factors, while very important, only partially

32. The fact that the industrial revolution was earlier in England than America and hence the transitions from rural to urban cultural patterns more nearly completed by the late nineteenth century helped also to reduce such cultural pockets. Cf. Harold Perkin, *The Origins of Modern English Society 1780–1880* (London, 1969).

33. Albert H. Newman, "Recent Changes in Theology of Baptists," *The American Journal of Theology* 10 (1906): 600–609, made essentially this point at the time.

explain its development.[34] First of all (as Ernest Sandeen has pointed out), fundamentalism was not necessarily rural; its principal centers were initially urban and Northern. Furthermore (as Sandeen has also argued), if fundamentalism were to be adequately explained by social tensions, rural-urban themes, problems of communication and the like, then fundamentalism should have generally disappeared, as many in the 1920s predicted it would, once the crises of social transitions were past. Since in fact fundamentalism survived the 1920s and continued to flourish, its roots must have been considerably deeper. Sandeen finds these deep roots particularly in the millenarian movement.[35] It remains to be explained why they took their strongest hold in America, and not in England where the fundamentalist forms of millenarianism in fact originated. The lasting appeal of fundamentalism must be explained by elements deep in the American religious and cultural traditions themselves.

Religious Traditions

The primary force in the American religious experience that prepared the way for fundamentalism is what can be called "the dynamics of unopposed revivalism."[36] Although revivalism has flourished in many other countries since the eighteenth century, in America it came to be almost unchallenged by other formidable traditions and institutions. The comparison with England is again instructive. While revivalism was long a transatlantic phenomenon, in England the universities, the established church, and the prerevivalist traditions of most of the Nonconformist groups were among the venerable forces promoting moderation and restraint. Tradition in general was much stronger in England than in America. The strength of resurgent evangelicalism in early nineteenth-century England, for instance, as a force for theological conservatism was substantially offset toward the middle of the century by the High

34. The classic statement of this interpretation is Stewart G. Cole, *History of Fundamentalism* (New York, 1931). In "From Fundamentalism to Evangelicalism," *The Evangelicals,* I have attempted to explain some social factors by suggesting that fundamentalism might involve a White Anglo-Saxon Protestant experience analogous to that of elements in immigrant groups.

35. Sandeen, *Roots,* esp. ix–xix, and his "Fundamentalism and American Identity," *The Annals of the American Academy of Political and Social Science* 387 (January 1970): 56–65. Paul A. Carter, "The Fundamentalist Defense of the Faith," in *Change and Continuity in Twentieth Century America: The 1920s,* ed. John Braeman et al., also offers an effective critique of primarily social and social-economic or political interpretations of fundamentalism, which he himself had endorsed in his earlier work.

36. This phrase is borrowed in part from Stanley Elkins, *Slavery: A Problem in American Institutional and Intellectual Life* (Chicago, 1959) who refers to "the dynamics of unopposed capitalism."

Church movement which made even stronger claims upon traditionalist sentiments.[37]

In America such forces either were absent or had little effect, thus leaving revivalism an almost open field for determining the distinctive characteristics of American religious life.[38] Many of these traits (such as individualism, biblicism, and primitivism) are conspicuous both in the mainstream of nineteenth-century American Protestantism and in twentieth-century fundamentalism. Such continuities suggest that fundamentalism can best be understood not primarily as an outgrowth of the movements promoting millenarianism and inerrancy (as Sandeen suggests), but rather to a large extent as a subspecies of revivalism in which certain types of new emphases became popular as part of the antimodernist reaction.

Unopposed revivalism often fostered anti-intellectualism, as Richard Hofstadter has described,[39] yet perhaps even more important for the development of fundamentalism was the revivalists' tendency to promote and reinforce a particular type of intellectual emphasis—that is, a tendency to think in terms of simple dichotomies. The universe was divided between the realm of God and the realm of Satan; the supernatural was sharply separated from the natural; righteousness could have nothing to do with sin. The central impulse of revivalism was to rescue the saved from among the lost, and its whole way of conceiving reality was built around this central antithesis. In such a dichotomized view of things, ambiguities were rare. Like the conversion experience itself, transitions were not gradual, but were radical transformations from one state to its opposite.

Such intellectual categories left almost no room for the motifs of thought that were characteristic of liberal theology and scientific naturalism in the later nineteenth century. Both Darwinism and higher criticism emphasized gradual natural development, and the new theology saw God working through such means, emphasizing the synthesis of the

37. Cf. Poole-Connor, *Evangelicalism,* 220. Well into the twentieth century Anglican conservative evangelicals had to deal with two fronts—the liberals and the High Church party.

38. Cf. Donald G. Mathews, "The Second Great Awakening as an Organizing Process 1780–1830: An Hypothesis," *American Quarterly* 21 (1969): 23–43. See also William G. McLoughlin, "Revivalism," in *The Rise of Adventism: Religion and Society in Mid-Nineteenth-Century America,* ed. Edwin S. Gaustad, 119–54, who goes so far as to suggest that revivalism is the key to understanding American life generally.

39. *Anti-Intellectualism in American Life* (New York, 1962). Cf. *The Paranoid Style of American Politics and Other Essays* (New York, 1965). Hofstadter is correct in seeing anti-intellectualism as an important component of fundamentalism, although this single emphasis obscures many other aspects.

natural and the supernatural rather than the antithesis. Wherever revivalism had been relatively unopposed in American religious life, there was virtually no preparation for the acceptance of the new categories—indeed there was hardly a way to discuss them. The reaction of many American Protestants, then, was not only to reject them outright as antithetical to the faith, but to assert the antitheses even more decisively. In reaction to naturalism, the supernatural aspects of the faith, such as the virgin birth, were emphasized in lists of fundamental doctrine. The three most distinctive doctrines of fundamentalism itself, inerrancy, opposition to evolution, and the premillennial return of Christ, all uncompromisingly accentuated the supernatural in the way God works, drawing the sharpest lines against any naturalistic or developmental explanations.

Although the dynamics of revivalism appear central to understanding the popularity of militant defenses of such doctrines in America, much of American revivalism and more broadly, pietism, had developed in the context of one other major religious tradition—that of Calvinism. From the beginning, Calvinism in America supported a tendency to demand, among other things, intellectual assent to precisely formulated statements of religious truth in opposition to all error.[40] Revivalists often modified and simplified the doctrines involved, yet many of them preserved both the emphasis on antitheses and the general point that assent to rightly-stated doctrine could be of eternal significance.

This tradition helps explain the paradox between Americans' reputation for religious tolerance and the actual intolerance in most of their ecclesiastical life. Both Calvinists and their revivalist heirs accepted and even endorsed civil tolerance of religious diversity by the eighteenth century, but civil tolerance was quite different from intellectual tolerance. One might allow Quakers or Roman Catholics full political equality and yet consider semi-Pelagianism to be legitimate grounds for fierce theological debate and separation. For Calvinists, separation of church and state often meant, among other things, that toleration did not have to extend to the churches.

Such tendencies, initiated in Calvinism, were preserved to some extent in American revivalism, and hence continued into twentieth-century fundamentalism. This point is confirmed by the fact that fundamentalism appeared primarily among groups with Reformed origins, such as Baptists and Presbyterians, but was rather rare on the side of American revivalism with Methodist origins where ethical rather than intellectual as-

40. Seventeenth-century Puritans, for instance, were fascinated by dichotomies and antitheses as the popularity of the Ramist method and their concerns over precisely distinguishing between the regenerate and the unregenerate indicate.

pects of Christianity tended to be emphasized.[41] Furthermore, in the late nineteenth and early twentieth centuries, the most natural allies of the revivalist fundamentalists were the Princeton theologians who for generations had been firing heavy theological artillery at every idea that moved and who were almost indecently astute at distinguishing biblical and Reformed truth from all error.

Intellectual Factors

The wide fundamentalist battle against the new ideas was fought with materials drawn from both the Bible and the common stockpile of American assumptions and concepts. The relative popularity of the fundamentalist account of things reveals something, therefore, about the character of American intellectual life generally. Continuing the comparison with England, it appears that the historical sensitivities of the mid-nineteenth century had inclined Englishmen toward a rather ready acceptance of new and sometimes startling ideas concerning biological evolution and the historical development of the Bible. Much the same might be said of some portions of America (such as New England) where many people were well-prepared to accept the new ideas; yet there were important countervailing forces as well.

Perhaps the best way to describe the difference on this point between America and Europe is to say that in America the romantic era was truncated. America came of age during the Enlightenment and remained generally content with mid-eighteenth-century modes of thought long after these had gone out of style in Europe. The American intellectual community remained rather isolated during the early national period; well into the second half of the nineteenth century the type of philosophy taught in almost all American colleges was the "common sense realism" of the Scottish Enlightenment. Although this philosophy was susceptible to a romantic interpretation in which persons could intuit truth, the truths involved were basically fixed aspects of reality from which could be derived rather definite law, so that there was little concept of development. Although it is difficult to document, a version of this common sense approach to reality appears to have been strong in shaping the popular philosophy of nineteenth-century America as well.

41. Pentecostalism is the movement of this tradition that parallels fundamentalism. Pentecostals also rejected modern culture but more in terms of intense personal piety that separated individuals from the world, rather than in terms of doctrinal warfare. The two movements should be kept distinct, I think, even though they sometimes overlapped and had some common origins in American revivalism and hence many common traits. W. J. Hollenweger, *The Pentecostals* (Minneapolis, 1972), comments on fundamentalist traits in Pentecostalism, 9 and elsewhere. Various Holiness teachings are likewise found among fundamentalists.

By the mid-century, of course, there were many manifestations of romanticism on the American philosophical, religious, and artistic scenes, yet even at that time these had to contend with strong counterforces that still embodied Enlightenment categories. Among evangelicals, who controlled most of American higher education, the tension between these two tendencies was far from resolved at mid-century. Theologians such as Horace Bushnell, Henry B. Smith, and John Nevin were just emerging, and those closer to the eighteenth-century tradition such as Charles Hodge or Nathaniel William Taylor were still strong influences.[42] Revivalism did provide a popular romanticism emphasizing personal sentiment and piety, but this had little if anything to do with the sort of romanticism that since before the beginning of the nineteenth century had been fostering among Europeans a sensitivity to the dynamics of change and a suspicion of rational and fixed definitions of experience.[43]

The result was that in the second half of the nineteenth century many Americans were only just beginning romantic explorations when the second scientific revolution, associated with Darwinism, demanded that the new historical and developmental views be placed on the theological agenda. Even the intellectual community, then, was not always thoroughly prepared for the post-romantic modes of thought. As a result some rather well-educated Americans were among those who met naturalist challenges with pre-romantic rationalistic defenses. Emerging fundamentalism at the popular level accordingly did not entirely lack intellectual leadership, especially from a number of older theological institutions. Its modes of thought were not simply shaped by revivalist eccentricities, but by the substantial pre-romantic and rather rationalistic intellectual trends that survived in the American academic and theological communities.

The fundamentalist response to Darwinism, for instance, generally was not an anti-intellectualistic one framed in terms of the incompatibility of science and religion. It was an objection rather to a *type* of science—a developmental type—which they almost always branded as "un-

42. The above generalizations about nineteenth-century American evangelicals are illustrated (among other places) in Marsden, *The Evangelical Mind and the New School Presbyterian Experience* (New Haven, Conn., 1970).

43. It is common practice to set the peak of European (including English) romanticism in the period from 1780 to 1830; e.g., Arthur O. Lovejoy, "The Meaning of Romanticism for the Historian of Ideas," *Journal of the History of Ideas* 2 (June 1941): 260–61 and Jacques Barzun, *Romanticism and the Modern Age* (Boston, 1943), 134–39. The tiny Mercersburg movement in America compared to the Anglo-Catholic movement in England during the same era suggests something of the contrast in the strength of romanticism in the religious life of the two countries; cf. James Hastings Nichols, *Romanticism in American Theology: Nevin and Schaff at Mercersburg* (Chicago, 1961).

scientific."[44] Seldom did they denounce science in principle. Fundamentalist theology likewise reflected high esteem for being "scientific" in the sense of organizing, classifying, and rationally ordering data.[45] Similarly their view of Scripture tended to be positivistic: the Bible contained only firm evidence and no error.[46]

There is in fact little reason to suppose that many Americans would be inclined to reject science outright as an authority. The opposite would be more likely in a highly technological society with strong Enlightenment roots. The fundamentalist view of science was thus not wholly incompatible with the American intellectual climate.

Perhaps even more striking in suggesting American cultural traits is the attitude toward history found in fundamentalism. Here the contrast to English evangelicalism is particularly instructive. The characteristic view of history among fundamentalists has been dispensational-premillennialism (although not every fundamentalist, especially in the 1920s, held this position). Dispensational-premillennialism originated in England in the early nineteenth century. Yet in the twentieth century it apparently has had relatively few adherents in England except among Plymouth Brethren while in America it remains tremendously popular.[47] What, then, accounts for the remarkable popularity in America of this imported British view?

Dispensationalism is essentially an antidevelopmental and antinaturalistic way of explaining historical change. History is divided into seven "dispensations," each representing "some change in God's method of dealing with mankind," and each involving "a new test of the natural man." Man fails these tests, so that each dispensation ends in judgment and catastrophe.[48]

44. For example, John Horsh, "The Failure of Modernism" (Chicago, 1925) (pamphlet), 22–23, says, "The science with which Scripture conflicts is unproved theory; it is science falsely so-called." William B. Riley defines science as "knowledge gained and verified by exact observation and correct thinking; especially as methodologically arranged in a rational system," which he takes to exclude "theory," "hypothesis," and "assumptions," p. 5, "Are the Scriptures Scientific?" (Minneapolis, n.d.) (pamphlet).

45. A good example is Reuben A. Torrey, *What the Bible Teaches*, 17th ed. (New York, 1933 [1898]), which he describes as ". . . simply an attempt at a careful, unbiased, systematic, thorough-going, *inductive* study and statement of Bible truth. . . . The methods of modern science are applied to Bible study—through analysis followed by careful synthesis," 1.

46. Cf. John Opie, "The Modernity of Fundamentalism," *Christian Century*, 12 May 1965, 608–11.

47. One example is the popularity of Hal Lindsey, *The Late Great Planet Earth* (Grand Rapids, 1970). As of the July 1974 printing the publisher claimed 4,300,000 copies in print.

48. These dispensations are 1) "Innocence," ending with the fall; 2) "Conscience," ending with the flood; 3) "Human Government," ending with Babel; 4) "Promise," ending in the bondage in Egypt; 5) "Law," ending with the death of Christ; 6) "Grace," which

Two general tendencies found in fundamentalist thought are particularly evident in this scheme. First is a fascination with dividing and classifying.[49] The second is a heightened supernaturalism. Human efforts and natural forces have almost nothing to do with historical change. Instead, God periodically intervenes with a series of spectacular supernatural events that suddenly transform one age into another. In fact, God and Satan are virtually the only significant historical forces, and they are armed forces at that. In contrast to any romantic and developmental interpretations, dispensationalism explains history as a series of supernatural impositions of highly abstract, logical, and almost legalistic principles that humans might either accept or reject.[50]

The popularity of such views in twentieth-century America reveal an important American thought pattern—that in comparison with other Western countries many Americans lacked certain typically modern concepts of history. In the views of history popular in America the elements that were missing were precisely the assumptions central to most modern historical scholarship. These were the assumption that history is a natural evolutionary development and the corollary that the present can be understood best as a product of developing natural forces from the past. American historiography had long been dominated by supernatural, or at least providential, interpretations.[51] Furthermore, even the secular histories frequently emphasized the newness of America, dwelling on the past only to accentuate progress and the future. To Americans, who had relatively little history of their own, their national experience often seemed like a new dispensation, discontinuous with the past.

This widespread absence of a sense of gradual or natural historical change had been reinforced and partly created by the revivalist tradition, and in many places preserved from encounters with developmental ideas by social and geographical factors. These influences combined to dispose many persons to declare every aspect of the new views to be anathema and to oppose them with various nonnegotiable logical antitheses. The

---

will end with a period of great tribulation, immediately followed by Christ's return to earth, victory at Armageddon; and 7) the millennium or personal reign of Christ, ending with Satan "loosed a little season" but quickly defeated. After the millennium is the "new heavens and new earth" of eternity. C. I. Scofield, *"Rightly Dividing the Word of Truth"* (Revell paper edition, New York, n.d. [1896]), 12–16.

49. Scofield says, "The Word of Truth . . . has right divisions . . . *so any study* of that Word which ignores these divisions must be in large measure profitless and confusion." Ibid., 3.

50. C. Norman Kraus, *Dispensationalism in America* (Richmond, 1958), 66–67 and 125–26 comments perceptively on this point.

51. Ernest Lee Tuveson, *Redeemer Nation: The Idea of America's Millennial Role* (Chicago, 1968) gives many examples of this point.

greater the claims and the greater the influence of the naturalistic developmental views, the more firmly the fundamentalists stressed the opposing paradigms.[52]

This observation should not be interpreted to mean that because modern developmental paradigms were newer they were for that reason necessarily superior to fundamentalist emphases on antitheses. Furthermore, it seems to me incorrect, at least as far as Christian thought is concerned, to regard antithesis and natural historical development as incompatible categories, since central to Christianity itself is the wholly-other God revealing himself and acting in history. In America in the early twentieth century both fundamentalists and liberals tended to oversimplify the issue on this point. Fundamentalists, seeing clearly that the Bible spoke of antitheses, would hear almost nothing of natural development; liberals, enamored of historical and developmental explanation, proclaimed that the old antitheses must be abandoned. Perhaps in part because of the novelty in America of the modes of thought associated with modernism, both sides oversimplified the issues and each overestimated the degree to which recognition of historical development necessitated the abandonment of traditional Christian teaching.

52. The total lack of communications between fundamentalists and modernists concerning both history and science fits well the now-familiar patterns of paradigm conflict described in Thomas S. Kuhn, *The Structure of Scientific Revolutions* (Chicago, 1962).

14

Christian Education and McMaster University

George A. Rawlyk

From George A. Rawlyk, "A. L. McCrimmon, H. P. Whidden and T. T. Shields, Christian Education, and McMaster University," in *Canadian Baptists and Christian Higher Education* (Montreal and Kingston, 1988), 31–62. Used by permission of McGill-Queen's University Press.

The granting of McMaster University's charter in 1887 was both a new beginning and a culmination "of Baptist educational ventures that reached far back into pre-Confederation Canada."[1] The McMaster of 1887, in other words, was as Professor Charles Johnston has persuasively argued, made up of historical segments from the Canada Baptist College in Montreal, the Canadian Literary Institute in Woodstock, and the Toronto Baptist College and Moulton College of Toronto. But, of course, McMaster University was also much more than this. It was also the creation of Senator William McMaster, a native of Tyrone County, Ireland, who had by the 1870s become one of Canada's most influential entrepreneurs and also a leading Reform politician. A staunch advocate of the commercial imperialism of Toronto, McMaster used his presidency of the Bank of Commerce to "establish a commercial dominion at

1. C. Johnson, *McMaster University: The Toronto Years,* 2 vols. (Toronto: University of Toronto Press, 1976), 1:3.

least the equal of Montreal's."[2] His ardent support of the Reform cause of George Brown and Alexander MacKenzie, led to McMaster's appointment to the Canadian Senate in 1867.

McMaster was more than an unusually successful Canadian entrepreneur and politician. He was also a pious and committed evangelical Baptist who was particularly concerned with doing everything humanly possible to improve the educational standards of his denomination's ministers as well as its laypeople. Like many other leading Canadian Baptists in the latter part of the nineteenth century, McMaster was obsessed with the desperate search for denominational respectability. One important way to achieve this end, it was felt, was to build a respectable Baptist university. Another way was to construct a Baptist cathedral—the new Jarvis Street Baptist Church—which took ostentatious new Gothic shape in Toronto in 1876 under the direction of Senator and Mrs. McMaster. According to William Davies, the founder of a famous Canadian packing firm and a bitter critic of the McMasters:

> this large Baptist Chapel, gothic, brown stone, spire pointing upward if not heavenward, marble baptistry etc. etc. Cost $100,000 and odd and the organ $7000 besides, and I believe it is all paid for, but it has been built regardless of the needs of the city. . . . One of the members . . . a Senator, very wealthy, married an American, natural result they soon had an American minister, then this new building also American, then the Lady and the minister lay their heads together and get a professional singer a sort of *prima donna* and she is paid $300.00 per year and many are very much hurt about it. . . . There appears to have been a spirit of centralization and aggrandizement about it which is hateful.[3]

Davies's caustic comments contain a ring of truth. The McMasters were indeed interested in "centralization and aggrandizement" and in the early 1880s they tended to think that what was good for them was excellent for their less fortunate coreligionists.

By 1879 the McMasters and some of their Toronto Baptist friends had come to the conclusion that a Baptist institution of higher learning had to be built in the capital of Ontario. The Canadian Literary Institute in Woodstock, they had to admit, was more than adequate in terms of its elementary and secondary programs. However, they were just as convinced that the institute's theological department had to be transferred to Toronto, since a respectable and progressive Baptist university had no real future in Woodstock. At the 1879 Baptist Convention at

2. Ibid., 19.
3. W. S. Fox, ed., *Letters of William Davies, Toronto, 1854–1861* (Toronto: University of Toronto Press, 1945), 112.

Guelph, it was decided, after a very heated debate, and with at least an implicit understanding that McMaster money would pay for the new Toronto institution and also significantly subsidize the ongoing Baptist educational effort in Woodstock, that a new "theological seminary" be established.

According to the 1 December 1880 Act incorporating the Toronto Baptist College, the college was under the control of a Board of Trustees carefully selected by Senator McMaster and his American-born pastor, the Reverend John Castle. According to the deed of trust, the trustees were

> to permit the use and occupation of said buildings . . . for the necessary and proper purposes of a theological college . . . for the education and training of students preparing for and intending to be engaged in pastoral, evangelical, missionary or other denominational work in connection with the Regular Baptist Denomination whereby is intended Regular Baptist Churches exclusively composed of persons who have been baptized on a personal profession of their Faith in Christ holding and maintaining *substantially* the following doctrines.[4]

It is important to note that the deed of trust does explicitly state, before listing its strong calvinist evangelical statement of faith, that those Baptists associated with the new "theological college" had only to hold and maintain "*substantially* the following doctrines." For some Baptists, even in 1880, "*substantially*" was not any kind of qualifier but rather the emphatic underscoring of orthodoxy.

The "following doctrines" were:

> The Divine Inspiration of the Scriptures of the Old and New Testaments and their absolute Supremacy and Sufficiency in matters of faith and practice; the existence of one living and true God, sustaining the personal relation of Father Son and Holy Spirit, the same in essence and equal in attributes, the total and universal depravity of mankind, the election and effectual calling of all God's people, the atoning efficacy of the Death of Christ, the free justification of believers in Him by His imputed Righteousness; the preservation unto eternal life of the Saints, the necessity and efficacy of the influence of the Spirit in regeneration and sanctification; the resurrection of the dead, both just and unjust; the general judgment, the everlasting happiness of the righteous and the everlasting misery of the wicked; immersion in the name of the Father the Son and the Holy Spirit, the only gospel "baptism," that parties so baptized are alone entitled to

4. See the confidential letter from N. W. Rowell to Chancellor H. P. Whidden, 30 May 1928, in the Whidden papers, Canadian Baptist Archives, McMaster Divinity College, Hamilton, Ontario. Hereafter the abbreviation for the archives will be CBA.

> Communion at the Lord's Table and that a Gospel Church is a Body of baptized believers voluntarily associated together for the service of God.[5]

What did the deed of trust, which was an integral part of the Toronto Baptist College Act of Incorporation, actually mean? Did it mean that everyone teaching or being taught in the college had to hold "substantially" to such a statement of faith? No, the widely accepted legal interpretation was quite different. As far as one noted legal expert—N. W. Rowell—was concerned the "theological tests or requirements set out in the Trust Deed" were not "tests or requirements" applied to the institution but were "tests or requirements applied to the Baptist Denomination entitled to control the University and have its theological students taught" there. Therefore, and this point needs to be stressed, because of its important implications for McMaster University in the 1920s, "the only way in which" McMaster's institution "could be affected" by anyone "challenging its theological teaching would be by their challenging the theological standing of the Baptist Denomination represented and in forming the Baptist Convention of Ontario and Quebec."[6]

McMaster carefully selected the trustees for the Toronto Baptist College and these men, on the whole, reflected the senator's commercial and political views. There were leading lawyers, businessmen, and politicians such as Alexander MacKenzie, the former Liberal prime minister of Canada. What these men seemed to have in common was a tremendous commitment to the Baptist cause in Ontario and Quebec as well as a profound belief in the efficacy of higher education. Moreover, led and inspired by McMaster, they were preoccupied with the quest for power and influence, not only in Canadian society but also within their own denomination.

By controlling the Baptist seminary in central Canada, which they hoped would quickly "emerge as a national institution for the denomination,"[7] they expected to control the entire denomination from the top down. According to Antonio Gramsci, cultural hegemony in a society being transformed by industrial capitalism is characterized by "the spontaneous consent given by the great masses of the population to the general direction imposed on social life by the dominant fundamental group; this consent is 'historically' caused by prestige (and consequent confidence) which the dominant group enjoys because of its position and function in the world of production."[8] For Gramsci, organized religion plays

5. Ibid.
6. Ibid.
7. Johnston, *McMaster University,* 1:30.
8. T. J. Jackson Lears, "The Concept of Cultural Hegemony: Problems and Possibilities," *American Historical Review* 90, 3 (June 1985): 568.

a crucially important role in the actual exercise of power of one group over another. It should not be forgotten that, as Tom Harpur has recently pointed out, "from one very important point of view, the whole of organized religion is a not-too-subtle form of power-seeking and control."[9] Christian feminists for years have been making this precise point about misogyny and the power structure of the Christian church. Their analysis and that of Gramsci and his disciples, in my view, can be powerfully applied to the development in the nineteenth and twentieth centuries of the Christian church in North America in general and to the Baptist denomination in Canada in particular.

It is Gramsci's contention that the new class of capitalistic entrepreneurs—the McMasters of this world—concern themselves with the creation of a new "strata of intellectuals" whose role it is "to win over the traditional strata to support . . . the new social, economic, and political order." For Gramsci, in new societies like that of Canada in the 1880s, the new group of intellectuals are expected to "fuse together in a single national crucible with a unitary culture the different forms of culture imported by immigrants of differing national origins."[10] This fusing process facilitates economic growth in a country like Canada and helps to explain why all Protestant churches in Canada in the pre-1914 period were so preoccupied with building an anglophile and Christian "Dominion from sea to sea."[11]

It was also Gramsci's contention that the new class of intellectuals, including, of course, the religious leaders, are locked into an integrative symbiotic relationship with a new social order thrown up by the fundamental changes affecting economic production. The intellectual-priest thus functions at two levels, which "correspond on the one hand to the function of 'hegemony' which the dominant group exercises throughout society and on the other hand to that of 'direct domination'—a command exercised through the state. . . . The functions in question are precisely organizational and connective. The intellectuals are the dominant group's 'deputies' exercising the subaltern functions of social hegemony and political government."[12]

Thus, if we use a Gramsci-like lens to view unfolding events in the Tor-

9. T. Harpur, *For Christ's Sake* (Toronto: McClelland and Stewart, 1986), 53. I am indebted to Mrs. Doris Odell for this quotation as well as the previous one.

10. See A. Gramsci, *Selections from the Prison Notebooks* (New York: International Publications Company, 1971). This quotation is from P. Craven, *'An Impartial Umpire': Industrial Relations and the Canadian State 1900–1911* (Toronto: University of Toronto Press, 1981), 15.

11. See N. K. Clifford, "His Dominion: A Vision in Crisis," *Studies in Religion* 2 (1973): 315–26.

12. Quoted in Craven, "An Impartial Umpire," *16.*

onto and Ontario Baptist community in the 1880s, a disconcerting picture suddenly emerges—McMaster and his Baptist business associates may be seen as calculating entrepreneurs determined to create their own battalion of ministerial "deputies," expertly trained to impose suitable hegemonic order and control over Canadian society.

Even though McMaster and his associates considered themselves to be staunch protectors of the pristine purity of evangelical calvinist Baptist orthodoxy, they were also committed advocates of the new North American consumer culture. And because of this, they offered what has been called "a new legitimization"[13] for the antitheses of calvinist evangelical orthodoxy—a narcissistic gospel of intense "therapeutic self-realization." In the 1880s and 1890s in North America "the leaders of the W.A.S.P. bourgeoisie," it has been observed, "felt cramped," overcivilized, "cut off from real life—threatened from without by an ungrateful working class, and from within by their own sense of physical atrophy and spiritual decay." Moreover,

> The old religious sanctions for the moral life, a life of sacrifice and toil, had begun to disintegrate in the face of both Darwin and the liberalization of Protestantism itself. A crisis of purpose, a yearning for a solid, transcendent framework of meaning, was not just Henry Adams' worry, but that of a much wider group. In this time of cultural consternation, the new professional-managerial corps appeared with a timely dual message. On the one hand, they preached a new morality that subordinated the old goal of transcendence to new ideals of self-fulfillment and immediate gratification. The late nineteenth-century link between individual hedonism and bureaucratic organization—a link that has been strengthened in the twentieth century—marks the point of departure for modern American consumer culture. The consumer culture is not only the value-system that underlies a society saturated by mass-produced and mass-marketed goods, but also a new set of sanctions for the elite control of that society.[14]

This inner transformation of North American society is of critical importance to any sophisticated understanding of late nineteenth- and early twentieth-century historical and theological development. The prevailing Whig scholarly concern with progress and modernity has meant, among other things, however, that most historians simply assume that by the turn of the century the North American evangelical consensus was being

13. See R. W. Fox and T. J. Jackson Lears, eds., *The Culture of Consumption* (New York: Random House, 1983), xi.

14. Ibid., xi–xii. See also T. J. Jackson Lears' brilliant book *No Place of Grace: Antimodernism and the Transformation of American Culture 1880–1920* (New York: Random House, 1981).

shattered by three powerful external forces. First, there was Darwin and evolution and the new science; then there was critical biblical scholarship; and third there was the impact of comparative religion which seemed to undermine, for many, the belief in the uniqueness of Christianity. Without question, these three forces certainly helped to reshape the contours of North American Protestantism.[15] Yet it may also be argued that in the long run American consumerism may have had a far greater negative impact on the nineteenth-century evangelical consensus than did the various manifestations of so-called modern scholarship. In other words, a convincing case may be put forward that the evangelical consensus suffered more from internal decay than from external attacks. And at the core of this decay, as D. W. Frank has recently contended, was the cancer of consumerism—"based on self-indulgence."[16] The testimony of a woman visiting some eighty years ago a department store, the key economic institution of the consumer society, cuts to the heart of the issue:

> I felt myself overcome little by little by a disorder that can only be compared to that of drunkenness, with the dizziness and excitation that are peculiar to it. I saw things as if through a cloud, everything stimulated my desire and assumed, for me, an extraordinary attraction. I felt myself swept along toward them and I grabbed hold of things without any outside and superior consideration intervening to hold me back. Moreover I took things at random, useless and worthless articles as well as useful and expensive articles. It was like a monomania of possession.[17]

Other women made similar comments—"my head was spinning," "I felt completely dizzy," "I am just as if I were drunk." These comments were made by middle-class women who had been arrested for shoplifting. They were, it has been observed, "an odd foreshadowing of Billy Sunday's contention that alcohol was the cause of virtually all crime." The women's addiction, however, was "to consumer gratification." "The pathological frenzy to which some women were driven," it is clear, "had become simply the seamier side of the new consumer society, where the old virtues of thrift and self-control were giving way to a culture of gratification."[18] These women, drunk on goods, were striking symbols of the new consumer society.

15. M. E. Marty, *Modern American Religion: The Irony of It All, 1893–1919*, 4 vols. (Chicago: University of Chicago Press, 1986), 1:17–90.

16. D. W. Frank, *Less Than Conquerors: How Evangelicals Entered the Twentieth Century* (Grand Rapids: Eerdmans, 1986), 222.

17. Quoted in ibid., 222.

18. Ibid., 223.

It seemed impossible for evangelical leaders—whether in Canada or in the United States—in the post-1880 period to attack frontally the insidious anti-Christian bias of consumerism. Instead, they became, the evidence seems to suggest, its ardent disciples and enthusiastic advocates of the fundamental goodness of economic growth and technological development. They were certainly unwilling to see what Karl Marx saw in "modern bourgeois society" in the 1880s and beyond. For Marx, such a society "has conjured up such gigantic means of production and of exchange" and has in the process become "like the sorcerer who is no longer able to control the powers of the subterranean which he has called up by his spells." Marx then went on: "Constant revolutionizing of production, uninterrupted disturbance of all social relations, everlasting uncertainty and agitation, distinguish the bourgeois epoch from all earlier ones. All fixed, fast-frozen relations, with their train of ancient and venerable prejudices and opinions, are swept away, all new-formed ones become antiquated before they can ossify. All that is solid melts into air, all that is holy is profane."[19] Marx had laid bare the essential nature of life in modernizing society and he had realized intuitively what had happened to North American evangelicalism. The "holy" had, in a profound sense, become "profane" and "all that" was "solid" had melted into nothingness.

Few, if any, central Canadian Baptists in the 1880s would have, or more accurately, could have, accepted the validity of Marx's penetrating prophetic insight into the essential nature of bourgeois-industrial society. And this was certainly the case with regard to McMaster and his Baptist business associates. Yet, as the nineteenth century blurred into the twentieth, and after McMaster's death in 1887, a few Baptists came to realize that something fundamentally destructive was beginning to undermine the theological and ideological underpinnings of their church and their society. But instead of focusing, as Marx had done, on the distinguishing features of the "bourgeois society" or, as others had done, on the evils of "consumerism," these disconcerted Baptists concentrated their concern on what to them was theological modernism—the way in which Darwinian scientific progress and biblical scholarship were significantly altering the older evangelical consensus. These Baptists and their supporters in other Protestant denominations would soon become known as fundamentalists and their growing obsession with preserving theological purity would be matched by a remarkable degree of "violence in thought and language."[20] These people would find it far easier to be judgmental than

19. Karl Marx and Friedrich Engels, *The Communist Manifesto* (New York: Washington Square Press, 1964), 63.

20. N. Furniss, *The Fundamentalist Controversy, 1918–1931* (New Haven, Conn.: Yale University Press, 1954), 36.

forgiving, destructive rather than constructive, and confrontational rather than accommodating. But these people, it should be stressed, were not the mainstream of evangelicalism at the turn of the century. They found themselves on one extreme of a broad theological spectrum which stretched all the way to the closed-minded liberalism of some who, in attempting to make Christianity especially relevant to the new age, made it virtually as irrelevant as themselves. At the center of the Baptist theological spectrum was to be found the evangelical mainstream—the vast majority of Baptists—who accepted basic evangelical truths and who were not really afraid of modernity. These people *felt* their religion—in other words, they experienced it—and they therefore saw no compelling need to intellectualize it. They expected their ministers to preach the old-time gospel but also to make it relevant to their situation.

Between the evangelical mainstream and the liberal extreme was to be found a very influential group that was eager to keep a foot in both camps. Its approach was permeated by an accommodationist spirit—what has been recently referred to as "a new hermeneutic" based on a "double commitment: to the biblical faith on the one hand and the modern outlook on the other."[21] Such individuals became the "intellectual-priests" of the emerging central Canadian Baptist commercial elite. In the 1880–1914 period, however, these men were not yet in complete control and found themselves challenged by yet another group—not as accommodating to modernity and somewhat more sympathetic to the theological underpinnings of fundamentalism—although certainly not to its increasing *hubris* and paranoia. Such individuals, some of whom were academics, were, like their fundamentalist friends, also fully aware of the contagion of change which was reshaping the boundaries of their society. Their answer to the problem was the careful constructing of intellectual barriers to protect the purity of the faith—but these barriers were put up in such a manner as to permit and to encourage the flow of new ideas. The barriers of the fundamentalists, however, left no space for these ideas. And the liberals, of course—their intense intellectual arrogance notwithstanding—prided themselves on having no barriers whatsoever.

The fundamentalists, the so-called liberal evangelicals, the conservative evangelicals, and the liberals were all concerned about higher education. And within the central Canadian Baptist community in the late nineteenth and early twentieth centuries the academic battle involved, in the beginning, the first three groups. But with the polarization of the theological debate in the years surrounding the First World War, the educational controversy began to involve only two sets of antagonists—the liberal

21. See C. H. Pinnock, "The Modernist Impulse at McMaster University, 1887–1927," in J. Zeman, ed., *Baptists in Canada* (Burlington: Welch, 1980), 195.

evangelicals (who were becoming almost more liberal than evangelical) and the fundamentalists—some of whom were former advocates of a more moderate conservative evangelical position. This ideological split, it should be stressed, was buttressed by growing class tensions between the two groups, what Dr. Walter Ellis has described as "class war in the churches."[22] Bourgeois liberal respectability was warring against what one Baptist liberal evangelical referred to as fundamentalist "bigotry, and fanaticism and obscurantism."[23] The perceived class differences existing between the two groups were superbly captured in a letter written to S. J. Moore, a Toronto Baptist millionaire in November 1926, by a shrewd observer of the fundamentalist-modernist split in the Convention: "I was impressed by the personnel of the majority. It included . . . nearly all the solid elements of the denomination. As the followers of Dr. Shields gathered about him at the close of the meeting, to join in their singing and other emotional manifestations, I could not but be impressed by the inferior personnel of the group. I am speaking of the general appearance."[24] It was a simple Manichean struggle between the "solid elements" and the "inferior personnel," between progress and backwardness, between the past and the future.

It is against this richly complex ideological and cultural backdrop that one must view evolving central Canadian Baptist attitudes toward Christian higher education at the turn of the century. To see the problem within strictly institutional or denominational parameters is to distort significantly historical reality and also to avoid some disconcerting problems relating to essential motivation. The Baptist educational experience, moreover, was not static but rather dynamic and constantly changing, influenced by people, events, and ideas, but always evolving within the context of what some might regard as Gramsci reality.

Senator McMaster and his Baptist friends were not satisfied for long merely with a "theological institute." During the early 1880s, they applied considerable pressure on their coreligionists and finally, on 15 March 1887, a bill was introduced at Queen's Park uniting the Toronto Baptist College and Woodstock College and incorporating them as McMaster University. On 22 April 1887, the Act of Incorporation became law; and exactly five months later Senator McMaster died, leaving close to one million dollars to his university. "The monumental irony of the sit-

22. W. E. Ellis, "Social and Religious Factors in the Fundamentalist-Modernist Schisms Among Baptists in North America, 1895–1934" (Ph.D. thesis, University of Pittsburgh, 1974), 284.

23. Quoted in the Toronto *Globe,* 21 October 1925 in an article entitled "Overwhelming Vote Cast in Convention for Professor Marshall."

24. O. C. S. Wallace to S. J. Moore, 9 November 1926, Whidden papers, CBA.

uation," McMaster University's historian has noted, "struck even the most insensitive." "At one stroke the university that McMaster had promoted was instantly financed but at the cost of his vigour, direction, and inspiration."[25]

Section 4 of McMaster University's Act of Incorporation made it clear that the university was definitely "a Christian school of learning." It went on:

> the study of the Bible, or sacred scriptures, shall form a part of the course of study taught by the professors, tutors, or masters appointed by the Board of Governors. And no person shall be eligible to the position of chancellor, principal, professor, tutor, or master, who is not a member in good standing of an Evangelical Christian Church; and no person shall be eligible for the position of principal, professor, tutor, or master in the faculty of theology who is not a member in good standing of a Regular Baptist Church, and the said Board of Governors shall have the right to require such further or other tests as to religious belief, as a qualification for any position in the faculty of theology, as to the said Board of Governors may seem proper; but no compulsory religious qualification, or examination of a denominational character shall be required from, or imposed upon any student whatever, other than in the faculty of theology.[26]

It is evident from the 1887 Act of Incorporation that, while McMaster University was to be a Christian institution, only its seminary was to be explicitly Baptist. There was to be no theological litmus test for McMaster students but all university teachers and officials were to be "Evangelical Christians"—and the faculty of theology were to be evangelical Baptists, broadly defined, who could be subjected by the Board of Governors to some kind of "test as to religious belief." Taking everything into account, the act, in many respects, was quite progressive in tone and content but so much, of course, depended on what was meant by the phrase "Christian school of learning" and "Evangelical Christian Church." The underlying assumption of the act, however, was crystal clear. Students at McMaster would be educated by evangelical Christian teachers in a Christian environment so that they would "be thoroughly equipped with all the resources of the best and most liberal culture to enable them to meet the polished shafts of a refined and subtle infidelity."[27]

The third chancellor of McMaster University, the Reverend O.C.S. Wallace, enunciated in his inaugural address in 1895 what he must have realized was a strong defense for Christian higher education. He was

25. Johnston, *McMaster University,* 1:40.
26. Rowell to Whidden, 30 May 1928, Whidden papers, CBA.
27. *Baptist Year Book,* 1883, 75.

widely regarded as a staunch defender of the evangelical *status quo* but he was also known as someone very concerned about preparing his "students for the challenges of life in the outer world."[28] Though a pious traditionalist in one sense, Wallace was also, as his later career would show, determined to make Christianity relevant for modern society. He was not opposed, therefore, to a shift in Protestant theology from a preoccupation with "salvation in the next world to therapeutic self-realization in this one."[29]

As far as Wallace was concerned, in 1895 McMaster University existed "for the teaching rather than the pursuit of truth." "Much of the educational work of the present day," he went on,

> is a menace to all that is holiest in faith and loftiest in morality because it is moulded in form and determined in spirit by the contrary of that principle. . . . We are not denying that there is truth to pursue, but we do most confidently and solemnly affirm that there is truth to teach. However vast may be the domain of the unexplored and the unknown, it is yet true that something is known [and is] ours by the . . . attestation of the ages [or] by the unequivocal revelation of God. . . . Before such truths as have been abundantly proven or clearly revealed we dare not take the attitude of the . . . doubter and the agnostic. . . . It is our aim to send forth . . . scholars whose opinions of truth and whose principles of conduct shall not be . . . a source and occasion of irreligion in the communities in which they live.[30]

Some of Wallace's friends, however, did not accept the new chancellor's point of view. One of them informed him:

> When once that spirit—that 'a university exists for the teaching rather than the pursuit of truth'—has laid hold of an institution its zenith has been reached. Like the perfectionists in character no advance is believed possible, no advance will be made . . . every truth that is not brought home to the individual conscience and judgment and there accepted as truth on its own merits is, to a student, a worse than useless incumbrance. . . . I believe in the scientific method, the method that is used in *all* good schools at the present day . . . and which the sentence quoted opposes. There is a wide difference between the scientific search for truth and the agnostic search for ignorance.[31]

28. See Johnston, *McMaster University,* 1:73.

29. Fox and Lears, *The Culture of Consumption,* xiii. The evolution of the theological and social views of Wallace may be seen in his popular writing in the *Canadian Baptist* and the *Maritime Baptist* in the first three decades of the twentieth century.

30. *McMaster University Monthly* 5 (1985): 100–105.

31. T. P. Hall to Wallace, 17 December 1895, Wallace papers, CBA. The quotation is to be found in Johnston, *McMaster University,* 1:72.

By the time of his resignation in 1905, Wallace had moved quite a distance in the direction of his friend's position of encouraging "the scientific search for truth" in order to make McMaster into a "good," modern university.[32] In his journey, the Nova Scotia-born educator was encouraged by some of his board members, as well as some of his faculty—especially those who were scientists. Yet Wallace would never abandon his commitment to the "development of a generous and noble" Christian character.[33]

Wallace's successor as chancellor was A. C. McKay, who for years had been the key administrative factotum at McMaster. He played a key role in keeping McMaster a separate educational institution by leading the fight against federation with the University of Toronto. McKay was enthusiastically committed to "the scientific search for truth" and he seemed to be amazingly indifferent to the growing theological civil war between so-called liberals and fundamentalists being fought in the Convention and in his theology faculty. What came to be known as the "Matthews Controversy" reached a crisis point in 1908 and 1909. The critics of Professor I. G. Matthews—the Chicago-trained Old Testament scholar—argued that Matthews was a pernicious modernist determined to destroy the orthodox faith of his theological students. To counter the growing fundamentalist movement in the Convention, McKay saw the need for McMaster's Senate to emphasize the institution's theological orthodoxy—but without abandoning his belief in the efficacy of science and modern scholarship. An investigating committee submitted its report to the Senate on 29 May 1909 and it declared Matthews innocent of the charges of unorthodoxy. Though he accepted many of the "results of critical scholarship" he nevertheless "held firmly to the inspiration and supernatural character of the Old and New Testaments." Then the Senate boldly declared:

> McMaster stands for freedom, for progress, for investigation. It must welcome truth from whatever quarter, and never be guilty of binding the spirit of free enquiry. As a Christian school of learning under Baptist auspices, it stands for the fullest and freest investigation, not only in the scientific realm but also in the realm of Biblical scholarship. Holding fast their historic position on the personal freedom and responsibility of the individual, refusing to bind or be bound by any human creed, rejecting the authority of tradition and taking their stand on the word of God alone as the supreme and all-sufficient rule of faith and practice, the Baptists have ever

32. The evolution of Wallace's thinking while he was chancellor, and afterwards, was not a major concern of Johnston in his Wallace chapter. See Johnston, *McMaster University*, 1:70–84.

33. Ibid., 73.

> been ready to accord to all students of the Sacred Scriptures the largest possible measure of freedom consistent with loyalty to the fundamentals of the Christian faith.[34]

At the 2 December 1909 Senate meeting, it was agreed that "while complete freedom should be accorded in the investigation and discussion of facts no theory should be taught in [the] University which fails to give their proper place to supernatural revelation . . . or which would impair in any way the supreme authority of the Lord Jesus Christ."[35]

When the "Matthews Controversy" was brought to the floor of the Convention in October 1910, the Senate position was endorsed by a large majority. A leader in this movement to prevent a Convention denunciation of McMaster and Matthews was the Reverend T. T. Shields, the minister of Jarvis Street Baptist Church and a leading fundamentalist in the Convention. Shields probably did not want to alienate in 1910 some of his key church members who were keen supporters of Matthews and McKay.

The Senate response to the "Matthews Controversy" is important in at least two ways with respect to Baptists and Christian higher education in central Canada. First, McMaster's Senate and also the Convention explicitly endorsed the key role of higher education in bringing about human "progress"—bourgeois progress and consumerism. Second, it was emphatically agreed that accommodation was indeed possible between the evangelical consensus and the new scholarship. And, moreover, it was contended that McMaster University had a special role in bringing about this accommodation which, for some, was merely the articulation of the liberal evangelical point of view.

By 1911, McKay had come to the realization that he was "not born to be in the midst of theological controversy."[36] He therefore resigned as chancellor to become principal of a new technical high school in Toronto. Many Baptists were genuinely sorry to see McKay leave McMaster. Others were not, feeling that he was too soft on modernism and liberalism. They looked for someone a little more spiritual, a little more pious, a little more evangelical, to replace him. They saw such a person in Abraham Lincoln McCrimmon.

McCrimmon was born in 1865 on a farm a mile north of Delhi in western Ontario. He graduated from the University of Toronto in 1890 as gold medalist in logic and philosophy. As a student at the University of Toronto, he excelled not only in his studies but also in athletics. A fine

34. Minutes of the McMaster University Senate, 29 May 1909, CBA.
35. Minutes of the McMaster University Senate, 2 December 1909, CBA.
36. W.S.M. McLay to McKay, 17 May 1911, McLay Papers, CBA.

pitcher, he once "struck out twelve men consecutively" and it was said "that he was one of the first exponents in Ontario of the curve ball."[37] When he graduated, therefore, McCrimmon had to choose between Christian service and a career in professional baseball. He gladly chose the former. In 1892, he became classics master at Woodstock College and five years later, he became its principal. While at Woodstock, McCrimmon showed that he "possessed one of the finest intellects among the educational leaders of America."[38] As a preacher and platform speaker, the former baseball star began to "rank with the most polished and forceful orators in the country."[39] He was widely perceived as an "intensely religious and ever zealous" Baptist, who always "sought to convey the message of God in clear and convincing language."[40] Until his death in 1925, McCrimmon regarded himself as an unreconstructed Baptist evangelical; an advocate of "soul-liberty," he always "made the necessity of regeneration . . . the centre of my message to a lost world."[41] Moreover, throughout his teaching career, he regarded, as he once put it, "my relationship to my students" as a "sacred relationship." It was based upon mutual confidence and respect and "spiritual power."[42]

During the 1903–4 academic year, McCrimmon pursued graduate studies at the University of Chicago. And on his return to Woodstock, he was appointed, while still principal of Woodstock College, to a lectureship in political economy at McMaster University. In 1906, he was persuaded to leave Woodstock and join the faculty of McMaster as a "full time Professor, occupying the Chair of Economics, Education and Sociology."[43]

In 1893, the year after he began teaching at Woodstock College, McCrimmon published a very brief description of his philosophy of Christian education. As far as the twenty-eight-year-old McCrimmon was concerned, "the Highest Type of Human Character is Therefore the Christian Character. The Ideal For the Christian [and for Christian Education] is Jesus Christ, As Revealed in the Word of God . . . .Here we have combined the absolute surrender of individuality and its most intense assertion."[44] Eight years later, McCrimmon developed his educational ideas at much greater length when he spoke at Brandon College, on 1 October 1901, on the topic "Christian Education."[45] According to Mc-

37. *Simcoe Reformer,* 15 April 1935.
38. Ibid.
39. Ibid.
40. Ibid.
41. "Baptists Facing the Future," undated, McCrimmon papers, CBA.
42. Ibid.
43. "McCrimmon Obituary," ibid., CBA.
44. *McMaster University Monthly,* February 1893.
45. McCrimmon papers, CBA.

Crimmon, "While it is the inalienable right of every man to have an education, it is the double emphasized responsibility for the Christian whose heart should be tender to God's teaching and whose will should be ready and anxious to do his work." Moreover, only Christian education molded the youthful mind in the image of Christ. The Woodstock principal then went on to assert that at the core of Christian education was the person of Christ:

> Our starting point is that we hold our connection with Christ as the supreme element in our lives. Identification with Him brings salvation to our souls. Identification with Him means that His thoughts are our thoughts and His work is our work. If we rear a structure whether of personal attainment or of objective work, which has not the purpose of Christ in it, it means that the work perishes. Not every education will do. We desire not knowledge alone but that knowledge rightly articulated to the work of Christ.

For McCrimmon, true "Christian Education" had to—as he expressed it—"Honour the Body" and "the Intellect." Christian education was not only concerned with shaping the minds of students but also with "the condition of the body." McCrimmon's Christian school was definitely not "some sort of goody-goody establishment where intellectual powers are at a discount." Rather, "The greatest intellects of this world are the intellects of Christian men. . . . It is only the Christian who has the proper motive to instigate him to the fullest development of the mind. It is the Christian alone who is in touch with the fountain of truth. In this age as in the preceding ones, the Christian teacher is the only safe one." "Daily intercourse with Christian teachers," was for McCrimmon the most "potent influence" for making students good moral citizens—even those who refused to become Christians.

Yet Christian education had more to it than the development of individual strengths within an evangelical environment. As far as McCrimmon was concerned, "The Christian college not only teaches how to develop the life but also instructs how to give that life for the benefit of mankind." He concluded his address on a powerful nationalistic note:

> When we view the opportunity before us our hearts warm with enthusiasm and inspiration. The desire to serve our country and our God, comes with ever increasing power. We are Canadians and we wish to see in Canada the highest type of manhood. Let us do our best to cultivate its people to nobility of character and purity of life. Let us grow them large because they are capable of such growth. Let us catch the sentiments of Dean Stanley when he said, "The heroes of mankind are the mountains, the highlands of the moral world. They diversify the monotony. They furnish the water shed of its history." The highest, holiest manhood must ever be our ideal.

For McCrimmon, Baptist education had a special role to play in creating Canadian "moral giants"—men and women who would tower over their contemporaries and be as "Cities upon the Hill" pointing in the direction of the New Jerusalem.

As chancellor of McMaster, from 1911 to 1922, McCrimmon attempted to implement what he called his "missionary conception" of higher education. He often would refer to the evangelical Baptist "view of Christian Education which has led many of the men who have joined the staff of our colleges to leave even the pastorate that they might weave their Christian influence into the lives of developing young men and women destined in different callings in life."[46] For McCrimmon, until his death, "The Christian college is the natural and inevitable complement to the Christian home, the church and the Sunday school. The state schools are worthy of all praise as they direct students to the truth, but after all any truth is unrelated truth, is truth without its meaning for life, until it is centred in Christ, the Son of God and the God of truth."[47]

For Baptists, however, just any Christian college would not do. It would have to be a Baptist institution because of what McCrimmon felt was the crucial significance of the denominational "matrix" in Christian education.[48] He stressed the fact that "our mission in education is with the adolescent in the uncertain years of his youth when he is trying out his tentatives, striving in this direction and that, criticizing his social and religious relations, seeking his ideals, discovering his life-work." It was therefore incumbent upon the Ontario and Quebec Baptist Convention to thrust

> Christ at the centre of [McMaster] life . . . so that His creative personality may organize and direct the developing powers; that to accomplish this purpose there are required Christian teachers, Christian conditions, continuous action of these personalities and conditions, and freedom to exercise such influences; that to furnish this continuous exercise of Christian influence, there must be adequate control so that there may be as great a guarantee as possible respecting the character of the teachers and the conditions; that as a Baptist denomination we must act consistently with our principles, or not act at all.[49]

For McCrimmon, these "principles" were obviously contained in McMaster University's 1887 Act of Incorporation.

46. See A. L. McCrimmon, *The Educational Policy of the Baptists of Ontario and Quebec* (Toronto, 1920), 9.
47. Ibid., 21.
48. Ibid., 22.
49. Ibid., 25.

He proudly described in 1920 the McMaster he had helped shape into what he called a leading "Christian University in this Canada of ours."[50] At McMaster, the unique Baptist blend of pietism, soul liberty, and missionary outreach greatly influenced each student "every day." The university, moreover,

> furnishes him with Christian teachers chosen because they are members of evangelical churches; it indoctrinates him with the principles of scholarship and civilization efficiently; it furnishes him with an atmosphere in which it is the natural and customary procedure to attend Church service; it gives the student a broad course of liberal culture in which to find himself and his sphere of work and at the same time gives an introduction to specialization . . . there is no thought too strenuous for its activity, no freedom too great for its chastened democracy; it is conducive to the cohesiveness and solidarity of our denomination and renders it a more effective fighting unit in the church militant; it furnishes . . . Christian leaders . . . it turns the thoughts of its Arts students to the ministry to keep them within calling distance; . . . it complements from a religious standpoint and under religious influences, the home, the church and the Sunday school, and at the same time complements from the educational standpoint the other universities of Canada.[51]

McMaster, in theory and in practice, was emphatically not an introverted, morbidly introspective, and defensive Baptist Bible college. Rather, it was a small Christian university, open to new scholarship, concerned with the preservation of Christian truth, but always within the context of "liberal culture." It, obviously, had the best of both worlds—orthodox evangelicalism on the one hand and "strenuous thought" and specialization on the other. McCrimmon sincerely believed that he could energize McMaster with the potent mix of orthodoxy and innovation. Instead of energizing the institution, however, and using it to strengthen the Convention, in the 1920s McCrimmon saw his beloved McMaster University help precipitate a furious denominational civil war, from which the Convention has still not yet fully recovered.

The First World War threatened to destroy McCrimmon's McMaster even before T. T. Shields endeavored to accomplish this end in the 1920s. Despite a myriad of external and internal problems, McCrimmon successfully steered his institution through the war years. In doing so, his already fragile health suffered and he found himself without the necessary physical and mental strength to deal constructively with the renewed and even more bitter fundamentalist-modernist controversy that engulfed the Convention at McMaster during the years immediately following the end

50. Ibid., 31.
51. Ibid., 26.

of hostilities. McCrimmon, in 1920, felt compelled to inform his dean of Arts that "owing to the persistent character of my sleeplessness and the fiendish delight it takes in making me super-nervous over the most trivial matters it was best that no further University correspondence should be sent to me."[52] The chancellor was immobilized. In 1921 the Senate began to look for a replacement and the next year Howard Primrose Whidden was named the new chancellor.

McCrimmon's illness may have had both physiological and psychological roots. He saw his idealized McMaster being transformed before his very eyes; the small "Christian university" intent upon making good pious Baptists was being transformed by the forces of change unleashed by the war into an increasingly secular institution of higher learning. Science and the social sciences were replacing Christian orthodoxy as the primary molders of student minds. McCrimmon found himself increasingly isolated. His conservative theology pushed him in the direction of fundamentalists like T. T. Shields—people he instinctively disliked because of their spiritual hubris, their violent language, and their vociferous alienation from Canadian cultural norms. McCrimmon's deep concern about education and learning pushed him towards those liberal Christians who were increasingly committed to intellectual accommodation at the expense of orthodoxy. It is not surprising that McCrimmon was immobilized in 1920 and 1921, incapable of providing leadership and direction to his much troubled Convention and university.

On his retirement from the chancellorship, McCrimmon returned to teaching at McMaster. He was president of the Baptist Convention of Ontario and Quebec for three terms between 1921 and 1932, and he also served as vice president of the Baptist World Alliance. When he died in 1935, McCrimmon was still teaching at McMaster—now located in Hamilton—where he had seen his small Baptist university transformed into a largely secular university and into an academic outpost of the new industrial order.[53]

Abraham Lincoln McCrimmon's obituary in the *Canadian Baptist* on 25 April 1935 captured the man as well as any contemporary analysis. According to the *Canadian Baptist*

> the deep secret of his life was found in Christ. That was the centre he sought for himself and to that centre he sought to lead others. . . . He rejoiced in

52. Quoted in Johnston, *McMaster University,* 1:166. The quotation was originally used in the *McMaster University Alumni News* obituary of McCrimmon, written by his friend Dean McLay, 4 May 1935.

53. For McCrimmon's critique, however muted, of the new McMaster, see his "The Preservation of the Christian Character and of the Denominational Control of McMaster University," 1930, McCrimmon papers, CBA.

> the intimations and certainties of immortality. How he loved in his classroom discussions to speak of the lines that went out into the unseen. His faith in his Saviour was as simple and humble as that of a child. In that faith he lived nobly, he laboured fruitfully, and he died triumphantly.

Such an obituary could never have been written about H. P. Whidden when he died in 1952. In fact, when his successor, G. P. Gilmour, wrote Whidden's official "Tribute," there was a remarkable absence of any references to spiritual and religious gifts and attributes. After discussing briefly Whidden's successful defense at McMaster during the turbulent 1920s, Gilmour maintained that

> Graduates remember Howard Primrose Whidden chiefly as a man of striking appearance, unusual dignity and broad educational outlook. A goodly number of them remember him as a helpful personal friend, for he had a gift for friendship and became the confidant and adviser of many. . . . His staff knew him as a man who chose men and women with care, who inspired faith in the work of a small university, and who guided them more by gentle hints and wise suggestions than by orders or interference.[54]

Whidden was born in Antigonish, Nova Scotia in 1870; after graduating from Acadia University in 1891 he studied theology at McMaster where he received his B.D. degree in 1894. He did further graduate work at the University of Chicago and then served as a Baptist minister in Morden, Manitoba and Galt, Ontario. In 1900 he was appointed professor of English and biblical literature at Brandon College. Three years later he accepted a call to the prestigious Northern Baptist Convention Church in Dayton, Ohio, where he served for almost nine years before returning in 1912 to Brandon as its president. He left Brandon in 1923 for McMaster. It should also be noted that he served as a Union member of Parliament from 1917 to 1921.

Whidden, as the *Winnipeg Tribune* correctly observed on 28 June 1939, was very "cool" and "suave" and handled pressure extremely well. "No matter how sharply he differed" from his critics "one never saw him ruffled to the point of sarcasm and unkindness in debate."[55] He was, without question, a consummate academic politician. A close friend and president of the University of Western Ontario, W. Sherwood Fox, once wrote that Whidden had, since his early Brandon days, "revealed a natural flair for administration and the handling of people."[56] And as far as Fox was concerned in 1941, Whidden had been chosen as McMaster's

54. *McMaster University Alumni News,* 23 May 1952.
55. *Canadian Baptist,* 15 April 1952.
56. Fox to McMaster University Alumni Office, 1 June 1941, CBA.

chancellor in 1922 because of his administrative gifts and not because of his spirituality. In fact, the evidence suggests that Whidden had definitely moved from a conservative evangelical position in the late 1890s to a liberal Christian position in the 1920s—far beyond McCrimmon's conservative evangelicalism.

A persistent and persuasive advocate of modernity and progress, and closely associated with the Ontario business elite, an active Mason and a committed Conservative, Whidden was perceived by many members of McMaster's Board of Governors—many of whom were key members of the Canadian business elite—as just the man to lead the university out of the dark forests of theological backwardness into the mainstream of North American bourgeois success and respectability. He was in so many ways the perfect "organic intellectual" determined to win the support of the traditional Canadian Baptists in what Gramsci has called "the new social, economic and political order." McCrimmon, who had tried to walk the knife edge between the nineteenth century and the twentieth—by finding his theological bearings in a distant past—had failed to solve McMaster's problems. Moreover, he was profoundly suspicious of various aspects of capitalism and consumerism. Perhaps, Whidden could influence McMaster positively, not by looking backwards but forward—his vision unencumbered either by embarrassing evangelical outcroppings or by seemingly outmoded rural values.

Whidden's insensitivity to the fundamentalist criticism of McMaster's apparent move towards modernism in the 1920s undoubtedly played a key role in bringing about the bitter split in the Convention. Whidden, of course, was not responsible for the split. A myriad of complex forces merged in the mid-1920s to bring it about.[57] Yet, he could have done more to placate the fundamentalists—but probably not enough. Perhaps only the replacement of Whidden by Shields would have persuaded the followers of Shields to remain in the Convention.

As might have been expected, Whidden said little and wrote little about Christian higher education. He, evidently, was far more interested in getting things actually done at McMaster than in talking about what might be done. He was always a pragmatic Nova Scotian far more concerned with present realities than with theories spinning off into the imagination.

In his inaugural address given in November 1923, Chancellor Whidden clearly revealed how his philosophy of education differed from that of his predecessor. It was a very brief address, and one of the few available statements that Whidden ever published about education.[58] There

57. See Ellis, "Social and Religious Factors" for the best available study on this topic.

58. Whidden's "What Is a Liberal Education?" *Canadian Journal of Religious Thought* 1 (1924): 39, is obviously a boiled-down version of the 1923 inaugural address.

were only eleven brief paragraphs in Whidden's speech.[59] The first seven dealt with his predecessors, McVicar, Rand, Wallace, McKay, and McCrimmon. There was also a passing mention of the "fine Christian idealism" and "rugged confidence" of Senator William McMaster. Then Whidden very briefly discussed what he referred to as the "Certain Essentials of Liberal Education." The word *Christian* or the word *Christ* was not even referred to once in the body of the new chancellor's speech. It was Whidden's contention that

> The chief business of the smaller university is to furnish a liberal education. If, as Kant said, 'Man's greatest concern is to know how he shall properly fill his place in the universe and understand what he must be in order to be a man,' then education is, as Galsworthy recently said, the sacred concern, indeed the only hope of the nation. *Liberal education should seek to relate the individual to his universe.* I refer more especially to the universe of things. Think of all that nature has in store for those who are willing to learn the simple yet sublime laws of nature.

It is noteworthy that Whidden underscored only one sentence in the first section of his speech. *"Liberal education should seek to relate the individual to the universe."* No mention was made of McMaster's motto "In Christ All Things Consist." No mention, moreover, was made of "Truth" being "centred in Christ." And Whidden was strangely silent about any special aspect of Christian education—either narrowly or broadly defined.

After discussing generally the rise of "the great newer sciences ... Physics ... Chemistry, Biology and Geology," Whidden suddenly declared "Through these four the modern world has largely become what it is." He then went on:

> As a result of the application of scientific knowledge the stellar spaces have been measured and brought near, the subtle forces hidden in air and earth and sea have been harnessed and made to serve man's need. The whole development and structure of material things in past ages is brought within our ken; the life of plant and animal is so much better understood that human life is conserved in previously unthought of ways. In connection with all this there has gone on steadily an emancipation of the mind of man with regard to the dominance of the material.

Thus, for Whidden, the "newer sciences," not the Bible, not Christ, not fundamentalism, had brought about the modern "emancipation of the

59. See the *Canadian Baptist*, 22 November 1923.

mind." Scientific knowledge and not evangelical orthodoxy—and not even experiential Christianity—had led to true freedom—the "emancipation of the mind."

Even though he did not expect that the "newer sciences" would produce great specialists at McMaster, Whidden nevertheless hoped that they would produce intelligent students aware of the basic rudiments of "modern scientific" life. But Whidden, building a bridge in his argument to other areas of the university, agreed with Tyndell that "it is not through science, nor through literature that human nature is made whole, but through a fusion of both." He developed this argument a little further:

> We see then how natural it is to urge that in a truly liberal educational programme recognition be given to the study of universal things in human life. *The mind of youth must be brought into sympathetic acquaintance with the best there is in the experience of man.* There is still need for the classics as well as for modern language and literature. If the coming leaders of thought and action are to know the best that has been thought or said in other days, the old humanities must not be thrown to the discard.

In the second part of his inaugural address, Whidden underlined one other sentence—a sentence he must have regarded as being especially heavy with meaning. "*The mind of youth*" he stressed "*must be brought into sympathetic acquaintance with the best there is in the experience of man.*" Whidden had thrown his knowledge net over the entire "experience of man"—not only a tiny section of it—and had urged all of his teachers to bring their students "into sympathetic acquaintance" with the best there was in the "experience of man."

McMaster's sixth chancellor then concluded his address with a call for a greater interest and awareness of the "New Humanities." "The historical, social and political sciences," he asserted, "must be more vitally understood and set forth if we are rightly to orient the student into his world of citizenship."

As Whidden came down from the platform after giving his inaugural address, he was confronted by one of T. T. Shield's lieutenants with a bitter complaint from his chief, not about the address, but about the honorary degree the university had granted to Dr. William H. P. Faunce, the president of Brown University, and a person Shields regarded as an unreconstructed modernist. The "Faunce Controversy" simmered into 1924 when, at the convention of that year, Whidden actually seconded Shields's motion that "this Convention relies upon the Senate to exercise care that honourary degrees be not conferred upon religious leaders whose theological views are known to be out of harmony with the cardinal principles of evangelical Christianity."[60] After being re-elected to the Board of Governors of McMaster University by the 1924 Convention, Shields was absolutely certain that he, at last, had the Convention modernists on the run. And, in particular, he felt that he had cowed Whidden into submission. Shields, however, not for the first time in his life, had completely misread not only the general theological situation but also the new chancellor.

Much to Shields's disgust, on 25 July 1925 the McMaster Senate endorsed the appointment of L. H. Marshall to the chair of pastoral theology. As far as Shields was concerned, the English Baptist theologian Marshall was a modernist and his appointment was convincing proof that Whidden and his supporters had abandoned evangelical principles. Eventually the "Marshall Controversy" resulted in a major split in the denomination and in late 1926 Shields and hundreds of supporters angrily quit the Convention.[61]

It is sometimes forgotten that during the first three decades of the twentieth century T. T. Shields probably had a greater impact—however negative—upon McMaster University than did any other person. A catalyst for denominational schism and theological warfare, Shields was either loved or hated, respected or detested. There was no middle ground for those who knew the extraordinarily gifted fundamentalist preacher and polemicist. One of his early disciples—Dr. Morley Hall—superbly captured this polarizing tendency in a story he once told about two women in the Jarvis Street Baptist Church who were struck by the special effect of a shaft of morning sunshine on the countenance of the Reverend Shields as he piously sat behind his pulpit. "One was impressed by the angelic look on her pastor's face," Hall recounted. "The other was certain that she saw traces of the demonic."[62] In 1931, Jean Graham, a perceptive *Saturday Night* reporter, also captured the almost Janus-like quality of Shields:

> Could this gentleman of benign countenance and mellifluous voice be the turbulent pastor who hated his enemies and loathed his theological opponents until he became wrathy and violent and longed for the Lord to destroy them? Surely there must be some mistake. As the sermon progressed the bewilderment increased. It was what would be called a simple gospel

60. *Baptist Year Book*, 1924, 43.

61. For an almost week-by-week and blow-by-blow account of unfolding events from a Shields' perspective, see the *Gospel Witness* for the 1924–27 period. For the Convention side, see G. W. Carder, "Controversy in the Baptist Convention, 1908–1929" (B.D. thesis, McMaster University, 1950).

62. Quoted in J. D. E. Dozois, "Dr. Thomas Todhunter Shields (1873–1955): In the Stream of Fundamentalism" (B.D. thesis, McMaster Divinity College, 1963), 57.

> sermon, with no reference to modernists or other monstrosities. . . . During the week following he appeared to go on a rampage of malice, hatred and uncharitableness. Who is the true Dr. Shields? Is he the kindly Christian or the peevish propagandist?[63]

Shields, it seems clear, was, in fact, both. He was an extraordinary mix of opposites—of love and hate, of gentleness and harshness, of sensibility and callousness. He was referred to by his enemies as "a dictator," as "a hypocrite," as "vain and egotistical," and as a "man without a Christian heart."[64] His friends, however, regarded him as a "man of God," "devastatingly honest" and absolutely "selfless."

Thomas Todhunter Shields was born in Bristol, England, in 1873, the fifth of eight children. His father, originally an Anglican priest, was eventually ordained a Baptist minister and emigrated with his family, in 1888, to pastor a small Baptist church in western Ontario. T. T. Shields, after his conversion in his father's church in 1891, was ordained a Baptist minister "without the benefit of either a college or a seminary education."[65] After serving a number of Baptist churches in western Ontario, T. T. Shields, in 1910, was called to the prestigious Jarvis Street pastorate. He remained there until his death in 1955.

A brilliant preacher, widely regarded as the "Spurgeon of Canada" since at least the first decade of the twentieth century, Shields had had serious reservations about McMaster University's special role within the Baptist denomination. Overly sensitive to his own lack of seminary training, he resented the way McMaster theology graduates leapfrogged into large urban churches over the careers of their less well educated fellow ministers. According to Shields, in his controversial book *The Plot That Failed,*

> Certain officials of McMaster University . . . had come to regard the Baptist denomination as McMaster's special preserve. Non-McMaster men were tolerated for the doing of rough work, even as the Chinese coolies were used to do rough work on the Western Front in the Great War. Train loads of coolies passed through Canada. But no one ever supposed that one of them could by any possibility become colonel of a regiment, or commander of a brigade, or of an army, to say nothing of the possibility of one's carrying a field-marshal's baton in his knapsack. To my personal knowledge certain of the Faculty of McMaster looked upon non-

63. *Saturday Night,* 11 July 1931.

64. G. Anglin, "The Battling Baptist," *MacLean's,* 15 June 1949. I am indebted to Ms. Lee Ann Purchace for some of this material about Shields.

65. C. A. Russell, "Thomas Todhunter Shields, Canadian Fundamentalist," *Ontario History* 70 (1978): 264.

> McMaster men as useful for preparing dugouts, lighting fires, and perhaps for carrying meals to the Graduates of McMaster University.[66]

Shields, however, did not explain in *The Plot That Failed* how he had become "commander" and "field-marshal" at Jarvis Street despite McMaster's policy of regarding, as he put it, "The Denomination" as its own "great estate."[67] Nor did Shields explain why he had been awarded an honorary D.D. by McMaster in 1918.

Shields's view of Christian education in the North American context underwent significant change in the 1920s. This point is sometimes not taken into account by scholars who merely see him as a closed-minded fundamentalist whose views of all issues had clicked into firm place by the turn of the century. From 1922 to 1925, for example, Shields was sharply ambivalent about McMaster's educational role. Despite his criticism of the denominational imperialism of the institution, nevertheless until at least 1925 Shields still felt that there was some hope for the institution, provided that Baptist fundamentalists were appointed to its theological department. The "Marshall Controversy" of 1925, however, provided Shields with convincing proof that the university and the denomination had irrevocably abandoned its orthodox Christian traditions and had, moreover, destroyed any remaining fundamentalist "hope" for theological renewal and spiritual revitalization.

In the 21 September 1922 issue of the *Gospel Witness*, Shields began his public discussion of McMaster University and Christian education. In a major article entitled "What About McMaster University?" Shields raised the question of whether the non-theology part of McMaster was, in any way, "serving the Denomination?" His response was that there was an unanswerable argument for a separate independent Baptist university but only if in such an institution "vital and vigorous Baptist principles" permeated the teaching of all courses. If such was not the case, he felt, it made a great deal of pedagogical and financial sense for Baptist students in arts and science to be sent to secular universities rather than McMaster. The large sums of money saved by the denomination would be far better used to support a vibrant, biblically based seminary.

In other articles in the *Gospel Witness* published late in 1922, Shields developed further his ideas concerning Christian education. For him

> The Baptist view is that a Christian is a Christian everywhere, and in all things; that if a man confesses that Jesus Christ is his Lord, his subjection

66. T. T. Shields, *The Plot That Failed* (Toronto: Gospel Witness, 1937), 10.
67. Ibid., 11.

> to Christ will color even his thinking, and that then, no matter what subject he may teach, whether it be history, or science, or language, or literature, or psychology, or sociology, or political economy, or theology he will view everything from a Christian standpoint, and there will be a savor of Christ in all his teaching: and his devotion to Christ will compound the principles of the gospel into a precious nard which will become diffused by His presence until the house is filled with the odor of the ointment: and the very atmosphere becomes charged with spiritual vitality.[68]

As had been the case with McCrimmon in 1920, Shields endorsed the view that the evangelical ideal of Christian education could, in fact, be realized at McMaster. And he, therefore, argued that any move toward "federation with the Provincial University" was "a retrograde step" and all Baptists were urged to "prevent it at all possible cost."[69]

Shields would stress over and over again in late 1922 that McCrimmon's successor as chancellor at McMaster had been to make the arts and science faculty into a "Baptist missionary educational institution,"[70] where students were not only converted to evangelical Christianity but also persuaded to sacrifice their lives and careers for their Savior. The appointment of Whidden, a man distrusted by Shields, seemed to provide convincing evidence to the Jarvis Street pastor that his ideal Christian institution would never be realized at McMaster. Consequently, in May 1923, he began to attack McMaster University because the "absolutely anti-Christian . . . doctrine of Evolution" was being taught there.[71] As Shields moved more and more into the premillennial camp in 1923, his criticism of McMaster intensified; and the Faunce honorary degree in November 1923, gave him the excuse to denounce Whidden and the Senate for abandoning "the faith once delivered to the saints."[72] By early January 1924, Shields was organizing special prayer meetings for McMaster University. At these, he announced to the readers of the *Gospel Witness* on 17 January:

> We shall ask the Lord to arise in His might and by His own power to deliver the University out of the hands of those whose principles have blighted the denomination for so long, and to deliver it to the management of those who will be true to "the faith once for all delivered to the Saints." . . . We who profess to believe in the supernatural must put our profession to the proof by invoking supernatural power to fight our battles.

68. *Gospel Witness*, 5 October 1922.
69. Ibid.
70. Ibid., 12 October 1922.
71. Ibid., 31 May 1923.
72. Ibid., 29 November 1923.

One month later Shields viciously attacked Whidden as the man responsible for the remarkable growth of modernism at Brandon College. And Shields warned his readers that the new chancellor of McMaster had also "encouraged" this "kind of teaching" at the Toronto institution.[73]

By November 1924, Shields's views about McMaster had changed, yet again. Encouraged by the Convention's endorsement of his criticism of the Faunce honorary degree and his contention that such degrees should not be "conferred upon religious leaders whose theological views are known to be out of harmony with the cardinal principles of evangelical Christianity,"[74] he resolved to give McMaster and the Convention another last chance. The other Shields—apparently seeking compromise—suddenly appeared from the bitter, bloody, internecine theological civil war.

Shields informed his shocked Toronto Baptist fundamentalist associates on 4 November 1924 that he was genuinely "sorry" if any of his anti-McMaster statements had, in fact, "hurt anyone."[75] He told them that he had

> given our hand to the Chancellor [Whidden] as the representative of our educational work; and we are prepared to trust him, to follow him, and to rely (to use the term in the resolution which we moved and which he seconded) upon him to carry out in spirit and letter and we all know to be the Convention's desire. We therefore in this public way . . . [Shields expected that his letter would be immediately published in the *Gospel Witness*] pledge our heart and hand to the support of our educational work.[76]

All of a sudden, Shields was now sympathetically describing McMaster as "our educational work." He obviously felt that the 1924 Convention had endorsed his fundamentalist position and that he was therefore in an unprecedented position to gain control, once and for all, over the strategically significant institution—McMaster University. He looked forward to the day when his McMaster men would make the old McMaster graduates "coolies" and "servants" of the fundamentalist elite.

In early November 1924, a euphoric Shields confidently expressed his new vision of "Christian Education." He first asserted that McMaster, as a Christian university, had "to resemble other universities" in conforming "to the highest standards of scholarship." But it had to be more than this as well. "Our view of the ideal for McMaster," Shields con-

73. Ibid., 14 February 1924.

74. Johnston, *McMaster University*, 1:180.

75. *Gospel Witness*, 23 September 1926. This important letter has not received the attention it certainly warrants.

76. Ibid.

tended, "is not that it should be like the State University-minus—but like the State University-plus." And for him the plus was the orthodox Christian dynamic. And this dynamic would be provided not only by committed evangelical faculty at McMaster, in arts, science and theology, but by a new "Baptist Bible Training College" administratively "in connection with McMaster University." Such a Bible college, Shields contended, would transform McMaster. "It would bring to its halls," he went on,

> hundreds of young people who would live every day, not with books about the Bible, but with the Bible itself. It would bring to the University a still more spiritual atmosphere than now obtains . . . for it is impossible that a great host of young people should engage in the study of God's word without filling the place with prayer and praise. Thus McMaster University would become more than ever a centre of evangelical teaching and evangelistic enthusiasm and effort.[77]

Shields was convinced that the Bible school, which he hoped would be associated in an intimate way with his own church, would strengthen and not weaken McMaster University. At the "Bible Training School," he argued, hundreds of students would "enlarge their minds" and thus be "inspire[d] . . . with a desire for higher learning" as they "would naturally pass from the Bible course of the College into the regular university courses." Such a Bible school, Shields prophesied, would encourage the fundamentalist Baptists, in particular, to "give the University a place in the[ir] hearts and . . . prayers . . . such as nothing else would do." He knew of many ministers, including himself, who would offer their services to the school at "a nominal cost." Shields then concluded with the declaration that it was incumbent upon his supporters to

> set up a standard of Christian learning which may be used to enlighten even those who count themselves wise. In other words, our duty is not to follow the example of other universities in these dark days but to set up a new standard of absolute loyalty to truth as revealed in Him who in all things consist. Hence, it is our duty to evangelize the rationalist university and to teach the rationalist scholar.[78]

Shields's proposal, as might have been expected, fell on deaf Convention ears. It was perceived as a fundamentalist Trojan Horse to capture McMaster for the Shields forces. And even Shields, by the summer of 1925, had lost his enthusiasm for it. Moving inexorably towards schism,

77. Ibid.
78. Ibid.

he proposed in late August a month after the Marshall appointment, to establish his own independent "Toronto Baptist Pastors College" based upon what he referred to as "the New Testament . . . educational ideal." "Christ must be put first," he declared in direct opposition to the liberal platitudes of Whidden's inaugural address. "The end of all education," Shields asserted, echoing McCrimmon, was "to know Him [the Christ] better." All true learning automatically centred on "a better knowledge of Christ."

> A pursuit of such an ideal can be maintained only in a healthy spiritual atmosphere. A man is not likely to develop an aesthetic taste in a coal mine; it is not probable that one would grow as a musician amid the din of a boiler making establishment. So to keep always in view this worthiest of all ideals, one must not only be possessed of a vigorous spiritual health himself but his soul must breathe the atmosphere of the heavenly places in Christ. Hence we believe that such an ideal is most likely to be realized in association with a New Testament church, founded upon New Testament principles, surcharged with the power of the Holy Spirit.[79]

Such a church was of course available—Jarvis Street Baptist Church—and here at his church and at his college the students would have their faith built up and not destroyed. The "Bible" would be "The Principal Text Book" and learning to preach the evangelistic gospel the only practical course. All faculty members were to be "required to subscribe" to the fundamentalist "Confession of Faith of the Baptist Bible Union of North America . . . publicly at the beginning of each term."[80] If they attempted to qualify in any way, any of these fundamentalist tenets, they would be immediately fired. Belonging to a so-called evangelical church was not enough; only a yearly fundamentalist litmus test, administered by Shields, would do.

Early in 1926, the Toronto Baptist Seminary opened its doors to its first students. A short time before, Shields had announced to his supporters that he was "at war" with McMaster and the Convention. Their "moderate Modernism"—as he spitefully called it—and their "spirit of the Spanish Inquisition" had compelled him to implement in the new year his August 1925 "College plan." He equated so-called Baptist liberty with a "mild attack of small pox or of leprosy."[81] By January 1927, Shields had organized his followers into a separate Baptist organization, the Regular Baptist Missionary and Educational Society of Canada. A

79. Ibid., 27 August 1925.
80. Ibid.
81. Ibid., 5 November 1925.

short time later this body was reorganized as "the Union of Regular Baptist Churches of Ontario and Quebec."[82]

Thus by 1927, Shields and his supporters had their own seminary, their own separate "Union," their own newspaper, the *Gospel Witness*, which had been started in 1922. They, therefore, possessed a smoothly running parallel Baptist organization to compete with their Convention opponents. And by May 1927, Shields had a university to compete with McMaster—Des Moines University, in Iowa—a financially troubled institution taken over by the fundamentalist Bible Baptist Union of North America, of which organization Shields was president from 1923 to 1930. Unable to put things right at McMaster, Shields enthusiastically turned to the task of transforming Des Moines into what McMaster had refused to be: "a great Christian institution of higher learning . . . absolutely free from the taint of modernism."[83]

But within two years, the Des Moines experiment had proven to be an embarrassing failure as a student revolt and a bitter American reaction against the anglophile Shields resulted in the closing of the university.[84] What happened with Des Moines University, a fundamentalist Baptist university which Shields ruled with an iron hand, might have also happened with McMaster, if Shields had had his way. During the period when Shields's Des Moines experiment was disintegrating into disaster, Whidden was carefully consolidating his position at McMaster and preparing the way for a move to Hamilton. In 1928, after much discussion, "The 'New McMaster Campaign' was launched which resulted two years later in the physical re-establishment" of McMaster in the west end of the "Steel City."[85] Whidden must have been delighted to have escaped the presence of Shields and also the bitter memories of what one of his associates referred to as "a lovely war."[86] He also must have been pleased to have been given the opportunity to build *his* kind of Baptist university. If he had lived to see the day when in 1957, the Convention cut its official ties with McMaster University and was content with the creation of McMaster Divinity College, Whidden would have been ecstatic indeed. This was the way he was leading McMaster when he led the move to Hamilton in 1930. Whidden would have agreed with his close friend John Gilmour, that "McMaster had only narrowly escaped being a glorified Woodstock rather than a univer-

82. L. K. Tarr, *Shields of Canada* (Grand Rapids: Baker, 1967), 99.

83. Johnston, *McMaster University,* 1:199.

84. For an excellent study of Shields and Des Moines, see G. S. May, "Des Moines University and Dr. T. T. Shields," *Iowa Journal of History* (July 1956): 193–232.

85. Johnston, *McMaster University,* 1:xii.

86. Quoted in ibid., 193, from a 1926 letter from the Reverend A. A. Cameron to Whidden.

sity."[87] McCrimmon's McMaster and also that of Shields was obviously a "glorified Woodstock"—a Baptist Bible college. The new McMaster, according to Whidden, must have been a real university—a place where the intellectual "deputies" of the new dominant class could help to impose on their society hegemonic control and order.

87. Quoted in ibid., 181. I am far less sympathetic to Whidden than is Johnston, largely because I do not feel that the McMaster of today is the only prism through which to view the events of the 1920s. In other words, McMaster could have become a small, reputable Christian college like Wheaton College, Illinois, rather than the large and secular science dominated institution of the 1980s. But the point still has to be made that the historian must deal with what actually happened and why and not what might have happened—*if*.

15

Youth for Christ and the New Evangelicals

Joel Carpenter

From Joel A. Carpenter, "Youth for Christ and the New Evangelicals' Place in the Life of the Nation," in *Religion and the Life of the Nation: American Recoveries,* edited by Rowland A. Sherrill (Urbana and Chicago: University of Illinois Press, 1991), 128–51.

On the evening of Memorial Day, 1945, 70,000 people gathered at the Soldier Field stadium in Chicago to witness an open-air pageant. Like other ceremonies on that day, this one remembered fallen servicemen and rededicated a nation still at war to a global mission. This rally had another major purpose, however. It celebrated the first anniversary of the Chicago-area chapter of "Youth for Christ," a rapidly growing evangelistic youth movement. By mid-1945, its leaders estimated that their Youth for Christ rallies thrived in three hundred to four hundred cities and towns, with nearly half a million attending, while soldiers and sailors held dozens of similar rallies in Europe and the Pacific.[1]

1. The accounts of Youth for Christ's rapid expansion in 1944–45 appear in Mel Larson, *Youth for Christ: Twentieth Century Wonder* (Grand Rapids: Zondervan, 1947), 84–95; J. Elwin Wright, "Youth for Christ," *United Evangelical Action* 6 (15 Febuary 1945): 8 (this periodical is cited hereinafter as *UEA*); James Hefley, *God Goes to High School* (Waco, Tex.: Word, 1970), 38–49, 69. Youth for Christ was comprised of a variety of evangelical ministries to "young people." The formation of Youth for Christ International

The Soldier Field rally reflected, in one spectacular event, the convergence of a renewed, exuberant evangelicalism and the war-inspired revival of the American civic faith. Its musical program praised God and country with a three-hundred-piece band, a choir of five thousand, and several well-known gospel singers, including George Beverly Shea. On the field, the religious and patriotic program began with a flag ceremony performed by high school cadets and four hundred marching nurses. Next followed a pageant featuring missionary volunteers in national costumes dramatizing the call to evangelize the world. Standing for America was a young evangelist named Billy Graham; he issued a summons for another great revival. On the platform, war heroes attested to their faith, as did intercollegiate boxing titlist Bob Finley. Track star Gil Dodds, the record-holder for the indoor mile, ran an exhibition lap before giving his testimony. The evening's preacher followed; he was Percy Crawford, director of the nationally broadcast "Young People's Church of the Air." At his gospel invitation, hundreds signed "decision cards." As the meeting drew to a close, a spotlight circled the darkened stadium, while a huge neon sign blazed "Jesus Saves" and the choir sang "We Shall Shine as Stars in the Morning."[2]

Indeed they did, for this extravaganza attracted major news coverage. The Chicago papers, the wire services, and *Newsweek* magazine carried stories of the rally, and, a few weeks later, William Randolph Hearst editorially blessed the youth movement and ordered his twenty-two newspapers to feature the rallies. Not since the Scopes trial had evangelical Christianity received such coverage, and, this time, most of it was friendly.[3]

---

in the summer of 1945 did not by any means bring all of these into one organization. Other significant groups included Percy Crawford's Young People's Church of the Air, centered in Philadelphia; Jim Rayburn's Young Life Campaign, first headquartered in Dallas; Jack Wyrtzen's Word of Life organization in greater New York; and many smaller groups. Additional youth-related ministries participated in this evangelistic surge, including Dawson Trotman's Navigators ministry to servicemen and the North American branch of Inter Varsity Christian Fellowship, organized in 1938.

2. "Wanted: A Miracle of Good Weather and 'Youth for Christ' Rally Got It," *Newsweek,* 11 June 1945, 84; and Mel Larson, "70,000 Attend Chicago Youth for Christ Rally Held on Memorial Day," *UEA* 6 (15 June 1945): 1, 8.

3. "Wanted: A Miracle"; "Youth's New Crusade," editorial reprinted from Hearst papers as "William Randolph Hearst's Editorial Endorsement of 'Youth for Christ,'" *UEA* 6 (16 July 1945): 13; "Hearst Papers Now Boost Youth for Christ," *UEA* 6 (2 July 1945): 1; *Minutes of the First Annual Convention,* Youth for Christ International, 22–29 July 1945, 6, 23–24, Youth for Christ Records, collection 48, box 13, folder 36, Billy Graham Center Archives. Other accounts of Youth for Christ in national publications during 1945–46 include William F. McDermott, "Bobby-Soxers Find the Sawdust Trail," *Colliers,* 26 May 1945, 22–23; Frank S. Mead, "Apostle to Youth," *Christian Herald* 68 (September 1945): 15–17; John Ray Evers, "Youth for Christ Meets Pittsburgh," *Christian Century* 63 (10 October 1945): 1171–72; "Youth for Christ," *Time,* 4 February 1946, 46–47; Clarence Woodbury, "Bobby-Soxers Sing Hallelujah," *American Magazine* 141 (March 1946): 26–27.

Youth for Christ was one of the most striking early signs of a rising new evangelical movement, which has remained a prominent factor in American life since then. By the late 1940s, rallies had grown to over one thousand in number, with an estimated weekly attendance of one million people: Youth for Christ evangelists had preached by then in forty-six countries. Too restless and visionary to settle down to the task of ministering to teenagers, many of the movement's early leaders, notably Billy Graham and Bob Pierce, founder of World Vision, infused a larger postwar evangelical coalition with their energy. These youthful evangelists created a variety of new organizations and communicated their message with popular broadcasts and publications. They merged their desire to be helpful contributors to the "American cause" with a renewed vision for world evangelization and revival in the United States.[4] Youth for Christ thus became the spearhead of a postwar evangelistic thrust and the first dramatic sign that American evangelicals were "coming in from the cold."[5]

The Youth for Christ sensation of 1944–47 has become a bit of trivia in American historical narrative, but it is worth recovering and examining. Historians are beginning to pay more attention to the World War II experience as a powerful shaper of contemporary America.[6] Likewise, they have devoted more interest recently to evangelical Christianity's role

4. "Youth for Christ Expands in Continent," *UEA* 4 (1 January 1946): 9, "Five YFC Leaders Will Fly to Europe," *UEA* 5 (March 1946): 10; "G.I. Missionaries to Manila," *Sunday* 7 (February 1946): 26–29, 49–52; Larson, *Youth for Christ,* 20–23, 60–63, 69–71, 80–81, 92–93; Hefley, *God Goes to High School,* 29–30, 34–40, 55–65, 66–68. See also Joel A. Carpenter, "From Fundamentalism to the New Evangelical Coalition," in *Evangelicalism and Modern America,* ed. George Marsden (Grand Rapids: Eerdmans, 1984), 3–16. For a helpful explanation of the distinction, assumed throughout this essay, between evangelical Christianity as a diverse family of movements which nonetheless share beliefs, influences, and tendencies and the more conscious coalition of "new evangelicals" being formed in the 1940s on the initiative of a "progressive" party in fundamentalism, see George Marsden, "The Evangelical Denomination," in ibid., vii–xvi. These more consistently self-identified "evangelicals," who Marsden suggests "have attempted to speak or to set standards for evangelicals generally," are the focus of this essay.

5. Richard John Neuhaus, *The Naked Public Square: Religion and Democracy in America* (Grand Rapids: Eerdmans, 1984), 260.

6. Charles C. Alexander, *Nationalism in American Thought, 1930–1945* (Chicago: Rand McNally, 1969); John Morton Blum, *V Was for Victory: Politics and American Culture during World War II* (New York: Harcourt Brace Jovanovich, 1976); and Geoffrey Perrett, *Days of Sadness, Years of Triumph: The American People, 1939–1945* (Baltimore: Penguin, 1974) remain the most insightful treatments of the war's impact on domestic cultural trends; while James Gilbert, *Another Chance: Postwar America, 1945–1968* (Philadelphia: Temple University Press, 1981) and Richard A. Pells, *The Liberal Mind in a Conservative Age: American Intellectuals in the 1940s and 1950s* (New York: Harper and Row, 1984) provide interpretations of the war's effect on postwar culture.

in American culture.[7] The Youth for Christ episode shows, moreover, that these two factors intersect, that the cultural and civic mood prompted by World War II and the early stages of the cold war encouraged the reinvigoration of evangelicalism.

Youth for Christ's public notoriety, then, helps illustrate evangelicals' ongoing struggle to find their place in modern American life. This episode shows very pointedly that the "new evangelicals" were re-visioning their mission to the nation. After years of alienation in the wake of the fundamentalists' defeats and public ridicule, a generation of postfundamentalist evangelical leaders was emerging, with the recovery of a "Christian America" as a prominent point on their agenda. This yearning to restore evangelicals' moral leadership continued as an important theme in the ensuing decades. Indeed, some conservative evangelicals, along with a newly politicized fundamentalist movement, have translated the "Christian America" myth into a political platform and have entered public affairs with considerable force. The surprising emergence of this "religious factor" in the American public arena has sent social analysts scrambling to find out how, in what has been considered a secular society, it could happen.[8]

The Youth for Christ story can shed some light on this "intrusion" of religion in the public square, for as an early manifestation of contemporary evangelicalism it displays some of this persuasion's distinctive traits in a particularly striking and protean form. Youth for Christ's sensational showing in the late 1940s illustrates evangelicalism's symbiotic relationship with modernity and with American culture in particular. Since their early days, evangelicals have been adept at converting communications technology to sustain their internal needs and send forth their message.[9] In a democratic and free-market religious milieu, they have been very audience conscious, as Nathan Hatch puts it, shaping their message

7. Leonard I. Sweet's masterful bibliographical essay, "The Evangelical Tradition in America," in *The Evangelical Tradition in America,* ed. L. I. Sweet (Macon, Ga.: Mercer University Press, 1984), 1–86, documents the recent flurry of scholarly interest in American evangelicals.

8. Works that assess the rise of the new religious right are legion already, and constantly growing. For a helpful guide to this literature through 1984, see Richard V. Pierard, "The New Religious Right in American Politics," in *Evangelicalism and Modern America,* 161–74 and 206–12 (bibliography).

9. Harry S. Stout, "Religion, Communications, and the Ideological Origins of the American Revolution," *William and Mary Quarterly,* 3d ser. 34 (October 1977): 419–544; Nathan O. Hatch, "The Christian Movement and the Demand for a Theology of People," *Journal of American History* 67 (December 1980): 545–67; Hatch, "Elias Smith and the Rise of Religious Journalism in the Early Republic," in *Printing and Society in Early America,* ed. William L. Joyce et al. (Worcester, Mass.: American Antiquarian Society, 1983), 250–77; and Joan Jacobs Brumberg, *Mission for Life: The Story of the Family of Adoniram Judson* (New York: Free Press, 1980), 44–78.

to address the desires and tastes of their hearers.[10] Evangelicals also find it easy to identify themselves and their message with the "mystic chords" of American collective memory and hope, since Puritan convenantal and evangelical revivalist and millennial motifs are mixed into the foundations of American cultural identity and mission.[11] Furthermore, evangelical values and the revival style became thickly embedded in national life during the nineteenth century.[12] These cultural strata now lie buried under much of twentieth-century American society but are still prominent in important parts of the landscape, such as the South, and often emerge elsewhere in the ideals and rhetoric of American politics.[13] In times when the terrain buckles, when newer ideological and institutional structures waver, the older values and myths may reemerge. The era of World War II was such a time, and Youth for Christ was a medium for the rebonding of evangelical religion and American civic faith. "In times like these, you need an anchor," sang the Youth for Christ rally crowds, one that "grips the Solid Rock."[14] They referred, of course, to Jesus, but accepting him, they assumed, meant taking on evangelical Christian piety and mores as well. These values, evangelicals believed, provided the best anchorage for their nation.

This essay will show, then, that Youth for Christ campaigners were given opportunities in wartime and early postwar America to move out of their religious ghettoes and into the national public arena. Their talent for grafting the tastes and techniques of popular communications onto evangelism and their efforts to leave behind some of the alienation of their sectarian background merged with three war-inspired trends: increased popular religiosity, revived faith in America's manifest destiny, and intensified concern for public morality—especially that of the emerging youth culture. As a result, Youth for Christ leaders found that their calls for the

10. Nathan O. Hatch, "Evangelicalism as a Democratic Movement," in *Evangelicalism and Modern America,* 71–82.

11. Ernest Lee Tuveson, *Redeemer Nation: The Idea of America's Millennial Role* (Chicago: University of Chicago Press, 1968); Nathan O. Hatch, *The Sacred Cause of Liberty: Republican Thought and the Millennium in Revolutionary New England* (New Haven, Conn.: Yale University Press, 1977); Alan E. Heimert, *Religion and the American Mind: From the Great Awakening to the Revolution* (Cambridge: Harvard University Press, 1966).

12. Perry Miller, *The Life of the Mind in America from the Revolution to the Civil War* (New York: Harcourt Brace, and World, 1965), vol. 1, *The Evangelical Basis;* Gordon S. Wood, "Evangelical America and Early Mormonism," *New York History* 61 (October 1980): 359–86; Martin E. Marty, *Righteous Empire: The Protestant Experience in America* (New York: Dial, 1970).

13. William Lee Miller, "The Seminarian Strain: Church and Statesmen in the Democratic Party," *New Republic,* 9 July 1984, 18–21.

14. Ruth Caye Jones, "In Times Like These," copyright 1944, assigned to Zondervan Publishing Company.

"spiritual revitalization of America" received a more congenial hearing than evangelicals had encountered for a generation. This success spurred on the postwar resurgence of evangelicalism, prompting the born-again to seek another Great Awakening with renewed confidence and anticipation. One simply cannot understand the new engagement of evangelicals in public discourse without seeing, first, the process by which they made their reentry a generation ago and, second, the triumphs and frustrations they have encountered since then. The aim of this essay is to recover the first half of that story, which is less well known, and to suggest that some of evangelicals' frustrations with public life in the ensuing years stemmed from the terms of admission they had accepted earlier.

In order to understand the full significance of Youth for Christ as a turning point for American evangelicals, it is important to know what was new about the rally movement. Most of the Youth for Christ pioneers were from fundamentalist backgrounds.[15] This may seem surprising, because only twenty years earlier fundamentalists were made the laughingstock of the cosmopolitan shapers of public opinion. Fundamentalists responded by nurturing feelings of alienation toward American culture and developing a network of religious institutions which allowed them to build a virtual subculture.

The same commitment and energy that insured fundamentalism's survival and growth as a grass-roots religious movement propelled it outward into increasing public exposure and activity, for like many sectarians fundamentalists felt compelled to make converts. The truth of their faith, they insisted, was validated as it transformed people. The institutional flourishing of fundamentalism in the 1930s meant not only the development of "shelter belts" from the winds of modern secularity but the provision of new tools for evangelization. Fundamentalists and other evangelicals developed radio broadcasting, journalism, and advertising techniques to retool mass evangelism and give it a contemporary idiom. Revived interest in evangelism and new organizational networks such as the National Association of Evangelicals and the Christian Business Men's Committees made the immense task of sustaining citywide campaigns possible once more. Radio preachers, mission and educational ex-

15. The notable exceptions were Charles Templeton, a Church of the Nazarene pastor in Toronto; Watson Argue, a pastor of an Assemblies of God congregation in Winnipeg; and Hubert Mitchell, of the International Church of the Foursquare Gospel in Los Angeles. Among those leaders who clearly were fundamentalist by training and affiliation were Torrey Johnson and Billy Graham of Chicago, Richard Harvey of St. Louis, Jack Wrytzen of New York, Percy Crawford and Walter Smyth of Philadelphia, John Huffman of Boston, George Wilson and Merv Rosell of Minneapolis, Roger Malsbary of Indianapolis, and Glenn Wagner of Washington, D.C. See Torrey Johnson and Robert Cook, *Reaching Youth for Christ* (Chicago: Moody, 1944), 31–34; Larson, *Youth for Christ,* 35, 45, 48–55, 59, 66–67, 86–87, 106–7, 112–13.

ecutives, evangelists, and publishers began to notice that their movement had created many thriving ministries and that they enjoyed a surprisingly receptive general audience. Perhaps, they surmised, the old, nearly forgotten dream of a nationwide revival could still come true.[16]

By the early 1940s, revival was becoming the fundamentalist watchword. Encouraged by their own success, fundamentalists were shifting from a separatistic, "pilgrim" stance toward a reformist, "puritan" pose, with revivalism as their major instrument for seeking national renewal. Under the leadership of the Moody Bible Institute president, Will H. Houghton, virtually every issue of the *Moody Monthly* carried an editorial or an article pleading for widespread repentance and conversion. Indeed, the theme of the Moody Bible Institute's annual Founder's Week Conference in 1942 was "America's God-given Opportunity for Worldwide Revival Today."[17] Editor Philip Howard's *Sunday School Times* conveyed the same expectancy, and in 1943 he helped launch the "Christ for America" evangelistic association to sponsor campaigns in major cities.[18] New hope for a revival was prominent in the messages of the first two conventions of the National Association of Evangelicals in 1942 and 1943. No doubt the wartime crisis summoned fundamentalists to recover these themes of covenant and revival. Said the NAE's first president Harold Ockenga in "Christ for America," his inaugural address, World War II had brought all of humanity to a crossroads. On one path lay "the rescue of western civilization by a . . . revival of evangelical Christianity," while the other led to "a return to the Dark Ages of heathendom."[19]

16. For more detailed exposition of these developments, see Carpenter, "From Fundamentalism to the New Evangelical Coalition," 3–16; and Carpenter, "The Fundamentalist Leaven and the Rise of an Evangelical United Front," in *Evangelical Tradition in America,* 257–88.

17. "Call to Founder's Week Conference," *Moody Monthly* (hereinafter *MM*) 42 (December 1941): 188; John R. Riebe, "Founder's Week Conference Report," *MM* 42 (March 1942): 407–10. On preoccupation with revival see G. Allen Fleece, "How Shall I Pray for Revival?" *MM* 42 (March 1942): 406, 410; "Editorial Notes," *MM* 43 (March 1943): 395; (June 1943): 560; (July 1943): 611; (August 1943): 663; Armin R. Geeswein, "How Does a Revival Begin?" *MM* 44 (October 1943): 61, 62, 86; "Editorial Notes," *MM* 44 (November 1943): 115; (December 1943): 184; (February 1944): 315.

18. Horace F. Dean, "Christ for America," *Sunday School Times* (hereinafter *SST*) 85 (1 May 1943): 351–52; Paul W. Rood, "A Statement to Fundamentalists," *SST* 84 (25 April 1942): 331; George T. B. Davis, "Nationwide Prayer for Revival and Victory," *SST* 84 (23 May 1942): 412–13; Dan Gilbert, "The Fundamentals Convention in Boston," *SST* 48 (4 July 1942): 539.

19. See addresses in the convention annuals *Evangelical Action! A Report of the Organization of the National Association of Evangelicals for United Action* (Boston: Fellowship Press, 1942); and *United We Stand, A Report of the Constitutional Convention of the National Association of Evangelicals,* Chicago, Ill., 3–6 May 1943. Ockenga's address quoted from ibid., 11.

To sum up this brief excursion, then, a new generation of fundamentalist leaders and their allies among other evangelicals were ushering in a major shift in outlook and activity. They were moving from alienation to engagement, from separatist sectarianism to panevangelical cooperation, and from the pose of a prophetic faithful remnant to that of the nation's evangelists and chaplains. Youth for Christ rode the crest of this new wave, and helped it break into the larger public's attention.

Internal development accounts for only part of the story, however. These "new evangelicals" drew powerful encouragement and assistance from the changing cultural climate during World War II and shortly thereafter. From their perspective, the nation showed a greater spiritual need and a greater religious interest than they had seen in a generation. America was "ripe for revival," they believed.[20] These perceptions have something of a corresponding reality behind them, for World War II was in many respects a tonic for Americans' faith in their nation's commonly stated ideals. Indeed, suggested one historian, the nation lived on the "accumulated social and political capital" of this experience long into the postwar years.[21] While the Depression had discouraged many people about ever realizing the American dream, war mobilization brought unprecedented opportunity—if not prosperity—to even the poorest. The Depression had generated internal strife, but the war brought a renewed sense of common purpose. True, millions experienced disrupted lives, pain and grief, or frustration at injustice. Yet the experiences of wartime prosperity and mobility and of defending their nation against anti-democratic enemies regenerated Americans' civic faith. Their nation's social, political, and economic institutions, many now affirmed, offered the fullest and freest way of life on earth. Popular entertainment, to give an example, unabashedly celebrated the American dream in these years, with *Oklahoma!* and *Our Town* evoking the same nostalgic reaffirmation of traditional values that inspired Norman Rockwell's magazine art. While Kate Smith made a hit of Irving Berlin's "God Bless America," the black bass Paul Robeson, though a committed socialist, performed the "Ballad for Americans" with gusto.[22]

Religious faith appeared to many to be one of the values most worth remembering and conserving. The critical, condescending tone of much

20. J. Elwin Wright, "Observations of the President," *New England Fellowship Monthly* 43 (April 1945): 8–9.

21. Perrett, *Days of Sadness,* 443.

22. Ibid., 196–99, 325–42, 350–56, 407–9, 441–43 (quote on p. 443); Alexander, *Nationalism in American Thought,* 190–201. Richard Pells, *Radical Visions and American Dreams: Culture and Social Thought in the Depression Years* (New York: Harper and Row, 1973), 116–50, 358–64. Alan Nevins, "How We Felt about the War," in *While You Were Gone: A Report of Wartime Life in the United States,* ed. Jack Goodman (New York: Simon and Schuster, 1946), 3–27; Philip Gleason, "Americans All: World War II and the Shaping of American Identity," *American Quarterly* 36 (fall 1984): 342–58.

public discussion of religion since the 1920s was now muted by the renewed respect for faith that emerged at all levels. Many thought the war effort required all the spiritual reserves the country could muster. Religious trends among liberal intellectuals included heightened respect for Reinhold Niebuhr's neo-orthodoxy and the neo-Thomist Catholic philosophy of Jacques Maritain, while many Jewish intellectuals recognized that their identity as a people needed a religious focus.[23] At the same time, piety became more fashionable along the Potomac. A syndicated columnist in Washington, D.C., praised fundamentalist Charles E. Fuller's "Old-Fashioned Revival Hour" for "bringing the new-old story of religion" to war-weary people; and Peter Marshall, the unctuous young Scot who pastored the city's New York Avenue Presbyterian Church, preached to overflowing crowds of government workers, congressmen, and soldiers. On a popular level, church attendance and membership swung sharply upward, and wartime stories of heroic chaplains, foxhole epiphanies, and interfaith fellowship abounded. For three years in a row, a religious novel was the nation's best-seller in fiction, and *Going My Way,* a gently inspiring story which portrayed Bing Crosby and Barry Fitzgerald as priests in New York City, won several Academy Awards in 1944.[24]

One might expect conservative evangelicals to be cheered by evidence of popular religious interest, but several spokesmen thought that the pervading moral climate contradicted these positive signs. As the war progressed, people were singing "Praise the Lord and Pass the Ammunition" and "God Bless America," but one fundamentalist editor thought that "passing the Lord and praising the ammunition" better described the national mood, as Americans boasted that their production of weaponry would win the war.[25] Conservative religious critics noticed that the war, as one historian later put it, "was a spur to both religious sentiment and permissiveness." Church attendance increased but so did alcohol and cigarette consumption. While women's fashions were skimpier, Hollywood grew more brazen, and live entertainment became more vulgar. In the boomtowns created by military camps and war in-

23. Pells, *Radical Visions,* 141–50, 358–61; Alexander, *Nationalism,* 155–56, 223–24, 229; Nathan Glazer, *American Judaism,* rev. ed. (Chicago: University of Chicago Press, 1972), 108.

24. Perrett, *Days of Sadness,* 384–85; Lewis Gannett, "Books," and Bosley Crowther, "The Movies," in *While You Were Gone,* 455, 516; Daniel P. Fuller, *Give the Winds a Mighty Voice: The Story of Charles E. Fuller* (Waco, Tex.: Word, 1972), 140–41; Catherine Marshall, *A Man Called Peter* (New York: McGraw-Hill, 1951).

25. "Passing the Lord and Praising the Ammunition," *The Voice* 21 (April 1943): 14; "'God Bless America,'" *Revelation* 12 (September 1942): 396, 426–28; "V for What-Have-You," ibid. (November 1942): 390, 490; "Prayer and Victory," *MM* 44 (June 1944): 543; William Ward Ayer, "The Pastor Says," *Calvary Pulpit* 3 no. 3 (1941): 2.

dustries, divorce, vice, and violent crime abounded.[26] While evangelist Hyman Appleman thought that it was good and proper for President Roosevelt to call for special days of prayer, he asked how God could answer these petitions when drunkenness and debauchery polluted the land. The nation should remember, Appleman wrote, that "If I regard iniquity in my heart, the Lord will not hear me."[27] Revival, not a rebirth of religiosity, was the need of the day, but the great religious awakening Appleman and other old-fashioned evangelists sought seemed to be eluding them.

The Youth for Christ campaigners, however, found currents which propelled their efforts past those of the older evangelists. The war-time focus on the nation's young people was stimulating a new "youth culture," with its own fashions and celebrities, and a new "young people's evangelism" seemed to be the instinctive response of young preachers and laymen who had grown up with this mass-media-generated popular culture. They emulated the entertainment world's stars and restyled gospel music to the "swing" and "sweet" sounds then popular. And like the radio newsmen, their messages were fast-paced, filled with late-breaking bulletins, and breathlessly urgent. Examples of these kinds of emulation abound, but here are two of the most striking: *Newsweek* labeled Torrey Johnson the "religious counterpart to Frank Sinatra," and Billy Graham patterned his preaching after the clipped cadences of news commentator Walter Winchell. Much more than their predecessors, the youth evangelists strove to be "geared to the times."[28]

Rising teenage crime had become one of the most worrisome domestic effects of the war, and here, too, Youth for Christ responded to its audience. To many, the fundamentalists' thunderings about gambling, smoking, drinking, and divorce sounded tedious and dated, no doubt, but everyone from J. Edgar Hoover of the FBI to the liberal sociologist Robert S. Lynd agreed with the preachers that teenage violence and vice had become national scourges. Crime-prone street gangs emerged in most big cities, and bus and train stations were full of teenage "Victory girls" who offered sexual favors to servicemen in exchange for a good time.[29]

26. Perrett, *Days of Sadness,* 384 (quote), 238–40, 385–87, 394–95.

27. Hyman J. Appleman, "America's First Line of Defense," *MM* 43 (July 1943): 615.

28. "Wanted: A Miracle," 84 (on Sinatra); Marshall Frady, *Billy Graham: A Parable of American Righteousness* (Boston: Little, Brown, 1979), 162; John Pollack, *Billy Graham: The Authorized Biography* (New York: McGraw-Hill, 1965), 85 (on Winchell); Johnson and Cook, *Reaching Youth for Christ,* 21.

29. Perrett, *Days of Sadness,* 238–40, 347–50, 385–87; 394–95; Anna W. M. Wolf and Irene Simonton Black, "What Happened to the Younger People," in *While You Were Gone,* 78–85; Agnes E. Meyer, *Journey through Chaos* (New York: Harcourt, Brace, and Co., 1944), 6, 60–65, 209–13, 250.

Thus, when Youth for Christ leaders claimed they had a spiritual antidote for juvenile delinquency, many community leaders gave them a hearing.[30]

The Youth for Christ movement, then, should be seen as an evangelical response to these three wartime trends: a rising concern about youth and public morality, an increase of popular religiosity, and the renewal of American civic faith. The best way to see the movement's accommodation to popular tastes and widely felt needs is in the context of its rallies. Rally evangelists hammered at the sins of youthful desire while creating an atmosphere of wholesome entertainment, patriotic affirmation, and religious commitment. Their meetings featured carefully orchestrated visions of innocence, heroism, and loyalty to a global cause, all wrapped in a contemporary idiom borrowed from radio variety shows and patriotic musical revues. Cosmetic-free girl ushers greeted the crowds while girl choirs dressed in white serenaded them; and the fast-paced program featured testimonies by decorated war veterans and sports stars, swing-tempo gospel music, and rousing prayer bulletins on the armed forces, Youth for Christ, and the worldwide missionary offensive. Sermons were short, rapid-fire, and laced with examples drawn from current events.[31] Young people "want something that challenges the heroic," Torrey Johnson explained. "They want something that demands sacrifice, . . . that appeals to the highest and holiest . . . that is worth living for and dying for."[32] In response to these perceived yearnings, rally leaders merged celebrations of the war effort and American civic ideals with calls for spiritual commitment. Allied offensives and missionary expansion shared the spotlight.

The evangelists often singled out young people's morals in order to convict them of their need for salvation. Youth for Christ evangelists, who often had sown a few wild oats before their conversions, spoke knowingly about teenage temptations—more, perhaps, as older brothers

30. Billy Graham, "Report of the Vice President at Large," *Minutes of the Second Annual Convention,* Youth for Christ International, Minneapolis, 22–29 July 1946, 38–39, Youth for Christ Records, collection 48, box 13, folder 37, Billy Graham Center Archives; and Torrey M. Johnson to Herbert J. Taylor, 25 October 1945, Herbert John Taylor Papers, collection 20, box 72, folder 2, Billy Graham Center Archives; both reveal that Youth for Christ evangelists actively courted the support of business and community leaders and were encouraged by the receptions they experienced.

31. "Youth for Christ," *Time,* 46–47; "Wanted: A Miracle," 84; "Bobby-Sox Hit Sawdust Trail," *News-Views: The Chicago Daily News Pictorial Section,* 3 February 1945, 2; Woodbury, "Bobby-Soxers Sing Hallelujah," 26–27, 121; McDermott, "Bobby-Soxers Find the Sawdust Trail," 22–23; Mel Larson, "Youth for Christ Movements," *MM* 45 (December 1944): 204–5; Evers, "'Youth for Christ' Meets Pittsburgh," 1171–72; Mead, "Apostle to Youth," 15–17.

32. Mel Larson, *Young Man on Fire: The Story of Torrey Johnson and Youth for Christ* (Chicago: Youth Publications, 1945), 112.

than as threatened parents—and then stressed that evangelical commitment and chastity were the better way. Jack Wyrtzen, leader of the "Word of Life" rally in New York, was particularly expert at stirring youthful consciences. He translated the parable of the prodigal son into contemporary (and perhaps autobiographical) terms; the young runaway "got to hanging about beer joints," began "playing fast and loose with women," and was soon "eating out of the garbage pails of sin." A reporter remarked that the youngsters listened with rapt attention, and that "some had grown a shade pale."[33]

By contrast, the music, the personal testimonies, and the evangelists' invitation to potential converts stressed the joy and satisfaction of commitment to Christ. At one Word of Life meeting, the all-girl choir and soloist George Beverly Shea sang "Jesus Can Satisfy the Heart," "Now I Belong to Jesus," and "What a Friend We Have in Jesus." When Wyrtzen told the audience that by confessing their sins and committing themselves to Christ they would start "the joy bells ringing in their hearts," a reporter said he saw an "almost pathetic eagerness" on many faces.[34] Youth for Christ evangelists unabashedly invited hearers to make a "decision for Christ," and many came forward; at the larger rallies, the penitents sometimes numbered in the hundreds.[35] Among the converts at Youth for Christ meetings were a large number of servicemen. One sailor testified, "I was a sinner, but now, praise the Lord, I am clean, through Christ." Said another young seaman attending the Chicago rally, "Ever since I left the protection of my home, I have felt almost adrift, with no sense of security. I don't want to get caught in the current of vice. I needed something to stabilize me and in my new faith in Christ, I have found it."[36] For many young people who were restless and eager for challenges but also uprooted, morally confused, and perhaps guilt-laden, Youth for Christ's message and invitation was compelling.

The Youth for Christ rallies evoked considerable public comment, and much of it was favorable. Civic leaders repeatedly praised Youth for Christ for its community service. Walter Anderson, chief of police in Charlotte, North Carolina, became the city's rally director, claiming that "Youth for Christ is doing more than anything else I know to stop juvenile delinquency." Governor Arthur B. Lainglie of Washington said that his job would be easier if there were more such youth ministries. Their combination of wholesome fun and religious challenge, he thought, was the best cure for juvenile crime. After Chicagoland Youth for Christ's Sol-

33. Woodbury, "Bobby-Soxers Sing Hallelujah," 121.
34. Ibid., 27, 121.
35. Graham, "Report of the Vice President at Large."
36. Woodbury, "Bobby-Soxers Sing Hallelujah," 27; McDermott, "Bobby-Soxers Find the Sawdust Trail," 23.

dier Field rally in 1945, Governor Dwight H. Green of Illinois wrote Torrey Johnson that "your Saturday night meetings are tremendous forces for alleviating juvenile delinquency," and he urged communities to support them. After viewing a Youth for Christ rally in the Washington state capitol, President Truman was said to have remarked that it was just what America needed.[37]

The rally leaders and publicists basked in this praise. At a time when the nation seemed to be pulling together as never before, they were encouraged that important people thought "born-again Christians" could render a valuable service to America. These young evangelists had wagered their reputations on the chance that their accommodation to worldly tastes and trends would bring positive results, and such praise as they received became ammunition for debate with their more sectarian opponents. Being despised in the world's eyes had been a badge of honor, but for many recruitment and conversion had higher priority. So the desire for evangelistic success was becoming a powerful acculturating force among evangelicals.

Youth for Christ rallies provoked critical responses as well. William Randolph Hearst's endorsement of the movement and its widespread support from conservative Protestant businessmen made some political and religious liberals suspicious. What was Youth for Christ really up to? The Department of Justice was at that time prosecuting a group of right-wing radicals who sympathized with the Nazis, and at least one of them, Gerald Winrod, was a fundamentalist. Many liberals believed that their conservative counterparts constituted a genuine threat to American security, and in this brief "Brown Scare," the liberal left hurled accusations at the fundamentalists in particular.[38] Rumors circulated that Youth for Christ was the stepchild of "fascist-minded" business interests, and gained some credence because of Hearst's favorable publicity. These allegations were quickly dispelled, however, by the liberal Protestant *Christian Century*, even though its editors were not sympathetic to Youth for Christ.[39]

Youth for Christ's spokesmen's answers to these allegations reveal a great deal about how the new evangelicals' strategy and motives were developing. The movement's leaders quickly denied any right-wing political connections or intentions. When a *Time* reporter asked about these charges, Torrey Johnson dissociated the movement from the fundamen-

37. Larson, *Youth for Christ,* 111; Willard M. Aldrich, "Young People Are a Crop," *MM* 45 (November 1944): 138, 140; Larson, *Young Man,* 91; *Minutes of the First Annual Convention,* 16.

38. Leo P. Ribuffo, *The Old Christian Right: The Protestant Far Right from the Depression to the Cold War* (Philadelphia: Temple University Press, 1983), 178–81.

39. "Has Youth for Christ Gone Fascist?" *Christian Century* 62 (14 November 1945): 1243–44.

talists of the far right, claiming that he did not know Winrod and disapproved of the demagogue's views. Johnson denied that Youth for Christ had any political motives. Its only goals, he claimed, were "the spiritual revitalization of America" and "the complete evangelization of the world in our generation."[40] He and other "new evangelicals" were spurred on by a revived sense of evangelicals' moral custodianship for America and new hope for the global expansion of their faith, but they avoided translating these themes into a political agenda. In a national climate which acknowledged religious needs, encouraged moderation and conformity, but punished extremism, Youth for Christ eagerly distanced itself from any tinge of radicalism. As part of the emerging "postfundamentalist" party, the youth evangelists sensed that evangelical politicization would dredge up memories of the fundamentalist political failures of the previous generation. Anxious to keep their welcome to the wider corridors of national life, the young evangelists eagerly assured the public that they would be civil. They had "no political axes to grind," Johnson said,[41] but wanted to contribute in a less controversial way to the well-being of their land. For the time being, the new evangelicals' politics remained latent or very general and spiritualized. A "Christian America" was still their goal, but their means would be revival.

After the war came to a close, Youth for Christ's leaders found yet another convergence between their concerns and those of national public leaders, which reinforced their belief that their revival campaigns were welcome. As the United States' interests clashed increasingly with those of the Soviet Union, concern for the nation's moral integrity took on a new element of urgency. Global intervention and victory had reawakened Americans' ideas of manifest destiny and directed them to see themselves as the free world's leaders in the struggle against totalitarianism. If America was to fulfill this role, her people must be rededicated to freedom and reformed in morals—or so went the postwar jeremiads.[42] The

40. "Anti-Semitism Is Denied," *New York Times,* 16 December 1945, 31; "Lauds Youth for Christ," *New York Times,* 27 October 1945, 44; Leslie Marston, "Youth for Christ or Moloch," *UEA* 4 (15 December 1945): 13, "Young Communists vs. Youth for Christ," *UEA* 5 (15 March 1946): 14, "Youth for Christ," *Time,* 46–47.

41. "Youth for Christ," *Time,* 47.

42. E. Stanley Jones, *The Christ of the American Road* (New York: Abingdon-Cokesbury, 1944); "Between War and Peace," *Catholic Action* 27 (December 1945): 27–28; Charles Clayton Morrison, *Can Protestantism Win America?* (New York: Harper and Brothers, 1948); Willard L. Sperry, *Religion in America* (New York: Macmillan, 1946), 258–63; Robert S. Alley, *So Help Me God: Religion and the Presidency, Wilson to Nixon* (Richmond: John Knox, 1972), 69–81; John F. Wilson, *Public Religion in American Culture* (Philadelphia: Temple University Press, 1979), 15, 50–51, 54–55; Robert T. Handy, *A Christian America: Protestant Hopes and Historical Realities,* 2d ed. (New York: Oxford University Press, 1984), 186–87.

growth of juvenile delinquency and rising divorce rates, many thought, were part of a larger spiritual malady that might make it easier for subversive forces to capture the hearts and minds of the people. Youth for Christ leaders latched onto this spiritual crisis motif. "Let me tell you something," Torrey Johnson cautioned, "America cannot survive another twenty-five years like the last. . . . If we have another lost generation, . . . America is sunk." Did the nation have the moral backbone to keep the world safe and free? Johnson told rally leaders that "we are headed either for a definite turning to God or the greatest calamity ever to strike the human race."[43]

For the first time in a generation, fundamentalists and evangelicals found that political leaders echoed such warnings. As the nation faced new crises as a global power, the old themes of "covenant people" and "redeemer nation" gained new currency. Only a day after he had heard Winston Churchill's grim "Iron Curtain" speech in 1946, President Truman told the Federal Council of Churches convened in Columbus, Ohio, that without "a moral and spiritual awakening" America would be lost. Likewise, General Dwight D. Eisenhower told a meeting of Army chaplains that there was no hope for mankind "except through moral regeneration." Eagerly quoting the politicians' jeremiads, Youth for Christ leaders offered to do their part.[44] But while Truman and Eisenhower were careful to keep their admonitions general enough to encompass all "Judeo-Christian" faiths,[45] evangelicals heard them as calls for revival. Their hopes for a "Christian America" produced by widespread personal repentance and conversion had been restored.

World War II and the postwar tensions heightened the global dimension of evangelicals' sense of mission. Fundamentalist and other evangelical foreign missionary agencies had been growing steadily in the previous decades,[46] but now born-again Christians in the armed forces and at home saw new opportunities and means to proclaim their gospel around the globe. The result was an explosion of new mission agencies and recruits. Filled with what they called a new "world vision," hundreds of missionary volunteers swamped the evangelical colleges and Bible schools, and others contributed to mission funds as never be-

43. Torrey Johnson, "God Is in It!" in *Minutes of the First Annual Convention,* 30.

44. Harry S. Truman, "The Need for Moral Analyzing," *New York Times,* 6 March 1946, 11; [Eisenhower], "Honoring Evangelical Chaplains of the Armed Forces," *New York Times,* 36, 41; Larson, *Youth for Christ,* 26; Hefley, *God Goes to High School,* 13.

45. Patrick Henry, "'And I Don't Care What It Is': The Tradition-History of a Civil Religion Proof-Text," *Journal of the American Academy of Religion* 49 (1981): 35–49; Mark Silk, "Notes on the Judeo-Christian Tradition in America," *American Quarterly* 36 (spring 1984): 65–85.

46. Joel A. Carpenter, "Fundamentalist Institutions and the Rise of Evangelical Protestantism, 1929–1942," *Church History* 49 (March 1980): 72–73.

fore.[47] The Youth for Christ movement poured its energy and personnel into this task. Hundreds of missionary volunteers were secured through the movement's "world vision" rallies, and its young evangelists founded major postwar missionary agencies. The armed forces' pursuit of global victory with all the resources of modern communications and transportation was challenging evangelicals, said youth evangelist Merv Rosell, to dare "greater conquests for Christ."[48] Visions of *Pax Americana* thus provoked a new global triumphalism among American evangelical missionaries.

While these missions' foremost aims were to preach the gospel, make converts, and establish new churches, the specter of communism propelled them as well. After hearing the famed anti-Nazi pastor Martin Niemoeller lament that German youth were a lost generation, Torrey Johnson wired him, offering the services of Youth for Christ. "If Germany goes communistic," Johnson warned, "then you can write France, Italy, Spain, and Portugal off . . . , and you can shove England down the road of socialism." But Christian revival and conversion, he believed, provided a peaceful counterforce to this trend.[49] As Youth for Christ rallies spread through the American occupation forces, the movement's leaders followed with what they called "invasion teams." These evangelists toured Great Britain, Scandinavia, France, The Netherlands, Germany, Greece, and Italy; the Caribbean and South America; and India and China. Meanwhile, General Douglas MacArthur had invited Youth for Christ and other missionaries to Japan to "provide the surest foundation for the firm establishment of democracy."[50] Such invitations made fundamentalists and evangelicals feel more welcome than ever before in their memory to become responsible, respectable contributors to the American mission.

Thus, as World War II and the early postwar experience seemed to

47. R. Arthur Mathews, *Towers Pointing Upward* (Columbia, S.C.: Columbia Bible College, 1973), 143–45; "Philadelphia Bible Institute Alumni Activities, Class of 1942 to 1953, Inclusive," paper in Alumni Office files, Philadelphia College of the Bible; Hefley, *God Goes to High School,* 65–68; Ralph D. Winter, *The Twenty-Five Unbelievable Years, 1945 to 1969* (South Pasadena, Calif.: Institute of Church Growth, 1970), 47–51.

48. Merv Rosell, "God's Global 'Go!'" *Winona Echoes* 51 (1945): 260–65; Torrey Johnson, "Almighty Challenge," ibid., 157–65; F. D. Whitesell, "God's Purposes in World War No. 2," *The Voice* 23 (September 1944): 8; Robert H. Glover, "Postwar Missions," *King's Business* 36 (March 1945): 84, 117; Glover, "What Should Be Our Postwar Evangelical Missionary Strategy?" *UEA* 4 (15 September 1945): 6, 19; Roy Ostreicher, "Post War Plans," *Brown Gold* 3 (June 1945): 4; Johnson, "Pressing on in Youth for Christ," 6–7.

49. Torrey Johnson, "Accepting the Challenge!" *Minutes of the First Annual Convention,* 18.

50. Larson, *Youth for Christ,* 22–23, 79–81, 91–94; Hefley, *God Goes to High School,* 13 (quote), 3–40.

offer the nation another chance to fulfill its manifest destiny at home and abroad, a new generation of fundamentalist and evangelical leaders reshaped their outlook according to these trends and looked forward to a fresh start. Perhaps "revival in our time" was on its way. Perhaps the mythic Christian past could be restored if enough people came to Christ. Eagerly they quoted 2 Chronicles 7:14 and applied it to the American situation: "If my people, which are called by my name, shall humble themselves, and pray, and seek my face, and turn from their wicked ways; then will I hear from heaven, and will forgive their sin, and will heal their land."[51]

What the Youth for Christ movement started, the new evangelical coalition carried forward. While evangelicals were still a long way from the centers of intellectual and political power in the 1950s and early 1960s, and they enjoyed the notice of news media only occasionally, their status was changing. Billy Graham emerged as evangelist to the nation, and then counsellor to presidents. Civic "leadership prayer breakfasts," led by evangelicals, sprang up in Washington, D.C., and across the country. A small group of evangelical theologians with doctorates from the nation's finest universities invigorated the coalition's intellectual life and dreamed of launching a new Christian university. With Graham's help, they launched instead a new periodical in 1956, *Christianity Today,* which became their voice in national public discourse. Clearly, the new evangelicals were enjoying a honeymoon with American culture.[52]

At a time when religious faith was generally considered "a good thing" and popular religious interest was high, the new evangelicals' call for revival in America did not seem very threatening. Indeed, the extent to which evangelical Christians' desire to restore "Christian America" clashed with the pluralistic reality of American public life had been masked. Billy Graham, the movement's leading prophet, pointedly in-

51. J. Elwin Wright, "Post-War Opportunity Requires Action Now," *New England Fellowship Monthly* 43 (March 1945): 8–9; James DeForest Murch, "The Church's Post-War Program," *UEA* 4 (1 September 1945): 12; "The Trouble Lies Deep," *UEA* 4 (15 September 1945): 12–13; Billy Graham, "We Need Revival" (sermon preached in 1949 Los Angeles meetings), in *Revival in Our Time: The Story of the Billy Graham Evangelistic Campaigns* (Wheaton, Ill.: Van Kampen, 1950), 69–80; Harold John Ockenga, "Is America's Revival Breaking?" *Evangelical Beacon,* 18 July 1950, 5–6.

52. Rudolph L. Nelson, "Fundamentalism at Harvard: The Case of Edward John Carnell," *Quarterly Review* 2 (summer 1982): 79–98; Edwin H. Rian, "The Plight of Protestantism in Education," *MM* 46 (October 1945): 76, 110–11; "Planning Curriculum for New University," *UEA* 5 (1 May 1946): 9; Wilbur M. Smith, *Before I Forget* (Chicago: Moody, 1971), 175–82, 283–95; Joel Carpenter, "The Moody Monthly," in *The Conservative Press in America,* ed. William Longton and Ronald Lora (Westport, Conn.: Greenwood Press, forthcoming). See Donald G. Bloesch, *The Evangelical Renaissance* (Grand Rapids: Eerdmans, 1973).

sisted that Americans had to be spiritually transformed if the nation was to be saved. And turning to God, in Graham's message, meant becoming a "born-again Christian." The apostle Paul warned that this message is an offense to the Jew and an absurdity to the Gentile, but Graham and his generation of evangelical leaders were often able to finesse the issue by sheer goodwill and their skillful evocation of the nation's evangelical legacy. While some pundits considered Graham's message scandalous, most found it eccentric, perhaps, but pretty much in line with the other, more generic calls for "moral and spiritual awakening" in a time of crisis. Martin Marty observed in 1959 that much as Graham tried to call the nation to repentance, his hearers seemed more charmed than convicted. This admirable, clean-cut young man seemed to many to embody American virtue, and his utterances comported well with the conventions of American folk piety.[53] And as Graham went, so went the movement. Sociologist James Hunter suggests that evangelicals' yearning for acceptance and respect has prompted many to adopt "no offense, but I'm an evangelical" as their public posture. Thus the Youth for Christ movement shows, in embryo, the new evangelicals' ability to mirror their audience's concerns, market their message with polish and civility, and affirm the "American Way of Life." These traits allowed them to avoid confrontation with American pluralism and secularity and to regain a place for themselves in national public life. That "place" has been a troubled one, however, for a variety of reasons, all derived from the character of the implicit bargains evangelicals made to gain it.

First, the new evangelicals' place on the public rostrum lacked substance. It seemed to be based not so much on a recognition that their distinctive religious perspective deserved a hearing, but because they were both effective communicators of the myth of American righteousness and die-hard supporters of a conservative strain of civic piety. Evangelicals' more particular message seemed to be selectively tuned out, or blandly tolerated, while presidential prayer breakfasts and "Honor America" rallies, rather, were the movement's admission tickets to the public arena.[54]

53. This paragraph owes much to the evaluation of Billy Graham in Martin Marty's *New Shape of American Religion* (New York: Harper and Brothers, 1959), 21–27. A. Roy Echardt, *The Surge of Piety in America: An Appraisal* (New York: Association Press, 1958), 42–67, notes Graham's basic affinity to the common concerns of American popular religion. See also Frady, *Billy Graham,* for a windy yet often insightful treatment of these themes. Hatch, "Evangelicalism as a Democratic Movement," reveals these character traits in the larger movement.

54. Richard V. Pierard, *The Unequal Yoke: Evangelical Christianity and Political Conservatism* (Philadelphia: Lippincott, 1970); Robert D. Linder and Richard V. Pierard, *Twilight of the Saints: Biblical Christianity and Civil Religion in America* (Downers Grove, Ill.: InterVarsity, 1978), 97–111, 140–43. Robert Booth Fowler, *A New Engagement: Evangelical Political Thought, 1966–1976* (Grand Rapids: Eerdmans, 1982), per-

For their part, the new evangelicals desired respect and admiration, so they blunted some of the jagged edges of their distinctiveness. These reformers of fundamentalism recovered a measure of civic responsibility, but at the same time they had become domesticated.[55] Fundamentalism's hairy-fisted, Bible-thumping condemnations of America's sins sounded impolitely shrill to the new evangelicals. Like the cosmopolitan German Jews in late nineteenth-century America, neo-evangelicals were often embarrassed by the tribalism of their less civil kinsmen.[56] Knowing that their own welcome was tenuous, they feared that the antics of the unreconstructed fundamentalists put their enterprise in jeopardy.

Evangelicals' role as civic chaplains made their place in public life particularly vulnerable to the powerful opposition to public piety that has mounted since the 1960s. A prominent cohort of government officials, political reform activists, jurists, journalists, and educators has generated this trend. This group's background has been the highly secular "culture of critical discourse" of the universities, the mass media, and the research-based industries. Their public service ideals are drawn more from a secular regard for humanity than traditional religious values. In the past two decades, this cultural group has succeeded remarkably in redirecting American public policy toward their position, which insists that religious conviction and expression have no legitimate public place. Dubbed the "New Class" by sociologists and "secular humanists" by conservative evangelicals, this group, evangelicals are convinced, threatens to privatize religion and smash evangelical hopes of restoring American righteousness.[57] By the late 1970s, with the rules of public civility seeming to tilt increasingly in favor of the secularists, conservative evangelicals seemed handcuffed in their attempts to reassert the legitimacy of their place.

---

ceptively surveys the conservative political loyalties of the "evangelical mainstream" in chapters 2 through 4.

55. James Davison Hunter, *American Evangelicalism: Conservative Religion and the Quandary of Modernity* (New Brunswick, N.J.: Rutgers University Press, 1983), chap. 6, "Accommodation: The Domestication of Belief."

56. Neo-evangelicals register their exasperation with fundamentalism in Harold J. Ockenga, "Can Fundamentalism Win America?" *Christian Life and Times* 2 (June 1947): 13–15; Edward John Carnell, "Post-Fundamentalist Faith," *Christian Century* 76 (26 August 1959): 971; Carnell, *The Case for Orthodox Theology* (Philadelphia: Westminster, 1959), 113–25; Ockenga, "Resurgent Evangelical Leadership," *Christianity Today* 4 (10 October 1960): 11–15; Harold Lindsell, "Who Are the Evangelicals?" *Christianity Today* 9 (18 June 1967): 3–6. On Jewish internal tensions, see John Higham, *Send These to Me: Jews and Other Immigrants in Urban America* (New York: Atheneum, 1975), 138–73.

57. Hunter, *American Evangelicalism,* 107–19; he cites a variety of sociological studies of the New Class phenomenon, and also evangelical and fundamentalist polemics against secular humanism.

The neo-evangelicals' country cousins, however, have come charging into the public arena. Militant fundamentalists and a host of Pentecostal allies, newly politicized, have emerged out of the cultural hinterlands and have refused to go away. Just at the time when some evangelical leaders, in the wake of Vietnam and Watergate, began to abandon large parts of the "Christian America" myth and to insist that God's covenants are both more individual and more transnational,[58] politicized fundamentalists reasserted the older vision, without the polite veneer the neo-evangelicals had carefully devised.[59]

Yet even the fundamentalists want to be liked. Jerry Falwell, Tim LaHaye, and others have tried to calm the intense fear and hatred they have encountered with assurances that they are not antidemocratic theocrats. They want, states LaHaye's platform, to "restore traditional moral and spiritual values" to American life and to reinforce, not undermine, religious freedom and democracy. They want to throw out the new public rules that seem to exclude religious values, but, granted those changes, they promise to behave.[60] Recently, in a very candid conversation, Tim LaHaye was asked what he would do if he could have his way completely in American politics. With scarcely a pause, he said he would be satisfied with the full incorporation of President Reagan's platform.[61] So much for the alarmist nonsense about a fundamentalist-inspired Brown Shirt movement. And so much for the new fundamentalism's ability to sustain any prophetic independence. Perhaps, as Garrison Keillor recently suggested, fundamentalists' "mission in this country" is to "shake us up ... with a very strong and very clear message."[62] But, having done some shaking, they are apparently very eager to beg pardon.

And so the assimilation process which domesticated much of sectarian

58. Mark A. Noll, Nathan O. Hatch, and George M. Marsden, *The Search for Christian America* (Westchester, Ill.: Crossway, 1983); John Warwick Montgomery, *The Shaping of America* (Minneapolis: Bethany Fellowship, 1976); Richard V. Pierard, "From Evangelical Exclusiveness to Ecumenical Openness: Billy Graham and Sociopolitical Issues," *Journal of Ecumenical Studies* 20 (summer 1983): 425–46.

59. Jerry Falwell, ed., *Listen America!* (New York: Doubleday, 1980); Peter Marshall and David Manuel, *The Light and the Glory* (Old Tappan, N.J.: Revell, 1977): John W. Whitehead, *The Second American Revolution* (Elgin, Ill.: David C. Cook, 1982); Francis Schaeffer, *A Christian Manifesto* (Westchester, Ill.: Crossway, 1981).

60. Richard John Neuhaus, "What Fundamentalists Want," *Commentary* 79 (May 1985): 41–46 (quote), informs this and the previous paragraph; see also Richard Lovelace, "Future Shock and Christian Hope," *Christianity Today* 27 (5 August 1983): 16; and "An Interview with the Lone Ranger of American Fundamentalism," *Christianity Today* 25 (4 September 1981): 22–23.

61. Tim LaHaye, in a discussion at the Center on Religion and Society's consultation, "The Bible, Politics, and Democracy," Billy Graham Center, Wheaton College (Ill.), 8 November 1985, audio tape.

62. "Door Interview: Garrison Keillor," *Wittenburg Door* 84 (April–May 1985): 18.

evangelicalism in the 1940s is at work again. The terms are not quite the same; notably, the new fundamentalism is adamantly political, and the occasion is not a friendly invitation to participate but the forcible intrusion of resentful, uninvited guests. Yet the parallels are striking: an internally vigorous, culturally responsive, and powerfully communicative evangelical movement has again found the opportunity to emerge from political, cultural, and religious obscurity. As a variety of cultural critics have asserted, the nation's cultural and spiritual landscape has buckled,[63] and, as in the days of World War II and the cold war, many Americans have been prompted to receive older verities. Once again, evangelical Christianity, with fulsome grass-roots support, has been a powerful medium for this resurgence, and again it appears that evangelicals—in this case the new fundamentalists—are being absorbed and tamed.

This essay has three major points to contribute, then, to the larger discussion about the role religion has played in the life of the United States. First, the Youth for Christ episode supports those who argue against the notion that modernization produces irresistible and progressive secularization. Religious faith and practice, as Theodore Caplow's Middletown III project has recently underscored, is a vital component of contemporary American culture.[64] Despite the powerful influence of secular institutions and ideologies, these deeply inscribed and vigorously maintained religious interpretations of American common life have repeatedly come welling up to rebaptize the nation's civic hopes and values.

Second, Youth for Christ and the postwar evangelical resurgence point to the accommodationist character of evangelicalism in the United States. To be sure, there is a genuine and paradoxical tension in these movements between a sojourner's alienation from the present age and what Grant Wacker calls a "custodial ideal," a proprietary responsibility for American national morality.[65] Evangelicals still feel that "this world is

63. On the decline of moral and political coherence, see Neuhaus, *Naked Public Square;* Christopher Lasch, "The Cultural Civil War and the Crisis of Faith," *Katallagete* 8 (summer 1982): 12–18; Lasch, *The Culture of Narcissism: American Life in an Age of Diminishing Expectations* (New York: W. W. Norton, 1978); Robert A. Nisbet, *The Twilight of Authority* (New York: Oxford, 1975); Daniel Yankelovich, *New Rules: Searching for Self-Fulfillment in a World Turned Upside Down* (New York: Random House, 1981); and Robert N. Bellah, Richard Madsen, William M. Sullivan, Ann Swidler, and Steven M. Upton, *Habits of the Heart; Individualism and Commitment in American Life* (Berkeley: University of California Press, 1985).

64. Theodore Caplow, Howard M. Bahr, and Bruce A. Chadwick, *All Faithful People: Change and Continuity in Middletown's Religion* (Minneapolis: University of Minnesota Press, 1983).

65. Grant Wacker, "Uneasy in Zion: Evangelicalism in Postmodern Society," in *Evangelicalism and Modern America,* 22–24. George Marsden, "Preachers of Paradox: The Religious New Right in Historical Perspective," in *Religion and America: Spiritual Life in a*

not my home," but they also identify strongly with the American nation. Their convictions and American republican ideology have been too closely joined for them to easily sever the relationship. And being thus drawn to public engagement, evangelicals want to be liked, to be accepted. Evangelicals' very adaptability, then, has limited the range of their ministry. Successful as evangelists and as chaplains to the nation's civic soul, they have much more trouble sustaining a prophetic role.

And finally, this story illumines the cultural hegemony of the American civic faith. In many respects, the United States is a radically pluralistic nation, composed of widely divergent peoples and regions. Common rootedness in the soil and common racial memory have slight power to bind its people as a body public. Rather, somewhat like some African peoples—and not unlike evangelicalism—the Americans are an assimilative tribe.[66] Lacking the cohesion of a single ethnic source, they manufacture their identity and ideology out of the mythic past. Consequently, any attempt to "re-vision" America faces serious constraints. American public life encourages a facile tolerance, but tends to absorb, approve, and domesticate traditions and movements on previously established, safe cultural terms. Youth for Christ and the new evangelicalism's emergence into the public square shows this powerful homogenizing tendency at work. Evangelical Christianity has been and still seeks to be a resource for the American moral imagination, but the scope of its vision and those of other religious traditions is narrowed by the limits of that imagination. Things could be worse, though. One alternative, all too common among nations that lack a focal point for public discourse, is religious civil war.

Secular Age, ed. Mary Douglas and Steven Tipton (Boston: Beacon, 1983), 150–68, explains this tension.

66. John Higham, "Hanging Together: Divergent Unities in American History," *Journal of American History* 61 (June 1974): 7–28; John Ngusha Orkar, "Patterns of Assimilation of the Tiv," paper presented to the Centre for African Studies, Dalhousie University, 1983, cited by Marsden, "Evangelicals, History, and Modernity," in *Evangelicalism and Modern America,* 97. Marsden ascribes this characteristic to American evangelicals.

16

Uneasy in Zion: Evangelicals in Postmodern Society

Grant Wacker

From Grant Wacker, "Uneasy in Zion: Evangelicals in Postmodern Society," in *Evangelicalism and Modern America* (Grand Rapids, Eerdmans, 1984), 17–28. Used by permission.

One of the fascinating questions facing students of American religion is why Protestant evangelicalism has flourished so remarkably since World War II and especially since the mid-1960s. Evangelicals themselves often say that the movement has prospered because people are fed up with secular humanism, which has led to, among other things, drugs in the public schools, sex on television, liberalism in the government, and weakness in foreign affairs. Historians and social scientists phrase it differently, but frequently they too end up saying pretty much the same—namely, that the evangelical surge has been a direct reaction to a long series of provocations in the external culture. And when we think about the developments of the last quarter century, it is difficult to doubt that there is a measure of truth in this interpretation.[1]

1. See, e.g., Jerry Falwell et al., eds. *The Fundamentalist Phenomenon: The Resurgence of Conservative Christianity* (Garden City, N.Y.: Doubleday, 1981), 12–26; James M. Wall, "What Future for the New Right?" *Christian Century*, 25 November 1981, 1219; Theodore Roszak, "In Search of the Miraculous," *Harper's* (January 1981): 54–62; David Martin, "Revived Dogma and New Cults," *Daedalus* 111 (1982): 54; and Dean M. Kelley, *Why Conservative Churches Are Growing: A Study in Sociology of Religion* (New

Even so, this stimulus-response model of explanation, which poses real or perceived secularism as the efficient cause of the evangelical revival, is inadequate for several reasons. In the first place, it does not account for the apparent vitality of what might be called (albeit very loosely) the "Evangelical Left." Although all evangelicals would dissociate themselves from "secular humanism"—if that term is defined as the ideology of human autonomy—many cherish the benefits of secularization, or what Richard Lovelace has called "Common Grace humanistic values," such as "freedom of inquiry, the open market of ideas, cultural and artistic liberty, and humane technologies." Further, many evangelicals approve of, or at least are not dismayed by, the trajectory of American politics during the last half century. They understand that an increasingly integrated political system—represented by the evolution from the New Deal to the Great Society—is necessary in order for them to enjoy the benefits of modern technology and democratic process. It is extremely difficult to know how large the evangelical left is, or even if it is growing or shrinking. Nonetheless, there are quantitative and impressionistic reasons to believe that most black and perhaps a fourth of white evangelicals fall into this category.[2]

A second and more serious flaw in the stimulus-response model is that it does not very well explain the expansion of the evangelical right, where, presumably, most of the numerical growth of recent years has been concentrated. The main difficulty is that the correlations between cause and effect are not very persuasive. This is a complicated problem, the kind that sociologists love to tinker with. Here it must suffice to say that the evangelical surge started in the early 1950s, long before external provocations like the death-of-God theology or the Vietnam debacle had started to rattle evangelical nerves, and the surge has continued without abatement ever since. Or to put it a bit differently, neither wars nor recessions nor Watergate nor Reaganomics nor fluctuations of the hemline

---

York: Harper and Row, 1972), 99, 110–11. Like many observers, Kelley assumes but does not prove that a demonstrable decline in the numerical strength of the mainline denominations is causally linked with a concurrent increase in the numerical strength of the conservative denominations.

2. Richard Lovelace, *Renewal* 2 (October 1982): 7–8. For impressionistic yet informed descriptions of the evangelical left, see Timothy L. Smith, "Protestants Falwell Does Not Impress," *New York Times,* 22 October 1980, op ed page, and Richard Quebedeaux, *The Young Evangelicals: Revolution in Orthodoxy* (New York: Harper and Row, 1974), 99–135. For a quantitative profile, see James Davison Hunter, "The New Class and the Young Evangelicals," *Review of Religious Research* 22 (1980): 160–63; Hunter, *American Evangelicalism: Conservative Religion and the Quandary of Modernity* (New Brunswick: Rutgers University Press, 1983), 56, 107–12, 118; Seymour Martin Lipset and Earl Raab, "The Election and the Evangelicals," *Commentary* (March 1981): 25–26.

have had discernible impact on the rate of evangelical expansion.[3] Moreover, there is no hint in the scanty poll data that is available that a significant number of persons have become evangelicals because they were appalled by the way things were going in the nonevangelical world.[4] And no one should really be surprised. The general history of movements of collective behavior, religious and otherwise, suggests that they are generated not by discrete provocations in the cultural environment but by fundamental realignments in the social system that create new needs and stir new aspirations.[5]

The magnitude and durability of the postwar evangelical movement seems to require, in short, a more systematic interpretation of its causes.

3. The complexity of the factors involved in church growth and decline is described in Dean R. Hoge, "A Test of Theories of Denominational Growth and Decline," in *Understanding Church Growth and Decline: 1950–1978,* ed. Hoge and David A. Roozen (New York: Pilgrim, 1979), 182–97. For the steady growth since the early 1950s of most major evangelical groups (as well as nonevangelical conservatives like Mormons), see Kelley, *Conservative Churches,* 24, 27–31, and Jackson W. Carroll et al., *Religion in America: 1950 to the Present* (San Francisco: Harper and Row, 1979), 14–15, 23. The growth of some conservative groups has tapered off since 1980, but overall there is little change. In 1976 Gallup indicated 18% of the adult population was evangelical; in 1980, 19%; in 1982, 17%. Princeton Religious Research Center, *Religion in America 1982: The Gallup Report* (Reports #201–202, June–July 1982), 31.

4. Luther P. Gerlach and Virginia H. Hine, *People, Power, Change: Movements of Social Transformation* (Indianapolis: Bobbs-Merrill, 1970), 84–87. C. Kirk Hadaway, "Changing Brands: Denominational Switching and Membership Change," in *Yearbook of the American and Canadian Churches 1980,* ed. Constant H. Jacquet, Jr. (Nashville: Abingdon, 1980), 264–67. Reginald W. Bibby and Merlin B. Brinkerhoff, "The Circulation of the Saints: A Study of People Who Join Conservative Churches," *Journal for the Scientific Study of Religion* 12 (1973): 273–83. Reginald W. Bibby, "Why Conservative Churches *Really* Are Growing: Kelley Revisited," *Journal for the Scientific Study of Religion* 17 (1978): 132–33; Wade Clark Roof and Christopher Kirk Hadaway, "Denominational Switching in the Seventies: Going Beyond Stark and Glock," *Journal for the Scientific Study of Religion* 18 (1979): 363–79. The Gerlach/Hine study shows that conversions result principally from positive pre-existing personal relationships. The other studies deal with switching from liberal to conservative groups (including but not restricted to evangelical groups). The Bibby and Bibby/Brinkerhoff studies minimize the significance of liberal to conservative switching as a factor in the latter's growth. The Hadaway and Roof/Hadaway studies do see liberal to conservative switching as a significant factor in the growth of some very conservative bodies, but they do not show that this accounts for more than a small fraction of the overall expansion of the evangelical movement. Moreover, the evidence offered by Roof/Hadaway (374, Table 4, "New Morality") actually suggests that liberal to conservative switchers do not measurably differ from mainline Protestants on key questions like abortion and legalization of marijuana.

5. Neil Smelser, *Theory of Collective Behavior* (New York: Free Press, 1962); John Wilson, *Introduction to Social Movements* (New York: Basic Books, 1973), esp. chaps. 1–3; Kenelm Burridge, *New Heaven, New Earth: A Study of Millenarian Activities* (New York: Schocken, 1969).

By this I simply mean that in order to understand why the movement has swelled in the last quarter century, we need to look beyond the immediate and transitory swings of contemporary culture and seek, instead, to set evangelicalism in the longer and broader contexts of American history and society. We need to see, in other words, how the movement fits into larger historical and structural dimensions of the American experience.

Fortunately we have not been left high and dry, as Perry Miller once said, in "a parched and barren land crying for deliverance from the hold of ideas that have served their purpose and died." Recently several historians have in fact fashioned impressively systematic interpretations of the sources of the postwar evangelical surge. In one way or another most have claimed that the distinctive structure of postmodern or postindustrial society, which arrived in the West in the 1920s and 1930s, and became an overwhelming force in American life after World War II, brought with it distinctive cultural forms, and the evangelical revival has been one of them. This is to say, in other words, that the roots of the revival must be sought in fundamental social transformations such as mass communications, high technology, and the triumph everywhere in American life of "impersonal structure[s] of expertise."[6]

With these developments in mind, some analysts of contemporary evangelicalism have taken an essentially reductionist approach, arguing that the evangelical upswing has been a negative reaction, not just to recent liberalizing trends in government and secularizing trends in the culture, but to the whole thrust of postmodern society itself. They have assumed, in short, that the revival has been an artifact, or epiphenomenon, of modern society, and that the fate of the former has been and will con-

6. Perry Miller, *The New England Mind: From Colony to Province* (Boston: Beacon, 1961 [1953]), 484–85; Robert H. Wiebe, "Modernizing the Republic, 1920 to the Present," in *The Great Republic: A History of the American People,* 2 vols., ed. Bernard Bailyn et al. (Lexington, Mass.: D.C. Heath, 1981 [1977]), 2:930. For the social and cultural consequences of modernization, especially in the United States since World War II, see Wiebe, "Modernizing the Republic," 857–77; Richard D. Brown, *Modernization: The Transformation of American Life, 1600–1865* (New York: Hill and Wang, 1976), chaps. 1, 8. For a lucid discussion of the way that modernization—commonly defined as "technologically inducted economic growth"—has altered and structured modern consciousness, see Peter L. Berger et al., *The Homeless Mind: Modernization and Consciousness* (New York: Random House, 1973), esp. chaps. 1–4. Berger's notions have been imaginatively used to interpret contemporary evangelicals by Hunter, *American Evangelicalism,* and nonevangelicals by James G. Moseley, *A Cultural History of Religion in America* (Westport, Conn.: Greenwood, 1981), chap. 8. See also Daniel Bell, *The Cultural Contradictions of Capitalism* (New York: Basic Books, 1976), 3–84, 146–71. The idea that social modernization is the vehicle of cultural modernity has not gone uncriticized, to say the least. See, for example, Mary Douglas, "The Effects of Modernization on Religious Change," *Daedalus* 111 (1982): 1–20.

tinue to be determined by the direction of the latter. Other analysts, on the other hand, have taken a more positive functionalist approach, arguing that the evangelical upswing has been an integral part of modernization, neither separable from nor reducible to the larger process. Both of these approaches have been construed and applied in various ways, but here it will suffice to look briefly at the work of two historians whose thinking illustrates the strengths and, I believe, the pitfalls of each approach.[7]

Perhaps the most distinguished representative of the view that the evangelical renaissance is essentially an artifact of postindustrial modernization is William G. McLoughlin. In his 1978 study *Revivals, Awakenings, and Reform,* which is, in a way, a distillation of several books and many years of research in evangelical history, McLoughlin distinguishes between evangelical revivals and cultural awakenings. In the eighteenth and nineteenth centuries, he argues, these were pretty much the same. In the early years of the twentieth century, however—and again and more clearly since World War II—evangelical revivals have been by-products or "effluvia" of cultural awakenings that followed fundamental transformations of the social system.[8]

In order to see why, in McLoughlin's estimation, this has been the case, we must first understand how he (and many students of religious history) sees the underlying social process. Drawing upon the work of anthropologist Clifford Geertz, McLoughlin contends that in a healthy society an awakening takes place whenever the society's ethos—its behavior, values, and attitudes—wobbles out of synchronization with its world view—the principles that ultimately undergird and legitimate the society's ethos. An awakening, then, is a long transformation, often lasting a

7. For a general discussion of the relation of phenomenological, reductionist, and functionalist models to the study of religion, see John H. Schütz, "Introduction," in Gerd Theissen, *The Social Setting of Pauline Christianity: Essays on Corinth,* ed. and trans. John H. Schütz (Philadelphia: Fortress, 1982), 15–20. For a general discussion of systemic analysis in history, and mechanistic (reductionist) and organic (functionalist) models therein, see Robert F. Berkhofer, Jr., *A Behavioral Approach to Historical Analysis* (New York: Free Press, 1969), chaps. 8, 9.

8. William G. McLoughlin, *Revivals, Awakenings, and Reform: An Essay on Religion and Social Change in America, 1607–1977* (Chicago: University of Chicago Press, 1978), esp. chaps. 1, 5–6. Quotation in next paragraph is on 10. For earlier formulations of the argument see McLoughlin, "Revivalism," in Edwin S. Gaustad, ed., *The Rise of Adventism: Religion and Society in Mid-Nineteenth Century America* (New York: Harper and Row, 1974), 119–53, and "Is There a Third Force in Christendom?" in *Religion in America,* eds. McLoughlin and Robert N. Bellah (Boston: Beacon, 1966), 45–72. "Effluvia" is on p. 47. For the most recent formulation of the argument, essentially unchanged, see McLoughlin, "The Illusions and Dangers of the New Christian Right," *Foundations* 25 (1982): 128–43.

generation or more, in which the core myths of a society are redefined or reformulated to legitimate new patterns of behavior. Thus McLoughlin contends that "great awakenings are periods when the cultural system has had to be revitalized in order to overcome jarring disjunctions between norms and experience, old beliefs and new realities, dying patterns and emerging patterns of behavior." Yet how does all this come about? What are the social mechanisms that trigger an awakening?

Guided by a model of cultural revitalization formulated by anthropologist Anthony F. C. Wallace, McLoughlin argues that when the tension between ethos and world view becomes sufficiently severe, individuals, then larger and larger groups, begin to crash through the old habits of thought and establish new legitimations for new patterns of behavior. Others, by contrast, invariably try to alleviate the tension by calling for a revival of traditional legitimations and behavior. This pressure to turn back is intense but futile. Like a nova, it is a flare-up that signals the demise of the old and the beginning of the new. In McLoughlin's view, this is precisely the role that evangelicals played in the 1900 awakening, and it is the role that they have played in the awakening that started to unfold again in the 1960s. They are the custodians of a tradition that was born long ago when the stable values of a predominantly rural society were normative. But in the increasingly pluralistic culture of postindustrial society that tradition is destined to become an anachronism at best, and an impediment to progress at worst.

Evangelicals are not likely to find McLoughlin's interpretation of their recent good fortune congenial, but unquestionably he has done his homework and offered a serious analysis of the way that the movement fits into the larger picture of American history and society. Nonetheless, McLoughlin's reductionist model creaks with problems. In the first place, if the postwar evangelical surge is essentially a backward-looking byproduct of a more fundamental social transformation, it is worth noting that that transformation has been going on for several decades but the evangelical revival shows no signs of sputtering, much less dying out. More significant is the fact, noted at the beginning of this chapter, that a large minority of evangelicals—the evangelical left—are remarkably in tune with the rhythms of social and cultural change. And among those who are not, or who claim that they are not, are many who have exhibited an uncanny aptitude for adapting to modern life. This is one of the reasons why a more flexibly functionalist interpretation of the wellsprings of the evangelical revival merits consideration.

Perhaps the most notable exponent of this approach is Martin E. Marty. In several books and articles Marty has thoroughly argued that contemporary evangelicalism is best understood not as a negative reaction to, but as an integral part of, the modernization process.

> Because Evangelicalism is the characteristic Protestant . . . way of relating to modernity, it has recently experienced a revitalization concurrent with the development of a new stage of modernity. This does not mean that Evangelicalism is epiphenomenal in relation to modernity, or that the modern condition predestines the outcome for passive religious adherents. . . . But there has been a symbiosis between unfolding modernity and developing Evangelicalism.[9]

In Marty's view, the first phase of modernization, the Industrial Revolution of the eighteenth century, was marked above all by structural differentiation. Life was chopped up into state, home, and job. By emphasizing worldly success, free church polity, and the values of domesticity, Protestant evangelicals sensitively registered these and other aspects of the transformation. The second phase, which overtook Western nations in the middle third of the twentieth century, has been marked by uniquely mobile and affluent styles of life and by a new sense of entitlement among large segments of the population. Again, Marty contends, evangelicals have been in the vanguard. Thus he points to their dextrous use of the media, their aptitude for forming cohesive cell groups, their facility for creating firm psychological boundaries, their fondness for born-again celebrities and authoritarian ministers, and, alas, their perennial willingness to confuse Christian faith with the accouterments of a tastefully appointed suburban lifestyle.

While most evangelicals are not likely to find Marty's interpretation much more palatable than McLoughlin's, Marty's is, I think, preferable because it is richer—because it takes seriously the subjective intentions as well as the objective consequences of evangelical faith. Or to put it more plainly, Marty's flexibly functionalist scheme, more than McLoughlin's rigorously reductionist scheme, ascribes causal, instrumental power to evangelical ideas. Marty's work suggests that evangelical religious and theological notions, though outmoded in the mainline seminaries and leading universities, have nonetheless been an indispensable part of the evolution of modern society. Indeed, when we use a model of this sort, other reasons for the movement's growth begin to appear. One thinks, for example, of the way evangelicals in the 1940s and 1950s instinctively

9. Martin E. Marty, "Religion in America Since Mid-century," *Daedalus* 111 (1982): 149–64, and "Forward" and "The Revival of Evangelicalism and Southern Religion," in *Varieties of Southern Evangelicalism,* ed. David Edwin Harrell, Jr. (Macon: Mercer University Press, 1981), ix–xii, 7–22, respectively. Quotation is on p. 9. See also Marty, *The Public Church: Mainline—Evangelical—Catholic* (New York: Crossroad, 1981), 11–12, 81, and *passim;* and Marty, *A Nation of Behavers* (Chicago: University of Chicago Press, 1976), chap. 4, esp. 105.

responded to the distinctive youth culture that emerged in the United States between the world wars.[10]

Even so, any attempt to account for the evangelical renaissance by linking it to the development of modern society, even in a positive and functional way, is complicated by the fact that evangelicalism is relatively localized,[11] while highly modernized societies obviously are not.[12] Evangelicalism, securely tied to its Wesleyan and Edwardsian roots, has always been a largely Anglo-American phenomenon, and the recent surge of evangelical fervor seems to have been a distinctively American phenomenon. I am not suggesting, of course, that the movement has been uniquely American, but its numerical magnitude and cultural influence do appear to have been measurably greater in the United States than in Canada or in the historically Protestant regions of Europe. (Journalistic hoopla notwithstanding, there is little reason to believe that the rise of religious traditionalism in nations like Iran is truly comparable, either religiously or socially.)[13]

Consequently, we need to search for distinguishing forces in the American experience that will explain, or at least help explain, evangelicalism's singular strength in the United States since World War II. While many ingredients might be profitably factored into the analysis, I suggest that two traditions, deeply rooted in the American past, have particularly influenced the relationship between evangelicals and modern society. The first

10. Gilman M. Ostrander, *American Civilization in the First Machine Age: 1890–1940* (New York: Harper and Row, 1970), 1–27, 237–74.

11. Martin, "Revived Dogma and New Cults," 59; John Crothers Pollock et al., *The Connecticut Mutual Life Report on American Values in the '80s: The Impact of Belief* (Hartford, Conn.: Ct. Mutual Life Ins. Co., 1981), 9. More generally, see Robert T. Handy, "Protestant Patterns in Canada and the United States: Similarities and Differences," in *In the Great Tradition: In Honor of Winthrop S. Hudson: Essays on Pluralism, Voluntarism, and Revivalism,* eds. Joseph D. Ban and Paul R. DeKar (Valley Forge: Judson, 1982), 33–52; George M. Marsden, "Fundamentalism as an American Phenomenon: A Comparison with English Evangelicalism," *Church History* 46 (1977): 215–32.

12. Berger, *Homeless Mind,* chaps. 5–6. Laurence Veysey, "The Autonomy of American History Reconsidered," *American Quarterly* 31 (1979): 455–77, esp. 473; John Kenneth Galbraith, *The New Industrial State* (Boston: Houghton Mifflin, 1967), 339; Daniel Bell, *The Coming of Post-Industrial Society: A Venture in Social Forecasting* (New York: Basic Books, 1973), x, 41, 99, 112–14. See also the review of the literature in Richard D. Brown, "Modernization and the Modern Personality in Early America, 1600–1865: A Sketch of a Synthesis," *Journal of Interdisciplinary History* 2 (1971/1972): 201–3.

13. The diversity and complexity of religious traditionalism (or apparent traditionalism) in nations like Iran make comparative generalizations with American evangelicalism virtually useless. See, for example, Edward Said, *Covering Islam: How the Media and the Experts Determine How We See the Rest of the World* (New York: Pantheon, 1981), 53–64, 94, 106; Michael M. J. Fischer, "Islam and the Revolt of the Petit Bourgeoisie," *Daedalus* 111 (1982): 101–25.

is the peculiar structure of church-state relations, and the second is the religious legacy of the American South.

The peculiarity of the American church-state tradition arises from the fact that it embraces two ideals which are, and always have been, essentially adversarial. One is what might be called the custodial ideal. It assumes that society is organic and that civil authorities have a custodial responsibility for the spiritual as well as the physical well-being of the organism. The custodial ideal was articulated with timeless eloquence in John Winthrop's *A Modell of Christian Charity,* which he wrote in 1630 aboard the *Arbella.* While other societies are expected to uphold only the usual ways of justice and mercy, Winthrop observed, we are an exceptional society, in covenant with each other and with God to live by the higher requirements of the gospel. Thus "we [dare not] think that the lord will beare with such faileings at our hands as hee dothe from those among whome wee have lived." The rolling cadences of Winthrop's prose should not obscure the blunt truth that the establishment of one or another form of Protestantism in most of the colonies was the legal articulation of this sense of corporate liability. The founder of Pennsylvania disdained an established church; "penal laws for religion," he wrote, "is a church with a sting in her tail." Nonetheless, Penn insisted that all citizens of the commonwealth were members of the realm of nature and therefore subject to the moral prescriptions of "General and Practical Religion." Even Virginia's Thomas Jefferson assumed the existence of universally normative moral absolutes; what he doubted was the expediency of trying to coerce lip service to these absolutes through legal sanctions. Throughout the nineteenth century, in the wake of disestablishment, the great tradition of the American churches was not unbridled freedom but "the coercion of voluntarism"—to use Winthrop S. Hudson's arresting phrase—the "compulsion to fulfill a distinctive and specific vocation in society," to nurture the common and enduring spiritual values and life of the republic. And even in the mid-twentieth century, the call for a transcendent civil religion or a refurbished religion of the republic has been, I suspect, a contemporary translation of John Winthrop's conviction that in a healthy society the cultivation of private and public virtue is the legitimate concern of government.[14]

14. John Winthrop, *A Modell of Christian Charity,* in *American Christianity,* 2 vols., eds. H. Shelton Smith et al. (New York: Charles Scribner's Sons, 1960), 1:97–102. For Penn, Jefferson, and civil religion, see Winthrop S. Hudson, ed., *Nationalism and Religion in America: Concepts of American Identity and Mission* (New York: Harper and Row, 1970), 138–52. See also Hudson, *The Great Tradition of the American Churches* (New York: Harper and Row, 1953); Edwin S. Gaustad, "The Great Tradition and the Coercion of Voluntarism," in *Great Tradition,* eds. Ban and DeKar, 161–72. The literature describing the custodial tradition is extensive. Good introductions to different dimensions of the

Yet always handcuffed to the custodial ideal has been another tradition, which might be called the plural ideal. This notion assumes that there is a critical difference between public interests and private concerns, and religion, for the most part, is a matter of private concern. The roots of the plural ideal stab just as deeply into the subsoil of American culture. Again, the primitive documents of Massachusetts are instructive. In the *Cambridge Platform* of 1648 the ecclesiastical and civil jurisdictions of the Commonwealth were separated. While it is undeniable that the clergy influenced civil affairs, it is also undeniable that the civil foundations of the colony were set not in Scripture but in the common law which was notoriously susceptible to the ferment of cultural and religious pluralism. The outcome is evident in the Constitution and First Amendment. Whatever the framers "really meant" when they stipulated that "Congress shall make no laws respecting the establishment of religion or prohibiting the free exercise thereof," it is clear that in the twentieth century the Supreme Court has progressively enlarged the proscriptions against government aid to organized religion. From time to time, of course, constitutional judgments have veered in a different direction. But the tendency has been to give nontraditional faiths equal standing with Judaism and Christianity and, concurrently, to make civil support of religion increasingly problematical. Besides these constitutional trends, the plural ideal has been undergirded by social changes such as the Eastern European immigration in the 1890s, the northward migration of American blacks in the 1920s, the democratization of higher education fostered by the G.I. Bill in the 1940s, and by the perennial leaven of nature religions involving magic, astrology, and shamanism. Taken together, these changes have differentiated American life, gradually transforming raw social diversity into a positive ideal of cultural and religious pluralism.[15]

---

tradition include Elwyn A. Smith, "The Voluntary Establishment of Religion," in *The Religion of the Republic,* ed. Smith (Philadelphia: Fortress, 1971), 154–82; Robert D. Linder, "Civil Religion in Historical Perspective: The Reality that Underlies the Concept," *Journal of Church and State* 17 (1975): 399–421; and Mark DeWolfe Howe, *The Garden and the Wilderness: Religion and Government in American Constitutional History* (Chicago: University of Chicago Press, 1965). It is almost needless to add that modern proponents of civil religion would not want to be uncritically linked with the custodial tradition. See, for example, Robert N. Bellah and Phillip E. Hammond, *Varieties of Civil Religion* (San Francisco: Harper and Row, 1980).

15. *Cambridge Platform,* in *American Christianity,* eds. Smith et al., 1:128–39. For the extensive literature on the plural tradition, the best place to start is Elwyn A. Smith, *Religious Liberty in the United States* (Philadelphia: Fortress, 1972), esp. part 3. For the relation between diversity and pluralism, see Martin E. Marty, "Interpreting American Pluralism," in Carroll et al., *Religion in America,* 78–90. More generally, see Edwin Scott Gaustad, *Dissent in American Religion* (Chicago: University of Chicago Press, 1973).

When the Constitution and Ten Amendments became the normative charter of the land in 1791, the custodial ideal was formally subordinated within the plural ideal. Still, both traditions have persisted as integral parts of American civilization. Indeed, the venerability of each is one of the reasons why the current debate between spokesmen like Jerry Falwell on one side and Norman Lear on the other is not readily resolved. Each has a firm foundation in American history, and each has broad support at the grass roots. And this is the critical point. The doubleness of the church-state tradition has prestructured the relationship between evangelicals and modern society, making that relationship inherently adversarial.

The structural nature of the tension between evangelicals and modern society becomes evident when we remember that over the years evangelicals have been the chief spokesmen for the custodial ideal. Their commitment to legal separation of church and state has been genuine, yet, as George Marsden and others have demonstrated, all but the most radically alienated of fundamentalists have embraced the notion that Christians, and especially evangelical Christians, ought to be the moral custodians of the culture. Some aspects of this self-assigned responsibility have been more commendable than others; but that is another matter. Here the important point is that since the early years of the nineteenth century, and more clearly and sharply since the 1920s, evangelicals have been locked in an adversarial relation with the dominant pluralistic tradition.[16]

Let us now return to the question of modernization. We are now able to understand why evangelicals in the United States, in particular, have been so restive and aggressive during the past quarter century. Although many scholars believe that modernization—and especially postindustrial modernization—has spurred secularization, some analysts, such as Talcott Parsons, have argued that modernization has simply forced people to express their religiousness in new and different ways. Whatever the exact nature of the relationship between modernization and secularization, it is clear that modernization has decisively benefited the plural rather than the custodial tradition, and it is not difficult to see why. The differentiation of the public and private spheres of life, the elaboration of occupational specialization, the triumph of technological rationality, and so forth, have forced religion in general—and Protestant evangelicalism in particular—to evacuate one public outpost after another. As a conse-

16. For the link between evangelicalism and the custodial tradition, see George M. Marsden, *Fundamentalism and American Culture: The Shaping of Twentieth Century Evangelicalism, 1870–1925* (New York: Oxford University Press, 1980), esp. chaps. 4 and 15. For the demonstrably adversarial nature of the relationship between the two traditions in contemporary America, see *Connecticut Mutual Life Report,* 86–87, 252.

quence, in Peter Berger's words, "different sectors of social life [have] now come to be governed by widely discrepant meanings and meaning systems."

> Not only [has] it become increasingly difficult for religious traditions . . . to integrate this plurality of social life-worlds . . . but even more basically, the plausibility of religious definitions of reality [has been] threatened . . . within the subjective consciousness of the individual.[17]

This, then, is the heart of my argument: an essentially ahistorical, transcultural structural development—namely, advanced modernization—has collided with and upset the historic balance between two immensely powerful traditions. The result has been that evangelicals, along with Mormons, conservative Catholics, orthodox Jews, and countless others who believe that American society cannot survive unbridled pluralism, have been aroused, like the proverbial sleeping dragon, to protect their place in the sun—and in the process to aggrandize as much enemy territory as possible.[18]

Most evangelicals probably do not have a very clear sense of the way in which the evolution of modern society has collided with and upset the precarious balance their values have long enjoyed in American culture. But the results have been serendipitous, for the modernity crisis has placed them in a surprisingly auspicious situation—the position of a young man or woman on the make who has not made it yet. In all sectors of society they have moved into positions of power, but they are not yet fashionable. They have pretty well learned how to fit into the rest of the culture, but in most places—at least most places outside the South—they are still a bit angular. Borrowing John Murray Cuddihy's terms, evangelicals have become civil enough to enjoy most of the trappings of the good

17. Berger, *Homeless Mind,* 79–80. Although the changes of the last twenty years have not been as radical as many people assume, the balance has unquestionably shifted toward an amplification of personal freedom. Sydney E. Ahlstrom, "The Traumatic Years: American Religion and Culture in the '60s and '70s," *Daedalus* 107 (1978): 13–29; Daniel Yankelovich, *New Rules: Searching for Self-Fulfillment in a World Turned Upside Down* (New York: Random House, 1981). For statistical documentation of growing religious pluralism, see Beth Spring, "The Changing Face of American Religion," *Christianity Today,* 22 October 1982, 64. To say that modernization has spurred pluralism is one thing, but to say that it has spurred secularization is quite another. For a critique of the latter assumption, see Talcott Parsons, "Christianity and Modern Industrial Society," in *Religion, Culture and Society,* ed. Louis Schneider (New York: John Wiley and Sons, 1964), 273–98.

18. Samuel S. Hill and Dennis E. Owen, *The New Religious Political Right* (Nashville: Abingdon, 1982); Wade Clark Roof, "America's Voluntary Establishment: Mainline Religion in Transition," *Daedalus* 111 (1982): 168–69.

life, but they are still uncivil enough to profit—and profit handsomely—from the psychic tension of the struggle.[19]

This advantageously adversarial position includes all or virtually all evangelicals who comprise the evangelical right. It probably includes the majority of evangelicals and evangelical sympathizers who are not particularly self-conscious or literate about economic and political matters, but who find themselves increasingly ill at ease in the Zion of postindustrial society. And to tell the truth, it also undoubtedly includes many within the evangelical left who consider themselves culturally sophisticated and politically liberal, yet who cannot countenance the loss of Jewish-Christian values in the public discourse and in the "reality defining" institutions of the land.[20]

There is, however, another important reason why evangelicals have survived and even won some major beachheads in their contest with modern society. They have been sustained, I think, by traditions deeply rooted in the American South—not the Old South, but the New South that came into existence in the 1880s and 1890s and that haunts the pages of writers like Flannery O'Connor and Erksine Caldwell. To be sure, I am not suggesting that Carl F. H. Henry begins each day by dipping into the works of Robert Lewis Dabney, nor that Confederate bumper stickers are likely to become hot items in the Wheaton College bookstore. Moreover, it is clear that the cultural diaspora of Southern evangelicalism has been facilitated by social changes such as the development of the interstate highway system in the 1950s and the unprecedented movement of folk into and out of the South during and after World War II. Yet measurable social changes help make less measurable

19. John Murray Cuddihy, *No Offense: Civil Religion and Protestant Taste* (New York: Seabury, 1978). For impressionistic yet informed descriptions of the status hungry, upwardly mobile, stable working, or lower middle class position of evangelicals, see Martin E. Marty, *Nation of Behavers,* chap. 4, esp. p. 104; Richard Quebedeaux, *The Worldly Evangelicals* (San Francisco: Harper and Row, 1978); Quebedeaux, *By What Authority: The Rise of Personality Cults in American Christianity* (San Francisco: Harper and Row, 1982), chap. 3. For quantitative data that strongly support this conclusion, see Hunter, *American Evangelicalism,* 46, 53–56, 117. For a sophisticated analysis of structural reasons why the evangelical right—and, by implication, the evangelical movement as a whole—is a potent force in the social system, see Michael Lienesch, "Right-Wing Religion: Christian Conservatism as a Political Movement," *Political Science Quarterly* 97 (1982): 403–25; see also McLoughlin, "Christian Right," 140–41.

20. For the ambivalence of the evangelical left, see Richard Lovelace, "Renewal and the Moral Majority," *Renewal* 1 (September 1981): 5–12. One 1982 poll of evangelical college students indicated that 57% believed that "people should be free to follow lifestyles very different from their own." On the surface, at least, this suggests that more than two-fifths of evangelical college students would *not* allow alternative lifestyles for others. *Pentecostal Evangel,* 13 March 1983, 25.

cultural transformations possible. So the point simply is this: since World War II, and especially since the early 1960s, ordinary evangelicals in the North and West—mainstream evangelicals, they might be called—have been increasingly predisposed to accept perceptual patterns and interpretations of reality long established in the Baptist and Methodist empire of the South.[21]

One indication of the growing coalescence of mainstream and Southern evangelical outlooks is the extent to which the former have accepted the public leadership of persons who have been associated with the evangelicalism of the New South. The most obvious example is, of course, Billy Graham, reared in Charlotte and for many years a resident of tiny Montreat, North Carolina, tucked in the Southern highlands. Although Graham's ministry is global, it is, as William Martin and others have shown, still profoundly Southern in style. Other superstars betray similar connections. A short list would include Jim Bakker, based in Charlotte; Pat Robertson in Virginia Beach; Jerry Falwell in Lynchburg, Virginia; James Robison in Forth Worth; Jimmy Swaggart in New Orleans; Oral Roberts in Tulsa; Bob Jones III in Greenville, South Carolina. Rex Humbard, though situated in Akron, Ohio, was reared and started his ministry in Arkansas. Most of the big-name independent faith healers of the last quarter century—A. A. Allen, William Branham, LeRoy Jenkins—have been, like Oral Roberts, rooted in or especially associated with the South. Among evangelical celebrities (or celebrities lionized by evangelicals) Southerners again predominate: Anita Bryant, Johnny Cash, Marabel Morgan, Tom Landry, Bobby Jones, Jesse Helms, Jeremiah Denton, and at one time, Jimmy Carter.[22] Moreover,

21. For the demographic shifts of the postwar period, and their cultural consequences, see Godfrey Hodgson, *America in Our Time: From World War II to Nixon* (New York: Random House/Vintage Books, 1978 [1976]), 54–64; Winthrop S. Hudson, *Baptists in Transition: Individualism and Christian Responsibility* (Valley Forge: Judson, 1979), 119. For the extraordinary economic and demographic growth of the South since 1940 and especially since 1970, and its impact upon the North and West, see Robert Estall, "The Changing Balance of the Northern and Southern Regions of the United States," *Journal of American Studies* 14 (1980): 365–86; Carl Abbott, *The New Urban America: Growth and Politics in Sunbelt Cities* (Chapel Hill, N.C.: University of North Carolina Press, 1981), 15–20. The assumption, evident in this paragraph, that culture is "the forms of things that people have in mind, their models for perceiving, relating, and otherwise interpreting them" is drawn form Ward H. Goodenough, "Cultural Anthropology and Linguistics," in *Language in Culture and Society: A Reader in Linguistics and Anthropology*, ed. Dell Hymes (New York: Harper and Row, 1964), 36.

22. Harrell, *Southern Evangelicalism,* 1–5. William Martin, "Billy Graham," *Southern Evangelicalism,* 71–88. For a survey of the rapidly expanding literature on Southern religion, and especially Southern evangelicalism, see John B. Boles, "The Discovery of Southern Religious History," in *Interpreting Southern History,* ed. John B. Boles and Evelyn Thomas Nolen (Baton Rouge: Louisiana State University Press, 1987), 510–45.

many of the leaders and celebrities not based in the South are clustered at the other end of the sunbelt. Here one thinks, for example, of Southern California luminaries like Bill Bright, Robert Schuller, Chuck Smith, and Pat Boone.

The prominence of these personalities is only the most obvious manifestation of the cultural diaspora of Southern evangelicalism. Less obvious but more influential is Southern evangelicalism's habitual involvement in "secular" politics—the myth of the spiritual church notwithstanding. From the late nineteenth century to the present, Southern evangelicals have been mired up to their hip boots in every major question of public policy, and their moral scorecard is more complex than most people think. Some fought—and some supported—Jim Crow codes and child labor regulations in the 1890s, alcohol prohibition and textbook censorship in the 1920s, civil rights laws and textile union restrictions in the 1950s, prayer in the schools and the Equal Rights Amendment in the 1970s. The point is, in short, that even in the "Christ-haunted" South, in Flannery O'Connor's marvelous phrase, evangelicals, seeking to be the moral custodians of the culture, have always known how to play political hardball when the prayer meeting let out.[23]

There is, moreover, a deeper dimension to all this. Southern evangelicals' propensity to vote their faith has grown from a distinctly premodern, if not antimodern, determination to fuse the public and the private, the legal and the moral.[24] Jimmy Carter's willingness to share his Southern Baptist faith with foreign heads of state appalled the Washington press corps, but it was perfectly natural for a Southern evangelical. This

23. Wayne Flynt, "One in the Spirit: Many in the Flesh," in *Southern Evangelicalism,* 23–44; John P. McDowell, *The Social Gospel in the South: The Woman's Home Mission Movement in the Methodist Episcopal Church, South, 1886–1939* (Baton Rouge: Louisiana State University Press, 1982); Charles Reagan Wilson, *Baptized in Blood: The Religion of the Lost Cause, 1865–1920* (Athens, Ga.: University of Georgia Press, 1980); John R. Earle et al., *Spindles and Spires: A Re-Study of Religion and Social Change in Gastonia* (Atlanta: John Knox, 1976); Donald G. Mathews and Jane DeHart Mathews, "The Cultural Politics of ERA's Defeat," *OAH Newsletter* (November 1982): 13–15. Robert F. Martin, "Critique of Southern Society and Vision of a New Order: The Fellowship of Southern Churchmen, 1934–1957," *Church History* 52 (1983): 66–80.

24. John Shelton Reed, *The Enduring South: Subcultural Persistence in Mass Society* (Chapel Hill, N.C.: University of North Carolina Press, 1974), 69–72, and *One South: An Ethnic Approach to Regional Culture* (Baton Rouge: Louisiana State University Press, 1982), 49–51, 54–55, 171–73. Conal Furay, *The Grass-Roots Mind in America: The American Sense of Absolutes* (New York: Franklin Watts/New Viewpoints, 1977), 90–92. Samuel S. Hill, "The South's Two Cultures," in *Religion and the Solid South,* ed. Hill (Nashville: Abingdon, 1972), 24–56. Grace Ann Emerson, "Jimmy Carter and Tension in the American Religious Dichotomy" (senior honor thesis, Department of Religion, University of North Carolina at Chapel Hill, 1983).

inclination to fuse (or confuse, depending on one's perspective) the public and private realms has led Southern evangelicals over the years to insist that the cultivation of expertness cannot be divorced from the cultivation of character. The ramifications of this conviction are not minor, for it means, on one hand, that the virtuous amateur is fit to judge the scientific merit of a biology textbook, or the economic merit of Keynesian fiscal theories, or the strategic merit of the SALT II treaty. On the other hand, Southern evangelical leaders, working from precisely these assumptions, have often exhibited a capacity for social realism and ethical growth that is difficult to criticize. One thinks, for example, of Billy Graham's long-standing position on race relations, his matured awareness of the dangers of ill-informed political involvements, and his recent courageous moves to alert evangelicals to the staggering moral implications of nuclear and environmental destruction.

Another characteristic of Southern evangelicalism that has become more visible in mainstream evangelicalism in recent years is the Southern white evangelical notion of history. Throughout the nineteenth century, evangelicals everywhere were prone to identify evangelical destiny with America's destiny. "If you converse with these missionaries of Christian civilization," Alexis de Tocqueville observed 150 years ago, "you will be surprised to . . . meet a politician where you expected to find a priest."[25] But there was a difference between Northern and Southern assumptions. In the North the coalescence of evangelical and American interests was tempered by the universalism of millennialism; in the South, white evangelicals took the opposite turn. There the identification of religion and soil was hardened by the humiliation of defeat. It was chastened by the necessity of extorting from Scripture a warrant for the segregation and subordination of half the population. And it was enriched by common memories, as Wilbur J. Cash said long ago, of the region's extraordinary natural beauty—"extravagant colors . . . proliferating foliage . . . the rich odors of hot earth and pinewood and the perfume of the magnolia in bloom." In a land where, in short, "the past is never dead, it's not even past," as one of Faulkner's characters puts it, critically verifiable history has imperceptibly blurred into a mythical history of sacred origins. And in the land of sacred origins, God's unique favor rested upon this soil, upon this band, upon these heroes. For the typical Southern evangelical,

25. Alexis de Tocqueville, *Democracy in America,* ed. Phillips Bradley, 2 vols. (New York: Random House/Vintage, 1945 [1835]), 1:317; Hudson, ed., *Nationalism and Religion,* chaps. 2 and 3; Robert T. Handy, *A Christian America: Protestant Hopes and Historical Realities* (New York: Oxford University Press, 1971), esp. chaps. 3, 4; Nathan O. Hatch and Mark A. Noll, eds., *The Bible in America: Essays in Cultural History* (New York: Oxford University Press, 1982), 39–78.

the land of cotton became the "last bulwark of Christianity," "the defender of the ark, its people . . . the Chosen People."[26]

The enduring significance of this religious Cult of the Lost Cause is that it bears an uncanny resemblance to the myth of sacred American origins that is heralded every day in the broadcasts of the Electronic Church and in evangelical bookstores across the land in tracts like Francis Schaeffer's *Christian Manifesto.* Scholars who hope to understand how these fictions emerge and what functions they serve may find the historiography of the Lost Cause instructive. Both myths have been tokens of a partly justifiable siege mentality, which is to say that in both instances the threat has been real: Yankee materialism and secular humanism have been palpable facts of life. Yet in both cases the threat has swelled to outlandish proportions, like night shadows on the walls of a child's bedroom. And the result has been a kind of Manichean dualism that has temporarily protected the familiar—this Christian American land, these Christian American schools—from the dangers of an alien world and a perplexing future.[27]

In summary, then, if we hope to understand the relationship between evangelicals and postmodern society, we need to scuttle the assumption that the contemporary revival is a direct reaction to the real or perceived encroachments of secular humanism. Instead, we must try to see how long-range processes have worked. Toward this end I have suggested that in the United States, especially since World War II, vast structural changes common to most Western societies have collided with and upset the historic balance between the custodial and the plural visions of American life. Not so much in reaction to, but as an integral part of this immense process of social and cultural readjustment, evangelicals have been aroused to fight for their accustomed place in the sun. But history works in unpredictable ways: this process seems to have driven evangelicals into an advantageously adversarial relation with the larger society. At the same time, for good or ill, they have been increasingly disposed to draw

26. Wilbur J. Cash, *The Mind of the South* (1941), 46, and William Faulkner, both quoted (the latter without attribution) in Furay, *Grass-Roots Mind,* 89, 94 respectively. "Bulwark," etc. in Reed, *Enduring South,* 57. For the main point of the paragraph, see Wilson, *Baptized in Blood;* Samuel S. Hill, Jr., *The South and the North in American Religion* (Athens, Ga.: University of Georgia Press, 1980), 90–106; C. Vann Woodward, *The Burden of Southern History* (Baton Rouge: Louisiana State University Press, 1960), chap. 8.

27. The recent evangelical formulation of the Christian America myth is described and critiqued in Mark A. Noll et al., *The Search for Christian America* (Westchester, Ill.: Crossway, 1983). See also Hill and Owen, *New Religious Political Right,* 109–13; George M. Marsden, "America's 'Christian' Origins: Puritan New England as a Case Study," in *John Calvin: His Influence in the Western World,* ed. W. Stanford Reid (Grand Rapids: Zondervan, 1982), 241–60, 386–87.

upon the tradition of cultural custodianship preserved in the religious subculture of the American South.

The last point is especially important. Now, more than ever, historians of evangelicalism need to understand the ways that this regional subculture has overflowed its sectional boundaries and permeated the mainstream. Long ago the prophet Amos foretold a day when many would "wander from sea to sea, and from the north even to the east," seeking the Lord in vain. "In these latter days," Southern sociologist John Shelton Reed has written, "the wayfaring stranger would be well-advised to forsake the secular North, abjure the mysterious East, and check out the South." Good advice, for the South, like the second coming, may be closer than most people think.[28]

28. Reed, *One South,* 135.

Epilogue

Taking the Measure of the Evangelical Resurgence, 1942–1992

Nathan O. Hatch
with Michael S. Hamilton

From "Can Evangelicalism Survive Its Success?" *Christianity Today,* 5 October 1992, 21–31.

Visiting my parents in Columbia, South Carolina, where I grew up in the early 1950s, always triggers a wealth of memories. Most vividly I recall what was absent from that world. Like much of America at the time, Columbia was then a town without a single fast-food restaurant or a single suburban shopping mall. It was also a place marked by the absence of that medley of religious influences that we associate with modern evangelicalism.

Columbia was a religious place, to be sure, with Baptist, Methodist, and Presbyterian spires punctuating almost every corner. But religious life had a one-dimensional quality being confined largely to church programs and activities. The broader culture was mildly supportive of Christian belief but churches had a virtual monopoly on winning the lost and sustaining the faithful.

When I was a boy, Columbia had no Christian radio and nothing on the airways comparable to Amy Grant, Sandi Patti, or Lionel Harris. When Elvis Presley became the rage in 1955, I still recall all of us in the fourth-grade class crooning "You Ain't Nothing but a Hound Dog." By contrast, the church's stodgy hymns and limp gospel songs could not compete for the hearts and minds of young people. While one could tune in Sunday church services on the radio, there was no Jim Dobson, Charles Swindoll, or John MacArthur offering insight for daily living—and nothing like the string of over one thousand Christian radio stations that blanket the country.[1] Television in the age of *I Love Lucy* and *The Wonderful World of Disney* was just gaining a foothold and did not seem menacing to serious Christians. But one could not look to television for daily Christian instruction and interpretation as cable television now permits. While midweek prayer meetings were a staple of church life, small group fellowships or care groups were unknown, as were Bible Study Fellowship and Walk-Through-the-Bible. Churches spoke of revival but had few means to bring the laity into the process, plans such as the Four Spiritual Laws or Evangelism Explosion. Churches had not yet developed specialized ministries to singles, to single parents, and to the divorced. Church growth seminars had not yet interrupted the weekly routine of pastors.

At local high schools there was no Young Life and at the University of South Carolina no Inter-Varsity, Campus Crusade, Navigators, or Fellowship of Christian Athletes. College students had nothing at their disposal like the popular apologetics of C. S. Lewis, Francis Schaeffer, or Josh McDowell. The eighty-five-member Christian College Coalition had not yet articulated its educational alternative to denominational colleges. Young people interested in pastoral ministry thought in terms of regional denominational seminaries rather than Fuller, Gordon-Conwell, or Trinity—seminaries yet to emerge. There was a Southern Baptist bookstore in Columbia with Bibles and Sunday school material but Christian publishers like Zondervan, Word, and Multnomah had not yet flooded the market with an array of books for Christian living—from child rearing to Christian fiction, from financial planning to biographies of Christian celebrities. And fundamentalists could boast no phenomenal best sellers like Hal Lindsey's *The Late Great Planet Earth* or Frank Peretti's *This Present Darkness*.[2]

There were no Christian grade schools or high schools, no Christian counseling centers, no *Christianity Today* , *Leadership*, or *Decision* magazines. There were no appeals to relieve Third World hunger from World

1. Quentin J. Schultze, "The Invisible Medium: Evangelical Radio," in *American Evangelicals and the Mass Media*, ed. Schultze (Grand Rapids: Academie/Zondervan, 1990), 171.

2. Hal Lindsey, *The Late Great Planet Earth* (Grand Rapids: Zondervan, 1970); Frank E. Peretti, *This Present Darkness* (Wheaton, Ill.: Crossway, 1986).

Vision, Samaritans Purse, or Bread for the Hungry. One could not join hands in service with other Christians through Habitat for Humanity or Prison Fellowship. None of my high school friends had the opportunity to serve overseas in summer missions projects. No mainline churches in Columbia had been touched by charismatic renewal and Pentecostal churches remained small and restricted largely to Olympia—the mill section of town.

These stark contrasts between the texture of evangelical life today and that which existed at the end of World War II serves as a useful introduction to the subject of this chapter: an attempt to assess what has happened to evangelicals in the last fifty years and to take stock of the current trajectory of the movement.

From Embattled Outposts to Flourishing Enterprises

Fifty years ago most learned interpreters of American religion expected revivalists, fundamentalists, and Pentecostals simply to wither and die.[3] As remnants of a bygone era, these expressions of old-fashioned orthodoxy and overt supernaturalism could not hope to keep pace with the modern world. They would continue to recede to the margins of American life. In the theological battles of the 1920s and 1930s, most mainline Protestant denominations had purged themselves of these reactionary forces. Protestants looked forward to growing religious influence in American life as they sought to reconcile faith and modern culture and to narrow the differences among themselves.

What neither scholars nor the leaders of mainline denominations counted on was the persistence of revivalistic Bible Christianity among ordinary American churchgoers and the furious organizational counteroffensive launched by those who spoke for them. Taking up positions in a variety of marginal denominations (Holiness, Pentecostal, Southern, ethnic-immigrant, Adventist, fundamentalist) and in transdenominational parachurch agencies, theological conservatives labored to organize Americans around alternative visions of Christian faith that stressed personal conversion, holy living, and direct experience of the divine in daily life.

Their unexpected achievements have surprised, and often flustered, outside observers. Church membership as a percent of population is up 10 percent in the past fifty years, despite the fact that mainline membership has dropped off. Half the increase is due to Roman Catholic growth, which has tapered off dramatically in the last decade. The other half is

3. Ernest R. Sandeen, *The Roots of Fundamentalism: British and American Millenarianism 1800–1930* (Chicago: University of Chicago Press, 1970), ix–xix.

the direct result of ongoing evangelical expansion.[4] Evangelicals also present the mainline with a renewed challenge from within. Most mainline denominations now host large grass-roots evangelical caucuses, which function as a kind of loyal opposition, and increasing numbers of mainline pastors have been trained at evangelical seminaries.

Denominational competition is not, however, the most important story of the past fifty years. The organizational structures that house the throbbing heart of evangelicalism are not denominations at all, but the special-purpose parachurch agencies that sometimes seem as numberless as the stars in the sky. These evangelistic agencies, missionary agencies, Bible societies, publishing houses, periodicals, radio and television programs, women's ministries, men's ministries, youth ministries, prison ministries, summer camps, colleges, Bible institutes, day schools, professional societies, avocational societies, charismatic groups, Bible study groups—even the categories seem numberless—stand outside America's denominational structure. Parachurch groups have picked the denominations' pockets, taking over denominational functions, inventing wholly new categories of religious activity to take into the marketplace, and then transmitting back into the denominations an explicitly nondenominational version of evangelical Christianity.[5]

Evangelical innovations have swept through America's increasingly permeable denominational walls. The church growth movement, and an emphasis on small groups and utilizing spiritual gifts, have colored a broad range of American churches since 1970. Similarly, a charismatic style of worship and singing has spread far beyond churches that speak in tongues.[6] Churches of long sectarian pedigree, like the Seventh-day Adventists and the Churches of Christ, increasingly take on an "evangelical" cast. (At a recent meeting of Church of Christ pastors in southern California, someone noted that several had taken time to go hear the preaching of Charles Swindoll.)

Liberated from denominational constraints, evangelicalism has turned loose its women and men of entrepreneurial bent upon American's spiritual problems. The movement's decentralized arrangement has encouraged people with a unique vision to tailor innovative outreach methods to specific groups of people in specific circumstances. Charles Colson's

4. Figures computed from Benson Y. Landis, ed., *Yearbook of American Churches: 1941 Edition* (Jackson Heights, N.Y.: Yearbook of American Churches Press); and Constance H. Jacquet, Jr., *Yearbook of American and Canadian Churches 1990* (Nashville: Abingdon, 1990).

5. Robert Wuthnow, *The Restructuring of American Religion: Society and Faith Since World War II* (Princeton, N.J.: Princeton University Press, 1988), 100–131.

6. Erling Jorstad, *Popular Religion in America: The Evangelical Voice* (Westport, Conn.: Greenwood, 1993), 167–201.

term in prison opened his eyes to prisoners' need for the good news of Jesus Christ, and it also gave him valuable insight into how to go about meeting that need. Evangelicalism's free-market structure gave him the freedom to build a new ministry around his vision, and it gave him mechanisms for selling it in the marketplace.[7] Like George Patton's tank brigades, evangelical parachurch groups can strike wherever and whenever a capable commander sees an opening.

But also like Patton's tank brigades, evangelicals are in constant danger of outrunning their supply lines. Their detachment from denominations has loosened their connection to the church and its two thousand years of Christian wisdom and experience. In their freedom to adapt ministries to the needs of a particular time and place, they are also at liberty to make the mistakes that Christians have made in the past.

Sophisticated in their use of all forms of mass media and highly attuned to their audience, evangelical entrepreneurs have transformed a popular religious movement into the most dynamic sector of modern religion. Nearly one-third of all Americans identify themselves as "born-again" Christians—a phrase given currency by transdenominational evangelicalism. The percentage is even higher for the young adults of the baby-boom generation, testimony to the evangelicals' unsurpassed ability to gather young people into the Christian fold.[8] Youth ministry continues to be a central and effective thrust of evangelicalism today—Young Life, for instance, will bring twenty-two thousand high schoolers into summer camps this year.

Nor has evangelical energy been contained by national boundaries. Evangelicals have virtually taken over the field of foreign mission. Forty years ago evangelical agencies sponsored less than half of all American missionaries; by 1980 the figure was over 90 percent. Wycliffe Bible Translators alone now has as many staff in the field as all American mainline agencies combined.[9]

Its decentralized structure, audience orientation, and what sociologist Nancy Ammerman has called its "willingness to confront strangers" have helped make evangelicalism remarkably adaptable to differing social contexts. Abroad, evangelical Christianity in various forms is the most rapid-

7. Charles W. Colson, *Born Again* (Lincoln, Va.: Chosen, 1976); and Colson, *Life Sentence* (Lincoln, Va.: Chosen, 1979).

8. George Gallup, Jr., and Jim Castelli, *The People's Religion: American Faith in the 90's* (New York: Macmillan, 1989), 92; Wade Clark Roof, "Return of the Baby Boomers to Organized Religion," in *Yearbook of American and Canadian Churches 1990*, ed. Jacquet, 288.

9. Robert T. Coote, "The Uneven Growth of Conservative Evangelical Missions," *International Bulletin of Missionary Research* 6 (1982): 120. The figure on Wycliffe is from Wycliffe's main office in a telephone interview with authors.

growing religion in many parts of the world, redrawing the religious maps of Latin America, sub-Saharan Africa, and Asia. In the U.S., evangelicalism has been able to translate its message into terms relevant across a wide ethnic and social spectrum, from Hispanic-Americans to African-Americans, from the impoverished underclass to the materialistic middle class. It has not, however, proven universally adaptable. The truly wealthy are noticeably absent from evangelical circles; and evangelicalism has yet to find a way to communicate with the ambitious and well-educated shapers of American culture who guide the mass media, the educational system, the universities, the courts, and the national government.[10]

The Influence of Billy Graham

It would be difficult to overestimate Billy Graham's importance in the last fifty years of evangelicalism. Raised in Southern fundamentalism and educated in Northern fundamentalism, he distilled out of those movements their positive thrusts and brought them onto the national stage.

Graham personally embodied most of the characteristics of resurgent evangelicalism. He stressed personal conversion and the importance of holy living, while de-emphasizing doctrinal and denominational differences that often divided Christians. He was a leader in postwar youth ministry. He worked not through any denomination but through independent parachurch organizations, releasing the gospel from ecclesiastical space and injecting it into the traffic-ways of everyday life—city stadiums, radio, television, newspapers, and movies.

Graham had strong ties to the National Association of Evangelicals, Fuller Theological Seminary, and *Christianity Today.* He supported the neo-evangelical intellectuals who sought to reform fundamentalism's dispensationalism, moralism, and anti-intellectualism, thereby legitimizing their efforts to a popular constituency that might have otherwise been quite suspicious. He recognized the worth of Pentecostals' and charismatics' forms of Christianity, and welcomed them into fellowship. He helped make it easier for evangelicals to return to the public square through his

10. Quotation from Nancy T. Ammerman, "Fundamentalists Proselytizing Jews: Incivility in Preparation for the Rapture," in *Pushing the Faith: Proselytism and Civility in a Pluralistic World*, ed. Martin E. Marty and Frederick E. Greenspahn (New York: Crossroad, 1988), 122. On the growth of evangelicalism worldwide, see David Barrett, ed., *World Christian Encyclopedia: A Comparative Study of Churches and Religions in the Modern World, A.D. 1900–2000* (Oxford: Oxford University Press, 1982). On growth in Latin America, see David Martin, *Tongues of Fire: The Explosion of Protestantism in Latin America* (Cambridge, Mass.: Basil Blackwell, 1990), and David Stoll, *Is Latin America Turning Protestant? The Politics of Evangelical Growth* (Berkeley: University of California Press, 1990).

association with major politicians, and by taking cautiously progressive positions on a few social issues like civil rights, poverty, and the nuclear arms race. He has been able to adapt his delivery to his audience—for instance, he preaches less about the terrors of hell than in his early years—without compromising his message of salvation through Jesus Christ.

It has often been written that Billy Graham thoroughly reflects the American middle class that attended his crusades. His politics, his language, his concerns, and most importantly, his religion, are pegged to the values and the aspirations of the middle sectors of American society. But Graham has also transcended the American middle class in his ability to speak to the spiritual aspirations of a broad spectrum of people in other societies. From Latin America to Asia he has been able to draw widespread cooperation and enormous crowds with the same message he preaches in the U.S. However, like evangelicalism generally, Graham has been less successful in winning over the educated classes, who have tended to regard him with skepticism and condescension.[11]

For evangelicalism, Billy Graham has meant the reconstitution of a Christian fellowship transcending confessional lines—a grass-roots ecumenism that regards denominational divisions as irrelevant rather than pernicious. Graham was at the storm center when separatist fundamentalists finally split off from the rest of evangelicalism, but he nevertheless led most American fundamentalists out of their sheltered enclaves into broader fields of fellowship and activity. In doing so, he gave popular American Christianity an enduring evangelical flavor. Today, Graham's is not the most frequently-heard voice on the American evangelical scene, but it is still the most respected, still the most winsome.

From the Theological to the Relational

The last five decades of American evangelicalism encompass stories of both continuity and change. Much remains the same—the indispensability of personal conversion, the quest to live lives pleasing to God and in line with his purposes, the firm belief that God acts in individual lives and in human history, the preference to read the Bible literally whenever possible, the centrality of lay leadership and parachurch groups for

11. The best of many books on Billy Graham is William Martin, *A Prophet with Honor: The Billy Graham Story* (New York: William Morrow, 1991), 128–30. On Graham as a representative of the middle class, see Grant Wacker, "'Charles Atlas with a Halo': America's Billy Graham," *The Christian Century* 109 (1 April 1992): 336–41. On the reaction of the mainline Protestant intelligentsia to Billy Graham, see Mark Silk, "The Rise of the 'New Evangelicalism': Shock and Adjustment," in *Between the Times: The Travail of the Protestant Establishment in America, 1900–1960*, ed. William R. Hutchison (New York: Cambridge University Press, 1989), 282–91.

transmitting the evangelical vision, the ambivalence toward churches belonging to mainline denominations, the democratic bias toward grassroots authority.

There have also been a number of changes that might be understood collectively as a shift away from the theological toward the relational.[12] Fifty years ago evangelicals were fully engaged in battling modernists' attempts to detach Christianity from historic orthodoxy. This kept evangelical concerns centered on the content of Christian belief—on the propositional truths of Scripture. Today, evangelicals seem far more interested in questions of worship. This has led in two different directions—a movement toward the liturgical by the intellectually inclined, and a movement toward the charismatic by the average churchgoer. Both represent a shift away from the knowledge about God toward the experience of God.[13]

Fifty years ago, evangelicals were taught that all Christians had a responsibility to witness to non-Christians about Christ at every opportunity. This was understood as plain, direct talk about every person's sinfulness and need of regeneration through faith in Jesus Christ. The corollary of this teaching was that anyone who could not testify to an evangelical-style conversion experience was presumed not to be a Christian. Today, however, the concept of witnessing has taken on more nu-anced forms, such as "life-style evangelism."[14] Human spiritual distortion seems more often discussed in terms of psychological maladjustment than as inbred sinfulness. Often it sounds as though the gospel is directed more toward personal well-being—health, financial security, and stable human relationships—than toward the eternal life of the soul.

Fifty years ago, evangelicals—not without reason—saw secular society as unremittingly hostile toward their faith. One response was to set up moral standards that would set evangelicals off from the rest of the world. Movies, dancing, swearing, and alcohol were strictly off limits; tobacco, mixed swimming, jewelry, makeup, and certain hairstyles and types of clothing might be locally prohibited. Associating with nonevangelicals for purposes other than evangelism was also usually regarded as worldly. Today, interest in hard-and-fast moral codes has moved a few notches down the scale of priorities. Fewer evangelical leaders call Christians to

12. One spirited exposition of this theme is David F. Wells's *No Place for Truth; Or, Whatever Happened to Evangelical Theology* (Grand Rapids: Eerdmans, 1993).

13. Robert E. Webber, *Evangelicals on the Canterbury Trail: Why Evangelicals Are Attracted to the Liturgical Church* (Waco, Tex.: Word, 1985); Richard Quebedeaux, *The New Charismatics II* (San Francisco: Harper and Row, 1983); Webber, *Signs of Wonder: The Phenomenon of Convergence in Modern Liturgical and Charismatic Churches* (Nashville: Star Song, 1992).

14. Joseph C. Aldrich, *Life-Style Evangelism: Crossing Traditional Boundaries to Reach the Unbelieving World* (Portland, Ore.: Multnomah, 1981).

self-denial; more provide roadmaps to self-esteem.[15] The original version of E. Margaret Clarkson's missionary hymn—"*So send I you to labor unrewarded / To serve unpaid, unloved, unsought, unknown, / to bear rebuke, to suffer scorn and scoffing. / So send I you to toil for Me alone*"—has been replaced in most hymnals by a more triumphal version.[16]

Fifty years ago, most evangelicals read the Bible through the dispensationalist lenses of the Scofield Bible. This stimulated keen interest in the fulfillment of prophecies preceding Christ's return; this, along with the tendency of their liberal opponents to emphasize the social obligations of Christians, gave evangelicals a second rationale for their lack of interest in social concerns. Now, however, dispensationalism does not seem nearly so widespread. Passion for the coming of the Holy Spirit today may have partially displaced passion for Christ's return tomorrow. Evangelicals have shown a new willingness to work in concert with nonevangelicals to effect social change—perhaps a sign that they now read in the prophets a call to work for justice as well as a timetable for the second coming.

Fifty years ago, a huge wave of missionaries traveled overseas with the single-minded goal of carrying the gospel to people groups around the globe that had never before heard it. The missionary focus was more on the next world than this—rescuing the souls of all who had never heard the gospel from an eternal death that was as certain as it was terrifying. Today, the concern for souls has not diminished, but evangelical missionaries now tend to go abroad with an equal concern for the physical well-being of their hosts. Modern mission agencies are as devoted to the relief of bodies as they are to the relief of souls.

Fifty years ago, evangelicals had virtually abandoned the life of the mind, concentrating instead on communicating their message to a popular audience. All the evangelical scholars in America would have, as historian George Marsden put it, "fit in one train car." Today, there is a sizable and growing contingent of evangelical scholars making their voices heard in intellectual circles, committed to the proposition that God can redeem even serious intellectual life.[17]

Many doubtless regard these changes as regress rather than progress, but it is clear that they have stemmed to a large degree from evangelicals' reactions to their experiences in spreading the gospel. Fifty years ago

15. James Davison Hunter, *Evangelicalism: The Coming Generation* (Chicago: University of Chicago Press, 1987), 50–75.

16. E. Margaret Clarkson, "So Send I You." Clarkson wrote the original version around 1940; she wrote the more upbeat version in 1962.

17. George M. Marsden, "The State of Evangelical Christian Scholarship," *The Reformed Journal* 37 (September 1987): 13.

evangelical subcultures were highly insular, equipping talented men and women with a clear and unambiguous ideology. But as they went out into the world to proclaim the Christian faith, they contacted human realities for which their ideology had not entirely prepared them.

Evangelists found that direct proclamation of the gospel sometimes hardened people against the gospel, but long-term personal relationships would sometimes soften those same hearts. They discovered many nonevangelicals—even Roman Catholics—who were true servants of Christ in every meaningful sense.[18]

Pastors found that conversion, sanctification, and baptism of the Holy Spirit did not automatically produce harmonious marriages, wise parents, respectful children, and merciful neighbors; and they discovered that strict moral codes could sometimes deflect emphasis from the weightier matters of the gospel.

Evangelicals of a scholarly bent found that the secular intellectual world spoke a virtually different language from that of evangelicals. Evangelicals inclined to activism realized that in abandoning social concern they had left the field to the secular state, which has steadily spread its influence into more and more areas of American life. Missionaries found that their Christian faith was partly shaped by their cultural heritage, and that other cultures possessed liberating insights at times more congruent with the biblical message.[19]

In addition, many of the changes in evangelicalism can be traced to the success of the movement. Fifty years ago, the movement had a distinct sense of itself as a small, outsider minority group, bunkered down against the assaults of a hostile society. Today, the phenomenal growth in numbers of evangelicals has permitted the growth of subcultural institutions that stretch across the spectrum of human activity. If the subculture is not as deep as it once was—if there is less obvious difference between evangelicals and nonevangelicals—the subculture is broader than it once was, making it easier for evangelicals to isolate themselves from the rest of society than ever before.

18. For one measurement of the shift in evangelical thinking regarding Roman Catholicism, compare John Carrara, *Catholicism Under the Searchlight of the Scriptures* (Grand Rapids: Zondervan, 1943) with James C. Hefley, *A Prejudiced Protestant Takes a New Look at the Catholic Church* (Old Tappan, N.J.: Revell, 1971).

19. On the vast gulf between evangelicalism and modern intellectual life, see Mark A. Noll, *The Scandal of the Evangelical Mind* (Grand Rapids: Eerdmans, 1994). On the advance of governmental influence and its impact on religion, see Robert Wuthnow, *The Struggle for America's Soul: Evangelicals, Liberals, and Secularism* (Grand Rapids: William B. Eerdmans, 1989), 97–114. For an example of the broadening of one well-known missionary's thinking, see Elisabeth Elliot, *The Savage My Kinsman* (New York: Harper and Brothers, 1961).

Evangelicalism and the Culture Wars

For most of this century, leaders of the mainline denominations have pilloried evangelicals for failing to recognize the social obligations of Christian faith. Large groups of evangelicals finally answered the call to social action in the 1970s—much to the dismay of their mainline critics. When they finally did take up social and political activism, evangelicals organized around a completely different agenda.

Evangelicals mostly worried about legal abortion, morality and family issues, religion and education, economic growth, and maintaining a defensive posture in the Cold War. Mainline activists were more concerned with civil rights, economic redistribution, nuclear peacemaking, curtailing U.S. military influence abroad, and environmental issues. As a result, the two groups found themselves at odds on virtually every issue. The mainline commitment to equal civil rights for women translated into support for legal abortion. Evangelical support for economic growth policies led them to oppose many environmental protection laws. And so forth.

By the 1980s, American society was marked by a sharp polarization on these and similar issues. Catholics, Jews, and all major Protestant denominations have split down the middle. The conservative agenda is championed by an interfaith coalition that sociologist James Davison Hunter has called the orthodox party. The liberal agenda is pursued by an interfaith coalition, joined by a secularist component, that Hunter has called the progressivist party.[20]

To a significant extent the polarization follows a division in American society between the lower middle classes, who tend to support the orthodox party, and the upper middle classes, who tend to be progressivist. Educational patterns are important—higher levels of education generally correlate with a progressivist orientation. Equally important has been the expansion of direct government influence into ever wider areas of daily life. This has naturally spawned a pitched battle over who will control the direction of that growing influence. It has also introduced the peculiar moral values of the government itself into debates that turn upon moral questions.[21]

The culture wars have shaken evangelicalism, just as they have the rest of society. Most evangelicals find themselves more or less in the orthodox camp, some gravitate toward the progressivist camp, but many sympathize with parts of both. The din of the debate has drowned out temperate

20. James Davison Hunter, *Culture Wars: The Struggle to Define America* (New York: Basic Books, 1991).

21. Wuthnow, *The Restructuring of American Religion*, 132–72.

voices, and the sharply dualistic views of both parties have made it difficult to find middle ground. This raises the possibility that the resurrection of evangelical social concern, earnestly called for by Carl F. H. Henry forty-five years ago, will further fragment the evangelical subculture.[22]

Can the Evangelical Center Hold?

The genius of American evangelicalism since World War II has been in transcending its own fragmentation and sectarianism and realizing a vital strain of "mere Christianity." Billy Graham, no doubt, has been the prime exemplar of this ideal of evangelical catholicity, of focusing on essentials and asking for reciprocal good will on less important matters. As standard bearer of evangelical unity, Graham has served much the same role that John Wesley ascribed to John Newton in the eighteenth century: "You appear to be designed by Divine Providence for a healer of breaches, a reconciler of honest but prejudiced men, and an uniter (happy work!) of the children of God that are needlessly divided from each other."[23]

A broad range of leaders, movements, and institutions have joined Graham in building a nonsectarian evangelical consensus. It has been the unswerving vision of the National Association of Evangelicals and of *Christianity Today* and leaders like Kenneth Kantzer, Charles Colson, and Robert Seiple. The same attention to essentials has also animated youth movements such as Inter-Varsity and Campus Crusade. It is a guiding principle of the eighty-five-member Christian College Coalition, and prominent in the writings of Philip Yancey, Elisabeth Elliot, James M. Boice, Os Guinness, R. C. Sproul, and Tony Campolo.

This sense of common purpose has fostered numerous concerted efforts among theologically conservative Protestants. Since the Berlin Congress on Evangelism in 1966, this has been an era characterized by evangelical congresses, conferences, caucuses, councils, and consultations. The evangelical community has also been blessed with certain formidable leaders who commanded ready respect and deference, persons such as Billy Graham, Bill Bright, Carl F. H. Henry, John Stott, and J. I. Packer.

The founding fathers of modern evangelicalism are in the twilight of their careers and the age which they inaugurated is swiftly coming to an

22. Carl F. H. Henry, *The Uneasy Conscience of Modern Fundamentalism* (Grand Rapids: Eerdmans, 1947).

23. *Letters of John Wesley*, ed. J. Telford, vol. 4 (London, 1931), 293, quoted in Bruce Hindmarsh, "'I Am a Sort of Middle-Man': The Politically Correct Evangelicalism of John Newton," paper given at a conference on "Evangelicalism in Trans-Atlantic Perspective," held 8–11 April 1992, at Wheaton College, Illinois, ms. p. 3.

end. The next generation simply does not have the same kind of recognized leaders. Nor will it have the Billy Graham Evangelistic Association, which has provided financial and organizational glue to make much common activity possible.

In the coming years it is likely that centrifugal forces will accelerate. That is the orientation of our fragmented culture and that is the core of American evangelical history: entrepreneurial, decentralized, and given to splitting, forming, and reforming. Evangelical ministries are dominated by self-appointed and independent-minded religious leaders. No one can predict the rise to authority of a James Dobson, a Becky Pippert, a John MacArthur, a Charles Colson, a John Wimber, or a Bill Hybels. The evangelical world is a competitive environment, dynamic and uncontrollable. Since 1989, for instance, nearly seven hundred different Christian ministries have poured into Eastern Europe and the former Soviet Union.[24] Yet these predominantly American efforts elude any overall coordination or mutual consultation about long-range strategy. They point to the dilemmas of a religious free market. How can we maintain theological integrity without veering into sectarian bickering? Can unity of purpose be achieved among charismatics and dispensationalists, Wesleyans and Reformed, Baptists and Episcopalians? What group or conclave should deliberate on knotty theological questions?

Most importantly, can evangelicals deflect the strong temptation to spend their energy on internal concerns rather than in engaging an intensely secular and materialistic culture? The task of relating to those who do not share evangelical assumptions may be more difficult than a generation ago. An elaborate evangelical subculture provides for many a safe haven from the storms of diversity. It is now possible to proceed from kindergarten to a Ph.D. within evangelical confines, to listen to evangelical media from morning until night, and to consume a steady diet of evangelical books and magazines. Studies show, for instance, that the burgeoning evangelical media empire—radio, television, and popular music—retains minimal audience beyond evangelical borders despite claims that the unchurched are being reached. By constructing a culture of their own, evangelicals run the risk of being less capable, and sometimes less interested, in communicating with neighbors different than themselves.[25]

24. Sharon Linzey, M. Holt Ruffin, and Mark R. Elliott, eds., *East-West Christian Organizations: A Directory of Western Christian Organizations Working in East Central Europe and the Newly Independent States Formerly Part of the Soviet Union* (Evanston, Ill.: Berry Publishing, 1993).

25. Schultze, ed., *American Evangelicals and the Mass Media*, 151, 176–78, 231.

Can Evangelicals Recover the Wisdom of the Church?

Someone recently quipped that referring to evangelical spirituality is to repeat oneself while referring to evangelical ecclesiology is to contradict terms. This comment, however exaggerated, does point to the characteristic evangelical reflex of prizing spiritual reality and disparaging church form and tradition.

The evangelical resurgence of the last half century has unintentionally chipped away at the power and influence of the institutional church. So much of evangelical life is freshly minted—new ministries, new publications, new seminaries, new churches. And those congregations emulated for their success typically reject ecclesiastical tradition for new and powerful ways of being "seeker friendly." The result is that fewer evangelicals than a generation ago stand in a religious tradition that can provide ballast and long-term orientation. In an increasingly rootless world, evangelicals need to draw sustenance from the church and its traditions.[26]

Never has this problem been more acute. Evangelicals in the past pictured themselves as a leavening influence within the church. Jonathan Edwards was self-consciously a part of New England's Calvinist churches and he wrestled within that tradition to solidify orthodox teaching and to renew spiritual vitality. John Wesley, for all his insistence upon evangelical reform, cherished the institutional church and worked within its structures. Too many evangelicals today divest themselves of being Presbyterian or Baptist, Disciple or Lutheran, Episcopalian or Methodist. We fall into reinventing the church every time a new vision seems workable, or anytime strong disagreement disturbs a congregation.

Devaluing the church enfeebles Christians in two respects: it cuts us off from the past and it relieves us of accountability. In an age when faith is often relevant, but shallow and self-centered, we must counter the bias that the newer it is, the better it is. Many traditions of faith in the market place today are not powerful enough intellectually or spiritually to provide an orienting vision for all of life. Many Americans, from a variety of denominational backgrounds, are historical orphans who have never reached back to recover a Christian heritage more profound than we know in the twentieth century. Evangelicals possess few solid vantage points from which to assess our own times and to exercise freedom from the whim of the moment.

Evangelicals also have difficulty seeing themselves as responsible and accountable to the church. The community of the redeemed, the very bride of Christ, is premised on bonds more durable than our fickle in-

26. Thomas Howard makes similar points in *Evangelical Is Not Enough* (Nashville: Nelson, 1984).

stinct to pick and choose. How else can the weak and the strong, the mature and the immature, interact to build up the entire body in good times and bad? The strength of modern evangelicalism is that it has evolved like a supermarket, a consumer-oriented, highly fragmented religious marketplace.[27] This buyer's market caters to the free will of the individual and exalts choice over commitment and continuity. The very structures of evangelical life are attuned to the intense individualism of American culture. To fulfill the scriptural ideal of the church, that Christ's fullest presence indwells the whole, not just the individual parts, evangelicals will have to cut against the grain of American culture—and against some of their own cherished assumptions.

Can Evangelicals Engage the Life of the Mind?

In recent years the United States has become more secular and more religious at the same time. The crucial point to note is the contrasting sectors of society in which these trends are taking place. Religion is abounding in the realm of popular culture and in ways that concentrate on breadth of audience rather than depth of insight.[28] In the realm of high culture—in the best universities, in the arts, in literary circles—the juggernaut of secularism rolls on, pressing religious belief into territory that is smaller and of less consequence.

Dan Quayle's "cultural elite" do manifest a decided secularism.[29]

While evangelicals decry the dangers of "secular humanism," they have rarely been in a position to do anything about it. For at least three reasons, evangelicals have not won the right to be heard by twentieth-century intellectuals. First, as pragmatic activists evangelicals have never revered the life of the mind. In fact, they often are suspicious of the methodical poking around of the scholar, and the intellectual's characteris-

27. R. Stephen Warner, "Work in Progress Toward a New Paradigm for the Sociological Study of Religion in the United States," *American Journal of Sociology* 98 (1993): 1004–93.

28. For scholarly discussions of American popular religion, see Peter W. Williams, *Popular Religion in America: Symbolic Change and the Modernization Process in Historical Perspective* (Englewood Cliffs, N.J.: Prentice-Hall, 1980); and Jorstad, *Popular Religion in America: The Evangelical Voice.* Though less well-balanced, religion travelogues often give a better idea of the amazing diversity of American popular religion than do scholarly treatments. Two of the better travelogue books are Malise Ruthven, *The Divine Supermarket: Shopping for God in America* (New York: William Morrow, 1989), which takes a broad sampling of American religiosity; and Randall Balmer, *Mine Eyes Have Seen the Glory: A Journey into the Evangelical Subculture* (New York: Oxford University Press, 1989), which focuses on evangelicalism.

29. Barbara Hargrove, *The Emerging New Class: Implications for Church and Society* (New York: Pilgrim, 1986).

tic nuance, qualification, and suspension of judgment. The most common evangelical depiction of the history of American higher education is that institutions like Yale and Princeton sold their spiritual birthright in the pursuit of academic excellence. To call for academic engagement in evangelical circles still raises the specter of the slippery slope.

The decentralized structure of the evangelical world also inhibits the expensive and painstakingly-slow task of Christian thinking. Amidst the scores of evangelical colleges and seminaries, none can provide faculty with the time for thought and writing provided at any good research university. Evangelicals simply have not made the investments necessary to compete on a level playing field.

The very success of evangelical institutions also works to make evangelicals more intellectually insular. Evangelicals have developed their own publishing houses, their own journals, their own media outlets, their own associations. The very success of these ventures make it all too easy for evangelical scholars to write books for the large, friendly—and commercially profitable—evangelical audience. Instead of engaging those who deny theistic assumptions, evangelicals spend most of their intellectual energies in intramural discussion.[30]

The vitality of evangelical life does little to reverse the pervasive secularization of American thought—a current that undermines the very possibility of theism in the next century. "The problem is not only to win souls but to save minds," Charles Malik said prophetically to evangelicals at the dedication of the Billy Graham Center at Wheaton College. "If you win the whole world and lose the mind of the world, you will soon discover you have not won the world. Indeed it may turn out that you have actually lost the world."[31]

Can Evangelicals Survive Their Own Success?

Over the course of the last half century evangelicals have come to know the good life. In Grand Rapids, Michigan, the First Assembly of God congregation just completed a five-thousand-seat sanctuary—the largest auditorium in Grand Rapids and twice the size of any church in western Michigan. This twelve-million-dollar facility stands in jarring contrast to the storefront chapels that characterized Pentecostalism be-

30. These points are elaborated in Noll, *The Scandal of the Evangelical Mind*; George Marsden, "The State of Evangelical Christian Scholarship,"*Christian Scholars Review* 17 (1988): 347–60; and Nathan O. Hatch, "Evangelical Colleges and the Challenge of Christian Thinking," *The Reformed Journal* 35 (September 1985): 10–18.

31. Charles Malik, "The Two Tasks," address given at Wheaton College, Ill., 13 September 1980.

fore World War II. In Charlotte, North Carolina, a once-modest congregation, Calvary Presbyterian, the church home of Billy Graham's late parents, Frank and Morrow Graham, left downtown for the growing suburbs in the early 1970s. Renamed Calvary Church, this bustling congregation of thirty-five hundred recently moved again, this time to a one-hundred-acre campus and forty-million-dollar showcase facility that includes a two-million-dollar organ, an award-winning preschool for six hundred children, and a Christian drama troupe.

Evangelical people and institutions have moved dramatically into the mainstream of American society. They enjoy more prosperity, education, and cultural sophistication; and they command greater attention from the media. Most importantly, evangelical endeavors now stand out as the success story in American religion. Even in the political realm, pollsters now identify them as the religious audience to be reckoned with.[32]

Evangelicals have become accustomed to versions of the gospel that do not give offense. There are still fundamentalists who relish separatism, and Churches of Christ who claim to be a faithful remnant. There are still evangelicals like Ron Sider, Doug Frank, Robertson McQuilken, and the Sojourners community that call for an ethic of sacrifice. Yet, by and large, the evangelical community has become comfortable with suburban mores and consumer culture. Having (for good reason) abandoned earlier definitions of worldliness that involve avoiding externals, evangelicals have been less successful in defining how the spirit of Christ might differ from that of success-oriented, upwardly mobile, American materialism.

We live in a culture that worships at the shrine of four related idols: pleasure, wealth, professional status, and physical appearance. It is a culture of convenience rather than duty and of avoiding pain rather than seeking to relieve the burdens of others. In an affluent culture these charms have deadly attraction.

Evangelicals are susceptible to the idols of materialism in part because evangelical success and commercial success are so easily intertwined. In an entrepreneurial, media-oriented environment, successful ministries become powerful financial engines. It becomes hard to distinguish between marketing the gospel and commercial success. At the 1989 Gospel Music Association Convention (representing an annual market of at least three hundred million dollars), one of singer Amy Grant's managers argued that the goals of ministry and business are "exactly the same—market share."[33]

32. James Davison Hunter, *American Evangelicalism: Conservative Religion and the Quandary of Modernity* (New Brunswick, N.J.: Rutgers University Press, 1983); and Hunter, *Evangelicalism: The Coming Generation.*

33. Quoted in William D. Romanowski, "Contemporary Christian Music: The Business of Music Ministry," in *American Evangelicals and the Mass Media*, ed. Schultze, 166.

To what extent have the idols of this age worked themselves into evangelical affections? To what extent has the goal of evangelical spirituality become self-fulfillment rather than self-denial, less a quest to know God and more a means to achieve the good life? To what extent has the church been stained by materialism, smug professionalism, and the quest for self-actualization? In short, have evangelicals so tamed the gospel to accord with American habits that it has been shorn of its radical power to convict and convert?

These are difficult and troubling questions. Fifty years ago Jim Elliot, a Wheaton student who would become a missionary martyr, could write to his mother: "Our silken selves must know denial."[34] That stern ethic was somewhat out of step even in the 1940s but today it sounds like advice from another planet. Evangelical belief has flourished typically at the margins of society among those who do not enjoy power, wealth, and station. That was the case in the early Methodist revivals and in the contemporary explosion of Protestantism in Latin America. More troubling is the fate of the gospel in an era, like our own, when Christians enjoy plenty and hunger for respectability. The advice of John Wesley to upwardly mobile Methodists two centuries ago is a pointed reminder of the dilemma of our own success:

> I fear, wherever riches have increased, the essence of religion has decreased in the same proportion. Therefore I do not see how it is possible, in the nature of things, for any revival of religion to continue long. For religion must necessarily produce both industry and frugality, and these cannot but produce riches. But as riches increase, so will pride, anger, and love of the world in all its branches. How then is it possible that Methodism, that is, a religion of the heart, though it flourishes now as a green bay tree, should continue in this state?[35]

34. Quoted in Elisabeth Elliot, *Shadow of the Almighty: The Life and Testament of Jim Elliot* (New York: Harper and Brothers, 1958), 94.

35. Quoted in Gertrude Himmelfarb, *The Idea of Poverty: England in the Early Industrial Age* (New York: Vintage, 1985 [1983]).

Bibliography

Edith Blumhofer, director, Institute for the Study of American Evangelicals, Wheaton, Illinois:

———. *Aimee Semple McPherson: Everybody's Sister*. Grand Rapids: Eerdmans, 1993.

———. *The Assemblies of God: A Chapter in the Story of American Pentecostalism*. 2 vols. Springfield, Mo.: Gospel Publishing House, 1989.

———. *Restoring the Faith: The Assemblies of God, Pentecostalism, and American Culture*. Urbana and Chicago: University of Illinois Press, 1993.

Joel A. Carpenter, former director, ISAE, and program director for religion, The Pew Charitable Trusts, Philadelphia, Pennsylvania:

———. *Revive Us Again: The Recovery of American Fundamentalism, 1930–1950*. Oxford University Press, 1994.

D. G. Hart, former director, ISAE, and librarian and associate professor of church history and theological bibliography, Westminster Theological Seminary, Philadelphia, Pennsylvania:

———. *Defending the Faith: J. Gresham Machen and the Crisis of Conservative Protestantism in Modern America*. Baltimore: The John Hopkins University Press, 1994.

Nathan O. Hatch, advisor, ISAE, and vice president for graduate studies and research, University of Notre Dame, Notre Dame, Indiana:

———. *The Democratization of American Christianity*. New Haven, Conn.: Yale University Press, 1989.

Hatch, Nathan O., John Woodbridge, and Mark A. Noll. *The Gospel in America: Themes in the Story of America's Evangelicals*. Grand Rapids: Zondervan, 1979.

———. *The Sacred Cause of Liberty: Republican Thought and the Millennium in Revolutionary New England*. New Haven, Conn.: Yale University Press, 1977.

Hatch, Nathan O., Mark A. Noll, and George M. Marsden. *The Search for Christian America*. Westchester: Crossway, 1983. Expanded edition, Colorado Springs: Helmers and Howard, 1989.

George M. Marsden, advisor, ISAE, and McAneney Professor of History, University of Notre Dame, Notre Dame, Indiana:

———. *The Evangelical Mind and the New School Presbyterian Experience: A Case Study of Thought and Theology in Nineteenth-Century America*. New Haven, Conn.: Yale University Press, 1970.

———. *Fundamentalism and American Culture: The Shaping of Twentieth-Century Evangelicalism, 1870–1925*. New York: Oxford University Press, 1980.
———. *Reforming Fundamentalism: Fuller Seminary and the New Evangelicalism*. Grand Rapids: Eerdmans, 1987.
———. *Religion and American Culture*. San Diego: Harcourt Brace Jovanovich, 1990.
Marsden, George M., Mark A. Noll, and Nathan O. Hatch. *The Search for Christian America*. Westchester: Crossway, 1983. Expanded edition, Colorado Springs: Helmers and Howard, 1989.
———. *The Soul of the University*. New York: Oxford University Press, 1994.
———. *Understanding Fundamentalism and Evangelicalism*. Grand Rapids: Eerdmans, 1991.

Mark A. Noll, senior advisor, ISAE, and McManis Professor of Christian Thought, Wheaton College, Wheaton, Illinois:
———. *Between Faith and Criticism: Evangelicals, Scholarship, and the Bible in America*. San Francisco: Harper and Row, 1986.
———. *Christians in the American Revolution*. Grand Rapids: Eerdmans, 1977.
Noll, Mark A., John Woodbridge, and Nathan O. Hatch. *The Gospel in America: Themes in the Story of America's Evangelicals*. Grand Rapids: Zondervan, 1979.
———. *A History of Christianity in the United States and Canada*. Grand Rapids: Eerdmans, 1992.
———. *One Nation Under God? Christian Faith and Political Action in America*. San Francisco: Harper and Row, 1988.
———. *Princeton and the Republic, 1768–1822: The Search for a Christian Enlightenment in the Era of Samuel Stanhope Smith*. Princeton, N.J.: Princeton University Press, 1989.
———. *The Scandal of the Evangelical Mind*. Grand Rapids: Eerdmans, 1994.
Noll, Mark A., Nathan O. Hatch, and George M. Marsden. *The Search for Christian America*. Westchester: Crossway, 1983. Expanded edition, Colorado Springs: Helmers and Howard, 1989.

George A. Rawlyk, advisor, ISAE, and professor of history, Queen's University, Kingston, Ontario:
———. *Champions of the Truth: Fundamentalism, Modernism and Maritime Baptists*. Kingston, Ont.: McGill-Queen's University Press, 1990.
———. *Ravished by the Spirit: Religious Revivals, Baptists, and Henry Alline*. Kingston, Ont.: McGill-Queen's University Press, 1984.
Rawlyk, George A., and Kevin Quinn. *The Redeemed of the Lord Say So: A History of Queen's Theological College, 1912–1972*. Kingston, Ont.: Queen's Theological College, 1980.

Harry S. Stout, advisor, ISAE, and Jonathan Edwards Professor of American Christianity, Yale University, New Haven, Connecticut:
———. *The Divine Dramatist: George Whitefield and the Rise of Modern Evangelicalism*. Grand Rapids: Eerdmans, 1991.

———. *The New England Soul: Preaching and Religious Culture in Colonial New England.* New York: Oxford University Press, 1986.

Grant Wacker, advisor, ISAE, and professor of the history of Christianity, The Divinity School, Duke University, Durham, North Carolina:

———. *Augustus H. Strong and the Dilemma of Historical Consciousness.* Macon, Ga.: Mercer University Press, 1985.

Index